MANHATTAN PREP

GMAT®

Integrated Reasoning & Essay

This guide covers the Integrated Reasoning section on the GMAT and Executive Assessment exams, as well as the Essay section on the GMAT. Master the IR question types and discover strategies for optimizing performance on the essay.

MW00799284

Acknowledgements

A great number of people were involved in the creation of the book you are holding.

Our Manhattan Prep resources are based on the continuing experiences of our instructors and students. The overall vision for this guide was developed by Whitney Garner and Stacey Koprince, who developed the strategies for each question type and wove them into a cohesive whole.

Stacey Koprince was the primary author and she was supported by a number of content experts. Whitney Garner and Emily Meredith Sledge served as a sounding board during the writing phase, developing and vetting ideas and editing new content. Mario Gambino managed production for the many complex images, with Derek Frankhouser and Israt Pasha lending their design expertise.

Matthew Callan coordinated the production work for this guide. Once the manuscript was done, Naomi Beesen and Ben Ku edited and Cheryl Duckler proofread the entire guide from start to finish. Carly Schnur designed the covers.

Retail ISBNs: 978-1-5062-1967-7, 978-1-5062-6253-6
Retail eISBN: 978-1-5062-4920-9
Course ISBN: 978-1-5062-4921-6
Course eISBN: 978-1-5062-4922-3

10 9 8 7 6 5 4 3 2

GMAT® Strategy Guides

GMAT All the Quant

GMAT All the Verbal

GMAT Integrated Reasoning & Essay

Strategy Guide Supplements

Math

GMAT Foundations of Math

GMAT Advanced Quant

Verbal

GMAT Foundations of Verbal

September 3, 2019

Dear Student,

Thank you for picking up a copy of *Integrated Reasoning & Essay*. I hope this book provides just the guidance you need to get the most out of your GMAT studies.

At Manhattan Prep, we continually aspire to provide the best instructors and resources possible. If you have any questions or feedback, please do not hesitate to contact us.

Email our Student Services team at gmat@manhattanprep.com or give us a shout at 212-721-7400 (or 800-576-4628 in the United States or Canada). We try to keep all our books free of errors, but if you think we've goofed, please visit manhattanprep.com/GMAT/errata.

Our Manhattan Prep Strategy Guides are based on the continuing experiences of both our instructors and our students. The primary author of the 7th Edition Integrated Reasoning & Essay guide was Stacey Koprince. Project management and design were led by Matthew Callan, Mario Gambino, and Helen Tan. I'd like to send particular thanks to instructors Whitney Garner, Ben Ku, and Emily Meredith Sledge for their content contributions.

Finally, we are indebted to all of the Manhattan Prep students who have given us excellent feedback over the years. This book wouldn't be half of what it is without their voice.

And now that you are one of our students too, please chime in! I look forward to hearing from you. Thanks again and best of luck preparing for the GMAT!

Sincerely,

Chris Ryan
Executive Director
Product Strategy

www.manhattanprep.com/gmat 138 West 25th Street, 7th Floor, New York, NY 10001 Tel: 212-721-7400
Fax: 646-514-7425

TABLE OF CONTENTS

The GMAT and the EA

The GMAT (Graduate Management Admission Test) and the EA (Executive Assessment) are computer-adaptive exams used for admission into graduate management education programs. MBA programs are more likely to use the GMAT, while the EA is most commonly used for EMBA programs (though both exams are used for both types of programs).

Both exams are made by GMAC (Graduate Management Admissions Council) and both test the same content via the same question types. The primary differences are in the scoring and the length of the exams.

Both exams have Quant, Verbal, and Integrated Reasoning (IR) sections; the GMAT also has an Essay section. The EA is 1.5 hours long, while the GMAT is about 3.5 hours long, including breaks.

Both exams provide individual scores for each section of the exam. The GMAT combines the Quant and Verbal section scores into one score, called the Total, on a 200–800 scale. The EA combines the IR, Quant, and Verbal section scores into a Total score on a 120–180 scale.

The IR section on the two exams is very similar, but time management strategies differ a bit. Where the two exams differ, this guide will specify what you need to know for the exam that you're planning to take.

The Executive Mindset

These exams are complex. They feel like academic tests—math, grammar, logical reasoning—but they're really not! At heart, these exams are a test of your executive reasoning skills.

Executive reasoning is the official term for your ability to make all kinds of decisions in the face of complex and changing information. It makes sense, then, that graduate management programs would want to test these skills. It's crucial for you to understand *how* they do so because that understanding will impact both how you study for the test and how you take the test.

You do need to know various math and grammar facts, rules, and concepts in order to do well on the exam—and this makes the GMAT and EA feel similar to tests that you took in school. There's one critical difference though: In school, your teachers tested you on material they expected you to know how to handle. Your teachers wouldn't put something on the test that they pretty much *expected* you to get wrong. That would be cruel!

Well, it would be cruel if the main point of the exam was to test your mastery of those facts, rules, and concepts. But that isn't the main point of the GMAT or the EA. These exams primarily measure your executive decision-making: when to invest your limited time and mental energy and when *not* to.

In other words, both the GMAT and the EA want to know how you make business decisions. And no good businessperson invests in every single opportunity placed in front of them, just because it's there. You'll invest in a majority of the problems presented to you, but you *will* say no to some—the ones that look too hard or seem like they'll take too long to solve. These are literally bad investments.

If you try to use a "school mindset" on the test, you'll keep trying to answer the current problem because you think that you're supposed to be able to do everything. You'll waste a bunch of time and then you'll have to rush on other questions in the section. As a result, you may miss questions that you actually do know how to answer and your score will be lower than it could have been.

Instead, use your "business mindset" to carry you through the exam. When the test finds your limit, acknowledge that! Call it a bad investment and let that problem go, ideally before you've spent very much time on it. Choose an answer—any answer—and move on.

As in the real world, you're going to have to decide what to do based upon incomplete information. At times, you'll decide to abandon a particular problem forever—knowing you can't come back to it even if you have extra time at the end. Practice being comfortable making decisions with that uncertainty.

(Note: The GMAT never lets you go back to any question that you've already answered. The EA allows you to go back within a limited subset of questions, but not all. You'll learn more about this in Chapter 8.)

Extend the business mindset to your studies as well. If there are certain topics that you really hate, don't study them in the first place. You're just going to bail (guess quickly and move on) when one of those "investment opportunities" comes up.

One caveat: You can't bail on huge swaths of content. For example, don't bail on all questions that test percents, fractions, and ratios, as these topics comprise a large portion of the IR section. You can, though, bail on a subset—perhaps you'll bail on fraction problems that require algebra, but choose to try fraction problems that contain real numbers.

Start orienting yourself around your business mindset today. You aren't going to do it all. You're going to choose the best opportunities for you, as you see them throughout the test. When you decide not to pursue a particular investment, you're going to say no as quickly as you can and forget about it—don't waste precious resources on a poor investment opportunity. Move on to the next opportunity, feeling good about making sound investment decisions about what to do and what *not* to do.

In short, embrace the executive mindset!

CHAPTER 1

How to Use This Guide

In This Chapter

- The Essay
- Integrated Reasoning

In this chapter, you will learn how to get the most out of this guide and other resources you may use as you prepare for these two sections.

CHAPTER 1 How to Use This Guide

The *GMAT Integrated Reasoning & Essay Strategy Guide* will help you prepare for the Integrated Reasoning (IR) section of the GMAT and Executive Assessment (EA), as well as the Analytical Writing Assessment (AWA, or Essay) section of the GMAT.

The Essay

The Essay is the least important section of the GMAT (and it doesn't appear on the Executive Assessment at all). You will just need to get a "good enough" score, and approximately 80% of test-takers cross that threshold. You probably won't need to spend very much time to get yourself ready for this section.

Still, you'll want to have a mental template in place to make it as easy as possible to write the essay; this guide will show you how.

For many students, working through the essay material in this guide will be enough to get ready for the Essay section. If you have access to our GMAT Interact™ essay lesson, you can use this resource in addition to or instead of the essay chapter in this guide.

If you are struggling to compose complex sentences, Appendix A of this guide will teach you how to write more advanced sentences. You may also find it useful to study the Sentence Correction unit of Manhattan Prep's *GMAT All the Verbal* or *GMAT Foundations of Verbal* guides.

You can test your skills using GMAC's GMAT Write™ program, the same software scoring system used on the real exam. For a small fee, you'll get a score and feedback on two essays. You'll be able to revise the essays and submit them again to see whether your score improves. If you're in one of our study programs, check your program details; you might already have access to GMAT Write™ for frcc.

Integrated Reasoning

On the GMAT, the Integrated Reasoning (IR) score is more important than the Essay score but usually less important than the Quant or Verbal score. As a result, you will likely spend more time studying Quant and Verbal than IR.

On the Executive Assessment, though, the IR score is about as important as the Quant and Verbal scores, so you will likely spend a similar amount of time getting ready for all three sections.

On both exams, the IR section tests you on a mix of quantitative and verbal skills. The problems don't resemble the kinds of problems you're used to seeing on standardized tests—and this unnerves some people at first. But IR more closely resembles the kind of real-world analysis that you already do every day at work, so as you learn how to handle each problem type, you may find that you end up preferring the IR section to the others.

IR tosses a whole bunch of data at you and expects you to figure out what information you do or don't need in order to solve the problem—just as you have to do every day in real life. IR also requires integration of quant, logic, and comprehension all in one problem—again, just like real life.

In short, IR is going to feel messy, chaotic, imprecise—in that sense, it won't feel like a typical standardized test. But if you orient yourself toward the idea that this is a real-life type of problem, you'll be *expecting* that information overload and so you'll be in a better position to handle this section.

Chapter 3, "Introduction to Integrated Reasoning," will give you an overview of the timing, scoring, and structure of this section, including the four types of IR problems. This chapter also introduces the UPS process: Understand, Plan, Solve. You'll use this process to answer every IR problem on the test.

Chapters 4–7 cover the four problem types, one per chapter. We think it is best to study the four types in the order they appear in this book.

Chapter 8 summarizes the strategies for each problem type and for the overall IR section. It also addresses decision-making strategies for both the GMAT and the EA.

Appendix A discusses how to write more complex sentences for the Essay section on the GMAT. Finally, Appendix B summarizes some of the common math topics that are tested on the IR section. For full treatment of these and other quant topics, as well as strategies that will help you solve more efficiently, see Manhattan Prep's *GMAT All the Quant* guide.

If you are studying for the EA, incorporate IR equally with your Quant and Verbal studies. Study all three types every week.

If you are studying for the GMAT, you will likely concentrate on Quant and Verbal for the first few weeks. That's fine, but don't wait until the end of your studies to look at the IR section; spread out the work relatively evenly over time. Plan to study one IR question type every few weeks, depending on the total length of your studies.

As you finish each chapter in this guide, practice your skills using the practice problems found in Atlas, Manhattan Prep's online study center. If you purchase any official materials, such as the *GMAT Official Guide* or the *EA Official Practice Questions* from GMAC® (the makers of both exams), you'll have access to additional online Question Banks of real IR problems from past administrations of the official test.

Finally, make sure to include the IR section when taking practice computer-adaptive tests (CATs). A lot of people studying for the GMAT skip the IR and Essay sections because they know that these sections are less important overall on that exam, but it's critical to practice under official test conditions.

You're ready to dive into the book. Good luck and happy studying!

CHAPTER 2

The Argument Essay

In This Chapter

- What Is the Argument Essay?
- The Physical Mechanics of Essay Writing
- What the Argument Essay Asks
- How to Manage Your Time
- How to Generate Good Ideas
- How to Structure the Essay
- Sample Essay
- How to Vary Sentence Structure and Content
- How to Prepare for the Essay
- Additional Preparation

In this chapter, you will learn how to write a GMAT essay that will get you a good enough score on the Analytical Writing Assessment (AWA) section of the exam. You'll also learn why you need only a good enough score, not a great score.

CHAPTER 2 The Argument Essay

The Analytical Writing Assessment (AWA) is also known as the Essay section. It appears either first or last on the GMAT, depending upon which section order you choose. (Note: The Executive Assessment does not have an Essay section.)

Schools just want to see a good enough essay score, so it won't take you long to get ready for this section.

What Is the Argument Essay?

This section of the GMAT consists of one 30-minute essay that you type into the computer. In this essay, you'll examine a flawed argument very similar to the flawed arguments you see on Critical Reasoning (CR) problems.

The schools want to ensure that you can write in English well enough to handle graduate-level academic coursework. This essay is the only thing that schools know that you wrote completely on your own, since you could have had help on your application essays. The Essay score provides admissions officers with a "fine" or "not fine" on your ability to communicate well in written English.

The scoring scale runs from 0 (lowest) to 6 (highest) in half-point increments. (The essay is separately scored—it does not factor into your GMAT Total score of 200–800.)

According to the *GMAT Official Guide*, a 6.0 essay "presents a cogent, well-articulated critique of the argument and demonstrates mastery of the elements of effective writing," though there may still be minor flaws. At the other end of the spectrum, *No score* (a 0) means you've left the essay blank, written something off topic or in a language other than English (including gibberish), or just recopied the topic.

You'll be assessed on three sets of skills:

1. *Logical analysis*: How well do you dissect and evaluate the argument?
2. *Persuasive writing*: How clearly and convincingly do you express your thoughts?
3. *Language usage*: grammar, syntax, variety of vocabulary

The Essay chapter in the *Official Guide* describes the essay task and provides a few useful example essays, as well as a list of possible essay topics and other useful material.

What Score Is Good Enough?

Here is the scoring scale for the AWA section, along with the GMAT's corresponding qualitative labels and the associated percentiles. (Note: Percentiles can change over time.)

AWA score	Label	Percentile
6.0	Outstanding	88
5.5		79
5.0	Strong	53
4.5		42
4.0	Adequate	17
3.5		11
3.0	Limited	4
2.5		3
2.0	Seriously Flawed	2
1.5		2
1.0	Fundamentally Deficient	1
0.5		1
0.0	No Score	0

As shown in the table, about half of all test-takers score a 5.0 or better. Most schools consider a 4.5 or better good enough, and even a 4.0 will probably be okay, as the GMAT calls this score *Adequate.*

A score of 3.5 or lower, though, may raise more serious concerns for the school. They will likely review the actual text of your essay in order to determine whether they think you can handle business-school-level communications.

So your goal is to score a 4.5 or higher on the essay. This gives you a little leeway to fall short (4.0) and still be okay.

Both a computer and a human grade your essay so, unlike your other scores, you won't receive your AWA score until a week or two after your test. You will receive your AWA score when you receive your official score report from GMAC®. If you score a 3.5 or lower, then you will need to consider whether to take the test again in order to raise this score.

If you score a 4.0 and the rest of your scores are good, don't retake the test just to lift your AWA score. If, though, you're going to retake the GMAT anyway, put in a little more time on your essay preparation to hit the 4.5 level.

If you are relatively confident that you'll score a 4.5 or higher, then you can do minimal preparation:

- Read the rest of this chapter and follow the instructions in "How to Prepare for the Essay."
  - Do the essay when taking practice computer-adaptive tests (CATs).
  - Possibly use GMAT Write™ (you'll learn what this is later in this chapter).

- Go in with a game plan. Know the process you want to follow.
- Write a decent amount. Longer essays generally score higher.

However, if you think you're at risk of a score below a 4.0, then you've got more work to do. To judge your risk, ask yourself these questions:

- *How much experience do you have writing academic English?*
  - Did you rarely write essays in English in school?
  - Were your grades in English classes low?
  - In your job, do you rarely write anything longer or more formal than short emails?
- *Is your command of written academic English weak?*

  If you're unsure, choose a long Reading Comprehension (RC) passage at random and read it with no time pressure, then consider these questions:
  - Are there many words that you didn't understand?
  - Did you fail to understand sentences when they got too long?
  - Did you take 10 minutes or more to finish the passage, only to find that you had little idea what it meant?
  - Did you frequently translate back into another language?
- *Is your command of spoken English weak?*
  - Do you struggle to keep up with a conversation among native English speakers?
  - Do you have a lot more trouble understanding English over the phone than in person?
  - Do you frequently strain to formulate new or complex ideas in English?

If you answered "yes" to several of these questions, work through this chapter carefully and follow up with Appendix A of this guide. You'll also need to do more practice with the essay outside of your practice tests.

The Physical Mechanics of Essay Writing

You will be typing your essay into a text box on the computer screen. You can enter as much text as you want, but you can only see about 10 lines at once.

The system feels like a clunky, old-fashioned word-processing program. You have just a few buttons with standard functions:

Button	Function	Keyboard shortcuts
Cut	Cuts text and puts it on a clipboard.	Ctrl-X or Alt-T
Copy	Copies text onto the clipboard.	Ctrl-C or Alt-C
Paste	Pastes text from the clipboard.	Ctrl-V or Alt-A
Undo	Undoes the last edit you made. You can undo your last 10 edits.	Ctrl-Z or Alt-U
Redo	Redoes something you just undid. You can redo the last 10 undone actions.	Ctrl-Y or Alt-R

Navigation keys on the keyboard act as you expect:

Arrow keys move the cursor up, down, left, or right.

Enter or *Return* inserts a paragraph break and moves you to a new line.

Page Up moves the cursor up one screen.

Page Down moves the cursor down one screen.

Backspace removes the character to the left of the cursor.

Delete removes the character to the right of the cursor.

Home moves the cursor to the beginning of the line.

End moves the cursor to the end of the line.

You will not have standard formatting options, such as underline, *italic*, or **bold**. Do not use any text-message substitutes, symbols, or abbreviations.

There is no tab or indent. To start a new paragraph, press *Enter* or *Return* a couple of times to insert a blank line between paragraphs. If you like to indent the beginning of paragraphs, hit the space bar a small, consistent number of times (say, five).

You will not have spelling or grammar check. You can make a few mistakes without impacting your score, but if you have so many mistakes that a reader would be distracted or possibly even unsure about your intended meaning, then your score will go down. Don't, though, get so caught up in being grammatically perfect that you write a much shorter essay than you're capable of writing in half an hour. Follow spelling and grammatical rules well enough to make your meaning clear, but keep writing.

What the Argument Essay Asks

The Argument Essay asks you to analyze an argument—something with a conclusion and premises. In fact, it will look very similar to the arguments you see in the Critical Reasoning (CR) section of the exam, and your CR tools will come in handy as you tackle the essay.

The argument that you need to analyze will contain a conclusion, or big claim, along with a few premises. Here's an invented, slightly extreme example:

> The country of Tarquinia has a much higher rate of traffic accidents per person than its neighbors, and in the vast majority of cases one or more drivers is found to be at fault in the courts. Therefore, Tarquinia should abolish driver-side seatbelts and airbags in all new cars and prohibit companies from developing other safety measures that protect the driver. These measures will eliminate traffic accidents in Tarquinia by motivating drivers to drive safely.

Here, the conclusion is that *these measures* (abolishing driver-side safety measures) *will eliminate traffic accidents in Tarquinia by motivating drivers to drive safely.* The premises are listed in the first sentence: the high rate of traffic accidents and the finding of driver fault. The second sentence describes the proposed measures and can be seen as part of the conclusion.

These are the official instructions for the essay:

> Discuss how well reasoned you find this argument. In your discussion, be sure to analyze the line of reasoning and the use of evidence in the argument. For example, you may need to consider what questionable assumptions underlie the thinking and what alternative explanations or counterexamples might weaken the conclusion. You can also discuss what sort of evidence would strengthen or refute the argument, what changes in the argument would make it more logically sound, and what, if anything, would help you better evaluate its conclusion.

Let's break these four sentences down. The first sentence is the most important:

Sentence 1: *Discuss how well reasoned you find this argument.*

The argument will *never* be very well reasoned! Your goal is to find the flaws and explain them clearly.

Sentence 2: *In your discussion, be sure to analyze the line of reasoning and the use of evidence in the argument.*

Line of reasoning:

- Does the conclusion follow completely logically from the premises? (It never does!) Why not?
- What and where are the gaps? Under what circumstances does the logic fail?
- What would help the author prove the conclusion?

Use of evidence:

- Does the evidence truly prove what the author wants it to? (It never does!) Why not?
- What does the given evidence actually prove? Under what circumstances?

Sentence 3: *For example, you may need to consider what questionable assumptions underlie the thinking and what alternative explanations or counterexamples might weaken the conclusion.*

Questionable assumptions:

- At each stage of the logic, what has the author assumed that is not necessarily justified?

Alternative explanations or counterexamples:

- What else might explain the facts?
- What situations, cases, or circumstances has the author overlooked?

Sentence 4: *You can also discuss what sort of evidence would strengthen or refute the argument, what changes in the argument would make it more logically sound, and what, if anything, would help you better evaluate its conclusion.*

The items listed in the fourth sentence are worthwhile but *less* important. You can get a 6.0 without including any of these aspects.

You are not asked to argue *for* or *against* the conclusion. Don't say whether you agree or disagree with it. Rather, pretend a friend has asked you to check his argument before he presents it to his boss. Help him analyze the logical strength of his argument: how well the conclusion is supported by the premises.

2

How to Manage Your Time

To write a decent essay in only 30 minutes, you'll need a clear process, such as the 5-step one below:

1. Read (1–2 minutes)
2. Brainstorm (2 minutes)
3. Outline (1–2 minutes)
4. Write (20 minutes)
5. Polish—a little (3–5 minutes)

Here's a short description of each step. You'll learn more about steps 2, 3, and 4 later in this chapter.

Step 1: Read (1–2 minutes)

First, clear your mind and read the argument slowly and carefully. Don't race through the reading. Thirty minutes is not very long, but if you don't take time to understand the argument, you won't write a very good essay.

As you read, identify the conclusion—the big claim that the author is making. The rest of the argument typically consists of background information and premises—facts and smaller claims made to support the conclusion. This support will always be flawed in some way, and those flaws will be based on gaps between the premises and the conclusion. Your job is to find those gaps.

Step 2: Brainstorm (2 minutes)

Some flaws will jump right out at you; others may take some thought. Jot down your ideas on your scratch paper or type them directly into the computer. Either way, don't write too much at this point—just enough to remind you of your thoughts.

Step 3: Outline (1–2 minutes)

Type a short placeholder into the text box for each paragraph, including an introduction, some body paragraphs, and a conclusion.

Step 4: Write (20 minutes)

Now, start writing. The three scored examples in the *Official Guide* show a clear pattern:

Score	Word count
6.0	335
4.0	260
2.0	108

The higher-scoring essays do tend to have more words. Aim for around 300 words.

Conveying complex information typically requires complex sentences. In fact, higher-scoring test-takers typically write longer sentences than lower-scoring ones, as noted in the table below:

Score	Word count	Sentences	Words per sentence
6.0	335	13	25.8
4.0	260	15	17.3
2.0	108	8	13.5

Train yourself to write approximately 20 words a sentence, not as a strict measure to apply in every case, but rather as a rough average. If you write 15 sentences averaging 20 words per sentence, you'll have 300 words (though one very short sentence can really stand out when you have an important point to make). Later in this chapter, you'll learn more about how to write better GMAT sentences.

Step 5: Polish—a little (3–5 minutes)

With a few minutes to go, turn off the spigot. Glance back over what you've written and smooth out the worst of the rough edges. Make sure you've removed any leftover text from your brainstorm or outline. Don't take too much time on any one sentence, gnawing your pen to find the *mot juste* (the "perfect word" in French); you only need a *good enough* score on the essay. Don't try to be Shakespeare.

When you're done, the test asks you to click next and submit, as on all sections. If you run out of time before you get to this, everything you've written will still be submitted.

If you're doing test order one, for which the essay is the first section, and you finish early, you may want to sit and let the timer run out. Use the extra time to close your eyes or gaze up at the wall, roll your shoulders around, and stretch in your seat.

How to Generate Good Ideas

As mentioned earlier, you'll need to brainstorm several flaws from the argument.

The key to brainstorming is to follow a method, four of which are described below. Try them out and use the method that works best for you.

Whichever method you use, jot down just enough to capture the idea; you don't have much time. Then, look for another idea. Here's how: Imagine that the flaw that you just spotted is now fixed. What *else* is wrong with the argument? Once you've identified three flaws, move to the outline phase.

Brainstorming Method 1: Line by Line

Start with the first sentence in the argument. What's wrong with it?

- If it's a piece of evidence, how does it fall short in proving the bigger point?
- If it's a claim, how is it not supported by the evidence?

Work your way, sentence by sentence, to the end of the argument.

2

Brainstorming Method 2: The CAST System

CAST is an acronym to remind you what you're looking for:

Counterexamples

- What situations would disprove the author's assertions?

Assumptions

- What is the author assuming, probably in an unjustified way?

Strengthen

- What would strengthen the argument?

Terms

- What specific words or terms in the argument create logical gaps or other problems?

Go letter by letter through CAST and jot down ideas.

Brainstorming Method 3: Use the Instructions

You'll always be provided with the same instructions, so you can use them as a checklist. The first sentence gives you the core task. The second sentence reminds you what to look *at*:

- Line of reasoning
- Use of evidence

The third sentence reminds you what to look *for*:

- Questionable assumptions
- Alternative explanations or counterexamples

Finally, the fourth sentence reminds you about other stuff you can add to your essay.

Brainstorming Method 4: Remember Common Fallacies

In the sample essay prompts (and in Critical Reasoning arguments), many of the same logical fallacies show up again and again. If you have trouble spotting flaws, here are some common ones to look for:

1. **Alternative Causes**

   If the author asserts that X causes Y, what *else* could be the cause of Y?

   Correlation ≠ Causation: If X and Y happen at the same time, it's not necessarily true that X causes Y. It could be that Y causes X, or some Z causes them both, or they just randomly happened together on this one occasion.

   After ≠ Because: If Y happens *after* X, it's not necessarily true that Y happens *because of* X. Some other cause could be at work.

   Future ≠ Past: If X did cause Y in the past, will X always cause Y in the future? Not necessarily. Circumstances could change.

2. **Unforeseen Consequences**

   If the author proposes plan A to achieve goal B, what could go *wrong*?

   Nothing's Perfect: How could the plan fail to achieve the stated goal? Does it go too far or not far enough? What implementation challenges has the author overlooked?

   Isn't It Ironic: What bad side effects of the plan could happen? These side effects might be bad on their own or they might directly prevent the plan from achieving its goal. Economic examples of the latter include customer attrition (e.g., if you raise prices to increase revenue, customers may flee) and price wars (e.g., if you cut your price to gain market share, your competition could cut prices in response). Think about who has been ignored by the author (such as customers and competitors) and what their negative responses to the plan might be.

   Skill & Will: If people are involved in implementing the plan (and they always are), you need the people to have both the *skill* to succeed and the *will* to succeed. Do they? Who benefits from the plan and are they the same people who need to carry it out?

3. **Faulty Use of Evidence**

   What is sketchy about the evidence?

   Limited Sample: Do you have too little data? How are the mentioned cases not representative of the wider world?

   Troubled Analogy: If the author draws a conclusion about M from facts about "similar" N, how are M and N different? What differing conditions has the author ignored?

   What It Really Means: The evidence simply may not imply what the author claims that it does.

4. **Faulty Use of Language**

   What ***extreme*** words does the author use? What ***vague*** terms are in the argument? You may even encounter a math fallacy, such as an argument that makes assumptions about real quantities when only percents have been given.

Now that you have plenty of ideas about possible flaws (and how to brainstorm them), look at the flaws described in an example essay: the 6.0 essay in the *Official Guide*. The given argument proposes an automatic early warning system to eliminate midair collisions between airplanes. Four flaws in this argument are pointed out in the second paragraph of the essay. Here's a brief list, as if they were brainstormed:

- Assumes cause of collisions = lack of knowledge
  - What if pilots don't pay attention to the warning system?
- Assumes pilots automatically obey the warning
  - What if they don't?
- Limited to commercial planes
  - What about other kinds of planes?
- What if the system fails?

The first two flaws are examples of the *Skill & Will* fallacy. The last two flaws are examples of *Nothing's Perfect*: The plan doesn't go far enough, and it ignores the possibility of failure.

Not every flaw in the argument is captured in the essay. That's fine! For instance, the author never criticizes the use of the extreme word *eliminate* in the conclusion (*reduce* would be more defensible). You do not need to address every last flaw in the argument.

Go ahead and brainstorm flaws in the Tarquinia argument. Take a few minutes and use any method you prefer in order to generate several specific flaws. Here is the prompt again; cover up the answers below the box until you have finished brainstorming.

> The country of Tarquinia has a much higher rate of traffic accidents per person than its neighbors, and in the vast majority of cases one or more drivers is found to be at fault in the courts. Therefore, Tarquinia should abolish driver-side seatbelts and airbags in all new cars and prohibit companies from developing other safety measures that protect the driver. These measures will eliminate traffic accidents in Tarquinia by motivating drivers to drive safely.

Here are some examples of flaws in this argument:

Higher accident rate = meaningful? • What if Tarquinia is not comparable to its neighbors? (car ownership, rural/urban mix might be different)	*Troubled Analogy*
Guilt in courts = true guilt? • What if courts are bad or just bureaucratic? Ignores other factors.	*What It Really Means*
Bad assumption: Drivers have the capability to prevent all or most accidents. (Maybe it's always icy in Tarquinia.)	*Skill & Will*
Removing safety features applies only to new cars. • System only works if all drivers are driving the cars made less safe.	*Nothing's Perfect*
Who would buy new cars? No one!	*Isn't It Ironic*

On first reading the argument, you may have felt that the proposed measures were extreme or impractical. However, you aren't supposed to talk about whether *you* yourself agree with the plan.

Instead, imagine how other people and companies would react. It would be nearly impossible to get car manufacturers, dealers, and the rest of the population to stick to the plan.

How to Structure the Essay

A good GMAT essay has three parts:

1. Introduction
2. Body
3. Conclusion

How you structure the body can vary, but your introduction and conclusion will be structured fairly similarly regardless of the specific argument you're given.

Introduction

First, briefly restate the argument's main claim or conclusion; if the argument is a plan, state the plan. Do not simply quote the argument; put it into your own words to show that you understood it:

> The author proposes plan X to accomplish goal Y...

Next, introduce your thesis statement: The argument is fundamentally flawed in some serious way.

For example, the thesis of the 6.0 example essay in the *Official Guide* is as follows:

> *The argument... omits some important concerns that must be addressed to substantiate the argument.*

Notice how general this thesis is. The essay writer is saying in a fancy way that the argument doesn't work. Here are some other examples:

> This plan is fundamentally flawed, in that the evidence provided fails to support the author's claim.
>
> The author makes several assumptions that are unlikely to be true, in which case her argument is seriously compromised.

To bulk up the intro paragraph, mention one or two of the most egregious flaws you discovered. Don't go into detail; you'll do that in the body of the essay.

If you'd like to give a positive nod to the argument, do so *before* your thesis, using a concession word such as *although*:

> Although the argument has some merits, a number of defects undermine the claim that...

Body

Describe and justify three to four specific flaws from the argument. If you brainstormed more than four flaws, pick the best and drop the rest. There are several ways to structure your body paragraph(s) to describe these flaws.

You can put all the flaws in one big paragraph, as the 6.0 example essay in the *Official Guide* does.

You can also describe each flaw in one sentence, then justify it in the next:

> The author fails to consider whether removing safety features in new cars will impact sales of new cars. If most potential customers decide to buy older used cars instead, then most cars will still have the safety features, derailing part of the author's plan.
>
> The author's evidence also falls short of establishing that drivers are actually capable of avoiding all accidents. Drivers are found to be at fault in "the vast majority" of cases, not all of them. In addition, even when someone is found to be at fault legally, it is not necessarily the case that she or he could have prevented the accident by driving more carefully.

In this case, save your discussion of improvements for the conclusion.

Alternatively, you can put each flaw in a separate body paragraph. Introduce the flaw, justify it, and then discuss how the author could address the flaw. For example:

> The author's evidence falls short of establishing that drivers are actually capable of avoiding all accidents. Drivers are found to be at fault in "the vast majority" of cases, not all of them. At least some drivers, then, could be seriously injured or even killed through no fault of their own, surely not the intended consequence of this law. In addition, the author appears to fail to realize that the safety features would be absent in both cars, so both the driver who caused the accident and the one who is the victim will be hurt or killed! Under those circumstances, the author may well achieve his stated goal, because it is unlikely that anyone will ever drive again.

You can even group a couple of flaws together in one paragraph, if they are related. For example, you could make one body paragraph about *poor use of evidence* (with two to three flaws) and another about *faulty line of reasoning* (with another two to three flaws).

Conclusion

1. Restate briefly *that* the argument is flawed and recap *why* this is the case:

   In summary . . .

2. Mention potential fixes to the line of reasoning used in the argument, if you haven't already:

   To address the problems in the argument, one would have to . . . (gather more data of XYZ kind) (run pilot projects to test the hypothesis) (etc.).

Use new language in your recap. You're saying, yet again, that the argument is flawed, but you need a novel way to say it. Replace particular words (e.g., flaw) with synonyms (error, gap, mistake, defect, fault, imperfection).

If you haven't already discussed possible improvements, do so here. If you are searching for still other things to say—and you have time—revisit the last sentence of the instructions. You can discuss possible new evidence or ways to evaluate the argument. Note that the 6.0 essay published in the *Official Guide* only briefly mentions potential improvements, so it's not necessary to do this. All that essay really does is explain the flaws; only the very last sentence gives a nod to fixes.

By the way, avoid humor in general; it can be easily misinterpreted in print. However, don't be afraid to let your personality shine through, if that helps you generate the volume of content you need.

Sample Essay

Had enough sentence analysis? Itching to get on with it and *write*?

Here's the Tarquinia essay again. On your computer, open up a basic word processor (WordPad or NotePad), one that doesn't have a spelling or grammar check. Alternatively, open up Microsoft Word (or a Google Doc) and disable automatic spelling/grammar check.

Set a timer for 30 minutes and write your essay.

> The country of Tarquinia has a much higher rate of traffic accidents per person than its neighbors, and in the vast majority of cases one or more drivers is found to be at fault in the courts. Therefore, Tarquinia should abolish driver-side seatbelts and airbags in all new cars and prohibit companies from developing other safety measures that protect the driver. These measures will eliminate traffic accidents in Tarquinia by motivating drivers to drive safely.

> Discuss how well reasoned you find this argument. In your discussion, be sure to analyze the line of reasoning and the use of evidence in the argument. For example, you may need to consider what questionable assumptions underlie the thinking and what alternative explanations or counterexamples might weaken the conclusion. You can also discuss what sort of evidence would strengthen or refute the argument, what changes in the argument would make it more logically sound, and what, if anything, would help you better evaluate its conclusion.

When you're done, cut and paste the results into Microsoft Word so that you can do a word count. Recall that you're aiming for approximately 300 words and about 15 sentences, for an average of 20 or so words per sentence. If your essay has substantially fewer than 300 words or an average of much less than 20 words per sentence, you'll need to bulk up.

Next, run the spelling and grammar check. Note any errors and figure out how you could fix them.

Now, take a look at a sample essay for the Tarquinia prompt. While this essay is not perfect, it would likely score a 5.5 or 6.0:

> In response to the comparatively high rate of traffic accidents in Tarquinia, the author argues that measures should be taken to compromise driver safety in order to motivate safer driving. This argument suffers from a number of flaws, ranging from flimsy use of evidence to ill-conceived elements of the proposal.
>
> First of all, the author cites two pieces of supporting evidence that, even if true, may not actually support the conclusion. Tarquinia may have a higher rate of accidents than its neighbors, but what if those neighbors have vastly different circumstances? Rates of car ownership, highway safety conditions (even including weather), and urban/rural divides could all contribute to the higher rate in Tarquinia. Likewise, it may be true that Tarquinian courts find one or more drivers at fault in most cases, but the degree to which these findings are driven by administrative necessity or other unrelated factors is unknown. Perhaps insurance law in the country demands that one or the other driver be found at fault, even if road conditions are largely to blame.
>
> Secondly, the design of the plan appears to be unworkable, even without consideration of the moral implications; for example, some accidents are the result of factors outside of anyone's control. Moreover, the fact that the proposal only applies to new cars creates another logical hole big enough to drive a truck through. Most car buyers would not willingly purchase a new car, and if anyone did, the presence of old cars (which would still have the old safety measures) would undermine the plan, since not all drivers would be subject to the same risk of harm for poor driving.
>
> In order to improve the proposal, the author would need to establish, first, that removing safety features would actually cause drivers to change their behavior and drive much more carefully. Second, the author would need to modify the plan such that all drivers were driving under the same conditions—perhaps older models would have their safety features removed. Even then, the fact that weather or road conditions will inevitably still cause some accidents renders this plan morally suspect.

Compare how you expressed a point with how the essay above expressed a similar point. Borrow or steal whatever you find useful—word choices, phrasing, sentence or paragraph structure. How can you do that? Retype the phrases or sentences you want to steal, making any tweaks you like to fit your writing style.

How to Vary Sentence Structure and Content

How could you improve this sample paragraph?

> The safety features are one major flaw in the argument. Safety features will only be removed from new cars. Only some drivers will have such a strong incentive to avoid all accidents. Some people may even avoid buying new cars. Removing the safety features may not be the deterrent that the author hopes.

The paragraph contains some good ideas, but the presentation of those ideas could be better. The sentences are pretty short, and three of the five use *safety features* as the subject. The ideas aren't very well connected to each other, and the last sentence could use a transition word to indicate more clearly that it is summarizing the paragraph.

Take a look at this example:

> The author fails to consider the potential ramifications of removing the safety features. The removal will take place only for new cars, so only a subset of drivers will have a very strong incentive to avoid all accidents, creating an imbalance among different drivers on the road. Some may counter that this drawback will disappear as more people buy new cars, but the safety feature mandate may actually cause people to prefer used cars to new ones, perpetuating the imbalance long-term. In short, removing the safety features from new cars may not be the deterrent that the author hopes.

In the second example, the author combines some sentences in order to better connect the ideas and varies the structure so that the subjects aren't always the same. The author also adds modifiers (e.g., *creating an imbalance... road*) to increase the complexity of the discussion and add nuance. Finally, the author uses a transition phrase, *in short*, to indicate that the last sentence summarizes the main point of the paragraph.

As you write, keep three aspects in mind:

1. A sentence should contain one clear, central thought.
2. Use modifiers to add complexity and nuance to the main thought.
3. Use signal words, such as *therefore*, *however*, and *in short*, to signal transitions to the reader.

For more, read Appendix A: "How to Write Better Sentences" at the end of this book.

An Analysis of the Sample Essay

Let's examine each sentence in the sample essay from earlier in this chapter.

Paragraph 1, Sentence 1:

In response to X...	*the author*	*argues*	*that*	*measures*	*should be taken to Y.*
Opening Modifier	Subject	Verb	THAT	Subject	Verb

The writer is summarizing the claim made by the author of the argument. This could have been spread across two sentences, but the writer collapses them into one through use of an opening modifier, a very effective way to write a more complex sentence.

Paragraph 1, Sentence 2:

This argument	*suffers*	*from a number of flaws*	*, ranging from A to B.*
Subject	Verb	Prepositional Phrase	Modifier

The writer then asserts a thesis—that the argument is flawed—and explains two parallel reasons why (A and B). The reader would expect later discussion in the essay to provide examples of these two reasons why.

Again the author adds a modifier to extend the sentence rather than write two separate sentences. This time, the modifier is at the end.

Paragraph 2, Sentence 1:

The author	*cites*	*evidence*	*that... may not... support the conclusion.*
Subject	Verb	Object	Modifier

Are you noticing a trend? Modifiers are an excellent mechanism for writing a more complex sentence. The first sentence of the essay had an opening modifier and the second used a comma *–ing* modifier. This third one uses a noun modifier that provides additional information about the *evidence* cited by the author.

Paragraph 2, Sentence 2:

Tarquinia may have a higher rate of accidents...	*, but*	*what if those neighbors have vastly different circumstances?*
Complete Sentence	, Conjunction	Complete Sentence

You can also create a compound sentence: two independent clauses, or complete sentences, connected by a comma and conjunction.

Also, asking a question can be an effective way to get the reader to consider a particular flaw in the logic.

Paragraph 2, Sentence 3:

Rates of ownership,	*highway conditions,*	*and*	*urban/rural divides...*
Subject	Subject	Conjunction	Subject

Parts of sentences can be compound in form as well. This sentence has a compound subject in the form of a list of three things.

Paragraph 2, Sentence 4:

It may be true that...	*, but*	*the degree... is unknown.*
Complete Sentence	, Conjunction	Complete Sentence

This is another compound sentence with an intricate second half:

... the degree	*to which these findings are driven by administrative necessity or other unrelated factors*	*is unknown.*
Subject	Modifier	Predicate

The modifier is a mouthful. It's actually a bit difficult to understand. (What is *administrative necessity*?) Your essay doesn't need to be perfect. The test writers understand that this is an impromptu writing exercise; they're willing to overlook some flaws.

Paragraph 2, Sentence 5:

Perhaps the law demands that one or the other be found at fault,	*even if road conditions are to blame.*
Independent Clause	Dependent Clause

2

You're now encountering a sentence-level subordinate clause: [*main sentence*], *even if* [*subordinate clause*]. The second part cannot stand alone as written; it has to be attached to an independent clause.

This sentence also begins with the word *perhaps*, signaling that the writer is speculating. This is another effective way to illustrate potential weaknesses in an argument.

Paragraph 3, Sentence 1:

The design appears unworkable	*, even without X*	*;*	*for example, some accidents are the result of Y.*
Complete Sentence	Modifier	Semicolon	Complete Sentence

Two related sentences can be connected with a semicolon, but don't just toss in this device anywhere. There should be a good reason to connect two sentences in this way. The first part of the sentence makes a particular claim; the second half provides an example to illustrate that claim.

Paragraph 3, Sentence 2:

The fact	*that the proposal only applies to new cars*	*creates another hole.*
Subject	Modifier	Predicate

You can put a complex noun modifier in between the main subject and verb. In this case, the *that* modifier introduces a clause with its own subject and verb.

Paragraph 3, Sentence 3:

Most buyers would not purchase a car	*, and*	*if anyone did*	*, the presence of old cars would undermine the plan*	*, since not all drivers would be subject to the same risk.*
Complete Sentence	, Conjunction	Subordinate Clause	Complete Sentence	Subordinate Clause

This is a long one—more than 30 words! The sentence is a little unwieldy; the writer should probably have broken it into two sentences. Still, this is a legitimate compound sentence, and the second sentence does have two legitimate subordinate clauses attached to it. The test is not going to penalize you for having a few sentences that go on a bit long, as long as the sentence is still intelligible.

Paragraph 4, Sentence 1:

In order to . . .	*the author would need to establish*	*, first, that removing A would cause drivers to B and C.*
Opening Modifier	Complete Sentence	Modifier

The ending modifier has a pretty complex structure. First, it has a cause–effect setup: Removing one thing would cause another. Second, there are in fact two effects, presented in parallel form: *change their behavior* and *drive much more carefully.*

The sentence also foreshadows, through the use of the word *first,* that the author would need to do two things *in order to improve the proposal.* The second thing should come in the next sentence.

Paragraph 4, Sentence 2:

Second,	*the author would need to modify the plan*	*such that . . .*	*—perhaps . . .*
	Complete Sentence	Subordinate Clause	Complete Sentence

You can also add a second complete sentence by setting that sentence off with a couple of hyphens (--) or an em-dash (—). For the latter, the keyboard shortcut is CTRL-Alt-Minus (on the numeric keypad).

Paragraph 4, Sentence 3:

Even then,	*the fact*	*that conditions will cause accidents*	*renders this plan suspect.*
	Subject	Modifier	Predicate

In the first two sentences of this paragraph, the writer does offer some ways for the author of the argument to improve the argument but this final sentence signals that the writer thinks the proposal is fundamentally flawed even if such fixes were to be made. You don't necessarily need to say something like this; you may think that the argument you're given could be fixed if certain flaws were appropriately addressed.

How to Prepare for the Essay

Now that you've gotten this far, do a few more practice essays to get ready:

1. **Do the Argument Essay section on all of your practice CATs.**

   You have a built-in chance to practice your essay writing when you take a practice test. You also want to make sure you're taking tests under full testing conditions, since mental stamina is an issue over the nearly 3.5-hour length of the exam. When you're done, check the essay in the same way described in this chapter: Paste it into Microsoft Word to check word count, spelling, and grammar, then take the time to rewrite any problematic parts to solidify your learning for next time.

2. **Do GMAT Write®.**

   You may or may not need to take this step. GMAT Write is a service offered by the makers of the GMAT. You practice with real prompts and are scored by the same computer algorithm as that used on the real exam.

   You can purchase access to GMAT Write on the mba.com website. If you are a Manhattan Prep student, check the details of your program, as it may already include this service.

   If you score a 4.5 or higher on GMAT Write, you're good to go (though still practice your essay on practice tests). If your score comes back as a 3.5 or lower, see the next section of this chapter. Finally, if you get a 4.0, you're on the cusp. Put a bit more time into your essay prep just to make sure that you don't fall below a 4.0 on the real test.

Additional Preparation

If you have scored a 3.5 or lower on GMAT Write or on the real Essay section—or you think you will—you need to put more time into preparing for the essay.

Here are practical steps to take:

Step 1: Work Through Manhattan Prep's *GMAT Foundations of Verbal Strategy Guide*

You may already be spending time with that book. Great—now you have another reason to focus. *GMAT Foundations of Verbal* covers all three Verbal problem types (Sentence Correction, Critical Reasoning, and Reading Comprehension), all of which come into play on the AWA essay. You need the parts of speech and other grammatical principles to strengthen the sentences you write. You need to spot missing assumptions and analyze other logical flaws to write an effective essay about a flawed argument. Finally, the better you *read* this kind of text (as in an RC passage), the better you can *write* this kind of text.

So focus on Verbal basics to build skill for the essay.

Step 2: Read and Write Summaries of High-Quality Articles in English

Find good source material. Use publications such as the *Economist*, the *Smithsonian*, the *Atlantic*, and the *New Yorker*. For daily newspapers, try the *New York Times*, the *Wall Street Journal*, the *Washington Post*, and the *Financial Times*. Go get *Scientific American*, the *Journal of American History*, the *Harvard Business Review*, or the *McKinsey Quarterly*. Pick up an alumni magazine from a top university. Visit MIT's Open-CourseWare site (ocw.mit.edu) to pick a course you find interesting and read materials from the syllabus.

Take note of sentences that strike you. Pick apart the core and examine how the author added modifiers or other bits of nuance and richness to the sentence. If you spot a particularly great sentence, you may even want to recopy it to solidify it in your brain.

If you get really ambitious, you can *rewrite* a piece, summarizing it or playing with language in some other way.

Step 3: Do a Few Sample Essays From the *Official Guide*

Pick a prompt at random. Give yourself 30 minutes and type an essay into a bare-bones word processor, as described earlier.

Now, without the pressure of time, analyze and rewrite each sentence in your essay. How could you have phrased your thoughts more precisely and more expressively? What words could you have chosen differently? How would you restructure the sentence?

At first, focus on polishing only the ideas that you were able to generate under time pressure. This way, the next time you have similar thoughts (as you will on other essays), the corresponding sentences will more easily and quickly coalesce.

Next, look for small gaps that you could close by adding material. Could you bulk up any existing sentences? What additional refinements could you add as modifiers? Could you provide better navigation and logical flow with signal words?

Finally, look for big gaps and other wholesale alterations. Did you miss any key flaws in the argument? If so, which kinds? Write and polish sentences corresponding to these flaws. Is there anything you'd cut or otherwise change drastically? If so, what?

Step 4: Learn to Type Faster

The faster and more easily you can type, the less brainpower you'll need for typing—and the more you can use on thinking and writing. If you type slowly, then your brain runs far ahead of your fingers and you lose your train of thought. In contrast, if you can get your thoughts down in near real time, you will simply write better.

Longer essays get higher scores, by and large. But that's far from the only reason to learn to type for real. If you spend more than 20 minutes a day at a computer keyboard, the time you invest in learning to type quickly by touch (without looking at the keys) will pay off more than any other investment you could possibly make.

Take a touch-typing course. There are many free resources on the web; google "learn to type" and see what you find.

CHAPTER 3

Introduction to Integrated Reasoning

In This Chapter

- The Four Types of Prompts
- Table Analysis
- Graphics Interpretation
- Multi-Source Reasoning
- Two-Part Analysis
- IR Connections to Quant and Verbal
- How to Tackle IR: Understand–Plan–Solve

In this chapter, you will learn the basics about the four Integrated Reasoning (IR) problem types, as well as the ways in which the content in the IR section overlaps with the content in the Quant and Verbal sections of the GMAT and EA. You'll also learn Understand–Plan–Solve (UPS), a process you'll use to tackle every IR problem.

CHAPTER 3 Introduction to Integrated Reasoning

The Integrated Reasoning (IR) section is one of four sections on the GMAT and one of three sections on the Executive Assessment (EA) exams. On the GMAT, it appears either second or third in the test order, depending on which order you choose at the beginning of the exam:

Option #1	Essay	IR	Quant	Verbal
Option #2	Quant	Verbal	IR	Essay
Option #3	Verbal	Quant	IR	Essay

On the EA, the IR section appears first, followed by the Verbal section and then the Quant section. (There is only one test order on the EA.)

As the name implies, Integrated Reasoning asks you to do both math and verbal analysis as you answer the 12 problems in the section. The good news: The quant and reasoning skills are the same ones that you're already studying for the Quant and Verbal sections of either exam. You do have some new skills to learn, though. Most IR problems have formats unique to this section of the test, including fill-in-the-blank statements, true/false statements, and other multipart formats.

Scoring on the GMAT

On the GMAT, the Integrated Reasoning section is scored separately from the rest of the test; your IR score does not affect your score on any other section. The IR score goes from 1 to 8 in integer increments; the lowest score is 1 and the highest score is 8.

As with the Quant and Verbal sections of the GMAT, you must answer IR problems in the order they appear; you must answer all parts of each problem, even if you have to guess, and you cannot go back to a problem you've already answered. However, unlike the Quant and Verbal sections of this test, the IR section is *not* adaptive, so your IR score is driven primarily by how many of the 12 problems you answer correctly, with slight adjustments for differences in problem difficulty.

Most schools weight the IR score more lightly than the Quant and Verbal scores in their admissions decisions. The mean score is between a 4 and a 5; for most schools, it's generally considered good enough to beat the mean. Aim for a score of 6 to give yourself a bit of leeway to fall short and still score a 5. (Of course, if IR is a strength for you, feel free to go for a higher score!)

Most of the major consulting and investment banking firms ask for GMAT scores when recruiting students from a master's program, and some do look at the IR score. If you hope to be hired by one of these firms, it's a good idea to aim for a score of 7 or 8 on the IR section.

Scoring on the EA

On the Executive Assessment, the Total score is equally weighted among your Integrated Reasoning, Verbal, and Quant subscores. For this test, you will want to focus your time and attention across all three sections relatively equally.

IR might even be a bit more important than the other two sections. On the EA, you will do the IR section first, and your performance on this section will determine your starting difficulty level for the subsequent Verbal and Quant sections of the test. (You'll learn more about this in Chapter 8.)

Overall, schools that take the EA aren't looking for the very high Total scores that people usually want on the GMAT. Since this test is relatively new, the standards are changing more quickly over time, but most programs find scores in the 150–160 range acceptable.

Whether you are taking the GMAT or the EA, do your research. First, check the school's website to see whether it publishes average scores for either exam. If it doesn't, ask the admissions department yourself.

Content

Most business schools use case studies to teach some or even most topics. Cases are true histories of difficult business situations; they include vast amounts of real information—both quantitative and verbal/logical—that you must sort through and analyze to glean insights and make decisions.

The IR section is designed to mirror two key aspects of case analysis that the Quant and Verbal sections of the GMAT and Executive Assessment don't address:

1. Math–verbal integration
2. The flood of real-world data

Problems on the Quant section of the test typically give you only what you need in order to solve and no more; the numbers often simplify cleanly, leaving you with an integer solution. In addition, the Quant section does not typically incorporate logical reasoning or other verbal skills, although it does require you to translate words into math. On the Verbal section, while Critical Reasoning (CR) and Reading Comprehension (RC) problems do include some extraneous information, they require only light mathematical understanding on occasion.

In contrast, IR may give you giant tables or graphics of ugly numbers or complex situations—but you'll never actually use most of the information (much like data in the real world). Further, you'll have to integrate the quant concepts with the kind of reasoning and analysis more typically found on the Verbal section of the exam.

In short, the IR section seeks to measure your ability to do case analysis in business school. Preparing for this section will be a challenge, but that work will actually help prepare you for grad school.

The Four Types of Prompts

Think of the layout of IR problems as similar to Reading Comprehension in the Verbal section: You're given a **Prompt** (or upfront information to process, similar to the RC passage), and you use that information to answer several questions.

Similarly, any IR problem will consist of two halves: a prompt and one or more questions associated with that prompt. The prompt is the collection of information you'll use to answer the question(s). On the IR section of both the GMAT and the Executive Assessment, you'll see 10 different prompts, accompanied by a total of 12 questions.

There are four types of IR prompts:

1. Table Analysis (aka Table)
2. Graphical Interpretation (aka Graph)
3. Multi-Source Reasoning (aka MSR)
4. Two-Part Analysis (aka Two-Part)

Table, Graph, and Two-Part prompts always have just one associated question. That is, for each Table prompt, you'll answer one question, and the same is true for each Graph prompt and each Two-Part prompt.

The MSR prompt, though, works like a full RC problem set: A single prompt typically comes with three associated questions. So that's how you will have only 10 prompts for 12 total questions.

The mix of questions on the IR section can vary. Here's one common mix of questions:

Prompt type	Total # of problems	Details
Table	2	2 prompts with 1 question each
Graph	3	3 prompts with 1 question each
MSR	3	1 prompt with 3 questions
Two-Part	4	4 prompts with 1 question each

Got all of that? Wait, there's one more thing to know. Most of those individual questions are multipart: You have to answer more than one thing for each question. The multipart questions all have either two or three parts that make up the full question.

Annoyed now? Yes, IR is complex. So is the real world! Once you gain some experience with IR, it will start to seem normal.

Table Analysis

The Table Analysis (Table) prompt is made up of two things: a sortable table and some additional text—also known as a **Blurb**—that gives you context about the information contained in the table. The blurb can be quite basic (e.g., a title); other times, the blurb may contain information necessary to answer the associated question.

The table will always appear on the left-hand side of the screen, and the question will always appear on the right-hand side. The blurb is sometimes above the table and sometimes above the question. In this example, the blurb is above the table:

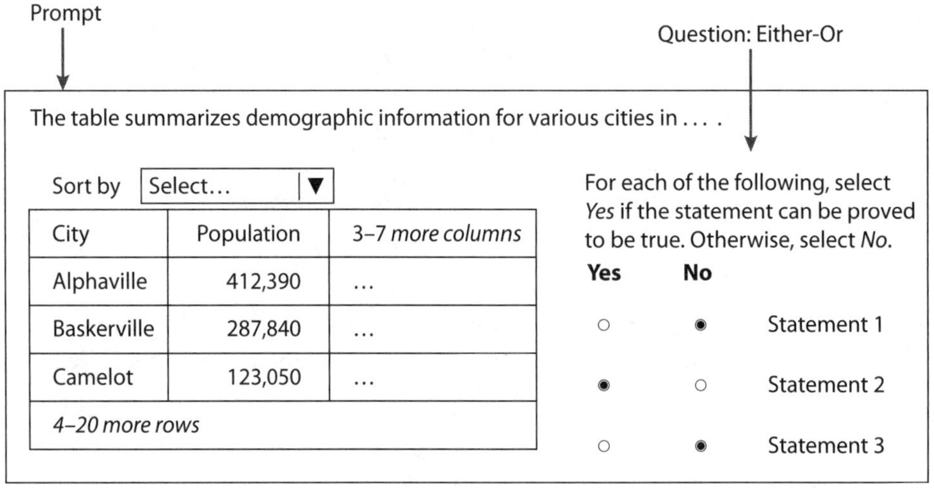

You will be able to sort the table by its columns; doing so will usually help you to save time and minimize careless mistakes. As you'll learn later in this guide, don't even think about trying to solve a Table problem without first considering the best sort to use.

Table prompts are always accompanied by one **Either-Or** question with three parts. The three parts will be in the form of three statements for which you will choose *either* the answer in the first column *or* the answer in the second column. In the example shown above, the choice is either Yes or No.

One more thing: There is no partial credit on the test. In order to get credit for the problem, you'll have to answer all three parts of the question correctly.

This has implications for test strategy. If you realize, for example, that you can answer one statement but you have no idea how to do the other two, then your best move might be to guess on all three and move on. Alternatively, if you feel confident that you can answer two parts in reasonable time but don't know how to do the third, you would likely still want to do that problem. A guess on the third part will still give you a 50/50 chance of answering the entire question correctly.

Essentially, the IR section is setting up the kinds of strategic decisions people have to make in the business world every day. How risky are the risks and how big are the rewards? You will often have to decide to let go of one business opportunity because you're betting that there will be some better opportunity down the line.

Graphics Interpretation

Graphics Interpretation (Graph) problems will present you with some kind of a graphic—anything from a classic pie chart or bar graph to some kind of unusual diagram created specifically for this test.

First, you'll see the graph or diagram and then you'll have a blurb describing the visual. As with tables, the blurb may just describe the visual or it may provide additional information that you'll need to use to answer the question. Here is an example:

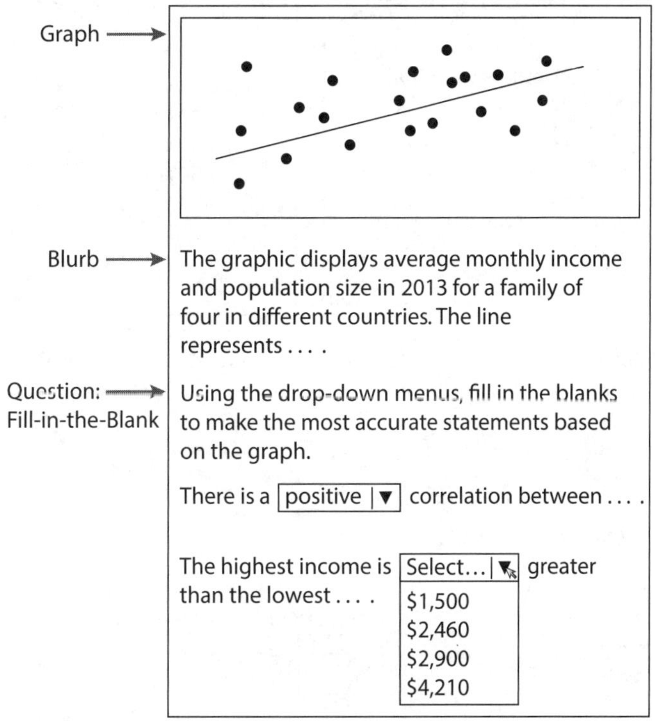
Graph
Blurb
The graphic displays average monthly income and population size in 2013 for a family of four in different countries. The line represents . . . .
Question: Fill-in-the-Blank
Using the drop-down menus, fill in the blanks to make the most accurate statements based on the graph.
There is a positive correlation between . . . .
The highest income is Select... greater than the lowest . . . .
$1,500
$2,460
$2,900
$4,210

Graph problems are accompanied by a **Fill-in-the-Blank** question with two separate parts to complete. You'll be given one or two sentences with two drop-down menus placed somewhere in the text, offering you multiple-choice options to fill in the blanks. You may have anywhere from three to five answer choices for each blank, and you will need to answer both parts correctly in order to earn credit for the given problem.

As the image shows, the answers could be numerical or in word form. Because you cannot see the multiple-choice answer options automatically, it's important to train yourself to click the drop-down arrows and view the answers very early in your process—before you even begin to try to understand the graph or process the statements. Knowing the form of the answers will help you to decide what approach to use when solving the problem.

Multi-Source Reasoning

Like Reading Comprehension prompts, Multi-Source Reasoning prompts will present you with a bunch of text along with a set of questions based on that text. Unlike RC passages, however, the information in MSR can include tables, charts, graphs, or other diagrams along with the text, and all of the information provided is spread across two or three tabs that can only be viewed one at a time. In order to answer the accompanying questions, you must integrate information from different tabs—many people dislike MSR for this reason.

MSR will feel like an RC passage: The prompt will stay on the left-hand side of the screen the whole time, but you will have a series of different questions appear on the right-hand side of the screen. Most of the time, you'll have a total of three separate accompanying questions. Here is an example:

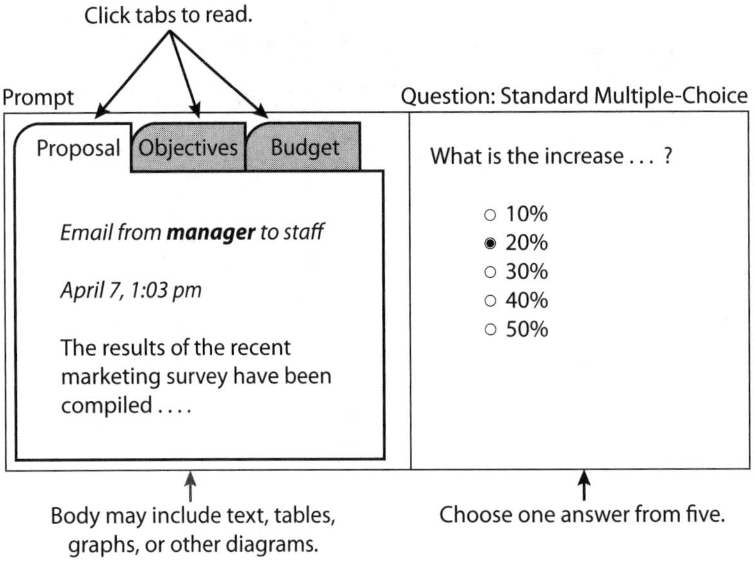

The image above is an example of one type of question for an MSR prompt. Here's an example of the other type of question, shown with the same prompt:

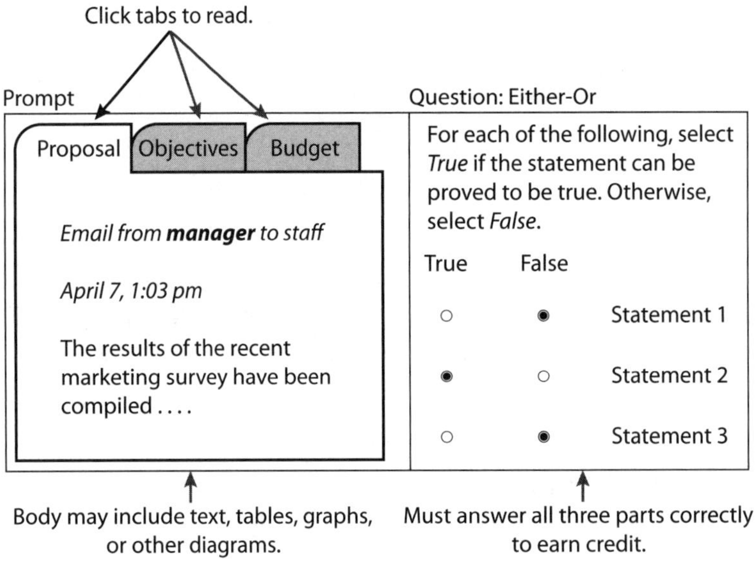

MSR questions always come in one of these two forms: standard multiple-choice or the same either-or form that you already saw with Table problems.

Each separate screen is its own question. Anything that appears on the same screen is a single (possibly multipart) question. The second example shows one either-or question with three parts (three statements); all three parts must be answered correctly in order to earn the point for that question.

Since there are three separate questions for an MSR prompt, you have the chance to earn three separate points, one for each question.

Most often, just one of the questions will be in typical multiple-choice format with five answer choices, among which you select one. This is the only type of IR question that is not multipart.

The other two MSR questions are usually either-or questions (each with three parts). These will work the same way either-or questions do for Tables, and you can use the same approaches to answer them.

Two-Part Analysis

Superficially, Two-Part Analysis (Two-Part) problems look very similar to multiple-choice problems from the Quant and Verbal sections of the test—until you get to the answers.

The example below fairly closely resembles a standard Quant problem, though as the name implies, you'll have to answer two questions (one in each column). The prompt appears first, typically in paragraph form, and the question is always below that:

3

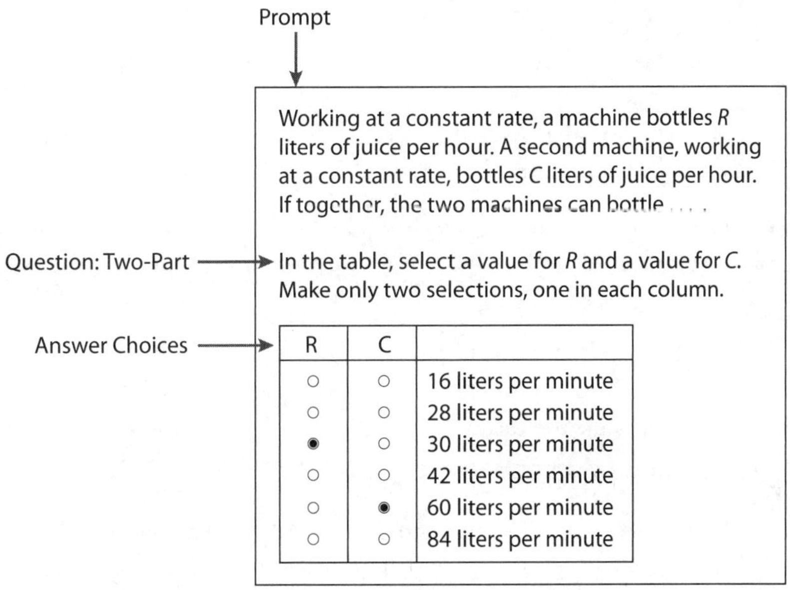
Prompt
Working at a constant rate, a machine bottles R liters of juice per hour. A second machine, working at a constant rate, bottles C liters of juice per hour. If together, the two machines can bottle . . .
Question: Two-Part
In the table, select a value for R and a value for C. Make only two selections, one in each column.
Answer Choices
R
C
16 liters per minute
28 liters per minute
30 liters per minute
42 liters per minute
60 liters per minute
84 liters per minute

Finally, you'll see a little table that contains your available answer choices in the right-hand column, along with two labeled columns on the left side. Those first two columns will be the two parts of the question you need to answer. Notice that the answer choices are the same for both parts; this will always be the case. As with all multipart questions, you'll need to answer all parts correctly in order to earn credit on Two-Part problems.

Two-Parts can also closely resemble classic Critical Reasoning problems—perhaps they'll ask you to both strengthen and weaken an argument. You may even see a logic-based problem, in which you're given a series of constraints and asked a scenario-based question. For example, you may be given various criteria for setting a time for a meeting (times that certain people are or are not available, people who must attend versus those whose attendance is optional, and so on), and then be asked to select the time that permits the maximum number of attendees—without leaving out anyone whose attendance is mandatory.

Two-Part prompts will often feel the least real-world and the most standardized-test-like of the IR question types. Two-Parts tend to be primarily quant-based, verbal-based, or logic-based; they don't often mix the three topic areas.

IR Connections to Quant and Verbal

The Integrated Reasoning section tests many of the same facts and skills tested on other sections of the GMAT and Executive Assessment.

Quant

For both Quant and IR, you'll need to know the same formulas, facts, and rules. The general problem-solving techniques you learn for the Quant section will also work on the IR section, but there is one key difference: The IR section includes lots of extra information, so you'll need to decide what to pay attention to and what to ignore. By contrast, problems in the Quant section rarely give information that you don't use.

Though any part of Quant is fair game on the IR section of the test, IR does emphasize two main content areas:

1. Fractions, Decimals, Percents, and Ratios
2. Statistics

You can find an overview of the two main Quant content areas in Appendix B of this guide. For more in-depth study of these and other topics, see the *GMAT All the Quant* guide.

A basic on-screen calculator is available during the IR section (but *not* during the Quant section). The calculator can be a blessing and a curse; it's important to learn when and how to use this tool (and when not to use it).

In the test screen window, click the link in the upper left corner to pull up the calculator. Note that the calculator will float above the problem on the screen; you can move it around, but you cannot click on the problem to answer the question while the calculator is still open.

The calculator includes the following limited functions:

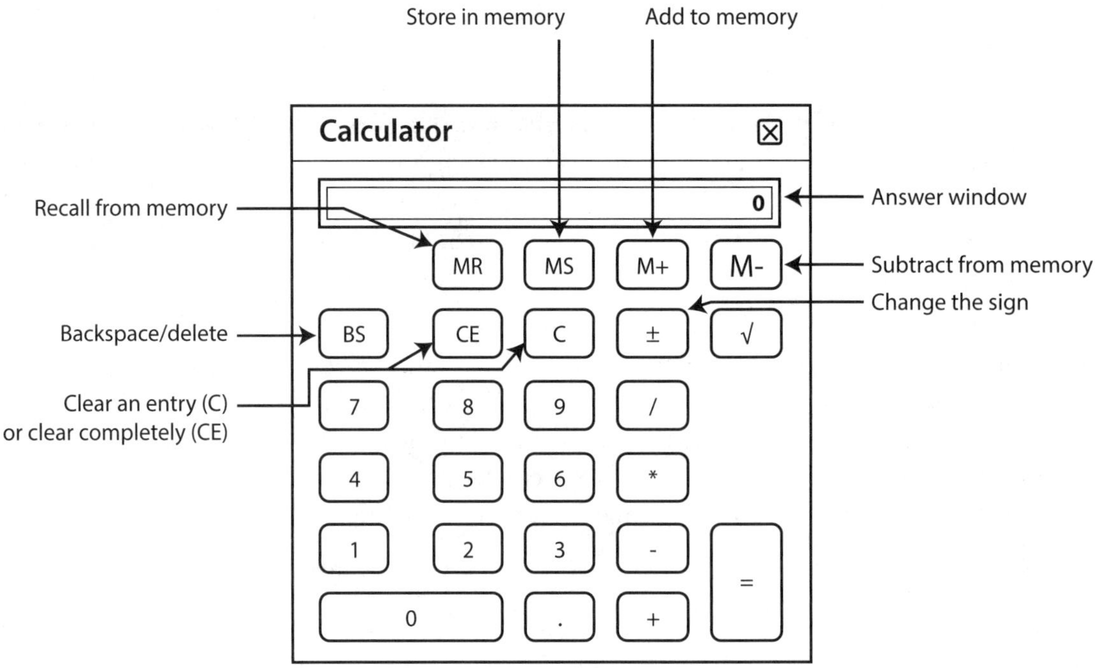

Have you ever panicked on a math problem during a test, picked up a calculator, and punched in some numbers, hoping inspiration would strike? If you ever find yourself doing this during the IR section, stop immediately, pick any random answer, and move on. The calculator is not a substitute for the actual solution process.

That said, don't hesitate to pull up the calculator when you do need it. The Quant section of the test often provides numbers that work pretty cleanly in calculations; the IR section, by contrast, won't hesitate to give you messy numbers. As long as you know what steps you want to take, the calculator can be a very helpful tool.

Verbal

The IR and Verbal sections overlap on reasoning and comprehension skills; the IR section does not include any grammar.

Some IR problems look very similar to Critical Reasoning problems. For instance, a Two-Part problem may ask you to find an assumption made by the argument and a flaw in the argument's reasoning.

CR, RC, and IR all have Inference problems, and you can use the same general approach for all three types.

The Executive Mindset

In order to do well on any test, you need to know how that test works. The Executive Mindset section at the beginning of this guide introduced you to the type of mindset that you want to take into both your studies and the exam itself.

Most people cannot answer all 12 problems in the 30 minutes given for the section; there is simply too much information thrown at you to answer each problem in an average of just 2.5 minutes. The vast majority of test-takers, then, will need to guess on at least one IR problem—and probably closer to two to four.

You'll learn more later in this guide about how to know when to bail (guess immediately and move on); just know for now that you will need to do this, whether you are taking the GMAT or the Executive Assessment.

GMAT Scoring

As you work through the section, you will earn points based upon the number of full problems you answer correctly. A full problem is one that appears on its own separate screen; it will have one, two, or three parts to answer. If there are multiple parts, you must answer all parts correctly in order to earn any credit for that problem.

While the exact scoring scale has never been published, research has uncovered the fact that you can miss a number of problems and still earn a good score on the test.

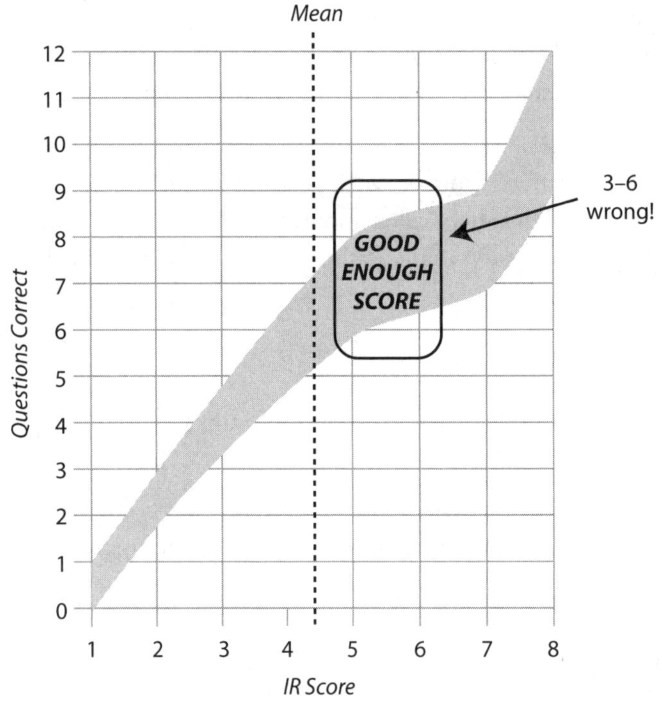

As shown in the graph above, the mean score is between a 4 and a 5, so it's recommended to aim for a score of 5 or higher. If you are applying to an especially competitive school, aim for a 6 or higher. (And if you would like to apply for internships or jobs with the top management consulting or investment banking firms, aim for a 7 or 8 on IR.)

If you're aiming for a score of 6 or higher, plan to bail (guess very quickly) on 2 problems in the section. You'll be able to spend an average of 3 minutes on the remaining 10 problems—and you'll be able to answer some of these incorrectly and still hit your target score.

If you're going for a score of 5, plan to bail on three problems in the section. You'll have nearly 3.5 minutes to spend on the remaining nine problems. Likewise, you'll be able to answer some incorrectly and still hit the target.

EA Scoring

Because the Executive Assessment is a relatively new exam, not as much is known about the scoring. The scoring range for the IR section is 0–20 points, but on the official practice test, someone who answers every single question correctly earns only 18 points, so that appears to be the practical upper limit. (The same is true for the Quant and Verbal sections of the EA.)

If you can hit a score of 10 on each of the three sections, your Total score will be 150, which is the minimum score many schools say they want to see. If you plan to bail on two or three problems, as recommended, you can still miss two to three additional problems and score at or close to a 10.

In Sum

By the time you're done studying for Integrated Reasoning, you should know two things:

1. Your weakest problem types and content areas
2. Your target score

You'll bail quickly on two or three harder problems in your weaker areas and allocate that saved time to other problems in the section.

As you work through the rest of this guide, you'll learn more about how and when to bail. While you study, keep in mind that you need to have a good handle on your own strengths and weaknesses in order to make good decisions about when to move on. (This is true for the whole test, not just IR!)

How to Tackle IR: Understand–Plan–Solve

Here is a universal 3-step process for Integrated Reasoning:

Step 1: Understand the prompt and question

Step 2: Plan your approach

Step 3: Solve the problem

At first glance, the process might seem pretty simple. Most test-takers, though, jump straight to solving and pay minimal attention to the earlier steps. If you want to get through IR with a minimum of stress and a good score, follow the process!

Step 1: Understand the Prompt and Question

Your first goal is just to comprehend the given information.

First, glance at the entire problem. What type is it? Do any clues jump out at you that tell you what this is testing overall? For example, if you see a pie chart, then you know you've got a Graph problem and there's a good chance you'll need to do some work with percentages. If you see any type of problem with answer choices in sentence form, then you know you've got a more verbal-focused problem.

Next, as you scan the given data, ask yourself *what* and *so what* questions:

***What* is this?**

- What is the title or accompanying text indicating?
- What is in this tab, this row, or this column?
- What kind of graph is this and what do these points on the graph represent?
- What kinds of numbers are these—percents or other relative values? Or absolute quantities, such as dollars or barrels?

***So what* about this?**

- How is this information organized?
- Why is this part here? What purpose does it serve, relative to everything else?
- How does it all fit together? What connections can you draw?

Finally, articulate the question to yourself in your own words. The wording is sometimes meant to trick you. For instance, the question might imply that you must use an advanced, time-consuming solution process when a much faster shortcut exists. You do have access to an on-screen calculator, but sometimes you can estimate aggressively and don't need to pull up the calculator at all.

Some people like to read the question first, before reading the prompt. If you like to do this, that's fine—just don't skip either step!

Step 2: Plan Your Approach

Next, you'll need to figure out what to *do* with the given information in order to solve the problem:

- What do you have to look up? Which portions should you reread?
- What pieces of information do you have to combine?
- What formulas will you need to use?
- What shortcuts can you use? Can you eyeball a figure or a list of numbers? Can you estimate?
- How should you organize your work?

You won't be able to determine every last step of your plan before you start to solve, but do think about the kind of information you need and how to organize it. Also think about the types of calculations you will need to do or steps you will need to take.

Step 3: Solve the Problem

Now, execute your plan of attack. If you've done the first two steps well, you'll make this step easier for yourself. And if you realize that you don't really understand some aspect of the prompt or question, or you can't devise a decent plan of attack, then you know that you should guess and move on. Save that time and mental energy for some other problem in this section!

When you do decide to move to the final step and solve, think about how to organize your work before you dive in. Be methodical; write notes and calculations clearly to minimize the chance of careless mistakes. Finally, if you get stuck at any step along the way, don't dwell. Go back and try to unstick yourself once. If you're still stuck, guess and move on to the next question. Remember: You can get a lot wrong and still get a good score!

As you work your way through the rest of this guide, you'll learn how to apply the Understand–Plan–Solve process to each of the four IR problem types.

CHAPTER 4

Table Analysis

In This Chapter

- UPS for Tables
- Sort, Eyeball, and Estimate
- Review and Improve on Tables

In this chapter, you will learn how to apply the Understand–Plan–Solve (UPS) process to Table problems. You'll also learn how to apply the SEE (sort, eyeball, estimate) approach to Tables.

CHAPTER 4 Table Analysis

Table Analysis (Table) problems, unsurprisingly, require you to analyze tables of information.

The table appears on the left side of the screen; the question appears on the right side of the screen. Table prompts are always accompanied by one three-part **Either-Or** question (e.g., true/false, yes/no).

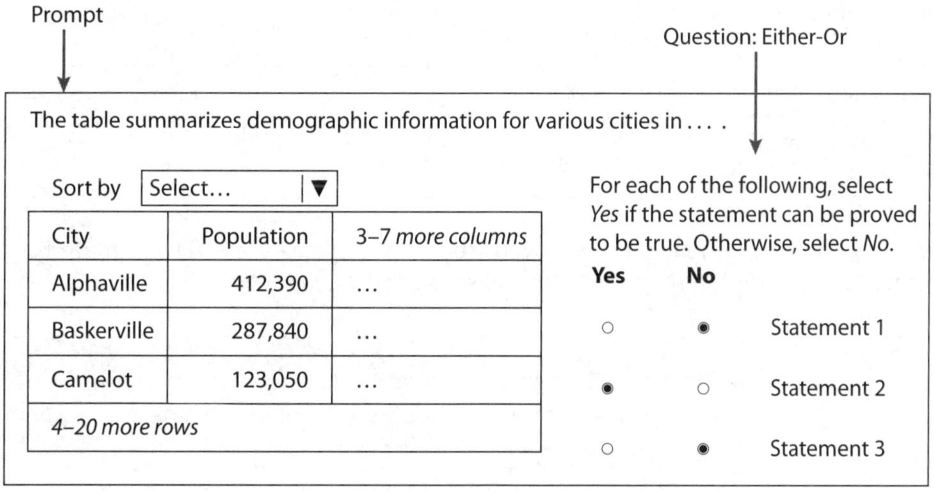

The table can be presented alone or with an associated blurb, which can range from a simple title to a full paragraph of information that you must understand in order to fully process the data in the table. The blurb is sometimes placed on the left side, above the table, and sometimes on the right side, above the question.

You'll be able to sort the data by column, but if you're an experienced Excel user, you'll find the sorting very limited. The sorts will always be ascending, and you can perform only one sort at a time (no secondary sorts).

UPS for Tables

As discussed in the Introduction to Integrated Reasoning chapter earlier in this guide, you'll use the UPS process to solve all IR problems, including Tables. UPS stands for Understand the prompt and question, Plan, and Solve. (If you skipped that section of Chapter 3, you may want to go back and read it now.)

Table problems usually have a quantitative focus, often testing general Statistics (mean, median, standard deviation, range, correlation, and so on) and Fractions, Decimals, Percents, and Ratios.

Take a look at the following Table problem:

The table displays data from the different divisions of Company X in 2011. Market shares are computed by dividing Company X's total sales (in dollars) for that division by the total sales (in dollars) made by all companies selling products in that category. Market shares are separately calculated for the world (global market share) and for the United States (U.S. market share). Ranks are based on Company X's position relative to other companies competing in the same market.

Division	Global market share	Global market rank	U.S. market share	U.S. market rank
Agriculture & Food	8%	6	12%	4
Health Care & Medical	12%	4	18%	2
Household Goods & Personal Care	5%	5	10%	4
Performance Plastics	30%	1	26%	1
Water & Process Solutions	19%	1	26%	1

Select *Yes* if the statement can be proved true for Company X in 2011 based on the information provided in the table. Otherwise, select *No*.

Yes	No	
○	○	There is a positive correlation between global market share and U.S. market share.
○	○	The same division of Company X is the median of Company X's five divisions by both U.S. market rank and global market rank.
○	○	The Performance Plastics division had greater market share in at least one other country than it had in the United States.

Step 1: Understand the Prompt and Question

The table and the blurb accompanying it are the prompt; focus on that first.

To understand the prompt, you're going to do three things: glance, read, and jot.

First, **Glance** at the table title (if applicable) and at the column and row headers. In this case, there is no title. The first column shows *divisions* that appear to be categories for different types of products. The next two columns provide global market data, and the final two provide U.S. market data. That data has to do with market share (in percent form) and market rank.

Next, **Read** the blurb (if any) given with the table. If the blurb explains specific parts of the table, examine the relevant parts as you read:

- In this case, the blurb indicates that the table contains data about the divisions of one specific company. Now you have the full context for the first column of the table.

- Next, the blurb explains how market share is calculated. Glance again to reinforce the message: The *Global market share* column shows market share for the entire global market and the *U.S. market share* column shows market share for just the U.S. They are both in percentage form. (Note: The U.S. market is a subset of the global market, since the global market is comprised of the markets of all countries.)
- Finally, the blurb indicates that the table shows how each division ranks against all other companies in that geographic region; again, glance at the table to reinforce the message.

Time to **Jot**. Take another glance over the full table to make sure you know the kind of data you have and how it is presented, then consider what you want to jot down. Your goal is not to make an inventory of everything you read. Rather, jotting at this stage can help to reinforce the major messages and keep you oriented properly as you try to solve the problem.

In this case, you might jot down something like this:

Global vs. U.S.
Share % + Rank for each

If you are not completely sure that you fully understand what you just reviewed, pick a cell or group of cells in the table and then articulate to yourself what the value or values represent. For example, the Household Goods & Personal Care division has a global market share of 5% and is ranked fifth in the global market in that category. There are four other companies that outrank this division of Company X in the global market (i.e., four other companies each make at least 5% of the global sales in that category).

If you can do this, great! Move on to the question. If you can't, consider whether you want to do this problem at all. If not, guess randomly—and immediately—and move on.

It is possible that a table blurb will contain complex additional information—that is, information about something other than the specific data in the table. For instance, in this example, the blurb provides some extra detail regarding how those numbers are calculated.

When this happens, you may not be able to fully understand or process this information until later. That's okay. You don't have to bail now if you don't understand that type of information. As long as you understand the basic information contained in the table, keep going.

Let's move to the question. It will first provide directions and then give you a box with three statements. Here is the question text for this problem again:

Select *Yes* if the statement can be proved true for Company X in 2011 based on the information provided in the table. Otherwise, select *No*.

Yes	No	
O	O	There is a positive correlation between global market share and U.S. market share.
O	O	The same division of Company X is the median of Company X's five divisions by both U.S. market rank and global market rank.
O	O	The Performance Plastics division had greater market share in at least one other country than it had in the United States.

This is an either-or problem; Table prompts always use this problem type. You will be asked to select one of two answers in either X or Y form: in this case, either *Yes* or *No.*

Three statements accompany the question; your task is to choose a single option for each statement. In order to earn credit for this problem, you have to answer all three statements correctly.

As with the prompt, your first goal is to understand the question asked. In this case, the question is whether you can *prove* each statement *true* based on the information provided. The *for Company X in 2011* language is given in order to avoid having to specify those details in each statement; they aren't going to try to trick you by asking a question about a random Company Y or a different year, for which no data is given, just to see whether you're paying attention.

Next, glance through the three statements.

First, are they more quant-based (you're asked about some actual math concept) or verbal/analytic-based (you're asked to infer or otherwise analyze in a way that doesn't involve computation)?

The first statement mentions correlation, a quant topic, but the other two are focused on your ability to read the table properly, so they are more verbal or analytical in nature.

Also note that the three statements look fairly different, so you will probably need to solve each one separately. This is the case most of the time on Table problems, but occasionally the statements are very similar and can be solved using the same process—sometimes even simultaneously.

Next, read the first statement. If it seems straightforward, go ahead to the next step in the process. If not, skip that statement for now and read the second one. You never need to solve the statements in order; you can start with whichever one seems easiest to you. (If you read all three statements and realize you don't want to start with any of them, guess immediately and move on.)

Step 2: Plan Your Approach

Assume that you decide to start with the first statement:

Yes	No	
○	○	There is a positive correlation between global market share and U.S. market share.

First, remind yourself of any math concepts, formulas, or rules you might need. In this case, what does *positive correlation* mean?

Two sets of data have a positive correlation when the two sets of numbers increase together or decrease together. For example, the age of a tree and the circumference of its trunk have a positive correlation: As age increases, so does the circumference of the trunk.

Next, on a Table problem, it is usually the case that sorting the table in some way will make it easier for you to find the answer. What kind of sort would be useful in this case?

The two relevant columns are *Global market share* and *U.S. market share*. Should you sort by the former or the latter? Sometimes, this will be obvious. Other times, you may have to think about this a bit or even try a couple of different sorts.

In this case, you can sort by either column. You'll be looking to see whether they "go in the same direction"—that is, they both generally increase or they both generally decrease.

Step 3: Solve the Problem

Here's the table sorted by *Global market share*:

Division	Global market share	Global market rank	U.S. market share	U.S. market rank
Household Goods & Personal Care	5%	5	10%	4
Agriculture & Food	8%	6	12%	4
Health Care & Medical	12%	4	18%	2
Water & Process Solutions	19%	1	26%	1
Performance Plastics	30%	1	26%	1

As global market share increases, U.S. market share does increase, indicating a positive correlation.

The answer to the first statement is *Yes*.

Evaluate the second and third statements in the same manner, repeating the Plan and Solve steps. Here's the second statement:

Yes	No	
O	O	The same division of Company X is the median of Company X's five divisions by both U.S. market rank and global market rank.

The median for five divisions would be the division in the third position when the numbers are placed in increasing order. You can sort either by global rank or by U.S. rank, your choice. Here is the sort by *U.S. market rank*:

Division	Global market share	Global market rank	U.S. market share	U.S. market rank
Performance Plastics	30%	1	26%	1
Water & Process Solutions	19%	1	26%	1
Health Care & Medical	12%	4	18%	2
Agriculture & Food	8%	6	12%	4
Household Goods & Personal Care	5%	5	10%	4

The Health Care & Medical division falls into the third-highest position for the U.S. rankings. Now, take a look at the *Global market rank* column. In a longer or more jumbled list, you might have to sort a second time by this column. In this case, though, the numbers are almost in order already; only the 5 and the 6 would need to be swapped. The Health Care & Medical division is again in the third position of the five divisions within Company X.

The answer to the second statement is *Yes*.

Here is the third statement:

Yes	No	
○	○	The Performance Plastics division had greater market share in at least one other country than it had in the United States.

In this case, you don't need to sort any columns; you can answer using just the Performance Plastics row:

Division	Global market share	Global market rank	U.S. market share	U.S. market rank
Performance Plastics	30%	1	26%	1

U.S. market share is 26% and global market share is 30%. In other words, this division had a higher market share globally than in the United States.

The U.S. market is a subset of the global market, so U.S. sales contribute to the company's global sales. What is the relationship between global market share and market share in just one country?

If the U.S. market were the global market—that is, these products were sold nowhere else in the world—the division's U.S. market share and global market share would be identical. The U.S. and global market shares are not the same, though, so there must be at least one other country in which the Performance Plastics division has sales.

Next, imagine that the division has 26% market share in every country where these products are sold. If that were the case, the company would have exactly 26% of the global market share as well. Its global share is greater, though—it has 30% of the market share globally. So it must have a greater share of the market somewhere other than the United States.

That scenario is what the third statement says: Company X's global market share, at 30%, is larger than its U.S. market share, so it must have a greater market share in at least one other country than it does in the United States.

The answer to the third statement is *Yes*.

The answers are as follows:

Yes	No	
◉	○	There is a positive correlation between global market share and U.S. market share.
◉	○	The same division of Company X is the median of Company X's five divisions by both U.S. market rank and global market rank.
◉	○	The Performance Plastics division had greater market share in at least one other country than it had in the United States.

Sort, Eyeball, and Estimate

On any Table problem, don't do any work at all until you've considered how to **SEE**: **Sort**, **Eyeball**, and **Estimate**. These steps will save you a lot of time and mental effort on the exam.

Try this problem:

The table presents the Q1 medical equipment sales figures for 9 regional sales teams and the forecasted changes in sales for each quarter (relative to the prior quarter). Q1 figures are in thousands of dollars.

		Forecast		
Sales team	**Q1 sales (in thousands)**	**Q2 (change from Q1)**	**Q3 (change from Q2)**	**Q4 (change from Q3)**
A	$ 902	−13.2%	8.6%	−8.3%
B	$1,301	−10.4%	−11.6%	−6.0%
C	$1,793	17.0%	−7.4%	13.2%
D	$ 877	−6.8%	−5.1%	−4.6%
E	$3,866	1.2%	3.5%	3.7%
F	$2,576	4.9%	4.2%	1.4%
G	$2,140	−5.4%	3.3%	2.2%
H	$3,214	15.6%	8.5%	−7.6%
I	$4,325	12.4%	−12.4%	16.8%

For each of the following statements, select *True* if the statement can be shown to be true using the information provided. Otherwise, select *False*.

True	False	
O	O	According to the forecasts, the team with the median sales in Q1 will also have the median sales in Q2.
O	O	Of the teams that are projected to see a quarterly increase in Q3, more than half are expected to see an additional quarterly increase in Q4.
O	O	The number of teams projected to see a quarterly decrease in both Q2 and Q3 is greater than the number of teams projected to see a quarterly decrease in both Q3 and Q4.

How did it go? Before continuing to read here, go back over your work to look for opportunities to answer any of the statements more efficiently. Pay close attention to any steps that seemed cumbersome; can you brainstorm any ideas to streamline or entirely avoid that part?

Step 1: Understand the Prompt and Question

The blurb is pretty basic; it just explains what's in the table.

Interestingly, actual quantities are given only in the Q1 column. The other three are all percentage increases or decreases from the immediately preceding quarter (the column to the left). Pick a row and follow the numbers to the right to see how they work.

How about row G? This team had Q1 sales of $2,140,000. Since all given numbers are in thousands, you can ignore the final three zeros and just call it $2,140. In Q2, sales are projected to decline: The forecast for Team G is a negative percent change. If you wanted to find the forecasted sales figure for Q2, you would either take 5.4% of the Q1 figure and subtract or you would multiply the Q1 figure by $(100 - 5.4)\% = 94.6\%$. Sales are projected to increase in Q3 and Q4, though: The forecast for Team G is a positive percent change in both quarters.

So you can see at a glance whether the team is predicted to do better or worse than the immediately previous quarter, based on whether the percentage change is positive or negative—but you would have to crunch the numbers to know the actual sales figures for Q2, Q3, and Q4.

Mini Math Lesson

Percentages do funny things. For example, in the final row, Sales Team I is forecast to have a 12.4% increase in Q2 and a 12.4% decrease in Q3. Does that mean that their sales figure in Q3 ends up back where it was in Q1, at $4,325K?

Think about that. If you're not sure, go ahead and calculate the steps to see what happens.

First, if you take any number and increase it by a certain percentage, then decrease the resulting number by the same percentage, you will never end up back at the same starting point (unless your starting point was 0 or your percentage was 0%). Why?

Try some real numbers to see. If you have $100 and increase by $20, you'll have $120. Now, take that new figure and decrease by 20%: $120 − $24 = $96.

It will always be the case that 20% of a smaller number is less than 20% of a greater number, so when you increase by a certain percentage and then decrease by that same percentage, you'll always end up lower than where you started. The same is true for Sales Team I: For Q3, they are forecast to have sales below their starting point of $4,325K.

By the way, do you think Team G did better or worse in Q4 than in Q1? Make your best guess, then do the math to check. The answer is at the end of this section.

Back to the problem. Here's the question stem again:

> For each of the following statements, select True if the statement can be shown to be true using the information provided. Otherwise, select False.

Essentially, can the statement be proven true using the data in the table? If so, call that one true. If you can't prove it true *using the given data*, call it false.

Here's the first statement:

True	False	
○	○	According to the forecasts, the team with the median sales in Q1 will also have the median sales in Q2.

The statement says that the same team has the median sales in both Q1 and Q2.

Glance back up at the blurb; how many sales teams are there? Nine. (You don't have to count—the blurb says that there are nine teams. Always check the blurb first before you try to count the total number of rows; if it's a longer table, chances are the blurb will tell you.)

Step 2: Plan Your Approach

To find the median, the numbers have to be listed in order, so you're definitely going to sort this thing. Finding the median for Q1 will be easy, since the Q1 column shows the actual sales figures.

Q2, though, is trickier, as it shows only the percentage increase or decrease from Q1. You do have a calculator, so maybe you just have to calculate the forecasted sales for each sales team in Q2?

There are nine rows. That's a lot of work.

So stop! Don't do annoying math. This is why you Plan before you Solve. First, sort by Q1 sales to find that median, then examine the data to think about the best approach for the Q2 data.

Step 3: (Start to) Solve the Problem

Here's the table sorted by Q1 (and without Q3 or Q4, since they don't matter for this statement):

Sales team	Q1 sales (in thousands)	Q2 (change from Q1)
D	$ 877	−6.8%
A	$ 902	−13.2%
B	$1,301	−10.4%
C	$1,793	17.0%
G	$2,140	−5.4%
F	$2,576	4.9%
H	$3,214	15.6%
E	$3,866	1.2%
I	$4,325	12.4%

The median for Q1 is the fifth one from the top or the bottom: Team G.

Go back to your Plan stage for a minute and remind yourself of the question: Does Team G have the median for *both* Q1 and Q2? In other words, does Team G stay in the fifth position or does its position change?

Team G's sales will decrease a little bit, but not that much—a little over 5%. The numbers for each team are far enough apart that you can use benchmarks to estimate the change:

10% of \$2,140 = \$214
Half of that = 5% = \$107
\$2,140 − \$107 ≈ \$2,000

Next, eyeball the data to see which other teams *might* change positions relative to Team G. (To *eyeball* is to look and think logically about the data; you won't be doing any actual calculations, even at an estimation level.)

Teams D, A, and B are already below $2,000 in Q1 and they all decrease further, so they will still stay below Team G in the Q2 list. No need to calculate anything for them.

Team C, by contrast, increases, so it could jump past Team G. You might have to do some calculations, so jot down Team C on your scratch paper as a reminder.

Next, take a look at the teams that have Q1 sales greater than those of Team G. They are already higher than $2,000 and all four increase in Q2, so they will stay above Team G in that quarter.

The only possibility is that Team C will swap places with Team G. Eyeballing the data saves a lot of time that would have been wasted with unnecessary calculations!

Jot down the numbers you need, then figure out how to do the calculations. Finally, plug the calculations into your calculator to solve:

4

	Q1 value	Q2 % change	Q2 value (rounded)
Team C	1,793	+17.0%	(1,793)(1 + 0.17) = $2,098
Team G	2,140	−5.4%	(2,140)(1 − 0.054) = $2,024

Team C does indeed pass Team G in Q2, so Team C is now the team with the median sales volume. Is it *not* true that the same team is in the median position for both quarters.

The correct answer for statement 1 is *False*.

Here is statement 2:

True	False	
O	O	Of the teams that are projected to see a quarterly increase in Q3, more than half are expected to see an additional quarterly increase in Q4.

This time, the statement focuses on Q3 and Q4. When you see something like *of the teams that* (fall into a certain category), the statement is giving you a qualifier: It wants you to consider only a subset of the categories given in the table.

In this case, the desired subset is those teams that will have a Q3 increase. You don't technically have to sort in order to see which teams have positive percentages in Q3, but do so anyway. Sorting by Q3 will group those teams together so that you don't inadvertently include teams that you don't want.

Before you do that, though, jot down what the statement wants you to find. Here's one way to do that:

$$\text{Is } \frac{(\text{Q3 AND Q4}) + \%}{\text{Q3} + \%\text{ only}} > \frac{1}{2}?$$

Here's another:

Do >50% of teams that ↑ in Q3 *also* ↑ in Q4?

Note it in any way that makes sense to you. Here's the data sorted by the Q3 column:

Sales team	Q3 (change from Q2)	Q4 (change from Q3)
I	−12.4%	16.8%
B	−11.6%	−6.0%
C	−7.4%	13.2%
D	−5.1%	−4.6%
G	3.3%	2.2%
E	3.5%	3.7%
F	4.2%	1.4%
H	8.5%	−7.6%
A	8.6%	−8.3%

Only five of the teams will have a quarterly increase in Q3: Teams G, E, F, H, and A. Of just those teams, three also have an increase in Q4: Teams G, E, and F.

Therefore, three out of five of the teams increase in both quarters. This is greater than 50%, so this statement is true.

The correct answer for statement 2 is *True*.

Here is the third statement:

True	False	
O	O	The number of teams projected to see a quarterly decrease in both Q2 and Q3 is greater than the number of teams projected to see a quarterly decrease in both Q3 and Q4.

This is very similar to statement 2: You're looking for two adjacent quarters with the same trend. You have to do it for two groupings this time, not just one. Jot this down in a form that makes sense for you; here's one way to do that:

Is # (Q2 and Q3) ↓ more than # (Q3 and Q4) ↓ ?

Make sure to evaluate each part separately so that you don't, for example, mistakenly carry over Q2 data into the examination of Q3 and Q4. And you'll again minimize your chances of a careless error if you sort as you go. First, sort by Q2:

Sales team	Q2 (change from Q1)	Q3 (change from Q2)
A	−13.2%	8.6%
B	−10.4%	−11.6%
D	−6.8%	−5.1%
G	−5.4%	3.3%
E	1.2%	3.5%
F	4.9%	4.2%
I	12.4%	−12.4%
H	15.6%	8.5%
C	17.0%	−7.4%

Two teams are projected to have a decrease in both Q2 and Q3: Teams B and D.

Next, sort by Q3:

Sales team	Q3 (change from Q2)	Q4 (change from Q3)
I	−12.4%	16.8%
B	−11.6%	−6.0%
C	−7.4%	13.2%
D	−5.1%	−4.6%
G	3.3%	2.2%
E	3.5%	3.7%
F	4.2%	1.4%
H	8.5%	−7.6%
A	8.6%	−8.3%

Again, two teams are projected to have a decrease in both Q3 and Q4; Teams B and D again.

It is *not* the case that the number of teams with decreased sales in both Q2 and Q3 is greater than that in both Q3 and Q4.

The correct answer for statement 3 is *False*.

The answers are:

True	False	
○	◉	According to the forecasts, the team with the median sales in Q1 will also have the median sales in Q2.
◉	○	Of the teams that are projected to see a quarterly increase in Q3, more than half are expected to see an additional quarterly increase in Q4.
○	◉	The number of teams projected to see a quarterly decrease in both Q2 and Q3 is greater than the number of teams projected to see a quarterly decrease in both Q3 and Q4.

Whenever you have to solve a Table problem, don't do any real work until you consider how you can SEE (sort, eyeball, estimate) to save yourself time and effort. On this problem, all three of these strategies made a big difference for the first statement. For the other two statements, sorting saved a small amount of time and—perhaps more important—helped to minimize the chances of a careless error.

Don't hesitate to pop up the on-screen calculator when you need it; just make sure that you know what you need to calculate before you start punching in numbers. It's a good idea to write out the calculations you want to do before you start using the calculator.

Mini Math Lesson Redux

So, what happened with Team G?

Most people will guess that Team G ends up with greater sales in Q4 than in Q1...but it doesn't! Why do people think this and why are they wrong?

Nobody wants to do tedious calculations, so most people will just compare the percentages. Sales are forecast to decrease by 5.4% in Q2, but then increase by 3.3% and 2.2% in Q3 and Q4, respectively. That seems like a 5.5% increase, since 3.3% + 2.2% = 5.5%, and 5.5% is greater than 5.4%, right?

Maybe. Would you rather have 5.5% of $10 or 5.4% of $1,000,000?

Why?

Here's how the calculations play out:

$$\begin{aligned} &Q1: && 2{,}140 \\ &Q2: -5.4\% = (2{,}140)(1-0.054) &&= 2{,}024 \\ &Q3: +3.3\% = (2{,}024)(1+0.033) &&= 2{,}091 \\ &Q4: +2.2\% = (2{,}091)(1+0.022) &&= 2{,}137 \end{aligned}$$

Since the first step is a decrease, that lowers the base figure that Team G is working from. The forecast is for an increase of 3.3% in Q3, but the increase is calculated from a lower base (2,024) than the initial 5.6% was taken away from. The same is true for the 2.2% increase.

So, for the same reason that you would much rather have 5.4% of a greater number than 5.5% of a smaller one, Team G finished the year a bit lower than it started.

Alternatively, you could use the calculator to find the cumulative change for Q4 in one combined step: cumulative change from Q1 to Q4 = (0.946)(1.033)(1.022) = 0.9987 = 99.87%.

In other words, the Q4 sales forecast is 99.87% of the Q1 sales figure. This is less than 100%, so Q4 sales will be less than Q1 sales.

Review and Improve on Tables

The Understand–Plan–Solve process will help you both solve the problem and review your work afterwards. Do review the problem regardless of whether you got it right or wrong.

If you answer a question incorrectly—or aren't fully confident about something you answered correctly—review each step of the process. Did you overlook, misunderstand, or fail to comprehend any information in the prompt? Did you inadvertently answer a different question than the one that was asked? Was there a better way to approach the problem? Did you make any mistakes at the solution stage?

If you answer it correctly, ask yourself whether there are any opportunities to do it better next time. Where could you streamline any steps of the process? (Consider both time and mental energy.) What if it took a long time to solve and you don't see a way to make it faster—do you really want to do this on the real test? It might be better to guess quickly and spend your time elsewhere.

Grab a timer and give yourself approximately 3 minutes to try this problem:

The table summarizes total sales information for a large production company for the first six months of 2014. The table also provides percent of total sales from the company's only three divisions (Electronics, Housewares, and Automotive). The company acquired the automotive division in March of that year.

2014 Monthly Sales by Product Line

Month	Total ($, thousands)	% Electronics	% Housewares	% Automotive
January	3,890	47.09	52.91	0.00
February	4,204	49.75	50.25	0.00
March	6,561	34.19	33.00	32.81
April	6,982	36.44	34.03	29.53
May	6,613	37.97	33.34	28.69
June	7,028	34.58	34.00	31.42

For each of the following statements, select *Would help explain* if the statement would, if true, help explain some of the information in the table. Otherwise, select *Would not help explain*.

Would help explain	Would not help explain	
○	○	Consumer purchases of electronics typically drop just after the month of December, but they revive within two to three months.
○	○	Companies that have electronics, housewares, and automotive product lines tend to have higher total sales in housewares than do companies that sell only one or two of these product lines.
○	○	The housewares division took a $1.1 million loss in March due to an accounting change.

How did it go? Before reading the explanations below (or even checking whether you got it right), ask yourself whether you're generally happy with how things went. If you want to try any part of the problem again, go ahead; you don't need to time yourself, and you can look up anything you want elsewhere in this guide.

Then, take a look at the correct answers (scroll to the end of this section—the answers are not immediately below so that the question isn't "spoiled" while you are working the problem). Does knowing the correct answer make you want to check or redo anything? Go ahead.

Finally, work your way through the official solution—but stop whenever you get a good idea about anything. See how far you can push that idea yourself before you continue reading the official solution. Make yourself work for it! You'll learn better that way.

Step 1: Understand the Prompt and Question

The accompanying blurb explains that the table provides total and percent of sales numbers across six months. It also explains why the Automotive division seemingly had no sales in January and February: because that division was acquired in March.

The Total column shows a significant jump in March, corresponding with the acquisition of the new division. Other than that, sales are generally increasing, though May shows a drop. The percentages for Electronics and Housewares drop in March, but this occurs because a third division is added; *sales in dollars* haven't necessarily dropped in the other two divisions, just their *share* of total sales.

This fact—that a new division was acquired partway through the period—means the data is going to be a little odd. Make a note to yourself to be especially careful with any questions that ask you to bridge the pre- and post-acquisition periods—perhaps jot down Feb and Mar on your scratch paper as your reminder. You may have to do some calculations in order to be able to compare the numbers in a meaningful way.

> For each of the following statements, select *Would help explain* if the statement would, if true, help explain some of the information in the table. Otherwise, select *Would not help explain*.

The *if true* language in the question stem sends a specific message: You are supposed to accept each statement as true. In other words, your job here is not to decide whether the statement is true. Rather, assuming already that the statement *is* true, does that statement help to explain some portion of the data that you see in the table?

This question is essentially the opposite of what you were asked to do on the last problem. You're not taking the table data and seeing whether you can prove that the statement is true. You're starting from the given statement and seeing whether it makes that data make sense.

Here's the first statement:

Would help explain	Would not help explain	
O	O	Consumer purchases of electronics typically drop just after the month of December, but they revive within two to three months.

Step 2: Plan Your Approach

Just after the month of December would be January, and January is included in the data. The statement is limited to the Electronics division.

Assume that this statement is true. If so, what would you expect to see in the data? It should be the case that January and possibly February Electronics revenues should be lower and then the numbers should increase possibly in February and certainly in March. Check the data to see whether this trend exists.

Ah, but the table doesn't show revenues just for the Electronics division. It shows total revenues and then the percentage of those revenues attributed to each division. So you are going to need to do some calculating to see what's happening with the revenues in this one division.

Step 3: Solve the Problem

From January to February, you have only the two data points (Electronics and Housewares), so you can eyeball the numbers. The Electronics percentage for February increased month-over-month, as did total sales, so Electronics purchases did go up from January to February. Did they go up in March as well?

4

In March, the Electronics percentage was 34.19%, or approximately $\frac{1}{3}$ of total revenues. Revenues were \$6,561, or approximately \$6,600, so a third is about \$2,200. (Note: The revenues are in thousands in the table—that is, revenue was really about \$6.561 million—but you can ignore that detail when you're just trying to figure out whether revenue increased or decreased.)

Total revenues in February were about \$4,200 and Electronics represented 49.75% of that, or about 50%. So February revenues were about \$2,100.

If you feel that the numbers are so close (\$2,100 and \$2,200) that your estimations could be in error, pop up the calculator and calculate the figure for which you had to estimate more heavily—in this case, March. Jot down the calculation first on your scrap paper: (6,600)(0.3419). The value is \$2,243 (and change), so yes, it is the case that revenue increased in March.

Overall, revenue went up both from January to February and from February to March.

For March to April, you now have all three divisions in the mix, so you can eyeball again. Electronics increased its percentage share *and* total revenues increased, so Electronics went up yet again in this period.

This statement does explain what's happening with the data for the Electronics division. The correct answer for statement 1 is *Would help explain*.

Repeat the UPS steps as you work through the second and third statements. Here's the second statement:

Would help explain	Would not help explain	
○	○	Companies that have electronics, housewares, and automotive product lines tend to have higher total sales in housewares than do companies that sell only one or two of these product lines.

Hmm. If a company sells all three lines, then it tends to sell more in housewares than does a company with only one or two of these lines. This prompt is only about one company, though, so how can you tell anything about a company that sells only one or two of these product lines?

Wait! For the first two months of the period shown in the table, this company did sell only two of these product lines. So compare the company to itself, pre- and post-acquisition.

In this case, it isn't necessary to sort the data at all, but you will have to do a little number crunching:

Month	Total ($, thousands)	% Electronics	% Housewares	% Automotive
January	3,890	47.09	52.91	0.00
February	4,204	49.75	50.25	0.00
March	6,561	34.19	33.00	32.81
April	6,982	36.44	34.03	29.53
May	6,613	37.97	33.34	28.69
June	7,028	34.58	34.00	31.42

In February, Housewares had about 50% of sales, or about $2,100 (you can continue to ignore the *thousands* designation). It had a slightly higher percentage share in January, but total sales were $300 lower that month, so the dollar amount for Housewares in January was lower than in February.

In March, the automotive business was acquired. Now, Housewares dropped to 33% of total sales, but of a larger base: $6,561. Approximately one-third of that figure is about $2,200, so Housewares sales did grow from February to March.

In April, Housewares increased its share of sales and total revenues increased, so housewares was again greater in April than in February. Likewise, in both May and June, Housewares had a greater share than in March and total revenues were greater than in March, so the trend continues.

The correct answer for statement 2 is *Would help explain.*

Here's the third statement:

Would help explain	Would not help explain	
O	O	The Housewares division took a $1.1 million loss in March due to an accounting change.

Don't jump straight to the data and start calculating anything. Understand first. This statement talks about a loss, but the data in the table is entirely about revenues. A loss is a cost; it would be reflected in profits, not in revenues. So the data in the table can't help to explain this cost.

Note: The GMAT doesn't expect you to know about accounting—you'll learn that in grad school!—but it does expect you to know that Profit = Revenue − Cost.

The correct answer for statement 3 is *Would not help explain.*

The answers are:

Would help explain	Would not help explain	
◉	○	Consumer purchases of electronics typically drop just after the month of December, but they revive within two to three months.
◉	○	Companies that have electronics, housewares, and automotive product lines tend to have higher total sales in housewares than do companies that sell only one or two of these product lines.
○	◉	The Housewares division took a $1.1 million loss in March due to an accounting change.

If you made a mistake at any step along the way, first try to isolate the error. If you fell into a trap because of the confusing data switch in March, when the Automotive division was acquired, the unusual data there was your clue to pause for a moment. The two 0.0% entries really stand out; something weird happened. Try to understand what happened and why before you get to the statements.

Note that when a table adds a set of data partway through, you can't compare the data sets as easily, particularly when the percentages have to add up to 100% (as in this case). Expect at least one of the statements to hinge on that change, and be prepared to do a little number crunching.

In this case, you had to deal with that change in multiple statements; in fact, that was the main focus of most of the problem. You didn't even have to sort on this table.

Don't hesitate to pop up the on-screen calculator when you need it—just make sure that you know what you need to calculate before you start punching numbers. Also, you can estimate a lot of the time; for example, 50.25% is close enough to 50% to estimate, and then you don't need to pull up the calculator at all.

Practice Your Skills

You're ready to practice and get better at Tables! Because most IR problems have some amount of interactivity (e.g., you need to sort on Table problems), your practice problems are located online in your Atlas study center. If you have access to Manhattan Prep's *GMAT All the Quant* guide, you may want to review the chapter on Statistics before doing more Table problems.

CHAPTER 5

Graphics Interpretation

In This Chapter

- UPS for Graphs
- Types of Graphs
- Review and Improve on Nonstandard Graphs
- Review and Improve on Standard Graphs

In this chapter, you will learn about the types of standard and not-so-standard graphs that can appear on the exams, and you'll learn how to apply the Understand–Plan–Solve (UPS) process to all Graph problems.

CHAPTER 5 Graphics Interpretation

Graphics Interpretation (Graph) problems can be built on a wide variety of types of graphs, charts, and diagrams, even non-math-based ones. You'll see many examples in this chapter, particularly of the "traditional" types of math graphs.

(Note: In the real world of data analysis, graphs and charts are not quite the same thing. But for the purposes of the exam, you can use these two terms interchangeably.)

Graph prompts consist of some sort of graphic with some accompanying text. The question always has two parts and always appears below the graph prompt. The example below shows a traditional type of math graph: a scatterplot:

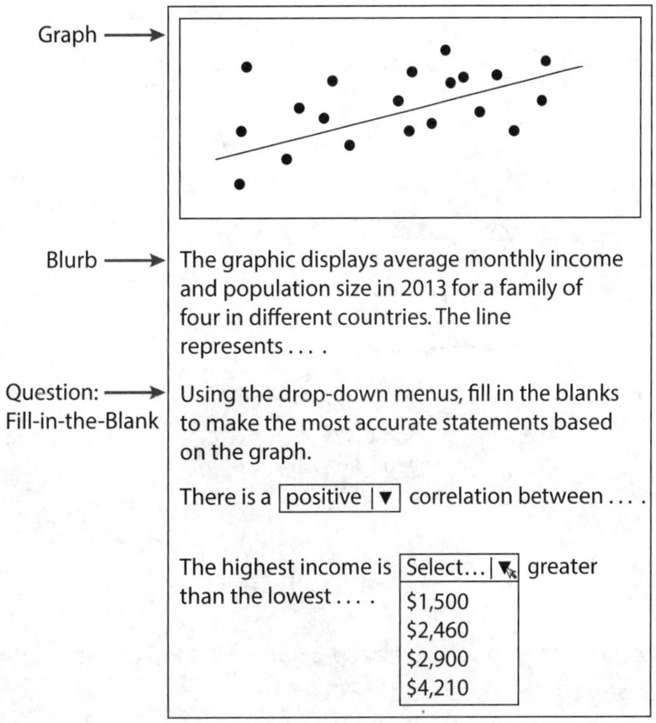
Graph
Blurb
The graphic displays average monthly income and population size in 2013 for a family of four in different countries. The line represents . . . .
Question: Fill-in-the-Blank
Using the drop-down menus, fill in the blanks to make the most accurate statements based on the graph.
There is a positive correlation between . . . .
The highest income is Select... greater than the lowest . . . .
$1,500
$2,460
$2,900
$4,210

Many graphs are common types that you've seen before: pie charts, bar charts, line graphs, and the like. The exam will expect you to know how to read these already; you'll learn how in this chapter. Other types could include Venn diagrams, timelines, organizational hierarchies, even geometry diagrams. If you are given a graph that doesn't fall into a standard math categorization, don't worry; you'll always be given instructions regarding what it is and how to read it.

The question consists of one or two sentences with two blanks. Your task is to fill in each blank with the best answer, chosen from a drop-down menu sitting right there in the blank. You'll have three to five answer choices for any one blank.

As on other Integrated Reasoning question types, this is considered a single multipart question, so you have to answer both parts correctly in order to earn credit for the problem.

The two blanks may be related to each other, in which case you'll need to solve both simultaneously. The two blanks may also be completely separate from each other.

UPS for Graphs

As discussed in the Introduction to Integrated Reasoning chapter, you'll use the UPS process to solve all IR problems, including Graphs. UPS stands for Understand the prompt and question, Plan, and Solve.

Graph questions most often have a quantitative focus, often testing general Statistics (mean, median, standard deviation, range, correlation, and so on) Fractions, Decimals, Percents, and Ratios. Some questions, though, are not quant-focused and instead revolve around your ability to figure out how to read the graph or diagram and think logically about the information presented.

Step 1: Understand the Prompt and Question

Take a look at this Graph prompt:

2013 Population 25 Years and Over

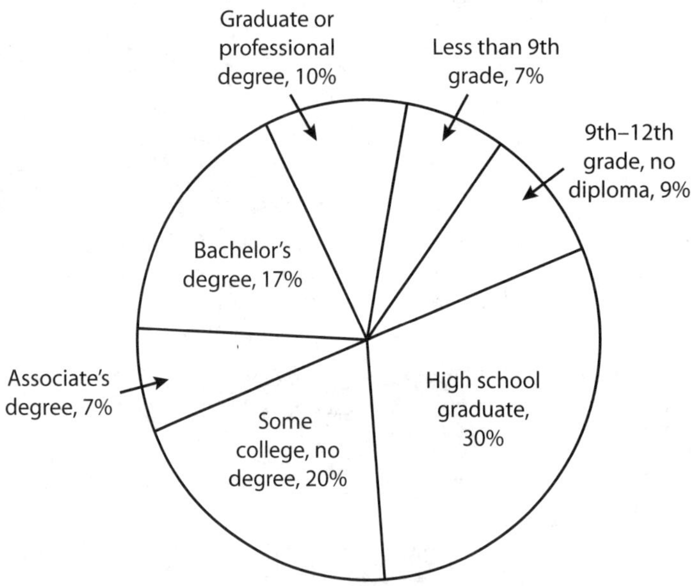

In 2013, the percent of the population aged 25 years and over that did NOT have a bachelor's, graduate, or professional degree is Select...

- 7%
- 16%
- 27%
- 59%
- 73%

(Note: Unlike this example, an official question will always have two blanks, each with its own set of options.)

What jumps out?

First, at a glance, this is a pie chart, one of the common types of math graphs. But don't start to look at the data yet. You have one other thing to do first.

As on Table problems, use SEE, with one slight change. This time, SEE stands for Select, Eyeball, and Estimate. On the actual test, you will see a box in each blank with the word *Select* and a little drop-down icon. Click on the word *Select* to glance at the multiple-choice options for that blank.

The form of the answers can completely change how you decide to approach a problem, so you want to glance at the answers very early in the process. In fact, glance at those answers right now. Notice anything?

The answers are in percent form, so math is involved. They are also spread pretty far apart. That's a clue that you may be able to estimate to solve. Now you know to examine the possibilities for estimation as you orient yourself to the prompt.

Now, go back to the graph. Read the title and any accompanying text in order to understand what the graph is all about. In this case, the title indicates that the chart provides information about a certain population in a certain year.

Next, dive into the graph itself. The wedges are labeled by type of schooling and show a percentage for each, but no real numbers. Since this is a pie chart, the percentages add up to 100%. (You don't need to check this. This is true for all pie charts.)

The answer choices are also in the form of percents, so you might need to add up some of the categories of the pie chart or maybe multiply some things together. The calculations could be tedious, but the answer choices are pretty spread apart, so you can estimate fairly aggressively. With luck, you won't even have to pull up the calculator.

Before you start to read the sentence, click on the first drop-down menu so that the multiple-choice options appear. Read the sentence with these options showing. (For a real question, which has two drop-downs, click on the second drop-down menu after you get past the part of the sentence that has the first blank.)

The question asks about certain categories of people: those with a bachelor's, graduate, or professional degree. Take careful note of that capitalized word NOT; the question is actually asking you to find the percentage of all others, *not* those three. You might even jot down that word.

Jotting down important information helps you to fix that information in your brain. You'll be less likely to forget or to make a careless mistake.

Step 2: Plan Your Approach

Given that there are five categories in the "wanted" group and only two in the "not wanted" group, it will be more efficient to add up the two "not wanted" categories and subtract from 100% in order to find the sum of the remaining five groups. That represents fewer math steps than adding up five numbers.

One more thing: The most common error is probably going to be that someone misses the word NOT and so solves for the "not wanted" group by accident. Expect to see that trap among the list of answers.

Further, since these two groups have to add up to 100%, if you have to guess, choose an answer that is part of a pair that adds to 100%. (In fact, only one pair of numbers fits this pattern: 27% and 73%.)

Step 3: Solve the Problem

Find the percentage for the two unwanted categories, bachelor's degree and graduate or professional degree:

$$17\% + 10\% = 27\%$$

Bingo! That's the "not wanted" group and that (trap) value is in the answers. Don't pick it. The correct answer is the other one in the pair, 73%.

In this case, it's not all that hard to add up the two numbers, 17 and 10. On another problem, with more cumbersome numbers, you could estimate at this stage, since the answers are pretty far apart.

Types of Graphs

Some graphs will be very familiar to you; others may seem unusual. You've probably seen a number of pie charts and bar graphs in your life, and you'll see these on Integrated Reasoning questions as well. On the other end of the spectrum, you might see a diagram that was completely made up for this test.

Here are some examples of more standard diagrams:

Column

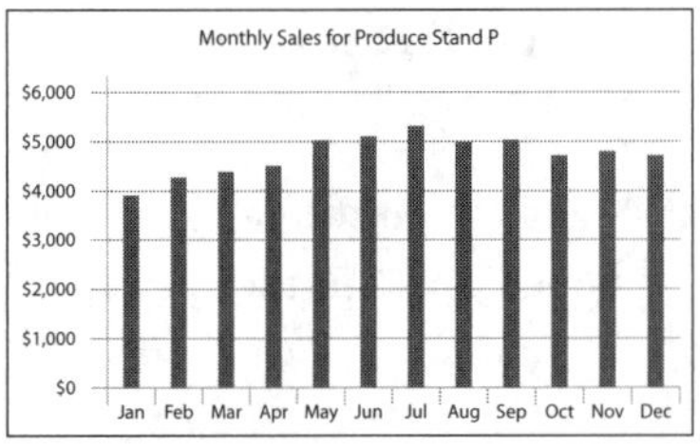

Stacked Column

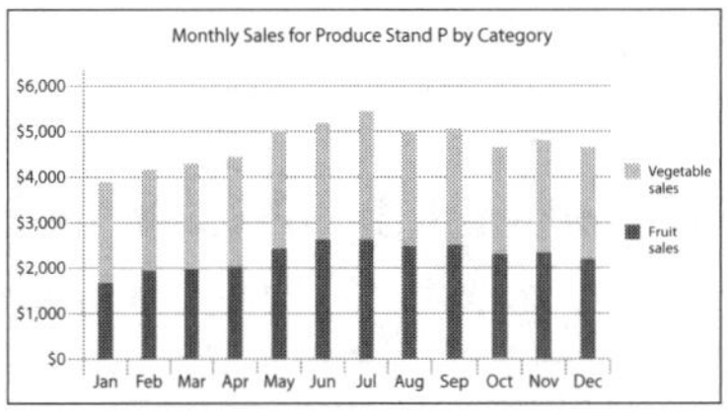

Clustered Column

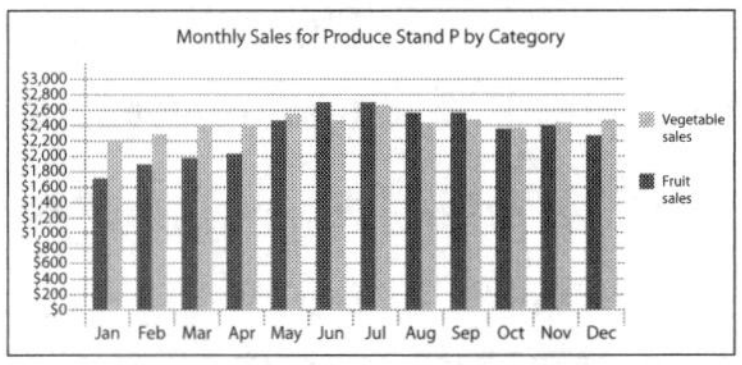

Bar

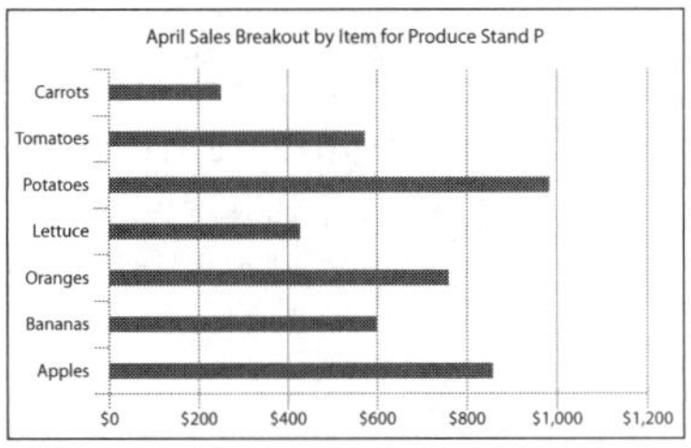

Line

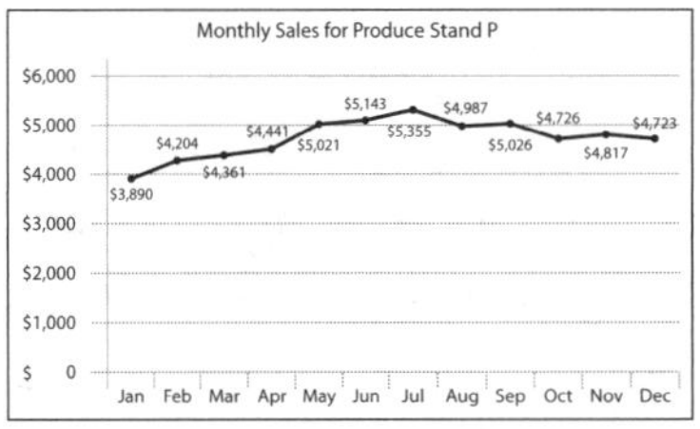

Scatterplot

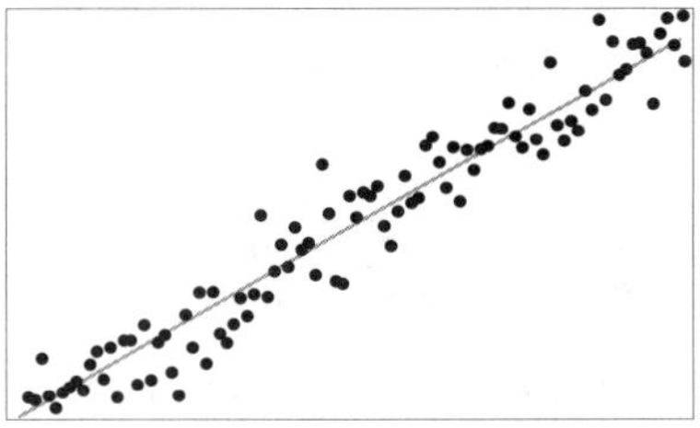

Pie Chart

April Sales Breakout for Produce Stand P

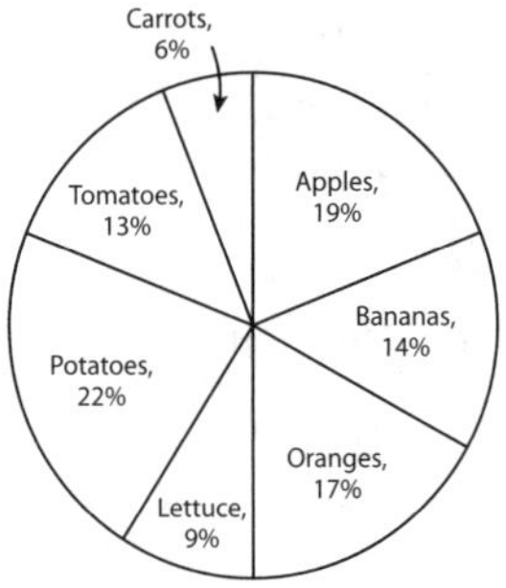

Total April Sales: $4,441

Bubble Chart

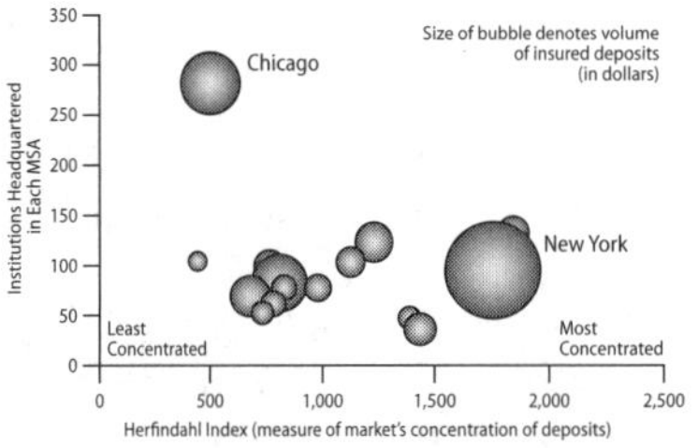

Venn Diagram

Students Taking French, Spanish, Both, or Neither

* Each square represents 5 students.

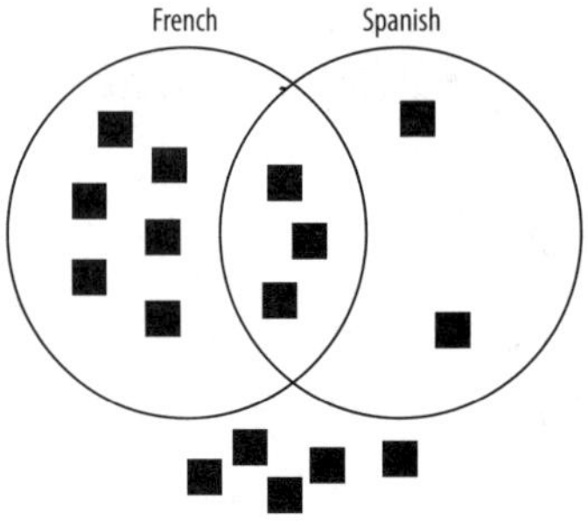

5

Organizational Chart

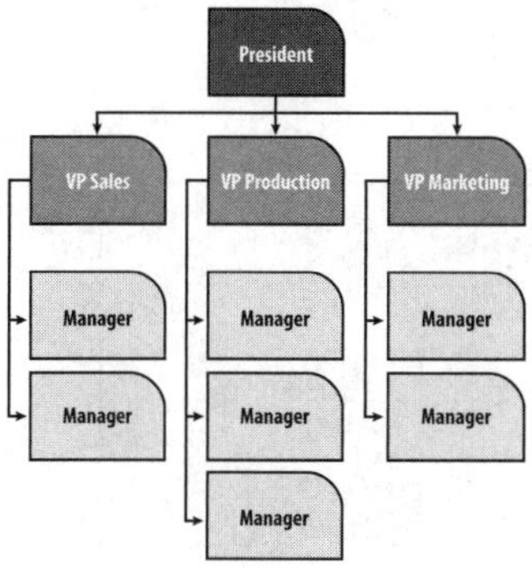

Timeline

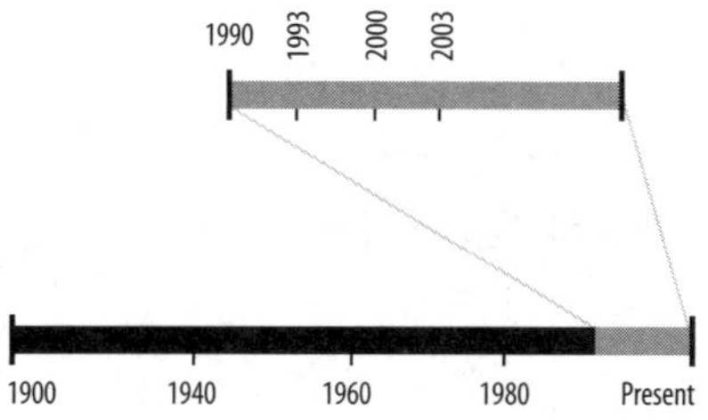

Others are possible!

Don't let all these columns, lines, and shapes scare you. These display formats are commonly used in business and academic settings today—and you've seen most, if not all, of the math-based ones before. When the exam does give a nonstandard visual, it will be the kind of diagram you might see in a company presentation, an annual report, or a business-school case study. You'll be given some kind of context to help you understand it.

The following are the most common types of standard math graphs that you're likely to see on the exam. As you review them, test yourself: See what you notice about a given chart before you read the chapter text explaining how that type of chart works. What kind of information can you glean? And what kind of analyses can you make?

Column and Bar Charts

A column chart shows amounts as heights, so you would scan for changes in the heights as you move from left to right. For example:

Column chart: Scan left to right.

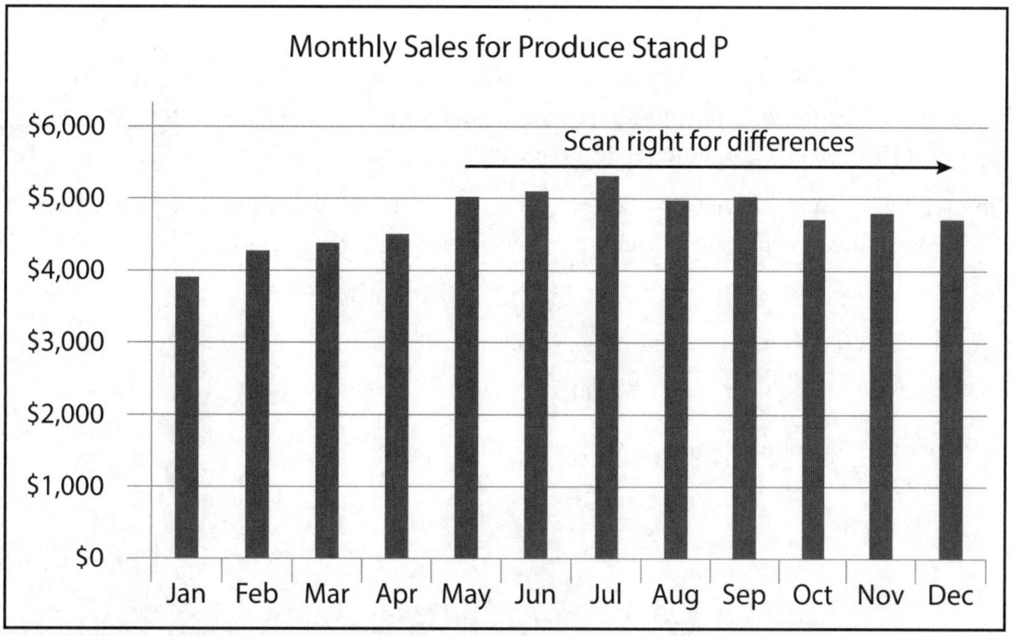

Similarly, bar charts show amounts as lengths, so you would scan for differences in those lengths as you move from top to bottom. For example:

Bar chart: Scan top to bottom.

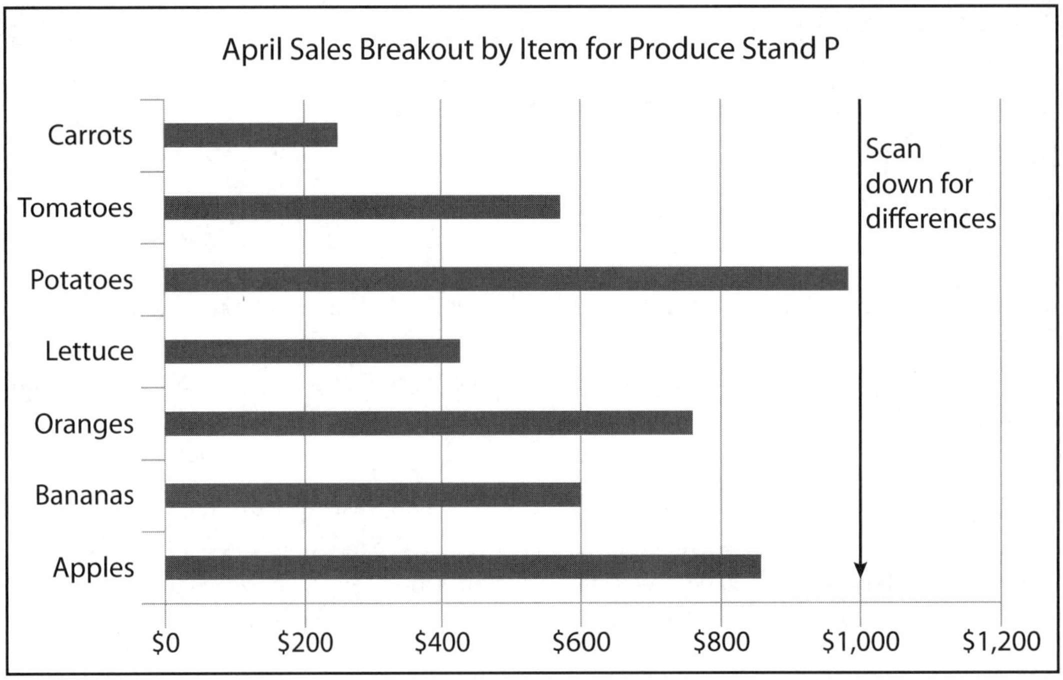

Column charts are often used to show trends over time, while bar charts are more frequently used for non-time comparisons (e.g., carrots vs. apples).

It can be difficult to read a value from a column or bar that ends *between* grid lines. The grid lines are those lighter grey lines that divide the graph into sections—for example, in the column chart, the grid lines show up at $1,000, $2,000, and so on up to $6,000.

If the column or bar does not end exactly on a grid line, you're going to have to estimate a little. Hold your finger, your pen, or even the edge of your scratch paper up to the screen to make a straight line, and take your best guess. (This will be close enough—don't worry!)

A question might ask you to calculate the percent increase or decrease from one time period to the next. Consider the Monthly Sales column graph given earlier, and answer the following:

What was the approximate percent increase in sales from April to May?

Estimate April sales to be $4,500 (the column ends about halfway between $4,000 and $5,000). May's column ends right on $5,000. Now use the percent change formula:

$$\frac{\text{May sales} - \text{April sales}}{\text{April sales}} \approx \frac{5{,}000 - 4{,}500}{4{,}500} = \frac{1}{9} \approx 11\%$$

Variations on Column and Bar Charts

If there is more than one series of numbers, the exam might use a stacked or clustered column chart. The stacked form places the two data points in the same column, one on top of the other, so it emphasizes the *sum* of the two series of numbers. For example:

Stacked column: Emphasizes *sums*.

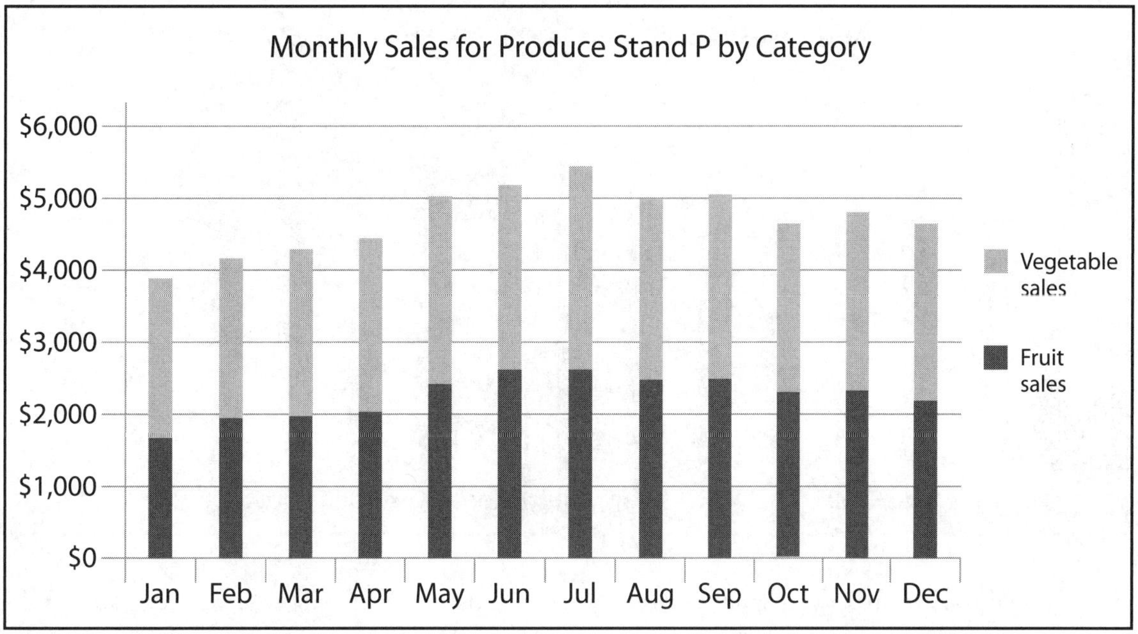

Note that, in the stacked column graph, it's easy to find the values for fruit sales and for total sales (fruit and vegetable together), but it's not easy to see the values for vegetable sales. You could use subtraction to find the value—for example, in January, vegetable sales were about $3,800 – $1,700 = $2,100.

You could also, though, eyeball by using the grid lines. The difference between any one set of grid lines is $1,000; call this one "segment" of the graph. Mentally take the entire lighter grey part of the column for January and move it up a little bit so that it starts right on the $2,000 grid line. (You can use your fingers to help eyeball this on the test screen.)

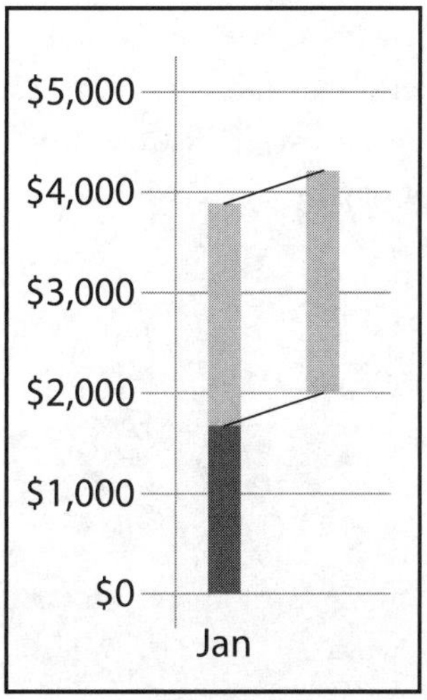

The lighter grey part of the column covers a little bit more than two segments of the graph, so the value is a little more than $2,000, or about $2,100.

The clustered column graph, by contrast, highlights which of the two values is greater at any point along the way. For example:

Clustered column: Emphasizes *differences.*

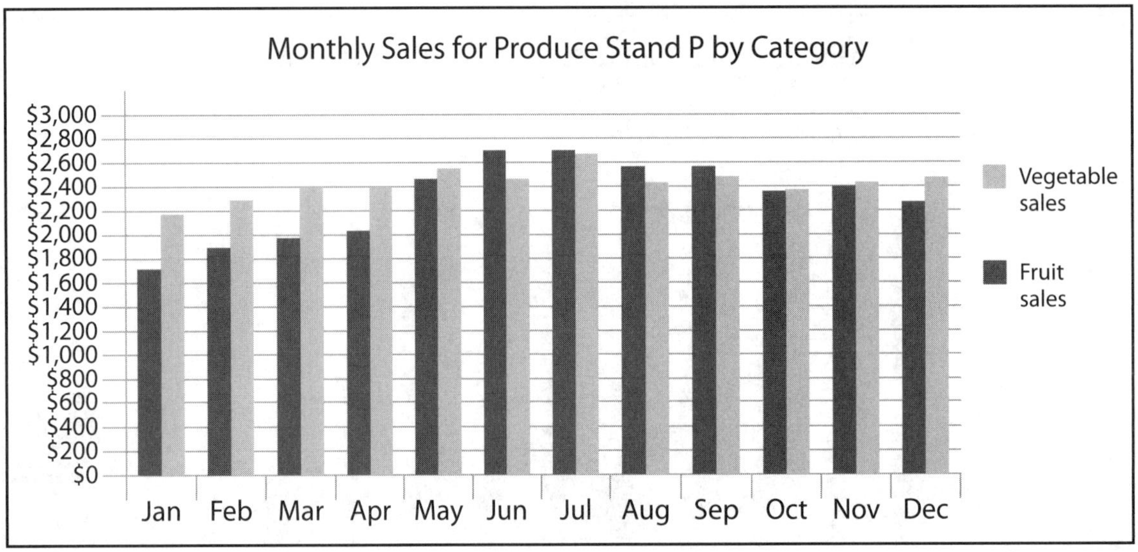

Now, finding the values for each individual category is straightforward, but you would have to add up the two paired columns to find the total sales for that month.

You might think that, if the test wants you to work with the total, it will give you the stacked column, since that shows the total—but not necessarily. And the test writers are not just being deliberately unhelpful to irritate you! The test wants to make sure that you know how to use the kinds of graphs you're likely to need to use in grad school, and you will often want to figure things out that don't fit perfectly with the type of graph given. They really are testing real-world skills with these problems.

Line Charts

Line charts are very similar to column charts. However, each number is shown as a floating dot rather than as a column, and the dots are connected by lines. The *x*-axis almost always represents time, since the lines imply connection. Although lines are continuous, do *not* assume that the data is itself continuous. If it is monthly data, for example, then the chart is showing just that one monthly data point—the line connecting one month to the next does not represent day-by-day data. For example:

Line

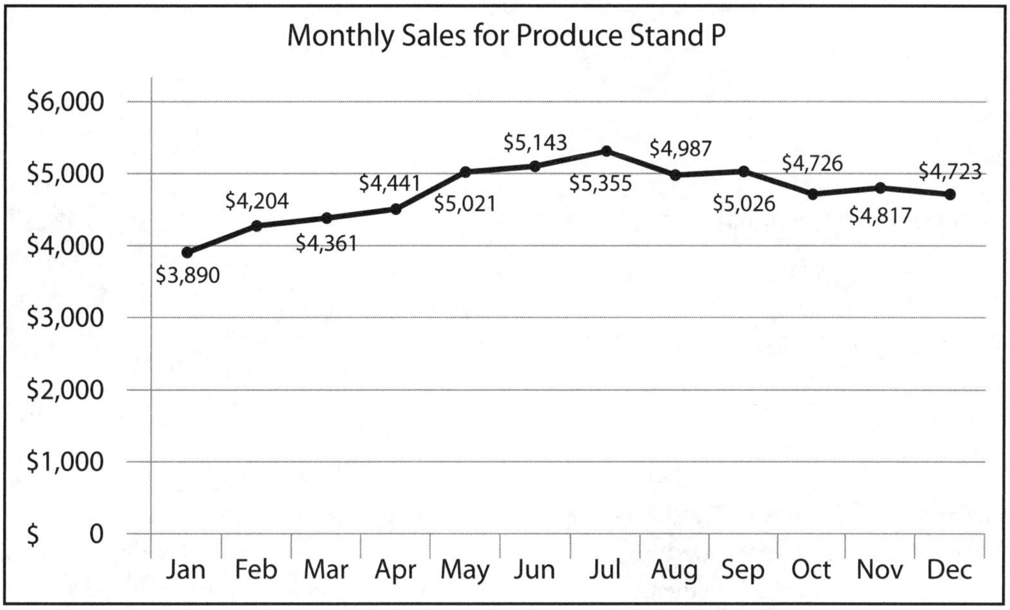

You could also have a line chart that contains multiple lines. Multiple lines are used to show multiple data series changing over time. When the desired emphasis is on the change within each set over time, this graph is more clear than a clustered column graph. For example:

Line (with two data series)

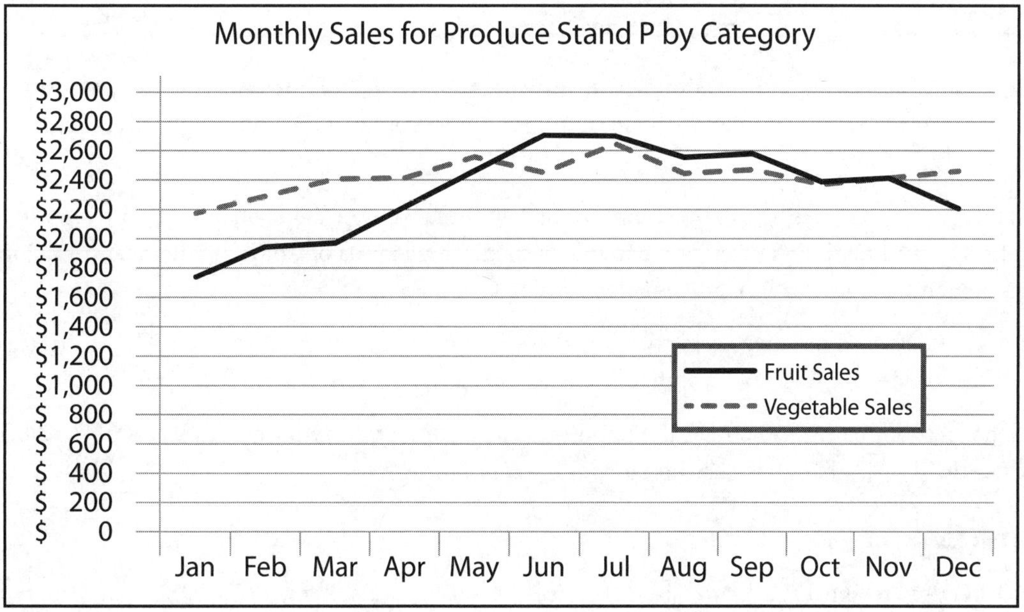

Compare this to the clustered column chart shown earlier. Both charts show how fruit sales compare to vegetable sales in any given month. Here, though, it's easier to see that fruit sales peak in the June–July time frame but are at their lowest in January, while vegetable sales are more steady throughout the year.

Scatterplots

A scatterplot is a more complex graph. It shows the relationship between two columns of data in a table. Each point on the plot represents a single record (a single row). For example:

Person	Age	Years since college
Amy	25	3
.	.	.
.	.	.
.	.	.

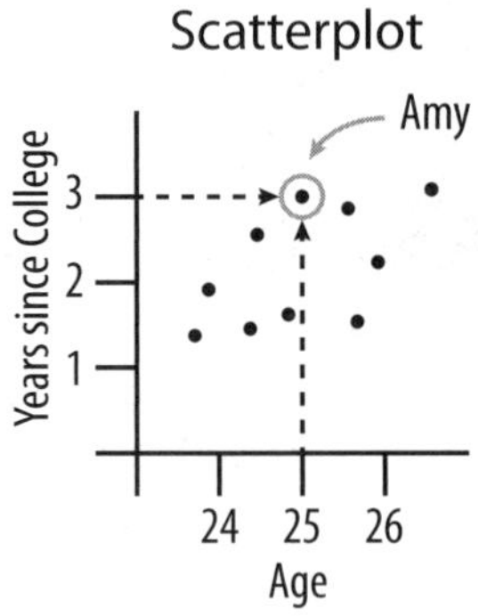

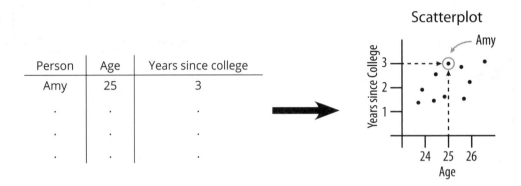

The overall pattern of the dots indicates how the two columns of numbers vary together, if at all. For example, glance back at the very first sample Graph problem shown at the beginning of this chapter. It shows a scatterplot. As you move to the right on the *x*-axis, the dots also tend to move up on the *y*-axis. In other words, as the *x* value increases, the *y* value also tends to increase.

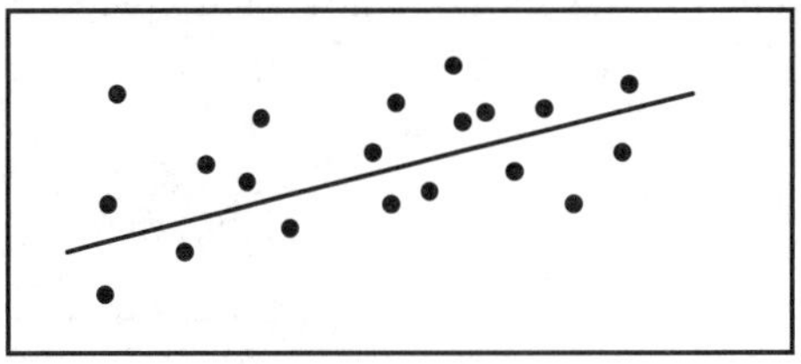

The graph above is showing a correlation between the two sets of data points—in this case, a positive correlation. If you draw a line showing the general trend of the points (as shown in the graphic), the line slopes upward from left to right.

If this sounds familiar, that's because you first learned about this in the Table chapter. Feel free to jump back there right now and remind yourself of what you learned. These kinds of callbacks are great for helping people to remember and recall the information they've learned.

A graph can also show a negative correlation: As one set of data points increases, the other set decreases. If you drew a trend line on such a graph, that line would slope downward from left to right.

If there's no trend—that is, sometimes the points go up and sometimes they go down, with no real connection—then the data in that graph has no correlation at all.

Pie Charts

A pie chart is used to show the relative sizes of "slices" as proportions of a whole, so pie charts are typically used when the test writers want to ask you about percents. The size of the angle of the pie slice is proportional to that item's percent of the whole, and all of the pieces of the pie add up to 100%.

Sometimes the pie chart shows real amounts and sometimes it directly shows percents, but even when there are real numbers, you will probably have to calculate something in terms of a percent. Percents on various slices will always be a percent of the whole.

Take a look at this example:

Pie

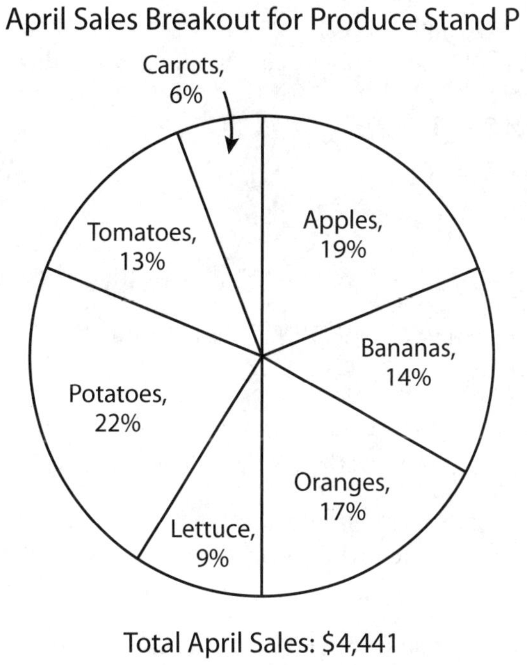

Since the total April sales figure is given ($4,441), you can calculate the dollar sales of any item, or any group of items, in the pie.

Try this problem:

> What is the total dollar value of lettuce and tomato sales for Produce Stand P in April?

Take a look at the following two sets of answers. How are they different? How might you approach the problem differently, depending on which set of answers you were actually given?

Set 1	Set 2
$103.52	$797.64
$514.91	$895.43
$977.02	$977.02
$1,348.37	$1,120.51

How would that change how you decide to solve?

In the first set, the answers are spread quite far apart, so you can estimate aggressively.

Lettuce and tomato sales are equal to 9% plus 13%, which sums to 22%, or about 20%.

You can take 20% of $4,400 (the approximate April sales) with a minimum of effort. First, take 10% by moving the decimal to the left one place. Then, multiply that number by 2 to get 20%:

$$20\% \times 4,400 = 440 \times 2 = 880$$

Is that close enough? Glance at the first set of answers. The calculation underestimated a bit, so the correct answer must be larger, and the only one that's close enough is $977.02.

That estimation is not quite good enough for the second set of answers, though, so make the calculation just a little more precise. You've already found 20%. Use that to find 2% and then add to get 22%:

$$\begin{array}{r} 20\% \times 4,400 = 440 \times 2 = 880 \\ 2\% \times 4,400 = 44 \times 2 = 88 \\ \hline 22\% \qquad\qquad\qquad = 968 \end{array}$$

Lettuce and tomato sales are approximately $968, so the correct answer is $977.02.

Note that you *under*estimated the starting number in the calculation. The value you calculate, therefore, will be too small but close enough.

If you don't spot the 22% shortcut—or if the numbers you're working with don't allow you to use that shortcut—you can try one other way. The first time, you underestimated a bit and got $880. Next, overestimate a bit: Find 25% of $4,400.

5

The fastest way to find 25% of a figure is to divide by 4 (or to divide by 2 twice). In this case, $4,400 divided by 4 is $1,100. This is an overestimation, so that last answer choice is too big. Only $977.02 works.

By the way, a pie chart can show only one series of data. If you see two pie charts, they represent two separate series of data.

Other Types of Charts

The test writers can draw any kind of diagram or visual they want. Don't panic. Read the title, read the labels, and try to understand how the graph is laid out visually. If you're stuck, focus on just one small part, such as a single data point. What does that point represent? What do you know about that piece of data? Then, work your way out from there.

(Or not! You will want to guess immediately on several Integrated Reasoning questions overall. If you see a graph that just doesn't make any sense, make this problem one of your guesses.)

Bubble charts look intimidating, but they are just scatterplots on steroids. Rather than two pieces of information about each point, you have three. In order to show that third dimension, all the little points are expanded to varying sizes—and those varying sizes give you a relative measure of that third dimension. For example:

Bubble

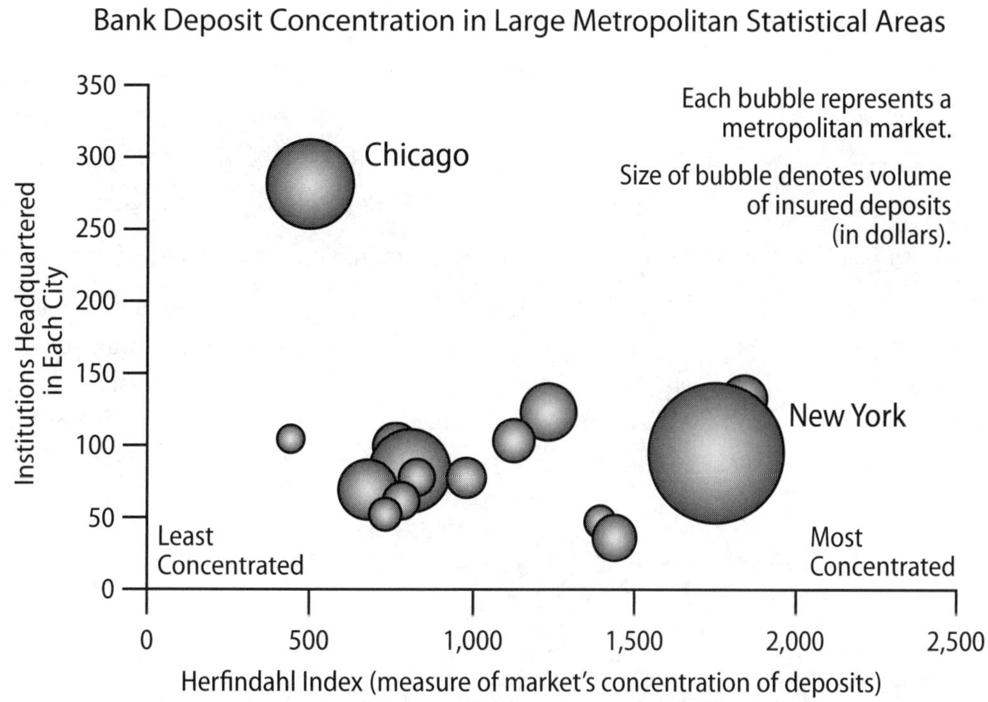

Sources: Summary of Deposits, June 2002; FDIC's Research and Information System, June 30, 2003.
Note: Fifteen largest markets shown, based on number of institutions headquartered there.

There are two really big bubbles labeled with city names, so compare them. New York has a bigger bubble than Chicago. What does that bubble represent? The *volume of insured deposits*. So more insured deposits are made in New York than in Chicago. (Not sure what insured deposits are? Don't worry about it—right now, it's enough to know that New York has more than Chicago does of whatever this thing is.)

The Chicago bubble is higher up the *y*-axis than the New York bubble. What does that mean? Look at the *y*-axis label: More companies of a certain type (banks in this case) are headquartered in Chicago. That's interesting.

Finally, the New York bubble is farther to the right along the *x*-axis. What does that mean? The *Herfindahl Index* is weird but the chart itself shows the text *Least Concentrated* and *Most Concentrated* at either end of the *x*-axis. So New York is more concentrated than Chicago—whatever *more concentrated* means.

You may only need to understand that New York has this characteristic, not what the label truly means, so don't spend any time now trying to "really" understand. Look at the question first and then decide what you need to try to understand more fully.

Speaking of the question, try this:

> There is ______ correlation between the value of insured deposits and the Herfindahl Index.
>
> (A) a positive
> (B) a negative
> (C) no

The question specifies two of the three dimensions: the Herfindahl Index (position along the *x*-axis) and the value of insured deposits (the size of the bubbles). A positive correlation would mean that the bubbles tend to increase in size the farther right you go on the *x*-axis. Is this the case?

Not really. The largest bubble is far to the right, but the next largest one is far to the left, as is the third largest and possibly the fourth or fifth largest.

Is this a negative correlation, then? In this case, the bubbles would be larger to the left and generally decrease as you move to the right—but the placement of New York absolutely kills this possibility.

The correct answer is *no* correlation. There isn't a consistent trend, or connection, between the placement of the bubble along the *x*-axis and the size of the bubble.

What else can the exam throw at you? You may have run across Venn diagrams during your study for the Quant portion of the exam. Venn diagrams consist of two (or three) overlapping circles, showing how two (or three) groups overlap. Here's a two-circle example showing the number of students in certain classes:

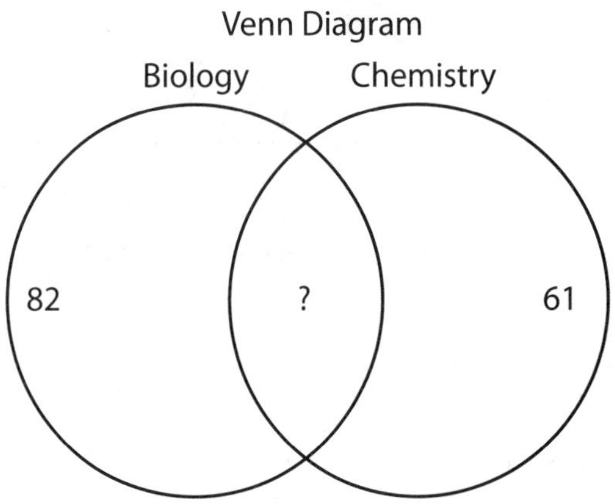

This Venn diagram indicates that there are 82 people in the biology-only group and 61 in the chemistry-only group, as well as an unknown number in the overlap between the two groups. The diagram would be accompanied by a blurb providing additional information, possibly asking you to calculate the number of people in both groups (or in neither group).

The organizational (org) chart and the expanded timeline shown below are good examples of non-math graphs. (Timelines don't have to run horizontally, by the way!)

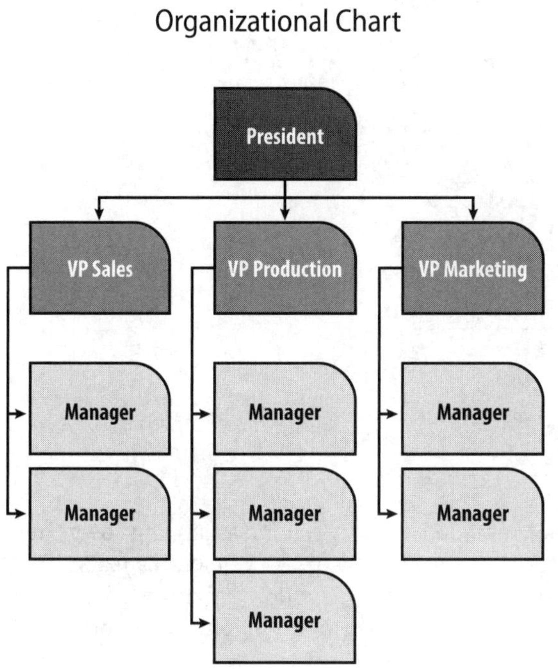

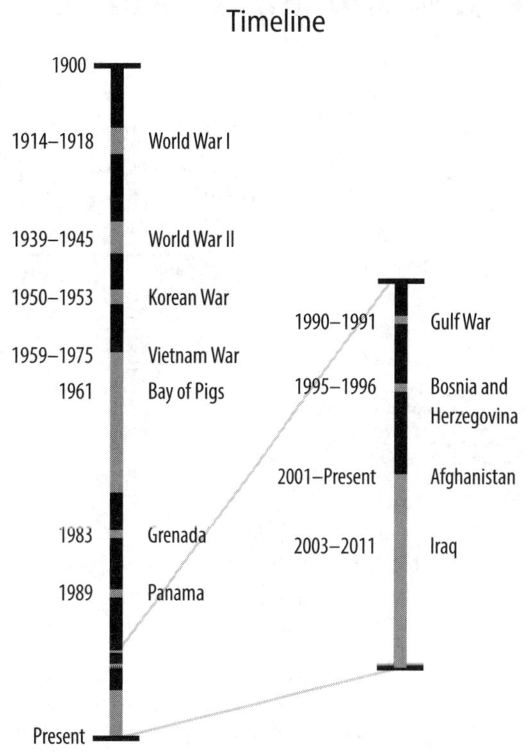

Typical org charts show hierarchical relationships within a business. Expanded timelines give you both a big picture of events in order and a "zoomed in" look at one part of the picture. Note that the scales in the different sections are different; be ready to make comparisons across those different scales.

Here are some other examples of nonstandard graphs, just to give you an idea:

- A diagram showing the workflow or set of steps a company uses to make a certain product
- A genealogy tree or other diagram to show inherited genetic traits or shared characteristics from one generation to the next
- A map showing data tied to different geographical regions
- A project schedule or timeline, possibly showing dependencies across different steps of the project

Anything is possible—which sounds more unsettling than it is. First, most of the nonstandard charts you see will specifically be designed to be read and used intuitively. After all, in the real world, poorly designed charts are rarely adopted for widespread use. Second, you will be given some direction in the blurb as to how to read the visual. Use the blurb to help you interpret the diagram.

Review and Improve on Nonstandard Graphs

Try out another problem, this time with a nonstandard graph:

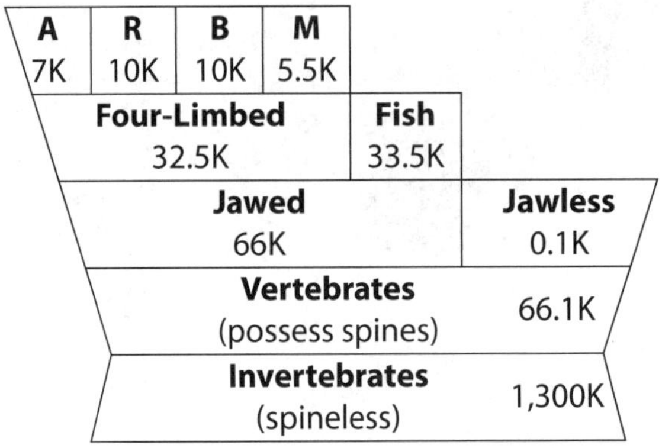

The diagram displays the number of living species represented by two nonoverlapping categories, Vertebrates and Invertebrates, which together comprise all animal species. The diagram also displays the various subcategories of Vertebrates and the approximate number of species in each (the abbreviation K stands for thousands). In the top row, A stands for amphibians, R stands for reptiles, B stands for birds, and M stands for mammals.

Based on the given information, use the drop-down menus to most accurately complete the following statements.

Four-limbed species represent approximately [Select... ▼] of all vertebrate species. Amphibians

- 2.5%
- 15%
- 35%
- 50%

and reptiles combined comprise approximately [Select... ▼] of all animal species.

- $\frac{1}{200}$
- $\frac{1}{100}$
- $\frac{1}{4}$
- $\frac{1}{2}$

How did it go? Before reading the explanation below (or even checking whether you got it right), review your work yourself. Is there anything you want to try calculating a different way? Do you want to double-check anything? Go for it.

Next, check just the correct answer. (Glance ahead. It's listed just before Step 1 of the walk-through.) Does knowing that give you any ideas for what to check or do a different way?

If you answered the question incorrectly—or aren't fully confident about something you answered correctly—review each step of the process thoroughly using the official solution. Did you overlook, misunderstand, or fail to comprehend any information in the prompt? Did you answer the question that was asked? Was there a better way to approach the problem? Did you make any mistakes at the solution stage?

If you answered the question correctly and were confident even before you saw the correct answer, then scan the walk-through below for any ideas about how to solve more efficiently. Are there any shortcuts or other methods you can use to make the job easier?

The correct answer for the first blank is fifty percent and the correct answer for the second blank is one one-hundredth. (These are written out in words so that you don't inadvertently spot the correct answers before you're ready to know!)

Step 1: Understand the Prompt and Question

The diagram is not a standard chart, so you will definitely use the blurb to help you understand it. Before doing that, though, take the first step in SEE: Click the *Select* drop-downs to see what the answers are. Both are math-focused. The answers for the first part of the question are in percentage form. They are far enough apart that you may be able to estimate at least enough to knock out some of the answers.

The answers for the second part of the question are in fraction form. The first two are clustered together and the final two are clustered together, so you may be able to eyeball enough to narrow down to two answers—that's a valid strategy if it looks like it may take too long to fully solve.

Now, examine the text. The blurb first mentions *two nonoverlapping categories, Vertebrates and Invertebrates.* Glance at the diagram itself: These two categories appear at the bottom.

Nonoverlapping means that no animal appears in both categories. Further, the first sentence also states that these two categories *together comprise all animal species,* so all animals are either V or Inv. Abbreviate as you jot down this information.

The blurb further explains that the boxes above the V box represent *subcategories* of V and that the numbers represent *the number (in thousands) of species.* Glance at the diagram again.

V's are split into the categories Jawed or Jawless. Total, there are 66K V's, most of which are jawed. Only a very small number are jawless. The jawed vertebrates can then be broken down into the categories Four-Limbed or Fish, and there are roughly equal numbers of each. Finally, the Four-Limbed group can be broken into four subgroups whose names appear only in the blurb: amphibians, reptiles, birds, and mammals. Reptiles and birds are the largest categories and mammals are the smallest category.

The question consists of two separate sentences. The first asks you to find Four-Limbed as a percent of Vertebrate. The second wants to know what fraction A's and R's represent of all species.

The two parts are not related, so you'll solve each individually.

Step 2: Plan Your Approach

In each case, the task is to make sure that you are working with the right categories. (In general, if you see a nonstandard diagram that has a bunch of subcategories of subcategories, chances are good that at least part of your job will be to make sure you're working with the right categories.) Organize your work carefully and double-check, before calculating, that you have pulled the data from the right groups.

Finally, keep an eye on the answer choices as you go; don't do more math than you have to do.

Step 3: Solve the Problem

The first part asks for Four-Limbed as a percent of Vertebrates. The Four-Limbed category has about 32.5K members and the Vertebrate category has about 66K members. Half of 66 is 33, so four-limbed species represent approximately 50% of all vertebrate species.

The second part asks for amphibians and reptiles as a fraction of all animal species. Jot down A + R for the top of the fraction. What about the bottom? Is that all vertebrates? Look back at the prompt.

No, it's not just the vertebrates. The blurb says that vertebrates and invertebrates *together* make up all animal species, so you'll need to add V and Inv. (Just double-check first that they didn't already tell you the total in the prompt—but they didn't.)

$$\text{Total animals} = 1{,}300\text{K} + 66\text{K} = 1{,}366\text{K}$$

That's the bottom of the fraction. What goes on top?

$$A + R = 7\text{K} + 10\text{K} = 17\text{K}$$

Here's the full fraction:

$$\frac{17}{1{,}366}$$

5

Hmm. That's much smaller than $\frac{1}{2}$ or $\frac{1}{4}$, so eliminate those two answers. But which of the other answers is it? One way to find out: Plug that fraction into the calculator. The decimal is 0.0124. The decimal value of $\frac{1}{100}$ is 0.01, and the decimal value of $\frac{1}{200}$ is half of that, or 0.005. The value 0.0124 is closer to 0.01, so the correct answer is $\frac{1}{100}$.

If you're not a fan of decimals, you can also simplify the fraction. The problem tells you that you can estimate and the two remaining answers are quite far apart, so you can estimate aggressively:

$$\frac{17}{1{,}366} = \frac{20}{1{,}400} = \frac{1}{70}$$

That fraction is closer to $\frac{1}{100}$, so that's the correct answer.

Here's one more way! Work backwards from the two remaining answers. If $\frac{1}{100}$ is the correct answer, then that fraction would approximately equal $\frac{17}{1{,}366}$. Does it? Use your calculator to find out (and do the same for the other remaining answer):

Is $\frac{1}{100} \approx \frac{17}{1{,}366}$?	Is $\frac{1}{200} \approx \frac{17}{1{,}366}$?
Is $1{,}366\left(\frac{1}{100}\right) \approx 17$?	Is $1{,}366\left(\frac{1}{200}\right) \approx 17$?
Is $14 \approx 17$?	Is $7 \approx 17$?

The fraction $\frac{1}{100}$ is a closer match.

Therefore, four-limbed species represent approximately $\boxed{50\%}$ of all vertebrate species. Amphibians and reptiles combined comprise approximately $\boxed{\frac{1}{100}}$ of all animal species.

Review and Improve on Standard Graphs

Try the process one more time:

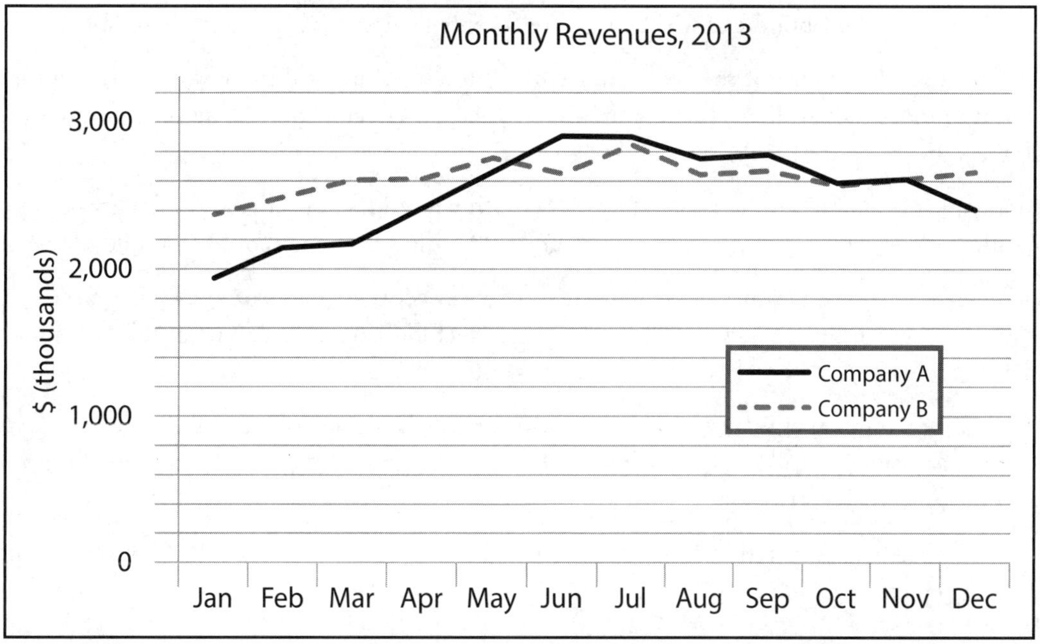

The chart shows 2013 monthly revenues reported by Company A and Company B, which compete in the cellphone market.

Based on the given information, use the drop-down menus to most accurately complete the following statement:

In 2013, Company A's annual revenues were [Select... ▾]. Company B's annual revenues and the positive difference between the two figures was approximately [Select... ▾].

First drop-down options:
- >
- <
- =

Second drop-down options:
- 0
- 250,000
- 750,000
- 1,250,000
- 3,000,000

How did it go? For your review, follow the same steps introduced for the problem about the Vertebrates and Invertebrates. First, take stock. How did you feel about the whole thing? Anything you want to try again?

Next, check just the correct answer. (It's at the very end of the explanation.) Does knowing that give you any ideas for what to check or do a different way?

Whether you answered the problem correctly or incorrectly, review each step of the process. Look for ways to do the problem better or faster next time, and look for clues to tell you when to guess and move on.

Step 1: Understand the Prompt and Question

This is a line chart. The first set of answers requires you only to be able to tell whether one thing is greater than, less than, or equal to something else; there's a good chance you'll be able to eyeball this. The second blank requires a real value, but the answer choices are far enough apart that you'll likely be able to estimate.

Also note that the answers for the second blank seem way too big compared to the y-axis given in the graph. The graph is in thousands as shown by the y-axis label. The answers show the real number, not the abbreviated numbers shown on the graph.

Use that as your segue into the chart itself. It shows monthly revenues in thousands of dollars during 2013 for two different companies. For example, a point at 2,000 indicates revenues of $2,000,000, or $2 million.

This is a line graph, so you may need to determine differences between points on the line. That's easiest to do by counting segments of the graph, so figure out what each horizontal line segment represents and jot down that figure. In this case, each segment represents 200, or $200,000.

In some months, Company A earned higher revenues; in other months, Company B did. Interestingly, Company B started higher and finished higher, while A jumped above B only in the middle of the year.

The two parts of the question ask for related information: which company had higher annual revenues and what that difference was. When this is the case, think about how to save yourself some time and effort by solving the statements simultaneously.

Step 2: Plan Your Approach

The first part asks whether Company A's revenues were greater, less than, or equal to Company B's, so plan to track the difference in terms of Company A.

The standard math way to solve would be to mark down every monthly figure and add them all up for both companies, then compare the two figures. That involves adding 24 numbers, though—way too much work! There has to be an easier way.

There is! Count only the differences between the figures. Further, use the segments to make your calculations easier. Count just by segments, then multiply by 200 (the value of one segment) to convert to the actual figure.

Finally, don't worry about the *thousands of dollars* part of things for now; solve using the y-axis scale and add in three zeros later.

Step 3: Solve the Problem

First, just eyeball the graph. For the first five months, Company A is significantly below Company B, enough to create quite a large negative differential. Company B does lose some ground in the middle of the chart, but not enough to offset the initial differential, especially considering that Company B rebounds at the end of the year.

So Company A should end up lower than Company B. You'll have to calculate more precisely to know how much, but expect the answer to the first blank to be *less than*.

In January, Company A is about two segments below Company B. For this month, the differential is −2. The February differential is −1.5, so the total differential is now −3.5. Continue counting:

	Jan	Feb	Mar	Apr	May	Jun	Jul	Aug	Sep	Oct	Nov	Dec
Diff	−2	−1.5	−2	−1	−0.5	1	0	0.5	0.5	0	0	−1
Total	−2	−3.5	−5.5	−6.5	−7	−6	−6	−5.5	−5	−5	−5	−6

Company A finishes the year with −6 segments, which translates to a total of $(-6) \times (200) = -1{,}200$ below Company B. Add in three zeros, and Company A's revenue is $1,200,000 below Company B's.

Thus, in 2013, Company A's annual revenues were $\boxed{<}$ Company B's annual revenues, and the positive difference between the two figures was approximately $\boxed{1{,}250{,}000}$.

Counting by segments is a bit strange at first, but it saves a lot of time. Practice until you feel comfortable working with the numbers in this way. You don't actually need to make a table and write everything down. If you feel comfortable counting on screen, you can. Use a finger to point to each month's data as you solve, and consider jotting down just the total at the end of each month so that, if you lose track, you can check your work without having to start from the beginning.

You can also go the long way: Pull up the calculator and plug in each actual value to find the sums for each company. Only do this, though, if you have plenty of time. Don't sacrifice other questions later in the section because you spent too much time adding up 24 numbers at this stage.

If you think the second part will take too long to solve and you're not willing to make that investment, you can invest a small amount of time to increase your odds in making a guess. If you eyeball the data, you can tell that the first part is *less than* without calculating anything. That's also enough information to know that the answer to the second part is not going to be 0. Then, guess from here; you would have at least a 25% chance of guessing correctly.

Practice Your Skills

If you have access to Manhattan Prep's *GMAT All the Quant* guide, your next task is to study the unit on Fractions, Decimals, Percents, and Ratios, as well as the chapter on Statistics. As you become more conversant with these topics, you can practice more Graph problems in your Atlas online syllabus.

CHAPTER 6

Multi-Source Reasoning

In This Chapter

- UPS for MSR
- Review and Improve on MSR

In this chapter, you will learn how to map the information from Multi-Source Reasoning (MSR) problems, as well as how to use Understand–Plan–Solve to approach the two types of questions that come with this problem type.

CHAPTER 6 Multi-Source Reasoning

Multi-Source Reasoning (MSR) problems are similar to Reading Comprehension (RC) passages, with two key differences: MSR can include mathematical data, graphics, and tables along with the text, and the information provided will be split across two or three tabs. Note: If you see a table in an MSR tab, you will *not* be able to sort the table.

Much like RC passages, the MSR prompts appear on the left side of the screen and the (typically) three accompanying questions appear on the right side of the screen, one at a time. These questions are of two different types: standard multiple-choice and either-or.

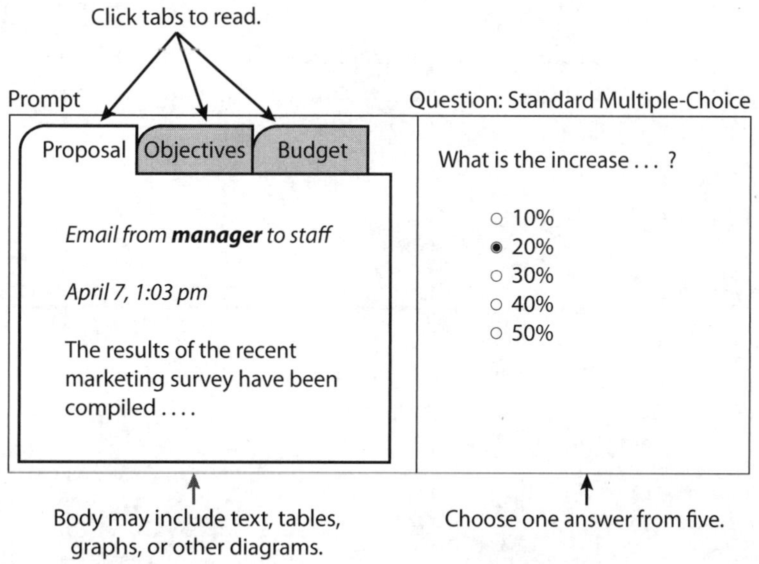

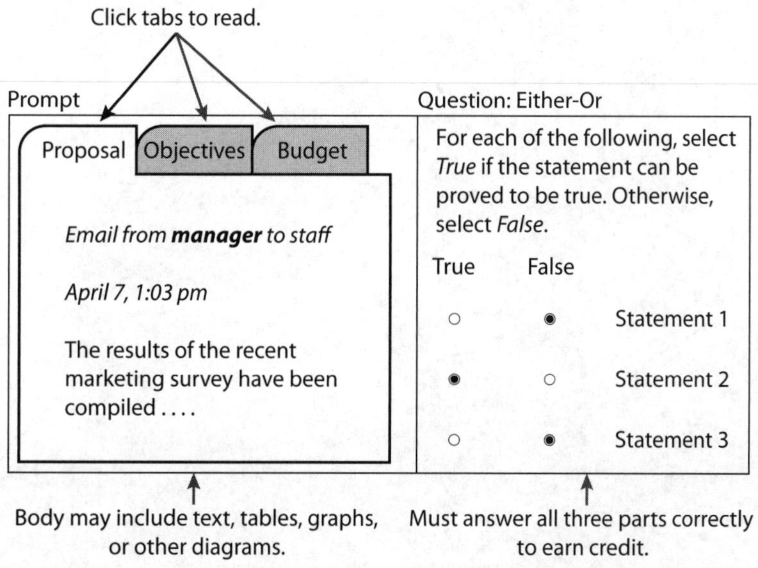

The most typical configuration for MSRs is one standard multiple-choice question and two separate either-or questions with three statements each. Occasionally, you might be given only two questions overall; more rarely, you might see four total questions.

The either-or questions will be in the same format that you've already seen on Table problems, and you can use the same techniques to solve.

The standard multiple-choice questions will be in the same format as problems in the Quant or Verbal sections of the exam, and you can often use the same techniques to solve. On a math-focused problem, you may be able to use smart numbers or work backwards. On a verbal-focused problem, you may be able to predict an answer (as on RC) or eliminate answers based on common traps that you've learned about for RC or Critical Reasoning.

As the word *multi-source* implies, the vast majority of questions will require you to integrate information from two or even all three of the tabs.

UPS for MSR

As with all Integrated Reasoning question types, you'll use the UPS process (Understand–Plan–Solve) to tackle MSR problems. Since there's quite a lot of information in the tabs, the Understand step is going to take some time. Because you will usually see three separate questions associated with the same MSR tabs, you can invest several minutes at the beginning to understand all of the information.

Step 1: Understand the Prompt and Question

Take a look at the two-tab MSR prompt below. Here's the first tab:

Sales Breakout | **Vitamin Content**

E-mail from Purchasing Supervisor to Sales Manager:

Total April sales for your produce stand were $4,441; the itemized data is below.

We already know that customers base their purchasing decisions on whether something is in season and how much it costs. Management believes that customers also care about the health factor, such as how high the vitamin content is for different types of produce. Do you have any data that could help us to evaluate this question?

We also need to think about pricing strategies in light of the fact that some items have a far longer shelf life. Potatoes will last weeks in cold storage, while the tomatoes won't last more than a few days without suffering a reduction in quality. Please send me any information you have about spoilage rates or other factors we should consider when setting prices.

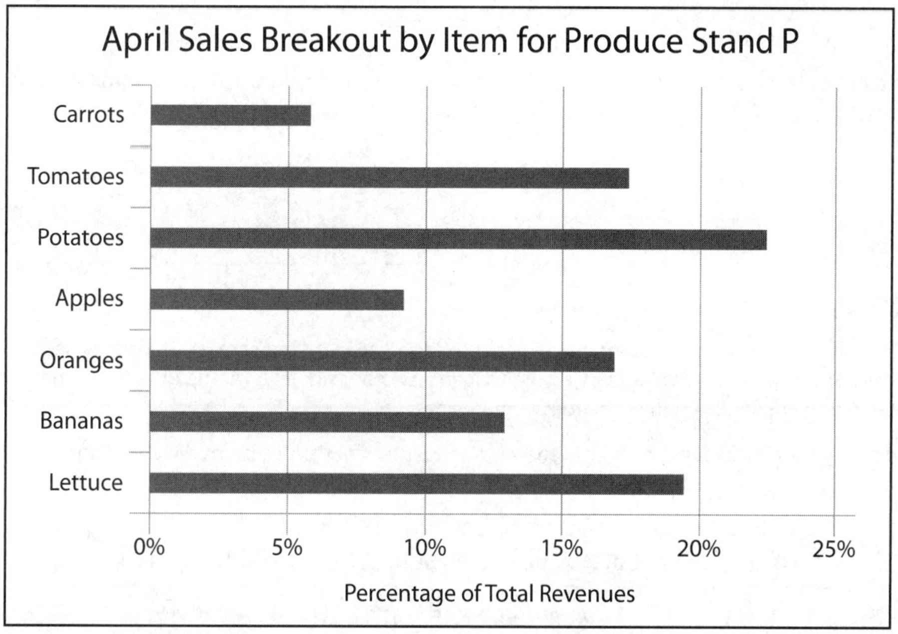

Glance first at the labels on the two tabs: *Sales Breakout* and *Vitamin Content*. You might also choose to click briefly on the second tab to see whether it's pure text or whether it also contains a graph, table, or other non-text information. Don't read anything; just glance. (In this case, you'd see some text and a table—more on this in a bit.)

Now, go back to the first tab and start reading. Think about the "So what?" Why is the blurb telling you this? The blurb first sets some context and provides overall sales figures for a produce stand. The first big paragraph then talks about the factors that customers consider when buying produce and asks an explicit question about vitamin content. The second tab's title is actually *Vitamin Content*, so presumably that tab will address this question.

The second big paragraph raises the issue of shelf life for their pricing strategy. Perhaps the supervisor is thinking that they will have to reduce prices on certain items with a shorter shelf life in order to make sure they sell before they spoil. (She doesn't actually say this, but go ahead and speculate a little. Put yourself in the story.) The text also mentions spoilage rates, so perhaps the second tab will address this as well.

Finally, the bar graph provides the percentage of sales by item; there may be some calculations coming soon.

As you understand what's going on, jot down information on your scrap paper, but as with RC, don't take very detailed notes. The test is open book; the source information will be in front of you the whole time. Rather, you are going to create a **Tab Map** that will help you figure out where to go in order to answer the various questions.

All of the thoughts above might condense down into this map:

#1 Sales

Apr $4,441

Buy in season. Cost. Care about V?

Pricing strat → spoilage

Ⓖ % sales by item

Use some kind of visual designation as a signal when you have a graph, a table, or some other visual or set of data. That way, you'll know at a glance which tab to click back to when you need that data.

Try it again with the second tab:

Sales Breakout | **Vitamin Content**

E-mail from Sales Manager to Purchasing Supervisor:

Carrots, apples, and potatoes last a very long time in cold storage. I am a bit concerned about the lettuce, though; our farmers generally produce a higher volume of lettuce than of any other single item. The other items generally sell within acceptable time frames, even the tomatoes and bananas.

Customers do sometimes ask about the vitamin and nutrient content of various items. Maybe I should post the data on the pricing signs? Here's some data on the vitamin A and vitamin C content of our produce:

Vitamin Content of Produce Items Sold at Produce Stand P in April

	Vitamin C content	***Vitamin A content***
Apples	low	low
Bananas	medium	low
Carrots	low	high
Lettuce	high	low
Oranges	high	medium
Potatoes	medium	low
Tomatoes	high	high

I also have research indicating that organic produce has a higher vitamin content than non-organic counterparts. I think that could be a very valuable marketing point.

In contrast to Table problems, MSR problems have static tables—you can't sort them. A map for the second tab might look like this:

> #2 Vit
>
> > Spoil: maybe lettuce
> >
> > Ⓣ Vit A + C
> >
> > Org = more Vit, +

So what? It sounds like lettuce might have spoilage or shelf-life issues, though the sales manager doesn't explicitly say so. Then there's a bunch of data on vitamin content; note that this data exists and that it's in the form high-medium-low (not numbers), but ignore the details until you get a question about it. Finally, the last couple of sentences introduce the idea that organic produce could be a positive selling point.

Take a moment to think about how the two tabs connect; feel free to click back and forth to glance at the info again. The supervisor asks some questions and the manager responds to those questions. The two visuals contain the same list of fruits and vegetables (though not in the same order—be careful). It isn't clear at this point how the sales data and the vitamin content data might otherwise connect, so wait to see what questions you're asked.

Here are the two tabs again, along with the first question:

Sales Breakout | **Vitamin Content**

E-mail from Purchasing Supervisor to Sales Manager:

Total April sales for your produce stand were $4,441; the itemized data is below.

We already know that customers base their purchasing decisions on whether something is in season and how much it costs. Management believes that customers also care about the health factor, such as how high the vitamin content is for different types of produce. Do you have any data that could help us to evaluate this question?

We also need to think about pricing strategies in light of the fact that some items have a far longer shelf life. Potatoes will last weeks in cold storage, while the tomatoes won't last more than a few days without suffering a reduction in quality. Please send me any information you have about spoilage rates or other factors we should consider when setting prices.

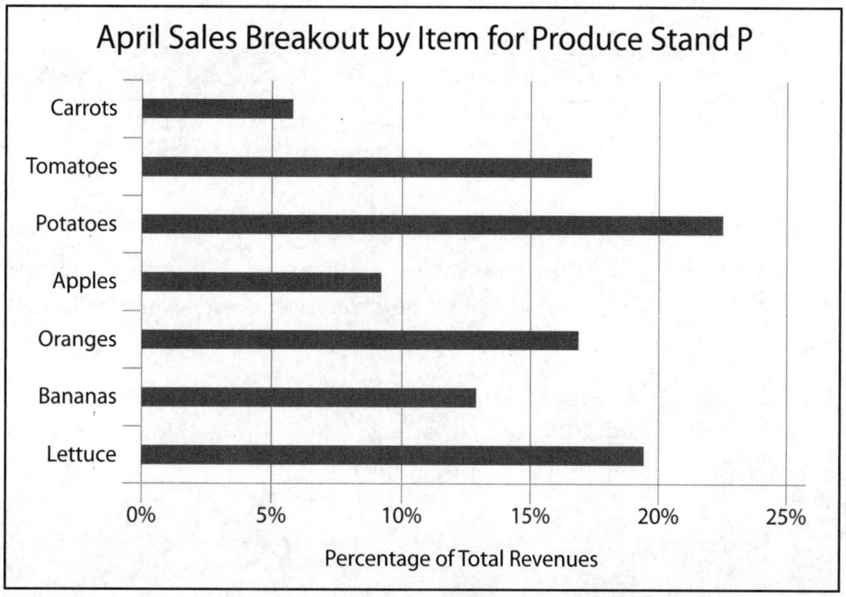

Sales Breakout	**Vitamin Content**

E-mail from Sales Manager to Purchasing Supervisor:

Carrots, apples, and potatoes last a very long time in cold storage. I am a bit concerned about the lettuce, though; our farmers generally produce a higher volume of lettuce than of any other single item. The other items generally sell within acceptable time frames, even the tomatoes and bananas.

Customers do sometimes ask about the vitamin and nutrient content of various items. Maybe I should post the data on the pricing signs? Here's some data on the vitamin A and vitamin C content of our produce:

Vitamin Content of Produce Items Sold at Produce Stand P in April		
	Vitamin C content	***Vitamin A content***
Apples	low	low
Bananas	medium	low
Carrots	low	high
Lettuce	high	low
Oranges	high	medium
Potatoes	medium	low
Tomatoes	high	high

I also have research indicating that organic produce has a higher vitamin content than non-organic counterparts. I think that could be a very valuable marketing point.

6

For each of the following, select *Justified* if it is a justified inference on the basis of the information provided. Otherwise, select *Not justified.*

Justified	Not justified	
O	O	Some of Produce Stand P's lettuce may spoil or be in danger of spoiling before it is all sold.
O	O	More bananas than apples are sold at Produce Stand P.
O	O	Produce high in vitamin A, vitamin C, or both accounted for more than half of April revenues at Produce Stand P.

This is an either-or question, the exact same format you saw for Table questions. These questions always present answers in the form *either X or Y*, such as true/false, yes/no, or, as in this case, justified/not justified. Three statements will accompany the question; your task is to choose a single answer for each statement. In order to earn credit for this question, you have to answer all three statements correctly.

This question specifically asks whether the statement is a *justified inference*. These statements will not be found directly in the tabs; rather, you will have to determine whether something is reasonably justified, or able to be proven, based upon related information from the prompt.

Next, scan through the three statements. On some problems, the statements are very similar and can be solved simultaneously or very similarly. On others, the statements are independent and must be solved separately.

In this case, the statements each address different aspects of the information provided, so work through them individually. Here's the first statement:

Justified	Not justified	
O	O	Some of Produce Stand P's lettuce may spoil or be in danger of spoiling before it is all sold.

This statement talks about lettuce spoilage. Where do you need to go to find this information? Glance at your map. Spoilage was mentioned in both tabs.

Step 2: Plan Your Approach

Sales Breakout | **Vitamin Content**

E-mail from Purchasing Supervisor to Sales Manager:

Total April sales for your produce stand were $4,441; the itemized data is below.

We already know that customers base their purchasing decisions on whether something is in season and how much it costs. Management believes that customers also care about the health factor, such as how high the vitamin content is for different types of produce. Do you have any data that could help us to evaluate this question?

We also need to think about pricing strategies in light of the fact that some items have a far longer shelf life. Potatoes will last weeks in cold storage, while the tomatoes won't last more than a few days without suffering a reduction in quality. Please send me any information you have about spoilage rates or other factors we should consider when setting prices.

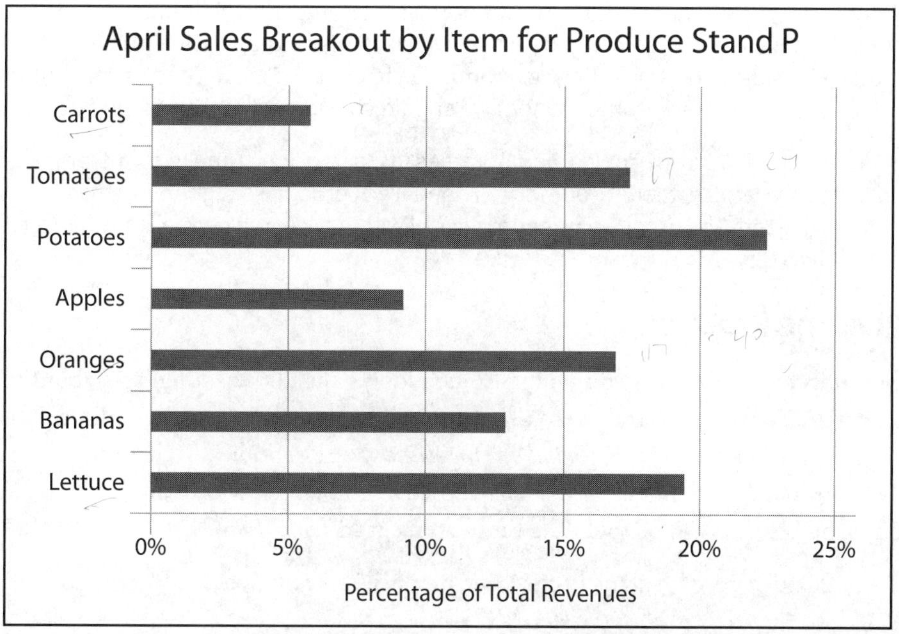

Sales Breakout	**Vitamin Content**

E-mail from Sales Manager to Purchasing Supervisor:

Carrots, apples, and potatoes last a very long time in cold storage. I am a bit concerned about the lettuce, though; our farmers generally produce a higher volume of lettuce than of any other single item. The other items generally sell within acceptable time frames, even the tomatoes and bananas.

Customers do sometimes ask about the vitamin and nutrient content of various items. Maybe I should post the data on the pricing signs? Here's some data on the vitamin A and vitamin C content of our produce:

Vitamin Content of Produce Items Sold at Produce Stand P in April		
	Vitamin C content	***Vitamin A content***
Apples	low	low
Bananas	medium	low
Carrots	low	high
Lettuce	high	low
Oranges	high	medium
Potatoes	medium	low
Tomatoes	high	high

I also have research indicating that organic produce has a higher vitamin content than non-organic counterparts. I think that could be a very valuable marketing point.

6

The *Sales Breakout* tab mentioned spoilage and the *Vitamin Content* tab specifically mentioned lettuce, so you'll need both to answer the question. Find and reread the relevant text:

> (Sales Breakout Tab): We also need to think about pricing strategies in light of the fact that some items have a far longer shelf life. Potatoes will last weeks in cold storage, while the tomatoes won't last more than a few days without suffering a reduction in quality. Please send me any information you have about spoilage rates or other factors we should consider when setting prices.
>
> (Vitamin Content Tab) Carrots, apples, and potatoes last a very long time in cold storage. I am a bit concerned about the lettuce, though; our farmers generally produce a higher volume of lettuce than of any other single item. The other items generally sell within acceptable time frames, even the tomatoes and bananas.

Step 3: Solve the Problem

The supervisor points out that some items will last much longer than others, then asks about spoilage rates, implying that some items may spoil or be in danger of spoiling. The sales manager indicates that certain items do last a long time, but he is *concerned about the lettuce*. He also indicates that the *other items generally sell within acceptable time frames*, implying that the lettuce might *not* sell within an acceptable time frame; that is, it might spoil before it can be sold. The first statement, then, is *Justified.*

Evaluate the second and third statements in the same manner, repeating your UPS steps each time:

Justified	Not justified	
O	O	More bananas than apples are sold at Produce Stand P.

Careful! The bar graph in the *Sales Breakout* tab shows information about sales *revenues*, not sales *volume*. While it is true that banana sales revenues were higher than apple sales revenues, the prompt does not indicate the relative number of items sold. It could be that more apples than bananas were sold, but the price per banana was higher, such that total banana revenue was higher. The second statement is *Not justified*. Now, here's the third statement:

Justified	Not justified	
O	O	Produce high in vitamin A, vitamin C, or both accounted for more than half of April revenues at Produce Stand P.

Note first that the question asks whether this group accounted for *more than half* of revenues. You will not necessarily have to calculate the exact figure; it will be enough if you can tell whether it is more or less than half. The *Vitamin Content* tab has the vitamin data; the *Sales Breakout* tab has the sales data. You're going to have to combine the two tabs.

First, go to *Vitamin Content* and look for the items that are high in either or both of the vitamins: carrots, lettuce, oranges, and tomatoes. The remaining items—apples, bananas, and potatoes—are not high in either vitamin. Jot the items in two clearly labeled lists: high-V and not-high-V. Since you are comparing to 50%, you could sum for either group.

Next, click on *Sales Breakout* and find the percentage of revenue for each item. It is easier to sum three categories than four, so eyeball the bars for the not-high-vitamin items: Do they sum to less than 50%?

$$\begin{array}{r} A < 10\% \\ B < 15\% \\ P < 25\% \\ \hline \text{sum} < 50\% \end{array}$$

The not-high-vitamin items account for less than half of revenues, so the high-vitamin items account for more than half of revenues.

Alternatively, eyeball the bars for the high-vitamin items. If you approximate or round down and the sum is still greater than 50%, the statement must be true.

$$\begin{array}{r} C > 5\% \\ L > 15\% \\ O > 15\% \\ T > 15\% \\ \hline \text{sum} > 50\% \end{array}$$

Even if you round each bar down to the closest grid line, the sum is still 50%. The longest bar is actually closer to 20%, so this sum will definitely cross the 50% threshold. Therefore, the third statement is *Justified*.

6

The answers are as follows:

Justified	Not justified	
◉	○	Some of Produce Stand P's lettuce may spoil or be in danger of spoiling before it is all sold.
○	◉	More bananas than apples are sold at Produce Stand P.
◉	○	Produce high in vitamin A, vitamin C, or both accounted for more than half of April revenues at Produce Stand P.

Here is a second question for the same prompt; try out the UPS process yourself.

In the month of April, Produce Stand P generated approximately how much revenue, in dollars, from items that were high in both vitamin A and vitamin C?

(A) $775
(B) $1,280
(C) $1,575
(D) $2,080
(E) $2,875

Sales Breakout | **Vitamin Content**

E-mail from Purchasing Supervisor to Sales Manager:

Total April sales for your produce stand were $4,441; the itemized data is below.

We already know that customers base their purchasing decisions on whether something is in season and how much it costs. Management believes that customers also care about the health factor, such as how high the vitamin content is for different types of produce. Do you have any data that could help us to evaluate this question?

We also need to think about pricing strategies in light of the fact that some items have a far longer shelf life. Potatoes will last weeks in cold storage, while the tomatoes won't last more than a few days without suffering a reduction in quality. Please send me any information you have about spoilage rates or other factors we should consider when setting prices.

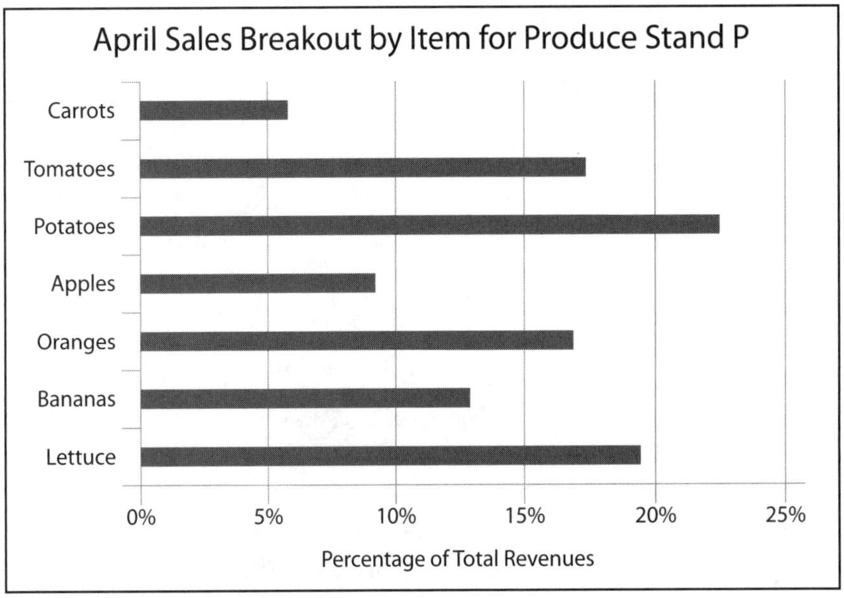

6

Sales Breakout | **Vitamin Content**

E-mail from Sales Manager to Purchasing Supervisor:

Carrots, apples, and potatoes last a very long time in cold storage. I am a bit concerned about the lettuce, though; our farmers generally produce a higher volume of lettuce than of any other single item. The other items generally sell within acceptable time frames, even the tomatoes and bananas.

Customers do sometimes ask about the vitamin and nutrient content of various items. Maybe I should post the data on the pricing signs? Here's some data on the vitamin A and vitamin C content of our produce:

Vitamin Content of Produce Items Sold at Produce Stand P in April		
	Vitamin C content	***Vitamin A content***
Apples	low	low
Bananas	medium	low
Carrots	low	high
Lettuce	high	low
Oranges	high	medium
Potatoes	medium	low
Tomatoes	high	high

I also have research indicating that organic produce has a higher vitamin content than non-organic counterparts. I think that could be a very valuable marketing point.

First, make sure you understand the question. You'll need to find items that are high in *both* vitamins A and C (*not* items high in just one or the other).

Second, plan how to answer the question. You'll need to use *Vitamin Content* to find those items high in both vitamin A and C. To calculate the revenue, add up the percentages of sales for the relevant items and then multiply by the dollar figure given for total sales in the first paragraph of the *Sales Breakout* tab. Lay these steps out on your scrap paper.

Finally, go ahead and solve. Only tomatoes are high in *both* vitamins A and C. Tomatoes accounted for approximately 17%–18% of total revenues (glance at those answers; you don't need to be very precise), so pull up the calculator and plug in this calculation: $0.17 \times 4{,}441 = 754.97$.

The closest match in the answers is $775. The correct answer is (A).

If you feel comfortable working by hand, the answers are far enough apart to estimate pretty roughly. For example, 10% of $4,441 is about $444, so 20% is about $888. The answer has to be close to but less than $888; only answer (A) matches.

Review and Improve on MSR

The Understand–Plan–Solve process will help you both to answer the question and to review your work afterwards. If you answer a question incorrectly—or aren't fully confident about something you answered correctly—review each step of the process.

First, did you properly understand everything? Did you overlook, misunderstand, or fail to comprehend any information in the prompt? How was your map; should you have included something that you didn't write down, or did you get too far into the detail? Did you miss any connections between different tabs or pieces of information? Did you answer the question that was asked?

What about your plan? Was there an easier or more efficient way to approach the problem? And did you make any mistakes at the solution stage?

Try another MSR problem set to test your skills. This time, you'll do all three questions first. A word of warning: The prompt is extremely technical. Often, when this happens, the questions themselves *don't* require you to dive very deeply into the technical details. Use that knowledge to your advantage as you work through this problem set.

Ready? Set a timer for 9 minutes and go!

Proposal | **Purpose** | **Budget**

The government of Storinia has proposed to conduct three particle physics experiments in Antarctica, as described below.

The *ultra-high-energy cosmic ray detector* (UHECR-D) will track a variety of subatomic particles with exceptionally high kinetic energy traveling from outer space by recording secondary showers of particles created by these UHECRs as they collide with the upper atmosphere of Earth.

The *polyethylene naphthalate neutrino observatory* (PEN-NO) will search for neutrinos, extremely light and fast subatomic particles that interact only weakly with normal matter. To prevent false-positive results from cosmic rays, PEN-NO will be buried deep below the ice.

The *magnetic monopole detector* (MaMoD) will attempt to verify the existence of magnetic monopoles, hypothetical subatomic particles that some physical theories postulate are left over from the creation of the universe.

6

Proposal | **Purpose** | **Budget**

The purpose of UHECR-D is to ascertain the identity, composition, and extraterrestrial origin of ultra-high-energy cosmic rays, which are much less prevalent and well-understood than lower-energy cosmic rays. PEN-NO will measure the mass and speed of neutrinos produced in particle accelerators and nuclear reactors, both to reduce uncertainty in the known mass of a neutrino and to contribute to the resolution of a recent challenge to Einstein's theory of relativity posed by the observation of neutrinos supposedly traveling slightly faster than light. PEN-NO will also measure the passage of solar and other neutrinos of astronomical origin. Finally, if MaMoD is successful in its search, it will provide experimental proof for Dirac's explanation of charge quantization and fix an asymmetry in Maxwell's equations of electromagnetism.

UHE - sub par
pen no - neutrinos, below ice
MaMod - magnetic monopole

Purpose	Proposal	**Budget**

The government of Storinia projects that it will cost $42 million in total and take 2 years to construct UHECR-D, PEN-NO, and MaMoD. The government also projects that once construction is finished, the annual operating budget for each experiment will be $3.6 million for UHECR-D, $4.3 million for PEN-NO, and $2.7 million for MaMoD. All these figures are in real 2015 dollars (removing the effect of predicted inflation).

1. For each of the following statements, select *Yes* if the statement is supported by the evidence provided. Otherwise, select *No*.

Yes	No	
○	○	With a construction budget of $30 million, the Storinian government will be able to search for proof of an explanation of charge quantization and help resolve a controversy by measuring the speed of neutrinos produced in nuclear reactors.
○	○	In its Antarctic experiments, the Storinian government will attempt to ascertain the mass and speed of cosmic rays.
○	○	If the PEN-NO experiment operates on the surface of the ice in Antarctica, its findings will be considered more valid than those produced by the experiment as currently envisioned.

2. According to the information provided, the proposed measurement of which of the following kinds of particles is intended to improve the estimate of the mass of these particles?

   (A) Ultra-high-energy cosmic rays

   (B) Particles created by UHECRs above the Earth

   (C) Neutrinos produced in nuclear reactors

   (D) Neutrinos that originate in the Sun

   (E) Magnetic monopoles

3. For each of the following particle types, select *Can conclude* if you can conclude from the information provided that the particles in question have a negligible effect on ordinary matter. Otherwise, select *Cannot conclude*.

Can conclude	Cannot conclude	
○	○	Ultra-high-energy cosmic rays
○	○	Neutrinos produced in particle accelerators
○	○	Magnetic monopoles

How did it go? Before reading the following explanations, review your work yourself.

Before you check the correct answers, evaluate how you think you did. Where are you confident and where are you unsure? What felt cumbersome to analyze or process, and can you think of any way to make that cumbersome part easier? Do you want to try any of the problems (or parts of problems) again? Go ahead. This time, you don't even need to time yourself. Take as much time as you want.

Next, check the correct answers but nothing else. (You'll have to scroll down a bit—we didn't want to give away the answers too soon.) Does knowing the answers give you any ideas about what else to try—or what might have gone wrong—on any part of any problem? If so, dig in to see whether you can figure things out on your own. Whenever you can do this, you'll remember the lesson a lot more easily.

Finally, use the explanations. Start to read through, but stop as soon as you read something that gives you an idea. Try to push that idea as far as you can before you go back to the explanation for more. Again, the more you figure out for yourself, the easier it will be for you to remember what you're learning.

Ready for the official explanations? Let's go!

Step 1: Understand the Prompt and Question

As you review the solution, check whether your reasoning and understanding were accurate, not just whether you answered the question correctly. Sometimes, you get lucky—it is a multiple-choice test, after all.

The long-hand text below summarizes what someone might think while reading each tab. A sample map is shown at the end.

Proposal tab:

> *Storinia is planning 3 experiments in Antarctica.*
>
> *I don't understand a lot of these words. That's okay—ignore them.*
>
> *(Glancing down.) One paragraph per experiment. Right now, I just need a basic understanding. Hopefully I won't ever need to really understand this detail.*
>
> *#1 is something about outer space coming to Earth.*
>
> *#2 will be buried in ice.*
>
> *#3 is something about magnetic something that has to do with the creation of the universe.*

Purpose tab:

> *The name of the tab is* Purpose, *so presumably they're going to tell me the purpose of at least some of these experiments.*
>
> *(Glancing down.) All three acronyms are listed in this paragraph.*
>
> *The details here are really hard. Big picture only.*
>
> *#1 is something about a certain type of cosmic ray that isn't well understood—what is it, what's it made of, where it comes from.*
>
> *#2 involves learning more about neutrinos and something about Einstein's theory of relativity.*
>
> *#3 is searching for something; if successful, it will prove one theory and fix another.*

Budget tab:

> *What the experiments will cost and how long they'll take to start.*
>
> *Also provides annual operating costs for each one.*

Here is one version of a map for this prompt. The first line of the first tab indicates that it will discuss three experiments, so consider using a table to organize the information by experiment and by tab.

Exp	T1 Prop	T2 Purp	T3 Budg
UHECR-D	space to Earth	made of? come from? high-energy cosmic ray	$3.6m annual
PEN-NO	neutrinos below ice	mass and speed Einstein th. relativity	$4.3m ann
MaMoD	exist? creation of universe	prove D's theory (CQ) fix M's eqns	$2.7m ann
All			$42m initial 2 yrs

You will likely gain additional understanding as you continue through the material. For instance, part of *UHECR-D* does stand for *high-energy cosmic ray*, but the significance of these words doesn't really become apparent until the *Purpose* tab—so you might not write them down until you get to that point. You could also go back and add them under the *Proposal* tab entry.

First, here are all of the correct answers:

Question 1: No, No, No

Question 2: (C)

Question 3: Cannot, Can, Cannot

6

Any ideas? Go test them out before you continue on with the explanations.

1. For each of the following statements, select *Yes* if the statement is supported by the evidence provided. Otherwise, select *No*.

The question asks whether, using information from the tabs, you can support, or prove true, the given statements.

Glance through them to see whether the statements are related in any way. They are not, so solve each one individually.

This kind of question is basically a "search and match" exercise. Read the statement first, then use your map to figure out where to look in the tabs to try to prove the statement. Here is the first statement:

Yes	No	
○	○	With a construction budget of $30 million, the Storinian government will be able to search for proof of an explanation of charge quantization and help resolve a controversy by measuring the speed of neutrinos produced in nuclear reactors.

The overall construction budget was $42m, so $30m is a subset of this budget. The question is asking whether this subset will be sufficient to accomplish just a certain part of the job. Which part?

Step 2: Plan Your Approach

Wait! Before you get into the annoying technical details, review the monetary information you were given. Tab 3 provides the *annual* budget to operate each separate experiment, but the initial *construction* budget was never split up by experiment—it's $42m for all three together. No information is given to allow you to assume, for example, that each will cost roughly the same to construct or, alternatively, that the ratio of construction costs will mirror the ratio of operating costs. The facilities for any one experiment could cost more or less than $30m to construct.

Step 3: Solve the Problem

That's it! The answer to the first statement is *No*: This is not supported by the given evidence.

If you messed anything up, pinpoint the specific mistake(s) and figure out what you could do differently to avoid that mistake in the future.

Alternatively, maybe you answered this correctly but realize in hindsight that you spent more time than necessary to do so. How could you save time next time? For instance, if you spent time digging into the detail on the experiments before realizing that you didn't need any of that to address the statement, then remind yourself next time to slow down and apply the process. Understand and plan before you try to solve.

Repeat your review of all three steps as you work through the second statement:

Yes	No	
○	○	In its Antarctic experiments, the Storinian government will attempt to ascertain the mass and speed of cosmic rays.

Hmm. All three experiments take place in the Antarctic. This question is asking whether one certain thing is planned for one of these experiments. Which one?

This time you do have to get a bit into the details. You've got two different sets of key words you could go with: either *mass and speed* or *cosmic rays*. Glance at your map.

And here's where your first big clue comes in! *Cosmic rays* are the first experiment, but *mass and speed* go with the second experiment. It looks like this choice might be a **Mix-Up** trap: It mixes up text from two different parts of the prompt, creating a statement that the passage didn't actually say.

Here's the sentence on cosmic rays:

> *The purpose of UHECR-D is to ascertain the identity, composition, and extraterrestrial origin of ultra-high-energy cosmic rays, which are much less prevalent and well-understood than lower-energy cosmic rays.*

This sentence says nothing about either *mass* or *speed*.

It's enough to check just the part that discusses cosmic rays, since the statement does specify this type of particle. But you can also check the part that describes the second experiment:

> *PEN-NO will measure the mass and speed of neutrinos produced in particle accelerators and nuclear reactors, both to reduce uncertainty in the known mass of a neutrino and to contribute to the resolution of a recent challenge to Einstein's theory of relativity posed by the observation of neutrinos supposedly traveling slightly faster than light. PEN-NO will also measure the passage of solar and other neutrinos of astronomical origin.*

Mass and speed are mentioned, but not *cosmic rays*. This part is all about something called a neutrino.

Indeed, this is a mix-up trap! They jammed together information about two different types of particles, hoping that people would remember reading about both *cosmic rays* and *mass and speed* and just assume that this meant the statement could be supported. If you fell for this trap, this is a good reminder to make sure that you check the proof in the source material—every time! Don't just rely on your memory; the test writers know people do this and they set traps accordingly.

The correct answer for the second statement is *No*: The statement is not supported by the given information.

Here's the third statement:

Yes	No	
○	○	If the PEN-NO experiment operates on the surface of the ice in Antarctica, its findings will be considered more valid than those produced by the experiment as currently envisioned.

This problem explicitly mentions the second experiment—great. The statement asks whether changing a certain condition (operating *on the surface of the ice*) would lead to a better outcome. Glance at your map. The first tab mentioned something about being *below the ice*. Go back and scan for that text.

To prevent false-positive results from cosmic rays, PEN-NO will be buried deep below the ice.

It was a conscious choice, then, to conduct the experiment below the ice: Doing so will prevent a certain bad outcome. If that is the case, then moving the experiment to the surface of the ice might allow that bad outcome to occur, so the results would *not* be better.

The correct answer for the third statement is *No*: This is not supported by the information given in the prompt.

6

The third statement was similar to an Inference question. The passage doesn't say outright that conducting the experiment on the surface wouldn't be as beneficial. Rather, you have to infer from the stated information to arrive at that conclusion.

Here are the correct answers for the first question:

1. For each of the following statements, select *Yes* if the statement is supported by the evidence provided. Otherwise, select *No*.

Yes	No	
○	◉	With a construction budget of $30 million, the Storinian government will be able to search for proof of an explanation of charge quantization and help resolve a controversy by measuring the speed of neutrinos produced in nuclear reactors.
○	◉	In its Antarctic experiments, the Storinian government will attempt to ascertain the mass and speed of cosmic rays.
○	◉	If the PEN-NO experiment operates on the surface of the ice in Antarctica, its findings will be considered more valid than those produced by the experiment as currently envisioned.

UPS Redux

Repeat the process with the second question. This one is a standard multiple-choice problem:

2. According to the information provided, the proposed measurement of which of the following kinds of particles is intended to improve the estimate of the mass of these particles?

   (A) Ultra-high-energy cosmic rays

   (B) Particles created by UHECRs above the Earth

   (C) Neutrinos produced in nuclear reactors

   (D) Neutrinos that originate in the Sun

   (E) Magnetic monopoles

This problem asks for a certain kind of particle that fits the question information. Glance at the answers—the first two are cosmic rays, the next two are neutrinos, and the last is magnetic monopoles. So the first thing to figure out is this: Which experiment is the question referring to?

The particles are going to be measured and that measurement is going to *improve the estimate of the mass.* That is, measure the particles and get a better idea of the mass of those particles.

Glance at your map. The second experiment, PEN-NO, talked about the mass of particles, so start there. The particles for this experiment are neutrinos, so it looks like the answer will probably be (C) or (D), but dive into the text to confirm this.

> *PEN-NO will measure the mass and speed of neutrinos produced in particle accelerators and nuclear reactors, both to reduce uncertainty in the known mass of a neutrino and to . . . PEN-NO will also measure the passage of solar and other neutrinos of astronomical origin.*

6

First, it is the neutrinos: *Reduce uncertainty in the known mass* is a synonym for *improve the estimate of the mass*. Eliminate answers (A), (B), and (E) for talking about the wrong type of particle. The next sentence does mention solar neutrinos but says only that the experiment will measure the *passage* of these neutrinos, not their mass.

The correct answer is (C): neutrinos produced in nuclear reactors.

While the answer choices for this question appear to imply that you have to get into all of the technical detail, you really don't have to go very far. The key word *mass* allows you to narrow down to two answers pretty quickly. And choosing between just two answers is not nearly as hard as evaluating all five.

You're back to either-or for the third problem:

3. For each of the following particle types, select *Can conclude* if you can conclude from the information provided that the particles in question have a negligible effect on ordinary matter. Otherwise, select *Cannot conclude*.

Each of the statements accompanying the question stem is one of the three types of particles discussed in the prompt. This question asks whether the information given in the prompt allows you to conclude that each type of particle has *a negligible effect on ordinary matter.*

What does *a negligible effect on ordinary matter* even mean? In general, if you don't really understand what's going on, don't move to plan or solve. Just guess and move on.

If you do want to tackle this problem, a *negligible* effect means an unimportant or minor effect. Next, where could that information be? The third tab was all about budget, so it won't be there. The first tab describes the particles themselves and the second describes the experiments. The desired information could be in either tab, so start with the first tab.

The first description is about cosmic rays but says nothing about ordinary matter. Flip over to the second tab. The first sentence provides more information about cosmic rays but still says nothing about ordinary matter, so you *cannot conclude* anything about the effect cosmic rays have on ordinary matter.

Go back to the first tab to see what it says about *neutrinos produced in particle accelerators*. This tab says that neutrinos in general *interact only weakly with normal matter*. That almost matches what the question stem says—it's not a very important effect. In this case, you *can conclude* that *neutrinos produced in particle accelerators* have a *negligible effect on ordinary matter*.

Finally, check what the text says about magnetic monopoles. The first tab doesn't mention ordinary matter in connection with these particles, nor does the second tab. As a result, you *cannot conclude* anything about the effect magnetic monopoles have on ordinary matter. Here are the correct answers for the third question:

3. For each of the following particle types, select *Can conclude* if you can conclude from the information provided that the particles in question have a negligible effect on ordinary matter. Otherwise, select *Cannot conclude*.

Can conclude	Cannot conclude	
○	◉	Ultra-high-energy cosmic rays
◉	○	Neutrinos produced in particle accelerators
○	◉	Magnetic monopoles

That was a very challenging MSR prompt. If you struggled with it, notice a couple of things that might help you next time around.

First, while the tabs did have extremely detailed scientific information, you didn't have to become an expert in particle physics in order to answer all of the questions. The technical language was often just window dressing. For instance, in problem 1, the first statement mentions all kinds of details (*charge quantization*??), but all you needed to know was that the prompt didn't provide any information regarding how much each of the three experiments would cost separately to build. Likewise, you can get through the second and third statements of the first question without having to understand all of the details.

The third question was pretty challenging—even the question stem itself was hard to parse. When you realize that you don't understand what the question is saying or asking, that's an excellent clue to get out. Guess randomly and move on!

If you feel okay with this subject matter, then even the third question requires only a medium understanding of the text. The one statement that did match used close synonyms (e.g., *ordinary matter* in the question and *normal matter* in the prompt). The descriptions for the other two particles don't mention any kind of interactions with any matter at all. The test writers want to see whether you can read around the scary technical language and still process the high-level information.

This fits a lot of what happens in the real world, too. You run up against some really technical detail at work, and you may have to understand it well enough to make a high-level business call about something—but you don't suddenly have to become an expert about this technical thing. Expect that to happen on MSR as well.

Finally, when you're done answering any question, your learning has just begun. Take the time to pick apart the prompt, the question, and your own reasoning in order to get better the next time you tackle an intricate science MSR question.

And remember: Getting better also involves knowing what *not* to do so that you can guess and move on quickly. Use that precious time to better advantage elsewhere in the section!

Practice Your Skills

Log into Atlas for additional practice problems. Give yourself a block of time to do an entire MSR prompt plus three problems—review after you're done with the whole set for that prompt, not after each problem.

CHAPTER 7

Two-Part Analysis

In This Chapter

- UPS for Quant Two-Parts
- UPS for Verbal Two-Parts
- UPS for Logic Two-Parts

In this chapter, you will learn how to Understand–Plan–Solve your way to the answer for all three types of Two-Part problems: quant-, verbal-, and logic-based.

CHAPTER 7 Two-Part Analysis

Two-Part Analysis problems closely resemble regular multiple-choice questions on the Quant and Verbal sections of the exam—with a twist. As the name implies, the question you will answer will have two parts to it, not just one.

The prompt will appear at the top of the screen, followed by the question. The multiple-choice answers will appear in a table below that, as shown here:

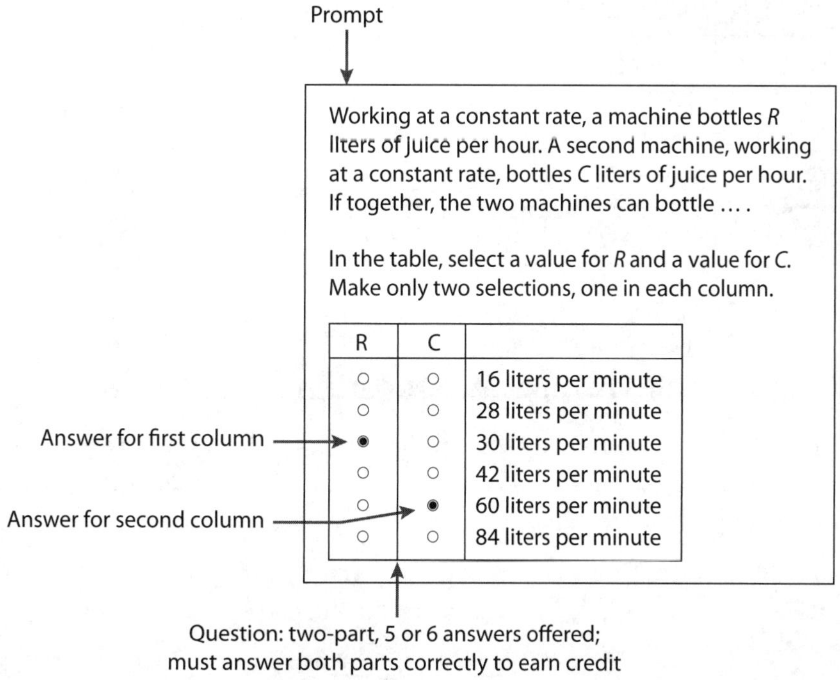
Prompt
Working at a constant rate, a machine bottles R liters of juice per hour. A second machine, working at a constant rate, bottles C liters of juice per hour. If together, the two machines can bottle ....
In the table, select a value for R and a value for C. Make only two selections, one in each column.
R
C
16 liters per minute
28 liters per minute
30 liters per minute
42 liters per minute
60 liters per minute
84 liters per minute
Answer for first column
Answer for second column
Question: two-part, 5 or 6 answers offered; must answer both parts correctly to earn credit

The prompt will often feel very similar to a standard quant or verbal problem, but will likely contain more information than the typical quant or verbal problem. In addition, the two questions will likely be related or adjacent in some way, since you have to choose from the same set of answers for each question. For example, you might be asked to strengthen *and* weaken an argument, and all of the answers would be statements. However, the questions could be quite different, as long as the set of answers logically follows both questions. For example, a set of numerical answers in units of *boxes per hour* might accompany two dissimilar rate questions, such as the rate at which machine X operated *and* the rate at which the night crew fell short of a production goal.

You'll be given five or six answer choices and the correct answer for each part could actually be the same answer (though this is rare). At times, you may be asked to solve for the answers simultaneously; for example, you may need to solve for the interest rate for Investment A and the interest rate for Investment B, which together earned a given amount of interest.

Two-Parts typically fall fairly cleanly into one of three categories: quant-, verbal-, or logic-based. Some problems incorporate elements from two categories, but it's usually the case that you can identify the problem as primarily quant-based or primarily verbal-based and work accordingly.

UPS for Quant Two-Parts

Here's how to apply the Understand–Plan–Solve process to a quant-based Two-Part.

Try this problem:

Two water storage tanks, Tank Alpha and Tank Bravo, can each hold more than 20,000 liters of water. Currently, Alpha contains 5,000 liters of water and Bravo contains 8,000 liters. Alpha will be filled at a constant rate of *A* liters per hour and Bravo will be filled at a constant rate of *B* liters per hour. If both tanks begin to be filled at the same time, after 15 hours, the two tanks will contain the same amount of water, though neither will be full.

In the table below, identify a value for *A* and a value for *B* that together are consistent with the given information. Make only one selection in each column.

A	*B*	
○	○	30
○	○	90
○	○	150
○	○	220
○	○	290

Ready? Let's go!

Step 1: Understand the Prompt and Question

7

Before you start to read a Two-Part prompt, glance at the answers. What form are they in? In this case, they're numbers. Glance also at the question stem; it asks for the value of *A* and the value of *B*. This quick glance will give you an early clue that you've got a quant-based problem.

Treat this as you would a standard math story problem and translate the information carefully on your scratch paper. A quick sketch can help keep the information straight:

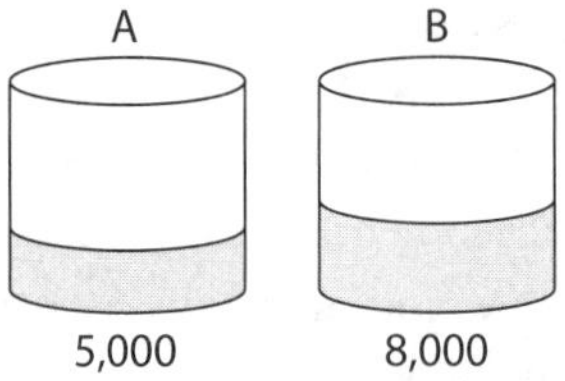

The two tanks are filling at different rates. In 15 hours, they'll have the same amount of water. What does that tell you about the rate for each tank?

Because Alpha has less water than Bravo to start, it must be filling at a faster rate—otherwise, Tank A couldn't catch up to Tank B. Jot a note on your scrap paper that $A > B$. If your answers don't match that idea, then you'll know you made a mistake somewhere.

The question stem contains an important clue: It specifically tells you to find values that *together are consistent* with the details given in the problem. As you move forward, look for opportunities to solve for the two values in tandem.

Step 2: Plan Your Approach

This is a work problem, so consider the RTW formula: Rate $\times$ Time $=$ Work.

How are you going to go from a starting point of 5,000 and 8,000 liters to an ending point of the same number of liters?

Alpha has 5,000 liters now and will be filled at a rate of A liters per hour for 15 hours... hmm. If you ignore Bravo, that's not enough to solve for A. It is the case that you're going to need to solve for the two variables simultaneously.

There are two possible approaches. First, you could do algebra. Use the given variables to set up a mathematical representation for the final number of liters for Tank Alpha, at a rate of A, and the final number of liters for Tank Bravo, at a rate of B. Then, set those two numbers equal.

Second, you could try the answer choices. You know rate A must be greater than rate B, so try setting $B = 30$, the smallest value in the answers, and work from there.

On this particular problem, it's possible for the value of B to be one of four answer choices (everything but 290). In addition, since the two rates are connected, you cannot solve just to find B. In other words, you might actually have to try all four possibilities before you find the answer. In this case, an algebraic approach is likely to be more efficient.

Step 3: Solve the Problem

Tank Alpha is filling at the rate of A liters per hour. Over 15 hours, it will add $15A$ liters. It started with 5,000 liters, so Alpha's final amount of water is equal to $5{,}000 + 15A$.

If Tank Bravo is filling at the rate of B liters per hour, then it will wind up with $8{,}000 + 15B$ liters. Now, set the equations equal to each other:

$$5{,}000 + 15A = 8{,}000 + 15B$$

That equation can't be solved for A and B individually—this is why you have to solve simultaneously. There are multiple possible solutions, but there is a consistent relationship between the two rates. Your task is to figure out what that relationship is. Only one *pair* of answer choices will fit that relationship.

$5{,}000 + 15A = 8{,}000 + 15B$	
$15A = 3{,}000 + 15B$	Subtract 5,000 from each side.
$15A - 15B = 3{,}000$	Subtract $15B$ from each side.
$A - B = 200$	Divide both sides by 15.

7

This is the relationship between the two rates: They have to differ by 200, and *A* must be greater than *B*. Look at the answers. The only pairing that works is 90 and 290:

A	*B*	
○	○	30
○	◉	90
○	○	150
○	○	220
◉	○	290

Double-check that you filled in the right columns with the appropriate numbers! Alpha has to fill faster, so *A* has to be the greater rate.

UPS for Verbal Two-Parts

Verbal Two-Parts most often feel similar to Critical Reasoning (CR) problems from the Verbal section.

As always, the UPS process will help you to both answer the question and review your work afterwards. Whether you answer the question correctly or incorrectly, use UPS to review each step of the process afterwards.

Try this problem:

> Software Company M accused Company S of intellectual property theft, citing as evidence similar user interface designs for the company's new operating system products, both of which launched this year, and the fact that Company M's chief designer defected to Company S nine months ago. Company S countered that the product was 90% completed by the time the former chief designer joined Company S and that the designer was not allowed to work on that product in order to avoid any potential conflicts of interest.
>
> Select the additional information that, if true, would provide the strongest evidence *For* Company S's claim that it did not illegally obtain information about Company M's products, and select the additional information that, if true, would provide the strongest evidence *Against* that claim.

For	Against	
○	○	A comparison with a third operating system company's user interface design shows overlap with Company M only in features that have been in industry-wide use for years.
○	○	Company S's former chief designer quit after a dispute over creative control.
○	○	Last year, another company released software that incorporates some of the same user interface designs at issue in the dispute.
○	○	Several key parts of the software code in Company S's product are nearly identical to code that Company M's former chief designer wrote for Company M.
○	○	It is quite common for software companies to accuse other companies of intellectual property theft.

How did it go? Before reading the explanations below, review your work yourself. Then, use the walk-through below to help you past any sticking points or to help you brainstorm more efficient approaches to your solution process.

Step 1: Understand the Prompt and Question

Glance at the answers: The fact that there are sentences indicate that this is likely either a verbal- or logic-based problem. The next clue: The question asks for evidence *For* something and evidence *Against* something. This is similar to a Critical Reasoning problem from the Verbal section, so tackle this in the same way that you tackle CR.

Read the argument and make a map:

M: S stole our design

1. Similar design
2. M's designer → S

S: 90% done; designer not allowed to work on it

The first part of the question asks you to strengthen Company S's claim that it did *not* steal anything from Company M; in other words, the question is oriented from S's point of view, not M's. The second part asks you to weaken Company S's claim.

Step 2: Plan Your Approach

You can use the same strategies you use for CR problems. A correct Strengthen answer makes the conclusion at least a little more likely to be valid, so the first column will validate (at least a little) the claim that Company S did *not* steal from Company M. Look through the answers now, concentrating just on this part of the question.

Step 3: Solve the Problem

If you're very good at CR, you can try to find the strengthen and weaken answers at the same time. If, on the other hand, you have ever accidentally picked a strengthen answer when you were supposed to weaken, or vice versa, then concentrate on finding the *For* answer first. Then, go through again for the *Against* answer.

The answer choices are labeled (A) through (E) for clarity. As you read each one, ask yourself whether it makes Company S's case any better:

> (A) *A comparison with a third operating system company's user interface design shows overlap with Company M only in features that have been in industry-wide use for years.*

A third company's system doesn't overlap much with Company M's system. A *lack* of overlap doesn't strengthen Company S's case. If a third company's system were super similar to M's system, that might help S's case—but that's not what this choice says. Eliminate this answer.

> (B) *Company S's former chief designer quit after a dispute over creative control.*

Careful! The argument is about Company M's designer, the one who moved over to Company S. The reason Company S's former designer (a different person) quit has no bearing on what happened when Company M's designer joined. Eliminate this choice.

> (C) *Last year, another company released software that incorporates some of the same user interface designs at issue in the dispute.*

7

A third company released software *last* year that contains some of the designs that are in dispute. The argument states that Company M released its own software *this* year, so this certainly bolsters Company S's claim that it did not steal anything from Company M (though maybe they both stole ideas from the third company!). This one looks good but check the final two answers.

(D) *Several key parts of the software code in Company S's product are nearly identical to code that Company M's former chief designer wrote for Company M.*

If some parts of the software code are identical to code written by Company M's former chief designer while working for that company, this definitely does not help Company S's claim that it didn't steal any ideas. This might even *weaken* S's claim. Note that down. Also, eliminate this choice.

(E) *It is quite common for software companies to accuse other companies of intellectual property theft.*

This may be true in general, but it does not provide any evidence as to what happened in the specific case discussed in the argument.

The correct answer for the first part, *For*, is answer (C).

Now, reuse your initial analysis to help narrow down the answers faster for the second part. Which choice goes *against* S's claim that it didn't steal any ideas?

Start with answer (D), the one that you already thought might be a weaken. If parts of the code written by the employee who switched companies are *nearly identical* in the two products, this definitely weakens S's claim that it did not steal anything from M. It would be pretty unlikely for someone else to have written code that is *nearly identical* in *several key parts.*

Do review the other answers, just to be sure. For answer (A), this third company's design overlaps with M only on commonly used features. What impact does that have on the claim that S stole some of M's features? It's not clear what features M is claiming S stole, so this information about a third company is not relevant to the argument.

Answers (B) and (E) are irrelevant one way or the other, so they can't be the *Against* answer. If answer (C) is the *For* answer, then it can't also be the *Against* answer; these two classifications are opposites. So answer (D) must be correct.

The answers are:

For	Against	
○	○	A comparison with a third operating system company's user interface design shows overlap with Company M only in features that have been in industry-wide use for years.
○	○	Company S's former chief designer quit after a dispute over creative control.
◉	○	Last year, another company released software that incorporates some of the same user interface designs at issue in the dispute.
○	◉	Several key parts of the software code in Company S's product are nearly identical to code that Company M's former chief designer wrote for that company.
○	○	It is quite common for software companies to accuse other companies of intellectual property theft.

When the two parts of the question are not connected, as in the first verbal example above, you could save time by thinking about the two parts simultaneously—but you are taking a risk. If you ever make mistakes with this (e.g., if you swapped the two answers on the last problem), then tackle the two questions separately in the future.

Some Two-Part questions will ask for two connected answers, as you saw in the quant-based question earlier, and this can happen on a verbal-based problem, too. For example, you might be asked to find a specific *Cause* and *Effect* sequence or a certain *Circumstance* that would lead to a specific *Prediction*. In these cases, you must think about the two parts of the question simultaneously.

Try another one:

> The Golden Age of Radio—the period of time during which radio broadcasting in the United States reached its widest audience—came to an end in the 1950s as radio was supplanted by television. World War II, which had caused widespread shortages of the technology used in television sets, ended in 1945. As a result of a greatly reduced cost of materials as well as a sudden influx of workers seeking employment after the war, television-manufacturing companies multiplied. Competition kept the price of television sets modest, compared to the relatively high income of many U.S. households during the post-war years; by the end of the decade, the number of households with a television had increased more than a hundredfold.
>
> Identify in the table one *Cause* and one *Effect* of that cause that together, according to the author, likely contributed to the end of the Golden Age of Radio. Make only two selections, one in each column.

Cause	Effect	
○	○	An increase in competition among television manufacturers
○	○	A decrease in the number of U.S. homes with a radio
○	○	A widespread shortage of television-manufacturing technology
○	○	A reduction in the number of available manufacturing workers during World War II
○	○	A decrease in the cost of television-manufacturing materials
○	○	The relatively high income of post-war U.S. households

Step 1: Understand the Prompt and Question

The sentences signal a verbal- or logic-based problem. The fact that the question asks for a *Cause* and an *Effect* signals a CR-type verbal problem. Further, a cause-effect setup will usually need to be solved simultaneously.

The prompt first makes a general claim: The Golden Age of Radio ended in the 1950s when TV took over.

Then it provides a series of events that led to this outcome. After World War II ended in 1945, raw costs for making TVs went down a lot, and a lot of people were looking for work. In addition, household income was relatively high. These facts meant that companies could make a lot of TVs and sell them cheaply, allowing the number of households with TVs to greatly increase.

7

The blurb basically explains why TV was able to overtake radio as the entertainment medium of choice in the 1950s. The question asks what *Cause* led to what *Effect* that together contributed to the rise of TV.

Step 2: Plan Your Approach

The various facts in the argument are a bit jumbled together. Since the question asks specifically about a cause and an effect, it's worth the effort to map the information logically:

WWII ends → workers avail + material costs decr.
→ more comp make more TVs
→ cheaper TVs

Also: more inc to buy

There is one big chain of information: the business reasons that led to more cheap TVs on the market. Anything in the chain except for the last piece of information could be the cause, and anything in that chain except for the first piece of information could be the effect.

Separately, household income also increased, but the blurb doesn't provide any information as to why or how that happened. As a result, this fact can't be part of any cause-effect chain in the answers.

Step 3: Solve the Problem

Examine the answers, looking for a cause that falls earlier in the chain of events and an effect that both falls later in the chain of events and can reasonably be called a result of the earlier cause. Take a look at answer choice (A):

(A) *An increase in competition among television manufacturers*

This is in the chain, so it is one of the potential pieces of the puzzle, though it's not possible to say whether it's the cause or the effect without reviewing the rest of the answers. Put a star next to this information in your map. Now, move to choice (B):

7

(B) *A decrease in the number of U.S. homes with a radio*

This one is tricky. Technically, the blurb says only that *radio was supplanted by television*; it does not specify what this means. It could be that people who already had radios kept those radios but also bought TVs and spent more time watching TV. So the *number* of radios didn't necessarily have to decrease. Here is choice (C):

(C) *A widespread shortage of television-manufacturing technology*

The shortage existed during the war; once the war ended in 1945, these shortages no longer existed, and that fact contributed to the greater number of TVs built. This choice is the opposite of one cause of the growth of the TV market. Move on to choice (D):

(D) *A reduction in the number of available manufacturing workers during World War II*

It is true that fewer workers were available during the war but, as with the last choice, this changed after the war. The fact that more workers were available after the war helped the TV market to thrive. This choice is the opposite of one cause of the growth of the TV market. Here is choice (E):

(E) *A decrease in the cost of television-manufacturing materials*

This is part of the argument given in the blurb. First, the cost of these materials decreased. That allowed more companies to make TVs, and that in turn increased competition in the market, which is what the first answer choice said. This choice is the *cause* and the first answer is the *effect*. And finally, look at choice (F):

(F) *The relatively high income of post-war U.S. households*

This was also mentioned, but it is not connected to any other pieces of information in the blurb, so it cannot be either the cause or the effect.

The answers are:

Cause	Effect	
○	●	An increase in competition among television manufacturers
○	○	A decrease in the number of U.S. homes with a radio
○	○	A widespread shortage of television-manufacturing technology
○	○	A reduction in the number of available manufacturing workers during World War II
●	○	A decrease in the cost of television-manufacturing materials
○	○	The relatively high income of post-war U.S. households

UPS for Logic Two-Parts

The third category is the logic problem. This is a type of verbal-based reasoning with some more formalized analytical thinking.

Try this problem:

A chemical plant operating continuously has two 12-hour shifts, a day shift and a night shift, during each of which as many as five chemicals can be produced. Equipment limitations and safety regulations impose constraints on the types of chemicals that can be produced during the same shift. No more than two oxidizers can be produced per shift; the same limit holds true for monomers. On either shift, the sum of the safety rating for all chemicals should be no greater than 13 for health risk and 9 for reactivity.

Four chemicals have already been chosen for each shift, as shown below:

Day Shift

Acrylonitrile	(health = 4, reactivity = 2, oxidizer = no, monomer = yes)
Chloroprene	(health = 2, reactivity = 0, oxidizer = no, monomer = yes)
Hydrogen peroxide	(health = 3, reactivity = 2, oxidizer = yes, monomer = no)
Titanium dioxide	(health = 1, reactivity = 0, oxidizer = no, monomer = no)

7

Night Shift

Ammonium nitrate	(health = 2, reactivity = 3, oxidizer = yes, monomer = no)
Phosphine	(health = 4, reactivity = 2, oxidizer = no, monomer = no)
Potassium perchlorate	(health = 1, reactivity = 1, oxidizer = yes, monomer = no)
Propylene	(health = 1, reactivity = 1, oxidizer = no, monomer = yes)

Select a chemical that *Could* be added to either shift. Then, select a chemical that *Cannot* be added to either shift. Make only two selections, one in each column.

Could be added to either shift	Cannot be added to either shift	
O	O	Chlorine (health = 3, reactivity = 0, oxidizer = yes, monomer = no)
O	O	Ethylene (health = 3, reactivity = 2, oxidizer = no, monomer = yes)
O	O	Nickel carbonyl (health = 4, reactivity = 3, oxidizer = no, monomer = no)
O	O	Phenol (health = 3, reactivity = 0, oxidizer = no, monomer = no)
O	O	Sulfuric acid (health = 3, reactivity = 2, oxidizer = yes, monomer = no)
O	O	Vinyl chloride (health = 2, reactivity = 2, oxidizer = no, monomer = yes)

Step 1: Understand the Prompt and Question

Glance at the answers: text *and* numbers. The complexity of the information in the answers, coupled with the tables of information in the question stem, indicate that this is likely a logic problem.

This is also a really technical problem. Don't get caught up in the language. You don't need to know what a *monomer* is or what *reactivity* means. You just need to be able to classify things.

Whenever you have a logic problem, list out the details in a clear and organized way:

2 shifts: D and N
Max 5 chem per shift

Four of the five slots on each shift are already filled, so you're looking to fill the fifth slot. Map the constraints:

Slot constraints:
– No more than 2 O's per shift
– No more than 2 M's per shift
– $H \leq 13$
– $R \leq 9$

You have to identify a single chemical that *Could* fit either shift (there's only one) and another chemical that *Cannot* fit either shift (again, there's only one). The characteristics of the chemicals you are to choose from are in the answer choices.

Since you are going to have to work with the information from the answers in order to solve, jot down a little table on your scratch paper, something like this:

COULD	CANNOT	Chemical
		Chl
		Eth
		NC
		Ph
		SA
		VC

Use this to keep track of your eliminations as you go.

Step 2: Plan Your Approach

Since this problem is about following a chain of logic, first figure out what *must* and *must not* be true about the fifth chemical based on the given constraints and the four chemicals that are already set for each shift. Then, armed with these more refined constraints about the fifth possibility for each shift, go through the list of chemicals in the answer choices to figure out whether the chemical in question could be added to the shift.

Step 3: Solve the Problem

First, lay out what each shift already has:

Day Has:	Night Has:
H = 10	H = 8
R = 4	R = 7
1 O	2 O's
2 M's	1 M

You're only allowed 2 M's total, which the day shift has, and 2 O's total, which the night shift has. So the fifth chemical can't be an M or an O. Glance through the answers. In the COULD column, write NO for chlorine, ethylene, sulfuric acid, and vinyl chloride. Four down, two to go!

You're also allowed only 13 H total, and the day shift already has an H of 10, so the H rating of the final chemical has to be ≤ 3. Likewise, R can't be more than 9 total, and the night shift already has an R of 7, so the R rating of the final chemical has to be ≤ 2.

Scan the two remaining answers. Nickel carbonyl fails on both counts—it has an H rating of 4 and an R rating of 3.

The only chemical that *could* be added to either shift is phenol.

Use the work you've already done to figure out which chemical cannot go on either shift. Of the rejected answers, start with nickel carbonyl, since you've looked most carefully at that one so far and it has the highest health and reactivity safety ratings. As noted above, nickel carbonyl can't go on the day shift because it has an H rating of 4. And it can't go on the night shift because it has an R rating of 3. This is the one that cannot be added to either shift!

Here are the answers:

7

Could be added to either shift	Cannot be added to either shift	Chemical
○	○	Chlorine (health = 3, reactivity = 0, oxidizer = yes, monomer = no)
○	○	Ethylene (health = 3, reactivity = 2, oxidizer = no, monomer = yes)
○	◉	Nickel carbonyl (health = 4, reactivity = 3, oxidizer = no, monomer = no)
◉	○	Phenol (health = 3, reactivity = 0, oxidizer = no, monomer = no)
○	○	Sulfuric acid (health = 3, reactivity = 2, oxidizer = yes, monomer = no)
○	○	Vinyl chloride (health = 2, reactivity = 2, oxidizer = no, monomer = yes)

When you see a quant- or verbal-based Two-Part, it will usually resemble the questions in the Quant and Verbal sections of the exam, and you can use many of the same strategies you're learning for those sections. Unlike the more quant- and verbal-based Two-Parts, logic problems are different from what you are already learning for the rest of the test. Take a little time to understand the story and make an organized map of the given constraints. Use that map to make any logical inferences you can to narrow down the possibilities further.

Practice Your Skills

Now that you've learned about each problem type, take a look at the next chapter, which summarizes each type and provides some additional strategies for time management on IR. Then, log into Atlas to practice more Two-Parts—and all problem types.

CHAPTER 8

Integrated Reasoning Strategies

In This Chapter

- Decision-Making on the GMAT
- Decision-Making on the EA
- How to Know When to Bail
- Table Analysis
- Graphics Interpretation
- Multi-Source Reasoning
- Two-Part Analysis
- When to Prioritize and When to Bail

In this chapter, you will review the Understand–Plan–Solve process and the specific strategies you learned for Tables, Graphs, MSRs, and Two-Parts. You will also learn how to optimize your test mindset and time management for the GMAT and the Executive Assessment.

CHAPTER 8 Integrated Reasoning Strategies

The four question types are identical on both the GMAT and the Executive Assessment (EA), so the solution process is the same no matter which test you take.

The sections work slightly differently on each test, though, so there are some differences in terms of your executive decision-making, depending upon which test you take.

Decision-Making on the GMAT

The section is 30 minutes long, and you'll need to solve a total of 12 problems. Unlike the Quant and Verbal sections, the Integrated Reasoning (IR) section is not adaptive; all 12 problems will be set before you start the section.

The vast majority of test-takers will not be able to address all 12 problems fully in that time, so plan to bail (guess *immediately*) on a number of problems in the section. (Also, if you are running low on time, just guess on every remaining problem. There are no penalties for wrong answers and you might get lucky!)

As on the Quant and Verbal sections, you must answer the current problem onscreen before you can move to the next one. In addition, as on Quant and Verbal, you cannot go back to a problem once you've answered it.

But that's okay! The test is constructed to allow you to get a number of problems wrong and still get a good score. Follow these guidelines depending upon your goal score:

If your goal score is...	Bail on this many problems	Per-problem time
6+	2	3 minutes
5	3	3 minutes 20 seconds
4	4	3 minutes 45 seconds

Decision-Making on the EA

The Integrated Reasoning section is 30 minutes long, and you'll need to solve a total of 12 problems. The section will come in two panels of 6 problems each.

Within one panel, you can move around as you choose among those six problems. When you finish the first panel and choose to move to the second panel, you will not be able to return to the first panel of problems.

Why do they do this? On the Executive Assessment, IR is section-adaptive (as are the Quant and Verbal sections). The first panel of six problems will be set in advance and will represent a range of difficulties. After you finish that panel, the test will give you a second panel of six problems that more closely targets the level at which you are performing, as illustrated below:

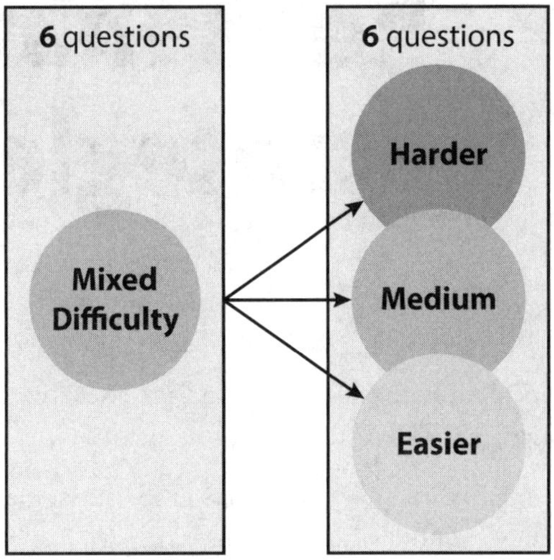

Further, your IR performance will determine your starting points for the Verbal and Quant sections, as illustrated below:

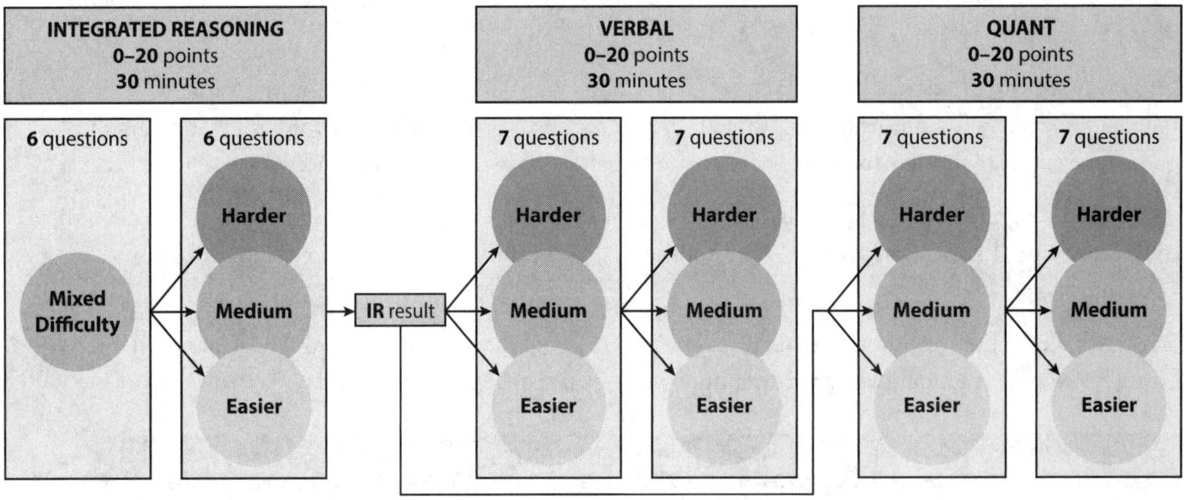

The vast majority of test-takers will not be able to fully complete all 12 IR problems in the 30 minutes provided, so plan to bail—guess immediately—on at least one problem in each panel. Because you can move around among the 6 problems in one panel, this decision is easier than it is on the GMAT. (Also, do answer everything. There are no penalties for incorrect answers and you might get lucky!)

Plan to use half of your time, 15 minutes, on the first panel. If you bail on one problem, that gives you 3 minutes for each of the remaining problems. If you decide to bail on a second one, you'll have 3 minutes and 45 seconds per problem on the four that you do answer.

In general, plan to bail on one problem in each panel and then give yourself one more "freebie" on top of that. You can choose whether to use the freebie in the first or second panel.

Move through each panel twice. The first time, solve the problems that seem straightforward to you. Mark the others with a flag as you go; these are your bail candidates. Once you've finished the ones that you find easier, scroll through the flagged problems to decide where you want to bail and what else you want to try.

How to Know When to Bail

First, a bail is a problem on which you guess immediately so that you save that time to use elsewhere. If you try a problem but can't find the answer, still guess on that problem—but don't count it as one of your bail problems.

Before test day (practice or the real thing!), take stock of your strengths and weaknesses. A low-ROI (return on investment) problem is one that combines both a topic area that you don't like and a weaker problem type for you. Know how to recognize these low-ROI questions quickly, so that you can get out right away when you see them.

Ask yourself some questions to help determine what to do and what *not* to do:

- Generally better at Quant or at Verbal?
- Comfortable with tables and/or graphs? (Do Table and/or Graph problems.)
- Good at piecing together information from different sources? (Then Multi-Source Reasoning is for you.)
- Comfortable with standard Critical Reasoning (CR) and/or Quant multiple-choice? (Look for these opportunities on Two-Part problems.)

When you finish a practice test, first review the section globally. Are you happy with the decisions that you made about where to invest time and effort and where *not* to? In hindsight, you might realize that you cut off one problem too quickly. What clues can help you to know next time that you actually can do this problem?

You may also realize that you spent too much time on another problem that you really had no idea how to do. Likewise, what are the clues that you want to spot next time so that you know to bail—guess and move on—right away?

Work out your decision-making processes before test day so that you can react appropriately to different scenarios on test day.

The four IR problem types are summarized on the following pages.

Table Analysis

Key details:

- Main feature: Table
- Type of problem: One Either-Or question
- Key Strategy: SEE (Sort, Eyeball, Estimate)

Table prompts will, of course, contain a table, along with one either-or question (e.g., true/false, yes/no). You'll answer three statements, each one of which must be answered correctly in order to earn credit on that problem.

The table may also be accompanied by a blurb: a separate paragraph of text that describes the information in the table and may even provide additional information you'll need to answer the question.

Before starting to solve the problem, glance through the three statements. If at least two look okay to you, go ahead and solve this problem. Even if you have to guess on one statement, you'll have a 50/50 chance if you were able to do the other two statements correctly.

If two or all three statements look hard enough that you're not sure you can do them or think they'll take too long, consider bailing on this problem.

Step 1: Understand the Prompt and Question

Glance at the title (if applicable), column headers, and rows. Read the blurb and examine the data in the table, thinking about the *what* and *so what*. What types of information do the different rows and columns contain? What connections (if any) exist between the columns? If appropriate, jot down a note or two.

Once you understand the basics, glance at the data in the table. Are there any surprising data points (e.g., some entries of 0 or some entries that are very different from the others)? Don't try to figure out why these entries are what they are; just notice them and keep them in mind for later.

You'll have one either-or question. Glance at all three statements before you read the question itself. Are they connected or unrelated? If connected, you can solve them simultaneously.

Next, read the question stem and jot down anything that will help keep you focused on what you need to do. If you don't understand what the question is asking you to do, guess and move on.

Step 2: Plan Your Approach

If you can solve some or all of the statements simultaneously, figure out which pieces you can solve together and in what order you want to tackle them.

If you are solving separately, start with whichever statement seems easiest to you. If they're all about the same, go in order. Use the SEE (sort, eyeball, estimate) strategy to guide your thinking.

For the first statement you tackle, how should you sort the table to make your job easier?

Can you eyeball any of the data—see what the trend is without calculating anything at all? If you do have to calculate anything, can you estimate at any point along the way? How heavily?

Step 3: Solve the Problem

Dive in! Sort the table and examine the data. Wherever you can, eyeball and estimate. If you have to perform a calculation, make sure to do so on your scrap paper, not in your head. You do have a calculator if you need a precise answer; write down the calculation you want to do before you plug it into the calculator. (But don't perform a precise calculation unless you really need to.)

If you get stuck, think about whether a different table sort might get you unstuck.

Finally, repeat the process for the other two statements.

Graphics Interpretation

Key details:

- Main feature: Graph, diagram or visual of some sort
- Content: Can be standard math or analytical
- Type of problem: One Fill-in-the-Blank question
- Key Strategy: SEE (Select, Eyeball, Estimate)

Graphs may consist of a standard math graph, a chart, a timeline, or even a geometry diagram. Anything is possible, but if you're given something nonstandard, you will also be given instructions as to how to read the graph.

The graph may also be accompanied by a blurb that describes the visual and may even provide additional information you'll need to solve the problem.

The question will consist of one or two sentences with a total of two blanks with drop-down menus for the answers. You may be given anywhere from three to six multiple-choice options for each blank.

If one of the two blanks looks too hard to answer, check how many answer choices it has. If it has only three or four and you can answer the other blank, then you'll still have pretty decent odds to make a lucky guess. If, on the other hand, that blank has five or six answer choices, you might want to bail on the entire problem.

Step 1: Understand the Prompt and Question

First, glance at the visual—is it a type of graph you recognize or something unusual? Then, take the first step of SEE (select, eyeball, estimate). Click on each drop-down menu (where you see the word *Select*) to see the answer choice options. Words? Numbers? If numbers, how spread out are they?

Next, read the title and blurb (if present) to orient you to the information given in the graph. Then, examine the graph, thinking about the *what* and *so what*. What types of information does it contain? What does each point, line, bar, box, arrow, or other visual represent?

If the graph type is completely unfamiliar to you, take a little more time to orient yourself. Jot down anything that will help you to remember the big picture. If you've read through the blurb and examined the graph carefully but still find yourself lost, guess and move on.

Once you understand the basics, glance at the data in the graph. Are there any surprising data points (e.g., some entries or parts that are very different from others)? Don't try to figure out why these entries are what they are; just notice them and keep them in mind for later.

Next, read the question stem and jot down anything that you may find useful. Then, click on the first blank to show the possible answer choices and read through the first part of the text that applies to that blank. When appropriate, click on the second blank to see those options.

Do not read the statement without looking at the multiple-choice options! The options may completely change the way you plan for and solve the problem. For instance, if the answers are values that are spread apart, you'll know you can estimate. Alternatively, you may have been expecting specific values but the blank actually contains qualifiers such as *greater than* and *less than*, allowing you to compare (either to a benchmark value or an estimate) rather than calculate.

The two blanks may be related, in which case you will solve simultaneously, or the two blanks may be independent. Know the relationship between the blanks before you start to solve.

Step 2: Plan Your Approach

Which blank is easier to answer first? Start there.

Which parts of the graph do you need in order to tackle your starting blank? You may need just one or two of the data points or one portion of the diagram given.

Do you just need to find or identify something, or will you need to perform a calculation? Can you eyeball or estimate values, or do you need to be more precise?

Step 3: Solve the Problem

Again, make sure that you are solving in a form that matches the drop-down answers given. Do any calculations on your scratch paper, and don't hesitate to pop up the calculator when needed. As always, write out the calculation you want to perform before plugging it into your calculator.

Wherever you can save time and effort by eyeballing or estimating, do so!

Multi-Source Reasoning

Key details:

- Main feature: Two or three tabs
- Types of problems: Typically three problems (though can be two or four)
  - 1 standard multiple-choice
  - 2 either-or problems

Multi-Source Reasoning (MSR) prompts contain two or three tabs of information and are typically accompanied by three separate problems. One of the problems is usually in standard multiple-choice format, while the other two are typically in either-or form (e.g., true/false, yes/no). On either-or problems, each of the three statements must be answered correctly in order to earn credit on that problem.

You'll need some additional time up front to process all of the MSR text, but this time is spread across the three problems you'll solve. Expect to spend about two to three minutes orienting yourself to everything in the tabs, then to spend about two additional minutes per problem.

On the Executive Assessment, a set of MSR problems will always appear together in one panel. Scroll through all three problems and do whichever one seems easiest first. It's generally not a good idea to decide to bail on the entire set of three, since they will appear in a single panel—missing three out of six would likely drop your score too low—but you could choose to bail on one of the three.

On the GMAT, you could choose to bail on all three MSRs. Just note that you can't view all three problems before deciding whether to bail—you'll have to decide what to do about the first problem before you can see the second. Glance at the problem itself before you try to process the information in the tabs. If it looks really hard, you might decide to bail on that immediately. In this case, guess randomly and move to the second question (still without looking at the tabs). If you also want to bail on the second problem, then bail on the entire MSR problem set; it's not worth it to learn the tabs if you're only going to do one problem. If you think you can answer the second problem, then dive into the tabs to learn the information.

Step 1: Understand the Prompt and Question

Glance at the tab titles for a hint of the topics covered. Use the titles to help you start creating your Multi-Source Reasoning map.

Dive into the first tab. As you read, create a map: Jot down high-level information on your scrap paper to help you figure out where to go when you get to the questions.

As you work your way through the tabs, think about the *what* and the *so what*: What does the tab say and what are the implications of that information? If a tab contains a table, diagram, or other visual, note that in your map. (Reminder: Tables in MSR tabs are *not* sortable.)

After you've looked at all of the tabs, take a moment to think about how they interconnect. You might even click through them all again to remind yourself.

MSRs come with two different kinds of questions: standard multiple-choice and either-or. Answer standard multiple-choice questions in the same way that you would answer a Reading Comprehension or quant problem. For either-or problems, use the same process you learned for Tables.

Step 2: Plan Your Approach

Which tabs are you likely to need in order to address this statement? What information do you need to review in those tabs? Reread the relevant information, jotting down notes if appropriate.

Will you need to do math? On multiple-choice questions, you can use the same strategies you learn for the Quant section of the exam: Smart Numbers, Work Backwards, Test Cases, and so on. Math-focused either-or statements can sometimes be solved in a similar way; if this is the case, take some time to figure out how to organize your scratch paper. Then you'll be able to run all three statements through the same process. (And don't forget to estimate wherever possible!)

On either-or questions, if you can solve some or all of the statements simultaneously, figure out which pieces you can solve together and in what order you want to tackle them.

Verbal- or logic-focused multiple-choice questions can be solved similarly to Reading Comprehension problems: Identify the source material you need to review, reread that material, formulate your own answer to the question, and look through the answer choices for a match.

Step 3: Solve the Problem

Finally, follow your plan! Don't hesitate to go back into the tabs to check or recheck any information you need. Multi-Source Reasoning is like an open-book test: The material is always in front of you. Take advantage of that fact, especially since there is so much information; don't just rely on your memory.

Two-Part Analysis

Key details:

- Main feature: Five or six answer choices displayed in a table at the bottom
- Content: Can be quant-, verbal-, or logic-based
- Type of problem: Two-Part multiple-choice
- Key Strategies: Same as for Quant and Verbal sections of exam

Two-Parts typically fall into one of three categories: quant, verbal, or logic. Quant-based Two-Parts will look very much like standard Problem Solving problems, and verbal-based Two-Parts will typically resemble Critical Reasoning problems. The logic variety doesn't show up elsewhere on the GMAT.

You'll choose from among the *same* five or six answers for each of the two parts of the question. Sometimes, the two parts will be connected and you'll solve for both simultaneously; other times, they'll be independent and you'll solve separately.

Step 1: Understand the Prompt and Question

Start by glancing at the answer choices. Do you have numbers? Words? Sentences? That will give you a quick idea of whether you have a quant-based question or whether it's verbal or logic.

Next, glance at the question stem (not the whole big paragraph—just the question stem after that). What is the question asking you to do?

Quant-based:	Asks you to calculate something
	Contains numbers, formulas, or similar
	May ask you to calculate connected values (such as an x and y that simultaneously make an equation true)
Verbal-based:	May ask you a Critical Reasoning–type question (strengthen, weaken, find an assumption)
	May ask you a connected question (such as cause and effect)
Logic-based:	Asks you to complete some kind of scenario
	May contain tables of information or lists of rules or constraints to follow

8

Now, read through the actual prompt and then reread the question stem. As always, jot down notes as you read to help orient yourself to the information.

Step 2: Plan Your Approach

For quant-based and verbal-based problems, you can use the same strategies that you use in the Quant and Verbal sections of the exam. If you need to solve the two parts simultaneously, figure out how to set up that solution or reasoning method before you start to solve.

For logic-based problems, you're essentially going to reason your way to the answer. First, use any constraints given in the prompt to narrow down the possibilities of whatever scenario you've been given. Do this narrowing *before* you dive into the main solution process.

Step 3: Solve the Problem

For quant- and verbal-based problems, use your standard solving techniques. For logic problems, take your narrowed-down constraints and play out the possible scenarios with the goal of eliminating incorrect answers. Most of the time, you can work from the answer choices, testing each one.

When to Prioritize and When to Bail

What are your IR strengths and weaknesses?

You may already have a good idea. If not, see how things go on your next practice exam. When you're done, analyze those problems and categorize into one of three buckets:

1. Bucket 1 Strengths: I can get these right and I don't need extra time to do them.
2. Bucket 2 Opportunities: I can learn to do this—correctly or faster or both. This is where I'll concentrate my practice until my next practice test.
3. Bucket 3 Bails: If I see something like this on my next practice test, I'm going to guess immediately and move on. (Later on, I might decide to study some of these—but not between now and my next practice test.)

Focus on Bucket 2

Your bucket 2 items (i.e., Opportunities) are your priorities for the next few weeks (or until your next practice exam). Maybe you got the problem right but took too long to do so. In that case, your focus will be on learning how to do that type of task more efficiently in future.

If you made a careless mistake, dig in to understand precisely *what* mistake you made and *why* you made it. Then, figure out what new habit you can implement that will minimize the chances of that type of mistake in the future. Finally, practice that new habit enough to make it your default process.

Sometimes, you will have missed the problem legitimately—you really didn't know how to do it—but when you review the solution, you feel comfortable learning this material. In that case, go for it!

Don't Focus on Bucket 3—for Now

You can't possibly study *everything* between now and your next practice test. There aren't enough hours in the day. Spend your precious study time on areas that are the most likely to pay off—and that doesn't include problems you took way too long to do and got wrong anyway. Likewise, when the official solution makes no sense to you, don't prioritize learning how to do that problem.

After your next practice test, you might return to some of your bucket 3 problem types or topic areas and realize that you feel more comfortable with them. At that point, you can move them up to bucket 2.

Or, you might still hate them! If so, leave them in bucket 3. By the time you get to the real test, the problem types or content areas still sitting in bucket 3 will be your bail problems. Then, you'll review how to recognize quickly that a particular problem is in this bail category so that you can guess right away during the test, saving you valuable time and mental energy for other problems.

APPENDIX A

How to Write Better Sentences

In This Appendix

- Structure Your Sentences—Then Flesh Them Out
- Pay Attention to Grammar (to a Degree)
- Choose Your Words—and Vary Them

In this appendix, you will learn how to write complex sentences in a clear and cogent manner.

APPENDIX A How to Write Better Sentences

Only the GMAT has an Essay section, but even if you're taking the Executive Assessment, why not learn how to make your sentences better in general? For one thing, your efforts will pay off on the rest of the exam, whether GMAT or EA: The more you understand about sentence construction, the better you'll be able to read on test day. And every part of the exam demands that you read sentences quickly and effectively.

By the way, if you're a non-native-English speaker, GMAC says that "in considering the elements of standard written English, readers are trained to be sensitive and fair in evaluating the responses of examinees whose first language is not English." In other words, you'll get a little consideration. Your language still needs to be intelligible, but they're not going to penalize you for messing up a few idioms.

Structure Your Sentences—Then Flesh Them Out

A sentence should represent a thought. Thus, the core structure of the sentence should represent the skeleton of that thought, stripped of all flesh.

To analyze a sentence quickly, break it into **Topic** and **Comment**:

Topic: what you're talking about

Comment: what you're saying about the topic

Here's a possible first sentence for the response to an essay question:

While the author makes several valid points, her conclusion that regular exercise has no benefits for losing weight fails to account for several factors that would serve to undermine that conclusion.

Strip that sentence down to its essentials to find the topic–comment structure:

Her conclusion . . .	fails to account for several factors.
Topic	*Comment*
"What are you talking about?"	"What are you saying about that conclusion?"

Good sentences have obvious—and intentional—core structures.

Now, how do you expand upon the core? How do you put flesh on the bones? You have many options.

1. Make Compounds with *and*, *or*, and Other Connecting Words

You can use these words to add a compound structure to the sentence. Here is a compound verb:

The argument fails to account for several factors and makes unwarranted assumptions.

2. Add Modifiers to Describe Parts of the Sentence

The simplest modifiers are single words (adjectives, adverbs, and possessives):

> The *author's* conclusion *completely* fails to account for several *important* factors.

Modifiers answer questions about parts of the sentence: *Whose* argument? *What kinds* of concerns? *To what degree* does the argument omit concerns?

Here is an example of a more complex modifier:

> The conclusion *that the author draws* fails to account for several factors *that must be addressed.*

Modifiers are a great way to lengthen and enrich sentences. To add modifiers, ask questions of the parts you already have in place:

What kind of points?	several valid points
Which conclusion?	that regular exercise has no benefits for losing weight
What would the factors do?	serve to undermine that conclusion

3. Add Sentence-Level Subordinate Clauses

Words such as *because*, *since*, *if*, *while*, and *although* indicate logical connections between your thoughts:

> *While the author makes valid points,* her conclusion . . . fails to account for several factors.

The author acknowledges that the argument isn't completely terrible but still asserts that it is flawed.

You can also use a semicolon to join two sentences, adding a relational word such as *therefore* or *moreover*:

> Her conclusion fails to account for several factors; *moreover, it downplays the importance of two relevant pieces of evidence.*

As you use all these tools, experimenting with lengthening sentences, you might find yourself going too far. Don't add just to add; make every word count.

If you have a cumbersome sentence, first try breaking it into more than one sentence. If that doesn't work, move the heavy stuff to the end. Shift the grammatical core up front, so that a reader doesn't have to wade through a whole lot of modifiers to understand the gist of what the sentence is saying.

Pay Attention to Grammar (to a Degree)

You need to know grammatical rules for Sentence Correction; you might as well apply this knowledge to sentence *construction*, too. Yes, you can make occasional mistakes with grammar in your writing; they aren't expecting a perfect essay. And remember that the essay scoring rewards volume. If you have a choice between writing a new sentence and polishing another sentence's grammar, you should generally write the new sentence.

All that said, the better your grammar, the clearer your thoughts. Pay attention to the following issues.

Parallelism: When you use parallel markers, make the parts logically and structurally parallel:

X and Y   X, Y, and Z   both X and Y   X or Y   not only X but also Y

For example:

> Her conclusion not only omits certain studies but also downplays the importance of evidence that she does cite.

Pronouns: The Deadly Five pronouns—*it, its, they, them,* and *their*—can cause serious problems in writing. Try to ensure that these words have clear, meaningful antecedents—the nouns that they refer to. For example:

Sloppy: If cars go too fast on the highway, it can cause crashes.

What does *it* refer to? The highway?

Better: If cars go too fast on the highway, crashes can occur.

Cars that go too fast on the highway can cause crashes.

Highway speeding can cause crashes.

Modifiers: Put modifiers next to the thing you want to modify.

Your essay does not have to exhibit perfect grammar to get a great score, let alone a decent score. Even 6.0 essays can have minor grammatical flaws. And you don't need a 6.0 anyway!

By the way, feel free to use the passive voice. For one thing, it's grammatically correct. More important, the passive voice in English provides a useful way of flipping sentences around so that you can control the topic–comment structure as you desire. Both of the sentences below are correct:

> Highway speeding can cause crashes.
>
> Crashes can be caused by highway speeding.

Choose Your Words—and Vary Them

Words are like notes on a piano. Play them and play around with them to appreciate their resonance. For the essay, it's worth distinguishing two categories of words: signal words and substance words.

Signal Words indicate relationships to previous text. Signals are super-handy as you *read* academic text (e.g., passages in Reading Comprehension). The same words are also super-handy as you *write* that kind of text. Don't be afraid to tell your readers exactly where they are and what's happening. Here are some good signal words to use in your writing:

Relationship	**Signal**
Focus attention	As for, Regarding, In reference to
Add to previous point	Furthermore, Moreover, In addition, As well as, Also, Likewise, Too
Provide contrast	On one hand/On the other hand, While, Rather, Instead, In contrast, Alternatively
Provide conceding contrast (author unwillingly agrees)	Granted, It is true that, Certainly, Admittedly, Despite, Although
Provide emphatic contrast (author asserts own position)	But, However, Even so, All the same, Still, That said, Nevertheless, Nonetheless, Yet, Otherwise, Despite *[concession]*, *[assertion]*

Relationship	**Signal**
Dismiss previous point	In any event, In any case
Point out similarity	Likewise, In the same way
Structure the discussion	First, Second, etc., To begin with, Next, Finally, Again
Give example	For example, In particular, For instance
Generalize	In general, To a great extent, Broadly speaking
Sum up, perhaps with exception	In conclusion, In brief, Overall, Except for, Besides
Indicate logical result	Therefore, Thus, As a result, So, Accordingly, Hence
Indicate logical cause	Because, Since, As, Resulting from
Restate for clarity	In other words, That is, Namely, So to speak
Hedge or soften position	Apparently, At least, Can, Could, May, Might, Should, Possibly, Likely
Strengthen position	After all, Must, Have to, Always, Never, etc.
Introduce surprise	Actually, In fact, Indeed
Reveal author's attitude	Fortunately, Unfortunately, So-called, *Other adverbs*

Substance Words contain real content. Our main suggestion here is to have a mini thesaurus up your sleeve for certain ideas that you are likely to express—and re-express—*no matter what particular essay you must write*. For instance, you will need to have more than one way of making this point: "The argument is flawed."

Simply memorizing a list of synonyms and spitting them back out will do you little good. The 2.0 (*Seriously Flawed*) essay published in the *Official Guide* is riddled with these terms, seemingly as a substitute for thought. But you don't want to spend a lot of time searching for another way to say that an argument is flawed. Use these lists to free your mind up to do real thinking:

Argument is good:	sound, persuasive, thorough, convincing, logical, compelling, credible, effective
Perfect:	airtight, watertight
Argument is bad:	flawed (of course!), defective, imperfect, faulty, fallacious, unpersuasive, unconvincing, ineffective; it overgeneralizes, makes an extreme claim, takes an unsupported logical leap, makes an unwarranted assumption, fails to justify X or prove Y or address Z
Really bad:	unsound, illogical, specious, erroneous, invalid, unfounded, baseless
Maliciously bad:	misleading, deceptive
Flaw:	defect, omission, fault, error, failing, imperfection, concern, issue, area, aspect, feature to be addressed, opportunity for improvement

Assess an argument:	judge, evaluate, critique, examine, scrutinize, weigh
Strengthen an argument:	support, bolster, substantiate, reinforce, improve, fortify, justify, address concerns, fix issues, reduce or eliminate defects, prove
Weaken an argument:	undermine, damage, harm, water down, impair, remove support for, disprove, destroy, demolish, annihilate, obliterate

Practice using some of these words in your emails or work documents. Don't go too wild—no word is precisely interchangeable with any other. Pick one word a day from the list above and find a way to use it. Keep an eye out for its use in print so that you learn the word's strength, spin, and tonal qualities.

In your essay, avoid slang and jargon. You risk confusing or even offending your readers. You don't have to stick to highly formal registers of English; feel free to use contractions (such as *don't*) and short, concrete words (such as *stick to*). However, only write what's appropriate for an academic paper.

APPENDIX B

Quantitative Topics

In This Appendix

- Decimals, Percents, and Ratios
- Statistics

In this appendix, you will learn about certain quant topics that are commonly tested on the Integrated Reasoning section of the GMAT and the Executive Assessment. Additional material on these and other topics can be found in Manhattan Prep's *GMAT All the Quant* guide.

APPENDIX B Quantitative Topics

Decimals, Percents, and Ratios

If you are not already very comfortable with solving percent and decimal problems, review core GMAT and EA Quant section materials, such as the Manhattan Prep *GMAT All the Quant* guide. (The Quant section of both exams tests the same material and has the same question types.) This section describes only the new wrinkles that Integrated Reasoning adds to these sorts of problems.

Here are the key differences in how the exam sections treat these topics:

Integrated Reasoning	Quant
Decimals and percents are encountered more often than fractions. Ratios are also important. *Example:* Which of the following stocks has the highest price-to-earnings ratio?	Fractions are as common as the others. *Example:* $\frac{1}{3x} + \frac{3}{4 + \frac{2}{x}} = ?$
Percent problems draw on real data in graph, chart, and paragraph form. *Example:* Was the percent increase in imports from China to the U.S. greater than the percent increase in imports from Brazil to the U.S.?	Percent problems can be more abstract. *Example:* If x is y% of z, what is y% of x in terms of z?

For both Quant and IR, you need to know standard percent formulas, such as the percent change formula: $\frac{\text{Change}}{\text{Original}} \times 100\% = \%$ Change. Be ready to compute percent increases and decreases using the calculator. For example, if you need to increase 107.5 by 17%, you will need to multiply 107.5 by 1.17, so punch the following into your calculator:

[1] [0] [7] [.] [5] [×] [1] [.] [1] [7] [=]

The result is 125.775.

How does this compare to the result of increasing 105.5 by 19%? Don't look for an estimation shortcut (slightly greater increase to a slightly smaller number—tough call). Just punch it in and see. The result is 125.545, so this calculated number is slightly less than the first one.

Common Percent Question Traps

Here are four percent traps that you are likely to see on the IR section:

1. **Percents vs. Quantities.** Some numbers are percents. Others are quantities. Don't mistake one for the other, especially when numbers are embedded in text:

    If a carrot has a higher percentage of vitamin A relative to its total vitamin composition than a mango does, does the carrot have more vitamin A than the mango does?

    It's impossible to tell because you don't know the total vitamin content of either the carrot or the mango. Perhaps carrots have a lot lower vitamin content overall than mangoes do. A big fraction of a small whole could possibly be less (in milligrams, say) than a smaller fraction of a bigger whole.

2. **Percent of what.** Don't assume that all of the percents given are percents of the same total. Some of the percents given may well be percents of something *other* than the grand total. If you miss that little detail, you will get the answer wrong:

    If 60% of customers at the produce stand purchased fruit and 20% of fruit purchasers purchased bananas, what percent of customers did not purchase bananas?

    A casual reader might see *20%...purchased bananas* and decide that the answer must be 80%. However, the problem says that 20% *of fruit purchasers* purchased bananas. Fruit purchasers are a subset of the total—only 60%. The banana-buying percent of *all* customers is just $0.60 \times 0.20 = 0.12$, or 12%. The answer is 100% – 12%, which is equal to 88%, not 80%.

3. **Percent *of* vs. percent *greater than*.** Try the following two questions:

    1. 10 is what percent of 8?
    2. 10 is what percent greater than 8?

    The first question asks for the percent *of*. The answer is $\frac{10}{8}$, or 125%.

    The second question asks for a percent *change*. The answer is $\frac{10-8}{8}$, or 25%.

    The wording is very similar. Pay attention to the details!

3. **Percent decrease and then increase. Consider this question:**

    If the price of lettuce is decreased by 20% and then the reduced price is increased by 22%, is the resulting final price less than, equal to, or greater than the original price?

    The resulting final price is less than the original price, not equal to it or greater than it. In fact, if you first decrease the price by 20%, you would have to increase the reduced price by 25% to get back to the original price.

    Plug in a number to see for yourself. If you decrease $100 by 20%, you'll have $80.

    You would have to increase $80 by $20 in order to get back to $100. Because $20 is 25% of $80, you would have to increase the price by 25%. Increasing $80 by 22% yields $97.60, which is less than $100.

Statistics

Statistics topics are important on Integrated Reasoning, since IR is all about analyzing real-world data.

Integrated Reasoning	Quant
Real-world statistical terms, including regression and correlation, are used to describe realistic data presented in tables and charts. *Example:* The mean age of the participants in the marketing study is 24.	Statistics terms, such as *mean* and *median*, are used primarily to create tricky problems based on contrived data, such as sets of consecutive integers. *Example:* How much greater than the mean is the median of the set of integers n, $n + 2$, $n + 4$, and $n + 6$?

When you have a lot of quantitative information, statistics can help boil it down to a few key numbers so that you can make good probabilistic predictions and better decisions.

This section covers essentially every statistics concept you need for IR. Most of the statistics problems on the IR section just require that you understand certain definitions.

Descriptive Statistics

Say there are 320 consultants at your company, all of whom graduated from business school, and you want to think about the *number of years* since each one graduated.

To make things simple, you'll probably round to the nearest whole number (instead of having data like 5.25 years, 7.8 years, etc.). Whole numbers are *discrete* (or able to be separated and counted), so with this information, you can make a *histogram* to display the count in each category. For example:

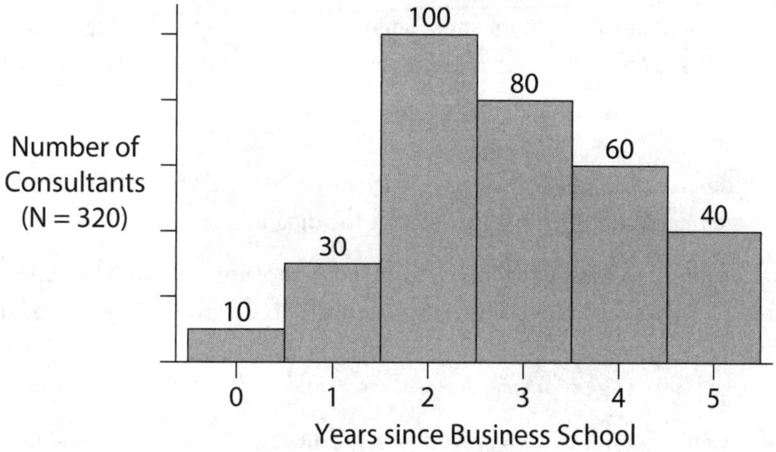

These three terms are very commonly tested on both IR and Quant:

1. Average (arithmetic mean)
2. Median
3. Mode

The **Average** (or **Arithmetic Mean**) is the most important. You may already know the formula from the Quant section:

$$\text{Mean} = \frac{\text{Sum of all terms}}{\text{Number of terms}}$$

Add up everyone's *Years since Business School,* and divide that total by 320, the number of consultants at the company:

$$\begin{aligned}\text{Mean years} &= \frac{\text{Total years}}{\text{Number of consultants}}\\ &= \frac{(10 \times 0) + (30 \times 1) + (100 \times 2) + (80 \times 3) + (60 \times 4) + (40 \times 5)}{320}\\ &= \frac{0 + 30 + 200 + 240 + 240 + 200}{320}\\ &= \frac{910}{320}\\ \text{Mean years} &= 2.84375\end{aligned}$$

The **Median** is the middle number, or the 50th percentile: Half of the people have more years since business school (or the same number) and half have fewer years (or the same number).

If you have an odd number of terms, say {101, 102, 103, 104, 105}, then the median is the middle number (in this case, 103). If you have an even number of terms, say {201, 202, 203, 204}, then the median is the average of the two middle terms (in this case, 202.5). In the earlier example, the median of the *Years since Business School* distribution is 3 years because both the 160th consultant and the 161st consultant are 3 years out of business school.

The **Mode** is the observation that shows up the most often, corresponding to the highest column on the histogram. The histogram for the consultants peaks at the 2-year bar, so the mode is 2 years since business school.

The Spread

Mean, median, and mode are all *central* measures—they answer the question, *Where's the center of all the data?* However, you often need to know how spread out the data is.

The crudest measure of spread is **Range**, which is just the largest value minus the smallest value. While range is easy to calculate, it's susceptible to **Outliers**—oddball observations that, rightly or wrongly, lie far away from most of the others. For example, if one person in your program is in her 70s and has been out of school for 50 years, then your range of *Years since College* would be huge because of that one outlier.

A better measure of spread is **Standard Deviation**. You will never have to calculate standard deviation on the exam because it is such a pain to do so without Excel or other software.

Roughly, standard deviation indicates how far, on average, each data point is from the mean. That's not the precise mathematical definition, but it's close enough for the exam.

For example, if your data points are {3, 3, 3, 3, 3}, then the standard deviation is 0, because every data point is 0 units away from the average of the set. If your data points are {1, 2, 3, 4, 5}, then your standard deviation is something greater than 0 (remember, you won't have to calculate it), because only one of the data points equals the average; the other four are more spread out. For example:

> Which data set has the higher standard deviation: {1, 2, 3, 4, 5} or {10, 20, 30, 40, 50}?

In the first data set, the numbers are very close to the mean of 3. In the second, the numbers are much farther away, on average, from the mean of 30. The second set has the higher standard deviation.

Standard deviation is incredibly important in finance, operations, and other subjects. For now, focus on an intuitive understanding. For instance, if you add outliers, the standard deviation increases. If you remove outliers, it decreases. If you just shift every number up by some constant value, the standard deviation stays the same.

Correlation

Up to now, everything has had to do with one variable—one measurement. For example, imagine that you were given data on the number of years since someone graduated from college:

Person	Years since college
You	4
Anika Atwater	2.5
Bao Yang	6
...	...

What if you get *two* pieces of data about each person? Now you can look at more interesting patterns:

Person	Years since college	Height
You	4	5 feet 7 inches
Anika Atwater	2.5	5 feet 10 inches
Bao Yang	6	5 feet 2 inches
...	...	...

To find a pattern, put all of these observations on a scatterplot:

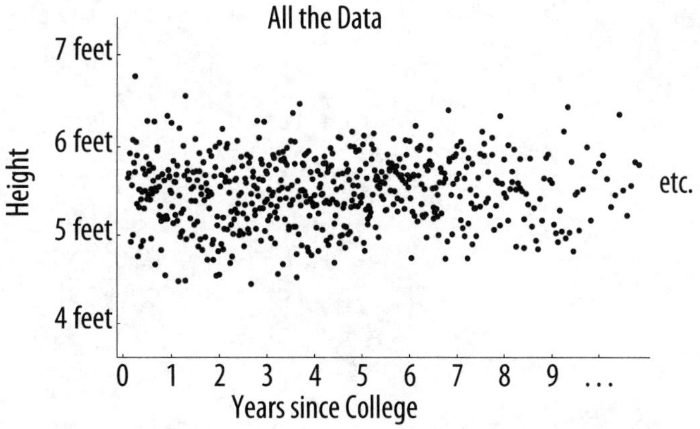

The disorganized jumble of data points shows that the two variables, *Years since College* and *Height*, are basically **Uncorrelated**. Numbers are correlated when they increase together or decrease together; in this case, there is **No Correlation** because no such pattern exists.

In contrast, if you plot *Years since College* versus *Age*, you'll get a pattern. Typically, older people have been out of college longer:

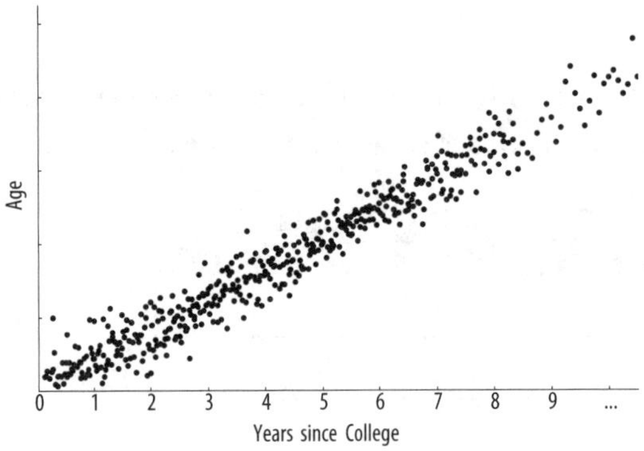

Most people are either high on both scales or low on both scales. This means that *Years since College* and *Age* are highly correlated. That is, there is a **Positive Correlation** between the two variables.

If the data is presented to you in a table, you'll have to sort by one of the two parameters and then compare the two columns. If the numbers mostly increase (or decrease) together, then there is a positive correlation. If one increases while the other decreases, the two have a negative correlation. If no such pattern exists, the two metrics have no correlation. To summarize:

Correlation	Pattern	Example
Positive	Points cluster around a line of positive slope	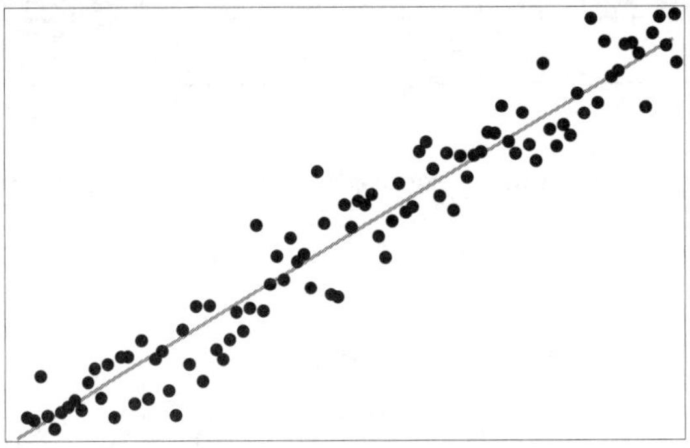

Correlation	Pattern	Example
None	No pattern (jumble) or a nonlinear pattern	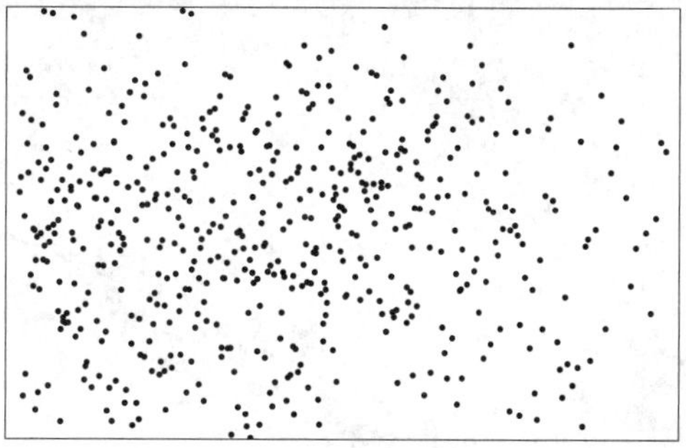 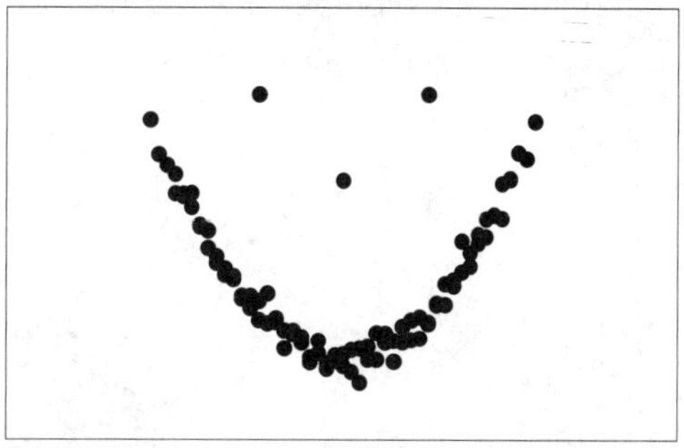
Negative	Points cluster around a line of negative slope	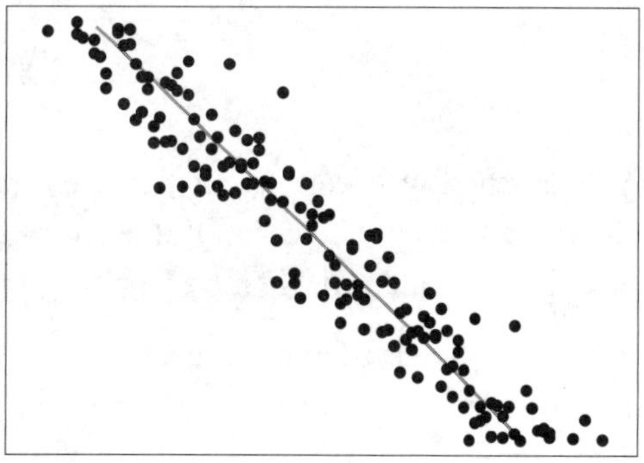

Regression

If you're asked to do a linear regression, you have to find the **Best-Fit Line**, or **Regression Line**, through a scatterplot. With such a line, you can describe the relationship between x and y more precisely and even predict values of y from values of x:

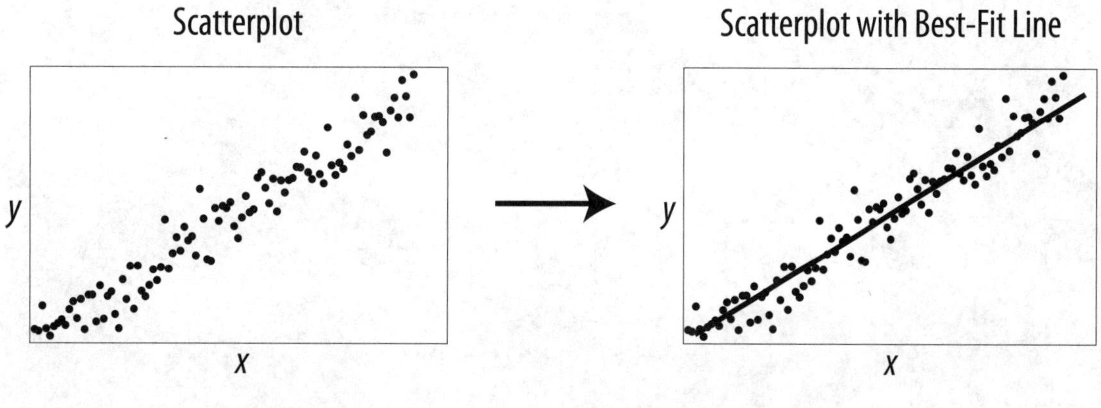

The best-fit regression line minimizes the distance, in some sense, between the points and the line. You can see this intuitively:

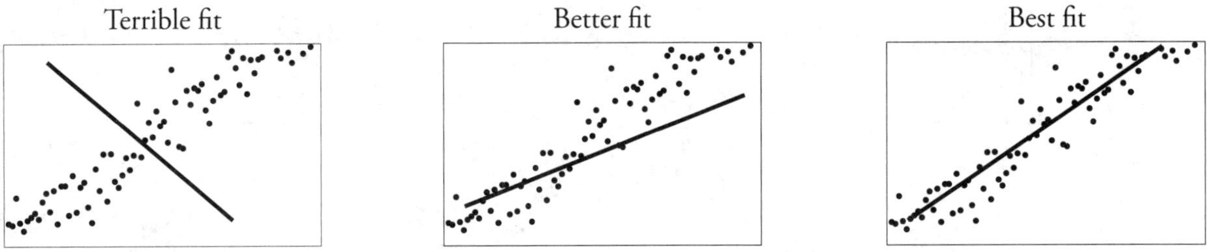

The exam will never ask you to compute a linear regression, but a graphical Integrated Reasoning problem might ask about the slope of a regression line:

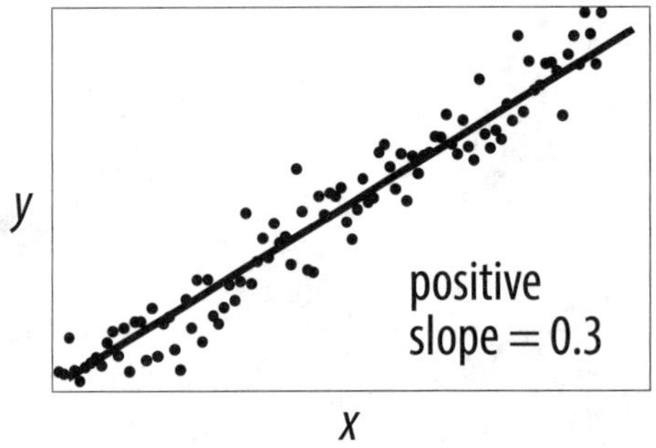

If the two variables are positively correlated, then the regression line will have positive slope (as one variable increases, so does the other one). Likewise, if the two variables are negatively correlated, the regression line will have negative slope (as one variable increases, the other decreases).

Remember that to find a line is to find its equation. The general equation of a line is $y = mx + b$. The letter m represents the **Slope** of the line, while b represents the ***y*-intercept**, where the line crosses the y-axis:

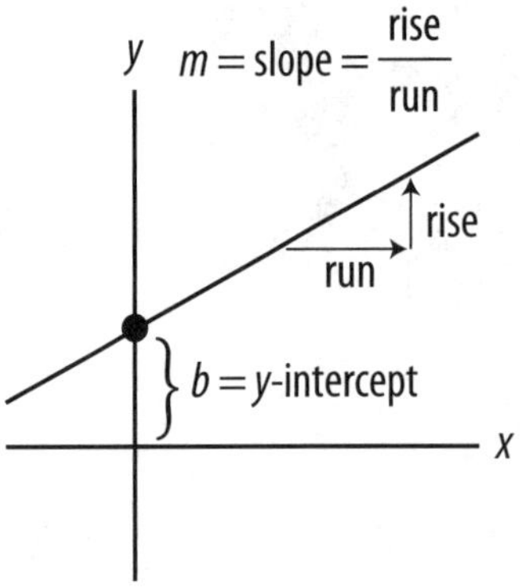

A line with the equation $y = 3x - 2$ intercepts the y-axis at $(0, -2)$. On this line, if x increases by 1, y increases by 3:

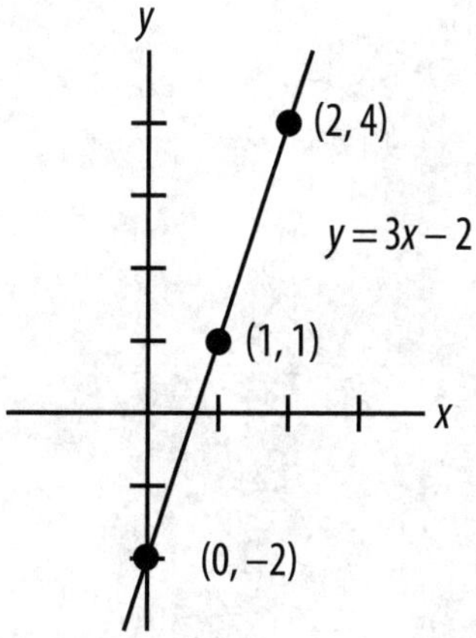

Finding the line means finding the values for the slope m and the y-intercept b.

MANHATTAN PREP

GMAT®

All the Verbal

This essential guide takes the guesswork out of grammar by presenting all of the major grammatical principles and minor grammatical points known to be tested on GMAT Sentence Correction. It also teaches you all of the critical and logical reasoning you need for the Reading Comprehension and Critical Reasoning sections of the GMAT.

Acknowledgements

A great number of people were involved in the creation of the book you are holding.

Our Manhattan Prep resources are based on the continuing experiences of our instructors and students. The overall vision for this edition was developed by Stacey Koprince and Andrea Pawliczek, who determined what strategies to cover and how to weave them into a cohesive whole.

Stacey Koprince (SC, RC), Andrea Pawliczek (CR), and Daniel Fogel (SC) were the primary authors; they were supported by a number of content experts. Chelsey Cooley and Daniel Fogel served as the primary editors during the writing phase. Mario Gambino, Helen Tan, and Patrick Tyrrell served as a sounding board during the writing phase, vetting both ideas and content. Patrick Tyrrell deserves special mention as the source of multiple new ideas for the CR unit of the guide. Mario Gambino managed production for all images, with Derek Frankhouser and Israt Pasha lending their design expertise.

Matthew Callan coordinated the production work for this guide. Once the manuscript was done, Naomi Beesen and Emily Meredith Sledge edited and Cheryl Duckler proofread the entire guide from start to finish. Carly Schnur designed the covers.

Retail ISBNs: 978-1-5062-4904-9, 978-1-5062-6255-0

Retail eISBN: 978-1-5062-4905-6

Course ISBN: 978-1-5062-4906-3

Course eISBN: 978-1-5062-4907-0

10 9 8 7 6 5 4 3 2

GMAT® Strategy Guides

GMAT All the Quant

GMAT All the Verbal

GMAT Integrated Reasoning & Essay

Strategy Guide Supplements

Math

GMAT Foundations of Math

GMAT Advanced Quant

Verbal

GMAT Foundations of Verbal

September 3, 2019

Dear Student,

Thank you for picking up a copy of *All the Verbal*. I hope this book provides just the guidance you need to get the most out of your GMAT studies.

At Manhattan Prep, we continually aspire to provide the best instructors and resources possible. If you have any questions or feedback, please do not hesitate to contact us.

Email our Student Services team at gmat@manhattanprep.com or give us a shout at 212-721-7400 (or 800-576-4628 in the United States or Canada). We try to keep all our books free of errors, but if you think we've goofed, please visit manhattanprep.com/GMAT/errata.

Our Manhattan Prep Strategy Guides are based on the continuing experiences of both our instructors and our students. The primary authors of the 7th Edition All the Verbal guide were Stacey Koprince, Andrea Pawliczek, and Daniel Fogel. Project management and design were led by Matthew Callan, Mario Gambino, and Helen Tan. I'd like to send particular thanks to instructors Chelsey Cooley, Emily Meredith Sledge, and Patrick Tyrrell for their content contributions.

Finally, we are indebted to all of the Manhattan Prep students who have given us excellent feedback over the years. This book wouldn't be half of what it is without their voice.

And now that *you* are one of our students too, please chime in! I look forward to hearing from you. Thanks again and best of luck preparing for the GMAT!

Sincerely,

Chris Ryan
Executive Director, Product Strategy
Manhattan Prep

www.manhattanprep.com/gmat 138 West 25th Street, 7th Floor, New York, NY 10001 Tel: 212-721-7400
Fax: 646-514-7425

TABLE OF CONTENTS

The GMAT Mindset

The GMAT is a complex exam. It feels like an academic test—math, grammar, logical reasoning—but it's really not! At heart, the GMAT is a test of your *executive reasoning skills.*

Executive reasoning is the official term for your ability to make all kinds of decisions in the face of complex and changing information. It makes sense, then, that graduate management programs would want to test these skills. It's crucial for you to understand *how* they do so because that understanding will impact both how you study for the GMAT and how you take the test.

You do need to know various math and grammar facts, rules, and concepts in order to do well on the GMAT—and this makes the test feel similar to tests that you took in school. There's one critical difference though: When your teachers gave you tests in school, they tested you on material they expected you to know how to handle. Your teachers wouldn't put something on the test that they *expected* you to get wrong. That would be cruel!

Well, it would be cruel if the main point of the exam was to test your mastery of those facts, rules, and concepts. But that isn't the main point of the GMAT. Rather, the GMAT wants to know how well you make decisions regarding when to invest your limited time and mental energy—and when *not* to.

In other words, the GMAT wants to know how you make business decisions. And no good businessperson invests in every single opportunity placed in front of them, just because it's there. A good businessperson evaluates each opportunity, saying yes to some and no to others. That's what you're going to do on the GMAT, too. You'll invest in a majority of the problems presented to you, but you *will* say no to some—the ones that look too hard or seem like they'll take too long to solve. These are literally bad investments.

So, the GMAT will offer you questions that it thinks you will not be able to do. How does it accomplish this? The GMAT is an adaptive test; that is, it adapts to you as you take it, offering easier or harder questions based on how you're doing on the test. Ideally, you'll do well on the material that you know how to answer in a reasonable amount of time. Your reward? You'll earn questions that are too hard for you to do—either they'll take too long to answer or they'll be so hard that you wouldn't be able to do them even if you had unlimited time.

Then what? If you try to use a "school mindset" on the test, you'll keep trying to answer the questions even though you really can't do them. You'll waste a bunch of time and then, later, you'll have to rush on other questions. As a result, you'll start to miss questions that you actually do know how to answer and your score will go down. This is the business equivalent of spending most of your annual budget by August...and then not having enough money left to run the business well from September through December.

Instead, use your "business mindset" to carry you through the exam. When the test finds your limit, acknowledge that! Call it a bad investment and let that problem go (ideally before you've spent very much time on it). Choose an answer, any answer, and move on.

Extend the business mindset to your studies as well. If there are certain topics that you really hate, decide that you're not going to study them in the first place. You're just going to bail (guess quickly and move on) when one of those "opportunities" comes up. (One caveat: You can't bail on huge swaths of content. For example, don't bail on all of grammar; that represents too great a portion of the Verbal section. You can, though, bail on a subset of grammar—say, pronouns and idioms.)

Start orienting yourself around your business mindset today. You aren't going to do it all. You're going to choose the best opportunities as you see them throughout the test. When you decide not to pursue a particular "investment," you're going to say no as quickly as you can and forget about it—don't waste precious resources on a poor investment opportunity! Move on to the next opportunity, feeling good about the fact that you're doing what you're supposed to do on the GMAT: making sound investment decisions about what to do and what *not* to do.

Verbal Reasoning on the GMAT

The Verbal Reasoning (or Verbal) section of the GMAT consists of three different question types: Sentence Correction (SC), Reading Comprehension (RC), and Critical Reasoning (CR).

Sentence Correction (SC) questions test the proper usage of grammar and meaning. Reading Comprehension (RC) questions test your ability to comprehend and to infer from complex information. Critical Reasoning (CR) questions test your ability to understand, analyze, critique, and infer from arguments.

You'll need to average a bit less than 2 minutes per question in the Verbal section, though your timing for individual questions will likely range from almost no time at all to approximately 3 minutes. The "almost no time at all" questions will be your *bail* questions: questions that look way too hard or that you know are a big weakness of yours (in other words, bad investment opportunities!). On other questions, you'll choose to invest some extra time—perhaps on a harder question in an area of strength.

You'll learn more about time management, as well as other test details, both in this guide and in the online resources associated with this guide. You can also test your skills using official GMAT problems that are published by the test makers in *The GMAT Official Guide* (also known as "the big OG" or "the OG"). These problems appeared on the official GMAT in the past, so they're a fantastic resource to help you get ready for the real test. (Note: The OG is sold separately from the Manhattan Prep strategy guides.)

UNIT ONE

Sentence Correction

In this unit, you will learn an efficient and effective solving process for all Sentence Correction problems. You will also learn the underlying grammar rules tested on the GMAT, as well as how to handle the various types of meaning issues (such as redundancy, ambiguity, and faulty logic) that come into play.

In This Unit:

CHAPTER 1

The Sentence Correction Process

In This Chapter:

- Question Format
- The Sentence Correction Process
- "Best" Does Not Mean Ideal
- Sentence Correction Timing
- Using and Improving Your Ear for Sentence Correction
- How to Get Better at the Sentence Correction Process

In this chapter, you will learn a 4-step process to use on all Sentence Correction (SC) problems. You'll also learn how to take advantage of the way SC works in order to save time and how to study to improve your SC skills.

CHAPTER 1 The Sentence Correction Process

Sentence Correction (SC) is one of three question types found in the Verbal section of the GMAT. Sentence Correction tests your mastery of both grammar and meaning as they apply to conventional written English.

SC questions typically comprise about one-third of the questions in the Verbal section. They tend to be the fastest of the three question types that appear in the Verbal section, so learning to work efficiently is especially important. To that end, you'll need to build a strong process for working through SC problems.

Question Format

Take a look at this SC problem:

> Although William Pereira first gained national recognition for his set designs for such movies as *Reap the Wild Wind* and *Jane Eyre*, he was more commonly remembered now as the architect of the Transamerica Tower and the designer of the master plan for the city of Irvine, California.
>
> (A) such movies as *Reap the Wild Wind* and *Jane Eyre*, he was more commonly remembered now
>
> (B) such movies as *Reap the Wild Wind* and *Jane Eyre*, he is now more commonly remembered
>
> (C) such movies as *Reap the Wild Wind* and *Jane Eyre*, but now he will be more commonly remembered
>
> (D) movies such as *Reap the Wild Wind* and *Jane Eyre*, he would be more commonly remembered now
>
> (E) movies such as *Reap the Wild Wind* and *Jane Eyre*, but he is now more commonly remembered

The question consists of a given sentence, part of which is underlined. The underlined segment may be short or it may comprise most or even all of the original sentence. The five answer choices are possible replacements for the underlined segment.

In all SC questions, choice (A) is exactly the same as the underlined portion of the sentence above it; in other words, you would select answer (A) if you think nothing is wrong with the original sentence. The other four choices will always offer different options. Your task is to select the answer that creates the best sentence *of the choices given*, in terms of both grammar and meaning. (It might not be the best way that you can think to write the sentence yourself.)

By the way, each of the five answer choices is correct approximately 20 percent of the time, including answer choice (A)—that is, the original sentence is correct approximately 20 percent of the time (though that's not the case on this particular problem). Because the original sentence is wrong about 80 percent of the time, you may find yourself unconsciously avoiding it closer to 100 percent of the time; just remember that every answer choice has an approximately equal chance of being the correct answer.

1

The Sentence Correction Process

Because the other two Verbal question types, Critical Reasoning (CR) and Reading Comprehension (RC), require so much reading, you're going to have to move quickly on Sentence Correction (SC). In fact, you'll need to average about 1 minute and 20 seconds per SC question.

As a result, you'll need a standard process to help you work through any SC question efficiently and effectively.

Here's the basic process:

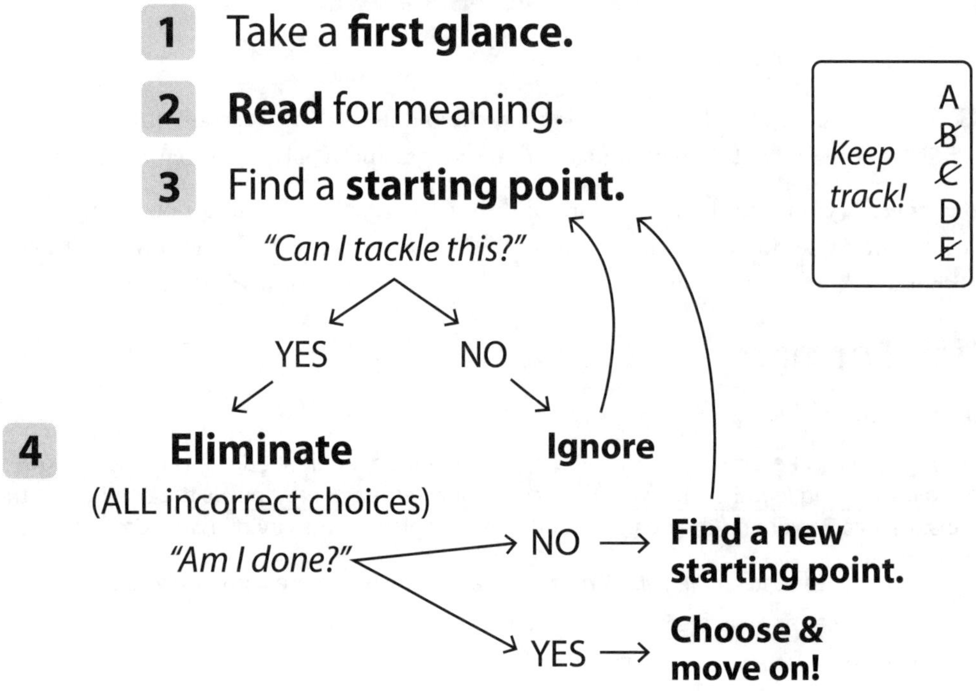

Try the process with the William Pereira example:

Although William Pereira first gained national recognition for his set designs for such movies as *Reap the Wild Wind* and *Jane Eyre*, he was more commonly remembered now as the architect of the Transamerica Tower and the designer of the master plan for the city of Irvine, California.

(A) such movies as *Reap the Wild Wind* and *Jane Eyre*, he was more commonly remembered now
(B) such movies as *Reap the Wild Wind* and *Jane Eyre*, he is now more commonly remembered
(C) such movies as *Reap the Wild Wind* and *Jane Eyre*, but now he will be more commonly remembered
(D) movies such as *Reap the Wild Wind* and *Jane Eyre*, he would be more commonly remembered now
(E) movies such as *Reap the Wild Wind* and *Jane Eyre*, but he is now more commonly remembered

Step 1: Take a First Glance

Don't start reading yet. Just take a *first glance* to spot clues that may help you answer the question. You may not notice much at first; you'll get better with practice!

How long is the underline? What's happening where the underline starts?

In the Pereira problem, the underline is relatively short. It starts after the word *for* and the first underlined word is *such*.

The word *such* by itself isn't a huge clue, so read a couple more words: *such movies as*. The phrase *such as* is used to introduce examples of something. Now you know that the sentence is going to give examples and discuss something about movies.

This is the equivalent of noticing right away on a quant question that there's a diagram of a triangle or that the problem text contains a quadratic equation. You don't have enough information to solve the problem, of course, but you have some context about what it is testing. In the Pereira problem, you now know something about the overall meaning and at least part of the organization of the sentence.

You can take this first glance one step further. On SC, the beginning of the five answers will *always* contain at least one difference, so glance at the first word or two of each choice. The "split," or difference among the answers, is *such movies as* vs. *movies such as*.

People more commonly say *movies such as*, but it's also acceptable to say *such movies as*, as long as that word in the middle (*movies*, in this case) is the category for which you're about to give examples. In other words, both variations are fine.

When the test gives you a split for which both variations are okay, it's called a **Red Herring**. A red herring is a distraction—the test is trying to get you to waste time debating two (or three or more!) variations, when the different forms are all acceptable.

So, you've taken your first glance; now what? The last word of the five answers will also always contain at least one difference. Most of the time, glancing at the beginning of the choices will be enough to give you your first clue and then you'd go to step 2. In this case, though, the beginning of the choices contained a red herring, so glance at the end of each choice as well.

At the end, the split is between *remembered now* and just plain *remembered*. It could be that the word *now* moves around in other choices or that the word *now* disappears entirely from some choices. The movement or disappearance of a time marker often affects the meaning of a sentence.

So, with the investment of perhaps 5 to 10 seconds, you know several things. The sentence is going to be about movies and give examples of movies. You won't waste time debating the *movies such as* and *such movies as* split, but you will keep an eye on the meaning of the sentence—in particular, *when* are things happening (now vs. some other time)?

Step 2: Read the Sentence for Meaning

Next, read the entire original sentence. It's natural to focus on grammar as you solve SC problems; the title of this step emphasizes meaning because most people forget to think about the meaning, even though meaning is just as important as grammar!

A sentence can be grammatically correct and yet illogical or ambiguous:

> Anne and Millie went to the movies in her car.

Wait a minute whose car did they take? Anne's? Millie's? Someone else's? The sentence is ambiguous.

As you read, pay attention to *both* the overall meaning and the underlying grammar. Don't think about how to fix anything yet; just notice what the possible issues are.

What does the William Pereira sentence say?

> Although William Pereira first gained national recognition for his set designs for such movies as *Reap the Wild Wind* and *Jane Eyre*, he was more commonly remembered now as the architect of the Transamerica Tower and the designer of the master plan for the city of Irvine, California.

The sentence begins with a contrast word (*although*), and that word is not part of the underline, so it can't change. As you read the rest of the sentence, pay attention to the contrast that it's trying to convey.

Extract the "core" of the sentence:

> Although WP first gained recognition for one thing, he was remembered for other, quite different things.

That basic meaning does make sense. Did anything else jump out at you? The end of the sentence says this:

> ... he was more commonly remembered now ...

Was remembered is in the past, but *now* is in the present. Using those two time markers together is illogical.

When something jumps out as a possible issue, jot down a word or two to help you remember, then keep reading. In this case, you might jot down something like "was ... now?"

Step 3: Find a Starting Point

Most SC problems test multiple issues, and those issues can appear anywhere in the sentence. Your task at this stage is to decide where to start.

If you've spotted an issue in the original sentence that you know for sure is incorrect, you can cross off answer (A), as that answer always repeats the text of the original sentence.

For example, let's say that you start with the "was ... now?" issue. It doesn't make sense to say that he *was remembered* in the present (*now*), so the original sentence is incorrect. Cross off answer (A).

Step 4: Eliminate All Incorrect Choices

Make that first issue keep working for you. Whenever you find an error in one choice, your next step is to check the remaining answer choices for that exact same error or a closely related error. Do any of the other choices have a similar illogical meaning?

Work efficiently. Scan the five answer choices vertically *only for that portion of the text.*
In other words, do *not* read the full text of all five answers:

(A) ... he was more commonly remembered now
(B) ... he is now more commonly remembered
(C) ... but now he will be more commonly remembered
(D) ... he would be more commonly remembered now
(E) ... but he is now more commonly remembered

~~A~~
B
~~C~~
~~D~~
E

The word *now* moves around, but it is always in the sentence, so the verb tense needs to be consistent with the meaning of *now.*

The hypothetical *he would be... remembered now* is illogical in this sentence, so answer (D) is incorrect. It's also not great to say *now he will be remembered,* as in answer (C). While you might hear someone say something like, "Now, I will go to the store," that person should really say, "I am leaving now" (as she leaves) or "In a few minutes, I will leave for the store."

So answers (A), (C), and (D) are out. Three down, two to go!

Repeat!

Find another starting point and repeat steps 3 and 4. After a repetition or two, you'll either get down to one answer or get stuck. Either way, pick an answer and move on to the next problem.

Now, where are you going to find these new starting points? You have two main options:

1. Tackle other errors that you've already spotted.
2. Compare the remaining answer choices vertically, looking for differences, or splits.

Spot a difference, then ask yourself whether you think that difference is straightforward to address. If so, go for it. If not, *ignore* that difference and look for a different one that you think is more straightforward—don't waste time agonizing over an annoying split. SC questions will almost always offer you multiple paths to the correct answer, so take the path that is easiest and fastest for you.

In the Pereira example, answers (B) and (E) remain. Compare them vertically—what's different? Answer (E) starts with the word *but*; this word is not present in answer (B).

But indicates a contrast; this is a meaning issue, so remind yourself of the big picture of the sentence:

> Although WP first gained recognition for one thing, he was remembered for other, quite different things.

The word *although* already conveys the contrast. A second contrast word would be redundant:

> Although WP first gained recognition for one thing, *but* he was remembered for other, quite different things. ??

Eliminate answer (E). The correct answer is (B).

Step 3 Redux

Let's go back to step 3 for a moment. What if you think a particular thing *may* be wrong but you're not sure?

Go straight to the answers and scan vertically for the text that you think might be an issue. Compare all five answers: What alternative wordings do the others contain for that text? These are your splits, or differences, for this particular issue. Use those splits to help you decide how to evaluate the issue (or whether to look for a different, easier issue).

Other times, you may spot a potential issue but not feel confident addressing it. In that case, forget about it—don't waste any time agonizing about it. Go look for something else that is easier for you. (Most SC problems offer at least three splits.)

What if you don't spot anything at all in the original sentence? (After all, that one is correct 20 percent of the time!) In this case, go straight to the answers and scan vertically to compare, looking for any splits. Use these splits to figure out what the sentence is testing. If you don't feel comfortable handling any particular split, move on to the next one.

Sometimes, you may think you've spotted an issue in the original sentence, but when you check the answers, all five are identical (for that specific issue). In that case, go look for something else.

In all of these scenarios, regardless of whether you spot an error in the original sentence, you'll always end up at the same next step: Compare the answers vertically, focusing on shorter "chunks" of the sentences to spot the differences. Use the splits to figure out your next steps.

There is one thing you do *not* want to do: Do not think about how you would rewrite the sentence yourself. There are many ways that a faulty sentence could be fixed, and you could waste a lot of time thinking of different ways to do so. Instead, let the splits drive your process.

The SC Process

Here's a summary of the process:

1. Take a First Glance

Look for an early clue that will help orient you to the problem—similar to noticing a certain math symbol on a quant problem. Don't spend more than 5 to 10 seconds on this step.

Glance at the beginning of the underline. Notice the word (including punctuation marks) just before the underline and the first one to three words of the underline itself. Then, glance at the beginning of each answer choice to see how the beginning of the underlined text changes.

Most of the time, this will be enough to give you an early clue. If it's not, try one more place: the end of the underline. Then, go to step 2, even if you still haven't found any early clue (you won't find a hint 100 percent of the time).

2. Read the Sentence for Meaning

Read the entire original sentence. Don't get so focused on grammar that you forget to process the meaning of the sentence.

Jot down words (possibly abbreviated) when something jumps out at you as a possible issue. Don't actually try to decide anything about that issue yet—just note the possibilities.

3. Find a Starting Point

Start with anything that feels straightforward to you. Often, you will spot something in the original sentence that you feel comfortable evaluating; immediately check the splits in the answer choices to see what your options are to fix the issue.

Sometimes, you will not spot anything in the original sentence that you want to use; in this case, scan the answers vertically to find the differences.

Make your first decision—most of the time, this will be a choice between keeping or eliminating answer choice (A)—and then...

4. Eliminate All Incorrect Choices

Reuse your work! Check all of the remaining answers to see whether they have the same error (or a very similar one). On occasion, you can cross off all four wrong answers based on your first issue!

Most of the time, though, you will still have more than one answer remaining after you address your first issue.

(As Needed) Repeat Steps 3 and 4

So, most of the time, you'll need another starting point. By this time, you will likely have spotted multiple potential issues to investigate. Don't review them in order. Choose whatever you think is easiest and repeat steps 3 and 4.

At some point, you'll either have one answer left (choose it—you're done!) or you'll have more than one answer left but you'll realize that you don't feel comfortable with any of the remaining splits. In the latter case, don't keep throwing time at this problem. Make the executive decision to pick an answer and move on. You'll likely have narrowed down your answers, so you'll be in position to make a strong guess.

"Best" Does Not Mean Ideal

SC questions ask for the best option *among those given*, not the best option in the universe. Sometimes you may feel—rightly so—that all the answers, including the correct one, aren't very good. Correct GMAT SC answers never break strict grammatical rules, but these answers can seem formal or even awkward. Expect that, at times, a correct answer won't sound or feel very good to you—it will merely be the best *of the options given*.

Sentence Correction Timing

In order to have adequate time for longer Reading Comprehension and Critical Reasoning questions, you'll need to average about 1 minute and 20 seconds per Sentence Correction problem. Some longer SCs might take up to 2 minutes, so you'll answer some SCs in a minute or less.

How can you possibly move that quickly and still reliably get the right answer? Here's how:

- Most wrong answers contain more than one error, but you only need one valid reason to cross off any wrong answer.
- The same error is often repeated in two or more choices.
- The SC process described earlier capitalizes on the first two points above to get you through the problem as efficiently as possible: Always work with whatever issue you find easiest, and when you do spot an error, eliminate as many answer choices as possible.

Although you have to work efficiently on SC, don't go so quickly that you make careless mistakes. Follow the process and you'll be able to work through the problem systematically, spending enough time but not too much.

If you're approaching the 2-minute mark, wrap up the problem. If you need longer than that to narrow down to one answer, chances are good that you're missing something and that this time would be better spent on another problem. Guess from among the remaining answers and move on.

In fact, if you can narrow it down to two answers, your 50-50 guess should barely be considered a guess. Because the GMAT is an adaptive test, you're only going to answer about 60 percent of Verbal questions correctly overall. Practically speaking, then, a 50 percent chance on any problem isn't bad; that's a legitimate answer on an adaptive test. Choose one of the remaining two answers and move forward with confidence.

Using and Improving Your Ear for Sentence Correction

When answering practice questions, if you are *completely confident* that an answer is wrong (as in, you'd bet someone $20 that you're right!), even though you can't articulate exactly why, go ahead and cross that answer off. When you review your work, ask yourself which specific words in the sentence sound funny or incorrect. Then, see whether you can articulate what was really going on—and make this open book (you can look up anything you want in the SC unit of this guide or any of your other study materials). Finally, check the solution.

First, were you right that that answer was wrong? Second, was your reason valid? If both of those things are true, then your "ear" may already be accurate for this specific type of issue—and now you know how to check whether it is. (Of course, if you want to improve your performance in this area, then you are still going to need to learn more than you know right now about the grammar or meaning of this issue.)

If you discover that you were wrong*, though, then you will need to dive into the grammar or meaning issues in that area, including possibly learning some technical grammar terminology and rules. Think of this process as retraining your ear so that you get that issue right the next time you see it.

**Wrong* can mean two things. It could mean that you thought (B) was the right answer when it was really (C). It could also mean that you correctly chose answer (B) but that your reason for choosing (B) was faulty—so the next time you see a similar issue, you might get that problem wrong. If this happens, consider the problem "wrong" for study purposes; that is, there's something here that you definitely need to learn in order to get a similar problem right in the future.

The first two chapters of this guide cover strategy and overall lessons for SC, while subsequent chapters teach specific grammar and meaning concepts that you need to know for the GMAT. The next section of this chapter provides you with some techniques to hone your SC process. As you progress through the guide, return to the next section periodically to remind yourself how to drill the process in the context of the grammar that you're learning.

Beginning with Chapter 2, the end of each chapter contains a problem set that tests your skills. Try some of the problems now and save some for later review. After you complete each problem, check the answer. Whenever necessary, return to the lessons in the chapter to solidify your understanding before trying the next problem.

You can also use *Official Guide* problems published by the makers of the official test, to further hone both your SC process and your SC ear. (Note: The *Official Guide* is sold separately from this guide.)

How to Get Better at the Sentence Correction Process

First Glance

Your first glance at a problem is, by definition, quick and superficial. If you get good at this step, though, you can pick up some useful clues that will help you read the original sentence with an idea already in mind of one topic the sentence may be testing.

For SC, pay attention to three issues during your first glance:

Clue	Possible Implication
1. Is the underline very long? Very short?	Very long underlines often signal issues with sentence structure, meaning, modifiers, or parallelism. Very short underlines (less than five words) may lead you to compare the answers in full before reading the original sentence.
2. What is the first underlined word? What is the word right before?	The nature of the first underlined word (or the word just before the underline) can give you a clue about one of the issues tested in the sentence. For example, if the word *has* is the first underlined word, the sentence is likely testing either subject–verb agreement or verb tense, since *has* is a verb.
3. What are the differences among the first word or two of each answer choice?	There will always be at least one difference at the beginning of the answers (as well as one at the end). Glance at the first word or two of each answer. For example, if the first word switches between *has* and *have*, then you know the sentence is testing singular vs. plural. Now, you can actively look for the relevant subject when you go to step 2 and read the original sentence.

After you've studied SC for a few weeks and tried some problems from the *Official Guide* material or other sources, add a first glance drill to your study regimen. Find some lower-numbered (easier) problems that you've already tried. Give yourself a few seconds (5 to 10 max!) to glance at a problem, then look away and say out loud what you noticed in those few seconds.

Afterwards, look at the full problem and remind yourself what it tests. Did your first glance unearth any of those issues? Examine the first underlined word, the one just before the underline, and the first one to three words of each choice more carefully, and ask yourself whether there are any clues, or markers, that you missed. If so, write them down on a flash card. Here's an example:

(front)	(back)
When I see: and	I'll think: Parallelism: X and Y X, Y, and Z Could be: a list, a modifier, compound subject or verb, two independent clauses

Sometimes, there are no good clues at the first glance level, so don't expect that this strategy will always help you. Still, don't skip this step; good clues exist for more than 50 percent of problems, so this quick step can be quite valuable.

Read the Sentence for Meaning

Your default strategy is to read the entire original sentence all the way to the period, noting possible grammar or meaning issues along the way. The non-underlined portion contains valuable information that can help you decide how to proceed. Once you're done reading, decide which issue to tackle first. If you think you've spotted an error in the original, verify, then cross off answer (A) as well as any other answers that repeat that error.

You might, though, choose to break this strategy for one very good reason: You spot an early error in a longer underline and you are 100 percent sure that you've found an error. In that case, go ahead and eliminate choice (A) immediately, then glance through the remaining answers to eliminate any with that same error. At that point, though, return to the original sentence and finish reading it, keeping an eye out for any additional errors that you could use to eliminate other answers.

Either way, read the entire original sentence so that you can spot overall issues with meaning or sentence structure. If you don't, you'll be much more likely to fall into a trap.

To drill yourself on meaning, pull out your *Official Guide* again and look at some problems you've done in the past. Read only the original sentence (not the answers), then look away and try to articulate aloud, in your own words, what the sentence is trying to say. (You don't need to limit your rephrase to a single sentence.)

Do actually talk out loud. You'll be able to hear the conviction in your own voice when you know what the sentence is trying to say, and when you don't know what the sentence means, you'll also be able to hear that you're not sure.

In the latter case, examine the problem again. Either you just didn't understand it, or there was actually an issue with the meaning of that sentence. Which is it? Check the solution: Does it say that there is a meaning problem? If so, great! No wonder you had trouble rephrasing it. If not, then the explanation itself may help you understand what the sentence is trying to say. (If you find the official solution hard to follow, you can find Manhattan Prep solutions to *Official Guide* problems in our *GMAT Navigator* program.)

Find a Starting Point

Most of the time, you'll have to find multiple starting points on SC problems—one of the annoying things about this problem type. There are two primary ways to find a starting point: 1) Read the original sentence and 2) compare answers.

To drill the latter skill, open up your *Official Guide* again and look at some problems you have done before. This time, do *not* read the original sentence. Instead, cover it up and go straight to the answers.

Compare the answers and, based on the splits that you spot, try to articulate all of the things that the problem might be testing.

You usually won't be able to pick the correct answer, but you can often tell *what* is being tested even when you can't tell *how* to answer. For example, you might see a verb switching back and forth between singular and plural. If the subject isn't underlined, then you can't know which verb form is required (because you haven't read the sentence!), but you do know that subject–verb agreement is an issue.

When you're done, read the full sentence or check the solution. How good were you at figuring out what the problem was testing? What clues did you miss? Consider making flash cards for those clues.

Eliminate All Incorrect Choices

One of the most frustrating moments in SC problems is when you've narrowed down the answers to two...and then you don't know how to decide. When this happens to you, don't waste time going back and forth repeatedly, agonizing over the answers. Pick one of the two and move on.

Afterward, review the problem to learn how to make that choice. Add the following analysis to your overall review of SC problems:

1. Why are each of the four wrong answers wrong?
2. How would someone (mistakenly) justify *eliminating* the right answer? What is the trap that would lead someone to cross out the correct answer?
3. How would someone (mistakenly) justify *picking* any of the wrong answers? What is the trap that would lead someone to pick a wrong answer?
4. Why is the right answer right? (Mostly, it's right because it doesn't make any of the mistakes made in the four wrong answers. But if you were tempted to eliminate it for some reason, make sure you understand why that part was actually okay.)

When you learn how you (or someone) would fall into the trap of thinking that some wrong answer looks or sounds or feels better than the right one, you'll be a lot less likely to fall into that same trap yourself in the future. In other words, you're getting into the minds of the test writers and figuring out how to avoid the traps that they're setting for you.

Throughout this guide, you will encounter both wrong and right examples to teach you the precise differences:

Wrong: SINCE the company failed to meet its earnings forecast, CONSEQUENTLY the stock dropped as soon as the numbers were released.

Right: SINCE the company failed to meet its earnings forecast, the stock dropped as soon as the numbers were released.

Right: The company failed to meet its earnings forecast; CONSEQUENTLY, the stock dropped as soon as the numbers were released.

Don't just glance over those examples. Cement the wrongness of the wrong options in your brain by saying aloud why they're wrong or adding a note:

Wrong: SINCE the company failed to meet its earnings forecast, CONSEQUENTLY the stock dropped as soon as the numbers were released.

This is redundant! Use *since* or *consequently*, not both.

There are many steps to the SC process—and so there are many opportunities to learn to work more efficiently and effectively. As you complete subsequent SC chapters, return to this section to remind yourself how to hone your process as you increase your SC expertise.

Advanced material for the SC unit can be found in Atlas, your online learning platform, on the Manhattan Prep website. Use the online material only if you feel that you have mastered everything in the SC unit of this strategy guide and you are aiming for a Verbal section score of 42 or higher.

CHAPTER 2

Grammar and Meaning

In This Chapter:

- Grammar: A Closer Look
- Meaning: A Closer Look
- Connect, or Match, the Words
- Say It Once: Avoid Redundancy
- Place Your Words
- Choose Your Words

In this chapter, you will learn how grammar and meaning work together on the GMAT, including the primary ways the GMAT will try to sneak errors past you.

CHAPTER 2 Grammar and Meaning

Sentence Correction (SC) appears on the GMAT because business schools want to be sure that their admitted applicants grasp the two principles of good business writing:

1. **Grammar:** Does the sentence adhere to the rules of standard written English?
2. **Meaning:** Does the sentence clearly indicate the author's intended meaning?

These principles are equally important and actually overlap quite a bit. Certain grammar rules exist in order to convey a logical and unambiguous meaning. You'll learn some of these principles in this chapter and others as you work your way through the SC unit.

Grammar: Much of the language that you hear in everyday speech actually violates one rule or another. The GMAT tests your ability to distinguish between good and bad grammar, even when the bad grammar seems natural.

Consider this example: *As a long-time member of this team, it's really gratifying that we won the championship.* You likely hear similar sentences all the time, but the sentence actually violates the rules of standard written English. It should read: *As a long-time member of this team, I am really gratified that we won the championship.* You'll learn why later in this unit.

Meaning: Confusing writing is bad writing. If you have to read a sentence more than once to figure out what the author is saying—or if the sentence lends itself to multiple interpretations—it is not a good sentence.

What about the often-cited principle of concision? It is true that the GMAT does not like to waste words. If an idea expressed in 10 words can be expressed clearly and grammatically in 6, the GMAT prefers 6. However, this is a *preference*, not a rule.

Often, test-takers focus far too much on concision. As a result, the GMAT often makes the right answer *less* concise than an attractive wrong answer. Furthermore, *Official Guide* explanations often label a sentence *wordy* or *awkward* without additional explanation. In fact, these sentences have a meaning problem or an idiom error—but the explanation does not spell out the specific issue. In general, focus your efforts on grammar and meaning; ignore concision by itself.

Grammar: A Closer Look

This unit will steer you through the major points of standard written English on the GMAT. Each chapter presents a major grammatical topic in depth: sentence structure, modifiers, parallelism, comparisons, pronouns, verbs, and idioms. You will learn the overarching principles of each grammatical topic. You will also learn the nitty-gritty details that will help you differentiate both correct grammar from poor grammar and clear and logical meaning from ambiguous or illogical meaning. In addition, you will complete practice exercises designed to hone your skills in the various topics.

For your reference, a glossary of common grammatical terms appears in Appendix B of this guide. Do not be overly concerned with memorizing the names of the grammatical terms, as the GMAT will never require you to know what the rules are called. Focus on understanding and applying these rules—that's what really matters. In fact, when the formal grammar term is obscure, this guide may substitute a made-up name, abbreviation, or nickname that will be easier to remember.

One more thing: For every grammar rule, there is an exception to the rule. This can be really annoying when you're studying grammar! The rules you will learn are valid in more than 90 percent of cases, so you really can rely on them. Every now and then, however, you'll run across an exception. If the exception is discussed in this guide, make an effort to remember it. If the exception is not mentioned in this guide (but you still see it in an *Official Guide* problem), we made the judgment that the exception is rare enough that learning it is not a good return on your investment. If SC is a stronger area for you, feel free to memorize such exceptions as you see them; if SC is not a strength, it's probably better to shrug and let that issue go. You don't need to get everything right to get a good score.

The Five Grammar Terms You Need to Know

We try to keep fancy terms to a minimum in this book, but there's no way to discuss grammar without using at least a few actual grammar terms. Here are the five terms you absolutely need to know:

1. Clause

A **Clause** is a set of words that contains a subject and a working verb. Here is an example of a clause:

She applied for the job.

She	*applied*
Who applied for the job? She did.	What did she do? She applied.

She is the **Subject** because she is the one performing the action. *Applied* is the **Working Verb** because it describes what the subject did. For any sentence, you could ask, "Who (or what) did what?" and the (correct) answer will point to the subject and working verb.

Together, the subject and working verb create a complete, stand-alone sentence, or an **Independent Clause**. Independent clauses have, at the very least, a subject and a working verb. Every correct sentence must have at least one independent clause.

More complex sentences will also include something else: a second independent clause, a dependent clause, or other modifiers.

A **Dependent Clause** also contains a verb but cannot stand alone as a sentence:

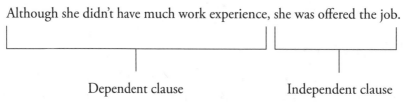

Although she didn't have much work experience, she was offered the job.

Although she didn't have much work experience,	she was offered the job.
Dependent clause	Independent clause

Only the second part of that sentence is independent: *She was offered the job.*

If you took just the first part by itself, you'd have a **Sentence Fragment**: *Although she didn't have much work experience.*

A sentence fragment is not a complete sentence. On the GMAT, the correct answer is always a complete sentence; if you spot a sentence fragment, cross off that answer.

You'll learn more about clauses in the Sentence Structure chapter of this unit.

2. Modifier

A **Modifier** provides additional information in a sentence, beyond the core subject and verb. The simplest example is an adjective. For example, in the phrase *the happy child*, the word *happy* is an adjective, modifying (or describing) the word *child*.

Modifiers can also be more complex:

> The large dog, which has black fur, is a Labrador.

The modifier *which has black fur* is called a **Nonessential Modifier**. If you remove it from the sentence, the core of the sentence still makes sense: The large dog is a Labrador.

Compare that to this sentence:

> The job that she started last week is much harder than her previous job.

In this sentence, *that she started last week* is called an **Essential Modifier**. Why is this one essential? Look what happens when you remove it from the sentence:

> The job is much harder than her previous job.

Which *job*? Her current job? Someone else's job? If you haven't already specified a particular job, then the meaning of the sentence is ambiguous. This is why *that she started last week* is an essential modifier: The modifier is necessary in order to understand the meaning of the core sentence.

You can find a full discussion of essential and nonessential modifiers in Chapter 4.

3. Sentence Core

The **Core** of a sentence consists of any independent clauses along with some essential modifiers. This is the bare minimum needed in order to have a coherent sentence.

Remember this sentence?

> Although she didn't have much work experience, she was offered the job.

The core sentence is *she was offered the job*. The part before the comma is a modifier—it's providing additional information about the core of the sentence. If you take that part out, you can still understand the basic meaning of the core (she got the job!), so this is a nonessential modifier. When you're looking for the core of the sentence, you can ignore any nonessential modifiers.

You'll learn more about the sentence core in the Sentence Structure and Modifiers chapters.

4. Conjunction

Conjunctions are words that help stick parts of sentences together. Here's an example:

> He worked hard, **and** a raise was his reward.

Coordinating conjunctions, or **Co-Conjunctions**, such as *and*, can glue two independent clauses together (among other things). Both *he worked hard* and *a raise was his reward* are independent clauses because each one can function as an independent sentence: He worked hard. A raise was his reward. Co-conjunctions connect two parts of a sentence that are at the same level or serve the same function (hence, the prefix *co*).

The most common co-conjunctions are the FANBOYS: *for, and, nor, but, or, yet, so.*

Modifiers can be connected to independent clauses by subordinating conjunctions, or **Sub-Conjunctions**. This is an example:

> **Although** she didn't have much work experience, she was offered the job.

The word *although* is a sub-conjunction. Other examples include *because, while, though, unless, before, after*, and *if.* Sub-conjunctions start a subordinate clause; the clause has a subject and verb but it cannot stand alone as its own sentence. As a result, these sub-clauses must be connected to an independent clause in order for you to have a valid sentence.

You'll learn more about conjunctions in the Sentence Structure and Modifiers chapters of this unit.

5. Marker

This one is not a grammar term, but it is important. A **Marker** is a clue that a certain grammatical topic is being tested. As you work through this unit, you will learn about various kinds of markers. For example, the word *unlike* is a comparison marker; when you see *unlike*, ask yourself what comparison is being made.

Let's say you read an explanation and think, "Hmm, I didn't know that that word was a marker for that topic." Immediately write that marker down! Keep a list, make flash cards, record it however you prefer—but do record the fact that when you see this particular marker, you should think about a particular grammar issue.

That's your quick-start grammar guide. (Yes, technically, we did sneak more than five terms into that list. The "extra" terms are all related, though.)

If you run across other unfamiliar terms, look them up in the glossary at the end of this guide.

Meaning: A Closer Look

For a sentence to be considered correct on the GMAT, it must be logical and unambiguous. If a choice is illogical or has more than one reasonable interpretation, cross it off. Consider this example:

> Tomorrow, she bought some milk.

This sentence doesn't violate any grammar rule, but it doesn't make any sense! Either she bought the milk in the past or she will buy the milk in the future. You know the sentence is wrong because the *meaning is illogical.*

Try another example:

> Animation filmmaker Hayao Miyazaki is arguably more famous than any animation filmmaker in the history of the art.

This sentence may appear to be just fine—in the real world, it probably would be—but there's something illogical about it. Miyazaki cannot be more famous than *any* animation filmmaker, because Miyazaki is himself a member of the group of animation filmmakers. The sentence currently says that he is more famous than anyone in a group that *includes himself.* Someone could claim that he is more famous than any *other* animation filmmaker, but not *all* animation filmmakers (including himself).

Consider this sentence:

> Falsehoods can be exposed using a polygraph device by a law enforcement professional.

Again, this sentence would probably be fine in the real world. Technically, though, the last part of the sentence is ambiguous: Was the *device* created *by a law enforcement professional*? Or can the falsehoods be exposed *by a law enforcement professional*? Remove the ambiguity by restructuring the sentence. Here's one possibility:

> Falsehoods can be exposed by a law enforcement professional using a polygraph device.

Now, the meaning is unambiguous: The law enforcement professional uses the device to expose the lie.

If the original sentence is confusing in some way, you will need to determine a logical and unambiguous meaning—but you don't have to come up with your own sentence from thin air! The possible answers will be sitting right in front of you, and they will help guide you to the proper meaning.

Most meaning issues fall into one of three major categories:

1. Words or phrases don't properly *match* in meaning (e.g., Yesterday she will buy milk).
2. Words are *redundant* (e.g., She loves movies, and she's a big fan of indie films in addition).
3. Words are in the wrong *place* (e.g., She tended to the gardens daily vs. She tended to the daily gardens).

Connect, or Match, the Words

Most sentences contain multiple words or groups of words that must connect, or match, in some way. For example, a singular subject must be paired with a singular verb in order to be grammatically correct. This requirement to pair certain words or phrases can also impact meaning; as you saw in an example earlier in this chapter, a verb tense must match the time frame of the overall sentence.

What's wrong with the following comparison?

> Unlike northern Canada, where the winter is quite cold, the temperature in Florida rarely goes below freezing.

Though it's probably clear that the author is trying to say that northern Canada and Florida are dissimilar, technically the sentence says that *Canada* and the *temperature* (in Florida) are dissimilar. It's illogical to compare a geographic location to the *temperature* in a different location.

A similar matching principle holds for other grammatical connections (e.g., pronouns and the nouns to which they refer). Future chapters will explore each type of connection in turn; for now, remember to test the *meaning* of any potential connection. Connected words must always make sense together.

Say It Once: Avoid Redundancy

Another aspect of meaning is redundancy. Each word in the correct choice plays some important role in the overall meaning of the sentence—but you don't need to say something twice. Redundancy can actually confuse the meaning, causing the reader to ask: Did I read that right? Is the author trying to say something other than what I first thought the sentence was trying to say?

A common redundancy trap on the GMAT is the use of two words or phrases that convey the same meaning:

Wrong:	The value of the stock ROSE by a 10 percent INCREASE.
Right:	The value of the stock INCREASED by 10 percent.
Right:	The value of the stock ROSE by 10 percent.

Since *rose* and *increase* both imply growth, only one is needed. Here's another example:

Wrong:	The three prices SUM to a TOTAL of $11.56.
Right:	The three prices SUM to $11.56.
Right:	The three prices TOTAL $11.56.

Pay attention to expressions of time. It is easy to sneak two redundant time expressions into an answer choice (especially if one expression is in the non-underlined part, or if the two expressions do not look like each other):

Past:	Previously	Formerly	In the past	Before now
Present:	Now	Currently	Presently	At present
Yearly:	Annual	Each year	A year (e.g., *three product launches a year*)	

If a sentence includes more than one time marker from the same category, check for redundancy:

Wrong:	AT PRESENT, the customer service department is NOW in the process of analyzing complaints.
Right:	AT PRESENT, the customer service department is in the process of analyzing complaints.
Right:	The customer service department is NOW in the process of analyzing complaints.

In the wrong example, *at present* and *now* are referring to the same action (*in the process of analyzing*), so it is redundant to use both time markers.

It is possible for there to be a valid reason to introduce a second time marker from the same category. For example:

Right:	AT PRESENT, the customer service department is in the process of analyzing complaints to determine how customer satisfaction has changed from last year until NOW.

In the final correct example, there are two present-tense time markers, but they are serving different functions. The first one indicates what the department is doing at the moment; the second one contrasts two different time frames (*last year* and *now*).

Also pay attention to transition words, such as contrast words. What is wrong with the sentence below?

> Although she studied night and day for three months, yet she did not do well on her exam.

The word *although* already conveys the coming contrast; it is redundant to introduce the contrast a second time with the word *yet*.

Throughout this unit, you will see additional examples of redundant language.

Place Your Words

Another common meaning issue has to do with where words are placed in a sentence. If you see that words are moving from one position to another in different answer choices, check the sentence for meaning issues.

The placement of a single word can alter the entire meaning of a sentence. For example:

> ALL the children are covered in mud.
>
> The children are ALL covered in mud.

In these sentences, changing the placement of *all* shifts the intent from *how many* children are covered in mud (all of them) to *how* the children are covered in mud (they have mud all over themselves). Consider another example:

> ONLY the council votes on Thursdays.
>
> The council votes ONLY on Thursdays.

In the first sentence, *only* indicates that the council alone votes on Thursdays (as opposed to the board, perhaps, which can vote any other day, but not Thursdays). According to that first sentence, the council could also vote any other day of the week. In the second sentence, however, the placement of *only* indicates that the council cannot vote on any day except for Thursday.

When a word changes its position in the answer choices, consider whether the change has an impact on the meaning of the sentence. Look out for short words (such as *only* and *all*) that quantify nouns or otherwise restrict meaning.

At a broader level, pay attention to overall word order. All of the words in a sentence could be well-chosen, but the sentence could still be awkward or ambiguous. For example:

> The council granted the right to make legal petitions TO CITY OFFICIALS.

What does the phrase *to city officials* mean? Did the city officials receive the right to make legal petitions? Or, did someone else receive the right to make petitions *to the officials*? Either way, the correct sentence should resolve the ambiguity:

> The council granted CITY OFFICIALS the right to make legal petitions.
>
> OR
>
> The right to make legal petitions TO CITY OFFICIALS was granted by the council.

You will learn more about how word placement affects meaning throughout the rest of this unit.

Choose Your Words

The GMAT doesn't explicitly test vocabulary, but on occasion, it may try to set a trap based on word choice.

An SC problem might try to mix up a particular word and its cousin. For example:

> My decision to drive a hybrid car was motivated by ECONOMIC considerations.
>
> ECONOMICAL considerations motivated my decision to drive a hybrid car.

The second sentence, which is shorter and in active voice, may sound preferable. Unfortunately, it is wrong! *Economical* means "thrifty, efficient." Notice that this meaning is not too distant from what the author intends to say: He or she wants an efficient automobile. But the appropriate phrase is *economic considerations*—that is, *monetary* considerations.

Consider the following pairs of "cousin" words and expressions, together with their distinct meanings:

> *aggravate* (worsen) vs. *aggravating* (irritating)
>
> *known as* (named) vs. *known to be* (acknowledged as) vs. *known for* (famous for a particular thing)
>
> *loss of* (no longer in possession of) vs. *loss in* (decline in value)
>
> *mandate* (command) vs. *have a mandate* (have authority from voters)
>
> *native of* (person from) vs. *native to* (species that originated in)
>
> *range of* (variety of) vs. *ranging* (varying)
>
> *rate of* (speed or frequency of) vs. *rates for* (prices for)
>
> *rise* (general increase) vs. *raise* (a bet or a salary increase in American English)
>
> *try to do* (seek to accomplish) vs. *try doing* (experiment with)

Some of these pairings are examples of idioms that can have different meanings depending upon the small word attached to the "main" word. For example:

> Charles "Buddy" Bolden, known as King Bolden, is considered one of the founders of jazz and was known for his improvisational skills and for combining elements from ragtime, blues, and gospel.

Bolden's nickname was King Bolden; he was *known as* this name; it would be incorrect to say he was *known for* this name. Similarly, he was *known for* certain musical traits; it would be incorrect to say he was *known as* these traits.

The list above is not comprehensive; English has plenty of pairs of cousin words whose meanings depend on context and the surrounding words. You'll learn more as you work your way through this unit, but if you run across unfamiliar examples in *Official Guide* problems, jot them down on a flash card.

Problem Set

In this chapter, you learned to avoid redundancy that muddles the meaning. In problems 1–4, circle the pair or pairs of redundant words.

1. Though canals have experienced a severe decline in barge traffic over the past several decades, yet with the rise in fuel costs, "shipping" by actual ships may once again become an important means of exporting goods outside the country.

2. After the test format was changed, scores subsequently dropped by more than a 25 percent decrease.

3. It is possible that the earthquake may have caused the building's collapse.

4. The retail sector has shrunk by a staggering margin each of the past five years, posting annual losses of at least 5 percent or more compared with the previous year.

Problems 5–7 are multiple choice with one correct answer. As on the real GMAT, answer (A) repeats the original sentence. Unlike the real GMAT, though, these problems have only two answer choices. Keep an eye out for issues with meaning discussed in this chapter.

5. <u>No matter how much work it may require</u>, getting an MBA is an investment that pays off for most people.

   (A) No matter how much work it may require

   (B) Though it does not require much work

6. <u>Many people believe that crime is on the rise but that, despite what is depicted on television, crime is actually at its lowest rate in decades.</u>

   (A) Many people believe that crime is on the rise but that, despite what is depicted on television, crime is actually at its lowest rate in decades.

   (B) Contrary to what many people believe and what is depicted on television, crime is at its lowest rate in decades.

7. Rising costs of raw materials may result in <u>fewer employees on the assembly line or product volume</u>.

   (A) fewer employees on the assembly line or product volume

   (B) a decrease in product volume or the number of employees on the assembly line

In this chapter, you learned about the importance of word placement as it relates to meaning. Modifiers, which you'll learn more about later, can completely change the meaning of the sentence as they move around. For example, these two sentences have very different meanings: 1) *Only* Ashanti plays tennis; 2) Ashanti plays *only* tennis.

8. In how many different places could you add the word *nearly* to the following sentence? How does the meaning change with each placement?

   The car did a 360-degree turn as it rolled off the track, colliding with some of the one thousand bystanders who had gathered to watch the race.

9. In how many different places could you add the phrase *in the first half* to the following sentence? How does the meaning change with each placement?

   The offense played well, and they showed significant progress even after they fell behind 23–0.

Solutions

1. Though canals have experienced a severe decline in barge traffic over the past several decades, yet with the rise in fuel costs, "shipping" by actual ships may once again become an important means of exporting goods outside the country.

   Using two contrast words such as *though* and *yet* is redundant. In this case, it is preferable to keep *yet* in order to delineate the contrast clearly; otherwise, a reader might mistakenly consider the phrase *with the rise of fuel costs* to be part of the first clause.

   Export means "to send goods *outside the country*"; using these phrases together is redundant.

2. After the test format was changed, scores subsequently dropped by more than a 25 percent decrease.

   The words *after* and *subsequently* convey the same idea. Similarly, you do not need both *dropped* and *decrease.*

3. It is possible that the earthquake may have caused the building's collapse.

   It is possible that and *may* both express the same level of uncertainty, so you can remove one of them without changing the intended meaning.

4. Sales for many stores in the retail sector have shrunk by staggering margins each of the past five years, posting annual losses of at least 5 percent or more compared with the previous year.

   Each of the past five years describes something that happens each year for a certain period of time. The word *annual* conveys part of that same meaning: Something happens each year. Since the word *annual* by itself does not also convey the idea of a five-year period, it would be preferable to drop this word from the sentence.

   At least 5 percent and *5 percent or more* both express the same idea, so you can remove one of them without changing the intended meaning.

5. **(A):** The original sentence indicates that getting an MBA might be a lot of work, but it still turns out to be a good investment for most people. Answer (B) loses this contrasting idea: Getting an MBA is not a lot of work, *though* (or *but*) it still turns out to be a good investment. It would be more logical to connect two positives with *and*, not the contrast word *though*: It's not a lot of work *and* it's a good investment.

6. **(B):** The original sentence indicates that people believe two things: 1) Crime is on the rise and 2) crime is at its lowest rate in decades. These two ideas are contradictory. While people can certainly believe contradictory things, if the sentence had intended to convey that meaning, it would have connected the two ideas with the word *and.* Instead, it uses the word *but*, signaling a different intended meaning: People believe one thing, but the opposite is actually true. Eliminate choice (A) for meaning issues.

   Choice (B) provides a logical and clear meaning: *Contrary* to popular belief, *crime is at its lowest rate* in a long time.

7. **(B):** The original sentence contains a subtle error; many people, in fact, will prefer answer (A) because it is more concise than (B). Try to avoid using concision to make your choice.

   Logically, the sentence is trying to convey two things that may result from rising costs: 1) The company will employ *fewer employees* or 2) the company will have to reduce *product volume*. The original sentence can be read in one of two ways. First, *rising costs... may result in... product volume.* This is illogical; the rising costs should result in some *change* in product volume. Second, *rising costs... may result in fewer... product volume.* This is an error; *product volume* is an uncountable noun, so it would have to be paired with an uncountable modifier (e.g., *lower product volume*). Either way, the original sentence is incorrect. You can learn more about countable and uncountable nouns in the Modifiers chapter.

8. There are (at least!) six different meanings that can be created by moving the word *nearly* around in the sentence:

   1. The car *nearly* did a 360-degree turn. The car came close to starting to spin, but it did not actually spin.
   2. The car did a *nearly* 360-degree turn. The car turned almost a full circle, but not quite.
   3. ... as it *nearly* rolled off the track. The car almost started rolling, but it didn't actually roll.
   4. ... as it rolled *nearly* off the track. The car did roll, and it rolled so far that it almost went off the track.
   5. ... off the track, *nearly* colliding with some... bystanders. The car came very close to the bystanders, but did not collide with them (thankfully!).
   6. ... some of the *nearly* one thousand bystanders. There were almost—but not quite!—one thousand bystanders at the track.

9. There are (at least) three different meanings that can be created by moving the words *in the first half* around in the sentence:

   1. *In the first half,* the offense played well. The offense played well *in the first half.* In both of these cases, the offense played well specifically for the first half of the game. It's not clear whether the action in the second part of the sentence (*showed significant progress...*) occurred in the first half or the second half.
   2. ... showed significant progress *in the first half.* The offense now appears to have played well for the entire game. The offense showed significant progress specifically during *the first half* of that game, which is also when they fell behind 23–0.
   3. ... they fell behind 23–0 *in the first half.* The offense played well for the entire game. The score was 23–0 at some point during the first half. Sometime after that, the offense showed significant progress, though it's not clear whether this was during the first half or the second (or both).

   In all of these cases, the time marker *in the first half* indicates when a particular action took place. The placement of a time marker can significantly change the meaning of a sentence because it changes when a specific event occurs.

CHAPTER 3

Sentence Structure

In This Chapter:

- Subject and Verb Must Both Exist
- Subject and Verb Must Agree in Number
- Eliminate the Middlemen and Skip the Warm-Up
- Use Structure to Decide
- Mid-Chapter Quiz: Test Your Skills
- The Sentence Core
- Two Independent Clauses
- Adding Modifiers

In this chapter, you will learn about core sentence structures, from the elements required in a valid sentence structure to the ways the GMAT attempts to camouflage sentences with invalid structure. You'll learn about complex sentence structures, subject–verb agreement, and punctuation, among other topics.

CHAPTER 3 Sentence Structure

Every sentence must have a **Subject** and a **Verb**. The subject is the noun that performs the action expressed by the verb:

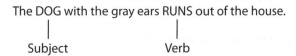

The DOG with the gray ears RUNS out of the house.

Subject — DOG; Verb — RUNS

The subject, the *dog*, performs the action of *running*. The subject and the verb must agree in number: In this case, both *dog* and *runs* are singular.

How does the GMAT make things more complicated?

Subject and Verb Must Both Exist

If a sentence is missing the subject or the verb, the sentence is a **Fragment**; in other words, it is not a complete sentence. On the GMAT, the correct answer must be a complete sentence, or **Independent Clause**. (The previous chapter introduced independent clauses; if you skipped or skimmed that chapter, go take a look now.)

The GMAT might disguise the error by dropping the verb:

Wrong: The cat sitting by the stairs.

Wait a minute, what about *sitting*? *Sitting* certainly looks like a verb. It is not, however, a **Working Verb**, a verb that can run a sentence by itself. Here's an example of a working verb:

Right: The cat sitting by the stairs WATCHED the mouse.

In this sentence, the word *watched* is a working verb. Here's another example of a working verb:

Right: The cat WAS SITTING by the stairs.

In this sentence, the words *was sitting* make up the full verb form. The word *sitting* is called a **Present Participle** and you'll see more of these ***–ing*** words throughout this book. For now, just remember that an *–ing* word is only a verb when it is preceded by a helping verb such as *is*, *was*, *will be*, and so on. *The cat sitting by the stairs* is not a complete sentence.

These are also not complete sentences:

Wrong: BECAUSE the dog was never mine.

Wrong: WHICH will be approved tomorrow.

Because and *which* are connecting words. They add extra information to a sentence, but they are not sentences by themselves. They're examples of **Modifiers**, which you will learn about in the next chapter.

The correct answer must contain at least one independent clause; if an answer choice does not, eliminate it!

Subject and Verb Must Agree in Number

A singular subject requires a singular verb form:

> The dog runs out of the house.

A plural subject requires a plural verb form:

> The dogs run out of the house.

You already know this; you would never write *the dog run out* or *the dogs runs out*. The GMAT, therefore, has to try to obscure these errors to get people to fall into a trap.

How? The GMAT might hide the subject so that you are unsure whether the subject is singular or plural. If you do not know the number of the subject, then you will not be able to select the verb form that agrees with it. Consider this example:

> The discovery of new medicines (was/were) vital to the company's growth.

What is the subject, *discovery* or *new medicines*? If you ask yourself, "What is/are vital to the company's growth?" you may be able to talk yourself into either choice. It makes as much sense to say the *discovery was vital* as it does to say the *new medicines were vital*.

In this case, *the discovery... was* is the correct subject–verb pair because the noun *medicines* is part of the **Prepositional Phrase** *of new medicines*. A noun in a prepositional phrase will *not* be the subject of the sentence. Note: There is an exception here, which you'll learn about in the advanced material associated with this chapter (located online in your Atlas learning platform). This is an example of one of those "for every grammar rule, there is an exception" cases mentioned earlier in this guide.

The plural *medicines* is a trap; the test writer deliberately inserts a noun that is both physically closer to the verb and the opposite in number from the actual subject, just hoping to catch you. Train yourself not to rely on physical proximity when finding the subject; check the actual sentence structure.

Are these sentences both correct?

> Lin and Guy drive to work.
>
> Lin, as well as Guy, drive to work every day.

The first sentence is a correct example of a **Compound Subject**: Lin and Guy together function as the subject of the sentence. Compound subjects are always plural because at least two nouns function together as the subject.

A compound subject *must* be connected by the word *and*, but the second sentence uses the modifier *as well as Guy*. This sentence, as written earlier, is incorrect because only Lin qualifies as the subject. It should read:

Right: LIN, as well as Guy, drives to work every day.

Subject (LIN) — Modifier (as well as Guy) — Verb (drives)

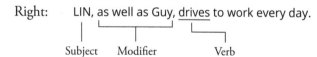

A sentence can also contain a **Compound Verb** (two or more verbs that all point to the same subject). For example:

Right: Lin *drove* to work *and said* hello to his coworker.

Subject Verb Conjunction Verb

Right: Lin and Guy *drive* to work together every morning *and greet* their coworkers cheerfully.

Subject Conjunction Subject Verb Conjunction Verb

That last sentence contains both a compound subject (*Lin and Guy*) and a compound verb (*drive and greet*). If the writer inserts enough distance between the two portions of a compound subject or verb, it could be easy to make a mistake. Read on to learn how the GMAT does this.

Eliminate the Middlemen and Skip the Warm-Up

The most common way to hide a subject is to insert words between the subject and the verb; we call these words the **Middlemen**. If you learn to ignore these words when looking for a subject, you'll be much less likely to pick the wrong noun as the subject.

To further obscure things, the GMAT often puts a significant number of words in front of the subject. In these cases, you have to ignore the **Warm-Up** that comes before the subject of the sentence.

There are a few common types of middlemen and warm-ups.

1. Prepositional Phrases

A prepositional phrase (or prep phrase, for short) is a group of words headed by a **Preposition**. For example:

of mice	for milk	by 1800
in Zambia	with her	at that level
to the store	on their orders	from the office

The underlined prepositions are among the most common in the English language. A list of common prepositions is included in the Glossary at the end of this guide. If you think something is a preposition but you're not sure, try making a prep phrase with *the house*:

dig under the house	fly over the house
the car by the house	walk to the house

Prepositions are followed by nouns or pronouns, which complete the phrase. Prep phrases modify or describe other parts of the sentence. A noun in a prep phrase will not be the main subject of the sentence. For example:

Near Galway, the houses on the road to Spiddle is/are gorgeous.

~~Near Galway~~, the HOUSES ~~on the road to Spiddle~~ ARE gorgeous.

In the example above, the subject is *houses* (plural) and the correct verb is *are* (also plural).

2. Dependent Clauses

Dependent clauses, which begin with connecting words such as *while* or *because*, cannot stand alone as sentences. They do not contain the main subject or main verb; rather, they are always attached to independent clauses. Look back at the first sentence in this paragraph: Can you find the dependent clause? (Hint: Examine the commas.)

> The dependent clause: which begin with connecting words such as *while* or *because*
>
> The independent clause: Dependent clauses cannot stand alone as sentences.

If a dependent clause is stripped out of a sentence, what remains is still a complete sentence.

Try another example:

> Because she studied hard, she earned a good score on the test.

What is the dependent clause? What is the independent clause (complete sentence)?

> Dependent: Because she studied hard
>
> Independent: She earned a good score on the test.

3. Other Modifiers

Other words can also function as modifiers, which add extra information to the sentence. Modifiers will be covered in depth in the next chapter.

Use Structure to Decide

Consider the following sentence:

> In the waning days of the emperor's life, the conquest of new lands on the borders of the empire was/were considered vital.

To find the subject of the verb *was* or *were considered*, you might be tempted to ask yourself, "What *was* or *were considered* vital?" This method will get rid of obviously inappropriate subjects, such as *the emperor's life* or *the waning days*, but you could fall into the trap of thinking that *new lands* is the subject. However, *new lands* is in a prep phrase modifying the noun *conquest*. Since a noun in a prep phrase cannot be the subject of the sentence (with very limited exceptions that you'll learn about later), the subject must be *conquest*:

> Wrong: ~~In the waning days of the emperor's life,~~ the CONQUEST ~~of new lands on the borders of the empire~~ WERE CONSIDERED vital.
>
> Right: ~~In the waning days of the emperor's life,~~ the CONQUEST ~~of new lands on the borders of the empire~~ WAS CONSIDERED vital.

Certain tempting nouns, such as *new lands*, will be inserted purposely to distract you. Use the structure of the sentence to eliminate the middlemen and find the subject.

Now consider this example:

> The tidal forces to which an object falling into a black hole is/are subjected is/are sufficient to tear the object apart.

You have to match up two subject–verb pairs in this one. First, find the main subject and match it with the appropriate verb:

> Better: The tidal FORCES ~~to which an object falling into a black hole is/are~~ ~~subjected~~ ARE sufficient to tear the object apart.

Next, match up the subject and the verb in the dependent clause:

> Right: The tidal forces to which an OBJECT ~~falling into a black hole~~ IS SUBJECTED are sufficient to tear the object apart.

3

Mid-Chapter Quiz: Test Your Skills

The following problems are multiple choice with one correct answer. As on the real GMAT, answer (A) repeats the original sentence. Unlike the real GMAT, though, these problems have only two answer choices. Keep an eye out for issues with sentence structure, discussed in this chapter.

When you're done, you may want to pause for a day or two to let this material sink in before you continue with the second half of this chapter.

1. The recent string of burglaries, in addition to poor building maintenance, have inspired the outspoken resident to call a tenants' meeting.

   (A) The recent string of burglaries, in addition to poor building maintenance, have

   (B) Recently, the string of burglaries, along with the poor building maintenance, has

2. The computer science instructor assigned a new textbook focused on recent advances in artificial intelligence.

   (A) The computer science instructor assigned a new textbook focused on recent advances in artificial intelligence.

   (B) A new textbook that is focused on recent advances in artificial intelligence assigned by our instructor.

3. Some of the earliest computer games designed to involve many players at once and first developed before the widespread availability of high-speed internet connections.

   (A) Some of the earliest computer games designed to involve many players at once and first developed before the widespread availability of high-speed internet connections.

   (B) First developed before the widespread availability of high-speed internet connections, some of the earliest computer games were designed to involve many players at once.

1. **(B):** Properly identifying the subject of this sentence can be tricky; remember to eliminate the middlemen!

   The recent string ~~of burglaries, in addition to poor building maintenance~~, have...

   The subject of the sentence is *string*, which is singular. Since the subject and verb must agree in number, the singular *has* is correct.

2. **(A):** The original sentence contains a correct subject (*instructor*) and verb (*assigned*) pair.

   In choice (B), however, the only verb (*is*) lies within a dependent clause (*that... intelligence*); no main verb exists, so this sentence structure is a fragment. The sentence could be fixed by adding *was* before *assigned* to turn that modifier into a working verb (*a textbook... was assigned*). You'll learn more about modifiers in the next chapter.

3. **(B):** Similar to choice (B) in question 2, answer (A) contains participles (*designed* and *developed*) that masquerade as verbs but are actually modifiers. There's no main verb at all in answer (A), so this sentence is a fragment. Choice (B) fixes this mistake by using the main verb *were designed.*

The Sentence Core

SC sentences can be very complex, so it is useful to learn how to strip out the extraneous text (mentally, since you can't write on the test screen) and get yourself down to the sentence core. You've already started to learn how to do this by stripping out middlemen and skipping the warm-up.

The core sentence consists of at least the main subject and verb—but more complex sentences, such as the ones found in SC, can have a lot more going on in the core. Take a look at this example:

> Despite some initial concerns, the teacher is confident that her students mastered the lesson.

The core structure of the sentence is this:

The teacher	is	confident	that	her students	mastered	the lesson.
Subject	Verb		THAT	Subject	Verb	Object

When the word *that* appears just after a working verb, it often acts as a reset button in the sentence: A new subject–verb(–object) structure will follow. When this occurs, both subject–verb pairs are part of the core sentence. (Not every sentence has an object.)

Note: The word *that* can also serve other roles, which you'll learn about throughout this guide.

In the real world, people will often drop the word *that* from the sentence structure:

> Wrong on the GMAT: The teacher is confident her students mastered the lesson.

This is acceptable in the real world, but it doesn't follow the strictest grammar conventions. Technically, the missing *that* can make the sentence ambiguous or confusing; consider these sentences:

Right:	I know Lupita Nyong'o, who won an Academy Award for her role in *12 Years a Slave*.
Wrong on the GMAT:	I know Lupita Nyong'o, who won an Academy Award for her role in *12 Years a Slave*, was born in Mexico City.
Right:	I know that Lupita Nyong'o, who won an Academy Award for her role in *12 Years a Slave*, was born in Mexico City.

Someone reading the middle sentence will initially think that you personally know Ms. Nyong'o. That reader will only realize much later in the sentence that you are trying to say that you know something *about* her. A good sentence is clear from start to finish; it doesn't make you change your interpretation of the meaning halfway through.

The word *that* signals to the reader that more information is coming—it's literally a signal to the reader to wait for that information before trying to interpret the meaning. The teacher isn't just confident in her students in general. She is confident *that they mastered the lesson*. You don't personally know Lupita Nyong'o; you know *that she is an actor*.

Two Independent Clauses

Two complete sentences can be connected into one extra-long sentence. For example:

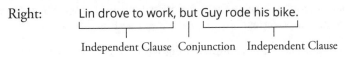

Right: Lin drove to work, but Guy rode his bike.

Independent Clause (Lin drove to work) | Conjunction (but) | Independent Clause (Guy rode his bike)

Lin drove to work is a complete sentence. So is *Guy rode his bike*. Two complete sentences can be connected using a comma plus a co-conjunction (such as *but*) to create a **Compound Sentence**. In this kind of sentence, you have two main subject–verb pairs and both are part of the core sentence.

But is part of a group of seven co-conjunctions called the FANBOYS:

For

And

Nor

But

Or

Yet

So

The English language contains many conjunctions; these seven are special because they are very common in the English language and because they can be used to connect two independent clauses into one complex, or compound, sentence.

It is not acceptable, however, to connect two sentences using only a comma:

Wrong: Lin drove to work, Guy rode his bike.

Independent Clause (Lin drove to work) | Comma without Conjunction! | Independent Clause (Guy rode his bike)

This is called a **Run-On Sentence** or a comma splice. Any GMAT answer choice that connects two independent clauses via only a comma is incorrect.

Pop quiz! What is the error in the sentence below?

Wrong: The latest statistics released by the Labor Department indicate that producer prices rose rapidly last month, despite a generally weakening economy, some analysts contend that the economic slowdown in the euro zone and in Asia will stem the rise in commodity prices, reducing inflationary pressures in the United States.

The sentence above is a run-on. The example below strips the sentence to its core subject and verb components and adds the necessary conjunction:

> Right: The latest statistics ~~released by the Labor Department~~ indicate that producer prices rose ~~rapidly last month, despite a generally weakening economy~~, BUT some analysts contend that the economic slowdown ~~in the euro zone and in Asia~~ will stem the rise in commodity prices~~, reducing inflationary pressures in the United States~~.

Here's just the core of the corrected sentence:

> Core: The latest statistics . . . indicate that producer prices rose, . . . BUT some analysts contend that the economic slowdown . . . will stem the rise in commodity prices.

3

Here's another type of error the GMAT might throw at you:

> Wrong: The term *Eureka*, which means "I have found it" in ancient Greek and was famously uttered by Archimedes, and ever since then, scientists have exclaimed the same word upon making important discoveries.

What's the problem with that sentence? It does contain a comma along with the conjunction *and* connecting the two parts.

Unfortunately, the first half is not a complete sentence. Try to make it stand alone:

> Wrong: The term *Eureka*, which means "I have found it" in ancient Greek and was famously uttered by Archimedes.

The term Eureka could be a subject, but the rest is only a modifier; it does not contain a working verb.

You could fix the sentence by turning the first part into an independent clause:

> Right: The term *Eureka*, which means "I have found it" in ancient Greek, WAS famously uttered by Archimedes, and ever since then, scientists have exclaimed the same word upon making important discoveries.

In sum, use a comma plus a co-conjunction to connect independent clauses. (The most common co-conjunctions are the FANBOYS.) Cross off any answers that connect two independent clauses using only a comma.

Semicolon

You can also connect two independent clauses with a semicolon. For instance:

> Right: Earl walked to school; he later ate his lunch.

Note that the part before the semicolon is a complete sentence, as is the part after the semicolon. Consider another example:

> Wrong: Arya and Nymeria are inseparable; doing everything together.

The second part of this sentence cannot stand on its own. Therefore, the two parts cannot be connected by a semicolon.

> Right: Arya and Nymeria are inseparable; they do everything together.

In the corrected example above, the two sentence parts can each stand alone. Therefore, you're allowed to connect them using a semicolon.

The semicolon is often followed by a transition expression, such as *however*, *therefore*, or *in addition*. For example, the two sentences in the previous paragraph can be combined in this way:

Right: In the corrected example above, the two sentence parts can each stand alone; therefore, you're allowed to connect them using a semicolon.

Note that these transitional elements are not co-conjunctions like *and*. As a result, you must use semicolons, not commas, to join the sentences:

Wrong: Arya and Nymeria are inseparable, THEREFORE, we never see them apart.

Right: Arya and Nymeria are inseparable; THEREFORE, we never see them apart.

From a practical standpoint, commas and semicolons are never interchangeable. If a sentence is correctly written using a comma, you can't replace that comma with a semicolon without making other changes. Likewise, if a sentence is correctly written using a semicolon, you can't replace that semicolon with a comma without making other changes.

When you see a split in the answers between a comma and a semicolon, check whether each half of the sentence can stand on its own. If one cannot, don't use a semicolon. If both can, the correct answer will use either a semicolon or a comma *plus* a co-conjunction. If a choice has two independent sentences connected only by a comma (with no co-conjunction), cross off that choice.

A rare but correct use of the semicolon is to separate a list of items that themselves contain commas:

Ambiguous: I listen to *Earth, Wind & Fire, Wow, Owls*, and *Blood, Sweat & Tears*.

Right: I listen to *Earth, Wind & Fire*; *Wow, Owls*; and *Blood, Sweat & Tears*.

The GMAT might also test colons and dashes; these punctuation marks are less common, so learn them if you are aiming for a higher score on the Verbal section of the GMAT. They are addressed in the additional material located online in your Atlas learning platform on the Manhattan Prep website.

Adding Modifiers

Quick quiz: What do you remember about dependent clauses? (You first learned about them in detail earlier in this chapter, in the Eliminate the Middlemen section.) Glance back through that section if you need to.

Dependent clauses are modifiers; they add extra information to the sentence. GMAT SC sentences will often include dependent clauses in order to make these sentences as complex as possible.

You'll learn all about these and other types of modifiers in the next chapter. For now, concentrate on learning the core sentence structures discussed in this chapter so that you are fully prepared to add even more complexity when you move to the Modifiers chapter.

3

Problem Set

For problems 1–4, box the verb and underline the subject. Then, determine whether the subject agrees in number with the verb. If there is a mistake, rewrite the sentence to correct the mistake. If the sentence is correct as it is, mark it with the word CORRECT.

1. Jack, along with some of his closest friends, is sharing a limo to the prom.

2. After all the gardening we did, the sun shining on the flowerbeds make a beautiful sight.

3. The decision to place the beautiful artifacts in out-of-the-way nooks around the mansion's various rooms was inspiring.

4. A national supermarket chain and a locally owned bakery, which has won awards for its croissants, has seen a significant decrease in revenues since the biggest employer in the area shut down.

Problems 5–7 are multiple choice with one correct answer. As on the real GMAT, answer (A) repeats the original sentence. Unlike the real GMAT, though, these problems have only two answer choices.

5. The sports governing body recently revamped the rules about hits to the head, a change intended to increase player safety, ever since then players have, somewhat paradoxically, suffered more concussions.

   (A) The sports governing body recently revamped the rules about hits to the head, a change intended to increase player safety, ever since then

   (B) Ever since the sports governing body revamped the rules about hits to the head, a change intended to increase player safety,

6. Disappointed by the narrow loss after a long and grueling campaign, Governor Schuster, with counsel from her family, is considering whether to run for Governor again next election.

   (A) Disappointed by the narrow loss after a long and grueling campaign, Governor Schuster, with counsel from her family, is

   (B) Although the narrow loss after a long and grueling campaign was disappointing, Governor Schuster and her family are

7. The lighthouse down by the bay overlooks both a vast stretch of coastline and a number of fisheries that are owned by the local government.

   (A) vast stretch of coastline and a number of fisheries that are owned by the local government

   (B) number of fisheries that are owned by the local government and a vast stretch of coastline

Bonus exercise! For problems 8–12, identify the error(s) and try to write a correct sentence. Note that there are many ways to fix any sentence, so on the GMAT itself, don't try to fix the sentence without examining your options in the answer choices.

8. The music company was afraid of the accelerating decline of sales of compact discs would not be compensated by increased internet revenue.

9. The petroleum distillates were so viscous, the engineers had to heat the pipe by nearly 30 degrees.

10. The municipality's back-to-work program has had notable success, nevertheless, it is not suitable for a statewide rollout for several reasons.

11. Historically, the Isle of Man had an economy based primarily on agriculture and fishing; now, one based on banking, tourism, and film production.

12. The Bentley trench, situated more than a mile and a half below sea level and completely covered by Antarctic glaciers, and it is the lowest point on the planet not under the oceans.

Solutions

1. **Correct.** The phrase *along with* is a middleman; don't count *some of his closest friends* as part of the subject. Only Jack is the subject.

   Jack, along with some of his closest friends, is sharing a limo to the prom.

2. **Incorrect.** The singular subject *the sun* must be paired with the singular verb *makes.*

   After all the gardening we did, the sun shining on the flowerbeds makes a beautiful sight.

3. **Correct.** Ignore prep phrases and other middlemen when looking for the subject. The sentence contains three middlemen in a row: 1) *to place the beautiful articles*, 2) *in out-of-the-way nooks*, and 3) *around the mansion's various rooms.*

   The decision to place the beautiful artifacts in out-of-the-way nooks around the mansion's various rooms was inspiring.

4. **Incorrect.** The word *and* creates a compound subject (the *supermarket chain* and the *bakery*), so the subject is plural, but the verb (*has*) is singular. There are two other subject–verb pairings in the sentence, both of which are correct: *bakery... has won* and *employer ... shut down.*

   A national supermarket chain AND a locally owned bakery, which has won awards for its croissants, have seen a significant decrease in revenues since the biggest employer in the area shut down.

5. **(B):** The original sentence is a run-on; it connects two independent clauses with nothing but a comma. Strip out the modifiers to find the (incorrect) core sentence: *The sports governing body revamped the rules, ever since then players have suffered more concussions.*

   Two independent clauses connected by a comma must also use a co-conjunction. Answer (B) corrects this error by changing *ever since then* to *ever since.* Now, the sentence begins with a dependent clause (*ever since... the head*); it's acceptable to connect a dependent clause to an independent clause with a comma and nothing else.

6. **(A):** Skip the middlemen and eliminate the warm-up to strip the sentence down to its core: *Governor Schuster is considering whether to run again next election.*

   The core of choice (B) says that *Governor Schuster and her family are considering whether to run for Governor again next election.* The subject changed from a singular subject (*Governor Schuster*) to a compound subject (*Governor Schuster and her family*), and the verb correctly changed from singular (*is*) to plural (*are*) to match. However, the compound subject introduces a meaning error: Governor Schuster is the person who ran for Governor last time and who may or may not run again this time. Her family members may have supported her, but they did not all run for Governor. You could fix this error by saying *Governor Schuster and her family are considering whether she should run* or by maintaining a singular subject, as the original sentence does.

7. **(B):** This is a tricky one. The original sentence is grammatically correct, but the meaning is ambiguous. What does the government own? *A number of fisheries*? Or both *a vast stretch of coastline and a number of fisheries*? That ending modifier (*that are owned by the local government*) could apply just to the second of the two parallel items, but it could also apply to both of the parallel items.

   The second sentence fixes this ambiguity by switching the order of the two phrases. Now, the sentence conveys a single, clear meaning. When more than one possible interpretation is acceptable, it doesn't matter which meaning the correct answer conveys; it matters only that the meaning is unambiguous. In this case, it's clear that the local government owns only the *fisheries*, not the *coastline*.

8. The original sentence has one independent clause (*the music company was afraid of* something) and then includes another main verb (*would not be... revenue*), but there is no conjunction to create a compound verb, so that second verb doesn't have the same subject (*company*). Logically, the subject for the second verb should be *the decline of sales*, but this noun is in a prep phrase, so it can't function as a subject of the sentence. One way to fix the sentence is to replace the preposition *of* with *that*:

   The music company was afraid THAT the accelerating decline of sales of compact discs would not be compensated by increased internet revenue.

9. Not sure what *viscous* means? It doesn't matter! Just think "they were so *something*" and keep going. The original sentence is a run-on. Here are some ways to fix it:

   The petroleum distillates were so viscous THAT the engineers had to heat the pipe by nearly 30 degrees.

   The petroleum distillates were EXTREMELY viscous; AS A RESULT, the engineers had to heat the pipe by nearly 30 degrees.

10. The word *nevertheless* is not a FANBOYS conjunction (such as *and*), so it cannot be used with a comma to connect two independent clauses. Here are two ways to fix the sentence:

    The municipality's back-to-work program has had notable success; nevertheless, it is not suitable for a statewide rollout for several reasons. [Change comma to semicolon.]

    The municipality's back-to-work program has had notable success, BUT it is not suitable for a statewide rollout for several reasons.

11. A semicolon connects two independent clauses. In the original sentence, the second part of the sentence does not form a valid independent clause. Here is one way to fix the sentence:

    Historically, the Isle of Man had an economy based primarily on agriculture and fishing; now, IT HAS one based on banking, tourism, and film production.

12. The original sentence begins with what could be the subject, followed by a modifier. After the modifier, the co-conjunction *and* starts a new independent clause; there is no main verb to pair with the first subject, *trench*. The first half of the sentence is a fragment. Here is one way to fix it:

    The Bentley trench, situated more than a mile and a half below sea level and completely covered by Antarctic glaciers, IS the lowest point on the planet not under the oceans.

CHAPTER 4

Modifiers

In This Chapter:

- Adjectives and Adverbs
- Modifier vs. Core Part 1
- Noun Modifiers
- Noun Modifier Markers: *Which, That, Who,* and More
- Adverbial Modifiers
- Modifier Markers: Prepositions
- Modifier Markers: *–ing* and *–ed* Words
- Modifier vs. Core Part 2
- Modifier Markers: Subordinators
- Quantity

In this chapter, you will learn about how modifiers—extra information—fit into and elaborate on the sentence core that you learned about in the previous chapter. You'll learn what markers indicate noun and adverbial modifiers and how to use these markers to spot and fix commonly tested GMAT modifier errors.

CHAPTER 4 Modifiers

A **Modifier** (or mod, for short) describes extra information about something else in the sentence. Although modifiers can be as simple as a single word (an adjective or an adverb), GMAT sentences often contain several complex modifiers. For example:

> Tired out from playing basketball, CHARLES DECIDED to take a nap.

The modifier *tired out from playing basketball* provides additional context as to *why* Charles decided to take a nap. Many modifiers answer the questions *who, what, which, when, where, how*, or *why*. Incorrectly used modifiers can lead to ambiguity or illogical meaning.

There are two broad categories of modifiers: **Noun** and **Adverbial**. Noun modifiers modify only a noun (including pronouns, a type of noun). Adverbial modifiers do *not* modify plain nouns or pronouns. Instead, they modify almost anything else: verbs, adjectives, prepositional phrases, even entire clauses. Note that adverbial modifiers can modify nouns + other stuff (such as a clause)—just not stand-alone nouns. Most of the time on the GMAT, adverbial modifiers modify some sort of action (and a noun could be part of that broader action).

Some types of words, such as adjectives, can only be noun mods; some types, such as adverbs, can only be adverbial mods.

Many structures, though, can be either noun or adverbial mods, depending upon how they're used. The three structures of this type that are most commonly used on the GMAT are prep phrases, *–ing* words, and *–ed* words. You will learn about all of these in this chapter.

Adjectives and Adverbs

Let's start with the most basic modifiers. An **Adjective** modifies *only* a noun, so these are always noun mods. An **Adverb**, on the other hand, modifies almost anything *but* a plain noun, so these are always adverbial mods. Neither of these is tested all that much on the GMAT, but they're a good introduction to help you understand the broader topic.

For example:

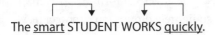

> The smart STUDENT WORKS quickly.

Here, the adjective *smart* modifies the noun *student*, while the adverb *quickly* modifies the verb *works*. Many adverbs are formed by adding *–ly* to the adjective.

Adjectives and adverbs are typically the simplest types of modifiers in a sentence—and perhaps that's why the GMAT doesn't test them all that frequently. Sometimes, you'll see a sentence in which an adverb (or occasionally an adjective) moves around in the different answer choices. For example:

> The company makes only one kind of bicycle.
>
> The company only makes one kind of bicycle.

In the first sentence, the company makes exactly one kind of bicycle, but it may also make other things (perhaps it makes scooters and skateboards as well). In this sentence, *only* modifies *one kind.*

In the second sentence, by contrast, the company makes exactly and only one thing: a kind of bicycle. It makes nothing else. In this sentence, *only* modifies *makes.*

The placement of a modifier is one of the most important things the GMAT tests, because the placement can completely change the meaning of the sentence. In some cases, as in the examples about the bicycles, the two meanings are both acceptable; they're just different.

Sometimes, though, one of the placements creates an ambiguous or outright illogical meaning. Compare these two sentences:

> The flower is so rare that it is found in only one type of habitat, rain forests at the highest humidity levels.

> The flower is so rare that it is found in one type of habitat, rain forests at only the highest humidity levels.

The first sentence conveys a clear and logical meaning: The *flower is so rare that it is found only* in a certain type of place. The second sentence, by contrast, is less clear. The word *only* now applies to the *humidity level* rather than the *type of habitat*, so the sentence appears to leave open the possibility that the flower can be found in other habitats, too. Logically, though, the word *only* should complete the *so rare that* meaning: It is *so rare that* it is found in *only* one area.

The GMAT will sometimes offer answers that use an adjective where an adverb is required, or vice versa. Consider this example:

> Max's great-grandmother, from whom he inherited his curly hair, is his supposed Irish ancestor.

> Max's great-grandmother, from whom he inherited his curly hair, is his supposedly Irish ancestor.

In the first option, the adjective *supposed* points to the noun *ancestor*, implying that Max's great-grandmother might not actually be his ancestor. In the second option, the adverb *supposedly* points to the adjective *Irish*, implying that Max's great-grandmother might not actually be Irish.

Max's great-grandmother is his relation, so she is by definition his ancestor. Only the second option has a sensible meaning: Max's grandmother is *supposedly Irish*, but she may not be after all.

Adjectives that have been observed alternating with their corresponding adverbs in released GMAT problems include *corresponding*, *frequent*, *independent*, *rare*, *recent*, *seeming*, *separate*, *significant*, *supposed*, and *usual.* If you spot an answer switching back and forth between the adjective and adverb forms of the same word, examine the meaning.

In order to do this, first decide what the word is modifying. If the choice uses the adjectival form of the word, the adjective must be modifying a noun; if the choice uses the adverbial form, the adverb must be modifying something other than a noun. Once you have that straightened out, you can decide which meaning is logical.

Modifier vs. Core: Part 1

Most modifiers are not part of the core sentence, so when you are trying to pay attention just to the core, you can mentally ignore many—but not all—modifiers.

Imagine a friend is giving you directions to her house. What's the difference between these two sets of directions?

> Turn left on Mayberry Street, and stop at the first house, which is red.
>
> Turn left on Mayberry Street, and stop at the first house that is red.

In the first example, the direction is to stop at the first house, period. The sentence also provides some extra information in the form of a modifier: That first house happens to be red. If you took that modifier out of the sentence, you would still know the proper meaning of the main part of the sentence and you'd stop at the correct house (the first one!). This is an example of a **Nonessential Modifier**, and these types of modifiers are *not* a part of the core sentence (since the information really is just extra).

The second sentence, by contrast, tells you to stop at the first red house. This is not necessarily the same house as the first house on the street. It could be that the first red house is actually the fifth one down the street. In other words, if you remove *that is red* from the sentence, you might show up at the wrong house. This is an example of an **Essential Modifier**, and you will usually want to keep these as part of the core sentence.

Why are these two meanings so different? In the second sentence, *that is red* is an essential mod, so it is part of the core description of the *house*. As a result, the adjective *first* applies to the whole description: First what? First *house that is red.*

By contrast, *which is red* is nonessential; it is not part of the core description of the house. In this case, the adjective *first* applies just to the *house* alone: First what? First *house* (which happens to be a certain color).

Nonessential mods are usually separated out from the rest of the sentence by commas, while essential mods typically are *not* separated out by commas, so you can use the presence or absence of a comma as a good clue as to whether the modifier is nonessential or essential. (You can also pay attention to the meaning.)

How do essential vs. nonessential modifiers map to noun vs. adverbial modifiers? These are two separate types of classifications. Both essential and nonessential modifiers can be either noun or adverbial mods. Whether there are commas will help you to classify essential vs. nonessential, but the distinction is a bit more intricate for noun vs. adverbial.

Start by noticing the specific marker that signals a modifier; the marker itself will usually tell you whether the modifier is noun vs. adverbial. For example, a *comma which* marker signals a nonessential noun mod. By contrast, when the word *that* is used to introduce a noun modifier, it is never set off by a comma; it is always an essential noun mod.

Next, scan the answers. If, for example, you see a *which* vs. *that* split, you now know that you need to think about whether this is essential or nonessential. (Since they're both noun modifiers, you don't need to think about the noun vs. adverbial issue.)

The three most commonly tested types of modifiers on the GMAT (prep phrases, *–ing* words, and *–ed* words) can be either noun or adverbial depending upon how they're used in a sentence.

Prep Phrases

For the first type, prep phrases, there isn't an easy clue as to whether the mod is noun or adverbial. It can be useful to ask a question about the modifier to figure out what it's modifying: What does (this modifier) describe? Take a look at these examples:

Marker	Example	What is it modifying? What does (the prep phrase) describe?
Prep Phrase (preposition + noun)	Three companies have made offers to buy the PLOT of land.	Noun: What does *of land* describe? A *plot* (plain noun).
	The ACQUISITION HAS BEEN APPROVED by regulators.	Adverbial: What does *by regulators* describe? How the *acquisition has been approved* (not just a noun).
	In some countries, MERGERS between the top two companies in an industry ARE NOT ALLOWED.	Adverbial: What does *in some countries* describe? Where *mergers are not allowed* (not just a noun).

When you see a prep phrase, but you're not sure what it's referring to, pull yourself back to the meaning of the sentence. What does (this mod) describe? If it describes a noun, it's a noun mod. If it describes anything other than a stand-alone noun, it's an adverbial mod. If it could refer to more than one thing or action in the sentence, cross that choice off for ambiguity. If whatever it refers to is illogical, cross off that choice for not making sense.

-ing and *-ed*

The other two types of commonly tested modifiers, *–ing* and *–ed* mods, have a simple clue you can use to identify whether they are noun or adverbial. If they are *not* set off from the rest of the sentence by commas, they are noun mods. If they *are* set off from the rest of the sentence by a comma or commas, they are adverbial mods. Here are some examples:

Marker	Example	What is it modifying?
-ing	The ENGINEER running this meeting fixed the problem.	Noun: An *-ing* mod without a comma is a noun mod.
	The ENGINEER FIXED THE PROBLEM, earning herself a promotion.	Adverbial: A *comma -ing* mod is an adverbial mod. The comma could be before the mod (as here), after, or both.
-ed	The CANDIDATE interviewed last week has accepted the job.	Noun: An *-ed* mod without a comma is a noun mod.
	Excited by the new opportunity, the CANDIDATE HAS ACCEPTED THE JOB.	Adverbial: A *comma -ed* mod is an adverbial mod. Again, the comma could be before, after (as here), or both.

As always, the first step is to spot the marker in the original sentence and then check the splits in the answers to see the given differences. If you have an *–ing* mod that is sometimes split out by a comma and sometimes not, then the problem is asking you to determine whether the modifier is referring to a noun (in which case, you don't want a comma) or an entire action (in which case, you do want a comma).

Bonus question: Which of the mods in the table are essential and which are nonessential? This quiz is open book; feel free to reread the earlier material to remind yourself how to distinguish between the two.

Ready? Okay: The *–ing* and *–ed* mods without any commas are essential mods. The ones with commas are nonessential mods. Most of the time, commas = nonessential and no commas = essential. (One tip: When stripping out the modifiers to get to the core sentence, you may sometimes be able to ignore all *–ing* and *–ed* mods, even if they are essential. Use meaning as your guide; if you can still understand the basic sentence without including the mod, go ahead and strip it out.)

Let's summarize the information about prep phrases, *–ing* mods, and *–ed* mods.

When you have a *comma prep phrase*, a *comma –ing*, or a *comma –ed*, then you have both an adverbial modifier and a nonessential modifier. (Note: The comma can appear before the mod, after the mod, or both before and after the mod.) You can ignore these mods when you are looking just for the sentence core.

When the modifier is *not* split out by a comma, things are a little more complicated. First, these are usually noun mods. (There are technically a decent number of exceptions here but, luckily, you can ignore the vast majority for the purposes of the GMAT.) Further, these no-comma mods are often essential—but they can also be nonessential. Use your best judgment based on the meaning of the sentence; when in doubt, call it essential and, if stripping to the core, leave it in.

You'll learn more about each of these forms throughout the rest of this chapter.

Which vs. *–ing*

Comma which modifiers and *comma –ing* modifiers serve different roles in a sentence; the former modifies nouns while the latter modifies actions. As such, they can't be used interchangeably. Sentences such as the following are common in speech, but they are actually grammatically incorrect:

Wrong: Crime has recently decreased in our neighborhood, which has led to a rise in property values.

A *comma which* mod has to refer to a very nearby noun—but the *neighborhood* didn't lead to a *rise in property values*. Rather the action *crime decreased* led to the *rise in property values*. A noun modifier won't work here.

One way to correct the sentence is to use an adverbial modifier to refer to the whole clause:

Right: CRIME HAS recently DECREASED in our neighborhood, <u>leading to a rise in property values</u>.

You could also flip it around, eliminating the *which* modifier altogether:

Right: The recent DECREASE in crime in our neighborhood HAS LED to a rise in property values.

In speech, people often break these rules, incorrectly using *which* to refer to a previous thought that is *not* a noun. In fact, the GMAT has made the same mistake in Sentence Correction explanations and even in a Reading Comprehension passage! Do not use your ear for this one. When you see a *comma which* vs. *comma –ing* split in the answers, examine the meaning. If the modifier should refer to a noun, use *comma which*. If the modifier should refer to an action, use *comma –ing*.

Noun Modifiers

Noun modifiers answer a specific question that you can ask about a noun. For example:

> The CAT on the couch loves dogs.

What does *on the couch* describe? The cat. When you ask the question What does (the modifier) describe? and the answer points to a stand-alone noun, you have a noun mod.

Long sentences typically have many nouns, so a noun modifier has to be placed in such a way that the reader knows exactly which noun is being modified. The practical result is that nouns and noun modifiers must be placed very close together (most of the time—though not always—they are right next to each other). Remember this rule:

> **Place a noun and its modifier as close together as the sentence allows.**

Adverbial modifiers are more flexible; they don't necessarily have to be placed near what they're modifying.

Here's what can happen when a noun and its modifier are separated by too much other text:

> Wrong: A hard worker and loyal team player, the new project was managed by Sue.

The sentence begins with an **Opening Modifier** set off from the rest of the sentence by a comma. You can identify it as a modifier because it cannot stand as its own sentence. Further, it's singled out as an *opening* mod not just because it starts the sentence but because it doesn't tell you who or what it's talking about.

What does *a hard worker and loyal team player* describe? Logically, it should refer to Sue, but Sue is as far away as she can get in the sentence.

It's possible to move Sue closer to her mod:

> Right: A hard worker and loyal team player, SUE managed the new project.

Since opening modifiers don't tell you who or what they're talking about, they need to refer to the main subject of the sentence. Most of the time, this noun will appear very soon after the comma at the end of the opening modifier.

More than half of the time, a noun and its modifier will be placed right next to each other, with no other words intervening. This isn't true 100 percent of the time, though. The most common exception occurs when you have two modifiers that both describe the same noun. For example:

> The BOX of nails, which is nearly full, belongs to Jean.

The noun *box* has two modifiers: *of nails* and *which is nearly full*. They can't both be placed right after the noun; one has to come before the other. The other order would look like this:

> Wrong: The BOX, which is nearly full, of nails belongs to Jean.

In general, an essential modifier takes precedence over a nonessential modifier. *Of nails* is an essential modifier—it is not separated out by a comma—so it is placed immediately after *box*. The *comma which* modifier is a nonessential modifier, so it is placed second, even though it also refers to *box*.

A *comma which* mod is always nonessential, so it will always come after a prep phrase if both modifiers are describing the same noun.

Which of the options below is better?

Jim biked along an old dirt road to get to his house, which cut through the woods.

To get to his house, Jim biked along an old dirt road, which cut through the woods.

A *comma which* mod is always a noun mod. What does *cut through the woods* describe? The *road*. The second option places *road* closer to its modifier, so it's the better option.

One more thing: The first option isn't just worse than the second. The first option is incorrect. Why isn't it okay for there to be a little separation between the noun and the *comma which* modifier, as there was in the box of nails example? In this example, *to get to his house* is not a noun modifier referring to *road*. What does *to get to his house* describe? Why *Jim biked*.

When the sentence places text that is referring to something other than a noun in between a noun and its modifier, it's generally better to move that text elsewhere so that the noun and its modifier can be closer together. The second option accomplished this by moving *to get to his house* to the beginning of the sentence.

4

SC questions are multiple choice; you will never have to rewrite the sentence yourself. If two options both appear correct, but one choice gives you the option to place the noun and its modifier closer together, go with that option.

Possessive Nouns Are Not Actually Nouns

Can you spot the error in the sentence below?

Wrong: Happy about his raise, Bill's celebration included taking his friends out to dinner.

Logically, the opening modifier *happy about his raise* should describe *Bill*. However, possessive nouns are technically adjectives, not nouns. (Whose celebration? Bill's celebration.) As it stands, the sentence technically says that *Bill's celebration* is *happy about his raise*. Here is one way to fix the sentence:

Right: <u>Happy about his raise</u>, BILL celebrated by taking his friends to dinner.

Noun Modifier Markers: *Which, That, Who,* and More

Noun modifiers are often introduced by **Relative Pronouns** such as the following:

Which That Who Whose Whom

The words in that list that start with *w* always signal noun modifiers; they are called *noun modifier markers*. Whenever you see this type of marker, think about noun modifiers.

The word *that* can also signal a noun modifier—but it doesn't always. A noun followed immediately by the word *that* signals a noun modifier. A verb followed immediately by the word *that* usually signals the more complex sentence structure subject–verb–THAT–subject–verb (see the Sentence Structure chapter for more).

The pronouns *who* and *whom* must modify people. On the other hand, the pronoun *which* cannot modify people.

Perhaps surprisingly, the pronoun *whose* can modify both people and things:

. . . the TOWN whose water supply was contaminated.

The words *which* or *whom* sometimes follow prepositions:

. . . the CANAL through which water flows.

. . . the SENATOR for whom we worked.

A lot of people think these types of structures (*through which, for whom*) sound "off" and, as a result, mistakenly cross off a correct answer. When you see this *preposition–which* or *preposition–whom* structure, check whether it is correct by inverting the text to create a complete sentence:

Original text: the CANAL through which water flows

Inverted text: Water flows through the canal.

The noun and verb inside the prepositional phrase (*water flows*) become the subject and verb of the inverted sentence. Then, use the preposition (*through*) and finish up with the noun that started the original phrase (*the canal*). (Note that the marker *which* is dropped from the inverted sentence.) If the inverted sentence is a valid sentence, then the original structure was also correct.

The words *where* and *when* can be noun or adverbial modifiers (and the test doesn't typically make you distinguish). The word *where* can be used to modify a noun that is a place, such as *area, site, state/province,* or *country*. For example:

Though most of the Nobel Prizes are awarded in Stockholm, where Alfred Nobel was born, the Peace Prize is awarded in Oslo.

However, *where* cannot modify a metaphorical place, such as a *condition, situation, case, circumstance,* or *arrangement*. In these cases, use *in which* rather than *where*:

Wrong: We had an arrangement WHERE he cooked and I cleaned.

Right: We had an arrangement IN WHICH he cooked and I cleaned.

Invert that second sentence to verify that the usage of *in which* is correct: *He cooked and I cleaned in* [the] *arrangement*. You may sometimes have to change the article (*a, an, the*) that leads into the final noun; that's okay.

The word *when* can be used to modify a noun that is an event or a time, such as *period, age, 1987,* or *decade*. In these circumstances, you can also use *in which* or *during which* instead of *when*:

Right: The three-century span of the Renaissance, a PERIOD when artists such as Leonardo da Vinci and Michelangelo thrived, marked the European transition from the middle ages to modern times.

Right: The three-century span of the Renaissance, a PERIOD during which artists such as Leonardo da Vinci and Michelangelo thrived, marked the European transition from the middle ages to modern times.

Adverbial Modifiers

Adverbial Modifiers answer a *how, when, where, why,* or *how much* question about some other information in the sentence. They do not have the same placement constraints as noun modifiers. A sentence typically contains only a few clauses, so adverbial modifiers can be placed more freely without creating meaning issues in the sentence. As long as the adverbial modifier clearly points to one particular verb or clause, the placement is acceptable.

It is still possible to place adverbial modifiers poorly, though. What's wrong with this sentence?

> Amar filled in his timesheet in order to make the payroll deadline rapidly.

Did he *fill in his timesheet rapidly* or did he *make the deadline rapidly*? The modifier is closer to the latter option, but that meaning doesn't make much sense—you either make a deadline or you don't. Here are two ways to fix the sentence:

> Right: Amar FILLED in his timesheet rapidly in order to make the payroll deadline.
>
> Right: Amar rapidly FILLED in his timesheet to make the payroll deadline.

In both cases, it's clear that *rapidly* modifies the first action—and this is a logical meaning.

Modifier Markers: Prepositions

Prepositions can signal noun or adverbial modifiers. On the GMAT, you'll most often be tested on the noun modifier form.

Here's an example of the noun form:

> The executive DIRECTOR of the company resigned three days ago.

What does *of the company* describe? The *director*. When a prepositional phrase is a noun modifier, it will almost always directly follow the noun that it is modifying.

One fairly common issue tested is whether a particular preposition is the right one to match the other words in the sentence. For example, you can say *the team is capable of succeeding* but not *the team is capable for succeeding*. These idioms (*capable of* but not *capable for*) have to be memorized; see the Idioms chapter for more on this topic.

You can have two prep phrases in a row. For example:

> The board of directors had a vigorous DEBATE about the EFFICACY of the new strategy.

The prep phrase *about the efficacy* modifies the noun *debate*. The prep phrase *of the new strategy* modifies the noun *efficacy*. It's fairly common to have two prepositional phrases in a row, but three or four in a row can be dangerous; the more you have, the more likely you are to create meaning issues.

A sentence can test meaning as the result of the placement of a prep phrase. For example:

> Wrong: The departmental director addressed the team's recent success in the memo.
>
> Right: In the memo, THE departmental DIRECTOR ADDRESSED the team's recent success.

What does *in the memo* describe? Because a prep phrase can be noun or adverbial, the first sentence could be read in one of two ways, one of which is that the team's recent success occurred *in* the memo. (They wrote a great memo? Logically, that's probably not what the sentence is trying to say.)

Ambiguity is bad. The second sentence separates out the modifier by a comma to create one logical meaning: The team had success and the director addressed that success in a memo.

In general, prep phrases that explain *how*, *when*, *where*, or *why* an action occurred or that answer a *how much* question are adverbial modifiers. Here's another example of an adverbial prep phrase:

> The TEAM ATTENDS staff meetings on Mondays.

What does *on Mondays* describe? When *the team attends* (the meetings).

The following sentence contains multiple *noun* modifiers. See how many you can spot:

> Researchers discovered that the most common risk factor resulting in cholera epidemics is the lack of a clean water supply.

The adjective *common* describes the *risk factor*. (The adverb *most* refers to *common*, so this is an adverbial modifier.) What about the more complex noun modifiers?

> Researchers discovered that the most common RISK FACTOR resulting in cholera epidemics is the LACK of a clean water supply.

The prepositional phrase *of a clean water supply* modifies the noun *lack*.

What about *resulting in cholera epidemics*? The word *resulting* is an *–ing* word and the word *in* is a preposition. When you see this, go with the first word first: the *–ing* word. This word is not preceded by a comma, so *resulting in cholera epidemics* signals a noun modifier; it refers to the *risk factor*.

Modifier Markers: *-ing* and *-ed* Words

When an *–ing* mod is not set off by a comma, then you have a noun modifier, as in this example from the previous section:

> Researchers discovered that the most common RISK FACTOR resulting in cholera epidemics is the lack of a clean water supply.

By contrast, when an *–ing* or *–ed* word is set off from the rest of the sentence by a comma, it is an adverbial modifier. Even though these are called *comma –ing* and *comma –ed* mods, it's also possible for that mod to be at the beginning of a sentence and followed by a comma.

Here's an example from earlier in this chapter:

> The ENGINEER FIXED THE PROBLEM, earning herself a promotion.

Both *–ing* and *–ed* words are called participles (though you don't need to know the official terms for the test):

Verb	Present Participle (*-ing*)	Past Participle (*-ed*)
to play	playing	played
to manage	managing	managed
to begin	beginning	begun

Present participles always end in *–ing*. Past participles most commonly end in *–ed*, but there are a number of irregular verb forms, such as the example shown in the table above (*begun*).

Most people are used to thinking of *–ing* words as verbs, but they only function as verbs in one specific circumstance. Most of the time, *–ing* words are modifiers; they can even be nouns! Here are some examples of *–ing* words:

She is running.	*is running* = verb
Running is fun.	*running* = subject (noun)
The GIRL playing soccer is my sister.	*playing soccer* (no commas) = noun modifier
SHE STAYED all day, playing soccer until she was the only one left on the field.	*, playing soccer... field* = adverbial modifier

Any *–ing* word functioning as a verb will always have another verb immediately before it, as shown in the *is playing* example. If no other verb is right next to the *–ing* word, then the *–ing* word is not a verb.

Any *–ing* words that are *not* verbs and *not* separated from the rest of the sentence by a comma will either be a noun, as in the example *playing soccer is fun*, or modify another noun, as in the example *the girl playing soccer is my sister.*

4

Any *–ing* words that are *not* verbs and *are* separated from the rest of the sentence by a comma will be an adverbial modifier. (There is one semi-common exception here: The structure *comma including* is a noun modifier. For example: *She likes many types of puzzles, including sudoku, hitori, and skyscrapers.* Synonyms for the word *including* can also trigger this exception.)

Past participles, or *–ed* words, are not tested as frequently as *–ing* words, but you will still probably see them on the GMAT. They can fall into one of three categories:

She played the lottery yesterday.	*played* = verb
She accidentally bought an expired lottery TICKET.	*expired* (no commas) = noun modifier
Exhausted from her job, SHE BOUGHT A lottery TICKET with hopes of winning big.	*exhausted... job,* = adverbial modifier

Unlike *–ing* words, *–ed* words are commonly used as verbs and they can be verbs all by themselves. The comma rule still holds though: When the *–ed* word is separated by commas from the rest of the sentence, it is an adverbial modifier.

When either a *comma –ing* or a *comma –ed* modifier is an opening modifier (at the beginning of a sentence), the modifier needs to refer to the main subject after the comma, as shown in the last example in the table.

The rest of the sentence matters, too, though. A sentence such as *exhausted from her job, she has red hair* would not be acceptable on the GMAT because the opening modifier does not have anything to do with the fact that she has red hair. Both *comma –ing* and *comma –ed* modifiers have to make sense with the whole clause that they modify: *She bought a lottery ticket* because she was *exhausted from her job*.

Check the Sequence in Participle Modifiers

The examples illustrate an additional requirement for *comma –ing* and *comma –ed* modifiers: The first piece of information leads to or results in the second piece of information.

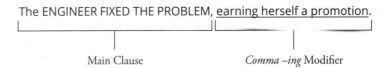

For example:

The ENGINEER FIXED THE PROBLEM, earning herself a promotion.

Main Clause | *Comma –ing* Modifier

Because the engineer fixed the problem, she earned a promotion. Fixing the problem resulted in earning the promotion. Consider this example:

Exhilarated by the successful product launch, the TEAM CELEBRATED after work.

Comma –ed Modifier | Main Clause

Because the launch was successful, the team celebrated. The exhilaration about the success led to the celebration.

Picture a woman ice skating. She loses her balance, crashes to the ice, and then clutches her ankle in pain. Which of these three sentences correctly describes this scenario?

> Slipping on the ice, she broke her ankle.
>
> Breaking her ankle, she slipped on the ice.
>
> She slipped on the ice, breaking her ankle.

The first and third sentences both correctly describe what happened: The woman slipped on the ice, and this action caused her to break her ankle.

The middle sentence is illogical because it implies that she broke her ankle first (for no reason at all, apparently!), and then slipped on the ice. While that may be possible, it's not very likely.

Modifier vs. Core: Part 2

What's going on in this sentence?

> The CEO declared that everyone had to work through the holidays to make the production deadline, but in calling for such an extreme measure, the company's employees were upset to the point of mutiny.

The phrase *in calling for such an extreme measure* is a modifier. Is it a prep phrase because it starts with *in* or a *comma –ing* because it has the word *calling*? Thankfully, you don't actually have to distinguish between those categories. What you do need to figure out is whether it's a noun or adverbial mod.

Since the text is separated out by a comma from the rest, it's an adverbial modifier. It needs to address the clause to which it is attached.

Which clause is that? The sentence has two:

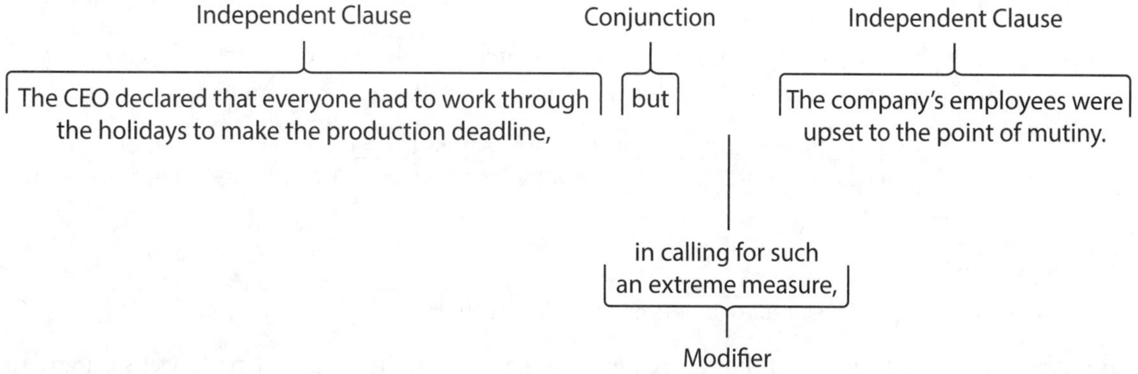

Because the *in calling* modifier falls after the conjunction connecting the two clauses (*but*), the modifier refers to the second part of the sentence—the *employees*, not the *CEO*. The employees didn't call for this extreme measure, though! The CEO did.

The sentence could be fixed in multiple ways:

Right: In an extreme measure, the CEO DECLARED that everyone had to work through the holidays to make the production deadline; her employees were upset to the point of mutiny.

Right: The CEO declared that everyone had to work through the holidays to make the production deadline, but in calling for such an extreme measure, SHE UPSET her employees to the point of mutiny.

Both of the correct sentences properly attribute the extreme move to the CEO, not to the employees.

Earlier, you learned that you can put two modifiers in a row. Remember this example?

The BOX of nails, which is nearly full, belongs to Jean.

This sentence is okay because both noun mods refer to the same noun, *box*. The essential mod (*of nails*) is placed closest to the noun and the nonessential mod (*which is nearly full*) is a little farther away.

What if you have one noun mod and one adverbial mod? Consider this sentence:

Wrong: George Carlin, both shocking and entertaining audiences across the nation, who also struggled publicly with drug abuse, influenced and inspired a generation of comedians.

The first modifier, *shocking and entertaining*, is an adverbial modifier referring to the core clause *George Carlin influenced and inspired*. The second modifier, *who also struggled*, is a noun modifier referring just to Carlin himself. Noun mods are supposed to be placed as close to the noun as they can get, while adverbial mods are less restricted. So placing the adverbial mod in between the noun mod and Carlin is not a good sentence structure.

Here's a better way to convey the same information:

Right: GEORGE CARLIN, who also struggled publicly with drug abuse, INFLUENCED AND INSPIRED a generation of comedians, both shocking and entertaining audiences across the nation.

In the better sentence, the adverbial modifier is moved to the end of the sentence; now, the noun modifier can be placed right after *Carlin*.

On harder questions, the GMAT might even rephrase the sentence so that one of the modifiers becomes part of the core of the sentence; that is, it is no longer a modifier at all. Here's an example:

Right: Both shocking and entertaining audiences across the nation, GEORGE CARLIN INFLUENCED AND INSPIRED a generation of comedians YET STRUGGLED publicly with drug abuse.

Here's the core sentence:

Carlin influenced and inspired (people) yet struggled (with drug abuse).

The *drug abuse* portion is now part of the core sentence, not a modifier. The sentence no longer separates the subject from the verbs *influenced and inspired*, making the opening modifier more clear as well.

If your first glance reveals a long underline, expect portions of the sentence to move around or even change roles completely in the answers. Here are two examples of correct sentences in which the core and modifier portions change:

4

Right: Employing the new lab equipment, the ENGINEER IDENTIFIED the problem within minutes.

Right: The ENGINEER EMPLOYED the new lab equipment, identifying the problem within minutes.

Both of these sentences convey the same information, but the first sentence begins with an opening modifier and then provides the core, while the second starts with the core and finishes with a modifier. Neither one is better than the other; both would be acceptable on the GMAT (and you won't have to choose between the two).

Here's another set of correct examples:

Right: Pushed to justify his decision, the MANAGER FROZE AND WAS UNABLE TO TALK, eventually breaking down in tears.

(Pushed to justify his decision = Modifier; the MANAGER FROZE AND WAS UNABLE TO TALK = Core; eventually breaking down in tears = Modifier)

Right: The MANAGER FROZE AND WAS UNABLE TO TALK when he was pushed to justify his decision; he eventually broke down in tears.

(The MANAGER FROZE AND WAS UNABLE TO TALK = Core; when he was pushed to justify his decision = Modifier; he eventually broke down in tears = Core)

In both of these sentences, the grammar is correct and the meaning is logical and unambiguous.

Modifier Markers: Subordinators

Take a look at this sentence:

Although the economy is strong, the RETAIL INDUSTRY IS STRUGGLING.

The first part of the sentence is called a **Subordinate Clause**, or sub clause. It is almost exactly like a complete sentence, but it has a subordinator (*although*) at the beginning.

Subordinate clauses are *not* complete sentences:

Wrong: Although the economy is strong.

Sub clauses modify the main clause to which they are attached; they are always adverbial modifiers. In the correct example presented first in this section, the subordinate clause provides additional information about the main clause: Despite the fact that the overall economy is doing well, one particular industry is not.

Sub clauses can look very similar to opening modifiers, but they are not actually opening mods for one specific reason. Sub clauses are actual clauses—they contain their own subjects. Openings mods do not. Compare these two correct examples:

Opening Mod: Although strong at the moment, the economy is showing signs that it may slow down soon.

Sub Clause: Although the economy is strong, the retail industry is struggling.

Take a look at just the portions of the sentence up to the comma:

Opening Mod: Although strong at the moment, . . .

Sub Clause: Although the economy is strong, . . .

In the opening mod example, you literally cannot tell what the sentence is talking about until you see the noun after that comma. An opening mod, by definition, does not tell you what noun it is talking about. Therefore, the noun has to be the subject/main word right after the comma; otherwise, you won't understand the meaning of the sentence.

By contrast, a sub clause tells you what noun it is talking about. Since you already know, the main clause can then start talking about a different subject.

If you see what looks like an opening mod at the beginning of a sentence, check whether it tells you what noun it's talking about. If not, that noun has to be the subject of the sentence, after the comma. If the opening text does tell you what noun it's talking about, though, then you don't have an opening mod after all, and you don't need to check whether the main subject matches.

Common subordinator markers include:

after	although	because	before	if	since
so that	that	unless	until	when	while

Pay attention to the meaning of the chosen word. If it indicates a contrast, for example, then make sure the sentence actually conveys a contrast:

Wrong: Although the economy is strong, the retail industry is doing well.

Use only one connecting word per "connection":

Wrong: ALTHOUGH I need to relax, YET I have so many things to do!

Right: ALTHOUGH I need to relax, I have so many things to do!

Right: I need to relax, YET I have so many things to do!

Subordinators are similar to the FANBOYS conjunctions: In both cases, make sure that the chosen word logically connects the two pieces of information. (The two types of conjunctions are not interchangeable, though; see the Sentence Structure chapter to remind yourself how to use FANBOYS.) The GMAT will test you to make sure that you are paying attention to this kind of meaning.

Here is a FANBOYS example that doesn't make sense:

Wrong: She is not interested in playing sports, AND she likes watching them on TV.

In this example, the word *and* is not sensible, because the two independent clauses are in opposition to each other. This meaning error can be corrected in multiple ways:

Right: She is not interested in playing sports, BUT she likes watching them on TV.

Right: ALTHOUGH she is not interested in playing sports, she likes watching them on TV.

The first example uses a different FANBOYS conjunction, one that has the appropriate meaning. The second example changes the sentence structure. Now, the first part of the sentence is a sub conjunction; the chosen word (*although*) conveys the correct meaning.

Finally, be on the lookout for sentences that join a main clause to something that should be a clause but is not:

Wrong: Citizens of many countries are expressing concern about the environmental damage—such as flooding and wildfires—caused by the widespread release of greenhouse gases may be impossible to reverse.

The main clause in this sentence is *citizens of many countries are expressing concern about the environmental damage caused by the widespread release of greenhouse gases*. There is nothing wrong with this main clause.

What about the rest of the sentence? The part between the dashes is okay, but the main verb at the end (*may be impossible to reverse*) has no subject. The GMAT wants you to think that *environmental damage* is the subject of *may be impossible to reverse*, but *environmental damage* is part of a prep phrase (*about the environmental damage*). Nouns in prep phrases cannot also be subjects.

One way to fix the sentence is to change the preposition *about* to the subordinator *that*:

Right: Citizens of many countries are expressing concern THAT the environmental damage—such as flooding and wildfires—caused by the widespread release of greenhouse gases may be impossible to reverse.

You learned about this sentence structure in the Structure chapter: subject–verb–THAT–subject–verb. In this correct version, the main clause is *citizens... are expressing concern*. The sub clause begins with the word *that* and extends to the end of the sentence.

Another way to fix the sentence is to put *may be impossible to reverse* inside a modifier:

Right: Citizens of many countries are expressing concern about the environmental damage—such as flooding and wildfires—caused by the widespread release of greenhouse gases, <u>DAMAGE THAT may be impossible to reverse</u>.

In this correct version, the main clause ends right before the comma. The words *damage that may be impossible to reverse* provide additional information about the damage mentioned earlier in the sentence.

This kind of structure sounds funny to many people (because no one talks this way), but it is a valid structure in more formal written English. The writer wants to provide additional information about *the environmental damage*, but that noun is pretty far away from the end of the sentence. In addition, there are other nouns (such as *release* and *gases*) between *damage* and the end of the sentence, so putting another noun mod referring to *damage* at the end of the sentence is likely to confuse the reader.

One way to get around that is to include a noun at the beginning of the mod. You can literally repeat the exact noun, as this sentence does: *the environmental DAMAGE... caused by the widespread release of greenhouse gases, DAMAGE that may be impossible to reverse.*

You may also be able to use a synonym for the original noun, such as: *the environmental DAMAGE... caused by the widespread release of greenhouse gases, DESTRUCTION that may be impossible to reverse.*

Quantity

In the English language, words and expressions of quantity are subject to strict grammatical rules.

Rule 1: Words Used for *Countable* Things vs. Words Used for *Uncountable* Things

Some nouns in the English language are countable, such as *hat(s)*, *feeling(s)*, and *person/people*. Other nouns are uncountable, such as *patience*, *water*, and *furniture*. During the test, if you are unsure whether a particular word is countable, literally try to count it out:

For *hat*: **One hat, two hats, three hats.** This works. *Hat* is countable.

For *patience*: **One patience (?), two patiences (?), stop.** This does not work. *Patience* is not countable.

Here are some examples of words and expressions that modify countable things and those that modify uncountable things:

Countable Modifiers	Uncountable Modifiers
MANY hats	MUCH patience
FEW stores	LITTLE merchandise
FEWER children	LESS money
FEWEST shoes	LEAST greed
NUMBER of chairs	AMOUNT of furniture
NUMEROUS books	GREAT courage

More, most, enough, and *all* work with both countable (plural) and uncountable (singular) nouns: *more hats, more patience, most people, most furniture, enough hats, enough patience, all people, all furniture.*

Do not use the word *less* with countable items. This error has become common in speech and in the signs above express lines in grocery stores: *10 items or less*. Since the noun *item* is countable, the sign should actually read *10 items or fewer*. For example:

Wrong: There were less Numidian KINGS than Roman emperors.

Right: There were fewer Numidian KINGS than Roman emperors.

Be careful with unit nouns, such as *dollars* or *gallons*. By their nature, unit nouns are countable: *one dollar, two dollars, three dollars*. Thus, they work with most of the countable modifiers. However, unit nouns represent uncountable quantities: *money, volume*. (You can count money, of course, but you cannot count the noun *money*: *one money* (?), *two moneys* (?), stop!) Use *less* with unit nouns when you really want to indicate something about the underlying quantity:

Right: We have less than 20 DOLLARS.

The amount of *money*, in whatever form, totals less than $20. If you write *we have FEWER THAN 20 dollars*, you would mean the actual pieces of paper. (You would probably say *fewer than 20 dollar bills*, to make the point even clearer.)

Rule #2: Words Used to Relate *Two* Things vs. Words Used to Relate *Three* or More Things

To relate two things, use comparative forms of adjectives and adverbs (*better, worse, more, less*). For example, the rabbit is *faster* than the toad. Use superlative forms (*best, worst, most, least*) to compare three or more things or people. For example, the rabbit is the *fastest* of all of the animals at the farm.

In addition, use *between* only with two things or people. When you are talking about three or more things or people, use *among*:

Right: I mediated a dispute BETWEEN Maya and Kalen.

Right: I mediated a dispute AMONG Maya, Logan, and Kalen.

Rule #3: The Word *Numbers*

4

If you wish to make a comparison using the word *numbers*, use *greater than*, not *more than* (which might imply that the quantity of numbers is larger, not the numbers themselves):

Right: The rare Montauk beaked griffin is not extinct; its NUMBERS are now suspected to be much GREATER than before.

Rule #4: *Increase* and *Decrease* vs. *Greater* and *Less*

The words *increase* and *decrease* are not the same as the words *greater* and *less*. *Increase* and *decrease* express the change of one thing over time. *Greater* and *less* signal a comparison between two things. For example:

Wrong: The price of silver is 10 dollars GREATER.
(Than what it used to be? Than the price of something else?)

Right: The price of silver INCREASED by 10 dollars.

Right: The price of silver is five dollars GREATER than the price of copper.

Watch out for redundancy in sentences with the words *increase* and *decrease*:

Wrong: The price of silver FELL by a more than 35 percent DECREASE.

Right: The price of silver DECREASED by more than 35 percent.

Right: The price of silver FELL by more than 35 percent.

Decrease already includes the notion of falling or lowering, so *fell* is redundant. Similarly, *increase* includes the notion of rising or growing, so *rise* or *growth* would be redundant as well.

Problem Set

Problems 1–6 contain one or more underlined modifiers. For each of these modifiers, 1) identify the word or words, if any, that it modifies, and 2) indicate whether the modifier is correct. If the modifier is incorrect, suggest one possible way to correct the error.

1. A recent formed militia, consisting of lightly armed peasants and a few retired army officers, is fighting a bitterly civil war against government forces.

2. Angola, which was ravaged by civil war for many years after it gained independence from Portugal, which is now one of Africa's success stories, has an economy that grew by 21 percent last year, where parliamentary elections are to be held later this week.

3. Mary buys cookies made with SugarFree, an artificial sweetener, which tastes as sweet as the corn syrup that her brother loves but having fewer calories than in an equivalent amount of corn syrup.

4. People that are well-informed know that Bordeaux is a French region whose most famous export is the wine which bears its name.

5. Unaccustomed to the rigors of college life, James's grades dropped.

6. The air conditioner broke in the middle of a heat wave, which caused great consternation.

Problems 7–10 contain boxed words or punctuation marks, some of which may be incorrect. Use the rules from this chapter to correct any errors that you can find in the boxed areas; do not change anything that is not boxed.

7. The negotiations between the company, the union, and the city government were initially contentious but ultimately amicable.

8. Jim is trying to reduce the number of soda that he drinks, at last night's party, however, his resolve to drink fewer soda was sorely tested, he found himself quaffing many of sodas.

9. Between 1998 and 2003, there was heavy fighting in Parthia between numerous armed factions yet this conflict, so much more complicated than a conventional war between two states, involved no less than 8 countries and 25 militias.

10. Most legislators—including much in the governor's own party—realize that the governor's budget would imperil the state's finances, nonetheless, the budget is likely to be approved, because few legislators want to anger voters by cutting spending or raising taxes.

Problems 11–13 are multiple choice with one correct answer. For the rest of this guide, any problems may test anything you have learned to this point in the guide. As on the real GMAT, answer (A) repeats the original sentence. Unlike the real GMAT, though, these problems have only three answer choices.

11. Upon setting foot in the Gothic cathedral, the spectacular stained-glass windows amazed the camera-wielding tourists.

    (A) Upon setting foot in the Gothic cathedral, the spectacular stained-glass windows amazed the camera-wielding tourists.

    (B) Upon setting foot in the Gothic cathedral, the camera-wielding tourists were amazed by the spectacularly stained-glass windows.

    (C) The camera-wielding tourists were, upon setting foot in the Gothic cathedral, amazed by the stained-glass windows, which were spectacular.

12. Mt. Everest, which is the tallest mountain on Earth, lies on the border of Nepal and Tibet, first summited by Tenzing Norgay and Edmund Hillary in 1953.

    (A) Mt. Everest, which is the tallest mountain on Earth, lies on the border of Nepal and Tibet, first summited by Tenzing Norgay and Edmund Hillary in 1953.

    (B) First summited in 1953 by Tenzing Norgay and Edmund Hillary, the tallest mountain on Earth, which is Mt. Everest, and lies on the border of Nepal and Tibet.

    (C) First summited by Tenzing Norgay and Edmund Hillary in 1953, Mt. Everest, the tallest mountain on Earth, lies on the border of Nepal and Tibet.

13. The population <u>of San Antonio increased more than it did in any other U.S. city in 2016, adding almost</u> 66 people per day.

    (A) of San Antonio increased more than it did in any other U.S. city in 2016, adding almost

    (B) increased more in San Antonio than it did in any other city in the United States in 2016, adding almost

    (C) of San Antonio increased more than the population of any other U.S. city in 2016, almost adding

Solutions

1. *Recent*: INCORRECT. The adjective *recent* modifies *militia*, whereas logic calls for an adverb, *recently*, to modify *formed*.

   Lightly: CORRECT. The adverb *lightly* modifies the past participle *armed*, which is being used as an adjective (*armed* modifies the noun *peasants*).

   Retired: CORRECT. *Retired* is an adjective that modifies *army officers*. (You can also argue that *retired* is a past participle being used as an adjective.)

   Bitterly: INCORRECT. The adverb *bitterly* modifies *civil*, but the writer surely meant to use an adjective (*bitter*) to modify the noun phrase *civil war*.

   Correction: A recently formed militia, consisting of lightly armed peasants and a few retired army officers, is fighting a bitter civil war against government forces.

2. *Which was ravaged…from Portugal*: CORRECT. This relative clause modifies the noun *Angola*.

   which is now one of Africa's success stories: INCORRECT. This relative clause illogically modifies *Portugal* (which is in Europe).

   where parliamentary… this week: INCORRECT. A relative clause that begins with *where* must modify a noun that names a physical place, so this clause cannot modify *year*. The clause is too far away from *Angola*, however, to perform its intended role of modifying *Angola*.

   Repairing this deeply flawed sentence involves rearranging its components and incorporating some of the modifiers into main clauses. Here is one possible way to fix it:

   Correction: Ravaged by civil war for many years after it gained independence from Portugal, Angola is now one of Africa's success stories; its economy grew by 21 percent last year, and parliamentary elections are to be held later this week.

3. *an artificial sweetener:* CORRECT, but could be better. This appositive noun phrase modifies *SugarFree*; it is the first of two nonessential modifiers in a row, both of which modify SugarFree.

   which tastes… brother loves: CORRECT, but could be better. This modifier also modifies *the artificial sweetener SugarFree*. If an option exists to allow you to have both modifiers closer to SugarFree, that would be ideal.

   having… corn syrup: INCORRECT. Bonus point! The *–ing* modifier *having… corn syrup* is meant to be parallel to the relative clause *which tastes… brother loves*. When relative clauses are parallel, they should start with the same relative pronoun. You'll learn more about parallelism in the next chapter.

   Correction: Mary buys cookies made with the artificial sweetener SugarFree, which tastes as sweet as the corn syrup that her brother loves but which has fewer calories than does an equivalent amount of corn syrup.

4. *that are well-informed*: INCORRECT. This clause uses the relative pronoun *that* to refer to people. Use *who* to refer to human beings.

   whose most famous… bears its name: CORRECT. This clause modifies *region*. Notice that *whose*, unlike *who* and *whom*, can correctly modify nonhuman entities.

which bears its name: INCORRECT. The context of this sentence calls for an essential clause to modify the wine, since the point of the clause is to identify *the wine*. If the sentence ended with the wine, it would be incomplete (*... whose most famous export is the wine.* Which wine?). The clause should therefore begin with *that* rather than *which*.

Correction: Well-informed people know that Bordeaux is a French region whose most famous export is the wine that bears its name.

5. *Unaccustomed to... college life*: INCORRECT. As an opening modifier, *unaccustomed... life* needs to refer to the main noun after the comma. Logically, however, James's *grades* are not *unaccustomed to college life*. James himself is.

   Correction: Because James was unaccustomed to the rigors of college life, his grades dropped.

6. *which caused great consternation*: INCORRECT. A *comma which* modifier refers to a noun, but the *heat wave* itself didn't cause the *consternation*. Rather, the trouble was the full action: that the *air conditioner broke* during the heat wave. This meaning requires some type of adverbial modifier.

   Correction: The air conditioner broke in the middle of a heat wave, causing great consternation.

7. Use the word *between* when talking about two things. Use the word *among* to describe relationships of three or more things. *Ultimately* is an adverb and correctly modifies the adjective *amicable*.

   Correction: The negotiations AMONG the company, the union, and the city government were initially contentious but ultimately amicable.

8. *Number*: Here *soda* is an uncountable substance—otherwise, *soda* would be *sodas*—so change *number* to something uncountable, such as *amount*. (In the real world, you could keep the word *number* and make *soda* plural, but the instructions said to change only circled items.)

   Commas: The sentence contains multiple independent clauses connected only by commas. For both circled commas, decide whether to connect the clauses by semicolons or by commas and appropriate conjunctions.

   Fewer: Once again, *soda* is singular so it is an uncountable substance. Change *fewer* to *less*.

   Many: This time, *sodas* is plural, so they are countable—presumably servings of soda. One possible fix is to use *a number of*.

   Correction: Jim is trying to reduce the AMOUNT of soda that he drinks; at last night's party, however, his resolve to drink LESS soda was sorely tested, AND he found himself quaffing A NUMBER of sodas.

9. *Between*: The first *between* is correct, since only two dates are mentioned. The second *between*, however, should be *among*, since the fighting involved more than two factions. The third *between* is correct, since only two states are mentioned.

   Yet: There are two problems here. First, *yet* is illogical because the action in the second clause (*this conflict... militias*) did not happen despite the action in the first clause (*Between... factions*), as the word *yet* suggests. Second, there are two independent clauses, but no comma before the conjunction (*yet*). Replace *yet* with either a comma plus a different conjunction or a semicolon.

Less: Countries and militias are countable entities, so change *less* to *fewer*.

Correction: Between 1998 and 2003, there was heavy fighting in Parthia AMONG numerous armed factions; this conflict, so much more complicated than a conventional war between two states, involved no FEWER than 8 countries and 25 militias.

10. *Much*: Legislators are countable, so change *much* to *many*.

Nonetheless: This word connects two clauses but it is not a co-conjunction or sub-conjunction. Use a semicolon, or change to a comma plus a FANBOYS with a contract meaning, such as *yet*.

Comma because: This is correct. *Because* is a subordinating conjunction; therefore, it can be separated from a main clause by a comma.

Correction: Most legislators—including MANY in the governor's own party—realize that the governor's budget would imperil the state's finances; nonetheless, the budget is likely to be approved, because few legislators want to anger voters by cutting spending or raising taxes.

11. **(C):** *Upon setting foot in the Gothic Cathedral* is an opening modifier; it describes something but doesn't tell you what it's describing, so it must describe the main noun following the comma. It is the *tourists*, not the *stained-glass windows*, who set foot in the cathedral, so eliminate answer (A).

Answer (B) contains the same opening modifier but fixes the mistake by putting the *camera-wielding tourists* after the comma. However, there is a subtle but important word change between answers (B) and (C): Choice (B) describes the *windows* as *spectacularly stained-glass*. Choice (C), on the other hand, describes the *windows* as *spectacular* (no *ly* at the end of that word).

Spectacular is an adjective; adjectives describe nouns (such as *window*). *Spectacularly* is an adverb—adverbs describe anything other than a stand-alone noun—so it can't apply to the noun *window*. You could say that something was spectacularly stained (as in, someone did a really good job of staining it). But it's not logical to say *spectacularly stained-glass* because stained-glass is just naming the type of window; it is not an action that could have been performed particularly well. Logically, the *windows* were *spectacular*.

12. **(C):** The full-sentence underline provides an early clue that the answer choices are likely to change pretty substantially in structure. Pay attention to the core vs. the modifiers, as well as the overall meaning of the sentence.

In the original sentence, two different modifiers (*which is the tallest mountain on Earth* and *first summited by...*) describe *Mt. Everest*. The first one is right next to *Everest*, but the second is so far away that it appears the two men summited *Tibet* (or perhaps *the border of Nepal and Tibet*). Eliminate choice (A) for faulty modifier placement.

Choice (B) fixes that initial error by rearranging the sentence but introduces a new error. The core sentence reads: *the tallest mountain AND lies on the border*. The subject and verb should not have a conjunction in between. It is also a bit clunky to set the subject as *the tallest mountain* and only later name it (*Mt. Everest*); while it is true that *the tallest mountain* was *first summited* by the two men, the meaning would be more immediately clear to the reader by using *Mt. Everest* as the subject, as correct answer (C) does.

13. **(B):** In the original sentence, the pronoun *it* refers back to the entire subject, *population of San Antonio*, implying that somehow the population of this city increased more than itself. Compare that to the structure in answer (B), which separates *population* from the city name; now *it* refers back just to the word *population*, and you can talk about the population of San Antonio separately from the population of any other U.S. city. (You'll learn more about both comparisons and pronouns later in this unit.)

Answer (C) also fixes the original illogical meaning, in this case by repeating the word *population*, but it introduces a different error at the end. *Adding almost 66 people* means that nearly 66 new people every day were in fact added to the population. *Almost adding 66 people* means that the city almost, but not quite, added people—so really, no new people were added at all. This doesn't fit with the meaning of the rest of the sentence; if the population increased more than that in other cities, then San Antonio must have added at least some people.

CHAPTER 5

Parallelism

In This Chapter:

- Markers and Elements
- The Root Phrase
- Closed vs. Open Markers
- The Many Parallel Structures of the Word *And*
- Idioms with Built-In Parallel Structure

In this chapter, you'll learn how to spot the markers that indicate parallelism in a sentence and how to confirm that the parallel elements really are parallel.

CHAPTER 5 Parallelism

Certain sentence structures require pieces of a sentence to be in the same form as, or parallel to, each other. One of the most common parallel structures is a list:

Damian traveled to Argentina, Uruguay, and the Galapagos Islands.

The sentence above provides a list of three places. Notice that all three are not countries; to be parallel to each other, the **Elements** just have to be matching parts of speech. Since all three elements in this list are nouns, the sentence satisfies the rules of parallelism.

Markers and Elements

Fortunately, parallel structures always have a **Marker** that tells you that parallelism is required. Spotting the marker is step 1 in the 3-step parallelism process. If you see a marker, check for parallelism. If you don't see a marker, then parallelism is not at issue. In the previous example sentence, *comma comma and* tells you that there are three parallel elements. In fact, the word *and* always indicates parallelism!

The first step in any SC question that tests parallelism is to recognize what's being tested. Memorize the common parallelism markers in the following table. (Use flash cards to help!)

	Marker	Structure	Example
Open	And	X and Y	Apples AND pears
		X, Y, and Z	Apples, pears, AND bananas
	Or	X or Y	Happy OR sad
	But	X but Y	She stumbled BUT kept her balance
	Rather than	X rather than Y	Play tennis RATHER THAN climb a mountain
Closed	Both/And	Both X and Y	BOTH men AND women
	Either/Or	Either X or Y	EITHER she works OR she plays
	Not/But	Not X but Y	NOT running BUT jogging
	Not only/ But also	Not only X but also Y	NOT ONLY the manager BUT ALSO her team
	From/To	From X to Y	FROM the house TO the end of the driveway

In the *not only X but also Y* marker, for example, the marker itself consists of the words *not only* and *but also*. *X* and *Y* represent the two elements that must be parallel to each other. When you see the structure *not only X but also Y*, parallelism is required.

Sometimes SC questions contain an error in the marker itself, such as: *either X and Y* or *both X as well as Y*. If you see a mistake in the marker itself, cross that answer off.

Some of the markers in the table are labeled "closed," while some are labeled "open." Closed markers are markers that have two (or more) separate parts, like *either* and *or*; sentences with closed markers tend to be less complicated, because the the markers tell you exactly where the *X* and *Y* elements are—directly after each marker.

Try the following sentence:

> The sales rep determined that she would either have to increase the number of calls per hour or she would have to earn more per customer interaction.

Step 1: Identify the Parallelism Marker

> Either *X* or *Y*

Step 2: Identify the Elements

Since this is a closed (two-part) marker, the elements come directly after each piece:

> The sales rep determined that she would EITHER *X* (have to increase the number of calls per hour) OR *Y* (she would have to earn more per customer interaction).

The *X* element is a verb (*have*); the *Y* element is a clause (*she would have*). This sentence breaks the rules of parallelism, which require the elements to be the same parts of speech.

This table contains examples of parallel nouns, adjectives, working verbs, and more.

Element	Example	Marker (open or closed)
Nouns	Her expression reflected BOTH anger AND relief.	*both X and Y* (closed)
Adjectives	The park was NEITHER accessible NOR affordable. We collected BOTH second- AND third-grade books.	*neither X nor Y* (closed) *both X and Y* (closed)
Working Verbs	The custodian cleaned the basement AND washed the windows.	*X and Y* (open)
Infinitive Verbs	We would like NOT ONLY to hear your side of the story BUT ALSO to provide a response.	*not only X but also Y* (closed)
Participle Modifiers	The actor left quickly, waving to fans BUT ducking into a car.	*X but Y* (open)
Prepositional Phrases	It was important to leave the money in the drawer RATHER THAN on the table. (Note: The prepositions do *not* necessarily have to be the same.)	*X rather than Y* (open)
Subordinate Clauses	They contended that the committee was biased BUT that it should not be disbanded.	*X but Y* (open)

The majority of parallelism errors on SC questions occur when elements are not parallel parts of speech. However, there can still be an error even if the elements are parallel to each other. Consider the sentence from earlier with a slight tweak:

> The sales rep determined that she would EITHER (have to increase the number of calls per hour) OR (would have to earn more per customer interaction).

Now, both elements are verbs, satisfying the first requirement of parallelism, but there's still a mistake. Can you find it?

The Root Phrase

The remaining error can be dealt with via the final step of the process.

Step 3: Identify the Root Phrase and Distribute It to Each Element

The **Root Phrase** is the portion of the sentence that leads up to the first word of the parallelism marker. The root phrase of this sentence is shown in capital letters:

> THE SALES REP DETERMINED THAT SHE WOULD either have to increase the number of calls per hour or would have to earn more per customer interaction.

The root phrase needs to properly lead in to each element:

> Root phrase + *X* element: *The sales rep determined that she would have to increase the number of calls per hour.*

This makes perfect sense. On the GMAT, the root phrase typically properly leads into the first element, because an error there would be easier to spot.

> Root phrase + *Y* element: *The sales rep determined that she **would would** have to earn more per customer interaction.*

Once you remove the first element, the word *would* effectively appears twice in a row. There are two ways to fix this classic GMAT error. You could keep *would* in the root phrase and remove it from the second element:

> The sales rep determined that she would either have to increase the number of calls per hour or have to earn more per customer interaction.

Alternatively, you could remove *would* from the root phrase and add it into the first element:

> The sales rep determined that she either would have to increase the number of calls per hour or would have to earn more per customer interaction.

As you saw with *would either have*, a marker (*either*) can fall in between two-word verb structures (*would have*). When you have this construction with an open marker, look at the totality of the sentence to determine what the root phrase is.

Consider these three versions of the same sentence:

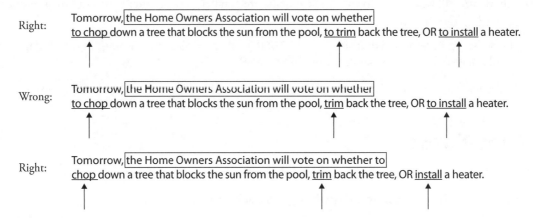

Right: Tomorrow, the Home Owners Association will vote on whether to chop down a tree that blocks the sun from the pool, to trim back the tree, OR to install a heater.

Wrong: Tomorrow, the Home Owners Association will vote on whether to chop down a tree that blocks the sun from the pool, trim back the tree, OR to install a heater.

Right: Tomorrow, the Home Owners Association will vote on whether to chop down a tree that blocks the sun from the pool, trim back the tree, OR install a heater.

Each sentence contains a 3-item list, but the form of the elements in the list varies a bit from sentence to sentence. In the first sentence, the root phrase *the Home Owners Association will vote on whether* leads properly into the three parallel elements *to chop*, *to trim*, and *to install.* The third sentence is also properly parallel, but it extends the root phrase to include the word *to*; in this case, the three parallel elements are *chop*, *trim*, and *install.*

The second sentence, though, messes up the structure. The first and third elements both include *to* (*to chop*, *to install*), but the second element is missing the *to* (*trim*). Either all three elements need to begin with the word *to*, as in the first sentence, or the word *to* is part of the root phrase and it can't be repeated in any of the three elements, as in the third sentence.

Closed vs. Open Markers

As shown in the last example (*X, Y, or Z*), open markers are trickier because the first element (*X*) has no marker word immediately preceding it to tell you exactly where it begins.

When working with open markers, start with the final element and work backwards from there. Use the 3-step process to evaluate the following sentence for parallelism issues:

> The doctor analyzed her patients' vital signs with a new device that simplified the process and logged the results in each patient's electronic medical records.

Step 1: Identify the Parallelism Marker

And

Step 2: Identify the Elements

Y element: *logged*

X element: *?*

Hmm. There are multiple verbs in the first part of the sentence; which verb is parallel to *logged*—*analyzed* or *simplified*?

> The doctor analyzed (?) her patients' vital signs with a new device that simplified (?) the process AND logged the results in each patient's electronic medical records.

Step 3: Identify the Root Phrase, and Distribute It to Each Element:

> Option 1 root phrase + elements: *the doctor analyzed . . . AND (the doctor) logged*

> Option 2 root phrase + elements: *a device that simplified . . . AND (a device that) logged*

Did *the doctor* log *the results in each patient's electronic medical records* or did the *new device* log *the results in each patient's electronic medical records*? Nothing about the sentence structure indicates which of these two reasonable interpretations is intended, so this sentence is ambiguous.

Here are some ways the GMAT might fix the sentence:

> The doctor analyzed her patients' vital signs with a new device that BOTH simplified the process AND logged the results in each patient's electronic medical records.

> Using a new device that simplified the process, the doctor analyzed her patients' vital signs AND logged the results in each patient's electronic medical records.

In the first example, the closed marker *both X and Y* removes any ambiguity about the root phrase. Now, it is the *new device that both simplified the process and logged the results.*

In the second example, the sentence structure flips completely. You may not have anticipated this sort of fix—remember, stay flexible! Now, *a new device* is part of an opening modifier. *The doctor* uses the *new device*, but it is *the doctor* herself who is the subject for *analyzed* and *logged.*

How about the following example?

> Every night after the lights go out, the campers attempt to sneak out of their bunks and steal candy from the kitchen.

Step 1: Identify the Parallelism Marker

> *And*

Step 2: Identify the Elements

> *Y* element: *steal*

> *X* element: *?*

Steal is a verb, so look for a verb in the first clause. Again, there are two: *attempt* and *sneak*. Which one is parallel to *steal*?

> The campers attempt (?) to sneak (?) out of their bunks AND steal candy from the kitchen.

Option 1:

> *X* element: *attempt*

> *Y* element: *steal*

5

Option 2:

X element: *sneak*

Y element: *steal*

Step 3: Identify the Root Phrase, and Distribute It to Each Element:

Option 1 root phrase + elements: *the campers attempt (one thing) . . . AND (the campers) steal (another)*

Option 2 root phrase + elements: *the campers attempt to sneak . . . AND (the campers attempt to) steal*

Option 2 says that the campers *attempt to . . . steal candy*—but it isn't clear that they succeed. The first option implies that the campers are successful. However, there's only one logical interpretation here: It's nonsensical to say that *the campers attempt to sneak out of their bunks*—implying that they don't necessarily succeed—but that they definitely *steal candy from the kitchen.* If they don't succeed in sneaking out, then they can't steal the candy!

Thus, Option 2 is the only coherent meaning; *the campers attempt to* do two things: 1) *sneak out* and 2) *steal candy.*

The Many Parallel Structures of the Word *And*

5

Many of the examples in this chapter contain the marker *and.* When *and* lacks a preceding comma, it can connect two of almost any part of speech, as shown in these correct sentences:

The manager AND her team were praised by the CEO.	→	compound subject
In one terrible day, the account manager lost a client AND greeted the CEO of her company by the wrong name.	→	compound verb
A rapid improvement in motor function AND in vision was observed.	→	prepositional phrase
Sal applied himself in his new job, arriving early every day AND leaving late every night.	→	adverbial modifier

When *and* is preceded by a comma, there are a few possible scenarios. If it's preceded by exactly one comma, the word *and* connects two independent clauses. Recall from the Sentence Structure chapter that to create a compound sentence, you need both a comma and a co-conjunction between the two independent clauses:

Right: The driver swerved to avoid the oncoming car, and he barely missed colliding with a tree.

When *and* is preceded by exactly two commas, there are two possibilities. Often, two commas will convey a list of three things:

Right: George Washington, John Adams, and Thomas Jefferson were the first three presidents of the United States.

However, the two commas may also be there to offset a modifier:

Right: The baker looked at the wedding cake, which stood over four feet high, and beamed proudly.

Strip out any modifiers before you evaluate the parallel structure.

The baker looked at the wedding cake~~, which stood over four feet high,~~ AND beamed proudly.

Finally, you may sometimes see three commas followed by *and*. This can introduce a list with four elements, but there is another tricky structure that the GMAT will sometimes test. Remember Sal from the earlier example, the one who was arriving early and leaving late every day? Take a look at what happens when a third modifier is added to *arriving* and *leaving*:

Sal applied himself in his new job, arriving early every day, skipping lunch regularly, and leaving late every night.

The first comma separates the core sentence from the modifiers; the other two commas separate the three items in the list (*X*, *Y*, and *Z*). Imagine that the test also provides you with this choice:

Sal applied himself in his new job, arrived early every day, skipped lunch regularly, and left late every night.

What's the difference between the two options? Is one preferable?

The second sentence is a list of four separate things that Sal did (*W*, *X*, *Y*, and *Z*), and the verbs are all properly parallel to each other. However, this version gives all four activities equal emphasis; at this level, the three latter activities do not need to have any connection to Sal's job. For example, the sentence could mean *Sal applied himself in his new job, arrived early every day at the gym, skipped lunch regularly on the weekend, and left the bar late every Saturday night.* While the sentence is grammatically correct, its meaning is less logical than the other option.

If you focus too rigidly on the *W*, *X*, *Y*, and *Z* structure, you might misinterpret the first sentence to be a list of four things, the first of which is not parallel to the three that follow. In fact, however, that first sentence contains a properly parallel list of three modifiers that all describe how *Sal applied himself in his new job*. The first comma separates the main clause (*Sal applied himself in his new job*) from the adverbial modifier (*arriving early every day*). The three *comma –ing* modifiers are all properly parallel to each other. As always, you can check the elements with the root phrase to verify that they all make sense:

Root phrase + *X* element: *Sal applied himself in his new job, arriving early every day.*

Root phrase + *Y* element: *Sal applied himself in his new job, skipping lunch regularly.*

Root phrase + *Z* element: *Sal applied himself in his new job, leaving late every night.*

This sentence is grammatically correct and conveys a more logical meaning than the other option, relating each part of the sentence to the fact that Sal applied himself in his new job. The structure *clause, adverbial modifier, adverbial modifier, and adverbial modifier* can be particularly tricky to parse. Identify the modifiers before you eliminate an answer that appears to break the rules of parallelism, and pay careful attention to the meaning of the sentence.

Idioms with Built-In Parallel Structure

Remember, check for parallelism *only* when you see a parallelism marker. A few examples of idioms with built-in parallel structure are shown below; you can find more in the chapters on Comparisons and Idioms.

Between *X* and *Y*	Distinguish *X* from *Y*	Neither *X* nor *Y*
Consider *X* *Y*	Estimate *X* to be *Y*	View *X* as *Y*
In contrast to *X*, *Y*	Mistake *X* for *Y*	Whether *X* or *Y*

What's wrong with the following sentences?

The launch of the new product line was neither a success or a failure.

Producing a paper bag requires between 20 to 25 times as much water as producing a plastic bag.

In the first sentence, the proper idiom is *neither X nor Y*. In the second sentence, the proper idiom is *between X and Y*. If an answer contains an idiomatic error in the parallelism marker itself, cross that choice off and save the 3-step process for the remaining answers.

Problem Set

In problems 1–4, box the open markers, circle the closed markers, put brackets around the [root phrase], and underline the elements in the parallel structure.

1. Researchers have found a correlation between exercising and earning good grades.

2. Although the nonprofit could not offer a high salary or a pension, it was able to offer not only four weeks of annual vacation but also full health benefits.

3. Many teachers choose to seek employment in the suburbs or private schools rather than face low salaries in the city.

4. A good night's sleep not only gives your body a chance to rest and to recover but also energizes you for the following day.

5

There is almost always more than one correct way to write a parallel structure. Problems 5–7 have at least one correct answer; some have more. Apply the 3-step process you learned about in the chapter, and select all the correct answers.

5. The corruption both at the city level and at the state level is dispiriting.

   (A) both at the city level and at
   (B) both at the city level and
   (C) at both the city level and at
   (D) at both the city level and

6. When the sales manager gets wind of the recent slump, she likely will fire some members of the sales team and blame the marketing team.

   (A) team and blame the marketing team
   (B) team and the marketing team
   (C) team, blaming the marketing team
   (D) and marketing teams

7. The recently hired director of marketing has been an abject failure; she neither understands principles of design nor search engine optimization.

   (A) failure; she neither understands principles of design nor
   (B) failure, understanding neither principles of design nor principles of
   (C) failure, lacking understanding in principles of design and
   (D) failure; she understands neither principles of design nor

Problems 8–10 are multiple choice with one correct answer. As on the real GMAT, answer (A) repeats the original sentence. Unlike the real GMAT, though, these problems have only three answer choices.

8. Voters want to elect a president who not only genuinely cares about health care, the environment, and the travails of ordinary men and women, but also has the experience, wisdom, and strength of character required for the job.

   (A) not only genuinely cares about health care, the environment, and the travails of ordinary men and women, but also has
   (B) genuinely cares about health care, the environment, and the travails of ordinary men and women, as well as
   (C) genuinely cares not only about health care, the environment, and the travails of ordinary men and women, but also about

5

9. The consultant is looking for a café where there are comfortable chairs and that provides free internet access.

   (A) where there are
   (B) that has both
   (C) that has

10. The blizzard deposited more than a foot of snow on the train tracks, which prompted the transit authority to shut down service temporarily and caused discontent among commuters who were left stranded for hours.

   (A) which prompted the transit authority to shut down service temporarily and caused
   (B) prompting the transit authority to shut down service temporarily, causing
   (C) prompting the transit authority to shut down service temporarily and causing

Solutions

1. [Researchers have found a correlation] between exercising and earning good grades.

2. [Although the nonprofit could not offer] a high salary or a pension, [it was able to offer] not only four weeks of annual vacation but also full health benefits.

3. This sentence has one parallel structure within another. The main pairing is [Many teachers choose to] seek rather than face. The parallelism within that is [in] the suburbs or private schools.

   [Many teachers choose to] seek employment [in] the suburbs or private schools rather than face low salaries in the city.

4. Like question 3, this sentence has one parallel structure within another. The main pairing is [A good night's sleep] not only gives but also energizes. The pairing within that is [a chance] to rest and to recover.

   [A good night's sleep] not only gives your body [a chance] to rest and to recover but also energizes you for the following day.

5. **(A) and (D):** The closed marker *both X and Y* requires the *X* and *Y* elements to be parallel parts of speech. Answer choices (B) and (C) commit a classic GMAT error, incorrectly placing a prep phrase (starting with *at*) parallel to a stand-alone noun. In choice (B), the given pairing is *both* (prep phrase) *and* (noun). In choice (C), the given pairing is *both* (noun) *and* (prep phrase).

   Answers (A) and (D) correct this error in different ways. In choice (A), the *X* and *Y* elements are parallel prep phrases (*at the city level* and *at the state level*). In choice (D), the *X* and *Y* elements are parallel nouns (*the city level* and *the state level*), as the preposition *at* has been moved to the root phrase, before the word *both*.

6. **(A), (B), and (D):** When you have an open parallelism marker such as *X and Y*, start with the element that follows the marker. Since *blame* is underlined in the original sentence, the final element can (and does) change from answer to answer.

   In answer choice (A), the verb *blame* is properly parallel to the verb *fire*: *She likely will fire... and blame.*

   The *Y* element in choice (B) is *the marketing team*, which is properly parallel to *the sales team*: *She likely will fire some members of... the marketing team.*

   Choice (C) changes up the structure, removing the word *and* as well as the parallel structure that comes with it. *Blaming* is now an adverbial modifier, pointing back to *she likely will fire*. However, this meaning is illogical; *blaming the marketing team* does not describe *how* the sales manager *will fire some members of the sales team*. The two actions are related but separate; the parallel structure in the other answers properly conveys this.

   Notice that answer (D) changes *team* to *teams*. In this correct sentence, the adjectives *sales* and *marketing* both modify *teams*. Adjectives come before the nouns that they modify, so in this construction, the root phrase comes after the elements, not before. For example, in the sentence *The black and white photograph is beautiful*, the parallel adjectives *black* and *white* both describe the root word *photograph*.

7. **(B), (C), and (D):** The closed parallelism marker *neither X nor Y* requires the *X* and *Y* elements to be parallel parts of speech. Answer choice (A) violates this requirement by placing a verb (*understands*) parallel to a noun (*search engine optimization*).

   Choice (B) correctly satisfies this parallel requirement, matching *principles of design* with *principles of search engine optimization.*

   In answer (C), the root phrase extends through the words *principles of.* The *X* and *Y* elements, *design* and *search engine optimization*, are both nouns.

   What about answer choice (D), in which *principles of design* is placed parallel to *search engine optimization*? The *X* and *Y* elements do not have to be exactly the same; they just need to be the same part of speech, and *X* and *Y* are both nouns here. The root phrase still logically leads into both elements: *She understands neither principles of design* and *she understands neither... search engine optimization.* Both elements are things the *director of marketing* does not understand.

8. **(A):** This tricky sentence contains a list within the parallel structure *not only X but also Y.* The list is the same in all three answers, so investigate the *not only X but also Y* structure in answers (A) and (C).

   The *X* and *Y* elements in answer (A) are *genuinely cares* and *has.* Even though the first element has an attached adverb (*genuinely*), that does not break the parallelism between these two verbs.

   Answer (C) shifts the placement of *not only*; the *X* element is now *about health care* and the *Y* element is *about the experience.* These prep phrases are parallel, too. However, the meaning of (C) is illogical: *Voters want to elect a president who genuinely cares... about the experience, wisdom, and strength of character required for the job*? That's not what the sentence intends to say; it's trying to say that voters want a president who, as answer choice (A) says, *has the experience, wisdom, and strength of character required for the job.* Eliminate answer choice (C) for this meaning error.

   Answer choice (B) removes the *not only X but also Y* structure, but it maintains the meaning error discussed in answer (C). Voters want a president who *has* experience, not one who *cares about* experience.

9. **(C):** The open marker *and Y* indicates parallelism. When you see an open marker, let the *Y* element guide you. Since *and* is in the non-underlined part of the sentence, the first element must be parallel to *that provides free internet access.*

   Answer choice (A) tries to make *where there are* parallel to *that provides*, but *where* introduces a full clause (*there are chairs*), while *that* has only a verb (*provides*), not a subject–verb pairing.

   Answer choice (B) does start with *that has*, but it adds in *both*, which is part of the closed parallelism marker *both X and Y.* The two elements in this marker are *comfortable chairs* and *that provides free internet access.* A noun cannot be parallel to a subordinate clause; eliminate this answer for violating parallelism.

   Answer (C) maintains the open parallel structure; *that has comfortable chairs* is properly parallel to *that provides free internet access.*

10. **(C):** In the original sentence, the *comma which* noun modifier incorrectly implies that *the train tracks* are what led to the discontinuation of service and angered the commuters. In fact, the entire situation (*the blizzard deposited more than a foot of snow on the train tracks*) is what *prompted the transit authority to shut down service*. Thus, the sentence requires the adverbial modifier *prompting*, used in answers (B) and (C).

The construction in answer choice (B), exactly two *comma –ing* modifiers in a row, is almost never acceptable because it leads to an ambiguous meaning. Is it the case that the *blizzard deposit[ing] snow* caused *discontent* or is it the case that the *transit authority shut[ting] down service* caused *discontent*? Either interpretation is logical. Answer (C) avoids this ambiguity by employing a parallel structure (*X and Y*), signaling that each modifier (*prompting* and *causing*) refers back to the main clause.

CHAPTER 6

Comparisons

In This Chapter:

- Comparison Markers
- Omitted Words
- *Like* vs. *As*
- The Many Uses of the Word *As*
- Comparative and Superlative Forms

In this chapter, you will learn about a subset of parallelism: comparisons. You'll learn the markers associated with comparisons and the stricter parallelism rules that comparisons must follow.

CHAPTER 6 Comparisons

Comparisons are a subset of parallelism, but they get their own chapter because they require an additional check in order to ensure that they are valid.

For example, what's wrong with the sentence below?

Wrong: Like Mary, Adam's car is green.

Poor Mary. She must be pretty sick if she's green, like Adam's car!

Right: LIKE Mary's car, Adam's car is green.

Comparisons require parallelism between the two elements being compared (nouns with nouns, for example), but that's rarely the mistake in an SC question that tests comparisons. Instead, the mistakes tend to be in the meaning (is it logical to compare the two elements?) or in the comparison marker itself. As soon as you see a comparison marker, check the meaning and the marker.

Comparison Markers

Like parallelism, comparisons always have a marker that alerts you to the comparison:

Right: John, LIKE his mother, has fiery red hair.

Right: LIKE his mother, John has fiery red hair.

This comparison can have the structure *X, like Y or like X, Y*. Here is a list of some common comparison markers and their associated structures:

Marker	Sample Structure
Like, Unlike	Jane, LIKE her parents, has green eyes. UNLIKE the cat, the dog is friendly.
As	Dhivya is smart, AS is Abby.
Than	You have earned a BETTER score THAN I have. Cisco's revenues are considerably HIGHER THAN Starbucks's.
As (adjective) as	Mira is AS likely AS Sam to win the promotion.
Different from, Similar to	My current job is quite DIFFERENT FROM my last one. (Pronoun *one* refers to *job*.) Ferraris are SIMILAR TO Lamborghinis.
In contrast to/with	Canada's housing market did not suffer many difficulties during the economic downturn, IN CONTRAST TO the housing market in the United States.

How can the GMAT break a comparison? Consider what's being compared in the following sentence:

John's hair, like his mother, is red and fiery.

Now *John's hair* is being compared to *his mother*, and that's illogical. The GMAT loves to trap students with these sorts of nonsensical comparisons, and the GMAT often fixes these broken comparisons by using a pronoun or apostrophe to stand in for the missing noun:

Right: John's hair, LIKE that of his mother, is red and fiery

Right: John's hair, LIKE his mother's, is red and fiery.

In fact, fixing a broken comparison with *that of* or *those of* is so common that you can think of these phrases as comparison markers!

In the correct examples, both the pronoun *that* and the apostrophe in *mother's* refer to *hair*. Note that it is acceptable for an apostrophe to imply a noun—you do not have to say *his mother's hair*.

What comparison is made in the sentence below?

Beethoven's music, which broke a number of established rules with its structure and melodic form, is considered more revolutionary than Bach.

The comparison structure in this sentence is *X more than Y*. As with open markers, comparisons are often most easily tackled by finding the second element first, since it follows the comparison marker: *more revolutionary than Bach*. So, what is more revolutionary than Bach? The subject of the sentence: *Beethoven's music*. This comparison is not parallel.

In everyday speech, this sentence would likely sound fine, since people often talk about the music of Bach as "Bach" (e.g., *I like to listen to Bach on the radio)*. Grammar rules demand, however, that if the sentence has referred to Beethoven's music with the word *music*, then the sentence should do the same with Bach's music:

Right: Beethoven's music, which broke a number of established rules with its structure and melodic form, is considered MORE revolutionary THAN BACH'S.

As before, you do not have to repeat the word *music*, as long as the second element, *Bach's*, clearly refers back to music. The sentence could also use *that of Bach* as the second element.

Omitted Words

As shown earlier in this chapter, comparisons can sometimes omit words in the *Y* element and still be considered properly parallel. Both of the following sentences are correct:

Right: My car is bigger than Brian's [*car*].

Right: My house is smaller than the Smiths' [*house*].

You can also omit units, verbs, and even whole clauses from the second term, as long as there is no ambiguity in the comparison:

Right: Whereas I drink two quarts of milk a day, my friend drinks three [*quarts of milk a day*].

Right: I walk faster than Brian [*walks*].

Right: I walk as fast now as [*I walked*] when I was younger.

In general, include the omitted words or appropriate helping verbs (such as *be*, *do*, and *have*) if the sentence would otherwise be ambiguous. For example:

Ambiguous: I like cheese more than Yvette.

Do you like cheese more than Yvette likes cheese? Or do you like cheese more than you like Yvette?

Right: I like cheese more than Yvette DOES. (*more than* Yvette *likes cheese*)

Right: I like cheese more than I DO Yvette. (*more than I like* Yvette)

The GMAT occasionally allows unnecessary helping verbs:

Right: Apples are more healthy to eat than caramels.

Right: Apples are more healthy to eat than caramels ARE.

The second sentence is not considered redundant or incorrect. If you see this on the test, ignore it and find some other difference on which to base your decision.

Like vs. *As*

Like and *as* are two very common comparison signals.

Like is used to compare nouns. Never put a clause or a prepositional phrase after *like*. (Reminder: A clause contains a working verb, one that can be the main verb in a sentence.)

Consider the following examples:

Right: LIKE her brother, Ava aced the test.

Wrong: LIKE her brother did, Ava aced the test.

6

Start with the easier element to spot: the one that directly follows the comparison marker. In the first sentence, *like* is followed by the noun phrase *her brother*, so *her brother* is the first element. The second element is the noun following the comma, *Ava*. It's logical to compare one person to another, so this choice is fine.

Note two things. First, the element immediately following the word *like* is a noun. This part should always have just a noun or noun phrase—no main verb. The incorrect example is incorrect precisely because the portion following *like* includes a verb (*her brother DID*).

Second, the other noun in the comparison (the one *not* following the word *like*) will be attached to a verb. In this case, the other element is the noun *Ava*, but *Ava* also functions as the subject of the main part of the sentence. Any legal sentence core does need a subject and verb; the part of the comparison that doesn't connect to the marker *like* will provide that subject and verb.

When you see *like*, think noun-to-noun comparison. The noun attached to *like* should never have its own verb.

As, on the other hand, can only be used to compare clauses, not nouns. In other words, each element of the comparison needs its own verb:

Right: AS her brother DID, Ava aced the test.

Wrong: AS her brother, Ava aced the test.

Notice that this comparison can be made correctly using either *like* or *as*, so stay flexible as you move through the answer choices. Don't assume that the correct answer will compare two nouns simply because the original sentence compares two nouns. It's not unusual for the GMAT to change the comparison marker in the correct answer—and that can change the form of the comparison elements as well.

Occasionally, you may see an *–ing* word that is functioning as a noun. For example:

Right: LIKE swimming, skiing is great exercise.

This comparison still pairs two nouns; the nouns just happen to be in *–ing* form. An *–ing* word is not a verb unless it has another verb directly attached to it (such as *is swimming*).

The Many Uses of the Word *As*

As is a remarkably versatile word. It can do more than just compare clauses. In fact, it has as many uses as almost any other word that you'll encounter. It can be used as a prepositional (prep) phrase. It has other uses, such as introducing examples. Did you notice all the different instances of the word *as* as you read this paragraph?

1. *As X as* (comparing clauses)

   One of the most common uses of *as* on the GMAT is in the two-part phrase *as X as*, where *X* is an adjective or adverb:

   Indian food is *as spicy as* Mexican food (is).

   Cheetahs can run almost three times *as fast as* the fastest human (can run).

   If you see a double-*as* on the GMAT, you've usually got a comparison; there are some other valid uses of *as X as*, though, so pay attention to the meaning. For example:

   The temperature may drop *as low as* 20 degrees.

   The words *as low as* convey a quantity, not a comparison. *As X as* can be a quantity modifier:

   The new product may be available *as soon as* next week.

   The words *as soon as* convey a time frame, not a comparison. *As X as* can also be a time marker.

2. Prep phrase (modifying clauses)

   As can also be the preposition that starts a prep phrase:

   Liat worked *as a consultant* for seven years.

   Barry Bonds retired *as the all-time home run leader.*

   When *as* starts a prep phrase, it's always an adverbial modifier.

3. Conjunction (connecting clauses)

   As can also function as a conjunction, connecting two clauses. In this context, it most often means *at the same time that*:

   He looked down at his phone *as he crossed the street.*

   Shoshana ate her breakfast *as she watched the news.*

4. Idioms

As can be used in a number of idioms; here are some that are common on the GMAT. See the Idioms chapter and the Idioms appendix for a more comprehensive list.

4a. *X such as/Such X as*

As can be used as part of the phrase *such as* to introduce examples:

Recent environmental regulations have banned *items such as* plastic straws and single-use plastic bags.

Recent environmental regulations have banned *such items as* plastic straws and single-use plastic bags.

The sentences are both correct. You can say *such X as* or *X such as*, where *X* is the category of examples (in this case, the category is *items*).

4b. *So as to*

The phrase *so as to* means *in order to*:

He made up an excuse so as to avoid suspicion.

4c. *As* vs. *than*

As discussed in the Parallelism chapter, the GMAT will sometimes use incorrect markers, such as *either X and Y*, rather than the correct *either X or Y*. This type of mistake is relatively common with comparison markers as well, and since *as* has so many uses, the GMAT will sometimes try to sneak it into places where it doesn't belong. For example:

Wrong: The speed limit is *higher* in the state of Texas *as* it is anywhere else in the United States.

The correct idiom is *higher... than*; the pairing *higher... as* is incorrect.

Comparative and Superlative Forms

When comparing two things, use the comparative form (*–er*) of an adjective or adverb. When comparing more than two things, use the superlative form (*–est*) of an adjective or adverb. For example:

Comparative:	She is SHORTER than her sister.
Superlative:	She is the SHORTEST of her five siblings.
Comparative:	You are MORE INTERESTING than he is.
Superlative:	You are the MOST INTERESTING person here.

Do not take an adverb that ends in *–ly* and make it a comparison by changing the ending to *–er*. This error is common in speech. Instead, add *more*:

Wrong:	Adrian runs QUICKLY. He runs QUICKER than Jacob.
Right:	Adrian runs QUICKLY. He runs MORE QUICKLY than Jacob.

However, some adverbs that do not end in *–ly* are made into comparatives by adding *–er*:

Right:	Adrian runs FAST. He runs FASTER than Jacob.

Do not use a comparative word, such as *higher*, unless the word *than* completes the comparison. The GMAT often incorrectly pairs comparative words with words besides *than*. Examples seen on SC include *more likely... as*, *higher... over*, and *less... compared to*. It is also incorrect to drop *than* entirely:

Wrong: With winter coming, I will have HIGHER energy bills.

The sentence *implies* the comparison *than before*. On the GMAT, however, you must make that comparison explicit, using the word *than*:

Right: With winter coming, I will have HIGHER energy bills THAN I did over the summer.

Problem Set

In problems 1–9, underline all comparison signals and all comparative or superlative forms. If the sentence is fine, write CORRECT. If not, correct the errors in the sentence. For an ambiguous sentence, express each possible meaning of the sentence with a correct sentence of your own.

1. Like many other states, Virginia is technically a commonwealth.

   Correct

2. I scored three goals in yesterday's game, as did Suzanne.

   As I scored three goals in yesterday's game, Suzanne did too.

   or Correct

3. The rapid development of India in the twenty-first century is like England in the eighteenth century.

   ~~the England~~'s . . .

   like that of

4. A leopard cannot run as fast as a cheetah.

   Correct

5. A leopard cannot catch a wildebeest as fast as a cheetah.

   . . . can.

6. In contrast to the trapeze artists, who fumbled their routine, the antics of the circus clowns kept the audience entertained for hours.

   , the clowns kept the audience entertain for hours with their antics.

7. The clothes looked more appealing inside the store than on the racks outside.

   Correct

8. The clothes inside the store looked more appealing than on the racks outside.

than the clothes on the racks outside

9. Hugo is widely acknowledged to be our best employee, because he works harder and more creatively than anyone else in the company.

Correct
anyone does

Problems 10–12 are multiple choice with one correct answer. As on the real GMAT, answer (A) repeats the original sentence. Unlike the real GMAT, though, these problems have only three answer choices.

10. Although the towers appear to be identical, the east tower is the tallest, reaching 20 feet higher than the west tower.

 (A) to be identical, the east tower is the tallest, reaching
 (B) to be identical heights, the taller east tower reaches
 (C) identical, the east tower reaches

11. Trends in popular music come and go, and the genres that are mainstream today are more likely to be forgotten tomorrow, as have many similar styles before them.

 (A) are more likely to be forgotten tomorrow, as have many similar styles
 (B) more likely will be forgotten tomorrow, as many similar styles have
 (C) are likely to be forgotten tomorrow, as were many similar styles

12. Courtney's experience at Haleford, a large research university with renowned professors, affluent students, and imposing buildings, were unlike her high school in a small town.

 (A) with renowned professors, affluent students, and imposing buildings, were unlike her
 (B) that employs renowned professors, affluent students, and imposing buildings, was unlike her experience at
 (C) known for its renowned professors, affluent students, and imposing buildings, was nothing like her experience at

Solutions

1. Like many other states, Virginia is technically a commonwealth.

   CORRECT. The noun phrase *many other states* follows the comparison signal *like*. This noun phrase is being compared to the noun *Virginia*, which is the subject of the sentence.

2. I scored three goals in yesterday's game, as did Suzanne.

   CORRECT. The word *as* sets up a comparison between two clauses: *I scored three goals in yesterday's game* and *did Suzanne*. The verb *did* in the second clause stands for the entire phrase *scored three goals in yesterday's game*, which thus does not need to be repeated.

3. The rapid development of India in the twenty-first century is like England in the eighteenth century.

   This sentence incorrectly compares the *rapid development of India* to *England*. The easiest way to fix the sentence is to include the phrase *that of* to make it clear that the comparison is between the rapid developments of both countries:

   Correction: The rapid development of India in the twenty-first century is like that of England in the eighteenth century.

4. A leopard cannot run as fast as a cheetah.

   CORRECT. The phrase *as fast as* sets up a comparison between two clauses. Since *can run* is implied after *as fast as a cheetah*, the clause *a leopard cannot run* is properly parallel to *a cheetah* (*can run*).

   Another acceptable version of this sentence is *a leopard cannot run as fast as a cheetah can*. Here the helping verb *can* stands for the full phrase *can run*.

5. A leopard cannot catch a wildebeest as fast as a cheetah.

   This sentence is ambiguous because it's unclear what is being compared to what. Does it mean that the wildebeest is as fast as a cheetah?

   Correction (1): A leopard cannot catch a wildebeest that runs as fast as a cheetah (runs).

   Or does it mean that the leopard catches the cheetah?

   Correction (2): A leopard cannot catch a wildebeest as fast as it can (catch) a cheetah.

   Or does it mean that the cheetah catches the wildebeest?

   Correction (3): A leopard cannot catch a wildebeest as fast as a cheetah can (catch a wildebeest).

   In these corrected versions, the text in parentheses is implied. The GMAT considers these sentences acceptable with or without the implied text.

6. In contrast to the trapeze artists, who fumbled their routine, the antics of the circus clowns kept the audience entertained for hours.

   This sentence makes an illogical comparison between *trapeze artists* and *antics*. A more logical comparison would be between *trapeze artists* and *circus clowns*.

   Correction: In contrast to the trapeze artists, who fumbled their routine, the circus clowns kept the audience entertained for hours with their antics.

7. The clothes looked more appealing inside the store than on the racks outside.

   CORRECT. This sentence compares how some clothes looked *inside the store* to how the same clothes looked *on the racks outside.*

8. The clothes inside the store looked more appealing than on the racks outside.

   This sentence seems to compare some clothes (*the clothes inside the store*) to a location (*on the racks outside*). It is hard to tell whether the author wants to compare two separate sets of clothes or one set of clothes in two display locations.

   One way to correct the sentence would be to rewrite it as the sentence in the previous question.

   Correction (1): The clothes looked more appealing inside the store than on the racks outside.

   This version makes sense because it puts the phrase *inside the store* after the comparison signal *more appealing*, making that phrase available for a comparison with *on the racks outside.* In this version, there is one set of clothes, and the comparison is between how these same clothes looked *inside the store* and how they looked *on the racks outside.* (Perhaps a customer brought the clothes into the store and is describing the different appearance of the same clothes before and after the move.)

   Correction (2): The clothes inside the store looked more appealing than (did) those on the racks outside.

   This version compares two sets of clothes: *the clothes inside the store* and *those on the racks outside.* The word *did* is optional.

9. Hugo is widely acknowledged to be our best employee, because he works harder and more creatively than anyone else in the company.

   CORRECT. In the first clause, Hugo is being singled out from among a group (employees), so use a superlative (*best*) to modify *employee.*

   In the second clause, there is a comparison between *X* and *Y*, so use the comparative forms rather than the superlative forms. (The comparison is between how *he works* and how *anyone else in the company works.*) The comparative form of the adverb *creatively* is *more creatively.* The comparative form of the adverb *harder* is simply *harder*, because *harder* is a short adverb that does not end in *–ly.*

10. **(C):** The original sentence says that *the east tower is the tallest*; this superlative form (*tallest*) indicates that there are at least three towers. However, the sentence describes only two towers—*the east tower* and *the west tower*—so the comparative form (*taller*) should be used instead.

    Answer choice (B) correctly replaces *tallest* with *taller*; however, the sentence already says that this *tower reaches 20 feet higher than* the other one. Describing *the east tower* as *taller* is redundant. Even the word *heights* is redundant in conjunction with *taller* and *higher than.* It might be acceptable to say that the two buildings were thought to be identical *heights* but one is actually *taller.* But all three descriptions (*heights, taller, higher than*) together are overkill.

    Choice (C) changes *appear to be identical* to *appear identical.* These idioms are both correct. This choice removes *taller* and *heights*, eliminating the redundancy.

11. **(C):** The word *more* indicates a coming comparison that should be in the form *X more than Y*. However, answers (A) and (B) use *more* without the second piece of the comparison idiom, *than*. *The genres that are mainstream today are more likely* than what *to be forgotten tomorrow*? Since there is no second piece of the comparison, eliminate answers (A) and (B) for this comparison error.

    Answer (C) fixes this by removing the word *more* altogether. Now, there's no comparison in the first half of the sentence, simply a statement that these mainstream genres *are likely to be forgotten*.

12. **(C):** This sentence is filled with modifiers, and there's no verb before the underline. Strip out the modifiers to find the core sentence: *Courtney's experience... were unlike her high school*. Since *experience* is singular, the verb must be singular to match. In addition, this choice compares *Courtney's experience* to *her high school*; these are not the same kind of thing. Eliminate choice (A) for a mismatched subject–verb and a mismatched comparison.

    Answers (B) and (C) correctly change the verb to *was*. Choice (B) uses *unlike*, while choice (C) uses *nothing like*. Although *unlike* is the more common comparison marker, these markers are both correct. Find another split.

    Both sentences have a list (*renowned professors, affluent students, and imposing buildings*), which requires parallelism, but the list is the same in each answer. The lead-in, however, is different. The root phrase in answer choice (B) is *that employs*. While Haleford *employs renowned professors*, it certainly does not *employ... imposing buildings*. Eliminate choice (B) for this meaning error.

CHAPTER 7

Pronouns

In This Chapter:

- The Antecedent Must Exist and Be Sensible
- The Antecedent and Pronoun Must Agree in Number
- The Deadly Five: *It, Its, They, Them, Their*
- *This, That, These*, and *Those*
- Some Ambiguity Is Acceptable

In this chapter, you will learn how to recognize pronouns and how to test that they are logical and reflect the appropriate number. You'll also learn how to deal with pronoun ambiguity—and when to ignore that issue and concentrate on something else instead.

CHAPTER 7 Pronouns

A **Pronoun** is a word that takes the place of a noun so that you do not have to repeat that noun elsewhere in the sentence. For example:

> GASOLINE has become so expensive that it now consumes as much as 16 percent of personal income in some rural areas.

In the sentence above, the pronoun *it* takes the place of the noun *gasoline*. In other words, *it* refers to *gasoline*. The noun that a pronoun replaces is known as its **Antecedent**.

On the GMAT, it is not unusual to think that a pronoun error exists, only to discover that the pronoun is correct after all. As soon as you think that you may have a pronoun issue, check the answer choices to see what the differences are.

Do the answers split between singular and plural? Between a pronoun and a regular noun? If there are differences, then you can apply the rules and possibly cross off some answers. Occasionally, you may discover that the pronoun does not change in all five answers; in this case, look for some other issue to tackle instead.

If you think a non-underlined pronoun may be problematic, find the antecedent (you'll learn how in this chapter). If the antecedent is also not underlined, then the pronoun is fine; look for some other split. If the antecedent is underlined, check the answers to see what other options are offered.

In short, whenever you think a pronoun might be problematic, immediately check the splits in the answers to see whether there is an issue at all.

The Antecedent Must Exist and Be Sensible

If the answer choices do offer different pronouns, then find the antecedent:

> Due to the ongoing drought, emergency wildfire prevention measures must be implemented immediately in all national parks in order to ensure that they don't inadvertently start fires.

What noun does *they* refer to? The *prevention measures*? That doesn't make sense. Logically, it should refer to the *visitors* or *people using the parks*. However, no noun exists in the sentence for those people. This answer choice would be incorrect on an SC problem because it never says who *they* are.

Be careful not to gloss over the meaning. For example:

> Although the term "supercomputer" may sound fanciful or exaggerated, it is simply an extremely fast mainframe that can execute trillions of calculations every second.

The antecedent appears to be *the term "supercomputer."* Look what happens when the pronoun is replaced with this noun:

> . . . the TERM "supercomputer" is simply an extremely fast mainframe . . .

The term is not a *mainframe* itself; rather, the term *refers to* a mainframe. In addition, the word *supercomputer* is not used to refer to an actual supercomputer; it is referring just to the term or class of item. Therefore, you must change the verb or make some other edit to refer to the term or class:

Right: Although the TERM "supercomputer" may sound fanciful or exaggerated, it simply *refers to* an extremely fast mainframe that can execute trillions of calculations every second.

Pronoun issues center around *meaning*. The GMAT tries to trick you into "assuming away" little wrinkles in meaning. Always replace the pronoun with its antecedent to make sure that the sentence still makes sense.

The Antecedent and Pronoun Must Agree in Number

If the answers switch between singular and plural *pronouns*, check the antecedent to see whether it is singular or plural. If the answers switch between singular and plural *nouns*, the issue could be one of two things: pronouns or verbs (for subject–verb agreement). Consider this example:

Confronted by radical changes in production and distribution, modern Hollywood studios are attempting various experiments in an effort to retain its status as the primary arbiter of movie consumption.

The antecedent of *its* is intended to be *studios*. However, *its* is singular, while *studios* is plural. Either the noun or the pronoun has to change (depending upon which portion is underlined in the problem):

Right: Confronted by radical changes in production and distribution, modern Hollywood STUDIOS are attempting various experiments in an effort to retain their status as the primary arbiters of movie consumption.

Right: Confronted by radical changes in production and distribution, THE modern Hollywood STUDIO is attempting various experiments in an effort to retain its status as the primary arbiter of movie consumption.

7

The GMAT tends to test number agreement when you can easily express the relevant concepts either in singular or in plural form (*studio* or *studios*). Use the underline placement and the differences in the answers as your guide.

As you learned in the Sentence Structure chapter, the GMAT can separate a subject from its verb in various ways in order to get you to miss a singular–plural mismatch. The same disguises apply to pronoun antecedents.

The Deadly Five: *It, Its, They, Them, Their*

The most common pronoun mistakes involve the singular *it* and *its*, as well as the plural *they*, *them*, and *their*. Whenever you see one of these five pronouns, check the answers; if differences exist, find the antecedent and check its viability.

it, its } singular

they, them, their } plural

If you see one of these words in the non-underlined portion, the sentence may or may not be testing pronouns. In that case, it's worth noting that the pronoun is there. If a noun switches from singular to plural in the answer choices, check whether that noun is the antecedent for the non-underlined pronoun. If so, the pronoun will dictate whether that noun must be singular or plural.

This, That, These, and *Those*

This, that, these, and *those* can be used as adjectives in front of nouns:

> New "NANO-PAPERS" incorporate fibers that give these materials strength.

You may also use *that* or *those* to indicate a "new copy" of the antecedent:

> The MONEY spent by Cersei's parents is less than that spent by her children.

In this example, *that spent by her children* means *the money spent by her children*, but the two pots of money are *not* the same. One pot of money is spent by the parents; another pot of money, spent by the children, is the new copy. In contrast, when you use *it*, *they*, or other personal pronouns, you mean the same actual thing as the antecedent. Consider this example:

> The MONEY SPENT BY CERSEI'S PARENTS is more than it was expected to be.

In this example, *it* refers to the actual money spent by her parents.

When a sentence uses *that* or *those* to indicate a new copy or copies, the pronoun must include a modifier that describes how the new copy is different from the previous version. For example:

> The MONEY spent by Cersei's parents is less than that spent by her children.
>
> The company's DIGITAL WATCH OFFERING is outperforming that of its competitor.

Official GMAT questions have required that this new-copy usage of *that* or *those* agree in number with the previous version:

Wrong: The company's DIGITAL WATCH OFFERING is outperforming those of its competitors.

Right: The company's DIGITAL WATCH OFFERING is outperforming the offerings of its competitors.

The correct option has a bonus pronoun lesson: The pronoun *its* refers to the possessive noun *company's*; technically, *company's* is an adjective, not a noun. This is an exception to the general rule that a pronoun refers to a noun: It is possible for a pronoun to refer to a possessive noun.

Finally, on the GMAT, do not use *this* or *these* in place of nouns. A sentence such as *This is great* is unacceptably vague to the GMAT. Also, do not use *that* or *those* in place of nouns, unless you modify *that* or *those* to make them new copies. Instead, use *it*, *they*, or *them*:

Wrong: Tal's PRODUCTS are unusual; many consider these unique.

Right: Tal's PRODUCTS are unusual; many consider them unique.

Some Ambiguity Is Acceptable

In theory, every pronoun in a well-written sentence should clearly refer to one antecedent. If a sentence uses the exact same pronoun multiple times, every instance should refer to the same antecedent. If the first *it* refers to one noun and the second *it* refers to another, the sentence is going to be confusing.

It is also preferable to have pronouns of the same class refer to the same noun. *It* and *its* are one class, and *they*, *them*, and *their* are another class. This is a preference, however, not an absolute rule; some correct GMAT sentences do use different pronouns of the same class to refer to different nouns. What are the antecedents for the pronouns in this sentence:

Researchers claim to have developed new "nano-papers" incorporating tiny cellulose fibers, which they allege give them the strength of cast iron.

Logically, the pronoun *they* refers to *researchers* (who *claim* something) and the pronoun *them* refers to the *nano-papers*. If another grammatically correct option exists without this mild ambiguity, choose the other option. If, however, the other four choices all contain other errors, then this choice would be correct.

An answer choice could avoid potential ambiguity by not using a pronoun in the first place:

Right: Researchers claim to have developed new "NANO-PAPERS" incorporating tiny cellulose fibers, which give these materials the strength of cast iron, according to the researchers.

In this example, the sentence inserts a new noun, *materials*, to refer back to the nano-papers, so it isn't necessary for the reader to find the antecedent. (It also repeats the word *researchers* to avoid using the pronoun *they*.)

If you spot a split between a sentence that uses a pronoun and one that inserts a regular noun instead, there's a good chance that the answer with the regular noun is correct. Removing the pronoun prevents any possible ambiguity around the antecedent.

What if the sentence contains more than one possible antecedent with the right plurality for a given pronoun? Sometimes, these answers are wrong; sometimes, the GMAT accepts a mild ambiguity. In general, if you run up against this issue, ignore it and use some other split to decide. If you are really gunning for a top score, your Atlas learning platform provides an advanced pronoun lesson on this topic.

Problem Set

In problems 1–8, box all the pronouns and underline each pronoun's antecedent, if there is one. If you notice any pronoun errors in a sentence, correct the sentence by altering the pronoun(s). Explain what rules are violated by the incorrect sentences. If a sentence is correct, mark it with the word CORRECT.

1. When the guests finished their soup, they were brought plates of salad.

2. Meg left all her class notes at school because she decided that she could do her homework without it.

3. Some people believe that the benefits of a healthy diet outweigh that of regular exercise.

4. Oil traders have profited handsomely from the recent increase in its price.

5. The players' helmets need to be repainted before they are used in Sunday's game.

6. A few Shakespearean scholars maintain that he borrowed some of his most memorable lines from Christopher Marlowe.

7. The Smiths avoid the Browns because they dislike their children.

8. Samantha took her laptop and her books with her on the airplane because she thought that she could use these to get some work done.

Problems 9–11 are multiple choice with one correct answer. As on the real GMAT, answer (A) repeats the original sentence. (Unlike the real GMAT, though, these problems have only three answer choices.)

9. When tetrapods developed lungs capable of surviving on land, they became the first amphibians.

    (A) lungs capable of surviving on land, they became the first amphibians
    (B) lungs capable of surviving on land, tetrapods became the first amphibians
    (C) lungs, they became the first amphibians capable of surviving on land

10. The bite of the king cobra delivers such strong neurotoxins that they can kill an Asian elephant.

    (A) bite of the king cobra delivers such strong neurotoxins that they
    (B) king cobra's bite delivers such strong neurotoxins that it
    (C) neurotoxins delivered by a king cobra's bite are so strong that it

11. Television writer Aaron Sorkin is known for writing dialogue that is wittier than that in most real-world interactions.

    (A) dialogue that is wittier than that in
    (B) wittier dialogue than
    (C) dialogue that is wittier than it is in

Solutions

1. When the guests finished their soup, they were brought plates of salad.

   CORRECT. *Guests* is the antecedent of *their* and *they*.

2. Meg left all her class notes at school because she decided that she could do her homework without them.

   Meg is the antecedent of *her* and *she*. *Notes* is the antecedent of *them*. (In the original sentence, the pronoun *it* is incorrect because *notes* is plural.)

3. Some people believe that the benefits of a healthy diet outweigh those of regular exercise.

   Benefits is the antecedent of *those*. (In the original sentence, *that* is incorrect, because *benefits* is plural.)

4. Oil traders have profited handsomely from the recent increase in the price of oil.

   This new, correct version of the sentence contains no pronouns. The original sentence is incorrect because *its* has no antecedent. *Oil* is an adjective in the expression *oil traders*, and therefore cannot be the antecedent of *its*.

5. The players' helmets need to be repainted before they are used in Sunday's game.

   CORRECT. *Helmets* is the antecedent of *they*. You need not worry that *they* could refer to *players'*. Since *helmets* and *they* are the subjects of their respective clauses, there is a structural pointer that *they* refers to *helmets*. (This pointer is not required; it just helps to reinforce the connection.) *Helmets* is also a logical antecedent for *they*, so there is no ambiguity.

6. A few Shakespearean scholars maintain that Shakespeare borrowed some of his most memorable lines from Christopher Marlowe.

   Shakespeare is the antecedent of *his*. The original sentence is incorrect because *he* has no antecedent. *Shakespearean* is an adjective that describes Shakespeare's works, so it cannot be the antecedent for *he*. One way to fix this sentence is to replace *he* with *Shakespeare*.

7. The original sentence is far too ambiguous: Which family dislikes the other family's children? The antecedent of *they* is almost certainly not meant to be the same as the antecedent of *their*, a confusing state of affairs. To correct this sentence, you could get rid of the pronouns. One possible version: *The Smiths avoid the Browns because the Browns dislike the Smiths' children*. Another possible version: *The Smiths avoid the Browns because the Smiths dislike the Browns' children*. Without knowing the author's original intent, it's impossible to say which meaning is the correct one.

8. Samantha took her laptop and her books with her on the airplane because she thought that she could use them to get some work done.

   Samantha is the antecedent of all three *her*'s and both *she*'s.

   *Her laptop and her book*s is the antecedent of *them*. (The original *these* is incorrect because *these* cannot be used as a stand-alone pronoun without a noun following.)

9. **(C):** The original sentence contains a meaning error: *Capable of surviving on land* is a noun modifier that describes the *tetrapods*. In answers (A) and (B), the sentence seems to say that the *lungs* themselves were capable of surviving on land. Instead, the noun modifier should be placed closer to the noun that it modifies (*tetrapods*). Eliminate choices (A) and (B) for this meaning error.

   Although choice (C) has two plural nouns (*tetrapods* and *lungs*) that seem like they could be the antecedent for the pronoun *they*, this sentence is not in fact ambiguous. First, *tetrapods* is the logical antecedent for *they*. Second, *tetrapods* and *they* are both the subjects of their respective clauses, so there is a structural pointer that reinforces the idea that *they* refers to *tetrapods*. (It is not required that both the noun and pronoun be subjects, but when they are, it reinforces the connection between the two.)

   Did the first half of the sentence in the previous set of parentheses sound awkward? It's a correct example of the subjunctive, a type of verb usage. You'll learn more about this in the next chapter.

10. **(B):** The original sentence intends to say that *the bite of the king cobra . . . can kill an Asian elephant.* However, the plural pronoun *they* can refer only to *neurotoxins*. While it is not illogical that *neurotoxins . . . can kill an Asian elephant*, the structure of the sentence indicates that the intent is to say that the *bite* does this. The idiom is as follows: *X (delivers) such Y that Z (occurs).* The *Z* and *X* elements can be the same thing, but *Y* and *Z* cannot be the same thing. Eliminate choice (A) for faulty meaning based on the idiom structure.

    Answer choice (B) corrects this error. The singular pronoun *it* now clearly refers to the singular antecedent *bite*.

    Answer choice (C) changes the subject of the sentence to *neurotoxins*, shifting the meaning to indicate that the *neurotoxins . . . can kill an Asian elephant*. It also, however, changes the pronoun to *it*. In this construction, the singular pronoun *it* cannot correctly refer to plural *neurotoxins*. Eliminate choice (C) for the same error as (A).

11. **(A):** The GMAT often uses the awkward-sounding but grammatically correct construction *that in* in comparisons to throw the reader off the scent. Whenever you want to test a pronoun, grab the noun antecedent (in this case, *dialogue*) and put it in place of the pronoun; if that works, the pronoun is fine. The original sentence correctly conveys that Sorkin writes *dialogue that is wittier than* the dialogue *in most real-world interactions*.

    Choice (B) illogically compares *dialogue* to *interactions*. The intended comparison is between *dialogue* and *dialogue*. Eliminate this choice for a faulty comparison.

    Unlike choice (A), which uses the pronoun *that*, answer (C) uses the pronoun *it*. The word *that* can refer to a different "copy" of the same noun, but the word *it* must refer to the exact original copy. Thus, the meaning in answer (C) gets jumbled: *Aaron Sorkin is known for writing dialogue that is wittier than* the exact same dialogue *is in most real-world interactions*. However, dialogue written specifically for a TV script is, by definition, not actual real-world dialogue.

CHAPTER 8

Verbs

In This Chapter:

- Simple Tenses
- Make Tenses Reflect Meaning
- The Perfect Tenses: An Introduction
- Past Perfect: The Earlier Action
- Present Perfect: Bridging Past and Present
- *–ing* Modifiers: Follow the Main Verb
- Present to Future or Past to Conditional
- Active and Passive Voice

In this chapter, you will learn the major verb tenses that are tested on the GMAT, as well as how to make the meaning clear and logical when a complex sentence talks about a sequence of several events.

CHAPTER 8 Verbs

The **Verb Tense** of a working verb indicates *when* the action of the verb takes place. In addition, certain modifiers adopt the time frame of the main verb in the sentence.

In sentences with one action, verb tense is relatively easy. Knowing this, the GMAT tries to complicate sentences by incorporating more than one action. As a result, you will need to pay close attention to the *sequence* of actions in GMAT sentences. This sequence will be driven by meaning, so think about meaning as you work through this chapter.

The GMAT also sometimes tests something called **Voice** and something else called **Mood**, both of which you'll learn about in this chapter.

If you are a native speaker of American English, your ear may already be well-attuned to the right use of tense. Incorrect uses of tense (e.g., *He has gone to France last year*) will (correctly) sound funny to you; your instinctive correction (*He went to France last year*) will be correct. As you review this chapter, if you find that learning what these tenses are called interferes with your ability to recognize correct usage of the tense, feel free to ignore the names. You just need to know how to use the tenses on the test; you don't need to name them.

If you are not a native speaker of American English, however, you may need to learn these rules more consciously, in which case knowing the names can help you distinguish among the tenses. Patterns of verb tense vary drastically among languages, even those related to English. For example, *He is gone to France last year* is correct when translated word-for-word into French, German, and Italian, but it is never correct in English.

Simple Tenses

The three simple tenses express three basic times:

1. Simple present: Sandy PLAYS well with her friends.
2. Simple past: Sandy PLAYED well with her friends yesterday.
3. Simple future: Sandy WILL PLAY well with her friends tomorrow.

The **Simple Present** tense is used to express both events happening now and "eternal" states or frequent events. In the simple present example, the sentence does not mean that Sandy is playing right now, but rather that, as a general rule, Sandy plays well with her friends.

The GMAT typically prefers the simple tenses, unless the sentence clearly requires one of the more complex tenses discussed later in this chapter. The more complex tenses each have particular circumstances in which they can be used; if those circumstances do not exist, then don't use a complex tense.

Make Tenses Reflect Meaning

Sometimes, all the tenses in a sentence are the same, because all the actions take place in the same time frame:

Right: She WALKED to school in the morning and RAN home in the afternoon.

Right: She WALKS to school in the morning and RUNS home in the afternoon.

Right: She WILL WALK to school in the morning and RUN home in the afternoon.

In each sentence, the verbs are in the same tense: simple past in the first, simple present in the second, and simple future in the third. (Note that, in the third example, *run* is understood as *will run*; *will* is part of the root phrase and applies to both verbs.) In these examples, changing tense midstream would be confusing and incorrect.

However, in some sentences, the author clearly intends to discuss different time periods. The tense can and should change to reflect that intention:

Right: He IS thinner now because he WENT on a strict diet six months ago.

(IS = Simple Present; WENT = Simple Past)

The switch from present to past is logical given the clear indications of time (*now* and *six months ago*).

You could also switch the order of the sentence:

Right: Because he WENT on a strict diet six months ago, he IS thinner now.

Look what happens in this example:

Wrong: Because he IS STARTING a strict diet, he LOST weight.

This sentence can't be correct. Logically, if he LOST the weight in the past, then STARTING his diet in the present cannot be the cause of his weight loss.

The GMAT might add in distracting modifiers to hide this tense mismatch:

Wrong: Because he IS STARTING a strict diet and an exercise regimen that he BEGAN more than a year ago, he LOST weight.

Notice that the sentence does include another past tense verb, *began*. In addition to the existing meaning error, the introduction of *began* creates another. Logically, he can't currently be *starting . . . an exercise regimen that he began more than a year ago*. Either he's starting it now or he started it more than a year ago.

The Perfect Tenses: An Introduction

The two most commonly tested complex tenses on the GMAT are the perfect tenses: past perfect and present perfect.

Past Perfect: The Earlier Action

If two actions in a sentence occurred at *different* times in the past, you can use the **Past Perfect** tense for the earlier action and simple past for the later action. The past perfect is the "past of the past."

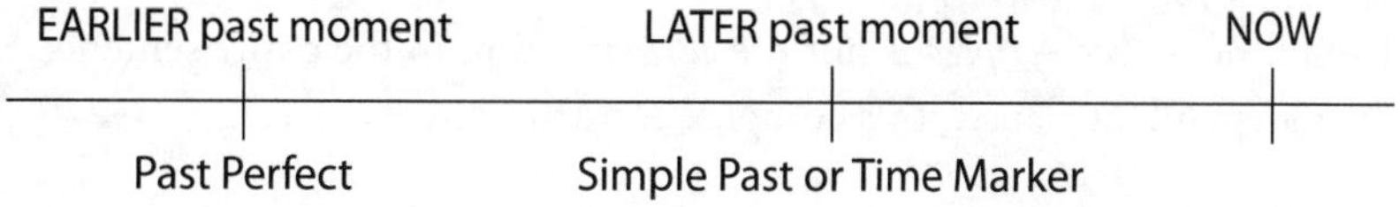

Here is an example:

Right: The film HAD STARTED by the time we ARRIVED at the theater.

The past perfect tense is formed as follows:

Past Perfect = HAD + Past Participle

In order to use past perfect for one event, the sentence must contain a second event that occurred later than the first event, but still in the past. One way to do this is via a verb in the simple past tense:

Right: The teacher THOUGHT that Jimmy HAD CHEATED on the exam.

The earlier past action, *had cheated*, pairs with a simple past action, *thought*: First, Jimmy took the exam (and possibly cheated on it!) and, later (but still in the past), the teacher began to suspect Jimmy.

Another option is to use a time marker. For example:

Right: BY 1970, four astronauts HAD WALKED on the moon.

In this sentence, the four astronauts walked on the moon sometime prior to 1970 (a past time marker). Common time markers include *by*, *before*, *after*, *until*, and *since*.

Even when the circumstances allow past perfect to be used, the sentence is not necessarily required to employ this more complex tense. Some sentences still make sense even when you stick with simple tenses:

Right: Laura LOCKED the deadbolt before she LEFT for work.

The word *before* indicates the sequence of events clearly; using past perfect is not necessary to convey the proper meaning. When the meaning of a sentence is already clear, the correct answer may or may not use past perfect to indicate an earlier action. In this case, do not cross off answers that use simple past. Instead, look for a different split to help you decide which answer to choose.

On hard questions, the GMAT may write a complicated sentence in which the past perfect verb is not the earliest action in the sentence—but it is still used correctly:

Right: The band U2 WAS just one of many new groups on the rock music scene in the early 1980s, but less than 10 years later, U2 HAD fully ECLIPSED its early rivals in the pantheon of popular music.

The first independent clause uses simple past (*was*). The second independent clause (after the word *but*) contains a time marker (*10 years later*) and then mentions another action (*had eclipsed*) that occurs before that time marker. Even though *had eclipsed* is not the *earliest* action in the entire sentence, it is the earlier of the two actions in its independent clause. This complex construction is correct.

Present Perfect: Bridging Past and Present

The **Present Perfect** tense is used for actions that started in the past but continue into the present or remain true. The present perfect tense effectively has one foot in the past and one foot in the present:

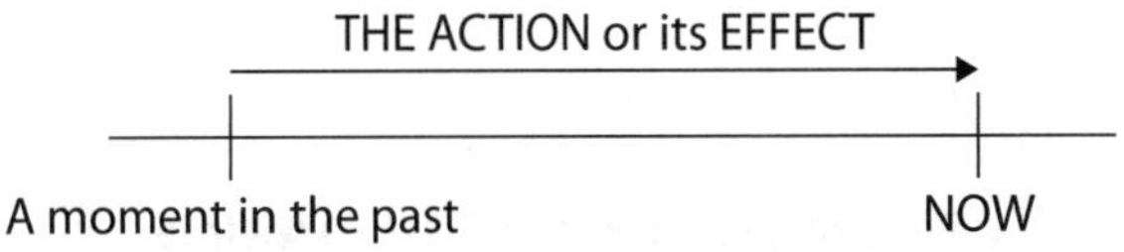

Consider this example:

Right: The Millers HAVE LIVED in a hut for three days.

The Millers began living in the hut three days ago and they are still living in that hut. In comparison, a sentence in the simple past conveys a different meaning:

Right: The Millers LIVED in a hut for three days.

At some point in the past, the Millers lived in a hut, but they no longer live in the hut now. How long ago did they live in the hut? The sentence doesn't tell you; it might have been a week ago or five years ago.

The present perfect tense is formed as follows:

Present Perfect = HAVE/HAS + Past Participle

For regular verbs such as *walk* or *live*, the past participle is the *–ed* form of the verb: *walked, lived.* Irregular verbs, such as *go* or *see*, have unique past participles (*gone, seen*). If you are a native English speaker, you likely already know the irregular forms. Otherwise, study the list of irregular past participles in the Glossary at the end of this guide.

Here are some examples of actions in the present perfect tense:

Right: This country HAS ENFORCED strict immigration laws for 30 years.

Right: They HAVE KNOWN each other since 1987.

Each example involves an action that began in the past and continues into the present. This country enforced strict immigration laws in the past and still enforces them today. They knew each other in the past and still know each other today. In each case, the idea of a continuing action is reinforced by a time phrase, such as *for 30 years* or *since 1987*, that states how long the action has been occurring (*enforced . . . for 30 years*) or for how long the information has been true (*have known . . . since 1987*).

Sometimes, the present perfect tense means that the action is definitely over, but its *effect* is still relevant to the present moment. For example:

Right: The child HAS DRAWN a square in the sand.

In this example, the child is no longer in the act of drawing a square. However, the square is still there.

Right: The child DREW a square in the sand, but the ocean ERASED it.

Right: The child DREW a square in the sand, but the ocean HAS ERASED it.

Wrong: The child HAS DRAWN a square in the sand, but the ocean HAS ERASED it.

The third example is incorrect because using the same tense for both actions implies that they took place at the same time. Logically, though, the ocean must have erased the square after it was drawn; the two events could not have happened simultaneously.

When using the word *since* as a time marker (since a certain time), use the present perfect to indicate an action or effect that continues to the present time:

Wrong: Since 1986, no one BROKE that world record.

Wrong: Since 1986, no one BREAKS that world record.

Right: Since 1986, no one HAS BROKEN that world record.

(Note: The word *since* can also mean *because*—in that case, it doesn't have an effect on the verb tense used in the sentence.)

Like *since*, the constructions *within the past . . .* or *in the last . . .* (such as *within the past five minutes* or *in the last 10 days*) also cross into the present, so use the present perfect with these terms. In contrast, a time phrase that does *not* cross over into the present (*last month, in 2007,* etc.) should not be used with the present perfect. Use the simple past instead:

Wrong: Veronica HAS TRAVELED all over the world in 2007.

Right: Veronica TRAVELED all over the world in 2007.

You could also write *Veronica has traveled all over the world* and omit any specific time reference. In this case, you are saying that it is still true today that *Veronica has traveled all over the world.*

Finally, the present perfect can be used in certain circumstances to clarify an ambiguous sequence in time. For example, the word *when* can mean either "at the same time" or "after." The use of present perfect eliminates any ambiguity. Consider these examples:

Right: The alarm WILL RING *when* the clock STRIKES 12. (no present perfect)

= The alarm will ring at the same time that the clock strikes 12.

Right: The company WILL REIMBURSE you *when* you HAVE SUBMITTED your expense report. (present perfect)

= The company will reimburse you after you submit the report.

–ing Modifiers: Follow the Main Verb

If you haven't already studied the Modifiers chapter or if your recall of *comma –ing* modifiers is a bit shaky, you may wish to review that material before proceeding here.

Comma –ing modifiers adopt the tense of the main working verb to which they are attached. For example:

Right: Peering out of the window, Bran WATCHED his direwolf frolic on the lawn.

The main verb, *watched*, is in past tense. Bran is not currently *peering* out of the window; rather, he peered out of the window while he watched the direwolf. The modifier *peering* picks up the time frame of the main verb.

Here's another example:

Right: The manager WILL SIGN the contract tomorrow, barring any unforeseen disruptions.

Again, the *–ing* word picks up the tense of the main verb. If any unforeseen disruptions occur *in the future*—between now and when the manager plans to sign the contract—then she might not sign after all.

Present to Future or Past to Conditional

Have you learned about **Conditional** in the past but felt confused about this tense? It turns out that there are two different—but overlapping—things that are called *conditional* (and neither one is technically a tense!).

One of these is the **Conditional Mood**. One way it is used is to talk about the future from the past. First, consider this sentence that talks about the future from the present:

Right: The scientist ANNOUNCES that the supercollider WILL PROVIDE new insights into the workings of the universe.

That example pairs present tense with future tense, a common construction. But what if the scientist made this announcement yesterday? Then, the sentence would look like this:

Right: The scientist ANNOUNCED that the supercollider WOULD PROVIDE new insights into the workings of the universe.

The scientist is talking about the future from the past. The conditional mood is formed by combining *would* with the base form of a verb: *would provide*. In the given sentence, the construction is used to express the future from the point of view of the past: At the point that the scientist made the announcement (in the past), new insights were expected to be provided at some time in the future.

The typical sequences for these types of sentences are either Present + Future or Past + Conditional:

Right: The scientist BELIEVES (Present) that the machine WILL BE (Future) wonderful.

Wrong: The scientist BELIEVES (Present) that the machine WOULD BE (Conditional) wonderful.

Right: The scientist BELIEVED (Past) that the machine WOULD BE (Conditional) wonderful.

Wrong: The scientist BELIEVED (Past) that the machine WILL BE (Future) wonderful.

The other usage you'll see for the term *conditional* is when writing conditional sentences, most commonly constructed in **If–Then** form: *If* you meet a certain condition, *then* some result will follow. For example, if you practice guitar chords daily, then you will become better at finger placement on the fretboard.

Some If–Then sentences will use the conditional mood in the sentence and some will not. This example uses the conditional: If you practiced guitar daily, you would be able to play the major chords by now.

You can learn more about both conditional sentences and conditional mood in the advanced materials located online in Atlas.

Verbs and Parallelism

One more thing. Remember learning about parallelism a few chapters ago? Let's make the supercollider sentence even more complicated:

> The scientist ANNOUNCED that the supercollider WAS ready, that it HAD not COST too much to build, and that it WOULD PROVIDE new insights into the workings of the universe.

The sentence uses multiple tenses in its *X, Y, and Z* list:

The scientist announced that...

...*the supercollider WAS ready.* (simple past)

...*it HAD not COST too much to build.* (past perfect)

...*it WOULD PROVIDE new insights.* (conditional mood)

A sentence can make multiple different verb tenses parallel, as long as each verb tense is appropriate for the meaning of that part of the sentence. Also note that all of the tenses have to pair appropriately with the starting tense in the root phrase, *announced*. The cost was incurred before the scientist *announced* anything, so the past perfect *had (not) cost* is appropriate. The prediction that it *would provide new insights* is an instance of future from the past, so the conditional mood is the right pairing.

Active and Passive Voice

Verbs are written in either **Active Voice** or **Passive Voice**. In the active voice, the subject of the sentence performs the action. In the passive voice, the subject of the sentence has an action performed on it by someone or something else. For example:

Active:	The hungry students ATE the pizza.
Passive:	The pizza WAS EATEN by the hungry students.

The passive voice is formed with a form of the verb *to be* (in this case, *was*), followed by the past participle (*eaten*).

Though passive voice has a reputation for sounding awkward, it is a valid construction:

Passive:	It HAS BEEN DECIDED by Jason that he will not attend college.
Active:	Jason HAS DECIDED not to attend college.

The active version may sound better to you than the passive one, but both are correct. People often think that the passive voice is inherently wrong, and the GMAT sometimes exploits this myth by making the awkward, passive answer *correct*. Meanwhile, the problem will also offer an answer in the active voice that sounds great but has a subtle error elsewhere. Consider the following example:

Passive:	It HAS BEEN DECIDED by Jason that he will not attend college next fall.
Active:	Jason HAS DECIDED next fall not to attend college.

The active voice example says that Jason *decided next fall*. This is illogical! He either already *decided* (in the past) or he *will decide next fall* (in the future). Meanwhile, the passive sentence is correct, even though it sounds awkward.

You could fix the active version this way: *Jason has decided not to attend college next fall*. But the GMAT might not offer you this option because it's too easy. The passive version shown earlier is a better trap—people will cross it off because it sounds clunkier than active voice, completely missing the error in the active version.

Don't be biased against the passive. Check what else is going on in the sentence. Sometimes, you're forced to have the sentence in passive voice simply due to the placement of the underline.

As a final note, you do not have to make active or passive voice parallel throughout a sentence. For example:

Right: The shuttle launch TOOK place flawlessly and WAS SEEN on television.

Both parallel elements work with the root phrase of the sentence: *The shuttle launch took place* and *the shuttle launch was seen on television.*

Problem Set

Problems 1–6 contain one or more underlined sections. If an underlined section contains no errors, mark it as CORRECT. Otherwise, write down a correct version of the underlined section. For extra credit, explain your decisions with respect to the tense, mood, and voice of the relevant verbs.

1. Mozart, who died in 1791, has lived in Salzburg for most of his life.

simple past

lived

2. The local government has built the school that was destroyed by the earthquake.

had built

or built

3. The editor of our local newspaper, who has earned much acclaim in her long career, has been awarded a Pulitzer Prize yesterday.

was

4. She already woke up when the phone rang.

had woken up   Past perfect

5. In the Fischer–Tropsch process, which developed in Germany by Franz Fischer and Hans Tropsch, coal is converted into a liquid fuel similar to petroleum.

Correct

6. Last Monday, Mary realized that she will have to spend all of that night rewriting her application because she did not back up her files.

would have

Problems 7–9 are multiple choice with one correct answer. As on the real GMAT, answer (A) repeats the original sentence. Unlike the real GMAT, though, these problems have only three answer choices.

7. By the end of the Apollo program, 12 Americans <u>had walked on the moon, but no one will have</u> reached the moon's surface since then.

    (A) had walked on the moon, but no one will have

    (B) walked on the moon, and no one has

    (C) had walked on the moon, though no one has

8. Water <u>freezes if it were</u> cooled to zero degrees Celsius.

    (A) freezes if it were

    (B) would freeze if it was

    (C) freezes if

9. <u>The art dealer, whose collection included works by a number of master painters, could not bring himself to part with his prized piece when he was asked to sell a painting by Picasso.</u>

    (A) The art dealer, whose collection included works by a number of master painters, could not bring himself to part with his prized piece when he was asked to sell a painting by Picasso.

    (B) When the art dealer was asked to sell his favorite Picasso painting, a prized piece from his collection of works by a number of master painters, he could not bring himself to do so.

    (C) When the art dealer has been asked to sell his favorite Picasso painting, which was a prized piece from his collection of works by a number of master painters, he could not bring himself to do so.

8

Solutions

1. Mozart, who died in 1791, has lived in Salzburg for most of his life.

   Has lived (present perfect tense) should be *lived* (simple past tense) or possibly *had lived* (past perfect). One possible reason to use the present perfect (*has lived*) is to indicate that an action or state of affairs is still in progress. Mozart is dead, so this reason does not apply here.

   The other possible reason to use the present perfect is to indicate that an action, though completed in the past, still has some continuing effect on the subject of the verb. Since Mozart is dead, this reason does not apply either.

   Since neither reason for using the present perfect applies to this sentence, use the simple past. There is no real need to use the past perfect (*had lived*), because the sequence of past events (Mozart's life and death) is obvious. Moreover, the actions are not contrasted (e.g., if he *lived* one place but *died* somewhere else). That said, to emphasize the sequence of events, you could choose to use the past perfect in this sentence:

Correction:	Mozart, who died in 1791, lived in Salzburg for most of his life.
OR	Mozart, who died in 1791, had lived in Salzburg for most of his life.

2. The local government has built the school that was destroyed by the earthquake.

   Has built (present perfect tense) should be *built* (simple past tense) OR *had built* (past perfect). Sometimes, the present perfect is used to indicate that an action or state of affairs is still in progress. However, the original process of building the school cannot be continuing now, because the school was destroyed by the earthquake. The government might be rebuilding the school now, but that is not the same as building the school. The other possible reason to use the present perfect is to indicate that an action, though completed in the past, still has some continuing effect on the subject and object of the verb. The effects of the action of building were essentially wiped out by the earthquake, because the earthquake destroyed the school. Since neither possible reason for using the present perfect applies to this sentence, you cannot use the present perfect.

   Either the simple past or the past perfect is possible. In the simple past version, the writer's mental time frame is concurrent with *built*. The following clause (*that was destroyed by the earthquake*) just serves to identify the school, and the writer might go on to discuss the building process. However, the past perfect emphasizes the sequence of events more than the simple past does. In the past perfect version, the writer's mental time frame is concurrent with *was destroyed*. The use of *had built* indicates that the writer is dipping back in time for only a moment to the building process. In fact, the writer might proceed to write more about the destruction (perhaps the consequences of shoddy construction methods). For example:

Correction:	The local government built the school that was destroyed by the earthquake.
OR	The local government had built the school that was destroyed by the earthquake.

3. The editor of our local newspaper, who has earned much acclaim in her long career, has been awarded a Pulitzer Prize yesterday.

   Has been awarded (present perfect tense) should be *was awarded* (simple past tense). The verb has to be in the simple past because you are told that the action occurred at a specific time in the past (*yesterday*):

   Correction: The editor of our local newspaper, who has earned much acclaim in her long career, was awarded a Pulitzer Prize yesterday.

4. She already woke up when the phone rang.

   Already woke up (simple past) should be *had already woken up* (past perfect). You need to use the past perfect here because the word *already* requires this use for a momentary action such as *wake up*, when placed prior to another past action. It would be fine to say *she was already awake when the phone rang*, because *was awake* is a state and thus takes up time. In that case, *already* would indicate that this state was in effect before the phone rang. However, when you use *already* with the simple past of a momentary action, you convey a present perfect meaning. As your spouse shakes you out of bed, you might say *I already woke up*, but in proper English, you should say *I HAVE already woken up*. In other words, the action is complete AND the effect (your wakefulness) continues to the present. In the sample sentence, since you want the subject's wakefulness to continue up through some point in the past (*when the phone rang*), you must use the past perfect of *wake up*:

   Correction: She had already woken up when the phone rang.

5. In the Fischer–Tropsch process, which developed in Germany by Franz Fischer and Hans Tropsch, coal is converted into a liquid fuel similar to petroleum.

   Developed (active voice) should be *was developed* (passive voice). The passive voice is required because the people who developed the process appear in the non-underlined phrase *by Franz Fischer and Hans Tropsch.*

   Is converted (passive voice) is correct. The passive voice is required because unnamed agent(s), rather than the coal itself, cause the conversion of the coal into a liquid fuel. Supposing that the whole sentence were underlined and that you were therefore free to rewrite it completely, should you change it into the active voice? No, because the passive voice is ideally suited to the purposes of this sentence. The author wants to tell you about the Fischer–Tropsch process, not to list the various parties who happen to use that process. It is therefore fitting for the words *Fischer–Tropsch process* to be in the subject position. To put *Fischer–Tropsch* in the subject position, the verb *to develop* must be in the passive voice:

   Correction: In the Fischer–Tropsch process, which was developed in Germany by Franz Fischer and Hans Tropsch, coal is converted into a liquid fuel similar to petroleum.

6. Last Monday, Mary realized that she will have to spend all of that night rewriting her application because she did not back up her files.

   Will have (simple future tense) should be *would have* (conditional tense). Mary made her realization on Monday. At that time, her sleepless night spent rewriting the application was in the future. However, last Monday night is now in the past. An action that was in the future (relative to the time of the main verb, *realized*), but is now in the past, must be rendered in the conditional tense. This tense is formed by replacing *will* with *would*.

   Did not back up (simple past tense) should be *had not backed up* (past perfect tense). The past perfect tense is required here because Mary's failure to back up her files must logically have occurred *before* Mary became aware of (*realized*) this failure:

   Correction: Last Monday, Mary realized that she would have to spend all of that night rewriting her application because she had not backed up her files.

7. **(C):** The original sentence contains two time markers: *by the end* and *since then*. The time marker *by the end of the Apollo program* indicates that the action in the main clause (12 Americans walking on the moon) occurred in the past prior to *the end of the Apollo program*. Thus, the proper tense is the past perfect *had walked*. The original sentence is correct on this point, but the simple past tense *walked* in answer choice (B) is incorrect.

   The time marker *since then* indicates an action that started in the past but continues (or is still true) in the present. The proper tense for the last verb is the present perfect *has reached*. Choice (A) incorrectly uses *will have reached*.

   Finally, there is a choice of conjunction after the comma. The meaning of the sentence requires a contrast. Twelve Americans walked on the moon previously; however, no one has since then. *But* or *though* has the correct meaning; *and* is incorrect.

8. **(C):** The original sentence is an if–then statement: If water becomes cold enough, then it *would freeze* (conditional) or *freezes* (present tense used to convey a general truth or a rule). Reordering the sequence of the verbs to an if–then order can help you check the verb sequence.

   Choice (A) says that if *it were cooled to zero degrees*, then *water freezes*. The hypothetical *were cooled* should be followed by the hypothetical *would freeze*, so the present tense *freezes* is incorrect.

   Choice (B) says that if *it was cooled to zero degrees*, then *water would freeze*. The past tense *was cooled* is factual, not hypothetical, so the logical outcome is that the *water froze* or the *water did freeze* in the simple past tense.

   Choice (C) says that if *cooled to zero degrees*, then *water freezes*. The first part implies the present tense (*if* it is *cooled*), and the second part uses the present tense *freezes*, both of which imply a general truth—a physical property of water.

9. **(B):** When the entire sentence is underlined, look for variations in meaning and sentence structure. The original sentence intends to say that the *art dealer . . . could not bring himself to part with his prized . . . painting by Picasso.*

   However, *when he was asked to sell a painting by Picasso* could be interpreted as *Picasso asked the dealer to sell a painting*. This subtle ambiguity is difficult to spot; notice the split between *Picasso painting* in (B) and (C) and *by Picasso* in (A). Eliminate (A) for ambiguous meaning.

   Compare answers (B) and (C) to spot the differences. They use different tenses for the first verb: *was asked* vs. *has been asked.* Either might be okay if that were the only clause, but only answer (B) works with the sequence of events in the rest of the sentence. Choice (C) says *When he has been asked to sell, . . . he could not bring himself to do so.* Since *has been asked* is in the present perfect, the second action (which takes place later in time) can't be in the past. For example, this would work: *When he has been asked to sell, . . . he has not been able to bring himself to do so.*

CHAPTER 9

Idioms

In This Chapter:

- Spot–Extract–Replace
- Idiom List

In this chapter, you'll learn how to spot some of the more common idioms tested on the GMAT. You will also learn a technique to help you identify the correct idiom that should be used in the sentence.

CHAPTER 9 Idioms

Idioms are expressions that have unique forms. There is no hard and fast rule for determining the form of an idiom; rather, it is just a form that you know or memorize. For example, *They tried to reach the summit and succeeded in doing so* is correct, but *They tried in reaching the summit and succeeded to do so* is not correct. The verb *to try* is followed by an infinitive, but the verb *to succeed* is followed by *in* and an *–ing* form of the verb. Why? There is no great reason. *Try to do* and *succeed in doing* are the accepted English idioms.

Many idioms are about meaning, at heart, so you can often use meaning to help you remember the proper form. It wouldn't make sense to say *both X or Y*, since the word *both* signals that you want to reference the two things together. It makes logical sense that the correct idiom is *both X and Y*.

If you are a native English speaker, most idiomatic expressions are already wired into your brain from years of hearing and speaking English. For non-native speakers, the task is more difficult. However, the GMAT does tend to focus on certain common idioms. Review the common idiom list in this chapter and memorize any that you do not know. If you want an especially high Verbal GMAT score, you can also spend some time learning some of the expressions listed in the Idioms appendix (Appendix A) of this guide (though there are enough that you may not want to try to memorize them all).

Spot–Extract–Replace

Your ear is your most valuable weapon as you try to figure out the proper form of an idiom. Here's how to use your ear well:

(A) Some historians attribute the eventual development of accurate methods for measuring longitude as the monetary prizes offered by various governments.

(B) Some historians attribute the eventual development of accurate methods for measuring longitude to the monetary prizes offered by various governments.

1. SPOT the suspect idiomatic expression. Compare answer choices to find the splits. In the choices above, the words that vary are *as* and *to*. What pairs with *as* or *to*? In this case, the idiom revolves around the use of the verb *attribute*.

2. EXTRACT the various forms of the idiom and put them into simpler sentences that you can easily compare. You can delete words, such as extraneous modifiers, or you can make up brand-new sentences. Either way, strip the sentence to a simple example:

   (A) Historians attribute the development AS the prizes.

   (B) Historians attribute the development TO the prizes.

   If you know this idiom, then the correct version will sound better to your ear. *Attribute TO* is the correct idiom. If neither version sounds better, then ignore this split and go find something else (or guess and move on).

3. REPLACE the corrected idiom in the sentence and confirm that it works:

   (B) Some historians attribute the eventual development of accurate methods for measuring longitude TO the monetary prizes offered by various governments.

The choice that your ear preferred should work in the entire GMAT sentence. If it does not work, either check your work or set aside this issue and move forward with something else.

Idiom List

The English language includes thousands of idioms. You can't possibly memorize them all, so concentrate on those that are tested most frequently. You've already seen many of the most common idioms earlier in this guide, particularly in the Parallelism and Comparisons chapters. The following list contains the next most commonly tested idioms, as seen on official GMAT test questions. The Idioms appendix contains additional idioms that have appeared on real questions but that are less common than the ones in this chapter.

Label	**Definition**
RIGHT:	Expressions that the GMAT considers correct
SUSPECT:	*Expressions that the GMAT seems to avoid if possible. These expressions are sometimes grammatically correct, but they may be wordy, controversial, or simply less preferred than other forms.*
WRONG:	*Expressions that the GMAT considers incorrect*

ABILITY

RIGHT: I value my ABILITY TO SING.

WRONG: *I value my ABILITY OF SINGING.*
I value my ABILITY FOR SINGING.
I value the ABILITY FOR me TO SING.

ALLOW

RIGHT: The holiday ALLOWS Maria TO WATCH the movie today. (permits an action)
Maria WAS ALLOWED TO WATCH the movie.
The demolition of the old building ALLOWS FOR new construction. (permits the existence of)

WRONG: *The holiday ALLOWED FOR Maria TO WATCH the movie.*
The holiday ALLOWED Maria the WATCHING OF the movie.
The holiday ALLOWS THAT homework BE done (or *CAN BE done*).
Homework is ALLOWED FOR DOING BY Maria.
The ALLOWING OF shopping TO DO (or *TO BE DONE*).

ALTHOUGH See BUT.

AND

RIGHT:

We are concerned about the forests AND the oceans.

We are concerned about the forests, the oceans, AND the mountains.

The company is profitable, AND the CEO is famous. (Note the comma before AND.)

SUSPECT:

We are concerned about the forests AND ALSO the oceans.

WRONG:

We are concerned about the forests, ALSO the oceans.

AS

RIGHT:

AS I walked, I became more nervous. (during)

AS I had already paid, I was unconcerned. (because, since)

AS we did last year, we will win this year. (in the same way)

JUST AS we did last year, we will win this year. (in the same way)

AS the president of the company, she works hard. (in the role of)

AS a child, I delivered newspapers. (in the stage of being)

My first job was an apprenticeship AS a sketch artist. (in the role of)

AS PART OF the arrangement, he received severance.

SUSPECT:

AS A PART OF the arrangement, he received severance. (Don't include the word *A*.)

WRONG:

My first job was an apprenticeship OF a sketch artist.

The students worked AS a sketch artist. (The nouns must agree in number.)

WHILE BEING a child, I delivered newspapers.

AS BEING a child, I delivered newspapers.

WHILE IN childhood, I delivered newspapers.

AS...AS

RIGHT:

Cheese is AS great AS people say.
Cheese is NOT AS great AS people say.
We have AS MANY apples AS need to be cooked.
We have THREE TIMES AS MANY pears AS you.
We have AT LEAST AS MANY apples AS you.
We have 10 apples, ABOUT AS MANY AS we picked yesterday.
His knowledge springs AS MUCH from experience AS from schooling.
His knowledge springs NOT SO MUCH from experience AS from schooling.
He wins frequently, AS MUCH because he plays SO hard AS because he cheats.

SUSPECT:

We have AS MANY apples AS OR MORE apples THAN you.
We have AS MANY apples AS THERE need to be cooked.

WRONG:

Cheese is SO great AS people say.
Cheese is NOT SO great AS people say.
Cheese is SO great THAT people say.
Cheese is AS great THAT people say.
We have AS MANY apples THAN you.
We have SO MANY apples AS you.
We have AS MANY OR MORE apples THAN you.
We have THREE TIMES AS MANY MORE pears AS you.
We have 10 apples, ABOUT EQUIVALENT TO what we picked yesterday.
His knowledge springs NOT from experience AS from schooling.

BECAUSE

RIGHT:

BECAUSE the sun shines, plants grow.
Plants grow BECAUSE the sun shines.
BECAUSE OF the sun, plants grow.
BY SHINING, the sun makes plants grow.
Plants grow, FOR the sun shines. (grammatically correct but very formal)

SUSPECT:

Plants grow BECAUSE OF the sun, which shines.
Plants are amazing IN THAT they grow in the sun. (correct but wordy)
The growth of plants IS EXPLAINED BY THE FACT THAT the sun shines. (correct but wordy)

WRONG: *Plants grow BECAUSE OF the sun SHINING.*
Plants grow AS A RESULT OF the sun SHINING.
BECAUSE OF SHINING, the sun makes plants grow.
ON ACCOUNT OF SHINING or ITS SHINING, the sun makes plants grow.
BECAUSE the sun shines IS the REASON that plants grow.
The ABILITY OF plants TO grow IS BECAUSE the sun shines.
BEING THAT the sun shines, plants grow.
The growth of plants IS EXPLAINED BECAUSE OF the shining of the sun.
The growth of plants IS EXPLAINED BECAUSE the sun shines.

BEING

RIGHT: BEING infected does not make you sick.
The judges saw the horses BEING led to the stables.

SUSPECT: *BEING an advocate of reform, I would like to make a different proposal.*

Note: The word BEING is often wordy or awkward. However, having caught on to the "BEING is wrong" shortcut, the GMAT problem writers have created a few problems that force you to choose BEING. It's true that BEING appears in many more wrong answers than right ones; however, the word can be used correctly as a gerund or as a participle.

BELIEVE

RIGHT: She BELIEVES THAT Gary IS right.
She BELIEVES Gary TO BE right.
IT IS BELIEVED THAT Gary IS right.
Gary IS BELIEVED TO BE right.

SUSPECT: *Gary IS BELIEVED BY her TO BE right.*

BOTH...AND

RIGHT: She was interested BOTH in plants AND in animals.
She was interested in BOTH plants AND animals.

WRONG: *She was interested BOTH in plants AND animals.*
She was interested BOTH in plants AS WELL AS in animals.
She was interested BOTH in plants BUT ALSO in animals.

BUT

RIGHT:

I STUDY hard BUT TAKE breaks.
I STUDY hard, BUT I TAKE breaks.
ALTHOUGH I TAKE frequent naps, I STUDY effectively.
DESPITE TAKING frequent naps, I STUDY effectively.
I TAKE frequent naps, YET I STUDY effectively.

SUSPECT:

DESPITE THE FACT THAT I TAKE frequent naps, I STUDY effectively.
ALTHOUGH a frequent napper, I STUDY effectively. (*ALTHOUGH* should generally be followed by a clause.)

WRONG:

I STUDY effectively ALTHOUGH TAKING frequent naps.
ALTHOUGH I TAKE frequent naps, YET I STUDY effectively.
ALTHOUGH I TAKE frequent naps, AND I STUDY effectively.
DESPITE TAKING frequent naps, YET I STUDY effectively.

CAN

RIGHT:

The manager CAN RUN the plant.
The plant CAN CAUSE damage.
The manager IS CAPABLE OF RUNNING the plant.

SUSPECT:

It is POSSIBLE FOR the plant TO CAUSE damage.
The plant POSSIBLY CAUSES damage.

WRONG:

The manager HAS THE CAPABILITY OF RUNNING the plant.
The manager HAS THE ABILITY OF RUNNING the plant.
The plant HAS THE POSSIBILITY OF CAUSING damage.

CONSIDER

9

RIGHT:

I CONSIDER her a friend.
I CONSIDER her intelligent.
(Note: You can switch the order of the two objects; if one is long, place it second, as in the next example.)
I CONSIDER illegal the law passed last week by the new regime.
The law IS CONSIDERED illegal.

SUSPECT: *The judge CONSIDERS the law TO BE illegal.*

....

WRONG: *The judge CONSIDERS the law AS illegal* (or *AS BEING illegal*).
The judge CONSIDERS the law SHOULD BE illegal.
The judge CONSIDERS the law AS IF IT WERE illegal.

....

EITHER...OR

RIGHT: I will take EITHER the subway OR the bus.

....

WRONG: *I will take EITHER the subway AND the bus.*

EXPECT

RIGHT: We EXPECT the price TO FALL.
The price IS EXPECTED TO FALL.
We EXPECT THAT the price WILL FALL.
IT IS EXPECTED THAT the price WILL FALL.
Inflation rose more than we EXPECTED.
There IS an EXPECTATION THAT the price will fall.

....

SUSPECT: *There IS an expectation the price WILL FALL.*
There IS an expectation OF the price FALLING.

....

WRONG: *The price IS EXPECTED FOR IT TO FALL.*
IT IS EXPECTED THAT the price SHOULD FALL.

FOR (conjunction) See BECAUSE.

FROM...TO

RIGHT: The price fell FROM 10 euros TO 3 euros.
The price fell TO 3 euros FROM 10 euros.

....

WRONG: *The price fell FROM 10 euros DOWN TO 3 euros.*
The price rose FROM 3 euros UP TO 10 euros.

IN ORDER TO

RIGHT: She drank coffee IN ORDER TO STAY awake.
She drank coffee TO STAY awake. (Infinitive TO STAY indicates purpose.)

SUSPECT: *She drank coffee IN ORDER THAT* (or *SO THAT*) *she MIGHT STAY awake.*
She drank coffee SO AS TO STAY awake.

WRONG: *She drank coffee FOR STAYING awake.*
Coffee was drunk by her TO STAY awake (or *IN ORDER TO STAY awake*). (The subject COFFEE is not trying TO STAY awake.)

INDICATE

RIGHT: A report INDICATES THAT unique bacteria LIVE on our skin.

SUSPECT: *A report IS INDICATIVE OF the presence of unique bacteria on our skin.*

WRONG: *A report INDICATES unique bacteria LIVE on our skin.* (*THAT* is needed.)
A report IS INDICATIVE THAT unique bacteria LIVE on our skin.
A report INDICATES unique bacteria AS present on our skin.
A report INDICATES unique bacteria TO LIVE on our skin.

INSTEAD OF See RATHER THAN.

LIKE See also SUCH AS.

RIGHT: LIKE his sister, Matt drives fast cars. (Both drive fast cars.)
Matt drives fast cars LIKE his sister's.
(Both drive similar cars; or, less optimally, one of the cars he drives is his sister's.)

WRONG: *Matt drives fast cars LIKE his sister does.*
LIKE his sister, SO Matt drives fast cars.

NOT…BUT

RIGHT: She DID NOT EAT mangoes BUT ATE other kinds of fruit.
She DID NOT EAT mangoes BUT LIKED other kinds of fruit AND later BEGAN to like kiwis, too.
A tomato is NOT a vegetable BUT a fruit.
A tomato is NOT a vegetable BUT RATHER a fruit.

WRONG: *She DID NOT EAT mangoes BUT other kinds of fruit.*

NOT ONLY...BUT ALSO

RIGHT: We wore NOT ONLY boots BUT ALSO sandals.
We wore NOT ONLY boots, BUT ALSO sandals. (The comma is optional.)
We wore NOT JUST boots BUT ALSO sandals.
We wore NOT ONLY boots BUT sandals.

SUSPECT: *We wore NOT ONLY boots BUT sandals AS WELL.*
We wore boots AND ALSO sandals.

WRONG: *We wore NOT ONLY boots AND ALSO sandals.*
We wore NOT ONLY boots BUT, AS WELL, sandals.

RATHER THAN

RIGHT: He wrote with pencils RATHER THAN with pens.

SUSPECT: *He wrote with pencils, BUT NOT pens.*

WRONG: *He wrote with pencils INSTEAD OF with pens.* (*OF with* is incorrect.)

SO...AS TO

SUSPECT: *The sauce was SO hot AS TO burn my mouth.*
Note: The GMAT has an inconsistent position on this idiom. At least one official explanation claims that this idiom is "incorrect" but provides no further explanation as to why. However, at least one official problem uses this idiom in a correct answer choice. Other authorities consider this idiom correct, and we agree. Nevertheless, you should be wary of its use.

WRONG: *The sauce had SUCH heat AS TO burn my mouth.*
The sauce had SO MUCH heat AS TO burn my mouth.

SO...THAT See also ENOUGH in Idioms appendix.

RIGHT: The book was SO SHORT THAT I could read it in one night.
The book was SHORT ENOUGH FOR me TO READ in one night.
Note: These two expressions have slightly different emphases, but it is unlikely that you will need to choose an answer solely on this basis.

SUSPECT: *The book was SO SHORT I could read it.* (*THAT* is preferred.)
The book was OF SUCH SHORTNESS THAT I could read it.
SUCH was the SHORTNESS of the book THAT I could read it.

WRONG: *The book had SO MUCH SHORTNESS THAT I could read it.*
The book was OF SUCH SHORTNESS, I could read it.
The book was SHORT TO SUCH A DEGREE AS TO ALLOW me to read it.

SO THAT

RIGHT: She gave money SO THAT the school could offer scholarships. (purpose)

SUSPECT: *She gave money, SO the school was grateful.* (result)

WRONG: *She gave money SO the school could offer scholarships.*

SUCH AS

RIGHT: Matt drives fast cars, SUCH AS Ferraris. (introducing examples)
Matt enjoys driving SUCH cars AS Ferraris.
Matt enjoys intense activities, SUCH AS DRIVING fast cars.

SUSPECT: *Matt drives fast cars LIKE Ferraris.* (intended to be an example)
Note: The GMAT has backed off from claiming that *like* cannot introduce examples, but it is probable that the GMAT will continue to avoid using *like* with examples, because *like* typically means *similar to*.

WRONG: *Matt drives Ferraris AND THE LIKE.*
Matt drives Ferraris AND OTHER cars SUCH AS THESE.
Matt trains in many ways SUCH AS BY DRIVING on racetracks.
Matt enjoys intense activities, SUCH AS TO DRIVE fast cars.

THAN

9

RIGHT: His books are MORE impressive THAN those of other writers.
This paper is LESS impressive THAN that one.
This paper is NO LESS impressive THAN that one.
This newspaper cost 50 cents MORE THAN that one.
MORE THAN 250 newspapers are published here.
Sales are HIGHER this year THAN last year.

WRONG:	*His books are MORE impressive AS those of other writers.* *This paper is MORE impressive RATHER THAN that one.* *This paper is MORE impressive INSTEAD OF that one.* *This paper is NO LESS impressive AS that one.* *This paper is NONE THE LESS impressive THAN that one.* *This newspaper cost 50 cents AS MUCH AS that one.* *AS MANY AS OR MORE THAN 250 newspapers are published here.* *Sales are HIGHER this year OVER last year.*
UNLIKE	See also CONTRAST in Idioms appendix.
RIGHT:	UNLIKE the spiny anteater, the aardvark is docile.
WRONG:	*UNLIKE WITH the spiny anteater, the aardvark is docile.*
WHETHER	
RIGHT:	I do not know WHETHER I will go.
SUSPECT:	*I do not know WHETHER OR NOT I will go.*
WRONG:	*I do not know IF I will go.* (*IF* requires a consequence.)
WHETHER...OR	
RIGHT:	I decided to eat the food, WHETHER it was tasty OR NOT. WHETHER trash OR treasure, the recyclables must be picked up.
WRONG:	*WHETHER trash OR ALSO treasure, the recyclables must be picked up.* *WHETHER THEY BE trash OR treasure, the recyclables must go.*
YET	See BUT.

Problem Set

Problems 1–3 contain at least one idiom. Underline correct idioms and box incorrect idioms. For idioms that are split up, be sure to identify both parts. Evaluate each idiom using the Spot–Extract–Replace method.

1. The ring-tailed squirrel is more adept at surviving harsh winter conditions as its cousin, the golden-mantled squirrel, so that the golden-mantled squirrel typically lives in warmer climates.

2. It is expected that advances in the production of high-temperature superconductors should increase the viability of so-called "maglev" trains that float on magnetic fields.

3. Faced with an increase of natural disasters, such as floods and wildfires, many state governments have imposed significant taxes on their citizens in order for raising funds in advance of the next calamity.

Problems 4–6 each contain a pair of correct sentences with slight variations in idioms that result in big changes in meaning. Describe the difference in meaning between the two sentences.

4. The robber served a shortened prison sentence so that he could receive proper medical treatment.

   The robber served a shortened prison sentence, so he could receive proper medical treatment.

5. In an attempt to reach a favorable plea deal, the defense attorney argued passionately with his client.

   In an attempt to reach a favorable plea deal, the defense attorney argued passionately for his client.

6. The patient asked for the doctor when the patient arrived at the hospital.

   The patient asked about the doctor when the patient arrived at the hospital.

Problems 7–9 are multiple choice with one correct answer. As on the real GMAT, answer (A) repeats the original sentence. Unlike the real GMAT, though, these problems have only four answer choices.

7. These results indicate the health of the marsh's ecosystem has seriously declined.

   (A) indicate the health of the marsh's ecosystem has seriously declined

   (B) indicate that the health of the marsh's ecosystem has seriously declined

   (C) are indicative that the health of the marsh's ecosystem has seriously declined

   (D) seriously indicate a decline in the health of the marsh's ecosystem

8. The conflict started both because of ethnic tensions as well as because of economic dislocations.

   (A) both because of ethnic tensions as well as

   (B) because of both ethnic tensions and

   (C) not because of ethnic tensions but also

   (D) as a result of ethnic tensions and worsened

9. Unlike humans and guinea pigs, most mammals have the ability of synthesizing vitamin C from glucose, a simple sugar.

   (A) Unlike humans and guinea pigs, most mammals have the ability of synthesizing vitamin C from glucose, a simple sugar.

   (B) Unlike humans and guinea pigs, most mammals have the ability for synthesis of vitamin C from glucose, a simple sugar.

   (C) Most mammals, unlike humans and guinea pigs, have the ability to synthesize vitamin C from glucose, a simple sugar.

   (D) Most mammals have the ability to synthesize vitamin C from glucose, a simple sugar, unlike humans and guinea pigs.

Solutions

1. Two-part idioms are in bold to show which two parts are connected.

   The ring-tailed squirrel is **more** adept at surviving harsh winter conditions **as** its cousin, the golden-mantled squirrel, so that the golden-mantled squirrel typically lives in warmer climates.

   Corrected sentence: The ring-tailed squirrel is **more** adept at surviving harsh winter conditions **than** its cousin, the golden-mantled squirrel, so the golden-mantled squirrel typically lives in warmer climates.

   The sentence contains two separate idioms. The correct comparison idiom is *more... than*; *more... as* is incorrect.

   The idiom *so that* indicates purpose, similar to *in order to*. For example, *I lift weights so that I can gain muscle*. In the sentence above, *so* is used as a synonym for *therefore* to convey a conclusion; the word *that* should be removed.

2. It is **expected that** advances in the production of high-temperature superconductors **should** increase the viability of so-called "maglev" trains that float on magnetic fields.

   Corrected sentence: It is **expected that** advances in the production of high-temperature superconductors **will** increase the viability of so-called "maglev" trains that float on magnetic fields.

   Expected that indicates what might or will happen. *Should*, on the other hand, indicates what ought to happen. The proper idiom is *expected that... will*.

3. Faced with an increase of natural disasters, such as floods and wildfires, many state governments have **imposed** significant taxes **on** their citizens in order for raising funds in advance of the next calamity.

   Corrected sentence: Faced with an increase in natural disasters, such as floods and wildfires, many state governments have imposed significant taxes on their citizens in order to raise funds in advance of the next calamity.

   The proper idiom is *increase in*.

   In order must be followed by an infinitive verb (*to X*) at some point in the sentence: *in order to raise*. The verb need not follow immediately—consider the following sentence:

   In order for students to succeed, they must study hard.

   Thus, *in order* can be followed by *for*, but what follows *for* must be the subject for the subsequent infinitive verb. This sentence lacks an infinitive verb altogether.

4. In the first sentence, *so that* indicates purpose. *The robber served a shortened prison sentence* in order to *receive proper medical treatment*.

   In the second sentence, *so* preceded by a comma indicates a consequence: Because *the robber served a shortened prison sentence*, he was able to *receive proper medical treatment*. In this case, *the shortened sentence* enabled the robber to *receive proper medical treatment*, but he didn't serve a shortened sentence for that specific purpose.

5. In the first sentence, the *defense attorney* argues *with his client*; the argument is taking place between these two people.

   The second sentence changes *with* to *for*. To argue *for* someone is to argue in that person's defense. Here, the *defense attorney* is arguing in support of his client, and that argument is taking place with someone else (perhaps the prosecutor or the judge).

6. The phrase *asked for* means to request someone's presence. In the first sentence, *the patient* requested to be seen by the doctor.

   In contrast, the phrase a*sked about* in the second sentence means that *the patient* wanted to know more information *about the doctor*.

7. **(B):** The original sentence incorrectly connects two independent clauses without the word *that*. Eliminate answer (A) for faulty sentence structure.

   In answer choice (C), *are indicative* should be followed by *of*.

   Answer choice (D) incorrectly places the adverb *seriously*. It is intended to modify how much the *health of the marsh's ecosystem has declined*. Its placement in this sentence incorrectly modifies *indicate*.

   Answer choice (B) correctly uses the subject–verb–that–subject–verb sentence structure and properly places *seriously* to modify how much the *health of the marsh's ecosystem has declined*.

8. **(D):** The original sentence contains an idiom error. *Both... as well as* is incorrect; the correct idiom is *both X and Y*.

   In answer choice (B), the idiom *both X and Y* requires the *X* and *Y* elements to be parallel. However, the noun *ethnic tensions* is not parallel to the conjunction *because*.

   Answer choice (C) fixes the parallelism issue in answer choice (B), but the comparison idiom is incorrect. The proper idiom is either *not only X but also Y* or *not only X but Y*.

   Answer choice (D) removes the idiom errors in previous answers and contains two verb structures that are properly parallel to each other: 1) *started as a result of ethnic tensions* and 2) *worsened because of economic dislocations*.

9. **(C):** The answer choices have a split around the preposition that follows the word *ability*: *of*, *for*, or *to*. *Ability for* is never correct; eliminate answer choice (B).

   Ability of and *ability to* can both be correct idioms, but they mean different things. *Ability of* refers to someone's ability, as in this example: *The sprinting ability of the cheetah is unmatched*. On the other hand, *ability to* introduces the ability that is being discussed: *The ability to sprint fast is vital to the cheetah's survival*. The original sentence uses *ability of* when it should use *ability to*. Eliminate answer choice (A).

   Answers (C) and (D) both correctly use *ability to*. However, choice (D) has a comparison error. The placement of *unlike humans and guinea pigs* after *a simple sugar* seems to say that *humans and guinea pigs* are not like *sugar*. The intended comparison is between *humans and guinea pigs* and *most mammals*. Correct answer (C) places *humans and guinea pigs* next to *most mammals*.

UNIT TWO

Reading Comprehension

In this unit, you will learn a process for reading passages effectively without getting too bogged down in the details and for keeping the information organized and accessible as you answer questions. You will also learn how to recognize the different Reading Comprehension (RC) question types, what steps to take to identify the correct answer, and how to avoid trap answers.

In This Unit:

CHAPTER 10

The Foundation

In This Chapter:

- How Reading Comprehension Works
- Find the Simple Story
- 4 Steps to the Simple Story
- Answer the Question

In this chapter, you will learn how to read passages efficiently in order to extract the main points you need without getting stuck in unnecessary detail.

CHAPTER 10 The Foundation

Picture this:

> You've just received an email from your boss, asking you to review the Summary of Acme Company's annual report before the two of you go into a conference call with Acme's CEO. The Summary is six pages long and the phone call starts in five minutes.
>
> The pressure is on! What do you do?
>
> (A) Speed-read your way through the entire thing. You won't actually remember or understand what you're reading, but hey, you did technically "read" it.
>
> (B) Start reading carefully, even though you won't be able to finish before the conference call starts.
>
> (C) Hand in your resignation.
>
> (D) Read the first paragraph carefully to get oriented, then start picking up the pace. Slow down for the big ideas, but speed up on the details.

The correct answer is (D), of course! You can't possibly read everything carefully in the allotted time, so you prioritize, looking for main ideas while minimizing the details for now. If the conversation does turn to a detail about one of those main ideas, then you'll have a rough idea where to look and can glance quickly through the summary to find the information. In fact, this whole exercise probably sounds a lot like decisions you make every day at work.

Reading Comprehension (RC) on the GMAT is a test of your real-world executive reasoning skills, even though it often feels like a school test. You typically won't have enough time to read everything thoroughly and carefully—the test literally doesn't give you enough time to do that—so you're going to need to prioritize. This unit will teach you how.

How Reading Comprehension Works

On the GMAT, you will probably see a total of four Reading Comprehension passages, most commonly accompanied by three questions, though occasionally you may be given four questions. (It's possible for these details to change slightly, but this is the most common configuration.)

The passage will always be on the left side of the screen and one question at a time will appear on the right, as depicted here:

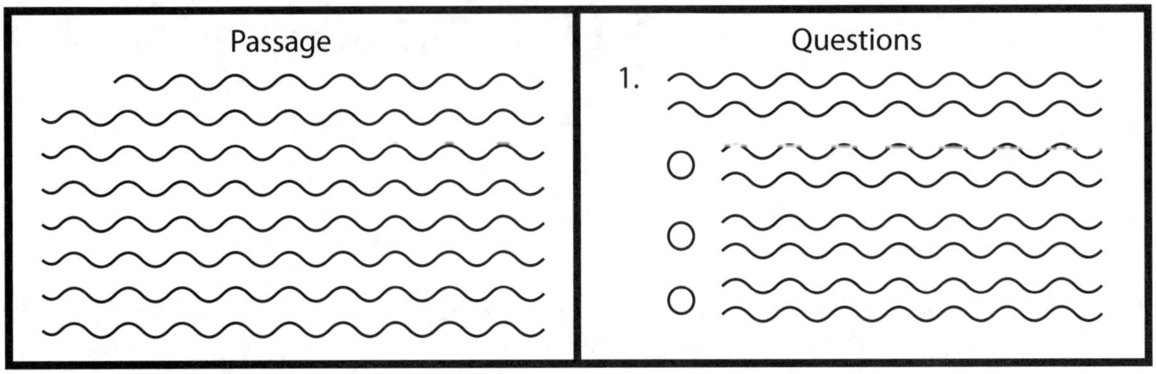

When you answer the first question, a new one will appear in its place. The passage will remain on the left-hand side of the screen. The GMAT will not tell you how many questions you're going to get; you'll know that you're done with the passage when the passage goes away and an entirely new question appears on the screen.

You'll want to spend about 2 to 3 minutes reading the passage (more on this later) and then an average of about 1.5 minutes per question. (You'll learn more about RC time management in Atlas, your online learning platform.)

The passages range from about 200 words up to about 350 words and from one to four paragraphs. Most people will see three shorter passages and one longer one, though this mix can change. The topics are fairly academic, covering areas in hard science, social science, history, and business.

You may see some topics that you enjoy, but you're also likely to see at least one that you don't like much. Try to resist the temptation to dismiss any of the passages as "boring" or "not my topic." If you can convince yourself that the passage is interesting, you'll fare much better on the questions. (Don't worry: This guide will help you to develop this active reading stance!) In the meantime, keep in mind that you're not expected to bring any outside knowledge to the task—whether the passage is about municipal bonds or polypeptide chains, you'll be provided with all of the information you need to answer the questions.

When you start to work through RC problems from *The Official Guide for GMAT Review*, you will see that the passages show line numbers on the left side of the paragraphs, and some questions will make direct reference to a line number. The actual GMAT exam does *not* number the lines in each passage. Instead, when the exam wants to draw your attention to a particular term or phrase in the passage, you will suddenly see that text highlighted in yellow when the relevant question pops up on the screen.

Find the Simple Story

Think back to the annual report challenge. You can't read everything carefully before the meeting. On the other hand, you don't want to just skim over the whole thing or you won't learn anything useful for the meeting.

The goal in situations like this is to find the **Simple Story**: the main points that you would use to summarize that annual report in just a few sentences for your boss. In order to do this, you really do need to read the text, but you do so selectively, paying attention to the main ideas while setting aside the details for now. Later, if you do need a detail, you can look it up; the report will be right in front of you for the whole meeting.

Try to find the simple story in the passage below. This is a shorter passage, so give yourself approximately 2 minutes to read through the passage. At the end, you'll need to answer a question about the main idea of the passage, so keep that in mind as you read; you want the big picture, not the details.

Take any notes that you like (or none at all—it's up to you), but resist the temptation to write on this page. Since the GMAT is administered on a computer, get used to taking notes on a separate piece of scratch paper and looking back and forth between the two.

<u>Bacteria</u>

> Recent research into antibiotic-resistant bacterial strains suggests the need for a reexamination of the frequency with which doctors prescribe antibacterial therapy. One study demonstrated, for example, that most minor bacterial infections will resolve without treatment within 5 to 14 days of onset of symptoms; a course of antibiotics might reduce that time frame by only 1 to 2 days. A second study indicated that the incidence of "superbugs," which have resistance to a wide variety of antibacterial agents, is increasing significantly and that these bugs are more likely to spread among those who have been treated with antibiotics within the past 5 years. In particular, researchers have become alarmed by NDM-1 (New Delhi metallo-beta-lactamase), which is not a single bacterial species, but a multiple-antibiotic-resistant enzyme capable of infecting other strains of bacteria.
>
> It is true that the proliferation of superbugs likely owes a great deal to the mistaken prescription of antibacterial treatment for viral infections, against which such treatment is ineffective, and to the routine addition of antibiotics to livestock feed in order to increase meat yields. Additionally, it is possible that ongoing research into the means by which resistance spreads among bacterial communities may lead to a new generation of antibiotics to which bacteria are unable to develop resistance. Yet these factors do not change the need for individual physicians to be more circumspect about drug therapy when treating cases of true bacterial infection.

Did you stick to the 2-minute time frame given? You have a little leeway (30 seconds or so extra), but resist the urge to spend much more time; the real test punishes those who don't manage their time well, and you'll build bad habits if you don't learn to work in the way that the GMAT requires.

If you feel a little panicky about the thought of having to read that fast, take a deep breath and remind yourself that you don't need to understand the annoying details—at least, not right now. You just need to get the big picture straight before the "meeting with your boss" starts.

Can you summarize, in one sentence, the overall idea of this passage? Go ahead and do so.

If you're struggling to do that, you may have gotten distracted by the details. If you took notes, glance at them. Do you have NDM-1 written down?

If so, then you probably got too pulled into the detail; that's very common at this stage. Now you know that you're going to need to retrain yourself to read at a higher level and actually let a lot of detail go (on your first read through).

Now, give yourself about a minute to try the following question:

The passage is primarily concerned with

(A) discussing research into the common symptoms associated with a particular medical condition
(B) explaining the frequency with which a certain medical condition is diagnosed
(C) contrasting the views of doctors and medical researchers with respect to the diagnosis of a particular medical condition
(D) questioning the current standard of treatment for a particular medical condition
(E) contending that physicians need to be more careful about distinguishing between two different, but related, medical conditions

Before reviewing the problem, let's talk about how to read the passage and find the simple story in the first place.

The first one to three sentences of a passage lay the groundwork for the entire passage, so at first, read carefully. Pay the most attention to the easier words that really tell you what's going on—not the technical ones that are just there to distract you.

Here's how a very strong test-taker might read the first paragraph. (The bold font represents text the reader pays close attention to.)

Passage Text	Reader's Thoughts
Recent research into antibiotic-resistant bacterial strains **suggests the need for a reexamination of the frequency with which doctors prescribe** antibacterial therapy.	*Hmm. I don't know much about* antibacterial therapy, *but I know that* suggests the need for a reexamination of the frequency *means something's not quite right about how often doctors are using it. Presumably the passage is about to tell me why.*
One study demonstrated, **for example**, that **most minor** bacterial infections will **resolve without treatment** within 5 to 14 days of onset of symptoms;	*Wait, so at least some of the time, you'd get better without even taking drugs?*
a course of antibiotics might reduce that time frame by only 1 to 2 days.	*If you do take drugs, they might not really have a huge impact. Interesting. Okay, so this whole example supports the idea that doctors use antibiotics too much.*
A **second study indicated** that the incidence of "**superbugs**," which have **resistance** to a wide variety of antibacterial agents, **is increasing significantly**	*I've read stuff before about antibiotic resistance; I'm pretty sure it's not a good thing. And* superbug *definitely doesn't sound good.*
and that **these bugs are more likely to spread among those who have been treated with antibiotics within the past 5 years**.	*Yay, no weird words here. So these superbug things are definitely bad for people who've been taking antibiotics.*
In particular, researchers have become alarmed by NDM-1 (New Delhi metallo-beta-lactamase), which is not a single bacterial species but a multiple-antibiotic-resistant enzyme capable of infecting other strains of bacteria.	*Uhh. Most of this makes no sense to me, but I get that NDM-1 is bad. It's also a detail, so I really don't care right now. Moving on!*

Right now, you may be thinking: Wait a second—what if I get a question about that detail?

The GMAT test writers might create as many as eight or nine questions for a passage, but you will be given only three or four of those questions. The passage will contain some details that you aren't asked about—and that might be the case for the NDM-1 detail. Do you want to learn about it just because you're very diligent and think it's the right thing to do, even if you never get asked about it?

Of course not! Don't waste time learning details that you might never need, especially when time is so tight. Rather, set the details aside for now. If you do get a question about NDM-1 later, you can return to this text and spend a little time working to understand it.

On to the second paragraph:

Passage Text	Reader's Thoughts
It is true that the proliferation of superbugs likely owes a great deal to the mistaken prescription of antibacterial treatment for viral infections, **against which such treatment is ineffective**,	It is true that—*you use that kind of language when you want to acknowledge some detail that doesn't fit with your overall point.* *The previous paragraph was about* bacterial *infections. Now, it's saying that there are also* mistaken prescriptions *for* viral *infections. And it's saying that this stuff doesn't even work against viruses anyway.*
and to the routine **addition of antibiotics to livestock feed** in order to increase meat yields.	*And a second reason there are superbugs... this is just another detail, so I can speed up a bit. I've got the big idea: It is true that there are other reasons for the proliferation of superbugs besides those given in the first paragraph.*
Additionally, it is possible that **ongoing research** into the means by which resistance spreads among bacterial communities **may lead to a new generation of antibiotics to which bacteria are unable to develop resistance**.	*An additional example... so this is more of the same? Research might solve the problem longer term.*
Yet these factors **do not change the need for individual physicians to be more circumspect about drug therapy** when treating cases of true bacterial infection.	Yet! *This is going against the ideas just presented. I'm not sure what* circumspect *means, but it looks like the author is coming back to the earlier point—doctors have to be more careful or thoughtful about prescribing these drugs so much.*

Here's the reader's simple story:

> *Something's not quite right about how often doctors are prescribing antibiotics for infections.*
> *Two studies support this idea: First, in some cases, the drugs don't help much, and second, something about superbugs.*
>
> *There are some other potential causes of these superbugs—prescribing antibiotics for infections isn't the only problem—but it's still the case that doctors have to be more careful about using these drugs even for legitimate reasons.*

Notice how much that simple story leaves out. There isn't even a mention of NDM-1, let alone what it is or how it works. That's perfectly fine—if you get a question about it, you can go back to find the relevant text and read in more detail. (Or you could decide that you disliked that detail enough that you would rather guess and move on.)

4 Steps to the Simple Story

Here's the basic process to find your simple story:

Step 1: Get oriented. Read the first sentence or two pretty carefully:

- Understand the topic under discussion and keep an eye out for any main ideas.
- Know the main idea of a paragraph by the time you're done reading that paragraph. You may want to jot down a note. (You'll learn more about taking notes in a later chapter.)
- Read the first paragraph of the passage more carefully than any of the others (when there is more than one paragraph in the passage).

Step 2: Find the main idea of each paragraph. When you start a new paragraph, pay close attention to (at least) the first sentence. Find the main idea of that paragraph—why was it included in the passage?

Step 3: Set aside the details. When you get to examples or other very specific details, focus on *why* the information is present. How does this example fit the overall story? Pay less attention to all of the nitpicky little details.

Step 4: Articulate the simple story. When you're done, pause for a moment to articulate the simple story to yourself. If you had to give someone a 10-second summary of the passage, what would you say?

In subsequent chapters, you'll learn techniques to help you develop the simple story and set yourself up to answer both general and specific detail questions. For now, take a look at how this approach can make the process of answering certain questions easier.

Answer the Question

Now that you have a better idea of how to find the simple story, feel free to try the problem again before you continue reading. Here it is:

The passage is primarily concerned with

(A) discussing research into the common symptoms associated with a particular medical condition

(B) explaining the frequency with which a certain medical condition is diagnosed

(C) contrasting the views of doctors and medical researchers with respect to the diagnosis of a particular medical condition

(D) questioning the current standard of treatment for a particular medical condition

(E) contending that physicians need to be more careful about distinguishing between two different, but related, medical conditions

This is a primary purpose question; you'll learn about this question type in more detail in the General Questions chapter. The correct answer will convey the overall point or main idea of the simple story. Before reading the answers, remind yourself of that story. Then, eliminate answers that go too far beyond the story, that focus too much on certain details without conveying the main idea, or that actually contradict the passage in some way.

The passage is primarily concerned with

(A) discussing research into the common symptoms associated with a particular medical condition

Incorrect. The passage mentions only that symptoms can resolve without treatment; the symptoms themselves are not discussed.

(B) explaining the frequency with which a certain medical condition is diagnosed

Incorrect. The first sentence does suggest that the frequency with which antibiotics are prescribed may need to change, but this is not the same as the frequency with which the medical condition is diagnosed in the first place.

(C) contrasting the views of doctors and medical researchers with respect to the diagnosis of a particular medical condition

Incorrect. The first paragraph does present information that might seem to imply a difference of opinion between doctors and researchers as to whether or how frequently antibiotics should be prescribed—but this is a difference in opinion about treatment. The passage doesn't indicate that the doctors and researchers might disagree about how to diagnose the condition.

(D) questioning the current standard of treatment for a particular medical condition

CORRECT. The first and last sentences of the passage together indicate that the author believes that doctors may be overprescribing antibiotics—in other words, that the current standard of treatment might not be appropriate. This fits the simple story: The first paragraph presents research to support this opinion, and the second acknowledges other causes of the "superbug" problem before reiterating that the frequency with which antibiotics are used for bacterial infections is still an issue.

(E) contending that physicians need to be more careful about distinguishing between two different, but related, medical conditions

Incorrect. This is tempting. The passage does mention two types of infections: viral and bacterial. However, the passage doesn't say that doctors are mistakenly diagnosing a bacterial infection when a patient actually has a viral infection. The passage says only that patients with viral infections are sometimes mistakenly treated with antibiotics; it could be that such patients are diagnosed correctly but given an inappropriate treatment.

The only answer that fits with the simple story is answer (D). Take a moment to review and summarize each answer:

(A) Symptoms? Not discussed.

(B) Passage is about frequency of the *treatment*, not frequency of the condition itself.

(C) The *treatment* is the issue, not the diagnosis.

(D) Correct!

(E) The *treatment* is the issue, not the diagnosis.

Note that answers (C) and (E) are incorrect for the same underlying reason, and answer (B) is incorrect for a very similar reason. If you can learn to "abstract" out the trap answers to this level on both Reading Comprehension and Critical Reasoning, you can get quite good at these two question types.

CHAPTER 11

Breaking Down the Passage

In This Chapter:

- Engage with the Passage
- Passage Components
- Language Clues
- Optional Strategy: Breaking Down Complex Sentences

In this chapter, you will learn how to break down the different parts of a passage in order to distill the simple story. You will also learn how to separate the big picture from the details and how to handle especially complex sentences.

CHAPTER 11 Breaking Down the Passage

Sometimes, you hit a passage that just speaks to you. You like the topic, the language doesn't seem as challenging, and you might even be somewhat familiar with the technical examples given. When this happens, go with it! Read the passage as though you're reading for pleasure and don't worry as much about building an explicit simple story. (Just be careful not to bring in outside knowledge.)

More often, though, you're not going to get that lucky. Remember the last time you started to read a passage and you wanted to groan aloud because you found the topic boring? Yet you still had to get through the passage and answer questions about it. What to do?

Engage with the Passage

The first step may seem minor, but it will be a real help. Think of someone you know who actually does like the topic. Pretend that you're going to tell her about it later: "Oh, Robyn would like this. I want to remember enough to tell her about the main gist of it." Who knows—you might actually discover that the topic isn't as boring as you thought.

What do you want to remember to tell Robyn? Certainly not some very specific detail four sentences into the second paragraph. Rather, you want to tell her the simple story. Having Robyn in mind will keep you focused on that task. Lean forward a bit in your seat, smile, and do your best to convince yourself that you are reading this passage by choice and not just because you have to.

Passage Components

Do you remember what a thesis statement is? When you were writing academic papers in school, you had to include a thesis statement and provide support for that thesis. You were expected to have an introduction and a conclusion. In many cases, you were even expected to raise questions or acknowledge contrasting points of view, while ultimately showing that your thesis still held.

GMAT passages are, for the most part, excerpts of academic papers. They are much shorter, of course, so they don't contain all of the expected components of an academic work, but certain components will be present.

You do not need to memorize the different components, nor do you need to explicitly label every sentence that you read. If you know what to look for, though, then you'll be better equipped to find the simple story.

The Point

The Point is the thesis statement: It is the single most important message of the passage and the heart of your simple story. The author has written the passage in order to convey the point, even if nothing else gets through to the reader.

Take a look back at the *Bacteria* passage from the last chapter. Where does the author express the point?

> Recent research into antibiotic-resistant bacterial strains suggests the need for a reexamination of the frequency with which doctors prescribe antibacterial therapy. One study demonstrated, for example, that most minor bacterial infections will resolve without treatment within 5 to 14 days of onset of symptoms; a course of antibiotics might reduce that time frame by only 1 to 2 days. A second study indicated that the incidence of "superbugs," which have resistance to a wide variety of antibacterial agents, is increasing significantly and that these bugs are more likely to spread among those who have been treated with antibiotics within the past 5 years. In particular, researchers have become alarmed by NDM-1 (New Delhi metallo-beta-lactamase), which is not a single bacterial species, but a multiple-antibiotic-resistant enzyme capable of infecting other strains of bacteria.
>
> It is true that the proliferation of superbugs likely owes a great deal to the mistaken prescription of antibacterial treatment for viral infections, against which such treatment is ineffective, and to the routine addition of antibiotics to livestock feed in order to increase meat yields. Additionally, it is possible that ongoing research into the means by which resistance spreads among bacterial communities may lead to a new generation of antibiotics to which bacteria are unable to develop resistance. Yet these factors do not change the need for individual physicians to be more circumspect about drug therapy when treating cases of true bacterial infection.

The point is encapsulated in the first and last sentences:

> Recent research into antibiotic-resistant bacterial strains suggests the need for a reexamination of the frequency with which doctors prescribe antibacterial therapy.
>
> Yet these factors do not change the need for individual physicians to be more circumspect about drug therapy when treating cases of true bacterial infection.

The basic idea is this: *The frequency with which doctors prescribe antibiotics is problematic and doctors have to be more careful.*

This is the single most important idea that the author was trying to convey in writing the passage. If you can't articulate the point, or if you think something else is the point, you are probably going to miss at least some of the questions associated with the passage.

Your simple story will always contain the point. The point can be anywhere in the passage, but it is most often found in the first paragraph or the beginning of the second paragraph. Most of the time, the point will be contained in a single sentence, but occasionally you'll have to combine two or three sentences to get it.

What about the rest of the information in the simple story? Read on.

Support and Background

Some amount of the information in any passage will serve to **Support** the author's point. This support is part of the story.

You may also think of some information as **Background**: It doesn't strongly support the point, but it sets the context for information presented in the passage. Although this information does not strictly support the point, you don't need to distinguish background information from support—you can group it all together. Certainly, you wouldn't want to brush past a whole paragraph without understanding it simply because it looks like background. You need to understand enough of the supporting and background information to build your simple story, but you do not have to thoroughly comprehend or memorize how these details work.

Looking back at the passage, where do you see information that supports the author's point?

The supporting information is contained in the second part of the first paragraph: Two studies support the point. In the simple story, these studies were compressed down to one sentence:

> *Two studies support this idea: First, in some cases, the drugs don't help much, and second, something about superbugs.*

The sentences in the passage contain a whole lot more detail than that, but it is enough to know that these examples support the point. If you are asked a question about any particular supporting detail, you'll know to go back to the latter part of the first paragraph.

Counterpoints, Acknowledgments, and Implications

Some passages will contain **Counterpoints**, information that goes against the author's point (or at least appears to). Passages might also **Acknowledge** a certain point or piece of evidence that does not support the point but that doesn't go against it either.

As with support and background, your goal is to know how the high-level information fits into the simple story, while leaving specific details for later.

Take a look at the passage one more time. Does it contain any counterpoints or acknowledgments?

The second paragraph of the passage begins by acknowledging that there are other possible factors (aside from the treatment of bacterial infections) that are contributing to the superbug problem.

Nevertheless, the author eventually concludes that the original point holds: Doctors have to be more careful about prescribing antibiotics even for legitimate purposes.

Whether you thought of these other factors as counterpoints or as acknowledgments is not all that important. It is important just to recognize that they did not ultimately support the author's point.

Occasionally, passages will contain **Implications** for the future, answering the question, "So what might happen from here or what should we do about the situation?" The *Bacteria* passage does not contain implications, but you could imagine that the author might have discussed a need to fund additional research to establish that the over-prescription of antibiotics for bacterial infections is contributing to resistant bacteria. Alternatively, the author might have proposed a government panel to study how to influence doctors to reduce the number of antibiotic prescriptions. Both of those would be implications.

Use all of these components to help you find your simple story.

Step 1: Get oriented. Read the first sentence or two pretty carefully.

- Understand the topic under discussion and keep an eye out for any main ideas.
- Know the main idea of a paragraph by the time you're done reading that paragraph.
- Read the first paragraph of the passage more carefully than any of the others (when there is more than one paragraph in the passage).

Step 2: Find the main idea of each paragraph. When you start a new paragraph, pay close attention to (at least) the first sentence. Find the main idea of that paragraph—why was it included in the passage?

11

Step 3: Set aside the details. When you get to examples or other very specific details, focus on *why* the information is present. How does this example fit the overall story? Pay less attention to all of the nitpicky little details.

Step 4: Articulate the simple story. When you're done, pause for a moment to articulate the simple story to yourself. If you had to give someone a 10-second summary of the passage, what would you say?

Language Clues

Sometimes, specific language in the passage will signal important categories of information that will help you to build your simple story. Keep an eye out for clues about four big categories:

1. Big Picture
2. Foreshadowing
3. Changes of Direction
4. Detail

Big Picture

Big-Picture language introduces or summarizes some kind of main idea. When you see words like these in a sentence, they should almost jump off the page. Don't get distracted by New Delhi metallo-beta-whatever. Pay attention to the big picture!

In the table below are some common language clues that signal a main idea:

Signal	Implication
In general; To a great extent; Broadly speaking; In conclusion; In sum; In brief; Therefore; Thus; So; Hence; As a result; Overall	A generalization or conclusion follows.
First, Second, etc.; To begin with; Next; Finally; Again	Two or more important points or examples are outlined. Pay attention to the overall purpose; *why* is the author mentioning these points or examples?
X argues that; *X* contends that; theory; hypothesis	A named person or group holds a specific theory or opinion.

Foreshadowing

When you watch a movie or television show, you don't just passively gaze at the screen. You are actively engaging with the story, anticipating what might be coming: Uh oh, the lawyer got distracted by the guy with the gun just as she was piecing together key arguments for the legal case—I bet she's going to make a mistake and mess up in court! Showing this distraction is a way for the director to foreshadow upcoming events.

Foreshadowing works the same way in writing: The author can drop a clue about something that he plans to say later in the passage. When you spot foreshadowing, you can use it to anticipate the point or other important ideas in the passage.

Given the following as the first sentence of an RC passage, where might you anticipate the passage could go next?

> Given recent company stumbles, it is important to ask: Is the potential return on investment worth the risk?

When an author asks a question in the beginning of a passage, she is almost certainly going to address that question in her passage. She may discuss how a company should weigh the risks and rewards of a potential investment; alternatively, she may provide examples of things that a company should *not* consider. She will probably provide at least one example of how a specific company messed this up or got this right.

How about this opener?

> For some time, government officials disagreed as to where to store high-level radioactive waste.

There are many possibilities for what immediately follows: Perhaps the author will describe the opinions held by different government officials, or perhaps he will explain what caused the disagreement in the first place. However, it seems certain that by the end of the passage the officials will have come to an agreement. The language *for some time*, coupled with the past tense verb *disagreed*, indicates that the problem existed in the past but no longer exists today. At some point, the passage will likely tell you that the officials came to an agreement and determined where to store that nuclear waste.

Here are some examples of common foreshadowing signals:

Signal	Implication
Traditionally; For some time; It was once believed; It had been assumed	Contrast coming up soon; now, things are different
Some (people) claim (believe, define, attribute, etc.); It is true that	Acknowledge a valid opposing point
Statement of a problem or question	Possible fix for problem or answer to question (or statement that it can't be fixed or answered, or more research needs to be done)
Current theory; conventional wisdom	New or different theory or idea coming up soon

The list above is meant to help you to start thinking about foreshadowing, but there are many possible language clues; don't just stick to that list. As you read the first paragraph, look for foreshadowing language to help you anticipate where the passage might be going. The sooner you start to have an idea of the big picture and the point, the better.

Changes of Direction

Change-of-Direction language can signal some kind of twist—a contrast or a qualification that could make for a good test question. In addition, twists can signal a counterpoint or a return to the main point.

In the *Bacteria* passage, the final sentence contains a change-of-direction signal:

> Yet these factors do not change the need for individual physicians to be more circumspect about drug therapy when treating cases of true bacterial infection.

The beginning of that same paragraph acknowledged some information that doesn't actually support the overall point. The appearance of the word *yet* signals that the author is about to change direction and jump back to that point.

Here are some common change-of-direction signals:

Signal	Implication
However; Yet; On one hand/On the other hand; While; Rather; Instead; In contrast; Alternatively	Indicate contrasting ideas
Granted; It is true that; Certainly; Admittedly; Despite; Although	Concede a point (author acknowledges or reluctantly agrees)
Actually; In fact; Indeed; Surprisingly	Indicate an unexpected result or phenomenon
Nevertheless; Nonetheless; That said; Even so	Assert a position after conceding a point
Supposedly; It was once thought; Seemingly; For some time	Something appeared to be a certain way, but it really wasn't that way at all

Detail

Certain clues will signal that you should pay less attention on your first read through. When you see these words, still run your eyes over the information, but change your goal: Understand why the information is there, but don't try to understand or remember every last detail given.

Signal	Implication
For example; As an example; In particular; For instance	Provide an example
Furthermore; Moreover; In addition; As well as; Also; Likewise; Too	Add to something that was already said
Likewise; In the same way	Provide a new example or detail that goes along with a previous one
In other words; That is; Namely; So to speak; a semicolon (;)	Restate something that was already said (in this case, you can use whichever set of words is easier for you to interpret!)

Optional Strategy: Breaking Down Complex Sentences

It is not unusual for a GMAT test-taker to read a sentence, pause for a moment, and think, "Huh? I have no idea what that means." The test writers are masters of the complex sentence, so it might be worth your while to take a few pages to practice in-depth reading on a sentence-by-sentence level.

You may or may not need this section. If you are a strong reader who often reads complex material for pleasure or for work, then you have likely already developed your own techniques for breaking down complex sentences into simpler thoughts so that you can digest the full meaning. If that is the case, don't feel that you have to change what already works for you.

If, on the other hand, you can think of at least one "Huh?" moment while reading RC passages, then read on.

What does this sentence mean?

> In a diachronic investigation of possible behavioral changes resulting from accidental exposure in early childhood to environmental lead dust, two sample groups were tracked over decades.

At this point, you may be distracted by the word *diachronic*. If you don't happen to know the meaning of that word, you have plenty of company! Believe it or not, you can ignore those kinds of words. When the test writers toss jargon words at you—scientific terms and the like—one of two things will happen. If you need to know what the word means, then the passage will give you a definition or a contrasting word that lets you figure out the weird word from context. If not, then the passage will just move on, and you should, too. Don't let one unfamiliar word prevent you from processing the rest of the material.

One way to move past such words is to turn them into single letters for ease of reading:

> *In a D investigation of possible behavioral changes . . .*

Here's how a reader might go about stripping that first sentence down to more manageable parts:

Passage Text	Reader's Thoughts
In a diachronic investigation of possible behavioral changes	*Someone was investigating behavior changes.*
resulting from accidental exposure in early childhood to environmental lead dust,	*I don't know what* environmental lead dust *is, specifically, but I've heard that lead is supposed to be bad for kids. Okay, this makes sense: Some kids were accidentally exposed to lead and someone then investigated some consequences.*
two sample groups were tracked over decades.	*Specifically, they investigated two groups of kids for a long time.*
	Put it all together: Kids were accidentally exposed to lead, and somebody investigated two groups of these kids to see whether their behavior changed over time. *Hmm, I wonder whether the lead did affect the kids? Presumably, the passage will get into that.*

Here are the steps that the reader took:

Steps	Example
1. Break the sentence down into smaller ideas; ignore technical jargon.	The reader above read just one idea, then she stopped to understand that one part before continuing to read and add new information. She also ignored the word *diachronic*.
2. Make connections to things you already know; simplify complex language.	The reader didn't get flustered by *environmental lead dust*. Instead, she made a connection to something she already knew: Lead is bad for kids. This knowledge went along with what the sentence was saying, helping her to wrap her head around the second part of the sentence.
3. Link to previous information.	As the reader understood each new idea, she linked it back to what she'd already read. At the end, she made sure that she had a handle on the entire sentence.
4. Anticipate.	Finally, the reader speculated about where the passage might be going. Such anticipation can help keep you actively engaged with the passage—even when the topic isn't your favorite!

As you might guess, breaking down sentences takes time. You won't be able to do this for every sentence in the passage.

Fortunately, you won't need to. First of all, you will actually understand many of the sentences just by reading them once. Second of all, think back to your overall goal: Find the simple story. You don't need to understand every sentence. You only need to understand the sentences that present the big ideas—the ideas that will help you to find the story. When you get to complex sentences about examples or other details, you can just read right over them and keep going.

Try another:

> While *Don Giovanni* is today widely considered Wolfgang Amadeus Mozart's greatest achievement, eighteenth-century audiences in Vienna—Mozart's own city—and the rest of Europe differed greatly in their opinion of a new work unexpectedly mixing traditions of moralism with those of comedy.

Passage Text	Reader's Thoughts
While *Don Giovanni* is today widely considered Wolfgang Amadeus Mozart's greatest achievement,	While *is a huge clue: contrast! I'm guessing that* today *is another important word: The contrast seems to be that DG is considered M's best work* today, *but maybe it wasn't in the past...?*
eighteenth-century audiences in Vienna—Mozart's own city—and the rest of Europe	*There are some details about location, but the important thing is that this part talks about 18th-century audiences. As I suspected, it's talking about the past now, specifically about people who were there when* Don Giovanni *was written.*
differed greatly in their opinion of a new work	*They didn't agree—did they all think it was bad? No, it says they* differed greatly *among each other: Some liked it and some didn't. Wait, so what's the contrast?* *Oh, I see. Today, it's widely considered his greatest achievement. Back then, some people liked it and some didn't.*
unexpectedly mixing traditions of moralism with those of comedy.	*This feels like detail. If I get questions about why some people liked it and some didn't, I'll come back here.*
	The basic message: Today, people think DG is M's greatest achievement. In the 18th century, though, the opinion was mixed.

Problem Set

For each of the four passages below, take 2 to 3 minutes to read the passage and tell yourself the simple story. Then, compare to the version in the solution. There are certainly many ways to convey the same content; just make sure that your version covers all of the big ideas of the passage.

Passage A: Animal Treatment

Over the course of the eighteenth and early nineteenth centuries, educated Britons came to embrace the notion that animals must be treated humanely. By 1822, Parliament had outlawed certain forms of cruelty to domestic animals, and by 1824 reformers had founded the Society for the Prevention of Cruelty to Animals.

This growth in humane feelings was part of a broader embrace of compassionate ideals. One of the great movements of the age was abolitionism, but there were many other such causes. In 1785, a Society for the Relief of Persons Imprisoned for Small Sums persuaded Parliament to limit that archaic punishment. The Society for Bettering the Condition of the Poor was founded in 1796 and a Philanthropic Society founded in 1788 provided for abandoned children. Charity schools, schools of midwifery, and hospitals for the poor were being endowed. This growth in concern for human suffering encouraged reformers to reject animal suffering as well.

Industrialization and the growth of towns also contributed to the increase in concern for animals. The people who protested against cruelty to animals tended to be city folk who thought of animals as pets rather than as live stock. It was not just animals, but all of nature, that came to be seen differently as Britain industrialized. Nature was no longer a menacing force that had to be subdued, for society's "victory" over wilderness was conspicuous everywhere. A new sensibility, which viewed animals and wild nature as things to be respected and preserved, replaced the old adversarial relationship. Indeed, animals were to some extent romanticized as emblems of a bucolic, pre-industrial age.

Passage B: Higher Education

Critics of our higher education system point out the often striking difference between the skills students develop in university courses and the skills desired by employers. Students generally enter university with the expectation that a degree will improve their job prospects, the argument goes, so why not give employers more direct control over the education process? Some commentators have even gone so far as to suggest that traditional postsecondary courses be replaced with short, standardized skills-training workshops.

However, the provision of vocational training is not the goal of most university programs. Rather, universities seek to provide students with experience in a particular field of inquiry, as well as exposure to a wide range of disciplines and worldviews. University students learn to situate themselves not only within the adult world of work and responsibility, but also within the broader streams of historical, social, and physical development that shape and are shaped by their actions and experiences.

It is certainly reasonable to ask whether this vision of education serves the interests of the roughly 2/3 of United States high school graduates who enroll immediately in 2- or 4-year programs after high school. Might some of these students' needs be better met by more narrowly focused vocational programs? Current research suggests that, rather than serving as a reliable engine of social mobility, the United States system of postsecondary education can actually reinforce existing inequalities. However, it is not at all clear that a more employer-oriented system, in which immediate economic need might deter many students from entering academically oriented degree programs, would be any more effective at producing opportunity for traditionally disadvantaged student populations. Further, it is worth considering that the kind of education traditionally provided by universities may confer benefits to society that are not as easily measured as an immediate boost in individual earnings. Before we make any sweeping changes on utilitarian grounds, we ought to consider the utility of the existing order.

11

Passage C: Rock Flour

Although organic agriculture may seem to be the wave of the future, some experts believe that the next stage in agricultural development requires the widespread adoption of something very inorganic: fertilizer made from powdered rocks, also known as "rock flour." The biochemical processes of life depend not only on elements commonly associated with living organisms, such as oxygen, hydrogen, and carbon, but also on many other elements in the periodic table. Specifically, plants need the so-called "big six" nutrients: nitrogen, phosphorus, potassium, calcium, sulfur, and magnesium. In modern industrial agriculture, these nutrients are commonly supplied by traditional chemical fertilizers.

However, these fertilizers omit trace elements, such as iron, that are components of essential plant enzymes and pigments. For instance, the green pigment chlorophyll, which turns sunlight into energy that plants can use, requires iron. As crops are harvested, the necessary trace elements are not replaced and become depleted in the soil. Eventually, crop yields diminish, despite the application or even over-application of traditional fertilizers. Rock flour, produced in abundance by quarry and mining operations, may be able to replenish trace elements cheaply and increase crop yields dramatically.

Not all rock flour would be suitable for use as fertilizer. Certain chemical elements, such as lead and cadmium, are poisonous to humans; thus, applying rock flour containing significant amounts of such elements to farmland would be inappropriate, even if the crops themselves do not accumulate the poisons, because human contact could result directly or indirectly (e.g., via soil runoff into water supplies). However, most rock flour produced by quarries seems safe for use. After all, glaciers have been creating natural rock flour for thousands of years as they advance and retreat, grinding up the ground underneath. Glacial runoff carries this rock flour into rivers and, downstream, the resulting alluvial deposits are extremely fertile. If the use of man-made rock flour is incorporated into agricultural practices, it may be possible to make open plains as rich as alluvial soils.

Passage D: Pro-Drop Languages

In many so-called "pro-drop" or "pronoun-drop" languages, verbs inflect for number and person. In other words, by adding a prefix or suffix or by changing in some other way, the verb itself indicates whether the subject is singular or plural, as well as whether the subject is first person (*I* or *we*), second person (*you*), or third person (*he, she, it,* or *they*). For example, in Portuguese, which is at least partially a pro-drop language, the verb *falo* means "I speak": the –o at the end of the word indicates first person, singular subject (as well as present tense). As a result, the subject pronoun *eu*, which means "I" in Portuguese, does not need to be used with *falo* except to emphasize who is doing the speaking.

It should be noted that not every language that drops its pronouns inflects its verbs. Neither Chinese nor Japanese verbs, for instance, change form at all to indicate number or person; however, personal pronouns are regularly omitted in both speech and writing, leaving the proper meaning to be inferred from contextual clues. Moreover, not every language that inflects its verbs drops subject pronouns in all non-emphatic contexts. Linguists argue about the pro-drop status of the Russian language, but there is no doubt that, although the Russian present-tense verb *govoryu* ("I speak") unambiguously indicates a first person, singular subject, it is common for Russian speakers to express "I speak" as *ya govoryu*, in which *ya* means "I," without indicating either emphasis or contrast.

Nevertheless, Russian speakers do frequently drop subject and object pronouns; one study of adult and child speech indicated a pro-drop rate of 40–80 percent. Moreover, personal pronouns must in fact be dropped in some Russian sentences in order to convey particular meanings. It seems safe to conjecture that languages whose verbs inflect unambiguously for person and number permit pronoun dropping, if only under certain circumstances, in order to accelerate communication without loss of meaning. After all, in these languages, both the subject pronoun and the verb inflection convey the same information, so there is no real need both to include the subject pronoun and to inflect the verb.

Solutions

Passage A: Animal Treatment

In the 18th and 19th centuries, people in Britain grew concerned about the humane treatment of animals. This was part of a general movement toward more compassionate treatment of others. Industrialization also shifted people's views: In the new industrialized world, nature no longer seemed like a threat.

Passage B: Higher Education

University education doesn't always fit with what employers want, so some people think schools should focus on more job-oriented skills. In the U.S., universities want to teach more than that, but what would be best for students? Maybe the current system doesn't help everyone, but the author thinks the new idea is not necessarily better and wants to be cautious about making changes.

Passage C: Rock Flour

Rock flour, a type of fertilizer made from powdered rocks, could provide a cheap source of nutrients for plants, significantly improving crop yields. While some rock flour might be dangerous, most of it should be safe to use.

Passage D: Pro-Drop Languages

In "pro-drop" languages, the speaker often drops pronouns (*I*, *you*, etc.) because the verb form makes the subject clear. However, these two things don't always go together: Some languages drop pronouns even though the verb doesn't indicate the subject, and some languages keep the pronoun even though the verb also makes the subject clear. The author thinks that some languages allow the speaker to drop the subject pronoun to accelerate communication.

CHAPTER 12

Mapping the Passage

In This Chapter:

- Why Use a Passage Map?
- Making the Passage Map
- Common Notations

In this chapter, you will learn how to make a passage map, a particular way of taking notes that makes you articulate the main points of the passage and prepares you to quickly find the information needed to answer the questions.

CHAPTER 12 Mapping the Passage

You have one more skill to develop before diving into the questions. These passages are complex; even the simple story is several sentences long. You wouldn't want to take the time to write the story out, but it is very useful to jot down certain things. So, you're going to create a **Passage Map**.

A caveat: Your goal is absolutely *not* to take notes the way that you took notes in school. You aren't going to be studying this same passage again weeks from now; once you're done with the passage, you can forget about it forever.

Instead, your goal is to jot down just a few words that will help you to develop and remember your simple story (including the point) and to remember where in the passage to look when you need support to answer a question.

Why Use a Passage Map?

You're going to have to answer two types of questions: general and specific. The passage map will help you to accomplish two important goals:

1. Predict the answers to general questions
2. Know where in the passage to find the details you'll need to answer specific questions

The two goals above will indicate whether you're creating an effective map. If you can't answer general questions based on the information in your map, then you didn't learn enough about the big picture on the first read through. You'll need to practice picking up on the main ideas and major changes in direction.

On specific questions, though, you actually do *not* want to be able to find the answers on your map. If you can, then you likely spent too much time diving into the detail on your read through. The GMAT will always include more detail in the passage than you will need to answer the questions; if you pay careful attention to all of that detail, you may run out of time on the test. You'll actually need to practice minimizing the attention you pay to details, possibly to the point of skimming some information.

Avoid relying too heavily on your memory when answering the detail questions. Remember, this is an "open book" test, and it is full of traps for those who are pretty confident that they remember the details. Check the passage! If you form good habits and apply a consistent and efficient process even on the easier-for-you questions, you'll have a better chance to answer the difficult questions correctly.

Making the Passage Map

Your passage map reflects the simple story, but it will be heavily abbreviated. Your map should include the following information (and not much more):

- The point
- The purpose of each paragraph
- Any other information you would include in the simple story, organized by paragraph

Every reader's map will be different. You have the flexibility to organize in a way that makes sense for you. Of course, this makes creating an answer key to passage mapping a little difficult, but this unit will model the process in a way that provides guidance while leaving your own passage map style up to you.

Try creating a map of the *Bacteria* passage that you saw earlier in this unit. Use any format you like as long as it reflects your simple story.

> Recent research into antibiotic-resistant bacterial strains suggests the need for a reexamination of the frequency with which doctors prescribe antibacterial therapy. One study demonstrated, for example, that most minor bacterial infections will resolve without treatment within 5 to 14 days of onset of symptoms; a course of antibiotics might reduce that time frame by only 1 to 2 days. A second study indicated that the incidence of "superbugs," which have resistance to a wide variety of antibacterial agents, is increasing significantly and that these bugs are more likely to spread among those who have been treated with antibiotics within the past 5 years. In particular, researchers have become alarmed by NDM-1 (New Delhi metallo-beta-lactamase), which is not a single bacterial species, but a multiple-antibiotic-resistant enzyme capable of infecting other strains of bacteria.
>
> It is true that the proliferation of superbugs likely owes a great deal to the mistaken prescription of antibacterial treatment for viral infections, against which such treatment is ineffective, and to the routine addition of antibiotics to livestock feed in order to increase meat yields. Additionally, it is possible that ongoing research into the means by which resistance spreads among bacterial communities may lead to a new generation of antibiotics to which bacteria are unable to develop resistance. Yet these factors do not change the need for individual physicians to be more circumspect about drug therapy when treating cases of true bacterial infection.

Here is the simple story:

> *Something's not quite right about how often doctors are prescribing antibiotics for infections. Two studies support this idea: First, in some cases, the drugs don't help much, and second, something about superbugs.*
>
> *There are some other potential causes of these superbugs—prescribing antibiotics for infections isn't the only problem—but it's still the case that doctors have to be more careful about using these drugs even for legitimate reasons.*

Here's one potential passage map for this story:

① Problem: Drs prescribe antiB a lot—too much?

1. Sometimes antiB don't help!
2. Superbugs ↑ = bad

② Other things cause superbugs, too

BUT Drs still have to be careful about using antiB Ⓟ

The map reflects the major elements of the story. It clearly delineates the point Ⓟ. It shows what information is in paragraph 1 versus paragraph 2. It mentions the support and the acknowledgment.

This map wouldn't take long to produce, but you can certainly abbreviate more heavily, depending on how strong your short-term memory is.

Here's a more abbreviated version:

① Prob: Drs use antiB a lot—too?

1. May not help!
2. Superbug ☹

② Other → superbugs

STILL Drs must be careful re: antiB Ⓟ

Someone with a great short-term memory and strong RC skills in general might abbreviate to the point that the map resembles hieroglyphics; only she or he would be able to read it. Here's an example:

① Prob: Drs AB too much

1. ≠ help
2. SB

② Other → SB

Drs must take care w/AB Ⓟ

Now, give yourself about 1.5 minutes to try this problem.

The research cited in the first paragraph suggests which of the following about antibacterial therapy?

(A) It frequently leads to infection with NDM-1.

(B) It is not generally used to treat minor bacterial infections.

(C) It may help to reduce the incidence of superbugs that are especially hard to treat.

(D) Reducing the rate at which such therapy is used would cause fewer bacteria to develop resistance to antibiotics.

(E) Its short-term benefits, if they exist, may not outweigh the potential harm to the broader population.

This question asks about the studies in the first paragraph. Some of the answers are very detailed, but it's certainly okay to make a quick pass to look for an answer that matches the simple story. If nothing turns up, then go back and analyze the details.

The studies cited in the first paragraph suggest which of the following about antibacterial therapy?

(A) It frequently leads to infection with NDM-1.

I don't know! I skimmed the info about NDM-1. Come back later.

(B) It is not generally used to treat minor bacterial infections.

They said it is used to treat minor infections—it only reduces treatment time by a couple of days. This one's wrong.

(C) It may help to reduce the incidence of superbugs that are especially hard to treat.

I don't know. Come back later.

(D) Reducing the rate at which such therapy is used would cause fewer bacteria to develop resistance to antibiotics.

I don't know. Come back later.

(E) Its short-term benefits, if they exist, may not outweigh the potential harm to the broader population.

CORRECT. *The paragraph does mention that such therapy might reduce the illness by one to two days. This could be a short-term benefit, but the author minimizes this benefit and goes on to discuss a much worse drawback (the superbug). That all fits with the simple story and the first paragraph.*

It's sometimes possible to find the right answer even if you don't yet know why some of the wrong ones are wrong. On the real test, pick (E) and move on. When you're studying, go back afterwards to learn why answers (A), (C), and (D) are wrong.

(A) It frequently leads to infection with NDM-1.

Incorrect. The passage does say that patients who have used antibiotics within the past five years are more likely to pick up superbugs, but it doesn't indicate how often this happens, especially in the case of NDM-1 in particular. Perhaps this bug is still very rare.

(C) It may help to reduce the incidence of superbugs that are especially hard to treat.

Incorrect. This paragraph mentions nothing about what causes the incidence of superbugs to decrease. In fact, the story hinges on the idea that these superbugs are *increasing*, so this answer contradicts the story.

(D) Reducing the rate at which such therapy is used would cause fewer bacteria to develop resistance to antibiotics.

Incorrect. This is tempting! The question points you specifically to the first paragraph, though, and the first paragraph does not discuss what causes bacteria to become antibiotic-resistant. (The second paragraph does touch on this a bit, but it does not discuss how *antibacterial therapy* might contribute to this phenomenon—read the question carefully!)

In this case, the wrong answers weren't necessarily easy to eliminate, but the right answer was definitely connected to the simple story.

If the correct answer didn't match your take on the passage, you may not have read carefully enough. This typically happens for one of two reasons:

1. You read so quickly that you aren't really taking in what you're reading. Have you ever read something and then realized that you have no idea what you just read and you have to read it again? You'll need to learn to read actively on RC; purposefully looking for the simple story will help.
2. You get distracted by the technical words, the examples, and the minutiae; you're paying so much attention to those details that you forget to tell yourself the simple story. In this case, you're going to have to learn how to strip out the details and concentrate on the big picture.

As this unit progresses, you'll learn techniques to help you overcome these (and other) problems by actively reading for the big picture and using that understanding to simplify the process of answering the questions.

Common Notations

You don't have much time to read the passage and make your passage map. The good news is that you'll only need your map for the few minutes it takes you to answer the questions. In fact, you may find that once your map has done its job and helped you to understand the passage, you don't end up looking back at it at all. With this in mind, don't try to create the kind of clear document you might study from in school; you're not really going to be using this map for very long.

Given that, you can abbreviate heavily in your map. Consider the following notations:

Tactic	Passage Language	Abbreviation
Abbreviate technical words or hard-to-pronounce names with a single letter, an acronym, or a much shorter version of the word.	serotonin Mihaly Csikszentmihalyi	S or sero C or MC
Use an arrow to show cause–effect or change over time.	Instability in interest rates can cause investors to avoid bonds.	IR unstable → ppl avoid bonds
Use a colon (:) to attribute an opinion or point of view to a specific person or group.	Many historians believe that economic interests can prolong a war.	H: $$ issues → longer war
Mark examples with parentheses or *eg.*	A classic example is the behavior of the female sphex wasp.	e.g., ♀S wasp
Use up and down arrows to indicate increases or decreases.	An increasing number of businesses are expected to reduce benefits for part-time employees.	↑ biz: ↓ ben part-time
Use math and science symbols that you already know.	greater than (or much greater than) less than (or much less than) change therefore	> (>>) < (<<) Δ ∴

Problem Set

For each of the four passages below, take 2 to 3 minutes to read and map the passage and articulate the simple story.

The solutions present one version of a passage map, but your version will vary; this is fine! The solutions also include simple stories, but you don't need to write these down when you are working a passage—the passage map should be enough to allow you to put together the simple story.

Passage E: Redlining

In the 1960s, Northwestern University sociologist John McKnight coined the term redlining, the practice of denying or severely limiting service to customers in particular geographic areas, areas often determined by the racial composition of the neighborhood. The term came from the practice of banks outlining certain areas in red on a map; within the red outline, banks refused to invest. With no access to mortgages, residents within the red line suffered low property values and landlord abandonment; buildings abandoned by landlords were then more likely to become centers of drug dealing and other crime, thus further lowering property values.

Redlining in mortgage lending was made illegal by the Fair Housing Act of 1968, which prohibited such discrimination based on race, religion, gender, familial status, disability, or ethnic origin, and by community reinvestment legislation in the 1970s. However, redlining has sometimes continued in less explicit ways and can also take place in the context of constrained access to health care, jobs, insurance, and more. Even today, some credit card companies send different offers to homes in different neighborhoods, and some auto insurance companies offer different rates based on zip code.

Redlining can lead to reverse redlining, which occurs when predatory businesses specifically target minority or low-income consumers for the purpose of charging them more than would typically be charged for a particular service. When mainstream retailers refuse to serve a certain area, people in that area can fall prey to opportunistic smaller retailers who sell inferior goods at higher prices.

Passage F: Tokugawa

The Tokugawa period in Japan (1603–1867) serves as a laboratory for organizational behavior historians for the same reason that Iceland is an ideal location for geneticists—isolation removes extraneous variables. The Tokugawa shoguns brought peace to a land of warring feudal lords. To preserve that tranquility, the Tokugawa shogunate forbade contact with the outside world, allowing only a few Dutch trading ships to dock at one restricted port. Domestically, in pursuit of the same goal, the social order was fixed; there were four classes—warriors [samurai], artisans, merchants, and farmers or peasants—and social mobility was prohibited. The ensuing stability and peace brought a commercial prosperity that lasted nearly two hundred years.

However, as psychologists and social historians have observed, in varying ways, humans often fail to anticipate unintended consequences. In the Tokugawa period, the fixed social hierarchy placed the samurai on top; they and the government were essentially supported by levies on the peasantry, as the other two classes were demographically and economically inconsequential. However, prosperity brought riches to the commercial classes and their numbers burgeoned. Eventually, their economic power dwarfed that of their supposed superiors, the samurai, but the social structure was so ingrained that it was unthinkable to change. By the early nineteenth century, this imbalance between social structure and economic reality eroded the stability of the society. This condition was one of the primary factors that led to the eventual collapse of the shogunate in 1867. In short, the success of the self-imposed order led to its undoing through consequences that were beyond the ken of the founders.

Passage G: Prescription Errors

In Europe, medical prescriptions were historically written in Latin. A prescription for eye drops written in Amsterdam could be filled in Paris, because the abbreviation *OS* meant "left eye" in both places. With the disappearance of Latin as a lingua franca, however, abbreviations such as *OS* can easily be confused with *AS* (left ear) or *per os* (by mouth), even by trained professionals. Misinterpretations of medical instructions can be fatal. In the early 1990s, two infants died in separate but identical tragedies: They were each administered 5 milligrams of morphine, rather than 0.5 milligrams, as the dosage was written without an initial zero. The naked decimal (.5) was subsequently misread.

The personal and economic costs of misinterpreted medical prescriptions and instructions are hard to quantify. However, anecdotal evidence suggests that misinterpretations are prevalent. While mistakes will always happen in any human endeavor, medical professionals, hospital administrators, and policymakers should continually work to drive the prescription error rate to zero, taking simple corrective steps and also pushing for additional investments.

Certain measures are widely agreed upon but may be difficult to enforce, given the decentralization of the healthcare system in the United States. For instance, professional organizations have publicly advocated against the use of Latin abbreviations and other relics of historical pharmacology. As a result, incidents in which *qd* (every day) and *qid* (four times a day) have been mixed up seem to be on the decline. Other measures have been taken by regulators. For instance, the Federal Drug Administration asked a manufacturer to change the name of Losec, an antacid, to Prilosec, so that confusion with Lasix, a diuretic, would be reduced. Unfortunately, there have been at least a dozen reports of accidental switches between Prilosec and Prozac, an antidepressant. As more drugs reach the market, drug-name "traffic control" will only become more complicated.

Other measures are controversial or require significant investment. For instance, putting the patient's condition on the prescription would allow double-checking but also compromise patient privacy. Computerized prescriber order entry (CPOE) systems seem to fix the infamous problem of illegible handwriting, but many CPOE systems permit naked decimals and other dangerous practices. Moreover, since fallible humans must still enter and retrieve the data, any technological fixes must be accompanied by substantial training. Ultimately, a multi-pronged approach is needed to address the issue.

Passage H: Ether's Existence

In 1887, an ingenious experiment performed by Albert Michelson and Edward Morley severely undermined classical physics by failing to confirm the existence of "ether," a ghostly massless medium that was thought to permeate the universe. This finding had profound results, ultimately paving the way for acceptance of Einstein's special theory of relativity.

Prior to the Michelson–Morley experiment, nineteenth-century physics conceived of light as a wave propagated at constant speed through the ether. The existence of ether was hypothesized in part to explain the transmission of light, which was believed to be impossible through "empty" space. Physical objects, such as planets, were also thought to glide frictionlessly through the unmoving ether.

The Michelson–Morley experiment relied on the fact that the Earth, which orbits the Sun, would have to be in motion relative to a fixed ether. Just as a person on a motorcycle experiences a "wind" caused by her own motion relative to the air, the Earth would experience an "ethereal wind" caused by its motion through the ether. Such a wind would affect our measurements of the speed of light. If the speed of light is fixed with respect to the ether, but the Earth is moving through the ether, then to an observer on Earth light must appear to move faster in a "downwind" direction than in an "upwind" direction.

In 1887, there were no clocks sufficiently precise to detect the speed differences that would result from an ethereal wind. Michelson and Morley surmounted this problem by using the wavelike properties of light itself to test for such speed differences. In their apparatus, known as an "interferometer," a single beam of light is split in half. Mirrors guide each half of the beam along a separate trajectory before ultimately reuniting the two half-beams into a single beam. If one half-beam has moved more slowly than the other, the reunited beams will be out of phase with each other. In other words, peaks of the first half-beam will not coincide exactly with peaks of the second half-beam, resulting in an interference pattern in the reunited beam. Michelson and Morley detected only a tiny degree of interference in the reunited light beam—far less than what was expected based on the motion of the Earth.

Solutions on next page. ▶ ▶ ▶

12

Solutions

Passage E: Redlining

Passage map:

① Redlining: deny/limit svc to minorities

② Now illegal, but still happens

③ Leads to reverse redL: charging more than typical

Simple story:

Redlining is denying or limiting services to minority customers. It's been illegal since the late '60s, but some businesses still do it. It can also lead to reverse redlining, where businesses do offer service to minority communities, but at a higher price than they would typically charge.

Passage F: Tokugawa

Passage map:

① T isolated; fixed social order; peace/stable.

② BUT merchants → wealthy, messed up social order, system collapsed. Fixed soc. order was once good, later bad.

Simple story:

The T period in Japan is good to study because it was isolated. The social order was fixed and it was a really stable era. Later, a "lower" group became wealthy, but the rigid social system stayed. So what helped make things stable at first eventually caused the system to collapse.

Passage G: Prescription Errors

Passage map:

① Eur. Rx in Latin, but now errors, dangerous

② DK how much error, but maybe lots. Try to ↓

③ Pop. measures: no Latin, no similar names

④ Other measures controv.: listing condition, computers

Simple story:

There are many ways to misinterpret medical prescriptions, and this can be dangerous. Some measures—such as eliminating the use of Latin and making names unambiguous—are agreed upon, but others are more controversial.

Passage H: Ether's Existence

Passage map:

① 1887, M&M—no ether; made way for Einstein

② Old: ether explained how light moved

③ Basis for exp: Earth "wind"

④ DTL: How M&M showed lack of ether

DTL is an abbreviation for the word *detail.*

Simple story:

Prior to 1887, scientists thought that space was not "empty," but filled with a substance called ether. In 1887, Michelson and Morley conducted an experiment that involved splitting a beam of light. There was less interference than there should have been if ether existed, so the experiment showed that ether might not actually exist.

CHAPTER 13

General Questions

In This Chapter:

- 4 Steps to the Answer
- Practice Passage: Insect Behavior
- Primary Purpose Questions
- Paragraph Questions
- Primary Purpose Cheat Sheet

In this chapter, you will learn how to handle general questions. These big-picture questions ask about the primary purpose or main point of the entire passage or of one paragraph in the passage.

CHAPTER 13 General Questions

Reading Comprehension questions can be grouped into two major categories:

1. **General** questions, such as Primary Purpose, Paragraph
2. **Specific** questions, such as Detail, Inference, Specific Purpose

This chapter will cover general questions, which may ask you about the overall purpose of the passage or about the purpose of a specific paragraph. The next chapter will cover specific question types.

You typically won't see more than one general question per passage; in fact, on some passages you won't see any. On average, expect to spend 30–60 seconds on each general question.

4 Steps to the Answer

In this chapter, you'll learn how to answer **Primary Purpose** and **Paragraph** questions using a standard 4-step process that you'll use for all RC questions.

Step 1: Identify the question. This chapter will tell you how to recognize that you have a Primary Purpose or a Paragraph question.

Step 2: Find the support. Your initial read of the passage and any map you make will give you a strong idea of the overall point and the purpose of each paragraph. At this stage, you may take a look at your passage map to remind yourself of the big picture, or you may feel comfortable not even doing that. (Note: On specific questions, you *will* have to go back to reread some part of the passage—more on this in the next chapter.)

Step 3: Predict an answer. Take a look at the question again and, using your map or memory, try to formulate a rough answer in your own words. You're not trying to match the correct answer exactly; rather, you're just trying to articulate the *kind* of information you would expect to find in the correct answer.

Step 4: Eliminate and find a match. Evaluate each answer, while keeping in mind your predicted answer. Eliminate any that definitely don't match. When you find a potential match, leave it in and continue to evaluate the remaining answers:

- If you eliminate four answers, great! Pick the remaining one and move on.
- If you still have two or three answers left, compare the answers to the relevant information in your map. If the answers are very similar, you may also compare them to each other.
- If you still have four or five answers left, make sure you are answering the right question! After that, it's probably best to cut your losses: Guess and move on.

Finally, one last word of advice. This might seem obvious, but *every single word* in the answer choice must be supported in order for that choice to be correct. Make sure that you are reading methodically. Don't rush just because you're stressed; saving 10 seconds is not worth the risk of missing a question due to a careless mistake.

Practice Passage: Insect Behavior

Give yourself approximately 4 minutes to read the passage below and answer the questions that follow.

At times, insect behavior appears to be explicable in terms of unconscious stimulus-response mechanisms; when scrutinized, it often reveals a stereotyped, inflexible quality. A classic series of experiments were performed on the female sphex wasp. The mother leaves her egg sealed in a burrow alongside a paralyzed grasshopper or other insect, which her larva can eat when it hatches. Typically, before she deposits the grasshopper in the burrow, she leaves it at the entrance and goes inside to inspect the burrow. If the inspection reveals no problems, she drags the grasshopper inside by its antennae. Once the larvae hatch, they feed on the paralyzed insects until ready to spin a cocoon and undergo metamorphosis.

Entomologist Jean-Henri Fabre discovered that if the grasshopper's antennae are removed while the wasp is inside inspecting the nest, the wasp will not drag it into the burrow, even though the legs or ovipositor could serve the same function as the antennae. Later Fabre found more evidence of the wasp's dependence on predetermined routine. While a wasp was performing her inspection of a burrow, he moved the grasshopper a few centimeters away from the burrow's mouth. The wasp brought the grasshopper back to the edge of the burrow, then began a whole new inspection. When Fabre took this opportunity to move the food again, the wasp repeated her routine. Fabre performed his disruptive maneuver forty times, and the wasp's response never changed.

1. The primary purpose of the passage is to

(A) demonstrate, based on examples, that insects lack awareness of their surroundings

(B) argue that insects are unique in their dependence on rigid routines

(C) analyze the maternal behavior of wasps

(D) contrast typical wasp behavior with unconscious behavior

(E) contend that insect behavior can rely on rigid routines that appear to be unconscious

2. Which of the following best describes the purpose of the second paragraph of the passage?

(A) To provide experimental evidence for the thesis articulated in the first paragraph

(B) To introduce a hypothesis about insect behavior

(C) To illustrate the ways in which grasshoppers are unsuitable for the wasp's purposes

(D) To explore the significance of the wasp's varied reactions to certain stimuli

(E) To acknowledge experimental evidence that does not support the author's thesis

Here's one example of a simple story, with the point noted:

The point	→	*Insect behavior is sometimes inflexible or unconscious. Normally, a wasp inspects the burrow and then brings the grasshopper inside. Later, the larvae feed on the grasshopper.*
		Fabre discovered that the wasp will only *drag a grasshopper by the antennae. He also found that, if the grasshopper is moved during the inspection phase, then the wasp will put the grasshopper back and inspect the burrow again, over and over.*
		Hmm. That sounds pretty inflexible—it's as though it can't think or adapt.

That last line is not stated in the passage, but a reader might summarize the simple story in this way.

Here's one example of a passage map:

① Insects: behavior inflex, unconsc
Typ: wasp inspect burrow, bring GH, larvae eat

② F: ONLY drag by antennae
If GH moves, wasp re-inspects, every time

Here's a much more abbreviated version:

① Insect: inflex
Normal behav

② F: weird behav

The second map is so abbreviated that it serves only as a quick reminder of things that the reader already remembers: The normal behavior is described in the first paragraph and the second paragraph has the weird behavior. If your short-term memory is strong, then feel free to use a hyper-abbreviated map like this one. (You might not even write anything at all, but only follow that path if you can maintain a strong mental sense of the passage throughout the process of reading and answering the questions. Don't avoid writing anything simply because you think it will save you time.)

Primary Purpose Questions

Step 1 on any question is to **identify the question type**:

1. The primary purpose of the passage is to

This is a **Primary Purpose** question—the test writers are asking for the point of the whole passage. These are also known as **Main Idea** questions.

Most of the time, these questions will ask you to identify the *primary purpose* of the passage or what the author is *primarily concerned with*. The correct answer should fit with the point that you have articulated to yourself.

Steps 2 and 3 merge for Primary Purpose questions: **Find the support** and **predict an answer**. For Primary Purpose questions, you don't need to go back to the passage. You will already have identified the point—if not, briefly review your map. In this passage, the point is that some insect behaviors seem to be inflexible; the insects can't adapt to changing situations.

Once you have that set in your head, it's time for step 4: **Eliminate and find a match**. For Primary Purpose questions, eliminate any choice that doesn't match the point. For example:

(A) demonstrate, based on examples, that insects lack awareness of their surroundings	*The insect is aware—she sees that the grasshopper has moved and she goes and gets it. The point is about insects' unconscious behavior, not their general awareness.*
(B) argue that insects are unique in their dependence on rigid routines	*The author does argue that insects are dependent on rigid routines but never claims that they are* unique *in this way. No other types of animals are mentioned.*
(C) analyze the maternal behavior of wasps	*The author uses a couple of examples of wasp behavior to make a more general point about insect behavior; the main point is not that these wasps are making a nest for their offspring.*
(D) contrast typical wasp behavior with unconscious behavior	*The author does not present* typical behavior *and* unconscious behavior *as different things. Rather, the typical behavior never changes, even when a disruption of the routine would seem to warrant changing a behavior.*
(E) contend that insect behavior can rely on rigid routines that appear to be unconscious	***CORRECT**. The author claims that,* at times, *insect behavior is* inflexible, *or rigid, and the insect may not always be capable of responding to an unexpected or changed situation.*

13

Several types of trap answers appeared in this question.

One word off:	These trap answers mostly look good, but one word isn't supported by the passage, taking the answer choice out of contention. Answer (B) was one word off (*unique*). (Note: This can stretch to a couple of words off!)
Extreme:	These trap answers contain an extreme word, such as *all* or *never*, that is not supported by the passage. It is certainly possible for extreme words to appear in a correct answer, but only if the passage provides direct support for such extreme language. Answer (B) contained an extreme word (*unique*) that was not supported by the passage (sometimes, a wrong answer can fit multiple trap categories!).
Out of scope:	These trap answers will typically touch on aspects of the passage, but will go further than what the passage actually discusses. Sometimes, these answers are just a bit too broad; other times, they are way off. Answer (A) talks about *awareness of their surroundings*, which isn't discussed in the passage.
True but not right:	These answers will typically reflect things that are true according to the passage, but they do not answer the specific question asked. Answer (C) falls into this category. The examples used in the passage *are* about maternal wasp behavior, but the overall point is about a broader topic: the inflexible nature of insect behavior in general.
Direct contradiction:	Answer (D) is an example of a direct contradiction: The passage says the opposite of what this answer choice conveys.

Paragraph Questions

In order to answer **Paragraph** questions correctly, you will need to have a strong grasp of the point of the passage as well as the purpose of each paragraph.

Most of the time, Paragraph questions will ask you for one of two things: 1) the purpose of a particular paragraph in the context of the whole passage or 2) the purpose of a particular paragraph in relation to another particular paragraph.

First, identify the question:

2. Which of the following best describes the purpose of the second paragraph of the passage?

In this case, the question asks for the purpose of the second paragraph in the context of the entire passage.

Second, find the support. Locate paragraph 2 in your map:

> ① Insects: behavior inflex, unconsc
> Typ: wasp inspect burrow, bring GH, larvae eat
>
> ② F: ONLY drag by antennae
> If GH moves, wasp re-inspects burrow, every time

Third, predict an answer. The second paragraph provides examples that support the overall point that insect behavior is inflexible.

Once you have that set in your head, eliminate and find a match. For Paragraph questions, try to disprove each answer. If the answer contains something that wasn't part of the passage, or was restricted to a different paragraph, cross it off.

Before you look at the explanations below, try to label some of the wrong answers using the trap categories you learned on the last problem.

(A) To provide experimental evidence for the thesis articulated in the first paragraph

CORRECT*. The second paragraph does talk about experiments, and those experiments do support what the author claimed in the first paragraph.*

(B) To introduce a hypothesis about insect behavior

The passage does introduce such a hypothesis, but it does so in the first *paragraph, not the second one. This is the overall point of the passage, but the question asks about only the second paragraph. (True but not right)*

(C) To illustrate the ways in which grasshoppers are unsuitable for the wasp's purposes

The passage doesn't say that the grasshoppers are unsuitable. This trap might be set for someone who is reading very quickly or superficially and draws an erroneous conclusion about the experiments with grasshoppers. (Out of scope)

(D) To explore the significance of the wasp's varied reactions to certain stimuli

The point of the passage is that the wasp does not *change her behavior even when the circumstances of her situation change; her reactions do not vary. (Direct contradiction)*

(E) To acknowledge experimental evidence that does not support the author's thesis

The evidence in the second paragraph does *support the author's thesis. (Direct contradiction)*

All of the traps here were discussed earlier in the chapter; flip back if you want a refresher on any of the categories.

If a question asks about the entire passage, then you have a Primary Purpose question. Remind yourself of the overall point, using your map as needed.

If the question asks specifically about one paragraph in the context of the whole, then use your map to remind yourself what that one paragraph is about and how it fits into the overall story of the passage.

Try to come up with your own answer to the question before you look at the answers. Then, dive into those answers and start eliminating anything that is too far from what you articulated. Do check all five answers, even after you think you've found the right one. Finally, verify that your final answer matches both the question asked and the answer you articulated to yourself up front.

Don't forget to keep an eye out for the common traps (summarized in your Cheat Sheet on the next page).

Primary Purpose Cheat Sheet

Identify the Question

Primary Purpose:
- The primary purpose (or function) of the passage is to . . .
- The author of the passage is primarily concerned with . . .
- Which of the following most accurately states the purpose of the passage?
- Which of the following titles best summarizes the passage?
- With which of the following would the author be most likely to agree?

Paragraph:
- What is the purpose of the second paragraph?
- Which of the following best describes the relationship of the third paragraph to the passage as a whole?

Find the Support

Use map or overall understanding of the passage.

Predict an Answer

Articulate the point or the purpose of the paragraph *before* looking at the answer choices.

Eliminate

Check all of the answers! Common traps:

Trap	**Characteristics**
Direct contradiction	The passage says the opposite
Extreme	Extreme word *without support* in the passage
One word off	Looks very tempting but one or two words are wrong
Out of scope	Goes beyond what the passage says
True but not right	The passage does say this, but it does not answer the question asked

Flash card the information on this page for future review. Don't copy down the exact language; put it in your own words and you'll remember it better.

Problem Set

The three passages in this problem set appear in both the General and Specific chapters, but different questions are presented in each chapter.

Give yourself 2 to 3 minutes to read each passage and up to 60 seconds to answer each question. After you're done, review your point and passage map before you check the solutions, thinking about ways to improve your process next time. If you come up with ways to improve your map, actually rewrite it to reinforce what you want to do differently next time. Then, check your work against the solution key.

Passage I: Japanese Swords

Historians have long recognized the Japanese sword, or *nihonto*, as one of the finest cutting weapons ever produced. But to regard the sword that is synonymous with the samurai as merely a weapon is to ignore what makes it so special. The Japanese sword has always been considered a splendid weapon and even a spiritual entity. The traditional Japanese adage "the sword is the soul of the samurai" reflects not only the sword's importance to its wielder but also its permanent connection to its creator, the master smith.

Master smiths may not have been considered artists in the classical sense, but each smith exerted great care in the process of creating swords, no two of which were ever forged in exactly the same way. Over hundreds of hours, two types of steel were repeatedly heated, hammered, and folded together into thousands of very thin layers, producing a sword with an extremely sharp and durable cutting edge and a flexible, shock-absorbing blade. It was common, though optional, for a master smith to place a physical signature on a blade; moreover, each smith's secret forging techniques left an idiosyncratic structural signature on his blades. Each master smith brought a high level of devotion, skill, and attention to detail to the sword-making process, and the sword itself was a reflection of his personal honor and ability. This effort made each blade as distinctive as the samurai who wielded it, such that today the Japanese sword is recognized as much for its artistic merit as for its historical significance.

1. The primary purpose of the passage is to

(A) challenge the observation that the Japanese sword is highly admired by historians

(B) introduce new information about the forging of Japanese swords

(C) discuss an obsolete weapon of great historical significance

(D) argue that Japanese sword makers were motivated by honor

(E) explain the value attributed to the Japanese sword

2. Which of the following is the primary function of the second paragraph?

(A) To present an explanation for a change in perception

(B) To determine the historical significance of Japanese swords

(C) To discuss the artistic aspects associated with creating Japanese swords

(D) To compare Japanese master smiths to classical artists

(E) To review the complete process of making a Japanese sword

Passage J: Polygamy

Polygamy in Africa has been a popular topic for social research over the past half-century; it has been analyzed by many distinguished minds and in various well-publicized works. In 1961, when Remi Clignet published his book *Many Wives, Many Powers*, he was not alone in his view that in Africa co-wives may be perceived as direct and indirect sources of increased income and prestige.

By the 1970s, such arguments had become crystallized and popular. Many other African scholars who wrote on the subject became the new champions of this philosophy. For example, in 1983, John Mbiti proclaimed that polygamy is an accepted and respectable institution serving many useful social purposes. Similarly, G.K. Nukunya, in his paper "Polygamy as a Symbol of Status," reiterated Mbiti's idea that a plurality of wives is a legitimate sign of affluence and power in the African society.

The colonial missionary voice, however, provided consistent opposition to polygamy. Invoking the authority of the Bible, missionaries argued that the practice was unethical and destructive of family life, and they propagated the view that Africans had to be coerced into abiding by the monogamous view of marriage favored by Western culture. In some instances, missionaries even dictated immediate divorce for newly converted men who had already entered into polygamous marriages. Unfortunately, neither the missionary voice nor the scholarly voice considered the views of African women important. Although there was some awareness that women regarded polygamy as both a curse and a blessing, the distanced, albeit scientific, perspective of an outside observer predominated both at the pulpit and in scholarly writings.

Contemporary research in the social sciences has begun to focus on the protagonist's voice in the study of culture, recognizing that the views and experiences of those who take part in a given reality ought to receive close examination. This privileging of the protagonist seems appropriate, particularly given that women in Africa have often used literary productions to comment on marriage, family, and gender relations.

1. Which of the following best describes the primary purpose of the passage?

   (A) To discuss scholarly works that view polygamy as a sign of prestige, respect, and affluence in the African society

   (B) To trace the origins of the missionary opposition to African polygamy

   (C) To argue for imposing restrictions on polygamy in African society

   (D) To explore the reasons for women's acceptance of polygamy

   (E) To discuss multiple perspectives on African polygamy and contrast them with contemporary research

2. The third paragraph of the passage plays which of the following roles?

   (A) It discusses the rationale for viewing polygamy as an indication of prestige and affluence in African society.

   (B) It supports the author's view that polygamy is unethical and destructive of family life.

   (C) It contrasts the views of the colonial missionaries with the position of the most recent contemporary research.

   (D) It describes the views on polygamy held by the colonial missionaries and indicates a flaw in this vision.

   (E) It demonstrates that the colonial missionaries were ignorant of the scholarly research on polygamy.

13

Passage K: Sweet Spot

Most tennis players strive to strike the ball on the racket's vibration node, more commonly known as the "sweet spot." However, many players are unaware of the existence of a second, lesser-known location on the racket face—the center of percussion—that will also greatly diminish the strain on a player's arm when the ball is struck.

In order to understand the physics of this second sweet spot, it is helpful to consider what would happen to a tennis racket if the player's hand were to vanish at the moment of impact with the ball. The impact of the ball would cause the racket to bounce backwards, resulting in a translational motion away from the ball. The tendency of this motion would be to jerk all parts of the racket, including the end of its handle, backward, or away from the ball. Unless the ball happened to hit precisely at the racket's center of mass, the racket would additionally experience a rotational motion around its center of mass—much as a penny that has been struck near its edge will start to spin. Whenever the ball hits the racket face, the effect of this rotational motion is to jerk the end of the handle forward, towards the ball. Depending on where the ball strikes the racket face, one or the other of these motions will predominate.

However, there is one point of impact, known as the center of percussion, which causes neither motion to predominate; if a ball strikes this point, the impact does not impart any motion to the end of the handle. The reason for this lack of motion is that the force on the upper part of the hand would be equal and opposite to the force on the lower part of the hand, resulting in no net force on the tennis player's hand or forearm. The center of percussion constitutes a second sweet spot because a tennis player's wrist is typically placed next to the end of the racket's handle. When the player strikes the ball at the center of percussion, her wrist is jerked neither forward nor backward, and she experiences greatly reduced vibration in the arm.

The manner in which a tennis player can detect the center of percussion on a given tennis racket follows from the nature of this second sweet spot. The center of percussion can be located via simple trial and error by holding the end of a tennis racket between the finger and thumb and throwing a ball onto the strings. If the handle jumps out of the player's hand, then the ball has missed the center of percussion.

1. What is the primary message the author is trying to convey?

   (A) A proposal for an improvement to the design of tennis rackets

   (B) An examination of the differences between the two types of sweet spot

   (C) A definition of the translational and rotational forces acting on a tennis racket

   (D) A description of the ideal area in which to strike every ball

   (E) An explanation of a lesser-known area on a tennis racket that reduces unwanted vibration

2. What is the primary function served by the second paragraph in the context of the entire passage?

   (A) To establish the main idea of the passage

   (B) To provide an explanation of the mechanics of the phenomenon discussed in the passage

   (C) To introduce a counterargument that elucidates the main idea of the passage

   (D) To explain the physics of tennis

   (E) To explain why the main idea of the passage would be useful for tennis players

Solutions

Passage I: Japanese Swords

Historians have long recognized the Japanese sword, or *nihonto*, as one of the finest cutting weapons ever produced. But to regard the sword that is synonymous with the samurai as merely a weapon is to ignore what makes it so special. The Japanese sword has always been considered a splendid weapon and even a spiritual entity. The traditional Japanese adage "the sword is the soul of the samurai" reflects not only the sword's importance to its wielder but also its permanent connection to its creator, the master smith.

Master smiths may not have been considered artists in the classical sense, but each smith exerted great care in the process of creating swords, no two of which were ever forged in exactly the same way. Over hundreds of hours, two types of steel were repeatedly heated, hammered, and folded together into thousands of very thin layers, producing a sword with an extremely sharp and durable cutting edge and a flexible, shock-absorbing blade. It was common, though optional, for a master smith to place a physical signature on a blade; moreover, each smith's secret forging techniques left an idiosyncratic structural signature on his blades. Each master smith brought a high level of devotion, skill, and attention to detail to the sword-making process, and the sword itself was a reflection of his personal honor and ability. This effort made each blade as distinctive as the samurai who wielded it, such that today the Japanese sword is recognized as much for its artistic merit as for its historical significance.

Sample passage map (yours will likely differ):

① J sword: not just weapon, spirit

② Master smith: skilled
how to make
artistic merit + history

The point (articulate to yourself; don't write): Japanese sword is a weapon *and* a work of art, important to both samurai and smith. The smiths were basically artists.

1. First, identify the question type:

The primary purpose of the passage is to

The wording here indicates that this is a Primary Purpose, or Main Idea, question. Glance at your map (find the support) and remind yourself of the point (predict the answer). Finally, go to the answers to find a match.

(A) *challenge the observation that the Japanese sword is highly admired by historians*

The passage does not challenge the idea that historians admired the swords; the entire passage reflects great admiration for the swords and their makers. (Direct contradiction)

(B) *introduce new information about the forging of Japanese swords*

The second paragraph does talk about how swords are forged, but does not present this information as *new*. Moreover, information about the forging process is only one part of the passage; it is not the overall point of the passage. (One word off)

(C) *discuss an obsolete weapon of great historical significance*

An *obsolete* weapon would no longer exist today; the passage does not indicate that Japanese swords are no longer used or no longer produced. (One word off)

(D) *argue that Japanese sword makers were motivated by honor*

The passage does indicate that the swords were a reflection of the master smith's personal honor, but this is a narrow detail; it is not the point of the entire passage. (True but not right)

(E) *explain the value attributed to the Japanese sword*

CORRECT. The passage does explain the value of the sword to the samurai (in the first paragraph—"*the sword is the soul of the samurai*" [lines 9–10]) and to the master smith (in the second paragraph).

2. First, identify the question type:

Which of the following is the primary function of the second paragraph?

This is a Paragraph question. Next, find the support (second paragraph of your map) and predict an answer. The master smith was an artist; the swords were effectively the smith's artwork. Sometimes, they even signed the swords!

Finally, check the answers to find a match.

(A) *To present an explanation for a change in perception*

The passage does not indicate that a general *change* in perception has occurred. Rather, the author is putting forth his own idea that smiths might be considered artists. (Out of scope)

(B) *To determine the historical significance of Japanese swords*

The last sentence of the paragraph does mention the historical significance, but the rest of the paragraph focuses on the forging process and the *artistic merit.* The paragraph does not discuss the historical significance. (Out of scope)

(C) *To discuss the artistic aspects associated with creating Japanese swords*

CORRECT. The paragraph begins by indicating that the smiths *may not have been considered artists in the classical sense* (lines 14–15), but goes on to underscore the uniqueness of the finished products (no two were forged the same way, the swords were often signed, the finished product was a reflection of the smith's personal honor and ability). The last sentence indicates that the swords are highly regarded for their *artistic merit* (line 36).

(D) *To compare Japanese master smiths to classical artists*

While the passage does imply that the smiths might be considered artists, there is no mention of actual classical artists, nor is any comparison made. (Out of scope)

(E) *To review the complete process of making a Japanese sword*

The passage does provide some details of the sword-making process, but it does not review the *complete* process. (Extreme)

Passage J: Polygamy

Polygamy in Africa has been a popular topic for social research over the past half-century; it has been analyzed by many distinguished minds and in various well-publicized works. In 1961, when Remi Clignet published his book *Many Wives, Many Powers*, he was not alone in his view that in Africa co-wives may be perceived as direct and indirect sources of increased income and prestige.

By the 1970s, such arguments had become crystallized and popular. Many other African scholars who wrote on the subject became the new champions of this philosophy. For example, in 1983, John Mbiti proclaimed that polygamy is an accepted and respectable institution serving many useful social purposes. Similarly, G.K. Nukunya, in his paper "Polygamy as a Symbol of Status," reiterated Mbiti's idea that a plurality of wives is a legitimate sign of affluence and power in the African society.

The colonial missionary voice, however, provided consistent opposition to polygamy. Invoking the authority of the Bible, missionaries argued that the practice was unethical and destructive of family life, and they propagated the view that Africans had to be coerced into abiding by the monogamous view of marriage favored by Western culture. In some instances, missionaries even dictated immediate divorce for newly converted men who had already entered into polygamous marriages. Unfortunately, neither the missionary voice nor the scholarly voice considered the views of African women important. Although there was some awareness that women regarded polygamy as both a curse and a blessing, the distanced, albeit scientific, perspective of an outside observer predominated both at the pulpit and in scholarly writings.

Contemporary research in the social sciences has begun to focus on the protagonist's voice in the study of culture, recognizing that the views and experiences of those who take part in a given reality ought to receive close examination. This privileging of the protagonist seems appropriate, particularly given that women in Africa have often used literary productions to comment on marriage, family, and gender relations.

Sample passage map (yours will likely differ):

① Polyg Afr
'61 Clignet: P = income, prestige

② 70s, 80s: positive dtls

③ Missionary: against
no one listened to W

④ Now listen to W

The point (articulate to yourself; don't write):
Some scholars thought polygamy was a good thing. Missionaries were against it. Now, people are actually paying attention to what the women think.

13

1. First, identify the question type:

   Which of the following best describes the primary purpose of the passage?

This is a Primary Purpose, or Main Idea, question. Check your passage map (or your memory!) to predict the kind of information the answer should include.

Finally, look for a match in the answers.

(A) *To discuss scholarly works that view polygamy as a sign of prestige, respect, and affluence in the African society*

The first two paragraphs do talk about works that portray polygamy positively, but the rest of the passage explores different viewpoints. This is one side of the story, not the overall point. (True but not right)

(B) *To trace the origins of the missionary opposition to African polygamy*

The passage does discuss missionary opposition to polygamy, but does not detail its origins; in addition, the missionary point of view is just one side of the story. (Out of scope)

(C) *To argue for imposing restrictions on polygamy in African society*

While it might be possible that the author would support a restriction on polygamy, the passage does not make such an argument. In fact, the passage never directly supports a particular position on polygamy—rather, it explores different perspectives on the topic. (Out of scope)

(D) *To explore the reasons for women's acceptance of polygamy*

The passage does indicate that women found polygamy *a curse and a blessing* (line 38), but it does not explore their reasons for thinking that polygamy might sometimes be a blessing. (Out of scope)

(E) *To discuss multiple perspectives on African polygamy and contrast them with contemporary research*

CORRECT. The first few paragraphs look at different past perspectives (scholars, missionaries). Then, the passage ends by indicating that contemporary researchers are paying attention to what women think (something the earlier groups didn't do).

2. First, identify the question type:

The third paragraph of the passage plays which of the following roles?

This is a Paragraph question. Glance at your map and articulate the purpose of the third paragraph to yourself before you look for a match in the answers.

The third paragraph begins by discussing the missionary view of polygamy (against) and goes on to say that both the missionaries and the scholars mentioned earlier failed to take into account the point of view of the women involved in these polygamous marriages.

(A) *It discusses the rationale for viewing polygamy as an indication of prestige and affluence in African society.*

This occurs in the first two paragraphs, not the third. (True but not right)

(B) *It supports the author's view that polygamy is unethical and destructive of family life.*

The author does not present a personal viewpoint in the passage. (Out of scope)

(C) *It contrasts the views of the colonial missionaries with the position of the most recent contemporary research.*

The third paragraph does discuss the missionary viewpoint, but contemporary research is discussed in the *fourth* paragraph, not the third. (True but not right and one word off)

(D) *It describes the views on polygamy held by the colonial missionaries and indicates a flaw in this vision.*

CORRECT. The paragraph does talk about the missionary view of polygamy. It also indicates a flaw in this thinking: that the missionaries failed to consider the views of women in polygamous marriages.

(E) *It demonstrates that the colonial missionaries were ignorant of the scholarly research on polygamy.*

The passage presents the missionary view separately from the views of the scholars mentioned earlier in the passage; it does not indicate whether the missionaries were familiar with the scholarly position. (Out of scope)

Passage K: Sweet Spot

Most tennis players strive to strike the ball on the racket's vibration node, more commonly known as the "sweet spot." However, many players are unaware of the existence of a second, lesser-known location on the racket face—the center of percussion—that will also greatly diminish the strain on a player's arm when the ball is struck.

In order to understand the physics of this second sweet spot, it is helpful to consider what would happen to a tennis racket if the player's hand were to vanish at the moment of impact with the ball. The impact of the ball would cause the racket to bounce backwards, resulting in a translational motion away from the ball. The tendency of this motion would be to jerk all parts of the racket, including the end of its handle, backward, or away from the ball. Unless the ball happened to hit precisely at the racket's center of mass, the racket would additionally experience a rotational motion around its center of mass—much as a penny that has been struck near its edge will start to spin. Whenever the ball hits the racket face, the effect of this rotational motion is to jerk the end of the handle forward, towards the ball. Depending on where the ball strikes the racket face, one or the other of these motions will predominate.

However, there is one point of impact, known as the center of percussion, which causes neither motion to predominate; if a ball strikes this point, the impact does not impart any motion to the end of the handle. The reason for this lack of motion is that the force on the upper part of the hand would be equal and opposite to the force on the lower part of the hand, resulting in no net force on the tennis player's hand or forearm. The center of percussion constitutes a second sweet spot because a tennis player's wrist is typically placed next to the end of the racket's handle. When the player strikes the ball at the center of percussion, her wrist is jerked neither forward nor backward, and she experiences greatly reduced vibration in the arm.

The manner in which a tennis player can detect the center of percussion on a given tennis racket follows from the nature of this second sweet spot. The center of percussion can be located via simple trial and error by holding the end of a tennis racket between the finger and thumb and throwing a ball onto the strings. If the handle jumps out of the player's hand, then the ball has missed the center of percussion.

Sample passage map (yours will likely differ):

① 2 SS (↓ strain), one less known

② if hand disappear?

③ center perc = no motion, ↓↓ vibration

④ find center perc

The point (articulate to yourself; don't write): People usually know about one sweet spot but not the other. Both reduce vibration in the arm. (Plus lots of technical details—ignore for now!)

1. First, identify the question type:

   What is the primary message the author is trying to convey?

This is a Primary Purpose, or Main Idea, question. Glance at your map to remind yourself of the point before you go to the answers.

(A) *A proposal for an improvement to the design of tennis rackets*

The passage doesn't talk about this at all. (Out of scope)

(B) *An examination of the differences between the two types of sweet spot*

It does talk about two different types of sweet spot. Leave this in for now.

(C) *A definition of the translational and rotational forces acting on a tennis racket*

One paragraph did mention these forces, but that was only one paragraph. This is not the point of the whole thing. (True but not right)

(D) *A description of the ideal area in which to strike every ball*

The passage does say that striking the ball at a sweet spot can reduce vibration, but it never says that spot is the ideal area in which to strike *every* ball. (Extreme)

(E) *An explanation of a lesser-known area on a tennis racket that reduces unwanted vibration*

It does talk about this. Leave this in.

Compare answers (B) and (E) to the support in the passage. The first paragraph mentions both sweet spots. After that, though, the passage focuses just on the lesser-known one; it doesn't go back-and-forth contrasting the two. Answer (E) is more appropriate than answer (B).

The correct answer is **(E)**.

2. First, identify the question type:

What is the primary function served by the second paragraph in the context of the entire passage?

This is a Paragraph question. Glance at your map and articulate the purpose of the second paragraph to yourself before you check the answers.

The second paragraph begins with the text *In order to understand the physics of this second sweet spot*. It then goes into lots of detail about what would happen if the player's hand vanished and various forces and... wait! Don't get sucked into the detail. The first sentence is probably enough: This is how the second sweet spot works. Check the answers.

(A) *To establish the main idea of the passage*

The first paragraph establishes the main idea. The second paragraph provides detail about how the second sweet spot works. (Out of scope)

(B) *To provide an explanation of the mechanics of the phenomenon discussed in the passage*

CORRECT. The second paragraph does explain the physics, or the *mechanics*, of the phenomenon (the second sweet spot) mentioned in the first paragraph.

(C) *To introduce a counterargument that elucidates the main idea of the passage*

The second paragraph does elucidate (or explain) the main idea, but it is not a counterargument to anything.
(One word off)

(D) *To explain the physics of tennis*

The paragraph does discuss the physical forces relevant to the sweet spot, but it does not explain all of the physics behind the game of tennis. That would be a very long paragraph! (Out of scope)

(E) *To explain why the main idea of the passage would be useful for tennis players*

The first and third paragraphs explain why the main idea is useful: to reduce vibration in the arm. The second paragraph does not do this. (True but not right)

CHAPTER 14

Specific Questions

In This Chapter:

- 4 Steps to the Answer
- Practice Passage: Electroconvulsive Therapy
- Detail Questions
- Inference Questions
- Specific Purpose Questions
- EXCEPT Questions
- Specific Question Cheat Sheet

In this chapter, you will learn how to handle the most commonly asked specific questions on the GMAT. You'll learn how to use your passage map to efficiently find relevant details, what analysis each type of question requires, and how to identify the correct answer and avoid trap answers.

CHAPTER 14 Specific Questions

Most of the questions you will see on the GMAT will ask you about specific details in the passage. On average, expect to spend about 1.5 minutes on each specific question.

Here are the three most common types of specific questions:

1. **Detail questions.** These questions ask you to find a specific detail explicitly stated in the passage.
2. **Inference questions.** On these, the correct answer will *not* be stated explicitly in the passage, but it can be proven true using information stated in the passage.
3. **Specific Purpose questions.** These questions ask you *why* the author mentions a specific piece of information or employs a particular example.

You may occasionally see another type, such as a Strengthen or Weaken question. These are more commonly given on Critical Reasoning questions; if you do see one on Reading Comprehension, you can use the same strategies that you use for CR.

4 Steps to the Answer

You'll use the same process you learned for general questions in order to answer specific questions:

Step 1: Identify the question. This chapter will tell you the common language to expect for the different question types.

Step 2: Find the support. Expect to go back into the passage for all specific questions. Use your map to quickly figure out where to go, then read the relevant one to three sentences. Do not skip this step! Many specific questions have trap answers designed specifically to catch people who don't look back at the passage.

Step 3: Predict an answer. Take a look at the question again and, using the relevant passage text, try to formulate a rough answer in your own words. But there's a caveat: This won't work 100 percent of the time. This chapter will explain what to do when you can't predict the answer.

Step 4: Eliminate and find a match. Do a first pass through the answers, crossing off anything that is definitely wrong. Leave in any potential matches for your predicted answer as well as any for which you're not sure (whether you think they might be right or wrong). Don't spend time debating an answer choice (yet). When you're done with your first pass, see what you have left:

- If you have eliminated four answers, great! Pick the remaining one and move on.
- If you still have two or three answers left, compare the answers to the relevant information in the passage. If the answers are very similar, you may also compare them to each other. Use this to narrow down to the best answer of the remaining options.
- If you still have four or five answers left, make sure you didn't misread the question! After that, it may be best to cut your losses: Guess and move on.

Practice Passage: Electroconvulsive Therapy

Give yourself approximately 8 minutes to read the passage below and answer the four questions that follow. Mimic real test conditions. Answer the questions in the order given; pick an answer before you move to the next one, and don't return to a question you've already answered.

Electroconvulsive therapy (ECT) is a controversial psychiatric treatment involving the induction of a seizure in a patient by passing electricity through the brain. While beneficial effects of electrically induced seizures are evident and predictable in most patients, a unified mechanism of action has not yet been established and remains the subject of numerous investigations. ECT is extremely effective against severe depression, some acute psychotic states, and mania, though, like many medical procedures, it has its risks.

Since the inception of ECT in 1938, the public has held a strongly negative conception of the procedure. Initially, doctors employed unmodified ECT. Patients were rendered instantly unconscious by the electrical current, but the strength of the muscle contractions from uncontrolled motor seizures often led to compression fractures of the spine or damage to the teeth. In addition to the effect this physical trauma had on public sentiment, graphic examples of abuse documented in books and movies, such as Ken Kesey's *One Flew Over the Cuckoo's Nest*, portrayed ECT as punitive, cruel, overused, and violative of patients' legal rights.

Modern ECT is virtually unrecognizable from its earlier days. The treatment is modified by the muscle relaxant succinylcholine, which renders muscle contractions practically nonexistent. Additionally, patients are given a general anesthetic. Thus, the patient is asleep and fully unaware during the procedure, and the only outward sign of a seizure may be the rhythmic movement of the patient's hand or foot. ECT is generally used in severely depressed patients for whom psychotherapy and medication prove ineffective. It may also be considered when there is an imminent risk of suicide, since antidepressants often take several weeks to work effectively. Exactly how ECT exerts its effects is not known, but repeated applications affect several neurotransmitters in the brain, including serotonin, norepinephrine, and dopamine.

ECT has proven effective, but it is not without controversy. Though decades-old studies showing brain cell death have been refuted in recent research, many patients do report loss of memory for events that occurred in the days, weeks, or months surrounding the ECT. Some patients have also reported that their short-term memories continue to be affected for months after ECT, though some doctors argue that this memory malfunction may reflect the type of amnesia that sometimes results from severe depression.

1. According to the passage, why has ECT been viewed negatively by the public?

   (A) Though ECT is effective in many cases, the medical community is not certain exactly how it works.

   (B) Early incarnations of ECT often resulted in physical trauma to the patient.

   (C) Effective use of ECT requires exposure to concerning medications, such as muscle relaxants and anesthesia.

   (D) ECT does not benefit individuals with anxiety disorders.

   (E) ECT cannot be performed without subsequent loss of memory in the patient.

14

2. Which of the following can be inferred about the way in which the modern form of ECT works?

   (A) Greater amounts of the neurotransmitters serotonin, norepinephrine, and dopamine seem to reduce symptoms of depression.

   (B) ECT cannot be used prior to attempting psychotherapy or medication.

   (C) Succinylcholine completely immobilizes the patient's body.

   (D) ECT often works faster than antidepressants.

   (E) One ECT treatment is often sufficient to reduce symptoms of depression significantly.

3. The author mentions amnesia as a possible side effect of severe depression in order to

   (A) acknowledge one of the possible negative side effects associated with ECT

   (B) emphasize the seriousness of severe depression as a debilitating disease

   (C) introduce a possible alternative cause for short-term memory loss reported by some patients

   (D) draw a connection between brain cell death and short-term memory loss

   (E) refute claims that ECT is responsible for any form of amnesia in patients

4. Each of the following is cited in the passage as a current or historical criticism of electroconvulsive therapy EXCEPT

   (A) ECT may cause the death of brain cells and memory loss

   (B) in certain cases, ECT was portrayed as a means to punish individuals

   (C) ECT had the potential to be used in inappropriate situations

   (D) early forms of ECT did not adequately protect patients from secondary harm brought on by the treatment

   (E) repeated applications of ECT affect several neurotransmitters in the brain

The questions above represent four distinct question types. The following sections will each cover one type and provide an explanation of the relevant question. First, here's what a reader might be thinking while reading the passage and jotting down a map:

ECT (electricity → seizure) has positives and negatives. Don't know how it works, but it is effective against depression and some other things.

Public doesn't like ECT. Early forms caused serious bodily trauma. Books and movies depicted it as cruel and abusive.

Modern ECT is much better. No trauma. Still don't know how it works but it helps really depressed people who can't get help in other ways.

It still has drawbacks, though, primarily around memory loss.

ECT + / −

	+	−
①	treats depression	how work?
②		public percep trauma cruel, etc.
③	Modern = no trauma helps v. depr. ppl	how work?
④		memory loss

Here's a simple story for the passage:

ECT was pretty bad at first but it's much better now. They don't really know how it works, but it does work for severe depression. Even though ECT is better now, it still has some drawbacks.

Detail Questions

Detail questions typically include the language *according to the passage* (or something very similar). If you see this language, then you are being asked to find a particular piece of information, explicitly stated somewhere in the passage, that answers that particular question. The first question is a Detail question:

1. According to the passage, why has ECT been viewed negatively by the public?

Most of the time, the question stem will provide enough information to tell you where in the passage to look for the answer. Where does this particular question stem signal that you should look?

The question stem specifically references the public's negative view of ECT. This concept is the topic sentence of the second paragraph, so your passage map would likely contain some reference to this idea.

Your map, then, tells you where to go for step 2 of the process (find the support). Return to paragraph 2 and read as far as you need to in order to get an idea of why people disliked ECT:

> Since the inception of ECT in 1938, the public has held a strongly negative conception of the procedure. Initially, doctors employed unmodified ECT. Patients were rendered instantly unconscious by the electrical current, but the strength of the muscle contractions from uncontrolled motor seizures often led to compression fractures of the spine or damage to the teeth. In addition to the effect this physical trauma had on public sentiment, graphic examples of abuse documented in books and movies, such as Ken Kesey's *One Flew Over the Cuckoo's Nest*, portrayed ECT as punitive, cruel, overused, and violative of patients' legal rights.

Use this information to try to predict the answer (step 3 of the process). First, people experienced some serious types of physical trauma (spinal fractures, damage to the teeth). Second, books and movies portrayed ECT as abusive and cruel. The correct answer should address one or both of those two topics.

Time for step 4: Eliminate and find a match! Try to identify any trap answer types that you have already learned.

(A) Though ECT is effective in many cases, the medical community is not certain exactly how it works.	*The passage does say this, but it does not say that this is why people dislike ECT. (True but not right)*
(B) Early incarnations of ECT often resulted in physical trauma to the patient.	***CORRECT.*** *This matches the first of the two reasons given in paragraph 2: Initially, people often experienced serious physical injuries when undergoing ECT treatment.*
(C) Effective use of ECT requires exposure to concerning medications, such as muscle relaxants and anesthesia.	*The passage does state that ECT now uses muscle relaxants and anesthesia, but the passage does not call these medications* concerning. *If anything, the passage seems to consider these advances positive because they allow the patient to be* asleep and fully unaware. *(Could be considered either One word off or True but not right)*
(D) ECT does not benefit individuals with anxiety disorders.	*The passage does not mention individuals with anxiety disorders. (Out of scope)*
(E) ECT cannot be performed without subsequent loss of memory in the patient.	*The last paragraph does mention that ECT can result in memory loss, but does not say that this side effect is always present. (Nor does the passage mention public perception with respect to memory loss.) (Extreme)*

As you work through the answers, your thought process might be something along these lines:

(A) *Not one of the two reasons I stated before.*

(B) *Yes, this was one of the reasons I stated. Leave in.*

(C) *Not one of the two reasons I stated before.*

(D) *Not one of the two reasons I stated before.*

(E) *Not one of the two reasons I stated before. I do remember the passage saying something about this though, and memory loss is obviously not good. Leave in for now.*

Hmm, (B) *vs.* (E). *Answer* (B) *is an exact match for what I said, so I'm going to go for it. If I didn't have such a good match, I'd go and check the part that talked about memory loss.*

If you do want to check the passage for the memory loss information, use the same process. Check your map; where was that info?

Paragraph 4. Reread the relevant text: *Many patients do report loss of memory for events that occurred in the days, weeks, or months surrounding the ECT. Some patients have also reported that their short-term memories continue to be affected for months after ECT.*

Check that against the choice. First, this text says *many*, not *all*, patients experience memory loss, so this is an *extreme* trap. Second, this paragraph is not where the passage discussed why the public has such a negative view of ECT.

The wrong answers represent several common traps, all of which were first presented in the General Questions chapter. For a quick review, reference your Cheat Sheet at the end of that chapter.

If you see a question that begins *According to the passage*, you almost certainly have a detail question. Use your map to figure out what paragraph you'll need; in this case, the concept of negative public perception was a good clue to look in the second paragraph.

Whenever possible, try to formulate an answer to the question before you look at the answer choices. Note that there may be more than one possibility. In this case, the correct answer could have talked about the bodily trauma or about the depictions in books and movies.

At times, you may struggle to understand certain parts of a passage, in which case you may not be able to predict an answer. In this case, do one of two things. If you think you understand the main points in the relevant text, use that to try to eliminate some answers before you guess. (Sometimes, you might be able to eliminate all four wrong answers!)

If you don't understand the text well enough to pick up the main points, then guess and move on. (Don't be stubborn and waste valuable time that you could use elsewhere; when you don't get it, admit that to yourself and move on right away.)

Inference Questions

Inference questions ask you to find an answer that must be true based on information presented in the passage—but the information in the correct answer will *not* be explicitly given to you in the passage.

For example, if your boss tells you that Acme Co is your company's most important client, what can you infer?

You might imagine that Acme Co is responsible for a larger chunk of the company's revenue than is any other client. This is a reasonable inference in the real world, but it will lead you to a wrong answer on the GMAT. Why? Because it doesn't *have* to be true. Perhaps Acme is the company's most prestigious client. Perhaps your boss is good friends with Acme's CEO.

In fact, you have no idea *why* Acme Co is the most important client. The boss just stated a fact and didn't give you any insight into the reason for that fact.

The GMAT is never asking you to come up with reasonable real-world inferences. Rather, it is asking you to deduce what *must be true* given the available evidence.

So if Acme Co is the company's most important client, what else has to be true?

For starters, your company has to have at least one other client. If Acme were the only client, then your boss couldn't call it the *most important* client.

If one of the company's other clients is Widget Inc, you could also correctly infer that Widget Inc is not the company's most important client—that spot is already taken by Acme!

Which problem in the *Electroconvulsive Therapy* set was the Inference problem? The wording of the question stem will tell you:

2. Which of the following can be inferred about the way in which the modern form of ECT works?

In this case, the word *inferred* is in the question stem. When you see any form of the words *infer*, *imply*, or *suggest*, you have an Inference question.

Now, find the support (step 2). *Modern ECT* is first mentioned in the third paragraph, so look there to find and reread the relevant text. Step 3 (predict an answer), however, is pretty tough: The paragraph is all about how ECT works. In this case, it would be tough for anyone to try to predict an answer in advance.

Instead, return to the third paragraph to remind yourself of the type of information it contains, then start to check the answers, crossing off anything you cannot prove to be true based on information from that paragraph. Here's the third paragraph:

> Modern ECT is virtually unrecognizable from its earlier days. The treatment is modified by the muscle relaxant succinylcholine, which renders muscle contractions practically nonexistent. Additionally, patients are given a general anesthetic. Thus, the patient is asleep and fully unaware during the procedure, and the only outward sign of a seizure may be the rhythmic movement of the patient's hand or foot. ECT is generally used in severely depressed patients for whom psychotherapy and medication prove ineffective. It may also be considered when there is an imminent risk of suicide, since antidepressants often take several weeks to work effectively. Exactly how ECT exerts its effects is not known, but repeated applications affect several neurotransmitters in the brain, including serotonin, norepinephrine, and dopamine.

Think big picture; don't get too caught up in the details. The modern form of ECT is much safer for patients—they're asleep and won't have the same issues that caused injuries before. Modern ECT can be very effective for depression and risk of suicide. Move to the answers and check them against the paragraph:

(A) Greater amounts of the neurotransmitters serotonin, norepinephrine, and dopamine seem to reduce symptoms of depression.	*The third paragraph does mention these neurotransmitters and that ECT is effective for depression. The technical detail is annoying, so leave this in for now; if you still have more than one choice left at the end, then you can examine this more closely.*
(B) ECT cannot be used prior to attempting psychotherapy or medication.	*Whenever you see an extreme word, check whether the passage justifies the usage. In this case, the third paragraph does not justify the use of the word* cannot*; it says only that those other therapies are tried first at least some of the time. (Extreme)*
(C) Succinylcholine completely immobilizes the patient's body.	*Another extreme word! Check it. The second sentence states that succinylcholine* renders muscle contractions practically nonexistent. *The qualifier* practically *means the muscle contractions are* almost *gone, but not* entirely. *The word* completely *is too extreme. (Extreme)*
(D) ECT often works faster than antidepressants.	*The third paragraph does mention antidepressants; leave this in for now.*
(E) One ECT treatment is often sufficient to reduce symptoms of depression significantly.	*The passage does not discuss the number of treatments necessary to reduce symptoms significantly. At one point, it does mention* repeated applications, *so, if anything, it appears that more than one treatment might be typical. (Out of scope)*

Compare (A) and (D)

(A) *Scan for these words; they appear in the last sentence. What's the message? Nobody really knows how ECT works, just that it affects these neurotransmitters—but it doesn't say that ECT results in* greater *amounts of these things, just that they are* affected. *The word* greater *in the answer choice isn't supported. (One word off)*

(D) ***CORRECT****. The third paragraph states that ECT* may also be considered when there is an imminent risk of suicide, since antidepressants often take several weeks to work effectively. *If ECT is used as an emergency intervention for suicide, because antidepressants take a while to work, then it must be true that ECT often works more quickly than antidepressants.*

If you see a question that contains some form of the words *infer*, *imply*, or *suggest*, then you know you have an Inference question. In most cases, the question stem will also contain some specific info that will help you to determine which paragraph you'll need. In this problem, a key term in the question stem (*modern ECT*) is mentioned for the first time at the beginning of the third paragraph.

If you can, try to formulate an answer to the question before you look at the answer choices. Note that, sometimes, the question stem will be too vague to predict a solid answer in advance (this can happen on any type of specific question). When this happens, remind yourself of the main points in any relevant paragraph(s) or sentences and then start to test the answers. (If you know that you don't understand the question well enough to formulate an answer for that reason, consider guessing and moving on.)

If you find yourself struggling with RC Inference questions, you may want to consider cross-training in Critical Reasoning. CR Inference questions work the same way, so you may find that you learn this more easily for CR and can then come back and apply your skills to RC.

On either question type, it can be helpful to analyze your work by comparing each answer choice carefully to the supporting text (after you have finished solving the problem). This will help you learn to distinguish a valid inference from an answer choice that goes too far.

Specific Purpose Questions

Specific Purpose questions are not as common as either Detail or Inference questions, but you can expect to see at least one on the Verbal section of the GMAT. These questions ask you for what purpose, or why, the author mentions a specific piece of information—so they are often called **Why** questions for short.

As with Inference questions, you can't just repeat back what the passage explicitly states. Instead, you have to do a little bit of processing. For example, consider this information:

> Silicon chip manufacturers struggle to maintain profit margins due to the exorbitantly high overhead costs associated with building semiconductor factories. Such factories typically cost a minimum of two billion dollars to build and may be obsolete within three to five years. As such, the manufacturers seek out customers who need very high volumes of products, allowing the overhead costs to be spread out over a large number of units.

Here's the question:

> The author states that semiconductor factories may become obsolete within three to five years of being built in order to

Why does the author talk about this particular detail? In the prior sentence, the author asserts that *chip manufacturers struggle to maintain profit margins* because these factories have *exorbitantly high overhead costs*, so she is providing information to support her contention that these costs really are so high as to impact profit significantly. The correct answer might say something like:

> emphasize the unusually high costs associated with manufacturing silicon chips

Here's the Specific Purpose question from the ECT passage:

3. The author mentions amnesia as a possible side effect of severe depression in order to

   What similarities can you spot between the semiconductor question stem and the one above? Both talk about the *author*. Both finish with *in order to*. Specific Purpose questions are typically structured to say *the author* (mentions some specific detail) *in order to*, and then you have to fill in the blank with the answer that explains *why* the author mentioned that particular detail.

So, where did the author of the ECT passage talk about amnesia and severe depression?

You may not have noted this very specific detail about amnesia in your map, so you may have to go on a hunt. The passage mentions *severe depression* in three out of the four paragraphs, so don't scan for those key words. Instead, scan for the word *amnesia.* One more clue: Amnesia is a type of memory loss. You might have noted or you may remember that the last paragraph talks about memory loss. Here's the relevant text from the fourth paragraph:

> Some patients have also reported that their short-term memories continue to be affected for months after ECT, though some doctors argue that this memory malfunction may reflect the type of amnesia that sometimes results from severe depression.

On to step 3: Formulate your own answer to the question. *Why* does the author bring up amnesia in the context of severe depression?

Some people appear to attribute short-term memory problems to ECT; this is consistent with much of the rest of the passage, which discusses negative side effects and risks associated with ECT. The second half of the quoted text, however, indicates that some doctors think that these symptoms might actually be caused by the depression itself. In other words, it's possible that this particular side effect is not actually a result of ECT.

The author, then, is pointing out that not every possible negative effect is definitely due to ECT. What answer choice goes along with this idea? (Also, try to identify any wrong answer traps that you have already learned.)

(A) acknowledge one of the possible negative side effects associated with ECT	*The passage does talk about many negative side effects associated with ECT, but the reference to amnesia is intended to introduce the idea that certain side effects actually might not be due to ECT. (Direct contradiction)*
(B) emphasize the seriousness of severe depression as a debilitating disease	*This choice sounds very tempting; in the real world, amnesia is a very serious issue and severe depression is a debilitating disease. However, depression is mentioned only as a possible alternative cause; the passage does not state that the amnesia is definitely a result of the depression. (True but not right)*
(C) introduce a possible alternative cause for short-term memory loss reported by some patients	***CORRECT.*** *The first half of the sentence brings up patient reports of memory loss due to ECT. The second half indicates a different potential cause: Some doctors think this memory loss might actually be due to amnesia from depression.*
(D) draw a connection between brain cell death and short-term memory loss	*The fourth paragraph mentions both brain cell death and short-term memory loss. The passage does not connect the two ideas, however. In fact, it says that reports of brain cell death have been refuted, though memory loss is still in evidence. (Mix-up)*
(E) refute claims that ECT is responsible for any form of amnesia in patients	*The sentence does offer a possible alternative cause, but ECT is not definitively ruled out as one possible cause. (Extreme)*

The wrong answers represent several common traps, one of which hasn't shown up in earlier problems. A **Mix-Up** is a tricky trap in which the test writers use wording straight from the passage to convey a different meaning than what is presented in the passage. They are expecting you to think it sounds familiar and jump on the choice without giving it too much thought, and in fact that's exactly what many test-takers do.

In answer (D) above, the keywords used are all straight from the passage. The meaning of the answer, however, does not fit with the author's reason for mentioning amnesia. In fact, the answer does not even convey what the passage really said.

In order to is the most common clue that you are facing a Specific Purpose question; if the question says the author brought up some detail *in order to* do something, then you're trying to figure out why the author brought up that detail.

As for all specific questions, use your map to figure out what paragraph you'll need; in this case, the words *amnesia* and *severe depression* indicated the fourth paragraph.

Whenever possible, try to formulate an answer to the question before you look at the answer choices. If you can't, remind yourself of the main points in any relevant sentences or paragraph(s) and then start to test the answers.

EXCEPT Questions

Any question type can also be written as an **EXCEPT question**; most of the time, when you see an EXCEPT question, you'll be dealing with a Detail question or an Inference question.

Here is the fourth question from the ECT passage. What question type is it?

4. Each of the following is cited in the passage as a current or historical criticism of electroconvulsive therapy EXCEPT

The language *each of the following is cited* indicates that this is a Detail question. The information in four of the answers is explicitly stated in the passage. The fifth answer, the one *not* cited in the passage, will be the correct answer.

Follow the same process you would normally use for a Detail question, with one twist.

It would be inefficient to try to find all of the criticisms of ECT in the passage first and only then go check the answers to find the matches. Instead, go straight to the answers and work backwards: Use the keywords to try to find the information in the passage. If you've spent more than about 20 seconds on an answer and still haven't found it in the passage, leave it and move to the next answer.

As you work, label the answers either True or False on your scrap paper. On this problem, true (or T) means that the answer is indeed cited in the passage as a criticism of ECT. False (or F) means that it is not. Cross off the four T answers and pick the odd one out, the lone F answer.

Also, note one important thing about the question: It asks for *current or historical criticism*, so something that was once criticized but is no longer considered problematic today would still count as a criticism of ECT.

(A) ECT may cause the death of brain cells and memory loss.	*T. The fourth paragraph mentions that very old research showed brain cell death (even though that research has been refuted today) and that memory loss is an ongoing concern.*
(B) In certain cases, ECT was portrayed as a means to punish individuals.	*T. Line 26 indicates that ECT was portrayed as* punitive.
(C) ECT had the potential to be used in inappropriate situations.	*T. Tricky! Line 26 indicates that ECT was portrayed as* overused. *If a treatment is overused, then at least some of those uses shouldn't be happening, or are inappropriate.*
(D) Early forms of ECT did not adequately protect patients from secondary harm brought on by the treatment.	*T. Lines 19–21 indicate that early forms of ECT* often led to compression fractures of the spine or damage to the teeth.
(E) Repeated applications of ECT affect several neurotransmitters in the brain.	***CORRECT****. F. Lines 45–47 do mention that ECT affects neurotransmitters, but this information is not presented as a* criticism *of ECT. Rather, it is presented as a partial means of understanding how ECT works.*

The standard wrong answer trap categories don't necessarily apply to EXCEPT questions. The four wrong answers are "right" in the sense that they were truly in the passage. The one correct answer on an EXCEPT question (the false one) can fall into one of the standard trap categories. Which trap does answer (E), above, represent?

According to the passage, it is true that ECT affects neurotransmitters, but it is false that this was *cited in the passage as a current or historical criticism* of ECT. So answer (E) is a variation of a true but not right trap answer.

EXCEPT questions are not a separate type of question; any of the main question types could be presented as an EXCEPT question. Use your usual clues to identify the question type. Then, work backwards: Go straight to the answers and try to find them in the passage. You're going to cross off the four true answers (for which you will find support in the passage) and select the one false answer.

Specific Question Cheat Sheet

Identify the Question

Detail:	Most common: *Accoring to the passage...*
	indicates explicitly...
	mentions (or proposes) which of the following...
Inference:	Most common: *infer, imply, suggest, provides support for...*
	author would be most likely to describe (or *predict*) X
Specific Purpose:	Most common clue: *in order to*
	The author's reference (to X) *serves primarily to...*
EXCEPT:	Any can also be EXCEPT questions. Use keywords from the answers to find the support in the passage.

14

Find the Support

Use your map to find specific paragraph of sentences needed. If you can't, go to answers to try to work backwards. If this doesn't work, guess and move on.

Predict an Answer

Try to formulate an answer in your own words. If you can't, go to anwers to try to work backwards. If this doesn't work, guess and move on.

Eliminate

Check all of the answers! Common traps include the following:

Trap	**Characteristics**
Direct contradiction	The passage says the opposite.
Extreme	Extreme word *without support* in the passage.
One word off	Looks very tempting but one or two words are wrong.
Out of scope	Goes beyond what the passage says.
Mix-up	Uses words directly from the passage, but the meaning is not what the passage says.
True but not right	The passage says this (or it's true in the real word), but it does not answer the question asked.

Flash card the information on this page for future review. Don't copy down the exact language; put it in your own words and you'll remember it better.

Problem Set

The three passages in this problem set appear in both the General and Specific chapters, but different questions are presented in each chapter.

Give yourself 2 to 3 minutes to read each passage and up to 60 seconds to answer each question. After you're done, review your point and passage map before you check the solutions, thinking about ways to improve your process next time. If you come up with ways to improve your map, actually rewrite it to reinforce what you want to do differently next time. Then, check your work against the solution key.

Passage I: Japanese Swords

Historians have long recognized the Japanese sword, or *nihonto*, as one of the finest cutting weapons ever produced. But to regard the sword that is synonymous with the samurai as merely a weapon is to ignore what makes it so special. The Japanese sword has always been considered a splendid weapon and even a spiritual entity. The traditional Japanese adage "the sword is the soul of the samurai" reflects not only the sword's importance to its wielder but also its permanent connection to its creator, the master smith.

Master smiths may not have been considered artists in the classical sense, but each smith exerted great care in the process of creating swords, no two of which were ever forged in exactly the same way. Over hundreds of hours, two types of steel were repeatedly heated, hammered, and folded together into thousands of very thin layers, producing a sword with an extremely sharp and durable cutting edge and a flexible, shock-absorbing blade. It was common, though optional, for a master smith to place a physical signature on a blade; moreover, each smith's secret forging techniques left an idiosyncratic structural signature on his blades. Each master smith brought a high level of devotion, skill, and attention to detail to the sword-making process, and the sword itself was a reflection of his personal honor and ability. This effort made each blade as distinctive as the samurai who wielded it such that today the Japanese sword is recognized as much for its artistic merit as for its historical significance.

1. Which of the following can be inferred about the structural signature of a Japanese sword?

   (A) It is an inscription that the smith places on the blade during the forging process.

   (B) It refers to the particular characteristics of a blade created by a smith's unique forging process.

   (C) It suggests that each blade can be traced back to a known master smith.

   (D) It reflects the soul of the samurai who wielded the sword.

   (E) It refers to the actual curved shape of the blade.

2. Each of the following is mentioned in the passage EXCEPT

   (A) Every Japanese sword has a unique structure that can be traced back to a special forging process.

   (B) Master smiths kept their forging techniques secret.

   (C) The Japanese sword was considered by some to have a spiritual quality.

   (D) Master smiths are now considered artists by most major historians.

   (E) The Japanese sword is considered both a work of art and a historical artifact.

14

3. The author explains the way in which swords were made in order to

    (A) establish that the Japanese sword is the most important handheld weapon in history

    (B) claim that the skill of the samurai is what made each Japanese sword unique

    (C) support the contention that the master smiths might be considered artists as well as craftsmen

    (D) illustrate that master smiths were more concerned with the artistic merit of their blades than with the blades' practical qualities

    (E) demonstrate that the Japanese sword has more historical importance than artistic importance

Passage J: Polygamy

Polygamy in Africa has been a popular topic for social research over the past half-century; it has been analyzed by many distinguished minds and in various well-publicized works. In 1961, when Remi Clignet published his book *Many Wives, Many Powers*, he was not alone in his view that in Africa co-wives may be perceived as direct and indirect sources of increased income and prestige.

By the 1970s, such arguments had become crystallized and popular. Many other African scholars who wrote on the subject became the new champions of this philosophy. For example, in 1983, John Mbiti proclaimed that polygamy is an accepted and respectable institution serving many useful social purposes. Similarly, G.K. Nukunya, in his paper "Polygamy as a Symbol of Status," reiterated Mbiti's idea that a plurality of wives is a legitimate sign of affluence and power in the African society.

The colonial missionary voice, however, provided consistent opposition to polygamy. Invoking the authority of the Bible, missionaries argued that the practice was unethical and destructive of family life, and they propagated the view that Africans had to be coerced into abiding by the monogamous view of marriage favored by Western culture. In some instances, missionaries even dictated immediate divorce for newly converted men who had already entered into polygamous marriages. Unfortunately, neither the missionary voice nor the scholarly voice considered the views of African women important. Although there was some awareness that women regarded polygamy as both a curse and a blessing, the distanced, albeit scientific, perspective of an outside observer predominated both at the pulpit and in scholarly writings.

Contemporary research in the social sciences has begun to focus on the protagonist's voice in the study of culture, recognizing that the views and experiences of those who take part in a given reality ought to receive close examination. This privileging of the protagonist seems appropriate, particularly given that women in Africa have often used literary productions to comment on marriage, family, and gender relations.

1. According to the passage, colonial missionaries and popular scholars shared which of the following traits in their approach to the issue of polygamy?

(A) Both considered polygamy a sign of social status and success.

(B) Neither accounted for the views of local women.

(C) Both attempted to limit the prevalence of polygamy.

(D) Both pointed out polygamy's destructive effects on family life.

(E) Both exhibited a somewhat negative attitude toward polygamy.

2. The author implies which of the following about Nukunya and Mbiti's works?

(A) From their point of view, a man who lacks wealth and influence is less likely to have many wives.

(B) They adjusted their initial views on polygamy, recognizing that the experiences of African women should receive closer attention.

(C) Their arguments represented a significant departure from those of Remi Clignet.

(D) Their analyses may have been tainted by the fact that both men practiced polygamy themselves.

(E) Their views reflected the majority opinion of the African population.

3. The passage mentions each of the following, EXCEPT

   (A) the year of publication of Remi Clignet's book *Many Wives, Many Powers*

   (B) the year in which John Mbiti made a claim that polygamy is an accepted institution

   (C) examples of African women's literary productions devoted to family relations

   (D) reasons for missionary opposition to polygamy

   (E) current-day perspectives with respect to studying polygamy

1) Polygamy = prestige

2) 1920 polygam affluent and power

3) church against polygamy
but women ignored

4) Now women are being listened

Passage K: Sweet Spot

Most tennis players strive to strike the ball on the racket's vibration node, more commonly known as the "sweet spot." However, many players are unaware of the existence of a second, lesser-known location on the racket face—the center of percussion—that will also greatly diminish the strain on a player's arm when the ball is struck.

In order to understand the physics of this second sweet spot, it is helpful to consider what would happen to a tennis racket if the player's hand were to vanish at the moment of impact with the ball. The impact of the ball would cause the racket to bounce backwards, resulting in a translational motion away from the ball. The tendency of this motion would be to jerk all parts of the racket, including the end of its handle, backward, or away from the ball. Unless the ball happened to hit precisely at the racket's center of mass, the racket would additionally experience a rotational motion around its center of mass—much as a penny that has been struck near its edge will start to spin. Whenever the ball hits the racket face, the effect of this rotational motion is to jerk the end of the handle forward, towards the ball. Depending on where the ball strikes the racket face, one or the other of these motions will predominate.

However, there is one point of impact, known as the center of percussion, which causes neither motion to predominate; if a ball strikes this point, the impact does not impart any motion to the end of the handle. The reason for this lack of motion is that the force on the upper part of the hand would be equal and opposite to the force on the lower part of the hand, resulting in no net force on the tennis player's hand or forearm. The center of percussion constitutes a second sweet spot because a tennis player's wrist is typically placed next to the end of the racket's handle. When the player strikes the ball at the center of percussion, her wrist is jerked neither forward nor backward, and she experiences greatly reduced vibration in the arm.

The manner in which a tennis player can detect the center of percussion on a given tennis racket follows from the nature of this second sweet spot. The center of percussion can be located via simple trial and error by holding the end of a tennis racket between the finger and thumb and throwing a ball onto the strings. If the handle jumps out of the player's hand, then the ball has missed the center of percussion.

1. The author mentions a penny that has been struck near its edge in order to

   (A) illustrate what happens at the lesser-known center of percussion

   (B) argue that a penny spins in the exact way that a tennis racket spins

   (C) illustrate the difference between two types of motion

   (D) draw an analogy to help explain a type of motion

   (E) demonstrate that pennies and tennis rackets do not spin in the same way

2. According to the passage, which of the following occurs when a ball strikes the racket strings on a sweet spot?

   (A) The jolt that accompanies most strokes will be more pronounced.

   (B) The racket experiences rotational motion but not translational motion.

   (C) The racket experiences translational motion but not rotational motion.

   (D) The player experiences less vibration in the arm holding the racket.

   (E) The center of mass and the center of percussion coincide.

3. Which of the following can be inferred about the forces acting on the racket handle?
   - (A) A player whose grip is anywhere other than at the end of the racket's handle will experience a jolting sensation when striking the ball.
   - (B) Striking a ball at the well-known sweet spot will result in fewer vibrations than striking it at the lesser-known sweet spot.
   - (C) Striking a ball on the vibration node will impart some amount of motion to the handle of the racket.
   - (D) Depending on where the ball strikes, the handle will experience either translational or rotational motion.
   - (E) If the player's hand could disappear at the moment of impact, the racket would drop straight to the ground.

Solutions

The solutions show a sample passage map and the point, as well as explanations for each answer choice. No simple story is provided, but do try to develop that level of understanding of the passage when creating your map. Where appropriate, wrong answers have been labeled by wrong answer category.

Passage I: Japanese Swords

Historians have long recognized the Japanese sword, or *nihonto*, as one of the finest cutting weapons ever produced. But to regard the sword that is synonymous with the samurai as merely a weapon is to ignore what makes it so special. The Japanese sword has always been considered a splendid weapon and even a spiritual entity. The traditional Japanese adage "the sword is the soul of the samurai" reflects not only the sword's importance to its wielder but also its permanent connection to its creator, the master smith.

Master smiths may not have been considered artists in the classical sense, but each smith exerted great care in the process of creating swords, no two of which were ever forged in exactly the same way. Over hundreds of hours, two types of steel were repeatedly heated, hammered, and folded together into thousands of very thin layers, producing a sword with an extremely sharp and durable cutting edge and a flexible, shock-absorbing blade. It was common, though optional, for a master smith to place a physical signature on a blade; moreover, each smith's secret forging techniques left an idiosyncratic structural signature on his blades. Each master smith brought a high level of devotion, skill, and attention to detail to the sword-making process, and the sword itself was a reflection of his personal honor and ability. This effort made each blade as distinctive as the samurai who wielded it such that today the Japanese sword is recognized as much for its artistic merit as for its historical significance.

Sample passage map (yours will likely differ):

① J sword: not just weapon, spirit

② Master smith: skilled
how to make
artistic merit + history

The point (articulate to yourself; don't write): Japanese sword is a weapon *and* a work of art, important to both samurai and smith. The smiths were basically artists.

1. First, identify the question type:

   Which of the following can be inferred about the structural signature of a Japanese sword?

The wording *can be inferred* indicates that this is an Inference question. Next, the question asks about the *structural signature* of a sword. Look at your map; in which paragraph would that information likely be found? The second paragraph talked about how the smiths forged the swords, so go to that paragraph and scan for the phrase *structural signature*.

The relevant sentence says:

> It was common, though optional, for a master smith to place a physical signature on a blade; moreover, each smith's secret forging techniques left an idiosyncratic structural signature on his blades. (lines 24–29)

The sentence references both a *physical signature* and a *structural signature*, so the structural signature must not be a literal signature. Further, the sentence indicates that each smith's structural signature is distinctive to the individual (*idiosyncratic*), a result of that smith's *secret forging techniques*.

(A) *It is an inscription that the smith places on the blade during the forging process.*

This refers to the physical signature, not the structural signature. (True but not right)

(B) *It refers to the particular characteristics of a blade created by a smith's unique forging process.*

CORRECT. This matches the information articulated in step 3 (predict an answer). Each smith's process resulted in a structural signature unique to that smith.

(C) *It suggests that each blade can be traced back to a known master smith.*

Tricky! The passage does say that a structural signature is unique to one smith, but it does not say that records survive indicating specifically who that smith was. A historian might be able to tell that three blades came from the same smith, but she may not be able to tell who that smith was. (Out of scope)

(D) *It reflects the soul of the samurai who wielded the sword.*

The first paragraph does include a quote about the soul of the samurai, but this information is not presented in relation to the information about the structural signature. (Mix-up)

(E) *It refers to the actual curved shape of the blade.*

Careful: If you have ever seen a samurai sword, then you may remember that it is curved—but the passage doesn't say so! In any case, since the signature is individual to the smith, something that all swords had in common wouldn't be helpful here.
(Out of scope)

2. First, identify the question type:

Each of the following is mentioned in the passage EXCEPT

The question indicates that four of the answers *are* mentioned in the passage, so this is a Detail EXCEPT question. The question is too vague to formulate an answer in advance, so work backwards: Go straight to the first answer choice and try to find it in the passage.

(A) *Every Japanese sword has a unique structure that can be traced back to a special forging process.*

True. This is mentioned in the second paragraph (lines 26–29): *each smith's secret forging techniques left an idiosyncratic structural signature on his blades.*

(B) *Master smiths kept their forging techniques secret.*

True. This is mentioned in the second paragraph (lines 26–27): *each smith's secret forging techniques.*

(C) *The Japanese sword was considered by some to have a spiritual quality.*

True. This is mentioned in the first paragraph (lines 6–8): the *sword has always been considered a splendid weapon and even a spiritual entity.*

(D) *Master smiths are now considered artists by most major historians.*

CORRECT. False. The passage does not say this. Some people may recognize the smiths as artists (see answer [E] below), but there is no indication that this view is held by *most major historians.* (Extreme)

(E) *The Japanese sword is considered both a work of art and a historical artifact.*

True. This is mentioned in the last sentence of the second paragraph (lines 35–37): the *sword is recognized as much for its artistic merit as for its historical significance.*

3. First, identify the question type:

The author explains the way in which swords were made in order to

The *in order to* language indicates that this is a Specific Purpose (Why) question. Paragraph 2 explains how the swords were made; why did the author include this information?

The beginning and end of the paragraph provide clues. First, the author says that smiths may not have been considered artists *in the classical sense*, foreshadowing the idea that perhaps they could still be considered artists. The end of the passage indicates that the forging process resulted in such a distinctive blade that the sword is now recognized for its artistic merit as well as its historical significance.

(A) *establish that the Japanese sword is the most important handheld weapon in history*

The passage does call the Japanese sword *one of the finest cutting weapons ever produced* (lines 2–3), but this is not quite as strong as calling it the most important handheld weapon in history. In any case, this is not the author's purpose in describing how the sword was made. (Extreme)

(B) *claim that the skill of the samurai is what made each Japanese sword unique*

The passage claims that the smith's secret forging techniques, not the skill of the samurai, made a blade unique. (Direct contradiction)

(C) *support the contention that the master smiths might be considered artists as well as craftsmen*

CORRECT. The default definition for the smiths is craftsmen, but the detailed information about the forging process, as well as the opening and closing sentences, indicate that the smiths might be considered artists as well.

(D) *illustrate that master smiths were more concerned with the artistic merit of their blades than with the blades' practical qualities*

The passage discusses both the artistic merits and the practical qualities of the swords, but the passage does not indicate whether the smiths thought one was more important than the other. (Out of scope)

(E) *demonstrate that the Japanese sword has more historical importance than artistic importance*

The last sentence does talk about both of these concepts, but it does not indicate that one is more important than the other. (Out of scope)

Passage J: Polygamy

Polygamy in Africa has been a popular topic for social research over the past half-century; it has been analyzed by many distinguished minds and in various well-publicized works. In 1961, when Remi Clignet published his book *Many Wives, Many Powers*, he was not alone in his view that in Africa co-wives may be perceived as direct and indirect sources of increased income and prestige.

By the 1970s, such arguments had become crystallized and popular. Many other African scholars who wrote on the subject became the new champions of this philosophy. For example, in 1983, John Mbiti proclaimed that polygamy is an accepted and respectable institution serving many useful social purposes. Similarly, G.K. Nukunya, in his paper "Polygamy as a Symbol of Status," reiterated Mbiti's idea that a plurality of wives is a legitimate sign of affluence and power in the African society.

The colonial missionary voice, however, provided consistent opposition to polygamy. Invoking the authority of the Bible, missionaries argued that the practice was unethical and destructive of family life, and they propagated the view that Africans had to be coerced into abiding by the monogamous view of marriage favored by Western culture. In some instances, missionaries even dictated immediate divorce for newly converted men who had already entered into polygamous marriages. Unfortunately, neither the missionary voice nor the scholarly voice considered the views of African women important. Although there was some awareness that women regarded polygamy as both a curse and a blessing, the distanced, albeit scientific, perspective of an outside observer predominated both at the pulpit and in scholarly writings.

Contemporary research in the social sciences has begun to focus on the protagonist's voice in the study of culture, recognizing that the views and experiences of those who take part in a given reality ought to receive close examination. This privileging of the protagonist seems appropriate, particularly given that women in Africa have often used literary productions to comment on marriage, family, and gender relations.

Sample passage map (yours will likely differ):

① Polyg Afr '61 Clignet: P = income, prestige

② 70s, 80s: positive dtls

③ Missionary: against no one listened to W

④ Now listen to W

The point (articulate to yourself; don't write): Some scholars thought polygamy was a good thing. Missionaries were against it. Now, people are actually paying attention to what the women think.

1. What type of question is this?

   According to the passage, colonial missionaries and popular scholars shared which of the following traits in their approach to the issue of polygamy?

The language *according to the passage* indicates that this is a Detail question. In general, the scholars' view was positive while the missionaries' view was negative, so these two groups would not appear to have many traits in common. The missionary viewpoint is not mentioned until the third paragraph, so begin searching there.

Halfway through the third paragraph, the author states that *neither the missionary voice nor the scholarly voice considered the views of African women important* (lines 33–36).

(A) *Both considered polygamy a sign of social status and success.*

This represents the position of the scholars, but not the missionaries. (Direct contradiction)

(B) *Neither accounted for the views of local women.*

CORRECT. This choice matches the relevant sentence from the passage.

(C) *Both attempted to limit the prevalence of polygamy.*

(D) *Both pointed out polygamy's destructive effects on family life.*

Choices (C) and (D) describe things that the missionaries did. The passage provides no information on this topic with respect to the scholars; since the scholars had a positive view of polygamy, they probably did not do these things. (Out of scope)

(E) *Both exhibited a somewhat negative attitude toward polygamy.*

The scholars cited had a positive attitude toward polygamy. (Direct contradiction)

2. First, identify the question type:

The author implies which of the following about Nukunya and Mbiti's works?

The word *implies* indicates that this is an Inference question. The two scholars were discussed in the second paragraph.

Both had positive views of polygamy. The question asks about both Mbiti and Nukunya's views, and only one view is attributed to both: Nukunya agreed with Mbiti's idea that polygamy is a *sign of affluence and power in the African society* (lines 20–21). The correct answer will be something that follows from that information.

(A) *From their point of view, a man who lacks wealth and influence is less likely to have many wives.*

CORRECT. If polygamy leads to affluence and power, then someone who does not have those two things is less likely to be practicing polygamy.

(B) *They adjusted their initial views on polygamy, recognizing that the experiences of African women should receive closer attention.*

The passage does not indicate that they adjusted their views. In fact, the third paragraph says that the *scholarly voice* did not consider women's views important. (Direct contradiction)

(C) *Their arguments represented a significant departure from those of Remi Clignet.*

Clignet was pro-polygamy, as were Mbiti and Nukunya; their views were not different from Clignet's. (Direct contradiction)

(D) *Their analyses may have been tainted by the fact that both men practiced polygamy themselves.*

The passage does not indicate whether the two men practiced polygamy themselves. (Out of scope)

(E) *Their views reflected the majority opinion of the African population.*

The passage indicates only that polygamy in Africa has been a popular research topic. The passage does not indicate whether a majority of Africans supported polygamy or considered it in a positive light. (Out of scope)

3. This is a Detail EXCEPT question.

The passage mentions each of the following, EXCEPT

Work backwards from the answers.

(A) *the year of publication of Remi Clignet's book* Many Wives, Many Powers

True. Clignet's book was published in 1961 (line 5).

(B) *the year in which John Mbiti made a claim that polygamy is an accepted institution*

True. Mbiti made this claim in 1983 (lines 14–16).

(C) *examples of African women's literary productions devoted to family relations*

CORRECT. False. Though the passage does mention that African women used literary productions in certain ways, it is false that the passage gives any examples of this.

(D) *reasons for missionary opposition to polygamy*

True. The second sentence of paragraph 3 provides specific reasons that the missionaries opposed polygamy.

(E) *current-day perspectives with respect to studying polygamy*

True. The final paragraph indicates that contemporary research has finally begun to recognize that it is important to focus on the voices of those who are actually in polygamous marriages, including women.

Passage K: Sweet Spot

Most tennis players strive to strike the ball on the racket's vibration node, more commonly known as the "sweet spot." However, many players are unaware of the existence of a second, lesser-known location on the racket face—the center of percussion—that will also greatly diminish the strain on a player's arm when the ball is struck.

In order to understand the physics of this second sweet spot, it is helpful to consider what would happen to a tennis racket if the player's hand were to vanish at the moment of impact with the ball. The impact of the ball would cause the racket to bounce backwards, resulting in a translational motion away from the ball. The tendency of this motion would be to jerk all parts of the racket, including the end of its handle, backward, or away from the ball. Unless the ball happened to hit precisely at the racket's center of mass, the racket would additionally experience a rotational motion around its center of mass—much as a penny that has been struck near its edge will start to spin. Whenever the ball hits the racket face, the effect of this rotational motion is to jerk the end of the handle forward, towards the ball. Depending on where the ball strikes the racket face, one or the other of these motions will predominate.

However, there is one point of impact, known as the center of percussion, which causes neither motion to predominate; if a ball strikes this point, the impact does not impart any motion to the end of the handle. The reason for this lack of motion is that the force on the upper part of the hand would be equal and opposite to the force on the lower part of the hand, resulting in no net force on the tennis player's hand or forearm. The center of percussion constitutes a second sweet spot because a tennis player's wrist is typically placed next to the end of the racket's handle. When the player strikes the ball at the center of percussion, her wrist is jerked neither forward nor backward, and she experiences greatly reduced vibration in the arm.

The manner in which a tennis player can detect the center of percussion on a given tennis racket follows from the nature of this second sweet spot. The center of percussion can be located via simple trial and error by holding the end of a tennis racket between the finger and thumb and throwing a ball onto the strings. If the handle jumps out of the player's hand, then the ball has missed the center of percussion.

Sample passage map (yours will likely differ):

① 2 SS (↓ strain), one less known

② if hand disappear?

③ center perc = no motion, ↓↓ vibration

④ find center perc

The point (articulate to yourself; don't write): People usually know about one sweet spot but not the other. Both reduce vibration in the arm. (Plus lots of technical details—ignore for now!)

14

1. First, identify the question type:

The author mentions a penny that has been struck near its edge in order to

The *in order to* language indicates that this is a Specific Purpose (Why) question. Paragraph 2 mentions the penny; why did the author include this information?

Here's the relevant text (lines 19–24):

> Unless the ball happened to hit precisely at the racket's center of mass, the racket would additionally experience a rotational motion around its center of mass—much as a penny that has been struck near its edge will start to spin.

The first part of the sentence talks about a certain motion that the tennis racket experiences—don't worry too much about exactly what it means. After the dash, the *much as a penny* language indicates that this example is an analogy: The racket is spinning in the same way that the penny would spin. The author uses this analogy to help the reader understand what is happening to the racket.

(A) *illustrate what happens at the lesser-known center of percussion*

This choice is tricky. The beginning of the third paragraph indicates that the motion described at the end of the second paragraph is *not* what happens at the center of percussion; if you spot that, you can eliminate this choice, but that's a pretty specific detail. Even if you miss that, though, it's enough to find another answer choice that does match your pre-stated idea—so keep looking. (Direct contradiction)

(B) *argue that a penny spins in the exact way that a tennis racket spins*

The author is trying to draw a parallel between the two but does not say that they spin in the *exact* same way. (Extreme)

(C) *illustrate the difference between two types of motion*

The paragraph does talk about two types of motion, but the penny example applies just to one of them. (True but not right)

(D) *draw an analogy to help explain a type of motion*

CORRECT. The penny analogy explains how the tennis racket spins.

(E) *demonstrate that pennies and tennis rackets do not spin in the same way*

The analogy indicates that they spin in a similar way. (Direct contradiction)

2. What type of question is this?

According to the passage, which of the following occurs when a ball strikes the racket strings on a sweet spot?

The language *according to the passage* indicates that this is a Detail question. A large portion of the passage talks about what happens when a ball strikes a racket on a sweet spot. Where should you look?

When the question is this broad, find the first mention of the topic. This first mention will give you the main idea and you can eliminate some answers. If you cannot eliminate all four, then you can go to the next mention of the topic and use that to eliminate until you get down to one answer (or you can decide that you'd rather guess and move on).

The first paragraph indicates that there are two sweet spots and that striking a ball there will *greatly diminish the strain on a player's arm.*

(A) *The jolt that accompanies most strokes will be more pronounced.*

This goes against the basic idea that the strain will *diminish*. (Direct contradiction)

(B) *The racket experiences rotational motion but not translational motion.*

(C) *The racket experiences translational motion but not rotational motion.*

Answers (B) and (C) talk about the same two forces, so deal with them together. The second paragraph does talk about these forces, but the details are pretty technical. Check the remaining answers first to see whether one matches your predicted answer; if so, you never have to check the technical detail.

(D) *The player experiences less vibration in the arm holding the racket.*

CORRECT. This is the basic benefit of the sweet spot: When a player hits a ball there, the strain, or vibration, felt in the arm is lessened.

(E) *The center of mass and the center of percussion coincide.*

Because answer (D) already works, dismiss this answer.

In the case of answers (B), (C), and (E), the test writer is trying to slow you down. You aren't required to assess each answer choice in order; when you hit something that requires a deeper dive, check the other answer choices first.

Striking the ball at a sweet spot can result in both translational and rotational motion, so answers (B) and (C) are both wrong. The passage never indicates a time when the center of mass and center of percussion would be in the same location, so answer (E) is also wrong.

3. First, identify the question type.

   Which of the following can be inferred about the forces acting on the racket handle?

The word *inferred* indicates that this is an Inference question. The forces acting on the racket handle are first discussed in paragraph 2.

Warning: This passage is a hard one and this question is seriously challenging. If you like the topic, feel free to delve into the technical details. If you don't, summarize only the high-level points, or just guess right now and move on. (And on the real test, be a little pleased—yes, pleased!—that you earned such a hard question.)

The question asks specifically about the *racket handle*. Scan the second paragraph for mentions of the handle. Translational motion moves the racket handle backward. Rotational motion jerks the handle forward.

The third paragraph adds that if a ball strikes the center of percussion, there will be *no* motion at the end of the handle.

(A) *A player whose grip is anywhere other than at the end of the racket's handle will experience a jolting sensation when striking the ball.*

The passage does not address what would happen if the player gripped the racket somewhere other than the end of the handle. The "sweet spot" describes where the ball strikes the strings, not where the player holds the racket. (Out of scope)

(B) *Striking a ball at the well-known sweet spot will result in fewer vibrations than striking it at the lesser-known sweet spot.*

The passage does not address which sweet spot might result in fewer vibrations. (Out of scope)

(C) *Striking a ball on the vibration node will impart some amount of motion to the handle of the racket.*

CORRECT. This is a very tricky answer! The third paragraph indicates that striking the ball at the center of percussion will result in no motion—and the author further specifies that this lack of motion occurs only when the ball is struck at this one location. If the ball strikes any *other* point on the racket, then the handle will experience some motion. The vibration node is the well-known sweet spot (see the first paragraph), so it qualifies as a spot other than the center of percussion.

(D) *Depending on where the ball strikes, the handle will experience either translational or rotational motion.*

If the ball is struck at the center of percussion, it will experience neither type of motion. If the ball is struck elsewhere, it will experience both types of motion. (Direct contradiction)

(E) *If the player's hand could disappear at the moment of impact, the racket would drop straight to the ground.*

The second paragraph states that, if the player's hand somehow disappeared, then the racket would bounce backward, among other motions. (Direct contradiction)

This last problem was incredibly hard. Even if you didn't find the support for (C), congratulate yourself if you were able to eliminate some of the incorrect answers. Also, notice that the second question in the set, while also a Detail question, was easier to answer because it did not require as much technical understanding of the passage. If you are having trouble following a very technical passage, you may get lucky and be offered a specific question that you can answer with only a high-level understanding. However, it's likely that at least one question will require enough technical understanding that the best choice may be to guess quickly and move on.

CHAPTER 15

Extra Problem Set

In This Chapter:

- Extra Problem Set

In this chapter, you will gain additional practice on all aspects of Reading Comprehension problems: reading and mapping the passage and answering questions of all types.

CHAPTER 15 Extra Problem Set

Time to put it all together! This chapter contains four passages with either four or five accompanying questions each. (Note: The real test will give you either three or four questions per passage.)

Each title is followed by a suggested length of time to give yourself to complete the passage and all questions. You can, of course, choose to spend extra time—but on the real test, that time will have to come from other questions. (If you receive extended time on the test, adjust accordingly.)

Problem Set

Passage L: The Invention of TV (8 minutes)

In the early years of television, Vladimir Zworykin was considered the device's inventor, at least publicly. His loudest champion was his boss, David Sarnoff, then president of RCA and a man regarded even today as "the father of television." Current historians agree, however, that Philo Farnsworth, a self-educated prodigy who was the first to transmit live images, was television's technical inventor.

In his own time, Farnsworth's contributions went largely unnoticed, in large part because he was excluded from the process of introducing the invention to a national audience. Sarnoff put televisions into living rooms, and Sarnoff was responsible for a dominant paradigm of the television industry that continues to be relevant today: advertisers pay for the programming so that they can have a receptive audience for their products. Sarnoff had already utilized this construct to develop the radio industry, and it had, within ten years, become ubiquitous. Farnsworth thought the television should be used as an educational tool, but he had little understanding of the business world, and was never able to implement his ideas.

Some argue that Sarnoff simply adapted the business model for radio and television from the newspaper industry, replacing the revenue from subscriptions and newsstand purchases with that of television set sales, but Sarnoff promoted himself as nothing less than a visionary. Some television critics argue that the construct Sarnoff implemented has played a negative role in determining the content of the programs themselves, while others contend that it merely created a democratic platform from which the audience can determine the types of programming it desires.

1. The primary purpose of the passage is to

   (A) correct public misconceptions about Farnsworth's role in developing early television programs

   (B) debate the influence of television on popular culture

   (C) challenge the current public perception of Vladimir Zworykin

   (D) chronicle the events that led from the development of radio to the invention of the television

   (E) describe both Sarnoff's influence on the public perception of television's inception and the debate around the impact of Sarnoff's paradigm

2. Which of the following best illustrates the relationship between the second and third paragraphs?

   (A) The second paragraph dissects the evolution of a contemporary controversy; the third paragraph presents differing viewpoints on that controversy.

   (B) The second paragraph explores the antithetical intentions of two men involved in the infancy of an industry; the third paragraph details the eventual deterioration of that industry.

   (C) The second paragraph presents differing views of a historical event; the third paragraph represents the author's personal opinion about that event.

   (D) The second paragraph provides details that are necessary to support the author's opinion, which is presented in the third paragraph.

   (E) The second paragraph presents divergent visions about the implementation of a technology; the third paragraph further explores one of those perspectives.

15

3. According to the passage, the television industry, at its inception, earned revenue from

   (A) advertising only
   (B) advertising and the sale of television sets
   (C) advertising and subscriptions
   (D) subscriptions and the sale of television sets
   (E) advertising, subscriptions, and the sale of television sets

4. The passage suggests that Farnsworth might have earned greater public notoriety for his invention if

   (A) Vladimir Zworykin had been less vocal about his own contributions to the television
   (B) Farnsworth had been able to develop and air his own educational programs
   (C) Farnsworth had involved Sarnoff in his plans to develop, manufacture, or distribute the television
   (D) Sarnoff had involved Farnsworth in his plans to develop, manufacture, or distribute the television
   (E) Farnsworth had conducted research into the type of programming the audience most wanted to watch

15

Passage M: Life on Mars (7 minutes)

Because of the proximity and likeness of Mars to Earth, scientists have long speculated about the possibility of life on Mars. As early as the mid-seventeenth century, astronomers observed polar ice caps on Mars, and by the mid-nineteenth century, scientists discovered other similarities to Earth, including the length of day and axial tilt. But in 1965, photos taken by the Mariner 4 probe revealed a Mars without rivers, oceans, or signs of life. Moreover, in the 1990s, it was discovered that Mars, unlike Earth, no longer possessed a substantial global magnetic field, allowing celestial radiation to reach the planet's surface and solar wind to eliminate much of Mars's atmosphere over the course of several billion years.

More recent probes have investigated whether there was once liquid water on Mars. Some scientists believe that this question is definitively answered in the affirmative by the presence of certain geological landforms. Others posit that alternative explanations, such as wind erosion or carbon dioxide oceans, may be responsible for these formations. Mars rovers *Opportunity* and *Spirit*, which began exploring the surface of Mars in 2004, have both discovered geological evidence of past water activity. In 2013, the rover *Curiosity* found evidence that the soil on the surface of Mars is approximately 2 percent water by weight. These findings substantially bolster claims that there was once life on Mars.

1. The passage is primarily concerned with which of the following?

   (A) Disproving a widely accepted theory
   (B) Initiating a debate about an unproven theory
   (C) Presenting evidence in support of a recently formulated claim
   (D) Describing various discoveries made concerning the possibility of life on Mars
   (E) Detailing the findings of the Mars rovers *Opportunity*, *Spirit*, and *Curiosity*

2. Each of the following discoveries is mentioned in the passage EXCEPT

   (A) Wind erosion and carbon dioxide oceans are responsible for certain geological landforms on Mars.
   (B) Mars does not have a substantial global magnetic field.
   (C) Mars had water activity at some point in the past.
   (D) The length of a day on Mars is similar to that on Earth.
   (E) The axial tilt of Mars is similar to that of Earth.

3. The passage suggests which of the following about polar ice caps?

   (A) Until recently, the ones on Mars were thought to consist largely of carbon dioxide.
   (B) By 1965, the ones on Mars had disappeared.
   (C) They are also found on Earth.
   (D) Their formation is tied to length of day and axial tilt.
   (E) They indicate that conditions on the planet Mars were once very different than they are at present.

4. Which of the following pieces of evidence, if found on Mars, would most support the claim that Mars once held life?

   (A) Carbon dioxide oceans

   (B) Celestial radiation and solar wind

   (C) High daily level of sunlight reaching the planet's surface

   (D) Volcanic eruptions

   (E) A significant global magnetic field

Passage N: Fossils (8.5 minutes)

In archaeology, as in the physical sciences, new discoveries frequently undermine accepted findings and give rise to new theories. This trend can be seen in the reaction to the recent discovery of a set of 3.3-million-year-old fossils in Ethiopia, the remains of the earliest well-preserved child ever found. The fossilized child was estimated to be about 3 years old at death, female, and a member of the *Australopithecus afarensis* species. The *afarensis* species, a major human ancestor, lived in Africa from earlier than 3.7 million to 3 million years ago. "Her completeness, antiquity, and age at death make this find unprecedented in the history of paleoanthropology," said Zeresenay Alemseged, a noted paleoanthropologist. Other scientists said that the discovery could reconfigure conceptions about the lives and capacities of these early humans.

Prior to this discovery, it had been thought that the *afarensis* species had abandoned the arboreal habitat of its ape cousins. However, while the lower limbs of this fossil supported findings that *afarensis* walked upright, its gorilla-like arms and shoulders suggested that it retained the ability to swing through trees. This has initiated a reexamination of many accepted theories of early human development. Also, the presence of a hyoid bone, a rarely preserved bone in the larynx that supports muscles of the throat, has had a tremendous impact on theories about the origins of speech. The fossil bone is primitive and more similar to that of apes than to that of humans, but it is the first hyoid found in such an early human-related species.

15

1. The primary purpose of the passage is to

(A) discuss a controversial scientific discovery
(B) contrast varying theories of human development
(C) support a general contention with a specific example
(D) argue for the importance of a particular field of study
(E) refute a widely believed myth

2. The passage quotes Zeresenay Alemseged in order to

(A) qualify the main idea of the first paragraph
(B) provide contrast to the claims of other scientists
(C) support the theory regarding the linguistic abilities of the *afarensis* species
(D) support the stated significance of the discovery
(E) provide a subjective opinion that is refuted in the second paragraph

3. It can be inferred from the passage's description of the discovery of the fossil hyoid bone that

(A) *Australopithecus afarensis* was capable of speech
(B) the discovered hyoid bone is less primitive than the hyoid bone of apes
(C) the hyoid bone is necessary for speech
(D) the discovery of the hyoid bone necessitated the reexamination of prior theories about speech
(E) the hyoid bone was the most important fossil found at the site

4. Each of the following is cited as a reason that the fossils discovered in Ethiopia were important EXCEPT

   (A) the fact that the remains were those of a child

   (B) the age of the fossils

   (C) the location of the discovery

   (D) the presence of a bone not usually discovered

   (E) the intact nature of the fossils

5. The impact of the discovery of the hyoid bone in the field of archaeology is most closely analogous to which of the following situations?

   (A) The discovery and analysis of cosmic rays lend support to a widely accepted theory of the origin of the universe.

   (B) The original manuscript of a deceased nineteenth-century author confirms ideas about the development of an important work of literature.

   (C) The continued prosperity of a state-run economy stirs debate in the discipline of macroeconomics.

   (D) Newly revealed journal entries by a prominent Civil War–era politician lead to a questioning of certain accepted historical interpretations about the conflict.

   (E) Research into the mapping of the human genome gives rise to nascent applications of individually tailored medicines.

Passage O: Chaos Theory (8.5 minutes)

Around 1960, mathematician Edward Lorenz found unexpected behavior in apparently simple equations representing atmospheric air flows. Whenever he reran his model with the same inputs, different outputs resulted, although the model lacked any random elements. Lorenz realized that tiny rounding errors in the initial data mushroomed over time, leading to erratic results. His findings marked a seminal moment in the development of chaos theory, which, despite its name, has little to do with randomness.

Lorenz's experiment was one of the first to demonstrate conclusively that unpredictability can arise from deterministic equations, which do not involve chance outcomes. In order to understand this phenomenon, first consider the non-chaotic system of two poppy seeds placed in a round bowl. As the seeds roll to the bowl's center, a position known as a point attractor, the distance between the seeds shrinks. If, instead, the bowl is flipped over, two seeds placed on top will roll away from each other. Such a system, while still not technically chaotic, enlarges initial differences in position.

Chaotic systems, such as a machine mixing bread dough, are characterized by both attraction and repulsion. As the dough is stretched, folded, and pressed back together, any poppy seeds sprinkled in are intermixed seemingly at random. But this randomness is illusory. In fact, the poppy seeds are captured by "strange attractors," staggeringly complex pathways whose tangles appear accidental but are in fact determined by the system's fundamental equations.

During the dough-kneading process, two poppy seeds positioned next to each other eventually go their separate ways. Any early divergence or measurement error is repeatedly amplified by the mixing until the position of any seed becomes effectively unpredictable. It is this "sensitive dependence on initial conditions" and not true randomness that generates unpredictability in chaotic systems, of which one example may be the Earth's weather. According to the popular interpretation of the "Butterfly Effect," a butterfly flapping its wings causes hurricanes. A better understanding is that the butterfly causes uncertainty about the precise state of the air. This microscopic uncertainty grows until it encompasses even hurricanes. Few meteorologists believe that we will ever be able to predict rain or shine for a particular day years in the future.

1. The primary purpose of this passage is to

(A) explain how non-random systems can produce unpredictable results

(B) trace the historical development of a scientific theory

(C) distinguish one theory from its opposite

(D) describe the spread of a technical model from one field of study to others

(E) contrast possible causes of weather phenomena

2. According to the passage, what is true about poppy seeds in bread dough, once the dough has been thoroughly mixed?

(A) They have been individually stretched and folded over, like miniature versions of the entire dough.

(B) They are scattered in random clumps throughout the dough.

(C) They are accidentally caught in tangled objects called strange attractors.

(D) They are bound to regularly dispersed patterns of point attractors.

(E) They are in positions dictated by the underlying equations that govern the mixing process.

3. According to the passage, the small rounding errors in Lorenz's model

   (A) rendered the results unusable for the purposes of scientific research
   (B) were deliberately included to represent tiny fluctuations in atmospheric air currents
   (C) had a surprisingly large impact over time
   (D) were at least partially expected, given the complexity of the actual atmosphere
   (E) shrank to insignificant levels during each trial of the model

4. The passage mentions each of the following as an example or potential example of a chaotic or non-chaotic system EXCEPT

   (A) a dough-mixing machine
   (B) atmospheric weather patterns
   (C) poppy seeds placed on top of an upside-down bowl
   (D) poppy seeds placed in a right-side-up bowl
   (E) fluctuating butterfly flight patterns

Solutions

The solutions show a sample passage map and the point, as well as explanations for each answer choice. No simple story is provided, but do try to develop that level of understanding of the passage when creating your map. Where appropriate, wrong answers have been labeled by wrong answer category.

Passage L: The Invention of TV

In the early years of television, Vladimir Zworykin was considered the device's inventor, at least publicly. His loudest champion was his boss, David Sarnoff, then president of RCA and a man regarded even today as "the father of television." Current historians agree, however, that Philo Farnsworth, a self-educated prodigy who was the first to transmit live images, was television's technical inventor.

In his own time, Farnsworth's contributions went largely unnoticed, in large part because he was excluded from the process of introducing the invention to a national audience. Sarnoff put televisions into living rooms, and Sarnoff was responsible for a dominant paradigm of the television industry that continues to be relevant today: advertisers pay for the programming so that they can have a receptive audience for their products. Sarnoff had already utilized this construct to develop the radio industry, and it had, within ten years, become ubiquitous. Farnsworth thought the television should be used as an educational tool, but he had little understanding of the business world, and was never able to implement his ideas.

Some argue that Sarnoff simply adapted the business model for radio and television from the newspaper industry, replacing the revenue from subscriptions and newsstand purchases with that of television set sales, but Sarnoff promoted himself as nothing less than a visionary. Some television critics argue that the construct Sarnoff implemented has played a negative role in determining the content of the programs themselves, while others contend that it merely created a democratic platform from which the audience can determine the types of programming it desires.

Sample passage map (yours will likely differ):

① VZ = inventor
S = father of TV
really F

② F not part of process, focus edu
S made comm (same as radio)

③ S just adapt? or visionary?
Some see S neg, some pos

The point (articulate to yourself; don't write): Farnsworth really invented TV, but he didn't know how to turn it into a business. Sarnoff used the radio model to make television big business. People have differing feelings about his role.

1. First, identify the question type:

The primary purpose of the passage is to

The wording indicates that this is a Primary Purpose question. Glance at your map and remind yourself of the point before you go to the answers.

(A) *correct public misconceptions about Farnsworth's role in developing early television programs*

The passage does correct the misconceptions about Farnsworth's role. This is only a detail of the passage, however; most of the passage talks about Sarnoff's development of the business model for television. (True but not right)

(B) *debate the influence of television on popular culture*

The passage does not delve into popular culture. (Out of scope)

(C) *challenge the current public perception of Vladimir Zworykin*

Zworykin is not the focus of the passage, nor does the passage say anything about *current* public perception of Zworykin; it only indicates that he was once considered the inventor of the technology. (Out of scope)

(D) *chronicle the events that led from the development of radio to the invention of the television*

The passage is not about the events that led to the invention of television, nor is it about radio. Radio is only mentioned because Sarnoff used a similar business model to launch the business of television. (Out of scope)

(E) *describe both Sarnoff's influence on the public perception of television's inception and the debate around the impact of Sarnoff's paradigm*

CORRECT. The passage does describe how Sarnoff made television popular; some critics think that his role was positive while others think that it was negative. Notice that this is the only answer choice that mentions Sarnoff. He is featured prominently in every paragraph, so any answer choice representing the point of the passage should not mention other people while ignoring him.

2. First, identify the question type:

Which of the following best illustrates the relationship between the second and third paragraphs?

This is a paragraph question. Glance at your map and articulate to yourself the relationship between the second and third paragraphs before you check the answers.

The second paragraph explains how Sarnoff made television a commercial success and why Farnsworth was not able to do so. The third paragraph expands on Sarnoff's work, indicating both positive and negative views.

(A) *The second paragraph dissects the evolution of a contemporary controversy; the third paragraph presents differing viewpoints on that controversy.*

Perhaps the fact that the wrong man was initially credited with television's invention could be considered a controversy, but that controversy is not contemporary, nor is it the purpose of the second or third paragraphs. (Out of scope)

(B) *The second paragraph explores the antithetical intentions of two men involved in the infancy of an industry; the third paragraph details the eventual deterioration of that industry.*

The second paragraph might be described in this way, but the third paragraph does not talk about the deterioration of television. Rather, the industry was (and is!) a success. Perhaps it didn't live up to Farnsworth's hopes, but the passage doesn't describe any decline—in fact, Farnsworth's vision didn't get off the ground. (Direct contradiction)

(C) *The second paragraph presents differing views of a historical event; the third paragraph represents the author's personal opinion about that event.*

The second paragraph provides historical details of the launch of television, not different views of the launch. The third paragraph does not present the author's personal opinion. (Out of scope)

(D) *The second paragraph provides details that are necessary to support the author's opinion, which is presented in the third paragraph.*

The author does not provide his own opinion; rather, he conveys the opinions of others (*some argue*; *some television critics argue*). (Out of scope)

(E) *The second paragraph presents divergent visions about a new technology; the third paragraph further explores one of those perspectives.*

CORRECT. The second paragraph does present the two different visions held by Farnsworth and Sarnoff. The third paragraph does provide additional information about Sarnoff's particular vision.

3. First, identify the question type:

According to the passage, the television industry, at its inception, earned revenue from

The language *according to the passage* indicates that this is a Detail question. The passage discusses television revenues in the second and third paragraphs. Search for the information.

Paragraph 2 (line 18): *advertisers pay for the programming*

Paragraph 3 (lines 29–31): *replacing the revenue from subscriptions and newsstand purchases with that of television set sales*

(A) *advertising only*

Revenue was also earned from the sale of TV sets. (True but not right)

(B) *advertising and the sale of television sets*

CORRECT. Revenue was earned from advertisers and the sale of TV sets.

(C) *advertising and subscriptions*

(D) *subscriptions and the sale of television sets*

(E) *advertising, subscriptions, and the sale of television sets*

Choices (C), (D), and (E) mention subscriptions. Subscriptions were used in the newspaper industry, not the television industry. (Mix-up)

4. First, identify the question type:

The passage suggests that Farnsworth might have earned greater public notoriety for his invention if

The word *suggests* signals that this is an Inference question, so you will need to go back to the passage. Farnsworth's contributions are discussed in the second paragraph:

> [Farnsworth] was excluded from the process of introducing the invention to a national audience . . . Farnsworth thought the television should be used as an educational tool, but he had little understanding of the business world, and was never able to implement his ideas. (lines 12–26)

If Farnsworth hadn't been excluded, maybe he would have earned more acclaim. Alternatively, if he had understood business better, then he might have earned more acclaim. Look for an answer with a similar meaning.

(A) *Vladimir Zworykin had been less vocal about his own contributions to the television*

The passage says that Sarnoff, not Zworykin himself, was vocal about Zworykin's contributions. (Mix-up)

(B) *Farnsworth had been able to develop and air his own educational programs*

It's possible that if Farnsworth had been able to follow through on his goal of using television for education, he would have earned public acclaim, but the passage says nothing to indicate this. Because he had little understanding of business, his programs might not have been great successes even if he had been able to produce them. (Out of scope)

(C) *Farnsworth had involved Sarnoff in his plans to develop, manufacture, or distribute the television*

There is no indication that Farnsworth had any such plans. Rather, it would have helped Farnsworth to be involved with Sarnoff's plans. (Mix-up)

(D) *Sarnoff had involved Farnsworth in his plans to develop, manufacture, or distribute the television*

CORRECT. If Farnsworth hadn't been excluded, then he might have garnered acclaim as Sarnoff and Zworykin did.

(E) *Farnsworth had conducted research into the type of programming the audience most wanted to watch*

The passage indicates that Farnsworth had little understanding of the business world; even if he knew what audiences wanted to watch, he wouldn't necessarily have known how to build a successful business model. (Out of scope)

Passage M: Life on Mars

Because of the proximity and likeness of Mars to Earth, scientists have long speculated about the possibility of life on Mars. As early as the mid-seventeenth century, astronomers observed polar ice caps on Mars, and by the mid-nineteenth century, scientists discovered other similarities to Earth, including the length of day and axial tilt. But in 1965, photos taken by the Mariner 4 probe revealed a Mars without rivers, oceans, or signs of life. Moreover, in the 1990s, it was discovered that Mars, unlike Earth, no longer possessed a substantial global magnetic field, allowing celestial radiation to reach the planet's surface and solar wind to eliminate much of Mars's atmosphere over the course of several billion years.

More recent probes have investigated whether there was once liquid water on Mars. Some scientists believe that this question is definitively answered in the affirmative by the presence of certain geological landforms. Others posit that alternative explanations, such as wind erosion or carbon dioxide oceans, may be responsible for these formations. Mars rovers *Opportunity* and *Spirit*, which began exploring the surface of Mars in 2004, have both discovered geological evidence of past water activity. In 2013, the rover *Curiosity* found evidence that the soil on the surface of Mars is approximately 2 percent water by weight. These findings substantially bolster claims that there was once life on Mars.

Sample passage map (yours will likely differ):

① Life on M?
+ sim to E
– diff too

② Water? debate
recent: yes, water

The point (articulate to yourself; don't write): Debate about life on Mars. Positives and negatives, but the big deal was the discovery of water, increasing the chance that there was life on Mars.

1. First, identify the question type:

The passage is primarily concerned with which of the following?

This is a Primary Purpose question. Glance at your map and remind yourself of the point before you go to the answers.

(A) *Disproving a widely accepted theory*

There is no widely accepted theory, just speculation. Plus, that speculation is more positive than negative! (Out of scope)

(B) *Initiating a debate about an unproven theory*

The passage does discuss a potential theory (that there may once have been life on Mars), but the passage itself does not initiate any debate. Rather, it reports on various findings and opinions of others. (Out of scope)

(C) *Presenting evidence in support of a recently formulated claim*

The earliest mentioned interest in Mars was in the mid-seventeenth century; this is not recent. (One word off)

(D) *Describing various discoveries made concerning the possibility of life on Mars*

CORRECT. The passage does describe various discoveries made in the mid-seventeenth and mid-nineteenth centuries, as well as, more recently, discoveries that concern the possibility of life on Mars.

(E) *Detailing the findings of the Mars rovers* Opportunity, Spirit, *and* Curiosity

The passage does discuss this, but the rovers are details; they are not the overall point of the passage. (True but not right)

2. First, identify the question type:

Each of the following discoveries is mentioned in the passage EXCEPT

The question indicates that four of the answers *are* mentioned in the passage, so this is a Detail EXCEPT question. The entire passage is about discoveries, so go straight to the first answer choice and try to find it in the passage.

(A) *wind erosion and carbon dioxide oceans are responsible for certain geological landforms on Mars*

CORRECT. False. The passage says only that wind erosion or carbon dioxide *may* be responsible for certain geological landforms, not that they *are*. This is an unusual form of an Extreme answer: Though the word *are* is not an extreme word itself, it is more extreme than *may*. (Extreme)

(B) *Mars does not have a substantial global magnetic field*

True. The first paragraph says that Mars *no longer possessed a substantial global magnetic field* (lines 12–13).

(C) *Mars had water activity at some point in the past*

True. The second paragraph says that *Mars rovers* Opportunity *and* Spirit*... discovered geological evidence of past water activity* (lines 25–29).

(D) *the length of a day on Mars is similar to that on Earth*

True. The first paragraph discusses Mars's *similarities to Earth, including the length of day* (lines 7–8).

(E) *the axial tilt of Mars is similar to that of Earth*

True. The first paragraph discusses Mars's *similarities to Earth, including the... axial tilt* (lines 7–8).

3. First, identify the question type:

The passage suggests which of the following about polar ice caps?

The word *suggests* points to an inference question. The passage mentions polar ice caps in the first paragraph:

> As early as the mid-seventeenth century, astronomers observed polar ice caps on Mars, and by the mid-nineteenth century, scientists discovered other similarities to Earth, including the length of day and axial tilt. (lines 3–8)

The second half of the sentence states that scientists discovered *other* similarities to Earth, implying that polar ice caps are also a similarity between the two planets.

(A) *Until recently, the ones on Mars were thought to consist largely of carbon dioxide.*

The passage does mention carbon dioxide, but not in the context of polar ice caps. (Mix-up)

(B) *By 1965, the ones on Mars had disappeared.*

The passage does mention that photos taken in 1965 showed that Mars was *without rivers, oceans, or signs of life* (line 10), but this sentence makes no reference to the polar ice caps. (Mix-up)

(C) *They are also found on Earth.*

CORRECT. The sentence says that scientists discovered *other* similarities to Earth, implying that the earlier discovery (polar ice caps) is also similar to what is found on Earth.

(D) *Their formation is tied to length of day and axial tilt.*

The passage mentions length of day and axial tilt as examples of other similarities to Earth, but it does not indicate that those had anything to do with the formation of polar ice caps. (Out of scope)

(E) *They indicate that conditions on the planet Mars were once very different than they are at present.*

It's possible that conditions were once very different, but the passage does not provide any information to indicate that this is the case. (Out of scope)

4. First, identify the question type:

Which of the following pieces of evidence, if found on Mars, would most support the claim that Mars once held life?

The words *most support the claim* indicate that this is a Strengthen question. Both paragraphs discuss characteristics that indicate the possibility of life. Because there are so many possible indicators, work backwards from the answers and try to find them in the passage. First, though, remind yourself that the passage also discusses characteristics that are incompatible with life. Read carefully!

(A) *Carbon dioxide oceans*

The second paragraph mentions that carbon dioxide oceans, rather than water, might be responsible for certain landforms, and the passage makes clear that water is an important indicator of possible life. Carbon dioxide oceans, then, would weaken the evidence for water presence and thus *decrease* the chances of life. (Weaken)

(B) *Celestial radiation and solar wind*

The first paragraph mentions celestial radiation and solar wind in the context of a scenario in which there is *not* life. (Weaken)

(C) *High daily level of sunlight reaching the planet's surface*

You might posit that abundant sunlight would improve the odds of life, but the passage does not provide any information about this. (Out of scope)

(D) *Volcanic eruptions*

The passage does not provide any information about volcanic eruptions. (Out of scope)

(E) *A significant global magnetic field*

CORRECT. The first paragraph says that scientists posited that life could exist on Mars due to the similarities between Earth and Mars. However, Mars, unlike Earth, does *not* have a substantial global magnetic field, and this difference between Mars and Earth is presented as a negative in the debate about life on Mars. The implication, then, is that a global magnetic field would be positive evidence in favor of life on Mars.

15

Passage N: Fossils

In archaeology, as in the physical sciences, new discoveries frequently undermine accepted findings and give rise to new theories. This trend can be seen in the reaction to the recent discovery of a set of 3.3-million-year-old fossils in Ethiopia, the remains of the earliest well-preserved child ever found. The fossilized child was estimated to be about 3 years old at death, female, and a member of the *Australopithecus afarensis* species. The *afarensis* species, a major human ancestor, lived in Africa from earlier than 3.7 million to 3 million years ago. "Her completeness, antiquity, and age at death make this find unprecedented in the history of paleoanthropology," said Zeresenay Alemseged, a noted paleoanthropologist. Other scientists said that the discovery could reconfigure conceptions about the lives and capacities of these early humans.

Prior to this discovery, it had been thought that the *afarensis* species had abandoned the arboreal habitat of its ape cousins. However, while the lower limbs of this fossil supported findings that *afarensis* walked upright, its gorilla-like arms and shoulders suggested that it retained the ability to swing through trees. This has initiated a reexamination of many accepted theories of early human development. Also, the presence of a hyoid bone, a rarely preserved bone in the larynx that supports muscles of the throat, has had a tremendous impact on theories about the origins of speech. The fossil bone is primitive and more similar to that of apes than to that of humans, but it is the first hyoid found in such an early human-related species.

Sample passage map (yours will likely differ):

① new disc → undermine old
new theories eg child fossil

② 2 things changed w/child
walking / limbs
speech / hyoid

The point (articulate to yourself; don't write): New discoveries change old ideas and give rise to new theories. A detailed archaeological example illustrates this overall point. The discovery of a particular skeleton led researchers to reexamine theories about early human life.

1. First, identify the question type:

The primary purpose of the passage is to

This is a Primary Purpose question. Glance at your map and remind yourself of the point before you go to the answers.

(A) *discuss a controversial scientific discovery*

The passage does not indicate that the discovery was in any way controversial. (Out of scope)

(B) *contrast varying theories of human development*

The passage does discuss how certain theories about early human development have changed over time, but it does not contrast different theories. (Out of scope)

(C) *support a general contention with a specific example*

CORRECT. The first sentence of the passage makes a general contention (*In archaeology . . . new discoveries frequently undermine accepted findings* [lines 1–3]). The rest of the passage provides a specific example (the Ethiopian fossils) that supports that contention.

(D) *argue for the importance of a particular field of study*

The author does not make a case about the *importance* of archaeology (or any other field) specifically. (Out of scope)

(E) *refute a widely believed myth*

A *myth* is something that people erroneously believe to be true, typically without any credible evidence. A *myth* is not what the passage describes: new evidence that led researchers to revise an existing theory. (Out of scope)

2. First, identify the question type:

The passage quotes Zeresenay Alemseged in order to

The *in order to* language indicates that this is a Specific Purpose (Why) question. Return to the passage and articulate in your own words why the author quoted Alemseged in paragraph 1.

> "Her completeness, antiquity, and age at death make this find unprecedented in the history of paleoanthropology," said Zeresenay Alemseged, a noted paleoanthropologist. Other scientists said that the discovery could reconfigure conceptions about the lives and capacities of these early humans. (lines 14–20)

The author is trying to use this example to support the point that discoveries can give rise to new theories. Alemseged's quote reinforces the idea that the discovery of this set of fossils is extremely significant (*unprecedented*), as does the fact that other scientists agree with Alemseged in this respect.

15

(A) *qualify the main idea of the first paragraph*

To qualify a piece of information is to limit or diminish it. Alemseged's quote does the opposite: It reinforces the point. (Direct contradiction)

(B) *provide contrast to the claims of other scientists*

Alemseged's quote emphasizes the importance of the discovery. The other scientists mentioned share this perspective. (Direct contradiction)

(C) *support the theory regarding the linguistic abilities of the* afarensis *species*

Linguistic abilities are mentioned at the end of the second paragraph, but Alemseged's quote is about the general significance of the find and it doesn't provide any support for a particular theory. (Mix-up)

(D) *support the stated significance of the discovery*

CORRECT. This choice matches the answer predicted above.

(E) *provide a subjective opinion that is refuted in the second paragraph*

Alemseged's opinion is reinforced, not refuted, by the second paragraph, which delves into the important consequences of the discovery. (Direct contradiction)

3. First, identify the question type:

It can be inferred from the passage's description of the discovery of the fossil hyoid bone that

This is an inference question. The hyoid bone was mentioned in the second paragraph:

> This has initiated a reexamination of many accepted theories of early human development. Also, the presence of a hyoid bone, a rarely preserved bone in the larynx that supports muscles of the throat, has had a tremendous impact on theories about the origins of speech. The fossil bone is primitive and more similar to that of apes than to that of humans, but it is the first hyoid found in such an early human-related species. (lines 28–37)

The first sentence sets up the idea that the hyoid discovery was an example of the need to reexamine some earlier theory. Specifically, it had a *tremendous impact on theories about the origins of speech* (lines 33–34). Since it was the earliest hyoid bone found in a human-related species, perhaps it indicates that speech may have arisen earlier than previously thought.

(A) Australopithecus afarensis *was capable of speech*

This is tempting but goes too far. The passage relates the hyoid to speech but does not provide information as to whether *afarensis* could actually speak. (Out of scope)

(B) *the discovered hyoid bone is less primitive than the hyoid bone of apes*

Check the last sentence of the paragraph. Tricky! The sentence calls the bone primitive and similar to that of apes, but does not say that it is less primitive than the ones found in apes. (Out of scope)

(C) *the hyoid bone is necessary for speech*

The passage does connect the hyoid bone to speech, but does not provide information that would imply that the bone is *necessary*. (Extreme)

(D) *the discovery of the hyoid bone necessitated the reexamination of prior theories about speech*

CORRECT. Leading into the hyoid example, the passage talks about discoveries leading to a reexamination of many accepted theories. The passage then says that the hyoid discovery has had a *tremendous impact* (line 33) on prior theories. The implication is that the hyoid discovery has also resulted in a reexamination of those prior theories.

(E) *the hyoid bone was the most important fossil found at the site*

The discovery of the hyoid was certainly important, but the passage provides no information about which discovery was the most important. (Extreme)

4. First, identify the question type:

Each of the following is cited as a reason that the fossils discovered in Ethiopia were important EXCEPT

The question indicates that four of the answers *are* mentioned in the passage, so this is a Detail EXCEPT question. Most of the passage discusses fossil discoveries, so go straight to the first answer choice and try to find it in the passage.

(A) *the fact that the remains were those of a child*

True. Alemseged's quote indicates that the *age at death* was important (lines 14–16).

(B) *the age of the fossils*

True. Alemseged's quote indicates that the *antiquity* of the bones was important (line 14).

(C) *the location of the discovery*

CORRECT. False. While the geographic location of the discovery is given in the passage, the location was not cited as a reason that the fossils were important.

(D) *the presence of a bone not usually discovered*

True. The hyoid example indicates that the bone is *rarely preserved* (line 31) and that it was the *first hyoid found in such an early human-related species* (lines 36–37). The passage says that the discovery of the hyoid bone had a *tremendous impact* (line 33).

(E) *the intact nature of the fossils*

True. Alemseged's quote indicates that the *completeness* of the bones was important (line 14).

5. First, identify the question type:

The impact of the discovery of the hyoid bone in the field of archaeology is most closely analogous to which of the following situations?

This is an unusual question that does not fall into one of the common categories; it's more like a Critical Reasoning question. It is asking you to make an analogy to the situation presented in the passage. You may or may not see an RC question like this on the test.

The hyoid is mentioned in the second paragraph, so read the appropriate text and ask yourself what the *impact of the discovery* was. Then, examine the answers to find a match.

The bone was the first hyoid found for this species, and it had a *tremendous impact on theories about the origins of speech* (lines 33–34). Find a similar situation in the answers.

(A) *The discovery and analysis of cosmic rays lend support to a widely accepted theory of the origin of the universe.*

The hyoid discovery led to a reexamination of an existing theory. In this answer, the new evidence supported the existing theory.

(B) *The original manuscript of a deceased nineteenth-century author confirms ideas about the development of an important work of literature.*

The hyoid discovery led to a reexamination of an existing theory. In this answer, the new evidence confirmed the existing theory.

(C) *The continued prosperity of a state-run economy stirs debate in the discipline of macroeconomics.*

The hyoid discovery inserted an important new piece of information into the conversation; this choice does not mention anything about new information or evidence.

(D) *Newly revealed journal entries by a prominent Civil War–era politician lead to a questioning of certain accepted historical interpretations about the conflict.*

CORRECT. The hyoid discovery, like the newly revealed journal entries in this choice, led to a questioning of certain interpretations or theories.

(E) *Research into the mapping of the human genome gives rise to nascent applications of individually tailored medicines.*

The hyoid discovery had an impact on previously formulated theories. This choice does not address previous applications or theories.

Passage O: Chaos Theory

Around 1960, mathematician Edward Lorenz found unexpected behavior in apparently simple equations representing atmospheric air flows. Whenever he reran his model with the same inputs, different outputs resulted, although the model lacked any random elements. Lorenz realized that tiny rounding errors in the initial data mushroomed over time, leading to erratic results. His findings marked a seminal moment in the development of chaos theory, which, despite its name, has little to do with randomness.

Lorenz's experiment was one of the first to demonstrate conclusively that unpredictability can arise from deterministic equations, which do not involve chance outcomes. In order to understand this phenomenon, first consider the non-chaotic system of two poppy seeds placed in a round bowl. As the seeds roll to the bowl's center, a position known as a point attractor, the distance between the seeds shrinks. If, instead, the bowl is flipped over, two seeds placed on top will roll away from each other. Such a system, while still not technically chaotic, enlarges initial differences in position.

Chaotic systems, such as a machine mixing bread dough, are characterized by both attraction and repulsion. As the dough is stretched, folded, and pressed back together, any poppy seeds sprinkled in are intermixed seemingly at random. But this randomness is illusory. In fact, the poppy seeds are captured by "strange attractors," staggeringly complex pathways whose tangles appear accidental but are in fact determined by the system's fundamental equations.

During the dough-kneading process, two poppy seeds positioned next to each other eventually go their separate ways. Any early divergence or measurement error is repeatedly amplified by the mixing until the position of any seed becomes effectively unpredictable. It is this "sensitive dependence on initial conditions" and not true randomness that generates unpredictability in chaotic systems, of which one example may be the Earth's weather. According to the popular interpretation of the "Butterfly Effect," a butterfly flapping its wings causes hurricanes. A better understanding is that the butterfly causes uncertainty about the precise state of the air. This microscopic uncertainty grows until it encompasses even hurricanes. Few meteorologists believe that we will ever be able to predict rain or shine for a particular day years in the future.

Sample passage map (yours will likely differ):

① L: diff results from rounding errors
chaos theory (not random)

② not chaos: bowl + poppy seeds

③ chaos: bowl + dough
attract, repulse

④ not random, depends on start cond
butterfly

The point (articulate to yourself; don't write): Lorenz discovered something about chaos theory (which is not really about randomness). Non-chaotic systems are predictable. Chaotic systems increase initial differences, so even though they are not actually random, they are hard to predict.

1. First, identify the question type:

   The primary purpose of this passage is to

This is a Primary Purpose question. Glance at your map and remind yourself of the point before you go to the answers.

(A) *explain how non-random systems can produce unpredictable results*

CORRECT. The passage does explain how chaotic (*non-random*) systems aren't actually predictable. The passage gives the example of poppy seeds kneaded into bread dough until their position *becomes effectively unpredictable* (lines 43–44).

(B) *trace the historical development of a scientific theory*

The passage does discuss some of Lorenz's contributions to chaos theory, but the passage does not trace the entire historical development of the theory. (Out of scope)

(C) *distinguish one theory from its opposite*

Only one theory (chaos theory) is mentioned in the passage. The passage does contrast two systems (non-chaotic and chaotic), but these are not both theories, nor is the overall point to contrast these two systems. (Out of scope)

(D) *describe the spread of a technical model from one field of study to others*

The passage does not discuss multiple fields of study. (Out of scope)

(E) *contrast possible causes of weather phenomena*

The end of the passage does mention the weather, but there is no mention of different possible causes of weather phenomena. Even if there were, this would be detail, not the point. (Out of scope)

2. First, identify the question type:

According to the passage, what is true about poppy seeds in bread dough, once the dough has been thoroughly mixed?

The language *according to the passage* indicates that this is a Detail question. The bread dough concept is introduced in the third paragraph and continued in the fourth paragraph. Start with the third paragraph:

> As the dough is stretched, folded, and pressed back together, any poppy seeds sprinkled in are intermixed seemingly at random. But this randomness is illusory. In fact, the poppy seeds are captured by "strange attractors," staggeringly complex pathways whose tangles appear accidental but are in fact determined by the system's fundamental equations. (lines 29–37)

After the dough is mixed, then, the seeds have separated based on some equations, but it's not possible to predict how. See whether there's a match in the answers; if not, try the fourth paragraph.

(A) *They have been individually stretched and folded over, like miniature versions of the entire dough.*

The paragraph indicates that the dough is stretched and folded over, not the seeds. (Mix-up)

(B) *They are scattered in random clumps throughout the dough.*

The paragraph specifically indicates that the movement is *not* random. (Direct contradiction)

(C) *They are accidentally caught in tangled objects called strange attractors.*

"Strange attractor" is a technical name for a complex, tangled pathway. There are no tangled objects. Moreover, there is nothing accidental about the movement. (Mix-up)

(D) *They are bound to regularly dispersed patterns of point attractors.*

The seeds are not in regularly dispersed patterns; the patterns are so complex that the outcome is *seemingly at random* (line 32). Later, in the fourth paragraph, the passage makes clear that the final positions are not predictable (and therefore not regularly dispersed) even though they are actually governed by equations. (Out of scope)

(E) *They are in positions dictated by the underlying equations that govern the mixing process.*

CORRECT. The final sentence of the third paragraph indicates that the system's fundamental equations determine the final position of the poppy seeds.

3. First, identify the question type:

According to the passage, the rounding errors in Lorenz's model

The language *according to the passage* indicates that this is a Detail question. The first paragraph introduces Lorenz's model and the rounding errors:

> Edward Lorenz found unexpected behavior in apparently simple equations representing atmospheric air flows. Whenever he reran his

model with the same inputs, different outputs resulted—although the model lacked any random elements. Lorenz realized that tiny rounding errors in his analog computer mushroomed over time, leading to erratic results. (lines 1–9)

The rounding errors were tiny at first but mushroomed (got much larger) over time, such that the final results of seemingly similar starting points could be quite different.

Since the question stem contains the first half of a sentence that the answer choices finish, remind yourself of the text before reading the answers: *The rounding errors in Lorenz's model . . .*

(A) *rendered the results unusable for the purposes of scientific research*

The passage does not indicate whether Lorenz was still able to use the results for his purposes. If anything, the errors led to a positive, not negative, result: The erratic results led to *a seminal moment in the development of chaos theory* (lines 10–11). (Out of scope)

(B) *were deliberately included to represent tiny fluctuations in atmospheric air currents*

Lorenz did not deliberately include the rounding errors. At first, he did not realize that they were present and couldn't understand why he kept getting different results. (Direct contradiction)

(C) *had a surprisingly large impact over time*

CORRECT. The rounding errors were so tiny that Lorenz did not notice them immediately, but they *mushroomed over time* until they produced different results even with seemingly the same inputs. The passage describes this behavior as *unexpected.*

(D) *were at least partially expected, given the complexity of the actual atmosphere*

The rounding errors were simply computer errors; the passage does not indicate that they resulted from the complexity of the atmosphere. (Mix-up)

(E) *shrank to insignificant levels during each trial of the model*

On the contrary, the rounding errors grew a great deal, or *mushroomed*, over time. (Direct contradiction)

4. First, identify the question type:

The passage mentions each of the following as an example or potential example of a chaotic or non-chaotic system EXCEPT

The question indicates that four of the answers *are* mentioned in the passage, so this is a Detail EXCEPT question. The entire passage talks about both chaotic and non-chaotic systems, so it's not possible to formulate an answer in advance. Go straight to the first answer choice and try to find it in the passage.

(A) *a dough-mixing machine*

True. The first sentence of the third paragraph indicates that a *machine mixing bread dough* (lines 27–28) is an example of a chaotic system.

(B) *atmospheric weather patterns*

True. The fourth paragraph mentions one possible example of a chaotic system as *Earth's weather* (lines 48–50).

(C) *poppy seeds placed on top of an upside-down bowl*

(D) *poppy seeds placed in a right-side-up bowl*

Answers (C) and (D) discuss the poppy seed examples. True. The second paragraph describes both examples as non-chaotic systems (lines 18–19).

(E) *fluctuating butterfly flight patterns*

CORRECT. False. While it is true that the passage discusses a *butterfly flapping its wings* (line 50), the passage does not mention anything about butterfly flight patterns.

UNIT THREE

Critical Reasoning

In this unit, you will learn a process for deconstructing arguments in order to understand how the information fits together logically. You will also learn how to recognize the different Critical Reasoning question types, what kind of analysis to do for each specific type, and how to avoid trap answers.

In This Unit:

CHAPTER 16

Argument Structure

In This Chapter:

- The Core
- Building Blocks of an Argument
- Signal Words
- Intermediate Conclusions and the Therefore Test
- Common Argument Types
- Answers to Pop Quiz
- Argument Structure Cheat Sheet

In this chapter, you will learn how to deconstruct arguments into their core components, or building blocks. You'll also learn how to recognize certain common types of arguments that will be discussed throughout the rest of this unit.

CHAPTER 16 Argument Structure

Here is an example of a typical GMAT argument in a Critical Reasoning (CR) problem:

> The expansion of the runways at the Bay City Airport will allow larger planes to use the airport. These new planes will create a lot of noise, a nuisance for residents who live near the airport. However, many of the residents in this neighborhood work in construction, and the contract to expand the runways has been awarded to a local construction company. Thus, the expansion of the runways will lead to an increased quality of life for the residents of this neighborhood.

In order to solve CR problems effectively and efficiently, you need to pay close attention to the specific information given for that problem, while keeping in mind how to reason through a problem of that type.

For every question, begin by understanding what you are *given*:

What is this author actually arguing?

What are the pieces of this argument?

How do they fit together?

Think about these questions in relation to the argument above before you keep reading.

On the GMAT:

1. All arguments contain at least one **Premise**. A premise is information used by the author to support some claim or conclusion. That information may be a fact or an opinion. In the example above, sentence 3 is a premise because it helps to support the author's conclusion.
2. Most (though not all) arguments contain a **Conclusion**, the primary claim the author is trying to prove or the outcome of a plan that someone is proposing. In the runway expansion example, sentence 4 is a conclusion.
3. Many arguments (though not all) contain **Background** information, which provides context to allow you to understand the basic situation. The information is true but does not either support or go against the conclusion. In the runway argument, sentence 1 provides background.
4. Some arguments contain a **Counterpoint** or **Counterpremise**—a piece of information that goes against the author's conclusion. In the example above, sentence 2 represents a counterpoint because it goes against the author's conclusion.
5. Many arguments rely on one or more **Assumptions**—something that is not stated in the argument but that the author *must believe to be true* in order to draw the given conclusion. Without the assumption, the argument fails. By definition, you will not be able to identify an assumption in the text of the argument because it is unstated. In the runway expansion argument, one assumption is that the construction jobs are more important to quality of life than the nuisance and noise of the increase in flights.

Collectively, these categories represent the **Building Blocks** of an argument. How do you know which sentences fall into which categories? Try to articulate your own thought process for the argument above, then take a look at the decision process of this fictional student:

Argument	Reader's Thoughts
The expansion of the runways at the Bay City Airport will allow larger planes to use the airport.	*Hmm. This is a fact. It could be a* ***premise*** *or it could just be background. I'm not sure yet.*
These new planes will create a lot of noise, a nuisance for residents who live near the airport.	*Now they're moving into claim territory. Something negative will come from this project. Why are they telling me this? I can't figure that out until I know the conclusion.*
However, many of the residents in this neighborhood work in construction, and the contract to expand the runways has been awarded to a local construction company.	*The word* however *indicates a contrast between sentences 2 and 3. What's the contrast? The noise is a negative consequence of the expansion, while winning a work contract is a positive consequence. Looks like I've got a* ***premise*** *and a* ***counterpoint*** *in these two sentences, but I don't know which one is which yet.*
Thus, the expansion of the runways will lead to an increased quality of life for the residents of this neighborhood.	*The word* thus *usually indicates a* ***conclusion****. Yes, this does seem like a conclusion—this project will have a certain outcome (better quality of life in this neighborhood), and I can now see how the previous two sentences fit into this conclusion. Sentence 3 is a* ***premise*** *because it provides one way in which the quality of life might be better for these people (they might make more money), and sentence 2 is a* ***counterpremise*** *because it tells me a negative consequence.*
After reading the argument: What is the author assuming?	*The author presents a cost of the plan (noise) and a benefit (construction jobs). In order for the expansion to increase quality of life, the author* ***assumes*** *that the benefit outweighs the cost.*

Notice how many times the reader thought, "I'm not sure yet" (or something along those lines). That will happen frequently while reading an argument. You're gathering information and trying to understand what each piece might be, but you won't really know how everything fits together until you know what the conclusion is—and that might not be until the end of the argument. Here's the argument again, with each sentence labeled:

Background

Counterpoint

The expansion of the runways at the Bay City Airport will allow larger planes to use the airport. These new planes will create a lot of noise, a nuisance for residents who live near the airport. However, many of the residents in this neighbourhood work in construction, and the contract to expand the runways has been awarded to a local construction company, Thus, the expansion of the runways will lead to an increased quality of life for the residents of this neighborhood.

Premise

Conclusion

The Core

The premise (or premises) and conclusion represent the **Core** of the argument. Remember that not all arguments will have a conclusion, but all will have at least one premise, so you will always have at least a partial core. The core represents what the author is trying to tell you or prove to you.

In this problem, the core consists of these two pieces:

However, many of the residents in this neighborhood work in construction, and the contract to expand the runways has been awarded to a local construction company.	Thus, the expansion of the runways will lead to an increased quality of life for the residents of this neighborhood.
Premise: provides one piece of evidence toward the conclusion	Conclusion: the claim supported by the given evidence

The argument is not airtight. For example, do you know for sure that residents of the neighborhood work for the local construction company that won the contract? If they don't, then perhaps residents won't benefit after all. As you'll see later in this book, that kind of reasoning will help when you get to the question-answering stage.

Building Blocks of an Argument

Here are the **building blocks** discussed so far:

Premise

- Is part of the **core** of the argument; present in every argument.
- Supports the author's conclusion.
- Can be a fact or an opinion; can be a description, historical information, data, or a comparison of things.
- Is often signaled by words or phrases such as *because of, since, due to,* or *as a result of.*

Conclusion

- Is part of the **core** of an argument; present in most arguments.
- Represents the author's main opinion or claim; can be in the form of a prediction, a judgment of quality or merit, a statement of causality, or the outcome of a plan.
- Is supported by at least one **premise**.
- Is often signaled by words such as *therefore, thus, so,* or *consequently* (although harder arguments might use such a word elsewhere in the argument in an attempt to confuse you).

Background

- Is not part of the **core**; not always present.
- Provides context to help understand the **core**; similar to premises but less important to the argument itself.
- Is almost always fact-based; can be in almost any form: historical information, data, descriptions of plans or ideas, definitions of words or concepts, and so on.

Counterpoint or Counterpremise

- Is not part of the **core**; only present occasionally.
- Opposes or goes against the author's **conclusion** in some way.
- Introduces multiple opportunities for traps: believing that the **conclusion** is the opposite of what it is, mistakenly thinking that a **counterpoint** is a **premise** (and vice versa), and so on.
- Is often signaled by a transition word such as *although*, *though*, *however*, *yet*, and *but* (recognize, though, that the counterpoint may come before such words).

Assumption

- Is not part of the **core**; is not written down in the argument.
- Is something that the author must believe is true in order to draw the given **conclusion**.

Argument Structure

The argument above used all four of the building blocks in this order:

Background–Counterpoint–Premise–Conclusion

The GMAT can vary the types of building blocks used in a particular argument, and it can also vary the order of those building blocks. Most arguments on the GMAT will contain at least one premise and one conclusion; you will see some arguments later on that contain only premises. If you can categorize the building blocks given in any particular argument, you're one step closer to answering the question correctly.

Pop Quiz

It's time to test your skills. You have three tasks. First, read the argument and try to identify the role of each sentence or major piece of information (note that one sentence could contain two different pieces of information). Use that information to jot down the premise(s) and conclusion. Second, try to articulate in your own words *how* the premise(s) support the conclusion. Third, identify any assumptions that must be true to draw the given conclusion.

1. Budget Fitness will grow its membership base by 10 percent in the next six months. Budget Fitness has recently crafted a clever ad campaign that it plans to air on several local radio stations.
2. Last year, the Hudson Family Farm was not profitable. However, the farm will be profitable this year. The farm operators have planted cotton, rather than corn, in several fields. Because cotton prices are expected to rise dramatically this year, the farm can expect larger revenues from cotton sales than it previously earned from corn.

Answers can be found on page 275.

Signal Words

Certain words can provide valuable clues as to whether you've got a conclusion, a premise, or a counterpoint. If an argument says, "Adnan will earn a high test score because he has studied hard," the word *because* signals a cause–effect relationship. One thing (he has studied hard) is supposed to lead to another (he will earn a high score on the test). The premise here is the cause that follows the *because*, and the conclusion is the claimed result.

Finish the following exchange:

> Sam: Can I borrow your car?
>
> Marie: Even though you don't have a driver's license . . .

What is Marie likely to say next? She has acknowledged a reason that she should *not* let Sam borrow her car, but her sentence implies that she's about to let him borrow it anyway. (Not very wise, Marie!)

What if the conversation had gone this way?

> Sam: Can I borrow your car?
>
> Marie: I like you, Sam. However, you don't have a driver's license, so . . .

This time, Marie's not falling for Sam's charming smile! She's about to deny him access to her car.

What's the difference? How do you know that, in the first case, Marie seems willing to lend Sam her car, while, in the second case, she isn't going to do so?

Signal words! The term *even though* signals an acknowledgment of or a concession to an opposing point of view. Even though it's true that Sam doesn't have a driver's license, Marie will still let him borrow her car. The contrast word *however*, on the other hand, flips a switch: Marie may like Sam, but she's not about to let him use her car when he doesn't even have a driver's license.

You can use these kinds of language clues to help you classify information in arguments:

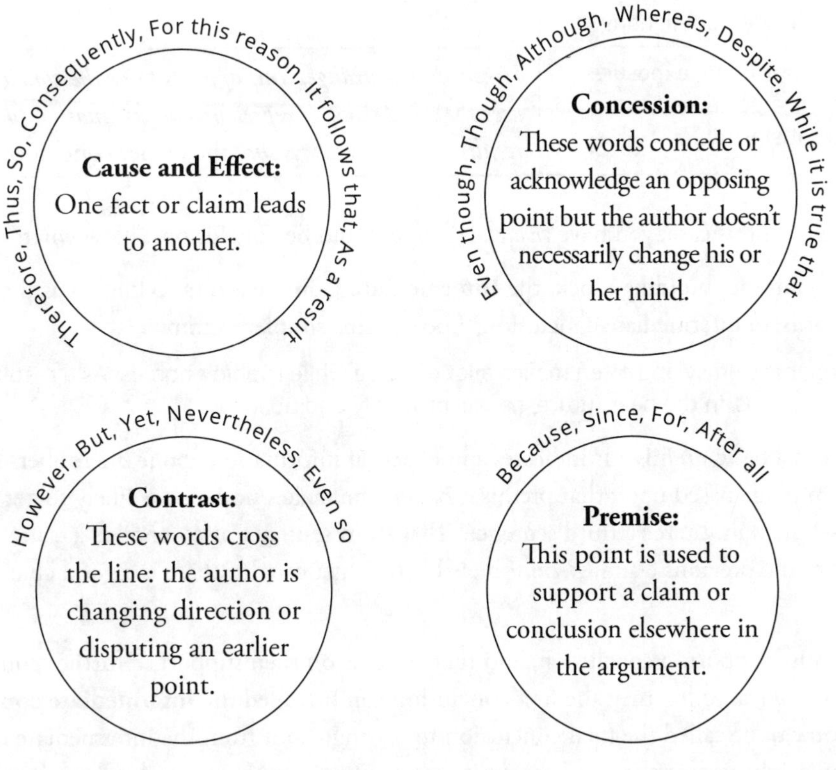
Therefore, Thus, So, Consequently, For this reason, It follows that, As a result
Cause and Effect:
One fact or claim leads to another.
Even though, Though, Although, Whereas, Despite, While it is true that
Concession:
These words concede or acknowledge an opposing point but the author doesn't necessarily change his or her mind.
However, But, Yet, Nevertheless, Even so
Contrast:
These words cross the line: the author is changing direction or disputing an earlier point.
Because, Since, For, After all
Premise:
This point is used to support a claim or conclusion elsewhere in the argument.

You likely know most or all of these words already, but you might not have consciously considered why they're used in certain contexts. Start paying attention! These signal words will make your job easier during the test.

Intermediate Conclusions and the Therefore Test

You have one more building block to learn in this chapter. Read and deconstruct the argument below:

> The owner of a small publishing company plans to lease a new office space that has floor-to-ceiling windows and no internal walls, arguing that the new space will enhance worker productivity. The owner cites a recent study showing that workers exposed to natural light throughout the day tended to report, on average, a higher level of job satisfaction than did those who worked in office spaces that used fluorescent lighting. Thus, the owner concluded, exposure to natural light has a positive effect on workers' job satisfaction.

The owner of a small publishing company plans to lease a new office space that has floor-to-ceiling windows and no internal walls,	*This is likely to be background information because it introduces a plan to do something but no actual claim (yet). The argument is probably about the plan, or a result of the plan.*
arguing that the new space will enhance worker productivity.	*This might be the conclusion because it describes the predicted future benefit of the company's plan.*
The owner cites a recent study showing that workers exposed to natural light throughout the day tended to report, on average, a higher level of job satisfaction than did those who worked in office spaces that used fluorescent lighting.	*This seems to be a premise in support of that conclusion. The workers will be more productive because the new space will provide exposure to natural light through the floor-to-ceiling windows.*
Thus, the owner concluded, exposure to natural light has a positive effect on workers' job satisfaction.	*Hmm, this is strange. This appears to be the conclusion as well. It uses the word* thus, *it represents an explanation for the study's results, and it even says that* the owner concluded *this!*

This is a tough one! In this case, you have *two* claims that could be conclusions. Now what?

This brings you to another building block, the **Intermediate Conclusion** (also known as the secondary conclusion). What is an intermediate conclusion? Look at this simpler example:

> The burglar is clumsy and often makes a lot of noise while robbing homes. As a result, he is likely to get caught. Thus, in the near future, he will probably end up in jail.

The first sentence is a basic premise: It indicates some factual information about the robber. The second sentence is a claim made based upon that premise: *Because* he makes noise, he is likely to get caught. This is a conclusion—but, wait, there's a third sentence! That third sentence also contains a claim, and this claim follows from the previous claim: *Because* he is likely to get caught, there is a good chance he will end up in jail.

Essentially, a premise supports a conclusion, and that conclusion then supports a further conclusion. If you place the events in logical order, then the first conclusion can be called the **intermediate conclusion**. The second conclusion can be called the final conclusion to distinguish it from the intermediate conclusion. Alternatively, you might reserve the word *conclusion* for the final conclusion and call the intermediate conclusion another premise—just recognize that it's a claim that is supported by other premises, and that in turn supports the (final) conclusion.

Either way, how do you figure out which is which? Use the **Therefore Test**. Call the two claims A (he's likely to get caught) and B (he will probably end up in jail). Plug the two claims into two sentences using *because* and *therefore*, and ask yourself which one is true:

> BECAUSE A (he's likely to get caught), THEREFORE B (he will probably end up in jail).
>
> OR
>
> BECAUSE B (he will probably end up in jail), THEREFORE A (he's likely to get caught).

(Using both *because* and *therefore* may seem like overkill, but it ensures that you keep the roles straight!) Which sentence makes more sense to you? The first scenario makes sense, but the second one doesn't. The fact that he will probably end up in jail should follow the *therefore*, so it is the final, real conclusion. The fact that he's likely to get caught follows the *because*, so it is only an intermediate conclusion.

In the burglar passage above, the three pieces were presented in logical progression: **premise–intermediate conclusion–final conclusion**. Arguments won't always follow this logical order, however; they might mix up the order and toss in additional information.

Try the Therefore Test with the job satisfaction argument. You have two possible conclusions:

1. (A)... arguing that the new space will enhance worker productivity.
2. (B) Thus, the owner concluded, exposure to natural light has a positive effect on workers' job satisfaction.

Which scenario makes more sense?

> BECAUSE the new space will enhance worker productivity, THEREFORE exposure to natural light has a positive effect on workers' job satisfaction.
>
> OR
>
> BECAUSE exposure to natural light has a positive effect on workers' job satisfaction, THEREFORE the new space will enhance worker productivity.

The second scenario makes more sense, so B is the intermediate conclusion and A is the final conclusion.

As is typical of arguments with an intermediate conclusion, the premise supports the intermediate conclusion, which then supports the final conclusion:

A study found a correlation between natural lighting and job satisfaction. ⇨ The owner concludes that exposure to natural light causes better job satisfaction. ⇨ The owner then concludes that the new, light-filled space will enhance productivity.

Here's the original argument again:

> The owner of a small publishing company plans to lease a new office space that has floor-to-ceiling windows and no internal walls, arguing that the new space will enhance worker productivity. The owner cites a recent study showing that workers exposed to natural light throughout the day tended to report, on average, a higher level of job satisfaction than did those who worked in office spaces that used fluorescent lighting. Thus, the owner concluded, exposure to natural light has a positive effect on workers' job satisfaction.

The argument begins with **background** information, then goes straight into the final **conclusion**. Next, you're given a **premise** followed by an **intermediate conclusion**.

As the argument above demonstrates, the logical structure of a GMAT argument can get a little complicated. If there is more than one logical step, make sure that your understanding is firm before you attempt to answer the question.

Common Argument Types

GMAT arguments cover a variety of topics from business to biology to traffic patterns of cities. Although the topics are varied, many arguments feature similar logic. Some of the most common argument types are presented in this section.

Approach all arguments on the GMAT as a skeptical reader. As you read, consider the "what if" questions you would want to ask the author when evaluating whether you believe the author's conclusion. In the discussion of argument types below, some of the issues and questions that are most relevant for each type are provided.

Causation

In causation arguments, circumstances are presented. The conclusion proposes a particular cause for that set of circumstances.

> In October, a local news station completed a redesign of its website. In November, the number of articles read on the website increased by 50 percent. Thus, the redesigned website clearly attracted more users or encouraged users to read more articles per visit.

For causation arguments, correct answer choices often relate to potential other causes for the observed result. In this case, the conclusion states that the redesign is responsible for the increase in articles read; you would want to consider what else might have caused the increase. For example, what if the news station provided extensive coverage of an important local election taking place in November?

Plan

A plan proposes a course of action to achieve a specific goal. In a plan, the conclusion is the goal of the plan. The words *in order to* or simply *to* frequently precede the goal of the plan.

> Metropolis has experienced an increase in the amount of trash in its city parks. In order to reduce the amount of litter in the parks, Metropolis plans to double the number of trash cans in each city park.

A plan must work as expected to achieve its aim. A plan may fail if the steps of the plan don't work as anticipated or there are unexpected costs or hindrances not discussed in the original argument. In this case, the plan seeks to limit people from littering in the park by making trash cans more accessible. What if the litter in the park is actually blowing into the park from the surrounding streets and sidewalks?

Prediction

Sometimes arguments conclude with a prediction of a future event.

> Rainfall totals were higher this year than they were last year in Eastown. Since wheat farmers rely on rain to irrigate their fields, yields of wheat per acre in Eastown will be higher than last year's yields.

In order for a prediction to come true, no other circumstances can intervene that might work against the prediction. In this case, the argument discusses only precipitation. How have temperatures this year affected wheat growth?

Profit

When arguments discuss profit, the conclusion often states that profits will increase or decrease—in other words, profit arguments are frequently a sub-category of predictions. You are expected to know that Profit = Revenue − Cost. Often, arguments will discuss only one element of profit (either revenues or costs), whereas the answer choice will focus on the other component.

Not every argument will fit into one of these categories, and sometimes the lines between categories get blurry. You might read an argument that seems like a plan to increase profit. Don't stress if you are not sure how to classify an argument; instead, think of the classification as another tool that can help you understand the argument and lead you toward the right answer. In subsequent chapters, you will learn what to expect in answer choices for each type of argument for different question types.

Answers to Pop Quiz

1.	Budget Fitness will grow its membership base by 10 percent in the next six months.	*This is a prediction about the future, so it is a claim, not a fact. This is a good candidate to be the conclusion.*
	Budget Fitness has recently crafted a clever ad campaign that it plans to air on several local radio stations.	*Budget Fitness already crafted the campaign—this is a fact. It is also a fact that the company currently "plans" to air the campaign (though whether it will actually air is uncertain, since that is a future event). This information supports the claim in the first sentence, so it is a premise.*

(Task 1) The order of the parts is **conclusion–premise**. If you rewrite it as premise → conclusion, then you have something like this:

BF has ad to air on radio → BF will grow members 10 percent in 6 mos

(Task 2) The author claims that the gym *will* increase its membership in the future *because* the company will launch an ad campaign. Presumably, the company thinks that this campaign will help attract new customers.

(Task 3) The argument assumes that the ad campaign will be effective in attracting new customers. (Note: There are often many assumptions contained in a given argument and many ways to word similar assumptions. The answer provided is just one example.)

2.	Last year, the Hudson Family Farm was not profitable.	*This is a fact; it already occurred in the past. This may be background info, a premise, or a counterpoint.*
	However, the farm will be profitable this year.	*The word* however *indicates a change in direction. This prediction is the* opposite *of what happened last year. This future prediction is a good candidate to be the conclusion, in which case the previous sentence would be a counterpoint.*
	The farm operators have planted cotton, rather than corn, in several fields.	*This is a fact. Hmm, why does it matter which crop the farm is planting?*
	Because cotton prices are expected to rise dramatically this year, the farm can expect larger revenues from cotton sales than it previously earned from corn.	*Okay, planting cotton will lead to more revenue than was earned last year. The author is using this information to support his conclusion in sentence 2.*

(Task 1) The order of the parts is **counterpoint–conclusion–premise–premise**. Reordering as premises → conclusion, you get this:

Cotton prices will be higher and the farm is planting cotton. → The farm will be profitable this year.

You might have been unsure about the third sentence. Does it really support the conclusion (**premise**) or does it just describe the situation (**background**)? Don't worry too much about this distinction. There are frequently sentences that could be classified either way. Your classification of this type of information is unlikely to influence your ability to answer the question correctly as long as you correctly identify the conclusion.

16

(Task 2) The argument predicts that an unprofitable farm *will* become profitable *because* a change in crops will result in higher revenues.

(Task 3) What about costs? The premise states that revenues will be higher, but revenues and profits are not the same thing. The author assumes the costs associated with cotton are not high enough to cancel out the increased revenues.

Argument Structure Cheat Sheet

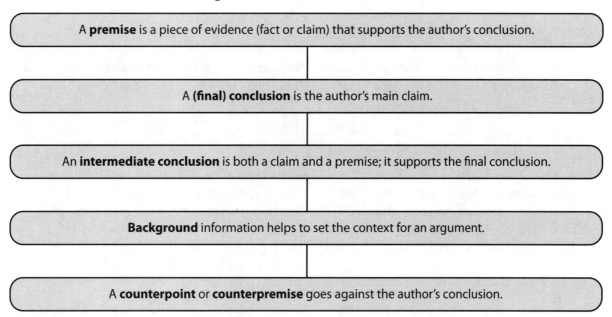

A **premise** is a piece of evidence (fact or claim) that supports the author's conclusion.

A **(final) conclusion** is the author's main claim.

An **intermediate conclusion** is both a claim and a premise; it supports the final conclusion.

Background information helps to set the context for an argument.

A **counterpoint** or **counterpremise** goes against the author's conclusion.

These building blocks will help you to understand the structure of an argument and answer the question.

When there is more than one conclusion or claim, use the **Therefore Test** to find the final conclusion. One of these two scenarios will work: either "*Because A* is true, *therefore B* is true" or "*Because B* is true, *therefore A* is true." The claim that follows the *therefore* in the working scenario is the final, real conclusion.

Problem Set

Identify the role of each sentence or major piece of information.

1. The school library currently depends heavily on donated books, which are often out of date or in poor condition. In order to encourage more students to use the library, the school administration has designated $10,000 of next year's budget to be used solely for the purchase of new books.

2. A program instituted by a state government to raise money allows homeowners to prepay their future property taxes at the current rate. Even if the government were to raise the tax rate in a subsequent year, any prepaid taxes would allow the homeowner to maintain taxes at the lower rate, lowering the overall property tax burden over time. For this reason, homeowners should participate in the program.

3. Tay-Sachs disease, a usually fatal genetic condition caused by the buildup of gangliocides in nerve cells, occurs more frequently among Ashkenazi Jews than among the general population. The age of onset is typically six months and generally results in death by the age of four.

4. The average level of physical fitness among students at North High School is likely to decline over the next few years. Due to recent changes in the way that the school calculates students' grades, earning a high grade in a physical education class will no longer improve a student's grade point average. Therefore, students who would otherwise have taken optional gym classes will be more likely to choose other electives in which earning a high grade is worth more points.

Determine whether each sentence or major piece of information is **part of the main argument** (a conclusion or premise) or **part of a counterargument** (a counterpoint). Then, determine what role the information plays in the main argument or counterargument: Is it a **conclusion** or a **premise**?

5. Some critics have argued that the price of food and drink at Ultralux, a restaurant, is too high for the quality offered. However, Ultralux features a beautiful interior and comfortable seating. Research has shown that consumers actually perceive food and drink as being of higher quality when they are consumed in such a setting. Thus, the food and drink at Ultralux are reasonably priced.

6. When compared to non-exercisers, people who exercise regularly also spend more time sitting or lying down in each 24-hour period. Because the risk of cancer and heart disease is higher among people who are more sedentary, doctors often recommend that their patients engage in regular physical exercise. However, since people who exercise are in fact often more sedentary than those who do not, this recommendation is counterproductive.

Solutions

1.	The school library currently depends heavily on donated books, which are often out of date or in poor condition.	***Background.*** *This is a statement of fact. It doesn't directly support the conclusion, which is that more students will use the library in the future. Instead, it helps to explain why a particular plan was chosen (rather than supporting the conclusion that the plan will work).*
	In order to encourage more students to use the library,	***Conclusion.*** *This argument describes a plan. When an argument describes a plan, the outcome of the plan is the conclusion of the argument.*
	the school administration has designated $10,000 of next year's budget to be used solely for the purchase of new books.	***Premise.*** *This statement explains why more students will use the library. Any statement that helps explain why the conclusion is true is a premise, since it supports the conclusion.*

2.	A program instituted by a state government to raise money allows homeowners to prepay their future property taxes at the current rate.	***Background.*** *This is a statement of fact. It isn't a premise, because it doesn't support the idea that homeowners should participate in the program—it just tells you what the program is.*
	Even if the government were to raise the tax rate in a subsequent year,	***Counterpoint.*** *In this part of the argument, the author is bringing up a potential problem with the argument: The government might raise taxes. Since this is something that might pose a problem for the argument, it's a counterpoint.*
	any prepaid taxes would allow the homeowner to maintain taxes at the lower rate, lowering the overall property tax burden over time.	***Premise.*** *The author now argues against the counterpoint. By showing that the counterpoint isn't actually a major issue, the author supports the main argument.*
	For this reason, homeowners should participate in the program.	***Conclusion.*** *This is what the author wants to convince you of. Notice that it has a* because . . . therefore *relationship with the rest of the argument: Because homeowners would have a lower tax burden, they should therefore participate in the program.*

3.	Tay-Sachs disease, a usually fatal genetic condition caused by the buildup of gangliocides in nerve cells, occurs more frequently among Ashkenazi Jews than among the general population.	***Premise (or Background).*** *This is a tricky one. There actually isn't a conclusion in this argument! Normally, the key to spotting premises is to find statements that support the conclusion. But if there isn't a conclusion, that won't work. You'd probably see this "argument" in an Inference problem, which we'll look at later. For now, if you see an argument that doesn't have a conclusion, treat all of the statements in it like premises.*
	The age of onset is typically six months and generally results in death by the age of four.	***Premise (or Background).*** *Like the sentence above, this is a statement of fact, so it can't be a conclusion. This "argument" just consists of two facts and doesn't draw a conclusion from either of them. You'd only see this in an Inference problem, which we'll learn about later on. For now, think of both of these sentences as premises.*

4.	The average level of physical fitness among students at North High School is likely to decline over the next few years.	***Conclusion.*** *When you first read this, it may not be obvious that it's the main conclusion. You can't necessarily spot the conclusion until you've read the entire argument. This is the main conclusion because everything else in the argument supports it. For instance, the fact that students will take fewer gym classes supports the belief that students will become less physically fit.*
	Due to recent changes in the way that the school calculates students' grades, earning a high grade in a physical education class will no longer improve a student's grade point average.	***Premise.*** *This is a statement of fact, so it can't be a conclusion. It supports the intermediate conclusion (in the next sentence), by explaining why students will take fewer gym classes.*
	Therefore, students who would otherwise have taken optional gym classes will be more likely to choose other electives in which earning a high grade is worth more points.	***Intermediate conclusion.*** *This sentence starts with* therefore, *and it's supported by the premise in the previous sentence. Don't be fooled! It isn't the main conclusion, because it supports the conclusion in the first sentence. If a statement is supported by part of the argument, but supports another part of the argument, it's an intermediate conclusion.*

5.	Some critics have argued that the price of food and drink at Ultralux, a restaurant, is too high for the quality offered.	***Counterargument.*** *This is the conclusion drawn by the critics, who the author of the argument disagrees with.*
	However, Ultralux features a beautiful interior and comfortable seating.	***Main argument.*** *This is one of the author's premises. It supports the point the author is making, which is that Ultralux actually isn't overpriced.*
	Research has shown that consumers actually perceive food and drink as being of higher quality when they are consumed in such a setting.	***Main argument.*** *This is another one of the author's premises. It helps to explain why the author believes that Ultralux has fair prices.*
	Thus, the food and drink at Ultralux are reasonably priced.	***Main argument.*** *This is the author's conclusion: It's the main point that the author's evidence supports.*

16

6.	When compared to non-exercisers, people who exercise regularly also spend more time sitting or lying down in each 24-hour period.	***Main argument.*** *It isn't obvious right away that this is part of the main argument. It's a fact, not an opinion, so it won't be the conclusion. Keep reading until you find the author's conclusion, which states that recommending exercise is counterproductive. Since this statement supports that conclusion, this is one of the author's premises.*
	Because the risk of cancer and heart disease is higher among people who are more sedentary,	***Counterargument.*** *This is the reasoning used by doctors, who the author disagrees with. It supports the doctors' conclusion, so it's being used as a premise.*
	doctors often recommend that their patients engage in regular physical exercise.	***Counterargument.*** *This is the doctors' recommendation. If an argument offers a recommendation and supports that recommendation with evidence, the recommendation itself is the conclusion. The author disagrees with this conclusion, so in this argument, this is a counterpoint.*
	However, since people who exercise are in fact often more sedentary than those who do not,	***Main argument.*** *This is basically the same thing that the author said in the first sentence! It's just restated to make it clear that sitting or lying down equates to being sedentary. Just like the first sentence, this is a premise belonging to the author.*
	this recommendation is counterproductive.	***Main argument.*** *This is what the author wants to convince you of! It's her conclusion. She disagrees with the doctors; her two premises explain why she disagrees.*

CHAPTER 17

Methodology

In This Chapter:

- Step 1: Identify the Question
- Step 2: Deconstruct the Argument
- Step 3: State the Goal
- Step 4: Work from Wrong to Right
- Exercise: Identify the Question
- Methodology Cheat Sheet

In this chapter, you will learn a 4-step process for use on all Critical Reasoning questions. The process will help you to identify the different question types, do the analysis required to reach the correct answer, and avoid trap answers.

CHAPTER 17 Methodology

In the previous chapter, you learned about argument building blocks and examined how to *deconstruct* an argument in order to understand how the pieces of information are related. These tasks represent the first two steps of the overall 4-step approach for any Critical Reasoning problem.

Before diving into the 4-step process, let's discuss what you *don't* want to do. While you have a lot of flexibility in how you work your way through the problem, there are some approaches that are downright bad, such as this one:

1. Read the argument pretty quickly, don't write anything down, don't understand the big picture.
2. Read the question.
3. Realize you need to read the argument again in order to answer; reread the argument.
4. Reread the question.
5. Examine the answers, eliminating one or several.
6. Read the argument for the third time.
7. Eliminate another answer.
8. Start checking each remaining answer against the argument and rereading the argument.
9. Repeat until one answer is left.

What's the problem? That's incredibly inefficient! If you've ever taken any standardized test before, you know that these tests have serious time pressure. The GMAT is no exception. In fact, you need to average about 2 minutes per CR question. So what do you do instead?

Use Manhattan Prep's 4-step approach for all CR questions:

Step 1: Identify the question.

Step 2: Deconstruct the argument.

Step 3: State the goal.

Step 4: Work from wrong to right.

Step 1: Identify the Question

Most arguments are followed by a question (you'll learn about one exception later). The wording of the question stem allows you to identify which type of question you're about to answer. You will need to employ different kinds of reasoning for different types of questions, so you want to know, right from the start, what kind of question you have.

There are three broad categories of Critical Reasoning questions: the **Structure-Based Family**, the **Assumption-Based Family**, and the **Evidence-Based Family**. Each of these families contains a few distinct question types. In later chapters, you'll learn how to identify all of the question types.

The Structure-Based Family

These questions ask you to determine something based upon the building blocks of the argument. What pieces are included in the argument and how do they fit together?

Question Type	Sample Question Phrasing	Goal
Describe the Role	In the argument given, the two boldface portions play which of the following roles?	Identify the roles (building blocks) of the boldface portions of the argument.
Describe the Argument	In the passage, the mayor challenges the council member's argument by doing which of the following?	Describe how a certain piece of information affects the argument.

The Assumption-Based Family

These questions all depend upon an understanding of the **assumptions** made by the author to reach a certain conclusion. As discussed in the last chapter, an assumption is something that the author *does not state* in the argument, but something that the author *must believe to be true* in order to draw the given conclusion. Without the assumption, the argument fails.

You'll learn much more about assumptions in future chapters; for now, take a look at this short example:

> Pedro received a higher score than Dan did on a recent algebra test. Therefore, Pedro is better at math than Dan.

You may have identified one or more logical jumps that the author had to make to get from the premise (higher score on an algebra test) to the conclusion (better at math). Assumptions fill these gaps in logic; they are what must be true for the conclusion to hold. Below are a couple examples of assumptions in this argument:

> Assumption: Scores on the algebra test are representative of overall math ability.

> Assumption: Dan and Pedro took the test under similar conditions (e.g., they were given the same amount of time).

If you were to insert an assumption into the argument, it would make the argument better:

> Pedro received a higher score than Dan did on a recent algebra test. Scores on the algebra test are representative of overall math ability. Therefore, Pedro is better at math than Dan.

An assumption should plug a hole in the argument. Most arguments on the GMAT rely on multiple assumptions, so inserting one assumption doesn't make the argument airtight. The assumption will be necessary to the argument; that is, if the assumption *isn't* true, the argument breaks down.

There are five types of Assumption Family questions, as shown below, which will be covered further in subsequent chapters:

Question Type	Sample Question Phrasing	Goal
Find the Assumption	The argument depends on which of the following assumptions?	Identify an unstated assumption.
Strengthen the Argument	Which of the following, if true, provides the most support for the argument above?	Identify a new piece of information that strengthens the author's argument.
Weaken the Argument	Which of the following, if true, most seriously weakens the argument?	Identify a new piece of information that weakens the author's argument.
Evaluate the Argument	Which of the following must be studied in order to evaluate the argument above?	Identify a piece of information that would help to determine the soundness of the argument.
Find the Flaw	Which of the following indicates a flaw in the reasoning above?	Identify something illogical in the argument.

The Evidence-Based Family

These arguments all lack conclusions; they consist entirely of premises. They also won't include any assumptions. You're asked to find something that *must be true* or something that *resolves a discrepancy* in order to answer the question. You'll learn more about both of these question types later in the book.

Question Type	Sample Question Phrasing	Goal
Inference	Which of the following can be logically concluded from the passage above?	Identify something that must be true based on the given information.
Explain a Discrepancy	Which of the following, if true, most helps to explain the surprising finding?	Identify a new piece of information that resolves some apparent paradox in the argument.

This book also discusses a variation called Complete the Argument. This variation is not a different question type; rather, it's a different way of presenting one of the other question types.

As you go through each of the families and their question types, you will learn what kind of language signals specific question types—and so you'll know how to identify the question, the first step in the process.

Step 2: Deconstruct the Argument

Now that you've identified the family and question type, you can use that information to deconstruct the argument. You began to learn how to do this in the prior chapter when you labeled arguments using the building block components.

At this stage, many people take a few light notes. If Critical Reasoning is already a strength for you and you don't write anything, then you may not need to start. If, on the other hand, you want to improve CR significantly, then making an argument map will likely be one of your necessary strategies.

Revisit the first argument from last chapter. As you deconstruct the argument, jot down an abbreviated map of the argument.

> The expansion of the runways at the Bay City Airport will allow larger planes to use the airport. These new planes will create a lot of noise, a nuisance for residents who live near the airport. However, many of the residents in this neighborhood work in construction, and the contract to expand the runways has been awarded to a local construction company. Thus, the expansion of the runways will lead to an increased quality of life for the residents of this neighborhood.

Here's one method of note-taking, idea by idea:

BC ↑ rnwy → ↑ P → > noise

BUT res work in constr [so work for them?]

© plan → better life for res

This map may seem cryptic by itself, but remember, you will always have access to the argument on your screen. You do not have to answer the question using only your notes. In fact, if you are taking too many notes, it can be helpful to imagine that you cannot use those notes to answer the question. The process of creating them is what matters.

Avoid writing down full sentences. Try to abbreviate dramatically, even reducing whole words to single letters on the fly, as was done above:

BC = Bay City Airport

↑ = expansion, larger

rnwy = runway

→ = therefore

> = more

P = planes

res = residents

constr = construction

If these abbreviations are too cryptic for you, of course, make them longer. But if you practice, you'll be amazed by how much you can abbreviate. Some of your abbreviations will be one-off creations; others you'll use all the time (e.g., a right arrow to mean *therefore*). The goal as you create these notes is not to re-create every detail of the argument, but rather to help your brain understand the argument in real time. An effective map will summarize the core of the argument, including the premises and the conclusion. Now that you've delineated the parts of the argument for yourself, you'll be in a better position to answer the question.

Here are a few tips for effective note-taking on the fly. First, most people would probably write down only the information from the first sentence first:

BC ↑ rnwy → ↑ P

Then, as you continue reading, you might realize that the second sentence follows from the first: Those bigger planes then cause more noise. As a result, you might choose to continue writing on the same line, even though the additional information is given in a separate sentence. In this fashion, you are linking together the parts of the argument.

Second, did you note the question in the brackets: *[so work for them?]* Why is that there? The argument says that many residents work in construction. It also says a local company was awarded the contract to do the work. Did you notice anything missing? The argument never actually said that the residents of this neighborhood work for the local construction company. That might be something to think about as you try to answer the question. Feel free to jot down any thoughts you have about the argument, in particular its holes, as you go. Just be sure to bracket those thoughts, so that you don't ever think they're part of the argument itself.

Not everyone writes this much; some people don't write anything at all. Throughout the examples in this book, you will see samples of sentence-by-sentence notes for a variety of arguments. Practice to determine what works best for you. At first, you might write down too much and get bogged down. Keep practicing for at least a few weeks; as you gain skill, you'll discover how quickly you can take useful, highly abbreviated notes.

Step 3: State the Goal

This is a crucial step: What exactly are you trying to do when you answer this question? What's your goal? At this stage, you know what kind of question you have, you (hopefully) understand the argument and how it fits together, and you know the conclusion (if there is one). What's next?

In stating your goal, consider how the question type applies to the specific argument. Each question type requires a certain kind of reasoning and demands certain characteristics from the correct answer. For example, imagine that the question for the Bay City Airport argument asked:

> Which of the following most strengthens the argument?

This is a **Strengthen the Argument** question; on these questions, you are looking for a new piece of information that makes the conclusion more likely to be true. You'll learn what to look for in correct answers for each question type as you work through this guide. What do you think of the following goal statements for the Bay City Airport argument?

- Which answer makes the conclusion more likely?
- Which answer makes it more likely that the runway expansion will improve quality of life in the neighborhood?

The first statement is too general; all it does is reiterate the general goal on Strengthen the Argument questions, and it provides no information about the conclusion you are trying to strengthen. The second, on the other hand, brings together the general goal with the specific conclusion of the argument. A more specific goal statement makes it easier to differentiate between answers that are related to the conclusion versus those that are not.

After you have stated your goal, spend a little time thinking about any issues you see in the argument. Are there any logical flaws? Are there other factors that are important to the conclusion but that the author has not mentioned? You may not identify issues on all arguments, but a little brainstorming can help as you move on to step 4.

Step 4: Work from Wrong to Right

Finally, the answer choices! On GMAT Verbal in general, you're asked to find the "best" answer. You're going to use a 2-step process to do so:

1. First, look through all five answers and eliminate as many "definitely wrong" answers as you can. Do *not* try to decide which is the *right* answer right now. Instead, concentrate on eliminating *wrong* answers.

2. If you have only one answer left after this first pass, great; you're done. If you have two or more answers left, then compare those remaining answers.

Why do you want to attack the answers this way, "working from wrong to right"? By definition, finding the *best* answer is a comparison; if you spot a tempting wrong answer, you might not be able to spot what is wrong with it until you've read the right answer. It's most efficient to dump all of the "No way!" answers as fast as you can, and then directly compare the remaining, more tempting answers. Of course, there will always be only one right answer, but your final choice will be made easier if you have already eliminated the bad wrong answers.

Finally, remember one last tip for Verbal questions: When you've narrowed it down to two answers, compare those two answers just once more. Then pick and move on. Going back and forth multiple times is a waste of time—either you know it after comparing the first time or you don't.

When you work from wrong to right, it's critical to keep track of your thinking on your scrap paper. You need to decide how to write down ABCDE and how to notate your thoughts.

Decision 1: How do I write down ABCDE?

Option 1	Pros	Cons
Write ABCDE for each question.	Can write on/cross off each letter; can keep letters right next to map about argument.	Have to write 36 separate times as you proceed through the Verbal section.

This option might look like this, if the first question is Weaken the Argument (noted with a W) and the second question is Strengthen the Argument (noted with an S):

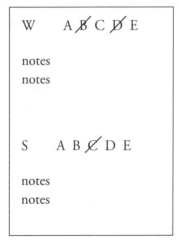

W A ~~B~~ C ~~D~~ E

notes
notes

S A B ~~C~~ D E

notes
notes

Option 2	Pros	Cons
Write ABCDE at the top of the page, then move to a new line for each question.	Only have to write once for each page (several times for entire test).	Have to keep track "below" each letter; map might not be right next to answer tracking row.

This option might look like the diagram below, in which the first question is Weaken and the second question is Strengthen. The scrap pad you'll be given is graph paper, so there will already be lines built in to separate the five answer choices.

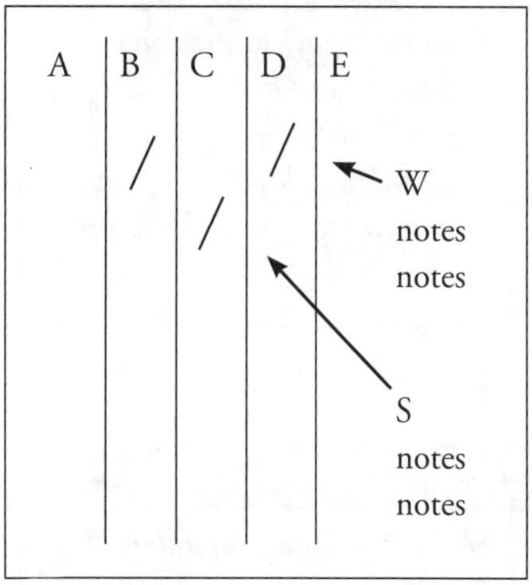

Decision 2: What symbols will I use to keep track of my thoughts?

You need four symbols. You can use any symbols you prefer as long as you consistently use the same symbols:

X or /	Definitely wrong
~	Maybe
?	I have no idea.
○	This is it!

Try using the this 4-step process on an actual problem:

Many companies use automated telephone services: Callers hear a machine-generated voice and are able to select options using the numbers on the telephone keypad. Research shows that callers are more patient when the machine-generated voice is that of a woman. Thus, smaller companies that cannot afford an automated service should consider hiring women, rather than men, to interact with customers by phone.

Which of the following, if true, would be most damaging to the conclusion above?

(A) Automated telephone services are becoming cheaper and cheaper every year.

(B) Patient customers tend to order more products and return fewer products than impatient customers.

(C) A separate study indicated that the extra patience exhibited by callers is limited to interactions with an automated system.

(D) Some customers prefer automated systems to talking with a live person.

(E) On average, callers are only slightly more patient when interacting with a female voice, rather than a male voice, in an automated telephone system.

How did you do with each step? Did you identify the question type? Do you feel comfortable with your map, and did you identify the conclusion (if there is one)? Did you remember to state the goal (briefly) before looking at the answers? Did you use the 2-step process to assess the answer choices, working from wrong to right?

Here's how someone might work through the problem above, step-by-step. The table displays text from the problem, the student's thoughts, and the relevant notes on scrap paper:

Step 1: Identify the Question

Argument	Thoughts	Paper
Which of the following, if true, would be most damaging to the conclusion above?	Most damaging to the conclusion *means this is a Weaken. I need to find the conclusion, and I need to think about what flaws or gaps might exist in the argument.*	W A B C D E

Step 2: Deconstruct the Argument

Argument	Thoughts	Paper
Many companies use automated telephone services:	*Sounds like background, but I'll jot down a note anyway.*	auto phone
Callers hear a machine-generated voice and are able to select options using the numbers on the telephone keypad.	*This is describing what an automated phone system is; I probably don't need to write that down.*	
Research shows that callers are more patient when the machine-generated voice is that of a woman.	*This is a fact, not a claim, so it has to be either a premise or counter-premise. It's probably a premise, since there's only one sentence left.*	Res: female = ↑ patience
Thus, smaller companies that cannot afford an automated service should consider hiring women, rather than men, to interact with customers by phone.	*This is the only claim, so it's the conclusion. Now I can go back and add a © to the conclusion in my map and a + to the premise.*	Small co's → use women phone

17

The final map might look something like this:

W A B C D E

auto phone

+ Res: female = ↑ patience

© Small co's → use women phone

Your map might look very different from the map above. That's perfectly fine as long as your map conveys to you the basic flow of information clearly and concisely as you put it together. Remember, the map is most useful as you make it, not as you look at it later.

Step 3: State the Goal

The question is a Weaken question, so briefly restate the main reasoning and conclusion of the argument. Once you have stated your specific goal, do a little brainstorming about any concerns you have with the argument.

> *Small companies should hire women to answer the phones, because callers are more patient when hearing automated female voices.*
>
> *How would I weaken this specific argument? What would make it less likely that companies should hire women to answer phones?*
>
> *Hmm. The evidence is about automated female voices, while the conclusion is about real women. Is there any kind of disconnect there?*

Step 4: Work from Wrong to Right

Now, attack the answers!

Argument	Thoughts	Paper
(A) Automated telephone services are becoming cheaper and cheaper every year.	*The conclusion discusses what companies should do when they* can't *afford automated services. This choice addresses those who can buy the service, so it's irrelevant to the argument.*	~~A~~
(B) Patient customers tend to order more products and return fewer products than impatient customers.	*This is a good reason for the company to do whatever it can to keep its customers in a patient mood. If anything, that would strengthen the argument.*	~~B~~
(C) A separate study indicated that the extra patience exhibited by callers is limited to interactions with an automated system.	*Hmm. This highlights a distinction between automated and live voices... Does that distinction have anything to do with the argument? Well, the conclusion only talks about hiring actual people, but it looks like all of the evidence is about automated systems. That could be a problem for the argument. Keep this one in.*	C ~
(D) Some customers prefer automated systems to talking with a live person.	*This argument is about only those companies that* can't *afford the system and are using real people. Nope, this isn't it.*	~~D~~
(E) On average, callers are only slightly more patient when interacting with a female voice, rather than a male voice, in an automated telephone system.	*This one seems to be telling me there isn't a huge difference between hearing male and female voices—but there is still a small positive effect for female voices. If anything, this strengthens the argument; after all, as a small business owner, I'll take any necessary steps that will get me more business! I've crossed off four answers, so (C) is the correct answer.*	~~E~~

At the end, the answer choice letters on your paper would look like this:

~~A~~ ~~B~~ (C) ~~D~~ ~~E~~

Exercise: Identify the Question

Warm up by matching each Critical Reasoning question stem to the type of question it's asking:

1. Which of the following indicates a vulnerability of the argument above? G
2. Which of the following, if true, most strongly suggests that the plan will fail to achieve its desired outcome? E
3. In the argument given, the boldfaced portion plays which of the following roles? A
4. In the passage above, the biologist responds to the journalist's claim by doing which of the following? B
5. Which of the following, if true, would best explain the garden snail's paradoxical behavior? I
6. Which of the following conclusions is most strongly supported by the statements given? H
7. Which of the following would be most useful to research in order to assess the likelihood that the teacher's claim is correct? F
8. Which of the following, if true, would provide the strongest justification for the mayor's conclusion? D
9. Which of the following is an assumption on which the school board's argument depends? C

(A) Describe the Role
(B) Describe the Argument
(C) Find the Assumption
(D) Strengthen the Argument
(E) Weaken the Argument
(F) Evaluate the Argument
(G) Find the Flaw
(H) Inference
(I) Explain a Discrepancy

17

Ready? Here are the answers to the exercise:

1. **(G):** The right answer to a Find the Flaw problem will point out, in general terms, a vulnerability or logical problem with the argument.
2. **(E):** If an argument describes a plan, the outcome of the plan is the conclusion of the argument. Weakening the argument means showing that the plan might fail.
3. **(A):** Describe the Role problems are the only problems in which parts of the argument appear in bold.
4. **(B):** A Describe the Argument problem asks you to describe the logic of someone's argument in more general terms.
5. **(I):** Explain a Discrepancy problems often refer to a surprise, paradox, or unusual finding in the question stem. Your task is to explain why it occurred.
6. **(H):** This question stem implies that the conclusion will be in the answer choices, not in the argument itself. This makes it an Inference problem. Be careful not to confuse this with a Strengthen the Argument question, which might also use the word *support*!
7. **(F):** Evaluate the Argument questions ask you to find the most useful question to ask or topic to research.
8. **(D):** Providing a justification for an argument is the same as strengthening that argument.
9. **(C):** Find the Assumption questions will ask you to find an assumption made by the author or something upon which the argument relies.

Methodology Cheat Sheet

Identify the Question	You'll learn how to do this in later chapters. The question type indicates what kind of information you can expect to find in the argument and what kind of reasoning will help to answer the question.
Deconstruct the Argument	Break the argument down into its building blocks. Make a very abbreviated map showing both the details and the "flow" of the information.
State the **Goal**	Very briefly articulate your goal based upon this question type (again, you'll learn the goals for each type in later chapters).
Work from **Wrong** to **Right**	Plan to go through the answers twice. On the first pass, focus on eliminating anything that is definitely wrong; leave everything else in. On the second pass, compare any choices that remain, then pick.

Know how you're going to keep track of your answers on your scrap paper. First, decide whether to have a separate ABCDE grid for each problem or whether to use the "write once per page" method described earlier in the chapter. Second, make sure you have four consistent symbols for these four labels:

1. Definitely wrong
2. Maybe
3. I have no idea.
4. This is it!

Problem Set

Map each argument on your paper, identifying the conclusion (if one exists) and the premise(s).

1. The overwhelming majority of advertisers prefer not to have their products associated with controversial content. In order to increase its advertising revenue, a large blogging platform plans to stop placing advertisements on blogs that deal with controversial topics, thus attracting advertisers who would otherwise be reluctant to advertise on the platform.

2. A series of research studies has reported that flaxseed oil can have a beneficial effect in reducing tumor growth in mice, particularly the kind of tumor found in human postmenopausal breast cancer. Thus, flaxseed oil should be recommended as an addition to the diets of all postmenopausal women.

3. During the past 30 years, the percentage of the population that smokes cigarettes has consistently declined. During the same time period, however, the number of lung cancer deaths attributed to smoking cigarettes has increased.

4. The Chinese white dolphin is a territorial animal that rarely strays far from its habitat in the Pearl River Delta. In recent years, increasing industrial and agricultural runoff to the delta's waters has caused many white dolphins to perish before they reach breeding age. Unless legislation is enacted to ensure there is no further decline in the delta's water quality, the Chinese white dolphin will become extinct.

5. Most doctors recommend consuming alcohol only in moderation, since the excessive intake of alcohol has been linked to several diseases of the liver. Drinking alcohol is no more dangerous for the liver, however, than abstaining from alcohol entirely. Last year, more nondrinkers than drinkers were diagnosed with liver failure.

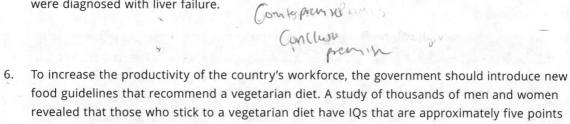

6. To increase the productivity of the country's workforce, the government should introduce new food guidelines that recommend a vegetarian diet. A study of thousands of men and women revealed that those who stick to a vegetarian diet have IQs that are approximately five points higher than those who regularly eat meat. The vegetarians were also more likely to have earned advanced degrees and hold high-paying jobs.

Solutions

Note: The sample maps shown below represent one style of map. Just make sure that your map is legible and concise and that it conveys the main points in a way that makes sense to you.

1.

Argument	Thoughts	Paper
The overwhelming majority of advertisers prefer not to have their products associated with controversial content.	*This is a fact. It could be background. Or, if it supports the conclusion, it's a premise.*	Adv: controv = bad
In order to increase its advertising revenue,	*Somebody is trying to increase revenue. That sounds like a goal. When the argument describes a plan, I can think of the goal of that plan as the conclusion.*	© Adv rev ↑
a large blogging platform plans to stop placing advertisements on blogs that deal with controversial topics,	*This is a premise describing how the goal will be achieved.*	Plan: no ads on controv blogs
thus attracting advertisers who would otherwise be reluctant to advertise on the platform.	*This is the result of the previous premise, and it supports the conclusion. This is an intermediate conclusion.*	Plan: no ads on controv blogs → more adv

The structure of this argument is **premise–conclusion–premise–intermediate conclusion**.

2.

Argument	Thoughts	Paper
A series of research studies has reported that flaxseed oil can have a beneficial effect in reducing tumor growth in mice, particularly the kind of tumor found in human postmenopausal breast cancer.	*This is a fact. It's either background or a premise.*	Res: flax helps ↓ tumor mice esp postmen b-cancer
Thus, flaxseed oil should be recommended as an addition to the diets of all postmenopausal women.	*Definitely the conclusion.*	© Postmen women shd take flax

The structure of this argument is **premise–conclusion**.

3.

Argument	Thoughts	Paper
During the past 30 years, the percentage of the population that smokes cigarettes has consistently declined.	*This is a fact. It's either background or a premise.*	30y: percent pop smoke cig ↓ steady
During the same time period, however, the number of lung cancer deaths attributed to smoking cigarettes has increased.	*Another fact, so another premise. There isn't a conclusion.*	Same time: lung canc dead from cig ↑

The structure of this argument is **premise–premise**. Remember, not all GMAT arguments contain conclusions.

4.

Argument	Thoughts	Paper
The Chinese white dolphin is a territorial animal that rarely strays far from its habitat in the Pearl River Delta.	*This is a fact. It's either background or a premise.*	Dolphin stays in delta
In recent years, increasing industrial and agricultural runoff to the delta's waters has caused many white dolphins to perish before they reach breeding age.	*This is also a fact—either background or premise.*	Recent: ind + ag in delta → dolphin dies b4 breed
Unless legislation is enacted to ensure there is no further decline in the delta's water quality, the Chinese white dolphin will become extinct.	*And here's the conclusion.* *[Note: H2O here is an abbreviation for water, based on the chemical formula H_2O.]*	IF govt doesn't fix H2O → dolphin extinct

The structure of this argument is **premise–premise–conclusion**.

5.

Argument	Thoughts	Paper
Most doctors recommend consuming alcohol only in moderation, since the excessive intake of alcohol has been linked to several diseases of the liver.	*This is a fact. It's either background or a premise.*	Drs rec ↓ alc bc ↑ alc → liver dis
Drinking alcohol is no more dangerous for the liver, however, than abstaining from alcohol entirely.	*Oh, this has the word* however*! The last sentence was a counterpremise, and this one sounds like the conclusion.*	© Drink not worse than abstain
Last year, more nondrinkers than drinkers were diagnosed with liver failure.	*This supports the previous sentence; it's a premise. (It also seems pretty flawed. What* ***percentage*** *of nondrinkers vs. drinkers had liver disease?)*	Last yr: more nondrink had liv dis

The structure of this argument is **counterpremise–conclusion–premise**.

17

6.

Argument	Thoughts	Paper
To increase the productivity of the country's workforce, the government should introduce new food guidelines that recommend a vegetarian diet.	*This is definitely a claim. It sounds like a conclusion, though I don't know for sure yet.*	Govt shd rec veg to ↑ wrkr prod
A study of thousands of men and women revealed that those who stick to a vegetarian diet have IQs that are approximately five points higher than those who regularly eat meat.	*This is a fact—the results of a study. It also supports the claim above, so it's a premise.*	Study: veg ↑ IQ than non-veg
The vegetarians were also more likely to have earned advanced degrees and hold high-paying jobs.	*This is another premise supporting the first sentence.*	Veg > better schl + high pay

The structure of this argument is **conclusion–premise–premise**.

Tip: When first learning this method, many people write too much. As part of your review, ask yourself, "Did I write this down in the most effective way? Did my map make sense? Did I write down something that I could have skipped, or did I use too many words when I could have abbreviated more?" If you were really off the mark, write out the map again in a more ideal way—and articulate to yourself why this new way is better than the old way.

CHAPTER 18

Structure-Based Family

In This Chapter:

- Describe the Role
- Describe the Argument
- Exercise: Understanding Answer Choices
- Describe the Role Cheat Sheet
- Describe the Argument Cheat Sheet

In this chapter, you will learn how to answer Critical Reasoning question types testing your ability to deconstruct arguments and to identify the role played by specific information or the logic underlying the argument.

CHAPTER 18 Structure-Based Family

In the first two chapters of this unit, you examined the building blocks of arguments and learned the 4-step approach for tackling any Critical Reasoning question:

Step 1: Identify the question.

Step 2: Deconstruct the argument.

Step 3: State the goal.

Step 4: Work from wrong to right.

Now, you're going to begin tackling the first of the three main Critical Reasoning families: the Structure-Based questions. As the name implies, these questions require you to understand the structure of the argument. What kinds of building blocks are present in the argument? What role does each building block play?

There are two main Structure question types: **Describe the Role** and **Describe the Argument**.

Describe the Role

Of the two types, Describe the Role is more common. These problems present a standard argument, with one or two portions in **boldface** font. You are asked to describe the *role* that each portion of boldface font plays.

Role is just another term for concepts you already know. A bolded portion could be a premise, a conclusion, a counterpremise, an intermediate conclusion, or background information. It could also be a counterconclusion or opposing conclusion, which goes against the author's main conclusion. You might think of this as the final claim of the *other* side of the argument.

These question types are easy to identify, because one or (usually) two statements will be presented in boldface font and the question stem will include the word *boldface*.

You're going to learn two methods to determine the role of each boldface statement. The Primary Method will always work, but it may be a little more complicated and time-consuming to use. The Secondary Method will allow you to narrow down the answer choices more easily but may not get you all the way to one answer—that is, you may have to guess from a narrowed set of answers. Regardless of the method you use, do still read and deconstruct the argument before moving on to classifying the boldface statements.

Primary Method
Classify each statement in boldface as one of the following three things: 1. (C) The author's **conclusion** 2. (P) A **premise** (it supports the author's conclusion) 3. (X) **Something else** (maybe a counterpremise, background information, acknowledgment of a weakness in the argument...)

In your notes, you'll classify each statement using the labels C, P, or X, as described above. When you evaluate the answer choices, you'll look for language that matches your labels.

Try this example:

> CEO: Now that Apex Corporation has begun to compete in our market, investors are expecting us to cut our prices to maintain market share. I don't believe this is necessary, however, because the market is growing rapidly and **a certain percentage of customers will always pay more for high-quality products**.
>
> In the argument above, the portion in boldface plays which of the following roles?

How does this argument work? First, the CEO states that investors are expecting a certain action, but she disagrees. She then provides two pieces of evidence intended to support her opinion: The market is growing and some number of customers are willing to pay higher prices. The boldface portion, then, is a premise: It supports the CEO's conclusion that the company does not need to cut prices in order to maintain market share.

Next, look for a P among the answer choices. The answer choices tend to be written in a difficult, abstract style. For example, some answers might read:

(A) The statement is evidence that has been used to weaken a claim made by the argument.

(B) The statement has been used to support a claim made by the argument.

(C) The statement is the primary claim made in the argument.

Start with the most basic piece: a building block. The word *claim* is typically a synonym for the conclusion. The first answer says that the statement weakens the conclusion. Something used to weaken the conclusion is a counterpremise; such a statement would be labeled X, not P. Choice (A) is not the correct answer.

The second answer talks about something that *supports a claim*. Since the claim is the conclusion, this answer choice does indeed describe a P, or premise, supporting the conclusion. This is probably the correct answer, but check choice (C) just to make sure.

The third answer describes the conclusion itself, not a premise supporting the conclusion. This choice is incorrect, so choice (B) is the correct answer.

You may have noticed that all the answer choices refer to how the statement relates to *the argument*. On the GMAT, when an answer choice refers to *the argument*, it refers to the perspective of the person making the argument. For instance, this argument is made by the CEO, even though it also describes the perspective of investors. If an answer choice says that a sentence *supports the argument*, it must support the perspective of the CEO, not the investors. Describe the Role questions often feature multiple perspectives; be careful to keep the different perspectives straight.

If you can use this method accurately, you will be able to eliminate the four wrong answers and get to the right answer. You might take too much time to do so, though, because of the strange format of the answers (and don't forget that the official questions typically have two boldface statements, not just one). The Secondary Method may allow you to get rid of some answers more quickly. Find the conclusion first, then ask yourself these three questions:

Secondary Method
1. Is the statement a *fact* or an *opinion*?
2. Is the statement *for* or *against* the conclusion?
3. If there are two statements, are they on the *same* side of the fence or *opposite* sides?

Strategy Tip: You can use the same side/opposite side trick with the Primary Method, too: C's and P's are on one side, while X's are on the other.

As with the Primary Method, you then look in the answer choices for matching language. How would this method work on the problem from above? The boldface statement is an *opinion* (she hasn't cited actual evidence from customers to support the claim). In addition, the statement is *for* the conclusion. The problem had only one statement, so the third question doesn't apply.

Next, check the answer choices. The word *evidence* typically indicates a fact, not an opinion, so answer (A) is likely incorrect. Answers (B) and (C) both describe claims, or opinions, and both are for the conclusion, so the Secondary Method wouldn't necessarily allow you to choose between the two. (In this case, you might notice the distinction between a conclusion and a premise and be able to choose the correct answer. This problem, though, is on the easier side.)

Common Trap Answers

The most tempting trap answers on Role questions tend to be "off" by just one word, often at the end of the sentence. For example, imagine that you've decided the first boldface is a premise in support of the author's conclusion. A tempting wrong answer might read:

> (A) The first **[boldface statement]** provides evidence in support of the position that the argument seeks to reject.

Every word of that answer matches what you want to find with the exception of the very last word, *reject*. In fact, if you changed that one word, the answer would be correct:

18

> (A) The first **[boldface statement]** provides evidence in support of the position that the argument seeks to establish.

The first version of the answer choice says that the first boldface is a premise in support of some *counter*conclusion. That's not the kind of premise you want! Read every word carefully, all the way to the end of each answer choice.

Putting It All Together

Try a full example:

Mathematician: Recently, Zubin Ghosh made headlines when he was recognized to have solved the Hilbert Conjecture. Ghosh posted his work on the internet, rather than submitting it to established journals. In fact, **he has no job, let alone a university position**; he lives alone and has refused all acclaim. In reporting on Ghosh, the press unfortunately has reinforced the popular view that mathematicians are antisocial loners. But **mathematicians clearly form a tightly knit community**, frequently collaborating on important efforts; indeed, teams of researchers are working together to extend Ghosh's findings.

In the argument above, the two portions in boldface play which of the following roles?

(A) The first is an observation the author makes to illustrate a social pattern; the second is a generalization of that pattern.

(B) The first is evidence in favor of the popular view expressed in the argument; the second is a brief restatement of that view.

(C) The first is a specific example of a generalization that the author contradicts; the second is a reiteration of that generalization.

(D) The first is a specific counterexample to a generalization that the author asserts; the second is that generalization.

(E) The first is a judgment that counters the primary assertion expressed in the argument; the second is a circumstance on which that judgment is based.

Step 1: Identify the Question

In the argument above, the two portions in boldface play which of the following roles?	*This is a Role question. The argument contains bold font, and the question stem contains the words* boldface *and* role.	R A B C D E

Step 2: Deconstruct the Argument

Mathematician: Recently, Zubin Ghosh made headlines when he was recognized to have solved the Hilbert Conjecture.	*A past fact—this is likely background. Still, jot down a note.*	M: Ghosh solved conjecture
Ghosh simply posted his work on the internet, rather than submitting it to established journals.	*Sounds like more background.*	posted on int
In fact, **he has no job, let alone a university position**; he lives alone and has refused all acclaim.	*Here's the first boldface. He's not a mathematician; that's surprising. Still, I don't know what the conclusion is, so I don't know what role this sentence is playing.*	No job

18

In reporting on Ghosh, the press unfortunately has reinforced the popular view that mathematicians are antisocial loners.	*So the first boldface is* evidence *of* the popular view *that mathematicians are loners... but the sentence also uses the word* unfortunately, *so it sounds like the author doesn't agree...*	Press: math = loners
But **mathematicians clearly form a tightly knit community**, frequently collaborating on important efforts; indeed, teams of researchers are working together to extend Ghosh's findings.	*I was right; the author disagrees. The author's conclusion is this second boldface statement, so I can label it with a* Ⓒ.	Ⓒ BUT math = commun, collab
	Now, what about that first boldface statement? It's not the conclusion, and it doesn't support the conclusion, so it must be an X: something else.	R A B C D E Ghosh solved conjecture posted on int Ⓧ No job Press: math = loners Ⓒ BUT math = commun, collab

Step 3: State the Goal

The first boldface statement is an X; that is, it is neither the conclusion nor a premise. In this case, it supports the alternate point of view, so call it a counterpremise. It goes against the conclusion. The second boldface statement is a C; it is the author's conclusion.

Remind yourself:

> *In the right answer, the first statement will be consistent with an X label and the second statement will be consistent with a C label. I'm looking for an XC combo, and those two labels are on opposite sides.*

18

Step 4: Work from Wrong to Right

(A) The first is an observation the author makes to illustrate a social pattern; the second is a generalization of that pattern.	*Hmm. I'm not 100 percent sure what they mean by* illustrate a social pattern, *but the description of the two statements here makes them sound like they're on the same "side"—the first illustrates something, and the second generalizes that same thing. I want an "opposite sides" answer.*	~~A~~
(B) The first is evidence in favor of the popular view expressed in the argument; the second is a brief restatement of that view.	*The first supports a popular view... okay, maybe. You could call the press view the popular view. Oh, but then it says that the second restates that same view. These two are on the same side again, and I want an opposite sides answer.*	~~B~~
(C) The first is a specific example of a generalization that the author contradicts; the second is a reiteration of that generalization.	*"The first is a [something] that the author contradicts." The [something] part confuses me, but I agree that the author contradicts the first one; this is a good description of a "label X" statement. Hmm. The second repeats* that generalization—*the same one mentioned in the first statement? No, I'm looking for opposite sides, not a repetition.*	~~C~~
(D) The first is a specific counterexample to a generalization that the author asserts; the second is that generalization.	*The first is a counterexample to something the author says? Yes, that accurately describes a "label X." The second is* that generalization. *I crossed off the last one for this same language. But wait... which generalization is this referring to this time? Oh, a generalization that the author* asserts; *that's the conclusion, which is a "label C." Leave this answer in.*	D~
(E) The first is a judgment that counters the primary assertion expressed in the argument; the second is a circumstance on which that judgment is based.	Counters *language—yes, the first statement does counter the conclusion, which is consistent with the label X.* That judgment = *the first boldface. The second is not something on which the first one is based—that would be same side, and I want opposite sides.*	~~E~~

~~A~~ ~~B~~ ~~C~~ (D~) ~~E~~

The correct answer is (D).

18

Common Trap Answers

Half Right

The test writers try to set some traps for you on incorrect Describe the Role answers. For example, one of the descriptions might match one of the boldface statements, but the other one won't match. Several of the wrong answers in the last problem were **Half Right** in this way.

One Word Off

In addition, a very tricky trap answer might be wrong by just one word; we call this the **One Word Off** trap. For example, you might be looking for a premise that supports the conclusion. The answer choice might say, "The first boldface supports a claim that the argument as a whole argues against."

What does that really mean? This choice says that the boldface supports a counterconclusion, not the author's conclusion—but you wouldn't know until you read the very last word of the sentence. In fact, if you changed the word *against* to the word *for*, then the choice would be describing a premise in support of the conclusion!

Describe the Argument

Describe the Argument questions can be similar to Role questions: Both often offer "abstract" answer choices based on the *structure* of the argument, perhaps referring to the various building blocks (conclusions, premises, and so on). The majority of these Argument questions will offer two competing points of view in a dialogue format. Then, you might be asked how the second person responds to the first person's argument.

Important note: Other question types can also be presented in this "two people speaking" format—the mere existence of two speakers does not make the problem a Describe the Argument problem. *Always identify the question type using the question stem.*

A minority of these questions will offer just one point of view and ask you how the author of that argument develops his or her point of view.

Common question formulations include:

> Baram responds to Sadie's argument by . . .
>
> Baram challenges Sadie's argument by . . .
>
> The author develops the argument by doing which of the following?

These all indicate that you have a Describe the Argument question.

Your task is to determine how a particular part of the text was constructed. When the text is a dialogue between two people, read and deconstruct the first person's complete argument just as you would do for any other GMAT argument. Next, examine the response and figure out which piece of the argument the response attacks.

Try an example:

> Baram: I need to learn the names of 100 muscles for the anatomy exam in two hours. I've just memorized 5 of them in 5 minutes, so I only need 95 more minutes to study. Therefore, I'll have plenty of time to memorize everything and get a perfect score on the test.
>
> Sadie: Are you sure? Perhaps the more you memorize, the harder it gets.
>
> Sadie responds to Baram by

What is Baram's argument? What is his conclusion and how does he support it?

> must learn 100 names in 2h
>
> mem 5 in 5m, so need 95m
>
> © will get 100 percent

Which part does Sadie attack? Does she attack the conclusion directly? No, but her words certainly cast doubt on Baram's eventual conclusion. She attacks Baram's assumption that he can maintain the same rate of learning, 1 name every minute, for all 100 names. He doesn't explicitly state that he can maintain that rate, but he clearly believes it to be true. The correct answer might be something like:

> Sadie calls into question an assumption Baram makes about the efficacy of his plan.

This answer addresses the appropriate part of the argument—an assumption that Baram makes about his plan. An incorrect answer might look something like:

> Sadie introduces new evidence that contradicts one of Baram's premises.

Sadie does say something new, but does it rise to the level of evidence? She only suggests that his memorization rate might not be constant; she doesn't prove that it is not. While you might be able to argue that the word *evidence* is okay, the word *contradicts* clearly takes things too far. Sadie does not definitively contradict Baram's premise that he will need only 95 more minutes; rather, she raises a question as to *whether* he can memorize the words in only 95 minutes.

Ultimately, the attack is designed to find fault with the conclusion, but don't assume that the second person is attacking the conclusion directly. Tearing down any piece of the argument would ultimately undermine the conclusion, so find the piece that the second person most directly attacks.

You probably won't be able to anticipate the exact wording of the correct answer, but if you can identify the part of the argument addressed, then you are in a much better position to identify the appropriate "matching" language in the correct answer.

Try a full example:

> Mayor: The recycling program costs us nearly $1 million to operate every year, and our budget shortfall this year is projected to be $5 million. Cutting the recycling program will help balance the budget.
>
> Consumer Advocate: It costs the city more to throw something out than to recycle it.
>
> The consumer advocate responds to the mayor by
>
> (A) establishing that the mayor's figures were incorrectly calculated
> (B) accepting the mayor's conclusion but questioning the legality of the plan
> (C) interpreting the mayor's evidence in a way that reduces the validity of the mayor's claim
> (D) introducing a new piece of information that calls into question the validity of the mayor's conclusion
> (E) pointing out that the mayor has not adequately considered the potential causes and effects of the budget shortfall

Step 1: Identify the Question

18

The consumer advocate responds to the mayor by	*This is a Describe the Argument question. Two people are talking, and I have to explain how one responds to the other.*	DA A B C D E

Step 2: Deconstruct the Argument

Mayor: The recycling program costs us nearly $1 million to operate every year, and our budget shortfall this year is projected to be $5 million.	*The mayor is stating a couple of facts—recycling costs $1m and they're going to miss their budget by $5m.*	M: Recyc cost $1m; this yr $5m short

Cutting the recycling program will help balance the budget.	*So the mayor suggests that they cut the R program in order to help balance the budget.*	→ Cut R → bal budg ©
Consumer Advocate: It costs the city more to throw something out than to recycle it.	*That's interesting. The advocate says that it costs even more to throw something out. Why does this matter? If you can't recycle something, what are you going to do with it instead? Probably throw it out.*	Advoc: Throw away costs > R

Step 3: State the Goal

For Describe the Argument questions, you have to address how some part of the argument is made: in this case, how the consumer advocate responds to the mayor. First, it sounds as if the advocate thinks that the mayor's plan isn't going to work since the advocate says that throwing stuff out is more costly than recycling it. If that's true, then the plan to cut the recycling program just got a bit worse—it might not actually achieve the ultimate goal, which is to save money and balance the budget.

State your goal briefly to yourself before going to the answers:

The answer I find should indicate that the consumer advocate disagrees with the mayor, specifically questioning whether the suggested action (cutting the recycling program) will result in the desired outcome (saving money, helping to balance the budget).

Step 4: Work from Wrong to Right

(A) establishing that the mayor's figures were incorrectly calculated	*The consumer advocate doesn't say anything about the mayor's figures—in fact, the advocate doesn't dispute the mayor's evidence at all. Rather, the advocate attacks the mayor's assumption that cutting the program will lead to balancing the budget.*	~~A~~
(B) accepting the mayor's conclusion but questioning the legality of the plan	*The advocate doesn't accept the conclusion, nor does the advocate say anything about legality. Rather, the advocate questions whether the plan will really lead to saving money.*	~~B~~
(C) interpreting the mayor's evidence in a way that reduces the validity of the mayor's claim	*Hmm. Maybe. The advocate does reduce the validity of the mayor's claim. I'm not 100 percent sure what* interpreting the evidence *means. I'll leave this in for now.*	C ~
(D) introducing a new piece of information that calls into question the validity of the mayor's conclusion	*The advocate does call the mayor's conclusion into question, yes. Oh, I see—this one is better than answer (C) because the advocate does introduce a new piece of info (that it costs more to throw something away).*	D ~
(E) pointing out that the mayor has not adequately considered the potential causes and effects of the budget shortfall	*This one is tricky. It's true that the mayor hasn't fully considered the potential effects of the plan to cut the recycling program—but that's not what this choice says. It talks about the causes and effects of the budget shortfall.*	~~E~~

~~A~~ ~~B~~ ~~C~~ ~ (D) ~ ~~E~~

18

On the first pass, choices (C) and (D) were left in, but a direct comparison showed that choice (D) was better than (C). The correct answer is (D).

Common Trap Answers

One Word Off

The most tempting trap answers on Describe the Argument questions are similar to those on Role questions: Most of the answer is fine, but one or two words will throw the answer off.

In addition, because most of these arguments will consist of a second person objecting to something the first person says, it will always be tempting to choose an answer that indicates that, for example, the consumer advocate rejects the mayor's conclusion. The advocate's comment does weaken the mayor's conclusion, but it may not directly attack the conclusion—and the question asks you to articulate what the advocate directly attacks.

Exercise: Understanding Answer Choices

One of the toughest things about Describe the Role problems is understanding the language in the answer choices. Before you do a full problem set, warm up by translating some answer choices for practice.

Each question gives you sample answer choice text from a Describe the Role problem. Your job is to determine what part of an argument that answer choice is actually referring to.

1. A claim upon which the author's argument depends
   (A) Author's premise
   (B) Author's conclusion
   (C) Premise of a counterargument
   (D) Conclusion of a counterargument
2. A conclusion that the author believes has been incorrectly drawn
   (A) Author's premise
   (B) Author's conclusion
   (C) Premise of a counterargument
   (D) Conclusion of a counterargument
3. Reasoning that has been used to support the claim made by the opposing scientists
   (A) Author's premise
   (B) Author's conclusion
   (C) Premise of a counterargument
   (D) Conclusion of a counterargument
4. A prediction supported by the author's interpretation of existing evidence
   (A) Author's premise
   (B) Author's conclusion
   (C) Premise of a counterargument
   (D) Conclusion of a counterargument
5. The desired outcome of a plan, which the author believes will be more successful than the previous approach
   (A) Author's premise
   (B) Author's conclusion
   (C) Premise of a counterargument
   (D) Conclusion of a counterargument

Answers to Exercise

1. **(A) Author's premise:** *Claim* usually refers to the conclusion of an argument. However, the author's argument *depends* on this claim. Something that an argument depends on is a premise: Conclusions always depend on premises.
2. **(D) Conclusion of a counterargument:** Since the author believes that this conclusion has been *incorrectly drawn*, it must be part of a counterargument that the author disagrees with.
3. **(C) Premise of a counterargument:** Something that *supports a claim* is a premise. Since this claim belongs to the *opposing scientists*, it's one that the author disagrees with, so it's part of a counterargument.
4. **(B) Author's conclusion:** A prediction is often a conclusion, and this one is *supported*: The rest of an argument always supports its conclusion. Since it's supported by the author's interpretation, it's part of the author's argument.
5. **(B) Author's conclusion:** When an argument discusses a plan, the desired outcome of that plan—even if it's just that the plan will succeed—is the conclusion of the argument.

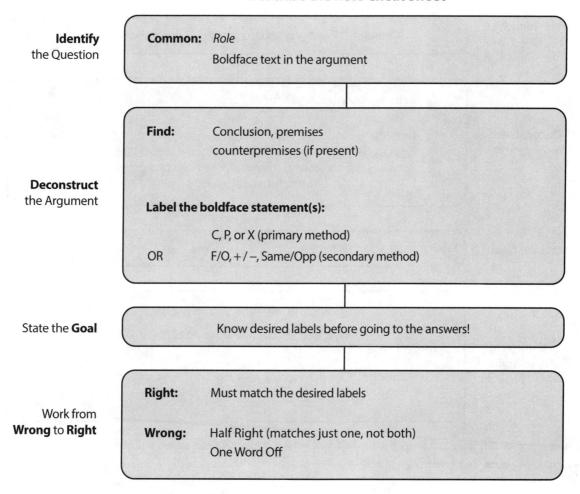

Describe the Role Cheat Sheet

Identify the Question

Common: *Role*
Boldface text in the argument

Deconstruct the Argument

Find: Conclusion, premises
counterpremises (if present)

Label the boldface statement(s):

C, P, or X (primary method)
OR F/O, + / –, Same/Opp (secondary method)

State the **Goal**

Know desired labels before going to the answers!

Work from **Wrong** to **Right**

Right: Must match the desired labels

Wrong: Half Right (matches just one, not both)
One Word Off

Take a photo of this page and keep it with the review sheets you're creating as you study. Better yet, use this page as a guide to create your own review sheet—you'll remember the material better if you write it down yourself.

Describe the Argument Cheat Sheet

Identify the Question

Common: How one person *responds* or *objects* to something.

Deconstruct the Argument

Find: Conclusion, premises

Does the second person flat-out contradict what the first one says? Or does the second person question whether the first's conclusion is relevant or accurate? Does the second person introduce new information?

State the **Goal**

What was attacked? How was it attacked?

Work from **Wrong** to **Right**

Right: Must match what the second person did

Must address the relevant part of the argument

Wrong: Doesn't address what the person directly attacks

One Word Off

Take a photo of this page and keep it with the review sheets you're creating as you study. Better yet, use this page as a guide to create your own review sheet—you'll remember the material better if you write it down yourself.

Problem Set

Answer each question using the 4-step Critical Reasoning process.

1. **Identify the question:** Is this a Describe the Role question or a Describe the Argument question?
2. **Deconstruct the argument:** Find the conclusion and map the argument on your paper.
3. **State the goal:** What will the right answer need to do?
4. **Work from wrong to right:** Eliminate four wrong answers. Watch out for common wrong answer types.

1. *Ad Revenues*

   Media Critic: Network executives allege that television viewership is decreasing due to the availability of television programs on other platforms, such as the internet and mobile devices. These executives claim that **declining viewership will cause advertising revenue to fall and networks will thus be unable to spend the large sums necessary to produce high-quality programming**. That development, in turn, will lead to a dearth of programming for the very devices that cannibalized television's audience. However, research shows that users of alternative platforms are exposed to new programs and, **as a result, actually increase the number of hours per week that they watch television**. This demonstrates that alternative platforms will not prevent networks from increasing advertising revenue.

   The portions in boldface play which of the following roles in the media critic's argument?

   (A) The first is a trend that weighs against the critic's claim; the second is that claim.

   (B) The first is a prediction that is challenged by the argument; the second is a finding upon which the argument depends.

   (C) The first clarifies the reasoning behind the critic's claim; the second demonstrates why that claim is flawed.

   (D) The first acknowledges a position that the network executives accept as true; the second is a consequence of that position.

   (E) The first opposes the critic's claim through an analogy; the second outlines a scenario in which that claim will not hold.

2. *Renaissance Masters*

Many people praise High Renaissance painting for creating very realistic images from observation, but **scholars have documented that some High Renaissance painters used pinhole cameras to project the likeness of their subjects onto the canvas and painted from there**. Thus, people who credit High Renaissance painters with superior artistic skills are misguided. **Painting from a projected image requires only an insignificant amount of additional skill beyond that needed to copy a picture outright**.

In the argument given, the two boldfaced portions play which of the following roles?

(A) The first is a finding that has been used to support a conclusion that the argument rejects; the second is a claim that supports that conclusion.

(B) The first is a finding that has been used to support a conclusion that the argument rejects; the second is that conclusion.

(C) The first is a claim put forth to support a conclusion that the argument rejects; the second is a consideration that is introduced to counter the force of that evidence.

(D) The first is evidence that forms the basis for the position that the argument seeks to establish; the second is a claim presented to solidify that position.

(E) The first is evidence that forms the basis for the position that the argument seeks to establish; the second is that position.

3. *Democracy*

As the United States demonstrated during its early development, it is not enough for citizens simply to have rights; the successful functioning of a democracy requires that they also know how to exercise those rights. Access to formal education was one necessary component that helped the U.S. citizenry learn how to exercise its rights. Therefore, in order for a democracy to function successfully, its citizens must have access to a formal education.

The author develops the argument by

(A) using an analogy to establish a precedent for a planned future event

(B) illustrating differences in the requirements for the functioning of a democracy depending upon the democracy in question

(C) introducing an example that illustrates a common principle

(D) forming a hypothesis that explains apparently contradictory pieces of evidence

(E) supplying an alternate explanation for a known phenomenon

4. *Malaria*

In an attempt to explain the cause of malaria, a deadly infectious disease, early European settlers in Hong Kong attributed the malady to poisonous gases supposedly emanating from low-lying swampland. In the 1880s, however, doctors determined that Anopheles mosquitoes were responsible for transmitting the disease to humans after observing that **the female of the species can carry a parasitic protozoan that is passed on to unsuspecting humans when a mosquito feasts on a person's blood**.

What function does the statement in boldface fulfill with respect to the argument presented above?

(A) It provides support for the explanation of a particular phenomenon.

(B) It presents evidence that contradicts an established fact.

(C) It offers confirmation of a contested assumption.

(D) It identifies the cause of an erroneous conclusion.

(E) It proposes a new conclusion in place of an earlier conjecture.

5. *Digital Marketing*

Sania: The newest workers in the workforce are the most effective digital marketing employees because they are more likely to use social networking websites and tools themselves.

Carlos: But effective digital marketing also requires very technical expertise, such as search engine optimization, that is best learned on the job via prolonged exposure and instruction.

Carlos responds to Sania by

(A) demonstrating that Sania's conclusion is based upon evidence that is not relevant to the given situation

(B) questioning the accuracy of the evidence presented by Sania in support of her conclusion

(C) reinforcing Sania's argument by contributing an additional piece of evidence in support of her conclusion

(D) pointing out differences in the qualifications desired by different employers seeking digital marketing employees

(E) providing an additional piece of evidence that undermines a portion of Sania's claim

6. *Innovative Design*

   Products with innovative and appealing designs relative to competing products can often command substantially higher prices in the marketplace. **Because design innovations are quickly copied by other manufacturers**, many consumer technology companies charge as much as possible for their new designs to extract as much value as possible from them. But large profits generated by the innovative designs give competitors stronger incentives to copy the designs. Therefore, **the best strategy to maximize overall profit from an innovative new design is to charge less than the greatest possible price**.

   In the argument above, the two portions in boldface play which of the following roles?

   (A) The first is an assumption that supports a described course of action; the second provides a consideration to support a preferred course of action.

   (B) The first is a consideration that helps explain the appeal of a certain strategy; the second presents an alternative strategy endorsed by the argument.

   (C) The first is a phenomenon that makes a specific strategy unlikely to be successful; the second is that strategy.

   (D) The first is a consideration that demonstrates why a particular approach is flawed; the second describes a way to amend that approach.

   (E) The first is a factor used to rationalize a particular strategy; the second is a factor against that strategy.

7. *Gray Wolf Population*

   Government representative: Between 1996 and 2005, the gray wolf population in Minnesota grew nearly 50 percent; the gray wolf population in Montana increased by only 13 percent during the same period. Clearly, the Minnesota gray wolf population is more likely to survive and thrive long term.

   Environmentalist: But the gray wolf population in Montana is nearly 8 times the population in Minnesota; above a certain critical breeding number, the population is stable and does not require growth in order to survive.

   The environmentalist challenges the government representative's argument by doing which of the following?

   (A) Introducing additional evidence that undermines an assumption made by the representative

   (B) Challenging the representative's definition of a critical breeding number

   (C) Demonstrating that the critical breeding number of the two wolf populations differs significantly

   (D) Implying that the two populations of wolves could be combined in order to preserve the species

   (E) Suggesting that the Montana wolf population grew at a faster rate than stated in the representative's argument

Solutions

1. Ad Revenues: The correct answer is **(B)**.

Step 1: Identify the Question

The portions in boldface play which of the following roles in the media critic's argument?	*This is a Role question. The question contains the word* boldface, *and I'm asked to find the* role *of each bold statement.*	R A B C D E

Step 2: Deconstruct the Argument

Media Critic: Network executives allege that television viewership is decreasing due to the availability of television programs on other platforms, such as the internet and mobile devices.	*The word* allege *tells me this is a claim. Also, the critic is talking about what other people claim, so I'm guessing the critic is going to contradict what they claim—so this is probably a counter-premise.*	Critic: Execs say TV ↓ b/c use other plats
These executives claim that **declining viewership will cause advertising revenue to fall and networks will thus be unable to spend the large sums necessary to produce high-quality programming**.	*More from the execs. More claims about bad things happening. Is the last thing the execs' conclusion? This is the 1st boldface. If the critic contradicts the execs later, then this first boldface will be labeled an X.*	Execs: TV ↓ → ad ↓ → no $ for qual prog
That development, in turn, will lead to a dearth of programming for the very devices that cannibalized television's audience.	*Ah, I see. Ironic. The fact that people are watching on other platforms will eventually lead to not having enough programming for those other platforms. Conclusion of the execs.*	→ No prog for other plats
However, research shows that users of alternative platforms are exposed to new programs and, **as a result, actually increase the number of hours per week that they watch television**.	*Here's the contradiction! I'll wait till I find the conclusion for sure, but the first boldface is probably an X, which would make this one a premise (P).*	BUT users of alt plats watch MORE TV
This demonstrates that alternative platforms will not prevent networks from increasing advertising revenue.	*Okay, the critic is concluding the opposite: that ad rates will go up. And if that's my conclusion, then the first boldface is indeed an X and the second one supports the critic's conclusion, so it's a P.*	© Ad rates Want: X P

Step 3: State the Goal

The question asks me to find the role of two boldface statements. The critic's conclusion is in the last line, and the second boldface, right before it, supports that conclusion. The second boldface is a premise (P). The first boldface is part of the executives' argument, which is the opposite of the critic's argument, so the first boldface is an X. I want to find the combo X P (in that order) in an answer choice.

Step 4: Work from Wrong to Right

(A) The first is a trend that weighs against the critic's claim; the second is that claim.	Weighs against the critic's claim—*yes, that's consistent with an X label. The second* is that claim, *meaning the critic's claim. No. The second one is a P, not a C.*	~~A~~
(B) The first is a prediction that is challenged by the argument; the second is a finding upon which the argument depends.	*That's true, the critic does challenge the first one. That's an X. And the second one is a P, so this could be something upon which the critic's argument depends. I'll keep it in.*	B ~
(C) The first clarifies the reasoning behind the critic's claim; the second demonstrates why that claim is flawed.	*Clarifies the critic's claim? No. The first one is something the execs claim. I don't even need to read the second half of the answer.*	~~C~~
(D) The first acknowledges a position that the network executives accept as true; the second is a consequence of that position.	*Yes, the execs do accept the first boldface as true—it's their premise. And they're on the opposite side of the critic, so something they think is an X. Okay, that's fine.* The second is a consequence of that position. *What position? Oh, they use* position *in the first half of the sentence... the execs' position. The second isn't something about the execs' position. It goes against the execs' position. No.*	~~D~~
(E) The first opposes the critic's claim through an analogy; the second outlines a scenario in which that claim will not hold.	*The first one does oppose what the critic concludes. I'm not quite sure whether it does so* through an analogy. *What about the second half? A scenario in which the critic's claim won't hold—meaning something that's on the opposite side of what the critic says. No! The second one outlines a scenario in which the execs' claim, not the critic's claim, won't hold.*	~~E~~

~~A~~ (B) ~ ~~C~~ ~~D~~ ~~E~~

2. Renaissance Masters: The correct answer is **(D)**.

Step 1: Identify the Question

In the argument given, the two boldfaced portions play which of the following roles?	*The word* boldfaced, *along with the boldface font in the argument, indicates that this is a Role question.*	R A B C D E

Step 2: Deconstruct the Argument

Many people praise High Renaissance painting for creating very realistic images from observation,	*The* many people *intro feels like there's a contrast coming... and there is! Okay, just get this piece down first.*	Many like Hi Ren pics b/c realistic
but **scholars have documented that some High Renaissance painters used pinhole cameras to project the likeness of their subjects onto the canvas and painted from there**.	*People think the High Renaissance painters could paint realistically just by observing, but actually some were just projecting the images onto a canvas and sort of tracing the image.*	BUT some painters just projected + traced
Thus, people who credit High Renaissance painters with superior artistic skills are misguided.	*The word* thus *might mean this is the conclusion. The previous sentence only said that* some *painters did the tracing thing, not all of them. But this sentence seems to be condemning all of them.*	People who like Hi Ren = misguided
Painting from a projected image requires only an insignificant amount of additional skill beyond that needed to copy a picture outright.	*Okay, the last sentence was definitely the conclusion. This sentence is supporting the conclusion. If this is true, then yes, painters who use this technique aren't that great.*	project = low skill
	I'm not 100 percent sure how to label the first boldface, but I did notice that the first one was a fact and the second one was an opinion. I could use the Secondary Method to solve.	

18

Step 3: State the Goal

I need to identify the role of the two boldfaced statements as they relate to the conclusion—which was that people who think High Renaissance painters are really skilled are misguided. The first one is a fact, and the second one is an opinion. The first one is FOR the conclusion. So is the second one.

Step 4: Work from Wrong to Right

(A) The first is a finding that has been used to support a conclusion that the argument rejects; the second is a claim that supports that conclusion.	A finding *could be a fact, and a* claim *is an opinion, so this one is okay so far.*	A ~
(B) The first is a finding that has been used to support a conclusion that the argument rejects; the second is that conclusion.	A finding *could be a fact, and the conclusion is technically an opinion. But the boldface opinion is FOR the conclusion; it's not actually the conclusion itself.*	~~B~~
(C) The first is a claim put forth to support a conclusion that the argument rejects; the second is a consideration that is introduced to counter the force of that evidence.	A claim *is not a fact. I can eliminate this one.*	~~C~~
(D) The first is evidence that forms the basis for the position that the argument seeks to establish; the second is a claim presented to solidify that position.	Evidence *can be a fact, and a* claim *is an opinion. This one has to stay in, too.*	D ~
(E) The first is evidence that forms the basis for the position that the argument seeks to establish; the second is that position.	Evidence *can be a fact, but the second boldface is an opinion supporting the conclusion, while this choice says that the second boldface is the* position, *or conclusion. I can eliminate this one.*	~~E~~
Compare (A) and (D)	*Based on the fact/opinion technique, I can't get any further; I just have to guess between (A) and (D).* *The main technique can distinguish between (A) and (D): Both boldfaces are premises used to support the author's conclusion. Answer (A) says that the first boldface is used "to support a conclusion that the argument rejects." Eliminate answer (A).*	~~A~~ ~ and D ~

~~A~~ ~~B~~ ~~C~~ (D) ~~E~~

18

3. Democracy: The correct answer is **(C)**.

Step 1: Identify the Question

The author develops the argument by	*The wording is similar to a Describe the Argument question, though it doesn't have the "two people talking" feature. This might be one of the rare variants that doesn't have two people talking. A quick glance at the abstract wording of the answer choices confirms: This is a Describe Arg question.*	DA A B C D E

Step 2: Deconstruct the Argument

As the United States demonstrated during its early development, it is not enough for citizens simply to have rights; the successful functioning of a democracy requires that they also know how to exercise those rights.	*Okay, specific example of a principle: the U.S. showed that citizens need to have rights AND need to know how to exercise those rights.*	US: not just have rights but know how to exercise → success democ
Access to formal education was one necessary component that helped the U.S. citizenry learn how to exercise its rights.	*More detail on the U.S. example. Access to formal education was needed to know how to exercise those rights.*	Need access to formal educ →
Therefore, in order for a democracy to function successfully, its citizens must have access to a formal education.	*Conclusion. The author's just sort of putting together the two "end" pieces of the argument here.*	© Need formal edu for success democ

Step 3: State the Goal

The author concludes that formal education is necessary in general for a democracy to be successful. The evidence: It happened this way in one country (the U.S.).

18

Step 4: Work from Wrong to Right

(A) using an analogy to establish a precedent for a planned future event	*The argument used an example. Is that the same thing as an analogy? Maybe. Oh, but what's the* planned future event*? There isn't anything; rather, the author concluded with a general statement, not a discussion of an event.*	~~A~~
(B) illustrating differences in the requirements for the functioning of a democracy depending upon the democracy in question	*I can imagine that it would be true that there are different requirements for different governments... but that's not what this argument says. The author only mentions the U.S. and then concludes something in general about that.*	~~B~~
(C) introducing an example that illustrates a common principle	*This looks decent. The argument did introduce an example and then used that to conclude a general principle.*	C ~
(D) forming a hypothesis that explains apparently contradictory pieces of evidence	*It would be reasonable to describe the conclusion as a hypothesis... but there aren't any contradictory things in the argument. Rather, the example given does illustrate the conclusion.*	~~D~~
(E) supplying an alternate explanation for a known phenomenon	*The author doesn't supply an* alternate explanation*; he isn't arguing against anyone. He just concludes something from the U.S. example.*	~~E~~

~~A~~ ~~B~~ (C ~) ~~D~~ ~~E~~

4. Malaria: The correct answer is **(A)**.

Step 1: Identify the Question

What function does the statement in boldface fulfill with respect to the argument presented above?	*This is a Role question. The question contains the word* boldface, *and I'm asked to find the* function *of each bold statement.*	R A B C D E

Step 2: Deconstruct the Argument

In an attempt to explain the cause of malaria, a deadly infectious disease, early European settlers in Hong Kong attributed the malady to poisonous gases supposedly emanating from low-lying swampland.	*This is a fact. Likely either background or premise.*	Euros in HK: Poison gas → malaria
In the 1880s, however, doctors determined that Anopheles mosquitoes were responsible for transmitting the disease to humans after observing that **the female of the species can carry a parasitic protozoan that is passed on to unsuspecting humans when a mosquito feasts on a person's blood**.	*Okay, this is still a fact, but it's the conclusion of the story. They used to think it was one thing, and then they figured out it was really the mosquitoes. The boldface language, in particular, is the evidence used to show that it was mosquitoes. That's a premise.*	But 1880s MDs: mosq bite, pass parasite blood Want: P

Step 3: State the Goal

The question specifically asks me what role this information plays: the female carries a parasite that is passed to humans when a mosquito bites someone. Because of that, the scientists decided that the mosquitoes were transmitting the disease. That's the most like a P—a premise that supports some further conclusion.

I need to find the abstract language that indicates some kind of premise or support.

Step 4: Work from Wrong to Right

(A) It provides support for the explanation of a particular phenomenon.	Support—*that's good—for a* phenomenon. *Okay, that's just fancy-speak for: Provides support for something that happened. That sounds okay. Leave it in.*	A ~
(B) It presents evidence that contradicts an established fact.	Evidence—*that's also good. And that evidence does contradict what the earlier settlers thought! Oh, wait—was that an established fact? Let me look at the first sentence again. No, they thought that, but the argument doesn't say it was an* established fact. *Cross this one off.*	~~B~~
(C) It offers confirmation of a contested assumption.	Confirmation *is also good... of a* contested assumption. *I'm not quite sure what they're referring to when they say* assumption, *but nothing was contested here. First, some people thought one thing, and later, new evidence led some doctors to conclude something else. No.*	~~C~~
(D) It identifies the cause of an erroneous conclusion.	*No—the only thing we might be able to describe as an erroneous conclusion is what the early settlers thought. But the bold stuff supports the doctors' conclusion.*	~~D~~
(E) It proposes a new conclusion in place of an earlier conjecture.	*Oh, yes, a new conclusion. Yes, that's exactly what the argument says! Oh, wait—I labeled the boldface stuff a P, not a C. Why was that? Oh, I see—tricky. The first half of the sentence, the non-bold part, is the new conclusion. The bold part is the evidence supporting that. This isn't it after all!*	~~E~~

(A) ~~B~~ ~~C~~ ~~D~~ ~~E~~

18

5. Digital Marketing: The correct answer is **(E)**.

Step 1: Identify the Question

Carlos responds to Sania by	*The "two person" structure and the focus on how Carlos responds indicate that this is a Describe the Argument question.*	DA A B C D E

Step 2: Deconstruct the Argument

Sania: The newest workers in the workforce are the most effective digital marketing employees because they are more likely to use social networking websites and tools themselves.	*Sania claims that the workers who use certain online tools are also the most effective at digital marketing and that those people are the newest workers.*	Sania: New empl use soc nw → most eff dig mktg ©
Carlos: But effective digital marketing also requires very technical expertise, such as search engine optimization, that is best learned on the job via prolonged exposure and instruction.	*Carlos doesn't dispute Sania's evidence, but he brings up a new point: You also need these other skills to be a good digital marketer... and those skills are learned on the job over a long* (prolonged) *time... which hurts Sania's claim that the* newest *workers are the most effective.*	Carlos: But eff dig mktg needs tech expertise, best learned on job

Step 3: State the Goal

I need to articulate how *Carlos responds to Sania. He doesn't say that she's wrong about the newest workers using social networking tools. Rather, he says that digital marketers also need this other skill that takes a long time to learn on the job. If that's the case, this weakens Sania's claim that the* newest *workers are the most effective.*

Step 4: Work from Wrong to Right

(A) demonstrating that Sania's conclusion is based upon evidence that is not relevant to the given situation	*Carlos doesn't say anything negative about Sania's evidence; rather, he introduces new evidence that attacks Sania's assumption that her piece of evidence is the most important thing to consider.*	~~A~~
(B) questioning the accuracy of the evidence presented by Sania in support of her conclusion	*This is similar to choice (A); Carlos doesn't question Sania's evidence.*	~~B~~
(C) reinforcing Sania's argument by contributing an additional piece of evidence in support of her conclusion	*Carlos does contribute an additional piece of evidence, but his new evidence hurts Sania's argument. Carlos doesn't support Sania's conclusion.*	~~C~~
(D) pointing out differences in the qualifications desired by different employers seeking digital marketing employees	*Carlos does point out a different way to assess the effectiveness of digital marketing employees, but he doesn't mention employers at all or differences among different employers.*	~~D~~
(E) providing an additional piece of evidence that undermines a portion of Sania's claim	*Bingo. This is exactly what Carlos does—a new piece of information that hurts the* newest workers *portion of Sania's claim.*	E ~

~~A~~ ~~B~~ ~~C~~ ~~D~~ (E)

18

6. Innovative Design: The correct answer is **(B)**.

Step 1: Identify the Question

In the argument above, the two portions in boldface play which of the following roles?	*This is a Role question. The question contains the word* boldface, *and I'm asked to find the* role *of each bold statement.*	R A B C D E

Step 2: Deconstruct the Argument

Products with innovative and appealing designs relative to competing products can often command substantially higher prices in the marketplace.	*Sort of between a fact and a claim. Probably a premise.*	Innov designs → ↑↑ $
Because design innovations are quickly copied by other manufacturers, many consumer technology companies charge as much as possible for their new designs to extract as much value as possible from them.	*Getting more toward claim-based material, with the first half of the sentence providing support for the second half. I'm not sure yet whether this is the conclusion though.*	Because others copy many co's charge ↑↑ $
But large profits generated by the innovative designs give competitors stronger incentives to copy the designs.	*BUT signals a contrast. Oh, so there's actually a drawback to making a lot of money: Competitors will copy even faster so I guess that could hurt market share. That's interesting.*	BUT ↑↑ prof → incent to copy
Therefore, **the best strategy to maximize overall profit from an innovative new design is to charge less than the greatest possible price**.	*Here we go, the conclusion. The person's claiming that companies actually* shouldn't *charge the largest possible price and this will actually help maximize profits in the end. The second boldface is the conclusion; that gets a C. The first boldface is a premise that supports a strategy the argument disagrees with (that companies should charge the greatest possible price for an ID).*	© to max prof charge < than max price Want: X C

Step 3: State the Goal

The question asks me to determine the role played by each of two boldface statements. I've decided the second one is the conclusion and the first is a premise supporting an alternate strategy, so I want to find an answer that gives this combo: X C (in that order).

Step 4: Work from Wrong to Right

(A) The first is an assumption that supports a described course of action; the second provides a consideration to support a preferred course of action.	*Hmm, they call the first an assumption, not a premise, but I suppose that's okay; they do say it* supports *something. The second, though, is the actual conclusion—but this answer choice makes the second sound like another premise. I don't think so.*	~~A~~
(B) The first is a consideration that helps explain the appeal of a certain strategy; the second presents an alternative strategy endorsed by the argument.	*The wording for the first statement is a little strange, but I suppose that could be considered a premise. And it does support the greatest possible price strategy. The second boldface is the strategy the argument supports. Keep this one.*	B ~
(C) The first is a phenomenon that makes a specific strategy unlikely to be successful; the second is that strategy.	*The first boldface provides support for the first strategy. It definitely doesn't weaken the author's strategy. Eliminate this answer choice.*	~~C~~
(D) The first is a consideration that demonstrates why a particular approach is flawed; the second describes a way to amend that approach.	*No, the first supports the alternate strategy—it doesn't illustrate a flaw. I don't even need to read the second half of this choice.*	~~D~~
(E) The first is a factor used to rationalize a particular strategy; the second is a factor against that strategy.	*Something used to* rationalize *a* strategy? *Yes, that could be describing a premise that supports the alternate strategy. Oh, but the second goes against the strategy? No! The second is actually the author's strategy.*	~~E~~

~~A~~ (B) ~~C~~ ~~D~~ ~~E~~

18

7. Gray Wolf Population: The correct answer is **(A)**.

Step 1: Identify the Question

The environmentalist challenges the government representative's argument by doing which of the following?	*There's a 2-person-talking structure, and I'm asked how the second person responds; this is a Describe the Argument question.*	DA A B C D E

Step 2: Deconstruct the Argument

Government representative: Between 1996 and 2005, the gray wolf population in Minnesota grew nearly 50 percent; the gray wolf population in Montana increased by only 13 percent during the same period.	*This is just a straight fact. The Minnesota wolf population grew a lot faster in that time period than the Montana wolf population.*	Gov rep: 96-05, wolf in Minn ↑ 50 percent, in Mont only ↑ 13 percent
Clearly, the Minnesota gray wolf population is more likely to survive and thrive long term.	*Conclusion! Claiming that Minnesota wolves are more likely to survive and thrive. Certainly, the Minnesota wolf population grew more... but does that automatically mean they're more likely to survive and thrive?*	© Minn > likely to survive/ thrive
Environmentalist: But the gray wolf population in Montana is nearly 8 times the population in Minnesota; above a certain critical breeding number, the population is stable and does not require growth in order to survive.	*Ah, okay. The environmentalist is pointing out that they're not necessarily the same thing. Once the population is large enough, it's already stable, so growth isn't necessarily critical to survival.*	Enviro: BUT Mont 8x Minn; when ↑ enough, pop = stable

Step 3: State the Goal

The gov rep concludes that the Minnesota wolves are more likely to survive and thrive because the growth rate was a lot higher, but the environmentalist responds that the Montana population was already a lot larger, so growth might not have been necessary to keep the population thriving. The Montana population might already have been stable in the first place.

I need to find something that explains this response in a more abstract way: A new piece of evidence changes the way someone would think about the issue addressed in the conclusion (surviving and thriving).

Step 4: Work from Wrong to Right

(A) Introducing additional evidence that undermines an assumption made by the representative	*This sounds pretty good. The environmentalist's statement is a new piece of evidence, and it does undermine the government rep's assumption that growth is a good indicator of likelihood to survive and thrive.*	A ~
(B) Challenging the representative's definition of a critical breeding number	*The environmentalist challenges the rep's assumption about what it takes to survive and thrive, but the environmentalist can't challenge the rep on* critical breeding number, *because the rep never mentions this concept.*	~~B~~
(C) Demonstrating that the critical breeding number of the two wolf populations differs significantly	*The environmentalist mentions the concept of* critical breeding number, *but establishes only that the number of wolves in each population differs significantly, not that the number of wolves needed to achieve the* critical breeding number *is different.*	~~C~~
(D) Implying that the two populations of wolves could be combined in order to preserve the species	*This might be an interesting strategy, but the environmentalist never mentions it.*	~~D~~
(E) Suggesting that the Montana wolf population grew at a faster rate than stated in the representative's argument	*This is tricky. The environmentalist introduces a new figure, but that figure has to do with the size of the two populations, not the rate of growth. The environmentalist does not dispute the rep's figures for rate of growth.*	~~E~~

(A) ~~B~~ ~~C~~ ~~D~~ ~~E~~

CHAPTER 19

The Assumption Family: Find the Assumption

In This Chapter:

- How Assumptions Work
- Excercise: Brainstorm Assumptions
- Assumption Family Questions
- Find the Assumption Questions
- The Negation Technique
- Find the Assumption Cheat Sheet

In this chapter, you will learn the role that assumptions play in arguments and how to answer the first of five question types that all rely on assumptions somehow.

CHAPTER 19 The Assumption Family: Find the Assumption

Assumptions were introduced briefly in the first two chapters of this unit, but did not play a role in Structure Family questions. They are the key to the largest family of questions, the Assumption Family; all five question types in this family contain arguments that involve at least one assumption made by the author. (The *author* refers to the hypothetical person who is "arguing" the argument and believes that argument to be valid.)

How Assumptions Work

An assumption is something that *the author must believe to be true* in order to draw a certain conclusion; however, the author *does not state* the assumption in the argument. The assumption itself might not necessarily be true in the real world; rather, the *author* believes that it is true in order to make his or her argument.

For example, what does the author of the following argument assume must be true?

> No athletes under the age of 14 can qualify for Country Y's Olympic team. Therefore, Adrienne can't qualify for Country Y's Olympic team.

therefore

No athlete under 14 can qualify for Olymp from Y. (premise) ⇨ Adrienne can't qual for Y's Olymp team. (conclusion)

The author assumes that this premise applies to Adrienne—in other words, that she is an athlete from Country Y and that she is under the age of 14. There may be other reasons she would not qualify for the Olympic team (perhaps her sport is not included), but if she can't qualify *for this reason*, then it must be because she is otherwise qualified (that is, she is an athlete from Country Y) but is too young.

The diagram above represents the **core** of the argument. The core consists of the conclusion and the main premise or premises that lead to that conclusion, as well as the unstated *assumption(s)*. You need assumptions as much as you need any other piece of the argument to make the whole thing work. After all, if Adrienne were *not* under 14, then the argument above would make no sense.

Assumptions fill at least part of a gap in the argument; the gap is represented by the arrow in the diagram above. If you insert a valid assumption into the argument, it makes the argument much better:

> No athletes under the age of 14 can qualify for Country Y's Olympic team. *Adrienne is an athlete from Country Y who is under the age of 14.* Therefore, Adrienne can't compete for Country Y's Olympic team.

therefore

No athlete under 14 can qualify for Olymp from Y.

(premise)

⇨

Adrienne can't qual for Y's Olymp team.

(conclusion)

Adrienne is an athlete from Country Y who is under the age of 14.

(assumption)

The argument above has a single obvious assumption that fills the gap on its own. Most GMAT arguments contain multiple assumptions, none of which individually fill the gap. Any one assumption will not automatically make the argument airtight, but it will make the argument more likely to be true, and the argument will depend on each of those assumptions. Take any assumption away and the argument collapses.

In order to train yourself to notice the presence of assumptions, think of the person in your life with whom you argue or disagree the most. Whenever you talk to him or her, your brain is already on the offensive. "Really? I'm not so sure about that. You've failed to consider…" Pretend this person is the one making the argument to you. How would you try to pick it apart? You'll be attacking assumptions.

Okay, are you ready? Brainstorm some assumptions for the following argument:

> Thomas's football team lost in the championship game last year. The same two teams are playing in the championship game again this year, and the players on Thomas's team have improved. Therefore, Thomas's team will win the championship game this year.

Picture that person with whom you argue; what would you say? Maybe something such as the following: "You're just *assuming* that Thomas's team has improved enough to be competitive with last year's winning team! You're also assuming that last year's winning team has *not* improved enough to keep themselves clearly ahead of Thomas's team!" As you brainstorm, however, remember that on the GMAT, you never have to come up with any assumption in a vacuum. After all, the test is multiple choice! If you are asked to find an assumption one of the choices will be a valid assumption and the other four choices will not be. So, while it's worth reading critically to poke holes in weak arguments, don't spend too much time thinking up assumptions on your own.

Here are a couple of important strategies for dealing with assumptions on the test:

Do		Don't
Notice gaps and articulate assumptions you can think of relatively easily.	**but**	Don't spend more than about 20 seconds brainstorming up front.
Look for your brainstormed assumptions in the answers.	**but**	Don't eliminate answers just because they don't match any of your brainstormed assumptions.
Choose an answer that the author must believe to be true in order to draw the conclusion.	**but**	Don't hold out for something that makes the conclusion "perfect" or definitely true.

Try inserting a brainstormed assumption into the football argument to see how it works:

> Thomas's football team lost in the championship game last year. The same two teams are playing in the championship game again this year, and the players on Thomas's team have improved enough to be competitive with the defending champion team. Therefore, Thomas's team will win the championship game this year.

If the author is going to claim that the improvement will lead to a victory for Thomas's team, then it is *necessary* for the author to believe that this improvement was enough to put that team at least at the same level as the defending champion team. Otherwise, it wouldn't make sense to say that, because these players have improved, they will win this year.

It is still not a foregone conclusion that Thomas's team will definitely win, even though the author clearly believes so. There are too many other potential factors involved; the author is making many assumptions, not just one. It is only necessary to find one assumption, though; it is not necessary to make the argument foolproof.

Exercise: Brainstorm Assumptions

Brainstorm at least one assumption that must be true. If you like, you can draw out the argument core.

1. Over 30 percent of students at an elementary school failed the state reading test last year. In order to reduce the failure rate, the school plans to offer free reading tutoring after school.
2. The employees of Quick Corp's accounting department consistently show a significant jump in productivity in the two weeks before taking vacation. Clearly, the knowledge that they are about to go on vacation motivates the employees to be more productive.
3. Mayor: The Acme Factory has developed a new manufacturing process that uses chemical Q, the residue of which is toxic to babies. In order to protect our children, we need to pass a law banning the use of this chemical.

Answers to Exercise

Possible assumptions are noted in italics below the arrow. You may brainstorm different assumptions from the ones shown. Other assumptions are acceptable as long as they represent something that MUST be true in order to make the given argument.

1.

therefore

Offer free tutoring ⇨ Reduce reading test failure

Student will go. Tutoring will help pass.

The author argues that offering free after-school tutoring will reduce the failure rate on the test. The plan must work as expected for that conclusion to hold. Students, especially those who are likely to fail the test, must actually attend the tutoring sessions. Also, the tutoring must help students pass the test. If, for example, the tutoring focused on material that was not on the test, it might not make much difference for failure rates.

2.

therefore

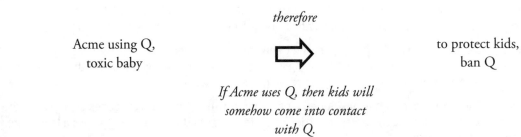

2 wks b4 vaca:
h ↑ prod ⇨ emp choose >> prod
b4 vaca

They didn't plan vacation to occur right after a big deadline or other busy time.

The author concludes that employees decide to be more productive *because* they'll be taking vacation soon; this is a **causation** argument. Perhaps it's the case, instead, that the employees choose to take vacation right after they know they'll be *forced* to work harder for some other reason. For example, maybe everyone in the accounting department takes vacation right after the annual financial report is due. The author is assuming that *other* causes of the jump in productivity don't apply in this case.

3.

therefore

Acme using Q,
toxic baby ⇨ to protect kids,
ban Q

If Acme uses Q, then kids will somehow come into contact with Q.

The mayor assumes that use of chemical Q in the production process will somehow eventually expose babies to the chemical residue. Maybe the chemical is used only for something that never comes into contact with the final product and will never come into contact with kids.

Assumption Family Questions

There are five types of Assumption questions. The first major type, Find the Assumption, is covered in this chapter. In the next chapter, you'll learn about the next two major types: Strengthen the Argument and Weaken the Argument. Later, you'll be introduced to the two remaining types in the Assumption Family: Evaluate the Argument and Find the Flaw.

Each type of question has its own key characteristics and goals, but some characteristics are common to all five types. There will always be a conclusion, so you definitely want to look for it. In addition, *while* you read, try to notice any gaps, indicating assumptions, that jump out at you (but don't take much longer than you normally take to read the argument itself).

Find the Assumption Questions

Find the Assumption (FA) questions ask you to, well, find an assumption that the author must believe to be true in order to make the argument. If the correct answer were *not* true, the argument would not be valid.

Your task is to figure out which answer choice represents something that must hold true according to the author. Note one especially tricky aspect of these problems: The assumption itself might only be true in the mind of the author. You might think, "Well, is that really true in the real world? I don't think that has to be true." Don't ask that question! The only issue is whether the *author* must believe it to be true in order to arrive at his or her conclusion. If the argument is "Planets are wonderful; therefore, Pluto is wonderful," then the assumption is that Pluto is a planet (whether you still think it is or not).

Identifying the Question

These questions are usually easy to identify, because the question stem will use some form of the noun *assumption* or the verb *to assume*. Occasionally, the question may ask for a new premise or a new piece of information that is required or necessary to draw the conclusion. Here are a couple of examples:

> Which of the following is an *assumption* on which the argument depends?
>
> Which of the following is *required* for the mayor's plan to succeed?

Try this sample argument:

> When news periodicals begin forecasting a recession, people tend to spend less money on nonessential purchases. Therefore, the perceived threat of a future recession decreases the willingness of people to purchase products that they regard as optional or luxury goods.
>
> Which of the following is an assumption on which the argument depends?

Do the first couple of steps before looking at the answer choices:

Step 1: Identify the Question

Which of the following is an assumption on which the argument depends?	*The question stem uses the word* assumption, *so it is the Assumption type. Write* FA *on the scrap paper and then the answer choice letters.*	FA A B C D E

Step 2: Deconstruct the Argument

When news periodicals begin forecasting a recession, people tend to spend less money on nonessential purchases.	*This sounds like a premise, though I suppose it could be a conclusion. The news periodicals predict a recession, and then people spend less money.*	Periodicals forecast recess → ppl spend ↓ \$ non-ess
Therefore, the perceived threat of a future recession decreases the willingness of people to purchase products that they regard as optional or luxury goods.	*This is the conclusion. The premise above tells what people do—spend less money. The conclusion tries to claim* why *they do it—a perceived future threat.*	© Perceived threat → ppl spend ↓ \$ lux
	What is the author assuming? That people are actually reading or hearing about the forecasts. That the recession hasn't already started and that's *why people are spending less money—maybe the periodicals are just slow in* forecasting *something that has already started. Also, the author assumes that* nonessential *and* luxury *mean the same thing.*	

Did you come up with any other assumptions? The key is to get your brain thinking about these things, but there are almost always multiple possible assumptions; you may not brainstorm the exact one that will show up in the answers.

Step 3: State the Goal

When you state your goal, you want to think about how the question type should be applied to the argument you just read. To do this, it can be helpful to articulate the core to yourself. You don't necessarily need to write/draw it out unless you want to.

therefore

Periodicals forecast:
recess! ↓ spend non-ess ⇨ Perceived threat → spend lux \$ ↓

People reading/hearing info from periodicals.
Threat only perceived today;
recession hasn't already started.

State your goal. What has to be true for the forecasts of a recession to result in decreased spending on luxury goods?

Take a look at the full problem now:

> When news periodicals begin forecasting a recession, people tend to spend less money on nonessential purchases. Therefore, the perceived threat of a future recession decreases the willingness of people to purchase products that they regard as optional or luxury goods.
>
> Which of the following is an assumption on which the argument depends?
>
> (A) People do not always agree as to which goods should be considered luxury goods.
>
> (B) Many more people read news periodicals today than five years ago.
>
> (C) Most people do not regularly read news periodicals.
>
> (D) Decreased spending on nonessential goods does not prompt news periodicals to forecast a recession.
>
> (E) At least some of the biggest spenders prior to the recession were those who curtailed their spending after the recession began.

Step 4: Work from Wrong to Right

As you move to the answer choices, look for the assumptions you brainstormed but also be flexible; you might not have thought of the assumption in the correct answer, or the assumption you thought of may be phrased differently than you imagined. On FA questions, traps often involve an answer that is not tied to the conclusion, an answer that makes the argument weaker, not stronger, or an answer that makes an irrelevant distinction or comparison. (Note: You'll learn more about trap answers later in the chapter.)

(A) People do not always agree as to which goods should be considered luxury goods.	*I can believe that this is true in the real world, but this is irrelevant to the conclusion. The argument is not based upon whether people agree as to how to classify certain goods.*	~~A~~
(B) Many more people read news periodicals today than five years ago.	*This sounds a little bit like one of my brainstormed assumptions—the argument assumes that people are actually reading those periodicals. I'm not so sure about the more* today than five years ago *part, though. You don't absolutely have to believe that in order to draw that conclusion. I'll keep it in for now, but maybe I'll find something better.*	B~
(C) Most people do not regularly read news periodicals.	*This is also about reading the periodicals... but it's the opposite of what I want! The argument needs to assume that people DO read the periodicals; if they don't, then how can they be influenced by what the periodicals forecast?*	~~C~~
(D) Decreased spending on nonessential goods does not prompt news periodicals to forecast a recession.	*Let's see. This choice is saying that the drop in spending is not* itself *causing the forecasts. That's good, because the argument is that the causality runs the other way: The forecasts cause the drop in spending. This one is looking better than answer (B). I can cross off (B) now.*	D~
(E) At least some of the biggest spenders prior to the recession were those who curtailed their spending after the recession began.	*Hmm. This one sounds good, too. Maybe if some of the biggest spenders keep spending during the recession, then the overall amount of money being spent won't go down that much... although the argument doesn't really seem to depend on how much it goes down. Oh, wait: This says* after the recession began—*but the conclusion is about a perceived threat of a* future *recession. Nice trap!*	~~E~~

~~A~~ ~~B~~~ ~~C~~ (D~) ~~E~~

There were a couple of good brainstormed assumptions, but none that matched the exact assumption contained in the correct answer, (D). That's okay; be prepared to be flexible!

Note that answer choice (C) contained an "opposite" answer: It weakened the conclusion rather than making it stronger.

The Negation Technique

On harder questions, you might find yourself stuck between two answer choices. To unstick yourself, try the **Negation Technique**.

On Find the Assumption questions, the correct answer will be something that the author must believe to be true in order to make his or her argument. As a result, if you were to turn the correct answer around to make the opposite point, then the author's argument should be harmed. Negating the correct answer should weaken the author's conclusion.

Try it out on the *News Periodicals* problem from above. Say that you narrowed the answers to (B) and (D):

(B) Many more people read news periodicals today than five years ago.

(D) Decreased spending on nonessential goods does not prompt news periodicals to forecast a recession.

Recall the argument itself as mapped out above:

Periodicals forecast recess → ppl spend ↓ $ non-ess

Perceived threat → ppl spend ↓ $ lux

The author argues that when the periodicals forecast a recession, people perceive a future threat, and so people choose to spend less money on luxury goods.

What if answer choice (B) were NOT true? It would say something like:

(B) The same number or fewer people read news periodicals today than five years ago.

Does this weaken the author's conclusion? Not really. While the argument does assume that at least some people are reading news periodicals, it doesn't discuss what used to happen five years ago, nor does it hinge on any sort of change over time.

Try negating answer (D):

(D) Decreased spending on nonessential goods DOES prompt news periodicals to forecast a recession.

Hmm. If spending goes down and then the news periodicals react by forecasting a recession…then the author has it backwards! The news periodicals aren't causing a behavior change in consumers. Rather, they're reacting to something the consumers are already doing. Thus, the argument no longer works. Negating this answer breaks down the author's argument, so this choice is the right answer.

A word of warning: Don't use this technique on every answer choice or you'll be in danger of spending too much time. However, when you're stuck, the Negation technique can be a big help. And if *that* doesn't work, as always, you know what to do: Guess and move on.

Right Answers

For Find the Assumption questions, the right answer is necessary to the conclusion. Generally, you will not see a lot of new language or new ideas different from what was in the argument: The exception is assumptions that exclude another possibility. Take a look at this argument you saw in a previous chapter:

Metropolis has experienced an increase in the amount of trash in its city parks. In order to reduce the amount of litter in the parks, Metropolis plans to double the number of trash cans in each city park.

Which of the following is an assumption on which the argument depends?

(A) Trash will not blow into the park from the streets and sidewalks surrounding the park.

(B) Some people still choose to litter even if there is a trash receptacle within 20 feet of their location.

This argument is a plan: put more trash cans in parks to reduce litter. You are looking for an assumption: What is necessary for the increase in trash cans to reduce litter in the parks?

Answer (A) might have given you pause because it introduces something not discussed in the argument: trash from the surrounding streets and sidewalks. But answer (A) is actually excluding the possibility. The plan presented can only reduce litter coming from inside the park because that is where there will be more trash cans. Answer (A) is the correct answer and an example of an assumption that excludes a possibility, and thus may have new ideas or language. If you were wondering, answer (B) actually makes the argument worse, suggesting people may still litter even with more trash cans.

Below are some common assumptions for different argument types. Note that some arguments will have unique assumptions that do not match the categories described:

- **Causation:** In an argument that concludes that X causes Y, assumptions often exclude reverse causation (Y causes X) or outside causes (Z causes both X and Y).
- **Plan:** In a plan, an assumption may validate that the steps of the plan will work as expected or exclude a previously unmentioned detriment to the plan (see park litter example above).
- **Prediction:** In order for a prediction to come true, you have to assume that no other future events beyond those mentioned in the argument will intervene.
- **Profit:** For profit to move in the direction predicted by the argument, there cannot be some other factor that outweighs the predicted outcome. For example, a conclusion that states profit will increase assumes there is not some hidden cost that exceeds the benefit.

Common Trap Answers

On many Find the Assumption questions, a trap answer won't actually address the conclusion. Because the question specifically asks you to find an assumption necessary to draw that conclusion, an answer that has **No Tie to the Conclusion** must be wrong. Answer (A) in the problem above is a good example. The conclusion does not depend upon whether different people would agree to classify the same item as a luxury good. Rather, the conclusion is about what causes someone to spend less money on anything that that individual believes to be a luxury good.

Trap answers can also use **Reverse Logic**, as in answer choice (C). Reverse logic does the opposite of what you want; in this case, answer (C) actually makes the argument worse, but an assumption should make the argument a bit stronger.

Answers (B) and (E) are examples of another trap: making an **Irrelevant Distinction or Comparison**. The argument does not hinge upon whether people read more now than they did five years ago. Nor does it depend upon the highest spending consumers doing something different from the rest of consumers. Rather, all consumers are lumped together in the argument.

Find the Assumption Cheat Sheet

Identify the Question	**Common:** *assumption* **Less common:** *assume, required* *more reasonably drawn*
Deconstruct the Argument	**Find:** Conclusion, premises counterpremises (if present) **Brainstorm:** Assumptions, gaps in argument
State the **Goal**	Something that must be true in order for the author to draw this conclusion
Work from **Wrong** to **Right**	**Right:** Must be true to draw conclusion; if *not* true, argument will be severely weakened (if stuck, try Negation technique). **Wrong:** No Tie to Conclusion Reverse Logic (makes conclusion weaker) Irrelevant Distinction or Comparison

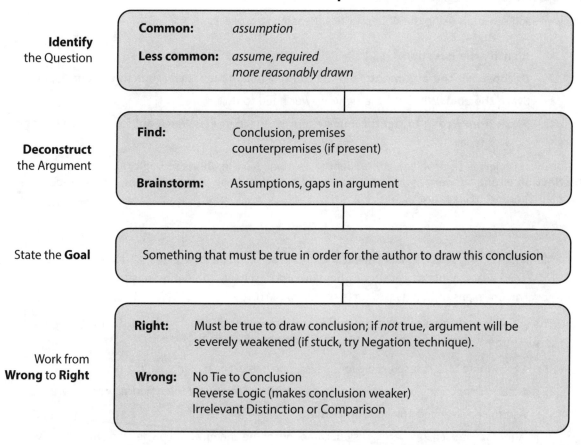

Take a picture of this page and keep it with the review sheets you're creating as you study. Better yet, use this page as a guide to create your own review sheet—you'll remember the material better if you write it down yourself.

Problem Set

Answer each question using the 4-step Critical Reasoning process.

1. **Identify the question.**
2. **Deconstruct the argument:** Find the conclusion and map the argument on your paper.
3. **State the goal:** What will the right answer need to do?
4. **Work from wrong to right:** Eliminate four wrong answers. Watch out for common wrong answer types.

Before you review each problem, try to identify as many **No Tie**, **Reverse Logic**, and **Irrelevant Distinction** wrong answers as you can. There will be at least one common wrong answer type in each problem, and probably more!

1. *MTC and Asthma*

Methyltetrachloride (MTC) is a chemical found in some pesticides, glues, and sealants. Exposure to MTC can cause people to develop asthma. In order to halve the nation's asthma rate, the government plans to ban all products containing MTC.

The government's plan to halve the nation's asthma rate relies on which of the following assumptions?

(A) Exposure to MTC is responsible for no less than half of the nation's asthma cases.

(B) Products containing MTC are not necessary to the prosperity of the American economy.

(C) Asthma has reached epidemic proportions.

(D) After MTC is used in an area, residual amounts of the chemical can be detected months or years later.

(E) Dust mites and pet dander can also cause asthma.

2. *Oil and Ethanol*

Country N's oil production is not currently sufficient to meet its domestic demand. In order to sharply reduce its dependence on foreign sources of oil, Country N recently began requiring all automobiles produced in the country to use a blend of gasoline and ethanol, rather than gasoline alone. Country N produces enough ethanol from agricultural by-products to make up for the gap between its domestic oil production and its current demand for energy.

Which of the following must be assumed in order to conclude that Country N will succeed in its plan to reduce its dependence on foreign oil?

(A) Electric power is not a superior alternative to ethanol in supplementing automobile gasoline consumption.

(B) In Country N, domestic production of ethanol is increasing more quickly than domestic oil production.

(C) Ethanol is suitable for the heating of homes and other applications aside from automobiles.

(D) In Country N, oil consumption is not increasing at a substantially higher rate than domestic oil and ethanol production.

(E) Ethanol is as efficient as gasoline in terms of mileage per gallon when used as fuel for automobiles.

3. *Exchange Student*

   Student Advisor: One of our exchange students faced multiple arguments with her parents over the course of the past year. Not surprisingly, her grade point average (GPA) over the same period showed a steep decline. This is just one example of a general truth: Problematic family relationships can cause significant academic difficulties for our students.

   Which of the following is required for the student advisor to conclude that problematic family relationships can cause academic difficulties?

   (A) Last year, the exchange student reduced the amount of time spent on academic work, resulting in a lower GPA.

   (B) The decline in the GPA of the exchange student was not the reason for the student's arguments with her parents.

   (C) School GPA is an accurate measure of a student's intellectual ability.

   (D) The student's GPA is lower than the average GPA for exchange students at the university.

   (E) Fluctuations in academic performance are typical for many students.

4. *Genetics*

   Two genes, BRCA1 and BRCA2, are linked to hereditary breast cancer. Genetic testing, which can detect these genes, is increasing in both accuracy and prevalence. The test is also less painful and invasive than a mammogram, which is typically used to detect early signs of breast cancer. Therefore, we can expect the percentage of women who undergo mammograms each year to decrease.

   Which of the following is an assumption on which the argument depends?

   (A) Some women who are tested for BRCA1 and BRCA2 will choose not to undergo a mammogram.

   (B) The percentage of women undergoing mammograms each year has remained consistent over the last decade.

   (C) Aside from BRCA1 and BRCA2, there are no other genes that are strongly linked to breast cancer.

   (D) Doctors will continue to recommend regular mammograms for all women at risk of breast cancer, regardless of the results of genetic testing.

   (E) A significant percentage of cases of breast cancer are linked to BRCA1 or BRCA2.

Solutions

1. MTC and Asthma: The correct answer is **(A)**. Try to spot any **No Tie to the Conclusion**, **Reverse Logic**, or **Irrelevant Distinction or Comparison** wrong answers before you keep reading!

Step 1: Identify the Question

The government's plan to halve the nation's asthma rate relies on which of the following assumptions?	*Asks for the* assumption*; this is a Find the Assumption question.*	FA A B C D E

Step 2: Deconstruct the Argument

Methyltetrachloride (MTC) is a chemical found in some pesticides, glues, and sealants.	*This is just a fact—background or maybe a premise.*	MTC = chem
Exposure to MTC can cause people to develop asthma.	*Another fact but it's specifically a bad fact. This is likely a premise.*	Can → asthma
In order to halve the nation's asthma rate, the government plans to ban all products containing MTC.	*Okay, the government has a plan to ban MTC, and the result will be (they claim) that the asthma rate will be cut in half. There are no numbers or anything to support that. Are a lot of people exposed now? What percentage of those who develop asthma were exposed? Etc.*	© Gov plan: ban MTC to ½ asthma rate

Step 3: State the Goal

The government claims that it can halve the asthma rate by banning MTC, but it gives absolutely no evidence or numbers to support halving *the rate.*

I need to find an answer that supports the idea that they can halve the asthma rate—maybe that a very large percentage of people who develop asthma were exposed to MTC or something like that.

Step 4: Work from Wrong to Right

(A) Exposure to MTC is responsible for no less than half of the nation's asthma cases.	*This sounds similar to what I said. Let's see. If MTC actually is responsible for at least half of asthma cases, then getting rid of it would get rid of all those cases as well. This one looks pretty good.*	A~
(B) Products containing MTC are not necessary to the prosperity of the American economy.	***No tie.*** *This is a deceptive wrong answer. It says that these products aren't economically important, but the conclusion isn't about economics! The conclusion talks about whether the plan will halve the asthma rate, regardless of the economic effects.*	~~B~~
(C) Asthma has reached epidemic proportions.	***No tie.*** *This answer choice explains why we might want to reduce the asthma rate. But it doesn't address the specific plan at all.*	~~C~~
(D) After MTC is used in an area, residual amounts of the chemical can be detected months or years later.	***Reverse logic.*** *This actually weakens the government's proposal. Since MTC sticks around long after the chemicals are actually used, banning the chemicals now may not reduce the asthma rate.*	~~D~~
(E) Dust mites and pet dander can also cause asthma.	***Irrelevant distinction.*** *Sure, there are other things that can cause asthma. But the argument isn't about these things—it's specifically about MTC. The fact that other things can also cause asthma doesn't change anything about the MTC situation.*	~~E~~

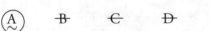

(A~) ~~B~~ ~~C~~ ~~D~~ ~~E~~

2. Oil and Ethanol: The correct answer is **(D)**. Try to spot any **No Tie to the Conclusion**, **Reverse Logic**, or **Irrelevant Distinction or Comparison** wrong answers before you keep reading!

Step 1: Identify the Question

Which of the following must be assumed in order to conclude that Country N will succeed in its plan to reduce its dependence on foreign oil?	*Contains the phrase* must be assumed—*this is a Find the Assumption question.*	FA A B C D E

Step 2: Deconstruct the Argument

Country N's oil production is not currently sufficient to meet its domestic demand.	*They produce oil but can't make enough for their own needs. That must mean they have to import some oil.*	N oil prod < dom demand
In order to sharply reduce its dependence on foreign sources of oil, Country N recently began requiring all automobiles produced in the country to use a blend of gasoline and ethanol, rather than gasoline alone.	*They're requiring cars to use ethanol, and they think that'll lead to having to use less foreign oil. It sounds like the cars can still use gas, though...*	To ↓ for. oil, N reqs ethanol in cars
Country N produces enough ethanol from agricultural by-products to make up for the gap between its domestic oil production and its current demand for energy.	*Okay, so they do make enough ethanol PLUS oil combined to satisfy their own needs currently. The question is whether people are actually going to use ethanol for their cars or whether they'll want to keep using gasoline. And what if demand changes in future?*	N eth + oil = curr demand

Step 3: State the Goal

Country N thinks it can sharply reduce *the amount of foreign oil it needs if it starts making people own cars that use ethanol. Will the plan really work that way? They're assuming people really will start to use the ethanol. They're also assuming they'll continue to produce enough oil and ethanol in the future.*

I need to find an answer that must be true in order to allow the author to draw the conclusion above.

Step 4: Work from Wrong to Right

(A) Electric power is not a superior alternative to ethanol in supplementing automobile gasoline consumption.	***Irrelevant distinction.*** *Comparing ethanol to electric power doesn't tell me anything useful about ethanol, which is what I really care about. We're supposed to find something that goes with the plan stated in the argument, and that plan mentions nothing about electric power.*	~~A~~
(B) In Country N, domestic production of ethanol is increasing more quickly than domestic oil production.	*If this is true, then switching stuff to ethanol seems like a good call. Does it have to be true in order to draw the conclusion? What if the two were increasing at the same rate? That would be fine, actually. This doesn't have to be true—so it isn't a necessary assumption.*	~~B~~
(C) Ethanol is suitable for the heating of homes and other applications aside from automobiles.	***Irrelevant distinction.*** *The argument only talks about a plan to have cars start using ethanol. Whether the plan will also work for homes doesn't have anything to do with cars.*	~~C~~
(D) In Country N, gasoline consumption is not increasing at a substantially higher rate than domestic oil and ethanol production.	*Hmm. The argument is assuming in general that the ethanol + oil production can keep up with the country's demand. So, yes, the author would have to assume that gas consumption isn't increasing at a much faster rate than production.* *Let's try negating this one: If gas consumption were increasing at a much higher rate, what would happen? Oh, they might have to get more from foreign sources—bingo! Negating this does weaken the conclusion.*	D ~
(E) Ethanol is as efficient as gasoline in terms of mileage per gallon when used as fuel for automobiles.	***No tie.*** *The conclusion isn't about gas mileage, it's about reducing foreign oil dependency. There isn't necessarily a link between those two things. Maybe people will use more ethanol than gas if it's less efficient, but maybe they won't.*	~~E~~

~~A~~ ~~B~~ ~~C~~ (D) ~ ~~E~~

19

3. Exchange Student: The correct answer is **(B)**. Try to spot any **No Tie to the Conclusion**, **Reverse Logic**, or **Irrelevant Distinction or Comparison** wrong answers before you keep reading!

Step 1: Identify the Question

Which of the following is required for the student advisor to claim that problematic family relationships can cause academic difficulties?	*This is an unusual question stem. It doesn't include the word* assumption, *but it does include a synonymous idea: What is* required *to draw the conclusion? This is an assumption question.*	FA A B C D E

Step 2: Deconstruct the Argument

Student Advisor: One of our exchange students faced multiple arguments with her parents over the course of the past year.	*This is a fact—background or a premise.*	Advisor: student had args w parents
Not surprisingly, her grade point average (GPA) over the same period showed a steep decline.	*Not only did the student's GPA go down, but the advisor says* not surprisingly. *Sounds like the advisor is going to conclude a causal relationship.*	GPA ↓↓
This is just one example of a general truth: Problematic family relationships can cause significant academic difficulties for our students.	*Here we go: The advisor claims that this student's family problems* caused *the academic problems. Maybe there was a different cause.*	↓ © Fam probs → acad probs

Step 3: State the Goal

I need to find an answer that the author must believe to be true in order to draw this conclusion. The only thing I can think of right now is very general: If the advisor is assuming the family problems were what caused the academic problems, then the advisor is also assuming there wasn't something else causing the academic problems.

19

Step 4: Work from Wrong to Right

(A) Last year, the exchange student reduced the amount of time spent on academic work, resulting in a lower GPA.	***Reverse logic.*** *This actually works against the advisor's conclusion. It suggests a different reason that the student's grades decreased. If this different reason is correct, then the advisor's reasoning is incorrect. An assumption always has to support the conclusion and can't work against it.*	~~A~~
(B) The decline in the GPA of the exchange student was not the reason for the student's arguments with her parents.	*Let's see. This is kind of what I said before—there is not a different cause for the decline of her GPA.* *Let's try negating this. If the student's GPA went down first and then her parents got mad at her for that reason, then you can't claim that the family problems caused the lower GPA. The advisor's argument would fall apart. This choice looks good.*	B ~
(C) School GPA is an accurate measure of a student's intellectual ability.	***No tie.*** *The conclusion has nothing to do with intellectual ability! It discusses academic difficulties and their relationship to GPA and does not draw any comparison to the student's intellectual ability.*	~~C~~
(D) The student's GPA is lower than the average GPA for exchange students at the university.	***Irrelevant distinction.*** *The argument deals with a decrease in a single exchange student's GPA. It isn't necessary to compare that student to other students in order to explain the decrease in her own GPA.*	~~D~~
(E) Fluctuations in academic performance are typical for many students.	***Reverse logic.*** *This actually works against the advisor's conclusion. The advisor argues that the problematic family relationship caused the student's difficulties. However, this answer choice suggests that the student's GPA decrease was actually due to random fluctuation. An assumption will never work against the conclusion.*	~~E~~

~~A~~ (B~) ~~C~~ ~~D~~ ~~E~~

4. Genetics: The correct answer is **(A)**.

Step 1: Identify the Question

Which of the following is an assumption on which the argument depends?	*The word* assumption *indicates that this is a Find the Assumption question.*	FA A B C D E

Step 2: Deconstruct the Argument

Two genes, BRCA1 and BRCA2, are linked to hereditary breast cancer.	*A fact about genes and cancer.*	2 genes linked to b-cancer
Genetic testing, which can detect these genes, is increasing in both accuracy and prevalence.	*We're getting better at testing for these genes, and we're doing it more often.*	testing: acc & freq ↑
The test is also less painful and invasive than a mammogram, which is typically used to detect early signs of breast cancer.	*Now the argument is comparing this testing to an alternative test for breast cancer. Looks like the genetic test has some advantages, although I still don't know if it's as good at detecting cancer.*	genetic test vs mammo.: less pain, less invasive
Therefore, we can expect the percentage of women who undergo mammograms each year to decrease.	*Here's the conclusion: It's a prediction about the future. Since genetic testing has these advantages, a smaller percentage of women will have mammograms in the future.*	© mammo. % ↓

Step 3: State the Goal

The author claims that the percentage of women who have mammograms will decrease. I know that mammograms have some disadvantages compared to genetic testing, but the author is making a big assumption in concluding that fewer people will actually have them! The right answer is something that must be true in order for the author to reach this conclusion.

Step 4: Work from Wrong to Right

(A) Some women who are tested for BRCA1 and BRCA2 will choose not to undergo a mammogram.	*If at least some women get tested and then don't have a mammogram, then that would help to reduce the percentage of mammograms. But does this have to be true? Actually, I think it does. For fewer women to have mammograms, at least some women must be changing their minds about having one.*	A ~
(B) The percentage of women undergoing mammograms each year has remained consistent over the last decade.	***No tie.*** *The conclusion deals with what will happen in the immediate future: The percentage of women undergoing mammograms each year will decrease. This answer choice describes something that happened in the past. I don't know whether the past and the future are related here.*	~~B~~
(C) Aside from BRCA1 and BRCA2, there are no other genes that are strongly linked to breast cancer.	***Irrelevant distinction.*** *Comparing those two genes to a third gene doesn't tell me anything about the mammogram situation. The argument is only about the results of genetic testing for those two genes, not about breast cancer more broadly.*	~~C~~
(D) Doctors will continue to recommend regular mammograms for all women at risk of breast cancer, regardless of the results of genetic testing.	***Reverse logic.*** *If anything, this suggests that the prevalence of mammograms will stay the same, since genetic testing won't change doctors' recommendations. An assumption always has to support the conclusion.*	~~D~~
(E) A significant percentage of cases of breast cancer are linked to BRCA1 or BRCA2.	***No tie.*** *This doesn't tell me anything about who will undergo a mammogram. If I assume that women who discover that they have this gene will choose not to have a mammogram, this might cause a decline in the number of mammograms. But I'd have to make my own assumptions in order to use that reasoning and that isn't allowed.*	~~E~~

(A) ~~B~~ ~~C~~ ~~D~~ ~~E~~

CHAPTER 20

The Assumption Family: Strengthen and Weaken

In This Chapter:

- Strengthen and Weaken: The Basics
- Strengthen the Argument Questions
- Weaken the Argument Questions
- EXCEPT Questions
- Strengthen the Argument Cheat Sheet
- Weaken the Argument Cheat Sheet

In this chapter, you will learn how to recognize and answer the second and third of the five question types in the Assumption Family: Strengthen and Weaken.

CHAPTER 20 The Assumption Family: Strengthen and Weaken

In the previous chapter, you learned about the first major question type in the Assumption Family: Find the Assumption. If you haven't read the previous chapter yet, please do so before reading this chapter.

To recap briefly:

- Assumptions are something an author must believe to be true in order to draw his or her conclusion. These assumptions are not stated explicitly in the argument.
- All assumption arguments will contain a "core": a conclusion and the major premise or premises that lead to it.
- All assumption arguments will include at least one (and probably more than one) unstated assumption.

This chapter addresses the next two Assumption Family question types: **Strengthen the Argument** and **Weaken the Argument**. Like Find the Assumption, these two types are commonly tested on the GMAT. They also hinge upon identifying an assumption.

Strengthen and Weaken: The Basics

Both Strengthen and Weaken questions ask you to find a *new* piece of information that, if added to the existing argument, will make the conclusion either more likely to be true (strengthen) or less likely to be true (weaken).

In the case of a Strengthen, the new piece of information will typically provide evidence to support an assumption. In the case of a Weaken, the new piece of info will attack an assumption: It will serve as evidence that the assumption is invalid.

How does this work? Let's look at one of the arguments from the last chapter again:

> Thomas's football team lost in the championship game last year. The same two teams are playing in the championship game again this year, and the players on Thomas's team have improved. Therefore, Thomas's team will win the championship game this year.

Last year's 2nd-place team has improved.	*therefore* ⇨	That team will win champ this year.
(premise)		(conclusion)

If you were asked a Find the Assumption question, the answer might be something like this: Thomas's team has improved enough to be competitive with the defending champions. In order for the author to draw this conclusion, that point must be assumed. If Thomas's team hasn't improved enough to be (at minimum) competitive with last year's first-place team, then it wouldn't make any sense to say that *because* they have improved, they will win this year.

If you're asked a Strengthen question, how does the answer change? A Strengthen answer provides some new piece of information that does not have to be true, but *if it is true*, that information does make the conclusion more likely to be valid. For example:

> The star quarterback on the defending champion team will miss the game due to an injury.

Must it be true that the star quarterback will miss the game in order for the author to believe that Thomas's team will win? No. If that information *is* true, though, then the conclusion is more likely to be true. Thomas's team is more likely to win if a star player on the opposing team can't play.

What happens if you're asked a Weaken question? Similarly, a Weaken answer provides a new piece of information that does not have to be true, but *if it is true*, then the conclusion is a bit less likely to be valid. For example:

> The players on the defending champion team train more than the players on any other team.

That specific fact does not have to be true in order for you to doubt the claim that Thomas's team will win—there are lots of reasons to doubt the claim—but *if it is true* that the defending champion team trains more than all of the other teams, then the author's conclusion just got weaker.

Note that Strengthen and Weaken question stems include the words *if true* or an equivalent variation. In other words, you are explicitly told to accept the information in the answer as true.

Finally, there are three possible ways that an answer choice could affect the argument on both Strengthen and Weaken questions: The answer *strengthens* the argument, the answer *weakens* the argument, or the answer *does nothing* to the argument. One of your tasks will be to classify each answer choice into one of these three buckets.

Strengthen the Argument Questions

Strengthen questions ask you to find a *new* piece of information that, if added to the existing argument, will make the argument somewhat more likely to be true.

Most often, Strengthen questions will contain some form of the words *strengthen* or *support*, as well as the phrase *if true*. Here are some typical examples:

> Which of the following, if true, most strengthens the argument above?
>
> Which of the following, if true, most strongly supports the mayor's claim?

Strengthen questions will sometimes use synonyms in place of the strengthen/support language. These synonyms may do the following:

- Provide the best basis *or* the best reason for
- Provide justification for
- Provide evidence in favor of (a plan or a conclusion)

Strengthen questions may occasionally lack the exact phrase *if true*, but some other wording will provide a similar meaning. That wording might be something quite similar, such as *if feasible* (in reference to a plan). Alternatively, the wording might indicate that the answer can be *effectively achieved* or *successfully accomplished* (indicating that the information would become true).

Try this short example:

> At QuestCorp, many employees have quit recently and taken jobs with a competitor. Shortly before the employees quit, QuestCorp lost its largest client. Clearly, the employees were no longer confident in QuestCorp's long-term viability.
>
> Which of the following, if true, most strengthens the claim that concerns about QuestCorp's viability caused the employees to quit?
>
> (A) Employees at QuestCorp's main competitor recently received a large and well-publicized raise.
>
> (B) QuestCorp's largest client accounted for 40 percent of sales and nearly 60 percent of the company's profits.
>
> (C) Many prospective hires who have interviewed with QuestCorp ultimately accepted jobs with other companies.

The question stem indicates that this is a Strengthen question. Deconstruct the argument. The core might be:

therefore

lost client, ppl quit → quit b/c concern about success

(premise) (conclusion)

Remember, you can write the core down or you can just articulate the core to yourself mentally. Whichever path works best for you is fine.

Make sure that you understand what the argument is trying to say. The author claims that, because the company lost its largest client, some employees lost confidence in the company, so they quit. The author assumes that losing that client will be a significant blow to the company. What if the company has many clients and the largest client only represented a very small fraction of the business? The author also assumes there aren't other reasons why employees quit.

State your goal: How would you strengthen this particular conclusion?

> *This is a Strengthen question, so I have to find some evidence that supports the claim that people quit specifically because they lost confidence in the company after it lost its largest client.*

(A) Employees at QuestCorp's main competitor recently received a large and well-publicized raise.	*Wouldn't that make QuestCorp's employees jealous—maybe they'd expect more money? That'd make it more likely that they quit because of pay issues rather than a loss of confidence in the company. If anything, this weakens the conclusion; I want a strengthen answer.*	~~A~~
(B) QuestCorp's largest client accounted for 40 percent of sales and nearly 60 percent of the company's profits.	*Ouch. Then losing this client would be a pretty serious blow to the company. This is a fact that helps make the conclusion a little more likely; I'll keep it in.*	B ~
(C) Many prospective hires who have interviewed with QuestCorp ultimately accepted jobs with other companies.	*Hmm.* Prospective hires *are not employees. I was asked to strengthen the part about* employees losing confidence in the company. I could speculate that maybe something is wrong with QuestCorp if people take other jobs...but the answer doesn't even tell me why *these people took other jobs. Maybe QuestCorp rejected them!*	~~C~~

The correct answer is (B).

Answer choice (A) represents one common trap on Strengthen questions: The answer does the opposite of what you want. That is, it weakens the conclusion rather than strengthening it.

Answer choice (C) represents another common trap: The answer addresses (and sometimes even strengthens) something other than what you were asked to address. In this case, the answer does seem to imply that there's something not so great about QuestCorp, but it discusses the wrong group of people (prospective hires) and doesn't actually provide any information that allows you to assess what they think of QuestCorp's viability. (Again, that last part doesn't matter in the end, because it's already talking about the wrong group of people.)

Putting It All Together

Try a full problem now:

Donut Chain, wishing to increase the profitability of its new store, will place a coupon in the local newspaper offering a free donut with a cup of coffee at its grand opening. Donut Chain calculates that the cost of the advertisement and the free donuts will be more than compensated for by the new business generated through the promotion.

Which of the following, if true, most strengthens the prediction that Donut Chain's promotion will increase the new store's profitability?

(A) Donut Chain has a loyal following in much of the country.

(B) Donut Chain has found that the vast majority of new visitors to its stores become regular customers.

(C) One donut at Donut Chain costs less than a cup of coffee.

(D) Most of the copies of the coupon in the local newspaper will not be redeemed for free donuts.

(E) Donut Chain's stores are generally very profitable.

Step 1: Identify the Question

Which of the following, if true, most strengthens the prediction that Donut Chain's promotion will increase the new store's profitability?	*The language* if true *and* most strengthens the prediction that... *indicates that this is a Strengthen the Argument question. Also, the question stem tells me the conclusion I need to address: The plan will lead to better profitability.*	S A B C D E Ⓒ promo → ↑ proof

Step 2: Deconstruct the Argument

Donut Chain, wishing to increase the profitability of its new store, will place a coupon in the local newspaper offering a free donut with a cup of coffee at its grand opening.	*Donut Chain thinks that giving away a free donut will lead to increased profitability.*	promo = free coupon
Donut Chain calculates that the cost of the advertisement and the free donuts will be more than compensated for by the new business generated through the promotion.	*It costs $ to place the ad and give away free donuts, but Donut Chain thinks it'll get enough new business to offset those costs. Still, does that lead to better profitability?*	$ spent < $ new biz
(brainstorm assumptions)	*The argument isn't 100 percent clear that the profitability part is the conclusion, but the question stem also said so. The author is assuming that giving away a free donut once will lead to increased revenues over time (what if they never come back?), and that will then lead to increased profits (more revenues don't necessarily equal more profits).*	

Step 3: State the Goal

I need to strengthen the claim that a particular plan is going to lead to increased profitability. The plan is to distribute coupons to give away free donuts.

I need to find an answer that makes it a little more likely that this plan will lead to more profits.

Step 4: Work from Wrong to Right

(A) Donut Chain has a loyal following in much of the country.	*This is good for Donut Chain. Does that mean it will* increase *profitability though? No. It's already an established fact. Plus, it only says that Donut Chain enjoys a loyal following in* much *of the country, not necessarily where the new store is located.*	~~A~~
(B) Donut Chain has found that the vast majority of new visitors to its stores become regular customers.	*So if Donut Chain can get people to visit once, they'll usually keep coming back. That sounds pretty good for Donut Chain's plan, which is all about getting people to visit the first time for that free donut.*	B
(C) One donut at Donut Chain costs less than a cup of coffee.	*This tells me nothing about profits or revenues or how much they could sell or anything, really. This doesn't address the argument.*	~~C~~
(D) Most of the copies of the coupon in the local newspaper will not be redeemed for free donuts.	*If this happens, then Donut Chain's plan is really unlikely to work—it spends money on the ads, but never gets the new customers to come in. That* weakens *the conclusion.*	~~D~~
(E) Donut Chain's stores are generally very profitable.	*It's good that Donut Chain stores are usually profitable; that means this new one is likely to be profitable, too. The conclusion, though, specifically talks about* increasing *the store's profitability—and the question specifically asks whether* this plan *will accomplish that goal. This choice looks tempting at first, but it doesn't address whether this plan will increase profitability.*	~~E~~

~~A~~ (B) ~~C~~ ~~D~~ ~~E~~

Where's the Conclusion?

In the Donut Chain argument above, you might have noticed the question provided additional information about the conclusion (that the coupon would increase profitability). Read this argument and question, and try to find the conclusion:

> Average customer wait times at the registry of motor vehicles (RMV) in Starton have increased by 30 minutes in the last year. The RMV recently developed a smartphone application that allows customers to view current wait times and predicted wait times later in the day.
>
> Which of the following, if true, most strengthens the claim that the smartphone application will decrease average wait times at the RMV?

The question asks you to support the claim that the app will decrease wait times. So that claim is the conclusion of the argument. But is that conclusion ever in the argument? No: The first statement says that wait times are a problem, but the possibility of reducing them is not in the argument.

Be aware that sometimes the conclusion of the argument is never stated in the argument but is instead found in the question. When you do step 1, look out for language in the question about a specific claim or prediction you are trying to support (or refute, depending on the argument type). Sometimes the GMAT hides the conclusion in the question, most frequently on Strengthen, Weaken, and Evaluate the Argument questions.

Right Answers

On Strengthen questions, right answers need to provide additional information that makes the conclusion more likely. Do not eliminate an answer just because you see a new word or idea; consider whether the answer is logically connected to the conclusion.

In the Donut Chain example, the right answer talked about *regular customers*. Although regular customers are not mentioned in the argument, such customers have a link to profitability and thus are relevant to strengthening the conclusion.

Common Trap Answers

One of the most common traps is the Reverse Logic answer: The question asks you to strengthen, but a trap answer choice weakens the conclusion instead. You saw an example of this with answer choice (D) in the Donut Chain problem. These can be especially tricky if you misread the conclusion or otherwise get turned around while evaluating the argument.

Most of the wrong answers will have no tie to the argument—they will neither strengthen nor weaken the argument. Some of these will be more obviously wrong, but these answers can also be quite tricky. A No Tie trap might address something in a premise without actually affecting the conclusion; answer choice (E) in the Donut Chain problem is a good example. Notice that it says something positive about Donut Chain, but not anything that addresses the specific chain of logic in the argument.

Strengthen Variant: Fill in the Blank

Contrary to popular belief, **Fill in the Blank (FitB) questions** are not actually a separate question type; rather, any of the existing question types can be presented in FitB format. In practice, most FitB questions are Strengthen questions; occasionally, they are Inference or Find the Assumption questions.

Look at an example:

> Which of the following most logically completes the argument below?
>
> XYZ Industries sells both a premium line of televisions and a basic line. The higher-end line sells at a 20 percent premium over the basic line and accounts for about half of the company's revenues. The company has announced that it will stop producing premium televisions and sell only the basic line in the future. This plan will help to improve profitability, since ______________.

Right away, you'll notice that there is no question stem after the argument—but there is a question above. The location of the question stem (and the blank at the end of the argument) indicates that you have the FitB structure. But which type of question is it?

The clue to help you identify the question will be just before the blank. In the vast majority of these problems, the word *since* or *because* will be just before the blank, in which case you have a Strengthen question.

The author claims that *this plan will help to improve profitability*. As with any Strengthen question, your task is to find an answer that will make this claim more likely to be true.

For the example above, for instance, a correct answer might read:

> premium televisions cost 40 percent more to produce and market than do basic televisions

If the company charges 20 percent more for a premium television, but has to pay 40 percent more to produce and market it, then it's more likely that the company makes less money on premium televisions than it does on basic ones. (This is not an absolute slam dunk, but that's okay. You just have to make the argument more likely to be valid.) Given this, the plan to drop the premium televisions and sell only the basic ones is more likely to improve profitability, strengthening the author's case.

On some FitB questions, the correct answer reinforces or even restates a premise already given in the argument. Most of the time, though, the correct answer will introduce a new premise, as with regular Strengthen questions. Either way, the result will be the same: The answer will make the author's argument at least a little more likely to be true.

Negatively Worded Claims

Many FitB questions introduce a negatively worded twist. Take a look at this variation on the original argument:

> Which of the following most logically completes the argument below?
>
> XYZ Industries sells both a premium line of televisions and a basic line. The higher-end line sells at a 20 percent premium but also costs 40 percent more to produce and market. Producing more televisions from the basic line, however, will not necessarily help to improve profitability, since ______________.

This is still a Strengthen question because the word *since* is just before the underline. The conclusion is that last sentence: A particular plan will *not* necessarily help to improve profitability. Why? Consider this possible correct answer:

> the market for basic televisions is shrinking

In other words, producing more TVs doesn't necessarily mean the company can *sell* more TVs, and it would have to sell them in order to make money. If the market for basic TVs is shrinking, then producing more of those TVs won't necessarily be beneficial for the company's profitability.

If you see *since* _______ in a FitB question, your goal is to strengthen the conclusion that comes before, even if that conclusion contains a *not* or is otherwise worded negatively.

Alternative Wording

The *since* _______ or *because* _______ variations are the two most common ways in which FitB questions can be presented. There are a few alternative examples, however, that might pop up. Students aiming for 90th percentile or higher on the Verbal section may want to be prepared for these rare variations; otherwise, it's fine to skip this section.

The rare variants will still typically include the conclusion or claim in the final sentence with the blank, but the "lead-in" wording to the blank will be different, signaling a different question type as shown below:

"Lead-In" Wording	Answer Choice Should	Question Type
If (some claim is true), "it should be expected that" ______________	represent something that must be true given the information in the argument	Inference
(In order for some claim to be true), "it must be shown that" ______________	represent something that must be true given the information in the argument	Inference
(Something is true) "assuming that" ______________	articulate an assumption used to draw the conclusion	Find the Assumption

Common Trap Answers

The common trap answers will mirror the trap answers given on the regular question type. For example, if the question is a Strengthen, then expect to see the same trap answers that you see on regular Strengthen questions: Reverse Logic (weakens rather than strengthens) and No Tie to the Argument.

Weaken the Argument Questions

Weaken the Argument questions ask you to find a *new* piece of information that, if added to the existing argument, will make the argument less likely to be valid. Your goal, then, is to *attack* the argument. The correct answer will generally attack some assumption made by the author.

Most Weaken question stems contain either the word *weaken* or a synonym of it. You will also typically see the phrase *if true* and question stems similar to these examples:

- Which of the following, if true, most seriously weakens the conclusion?
- Which of the following, if true, would cast the most serious doubt on the validity of the argument?
- Which of the following, if true, would raise the most serious doubt regarding the conclusion of the argument?
- Which of the following, if true, most strongly calls into question the author's conclusion?
- Which of the following, if true, most seriously undermines the mayor's claim?

Sometimes, the question stem will contain more unusual language, such as the words in quotes below:

- Find a "disadvantage" or what is "damaging" to the argument
- A plan is "ill-suited" or otherwise unlikely to succeed
- Find a "criticism" of the argument

Now, try the same short argument about QuestCorp from earlier in the chapter, but with a different question stem and answers:

> At QuestCorp, many employees have quit recently and taken jobs with a competitor. Shortly before the employees quit, QuestCorp lost its largest client. Clearly, the employees were no longer confident in QuestCorp's long-term viability.
>
> Which of the following, if true, most seriously undermines the claim that concerns about QuestCorp's viability caused the employees to quit?
>
> (A) A new competitor in the same town provides health insurance for its employees, a benefit that QuestCorp lacks.
>
> (B) QuestCorp is unlikely to be able to replace the lost revenue via either an increase in existing client sales or the attraction of new clients.
>
> (C) Many prospective hires who have interviewed with QuestCorp ultimately accepted jobs with other companies.

The question stem indicates that this is a Weaken question. In your mind or on your paper, the argument core might look like this:

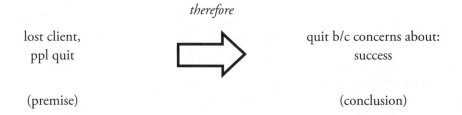

lost client, ppl quit	*therefore* ⇨	quit b/c concerns about: success
(premise)		(conclusion)

As always, make sure that you understand what the argument is trying to say. The author claims that losing this client caused employees to lose confidence in QuestCorp, leading them to quit. The author is assuming that losing this one client was serious enough to result in a major problem for the company. Is that necessarily the case?

Remind yourself of your goal:

This is a Weaken question, so I have to find some evidence that makes it less *likely that people quit for that reason. That could be because it wasn't really a big problem, or it could be that there was some other reason that people quit.*

(A) A new competitor in the same town provides health insurance for its employees, a benefit that QuestCorp lacks.	*The argument claims that people left for one reason, but this answer actually provides an alternative. Maybe people quit because they could get better benefits at the other company. This would weaken the claim that people quit specifically because of concerns over QuestCorp's viability as a company.*	A~
(B) QuestCorp is unlikely to be able to replace the lost revenue via either an increase in existing client sales or the attraction of new clients.	*So QuestCorp lost its largest client, which means a loss of revenue, and the company probably can't find a way to make up that revenue through other sales. That definitely reinforces the problem described in the argument. This actually strengthens the argument; that's the opposite of what I want.*	~~B~~
(C) Many prospective hires who have interviewed with QuestCorp ultimately accepted jobs with other companies.	*Hmm.* Prospective hires *are not* employees. *I was asked to weaken the part about employees losing confidence in QuestCorp. I could speculate that maybe something is wrong with the company if people take other jobs… but the answer doesn't even tell me* why *these people took other jobs. Maybe QuestCorp rejected them!*	~~C~~

(A~) ~~B~~ ~~C~~

The correct answer is (A).

Answer (B) repeats the common Reverse Logic trap discussed earlier: It strengthens the argument. Answer (C) attempts to distract you by talking about a different part of the argument—perhaps you'll reason that, if interviewees took different jobs, then they didn't believe QuestCorp was a good company. You have no idea why these prospective hires ended up working for another company, though—it's entirely possible that QuestCorp didn't extend a job offer to these people.

Note that the problem used the exact same answer choice (C) for both the Strengthen and Weaken versions of this QuestCorp problem. If a choice is irrelevant to the argument, as choice (C) is, then it doesn't matter whether you're asked to strengthen or weaken the argument. An irrelevant choice doesn't affect the argument at all.

Try this full example:

> The national infrastructure for airport runways and air traffic control requires immediate expansion to accommodate the increase in smaller private planes. To help fund this expansion, the Federal Aviation Authority has proposed a fee for all air travelers. However, this fee would be unfair, as it would impose costs on all travelers to benefit only the few who utilize the new private planes.
>
> Which of the following, if true, would cast the most doubt on the claim that the proposed fee would be unfair?
>
> (A) The existing national airport infrastructure benefits all air travelers.
>
> (B) The fee, if imposed, will have a negligible impact on the overall volume of air travel.
>
> (C) The expansion would reduce the number of delayed flights resulting from small private planes congesting runways.
>
> (D) Travelers who use small private planes are almost uniformly wealthy or traveling on business.
>
> (E) A substantial fee would need to be imposed in order to pay for the expansion costs.

Step 1: Identify the Question

Which of the following, if true, would cast the most doubt on the claim that the proposed fee would be unfair?	*The language* cast the most doubt on the claim *indicates that this is a Weaken question. Attack: The proposed fee would be unfair.*	W A B C D E Ⓒ fee = unfair

Step 2: Deconstruct the Argument

The national infrastructure for airport runways and air traffic control requires immediate expansion to accommodate the increase in smaller, private planes.	*This is written as a fact and appears to be stating something that has already been established; I'm guessing it's background info, not the conclusion, but I'm not 100 percent sure.*	To handle more small priv planes → must expand infra
To help fund this expansion, the Federal Aviation Authority has proposed a fee for all air travelers.	*Okay, here's a plan. It could be the conclusion. The FAA wants to charge a fee to pay for the expansion.*	FAA: fee → fund exp
However, this fee would be unfair, as it would impose costs on all travelers to benefit only the few who utilize the new private planes.	*Change of direction! The author disagrees with the plan, claiming it's unfair. The author's reasoning: Everyone would have to pay the fee, but only a few people would benefit.* *Why wouldn't everyone benefit? If there's more space, then all the planes will be able to take off more quickly. The author is assuming the benefit is only for the people flying in small planes.*	BUT fee = unfair b/c all pay to benef few

Step 3: State the Goal

The airports are congested because there are so many small planes, and the FAA wants to charge a fee to expand the airports. The author claims that this is unfair because the fee would be paid by all but the expansion would only benefit a few.

I want to weaken the author's conclusion, so I need to find some reason why it really isn't unfair. One possibility: Maybe more people will benefit than just the small plane people.

20

Step 4: Work from Wrong to Right

(A) The existing national airport infrastructure benefits all air travelers.	*This sounds like what I was thinking before—everyone benefits, so why is it unfair for everyone to pay? Great; I'll leave it in.*	A ~
(B) The fee, if imposed, will have a negligible impact on the overall volume of air travel.	A negligible impact *means it won't really change anything. The fee won't change the volume of planes trying to fly...but that was never the plan. The plan was to raise money to expand the infrastructure—then they'll be able to handle more volume. This answer doesn't address the right thing.*	~~B~~
(C) The expansion would reduce the number of delayed flights resulting from small private planes congesting runways.	*Hmm. This is another potential benefit for everyone—a reduction in the number of flight delays. I'll leave this one in, too.*	C ~
(D) Travelers who use small private planes are almost uniformly wealthy or traveling on business.	*That's nice for them, but what does it have to do with this argument? Maybe you could say, "So they can afford to pay more," but that isn't the point of the argument. The point of the argument is that it's unfair to make the regular travelers pay for something that doesn't benefit them (according to the author).*	~~D~~
(E) A substantial fee would need to be imposed in order to pay for the expansion costs.	*So the fee would have to be pretty large. If anything, doesn't that make it even more unfair? Though, actually, I don't think it really addresses the fairness at all. Either it is fair, in which case the size of the fee doesn't matter, or it isn't fair...in which case the size of the fee still doesn't matter.*	~~E~~
Examine (A) and (C) again.	*Compare choices (A) and (C). Both say that this expansion would benefit everyone...wait a second. Choice (C) does explicitly mention the expansion, but (A) says* the existing...infrastructure. *Existing? Of course, the existing structure benefits everyone who uses it—the argument isn't about that. It's about whether the* expansion *would benefit everyone. Only choice (C) actually says that; I missed that the first time around.*	~~A~~ ~ Ⓒ

~~A~~ ~~B~~ Ⓒ ~~D~~ ~~E~~

Right Answers

As discussed with Strengthen questions, for Weaken questions, look for an answer that has a logical connection to the conclusion, in this case one that makes the conclusion less likely to be true. You will often see new language and ideas in correct answers because one way to weaken an argument is to bring up an issue that the author did not discuss. For example, in the previous example, the author had not discussed flight delays in the original argument. Below are some common ways to weaken different argument types:

- **Causation:** Provide an alternate cause for the situation.
- **Plan:** Present an unexpected cost of the plan or reason the plan will not work as expected.
- **Prediction:** Discuss additional circumstances or future changes that might affect the prediction.
- **Profit:** Provide additional information about costs or revenues (often the one not discussed in the argument). Be careful about how the direction of a change relates to the conclusion (e.g., an answer that provides a reason that costs may increase weakens an argument that profits will increase).

An argument of each of type is provided below. For each argument, first identify the argument type. Second, find a way to weaken the argument in the manner described above.

1. This year's spring festival takes place next weekend. A large number of attendees at last year's festival have recently shared positive posts about the festival on social media. Also, the advertising budget for the festival is 50 percent higher than last year's budget. Therefore, attendance at this year's spring festival will exceed attendance at last year's festival.
2. Jitters Coffee Shop offers free WiFi for use by its customers. The manager is concerned that the free WiFi results in customers sitting at tables for extended periods, driving away new customers who cannot find a table. In order to increase sales, the manager plans to limit WiFi use to 30 minutes per session.
3. A teacher observed that students who consistently sat in the first three rows of the classroom scored an average of 12 points higher on the final exam than students who consistently sat in the last three rows. Thus, sitting in the front of the classroom causes enhanced retention of course material.
4. Workers at Tangerine Corporation receive overtime pay equal to one and a half times their normal hourly pay when they work more than 40 hours in a given week. Recently, Tangerine implemented a policy requiring approval from a manager for any employee to exceed the 40-hour threshold. By limiting overtime pay, this policy will increase profits for Tangerine.

Take a look at the suggested answers below. There are multiple ways to weaken any argument, so you may have thought of a different answer.

1. **Prediction.** This conclusion is a prediction about increased attendance at the festival. The premises in the argument only discuss publicity via both social media and advertising. You can weaken this argument by providing any other issue that might decrease attendance (bad weather, fewer attractions at this year's festival). For example, a major snowstorm is predicted for the weekend of the festival this year.
2. **Plan.** The manager provides a plan to increase sales: limit WiFi to 30 minutes so more customers can sit down. You can weaken this argument by providing reasons this plan might not increase sales or even decrease sales. For example, most customers who use the WiFi for over an hour make multiple purchases during their stay. If this were the case, the plan could actually lead to losing some sales.

3. **Causation.** The teacher has made an observation that two things occur together: sitting in the front and higher test scores. The conclusion introduces causation: Sitting in front causes enhanced retention of the course material. You can weaken this argument by providing another cause for the teacher's observation: either reverse causation or an outside cause for both factors. Reverse causation in this case would mean high test grades are causing students to sit in the front of the room. While that idea doesn't make complete sense, it might get you thinking about what types of students might choose to sit in the front. For example, students who report studying more hours per week tend to select seats in the front of the classroom.
4. **Profit** (also a Plan). The argument states that profits will increase, but the information provided only discusses potentially reducing costs through limiting overtime pay. You can weaken this plan by providing a reason that the plan may reduce revenues (or a reason it might not reduce costs). For example, most overtime work results in additional sales to new clients.

Common Trap Answers

Weaken questions contain the same kind of common trap answers that show up on Strengthen questions.

One of the trickiest types is the Reverse Logic trap: The question asks you to weaken, but a trap answer choice strengthens the argument instead. You will also again see the No Tie to the Argument traps—choices that might discuss something in a premise but don't affect the argument.

The most tempting wrong answer in the last problem, answer choice (A), is actually a No Tie trap. Almost everything in the choice was addressing the right thing, but one word made it wrong: *existing*. The conclusion was about the future infrastructure, after an expansion, so limiting the answer to the existing infrastructure meant that the information didn't affect the conclusion after all.

EXCEPT Questions

Assumption Family questions may also be presented in a "negative" form that is commonly referred to as EXCEPT questions.

A regular Weaken question might read:

> Which of the following, if true, most seriously weakens the conclusion?

A Weaken EXCEPT question might read:

> Each of the following, if true, weakens the conclusion EXCEPT:

What is the difference in wording between those two questions?

The first one indicates that one answer choice, and only one, weakens the argument. You want to pick that choice.

The second one indicates that four answer choices weaken the argument. These four are all wrong answers. What about the fifth answer—what does that one do?

Many people assume that the fifth one must do the opposite: strengthen the argument. *This is not necessarily true.* The fifth one certainly does not weaken the argument, but it may not strengthen the argument either. It might have no impact whatsoever on the argument.

For these negatively worded questions, use the "odd one out" strategy. Four of the answer choices will do the same thing; in the case of the example above, four answers will weaken the argument. The fifth choice, the correct one, will do something else. It doesn't matter whether the fifth one strengthens the argument or does nothing—all that matters is that it is the odd one out, the one that does *not* weaken. In order to keep track of the four similar answers versus the odd one out, label the choices as you assess them with an S for Strengthen, a W for Weaken, and an N for Neutral or "does Nothing."

Try this example:

> Supporters of a costly new Defense Advanced Research Projects Agency (DARPA) initiative assert that the project will benefit industrial companies as well as the military itself. In many instances, military research has resulted in technologies that have fueled corporate development and growth, and this pattern can be expected to continue.
>
> Each of the following, if true, serves to weaken the argument above EXCEPT:
>
> (A) The research initiative will occupy many talented scientists, many of whom would otherwise have worked for private corporations.
>
> (B) In the past decade, DARPA has adopted an increasingly restrictive stance regarding the use of intellectual property resulting from its research.
>
> (C) If the DARPA initiative hadn't been approved, much of the funding would instead have been directed toward tax breaks for various businesses.
>
> (D) At any given time, DARPA is conducting a wide variety of costly research projects.
>
> (E) The research initiative is focused on specific defense mechanisms that would be ineffective for private corporations.

Step 1: Identify the Question

Each of the following, if true, serves to weaken the argument above EXCEPT:	*The language* serves to weaken *indicates that this is a Weaken question. The word* EXCEPT *indicates that the four wrong answers will weaken, and I want to pick the "odd one out" answer.*	WEx A B C D E

Step 2: Deconstruct the Argument

Supporters of a costly new Defense Advanced Research Projects Agency (DARPA) initiative assert that the project will benefit industrial companies as well as the military itself.	*The supporters of DARPA think that this costly project will be good for companies and for the military.*	© Supporters: Costly proj will benef co's & mil
In many instances, military research has resulted in technologies that have fueled corporate development and growth, and this pattern can be expected to continue.	*Research has helped companies in the past, and the author claims this will keep happening in the future. That all supports the claim of the supporters: that the specific DARPA project will be beneficial for companies.*	Past: mil research → techs help co's, will cont

20

Step 3: State the Goal

In the past, military research has helped companies, and the claim is that this DARPA project will also help companies.

I want to find four answers that weaken the argument. The answer that doesn't weaken—the odd one out—is the correct answer.

Step 4: Work from Wrong to Right

(A) The research initiative will occupy many talented scientists, many of whom would otherwise have worked for private corporations.	*This benefits the military and specifically does not benefit the companies. That does weaken the idea that companies will benefit.*	~~A~~ *W*
(B) In the past decade, DARPA has adopted an increasingly restrictive stance regarding the use of intellectual property resulting from its research.	*Hmm.* Restrictive *makes it sound like DARPA doesn't let others use its research as much. If that's the case, then that would weaken the idea that companies will benefit. I'm not totally sure that's what this means though—the wording is tricky—so I'm going to give this a question mark and come back to it later.*	B *W?*
(C) If the DARPA initiative hadn't been approved, much of the funding would instead have been directed toward tax breaks for various businesses.	*A tax break is a good thing. This choice is saying that the funding for the DARPA project would instead have been spent on tax breaks, which is a definite benefit. So not giving those tax breaks is a bad thing for the companies; this does weaken the argument.*	~~C~~ *W*
(D) At any given time, DARPA is conducting a wide variety of costly research projects.	*This choice talks about all research projects DARPA is conducting. Hmm. The argument makes a claim only about one specific project. Does this information make that claim more or less likely to be valid? I can't really see how it affects the argument's conclusion at all.*	D *N*
(E) The research initiative is focused on specific defense mechanisms that would be ineffective for private corporations.	*The key here is the language* ineffective for private corporations. *If the private companies can't make effective use of the results of this particular research, then that weakens the claim that the DARPA research will benefit companies.*	~~E~~ *W*
Examine (B) and (D) again.	*I need to compare answers (B) and (D). I thought (B) might weaken a little bit, and I thought (D) didn't do anything to the argument. Between those two, I should choose the one that doesn't weaken at all, so I'm going to choose choice (D).*	~~B~~ (D) *W N*

The correct answer is (D).

The biggest trap answer on an EXCEPT question is simply to forget halfway through that you're working on an EXCEPT question. If this happens, you might accidentally pick a Weaken answer or pick the answer that you think *most* weakens the argument. The *W* labels under your weaken answers will help to remind you that multiple answers weaken, so that is not what you want to pick.

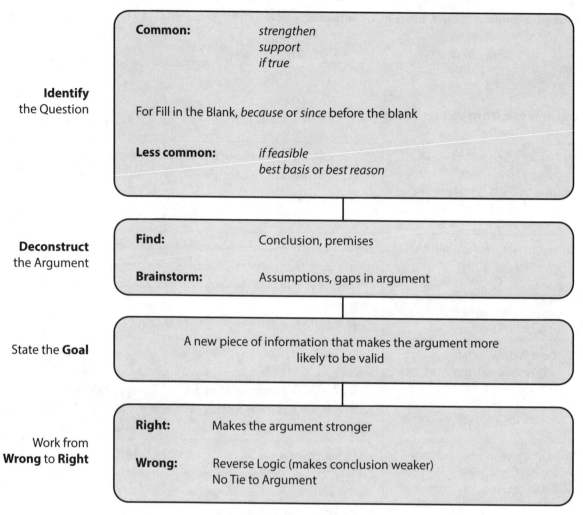

Strengthen the Argument Cheat Sheet

Identify the Question	**Common:** *strengthen*, *support*, *if true* For Fill in the Blank, *because* or *since* before the blank **Less common:** *if feasible*, *best basis* or *best reason*
Deconstruct the Argument	**Find:** Conclusion, premises **Brainstorm:** Assumptions, gaps in argument
State the **Goal**	A new piece of information that makes the argument more likely to be valid
Work from **Wrong** to **Right**	**Right:** Makes the argument stronger **Wrong:** Reverse Logic (makes conclusion weaker); No Tie to Argument

Note: Fill in the Blank is almost always Strengthen, because the blank is usually preceded by *since* or *because*. When in doubt, assume that the question type is Strengthen.

Take a picture of this page and keep it with the review sheets you're creating as you study. Better yet, use this page as a guide to create your own review sheet—you'll remember the material better if you write it down yourself.

Weaken the Argument Cheat Sheet

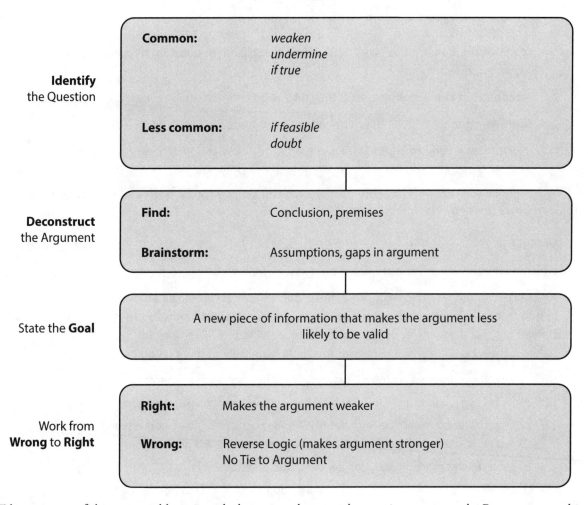

Identify the Question	**Common:**	*weaken* *undermine* *if true*
	Less common:	*if feasible* *doubt*
Deconstruct the Argument	**Find:**	Conclusion, premises
	Brainstorm:	Assumptions, gaps in argument
State the **Goal**	A new piece of information that makes the argument less likely to be valid	
Work from **Wrong** to **Right**	**Right:**	Makes the argument weaker
	Wrong:	Reverse Logic (makes argument stronger) No Tie to Argument

Take a picture of this page and keep it with the review sheets you're creating as you study. Better yet, use this page as a guide to create your own review sheet—you'll remember the material better if you write it down yourself.

Problem Set

Answer each question using the 4-step Critical Reasoning process.

1. **Identify the question:** Is this a Strengthen the Argument question or a Weaken the Argument question?
2. **Deconstruct the argument:** Find the conclusion and map the argument on your paper.
3. **State the goal:** What will the right answer need to do?
4. **Work from wrong to right:** Eliminate four wrong answers. Watch out for common wrong answer types.

Before you check your answers, identify as many Reverse Logic wrong answers as you can in each problem. Every problem has at least one!

1. *Motor City*

   Which of the following best completes the passage below?

   A nonprofit organization in Motor City has proposed that local college students be given the option to buy half-price monthly passes for the city's public transportation system. The nonprofit claims that this plan will reduce air pollution in Motor City while increasing profits for the city's public transportation system. However, this plan is unlikely to meet its goals, since ___________.

   (A) most college students in Motor City view public transportation as unsafe
   (B) most college students in Motor City view public transportation as prohibitively expensive
   (C) college students typically do not have the 9-to-5 schedules of most workers, and can thus be expected to ride public transportation at times when there are plenty of empty seats
   (D) a bus produces more air pollution per mile than does a car
   (E) a large proportion of the college students in Motor City live off campus

2. *Smithtown Theatre*

   The Smithtown Theatre, which stages old plays, has announced an expansion that will double its capacity along with its operating costs. The theatre is only slightly profitable at present. In addition, all of the current customers live in Smithtown, and the population of the town is not expected to increase in the next several years. Thus, the expansion of the Smithtown Theatre will prove unprofitable.

   Which of the following, if true, would most seriously weaken the argument?

   (A) A large movie chain plans to open a new multiplex location in Smithtown later this year.
   (B) Concession sales in the Smithtown Theatre comprise a substantial proportion of the theatre's revenues.
   (C) Many recent arrivals to Smithtown are students who are less likely to attend the Smithtown Theatre than are older residents.
   (D) The expansion would allow the Smithtown Theatre to stage larger, more popular shows that will attract customers from neighboring towns.
   (E) The Board of the Smithtown Theatre often solicits input from residents of the town when choosing which shows to stage.

3. *Books and Coffee*

The owners of a book store and a nearby coffee shop have decided to combine their businesses. Both owners believe that this merger will increase the number of customers and therefore the gross revenue, because customers who come for one reason may also decide to purchase something else.

Which of the following, if true, most weakens the owners' conclusion that a merger will increase revenue?

(A) Books and drinks can both be considered impulse purchases; often, they are purchased by customers without forethought.

(B) Profit margins at a coffee shop are generally significantly higher than profit margins at a book store.

(C) People who are able to read the first chapter of a book before buying are more likely to decide to buy the book.

(D) A large majority of the book store's current customer base already frequents the coffee shop.

(E) A combination book store and coffee shop that opened in a neighboring city last year has already earned higher than expected profits.

4. *Teacher Compensation*

Traditionally, public school instructors have been compensated according to seniority. Recently, education experts have criticized the system as one that rewards lackadaisical teaching and reduces motivation to excel. Instead, these experts argue that, to retain exceptional teachers and maintain quality instruction, teachers should receive salaries or bonuses based on performance rather than seniority.

Which of the following, if true, most weakens the argument of the education experts?

(A) Some teachers express that financial compensation is not the only factor contributing to job satisfaction and teaching performance.

(B) School districts will develop their own unique compensation structures that may differ greatly from those of other school districts.

(C) Upon leaving the teaching profession, many young, effective teachers cite a lack of opportunity for more rapid financial advancement as a primary factor in the decision to change careers.

(D) In school districts that have implemented pay for performance compensation structures, standardized test scores have dramatically increased.

(E) A merit-based system that bases compensation on teacher performance reduces collaboration, which is an integral component of quality instruction.

5. *Machu Picchu*

In 2001, the Peruvian government began requiring tourists to buy permits to hike the Inca Trail to the ancient city of Machu Picchu. Only 500 people per day are given permission to hike the Inca Trail, whereas before 2001 daily visitors numbered in the thousands. The Peruvian government claims that this permit program has successfully prevented deterioration of archaeological treasures along the Inca Trail.

Which of the following, if true, most strengthens the argument above?

(A) Since 2001, Incan ruins similar to Machu Picchu but without a visitor limit have disintegrated at a significantly greater rate than those on the Inca Trail.

(B) Villages near Machu Picchu have experienced declines in income, as fewer tourists buy fewer craft goods and refreshments.

(C) Many of the funds from the sale of Inca Trail permits are used to hire guards for archaeological sites without permit programs.

(D) Since 2001, tourist guides along the Inca Trail have received 50 percent to 100 percent increases in take-home pay.

(E) Due to limited enforcement, the majority of tourists hiking the Inca Trail currently do so without a permit.

6. *Digital Video Recorders*

Advertising Executive: More than 10 million households now own digital video recorders that can fast-forward over television commercials; approximately 75 percent of these households fast-forward over at least one commercial per 30-minute program. Because television commercials are not as widely watched as they used to be, they are much less cost-effective today.

Which of the following is required in order for the advertising executive to claim that television commercials are less cost-effective today?

(A) Product placement within television programs is a viable alternative to traditional television commercials.

(B) The television programs preferred by consumers without digital video recorders are similar to those preferred by consumers with the devices.

(C) Prior to the advent of digital video recorders, very few television viewers switched channels or left the room when commercials began.

(D) The cost-effectiveness of television advertising is based less upon how many people watch a particular commercial and more upon the appropriateness of the demographic.

(E) The amount that television channels charge for advertisers to air commercials on their channel has increased steadily over the last decade.

7. *APR*

CEO: Over the past several years, we have more than doubled our revenues, but profits have steadily declined because an increasing number of customers have failed to pay their balances. In order to compensate for these higher default rates, we will increase the interest charged on outstanding balances from an annual percentage rate (APR) of 9.5 percent to an APR of 12 percent. This increase will be sufficient to compensate for the current rate of defaults and allow us to increase our profits.

Which of the following statements, if true, would most seriously undermine a plan to increase interest rates in order to spur profitable growth?

(A) Many other companies have experienced a similar trend in their default rates.

(B) The company's operating expenses are above the industry average and can be substantially reduced, thus increasing margins.

(C) The increase in default rates was due to a rise in unemployment, but unemployment rates are expected to drop in the coming months.

(D) The proposed increase in the APR will, alone, more than double the company's profit margins.

(E) An increase in the APR charged on credit card balances often results in higher rates of default.

8. *Jupiter vs. Mars*

Scientists suspect that Europa, a moon orbiting Jupiter, may contain living organisms. However, the government recently scrapped an unmanned science mission to Europa and replaced it with a project aimed at landing an astronaut on Mars. Polls show that the public is far more fascinated by space travel than by discovering life elsewhere in the universe. Critics argue that the government's decision-making process places a greater emphasis on popularity than it does on the importance of scientific research.

Which of the following, if true, would most strengthen a contention by the government that the critics' accusation is incorrect?

(A) In the first year of the project, the government will spend 30 percent of its total budget on developing a space shuttle that can travel to Mars; that figure is expected to drop to 0 percent after five years.

(B) The government cannot be absolutely certain of the chances for success of either project.

(C) Some scientists are convinced that a mission to Europa would add immeasurably to our understanding of the universe.

(D) A new telescope that has just become available to scientists promises to yield more information than the planned mission to Europa was designed to provide.

(E) Most people feel that a shuttle to Mars would represent a first step toward an extensive program of space travel.

20

9. *Deep-Brain Stimulation*

Which of the following most logically completes the argument given below?

Deep-brain stimulation is a new technique for combating severe depression. In a recent experiment, electrodes were implanted into the brains of six patients who had not responded to any currently approved treatment for depression. When an electrical current to the electrodes was switched on, four of the patients reported feeling a dramatic reduction in depressive symptoms. The long-term prospects of the new treatment are not promising, however, because ________.

(A) other treatments for depression may also be effective

(B) the other two patients reported only a slight reduction of depressive symptoms during the treatment

(C) deep-brain stimulation relies on the expertise of highly skilled physicians

(D) when the electrical current is interrupted, the effects of the treatment are reversed

(E) in a subsequent experiment, a one-hour treatment with the electrodes resulted in a sustained remission from depression in the four patients for six months

Solutions

1. Motor City: The correct answer is **(A)**. Remember to identify any Reverse Logic answers before you read the explanation!

Step 1: Identify the Question

Which of the following best completes the passage below?	*The blank at the end signals a Fill in the Blank format. The word* since *just before the blank indicates that this is a Strengthen question.*	S A B C D E

Step 2: Deconstruct the Argument

A nonprofit organization in Motor City has proposed that local college students be given the option to buy half-price monthly passes for the city's public transportation system.	*This is a fact—the organization has proposed this plan.*	Nonprof: give coll stud 1/2 off pub trans
The nonprofit claims that this plan will reduce air pollution in Motor City while increasing profits for the city's public transportation system.	*Okay, the nonprofit claims something, but I'm not labeling this the conclusion, because the conclusion is supposed to be in the final sentence of CA questions.*	→ ↓ air poll, ↑ prof
However, this plan is unlikely to meet its goals, since______________.	*This is the conclusion. The author thinks the plan won't work. Why?*	Ⓒ BUT unlikely to work

Step 3: State the Goal

The author believes that the nonprofit's plan is not going to work, and I need to find a reason that supports this author's belief. The plan is to let college students buy public transportation passes for half price in order to reduce air pollution and increase profits. Which answer choice supports the idea that this plan will not *work?*

Step 4: Work from Wrong to Right

(A) most college students in Motor City view public transportation as unsafe	*If this is the case, then the students wouldn't want to use public transport at all, even if they were given a discount. That would make the plan unlikely to succeed. This might be it!*	A ~
(B) most college students in Motor City view public transportation as prohibitively expensive	***Reverse logic.*** *Giving the students a discount is likely to make them use public transport more. This makes the plan more likely to succeed, not less likely.*	~~B~~
(C) college students typically do not have the 9-to-5 schedules of most workers, and can thus be expected to ride public transportation at times when there are plenty of empty seats	***Reverse logic.*** *If this were true, it'd be good news for the public transport's profits—the students would be filling what are currently empty seats.*	~~C~~
(D) a bus produces more air pollution per mile than does a car	*At first, this sounds good—if a bus produces more air pollution than a car, then using more buses would create more air pollution, which would hurt the plan. But the plan isn't to add more buses; it's to put more people on the already-running buses. Plus, one car won't be replaced with one bus! A bus might replace 10 or more cars.*	~~D~~
(E) a large proportion of the college students in Motor City live off campus	***Reverse logic.*** *This makes it likely that the students need some method of transportation to get to school—if they're using cars now and switch to buses, then the plan just might work.*	~~E~~

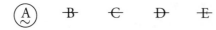

(A ~) ~~B~~ ~~C~~ ~~D~~ ~~E~~

2. Smithtown Theatre: The correct answer is **(D)**. Remember to identify any Reverse Logic answers before you read the explanation!

Step 1: Identify the Question

Which of the following, if true, would most seriously weaken the argument?	*The words* if true *and* weaken *tell me that this is a Weaken question.*	W A B C D E

Step 2: Deconstruct the Argument

The Smithtown Theatre, which stages old plays, has announced an expansion that will double its capacity along with its operating costs.	*They have a plan. It's future, so it could be the conclusion, but I'm guessing there'll be more of a claim like "The theatre will (or will not) be successful with its plan" or something like that.*	Theatre: expand to ↑↑ cap & cost
The theatre is only slightly profitable at present.	*This is a fact. I wonder: If the theatre expands, will it get enough new business to continue covering costs?*	Now: barely prof
In addition, all of the current customers live in Smithtown, and the population of the town is not expected to increase in the next several years.	*The first half is a fact; the second half is a future prediction. So far, the case for the theatre's new plan doesn't sound very good.*	Cust live in S, prob won't be more from S
Thus, the expansion of the Smithtown Theatre will prove unprofitable.	*Okay, here's the conclusion. The author thinks the plan will fail and provides some pieces of evidence to support that claim.*	© Theatre expansion unprof

Step 3: State the Goal

The theatre has a plan to expand, but the author claims that the plan will fail. The author reasons that the theatre is only barely profitable right now, and it doesn't seem like there are a lot more opportunities to get new customers.

I want something that will weaken the author's claim. I have to be careful here: I should weaken the idea that the plan will fail, not weaken the plan itself. The right answer will actually strengthen the plan and show that the expansion may work.

Step 4: Work from Wrong to Right

(A) A large movie chain plans to open a new multiplex location in Smithtown later this year.	***Reverse logic.*** *If anything, you'd have to say that the new movie theatre would take business from the theatre, which would strengthen the author's claim that the theatre will fail.*	~~A~~
(B) Concession sales in the Smithtown Theatre comprise a substantial proportion of the theatre's revenues.	*How would this change if the theatre expanded? That still depends upon whether they can get more people to come to the theatre, so this doesn't really tell me anything new.*	~~B~~
(C) Many recent arrivals to Smithtown are students who are less likely to attend the Smithtown Theatre than are older residents.	***Reverse logic.*** *The new people moving to town are people who aren't likely to start going to the theatre. That strengthens the author's claim that ST's expansion is going to fail.*	~~C~~
(D) The expansion would allow the Smithtown Theatre to stage larger, more popular shows that will attract patrons from neighboring towns.	*Hmm. This basically means that the expansion would attract a greater audience—that helps! If they have more people, they can fill the larger theatre and make more money. This one is looking good as a weakener for the claim that the expansion will fail.*	D ~
(E) The Board of the Smithtown Theatre often solicits input from residents of the town when choosing which shows to stage.	*This is how they do things now. Would it stay the same or change when they expand? I have no idea.*	~~E~~

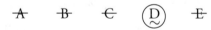

~~A~~ ~~B~~ ~~C~~ (D ~) ~~E~~

3. Books and Coffee: The correct answer is **(D)**. Remember to identify any Reverse Logic answers before you read the explanation!

Step 1: Identify the Question

Which of the following, if true, most weakens the owners' conclusion that a merger will increase revenue?	*The words* if true *and* weakens *tell me that this is a Weaken question. Further, I now know the conclusion: Some merger will result in increased revenue.*	W A B C D E Ⓒ Merger → ↑ rev

Step 2: Deconstruct the Argument

The owners of a book store and a nearby coffee shop have decided to combine their businesses.	*This is a fact; they have already made this decision, although it sounds like they haven't actually merged yet.*	Book + coffee combining
Both owners believe that this merger will increase the number of customers and therefore the gross revenue,	*This is the same thing the Q stem said: The merger will increase revenue.*	Will → ↑ cust, rev
because customers who come for one reason may also decide to purchase something else.	*According to the owners, the individual customers of each store will end up buying both books and coffee, so there'll be more customers for both, which means more revenue for both.*	B/c cross-sell

Step 3: State the Goal

The owners think that merging will lead to increased revenue because it'll increase the number of customers and the customers will buy more stuff. This assumes that the same customers weren't already going to both stores and buying stuff.

This is a Weaken question, so I need to find something that will make the conclusion less likely to be valid. The right answer will show that revenue might not increase.

Step 4: Work from Wrong to Right

(A) Books and drinks can both be considered impulse purchases; often, they are purchased by customers without forethought.	***Reverse logic.*** *If people normally just buy coffee but see a book they like, maybe they'll be more likely to buy. That would strengthen the plan to merge, but I want to weaken the plan.*	~~A~~
(B) Profit margins at a coffee shop are generally significantly higher than profit margins at a book store.	*That might make the coffee shop owner not want to merge, but it doesn't address the revenue side of the equation at all—and the conclusion has to do with revenues, not profits.*	~~B~~
(C) People who are able to read the first chapter of a book before buying are more likely to decide to buy the book.	***Reverse logic.*** *This helps the owners' argument again! If I can sit there and read while having my coffee, then I'm more likely to buy the book, which would increase revenues.*	~~C~~
(D) A large majority of the book store's current customer base already frequents the coffee shop.	*Most of the people who shop at the book store also already go to the coffee shop. That's bad for the owner's plan—it means that they're not going to pick up as many new customers as I might have thought before.*	D ~
(E) A combination book store and coffee shop that opened in a neighboring city last year has already earned higher than expected profits.	*Two problems here. One, the author's not talking about the same book store and coffee shop. Two, this choice talks about profits, not revenues.*	~~E~~

~~A~~ ~~B~~ ~~C~~ (D) ~~E~~

20

4. Teacher Compensation: The correct answer is **(E)**. Remember to identify any Reverse Logic answers before you read the explanation!

Step 1: Identify the Question

Which of the following, if true, most weakens the argument of the education experts?	*The language* if true *and* weakens *tells me this is a Weaken question. In addition, the question tells me that I need to look for a reference to* education experts *because whatever they claim is the conclusion.*	W A B C D E

Step 2: Deconstruct the Argument

Traditionally, public school instructors have been compensated according to seniority.	*Fact: Teachers have been getting paid based upon how long they've worked.*	Trad: Pub school teachers = $ by seniority
Recently, education experts have criticized the system as one that rewards lackadaisical teaching and reduces motivation to excel.	*Supposedly, paying teachers by seniority makes them less likely to work hard.*	Experts: ↓ motiv
Instead, these experts argue that, to retain exceptional teachers and maintain quality instruction, teachers should receive salaries or bonuses based on performance rather than seniority.	*The experts want to base compensation on performance, and they claim this will lead to better teachers and instruction. This is the conclusion.*	Ⓒ Base comp on perform → keep great teachers

Step 3: State the Goal

Teachers normally get paid based on seniority, but these experts think that paying them based on performance will help teacher quality.

I need to find something that weakens this plan. The right answer should show that paying teachers based on performance won't *get us better teachers.*

Step 4: Work from Wrong to Right

(A) Some teachers express that financial compensation is not the only factor contributing to job satisfaction and teaching performance.	*This answer is going in the right direction. If financial compensation isn't the only factor, then maybe paying teachers based on performance won't make them perform better. But there are a few problems: First, this answer says it isn't the only factor. But if it isn't the only factor, that means compensation is still* a *factor! Plus, this is just about what some teachers say. Even if some teachers claim to disagree, they might not be right, and they might not represent the majority.*	~~A~~
(B) School districts will develop their own unique compensation structures that may differ greatly from those of other school districts.	*The argument isn't claiming that every school district has to be identical. It just makes a recommendation that compensation be tied to performance in general.*	~~B~~
(C) Upon leaving the teaching profession, many young, effective teachers cite a lack of opportunity for more rapid financial advancement as a primary factor in the decision to change careers.	***Reverse logic.** This shows that teachers do care about the financial side of things. So, paying effective teachers more will probably help schools hang on to them.*	~~C~~
(D) In school districts that have implemented pay for performance compensation structures, standardized test scores have dramatically increased.	***Reverse logic.** If paying for teacher performance helps the students, then the experts' plan is probably a good one.*	~~D~~
(E) A merit-based system that bases compensation on teacher performance reduces collaboration, which is an integral component of quality instruction.	*The experts' plan has a drawback: It reduces something that is considered an* integral component *of good teaching. If that's true, it could hurt the idea that basing compensation on performance will result in maintaining good instruction.*	E ~

~~A~~ ~~B~~ ~~C~~ ~~D~~ (E ~)

20

5. Machu Picchu: The correct answer is **(A)**. Remember to identify any Reverse Logic answers before you read the explanation!

Step 1: Identify the Question

Which of the following, if true, most strengthens the argument above?	*The words* if true *and* strengthens the argument *indicate that this is a Strengthen question.*	S A B C D E

Step 2: Deconstruct the Argument

In 2001, the Peruvian government began requiring tourists to buy permits to hike the Inca Trail to the ancient city of Machu Picchu.	*This is a fact. People now have to pay to hike the Inca Trail.*	2001 Peru gov: req permits to hike Inca Trail
Only 500 people per day are given permission to hike the Inca Trail, whereas before 2001 daily visitors numbered in the thousands.	*More facts. Now, only 500 people a day are allowed; before, there were thousands a day.*	Now: 500/day (old = 1000's)
The Peruvian government claims that this permit program has successfully prevented deterioration of archaeological treasures along the Inca Trail.	*Here's the claim: The PG specifically says that the permit program is responsible for preventing deterioration along the trail.*	Ⓒ Gov: permits → ↓ damage

Step 3: State the Goal

The Peruvian government claims that its permit program has been responsible for preventing deterioration along the Inca Trail. This is a cause-and-effect relationship. Since I need to strengthen the argument, the right answer should show that the permit program probably has reduced the damage.

Step 4: Work from Wrong to Right

(A) Since 2001, Incan ruins similar to Machu Picchu but without a visitor limit have disintegrated at a significantly greater rate than those on the Inca Trail.	*This sounds promising. The government's assumption was that the visitor limit helped prevent deterioration, so showing that other sites without limits did experience deterioration would make it more likely that the government's reasoning is valid. I'll definitely keep this one in.*	A ~
(B) Villages near Machu Picchu have experienced declines in income, as fewer tourists buy fewer craft goods and refreshments.	*This sounds bad for the villages, but it doesn't impact the specific claim about preventing deterioration along the trail.*	~~B~~
(C) Many of the funds from the sale of Inca Trail permits are used to hire guards for archaeological sites without permit programs.	*All this tells me is that* other *sites are better protected due to the guards. It doesn't tell me whether the program is protecting the Inca Trail itself.*	~~C~~
(D) Since 2001, tourist guides along the Inca Trail have received 50 percent to 100 percent increases in take-home pay.	*This doesn't tell me anything about the damage to the trail.*	~~D~~
(E) Due to limited enforcement, the majority of tourists hiking the Inca Trail currently do so without a permit.	***Reverse logic.*** *This one makes me think that even though only 500 people per day are allowed on the trail, the actual number is much higher. So, the permit program probably isn't working very well.*	~~E~~

(A) ~ ~~B~~ ~~C~~ ~~D~~ ~~E~~

20

6. Digital Video Recorders: The correct answer is **(C)**.

Did this one seem a little different from all of the others? We set a trap for you! This is a Find the Assumption question, not a Strengthen or a Weaken. We discussed Find the Assumption questions in the previous chapter (though we used a less common variant for the question wording, just to see whether you were paying attention). We did warn you at the beginning of this chapter to read the previous chapter first!

On the real test, you'll never have the luxury of knowing that the next question will be a certain type. Be prepared for *anything*.

Step 1: Identify the Question

Which of the following is required in order for the advertising executive to claim that television commercials are less cost-effective today?	*The words* required in order to claim *indicate that this is a Find the Assumption question.*	FA A B C D E

Step 2: Deconstruct the Argument

Advertising Executive: More than 10 million households now own digital video recorders that can fast-forward over television commercials;	*This is just a fact.*	Exec: 10 mill + HH's = DVR
approximately 75 percent of these households fast-forward over at least one commercial per 30-minute program.	*Another fact. I don't think I need to write down the exact numerical details right now, but I'll note that there are numerical details with a # just to remind myself.*	75 percent skip ads (#)
Because television commercials are not as widely watched as they used to be, they are much less cost-effective today.	*This contains another premise and the conclusion. The premise: TV ads aren't as widely watched today. The conclusion: TV ads are much less cost-effective than they used to be.*	B/c ads now watched less, ads = less cost eff

Step 3: State the Goal

Okay, the advertising executive claims that TV ads are not as cost-effective specifically because people aren't watching them as much, and that is specifically because a lot of people fast-forward over at least some commercials. I want an answer that the author must believe to be true in order to draw that conclusion. What assumptions are being made?

Let's see. They're assuming that people really did watch TV commercials more before, instead of changing channels or something. They're also assuming that if fewer people are watching, that's actually hurting the cost-effectiveness. Maybe commercials are worth more per viewer these days?

Step 4: Work from Wrong to Right

(A) Product placement within television programs is a viable alternative to traditional television commercials.	*That's nice for the advertisers who want to make money, but this doesn't have to be true in order to claim that TV commercials are less cost-effective now.*	~~A~~
(B) The television programs preferred by consumers without digital video recorders are similar to those preferred by consumers with the devices.	*The DVR thing was used as evidence to show how some people are skipping commercials. I don't think making a distinction about people with or without the DVRs really tells us anything. The conclusion is about commercials, not what programs people watch.*	~~B~~
(C) Prior to the advent of digital video recorders, very few television viewers switched channels or left the room when commercials began.	*That's interesting. People didn't used to change channels or leave the room, so maybe they really were watching more TV commercials. If I negate this answer, then it would say that people* did *switch channels or leave the room. If that were the case, then it'd be tough to claim that people watch fewer commercials nowadays. This choice looks good.*	C ~
(D) The cost-effectiveness of television advertising is based less upon how many people watch a particular commercial and more upon the appropriateness of the demographic.	*Hmm. They're saying that cost-effectiveness isn't measured based on how many people watch the commercials. That actually hurts the argument! If viewing doesn't matter for cost-effectiveness, then cost-effectiveness probably isn't going down. An assumption will never hurt the argument, so I can eliminate this.*	~~D~~
(E) The amount that television channels charge for advertisers to air commercials on their channel has increased steadily over the last decade.	*This definitely helps the argument, since it makes it seem like the commercials are less cost-effective now. But it isn't an assumption, because it doesn't have to be true for the argument to make sense. It would be helpful if it* was *true, but it's not a big deal if it isn't.*	~~E~~

~~A~~ ~~B~~ (C) ~~D~~ ~~E~~

7. APR: The correct answer is **(E)**. Remember to identify any Reverse Logic answers before you read the explanation!

Step 1: Identify the Question

Which of the following statements, if true, would most seriously undermine a plan to increase interest rates in order to spur profitable growth?	*The* undermine *and* if true *language indicates that this is a Weaken question. Further, the question stem tells me the conclusion: There's a plan to increase interest rates that will supposedly cause profits to grow.*	W A B C D E Ⓒ Plan: ↑ int rats → ↑ prof growth

Step 2: Deconstruct the Argument

CEO: Over the past several years, we have more than doubled our revenues, but profits have steadily declined because an increasing number of customers have failed to pay their balances.	*Several facts here. Revenues have gone up but profits have gone down because the customers aren't paying what they owe.*	CEO: 2x rev but ↓ prof b/c cust not pay bills
In order to compensate for these higher default rates, we will increase the interest charged on outstanding balances from an annual percentage rate (APR) of 9.5 percent to an APR of 12 percent.	*Okay, here's the plan. They'll charge more interest to everyone to compensate for the people who aren't paying their bills.*	↑ percent int rate to comp
This increase will be sufficient to compensate for the current rate of defaults and allow us to increase our profits.	*Hmm. They're claiming that 12 percent will be enough to compensate for the* current *rate of people who don't pay so that they can increase profits (which is the conclusion I already wrote down). They're assuming that the current rate isn't going to get worse in the future.*	12 percent will be enough

Step 3: State the Goal

The company plans to charge higher interest rates in order to become profitable again. This is a Weaken question, so the right answer should show that this might not actually help profits.

Step 4: Work from Wrong to Right

(A) Many other companies have experienced a similar trend in their default rates.	*This doesn't address the company's plan to fix the problem: increasing the interest rate. This doesn't impact the conclusion at all.*	~~A~~
(B) The company's operating expenses are above the industry average and can be substantially reduced, thus increasing margins.	*If the company does this, it could increase profits, which is the company's goal. . .but the conclusion is that the plan to increase interest rates will improve profits. The right answer needs to weaken that specific plan, not the company's goal in general.*	~~B~~
(C) The increase in default rates was due to a rise in unemployment, but unemployment rates are expected to drop in the coming months.	***Reverse logic.*** *If unemployment caused people not to pay their bills, and fewer people are going to be unemployed, then maybe more will pay their bills? That would help the company, but I want something that will weaken the conclusion. This isn't even a great strengthener, since it doesn't talk about the actual plan in the argument.*	~~C~~
(D) The proposed increase in the APR will, alone, more than double the company's profit margins.	***Reverse logic.*** *This supports the company's claim that increasing the interest rate will help raise profits. I want something that weakens that claim.*	~~D~~
(E) An increase in the APR charged on credit card balances often results in higher rates of default.	*Okay, if they do increase the APR, then more people may stop paying their bills as a result! The conclusion specifically said that raising the APR would compensate for the* current rate of defaults, *so if the rate goes up, then the company is less likely to increase its profits. This does weaken the conclusion.*	E ~

~~A~~ ~~B~~ ~~C~~ ~~D~~ (E ~)

20

8. Jupiter vs. Mars: The correct answer is **(D)**. Remember to identify any Reverse Logic answers before you read the explanation!

Step 1: Identify the Question

Which of the following, if true, would most strengthen a contention by the government that the new project is a better use of its funds?	*The words* if true *and* strengthen a contention *indicate that this is a Strengthen question. The conclusion is also in the question stem: that the critics are wrong.*	S A B C D E Ⓒ Gov: critics wrong

Step 2: Deconstruct the Argument

Scientists suspect that Europa, a moon orbiting Jupiter, may contain living organisms.	*There is a fact: Scientists suspect something is true. I don't actually know whether it's true, though.*	Sci: Europa may have life
However, the government recently scrapped an unmanned science mission to Europa and replaced it with a project aimed at landing an astronaut on Mars.	*There was a project to send an unmanned mission to Europa, but that was replaced by another project to send a person to Mars. More facts.*	Ⓒ BUT gov replaced w/ Mars proj
Polls show that the public is far more fascinated by space travel than by discovering life elsewhere in the universe.	*More facts—a survey showed that people like space travel more.*	Ppl like space travel more
Critics argue that the government's decision-making process places a greater emphasis on popularity than it does on the importance of scientific research.	*This is a counterconclusion. The critics say that the government is just paying attention to popularity of projects, but the question stem told me that the government claims that the new project is a better use of funds.*	Critics: gov cares more ab popularity

Step 3: State the goal.

There are two opposing points of view, the government and the critics. The government claims that the critics are wrong. So, the government is claiming that it doesn't actually care more about popularity than about science. I need to strengthen that claim by showing that the government actually does care about science. I should be really careful not to strengthen the critics' claim, which is that the government cares more about popularity!

Step 4: Work from wrong to right.

(A) In the first year of the project, the government will spend 30 percent of its total budget on developing a space shuttle that can travel to Mars; that figure is expected to drop to 0 percent after five years.	*This doesn't give me any additional information as to why the Mars project is better than the Europa project. I don't know whether they'd be spending more or less on the Europa project, nor do I know what kind of good research they'll expect to get in return.*	~~A~~
(B) The government cannot be absolutely certain of the chances for success of either project.	*Was there anything in the argument that hinged on being absolutely certain of success? No. If they told me that the Mars project has a greater chance for success, that would be good—but knowing that, I* don't *know the chances for either project...that doesn't add anything.*	~~B~~
(C) Some scientists are convinced that a mission to Europa would add immeasurably to our understanding of the universe.	***Reverse logic.*** *This one tells me that the Europa mission is important for science. But, the government didn't fund it! That makes it more likely that the government only cares about popularity. So, this strengthens the critics' argument, not the government's.*	~~C~~
(D) A new telescope that has just become available to scientists promises to yield more information than the planned mission to Europa was designed to provide.	*Now they have a new telescope that they can use to get even more research than they would have if they sent an unmanned mission? It looks like the government canceled the Europa mission because it wasn't the best choice for science, not because it was less popular! Maybe the government really does care about science.*	D ~
(E) Most people feel that a shuttle to Mars would represent a first step towards an extensive program of space travel.	*This explains why people find the shuttle to Mars interesting, but it doesn't actually tell me anything new about the government's decision. It still looks like the government picked this program because it was popular with many people, regardless of the reason that it was popular.*	~~E~~

~~A~~ ~~B~~ ~~C~~ (D) ~~E~~

20

9. Deep-Brain Stimulation: The correct answer is **(D)**. Remember to identify any Reverse Logic answers before you read the explanation!

Step 1: Identify the Question

Which of the following most logically completes the argument given below?	*The blank at the end signals a Fill in the Blank format. The word* because *just before the blank indicates that this is a Strengthen question.*	S A B C D E

Step 2: Deconstruct the Argument

Deep-brain stimulation is a new technique for combating severe depression.	*Straight fact.*	Deep-brain stim combats depression
In a recent experiment, electrodes were implanted into the brains of six patients who had not responded to any currently approved treatment for depression.	*This tells me how it works and that they tested it on six people.*	Tested on 6 ppl
When an electrical current to the electrodes was switched on, four of the patients reported feeling a dramatic reduction in depressive symptoms.	*And four of the people got a lot better.*	4 better
The long-term prospects of the new treatment are not promising, however, because ______________.	*Oh, but the author thinks the treatment's not really going to work long-term. Why?*	Ⓒ BUT probably won't work, b/c . . .

Step 3: State the Goal

The author describes a new medical treatment but says it's probably not going to be good long-term; I need to find a reason why. The right answer should say something negative about the treatment's long-term prospects.

Step 4: Work from Wrong to Right

(A) other treatments for depression may also be effective	*Talking about other treatments doesn't explain why deep-brain stimulation won't be a good treatment long-term. The conclusion is only about deep-brain stimulation, not about depression treatment in general.*	~~A~~
(B) the other two patients reported only a slight reduction of depressive symptoms during the treatment	*This looks like a negative at first glance, but then I remembered that the first four patients were helped dramatically. Technically, the treatment helped every patient! That doesn't hurt the treatment's prospects.*	~~B~~
(C) deep-brain stimulation relies on the expertise of highly skilled physicians	*This is probably true, but the right answer needs to be a downside of the treatment. Is relying on the expertise of physicians a downside? Possibly, but it's a real stretch. I'd have to assume that requiring skilled physicians has other consequences, like increasing the cost—and I don't know that.*	~~C~~
(D) when the electrical current is interrupted, the effects of the treatment are reversed	*When the current is on, the symptoms go away, but when the current is off, the depression comes back. That means they'd have to be connected to some machine all the time—they couldn't just get a treatment once a week or once a month. That definitely makes the treatment less practical and promising. Unless choice (E) is better, this looks like the answer.*	D ~
(E) in a subsequent experiment, a one-hour treatment with the electrodes resulted in a sustained remission from depression in the four patients for six months	***Reverse logic.*** *This is almost the opposite of choice (D). If you get a one-hour treatment, then the symptoms go away for 6 months—that's great for deep-brain stimulation! This can't be the right answer.*	~~E~~

~~A~~ ~~B~~ ~~C~~ (D ~) ~~E~~

20

CHAPTER 21

The Assumption Family: Evaluate the Argument and Find the Flaw

In This Chapter:

- Evaluate the Argument Questions
- The Strengthen/Weaken Strategy
- Find the Flaw Questions
- Evaluate the Argument Cheat Sheet
- Find the Flaw Cheat Sheet

In this chapter, you will learn how to apply your knowledge of Strengthen and Weaken questions to the fourth type of Assumption question: Evaluate. You will also learn how to address the final (and not very common) Assumption question type: Flaw.

Chapter 21 The Assumption Family: Evaluate the Argument and Find the Flaw

In the previous two chapters, you learned about the three major question types in the Assumption Family: Find the Assumption, Strengthen, and Weaken. If you haven't read those chapters yet, please do so before reading this chapter.

In addition, think about how much time you want to put into this chapter. **Evaluate the Argument** questions are somewhat uncommon—you'll most likely see just one or two. **Find the Flaw** questions are even rarer. If you have a very high Verbal goal (90th percentile or higher), then study these two question types. If your Verbal score goal is lower, consider guessing on Flaw questions. If you struggle with Evaluate questions, you might want to guess on those as well.

The Assumption lessons you learned earlier still apply to Evaluate and Flaw questions:

- Assumptions are something an author must believe to be true in order to draw his or her conclusion. These assumptions are not stated explicitly in the argument.
- All assumption arguments will contain a core: a conclusion and the major premise or premises that lead to it.
- All assumption arguments will include at least one (and probably more than one) unstated assumption.

Evaluate the Argument Questions

For Evaluate questions, your first step is still to find an assumption, but you have to do a little more work to get to the answer. At heart, you are asked what additional information would help to determine whether the assumption is valid or invalid.

Most Evaluate question stems will contain one or more of the following:

- The word *evaluate* or a synonym
- The word *determine* or a synonym
- Language asking what would be *useful to know* (or *establish*) or *important to know*

For example, an Evaluate question stem might ask:

> Which of the following must be studied in order to evaluate the argument?
>
> Which of the following would it be most useful to know in determining whether the mayor's plan is likely to be successful?

Occasionally, an Evaluate question will use other wording, but the question will still get at the same overall idea—what information would help to evaluate the given argument? That information, if made available, would either strengthen or weaken that argument.

The Strengthen/Weaken Strategy

Evaluate answer choices will often be in the form of a question or in the form of a "one way or the other" statement. Imagine you have to take a stand on whether you agree with the conclusion of the argument: What question would you ask the author to help your decision? For example, say you're asked to evaluate this argument:

> In order to increase its profits, MillCo plans to reduce costs by laying off any nonessential employees.

Hmm. According to the argument:

> MillCo will lay off nonessential employees → reduce costs → increase profits

Does that sound like a good plan? What additional information would help you evaluate this plan?

Profits are equal to revenues minus costs. The argument says costs will go down, but no information is given about revenues. It seems pretty important to have some information about revenues to draw a conclusion about profits. One question might be: How will revenues be affected by this plan?

The question associated with the argument and the correct answer might read:

> Which of the following would be most important to determine to evaluate the argument?
>
> Whether revenues will be affected adversely enough to threaten MillCo's profit structure

This *whether* does something very interesting to the argument. Imagine that you could find out whether revenues will be affected adversely. The argument would be strengthened one way and weakened the other. Take a look:

> Yes, the plan *will* affect MillCo's revenues adversely enough to threaten profits. In this case, the plan to increase profits is less likely to work, so the argument is weakened.
>
> No, the plan *won't* affect MillCo's revenues adversely enough to threaten profits. In this case, the plan to increase profits is a little more likely to work, so the argument is strengthened.

If the answer goes one way, the argument is strengthened, and if it goes the other way, the argument is weakened.

The correct answer will be structured in such a way that these two possible "paths" exist, one strengthening and one weakening the argument.

The incorrect answers will be presented in a similar format, but won't actually test the strength of the argument. What if you had the following answer choice?

> Whether MillCo might reduce its costs more by eliminating some health insurance benefits for the remaining employees

Evaluate the two paths:

> Yes, MillCo can reduce costs more by eliminating some health benefits. How will this affect the given plan to lay off employees? Technically, this doesn't impact whether laying off certain employees will improve profits. It is true that reducing costs could help to increase profits, but the argument specifies that MillCo will reduce costs specifically by laying off nonessential employees. Whether the company could also reduce costs in some other way has no bearing on this specific argument.
>
> No, MillCo cannot reduce costs more by eliminating some health benefits. This certainly doesn't strengthen the argument. It doesn't weaken the argument either, though, since the argument hinges on laying off employees. This path does nothing to the argument.

This incorrect answer choice is trying to distract you by offering a different way to increase profits, but you aren't asked to find alternative ways to increase profits. You're asked to evaluate whether the *existing argument* involving this particular path to profits is valid. The answer doesn't provide a strengthen/weaken pair here, so the choice cannot be the right answer.

On Evaluate questions, after reading the question, you're going to focus on the argument:

> First, find the core (conclusion plus major premises).
>
> Second, briefly think about the questions you have or additional information you would want in order to evaluate the conclusion.

As you move to the answer choices, look for an answer similar to the questions you identified. Make sure to be flexible because the correct answer may not be something you identified. The correct answer should offer two different paths: one that would make the argument stronger and one that would make the argument weaker.

Try a full example; set your timer for 2 minutes. If you get stuck, pick an answer before you read the explanation. During the real test, you'll have to pick an answer in order to move on, so practice letting go and guessing.

> Food allergies account for more than 30,000 emergency room visits each year. Often, victims of these episodes are completely unaware of their allergies until they experience a major reaction. Studies show that 90 percent of food allergy reactions are caused by only eight distinct foods. For this reason, parents should feed a minuscule portion of each of these foods to their children to determine whether the children have these particular food allergies.
>
> Which of the following must be studied in order to evaluate the recommendation made in the argument?
>
> (A) The percentage of allergy victims who were not aware of the allergy before a major episode
> (B) The percentage of the population that is at risk for allergic reactions
> (C) Whether some of the eight foods are common ingredients used in cooking
> (D) Whether an allergy to one type of food makes someone more likely to be allergic to other types of food
> (E) Whether ingesting a very small amount of an allergen is sufficient to provoke an allergic reaction in a susceptible individual

Step 1: Identify the Question

Which of the following must be studied in order to evaluate the recommendation made in the argument?	*The words* must be studied *and* evaluate *indicate that this is an Evaluate question.*	Ev A B C D E

Step 2: Deconstruct the Argument

Food allergies account for more than 30,000 emergency room visits each year.	*This is a fact.*	Food allerg → 30k ER/yr
Often, victims of these episodes are completely unaware of their allergies until they experience a major reaction.	*Fact, but more fuzzy. A lot of people don't know they're allergic till they have a major reaction.*	Ppl unaware till have rxn
Studies show that 90 percent of food allergy reactions are caused by only eight distinct foods.	*More facts! That's interesting. Only eight foods cause most allergic reactions.*	Only 8 foods → 90 percent rxn
For this reason, parents should feed a minuscule portion of each of these foods to their children to determine whether the children have these particular food allergies.	*This is the conclusion. The author's saying parent should give a tiny bit of these eight foods to see what happens.*	Ⓒ Give child tiny bit of 8 foods to test

Step 3: State the Goal

This is an Evaluate question, so I need to find an answer that will help to determine whether or not the conclusion is likely to be valid. The correct answer will have two paths: one path will make the conclusion a little more likely to be valid and the other will make the conclusion a little less likely to be valid.

In this case, the author recommends that we all try tiny bits of these eight foods to see whether we're allergic. What will help determine if this is a good idea? Could these tests actually cause harm if children have severe reactions to the sample amounts? Will these tests actually work? How much do you need to eat to cause an allergic reaction (are the minuscule bits enough)?

Step 4: Work from Wrong to Right

(A) The percentage of allergy victims who were not aware of the allergy before a major episode	*The argument said that victims* often *aren't aware of the allergy beforehand. If I knew that 90 percent weren't aware, that would go along with what the argument already says. If I knew that 50 percent weren't aware...hmm, that wouldn't change the argument. In general, knowing the exact percentage doesn't change anything.*	~~A~~

(B) The percentage of the population that is at risk for allergic reactions	*If a really high percentage is at risk for allergies, then it's probably important to figure out whether people are allergic...but that doesn't mean that the specific recommendation in the conclusion here is a good one or bad one. Also, this answer choice doesn't specifically limit itself to food allergies; it mentions all allergies in general.*	~~B~~
(C) Whether some of the eight foods are common ingredients used in cooking	*If yes, then many people may have already tried small amounts of these foods. That doesn't actually tell me, though, whether the recommendation is a good one. If no, then it doesn't affect the conclusion at all—I still don't know whether it's a good recommendation.*	~~C~~
(D) Whether an allergy to one type of food makes someone more likely to be allergic to other types of food	*If yes or if no, I'd still want to test people to see whether they're allergic to anything. This choice doesn't have two paths that lead to alternate outcomes.*	~~D~~
(E) Whether ingesting a very small amount of an allergen is sufficient to provoke an allergic reaction in a susceptible individual	*If yes, then the author's plan will work: Children will be able to try small amounts and determine whether they're allergic. If no, then the author's plan is not a good one: Trying small amounts won't actually help you tell whether a child is allergic.*	E ~

~~A~~ ~~B~~ ~~C~~ ~~D~~ (E)

In the prior example, although the student brainstormed a relevant question in step 3, it was not available as an answer choice. Make sure not to get hung up on the specific questions you thought of when working through the answers; most arguments have multiple relevant questions and only one will be in the answer choices.

Correct Answers

The correct answer will be information important to determining if the the conclusion is valid. You don't get follow-up questions on the GMAT. The answer to the question in the correct answer choice must help you evaluate the conclusion on its own without any additional information or clarification. One answer to the question posed in the correct answer will clearly strengthen the argument and the other will clearly weaken it.

Common Trap Answers

The incorrect answers are very tricky. How do the test writers get you to pick trap answers on Evaluate questions?

No Effect on the Conclusion

Answer (C) presented something that seemed like it would matter: Maybe lots of people have already tried the eight foods. What does that mean for the recommendation? Maybe some people have already had reactions to some foods. But some people might have tried only six of the eight, so maybe they should still try the other two. Or, maybe...You could speculate endlessly, but all paths lead to the same place: This choice doesn't impact whether the specific recommendation made is good or bad.

The correct answer should *clearly strengthen* the conclusion if it goes one way and *clearly weaken* if it goes the other. Be careful of answers that only *might strengthen* or *might weaken* or *might do nothing*, especially if you need additional information to make the determination.

Irrelevant Distinction or Comparison

You saw this trap for the first time in the Find the Assumption chapter. In the problem above, answer (D) does discuss something mentioned by the argument—allergies—but tries to talk about whether someone might have more than one allergy; this is not at issue in the argument. The argument only distinguishes those with allergies and those without.

Find the Flaw Questions

Find the Flaw questions are the least common of the five Assumption Family question types. The question stems will almost always contain some form of the word *flaw*, but be careful: Weaken the Argument questions also might contain the word *flaw* in the question stem.

Here's how to tell the difference. Weaken questions will also contain *if true* language. Flaw questions will *not* contain this language. Take a look at the chart below:

Flaw	Weaken
Look for this first:	
Contains the word *flaw* but NOT *if true* language.	Contains the word *flaw* AND the words *if true* (or an equivalent synonym).
If you're still not sure, try this:	
Answer choices are a bit more abstract, similar to but not as abstract as Structure Family questions.	Answer choices represent a new piece of information (as described in the discussion of the Weaken question type).
Example:	
Which of the following indicates a *flaw* in the reasoning above?	Which of the following, *if true*, would indicate a *flaw* in the teacher's plan?

On occasion, a Flaw question may contain a synonym of the word *flaw*, such as *vulnerable to criticism.*

As with the other Assumption Family questions, Find the Flaw questions will contain an argument core, and it's great if you notice assumptions that the author makes. The correct answer, though, will be essentially the opposite of the correct answer on a Find the Assumption question. On Find the Assumption, you pick an answer that articulates an assumption that is necessary to the argument. On Flaw questions, by contrast, you are looking for wording that indicates why it is *flawed* thinking to believe that this assumption is true.

For example:

> Pierre was recovering from the flu when he visited Shelley last week, and now Shelley is showing signs of the flu. If Pierre had waited until he was no longer contagious, Shelley would not have become ill.

The author is assuming that Pierre was definitely the one to infect Shelley. The author is also assuming that there is no other way Shelley could have gotten sick. Perhaps it is flu season, and many people with whom Shelley came in contact had the flu!

The correct answer might be something like:

> The author fails to consider that there are alternate paths by which Shelley could have become infected.

Contrast that language with the assumption itself: The author assumes that only Pierre could have infected Shelley. If that's true, then that piece of information at least partially fixes the author's argument. When you take the same information, though, and flip it around into a flaw, you harm the author's argument:

Pierre was recovering from the flu when he visited Shelley last week, and now Shelley is showing signs of the flu. If Pierre had waited until he was no longer contagious, Shelley would not have become ill.	
Assumption	*Flaw*
Only Pierre could have infected Shelley.	The author fails to consider that there are alternate paths by which Shelley could have become infected.
The argument is made stronger.	*The argument is made weaker.*

In sum, think of Flaw questions as the "reverse" of Assumption questions. The answer still hinges on an assumption, but the correct answer will word that assumption in a way that hurts the argument.

In addition, the answer choice language may be a bit more abstract than the answer choices on other Assumption Family questions. Often, the answer choices will talk about what the author "fails to consider (or establish)," "does not specify (or identify)," or something along those lines.

Try this full example:

> Environmentalist: Bando Inc.'s manufacturing process releases pollution into the atmosphere. In order to convince the company to change processes, we will organize a boycott of the product that represents its highest sales volume, light bulbs. Because Bando sells more light bulbs than any other product, a boycott of light bulbs will cause the most damage to the company's profits.
>
> The environmentalist's reasoning is flawed because it fails to
>
> (A) allow for the possibility that Bando may not want to change its manufacturing process
> (B) supply information about other possible ways for Bando to reduce pollution
> (C) consider that the relative sales volumes of a company's products are not necessarily proportional to profits
> (D) identify any alternate methods by which to convince Bando to change its manufacturing process
> (E) consider that a boycott may take too long to achieve its purpose

Step 1: Identify the Question

The environmentalist's reasoning is flawed because it fails to	*The word* flawed *indicates that this is either a Flaw or a Weaken question.* If true *does not appear, so this is a Flaw question. I'll write down "Fl" on my scrap paper.*	Fl A B C D E

Step 2: Deconstruct the Argument

Environmentalist: Bando Inc.'s manufacturing process releases pollution into the atmosphere.	*This is a fact (assume the environmentalist is telling the truth).*	Environ-ist: manuf → atmo pollutn
In order to convince the company to change processes, we will organize a boycott of the product that represents its highest sales volume, light bulbs.	*Okay, here's a plan, so it's likely a conclusion. They think if they boycott something, this company might change its manufacturing process. So they're going to boycott light bulbs because Bando sells more light bulbs than anything else.*	boyc bulbs (↑ sales) → so company Δ manuf
Because Bando sells more light bulbs than any other product, a boycott of light bulbs will cause the most damage to the company's profits.	*Another claim. Because they sell more light bulbs than anything else, the environmentalist figures that a boycott of light bulbs will do the most damage to profits. Profits? How profitable are the light bulbs?* *Okay, the conclusion was the previous sentence, because all of this is designed to convince Bando to change its manufacturing process.*	Bando sells ↑ bulbs → boyc → ↑ damage to prof

Step 3: State the Goal

The environmentalist doesn't like that Bando pollutes. Bando sells more light bulbs than any other product, so the environmentalist wants to boycott those bulbs to do the most damage to Bando's profits (according to this environmentalist, anyway), and then the hope is that this will all cause the company to change its manufacturing process.

I need to find an answer that will articulate a flaw in that reasoning. I've already thought of one. The environmentalist is assuming that just because Bando sells more light bulbs than anything else, the company is also earning the most profits from those products. But there's no evidence to support that. Also, consumers might not actually agree to boycott Bando.

Step 4: Work from Wrong to Right

(A) allow for the possibility that Bando may not want to change its manufacturing process	*If anything, it could be argued that the environmentalist is already assuming the company* will not *want to change—that's why the environmentalist thinks he or she has to organize a boycott to change the company's mind!*	~~A~~
(B) does not supply information about other possible ways for Bando to reduce pollution	*In the real world, I agree that environmentalists should explore all possible ways...but the question asks me to find a flaw in this particular plan about the boycott. This doesn't apply to that plan.*	~~B~~

(C) consider that the relative sales volumes of a company's products are not necessarily proportional to profits	*This sounds kind of like what I said before. It's a little abstract, so I'm not sure I fully understand all of it, but it does say that sales aren't necessarily proportional to profits. I'll keep this one in.*	C ~
(D) identify any alternative methods by which to convince Bando to change its manufacturing process	*This is like choice (B). It'd be good in general for the environmentalist to do this...but this doesn't help me figure out a flaw in the boycott plan specifically.*	~~D~~
(E) consider that a boycott may take too long to achieve its purpose	*I think what really matters is whether the plan is going to work at all, not how long it takes. The argument doesn't have any requirements about how long it will take to get Bando to change its process.*	~~E~~

~~A~~ ~~B~~ (C) ~~D~~ ~~E~~

Common Trap Answers

Irrelevant Distinction or Comparison

This trap discusses alternative plans or paths when you were asked to comment on the given plan, similar to answers (B) and (D) in the example above. A choice can also bring up a detail or distinction that does not actually affect the argument, similar to choice (E) in the problem above.

Flaw questions may also occasionally use Reverse Logic, similar to answer choice (A) in the example above.

Evaluate the Argument Cheat Sheet

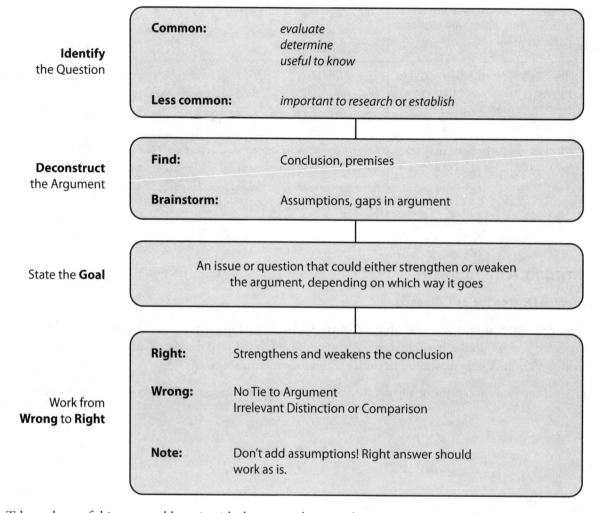

Identify the Question	**Common:**	*evaluate* *determine* *useful to know*
	Less common:	*important to research* or *establish*
Deconstruct the Argument	**Find:**	Conclusion, premises
	Brainstorm:	Assumptions, gaps in argument
State the **Goal**		An issue or question that could either strengthen *or* weaken the argument, depending on which way it goes
Work from **Wrong** to **Right**	**Right:**	Strengthens and weakens the conclusion
	Wrong:	No Tie to Argument Irrelevant Distinction or Comparison
	Note:	Don't add assumptions! Right answer should work as is.

Take a photo of this page and keep it with the review sheets you're creating as you study. Better yet, use this page as a guide to create your own review sheet—you'll remember the material better if you write it down yourself.

Find the Flaw Cheat Sheet

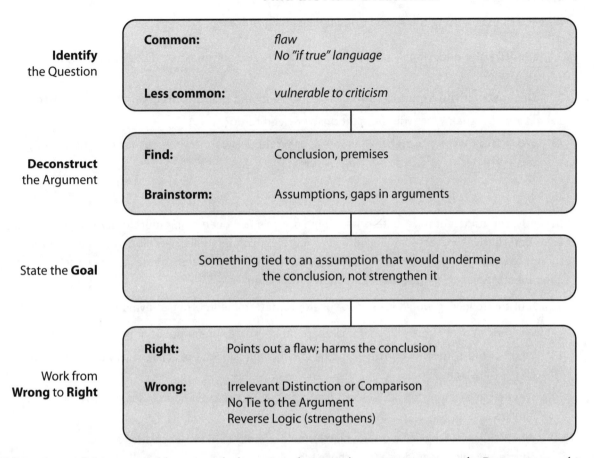

Step		
Identify the Question	**Common:**	*flaw* *No "if true" language*
	Less common:	*vulnerable to criticism*
Deconstruct the Argument	**Find:**	Conclusion, premises
	Brainstorm:	Assumptions, gaps in arguments
State the **Goal**		Something tied to an assumption that would undermine the conclusion, not strengthen it
Work from **Wrong** to **Right**	**Right:**	Points out a flaw; harms the conclusion
	Wrong:	Irrelevant Distinction or Comparison No Tie to the Argument Reverse Logic (strengthens)

Take a photo of this page and keep it with the review sheets you're creating as you study. Better yet, use this page as a guide to create your own review sheet—you'll remember the material better if you write it down yourself.

Problem Set

Answer each question using the 4-step Critical Reasoning process.

1. **Identify the question:** Is this an Evaluate the Argument question or a Find the Flaw question?
2. **Deconstruct the argument:** Find the conclusion and map the argument on your paper.
3. **State the goal:** What will the right answer need to do?
4. **Work from wrong to right:** Eliminate four wrong answers. Watch out for common wrong answer types.

1. *Tuition*

Recently, the tuition at most elite private high schools has been rising more quickly than inflation. Even before these increases, many low- and middle-income families were unable to afford the full tuition costs for their children at these schools. With the new tuition increases, these schools will soon be attended solely by students from affluent families.

Which of the following would it be most useful to determine in order to evaluate the argument?

(A) Whether students from affluent families are more likely to prefer public or private high schools

(B) Whether most students from low- and middle-income families are academically qualified to attend elite private high schools

(C) Whether low-income families are less likely to be able to afford tuition costs than middle-income families

(D) Whether graduates of elite private high schools typically earn higher salaries as adults than do people who did not graduate from these schools

(E) Whether grants or scholarships are available for students from economically disadvantaged families

2. *Charity*

Studies show that impoverished families give away a larger percentage of their income in charitable donations than do wealthy families. As a result, fundraising consultants recommend that charities direct their marketing efforts toward individuals and families from lower socioeconomic classes in order to maximize the dollar value of incoming donations.

Which of the following best explains why the consultants' reasoning is flawed?

(A) Marketing efforts are only one way to solicit charitable donations.

(B) Not all impoverished families donate to charity.

(C) Some charitable marketing efforts are so expensive that the resulting donations fail to cover the costs of the marketing campaign.

(D) Percentage of income is not necessarily indicative of absolute dollar value.

(E) People are more likely to donate to the same causes to which their friends donate.

3. *CostMart*

Editorial: To avoid increasing the unemployment rate in the city of Dorwall, a CostMart warehouse department store should not be permitted to open within city limits. In the past, when CostMart has opened a new warehouse department store in a city, up to 20 percent of local retailers—which, in Dorwall, primarily employ local residents—have closed within the next three years.

Which of the following questions would be most useful for evaluating the conclusion of the editorial?

(A) Does the bankruptcy rate of local retailers in a city generally stabilize several years after a CostMart warehouse department store opens?

(B) Are the majority of residents of Dorwall currently employed within the city limits?

(C) Will the number of jobs created by the opening of the CostMart warehouse store be greater than the number of jobs that will be lost when local retailers close?

(D) Have other cities that have permitted CostMart warehouse stores to open within city limits experienced an increase in unemployment within the city?

(E) Does CostMart plan to hire employees exclusively from within Dorwall for the proposed warehouse department store?

4. *Bicycle Manufacturing*

Bicycle Manufacturer: Switching our focus from building aluminum bicycles to primarily building carbon-fiber bicycles will reduce the time taken by our manufacturing process. Although the initial construction of aluminum bicycle frames was significantly faster and simpler than the construction of carbon-fiber frames, each weld in an aluminum frame then needed to be individually checked for integrity. This required that substantial time be spent on quality control to avoid shipping out any defective frames.

Which of the following would be most useful in evaluating the claim made in the argument?

(A) Whether factory workers will require additional training in order to manufacture carbon bicycle frames

(B) Whether the carbon manufacturing process is likely to require time-consuming quality checks

(C) Whether aluminum bicycle frames with defective welds can be fixed or must be thrown away

(D) Whether there are improvements that could be introduced that would significantly reduce the rate of defects in aluminum bicycle frames

(E) Whether the demand for carbon-fiber bicycles is as high as the demand for aluminum bicycles

5. *Ethanol*

Ethanol, a fuel derived from corn, can be used alone to power vehicles or along with gasoline to reduce the amount of gasoline consumed. Compared with conventional gasoline, pure ethanol produces significantly less pollution per gallon used. In order to combat pollution, many individuals advocate the increased usage of ethanol as a fuel source for vehicles in conjunction with or in place of gasoline.

In evaluating the recommendation to increase the use of ethanol, it would be most important to research which of the following?

(A) Whether the majority of existing vehicles are capable of using ethanol for fuel, either alone or in conjunction with gasoline

(B) Whether the process of growing corn to produce ethanol results in significant amounts of pollution

(C) Whether completely replacing gasoline with ethanol results in less pollution than using ethanol in conjunction with gasoline

(D) Whether ethanol is more expensive to produce than conventional gasoline

(E) Whether there are some vehicles in which using ethanol fuel would not result in a significant reduction in pollution compared to conventional gasoline

21

Solutions

1. Tuition: The correct answer is **(E)**.

Step 1: Identify the Question

Which of the following would it be most useful to determine in order to evaluate the argument?	*Contains the words* evaluate *and* useful to determine—*this is an Evaluate question.*	Ev A B C D E

Step 2: Deconstruct the Argument

Recently, the tuition at most elite private high schools has been rising more quickly than inflation.	*Fact: Tuition at this specific type of school has been going up even faster than inflation.*	↑ priv HS tuit > infl
Even before these increases, many low- and middle-income families were unable to afford the full tuition costs for their children at these schools.	*And many people without much money already couldn't afford these schools, even before the tuition went up. Another fact.*	B4: mid inc fams can't afford
With the new tuition increases, these schools will soon be attended solely by students from affluent families.	*This must be the conclusion because the other two were facts, and this is a prediction about the future. Basically, they're saying that only wealthy students are going to be able to afford these schools now.*	© Priv HS will have only rich students

Step 3: State the Goal

This is an Evaluate question, so I need to find an answer that will help to determine whether or not the conclusion is likely to be valid. The correct answer will have two paths: One path will make the conclusion a little more likely to be valid and the other will make the conclusion a little less likely to be valid.

The conclusion is that only *wealthy students are going to be able to go to these elite private high schools. What is the author assuming? That there's no way that students from lower-income families can attend these schools: Their families can't take out loans, they can't receive scholarships, etc.*

21

Step 4: Work from Wrong to Right

(A) Whether students from affluent families are more likely to prefer public or private high schools	*The conclusion is that private high schools will only have wealthy students, not that all wealthy students will go to private schools. Even if most wealthy students go to public schools, private schools won't suddenly become affordable for other students. So, this doesn't affect the conclusion.*	~~A~~
(B) Whether most students from low- and middle-income families are academically qualified to attend elite private high schools	*This is interesting. Maybe the lower-income students aren't actually qualified to go to these schools. But on the other hand, regardless of whether they're qualified, they won't be able to afford them! So the conclusion is equally strong either way: If the low-income students are qualified, they can't afford the schools, so they won't attend. And if they aren't qualified, they also won't attend. Either way, these high schools will only be attended by students from wealthy families.*	~~B~~
(C) Whether low-income families are less likely to be able to afford tuition costs than middle-income families	*This answer makes a distinction between low- and middle-income families, but the argument doesn't distinguish between these two groups—it combines them. Logically, it would make sense that the less money a family has, the less likely it could afford the tuition...but this doesn't change anything about the basic argument that low- and middle-income families can't afford the tuition.*	~~C~~
(D) Whether graduates of elite private high schools typically earn higher salaries as adults than do people who did not graduate from these schools	*This answer choice discusses the consequences of attending one of these private high schools. However, the conclusion deals with whether certain students can attend these schools in the first place. The outcome of attending a private school doesn't influence whether a student will be able to afford to attend.*	E ~
(E) Whether grants or scholarships are available for students from economically disadvantaged families	*If there are grants and scholarships for lower-income students, then perhaps they can afford to attend these schools—this hurts the argument's conclusion. If there are no grants and scholarships for these students, then the argument's conclusion is more likely to be true: These students won't be able to afford these schools. This answer can either strengthen or weaken the argument, so it's correct.*	E ~

~~A~~ ~~B~~ ~~C~~ ~~D~~ (E)

2. Charity: The correct answer is **(D)**.

Step 1: Identify the Question

Which of the following best explains why the consultants' reasoning is flawed?	*The word* flawed *indicates that this is either a Flaw or Weaken question. The lack of the words* if true *(or an equivalent) means that this is a Flaw question.*	F A B C D E

Step 2: Deconstruct the Argument

Studies show that impoverished families give away a larger percentage of their income in charitable donations than do wealthy families.	*This is a fact. It's impressive that the poor donate anything, but if they do donate anything, then this fact makes sense because donating $100 is a much greater percentage of your income if you don't have much income.*	Poor donate > % inc than rich
As a result, fundraising consultants recommend that charities direct their marketing efforts toward individuals and families from lower socioeconomic classes in order to maximize the dollar value of incoming donations.	*This is the conclusion. Based on the percentage info, the consultants are saying that the charities should focus on lower-income people...but the consultants are assuming that* greater percentage *equals* more money*. A very rich person might donate $10 million, a small percentage of income but a very large sum.*	© Consultants: to get most $, char shld focus on ↓ inc ppl

Step 3: State the Goal

For Flaw questions, it's important to find the conclusion and brainstorm any assumptions, if I can. I need to find an answer that hurts the argument or shows why the argument is not a good argument.

In this case, the fundraising consultants are recommending that the charities target lower-income families in order to maximize the number of dollars they get in donations. I've identified one potential assumption: The consultants assume that donating a greater percentage of income also means donating a greater dollar amount collectively. If that's not actually the case, then that's a flaw.

Step 4: Work from Wrong to Right

(A) Marketing efforts are only one way to solicit charitable donations.	*This might be true, but it just indicates that there might be other ways, in addition to marketing efforts, to raise money. That doesn't affect the consultants' recommendation to target lower-income families in particular.*	~~A~~
(B) Not all impoverished families donate to charity.	*I'm sure this is true, but how does it affect the conclusion? It doesn't. The argument never claims that ALL impoverished families donate to charity—only that, in general, they donate a larger percentage of income to charity.*	~~B~~
(C) Some charitable marketing efforts are so expensive that the resulting donations fail to cover the costs of the marketing campaign.	*Oh, maybe this is it. If you spend more on the marketing than you make from donations, that can't be a very successful marketing campaign. What was the conclusion again? Oh, wait,* to maximize the dollar value of donations. *Whether the marketing covered costs isn't part of the conclusion—it just depends on how much money they get in donations. Tricky, but not correct.*	~~C~~
(D) Percentage of income is not necessarily indicative of absolute dollar value.	*This is what I was saying before about the really rich person donating $10 million! You can have a bunch of low-income people give 10 percent of their income and one billionaire give 9 percent of her income...and the billionaire could be giving more in terms of absolute dollars. This indicates the flawed assumption made by the fundraising consultants.*	D~
(E) People are more likely to donate to the same causes to which their friends donate.	*I can believe that this is true, but the argument doesn't address which causes people choose for charity. Rather, the argument talks about amount of money donated.*	~~E~~

~~A~~ ~~B~~ ~~C~~ (D~) E

3. CostMart: The correct answer is **(C)**.

Step 1: Identify the Question

Which of the following questions would be most useful for evaluating the conclusion of the editorial?	*The language* most useful *and* evaluating *indicates that this is an Evaluate question.*	Ev A B C D E

Step 2: Deconstruct the Argument

Editorial: To avoid increasing the unemployment rate in the city of Dorwall, a CostMart warehouse department store should not be permitted to open within city limits.	*This seems like the conclusion: It's telling me what Dorwall* should *do. Also, it doesn't just say that Dorwall should ban CostMart. The conclusion is specifically about unemployment.*	© Dorwall shld ban CostMart in city → unempl. not ↑
In the past, when CostMart has opened a new warehouse department store in a city, up to 20 percent of local retailers—which, in Dorwall, primarily employ local residents—have closed within the next three years.	*The author is explaining why CostMart will increase unemployment. A lot of local stores will close, so locals will lose their jobs.*	new store → 20 percent of local stores close

Step 3: State the Goal

I need to find an answer that will have two possible paths—one way will strengthen the author's claim and the other way will weaken it. The author's claim is that banning CostMart will prevent an increase in unemployment. One path will show that CostMart might cause unemployment and the other path will show that it might not.

Step 4: Work from Wrong to Right

(A) Does the bankruptcy rate of local retailers in a city generally stabilize several years after a CostMart warehouse department store opens?	*If yes, then unemployment wouldn't continue to worsen over time...but it would still happen in the first place! Even if the bankruptcy rate stabilizes, the editorial still has a good point.*	~~A~~
(B) Are the majority of residents of Dorwall currently employed within the city limits?	*If yes, then...I'm not sure what this has to do with the conclusion. The argument says that local retailers primarily employ Dorwall residents. Even if most of the other residents are employed outside of the city, the ones who work at local retailers are at risk of losing their jobs.*	~~B~~
(C) Will the number of jobs created by the opening of the CostMart warehouse store be greater than the number of jobs that will be lost when local retailers close?	*If yes, then the opening of CostMart will result in a net gain in jobs within the Dorwall city limits. That weakens the author's point about unemployment. If no, then some of the residents who lose their jobs might not be able to find new ones, which makes the author's point stronger.*	C ~
(D) Have other cities that have permitted CostMart warehouse stores to open within city limits experienced an increase in unemployment within the city?	*This could be right. If CostMart has increased unemployment in other cities, isn't it more likely to increase unemployment in Dorwall? Well, not necessarily—there's no way to know whether the other cities had the same economic situation as Dorwall. We just knew that their local retailers closed; if that happened in Dorwall, jobs would be lost.*	~~D~~
(E) Does CostMart plan to hire employees exclusively from within Dorwall for the proposed warehouse department store?	*This one could be good, too. If yes, then that would reduce unemployment! If no, then...hmm...it's not bad necessarily but it's not good either, so I'll have to be sure.*	E ~
Compare (C) and (E).	*Wait. (C) specifically says that the number of jobs created will be greater than the ones that are lost. (E) doesn't demonstrate this. Maybe CostMart will only hire Dorwall employees, but there still won't be enough jobs for all of them. Or, maybe CostMart will hire a few people from outside of Dorwall, but there will be enough jobs for the Dorwall residents, too.*	C ~~E~~ ~ ~

~~A~~ ~~B~~ (C) ~~D~~ ~~E~~

4. Bicycle Manufacturing: The correct answer is **(B)**.

Step 1: Identify the Question

Which of the following would be most useful in evaluating the claim made in the argument?	*The language* most useful in evaluating *indicates that this is an Evaluate question.*	Ev A B C D E

Step 2: Deconstruct the Argument

Bicycle Manufacturer: Switching our focus from building aluminum bicycles to primarily building carbon-fiber bicycles will reduce the time taken by our manufacturing process.	*This looks like a prediction. It's probably the manufacturer's conclusion.*	Ⓒ Alum → CF = time ↓
Although the initial construction of aluminum bicycle frames was significantly faster and simpler than the construction of carbon-fiber frames, each weld in an aluminum frame then needed to be individually checked for integrity.	*Now I know why it took longer to make the aluminum bikes. They were faster to make, but the quality control took a long time.*	Alum: faster originally, but QC = time ↑
This required that substantial time be spent on quality control to avoid shipping out any defective frames.	*This really just confirms what we found out in the last sentence! Since we had to check all of those welds, QC took forever.*	

Step 3: State the Goal

The right answer will have two possible paths. One should show that switching to carbon manufacturing might save time. The other should show that it won't actually save time. There might be a drawback to the carbon manufacturing process: Maybe some other part of it actually takes extra time?

Step 4: Work from Wrong to Right

(A) Whether factory workers will require additional training in order to manufacture carbon bicycle frames	*This seems reasonable. If it takes extra training to make the new frames, it'll probably take more time.*	A ~
(B) Whether the carbon manufacturing process is likely to require time-consuming quality checks	*Okay, this directly addresses the time issue! If it goes one way, then carbon manufacturing might actually take longer. If it goes the other way, carbon should save time. This is stronger than (A), because it definitely affects the time spent. I don't have to just guess that it'll take more time.*	B ~
(C) Whether aluminum bicycle frames with defective welds can be fixed or must be thrown away	*This might explain why aluminum manufacturing took a long time, but it doesn't say anything about whether switching to carbon would help.*	~~C~~
(D) Whether there are improvements that could be introduced that would significantly reduce the rate of defects in aluminum bicycle frames	*Interesting. If this is true, then maybe the aluminum process could be made faster. But the problem is, the conclusion is about whether switching to carbon would help or not. It's not about whether something else could help.*	~~D~~
(E) Whether the demand for carbon-fiber bicycles is as high as the demand for aluminum bicycles	*This doesn't mention manufacturing time at all. If I wanted to relate it to time, I'd need to make some serious assumptions.*	~~E~~

~~A~~ ~ (B) ~ ~~C~~ ~~D~~ ~~E~~

5. Ethanol: The correct answer is **(B)**.

Step 1: Identify the Question

In evaluating the recommendation to increase the use of ethanol, it would be most important to research which of the following?	*This question asks me to evaluate a recommendation, so it's an Evaluate question.*	Ev A B C D E

Step 2: Deconstruct the Argument

Ethanol, a fuel derived from corn, can be used alone to power vehicles or along with gasoline to reduce the amount of gasoline consumed.	*This is a fact. Ethanol, alone or with gas, can power vehicles.*	Eth OR eth + gas can power veh.
Compared with conventional gasoline, pure ethanol produces significantly less pollution per gallon used.	*Another fact. This is just about pure ethanol, though. Weren't we just talking about combining it with gasoline?*	PURE eth = pollution < than gas
In order to combat pollution, many individuals advocate the increased usage of ethanol as a fuel source for vehicles in conjunction with or in place of gasoline.	*Here's the conclusion. It's very specific: In order to* combat pollution, *we should use more ethanol, alone or with gas.*	© Eth or eth + gas → pollution ↓

Step 3: State the Goal

This is an Evaluate question, so the right answer will be able to both strengthen and weaken the argument. It has to show that the ethanol plan might decrease pollution, but on the other hand, it might not. I'll have to avoid trap answer choices that don't mention pollution, though.

21

Step 4: Work from Wrong to Right

(A) Whether the majority of existing vehicles are capable of using ethanol for fuel, either alone or in conjunction with gasoline	*If most vehicles can use ethanol, the plan is good to go. What if most vehicles can't use ethanol? Well, switching as many as possible over to ethanol would still reduce pollution. This doesn't say that switching wouldn't reduce pollution! It just says that switching might be difficult.*	~~A~~
(B) Whether the process of growing corn to produce ethanol results in significant amounts of pollution	*This is a drawback to using ethanol! If making ethanol fuel produces a lot of pollution, then switching won't actually cut down on pollution. But if it can be produced cleanly, the switch will cut pollution a lot. It can go either way, so it might be right.*	B ~
(C) Whether completely replacing gasoline with ethanol results in less pollution than using ethanol in conjunction with gasoline	*The conclusion combines these two things together, but the answer choice splits them up. Even if one produces less pollution than the other, they might or might not make less pollution than pure gasoline. There's no way to know, so it's wrong!*	~~C~~
(D) Whether ethanol is more expensive to produce than conventional gasoline	*Cost might be a drawback to ethanol in general, but the conclusion is about pollution, not cost.*	~~D~~
(E) Whether there are some vehicles in which using ethanol fuel would not result in a significant reduction in pollution compared to conventional gasoline	*This talks about* some *vehicles. Okay, if switching won't cut pollution from some vehicles, will the overall switch still cut pollution? I don't know, since I don't know how many vehicles we're talking about. This doesn't tell me that the switch would or wouldn't work.*	~~E~~

~~A~~ (B ~) ~~C~~ ~~D~~ ~~E~~

CHAPTER 22

Evidence Family

In This Chapter:

- What Are Inferences?
- Inference Questions
- Explain a Discrepancy
- EXCEPT Questions
- Inference Cheat Sheet
- Explain a Discrepancy Cheat Sheet

In this chapter, you will learn how to recognize and answer two question types that differ from the rest in one crucial way: Evidence Family arguments typically do *not* contain conclusions. You will also learn how to distinguish Inference questions from Strengthen questions, allowing you to avoid traps.

CHAPTER 22 Evidence Family

The **Evidence Family** of questions is the third main family. Here's a short recap of what you learned about this family earlier in the book:

- There are no conclusions. Evidence Family questions are made up entirely of premises.
- There are no assumptions either! Just premises.
- There are two main question types: **Inference** and **Explain a Discrepancy**.

Inference questions require you to find a piece of information that *must be true* according to the premises given in the argument.

Explain a Discrepancy questions require you to identify some kind of paradox or puzzling result in an argument and find an answer that explains, or resolves, the puzzling part of the argument. Before delving further into each type, let's talk about what inferences are on the GMAT.

What Are Inferences?

In GMAT world, an inference is something that absolutely *must* be true according to the evidence given in the argument. You don't usually think of inferences this way; rather, in the real world, inferences are *likely* to be true based on the available evidence, but they don't absolutely have to be true. In the real world, an inference is a good guess or conjecture. In GMAT world, an inference is a bulletproof logical consequence.

For example, if a friend tells you that chocolate is her favorite flavor of ice cream, what kind of real-world inferences might you make? You might infer that she likes chocolate in general and that she likes ice cream in general. Maybe she likes all desserts in general—perhaps she has a sweet tooth. All of these things are perfectly reasonable to infer in the real world, but not a single one *has* to be true. It's possible that she likes chocolate only when it's in the form of ice cream or that she likes ice cream only when it's chocolate. The kinds of answers discussed in this paragraph would be tempting *incorrect* answers on the GMAT.

What would be good GMAT inferences? Well, what *must* be true? She can't like vanilla ice cream better than she likes chocolate ice cream—if chocolate is her *favorite* flavor of ice cream, then by definition she doesn't like any other flavor better. She has to have tried at least one other flavor of ice cream at some point in her life—she has to have had the ability to compare with at least one other flavor in order to decide that chocolate is her *favorite* flavor. These kinds of inferences would be correct answers on the GMAT.

All inference lessons refer to the GMAT's definition: something that *must* be true based on the available evidence.

Inference Questions

Inference questions require you to find an answer that must be true according to the information in the argument.

Most Inference question stems contain some form of the words *conclude* or *infer*, although some variations don't include those specific words. Here are examples of phrasing in Inference questions:

Which answer can be "logically concluded"?

The "statements above most strongly support which of the following conclusions"?

Which answer can be "properly inferred"?

The statements above "best support" which of the following "assertions"?

Which answer "must be true" based upon the statements above?

Note: Inference question stems can contain the language "most strongly support," which you also saw on Strengthen questions.

The diagram below shows how to tell whether the word *support* indicates Strengthen or Inference. On Inference questions, the argument (above) is used to support the correct answer (below). On Strengthen questions, the correct answer (below) is used to support the conclusion of the argument (above):

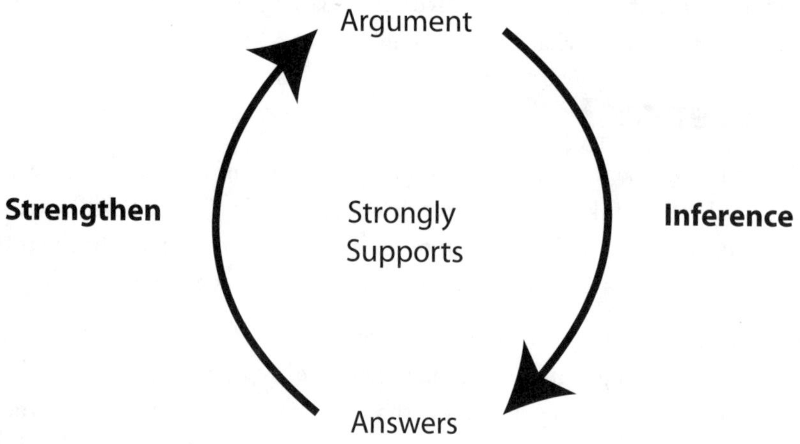

Inference questions will ask you to **use the argument to support an answer choice.** Also, Inference arguments will *not* contain a conclusion in the argument or question stem; they will consist only of premises.

By contrast, Strengthen questions will ask you to **use an answer to support the argument.** The correct answer would serve as an additional premise to support the argument's conclusion. Also, Strengthen questions will contain a conclusion in the argument or question stem.

Try this short example:

> Both enrollment and total tuition revenue at Brownsville University have increased during each of the last four years. During the same period, enrollment at Canterbury University has steadily decreased, while total tuition revenue has remained constant.
>
> Which of the following hypotheses is best supported by the statement given?
>
> (A) Brownsville University now collects more total revenue from tuition than does Canterbury University.
>
> (B) The per-student tuition at Canterbury University has risen over the last four years.
>
> (C) Brownsville University will continue to increase its revenues as long as it continues to increase enrollment.

The question stem uses the word *hypotheses* instead of the more common *conclusions*, but it signals the same thing: an Inference question. Your notes might look like this:

4 yrs:

BU: enrol, tuit ↑

CU: enrol ↓, tuit =

(premise)

There are two schools but different trends are happening. BU's enrollment and tuition revenues are both going up. CU's enrollment is going down, but tuition revenues are the same.

State your goal: *This is an Inference question, so I have to find an answer that must be true according to the premises.*

(A) Brownsville University now collects more total revenue from tuition than does Canterbury University.	*Things have certainly been looking up for BU lately, but the argument says nothing about the actual dollar values that the schools are collecting. It's entirely possible that CU still collects more money than BU.*	~~A~~
(B) The per-student tuition at Canterbury University has risen over the last four years.	*Let's see.* Per-student tuition = *revenues/# of students. CU has the same revenues today, so the numerator stays the same, but fewer students, so the denominator gets smaller. Dividing by a smaller number = a larger number. This must be true! I'll check (C), just in case.*	B~
(C) Brownsville University will continue to increase its revenues as long as it continues to increase enrollment.	*This might be reasonable to believe in the real world, but it doesn't have to be true. A trend never absolutely has to continue in the future.*	~~C~~

~~A~~ (B~) ~~C~~

The argument provides several fact-based premises. (It is also possible to have premises that are somewhat more claim-based.) The correct answer must be true based on those premises, though in this case, you only needed to use the information about Canterbury in order to draw the correct conclusion. Answer (B) didn't use the Brownsville data at all. That's perfectly acceptable; you may need to use only some of the information in the argument, not all of it.

Answer (A) tried to trap you into concluding something based on information you don't have (actual dollar values). Answer (C) is a classic Real-World Distraction trap—it might be reasonable to believe that the trend will continue, but nothing says that a trend must continue in the future.

Quick quiz! What can you infer in the situation described below?

> Imagine two ice cream companies, X and Y. Chocolate ice cream represents 60 percent of Company X's sales and 50 percent of Company Y's sales. Clearly, Company X sells more chocolate ice cream than Company Y.

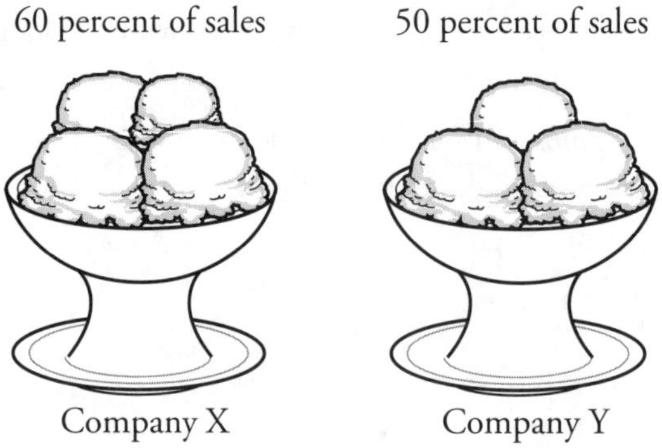

The conclusion above is not necessarily true. You know nothing about the actual sales' numbers, nor about how those percentages relate to each other. What if company Y has $1 million in annual revenues and company X has only $10,000 in annual revenues? In that case, company Y sells a lot more chocolate ice cream than company X. You can't conclude anything about actual dollar amounts from this limited information about percentages.

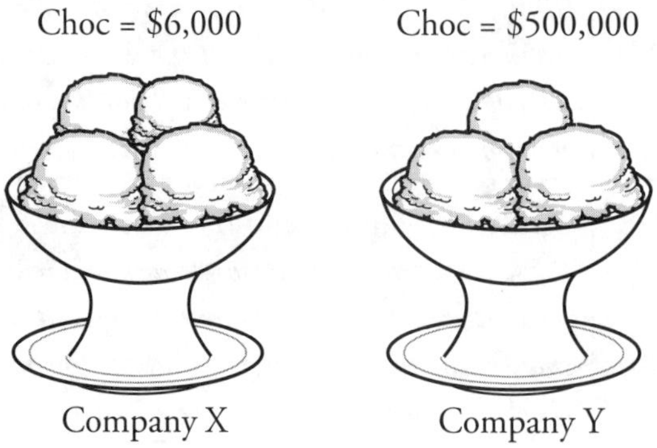

Try this problem:

> A particular company sells only vanilla and chocolate ice cream. Last year, 55 percent of the company's profits were derived from chocolate ice cream sales and 40 percent of the revenues were derived from vanilla ice cream sales. What can you infer?
>
> (A) Chocolate ice cream is more popular than vanilla ice cream.
>
> (B) The company's vanilla ice cream produces more profit per dollar of sales than does the company's chocolate ice cream.

Yes, they might actually test your math skills on critical reasoning! Because you know that the company sells only these two products, you can figure out two additional percentages. If 55 percent of profits came from chocolate, then 45 percent of profits came from vanilla. If 40 percent of revenues came from vanilla, then 60 percent of revenues came from chocolate. These things must be true, but these inferences are probably too easy for any GMAT question. What else can you infer?

The company earned 60 percent of its revenues, but only 55 percent of its profits, from chocolate. By contrast, the company earned 40 percent of its revenues and a *higher* percentage of its profits, 45 percent, from vanilla. That's interesting. The company made more profit on vanilla and less profit on chocolate than you might have expected based on the percentage of revenues that each product generates. *Profitability* is a measure of profit per dollar of revenues. The vanilla ice cream product is more *profitable* than the chocolate ice cream product. That must be true, so answer (B) is correct.

What doesn't have to be true? It doesn't have to be true that vanilla will continue to be more profitable in the future. The trend might not continue. It also doesn't have to be true that more chocolate ice cream is more popular or even that more is sold by the industry in general—maybe this company makes a fantastic chocolate ice cream, but some other company makes a much better vanilla. Notice that answer (A) focuses on how popular chocolate ice cream is in general, not just this company's chocolate ice cream. You don't have any information about how popular chocolate ice cream is overall.

When you are given numbers, proportions, or any other mathematical information, do two things:

1. Confirm whether you have real numbers or percentages.
2. Figure out any other values or relationships that must be mathematically true.

Try a full example. Set your timer for 2 minutes:

> Reducing government spending has been demonstrated to raise the value of a country's currency over time. However, many economists no longer recommend this policy. A currency of lesser value causes a country's exports to be more competitive in the international market, encouraging domestic industries and making the economy more attractive to foreign investment.
>
> The statements above most strongly support which of the following inferences?
>
> (A) Limited government spending can also lead to a reduction in the national deficit.
> (B) Reducing government spending can make a country's exports less competitive.
> (C) Many economists now recommend higher levels of government spending.
> (D) An increase in the value of a currency will result in reduced government spending.
> (E) Competitive exports indicate a weak currency.

Step 1: Identify the Question

The statements above most strongly support which of the following inferences?	*They're asking to support something below (in the answers), and they use the word* inference. *This is an Inference question.*	In A B C D E

Step 2: Deconstruct the Argument

Reducing government spending has been demonstrated to raise the value of a country's currency over time.	*This is a fact (that is, I should take it as one in the world of this argument). One thing demonstrably leads to another.*	↓ gov spend → ↑ val curr
However, many economists no longer recommend this policy.	*Hmm. According to the first sentence, raising the value of currency sounds like a good thing, so why wouldn't the economists want to do that?*	BUT econs no longer rec
A currency of lesser value causes a country's exports to be more competitive in the international market, encouraging domestic industries and making the economy more attractive to foreign investment.	*Oh, okay, so there are some good reasons to have a lower currency value. I guess the economists think these benefits outweigh the lower value.*	↓ val curr → exports more > compet → various benefits

Step 3: State the Goal

Reducing government spending will increase currency value. It seems like it would be good to have a high currency value, but some economists disagree, because there are other benefits involved in having a lower currency value.

I need to find an answer that must be true given the information in the argument. I don't need to use all of the info in the argument, though I may.

Step 4: Work from Wrong to Right

(A) Limited government spending can also lead to a reduction in the national deficit.	*Deficit? This might be reasonable to believe in the real world, but there was nothing about the deficit in the argument—there's no evidence to support this statement.*	~~A~~
(B) Reducing government spending can make a country's exports less competitive.	*Let's see. The author said that reducing spending leads to a higher currency value. And then the economists said that a lower currency value makes exports more competitive. If that's true, then a higher currency value could make exports less competitive . . . so it is actually the case that reducing spending might lead to less competitive exports! Keep this one in.*	B ~
(C) Many economists now recommend higher levels of government spending.	*The argument says* many economists *and the answer says* many economists, *so that part is okay. If you tell someone not to lower their spending, is that the same thing as telling them to increase their spending? No. You could also recommend spending the same amount. Tricky! This one isn't a "must be true" statement.*	~~C~~
(D) An increase in the value of a currency will result in reduced government spending.	*This one feels similar to (B)—language pretty similar to the argument, and I have to figure out what leads to what. The author said that X (reducing spending) will lead to Y (a higher currency value). This answer reverses the direction: Y will lead to X. That's not what the author said!*	~~D~~

(E) Competitive exports indicate a weak currency.	*The economists said that a lower currency value leads to more competitive exports. Hmm. These things do seem to go together, according to the argument. I'll leave this one in and compare it to answer (B).*	E
Compare (B) and (E).	*Now I need to compare (B) and (E). I'll check the wording of the answers to make sure I'm reading them correctly. Oh, I see. Answer (B) says that reducing spending* can make *exports less competitive, which is true, while (E) says that competitive exports indicate a weak currency. The argument says that a weaker currency leads to more competitive exports, but it doesn't say that the ONLY way to competitive exports is to have a weak currency. Maybe you can have competitive exports by investing in great research and development nationally or in some other fashion, so (E) isn't necessarily true and I can eliminate it.*	B ~~E~~

Right Answers

Right answers on Inference questions must be entirely supported by the information provided in the argument. Often, the right answer will bring together two or more of the premises in the argument, but not necessarily all the premises. This was the case in the prior example where the right answer linked reduced government spending (first sentence) to exports (last sentence). Occasionally, you may see a right answer that only draws from one premise in the argument.

Common Trap Answers

Real-World Distraction

The most tempting wrong answers on Inference questions tend to revolve around Real-World Distractions—things that you would reasonably assume to be true in the real world, but that don't absolutely have to be true. Some of these trap answers may quite obviously go way too far, but the trickiest ones will seem very reasonable... until you ask yourself whether that answer must be true.

Choices (C) and (E) from the last problem both seem reasonable in the real world, but neither one has to be true. The argument said merely that economists no longer recommend a policy to *reduce* spending. That doesn't necessarily mean that the economists recommend *higher* spending, as choice (C) says. There's also a third option: maintaining the same level of spending. Choice (E) didn't qualify the claim with a *could* or *can*. It isn't the case that competitive exports must always indicate a weak currency; they might have been caused by something else.

Reverse Logic

Other trap answers will use language very similar to the language in the argument but will reverse the proper direction of the information. If you're told that eating honey causes people to hiccup, then a wrong answer might say that hiccupping causes people to eat honey. In the last problem, choice (D) used Reverse Logic, as did answer choice (E).

Too Broad

If you're told that the flu often results in weight loss, then a trap answer might say that illness causes people not to be hungry. All illnesses? The flu is just one example; it isn't reasonable to conclude something about illnesses in general. (In addition, perhaps people are hungry when they have the flu, but they feel so nauseous that they can't eat!). Often, wrong answers on the GMAT will include a claim that is broader than the information in the argument; these broader claims, although common when making inferences in the real world, are not valid GMAT inferences.

Explain a Discrepancy

As with Inference questions, **Discrepancy questions** consist only of premises, mostly on the fact-based side (though it is possible to have more claim-like premises). Most of the time, two sets of premises will be presented, and those premises will seem to be contradictory in some way. They won't "make sense" together. Sometimes, the argument will include indicator words such as *surprisingly* or *yet*.

Most Discrepancy question stems will include some form of the words *explain* or *resolve*, and the vast majority will also contain the words *if true*. Here are two typical examples:

> Which of the following, if true, most helps to resolve the paradox described above?
>
> Which of the following, if true, best explains the fact that many economists no longer recommend reducing spending in order to increase currency values?

Your task on Discrepancy questions is to find an answer that *resolves* or *fixes* the discrepancy—that is, all of the information now makes sense together. If you leave the argument as is, people should say, "Wait. That doesn't make sense." If you add the correct answer into the argument, people should say, "Oh, I see. That makes sense now."

Take a look at this short example:

> According to researchers, low dosages of aspirin taken daily can significantly reduce the risk of heart attack or stroke. Yet doctors have stopped recommending daily aspirin for most patients.
>
> Which of the following, if true, most helps to explain why doctors no longer recommend daily low dosages of aspirin?
>
> (A) Only a small percentage of patients have already experienced a heart attack or stroke.
>
> (B) Patients who are at low risk for heart attack or stroke are less likely to comply with a doctor's recommendation to take aspirin daily.
>
> (C) Aspirin acts as a blood thinner, which can lead to internal bleeding, particularly in the stomach or brain.

The question stem asks you to *explain* something that doesn't make sense: Aspirin is apparently beneficial, but "doctors have *stopped* recommending" its use for most people (implying that they used to recommend it more). Why would they do that? You might sketch or think of the info visually in this way:

daily aspirin ↓ heart attack, stroke	*BUT* WHY?	Drs stop recomm for most

You're trying to highlight the apparent discrepancy between the two facts: On the one hand, daily aspirin is beneficial, and, on the other, doctors have stopped recommending it.

Go back to step 3, and state the goal:

So far, they've told me something really good about taking aspirin daily: It significantly reduces the risk of some pretty bad things. The fact that the doctors have stopped *recommending it means that they used to recommend it, so why would they stop doing so? Maybe there's something else that's bad about taking aspirin daily.*

(A) Only a small percentage of patients have already experienced a heart attack or stroke.	*So maybe this means the doctors think it won't help that many people? Wait. The purpose of taking the aspirin is to try to prevent a heart attack or stroke. If most people haven't had a heart attack or stroke, you'd want them to do something that would help lower the risk.*	~~A~~
(B) Patients who are at low risk for heart attack or stroke are less likely to comply with a doctor's recommendation to take aspirin daily.	*I can believe this is true in the real world, but is a doctor really going to say, "Oh, I know a lot of people won't take the life-saving medication properly, so I just won't bother to prescribe it." I hope not! Plus, why would they recommend aspirin to people who are at low risk?*	~~B~~
(C) Aspirin acts as a blood thinner, which can lead to internal bleeding, particularly in the stomach or brain.	*Oh, this is a bad thing about aspirin—it can cause you to bleed! Yeah, if it could make your brain start bleeding, I can imagine that doctors would want to avoid prescribing it unless there was a really good reason to do so.*	C~

~~A~~ ~~B~~ (C~)

Answer (C) indicates a bad consequence that can result from taking aspirin. If you add it to the argument, now it's understandable why doctors might be reluctant to have people take aspirin regularly.

Answer (A) talks about the wrong group. The argument talks about preventing heart attacks or strokes in the general population, not only among those who have already experienced these maladies.

Answer (B) might be true, but this doesn't explain why doctors would stop recommending aspirin in general. In addition, this choice limits itself to those who are at low risk for heart attack or stroke—why would doctors need to recommend daily aspirin for a group that doesn't have the risk factors?

As you read that argument, the surprising finding (aspirin no longer recommended) may have seemed a lot like what has previously been classified as a conclusion. It is not actually a conclusion because there was nothing in the existing argument to support that claim; a claim is only a conclusion if it is supported by at least one premise. In fact, the only information in the argument went against that claim. Once you add the answer choice, you actually do have an argument with a counterpremise, premise (the answer), and conclusion. This approach provides another way to think about answering Discrepancy questions: Find a premise to support the surprising claim in the argument.

Try another example:

> In a recent poll, 71 percent of respondents reported that they cast votes in the most recent national election. Voting records show, however, that only 60 percent of eligible voters actually voted in that election.
>
> Which of the following pieces of evidence, if true, would provide the best explanation for the discrepancy?
>
> (A) The margin of error for the survey was plus or minus 5 percentage points.
>
> (B) Fifteen percent of the survey's respondents were living overseas at the time of the election.
>
> (C) Prior research has shown that people who actually do vote are also more likely to respond to polls than those who do not vote.
>
> (D) Some people who intend to vote are prevented from doing so by last-minute conflicts or other complications.
>
> (E) People are less likely to respond to a voting poll on the same day that they voted.

Step 1: Identify the Question

Which of the following pieces of evidence, if true, would provide the best explanation for the discrepancy?	*The question stem uses the word* explanation *and explicitly mentions a* discrepancy, *so this is an Explain the Discrepancy question.*	ED A B C D E

Step 2: Deconstruct the Argument

In a recent poll, 71 percent of respondents reported that they cast votes in the most recent national election.	*Pure fact. There was a poll, and 71 percent of the people who responded said they voted in the last election.*	Poll: 71 percent voted
Voting records show, however, that only 60 percent of eligible voters actually voted in that election.	*Okay, that's strange. Records show that only 60 percent of people who were allowed to vote actually voted.*	BUT records: only 60 percent of elig voters voted

Step 3: State the Goal

How can it be the case that, when asked, 71 percent of the people said they voted, but records show only 60 percent of those who were allowed to vote actually voted? I don't think it would be because some people voted who weren't allowed to—that would technically resolve the discrepancy, but I doubt the GMAT is going to say that. So what could it have been? Maybe some people are remembering incorrectly or mixing up the election in question. Oh, I know! Polls always have a margin of error, so maybe the margin of error accounts for the discrepancy.

Okay, I need to find something that will make the whole thing make sense—it'll explain why 71 percent said they voted but records showed that only 60 percent actually voted.

Step 4: Work from Wrong to Right

(A) The margin of error for the survey was plus or minus 5 percentage points.	*Margin of error, bingo! Excellent. So the real percentage could've been anywhere from...71 percent + 5 percent to 71 percent − 5 percent, which is still 66 percent. This doesn't go far enough. Still, it's about margin of error. I'm going to keep this one and come back to it later.*	A ~
(B) Fifteen percent of the survey's respondents were living overseas at the time of the election.	*This percentage is larger than the 11 percent discrepancy mentioned in the argument. But what group are they talking about? Are these the people who did vote, or didn't vote, or some mix of the two? And what does* living overseas *imply? This country might allow people to vote by absentee ballot. This doesn't resolve anything.*	~~B~~
(C) Prior research has shown that people who actually do vote are also more likely to respond to polls than those who do not vote.	*People who vote are also more likely to respond to a survey. What does that mean? Of the people who responded, more were likely to have been voters than is represented in the overall population. Oh, I see—the survey group was skewed toward those who voted. That's why 71 percent of that subgroup could have voted while only 60 percent of the overall population of eligible voters voted. That's better than (A)—I'll get rid of (A).*	C ~
(D) Some people who intend to vote are prevented from doing so by last-minute conflicts or other complications.	*I'm sure this is true in the real world. How does it affect this argument? The survey took place after the election; it asked people whether they had voted in the past. It doesn't address what people intended to do before the election.*	~~D~~
(E) People are less likely to respond to a voting poll on the same day that they voted.	*I have no idea when the poll was taken, so I can't do much with this. Even if the poll was done the same day as the election, this just highlights the discrepancy—it's even more puzzling now. I would expect the percentage of people who said they voted to be lower than the real percentage because those who didn't vote that day would be more likely to agree to participate in the poll.*	~~E~~

On the first pass through the answers, both (A) and (C) seemed possible, but choice (A) didn't explain far enough, especially when compared with (C). The correct answer is (C).

~~A~~ ~~B~~ (C) ~~D~~ ~~E~~

Right Answers

The right answer on a Discrepancy question should provide an explanation for the surprising finding presented in the argument. New language, information, and ideas are common in right answers because the finding was not explained by the original information in the argument.

Common Trap Answers

Half Way

One common wrong answer trap will seem to be on topic because it will address one of the premises, but it won't actually resolve the discrepancy between the two premises. Thus, this trap answer only goes Half Way. Some of these will more obviously fall short, such as answer (D), while others will be trickier because they just don't go quite far enough, such as answer (A). If answer (A) had said that the margin of error was plus or minus 15 percentage points, it could have been the correct answer.

Reverse Logic

You may also see Reverse Logic traps, where the answer choice actually highlights or even heightens the discrepancy—that is, the choice makes the surprise even more surprising. Answer (E) could fall into this category: If the poll was taken the same day as the election, then the fact that the numbers don't match would be even more puzzling. People probably wouldn't have forgotten how they just voted, so did some of them lie?

EXCEPT Questions

As with Assumption Family questions, Evidence Family questions can also be presented in the negative EXCEPT format. These are more likely to occur on Discrepancy questions than on Inference questions.

A regular Discrepancy question might read:

> Which of the following, if true, would best help to explain the surprising finding?

An EXCEPT Discrepancy question might read:

> Each of the following, if true, could help to explain the surprising finding EXCEPT

What is the difference in wording between those two questions?

The first one indicates that one answer choice, and only one, explains the discrepancy. That is the answer choice that you want to pick.

The second one indicates that four answer choices explain the discrepancy. These four are all wrong answers. The fifth answer will *not* explain or resolve the discrepancy. This is the odd one out and the correct answer.

Similarly, on an Inference EXCEPT question, four answer choices will represent things that must be true according to the argument; eliminate these four. One answer will represent something that does not have to be true. This is the odd one out; pick it.

22

Inference Cheat Sheet

Identify the Question

Common: *conclude*
infer

Less common: *assertion*
hypothesis
must be true

Infer: Use argument to support answer.

Strengthen: Use answer to support conclusion in argument.

Deconstruct the Argument

Find: Premises
(No conclusion! No assumptions!)

If not sure whether Infer or Strengthen, check the argument for a conclusion. No conclusion = infer.

State the **Goal**

Must be true based on the information given in the argument.
Does not need to use all of argument info.

Work from **Wrong** to **Right**

Right: Must be true given the info in the argument.

Wrong: Real-World Distraction (logical in real world, but not necessarily true based on argument)

Reverse Direction (says X leads to Y, when really Y leads to X)

Switch Terms (leads to different meaning: not the right group, object, or idea)

Take a picture of this page and keep it with the review sheets you're creating as you study. Better yet, use this page as a guide to create your own review sheet—you'll remember the material better if you write it down yourself.

22

Explain a Discrepancy Cheat Sheet

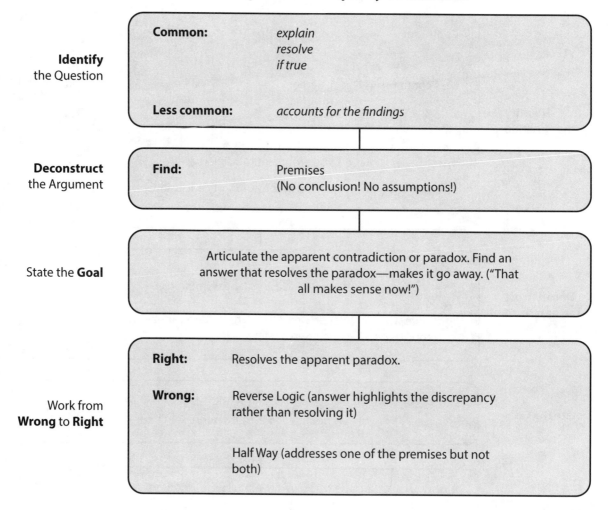

Identify the Question	**Common:**	*explain* *resolve* *if true*
	Less common:	*accounts for the findings*
Deconstruct the Argument	**Find:**	Premises (No conclusion! No assumptions!)
State the **Goal**		Articulate the apparent contradiction or paradox. Find an answer that resolves the paradox—makes it go away. ("That all makes sense now!")
Work from **Wrong** to **Right**	**Right:**	Resolves the apparent paradox.
	Wrong:	Reverse Logic (answer highlights the discrepancy rather than resolving it) Half Way (addresses one of the premises but not both)

Take a picture of this page and keep it with the review sheets you're creating as you study. Better yet, use this page as a guide to create your own review sheet—you'll remember the material better if you write it down yourself.

Problem Set

Answer each question using the 4-step Critical Reasoning process.

1. **Identify the question:** Is this an Inference question or an Explain the Discrepancy question?
2. **Deconstruct the argument:** Map the argument on your paper. Remember that there won't be a conclusion.
3. **State the goal:** What will the right answer need to do?
4. **Work from wrong to right:** Eliminate four wrong answers. Watch out for common wrong answer types.

1. *Mycenaean Vase*

Museum A will display only objects that are undamaged and that have been definitively proven to be authentic. Doubts have been raised about the origins of a supposedly Mycenaean vase currently on display in the museum's antiquities wing. The only way to establish this vase's authenticity would be to pulverize it, then subject the dust to spectroscopic analysis.

The claims above, if true, most strongly support which of the following conclusions?

(A) Authentic Mycenaean vases are valuable and rare.

(B) Museum A was not sufficiently diligent in establishing the authenticity of the vase before displaying it.

(C) The vase in question will no longer be displayed in Museum A.

(D) Spectroscopic analysis is the only method used by Museum A to establish the authenticity of objects.

(E) Many of the world's museums unknowingly display forgeries.

2. *Gas Mileage*

The average fuel efficiency of vehicles sold nationwide during the period 2000–2004 was 25 miles per gallon; the corresponding figure during the period 1995–1999 was 20 miles per gallon. The national average price of gasoline during the period 2000–2004 was $2 per gallon; the corresponding figure during the period 1995–1999 was $1.60 per gallon.

The statements above, if true, best support which of the following conclusions?

(A) The average fuel efficiency of vehicles sold nationwide should reach 30 miles per gallon for the period 2005–2009.

(B) The cost of gasoline for an average trip in a vehicle was higher during the period 1995–1999 than during the period 2000–2004.

(C) Rising gasoline prices lead consumers to purchase more fuel-efficient cars.

(D) The ratio of average fuel efficiency to average price of gasoline from the 1995–1999 period was roughly equal to the ratio from the 2000–2004 period.

(E) Consumers spent more money on gasoline during the period 2000–2004 than during the period 1995–1999.

3. *CarStore*

CarStore's sales personnel have an average of 15 years' experience selling automobiles, and for the last 5 years, they have sold more cars each year than other local dealers. Despite this, CarStore management has decided to implement a mandatory training program for all sales personnel.

Which of the following, if true, best explains the facts given above?

(A) Sales personnel at CarStore earn significantly more money than those who work for other local dealers.

(B) Within the last 5 years, a number of other local dealers have implemented mandatory training programs.

(C) It is common for new or less experienced employees to participate in training programs.

(D) A website has recently released confidential pricing information for the cars sold by CarStore, and customers have begun trying to negotiate lower prices using this data.

(E) Several retailers that compete directly with CarStore use "customer-centered" sales approaches.

4. *Stem Cell Research*

Government restrictions have severely limited the amount of stem cell research U.S. companies can conduct. Because of these restrictions, many U.S. scientists who specialize in the field of stem cell research have signed long-term contracts to work for foreign companies. Recently, Congress has proposed lifting all restrictions on stem cell research.

Which of the following statements can most properly be inferred from the information above?

(A) Some foreign companies that conduct stem cell research work under fewer restrictions than some U.S. companies do.

(B) Because U.S. scientists are under long-term contracts to foreign companies, there will be a significant influx of foreign professionals into the U.S.

(C) In all parts of the world, stem cell research is dependent on the financial backing of local government.

(D) In the near future, U.S. companies will no longer be at the forefront of stem cell research.

(E) If restrictions on stem cell research are lifted, many of the U.S. scientists will break their contracts to return to U.S. companies.

5. *Hunting Season*

In an effort to reduce the number of deer, and therefore decrease the number of automobile accidents caused by deer, the government lengthened the deer hunting season earlier this year. Surprisingly, the number of accidents caused by deer has increased substantially since the introduction of the longer hunting season.

All of the following, if true, help to explain the increase in traffic accidents caused by deer EXCEPT

(A) The presence of humans in the woods causes the deer to move to new areas, which causes the deer to cross roads more frequently than normal.

(B) In the area where the deer live, the lengthened hunting season attracted a significantly greater amount of traffic than usual this year.

(C) Most automobile accidents involving deer result from cars swerving to avoid deer, and they leave the deer in question unharmed.

(D) Deer tend to bolt when hearing gunshots or other loud sounds and are more likely to run across a road without warning.

(E) A new highway was recently built directly through the state's largest forest, which is the primary habitat of the state's deer population.

6. *World Bank*

In 2010, China comprised about 10 percent of the world's gross domestic product (GDP), and its voting share in the World Bank was increased from less than 3 percent to 4.4 percent. During the same time frame, France comprised about 4 percent of the world's GDP and saw its voting share in the World bank drop from 4.3 percent to 3.8 percent.

Which of the following can be logically concluded from the passage above?

(A) Prior to 2010, China comprised less than 10 percent of the world's GDP.

(B) Voting share in the World Bank is not directly proportional to each country's share of the world's GDP.

(C) China's share in the world's GDP is increasing more rapidly than France's share.

(D) The Chinese government is likely to be dissatisfied with the degree of the increase in its voting share.

(E) World Bank voting shares are allocated based upon each country's share of the world's GDP during previous years, not during the present year.

7. *Barcodes*

Two-dimensional barcodes are omni-directional; that is, unlike one-dimensional barcodes, they can be scanned from any direction. Additionally, two-dimensional barcodes are smaller and can store more data than their one-dimensional counterparts. Despite such advantages, two-dimensional barcodes account for a much smaller portion of total barcode usage than one-dimensional barcodes.

Which of the following, if true, most helps to resolve the apparent paradox?

(A) Many smaller stores do not use barcodes at all because of the expense.

(B) For some products, the amount of data necessary to be coded is small enough to fit fully on a one-dimensional barcode.

(C) Two-dimensional barcodes are, on average, less expensive than one-dimensional barcodes.

(D) Two-dimensional barcodes can also be scanned by consumer devices, such as cell phones.

(E) One-dimensional barcodes last longer and are less prone to error than two-dimensional barcodes.

Solutions

1. Mycenaean Vase: The correct answer is **(C)**.

   Step 1: Identify the Question

The claims above, if true, most strongly support which of the following conclusions?	*The language* strongly support *could indicate an Inference or a Strengthen question. Since the question stem says* which of the following conclusions, *the conclusion will be in the answer choices, not in the argument. This is an Inference problem.*	In A B C D E

   Step 2: Deconstruct the Argument

Museum A will display only objects that are undamaged and that have been definitively proven to be authentic.	*This is a fact—all objects have to be perfect and authenticated for this museum to display them.*	Mus: only perfect, auth objects
Doubts have been raised about the origins of a supposedly Mycenaean vase currently on display in the museum's antiquities wing.	*Another fact: They're not sure whether this vase is authentic.*	Doubts about Myc vase
The only way to establish this vase's authenticity would be to pulverize it, then subject the dust to spectroscopic analysis.	*That's interesting and kind of sad. In order to prove whether the vase is authentic, they've got to destroy it!*	To auth, must destroy!

   Step 3: State the Goal

   This is an Inference question; I need to find something that must be true according to the info given in the argument. In this case, they're not sure whether this vase is authentic and the only way to establish its authenticity is to destroy it. What follows logically from that? They can't display a fake vase, and they can't display a pulverized vase, so they won't be able to display it at all.

22

Step 4: Work from Wrong to Right

(A) Authentic Mycenaean vases are valuable and rare.	*This might be true, but I can't prove it using only what's in the argument.*	~~A~~
(B) Museum A was not sufficiently diligent in establishing the authenticity of the vase before displaying it.	*That seems a little judgmental, but reasonable. The museum only wants to display authentic objects, so why were they displaying this vase?*	B ~
(C) The vase in question will no longer be displayed in Museum A.	*I can prove that this answer choice is true! Since they only display objects they know are authentic, if they want to display the vase, they have to authenticate it. But to authenticate it, they have to destroy it! No matter what, they won't be able to display the vase. This is better than (B), since it's something I can prove using logic, not a value judgment.*	C ~
(D) Spectroscopic analysis is the only method used by Museum A to establish the authenticity of objects.	*That's not necessarily true. They have to use it for this vase, but they might have other methods for other objects.*	~~D~~
(E) Many of the world's museums unknowingly display forgeries.	*This makes sense in the real world, but I can't prove it using only the information here. I only know about one museum and one object, not many of the world's museums.*	~~E~~

~~A~~ ~~B~~ ~ (C) ~ ~~D~~ ~~E~~

2. Gas Mileage: The correct answer is **(D)**.

Step 1: Identify the Question

The statements above, if true, best support which of the following conclusions?	*The language* best support *could indicate an Inference or a Strengthen question. The rest of the question says that the conclusion will be one of the answer choices, so this is an Inference question.*	In A B C D E

Step 2: Deconstruct the Argument

The average fuel efficiency of vehicles sold nationwide during the period 2000–2004 was 25 miles per gallon; the corresponding figure during the period 1995–1999 was 20 miles per gallon.	*These are all facts, which I'm expecting because this is an Inference question. They're talking about time periods and figures, so maybe a table is the best way to keep track.*	**95–99** / **00–04** Fuel eff 20 mpg / 25
The national average price of gasoline during the period 2000–2004 was $2 per gallon; the corresponding figure during the period 1995–1999 was $1.60 per gallon.	*Yep, a table was a good idea! More facts and figures for the same time frame.*	$1.60 per gal / $2

Step 3: State the Goal

This is an Inference question, so I'm looking for something that must be true based on all this data. I was given specific figures for average fuel efficiency and average gas price for two time periods. Both went up over time. I imagine that I'll need to make a mathematical inference.

Step 4: Work from Wrong to Right

(A) The average fuel efficiency of vehicles sold nationwide should reach 30 miles per gallon for the period 2005–2009.	Should reach? *That doesn't have to be true. Who knows what's going to happen in the future?*	~~A~~
(B) The cost of gasoline for an average trip in a vehicle was higher during the period 1995–1999 than during the period 2000–2004.	*Interesting. Gas efficiency was lower in the first time period, but gas also cost less. On top of that, I don't know whether the number or length of trips changed. I don't have enough information to prove this.*	~~B~~
(C) Rising gasoline prices lead consumers to purchase more fuel-efficient cars.	*This statement is logical, but I can't prove it using only what's in the argument, and I'm not allowed to use outside knowledge. The argument doesn't say anything about why consumers decide to purchase certain cars.*	~~C~~
(D) The ratio of average fuel efficiency to average price of gasoline from the 1995–1999 period was roughly equal to the ratio from the 2000–2004 period.	*The ratio? Hmm. I don't know, but I can calculate based on the figures I was already given. In the first period, the fuel efficiency number was 20 miles per gallon, and the cost of gas was \$1.60. 20/\$1.60 = 20/(8/5) = 400/8 = 12.5. In the second period, the numbers were 25 and \$2. That's also a ratio of 12.5. They're equal!*	D ~
(E) Consumers spent more money on gasoline during the period 2000–2004 than during the period 1995–1999.	*Tricky! This one seems pretty good at first glance, but average price per gallon is not the same thing as total amount of money spent. It's true that the average price was higher, but maybe people bought fewer gallons of gasoline (especially because fuel efficiency was better!). This one might be true, but it doesn't have to be.*	~~E~~

~~A~~ ~~B~~ ~~C~~ (D) ~~E~~

3. CarStore: The correct answer is **(D)**.

Step 1: Identify the Question

Which of the following, if true, best explains the facts given above?	*The language* best explains the facts *is slightly unusual. But since I need to explain something, it's a Discrepancy problem.*	ED A B C D E

Step 2: Deconstruct the Argument

CarStore's sales personnel have an average of 15 years' experience selling automobiles, and for the last 5 years, they have sold more cars each year than other local dealers.	*CarStore's people have 15 years' experience on average, and they sell more cars than the competition. These are facts.*	Sales ppl: avg 15y exper, sell more than comp ~
Despite this, CarStore has recently implemented a mandatory training program for all sales personnel.	*Here's the contrast. Why are they going to make them all go through training? Maybe something has changed in the marketplace?*	BUT store now req training for all

Step 3: State the Goal

This is a Discrepancy question, so I need to find an answer that explains the surprise. What is the reason for the new training?

Step 4: Work from Wrong to Right

(A) Sales personnel at CarStore earn significantly more money than those who work for other local dealers.	*Maybe they want to train their employees because they're investing a lot of money into them? No, that's too much of a stretch. It doesn't clearly explain why management suddenly made this decision.*	~~A~~
(B) Within the last 5 years, a number of other local dealers have implemented mandatory training programs.	*This would be a good explanation if I didn't know that CarStore employees were selling more cars than employees at other dealers. But, the argument makes it sound like if this is true, then the training programs at the other dealerships don't work. Why would CarStore copy them?*	~~B~~
(C) It is common for new or less experienced employees to participate in training programs.	*This makes sense, but doesn't explain why the employees who average 15 years' experience need training. The argument said that all sales personnel have to undergo the training, not just the new ones.*	~~C~~
(D) A website has recently released confidential pricing information for the cars sold by CarStore, and customers have begun trying to negotiate lower prices using this data.	*This describes a change, which is promising. A change in the situation might explain why management wants to train the sales personnel now. And this change makes sense, too: Customers are using a new negotiating tactic, so CarStore employees should be trained to respond to it.*	D
(E) Several retailers that compete directly with CarStore use "customer-centered" sales approaches.	*The other retailers aren't doing as well as CarStore is, so this doesn't explain why the CarStore employees need training. We also don't know whether CarStore already uses this approach or whether it has something better.*	~~E~~

~~A~~ ~~B~~ ~~C~~ (D) ~~E~~

4. Stem Cell Research: The correct answer is **(A)**.

Step 1: Identify the Question

Which of the following statements can most properly be inferred from the information above?	*The word* inferred *indicates that this is an Inference question.*	In A B C D E

Step 2: Deconstruct the Argument

Government restrictions have severely limited the amount of stem cell research U.S. companies can conduct.	*This is a fact. The U.S. government restricts this stem cell research.*	In A B C D E Stem cell res restrict by U.S. gov
Because of these restrictions, many U.S. scientists who specialize in the field of stem cell research have signed long-term contracts to work for foreign companies.	Because of *that—so the first sentence leads to the second sentence.*	→ U.S. sci work foreign coms instead
Recently, Congress has proposed lifting all restrictions on stem cell research.	*Still a fact: The government is considering lifting the restrictions. Maybe that'll bring the scientists back to work for U.S. companies?*	U.S. gov: maybe lift restrict?

Step 3: State the Goal

This is an Inference question, so I need to find something that's definitely true based on the information so far. The U.S. government restricts a certain kind of research, so many U.S. scientists who do this type of research are working for foreign companies instead. Congress might lift the restrictions.

Step 4: Work from Wrong to Right

(A) Some foreign companies that conduct stem cell research work under fewer restrictions than some U.S. companies do.	*If the researchers decided to work for foreign companies specifically* because *the U.S. companies had restrictions, then that would mean that at least some foreign companies did have fewer restrictions. Yes, this one must be true! I'll check the other answers just in case, though.*	A
(B) Because U.S. scientists are under long-term contracts to foreign companies, there will be a significant influx of foreign professionals into the U.S.	*This might be true, but it certainly doesn't have to be true. The argument doesn't say anything about foreign professionals coming into the United States.*	~~B~~
(C) In all parts of the world, stem cell research is dependent on the financial backing of local government.	*The argument doesn't say anything about how this type of research gets its financial backing. This doesn't have to be true.*	~~C~~
(D) In the near future, U.S. companies will no longer be at the forefront of stem cell research.	*Irrelevant. The argument doesn't discuss who is or will be at the forefront of this kind of research.*	~~D~~
(E) If restrictions on stem cell research are lifted, many of the U.S. scientists will break their contracts to return to U.S. companies.	*This might happen, but we can't necessarily predict what will happen in the future.*	~~E~~

(A) ~~B~~ ~~C~~ ~~D~~ ~~E~~

5. Hunting Season: The correct answer is **(C)**.

Step 1: Identify the Question

All of the following, if true, help to explain the increase in traffic accidents caused by deer EXCEPT	*The language* help to explain *indicates that this is a Discrepancy question. This is also an EXCEPT question.*	ED Ex A B C D E

Step 2: Deconstruct the Argument

In an effort to reduce the number of deer, and therefore decrease the number of automobile accidents caused by deer, the government lengthened the deer hunting season earlier this year.	*Multiple levels here. First, the government lengthened the hunting season, which is supposed to reduce the number of deer, which is then supposed to reduce the number of car accidents caused by deer.*	Gov: ↑ hunt seas → ↓ deer → ↓ car acc
Surprisingly, the number of accidents caused by deer has increased substantially since the introduction of the longer hunting season.	*That's weird. The exact opposite has happened: There have been more car accidents caused by deer!*	BUT # car acc ↑

Step 3: State the Goal

This is a Discrepancy EXCEPT question. Normally on Discrepancy questions, I'm looking for the answer that makes the contradictory evidence make sense. On this one, though, all four wrong answers will fix the discrepancy. The odd one out—the one that doesn't fix the discrepancy—will be the right answer.

So I need to find (and cross off) four things that explain why there have been even more car accidents caused by deer.

22

Step 4: Work from Wrong to Right

(A) The presence of humans in the woods causes the deer to move to new areas, which causes the deer to cross roads more frequently than normal.	*If hunting season is lengthened, then there will be people in the woods for a longer period of time. According to this choice, that means the deer are going to cross the roads more frequently than they otherwise would have. That could increase the likelihood of accidents due to deer, which explains the discrepancy. Cross this one off.*	~~A~~
(B) The lengthened hunting season attracted a significantly greater amount of traffic than usual to the area this year.	*Oh, this makes sense. The lengthened hunting season actually caused more traffic, so there are more chances for accidents between cars and deer where the deer live. This explains the discrepancy, too.*	~~B~~
(C) Most automobile accidents involving deer result from cars swerving to avoid deer, and they leave the deer in question unharmed.	*This one is tricky! It explains how the accidents happen, which makes sense. But the right answer has to explain why there are* more *accidents. This doesn't show anything about the number of accidents.*	C ~
(D) Deer tend to bolt when hearing gunshots or other loud sounds and are more likely to run across a road without warning.	*If there are gunshots for a longer length of time, then there are more chances for the deer to bolt and cross the road suddenly. . .increasing the chances of an accident.*	~~D~~
(E) A new highway was recently built directly through the state's largest forest, which is the primary habitat of the state's deer population.	*The situation has changed from the year before: A new highway was built right through the area where the deer live. So it would make sense that there are now more accidents caused by deer.*	~~E~~

~~A~~ ~~B~~ (C) ~~D~~ ~~E~~

6. World Bank: The correct answer is **(B)**.

Step 1: Identify the Question

Which of the following can be logically concluded from the passage above?	*The language* logically concluded *indicates that this is an Inference question.*	In A B C D E

Step 2: Deconstruct the Argument

<table>
<tr>
<td>In 2010, China comprised about 10 percent of the world's gross domestic product (GDP), and its voting share in the World Bank was increased from less than 3 percent to 4.4 percent.</td>
<td>A bunch of stats about China in 2010. I just need to keep this straight because, glancing down, I can see the next sentence has more numbers.</td>
<td><table><tr><td>2010</td><td>GDP</td><td>Vote Share</td></tr><tr><td>China</td><td>10</td><td><3 → 4.4</td></tr></table></td>
</tr>
<tr>
<td>During the same time frame, France comprised about 4 percent of the world's GDP and saw its voting share in the World bank drop from 4.3 percent to 3.8 percent.</td>
<td>Same type of stats, but about France this time. Same time frame.</td>
<td><table><tr><td>Fra</td><td>4</td><td>4.3 → 3.8</td></tr></table></td>
</tr>
</table>

Step 3: State the Goal

This is an Inference question, so I need to find something that must be true based upon the info given so far. There are a lot of numbers to keep straight, but generally, China has a larger share of the world GDP than France. China used to have a lower voting share than France, but now it has a higher share.

22

Step 4: Work from Wrong to Right

(A) Prior to 2010, China comprised less than 10 percent of the world's gross domestic product.	*China's voting share increased in 2010. Maybe that happened because its GDP was lower than 10 percent, and then it increased? On the other hand, I don't actually know that the voting share is based on the GDP. They could have nothing to do with each other. This doesn't have to be true.*	~~A~~
(B) Voting share in the World Bank is not directly proportional to each country's share of the world's GDP.	*If they were directly proportional, a country with twice the GDP would also have twice the voting share. But China's GDP is more than twice France's and their voting shares are almost the same. The voting share must not be directly proportional! This is probably right.*	B ~
(C) China's share in the world's gross domestic product is increasing more rapidly than France's share.	*China's share is higher now, but I don't actually know whether France's share is increasing or how quickly.*	~~C~~
(D) The Chinese government is likely to be dissatisfied with the degree of the increase in its voting share.	*There's no way to know this using only the information in the argument. I don't even know whether an increase from 3 percent to 4.4 percent is considered small or large.*	~~D~~
(E) World Bank voting shares are allocated based upon each country's share of the world's GDP during previous years, not during the present year.	*I could speculate that this was true, but I can't prove it. I don't have enough information to tell where these numbers came from.*	~~E~~

~~A~~ (B ~) ~~C~~ ~~D~~ ~~E~~

7. Barcodes: The correct answer is **(E)**.

Step 1: Identify the Question

Which of the following, if true, most helps to resolve the apparent paradox?	*The word* paradox *indicates that this is a Discrepancy question.*	ED A B C D E

Step 2: Deconstruct the Argument

Two-dimensional barcodes are omni-directional; that is, unlike one-dimensional barcodes, they can be scanned from any direction.	*Okay, so 2D barcodes have a better feature than 1D barcodes.*	2D barcodes scan any dir, unlike 1D
Additionally, two-dimensional barcodes are smaller and can store more data than their one-dimensional counterparts.	*Even more advantages for the 2D barcodes.*	Also 2D smaller, more data
Despite such advantages, two-dimensional barcodes account for a much smaller portion of total barcode usage than one-dimensional barcodes.	*But the 1D barcodes are used a lot more—why? There must be some advantages to the 1Ds or disadvantages to the 2Ds that I don't yet know about.*	BUT 1D is used >>

Step 3: State the Goal

I need to find something that fixes the discrepancy described in the argument: The 2D barcodes have a bunch of advantages, but people mostly still use the 1D barcodes. Why? Maybe the 2D ones are super-expensive or something like that.

22

Step 4: Work from Wrong to Right

(A) Many smaller stores do not use barcodes at all because of the expense.	*Expense—does this explain why 1D barcodes are still being used? No, wait—this says the stores aren't using any type of barcode at all. So that doesn't explain why the ones that do use barcodes seem to prefer the 1D models.*	~~A~~
(B) For some products, the amount of data necessary to be coded is small enough to fit fully on a one-dimensional barcode.	*Okay, so some products might not need the 2D barcodes. Except, this only mentions* some products, *while the argument says that the 2D barcodes are a* much smaller *portion of total usage. This doesn't fully explain the discrepancy.*	~~B~~
(C) Two-dimensional barcodes are, on average, less expensive than one-dimensional barcodes.	*Less expensive, this is it! Wait a second. No, this says the 2D barcodes are less expensive—that gives them yet another advantage! If they're less expensive, I'd expect people to use them more. This isn't it.*	~~C~~
(D) Two-dimensional barcodes can also be scanned by consumer devices, such as cell phones.	*This sounds like yet another advantage of the 2D barcodes. This isn't it either!*	~~D~~
(E) One-dimensional barcodes last longer and are less prone to error than two-dimensional barcodes.	*Here are two advantages of the 1D barcodes. If it's true that they last longer and are less prone to error, then that would explain why people would want to use them rather than the 2D barcodes.*	E ~

~~A~~ ~~B~~ ~~C~~ ~~D~~ (E)

APPENDIX A

Idioms

APPENDIX A

Idioms

This appendix contains idioms that have been tested on the GMAT in the past but that are not among the most commonly tested idioms. The list is quite long; we don't recommend memorizing every idiom here.

Rather, use this appendix as a reference. If you miss a problem that uses one of these idioms, check the entry to learn the acceptable uses of the idiom.

Label	**Definition**
RIGHT:	Expressions that the GMAT considers correct.
SUSPECT:	*Expressions that the GMAT seems to avoid if possible. They occasionally show up in a correct answer, but only when the other four choices are clearly wrong. These expressions are sometimes grammatically correct, but they may be wordy, controversial, or simply less preferred than other forms.*
WRONG:	*Expressions that the GMAT considers incorrect.*

ACT

RIGHT: The bay ACTED AS a funnel for the tide. (functioned as)
My friend ACTED LIKE a fool. (behaved in a similar manner)

SUSPECT: *The bay ACTED LIKE a funnel for the tide.*
Note: At least one official explanation for an *Official Guide* problem claims that ACT LIKE must be used only with people. This claim is contradicted by other published problems. The way to resolve this issue is to ask whether the author intends *metaphorical comparison* (LIKE) or *actual function* (AS). If actual function is possible, use AS.

AFFECT/EFFECT

RIGHT: The new rules will AFFECT our performance.

WRONG: *The new rules will CAUSE AN EFFECT ON our performance.*

AFTER

RIGHT: AFTER the gold rush, the mining town collapsed.

SUSPECT: *FOLLOWING the gold rush, the mining town collapsed.* (Ambiguous: Could be interpreted to mean that the mining town was following the gold rush in a metaphorical way.)

AGGRAVATE

RIGHT: His behavior AGGRAVATED the problem. (made worse)

WRONG: *His behavior WAS AGGRAVATING TO the problem.* (was annoying to)

AGREE

RIGHT: They AGREE THAT electrons EXIST.
Electrons are particles THAT physicists AGREE EXIST.

WRONG: *They AGREE electrons EXIST.* (*THAT* is required.)
There is AGREEMENT AMONG them TO THE FACT THAT electrons exist.
Electrons are particles physicists AGREE THAT EXIST.
Electrons are particles physicists AGREE TO EXIST.
Electrons are particles THAT physicists AGREE ON AS EXISTING.

AID

RIGHT: She AIDS her neighbor.
She provides AID TO victims.
AID FOR victims is available.
Her AID IN WALKING the dog was appreciated.

WRONG: *Her AID TO WALK the dog was appreciated.*

AIM

RIGHT: We adopted new procedures AIMED AT REDUCING theft.
We adopted new procedures WITH THE AIM OF REDUCING theft.

WRONG: *We adopted new policies WITH THE AIM TO REDUCE theft.*

AMONG See BETWEEN.

<u>ANXIETY</u>

RIGHT: His ANXIETY ABOUT his company's future is ill-founded.
His ANXIETY THAT his company MAY BE SOLD is ill-founded.

WRONG: *His ANXIETY ABOUT his company MAY BE SOLD is ill-founded.*

<u>APPEAR</u>

RIGHT: Imperfections APPEAR AS tiny cracks. (show up as)
He APPEARS CONFUSED. (seems)
The dinosaurs APPEAR TO HAVE BEEN relatively smart.
IT APPEARS THAT the dinosaurs WERE smart.

WRONG: *He APPEARS AS confused.*
The dinosaurs APPEARED AS smart.

<u>APPLY</u>

RIGHT: The rules APPLY TO all of us.

WRONG: *All of us ARE SUBJECT TO THE APPLICABILITY OF the rules.*

<u>AS LONG AS</u>

RIGHT: I will leave, AS LONG AS it IS safe.
I will leave, SO LONG AS it IS safe.
I will leave, PROVIDED THAT it IS safe.

SUSPECT: *I will leave, BUT it HAS TO BE safe.*

WRONG: *I will leave, BUT it BE safe.*
I will leave, AS (or *SO*) *LONG AS it BE safe.*

<u>AS ... SO</u>

RIGHT: AS you practice, SO shall you play. (in the same way or manner)
JUST AS you practice, SO shall you play. (in the same way or manner)
JUST AS you practice piano regularly, you should study regularly. (in the same way; the situations are analogous)

WRONG: *You practice, SO shall you play.*
JUST LIKE you practice, SO shall you play.

ASK

RIGHT: I ASKED FOR his AID.
He ASKED her TO GO to the store.
He ASKED THAT she GO to the store. (subjunctive)

WRONG: *He ASKED THAT she SHOULD GO to the store.*

ATTRIBUTE

RIGHT: We ATTRIBUTE the uprising TO popular discontent.

WRONG: *We ATTRIBUTE the uprising AS popular discontent.*

AVERAGE

RIGHT: Tech COMPANIES are as likely as the AVERAGE COMPANY to fail.
ON AVERAGE, 3 out of 10 new small businesses fail during their first two years.

WRONG: *AT AVERAGE, 3 out of 10 new small businesses fail during their first two years.*

AWARE

RIGHT: AWARE OF the danger, he fled.
AWARE THAT danger was near, he fled.

WRONG: *WITH AN AWARENESS THAT danger was near, he fled.*
WITH AN AWARENESS OF the danger, he fled.

BAN

RIGHT: They passed a BAN PROHIBITING us FROM CARRYING bottles.

WRONG: *They passed a BAN that we CANNOT CARRY bottles.*

BASED ON

RIGHT: The verdict was BASED ON the evidence.
The jury reached a verdict BASED ON the evidence.

WRONG: *BASED ON the evidence, the jury reached a verdict.* (The jury was not itself BASED ON the evidence.)

BEGIN

RIGHT: The movement BEGAN AS a protest. (started as a protest, became a movement)

The movement BEGAN WITH a protest. (A protest was the first event of the movement.)

The protest BEGAN a movement. (The protest caused a movement.)

....

WRONG: *The movement WAS BEGUN FROM a protest.*

BETWEEN

RIGHT: An argument ensued BETWEEN the CEO AND the marketing director.

A skirmish ensued AMONG the attendees of the game. (Use AMONG for more than two parties.)

....

WRONG: *An argument ensued BETWEEN the CEO WITH the marketing director.*

An argument ensued AMONG the CEO AND the marketing director.

An argument ensued AMONG the CEO WITH the marketing director.

BORDERS

RIGHT: WITHIN the BORDERS of a country.

....

WRONG: *IN the BORDERS of a country.*

INSIDE the BORDERS of a country.

CHANCE

RIGHT: I have ONE CHANCE IN A THOUSAND OF WINNING tonight.

....

WRONG: *I have ONE CHANCE IN A THOUSAND FOR WINNING tonight.*

I have ONE IN A THOUSAND CHANCES TO WIN tonight.

I have ONE CHANCE IN A THOUSAND THAT I WILL WIN tonight.

I have ONE CHANCE IN A THOUSAND FOR ME TO WIN tonight.

CLAIM

RIGHT: They CLAIM THAT they CAN read minds.

They CLAIM TO BE ABLE to read minds.

....

WRONG: *They CLAIM BEING ABLE to read minds.*

COMPARABLE

RIGHT: Costs are rising, but incomes have not increased COMPARABLY.

SUSPECT: *Costs are rising, but incomes have not increased TO A COMPARABLE EXTENT.*

COMPARED/COMPARISON

RIGHT: IN COMPARISON WITH (or TO) horses, zebras are vicious.

A zebra can be COMPARED TO a horse in many ways.

COMPARED WITH a horse, a zebra is very hard to tame.

Note: The GMAT ignores the traditional distinction between COMPARED TO (emphasizing similarities) and COMPARED WITH (emphasizing differences).

WRONG: *WHEN COMPARED TO horses, zebras are vicious.*

Zebras are MORE vicious COMPARED TO horses.

CONCEIVE

RIGHT: He CONCEIVES OF architecture AS a dialogue.

SUSPECT: *His CONCEPTION OF architecture IS AS a dialogue.*

WRONG: *He CONCEIVES OF architecture TO BE a dialogue.*

CONFIDENCE

RIGHT: We have CONFIDENCE THAT the market WILL RECOVER.

SUSPECT: *We have CONFIDENCE IN the market's ABILITY TO RECOVER.*

WRONG: *We have CONFIDENCE IN the market TO RECOVER.*

CONNECTION

RIGHT: There is a strong CONNECTION BETWEEN his grades AND his effort.

WRONG: *There is a strong CONNECTION OF his grades AND his effort.*

CONTEND

RIGHT: They CONTEND THAT they can decipher the code.

WRONG: *They CONTEND they can decipher the code.* (*THAT* is required.)
They CONTEND the code TO BE decipherable.
They CONTEND the ABILITY to decipher the code.

CONTRAST

RIGHT: IN CONTRAST WITH the zoo, the park charges no admission.
IN CONTRAST TO the zoo, the park charges no admission.
UNLIKE the zoo, the park charges no admission.

WRONG: *AS CONTRASTED WITH the zoo, the park charges no admission.*
IN CONTRAST TO the zoo CHARGING admission, the park does not.

CONVINCE

RIGHT: She was CONVINCED THAT she had been robbed.

SUSPECT: *She was OF THE CONVICTION THAT she had been robbed.*

COST

RIGHT: Pollution COSTS us billions IN increased medical bills.

WRONG: *The COST OF pollution TO us is billions IN increased medical bills.*
Increased medical bills COST us billions BECAUSE OF pollution.

COULD

RIGHT: You COULD DO anything you want.

SUSPECT: *You HAVE* (or *MAY HAVE*) *THE POSSIBILITY OF DOING anything you want.*

WRONG: *You COULD POSSIBLY DO anything you want.* (redundant)

CREATE

RIGHT: We WILL CREATE a team TO LEAD the discussion.

WRONG: *We WILL CREATE a team FOR LEADING the discussion.*

CREDIT

RIGHT: Hugo CREDITS Sally WITH good taste.
Sally IS CREDITED WITH good taste.

WRONG: *Sally IS CREDITED FOR good taste.*
Sally IS CREDITED FOR HAVING good taste.
Sally IS CREDITED AS a person with good taste.
Sally IS CREDITED AS HAVING good taste.
Sally IS CREDITED TO BE a person with good taste.

DANGER

RIGHT: We ARE IN DANGER OF FORGETTING the past. (Forgetting is possible or likely.)

SUSPECT: *We ARE ENDANGERED BY FORGETTING the past.* (Forgetting causes us to be in danger.)

WRONG: *We ARE IN DANGER TO FORGET the past.*
We HAVE A DANGER OF FORGETTING the past.
We HAVE A DANGER TO FORGET the past.

DATE

RIGHT: They DATED the artifact AT three centuries old.
The artifact WAS DATED AT three centuries old.

WRONG: *The artifact WAS DATED TO BE three centuries old.*
The artifact WAS DATED AS BEING three centuries old.

DECIDE

RIGHT: She DECIDED TO START a company.

SUSPECT: *Her DECISION WAS TO START a company.*

DECLARE

RIGHT: I DECLARED the election a fraud.
I DECLARED the referendum invalid.
I DECLARED invalid the referendum that the new regime imposed.
They DECLARED THAT the election was a fraud.

SUSPECT: *They DECLARED the election was a fraud.* (*DECLARE THAT* is preferred.)
The judge DECLARED the election TO BE a fraud.

WRONG: *The judge DECLARED the election AS a fraud.*

DECLINE See also NUMBER.

RIGHT: The DECLINE IN the price of oil was unexpected.
Bee populations are IN DECLINE.
Oil DECLINED in price.
My friend's reputation DECLINED.

WRONG: *My friend DECLINED in reputation.*

DEMAND

RIGHT: They DEMANDED THAT the store BE closed.
Their DEMAND THAT the store BE closed was not met.

WRONG: *They DEMANDED the store TO BE closed.*
They DEMANDED THAT the store SHOULD BE closed.

DESIGN

RIGHT: This window IS DESIGNED TO OPEN.

WRONG: *This window IS DESIGNED SO THAT IT OPENS.*
This window IS DESIGNED SO AS TO OPEN.

DETERMINE

RIGHT: The winner was DETERMINED BY a coin toss.

WRONG: *The winner was DETERMINED THROUGH a coin toss.*
The winner was DETERMINED BECAUSE OF a coin toss.
The winner was DETERMINED FROM a coin toss.
The winner was DETERMINED AS A RESULT OF a coin toss.

DEVELOP

RIGHT: The executive DEVELOPED her idea INTO a project.
The idea DEVELOPED INTO a project.

WRONG: *An idea DEVELOPED ITSELF INTO a project.*

DIFFER/DIFFERENT

RIGHT: My opinion DIFFERS FROM yours.
My opinion IS DIFFERENT FROM yours.

WRONG: *My opinion IS DIFFERENT IN COMPARISON TO yours.*

DIFFERENCE

RIGHT: There is a DIFFERENCE IN ability BETWEEN us.
There is a DIFFERENCE BETWEEN what you can do AND what I can do.
There are DIFFERENCES IN what you and I can do.

WRONG: *There are DIFFERENCES BETWEEN what you and I can do.*

DIFFICULT

RIGHT: Quantum mechanics is DIFFICULT TO STUDY.

WRONG: *Quantum mechanics is DIFFICULT FOR STUDY.*

DISCOVERY

RIGHT: I love the DISCOVERY THAT carbon CAN form soccer-ball molecules.

SUSPECT: *I love the DISCOVERY OF carbon's ABILITY TO form soccer-ball molecules.*

WRONG: *I love the DISCOVERY OF carbon BEING ABLE TO form soccer-ball molecules.*

DISINCLINED

RIGHT: She IS DISINCLINED TO WRITE to her parents.

WRONG: *She HAS A DISINCLINATION TO WRITE to her parents.*
There IS A DISINCLINATION ON HER PART TO WRITE to her parents.
Her busy schedule BRINGS OUT A DISINCLINATION IN HER TO WRITE to her parents.

DISTINGUISH/DISTINCTION

RIGHT: The investor DISTINGUISHED BETWEEN trends AND fads.
There is a DISTINCTION BETWEEN trends AND fads.

WRONG: *The investor DISTINGUISHED trends AND fads.*
The investor DISTINGUISHED BETWEEN trends FROM fads.
There is a DISTINCTION BETWEEN trends WITH fads.
There is a DISTINCTION OF trends TO fads.
Trends HAVE a DISTINCTION FROM fads.

DO

RIGHT: I did not eat the cheese, but my mother DID (or DID SO).

WRONG: *I did not eat the cheese, but my mother DID IT* (or *DID THIS*).

DOUBLE See TWICE.

DOUBT

RIGHT: We DO NOT DOUBT THAT the apples are ripe.
We HAVE NO DOUBT THAT the apples are ripe.
She DOUBTS WHETHER Jan will arrive on time.

SUSPECT: *She DOUBTS THAT Jan will arrive on time.*
Note: An official GMAT explanation states that DOUBT, used in a positive statement without NOT or NO, should be followed by WHETHER or IF, not THAT. It is unclear, however, whether the GMAT always holds to this statement.

WRONG: *We DO NOT DOUBT WHETHER the apples are ripe.*
We HAVE NO DOUBT WHETHER the apples are ripe.

DUE TO

RIGHT: The deficit IS DUE TO overspending. (results from)
Our policy will not cover damage DUE TO fire. (resulting from)
BECAUSE politicians SPEND money, we have a deficit.

WRONG: *DUE TO politicians SPENDING money, we have a deficit.*
DUE TO THE FACT THAT politicians SPEND money, we have a deficit.

<u>ECONOMIC and ECONOMICAL</u>

RIGHT: The rise in gasoline prices has an ECONOMIC impact on consumers. (financial)
Our new car is more ECONOMICAL than our last. (efficient)

WRONG: *The rise in gasoline prices has an ECONOMICAL impact on consumers.*

<u>EFFECT</u> See AFFECT.

<u>ELECT</u>

RIGHT: She ELECTED TO WITHDRAW her money early.

SUSPECT: *She ELECTED early WITHDRAWAL OF her money.*

WRONG: *She ELECTED WITHDRAWING her money early.*

<u>ENOUGH</u> See also SO/THAT.

RIGHT: The book was SHORT ENOUGH TO READ in a night.
The book was SHORT ENOUGH FOR me TO READ in a night.
The power plant manager has found a way to generate more energy, ENOUGH TO POWER an entire city.

SUSPECT: *The power plant manager has found a way to generate energy at an unprecedented scale, ENOUGH FOR powering an entire city.*

WRONG: *The book was SHORT ENOUGH THAT I could read it in a night.*
The book was SHORT ENOUGH FOR IT TO BE read in a night.
The book was SHORT ENOUGH SO THAT I could read it in a night.
The book was SHORT ENOUGH AS TO BE read in a night.

<u>ENSURE</u>

RIGHT: He ENSURES THAT deadlines ARE met.
He ENSURES THAT deadlines WILL BE met.

WRONG: *He ENSURES THAT deadlines MUST BE met.*
He ENSURES THAT deadlines SHOULD BE met.

EQUIPPED

RIGHT: They are EQUIPPED TO FIGHT on any terrain.

WRONG: *They are EQUIPPED FOR FIGHTING on any terrain.*

ESTIMATE

RIGHT: She ESTIMATES the cost TO BE 10 dollars.
The cost IS ESTIMATED TO BE 10 dollars.
With a temperature ESTIMATED AT 100 degrees, boiling water can cause severe burns.
She ESTIMATES the cost TO BE 10 percent less than it was last year.

WRONG: *She ESTIMATES the cost AT 10 percent less than it was last year.*

EVEN

RIGHT: The company is EVEN MORE PROFITABLE THAN Apple.
I earn AS MUCH acclaim AS EVEN the most famous athlete.

WRONG: *The company is MORE PROFITABLE EVEN THAN Apple.*
I earn EVEN AS MUCH acclaim AS the most famous athlete.

EVER

RIGHT: The economy is MORE fragile THAN EVER BEFORE.

WRONG: *The economy is MORE fragile THAN NEVER BEFORE.*
The economy is MORE fragile AS NEVER BEFORE.
The economy is MORE THAN EVER BEFORE fragile.

EVERY

RIGHT: FOR EVERY dollar SAVED, THREE dollars ARE WASTED.

SUSPECT: *FOR EVERY dollar SAVED, you WASTE THREE dollars.*

WRONG: *FOR EVERY dollar SAVED WASTES THREE dollars.*

EXCEPT

RIGHT: EXCEPT FOR a final skirmish, the war was over.

SUSPECT: *BESIDES a final skirmish, the war was over.*
WITH THE EXCEPTION OF a final skirmish, the war was over.
EXCEPTING a final skirmish, the war was over.

EXPEND

RIGHT: We EXPEND energy ON neighborhood development.

WRONG: *We EXPEND energy FOR neighborhood development.*

EXTENT

RIGHT: We enjoyed the film TO some EXTENT.
The EXTENT TO WHICH we enjoyed the film was moderate.
TO the EXTENT THAT your example is relevant, it supports my conclusion.

WRONG: *The EXTENT THAT we enjoyed the film was moderate.*

FAULT

RIGHT: The criminals ARE AT FAULT FOR BREAKING the law.

SUSPECT: *BREAKING the law IS THE FAULT OF the criminals.*

WRONG: *THAT the criminals BROKE the law IS AT FAULT.*
IT IS THE FAULT OF the criminals WHO BROKE the law.

FIND

RIGHT: The scientist FOUND THAT the reaction WAS unusual.

SUSPECT: *The scientist FOUND the reaction TO BE unusual.*

WRONG: *The scientist FOUND the reaction WAS unusual.* (*THAT* is required.)

FORBID

RIGHT: The law FORBIDS any citizen TO VOTE twice.

WRONG: *The law FORBIDS any citizen FROM VOTING twice.*

GOAL

RIGHT: The GOAL IS TO EXPAND the company.

SUSPECT: *The GOAL IS EXPANSION OF the company.*

WRONG: *The GOAL IS EXPANDING the company.*

HEAR

RIGHT: She HEARD THAT her investment HAD PAID off.

WRONG: *She HEARD OF her investment PAYING off.*

HELP

RIGHT: He HELPS RAKE the leaves.
He HELPS TO RAKE the leaves.
He HELPS me RAKE the leaves.
He HELPS me TO RAKE the leaves.
His HELP IN RAKING the leaves has been appreciated.

WRONG: *He HELPS me IN RAKING the leaves.*
I need him AS HELP TO RAKE the leaves.

HOLD

RIGHT: The law HOLDS THAT jaywalking is illegal.

SUSPECT: *The law HOLDS jaywalking TO BE illegal.*

WRONG: *The law HOLDS jaywalking is illegal.*

INFLUENCE

RIGHT: His example INFLUENCED me.

WRONG: *His example WAS AN INFLUENCE ON me.*
His example WAS INFLUENTIAL ON me.

INSTANCE

RIGHT: We cook often; FOR INSTANCE, last week we cooked every night.

WRONG: *We cook often; AS AN INSTANCE, last week we cooked every night.*

INSTEAD

RIGHT: They avoided the arcade and INSTEAD went to a movie.

WRONG: *They avoided the arcade and RATHER went to a movie.*
They avoided the arcade, RATHER going to a movie.

INTERACT

RIGHT: These groups often INTERACT WITH ONE ANOTHER (or EACH OTHER).

WRONG: *These groups often INTERACT AMONG ONE ANOTHER.*
These groups often INTERACT WITH THEMSELVES.

INTERACTION

RIGHT: The INTERACTION OF two nuclei COLLIDING releases energy.

SUSPECT: *The INTERACTION BETWEEN two nuclei COLLIDING releases energy.*

WRONG: *The INTERACTION WHERE two nuclei COLLIDE releases energy.*

INVEST

RIGHT: She INVESTED funds IN research TO STUDY cancer.

WRONG: *She INVESTED funds INTO research TO STUDY cancer.*
She INVESTED funds FOR research TO STUDY cancer.
She INVESTED funds IN research FOR STUDYING cancer.

ISOLATED

RIGHT: The culture was ISOLATED FROM outside contact.
IN ISOLATION, his reaction is puzzling, but it makes sense in context.

SUSPECT: *The culture was IN ISOLATION.*

WRONG: *The culture was IN ISOLATION FROM outside contact.*

JUST AS ... SO See AS ... SO.

KNOW

RIGHT: We KNOW her TO BE brilliant.
She is KNOWN TO BE brilliant.
We KNOW him AS "Reggie."
He is KNOWN AS "Reggie."

WRONG: *We KNOW her AS brilliant.* (*KNOW AS* means named; not used for a description.)

LACK

RIGHT: Old gadgets ARE LACKING IN features.
Old gadgets LACK features.
The LACK OF features is upsetting.

SUSPECT: *There is A LACK OF engineers TO BUILD new gadgets.*

WRONG: *Old gadgets LACK OF features.*
It is hard to build bridges LACKING engineers.

LESS See also THAN.

RIGHT: Our utility bills add up to LESS THAN 10 percent of our income.

WRONG: *Our utility bills add up to LOWER THAN 10 percent of our income.*

LET

RIGHT: My doctor LETS me SWIM in the ocean.

WRONG: *My doctor LEAVES me SWIM in the ocean.*
The surgery WILL LEAVE me TO SWIM in the ocean.

LIE

RIGHT: Our strength LIES IN numbers. (resides in/comes from)
Yesterday, our strength LAY IN numbers.
Tomorrow, our strength WILL LIE IN numbers.
I lose my books whenever I LAY them down. (present tense of different verb)

WRONG: *Tomorrow, our strength WILL LAY IN numbers.*

LIKELY

RIGHT: My friend IS LIKELY TO EAT worms.
IT IS LIKELY THAT my friend WILL EAT worms.
My friend is MORE LIKELY THAN my enemy [is] TO EAT worms.
My friend is TWICE AS LIKELY AS my enemy [is] TO EAT worms.
MORE THAN LIKELY, my friend WILL EAT worms.

WRONG: *My friend IS LIKELY THAT he WILL EAT worms.*
RATHER THAN my enemy, my friend is THE MORE LIKELY to EAT worms.

LOSS

RIGHT: I have suffered a LOSS OF strength. (decline of a quality)
They have suffered a LOSS IN the euro. (decline of an investment)

WRONG: *I have suffered a LOSS IN strength.*

MAKE

RIGHT: The leader MADE the resistance POSSIBLE.
The leader MADE IT POSSIBLE TO RESIST oppression.
The leader MADE IT POSSIBLE FOR us TO RESIST oppression.
Windshields ARE MADE resistant to impact.

SUSPECT: *The leader MADE POSSIBLE the resistance.*

WRONG: *The leader MADE POSSIBLE TO RESIST oppression.*

MANDATE

RIGHT: The general MANDATED THAT a trench BE dug. (subjunctive)

SUSPECT: *We HAVE A MANDATE TO CALL an election soon.* (have authority)

WRONG: *The general MANDATED a trench TO BE dug.*
The general MANDATES THAT a trench WILL BE dug.
We HAVE A MANDATE FOR an election in the near future.

MASS

RIGHT: The truck HAS 10 TIMES THE MASS of a small car.

WRONG: *The truck IS 10 TIMES THE MASS of a small car.*

MAYBE See PROBABLY.

MEANS

RIGHT: Music education is A MEANS TO improved cognition.

WRONG: *Music education is A MEANS OF improved cognition.*
Music education is A MEANS FOR improved cognition.

MISTAKE

RIGHT: My waiter HAS MISTAKEN me FOR a celebrity.

WRONG: *My waiter HAS MISTAKEN me AS a celebrity.*
My waiter HAS MISTAKEN me TO a celebrity.

MORE See also THAN.

RIGHT: We observed A 10 percent INCREASE IN robberies last month.
MORE AND MORE, we have observed violent robberies on weekends.
INCREASINGLY, we have observed violent robberies on weekends.

SUSPECT: *We observed 10 percent MORE robberies last month.*

MOST

RIGHT: OF ALL the Greek gods, Zeus was THE MOST powerful. (superlative)
He was THE SECOND MOST attractive AND THE MOST powerful.

WRONG: *OF ALL the Greek gods, Zeus was THE MORE powerful.*
He was THE SECOND MOST attractive AND MOST powerful.

NATIVE

RIGHT: The kangaroo is NATIVE TO Australia. (said of animals, plants)
My friend is A NATIVE OF Australia. (said of people)

WRONG: *The kangaroo is NATIVE IN Australia.*

NUMBER

RIGHT: A NUMBER OF dogs ARE barking.
THE NUMBER OF dogs IS large.
THE NUMBER OF dogs HAS FALLEN, but THE NUMBER OF cats HAS RISEN.
The grey oyster nearly vanished, but ITS NUMBERS have rebounded.

WRONG: *THE NUMBERS OF dogs HAVE fallen.*
Dogs HAVE FALLEN IN NUMBER, but cats HAVE RISEN IN NUMBER.

ONCE

RIGHT: We might ONCE have seen that band.

WRONG: *We might AT ONE TIME have seen that band.*

ONLY

RIGHT: Her performance is exceeded ONLY by theirs. (modifies *by theirs*)

WRONG: *Her performance is ONLY exceeded by theirs.* (technically modifies *exceeded*)

Note: ONLY should be placed just before the words it is meant to modify. In both speech and writing, ONLY is often placed before the verb, but this placement is generally wrong, according to the GMAT, since we rarely mean that the verb is the only action ever performed by the subject.

OR

RIGHT: I do NOT want water OR milk.

SUSPECT: *I do NOT want water AND milk.* (implies the combination)

ORDER

RIGHT: The state ORDERS THAT the agency COLLECT taxes. (subjunctive)
The state ORDERS the agency TO COLLECT taxes.

WRONG: *The state ORDERS THAT the agency SHOULD COLLECT taxes.*
The state ORDERS the agency SHOULD COLLECT taxes.
The state ORDERS the agency WOULD COLLECT taxes.
The state ORDERS the agency COLLECTING taxes.
The state ORDERS the agency the COLLECTION OF taxes.
The state ORDERS the COLLECTION OF taxes BY the agency.
The state ORDERS taxes collected.

OWE

RIGHT: He OWES money TO the government FOR back taxes.

SUSPECT: *He OWES money TO the government BECAUSE OF back taxes.*

PAY

RIGHT: The employer PAYS the same FOR this JOB as for that one.

WRONG: *The employer PAYS the same IN this JOB as in that one.*

PERHAPS See PROBABLY.

PERSUADE

RIGHT: He PERSUADED her TO GO with him.

WRONG: *He PERSUADED her IN GOING with him.*
He PERSUADED THAT she GO with him.
He PERSUADED THAT she SHOULD GO with him.

POTENTIALLY

RIGHT: A tornado IS POTENTIALLY overwhelming.

WRONG: *A tornado CAN POTENTIALLY BE overwhelming.* (redundant)

PROBABLY

RIGHT: This situation IS PROBABLY as bad as it can get.
This situation MAY BE as bad as it can get. (less certain than PROBABLY)
PERHAPS (or MAYBE) this situation IS as bad as it can get.

SUSPECT: *IT MAY BE THAT this situation IS as bad as it can get.*

WRONG: *This situation IS MAYBE as bad as it can get.*

PROHIBIT

RIGHT: The law PROHIBITS any citizen FROM VOTING twice.

WRONG: *The law PROHIBITS any citizen TO VOTE twice.*
The law PROHIBITS THAT any person VOTE (or *VOTES*) *twice.*

PRONOUNCE

RIGHT: She PRONOUNCED the book a triumph.

SUSPECT: *She PRONOUNCED the book AS a triumph.*

PROPOSE

RIGHT: The attorneys PROPOSED THAT a settlement BE reached. (subjunctive)
The attorneys PROPOSED a new venue.
The attorneys PROPOSED TO MEET for lunch.

WRONG: *The attorneys PROPOSED THAT a settlement IS reached.*
The attorneys PROPOSED a settlement BE reached.
The attorneys PROPOSED a settlement TO BE reached.
The attorneys PROPOSED a settlement IS TO BE reached.

PROVIDED THAT See IF.

RAISE See RISE.

RANK

RIGHT: This problem RANKS AS one of the worst we have seen.

WRONG: *This problem HAS THE RANK OF one of the worst we have seen.*

RATE

RIGHT: The RATES FOR bus tickets are good for commuters. (prices)
The RATE OF theft has fallen. (frequency or speed)

WRONG: *The RATES OF bus tickets are good for commuters.*
The RATE FOR theft has fallen.

REASON

RIGHT: I have A REASON TO DO work today.
She has A REASON FOR the lawsuit.
This observation indicates a REASON THAT he is here.

SUSPECT: *This observation indicates a REASON WHY he is here.*

WRONG: *This observation indicates a REASON he is here.*
The REASON he is here IS BECAUSE he wants to be.

REBEL

RIGHT: The colonists REBELLED AGAINST tyranny.

SUSPECT: *The colonists' REBELLION WAS AGAINST tyranny.*

RECOGNIZE

RIGHT: They RECOGNIZED THAT the entrance fee WAS a bargain.
They RECOGNIZED the entrance fee TO BE a bargain.
They RECOGNIZED the entrance fee AS a bargain.

WRONG: *They RECOGNIZED the entrance fee AS BEING a bargain.*

RECOMMEND

RIGHT: We RECOMMENDED THAT the shelter BE opened. (subjunctive)

WRONG: *We RECOMMENDED THAT the shelter SHOULD BE opened.*

REDUCE

RIGHT: The coalition REDUCED prices.
The coalition was considering A REDUCTION IN prices.

SUSPECT: *The coalition MADE A REDUCTION IN prices.*
The coalition CAUSED A REDUCTION IN prices.

WRONG: *The coalition MADE A REDUCTION OF prices.*

REFER

RIGHT: This term REFERS TO a kind of disease.
REFERRING TO the controversy, the politician asked for calm.

SUSPECT: *This term IS USED TO REFER TO a kind of disease.*

WRONG: *This term IS IN REFERENCE TO a kind of disease.*
IN REFERENCE TO the controversy, the politician asked for calm.

REGARD

RIGHT: He REGARDS the gold ring AS costly.
The gold ring IS REGARDED AS costly.
He IS REGARDED AS HAVING good taste.

WRONG: *The gold ring IS REGARDED THAT IT IS costly.*

RELUCTANT

RIGHT: They were RELUCTANT TO SAY anything.

WRONG: *They were RELUCTANT ABOUT SAYING anything.*

REPORT

RIGHT: A study HAS REPORTED THAT bees ARE DISAPPEARING rapidly.

.....

WRONG: *A study HAS REPORTED bees AS DISAPPEARING rapidly.*

REQUEST

RIGHT: I REQUEST THAT he BE removed. (subjunctive)

.....

WRONG: *I REQUEST him TO BE removed.*

REQUIRE

RIGHT: She REQUIRES time TO WRITE (or IN ORDER TO WRITE).
She REQUIRES her friend TO DO work.
Her friend IS REQUIRED TO DO work.
She REQUIRES THAT her friend DO work. (subjunctive)
She REQUIRES OF her friend THAT work BE done. (subjunctive)

.....

SUSPECT: *In this hostel, there is a REQUIREMENT OF work.*
There is a REQUIREMENT THAT work BE done.

.....

WRONG: *She REQUIRES her friend DO work* (or *MUST DO work*).
She REQUIRES her friend TO HAVE TO DO work.
She REQUIRES OF her friend TO DO work.
She REQUIRES THAT her friend DOES work (or *SHOULD DO work*).
She REQUIRES THAT her friend IS TO DO work.
She REQUIRES DOING work (or *THE DOING OF work*).
She REQUIRES her friend DOING work.
In this hostel, there is a REQUIREMENT OF work BY guests.

RESEMBLE

RIGHT: A neighbor of mine RESEMBLES my father.

.....

SUSPECT: *A neighbor of mine HAS A RESEMBLANCE TO my father.*

RESTRICTION

RIGHT: The government imposed RESTRICTIONS ON the price of gasoline.

.....

WRONG: *The government imposed RESTRICTIONS FOR the price of gasoline.*

RESULT

RIGHT: Success RESULTS FROM hard work.
Hard work RESULTS IN success.
Success IS A RESULT OF hard work.
Success comes AS A RESULT OF hard work.
AS A RESULT OF our hard work, we became successful.
The RESULT OF our hard work WAS THAT we became successful.

WRONG: *We worked hard WITH THE RESULT OF success.*
We worked hard WITH A RESULTING success.
RESULTING FROM our hard work, we became successful.
BECAUSE OF THE RESULT OF our hard work, we became successful.
The RESULT OF our hard work WAS we became successful. (*THAT* is needed.)

REVEAL

RIGHT: The analysis REVEALED THAT the comet WAS mostly ice.

WRONG: *The analysis REVEALED the comet WAS mostly ice.* (*THAT* is needed.)
The analysis REVEALED the comet TO HAVE BEEN mostly ice.

RISE

RIGHT: Oil prices ROSE sharply last year.
A RISE IN oil prices has led to inflation. (The article *A* before *RISE* signals a noun, not a verb.)
RISING prices at the gas pump are hurting consumers.
The RISING OF the SUN always lifts my spirits.

WRONG: *A RAISE IN oil prices has led to inflation.*
A RISING OF PRICES at the gas pump is hurting consumers.

RULE

RIGHT: The judge RULED THAT the plaintiff WAS in contempt.

SUSPECT: *The judge RULED the plaintiff WAS in contempt.*

WRONG: *The judge RULED the plaintiff TO BE in contempt.*
The judge RULED ON the plaintiff WHO WAS in contempt.

SAME

RIGHT: The car looks THE SAME TO me AS TO you.
I drove to the store AT THE SAME TIME AS you [did].

WRONG: *The car looks THE SAME TO me AS you.* (ambiguous)
I drove to the store AT THE SAME TIME you did.

SECURE

RIGHT: Our authority IS SECURE.

WRONG: *We ARE SECURE ABOUT our authority.*

SEEM

RIGHT: This result SEEMS TO DEMONSTRATE the new theory.
IT SEEMS THAT this result DEMONSTRATES the new theory.
IT SEEMS AS IF this result DEMONSTRATES the new theory.

SUSPECT: *This result SEEMS TO BE A DEMONSTRATION OF the new theory.*
This result SEEMS DEMONSTRATIVE OF the new theory.
This result SEEMS LIKE A DEMONSTRATION OF the new theory.

WRONG: *This result SEEMS AS IF IT DEMONSTRATES the new theory.*
This result SEEMS LIKE IT DEMONSTRATES the new theory.

SHOULD

RIGHT: A car SHOULD BE TAKEN to the mechanic frequently. (obligation)

WRONG: *A car SHOULD PASS every two hours.* (probability)
The owner REQUESTED THAT the car SHOULD BE TAKEN to the mechanic. (Use the subjunctive *BE TAKEN* instead.)

SHOW

RIGHT: A discovery SHOWS THAT an object IS strange.
A discovery SHOWS an object TO BE strange.

SUSPECT: *A discovery SHOWS an object IS strange.*

WRONG: *A discovery SHOWS an object AS strange* (or *AS BEING strange*).

SIGNIFICANT

RIGHT: Your edits HAVE SIGNIFICANTLY IMPROVED the book.

SUSPECT: *Your edits HAVE MADE A SIGNIFICANT IMPROVEMENT IN the book.*

WRONG: *Your edits HAVE BEEN SIGNIFICANT IN IMPROVING the book.*
Your edits HAVE BEEN SIGNIFICANT IN AN IMPROVEMENT OF the book.

SIMILAR

RIGHT: ALL companies HAVE SIMILAR issues. (Comparison requires plural.)

WRONG: *EACH company HAS SIMILAR issues.*
EVERY company HAS SIMILAR issues.

SINCE

RIGHT: Xingo is THE MOST successful new product SINCE 1997. (up to now)
It is the best new beverage SINCE Prune Cola.

SUSPECT: *Xingo is the best new beverage FOLLOWING Prune Cola.*

WRONG: *Xingo is THE MOST successful new product AFTER 1997.*

SO LONG AS See AS LONG AS.

SO TOO

RIGHT: Bellbottoms ARE coming back in style, and SO TOO ARE vests.

SUSPECT: *Bellbottoms ARE coming back in style, and ALSO vests.*

WRONG: *Bellbottoms ARE coming back in style, and SO TOO vests.*

SUBSTITUTE

RIGHT: We SUBSTITUTED Parmesan cheese FOR mozzarella.

WRONG: *We SUBSTITUTED Parmesan cheese IN PLACE OF mozzarella.*

SUCCEED

RIGHT: She SUCCEEDED IN REACHING the summit.

WRONG: *She SUCCEEDED TO REACH the summit.*

SUCH

RIGHT: You may enjoy chemistry and physics, but I hate SUCH subjects.
You may enjoy chemistry and physics, but I hate THESE subjects.
Note: THESE means "these specifically." SUCH is more general.

WRONG: *You may enjoy chemistry and physics, but I hate subjects OF THIS KIND.*
You may enjoy chemistry and physics, but I hate subjects LIKE THESE.

SUGGEST

RIGHT: A study SUGGESTS THAT more work IS needed.
A study SUGGESTS THAT more work WILL BE needed.
We SUGGEST THAT he BE promoted. (subjunctive)
This artwork SUGGESTS great talent.

SUSPECT: *This artwork IS SUGGESTIVE OF great talent.*

SURFACE

RIGHT: Craters have been seen ON THE SURFACE OF the moon.

SUSPECT: *Craters have been seen AT THE SURFACE OF the moon.*

TARGETED

RIGHT: This intervention is TARGETED AT a specific misbehavior.

WRONG: *This intervention is TARGETED TO a specific misbehavior.*

THINK

RIGHT: She THINKS OF them AS heroes.
She IS THOUGHT TO BE secretly wealthy.

WRONG: *They ARE THOUGHT OF BY her AS heroes.*
She THINKS OF them TO BE heroes.
She THINKS OF them BEING heroes.

TO + verb See IN ORDER TO.

TRAIN

RIGHT: She WAS TRAINED TO RUN a division.

WRONG: *She WAS TRAINED FOR RUNNING a division.*
She WAS TRAINED IN RUNNING a division.

TRY

RIGHT: They WILL TRY TO BUILD a company. (intent or purpose)

SUSPECT: *We TRIED BREAKING the door down.* (experiment)

WRONG: *They WILL TRY AND BUILD a company.*
They WILL TRY THAT THEY BUILD a company.

TWICE

RIGHT: He is TWICE AS tall AS Alex [is].
Leaves fall TWICE AS quickly AS they grow.
Naomi wrote TWICE AS MANY letters AS Sara [did].
Naomi wrote 10 letters, DOUBLE THE NUMBER THAT Sara wrote.
Naomi's income DOUBLED in three years.
Naomi DOUBLED her income in three years.

WRONG: *He is TWICE AS tall THAN Alex [is].*
Leaves fall TWICE AS quickly AS their rate of growth.
Naomi wrote DOUBLE THE LETTERS THAT Sara did.
Naomi's income INCREASED BY TWICE in three years.

USE

RIGHT: He USES the hammer AS a weapon.
He USES the hammer TO BREAK a board.
He BREAKS a board WITH the hammer.

WRONG: *He USES a hammer FOR BREAKING a board.*
He USES the hammer LIKE a weapon.
He USES the hammer TO BE a weapon.

VARIATION

RIGHT: There are VARIATIONS IN sunspot frequency and strength over time.

WRONG: *There are VARIATIONS OF sunspot frequency and strength over time.*
There are VARIATIONS AMONG sunspot frequency and strength over time.

VIEW

RIGHT: I VIEWED this process AS a mistake.

WRONG: *I VIEWED this process TO BE a mistake.*
I VIEWED this process LIKE a mistake.

<u>WAY</u>

RIGHT: We proposed a WAY OF REACHING the goal.
The WAY IN WHICH we discussed the idea was positive.
The best WAY TO REACH the goal IS TO FOCUS one's energy.
This process was developed TO ACHIEVE the target.

SUSPECT: *This process was developed AS A WAY OF ACHIEVING the target.*

WRONG: *We proposed a WAY FOR REACHING the goal.*
The best WAY TO REACH the goal IS FOCUSING one's energy.

<u>WEIGH</u>

RIGHT: My laptop WEIGHS LESS THAN a suitcase.
My laptop IS LIGHTER THAN a suitcase.

WRONG: *My laptop WEIGHS LIGHTER THAN a suitcase.*

<u>WHERE</u>

RIGHT: Sussex is the only county WHERE pomegranates grow in this state.
Sussex is the only county IN WHICH pomegranates grow in this state.
This incident represents a case IN WHICH I would call the police.

WRONG: *This incident represents a case WHERE I would call the police.*

<u>WHOSE/WHOM</u>

RIGHT: The officer WHOSE task was to be here did not show up.
The company WHOSE growth leads the industry is XYZ, Inc.
The board consists of 12 members, EACH OF WHOM is responsible for following the law and supervising the management team.
The teachers, MOST OF WHOM have tenure, are negotiating their contract.

WRONG: *The officer, THE task OF WHOM was to be here, did not show up.*

WITH

RIGHT: The lions growled, WITH their fur STANDING on end.

WRONG: *WITH only 25 percent of the student body, seniors get 50 percent of the resources.*

WORRY

RIGHT: The committee was WORRIED ABOUT increased prices.

WRONG: *The committee was WORRIED OVER increased prices.*

APPENDIX B

Glossary

APPENDIX B

Glossary

The following is a list of grammatical terms used in this guide.

Absolute Phrase

A phrase is a group of words that modifies a whole clause or sentence. An absolute phrase cannot stand alone as a sentence, but it often expresses an additional thought. An absolute phrase is separated from the main clause by a comma; it may come before or after that main clause. See also **Modifier**.

> The car fell into the lake, the cold water filling the compartment.
>
> His arm in pain, Guillermo strode out of the building.

Action Noun

A noun that expresses an action. Action nouns are often derived from verbs. In general, action nouns can be parallel to other action nouns (including gerunds), but not to person-place-thing nouns. Also, if a particular noun has both action and gerund forms, the action form is typically preferred (e.g., *the eruption of the volcano* is typically preferred over *the erupting of the volcano*).

verb + –TION:	construction, pollution, redemption
verb + –AL:	arrival, reversal
verb + –MENT:	development, punishment
Same as verb:	change, rise, struggle

Active Voice

The form of a verb in which the subject is doing the action expressed by the verb.

> The driver swerved.
>
> The tires exploded.
>
> They broke the lamp.

Additive Phrase

Modifier phrases that add nouns onto another noun. However, additive phrases are not part of the main subject of a sentence.

along with me	in addition to the memo	as well as a dog
accompanied by her	together with the others	including them

Adjective

A word that modifies a noun.

wonderful food	forest fire
green eyes	the changing seasons

Adverb

A word that modifies a verb, an adjective, another adverb, or even a whole clause. Most adverbs end in *–ly*, but not all.

The stone fell slowly.

A swiftly frozen lake appears cloudy.

We ran very quickly.

Adverbial Modifier

A word, phrase, or clause that describes a verb or clause.

Adverb:	He walked energetically.
Prepositional phrase:	He walked toward the building.
Subordinate clause:	He walked because he was thirsty.
Present participle:	He walked ahead, swinging his arms.
Infinitive:	He walked to buy a drink.
Preposition + simple gerund:	He walked by putting one foot in front of the other.

Antecedent

The noun that a pronoun refers to.

The ROWERS lifted the BOAT and flipped it over their heads.

(*Rowers* is the antecedent of *their*. *Boat* is the antecedent of *it*.)

Appositive

A noun or noun phrase that is placed next to another noun to identify it. Often separated from the rest of the sentence by commas.

The coach, an old classmate of mine, was not pleased.

(*An old classmate of mine* is an appositive phrase to the noun *coach*.)

Article

The words *a*, *an*, or *the*. An article must be followed by a noun (perhaps with modifiers in between). Articles can be considered special adjectives.

a CAT	the board MEETING
an APPLE	an important but often overlooked RULE

Bare Form (of verb)

The dictionary form of a verb (what you would look up in a dictionary). A bare form has no endings added on, such as *–s*, *–ed*, or *–ing*. The bare form is the infinitive without the *to* in front.

assess	call	command
decide	furnish	gather

Bossy Verb

A verb that tells someone to do something. Bossy verbs are paired with one of two tenses, depending on the specific verb: the command subjunctive or an infinitive. (Some bossy verbs are flexible and can be paired with either of those forms.)

Bossy + infinitive:	I TOLD him to run.
Bossy + subjunctive:	He REQUESTED that the bus wait another minute.
Bossy + either form:	I ASKED him to finish the report by tomorrow.
	I ASKED that he finish the report by tomorrow.

Case

The grammatical role that a noun or pronoun plays in a sentence.

Subject case (subject role):	I, you, she, he, it, we, they
Object case (object role):	me, you, her, him, it, us, them
Possessive case (ownership role):	my/mine, your(s), her(s), his, its, our(s), their(s)

Nouns show the possessive case by adding *'s* for singular nouns (Mary's car) or *s'* for plural nouns (the executives' conference call).

Clause

A group of words that contains a subject and a working verb.

Main or independent clause:

The company is successful.

Yesterday I ate a pizza in haste.

Subordinate or dependent clause:

Yesterday I ate a pizza that I did not like.

When I think about that pizza, I feel ill.

Collective Noun

A noun that looks singular (it does not end in *–s*) but that refers to a group of people or things. Usually considered singular on the GMAT (but look for clues in the sentence!).

The army is recruiting again.

This team was eliminated during the semifinal round.

Command Subjunctive

Subjunctive form used with certain bossy verbs and similar constructions. Same in form as a direct command. See also **Subjunctive Mood** and **Bossy Verb**.

The draft board required that he register for selective service.

Comparative Form

Form of adjectives and adverbs used to compare two things or people. Regular comparative forms are either the base word plus *–er* (e.g., *greener*) or the base word preceded by *more* (e.g., *more intelligent*). Common irregular forms are listed in the table:

Adjective or Adverb	Comparative
good/well	better
bad/badly	worse
much, many	more
little, few	less, fewer
far	farther, further

Comparisons

Structures by which we compare things or people in sentences. Usually marked with signal words such as *like*, *unlike*, *as*, or *than*. Comparisons can be between two things or people (comparative) or among three or more things or people (superlative).

Complex Gerund

A gerund is an *–ing* form of a verb that functions as a noun; a complex gerund includes an article or something similar to indicate that the *–ing* word is definitely functioning as a noun. In general, complex gerunds can be put in parallel with action nouns, but simple gerunds should not be. See also **Simple Gerund**.

The running of the bulls is a tradition in Spain.

The volcanic eruption resulted in the melting of the iceberg.

Concrete Noun

A noun that does not represent an action. Concrete nouns refer to things, people, places, and even time periods or certain events. Generally, concrete nouns are not logically parallel to action nouns.

hole	manager	month
proton	area	inauguration

Conditional Tense

A verb tense formed by combining the helping verb *would* with the base form of the verb. See also **Tense**.

Future as seen from the past:

He said that he would write.

Hypothetical result of unlikely condition:

If she liked pizza, she would like this restaurant.

Conjunction

A word that joins two parts of a sentence together. Coordinating and correlative conjunctions give the two parts equal weight. Subordinating conjunctions put one part in a logically junior role, in relation to the other part.

Coordinating (Co):	and, but, or (less common: for, nor, so, yet)
Correlative (Cor):	either X or Y; neither X nor Y; not X but Y; not only X but also Y
Subordinating (Sub):	after, although, because, before, if, since, when

Conjunctive Adverb

A transition word or phrase that is used after a semicolon to help connect two main clauses. Conjunctive adverbs are not true conjunctions.

therefore, thus, consequently, however, nevertheless, furthermore, etc.

The general was stuck in traffic; therefore, the ceremony started late.

Connecting Punctuation

The comma (,), the semicolon (;), the colon (:), and the em dash (—). Used to link parts of a sentence.

Connecting Words

Conjunctions, conjunctive adverbs, and relative pronouns. Used to link parts of a sentence.

Countable Noun

A noun that can be counted in English. For example, you can say *one hat, two hats, three hats.* Countable nouns can be made singular or plural.

hat/hats	thought/thoughts
month/months	person/people

Dangling Modifier

A noun modifier that does not properly modify or describe any noun in the sentence. In fact, the noun that should be modified has been omitted from the sentence. Likewise, a verb modifier that requires a subject but lacks one in the sentence is considered dangling. Dangling modifiers are always incorrect. See also **Modifier**.

> Walking along the river bank, the new tower can be seen.
>
> (The modifier *walking along the river bank* has no subject. The sentence could be rewritten as follows: *Walking along the river bank, one can see the new tower.*)

Demonstrative Pronoun

The pronouns *this, that, these,* and *those*. Demonstrative pronouns can be used as adjectives (*these plants, that company*). They can also be used in place of nouns, but they must be modified in some way, according to the GMAT. See also **Pronoun**.

> The strategy taken by Livonia is preferable to that taken by Khazaria.
>
> (The demonstrative pronoun *that* properly stands for the noun *strategy*. The pronoun *that* is modified by the phrase *taken by Khazaria.*)

Dependent Clause

A clause that cannot stand alone without a main or independent clause. A dependent clause is led by a subordinator. Also known as a subordinate clause. See also **Clause** and **Subordinator**.

Direct Object

The noun that is acted upon by a verb in the active voice. Can be a pronoun, a noun phrase, or a noun clause.

> I broke the lamp.
>
> Who let the big dogs out?
>
> I believe that you are right.

Essential Modifier

A modifier that provides necessary information. Use an essential modifier to identify the particular noun out of many possibilities or to create a permanent description of the noun. Do not use commas to separate an essential modifier from the modified noun. See also **Modifier**.

I want to sell the car that my sister drove to the city.

Fragment

A group of words that does not work as a stand-alone sentence, either because it is begun by a subordinator or because it lacks a subject or a verb. See also **Subordinator**.

Although he bought a pretzel. (*Although* is a subordinator.)

The device developed by scientists. (*Developed by scientists* is a noun modifier; the subject *the device* lacks a verb.)

Future Tense

The form of a verb that expresses action in the future. Also known as simple future. See also **Tense**.

The driver will swerve.

The tires will be punctured.

They will break the lamp.

Gerund

An *–ing* form of a verb used as a noun.

Skiing is fun.

She enjoys snowboarding.

She often thinks about sledding.

Gerund Phrase

A phrase centered on an *–ing* form of a verb used as a noun.

Simple:	Skiing difficult trails is fun.
Complex:	We discussed the grooming of the horses.

Helping Verb

A verb used with another verb. Helping verbs create various grammatical structures or provide additional shades of meaning. The most common are the three primary helping verbs.

be:	I am working.
do:	The company does follow safety rules.
have:	The team has succeeded.

There are also modal helping verbs, such as *can*, *could*, *may*, *might*, *must*, *shall*, *should*, *will*, and *would*. These words qualify the main verb (He *may* accept the job) or convey a judgment (He *should* accept the job).

Hypothetical Subjunctive

Subjunctive form that indicates unlikely or unreal conditions. This form is used in some cases after the words *if*, *as if*, or *as though*, or with the verb *to wish*. The hypothetical subjunctive is equivalent to the simple past tense of every verb, except the verb *to be*: The hypothetical subjunctive of *be* is *were* for every subject. See also **Subjunctive Mood**.

If he were in better shape, he would win the race.

Idiom

An expression that has a unique form. Idioms do not follow general rules; rather, they must simply be memorized.

If–Then Statement

A sentence that contains both a condition (marked by an *if*) and a result (possibly marked by a *then*). Either the condition or the result may be written first in the sentence. The verbs in *if–then* statements follow particular patterns of tense and mood.

If he were in better shape, he would win the race.

They get sick if they eat dairy products.

If she swims, then she will win.

Imperative Mood

The form of a verb that expresses direct commands. Identical to the bare form of the verb as well as to the command subjunctive. See also **Mood**.

Go to the store and buy me an ice cream cone.

Indefinite Pronoun

A pronoun that does not refer to a specific noun. Most indefinite pronouns are singular.

anyone, anybody, anything	no one, nobody, nothing
each, every (as pronouns)	someone, somebody, something
everyone, everybody, everything	whatever, whoever

either, neither (may require a plural verb if paired with *or*/*nor*)

A few indefinite pronouns are always plural.

both, few, many, several

The SANAM pronouns (some, any, none, all, more/most) can be either singular or plural, depending on the noun in the *of* phrase that follows the pronoun.

None of the RECORDS have been updated. (plural)

Most of the COFFEE was spilled down the stairs. (singular)

Independent Clause

A clause that can stand alone as a grammatical sentence. Contains its own subject and verb. Also known as a Main Clause.

Indicative Mood

The form of a verb that expresses facts or beliefs. Most verbs in most English sentences are in the indicative mood. See also **Mood**.

I went to the store and bought an ice cream cone.

I will do so again.

Indirect Object

The noun that expresses the recipient or the beneficiary of some action. Can be a Pronoun, a Noun Phrase, or a Noun Clause.

I gave him the lamp.

She found the man a good book.

Infinitive

The bare form of the verb plus the marker *to*. Used as a noun or as a modifier within a sentence.

I prefer to read novels.

She drove many miles in order to see her uncle.

–ing Form

The bare form of the verb plus the ending *–ing*. When used as a noun, the *–ing* form is called a gerund. When used as a modifier or as part of the progressive tense, the *–ing* form is called a present participle.

Present participle (part of verb):	I am eating an apple.
Gerund (noun):	Eating an apple is good for you.
Present participle (noun modifier):	The man eating an apple is my friend.
Present participle (adverbial modifier):	I sat on the porch, eating an apple.

Intransitive Verb

A verb that does not take a direct object. Intransitive verbs cannot be put in the passive voice.

I went to the library.

The driver swerved.

(Intransitive verb *–ing* forms followed by nouns are usually adjectives: *The swerving driver came to a stop on the sidewalk.*)

Linking Verb

A verb that expresses what a subject is, rather than what it does. The most important linking verb is *to be*. Often, linking verbs are followed by adjectives that describe the subject.

Our academic adviser is happy.

My sister's dog is devoted to her.

Main Clause

A clause that can stand alone as a grammatical sentence. A main clause contains its own subject and verb and is not introduced by a subordinator. Also known as an Independent Clause.

I prefer to read novels.

While eating lunch, she finished reading the report.

Marker

Words that serve as clues that the GMAT is testing a particular issue. For example, *and* is a parallelism marker and *which* is a modifier marker.

Middleman

Words that the GMAT inserts between the subject and the verb to hide the subject. Middlemen are usually modifiers of various types.

Misplaced Modifier

A noun modifier that is not positioned next to the noun it needs to describe in the sentence. Misplaced modifiers are incorrect. See also **Modifier**.

Misplaced: I collapsed onto the sofa exhausted by a long day of work.

Corrected: *Exhausted by a long day of work, I collapsed on the sofa.*

(In the misplaced example, the modifier *exhausted by a long day of work* refers to *sofa*, but a sofa can't be exhausted.)

Modal Helping Verb

See **Helping Verb**.

Modifier

Words, phrases, or clauses that describe other parts of the sentence. Noun Modifiers modify nouns. Adverbial Modifiers modify anything other than nouns (verbs, clauses, adjectives, etc.).

Mood

The form of the verb that indicates the attitude of the speaker toward the action.

> Indicative: I drive fast cars. We drove to Las Vegas.
>
> Imperative: Drive three blocks and turn left.
>
> Command Subjunctive: I suggested that he drive three blocks.
>
> Hypothetical Subjunctive: If he drove three blocks, he would see us.

Nonessential Modifier

A modifier that provides extra information. If this modifier were removed from the sentence, the core meaning of the sentence would still make sense. Use commas to separate a nonessential modifier from the modified noun. See also **Modifier**.

> I want to sell this beat-up old car, which my sister drove to the city.

Noun

A word that means a person, place, or thing. Nouns can be the subject of a verb, the direct or indirect object of a verb, or the object of a preposition. Nouns can be modified by an adjective or another noun modifier.

Noun as Adjective

A noun that is placed in front of another noun and that functions as an adjective.

> A government survey; the stone wall
>
> (*A government survey* is a type of survey; a *stone wall* is a type of wall.)

Noun Clause

A subordinate clause (with its own subject and verb) that acts as a noun in the sentence. That is, it is the subject of a verb, the object of a verb, or the object of a preposition. Led by relative pronouns *which*, *what*, *when*, *why*, *whether*, or *that*.

> I care about what he thinks. (object of the preposition *about*)
>
> Whether I stay or go is unimportant. (subject of the verb *is*)
>
> I believe that you are right. (object of the verb *believe*)

Noun Modifier

A word, phrase, or clause that describes a noun.

Adjective:	This big window needs to be replaced.
Past participle:	The window broken during the storm needs to be replaced.
Present participle:	The window rattling against the sill needs to be replaced.
Prepositional phrase:	The window on the right needs to be replaced.
Appositive:	This window, an original installation, needs to be replaced.
Infinitive:	The window to replace is on the second floor.
Relative clause:	The window that needs to be replaced has a missing pane.

Noun Phrase

A phrase that acts as a noun in the sentence. A noun phrase typically consists of a noun and its modifiers.

A new government SURVEY of taxpayers is planned.

(The subject of the sentence is the noun phrase consisting of the noun *survey* and its modifiers: *a*, *new*, *government*, and *of taxpayers*.)

Object Case

The form of a pronoun used as the object of a verb or of a preposition. Nouns do not change form in the object case. See also **Case**.

Opening Modifier

A phrase or clause at the beginning of a sentence that does not contain the noun or subject it refers to. An opening modifier is always followed by a comma. The main noun/subject after the comma has to be the noun to which the opening modifier was referring.

Intrigued by the opportunity, the manager approached her supervisor to inquire about the requirements for the new position.

Parallel Element

A part of a sentence made parallel to another part or parts of the sentence through the use of parallel markers.

We will invite both his friends and her family.

Parallel Marker

The words that link or contrast parts of a sentence, forcing them to be parallel.

We will invite both his friends and her family.

Parallelism Category

A type of word, phrase, or clause. Something in one parallelism category can be made parallel to something else of the same type, but it should not be made parallel to anything in another category.

Concrete nouns:	I like to eat peanut butter and ice cream.
Action nouns and complex gerunds:	I like to watch the release of the doves and the changing of the guard.
Simple gerunds:	I like eating ice cream and watching birds.
Working verbs:	I like eating ice cream and watching birds.
Infinitives:	I prefer either to eat ice cream or to watch birds.
Adjectives and participles:	I like ice cream, either frozen or warm.
Clauses:	She knows that I like ice cream and that I hate sorbet.

Participle

One of two kinds of words derived from verbs. Present participles typically end in *–ing* and can be used as a verb, a noun, a noun modifier, or an adverbial modifier. Present participles typically indicate ongoing action (though not necessarily in the present). Past participles typically end in *–ed* (though there are lots of irregular forms) and can be used as a verb, a noun modifier, or an adverbial modifier. Past participles tend to indicate a completed action relative to the given time frame in the sentence.

	Form	Example
Present Participle	Verb:	She will be hiking next week.
	Noun:	Studying for the GMAT is fun.
	Noun mod:	The man running down the hall is late for his meeting.
	Adverbial mod:	He missed the deadline, hurting his standing with his boss.
Past Participle	Verb:	The tires were punctured.
	Noun mod:	The tire punctured by the nail needs to be repaired.
	Adverbial mod:	Punctured by a nail, the tire slowly deflated.

Parts of Speech

The basic kinds of words. A word's part of speech is determined both by what the word means and by what role or roles the word can play in a sentence.

Noun:	peanut, lake, vacuum, considerations, opportunity
Verb:	swim, proceed, execute, went, should
Adjective:	wonderful, blue, helpful
Adverb:	slowly, very, graciously
Preposition:	of, for, by, with, through, during, in, on
Conjunction:	and, but, or, although, because

Passive Voice

The form of a verb in which the subject is receiving the action expressed by the verb.

The driver was thrown from the car.

The crystal vases have been broken by the thieves.

Past Participle

The participle used in perfect tenses and passive voice. A past participle may also be used as an adjective. Past participles tend to indicate completed action, although not necessarily in the past (relative to now).

The tires will be punctured. (passive voice)

They have broken the lamp. (present perfect tense)

A frozen lake. (adjective)

Regular past participles are formed by adding *–d* or *–ed* to the base form of the verb. Many irregular past participles are listed below, together with irregular past tense forms. Sometimes the past tense form and the past participle are identical. Non-native English speakers should study this list. Native English speakers likely already know most or all of these forms.

Base Form	Past Tense	Past Participle
be	was, were	been
become	became	become
begin	began	begun
break	broke	broken
bring	brought	brought
build	built	built
buy	bought	bought
catch	caught	caught
choose	chose	chosen
come	came	come
cost	cost	cost
cut	cut	cut
do	did	done
draw	drew	drawn
drink	drank	drunk
drive	drove	driven
eat	ate	eaten
fall	fell	fallen
fight	fought	fought
find	found	found
forget	forgot	forgotten

Base Form	Past Tense	Past Participle
freeze	froze	frozen
give	gave	given
go	went	gone
grow	grew	grown
hold	held	held
keep	kept	kept
know	knew	known
lead	led	led
lose	lost	lost
make	made	made
pay	paid	paid
put	put	put
rise	rose	risen
say	said	said
see	saw	seen
seek	sought	sought
sell	sold	sold
send	sent	sent
set	set	set
show	showed	shown
shrink	shrank	shrunk
speak	spoke	spoken
spend	spent	spent
spread	spread	spread
stand	stood	stood
steal	stole	stolen
strike	struck	struck
sweep	swept	swept
take	took	taken
teach	taught	taught
tell	told	told
think	thought	thought
throw	threw	thrown
understand	understood	understood
win	won	won
write	wrote	written

Past Perfect Tense

The form of a verb that expresses action that takes place before another past action or time marker. The past perfect tense is formed with the verb *had* and the past participle.

The officer said that the driver had swerved.

By 2005, she had visited India three times.

Past Tense

The form of a verb that expresses action in the past. See also **Tense**.

The driver swerved.

The tires were punctured.

They broke the lamp.

(Common irregular past tense forms are listed under the entry for Past Participles.)

Person

Indicates whether the word refers to the speaker or writer (first person), the listener or reader (second person), or someone/something else (third person). Personal pronouns are marked for person. Present tense verbs in the third person singular add an *–s*: *The doctor writes.*

First person: I, me, my, we, us, our

Second person: you, your

Third person: she, he, it, its, they, them, their

Phrase

A group of words that has a particular grammatical role in the sentence. The type of phrase is often determined by one main word within the phrase. A phrase can contain other phrases. For example, a noun phrase can contain a prepositional phrase.

Noun phrase:	The short **chapter** at the end of the book is important.
Verb phrase:	The computer must have been **broken** in the move.
Adjective phrase:	The employee most **reluctant** to volunteer was chosen.
Prepositional phrase:	The wolf **in** the cage has woken up.

Plural

A category of number that indicates more than one. Nouns, pronouns, and verbs can be made plural. See also **Singular**.

Many dogs are barking; they are keeping me awake.

Possessive Case

The form of a pronoun or a noun that owns another noun. In possessive case, nouns add *–'s* or *–s'*. See also **Case**.

Preposition

A word that indicates a relationship between the object (usually a noun) and something else in the sentence. In some cases, prepositions can consist of more than one word.

of, in, to, for, with, on, by, at, from, as, into, about, like, after,

between, through, over, against, under, out of, next to, upon

Prepositional Phrase

A prepositional phrase consists of a preposition and an object (a noun). The preposition indicates a relationship between that object and something else in the sentence.

I would like a drink of water. (*Of water* modifies *drink*.)

The man in the gray suit is the CEO. (*In the gray suit* modifies *man*.)

Present Participle

The participle used in progressive tenses. A present participle may also be used as a noun, a noun modifier, or a verb modifier. Present participles tend to indicate ongoing action, although not necessarily at the present moment. To form a present participle, add *–ing* to the base form of the verb, possibly doubling the verb's last consonant.

The tires were rolling.

She jumped into the swimming pool.

Hiking is great.

Present Perfect Tense

The form of a verb that expresses action that began in the past and continues to the present or whose effect continues to the present. The present perfect tense is formed with the verb *has* or *have* and the past participle.

The tires have been punctured. (The tires were punctured in the past, and it is still true in the present that they are punctured.)

You have broken my lamp! (The lamp was broken in the past, and it is still broken now.)

Present Tense

The form of a verb that expresses action in the present. The simple present (nonprogressive) often indicates general truths. See also **Tense**.

The driver swerves.

The tires are on the car.

They speak English. (general truth; not necessarily speaking English right now)

Primary Helping Verb

See **Helping Verb**.

Progressive Tense

The form of a verb that expresses ongoing action in the past, present, or future. See also **Tense**.

> The driver is swerving.
>
> The tires were rolling.
>
> They will be running.

Pronoun

A pronoun stands in for another noun elsewhere in the sentence or for an implied noun. The noun is called the antecedent.

> When Amy fell, she hurt her knee. (*She* and *her* refer to the antecedent *Amy*.)
>
> When it started to rain, the tourists pulled out their umbrellas. (*Their* refers to *tourists*.)
>
> The term bibliophile refers to someone who loves books. (*Someone* is a pronoun but does not need to have a specific antecedent; *who* refers to *someone*.)

Relative Clause

A subordinate clause headed by a relative pronoun. Relative clauses may act as noun modifiers or, more infrequently, as nouns.

> The professor who spoke is my mother.
>
> What you see is what you get.

Relative Pronoun

A pronoun that connects a subordinate clause to a sentence. The relative pronoun plays a grammatical role in the subordinate clause (e.g., subject, verb, object, or prepositional object). If the relative clause is a noun modifier, the relative pronoun also refers to the modified noun. If the relative clause is a noun clause, then the relative pronoun does not refer to a noun outside the relative clause.

> The professor who spoke is my mother.
>
> (The relative pronoun *who* is the subject of the clause *who spoke*. *Who* also refers to *professor*, the noun modified by the clause *who spoke*.)
>
> What you see is a disaster waiting to happen.
>
> (The relative pronoun *what* is the object of the clause *what you see*. *What* does not refer to a noun outside the clause; rather, the clause *what you see* is the subject of the sentence.)

Reporting Verb

A verb, such as *indicate*, *claim*, *announce*, or *report*, that in fact reports or otherwise includes a thought or belief. A reporting verb should be followed by *that* on the GMAT.

> The survey indicates that CFOs are feeling pessimistic.

Run-On Sentence

A sentence incorrectly formed out of two main clauses joined without proper punctuation or a proper connecting word, such as a coordinator or subordinator. Also called a comma splice.

Wrong:	The film was great, I want to see it again.
Right:	The film was great; I want to see it again.
Right:	The film was great, and I want to see it again.
Right:	Because the film was great, I want to see it again.

SANAM Pronouns

An indefinite pronoun that can be either singular or plural, depending on the object of the *of* phrase that follows. The SANAM pronouns are *some, any, none, all, more/most.*

Some of the milk has gone bad.

Some of the children are angry.

Sentence

A complete grammatical utterance. Sentences contain a subject and a verb in a main clause. Some sentences contain two main clauses linked by a coordinating conjunction, such as *and.* Other sentences contain subordinate clauses tied to the main clause in some way.

My boss is angry. (This sentence contains one main clause. The subject is *boss*; the verb is *is.*)

He read my blog, and I saw the comments that he posted. (This sentence contains two main clauses linked by *and.* In the first, the subject is *he* and the verb is *read.* In the second, the subject is *I* and the verb is *saw.* There is also a subordinate clause, *that he posted*, describing *comments.*)

Simple Gerund

A gerund is an *–ing* form of a verb that functions as a noun. A simple gerund typically does not include an article or something similar (as a complex gerund does).

Swimming is fun.

She likes running and hiking.

(In general, simple gerunds should not be put in parallel with action nouns. Complex gerunds can be put in parallel with action nouns. See also **Complex Gerund**.)

Singular

A category of number that indicates one. Nouns, pronouns, and verbs can be made singular. See also **Plural**.

A dog is barking; it is keeping me awake.

Split

Differences in the answer choices. When working on a Sentence Correction problem, compare the answers to find splits; these differences will help you determine what the problem is testing.

State Verb

A verb that expresses a condition of the subject, rather than an action that the subject performs. State verbs are rarely used in progressive tenses.

> Her assistant knows Russian.
>
> I love chocolate.
>
> This word means "hello."

Subgroup Modifier

A type of modifier that describes a smaller subset within the group expressed by the modified noun.

> French wines, many of which I have tasted, are superb.

Subject

The noun or pronoun that goes with the verb and that is required in every GMAT sentence. The subject performs the action expressed by an active-voice verb; in contrast, the subject receives the action expressed by a passive-voice verb. The subject and the verb must agree in number (singular or plural).

> The market closed.
>
> She is considering a new job.
>
> They have been seen.

Subjunctive Mood

One of two verb forms indicating desires, suggestions, or unreal or unlikely conditions.

> Command subjunctive: She requested that he stop the car.
>
> Hypothetical subjunctive: If he were in charge, he would help us.

Subordinate Clause

A clause that cannot stand alone without a main or independent clause. A subordinate clause is led by a subordinator. Also known as a dependent clause. See also **Clause**.

> Her dog, which is brown, is friendly.
>
> Although he barely studied, he scored well on the test.

Subordinator

A word that creates a subordinate clause. Relative pronouns typically introduce noun modifiers. Subordinating conjunctions typically introduce adverbial modifiers.

Relative pronoun:	which, that, who, whose, whom, what
Subordinating conjunction:	although, because, while, whereas

Superlative Form

Form of adjectives and adverbs used to compare three or more things or people. The reference group may be implied. Regular superlative forms are either the base word plus *–est* (e.g., *greenest*) or the base word preceded by *most* (e.g., *most intelligent*). Irregulars are listed below.

Adjective or Adverb	Superlative
good/well	best
bad/badly	worst
much, many	most
little, few	least, fewest
far	farthest, furthest

Tense

The form of the verb that indicates the time of the action (relative to the present time). The completed or ongoing nature of the action may also be indicated.

Present:	She speaks French.
Past:	She spoke French.
Future:	She will speak French.
Present progressive:	She is speaking French.
Past progressive:	She was speaking French.
Future progressive:	She will be speaking French.
Present perfect:	She has spoken French.
Past perfect:	By 2018, she had spoken French for half her life.

That Clause

A clause that begins with the word *that*. The *that* clause can be a standard noun modifier.

The suggestion that he made is bad.

A *that* clause can also be part of a Subject–Verb–THAT–Subject–Verb(–Object) sentence structure. In this case, the entire *that* clause is considered the object of the first subject–verb pairing

He suggested that the world is flat.

Transitive Verb

A verb that takes a direct object; if the sentence doesn't have that object, it is incomplete.

Wrong: The company makes.

Right: The company makes computer chips.

Some verbs can be either transitive or intransitive. In particular, verbs that indicate changes of state can be either.

The lamp broke.

I broke the lamp.

Transitive verbs can usually be put in the passive voice, which turns the object into the subject.

The agent observed the driver.

The driver was observed by the agent.

Transitive verb *–ing* forms followed by nouns are usually simple gerund phrases.

The agent was paid for observing the driver.

This duality means that some *–ing* forms in isolation can be ambiguous. The phrase *melting snow* could mean "the act of causing snow to melt" or "snow that is melting." Use context to resolve the ambiguity.

Uncountable Noun

A noun that cannot be counted in English. For instance, you cannot say *one patience, two patiences, three patiences*. Most uncountable nouns exist only in the singular form and cannot be made plural.

patience	milk	information
furniture	rice	chemistry

Verb

The word or words that express the action of the sentence. The verb indicates the time of the action (tense), the attitude of the speaker (mood), and the role of the subject (voice). The verb may also reflect the number and person of the subject. Every sentence must have a verb.

Verbal

A word or phrase that is derived from a verb and that functions as a different part of speech in the sentence: as a noun, as an adjective (noun modifier), or as an adverb (verb modifier).

Infinitive:	He likes to walk to the store.
Gerund:	I enjoy walking.
Present participle:	The man walking toward us is my father.
Past participle:	The facts given in the case are clear.

Voice

The form of the verb that indicates the role of the subject as performer of the action (active voice) or recipient of the action (passive voice).

Active voice:	She threw the ball.
Passive voice:	The ball was thrown by her.

Warm-Up

Words that the GMAT inserts at the beginning of the sentence to hide the subject in question. Warm-ups are modifiers of various types, including Opening Modifiers.

Working Verb

A verb that could be the main verb of a grammatical sentence. A working verb shows tense, mood, and voice, as well as number and person in some circumstances. The use of this term helps to distinguish working verbs from verbals, which cannot by themselves be the main verb of a sentence.

MANHATTAN PREP

GMAT®

All the Quant

This guide provides an in-depth look at the variety of GMAT questions that test your knowledge of fractions, decimals, and percents. Learn to see the connections among these part–whole relationships and practice implementing strategic shortcuts.

Acknowledgements

A great number of people were involved in the creation of the book you are holding.

Our Manhattan Prep resources are based on the continuing experiences of our instructors and students. The overall vision for this edition was developed by Stacey Koprince, who determined what strategies to cover and how to weave them into a cohesive whole.

Stacey Koprince was also the primary author and she was supported by a number of content experts. Chelsey Cooley, Daniel Fogel, Mario Gambino, Whitney Garner, David Mahler, Andrea Pawliczek, and Helen Tan served as a sounding board during the writing phase, vetting ideas and editing new content. Chelsey Cooley also wrote a number of new problems for the guide and David Mahler proofed them all. The handwritten solutions were all the work of Helen Tan. Mario Gambino managed production for all images, handwritten and otherwise, with Derek Frankhouser and Israt Pasha lending their design expertise.

Matthew Callan coordinated the production work for this guide. Once the manuscript was done, Naomi Beesen and Emily Meredith Sledge edited and Cheryl Duckler proofread the entire guide from start to finish. Carly Schnur designed the covers.

Retail ISBNs: 978-1-5062-4854-7, 978-1-5062-6254-3
Retail eISBN: 978-1-5062-4855-4
Course ISBN: 978-1-5062-4859-2
Course eISBN: 978-1-5062-4860-8

10 9 8 7 6 5 4 3 2

GMAT® Strategy Guides

GMAT All the Quant

GMAT All the Verbal

GMAT Integrated Reasoning & Essay

Strategy Guide Supplements

Math

GMAT Foundations of Math

GMAT Advanced Quant

Verbal

GMAT Foundations of Verbal

September 3, 2019

Dear Student,

Thank you for picking up a copy of *All the Quant*. I hope this book provides just the guidance you need to get the most out of your GMAT studies.

At Manhattan Prep, we continually aspire to provide the best instructors and resources possible. If you have any questions or feedback, please do not hesitate to contact us.

Email our Student Services team at gmat@manhattanprep.com or give us a shout at 212-721-7400 (or 800-576-4628 in the United States or Canada). We try to keep all our books free of errors, but if you think we've goofed, please visit manhattanprep.com/GMAT/errata.

Our Manhattan Prep Strategy Guides are based on the continuing experiences of both our instructors and our students. The primary author of the 7th Edition All the Quant guide was Stacey Koprince. Project management and design were led by Matthew Callan, Mario Gambino, and Helen Tan. I'd like to send particular thanks to instructors Chelsey Cooley, Daniel Fogel, Whitney Garner, David Mahler, Andrea Pawliczek, and Emily Meredith Sledge for their content contributions.

Finally, we are indebted to all of the Manhattan Prep students who have given us excellent feedback over the years. This book wouldn't be half of what it is without their voice.

And now that *you* are one of our students too, please chime in! I look forward to hearing from you. Thanks again and best of luck preparing for the GMAT!

Sincerely,

Chris Ryan
Executive Director
Product Strategy

www.manhattanprep.com/gmat 138 West 25th Street, 7th Floor, New York, NY 10001 Tel: 212-721-7400
Fax: 646-514-7425

TABLE OF CONTENTS

UNIT TWO: Algebra

UNIT FIVE: Geometry

The GMAT Mindset

The GMAT is a complex exam. It feels like an academic test—math, grammar, logical reasoning—but it's really not! At heart, the GMAT is a test of your *executive reasoning skills.*

Executive reasoning is the official term for your ability to make all kinds of decisions in the face of complex and changing information. It makes sense, then, that graduate management programs would want to test these skills. It's crucial for you to understand *how* they do so because that understanding will impact both how you study for the GMAT and how you take the test.

You do need to know various math and grammar facts, rules, and concepts in order to do well on the GMAT—and this makes the test feel similar to tests that you took in school. There's one critical difference though: When your teachers gave you tests in school, they tested you on material they expected you to know how to handle. Your teachers wouldn't put something on the test that they *expected* you to get wrong. That would be cruel!

Well, it would be cruel if the main point of the exam was to test your mastery of those facts, rules, and concepts. But that isn't the main point of the GMAT. Rather, the GMAT wants to know how well you make decisions regarding when to invest your limited time and mental energy—and when *not* to.

In other words, the GMAT wants to know how you make business decisions. And no good businessperson invests in every single opportunity placed in front of them, just because it's there. A good businessperson evaluates each opportunity, saying yes to some and no to others. That's what you're going to do on the GMAT, too. You'll invest in a majority of the problems presented to you, but you *will* say no to some—the ones that look too hard or seem like they'll take too long to solve. These are literally bad investments.

So the GMAT will offer you questions that it thinks you will not be able to do. How does it accomplish this? The GMAT is an adaptive test; that is, it adapts to you as you take it, offering easier or harder questions based on how you're doing on the test. Ideally, you'll do well on the material that you know how to answer in a reasonable amount of time. Your reward? You'll earn questions that are too hard for you to do—either they'll take too long to answer or they'll be so hard that you wouldn't be able to do them even if you had unlimited time.

Then what? If you try to use a "school mindset" on the test, you'll keep trying to answer the questions even though you really can't do them. You'll waste a bunch of time and then, later, you'll have to rush on other questions. As a result, you'll start to miss questions that you actually do know how to answer and your score will go down. This is the business equivalent of spending most of your annual budget by August. . .and then not having enough money left to run the business well from September through December.

Instead, use your "business mindset" to carry you through the exam. When the test finds your limit, acknowledge that! Call it a bad investment and let that problem go (ideally before you've spent very much time on it). Choose an answer, any answer, and move on.

Extend the business mindset to your studies as well. If there are certain topics that you really hate, decide that you're not going to study them in the first place. You're just going to bail (guess quickly and move on) when one of those "opportunities" comes up. (One caveat: You can't bail on huge swaths of content. For example, don't bail on all of algebra; that represents too great a portion of the Quant section. You can, though, bail on a subset—say, absolute values and sequences.)

Start orienting yourself around your business mindset today. You aren't going to do it all. You're going to choose the best opportunities as you see them throughout the test. When you decide not to pursue a particular "investment," you're going to say no as quickly as you can and forget about it—don't waste precious resources on a poor investment opportunity! Move on to the next opportunity, feeling good about the fact that you're doing what you're supposed to do on the GMAT: making sound investment decisions about what to do and what *not* to do.

Quantitative Reasoning on the GMAT

The Quantitative Reasoning (or Quant) section of the GMAT consists of two different question types: Problem Solving and Data Sufficiency.

Problem Solving (PS) problems are standard, multiple-choice math questions with five answer choices. Data Sufficiency (DS) problems are unique to the GMAT. These also have five multiple-choice answers; you'll learn how DS works in this guide.

You'll need to average approximately two minutes per question in the Quant section, though your timing for individual questions will likely range from almost no time at all to approximately three minutes. The "almost no time at all" questions will be your *bail* questions: questions that look way too hard or that you know are a big weakness of yours (in other words, bad investment opportunities!). On other questions, you'll choose to invest some extra time—perhaps on a harder question in an area of strength.

You'll learn more about time management, as well as other test details, both in this guide and in the online resources associated with this guide. You can also test your skills using official GMAT problems that are published by the test makers in The GMAT Official Guide (also known as "the big OG" or "the OG"). These problems appeared on the official GMAT in the past, so they're a fantastic resource to help you get ready for the real test. (Note: The OG is sold separately from the Manhattan Prep strategy guides.)

UNIT ONE

Fractions, Decimals, Percents, and Ratios

In this unit, you will learn about the relationships between fractions, decimals, percents, and ratios and how to manipulate and solve for all forms. This unit also includes the basics of the Data Sufficiency question type, as well as an introduction to two important strategies for the GMAT: when and how you can use real numbers rather than algebra to solve (via three methods: Test Cases, Choose Smart Numbers, and Work Backwards) and when and how you can estimate.

In This Unit

CHAPTER 1

FDPs

In This Chapter

In this chapter, you will learn the basic usage of fractions, decimals, and percents, as well as how to move back and forth quickly among the three. You'll also learn what kinds of calculations are most easily performed in which form.

CHAPTER 1 FDPs

FDPs stands for fractions, decimals, and percents. These three forms are grouped together because they are different ways to represent the same number. For example:

A **fraction** consists of a numerator and a denominator:	$\frac{1}{2}$
A **decimal** uses place values:	0.5
A **percent** expresses a relationship between a number and 100:	50%

All three are equal to each other and represent the same number: $\frac{1}{2} = 0.5 = 50\%$.

Ratios are closely related to fractions but not quite the same; you'll learn more about ratios in a couple of chapters.

The GMAT often mixes fractions, decimals, and percents in a single problem, and certain kinds of math operations are easier to perform on one form compared to the others. In order to achieve success with FDP problems, you need to shift amongst the three accurately and quickly. Try this problem:

A sum of money is divided among three sisters. The first sister receives $\frac{1}{2}$ of the total, the second receives $\frac{1}{4}$ of the total, and the third receives the remaining \$10. How many dollars do the three sisters split?

(A) \$10
(B) \$20
(C) \$30
(D) \$40
(E) \$50

To solve, you have to figure out what proportion of the money the first two sisters get so that you know what proportion the third sister's \$10 represents. The information is provided in fractions, and it's not too difficult to add up the relatively simple fractions $\frac{1}{2}$ and $\frac{1}{4}$. However, harder fractions would make the work a lot more cumbersome. In general, adding fractions is annoying because you have to find a common denominator.

Decimals and percentages are much easier to add. Because the problem talks about parts of a whole, convert to percentages. The first sister receives 50% of the money and the second receives 25%, leaving 25% for the third sister. That 25% represents \$10, so 100% of the money is 4 times as much, or \$40. The correct answer is (D).

In order to do this kind of math quickly and easily, you'll need to know how to convert among fractions, decimals, and percents. Luckily, certain common conversions are used repeatedly throughout the GMAT. If you memorize these conversions, you'll get to skip the calculations. The next two sections of this chapter cover these topics.

Common FDP Equivalents

Save yourself time and trouble by memorizing the following common equivalents:

Fraction	Decimal	Percent
$\frac{1}{1}$	1	100%
$\frac{1}{2}=\frac{2}{4}=\frac{3}{6}=\frac{4}{8}=\frac{5}{10}$	0.5	50%
$\frac{3}{2}$	1.5	150%

$\frac{1}{4}=\frac{2}{8}$	0.25	25%
$\frac{3}{4}=\frac{6}{8}$	0.75	75%
$\frac{5}{4}$	1.25	125%
$\frac{7}{4}$	1.75	175%

$\frac{1}{8}$	0.125	12.5%
$\frac{3}{8}$	0.375	37.5%
$\frac{5}{8}$	0.625	62.5%
$\frac{7}{8}$	0.875	87.5%

$\frac{1}{5}=\frac{2}{10}$	0.2	20%
$\frac{2}{5}=\frac{4}{10}$	0.4	40%
$\frac{3}{5}=\frac{6}{10}$	0.6	60%
$\frac{4}{5}=\frac{8}{10}$	0.8	80%

Fraction	Decimal	Percent
$\frac{1}{10}$	0.1	10%
$\frac{3}{10}$	0.3	30%
$\frac{7}{10}$	0.7	70%
$\frac{9}{10}$	0.9	90%

$\frac{1}{3}=\frac{2}{6}$	$0.\overline{3}\approx 0.333$	$\approx$33.3%
$\frac{2}{3}=\frac{4}{6}$	$0.\overline{6}\approx 0.666$	$\approx$66.7%
$\frac{4}{3}$	$1.\overline{3}\approx 1.333$	$\approx$133.3%

$\frac{1}{6}$	$0.1\overline{6}\approx 0.167$	$\approx$16.7%
$\frac{5}{6}$	$0.8\overline{3}\approx 0.833$	$\approx$83.3%
$\frac{1}{9}$	$0.1\overline{1}\approx 0.111$	$\approx$11.1%

$\frac{1}{100}$	0.01	1%
$\frac{1}{50}$	0.02	2%
$\frac{1}{25}$	0.04	4%
$\frac{1}{20}$	0.05	5%

Converting among Fractions, Decimals, and Percents

If you see a number that isn't on the Common Equivalents list to memorize, you can convert among fractions, decimals, and percents. The table below shows how:

FROM ↓ TO→	Fraction	Decimal	Percent
Fraction $\frac{1}{4}$		Divide the numerator by the denominator: $1 \div 4 = 0.25$ Alternatively, multiply the top and bottom to get the denominator to equal 100: $\frac{1}{4} \times \frac{25}{25} = \frac{25}{100} = 0.25$ Note: These operations are hard if the fraction is annoying; in that case, see whether you can estimate.	Divide the numerator by the denominator and move the decimal two places to the right: $1 \div 4 = 0.25 \rightarrow 25\%$
Decimal 0.375	Use the place value of the last digit in the decimal as the denominator and put the decimal's digits in the numerator. Then, simplify: $\frac{375}{1{,}000} = \frac{3}{8}$		Move the decimal point two places to the right: $0.375 \rightarrow 37.5\%$
Percent 65%	Use the digits of the percent for the numerator and 100 for the denominator. Then, simplify: $\frac{65}{100} = \frac{13}{20}$	Find the percent's decimal point and move it two places to the left: $65.0\% \rightarrow 0.65$	

Think before you convert, though. If the conversion is annoying—you have to do long division or similar—don't do it. Instead, see whether you can estimate or use some other approach. For example, converting 0.65 to a percent or fraction isn't too bad. But converting $\frac{7}{13}$ to a decimal or percent would be very annoying.

Instead, can you estimate? The fraction is almost $\frac{7}{14}$, or 0.5.

Pop quiz: Is $\frac{7}{13}$ a little larger or a little smaller than $\frac{7}{14}$? Play around with that a little bit. Later in this guide, you'll learn how to estimate this quickly.

You'll get plenty of practice with these skills throughout this book, but if you'd like some more, see Manhattan Prep's *GMAT Foundations of Math*.

When to Use Which Form

As you saw in the "three sisters" problem, when you have to add or subtract, percentages (or decimals) tend to be easier. By contrast, fractions work very well with multiplication and division.

If you have already memorized the given fraction, decimal, and percent conversions, you can move among the forms quickly. If not, you may have to decide between taking the time to convert from one form to the other and working the problem using the less convenient form (e.g., in order to add, you could convert fractions to decimals or you could leave them in fraction form and find a common denominator).

Try this problem:

> What is 37.5% of 240 ?

If you convert the percent to a decimal and multiply, you will have to do a fair bit of arithmetic, as shown on the left:

$$\begin{array}{r} 0.375 \\ \times\ 240 \\ \hline 0 \\ 15000 \\ 75000 \\ \hline 90.000 \end{array}$$

Alternatively, recognize that $0.375 = \frac{3}{8}$.

$$(0.375)(240) = \frac{3}{\cancel{8}}\ \overset{30}{\cancel{240}} = 3(30) = 90$$

This is much faster!

Try something a bit harder:

> A dress is marked up $16\frac{2}{3}\%$ to a final price of \$140. What was the original price of the dress?

$16\frac{2}{3}\%$ is on the memorization list; it is equal to $\frac{1}{6}$. In order to increase a number by $\frac{1}{6}$, add a sixth of the number to itself: $1 + \frac{1}{6} = \frac{7}{6}$. Call the original price x and set up an equation to find x:

$$x + \frac{1}{6}x = 140$$

$$\frac{7}{6}x = 140$$

$$x = \left(\frac{6}{7}\right)140 = \frac{6}{\cancel{7}}\ \overset{20}{\cancel{140}} = 120$$

Therefore, the original price was \$120.

Decimals and percents work very well with addition and subtraction because you don't have to find common denominators. For this same reason, decimals and percents are often preferred when you want to compare numbers or perform certain estimations. For example, which is larger, $\frac{3}{5}$ or $\frac{5}{8}$?

You could find common denominators, but both fractions are on the "conversions to memorize" list:

$$\frac{3}{5} = 60\% \qquad\qquad \frac{5}{8} = 62.5\%$$

The larger fraction is $\frac{5}{8}$.

In some cases, you may decide to stick with the given form rather than convert. If you do have numbers that are easy to convert, though, then use fractions for multiplication and division and use percents or decimals for addition and subtraction as well as for estimating or comparing numbers.

Advanced material for the FDPRs unit (primarily covering additional strategies for decimals and digits) can be found in Atlas, Manhattan Prep's online learning platform. Use the online material only if you feel that you have mastered everything in the FDPR unit of this strategy guide and only if you are aiming for a Quant section score of 48 or higher.

Problem Set

Now that you've finished the chapter, try these problems. On the GMAT, quant problems will always provide five answer choices. In this guide, you will sometimes have fewer than five answer choices (and sometimes none at all).

1. Express the following as fractions and simplify: 0.4 0.008

2. Express the following as fractions and simplify: 420% 8%

3. Express the following as decimals: $\frac{9}{2}$ $\frac{3,000}{10,000}$

4. Express the following as percents: $\frac{83}{1,000}$ $\frac{25}{8}$

5. Express the following as percents: 80.4 0.0007

6. Order from least to greatest: $\frac{8}{18}$ 0.8 40%

7. 20 is 16% of what number?

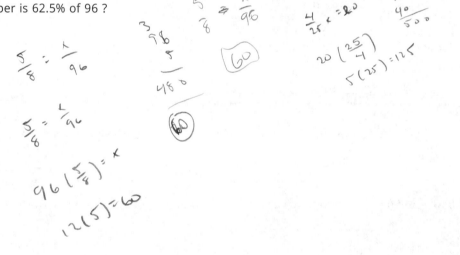

8. What number is 62.5% of 96 ?

1

Solutions

1. **$\frac{2}{5}$ and $\frac{1}{125}$:** To convert a decimal to a fraction, write it over the appropriate power of 10 and simplify:

$$0.4 = \frac{4}{10} = \frac{2}{5}$$

$$0.008 = \frac{8}{1000} = \frac{1}{125}$$

2. **$\frac{21}{5}$ or $4\frac{1}{5}$ and $\frac{2}{25}$:** To convert a percent to a fraction, write it over a denominator of 100 and simplify:

$$420\% = \frac{420}{100} = \frac{21}{5} \text{ (improper)} \quad \text{OR} \quad 4\frac{1}{5} \text{ (mixed)}$$

$$8\% = \frac{8}{100} = \frac{2}{25}$$

3. **4.5 and 0.3:** To convert a fraction to a decimal, divide the numerator by the denominator:

$$\frac{9}{2} = 9 \div 2 = 4.5$$

It often helps to simplify the fraction *before* you divide:

$$\frac{3{,}000}{10{,}000} = \frac{3}{10} = 0.3$$

4. **8.3% and 312.5%:** To convert a fraction to a percent, rewrite the fraction with a denominator of 100:

$$\frac{83}{1{,}000} = \frac{8.3}{100} = 8.3\%$$

Alternatively, convert the fraction to a decimal and shift the decimal point two places to the right:

$$\frac{25}{8} = 25 \div 8 = 3\frac{1}{8} = 3.125 = 312.5\%$$

5. **8,040% and 0.07%:** To convert a decimal to a percent, shift the decimal point two places to the right:

$$80.4 = 8{,}040\%$$

$$0.0007 = 0.07\%$$

6. **$40\% < \frac{8}{18} < 0.8$:** To order from least to greatest, express all the terms in the same form (your choice as to which form!):

$$\frac{8}{18} = \frac{4}{9} = 0.4444... = 0.\overline{4}$$

$$0.8 = 0.8$$

$$40\% = 0.4$$

$$0.4 < 0.\overline{4} < 0.8$$

7. **125:** The sentence translates as $20 = (16\%)x$. Fraction form is better for multiplication or division, so convert 16% into a fraction first: $16\% = \frac{16}{100} = \frac{4}{25}$. Then solve for x:

$$20 = \frac{4}{25}x$$
$$20\left(\frac{25}{4}\right) = x$$
$$(5)(25) = x$$
$$x = 125$$

8. **60:** The sentence translates as $x = (62.5\%)(96)$. 62.5% is one of the common FDP equivalents to memorize; the fraction form is $\frac{5}{8}$. Solve for x:

$$x = \left(\frac{5}{8}\right)96$$
$$x = (5)(12)$$
$$x = 60$$

CHAPTER 2

Data Sufficiency 101

In This Chapter

- How Data Sufficiency Works
- The Answer Choices
- Starting with Statement (2)
- Value vs. Yes/No Questions
- The DS Process
- Testing Cases

In this chapter, you will learn how to tackle Data Sufficiency (DS) problems, including an overall process to help you solve the problems efficiently. You'll also learn how to test cases on DS; this strategy will help you handle more complicated problems as you advance in your studies.

CHAPTER 2 Data Sufficiency 101

The GMAT invented its own type of math problem, **Data Sufficiency** (DS), that tests how you think logically about mathematical concepts. DS problems are a cross between math and logic. Imagine that your boss just dumped a bunch of papers on your desk, saying, "I'm wondering whether we should raise the price on this product. Can you answer that question from this data? If so, which pieces do we need to prove whether we should or should not raise the price?" What would you do?

Your boss has asked a specific question: Should you raise the price? You have to decide which pieces of information will allow you to answer that question—or, possibly, that you don't have enough information to answer the question at all.

This kind of logical reasoning is exactly what you use when you answer DS questions.

How Data Sufficiency Works

You will certainly need to know math in order to answer Data Sufficiency questions, but you also need to know how DS works in the first place. And you need to know certain strategies that will help you to work through DS problems efficiently and effectively.

Consider this question: How old is Farai?

Obviously, you can't answer that question right now—you have no information about Farai or Farai's age. Imagine that you're also told a fact: Farai is 10 years older than Dmitry.

But you don't know anything about Dmitry's age either! The GMAT would say that this fact—Farai is 10 years older than Dmitry—is *not sufficient* (i.e., not enough) to answer the question. If you do know this fact, though, then what additional information would allow you to be able to answer the question?

Well, if you knew how old Dmitry was, then you could figure out how old Farai was. For example, if Dmitry is 10, then Farai would have to be 20.

So if you know *both* that Farai is 10 years older than Dmitry *and* that Dmitry is 10 years old, then you have *sufficient* (i.e., enough) information to answer the question: How old is Farai?

Every DS problem has the same basic form. It will ask you a question. It will provide you with some facts. And it will ask you to figure out what combination of facts is *sufficient* to answer the question.

Take a look at another example, in full DS form:

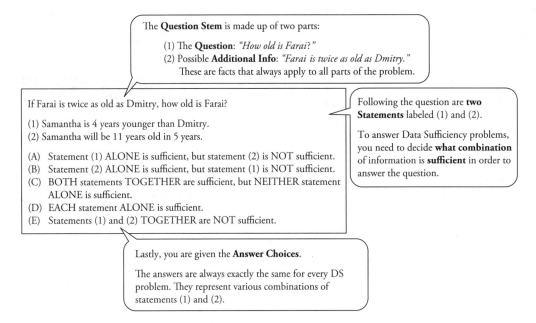

The **Question Stem** is made up of two parts:

(1) The **Question**: *"How old is Farai?"*
(2) Possible **Additional Info**: *"Farai is twice as old as Dmitry."* These are facts that always apply to all parts of the problem.

If Farai is twice as old as Dmitry, how old is Farai?

(1) Samantha is 4 years younger than Dmitry.
(2) Samantha will be 11 years old in 5 years.

(A) Statement (1) ALONE is sufficient, but statement (2) is NOT sufficient.
(B) Statement (2) ALONE is sufficient, but statement (1) is NOT sufficient.
(C) BOTH statements TOGETHER are sufficient, but NEITHER statement ALONE is sufficient.
(D) EACH statement ALONE is sufficient.
(E) Statements (1) and (2) TOGETHER are NOT sufficient.

Following the question are **two Statements** labeled (1) and (2).

To answer Data Sufficiency problems, you need to decide **what combination** of information is **sufficient** in order to answer the question.

Lastly, you are given the **Answer Choices.**

The answers are always exactly the same for every DS problem. They represent various combinations of statements (1) and (2).

The **Question Stem** always contains the **Question** you need to answer. It may also contain **Additional Info** (also known as *givens*) that you can use to help answer the question.

Below the question stem, the two **Statements** provide additional facts or given information—and you are specifically asked to determine what combination of those two statements would be sufficient to answer the question.

The **Answer Choices** describe various combinations of the two statements: For example, statement (1) is sufficient, but statement (2) is not. Note that the answer choices don't contain any possible ages for Farai. DS questions aren't asking you *to* solve; they're asking *whether* you *can* solve. (No need to try to figure out what all of those answer choices mean right now; you'll learn as you work through this chapter.)

DS questions look strange but you can think of them as deconstructed Problem Solving (PS) questions—the "regular" type of multiple-choice math problem. Compare the DS-format problem shown earlier to the PS-format problem below:

> Samantha is 4 years younger than Dmitry, and Samantha will be 11 years old in 5 years. If Farai is twice as old as Dmitry, how old is Farai?

The two questions contain exactly the same information; that information is just presented in a different order. The PS form puts all of the givens as well as the question into the question stem. The DS problem moves some of the givens down to statement (1) and statement (2).

As is true for the given information in PS problems, the DS statements are always true. In addition, the two statements won't contradict each other. In the same way that a PS question wouldn't tell you that $x > 0$ and $x < 0$ (that's impossible!), the two DS statements won't do that either.

In the PS format, you would need to calculate Farai's age. In the DS format, you typically will *not* need to solve all the way to the end; you only need to go far enough to know whether Farai's age can be calculated. Since every DS problem works in this same way, it is critical to learn how to work through all DS questions using a systematic, consistent process. Take a look at how this plays out:

If Farai is twice as old as Dmitry, how old is Farai?

(1) Samantha is 4 years younger than Dmitry.
(2) Samantha will be 11 years old in 5 years.

(A) Statement (1) ALONE is sufficient, but statement (2) is NOT sufficient.
(B) Statement (2) ALONE is sufficient, but statement (1) is NOT sufficient.
(C) BOTH statements TOGETHER are sufficient, but NEITHER statement ALONE is sufficient.
(D) EACH statement ALONE is sufficient.
(E) Statements (1) and (2) TOGETHER are NOT sufficient.

The goal: Figure out which pieces of information *would* allow you to answer the question (How old is Farai?).

Your first task is to understand what the problem is saying and jot down the information in math form. Draw a T on your page to help keep the information organized; write information from the question stem above the horizontal line. Make sure to include a question mark to indicate the question itself (later, you'll learn why this is important):

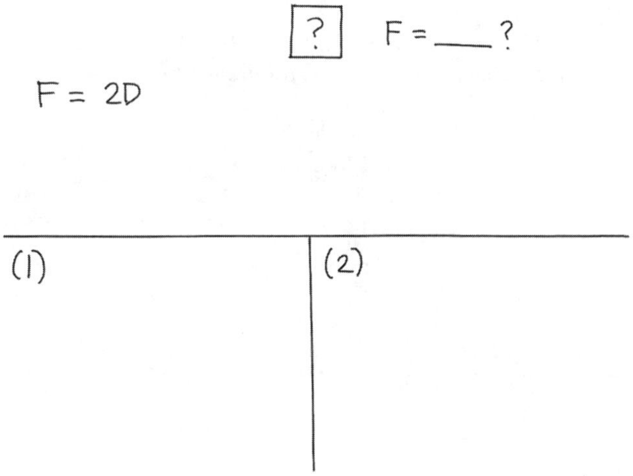

Hmm. Reflect for a moment. If they tell you Dmitry's age, then you could just plug it into the given equation to find Farai's age. Remember that!

Take a look at the first statement. Also, write down $\frac{\text{AD}}{\text{BCE}}$ off to the right of your scratch paper, above the line (you'll learn what this is as you work through this chapter):

(1) Samantha is 4 years younger than Dmitry.

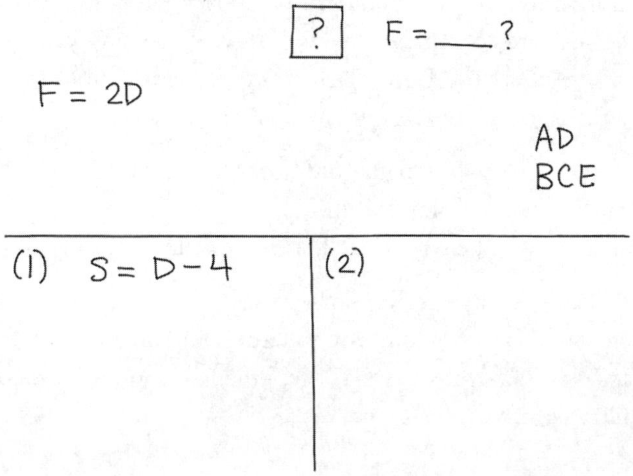

Translate the first statement and jot down the information below the horizontal line, to the left of the T. (Not confident about how to translate that statement into math? Use Manhattan Prep's *GMAT Foundations of Math* to practice translating.)

The first statement doesn't allow you to solve for either Samantha or Dmitry's real age. Statement (1), then, is *not sufficient.* Cross off the top row of answers, (A) and (D).

Why? Here's the text for answers (A) and (D):

(A) Statement (1) ALONE is sufficient, but statement (2) is NOT sufficient.

(D) EACH statement ALONE is sufficient.

These two answers indicate that statement (1) *is* sufficient to answer the question. But statement (1) is *not* sufficient to find Farai's age, so both (A) and (D) are wrong.

The answer choices will always appear in the order shown for the above problem, so any time you decide that statement (1) is not sufficient, you will always cross off answers (A) and (D) at the same time. That's why the AD/BCE answer grid groups these two answers together on the top row.

Next, consider statement (2), but wait! First, forget what statement (1) told you. Because of the way the DS answers are constructed, you must evaluate the two statements *separately* before you look at them together. So here's just statement (2) by itself:

(2) Samantha will be 11 years old in 5 years.

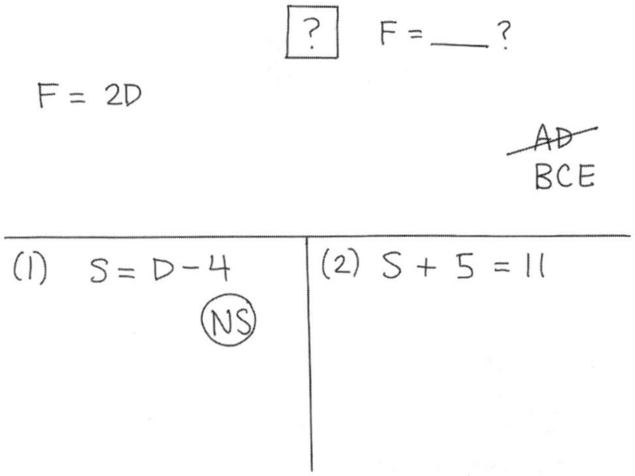

In your T diagram, write the information about statement (2) below the horizontal line and to the right. It's useful to separate the information this way in order to help remember that statement (2) is separate from statement (1) and has to be considered completely by itself first. (You'll always organize the information in this way: The question stem goes above the T, statement (1) goes below and to the left of the T, and statement (2) goes below and to the right.)

Back to statement (2). This one allows you to figure out how old Samantha is now, but *alone* the info doesn't connect back to Farai or Dmitry. By itself, statement (2) is *not* sufficient. Of the remaining answers (BCE), answer (B) says that statement (2) is sufficient by itself. This isn't the case, so cross off answer (B).

When you've evaluated each statement by itself and haven't found sufficient information, you must look at the two statements together. Statement (2) allows you to figure out Samantha's age. Statement (1) allows you to calculate Dmitry's age if you know Samantha's age. Finally, the question stem allows you to calculate Farai's age if you know Dmitry's age!

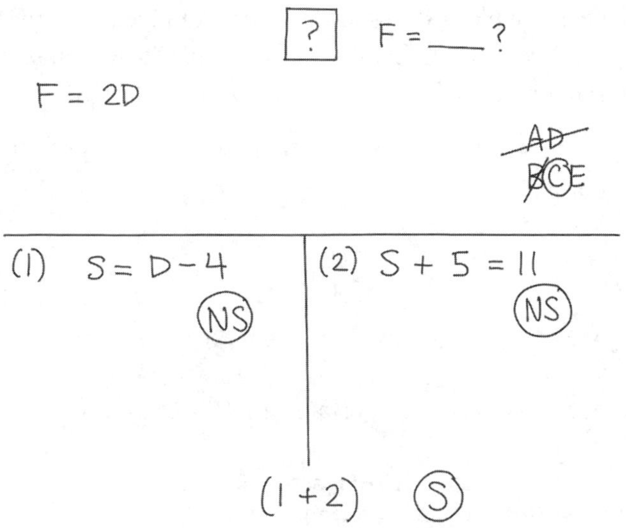

As soon as you can tell that you *can* find Farai's age, write an S with a circle around it to indicate *sufficient*. Don't actually calculate Farai's age; you only need to know that you *can* calculate it. Save that time and mental energy for other things on the test.

The correct answer is (C): both statements together are sufficient to answer the question but neither statement alone is sufficient.

The Answer Choices

The five Data Sufficiency answer choices will always be exactly the same (and presented in the same order), so you won't even need to read them on the real test. By then, you'll have done enough DS problems to have them memorized. (In fact, to help you memorize, this book won't even show the DS answer choices in end-of-chapter problem sets.)

Here are the five answers written in an easier way to understand:

(A) Statement (1) *does* allow you to answer the question, but statement (2) *does not*.

(B) Statement (2) *does* allow you to answer the question, but statement (1) *does not*.

(C) Neither statement works on its own, but you can use them *together* to answer the question.

(D) Statement (1) works by itself *and* statement (2) works by itself.

(E) Nothing works. Even if you use both statements together, you still can't answer the question.

Answer (C) specifically says that neither statement works on its own. For this reason, you are required to look at each statement by itself first *and decide that neither one works alone* before you are allowed to evaluate the two statements together.

Here's an even shorter way to remember the five answer choices, the "12-TEN" mnemonic (memory aid):

1	only statement 1
2	only statement 2
T	together
E	either one
N	nothing works

As you practice DS over the next couple of weeks, make an effort to memorize the five answers. If you do a couple of practice DS problems every day in that time frame, you'll likely memorize the answers without conscious effort—and you'll solidify the DS lessons you're learning right now.

Speaking of solidifying the lessons you're learning, set a timer for 2 minutes and try this problem:

What is the value of 20% of x ?

(1) 30 is $\frac{1}{2}$ of x.

(2) x is 0.25 of 240.

(A) Statement (1) ALONE is sufficient, but statement (2) alone is not sufficient to answer the question asked.

(B) Statement (2) ALONE is sufficient, but statement (1) alone is not sufficient to answer the question asked.

(C) BOTH statements (1) and (2) TOGETHER are sufficient to answer the question asked, but NEITHER statement ALONE is sufficient.

(D) EACH statement ALONE is sufficient to answer the question asked.

(E) Statements (1) and (2) TOGETHER are NOT sufficient to answer the question asked.

Ready? What did you get? (If you got stuck and didn't get to an answer, pick one anyway. That's what you'll have to do on the real test, so you might as well practice that now.)

Start with the question stem: What is 20% of x ? Pause. Your first goal is to understand the significance of the question. This is DS—you don't have to find the actual value. What would you need to know in order to be confident that you *could* calculate that value?

If you can find a single value for x, then you can find 20% of that value, so the real question is a bit simpler: What is x ?

Congratulations! You've just rephrased a DS question. Rephrasing a question allows you to get right down to the heart of the question—and save yourself time and mental energy as you solve.

Now, you can dive into the statements with a simpler plan: Will this statement allow you to find a single value for x ? Jot down your answer grid $\begin{matrix}\text{AD}\\\text{BCE}\end{matrix}$ and look at the first statement:

(1) 30 is $\frac{1}{2}$ of x.

Some people may be able to evaluate this statement without writing anything down. Others will want to jot it down in "real math" terms—as an equation, not a sentence.

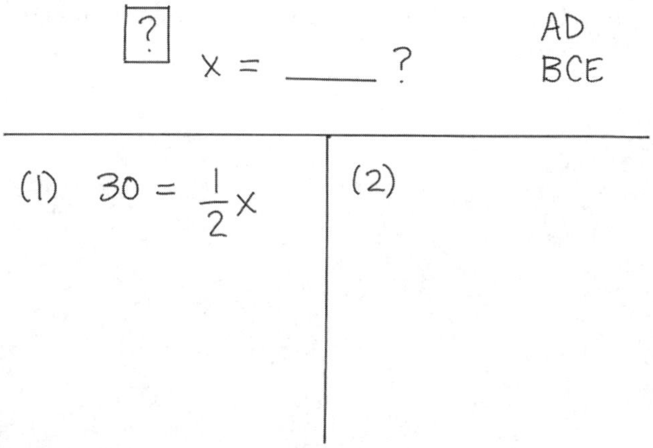

Statement (1) is a linear equation with just one variable. This equation can indeed be solved for a single value of x, so this statement is sufficient to answer the question. Which row should you cross off in the grid, AD or BCE?

Think of statement (1) as associated with answer choice (A). If statement (1) is sufficient, then answer (A) needs to stay in the mix; cross off the bottom row, BCE.

What's next? Pause and try to remind yourself before you keep reading.

Now, forget about statement (1) and take a look at statement (2):

(2) x is 0.25 of 240.

If you feel confident that this statement will also translate into a linear equation with just one variable, then you may choose not to write anything down. If you're not sure, though, write it down to confirm.

This equation will also allow you to solve for a single value for x, so statement (2) is sufficient to answer the question.

Since statement (2) is also sufficient, cross off answer (A) and circle answer (D): Either statement alone is sufficient to answer the question. Do actually take the time to do this on your scratch paper before you select your answer on screen. It won't take you more than a second and this action will help to minimize careless mistakes on the test.

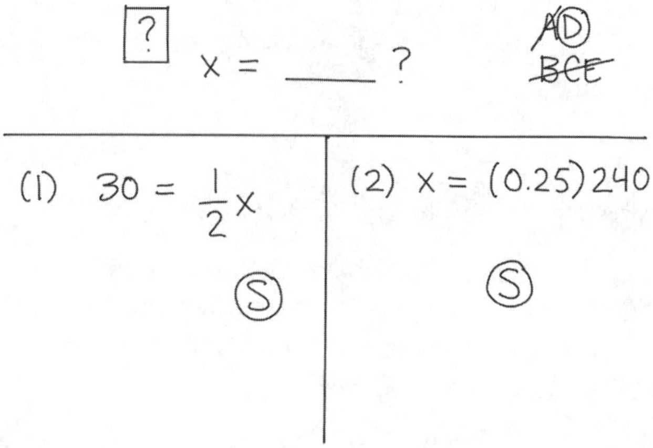

2

Here's a summary of the answer choice process when starting with statement (1):

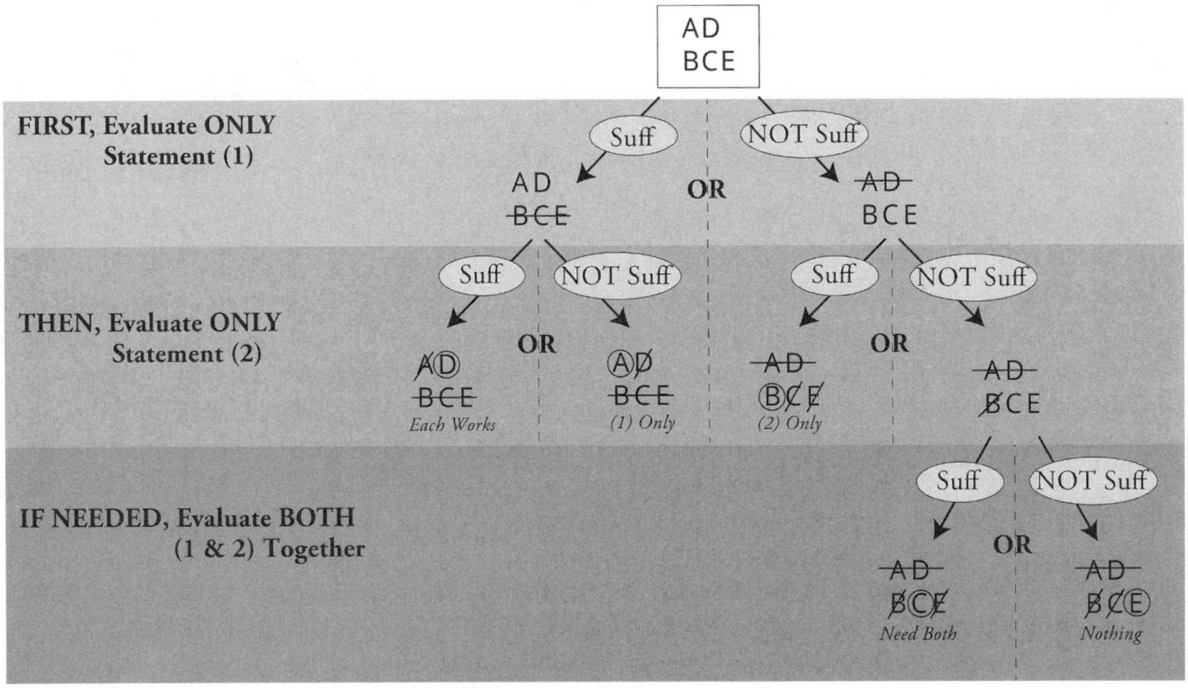

Starting with Statement (2)

If statement (1) looks hard or annoying, you can start with statement (2) instead. Your process will be the same; you'll just make one small change in your answer grid.

Try this problem:

If Farai is twice as old as Dmitry, how old is Farai?

(1) Two years ago, Dmitry was twice as old as Samantha.

(2) Samantha is 6 years old.

1
2
T
E
N

(From now on, the full answer choices won't be shown. Start memorizing! You can also glance back at earlier pages until you know the answers by heart.)

First, what to do with that question stem? You can write it down the same way you did before, but now that you've learned about rephrasing, add one more thing. If you found *D*'s age, you could find *F*'s age, so the question can be rephrased as "$D = ?$"

Next, statement (1) is definitely more complicated than statement (2), so start with statement (2) this time. Lay out your scratch paper in the same way—statement (1) on the left and statement (2) on the right—but this time write $\begin{matrix}\text{BD}\\ \text{ACE}\end{matrix}$ for your answer grid (you'll learn why in a minute):

(2) Samantha is 6 years old.

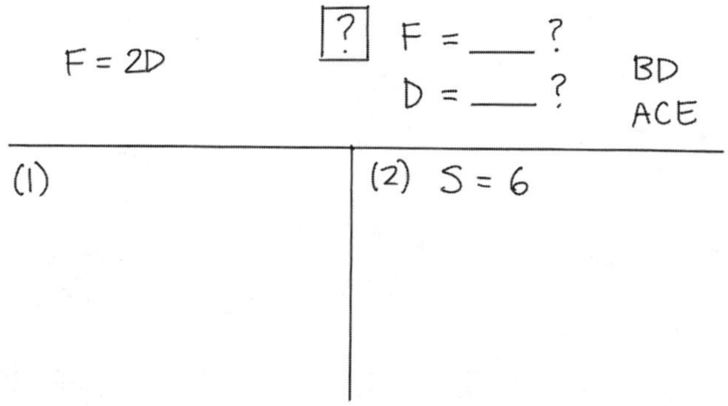

Statement (2) is not sufficient to determine Farai's age. Think of this statement as associated with answer (B). Since the statement is *not* sufficient, you *don't* want to keep (B), so cross off the row that contains that answer: the top row (BD).

Whenever you decide to start with statement (2), you'll always use the $\frac{\text{BD}}{\text{ACE}}$ answer grid, and you'll always cross off either the entire top row or the entire bottom row, depending on whether statement (2) is sufficient.

Now, forget about statement (2) and assess statement (1):

(1) Two years ago, Dmitry was twice as old as Samantha.

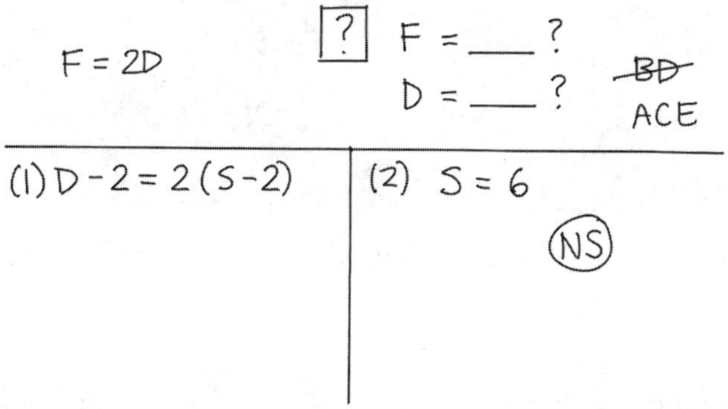

That translation is tricky. Since it's talking about the time period 2 years ago, subtract 2 from each of *D* and *S*. Then translate and write the rest of the equation. By itself, is statement (1) sufficient?

Nope! This isn't enough to find a specific age for Farai, Dmitry, or Samantha. Cross off (A), the first of the remaining answers in the bottom row, and now assess the two statements together:

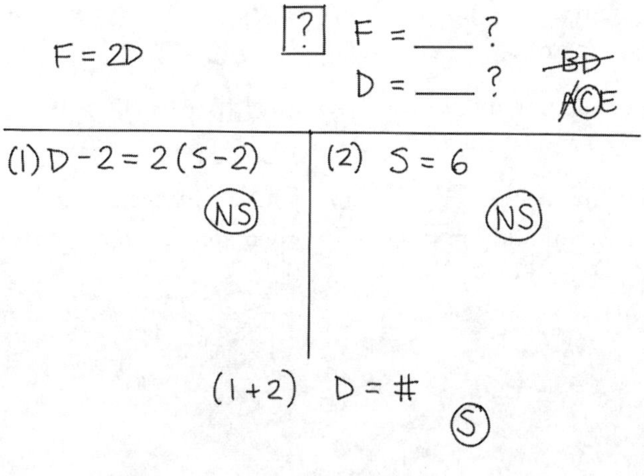

You can plug Samantha's age (from the second statement) into the formula from statement (1) to find Dmitry's age, and Dmitry's age is sufficient to answer the question. Together, the statements are sufficient.

The correct answer is (C): Neither statement works alone, but *together* the information is sufficient to answer the question.

Here's a summary of the answer grid process when starting with statement (2):

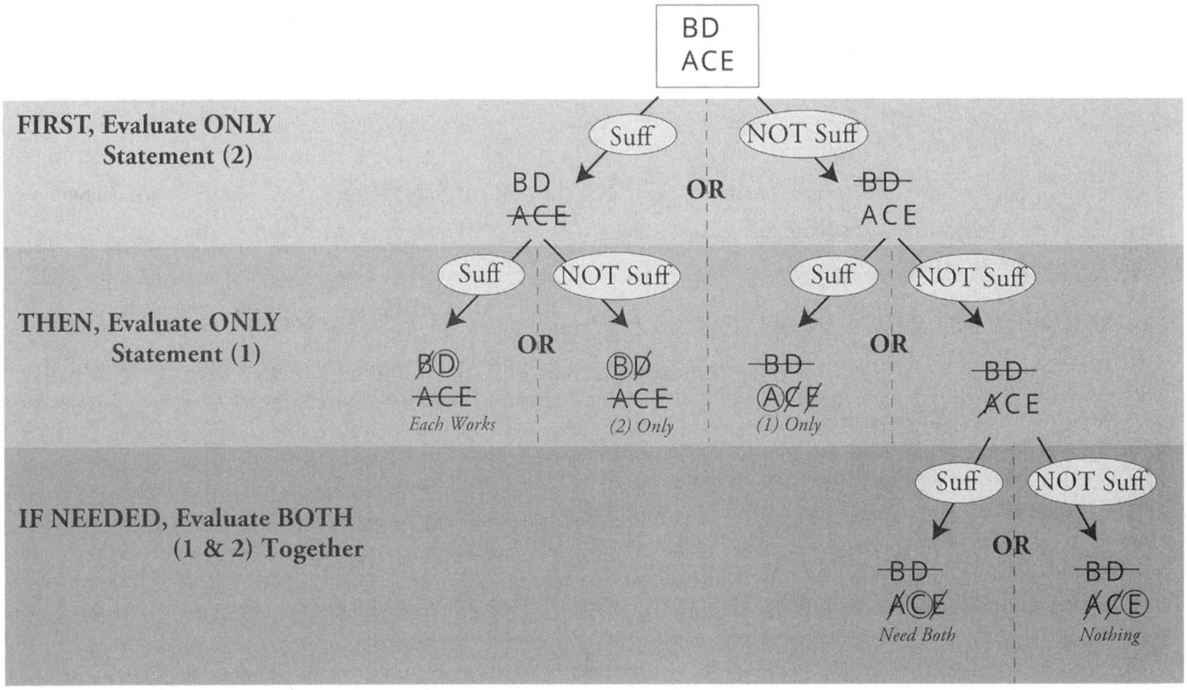

The two answer grids work the same way, regardless of which one you use. When starting with statement (1), always use the AD/BCE grid. Think of statement (1) as associated with the first answer letter in that grid, (A).

When starting with statement (2), always use the BD/ACE grid and think of this statement as associated with the first answer letter, (B).

In either case, when assessing your starting statement, you will get to cross off an entire row:

- If the first statement you try *is* sufficient, cross off the *bottom row* (the row that does *not* contain the letter associated with that statement).
- If the first statement you try is *not* sufficient, cross off the *top row* (the row containing the letter associated with that statement).

Once you've crossed off an entire row and have just one row left, assess the answers in the remaining row, one answer at a time.

Finally, you must assess the statements separately before you can try them together—and you'll only try them together if neither one is sufficient on its own. In other words, you will only consider answers (C) and (E) if you have already crossed off answers (A), (B), and (D).

Value vs. Yes/No Questions

Data Sufficiency questions come in two "flavors": Value or Yes/No.

So far, you've done Value questions. On these, it is necessary to find a single value in order to answer the question. If you can't find any value or you can find two or more values, then the information is not sufficient.

Here's an example of a Value question with one accompanying statement:

> How old is Farai?
>
> (1) Farai's age is a multiple of 4.

Farai could be 4 or 8 or 12 or any multiple of 4. Because it's impossible to determine one particular value for Farai's age, the statement is not sufficient to answer the Value question: How old is Farai?

Now, consider this question:

> Is Farai's age an even number?
>
> (1) Farai's age is a multiple of 4.
>
> (2) Farai is between 19 and 22 years old.

This question is fundamentally different. It's not asking for a value; it's asking *whether* something is true. These are called Yes/No questions and there are three possible answers to this type of question:

1. Always Yes: Sufficient!
2. Always No: Sufficient!
3. Maybe (or Sometimes Yes, Sometimes No): Not Sufficient

It may be a surprise that Always No is sufficient to answer the question. Imagine that you ask a friend to go to the movies with you. If she says, "No, I'm sorry, I can't," then you did receive an answer to your question (even though the answer is negative). You know she can't go to the movies with you.

Apply this reasoning to the Farai question. Is statement (1) sufficient to answer the question: Is Farai's age an even number?

> (1) Farai's age is a multiple of 4.

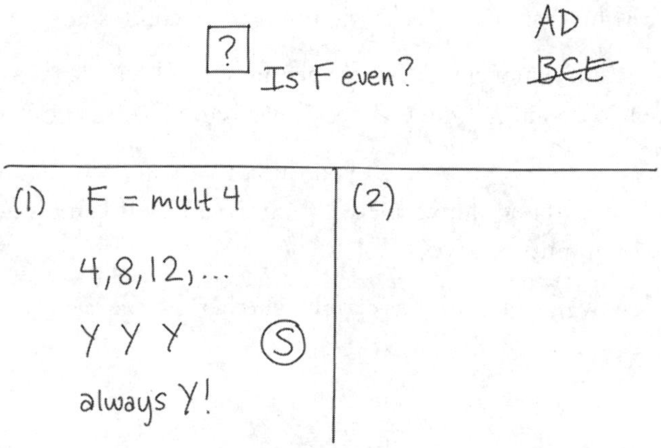

If Farai's age is a multiple of 4, Farai could be 4, 8, 12, ... but in *every* case, the answer to the question is Yes. Even though you don't know how old Farai is, the information is sufficient to answer the specific question asked: Yes, Farai must be an even number of years old.

Because statement (1) is sufficient, keep answer (A) in the mix. Cross off the bottom row of answers (BCE).

In the sample notes above, notice that the question is jotted down with the question mark included: *Is F even?* It's crucial to include both the starting "question word" (*Is*) and the question mark; if you omit these, then later you might mistakenly think that the problem is telling you that *F is even*—and, if that happens, you're much more likely to get this question wrong.

You might not make that mistake on this particular problem, but this is a potential source of error on *any* Yes/No problem (and sometimes on Value problems), so get into the habit of writing that question mark every time. Always distinguish between *facts* (things you know to be true) and *questions*.

Okay, back to the problem. Next, check statement (2):

(2) Farai is between 19 and 22 years old.

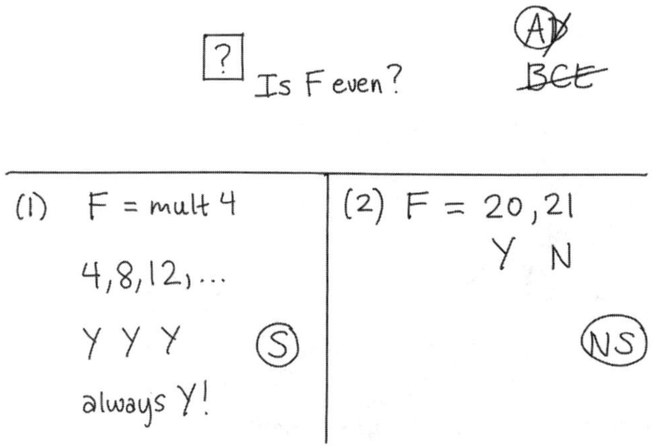

Farai could be 20, in which case the age is even. However, Farai could also be 21, in which case the age is odd. The result here is Sometimes Yes, Sometimes No, so the information in statement (2) is *not* sufficient to answer the question. Cross off answer (D).

The correct answer is (A): The first statement is sufficient but the second is not.

Note two common traps. First, for statement (2), someone might think that Farai must be 20, not 21, because the age is even. But the problem doesn't *tell* you that Farai's age is even; it asks *whether* Farai's age is even.

Answer (C) is also a trap answer on this problem. If you think that you need to find one specific value for Farai's age, then you'll think that you need both pieces of information: If Farai is *between* 19 and 22 *and* the age is a multiple of 4, then Farai must be 20 years old.

But the problem doesn't ask how old Farai is. It asks only whether the age is an even number—and the first statement is sufficient to answer that question.

The DS Process

This section summarizes each step that you've learned in one consistent DS process. You can use this on every DS problem on the test. (You can even use the overall framework on regular Problem Solving problems!)

Your process consists of three distinct stages: Understand, Plan, and Solve. Most people dive straight into the third step, Solve, but this can create all kinds of issues. You may find yourself halfway through a solution and it then falls apart on you. Or you'll realize most of the way through that there was some easier, faster way you could have approached this.

The Understand and Plan steps help you to make sure that you actually want to do this problem in the first place (business mindset—don't do them all!) and they help you to settle on a solution process that is efficient and effective.

Step 1: Understand

First, just *glance* at the problem to note the overall type—in this case, it's a DS. Where does it look messy or complex? Include the question stem and both statements in your glance.

Next, *read* the problem and decide: Is this a Value or a Yes/No?

Value: The question asks for the value of an unknown (e.g., What is x ?).

A statement is **Sufficient** if it provides **exactly one possible value**.

A statement is **Not Sufficient** if it provides **more than one possible value**.

Yes/No: The question asks whether a given piece of information is true (e.g., Is x even?). Most of the time, these will be in the form of Yes/No questions.

A statement is **Sufficient** when the answer is **Always Yes** *or* **Always No**.

A statement is **Not Sufficient** when the answer is **Sometimes Yes, Sometimes No**.

Jot down both the given information and the question itself. If the information is straightforward, it's fine to jot as you read. If the information is at all complex (especially if it's a story!), you may want to read the whole thing before you jot anything down.

Finally, *given* information—that is, any information in the question stem other than the question itself—is true information that you must consider or use when answering the question. Write this information separately from the question itself. It's important to distinguish between what you were *told* is true and what you were *asked* to find.

Step 2: Plan

Reflect on the question and the givens, and rephrase the question if you can. If you have a lot of information, you may also need to decide how to *organize* your work.

At the least, you'll usually be able to simplify what is written on screen. For example, if the question stem asks, "What is the value of x ?" then you might write down something like $x = ?$

For more complicated question stems, you will likely have more work to do to rephrase the question—but rephrasing will make your job easier when you get to the next step. Ideally, before you go to the statements, you will be able to articulate a fairly clear and straightforward question (or, at least, one that's a little more clear than the original question).

Consider this problem:

Is $\frac{3x}{2} + y = \frac{x}{2} + y + 1$?

(1) $x = 1$

(2) $x + y = 1$

Do you need to know the individual values of *x* and *y* in order to answer the question? Or is there some simpler thing you could find? It's tough to tell when the equation is that annoying.

If you're given an equation, the first task is to put the "like" variables together. Also, when working with the question stem, make sure to carry the *Is* and the question mark through your work:

Is $\frac{3x}{2} + y = \frac{x}{2} + y + 1$?

Hmm. There are *x* variables on both sides of the equation. Ditto for the *y* variables. Get them together on one side and keep simplifying:

$$\text{Is } \left(\frac{3x}{2} - \frac{x}{2}\right) + y + (-y) = 1\text{ ?}$$

$$\text{Is } \frac{2x}{2} = 1\text{ ?}$$

$$\text{Is } x = 1\text{ ?}$$

Check it out: The variable *y* drops out completely! That whole thing is really just asking whether $x = 1$. The rephrased question is a lot better than the original one. (Note: You may need to write out more steps of math to simplify. Write it out—don't do math in your head and open yourself up to careless mistakes!)

It might seem silly to keep writing *Is* and the question mark on each line, but don't skip that step or you'll be opening yourself up to a careless error (you'll see how later in this book). By the time you get to the end, you don't want to forget that this is still a *question*, not a statement or a given. You don't actually know whether $x = 1$.

Step 3: Solve

Now that you've got the question you want to answer, use the answer grid to evaluate the statements.

If you start with statement (1), then write the AD/BCE grid on your scrap paper. If you start with statement (2), then write BD/ACE instead.

Here is the rephrased problem:

Is $x = 1$?

(1) $x = 1$

(2) $x + y = 1$

Statement (1) is sufficient to answer the question: Yes, $x = 1$. Keep answer (A) in the mix, so cross off the bottom row of answers:

AD
~~BCE~~

Statement (2) might have looked more promising before you rephrased the question. Now, though, you know that the value of *y* doesn't matter. Can you tell whether $x = 1$ from this statement?

If $x = 1$ and $y = 0$, then $x + y = 1$ and the answer is Yes, $x = 1$.

However! If $x = 0$ and $y = 1$, then $x + y = 1$ and the answer is No, $x \neq 1$.

Since this is a Sometimes Yes, Sometimes No answer, statement (2) is not sufficient to answer the question.

Cross off answer (D) and circle correct answer (A) on your grid:

Ⓐ ~~D~~
~~BCE~~

If you decide to start with statement (2), your overall process is almost identical, but you'll use the BD/ACE grid instead.

Whether you use AD/BCE or BD/ACE, you will always:

- Cross off the *top* row if the first statement you try is *not* sufficient
- Cross off the *bottom* row if the first statement you try *is* sufficient

Finally, remember to forget the first statement you try when moving to the next statement! Try each statement by itself first. Only evaluate the two statements together if you've already crossed off answers (A), (B), and (D), so that only answers (C) and (E) are left.

Here's a summary of the 3-step process:

Step 1: Understand

Glance at the problem. Note that it's DS and also notice which parts look annoying or complex. (Don't think about this yet. Just notice.)

Read the problem. Don't rush it. Your goal right now is just to understand what it's asking. Is it Value or Yes/No?

Jot down information. Don't do anything with this info yet.

Step 2: Plan

Reflect on what you know so far. Any ideas about how to rephrase (simplify) the complex parts in the question stem or even in the statements, if applicable?

Organize your information, if needed, and organize your thoughts. Do you have a decent idea for how to solve in a reasonable amount of time?

If so, proceed. If not, make the call to bail: Pick a random answer and move on.

Step 3: Solve

If you make it to this stage, go ahead and do whatever work is needed to solve this problem. Note that even the best laid plans sometimes fail. If things aren't working the way you thought they would or you're realizing that this is taking a lot more time than you'd planned, get out of the problem. Have a business mindset—don't use up too many of your resources on any one business opportunity!

Testing Cases

Data Sufficiency problems often allow for multiple possible scenarios, or cases—in fact, this occurred on statement (2) of the last problem. There are an infinite number of possible values for x and y, as long as $x + y = 1$.

When a statement is set up to allow multiple cases, you can use the **Test Cases** strategy to determine whether a statement is sufficient or not sufficient. This process can feel a little different for Yes/No vs. Value questions, so you'll get a chance to try both in this section.

When you're doing this, your goal is to try to prove the statement *insufficient*, if possible. Why? As soon as you find both one Yes answer and one No answer, you're done! Then it's Sometimes Yes/Sometimes No, which is not sufficient to answer the question. Think of this as trying to find contradictory answers.

If you keep getting a Yes answer every time, even when you're actively trying hard to find a No answer (or vice versa), then you can feel pretty confident that this statement is giving you a definitive answer—that is, that the statement is sufficient to answer the question.

Consider this problem:

> If x and y are positive integers, is the sum of x and y between 50 and 60, inclusive?
>
> (1) $x - y = 6$

First, **Understand**. This is a DS Yes/No problem. It tells you that x and y are positive integers and asks whether $x + y$ is between 50 and 60, inclusive. (*Inclusive* is math-speak for *include the endpoints—50 and 60—in the range.*)

Glance at the statement. You aren't given enough information to be able to solve definitively for specific values of x and y; there are many possible values. So you can test cases on this problem. You'll need to pick positive integers (given by the question stem) and you'll be trying to prove or disprove a sum in the 50–60 range.

Use that understanding to **Plan**. You also need to follow any constraints given in the statement. In this case, the two numbers have to be positive integers and $x - y$ must equal 6. Go ahead and try any two numbers that fit these constraints, then see what happens.

Solve. Case 1: $x = 10$ and $y = 4$.

These numbers are both positive integers and are valid based on the constraint from the first statement ($10 - 4 = 6$). Now, try to answer the Yes/No question: $10 + 4 = 14$, so in this case No, the sum is not between 50 and 60, inclusive.

You now have a No answer. Go back to the Plan step for a second. Can you think of another set of numbers that will give you the opposite, a Yes answer? What kind of numbers would you need?

Think about what a Yes answer means. The sum would have to be in the 50–60 range, so you'll need larger starting numbers. You might have to play with the numbers a bit to find a good pairing.

Solve. Case 2: $x = 30$ and $y = 24$.

These numbers are both positive integers and valid for the first statement ($30 - 24 = 6$). Now, answer the Yes/No question: $30 + 24 = 54$, so in this case, Yes, the sum is between 50 and 60, inclusive.

Because you have found both a Yes case and a No case, you have proved that this statement is not sufficient to answer the question.

Here's a summary of the process:

1. In the Understand phase of the DS process, notice that you *can* test cases on a particular problem. You can do this when the problem and the statement allow for multiple possible values. Also think to yourself, "What would contradictory answers look like on this problem?" For instance, in the above problem, a sum between 50 and 60 (inclusive) would be a Yes, while any other sum would be a No.

2. Come up with a Plan. Consider two things:
   - First, what kinds of numbers are you *allowed* to pick? Any numbers you use must fit the facts given in the question stem and in the statement that you're testing right now.
   - Second, what kinds of numbers would be likely to give you a *different* or contradictory answer?
3. Solve. Process your first case:
   - Choose your first set of numbers.
   - Double-check that the numbers work with all of the given facts. If your chosen numbers "break" any of the facts—that is, make any fact in the question stem or the statement on which you're working right now false—*discard* that case. Cross that case out on your scratch paper and start again.
   - Solve and find the specific answer for this case. On a Yes/No problem, you'll get either Yes or No. On a Value problem, you'll get a numerical value.
4. Solve again! Try to find a second case that gives you a *different* answer. Before you choose numbers, remind yourself of what a contradictory answer looks like for this problem. On a Yes/No problem, you'll be looking for the opposite of what you found for the first case (if you found a Yes the first time, you're looking for a No, or vice versa). For a Value problem, you'll be looking for a different numerical answer (if you found a value of 3 the first time, then the second time you're looking for any number other than 3).

If you can find two contradictory answers, you're done! That statement is not sufficient to provide one consistent answer, so you can cross off the relevant answer(s) on your grid and move to the next step in your DS process.

What if you try to find a different answer but keep finding the same answer? Try this problem:

> If x and y are positive integers, is the product of x and y greater than 20 ?
>
> (1) x is a multiple of 11 and y is divisible by 2.

Math vocab alert: *Product* means *multiply*. A *multiple* of a number is that number multiplied by a series of integers. For example, the positive multiples of 4 are 4, 8, 12, 16, and so on. And *divisible by 2* means that you'll get an integer when you divide that number by 2.

Understand. The two variables are positive integers and the question is a Yes/No: Is $xy > 20$?

Plan. Many possible values are allowed, so test cases. Look for contradictory answers.

Solve. Case 1: Test $x = 11$ and $y = 2$. The product is $(11)(2) = 22$, which is greater than 20. The answer to the question in this case is Yes. Now, can you find a No answer?

Solve. Case 2: How about $x = 11$ and $y = 4$? Then xy will be 44...hmm. Increasing the value of either variable just makes the product even greater. Can you go smaller?

It's not possible. The smallest multiple of 11 is 11 and the smallest positive integer divisible by 2 is the number 2, so the smallest product of the two is 22.

You've just proved the statement sufficient. The given information leads to an Always Yes answer; it is impossible to find a No case, no matter what you try. The Test Cases strategy can help you figure out the "theory" behind the answer, or the mathematical reasoning that proves the statement is sufficient.

This won't always work so cleanly. Sometimes, you'll keep getting all Yes (or all No) answers but you won't be able to figure out the theory behind it all. If you test three or four different cases, and you're actively seeking out a contradictory answer but never find it, then go ahead and assume that the statement is sufficient, even if you're not completely sure why.

Here's how testing cases would work on a Value problem:

> If x and y are prime numbers, what is the product of x and y?
>
> (1) The product xy is even.

Math vocab alert: *Prime* numbers are numbers that are divisible by exactly two numbers: themselves and 1. The number 2 is the smallest prime number (and the only even prime!). Other examples include 3, 5, 7, 11, 13, and 17.

Understand. Theory problem—no real numbers given. Can only choose primes for x and y. What is the value of xy? The statement contains the word *even*...

Plan. Think about even and odd—*and* prime. The only even prime number is 2. All other prime numbers are odd. Whenever you multiply anything by 2, the result is even, so if the product xy is even and those numbers are both prime, one of those numbers has to be 2.

Solve. Case 1: $x = 2$ and $y = 3$. Both numbers are prime numbers and their product is even, so these are legal numbers to try. In this case, the product is 6. Are you allowed to choose numbers that will give a different product?

Solve. Case 2: $x = 2$ and $y = 5$. Both numbers are prime numbers and their product is even, so these are legal numbers to try. In this case, the product is 10.

The statement is not sufficient because there are at least two different values for the product of x and y.

When you're testing cases on DS, take an "I'm going to try to find different answers" mindset:

- After you try your first case, think about how that math worked. What kind of number would be a good one to try for your second case in order to try to get a different answer?
- If you do find two different answers (Yes and No, or two different numbers), then immediately declare that statement not sufficient.
- If, after several tries, you keep finding the same answer despite actively trying to use numbers that will give a different answer, that statement is likely sufficient. By now, you may even be able to say why (because you've seen why different kinds of numbers keep giving the same result). Even if you can't articulate why, go ahead and assume that the statement is sufficient.

Now, you're ready to test your DS skills in this chapter's problem set. As a reminder, the problem sets in this book will not include the DS answer choices; if you forget what they are, you can look them up in this chapter.

As you continue to work through the chapters in this book, you can also continue practicing DS via *Official Guide* problems (if you have that book). Start with lower-numbered problems first, in order to practice the process, and work your way up to more difficult problems as you gain expertise.

Problem Set

As you solve each problem, focus on solidifying your DS process. Before you check your answers, review your work. Did you write down (and use) your answer grid? Did you look at each statement separately before looking at them together? Did you mix up or skip any of the steps of the process? You may want to rewrite your work before you review the answers.

The five answer choices for every problem are as follows. (Note: In future problem sets, the answer choices for DS problems will *not* be given.)

(A) Statement (1) ALONE is sufficient, but statement (2) alone is NOT sufficient to answer the question asked.

(B) Statement (2) ALONE is sufficient, but statement (1) alone is NOT sufficient to answer the question asked.

(C) BOTH statements (1) and (2) TOGETHER are sufficient to answer the question asked, but NEITHER statement ALONE is sufficient.

(D) EACH statement ALONE is sufficient to answer the question asked.

(E) Statements (1) and (2) TOGETHER are NOT sufficient to answer the question asked, and additional data are needed.

1. If $2x + y = 7$, what is the value of x ?

   (1) $y = 3$

   (2) $3x + y = 9$

2. If x is a positive integer, is x less than 10 ?

   (1) x is a multiple of 8.

   (2) $x < 15$

3. A certain bag contains only red and blue marbles. Are there at least 25 red marbles in the bag?

   (1) Fewer than 40% of the marbles in the bag are red.

   (2) There are at least 90 marbles in the bag.

Now that you've practiced the DS process, test out your skills on a couple of lower-numbered *Official Guide* problems. When you review, ask yourself what you need to do to make the process smoother (including how you set up your scratch paper).

Solutions

2

1. **(D):** First, understand. This is a DS Value problem. The question stem provides a given equation and asks for the value of x. What would you need to know in order to be able to find the one and only value for x ?

   Plan. Since the question stem also provides an equation, $2x + y = 7$, you could find x if you know the value for y. Jot that down on your scratch paper. Also, statement (1) looks easier, so start there.

   (1) SUFFICIENT: If you know the value of y, then you can plug it into the equation given in the question stem to find the value of x. Eliminate answers (B), (C), and (E).

   (2) SUFFICIENT: The question stem provides one linear equation (no squares or similar complications). The statement provides a different linear equation. You can use the two equations to solve for the individual values of the two variables. Eliminate answer (A).

   The correct answer is **(D)**: Each statement works alone.

2. **(C):** First, understand. The question stem indicates that x is a positive integer; jot that down. Yes/No question: Is $x < 10$? If x is between 1 and 9 inclusive, the answer is Yes. If x is 10 or greater, the answer is No. If you can't place x definitively into one of those two categories, the answer is Maybe/Who Knows?/Not Sufficient. And since the problem allows many possible values, test cases.

   Plan. You're only allowed to use positive integers for x. The "change point" is whether x is <10 or ≥ 10, so think about both groups of values when testing cases.

   (1) INSUFFICIENT: x could be 8, in which case the answer is Yes. But x could also be 16, in which case the answer is No. Since there are two different answers, this statement is not sufficient; cross off answers (A) and (D).

   (2) INSUFFICIENT: x could be 14, in which case the answer is No. But x could also be 8, in which case the answer is Yes. Since there are two different answers, this statement is not sufficient; cross off answer (B).

   (1) AND (2) SUFFICIENT: Return to the Plan step and remind yourself of the combined constraints. Positive integers only. Multiple of 8. Less than 15. What cases can you test?

   x could be 8, in which case the answer is Yes. The next multiple of 8 is 16...but this fails the constraint that $x < 15$. There's no other case to test; the only answer is Yes, so together, the two statements work.

   The correct answer is **(C)**: The two statements work together but neither one works alone.

3. **(E):** First, understand. There are only red and blue marbles in the bag—but there's no indication in the question stem as to the number of each color or the total number of marbles. The question is Yes/No: Is red ≥ 25 ?

   Glance at the statements. One contains a percent sign and one has a real number.

   Plan. Remind yourself of an important point on the GMAT when dealing with percents vs. real numbers. If you only know information about a percentage of something, you can't figure anything out about the real numbers associated with that something.

(1) INSUFFICIENT: This statement provides information about the percentage of red marbles. Percentages alone cannot give you the real number. Eliminate answers (A) and (D).

(2) INSUFFICIENT: This statement does provide a real number: There are 90 marbles total. But there could be just 1 red marble or 89 red marbles. This isn't enough to know whether at least 25 are red. Eliminate answer (B).

(1) AND (2) INSUFFICIENT: The combined information is complicated; time to do a little calculation. Fewer than 40% of the marbles are red. There are at least 90 marbles total. To simplify testing cases, use 90 as the total for now. To find 40% of 90, take 10% and multiply by 4; 10% is 9, so 40% is (9)(4) = 36.

Fewer than 36 marbles are red. There could be 35 red marbles, in which case the answer is Yes. But there could also be 20 red marbles, in which case the answer is No. Even together, the two statements aren't enough to solve.

The correct answer is **(E)**: Even together, the two statements aren't sufficient to answer the question.

CHAPTER 3

Fractions and Ratios

In This Chapter

- Ratio Labels
- Types of Fractions
- Numerator and Denominator Rules
- Simplifying Fractions and Ratios
- Simplify before You Multiply
- Add and Subtract: Use a Common Denominator
- Dividing Fractions: Use the Reciprocal
- Split Up Double-Decker Fractions
- The Unknown Multiplier
- Comparing Fractions: The Double-Cross
- Multiple Ratios: Make a Common Term
- Complex Fractions: Don't Split the Denominator
- Relative Values and Data Sufficiency

In this chapter, you will learn the relationship between fractions and ratios and how to use either form to solve problems. You'll also learn all of the needed computation skills to manipulate fractions and ratios.

CHAPTER 3 Fractions and Ratios

Fractions are most often used to express numbers that fall in between integers. For example, the fraction $\frac{13}{2}$, which equals 6.5, falls between the integers 6 and 7:

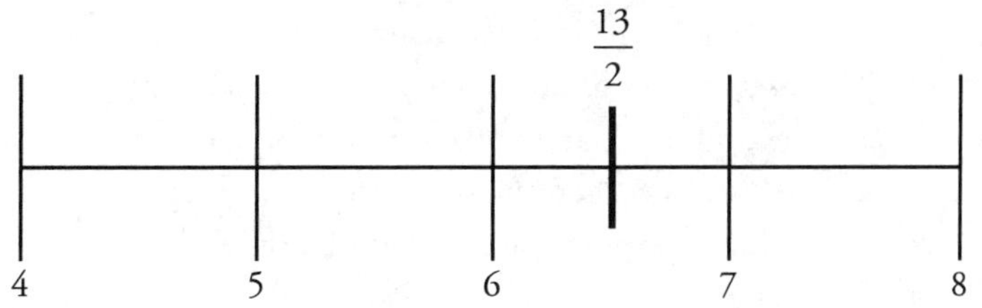

All fractions express what's called a **part-to-whole relationship**. The top number (the numerator) is the *part* and the bottom number (the denominator) is the *whole*. For example, if you eat 5 of the 8 slices in a pizza, you have eaten 5 parts out of 8 (the whole pizza), or $\frac{5}{8}$ of the pizza. You left $\frac{3}{8}$ of the pizza for your friend Sam.

Ratios, on the other hand, express what's called a **part-to-part relationship.** In the pizza example, you ate 5 parts and Sam ate 3 parts. The ratio of pizza that you ate to pizza that Sam ate is 5 to 3.

Something interesting happens here: Notice that the 5 and the 3 are the numerators of the two fractions from the prior paragraph. A ratio consists of all of the parts of a whole—and you can actually create the whole by adding up the parts! In this case, $5 + 3 = 8$, which is the whole, or the denominator, of the fractions. When talking about ratios, this *whole* is called the **ratio total**.

You can convert any fraction to a ratio and vice versa. If a bouquet of flowers has 1 rose for every 3 tulips, then the ratio of roses to tulips is 1 : 3. The *whole* is $1 + 3 = 4$. Therefore, $\frac{1}{4}$ of the bouquet consists of roses and $\frac{3}{4}$ consists of tulips.

Ratios can be written in three different ways:

1. 1 to 3
2. 1 : 3
3. $\frac{1}{3}$

In the third case, you'll need to learn how to read the sentence to know whether it's talking about a fraction or a ratio. The following are examples of ratios:

- The ratio of dogs to cats is $\frac{3}{4}$.
- This bouquet contains $\frac{3}{4}$ as many roses as daisies. (For every 3 roses, there are 4 daisies.)
- For every 3 blue cars sold, there are 4 red cars sold. (The ratio of blue cars sold to red cars sold is 3 : 4.

In the first example, the sentence outright tells you that the number that looks like a fraction is really a ratio. The second and third, though, make you interpret the information. In each case, the information conveyed is part-to-part. If you can write a sentence that fits the pattern "For every *X* of the first thing, there are *Y* of the second thing," then you know you have a ratio.

Fractions will always have two portions (with the *part* on top and the *whole* on the bottom), but ratios can have two or more portions. For example, you could have 2 horses to 3 rabbits to 7 llamas, or a ratio of 2 : 3 : 7.

Finally, fractions and ratios both express a *relationship* between two (or more, for ratios) items, but by themselves they do not tell you the exact quantities in question—knowing that someone ate $\frac{1}{2}$ of a pizza does not indicate how many slices that person ate. If the pizza had 8 slices, then that person ate 4 of them, but if the pizza had 10 slices, then that person ate 5.

3

Similarly, knowing that the ratio of dogs to cats is 2 to 3 does *not* indicate the actual number of dogs and cats. There could be 2 dogs and 3 cats, or 6 dogs and 9 cats, or any other combination that works out to 2 dogs for every 3 cats. (Note: If the problem is talking about something that can't reasonably come in non-integer quantities, such as dogs and cats, then the problem is assuming what's called an *integer constraint*: Only integer values are allowed for the real number of dogs and cats.)

Ratio Labels

It's vital to jot down the order in which the ratio information is given. After all, "the ratio of dogs to cats is 2 : 3" is very different from "the ratio of dogs to cats is 3 : 2."

It is very easy to accidentally reverse the order of a ratio—especially on a timed test like the GMAT. In order to avoid these reversals, write units on either the ratio itself or on the variables you create, or on both.

Thus, if the ratio of dogs to cats is 2 : 3, you might write any of the below:

D : C 2 : 3	$\frac{D}{C} = \frac{2}{3}$	$\frac{2 \text{ dogs}}{3 \text{ cats}}$

However you choose to jot down this information, label the ratio on your scratch paper carefully—every time.

Types of Fractions

It's useful to know certain terms in order to study for the GMAT, but you don't need to memorize these names for the test. You just need to know that these different categories exist.

Proper fractions are those that fall between 0 and 1. In proper fractions, the numerator is always smaller than the denominator. For example:

$$\frac{1}{4}, \frac{1}{2}, \frac{2}{3}, \frac{7}{10}$$

Improper fractions are greater than or equal to 1. In improper fractions, the numerator is always greater than or equal to the denominator. For example:

$$\frac{5}{4}, \frac{13}{2}, \frac{11}{3}, \frac{101}{10}$$

An improper fraction can be rewritten as a mixed number (an integer and a proper fraction together). For example:

$$\frac{5}{4}=\frac{4}{4}+\frac{1}{4}=1\frac{1}{4} \qquad \frac{11}{3}=\frac{9}{3}+\frac{2}{3}=3\frac{2}{3}$$

Most of the time, you'd only need to convert to a mixed number at the end of the problem, in order to match the format of the answers. If you are still in the middle of the problem, don't convert to a mixed number unless you absolutely have to, because you can't use mixed numbers easily in normal math operations (e.g., multiplying by another number).

Numerator and Denominator Rules

In fractions, certain key rules govern the relationship between the **numerator** (the top number) and the **denominator** (the bottom number) of proper fractions. The following rules apply only to positive numbers.

If you increase the numerator of a fraction, while holding the denominator constant, the value increases:

$$\frac{1}{8}<\frac{2}{8}<\frac{3}{8}<\frac{4}{8}<\cdots$$

You are increasing the *part* while keeping the *whole* constant. Increasing only the numerator is like eating more slices of the same pizza: You eat 1 out of 8 slices, then 2 out of 8 slices, and so on.

If you increase the denominator of a fraction, while holding the numerator constant, the value gets smaller and smaller as it approaches 0:

$$\frac{1}{2}>\frac{1}{3}>\frac{1}{4}>\frac{1}{5}\cdots>\frac{1}{1{,}000}\cdots\to 0$$

This time, you're increasing the *whole* but leaving the *part* constant. Imagine that you have one slice of a whole pizza and, magically, the rest of the pizza (but not your slice!) keeps getting bigger and bigger. Your one part (one slice) becomes a smaller and smaller portion of the entire pizza.

Pop quiz: Is $\frac{7}{13}$ a little greater or a little less than $\frac{7}{14}$, or 0.5 ? The denominator gets a little *smaller* in this example, not larger.

When you *increase* the denominator, the fraction gets *smaller*. So when you *decrease* the denominator, the opposite happens: The value of the fraction *increases* a little. Therefore, $\frac{7}{13}$ is a little greater than 0.5.

Finally, consider this lesser-known rule that the GMAT likes to employ (still for positive numbers only): Adding the exact same number to *both* the numerator and the denominator brings the fraction *closer* to 1, regardless of the fraction's value.

If the starting fraction is *less* than 1, the fraction gets closer to 1 (it *increases*) as you add the same number to the top and bottom:

$$\frac{1}{2}<\frac{1+1}{2+1}, \text{ or } \frac{1}{2}<\frac{2}{3}$$

$$\frac{2}{3}<\frac{2+9}{3+9}, \text{ or } \frac{2}{3}<\frac{11}{12}$$

$$\frac{11}{12}<\frac{11+988}{12+988}, \text{ or } \frac{11}{12}<\frac{999}{1{,}000}$$

$$\text{Thus: } \frac{1}{2}<\frac{2}{3}<\frac{11}{12}<\frac{999}{1{,}000}\cdots\to 1$$

And if the starting fraction is *greater* than 1, the fraction gets closer to 1 (it *decreases*) as you add the same number to the top and bottom:

$$\frac{3}{2} > \frac{3+1}{2+1}, \text{ or } \frac{3}{2} > \frac{4}{3}$$

$$\frac{4}{3} > \frac{4+9}{3+9}, \text{ or } \frac{4}{3} > \frac{13}{12}$$

$$\frac{13}{12} > \frac{13+988}{12+988}, \text{ or } \frac{13}{12} > \frac{1{,}001}{1{,}000}$$

$$\text{Thus: } \frac{3}{2} > \frac{4}{3} > \frac{13}{12} > \frac{1{,}001}{1{,}000} \cdots \rightarrow 1$$

3

Simplifying Fractions and Ratios

Simplifying a fraction is a way to express a fraction or ratio in its lowest terms. Answers in fraction or ratio form on the GMAT will always be presented in fully simplified terms. If you multiply or divide both the numerator and the denominator by the same number, you don't actually change the value of the fraction because you're actually multiplying or dividing by 1. You're always allowed to do this as long as you do the same thing to the top and bottom of the fraction or all parts of the ratio. For example:

Fraction:

$$\frac{24}{30} = \frac{24 \div 6}{30 \div 6} = \frac{4}{5}$$

Ratio:

$$4 : 12 : 16$$

$$\frac{4}{4} : \frac{12}{4} : \frac{16}{4}$$

$$1 : 3 : 4$$

You can simplify (or reduce) a fraction or ratio by dividing both the numerator and the denominator by any common factors until no common factors remain (either one at a time, or in a single step):

Two steps: $$\frac{75}{45} = \frac{75 \div 5}{45 \div 5} = \frac{15}{9} = \frac{15 \div 3}{9 \div 3} = \frac{5}{3}$$

One step: $$\frac{75}{45} = \frac{75 \div 15}{45 \div 15} = \frac{5}{3}$$

Simplify before You Multiply

When multiplying fractions, you could first multiply the numerators together, then multiply the denominators together, and finally simplify the resulting product. For example:

$$\frac{8}{15} \times \frac{35}{72} = \frac{8(35)}{15(72)}$$

Next step? You don't have a calculator on the GMAT, so time to do long multiplication...

$$\frac{8(35)}{15(72)} = \frac{280}{\ldots}$$

Wait! Stop! Don't even do that first step. If the math is that annoying, pause and think about what else you could do. In this case, you'd eventually have to simplify that fraction, so why not do that first?

In general, always try to simplify before you multiply: Cancel common factors from the top and bottom of the fractions.

For example, the **8** in the numerator and the **72** in the denominator both have 8 as a factor. Thus, the 8 can be simplified to 1 and the 72 can be simplified to 9:

$$\frac{{}^{1}\cancel{8}}{15} \times \frac{35}{\cancel{72}_{9}}$$

3

It doesn't matter that the numbers appear in two different fractions. When multiplying fractions together, you can treat all of the numerators as one group and all of the denominators as another. You can cancel anything in the top group with anything in the bottom. (You can't do this when you're adding or subtracting two fractions—just when you're multiplying.)

What next? The **35** and **15** both have 5 as a factor, so simplify those two numbers as well:

$$\frac{{}^{1}\cancel{8}}{{}_{3}\cancel{15}} \times \frac{\cancel{35}^{7}}{\cancel{72}_{9}} = \frac{1(7)}{3(9)} = \frac{7}{27}$$

Make your life easier: Always simplify before you multiply! These numbers are a lot nicer than what you would have gotten by multiplying first.

Add and Subtract Fractions: Use a Common Denominator

If you're asked to add or subtract fractions, first consider whether it would be better to convert to percents or decimals instead. If you see common conversions that you have memorized, it's likely going to be easier to convert from fractions to percents or decimals first.

If you do decide to add or subtract in fraction form, follow these steps:

1. Find a common denominator.
2. Rewrite each fraction so that it is expressed using this common denominator.
3. Add up the numerators only.

Here's an example:

$$\frac{3}{8} + \frac{7}{12}$$

$$\frac{9}{24} + \frac{14}{24}$$ A common denominator is 24. Thus, $\frac{3}{8} = \frac{9}{24}$ and $\frac{7}{12} = \frac{14}{24}$.

$$\frac{9}{24} + \frac{14}{24} = \frac{23}{24}$$ Finally, add the numerators to find the answer.

Why don't you also add up the denominators? Think back to the pizza you shared with your friend Sam at the beginning of this chapter. You ate 5 of the 8 slices, or $\frac{5}{8}$ of the pizza, and Sam ate 3 of the 8 slices, or $\frac{3}{8}$ of the pizza. Together, you ate $\frac{8}{8}$ of the pizza—that is, the whole thing!—not $\frac{8}{16}$, or half of the pizza.

In this example, you have to simplify the fraction at the end:

$\frac{11}{15} - \frac{7}{30}$	
$\frac{22}{30} - \frac{7}{30}$	A common denominator is 30: $\frac{11}{15} = \frac{22}{30}$. Leave $\frac{7}{30}$ the same.
$\frac{22}{30} - \frac{7}{30} = \frac{15}{30}$	Subtract the numerators.
$\frac{15}{30} = \frac{1}{2}$	Simplify $\frac{15}{30}$ to find the answer: $\frac{1}{2}$.

Dividing Fractions: Use the Reciprocal

What if you're asked to do the following math?

$$\frac{1}{2} \div \frac{3}{4}$$

If you're asked to divide by a fraction (in this case, you're asked to divide by $\frac{3}{4}$), instead multiply by the reciprocal. The reciprocal of a fraction is the *flip* of that fraction. For example:

The reciprocal of $\frac{3}{4}$ is $\frac{4}{3}$. The reciprocal of $\frac{2}{9}$ is $\frac{9}{2}$.

What is the reciprocal of an integer? Think of an integer as a fraction with a denominator of 1. For example, the integer 5 is the fraction $\frac{5}{1}$. To find the reciprocal, flip it:

The reciprocal of 5, or $\frac{5}{1}$, is $\frac{1}{5}$. The reciprocal of 8 is $\frac{1}{8}$.

In order to divide by a fraction, follow these steps:

1. Change the divisor (the second number) into its reciprocal.
2. Multiply the fractions.

For example:

$\frac{1}{2} \div \frac{3}{4}$	First, change the divisor $\frac{3}{4}$ into its reciprocal $\frac{4}{3}$.
$\frac{1}{2} \times \frac{4}{3}$	Rewrite the problem as multiplication.
$\frac{1}{{}_1\cancel{2}} \times \frac{\cancel{4}^2}{3} = \frac{2}{3}$	Solve. Simplify before you multiply!

Split Up Double-Decker Fractions

The division of fractions can be shown by putting the fractions themselves into a **double-decker fraction**. Consider one of the previous examples:

$\frac{1}{2} \div \frac{3}{4}$ can also be written as a double-decker fraction this way: $\dfrac{\frac{1}{2}}{\frac{3}{4}}$

You can rewrite this as the top fraction divided by the bottom fraction. Then, solve normally by using the reciprocal of the second fraction and then multiplying:

$$\frac{\frac{1}{2}}{\frac{3}{4}} = \frac{1}{2} \div \frac{3}{4} = \frac{1}{\cancel{2}} \times \frac{\cancel{4}}{3} = \frac{2}{3}$$

3

In addition, you can often simplify more quickly by multiplying both top and bottom by a common denominator of the "fractions within the fraction":

$$\frac{\frac{1}{2}}{\frac{3}{4}} = \frac{\frac{1}{2} \times 4}{\frac{3}{4} \times 4} = \frac{2}{3}$$

In this case, the common denominator of 2 and 4 is 4, so multiply both the top and bottom by 4 to make the fractions within the fraction drop out.

The Unknown Multiplier

You've already learned that if you multiply the top and the bottom of a fraction by the same number, you will end up with an equivalent fraction. For example:

$$\frac{4}{7} = \frac{8}{14} = \frac{12}{21}$$

A ratio is equivalent to the most-reduced fraction, $\frac{4}{7}$, in the above example. For example, you might be told that there are 4 dogs for every 7 cats. That ratio doesn't (necessarily) tell you the actual number of dogs and cats, though. You could have exactly 4 dogs and 7 cats, but you could also have 8 dogs and 14 cats, or 12 dogs and 21 cats, and so on.

The $\frac{8}{14}$ fraction is the result of multiplying the top and bottom of the base ratio, $\frac{4}{7}$, by 2.

The $\frac{12}{21}$ fraction is the result of multiplying the base ratio by 3.

The number by which you multiply the ratio to find the actual number of things is called the **unknown multiplier**. Every ratio has an unknown multiplier, and that multiplier is the same for every part of the ratio.

Recall from earlier in this chapter that every ratio has a ratio total, calculated by adding up the parts of the ratio.

If the ratio of dogs to cats is 4 to 7 and there are 8 actual dogs, what else can you figure out? Lay out the information in a table—and always include the ratio total as one column in the table:

	Part	Part	Whole
	Dogs	**Cats**	**Total**
Ratio	4	7	
Multiplier			
Actual	8		

The multiplier for dogs must be $\frac{8}{4} = 2$. Since the multiplier is always the same for all parts of a ratio, write 2 in all of the multiplier boxes. (Note: The multiplier must be an integer for this problem, because you must have whole numbers of dogs and cats.)

	Dogs		Cats		Total
Ratio	4	+	7	=	11
	×		×		
Multiplier	**2**	=	**2**	=	**2**
	=		=		
Actual	8	+		=	

Now, you can determine that there are 14 cats. You can even calculate the total number of animals, either by adding dogs and cats $(8 + 14 = 22)$ or by multiplying the ratio total $(4 + 7 = 11)$ by the multiplier, 2.

If you know the ratio and you know any one of the actual values, then you can calculate everything in the table.

Try this problem:

> A display holds 56 devices, all of which are either phones or tablets. If the ratio of phones to tablets is 3 : 4, how many of the devices in the display are phones?

Draw a table and begin to fill it in:

	Phones	Tablets	Total
Ratio	3	4	7
Multiplier	8	8	8
Actual	24	32	56

Add the top row to obtain a total of 7. The ratio of phones to tablets to total is 3 : 4 : 7. The multiplier for the total is $\frac{56}{7} = 8$, so 8 is the multiplier across the board.

	Phones	Tablets	Total
Ratio	3	4	7
Multiplier	8	8	8
Actual	(24)		56

There are $3 \times 8 = 24$ phones in the display. (Again, the multiplier must be an integer for this problem.)

If you prefer, you can also solve algebraically. Call the unknown multiplier x. The ratio is 3 : 4 and the actual numbers of phones and tablets are $3x$ and $4x$, respectively.

The problem indicates that the total number of devices equals 56:

$$\begin{aligned} \text{Phones} + \text{Tablets} &= \text{Total} \\ 3x + 4x &= 56 \\ 7x &= 56 \\ x &= 8 \end{aligned}$$

Plug the multiplier into the expression for phones ($3x$) to determine how many phones are in the display: $(3)(8) = 24$. There are 24 phones in the display.

The unknown multiplier is particularly useful with three-part ratios. For example:

> A recipe calls for amounts of lemon juice, orange juice, and water in the ratio of 2 : 5 : 7. If the mixture yields 35 milliliters of liquid, how much orange juice was included?

First, set up the given information, including the total for the base ratio:

	L	O	W	Tot
R	2	5	7	14
M				
A		( )		35

Next, begin calculating what you need in order to find the value for the Orange-Actual cell. Compare the actual total to the ratio total to find the multiplier.

	L	O	W	Tot
R	2	5	7	14
M		2.5		2.5
A		(12.5)		35

In this problem, the unknown multiplier turns out not to be an integer. This result is fine, because the problem deals with continuous quantities (milliliters of liquids).

Here's how to set up the problem algebraically:

$$\begin{array}{ccccccc} \text{Lemon} & + & \text{Orange} & + & \text{Water} & = & \text{Total} \\ 2x & + & 5x & + & 7x & = & 14x \end{array}$$

Now, solve: $14x = 35$, or $x = 2.5$. Thus, the amount of orange juice is $5x = 5(2.5) = 12.5$ milliliters.

Comparing Fractions: The Double-Cross

Which fraction is greater, $\frac{7}{9}$ or $\frac{4}{5}$?

3

The traditional method of comparing fractions involves finding a common denominator and comparing the two fractions. The common denominator of 9 and 5 is 45.

Thus, $\frac{7}{9} = \frac{35}{45}$ and $\frac{4}{5} = \frac{36}{45}$. In this case, $\frac{4}{5}$ is slightly greater than $\frac{7}{9}$.

Why? Because the numerator 36 is greater than the numerator 35. Once you find a common denominator, the only thing you need to compare is the numerator—so take advantage of that fact to make the work go faster:

$(7 \times 5) = 35 \quad (4 \times 9) = 36$

Set up the fractions next to each other. Multiply the numbers across the arrows and put each answer by the corresponding numerator (*not* the denominator!).

$35 < 36$

$\frac{7}{9} < \frac{4}{5}$

Since 35 is less than 36, the first fraction must be less than the second one.

Essentially, you have done the same thing as before—you just didn't bother to write down the common denominator of 45. This process can save you time when comparing fractions on the GMAT.

You can even use the double-cross method to add or subtract fractions, with one more step: Draw a third arrow straight across the bottom. All three arrows mean *multiply*. For example:

$\frac{7}{9} + \frac{4}{5}$

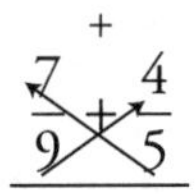

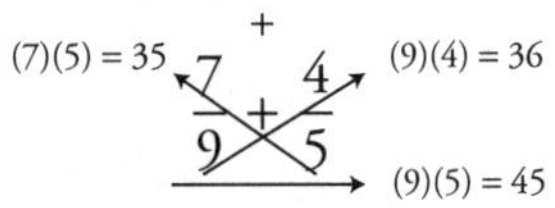

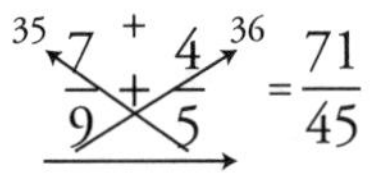

Essentially, multiply across all three arrows, as shown. Add the two results for the numerators (or subtract, if the problem asks you to subtract). For the denominator, just use the single number from the bottom multiplication.

Since this method involves multiplying, check the numbers before you start. If they're large enough to annoy you, you might want to use the traditional method of finding a common denominator.

Multiple Ratios: Make a Common Term

You may encounter two separate ratios containing a common element (e.g., dogs to cats and cats to birds). To combine the ratios, you can use a process remarkably similar to creating a common denominator for fractions.

Consider the following problem:

> In a box containing action figures from Game of Thrones, there are 3 figures of Arya for every 2 figures of Brienne, and 5 figures of Arya for every 4 figures of Daenerys. What is the ratio of Daenerys figures to Brienne figures?

Jot down the given info as you try to understand the story:

$A : B$	$A : D$
3 : 2	5 : 4

The question asks for the ratio of D to B, but neither of the given ratios contains both of these variables. What now?

Just as you can change *fractions* to have common *denominators*, you can change ratios so that the common *terms* correspond to the same quantity. Once you do this, you can put everything together in one big three-part ratio.

The two ratios have Arya in common, but the two values for Arya are different. In order to combine the two ratios, the values for Arya must be the same.

$A : B : D$		$A : B : D$
3 : 2 : ?	→ Multiply by 5 →	15 : 10 : ?
5 : ? : 4	→ Multiply by 3 →	15 : ? : 12
	This is the combined ratio:	**15 : 10 : 12**

Once the A's are the same (15), combine the two ratios into one big three-part ratio. Note: Do not add the two A's together. Just use the base number, 15.

Now, answer the question. Pull out just the parts that you are asked for: D and B. The ratio D to B is 12 to 10, which simplifies to 6 to 5.

Try this same problem but with a different question:

> In a box containing action figures from Game of Thrones, there are 3 figures of Arya for every 2 figures of Brienne, and 5 figures of Arya for every 4 figures of Daenerys. What is the least number of action figures that could be in the box?

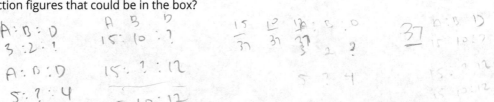

First, you still want to combine the two separate ratios into one big ratio, as you did for the first version of the problem. So $A : B : D$ is 15 : 10 : 12.

Next, what could the *actual* number of action figures be, not just the ratio? The actual values for the action figures are the ratio numbers multiplied by an unknown multiplier (which must be a positive integer, since you need whole action figures). The question asks for the *least* number of action figures, so use the least possible multiplier, 1. In other words, the ratio itself represents the least number of action figures.

Therefore, the least possible number of action figures is $15 + 10 + 12 = 37$.

Complex Fractions: Don't Split the Denominator

3

A complex fraction is a fraction in which there is a sum or a difference in the numerator or the denominator. For example:

$$\frac{x+y}{z}$$

When simplifying fractions that incorporate sums or differences, remember this rule: You may split up the terms of the numerator, but you may *never* split the terms of the denominator.

For example, you can add up the two terms in the numerator in this example, but you may decide it's easier to split it into two fractions first and add after:

$$\frac{480+165}{10} = \frac{480}{10} + \frac{165}{10} = 48 + 16.5 = 64.5$$

By contrast, the terms in this example may *not* be split:

$$\frac{5}{15+10} \neq \frac{5}{15} + \frac{5}{10} \quad \textbf{NO!}$$

Instead, simplify the denominator first:

$$\frac{5}{15+10} = \frac{5}{25} = \frac{1}{5}$$

Often, GMAT problems will involve complex fractions with variables. On these problems, it is tempting to split the denominator. Do not fall for it!

$$\frac{5x-2y}{x-y} \neq \frac{5x}{x} - \frac{2y}{y} \quad \textbf{NO!}$$

Unfortunately, $\frac{5x-2y}{x-y}$ cannot be simplified further, because neither of the terms in the numerator shares a factor with the entire denominator.

On the other hand, the expression $\frac{6x-10}{10}$ can be simplified by splitting the numerator. Both terms in the numerator share a factor with the denominator, and by splitting into two fractions, you can write each part in simplified form:

$$\frac{6x-10}{10} = \frac{6x}{10} - \frac{10}{10} = \frac{3}{5}x - 1$$

Relative Values and Data Sufficiency

Some problems will give you concrete values while others will provide only relative values:

> **Concrete values** are actual amounts (# of tickets sold, liters of water, etc.).
>
> **Relative values** relate two quantities using fractions, ratios, percents, or decimals (twice as many, ratio of 2 : 3, 60% less, etc.).

Try this Data Sufficiency problem:

> A company sells only two kinds of pie: apple pie and cherry pie. What fraction of the total pies sold last month were apple pies?
>
> (1) The company sold 460 pies last month.
>
> (2) The company sold 30% more cherry pies than apple pies last month.

3

When a question asks for a relative value, not a concrete or actual value, you don't need as much information in order to solve.

The question asks what fraction of the total pies sold were apple pies:

$$\frac{\text{apple pies}}{\text{total pies}} = ? \quad \text{or} \quad \frac{a}{a+c} = ?$$

Statement (1) indicates that the total number of pies sold was 460, so $a + c = 460$:

$$\frac{a}{460} = ?$$

The value of a is still unknown, so this statement is not sufficient. Eliminate answer choices (A) and (D).

Statement (2) indicates that the company sold 30% more cherry pies than apple pies; in other words, the number of cherry pies sold was 130% of the number of apple pies sold:

$$1.3a = c$$

On the surface, this may not seem like enough information. But watch what happens when you replace c with $1.3a$ in the rephrased question.

$$\frac{a}{a+c} = ?$$

$$\frac{a}{a+1.3a} = ?$$

$$\frac{\cancel{a}}{2.3\cancel{a}} = \frac{1}{2.3}$$

The a variables drop out. Statement (2) actually does provide enough information to find the value of the fraction. The correct answer is (B).

How could you recognize that statement (2) is sufficient without having to do that algebra?

This DS question stem was asking for a relative value (*What* fraction *of the total pies*...). Relative values are really just ratios in disguise. The ratio in this question is as follows:

> apple pies sold : cherry pies sold : total pies sold

The question asks for the ratio of apple pies sold to total pies sold, or apple : total. Statement (2) provides the ratio of apple pies sold to cherry pies sold. You could write it this way:

$a : c$

$10 : 13$

The number 13 is 30% greater than the number 10, so this ratio fits the given information. And, if you know the two parts of the ratio, then you can find the ratio total:

$a : c : t$

$10 : 13 : 23$

As a result, the ratio of apple pies to total pies ($a : t$) is 10 : 23. Statement (2) is sufficient to answer the question.

If you know a ratio, you can find a fraction based on using the ratio total. For example, 10 out of 23 total pies are apple, so the fraction of apple pies is $\frac{10}{23}$.

Also note that, although statement (2) allows you to determine the *relative* value, it does not provide enough information to calculate the *actual* number of pies. If the question had asked for a concrete number, such as the number of apple pies, you would have needed to use both statements to solve.

Problem Set

Note: On quant problems, the GMAT will always provide exactly five answer choices. In this guide, you will sometimes encounter multiple-choice problems with fewer than five answer choices.

For problems 1–5, decide whether the given operation will cause the original value to **increase**, **decrease**, or **stay the same**.

1. Multiply the numerator of a positive fraction by $\frac{3}{2}$.

2. Add 1 to the numerator of a positive fraction and subtract 1 from its denominator.

3. Multiply both the numerator and denominator of a positive fraction by $3\frac{1}{2}$.

4. Multiply a positive fraction by $\frac{3}{8}$.

5. Divide a positive fraction by $\frac{3}{13}$.

6. If 48 : 2x is equivalent to 144 : 600, what is x ?

7. Simplify: $\frac{8(3)(x)^2(3)}{6x}$

8. Simplify: $\frac{\frac{3}{5}+\frac{1}{3}}{\frac{2}{3}+\frac{2}{5}}$

9. Simplify: $\frac{12ab^3 - 5a^2b}{3ab}$

10. Initially, the markers and pens in a drawer were in the ratio of 5 : 7. Then, 6 pens were removed. If there are 35 markers in the drawer, how many pens are left?

    (A) 29
    (B) 43
    (C) 49

3

Save the problem set below for review after you finish this entire guide.

11. Which of the following fractions has a value between $\frac{3}{5}$ and $\frac{2}{3}$?

    (A) $\frac{9}{14}$

    (B) $\frac{8}{18}$

    (C) $\frac{16}{21}$

12. A cleaning solution mixture calls for a ratio of 1 part bleach for every 4 parts water. When mixing the solution, Aki made a mistake and mixed in half as much bleach as was required by the ratio. The total solution consisted of 27 milliliters. How much bleach did Aki put into the solution, in milliliters?

    (A) 3

    (B) 4

    (C) 6

13. The amount of time that three people worked on a certain project was in the ratio of 2 : 3 : 5. If the project took 110 hours, what is the difference between the number of hours worked by the person who worked for the longest time and the person who worked for the shortest time?

    (A) 22

    (B) 33

    (C) 55

14. Challenge! Every game of chess that Artem played this month resulted in a win, a loss, or a tie. What fraction of the chess games that Artem played this month did he win?

    (1) The number of games that resulted in a tie was $\frac{1}{4}$ of the number of games that Artem won.

    (2) Artem lost $\frac{2}{5}$ of the games.

Solutions

1. **Increase:** Multiplying the numerator of a positive fraction by a number greater than 1 increases the numerator. As the numerator of a positive fraction increases, its value increases.

2. **Increase:** As the numerator of a positive fraction increases, the value of the fraction increases. As the denominator of a positive fraction decreases, the value of the fraction also increases. Both actions will work to increase the value of the fraction.

3. **Stay the same:** Multiplying or dividing the numerator and denominator of a fraction by the same number is equivalent to multiplying by 1, so doing this will not change the value of the fraction.

4. **Decrease:** Multiplying any positive number by a positive, proper fraction (a fraction between 0 and 1) decreases the number.

5. **Increase:** Dividing a positive number by a positive, proper fraction (a fraction between 0 and 1) increases the number.

6. **100:** Consider the first given, $48 : 2x$, the ratio, and the second given, $144 : 600$, the actual. Put the info in a ratio table and find the multiplier:

	Part 1	Part 2
R	48	$2x$
M		
A	144	600

Try some numbers to see what you'd need to multiply 48 by to get to 144. How about 48×2? Not enough; that's only 96. What about 48×3? $50 \times 3 = 150$, so 48×3 has to be 6 less. . .Yes, that's 144! Plug the info into the table and solve for x:

	Part 1	Part 2
R	48	$2x$
M	3	3
A	144	600

For the second part, the ratio number times the multiplier gives the actual value: $(2x)(3) = 600$, so $x = 100$.

3

7. **12x:** First, cancel terms in both the numerator and the denominator. Then, combine terms:

$$\frac{8(3)(x)^2(3)}{6x}$$
$$=\frac{8(\not{3})(x)^2(3)}{{}_2\not{6}x}$$
$$=\frac{{}^4\not{8}(x)^2(3)}{\not{2}x}$$
$$=\frac{4(x)^{\not{2}}(3)}{\not{x}}$$
$$=4(x)(3)$$
$$=12x$$

3

8. $\mathbf{\frac{7}{8}}$**:** To get rid of the fractions within fractions, first find the common denominator of all the fractions-within-fractions. The denominators are all 5 or 3, so the common denominator is 15. Next, multiply everything by the fraction $\frac{15}{15}$:

$$\left(\frac{\frac{3}{5}+\frac{1}{3}}{\frac{2}{3}+\frac{2}{5}}\right)\left(\frac{15}{15}\right)=\frac{9+5}{10+6}=\frac{14}{16}=\frac{7}{8}$$

Alternatively, add the fractions in the numerator and denominator:

$$\frac{\frac{14}{15}}{\frac{16}{15}}=\frac{{}^7\not{14}}{{}_1\not{15}}\times\frac{{}^1\not{15}}{{}_8\not{16}}=\frac{7}{8}$$

9. $\mathbf{4b^2-\frac{5}{3}a}$**:** Split the numerator. Then, cancel terms in both the numerator and denominator:

$$\frac{12ab^3-5a^2b}{3ab}=\frac{12ab^3}{3ab}-\frac{5a^2b}{3ab}=4b^2-\frac{5}{3}a$$

10. **(B) 43:** Find the unknown multiplier, then use it to calculate the initial number of pens in the drawer. Include the Total column when you make the table, but only use it if the problem requires you to. (Note: The given information is shown in bold; the calculated information is not bold.)

	M	P	Tot
R	**5**	**7**	
M	7	7	
A	**35**	49	

There were initially 49 pens in the drawer but 6 were removed, so 43 pens remain.

11. (A) $\frac{9}{14}$: The two starting fractions are both on the "common conversions" list, so consider converting to percentages or decimals:

$$\frac{3}{5} = 0.6 = 60\% \text{ and } \frac{2}{3} = 0.6\overline{6} = 66\frac{2}{3}\%$$

Take a look at the answers. Are there any that are well below or above that range?

Answer (B), $\frac{8}{18}$, is less than 0.5 (since $\frac{9}{18}$ is 0.5), so eliminate this answer. What about the other two?

Answer (C), $\frac{16}{21}$, is close to $\frac{15}{20}$, which is 0.75. But is $\frac{16}{21}$ greater than or less than 0.75? In order to go from $\frac{15}{20}$ to $\frac{16}{21}$, you have to add 1 to both the numerator and denominator. If you start with a positive fraction less than 1 and add the same positive number to both the top and bottom, the fraction will get closer to 1—that is, it will increase. Therefore, $\frac{16}{21}$ must be greater than 0.75. It cannot be correct; the only answer remaining is **(A)**.

3

12. (A) 3 mL: The proper ratio of bleach to water is 1 : 4. However, Aki accidentally put in half as much bleach as the ratio called for. Sketch out the given info in a ratio box and think about how to proceed:

	B	W	Total
R	orig: 1 oops: 0.5	4	
M			
A	?		27

The actual ratio Aki used was 0.5 : 4, and the total volume of the mixture was 27 milliliters. This would be a lot easier to solve if you knew the unknown multiplier or if you knew how much bleach or water Aki actually used. In fact, you (sort of) do: The answer choices represent three possible values for the amount of bleach used. Work backwards!

If Aki used 4 milliliters of bleach, then the mixture would have had 23 milliliters of water (since the whole thing is 27 mL). The ratio, then, would be 4 : 23. Does that reduce to a ratio of 0.5 : 4?

$$4 : 23 \rightarrow 0.5 : \frac{23}{8}$$

Divide 4 by 8 to get 0.5. Do the same thing to the 23. Nope, that value is not 4. Eliminate answer (B).

Is that answer too big or too small? $\frac{23}{8}$ is just a bit smaller than $\frac{24}{8}$, or 3. But the water part of the ratio is supposed to be 4, not 3, so there isn't enough water in this mixture. In order for more of the 27 milliliters of mixture to be water, you need less bleach, so the answer must be the smaller number, 3 milliliters.

If you're not sure, you can check (but don't do more math than you need to do!). If Aki used 3 milliliters of bleach, then the mixture contained 27 − 3 = 24 milliliters of water. The ratio 3 : 24 does reduce to the ratio 0.5 : 4.

13. **(B) 33:** The ratio is 2 : 3 : 5. Call x the unknown multiplier, so the actual number of hours for each person are $2x$, $3x$, and $5x$. Use this to set up an equation and solve for x:

$$2x + 3x + 5x = 110$$
$$10x = 110$$
$$x = 11$$

Therefore, the person who worked for the longest time put in $5(11) = 55$ hours, and the person who worked for the shortest time put in $2(11) = 22$ hours. This represents a difference of $55 - 22 = 33$ hours.

14. **(C):** There are three possible outcomes for each game: W, L, or T. The question asks for the fraction of games won, or $\frac{W}{W+L+T}$. Note that the question is asking for a relative value, not the actual numbers involved; it may be possible to find this fraction without knowing the actual number of wins and the total number of games.

3

The first statement mentions both ties and wins, while the second mentions only losses. Since the second statement is less complex, start there and write $\frac{\text{BD}}{\text{ACE}}$ on your scratch paper.

(2) INSUFFICIENT: Artem lost 2 out of every 5 games. At most, then, Artem won 3 out of every 5 games, but he could have won fewer. All you can tell for sure is that Artem won or tied 3 out of 5 games. Eliminate answers (B) and (D).

(1) INSUFFICIENT: This statement can be interpreted as a ratio. For every 1 game tied, Artem won 4 games. The ratio of ties to wins is 1 : 4. No information is given about losses, however, so this information is not enough to determine the fraction of games won out of the total number of games. Eliminate answer (A).

(1) AND (2) SUFFICIENT: Set up a partial ratio box. Since the question asks for a fraction and never provides real numbers, you only need the first row (the Ratio row). The ratio of T : W is 1 : 4.

	T	*W*	*L*	**Total**
R	1	4	*L*	5 + *L*

The second statement indicates that L represents 2 parts out of a total of 5 parts. That information is the equivalent of providing a second equation so that you can solve for the two unknowns (L and the ratio total). If you like, you can just memorize the idea that if there is only one unknown part of the ratio (L in this case) *and* you're also told the relationship between that unknown and the ratio total, then you can always find the relationship between any of the three individual parts and the total. If you want to understand why this is true, read on (understanding why may help you to remember this fact).

Statement (2) can be written algebraically as $\frac{L}{Total} = \frac{2}{5}$. The ratio box indicates that the total is $5 + L$. You can substitute that into the statement (2) equation to solve for the L part of the ratio. (This is DS, so don't actually solve. Just know that you can.) If you know the ratio value of L, you know all three parts of the ratio, so you can find $\frac{W}{W+L+T}$.

The correct answer is **(C)**: Both statements together are sufficient, but neither one works alone.

CHAPTER 4

Strategy: Arithmetic vs. Algebra 1

In This Chapter

- Test Cases
- Choose Smart Numbers
- Work Backwards

In this chapter, you will learn three strategies for avoiding algebra and using real numbers (arithmetic) instead. You can use these strategies on both the Quantitative and Integrated Reasoning sections of the GMAT.

CHAPTER 4 Strategy: Arithemetic vs. Algebra 1

When you first learned how to do math, you started with arithmetic—that is, you did math stuff with real numbers. Later on sometime, you learned about variables (or unknowns) and started to do algebra.

Which of these problems is easier for you to solve?

What percent of a number is 50% of 10% of that number?	What percent of 100 is 50% of 10% of 100 ?
(A) 1%	(A) 1%
(B) 5%	(B) 5%
(C) 10%	(C) 10%

The setup of the two problems is identical—one just has real numbers rather than unknowns. In the first problem, you would assign a variable to the unknown *number* mentioned, and then you would use algebra to solve. You may think that this version is not particularly difficult, but no matter how easy you think it is, it's still easier to work with the real numbers given in the second problem.

In general, arithmetic is easier than algebra—for everyone. Our brains just work better with real numbers.

So take this mantra into the test with you: Don't just do the math presented to you, in the form it is presented. Pause to evaluate—make a conscious choice! If the algebra on a particular problem is really easy for you, go for it. Often, though, using real numbers will be faster and easier—and that means more time and mental energy to spend elsewhere on the test.

Here's the exciting thing: There are a number of ways to turn GMAT algebra into arithmetic. You've already learned about one strategy in the Data Sufficiency chapter: Test Cases.

In those DS problems, some theoretical question was asked, and multiple possible values were allowed to be used in the problem. . .in other words, the question involved some algebra. But algebra is annoying—so, where possible, try some real numbers (test cases) to see whether you can get different answers (not sufficient!) or whether you keep getting the same answer (sufficient!).

This general principle (try some real numbers/do arithmetic instead of algebra) can apply to Problem Solving (PS) problems as well. The details just change a bit in terms of how you execute.

There are three main main strategies that you can use to turn algebra into arithmetic on PS problems:

1. Test Cases (TC)
2. Choose Smart Numbers (SN)
3. Work Backwards (WB)

In this chapter, you'll learn the basics for each question type. As you continue your studies, you'll continue to learn more about these strategies until you're an expert for the real test.

Test Cases

You can actually **Test Cases** (TC) on Problem Solving problems, too—in one specific circumstance. When the problem asks which answer choice *must be* or *could be* something (true or false or have some certain characteristic), you can use this strategy.

Consider this problem:

> If x and y are integers and $xy = 6$, which of the following must be true?
>
> (A) x is even.
>
> (B) x equals either 2 or 3.
>
> (C) Either x or y is even.

Understand. Both are integers. The product xy equals 6. *Must be* signals that you could test cases. According to this question stem, one (and only one) of the answers *must be true* all the time.

Plan. If the numbers are both integers and multiply to 6, then they could be 2 and 3, or 1 and 6, or... anything else? They could also be negative, such as -2 and -3. Feel free to start with a positive case, but see how the math plays out; you may want to try a negative later.

Solve. Case 1: $x = 2$ and $y = 3$. In this case...hmm, all of the answers are true. Can you think of a case to test that would give you a different response for answer (A)? In other words, can you choose a value for x that is *not* even?

Case 2: Swap the two numbers. If $x = 3$ and $y = 2$, then you can eliminate answer (A). Answers (B) and (C) are still in. Take a look at the text of those two answers; what do you want to try next?

Case 3: Try something other than 2 and 3. If $x = 1$ and $y = 6$, then you can eliminate answer (B).

The correct answer is **(C)**, the only remaining answer.

These *must be* questions aren't super common on the GMAT, so more often, you'll test cases on DS problems—but it's good to know that you can use this strategy on certain PS problems, too.

Let's summarize that process.

U: First, during the Understand step, **recognize** that you can test cases on a PS problem. The question will ask what *must* or *could be* a certain thing (true, false, or a certain characteristic).

P: During the Plan step, **think about** any **constraints** you're given; this determines what kinds of numbers you are allowed to try. Also think about what kinds of numbers might give you a different answer. You'll learn more strategies for this step later in this guide.

S: Then, **choose one set of numbers**, following any constraints given in the problem, and test the answers. Cross off any answers that fail the test. **Decide what to test next:** Look at the remaining answer choices and think about what kind of case might help you to knock out one (or more) of the choices. Repeat until you're down to one answer (or you get stuck; in that case, guess from the remaining answers and move on).

Choose Smart Numbers

The next two strategies, **Choose Smart Numbers** (SN) and **Work Backwards** (WB) apply only to PS problems. On the real test, expect to see one to three PS problems for *each* of these two strategies. (And you can use all three of these strategies on the Integrated Reasoning section, too!)

When the problem asks you to find either a variable expression or a relative number (such as a percentage, a fraction, or a ratio), you can choose smart numbers. This strategy is similar to testing cases, but not quite the same.

Remember this problem?

> What percent of a number is 50% of 10% of that number?
>
> (A) 1%
>
> (B) 5%
>
> (C) 10%

Understand. It keeps talking about *a number* but never offers a real value for that number. Even the answer choices aren't actual values—they're just percentages, or relative values. In this case, you can pick your own value for the problem.

So far, this probably feels similar to testing cases. Here's the great part: Unlike DS, this problem type has specific answer choices, so you only need to try one case when you use SN. That one case will lead to one of the answers and then you're done! (The only exception to this on PS is the *must be* or *could be* problem type shown in the prior section, for which you may need to test multiple cases.)

Plan. Since the problem deals with percentages, 100 is a nice number to pick.

= 100

Jot this down and put a big box around it—you may need to use it multiple times, so you want to find it again easily.

Now, anywhere the problem talks about *that number*, you're going to use 100. Let's see how that works:

> What percent of a number is 50% of 10% of that number?

Solve. Start with the concrete numbers in the question:

= 100

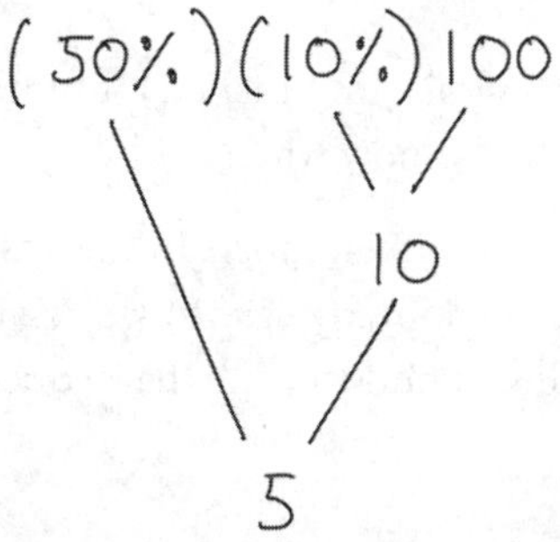

Note: Since it's all multiplication, you can do that math in either order. It's your choice whether to take 10% first or 50% first. Either way, 50% of 10% of 100 equals 5.

The starting number is 100 and the *50% of 10% of that number* portion of the question now equals 5. Plug this information into the original question:

> **Original:** What percent of a number is *50% of 10% of that number*?
>
> **Rephrased:** What percent of 100 is 5 ?

Since it asks for the percent and gives you the two real numbers, put the *of* number on the bottom of a fraction and the other number on top: $\frac{5}{100} = 5\%$. You can also think it through logically if you prefer: 5 is 5% of 100. Go find a match in the answers.

The correct answer is (B).

Let's summarize that process.

U: During the Understand step, **recognize** that you can use smart numbers. It's a PS problem. The problem will keep talking about a certain thing but will never give a real number for that thing, in the question stem or in the answer choices. The answers will contain variables or relative values, such as fractions, percents, or ratios.

P: During the Plan step, think about **what kind of number will work nicely** in the problem. You'll learn more strategies for this step later in this guide.

S: Finally, **use your chosen number to work through the math** until you find a numerical answer, then find the choice that matches your numerical answer.

Work Backwards

On certain problems, you can also work backwards from the answer choices. Some problems do give you real numbers for everything; in this case, you can't choose your own numbers to try as you did for the first two strategies.

Consider this problem:

> Flannery is 28 years old and Harumi is 11 years old. In how many years will Flannery's age be twice Harumi's age?
>
> (A) 3
> (B) 4
> (C) 6
> (D) 8
> (E) 9

There are ways to solve this problem algebraically, but that's a lot more annoying than doing some arithmetic. But this problem has real numbers already...so now what?

The problem is asking you to solve for one of the numbers in the answer choices. The numbers in the answer choices are "nice" numbers—they look pretty easy to work with. So you could just do the problem backwards, trying each answer choice till you find the one that works.

That might seem like it could take a long time. What if you have to try all five answers?

The good news: You won't have to. The GMAT will put numerical answers in increasing order or decreasing order (so, in this case, either 3, 4, 6, 8, 9 or 9, 8, 6, 4, 3). This little feature means that you'll likely never have to try more than two answer choices when working backwards.

Understand. $F = 28$ and $H = 11$. In how many years will $F = 2H$? The answer choices represent that actual number of years and they're "nice" numbers, so work backwards.

Plan. When working backwards, start with answer (B) or (D). In this case, answer (B) is smaller, so start there. (Why not answer (C)? You'll learn a little later.) Start a chart on your scratch paper showing answer (B) and what it represents. You're going to keep adding new columns to this chart as you perform each step.

Solve. Work through the problem, using answer (B). When you get to the last piece of information given in the question stem, check whether your math matches what the problem says:

> Flannery is 28 years old and Harumi is 11 years old. In how many years will Flannery's age be twice Harumi's age?

F = 28 now
H = 11 now

Yrs from now:	F will be:	H will be:	F is 2H?
(B) 4	32	15	No

The very last piece of given information is that *F* will be twice *H*'s age. But this isn't what happens with answer (B)—15 times 2 is 30, not 32. So this answer cannot be correct. Cross it off.

Next, look at the way that math played out. Do you need a larger value for "years from now" or a smaller one? How can you tell?

If you aren't sure (it's not easy to tell on this problem!), try answer (D)—by comparing the results from testing (B) and (D), a pattern in the answer choices will emerge:

Yrs from now:	F will be:	H will be:	F is 2H?
(B) 4	32	15	No $H < \frac{1}{2}$
(D) 8	36	19	No, $H > \frac{1}{2}$

In 8 years, *H* will be 19 and F will be 36. Once again, *F* is not double *H*'s age. This answer is still not the right one. But something's different this time. Using choice (B), *H* was *less* than half of *F.* That is, answer (B) was too small. But using answer (D), *H* is now *more* than half of *F.* Answer (D) goes too far! What does that mean?

You need a number that's greater than 4 and less than 8. Only answer choice (C) qualifies. You can check the math if you're not sure—but the GMAT is a timed test, so don't do work that you don't need to do.

The correct answer is **(C)**.

Here's how you *can* figure out directly that you needed a larger number on this problem (though it's not easy—so feel free not to go this far with it!). In the original scenario, twice *H*'s age is 22, which is 6 years less than *F* at 28. Jot down what you know:

Using answer (B): In 4 years, *F* will be 32 and *H* will be 15. Double 15 to get 30, which is 2 years less than 32. So the 2*H* value has gotten *closer* to half of *F*'s age but is still *less* than half of *F*'s age.

F = 28 now
H = 11 now

Yrs from now:	F will be:	H will be:	F is 2H ?	now H x 2 = 28 → 3y less
(B) 4	32	15	No $H < \frac{1}{2}$	H x 2 = 30 → 2y less

In other words, more time needs to pass before *H* will be half of *F*, so you'd need to try a larger number. Your test for (D) would show that it was too large, and so again, you'd choose (C).

4

The fact that the answers are in order is exactly what allows you to "follow the pattern" when working backwards. You'll always start with either answer (B) or answer (D).

Imagine you have the same problem but the five answers are (A) 6, (B) 8, (C) 9, (D) 10, and (E) 12. You'd try (B), 8, first and, as above, you'd figure out that 8 was incorrect. What would that mean?

If you were able to analyze the math, you'd realize that (B) was *too large*, so the correct answer must be (A), the only smaller choice. You'd never have to try answer (D).

Don't spend a ton of time trying to figure that out though. If you don't see a quick way to tell whether you need to go larger or smaller, just test (D) and compare it to (B) to find the pattern. Here's what would happen for the new answer choices:

> (B): In 8 years, *F* will be 36 and *H* will be 19. Double *H* is 38, not 36. This is too big and off by 2 years.
>
> (D): In 10 years, *F* will be 38 and *H* will be 21. Double *H* is 42, not 38. This is too big and off by 4 years.

Both (B) and (D) are wrong in the same direction, but (D) is even farther off. Choosing a bigger answer choice made things worse! So you now know that (A) is the correct answer.

Consider these three possible patterns of answers; what does each one mean? For each example, assume you've tried answers (B) and (D) and determined that they're incorrect.

Example 1	Example 2	Example 3
(A) 1	(A) 1	(A) 5
(B) 2 too small	(B) 2 too small	(B) 4 not right; can't tell which way to go
(C) 3	(C) 3	(C) 3
(D) 4 too big	(D) 4 too small, but closer	(D) 2 still wrong in the same direction as (B), but closer
(E) 5	(E) 5	(E) 1

In the first example, answer (B) is too small but (D) is too big. The correct answer must be in between, so the only possible choice is answer (C).

In the second example, answers (B) and (D) are both too small, but answer (D) gets *closer* to the right answer. The pattern is sending you to answer (E).

The third example is more complex. You can tell answer (B) is wrong but you're not sure which way to go, so you try answer (D) next. Once you've tried (D), you can see the pattern: Answer (D) is still "off" in the same way as (B) but is getting closer. In this case, the pattern is pointing you to go further to answer (E).

This pattern idea is why you want to try answers (B) and (D) vs. answer (C). Starting with answers (B) and (D) will show you the "spaced-out" pattern among all five answers.

Here's a summary of the working backwards process.

U: First, **recognize** that you can work backwards. It's a PS problem and the answers represent a single variable in the problem (for example, they represent one person's age, not the difference between the ages of two people). The answers will contain actual values—no variables or relative values—and those values should be pretty "nice" to work with for that type of problem, whatever it is.

P: Second, glance at the answers; do they increase or decrease? **Start with answer (B) or (D).** Note: This summary will assume that the answers increase and that you start with answer (B).

Set up a little table on your scratch paper. **Organize to make it easier** to run through the math again with another answer, just in case.

S: Do the math from the beginning of the problem to the last fact given in the problem. **If the answer you started with, (B), is correct, the last fact will match,** so this will be the correct answer. If it doesn't match, cross off answer (B).

Is there an easy way to tell whether to go larger or smaller? If not, try answer (D).

If you can tell that you need a *smaller* number, then the answer must be (A). Pick it and move on. If you can tell that you need a *larger* number, cross off answer (A) and try answer (D).

If you try (D) and it's correct, you're done. If not, cross it off. Then, **examine the pattern created by answers (B) and (D)** and make your choice among the remaining answers accordingly.

Note: As you practice working backwards, you will get better at being able to decipher the pattern shown by answers (B) and (D). But if you aren't sure, you'll have to decide between trying more answers and just guessing and moving on. If you've already spent 2+ minutes, it's probably best just to guess and move on unless the math is very fast. You've eliminated two answers, so your chances of guessing correctly are pretty good.

You'll continue to learn more advanced techniques for each of these three strategies as you work your way through this guide. Now, practice what you just learned in the following problem set.

Problem Set

Practice your test-taking strategies: Smart Numbers, Test Cases, Work Backwards. Try the algebraic/textbook way as well to compare methods. When you're done, ask yourself which way you prefer to solve *this* problem and why.

On the real test, you won't have time to try both methods; you'll have to make a decision and go with it. Learn *how* to make that decision while studying; then, the next time a new problem pops up in front of you, you'll be able to make a quick (and good!) decision about what to do.

1. If $a < 0$ and $b < c$, which of the following must be true?

   (A) $ab < c$

   (B) $ac > b$

   (C) $ab > 0$

   (D) $ac < 0$

   (E) $ab > ac$

2. At the beginning of the day, the ratio of \$5 bills to \$10 bills in Thom's wallet was 2 to 3. Thom then paid for a purchase with one \$5 bill and four \$10 bills, and did not receive change. Afterwards, Thom observed that the ratio of \$5 bills to \$10 bills in the wallet was 3 to 2. How many \$5 bills were in Thom's wallet at the beginning of the day?

   (A) 4

   (B) 6

   (C) 8

   (D) 10

   (E) 12

3. Two libraries are planning to combine a portion of their collections in one new space. The new space will house $\frac{1}{3}$ of the books from Library A, along with $\frac{1}{4}$ of the books from Library B. If there are twice as many books in Library B as in Library A, what proportion of the books in the new space will have come from Library A?

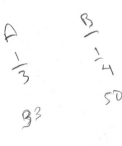

   (A) $\frac{1}{3}$

   (B) $\frac{2}{5}$

   (C) $\frac{1}{2}$

   (D) $\frac{7}{12}$

   (E) $\frac{3}{5}$

Answers and explanations follow on the next page. ▶ ▶ ▶

Solutions

1. **(E) $ab > ac$:** The question stem asks a *must be* question, so test cases on this problem. The stem also indicates that a is negative and that b is less than c. Since the first piece of information makes a distinction between positive and negative, think about the second piece of information in that same context. If b is less than c, then they could both be positive or both be negative, or b could be negative while c is positive.

Glance at the answers. They all involve multiplication of various combinations of the variables. Answers (C) and (D) also include > 0 or < 0, which are shorthand for positive and negative, respectively. What do you know about rules around positive and negative when multiplying two numbers together? If you're not sure, try a couple of small numbers to see what happens.

If the two numbers have the same sign, such as $(1)(2) = 2$ or $(-1)(-2) = 2$, then the product will be positive. If the two numbers have the opposite sign, such as $(1)(-2) = -2$, then the product will be negative.

4

Given that, test answers (C) and (D) first.

(C) $ab > 0$. The variable a is negative, but b could be negative or positive. If b is positive, then this choice is false; that is, it is not always true. Eliminate.

(D) $ac < 0$. The variable a is negative, but c could be negative or positive. If c is negative, then this choice is false; that is, it is not always true. Eliminate.

For the other three choices, try real values. Remember: a must be negative and $b < c$. Try whatever comes to mind first for your first test, then think about how to alter the first test in order to get another answer to drop out.

	Test 1 $a = -1$ $b = -2$ $c = 3$	Test 2 $a = -1$ $b = -2$ $c = -1$
(A) $ab < c$	$(-1)(-2) < 3$ $2 < 3$ True	$(-1)(-2) < -1$ $2 < -1$ False
(B) $ac > b$	$(-1)(3) > -2$ $-3 > -2$ False	(already eliminated)
(E) $ab > ac$	$(-1)(-2) > (-1)(3)$ $2 > -3$ True	$(-1)(-2) > (-1)(-1)$ $2 > 1$ True

Answer (B) drops out in the first test. For the second, look at how the math worked. You can make the value for c negative, so it cannot be greater than the positive ab product, making choice (A) false.

2. **(A) 4:** Thom started with a certain ratio of bills, used some of those bills, and then finished with a different ratio of bills. Annoyingly, the problem doesn't offer any real numbers as a starting point. You could solve algebraically—but you could also just use the answer choices as your starting point and work backwards. Start with answer (B):

$5 at start	**Start ratio** $5 : $10 2 : 3	**Pay** –1 $5 –4 $10	**New ratio** $5 : $10 = 3 : 2?
(B) 6	Actual 6 : 9	New 5 : 5	No

If Thom started with six $5 bills, and the starting ratio was 2 : 3, then the unknown multiplier is 3 and there were nine $10 bills to start. After paying out the given amounts, Thom would be left with a new ratio of 5 : 5, or 1 : 1, but the problem specifies that the new ratio should be 3 : 2, so (B) is not correct. Try (D) next:

$5 at start	**Start ratio** $5 : $10 2 : 3	**Pay** –1 $5 –4 $10	**New ratio** $5 : $10 = 3 : 2?
(B) 6	Actual 6 : 9	New 5 : 5	No
(D) 10	Actual 10 : 15	New 9 : 11	No

This time, the new ratio would be 9 : 11, which still doesn't match the given ratio of 3 : 2, so answer (D) is also incorrect.

Now, what's the pattern between the two choices? It might help to view the ratios as fractions (you can always "read" ratios as fractions without literally rewriting them):

Answer (B) ratio	Answer (D) ratio	Desired new ratio
$\frac{5}{5}$ or $\frac{1}{1}$	$\frac{9}{11}$	$\frac{3}{2}$

The ratio given by answer (B) is 1. Answer (D) got smaller. But the desired ratio, $\frac{3}{2}$, is larger than both, so moving from answer (B) to answer (D) was the wrong direction. The answer must be **(A)**.

If you don't feel confident in that reasoning, go ahead and try answer (A). It will work!

3. (B) $\frac{2}{5}$: The answers are in relative form, so you can use smart numbers. When working with fraction problems, choose a common denominator of the fractions given in the problem, in case you have to divide by either of those denominators. In this case, the problem contains the fractions $\frac{1}{3}$ and $\frac{1}{4}$, so use the common denominator of 12. Any multiple of 12 will work, but keep things simple and use 12 itself.

Assign the value 12 to the total for the *smaller* library—in this case, Library A—because the other library has twice as many books. As a result, Library B's capacity, 24, is also a multiple of the denominators 3 and 4:

$(12)\left(\frac{1}{3}\right) = 4$ of Library A's books will move to the new space.

$(24)\left(\frac{1}{4}\right) = 6$ of Library B's books will move to the new space.

The new space will therefore contain 10 books total. Because 4 out of 10 of those books came from Library A, 40%, or $\frac{2}{5}$, of the books in the new space will have come from Library A.

The correct answer is **(B)**.

Bonus Exercise: Take a look at the wrong answers. Can you figure out how someone would have gotten to any of them?

Answer (A), $\frac{1}{3}$, is one of the numbers given in the question. Also, it's the proportion of the books in the combined original libraries that are Library A's (that is, all books, not just the moved books).

Answer (D), $\frac{7}{12}$, represents the sum of $\frac{1}{3}$ and $\frac{1}{4}$, which is a simple—too simple!—arithmetic combination of two of the given numbers.

Answer (E), $\frac{3}{5}$, represents the proportion of Library B's books in the new space. If you calculated this answer, then you may have solved correctly, but for the wrong thing. How can you avoid making that kind of mistake in future?

CHAPTER 5

Percents

In This Chapter

- Percents as Decimals: Move the Decimal
- Percent, Of, Is, What
- Fast Math: Percent Benchmarks
- Percent Increase and Decrease
- Increasing or Decreasing from the Original
- Successive Percent Change

In this chapter, you will learn how to translate and solve percent problems, as well as how to approach more advanced percent topics such as percent increase and decrease. You'll also learn how to benchmark percents—a strategy that will allow you to perform computations much more quickly.

CHAPTER 5 Percents

Percent literally means "per one hundred." You can think of a percent as a special type of fraction (or decimal) that involves the number 100:

Of the students, 75% like chocolate ice cream.

This means that, out of every 100 total students, 75 like chocolate ice cream.

In fraction form, this is written as $\frac{75}{100}$, which simplifies to $\frac{3}{4}$.

In decimal form, this is written as 0.75.

One common mistake is the belief that 100% equals 100. In fact, 100% means $\frac{100}{100}$. Therefore, 100% = 1.

A multiplier greater than 1, in percent terms, is greater than 100%. For example, if your salary this year is 1.2 times your salary last year, then your salary is now 120% of what it was last year. (Nice!)

A multiplier less than 1 is less than 100%. For example, if your expenses this year are 0.78 of last year's expenses, then your current expenses are 78% of your previous expenses.

Percents as Decimals: Move the Decimal

You can convert percents into decimals by moving the decimal point two spaces to the left:

$525\% = 5.25$ $\quad 52.5\% = 0.525$ $\quad 5.25\% = 0.0525$ $\quad 0.525\% = 0.00525$

A decimal can be converted into a percent by moving the decimal point two spaces to the right:

$0.6 = 60\%$ $\quad 0.28 = 28\%$ $\quad 0.459 = 45.9\%$ $\quad 1.3 = 130\%$

> **Strategy Tip:** Remember, the percent always looks "bigger" than the decimal!

Percent, Of, Is, What

These four words are by far the most important when translating percent questions. In fact, many percent word problems can be rephrased in terms of these four words:

Percent	=	divide by 100	$\overline{100}$
Of	=	multiply	$\times$
Is	=	equals	=
What	=	unknown value	*x*, *y*, or any variable

For example, try this problem:

What is 70 percent of 120 ?

First, as you read left to right, translate the question into an equation:

x	$=$	70	$\overline{100}$	$\times$	120
What	is	70	percent	of	120 ?

Now, solve the equation:

$$x = \frac{70}{100} \times 120$$

$$x = \frac{7}{10} \times 120$$

$$x = 7 \times 12$$

$$x = 84$$

This translation works no matter what order the words appear in. Try another example:

30 is what percent of 50 ?

This statement can be translated directly into an equation:

30	$=$	x	$\overline{100}$	$\times$	50
30	is	what	percent	of	50 ?

In the examples above, x represents the unknown value that you have been asked to find. If you have a Data Sufficiency problem, you might be done already; because the equation has only one variable, and that variable is not a square or in any kind of weird form, you can find a single value for x. That would be sufficient if, for example, the problem asked you to find x.

If you are doing a Problem Solving problem, you may need to solve for x, which means "get x by itself on one side." For example:

$$30 = \frac{x}{100} \times 50$$

$$30 = \frac{x}{2}$$

$$60 = x$$

Look for *percent*, *of*, *is*, and *what* as you translate percent problems into equations; those four words should provide the necessary structure for each equation.

As you get better with translation, you may eventually feel comfortable using a shortcut. Take a look at this example:

Thirty is what percent of 50 ?

First, note that this problem *gives* you two real numbers and asks you to *find* a percent. When this is the setup, you can use the following shortcut.

Think of the *what percent of 50* portion as saying *what percent* ***out of*** *50*. Put the *out of* number in the denominator. Put the other number in the numerator. The *what percent* part goes by itself on the other side of the equation as shown here:

$$\frac{30}{50} \times 100 = x\%$$

Whenever you see *what percent of a number*, you can think of this as "percent out of" that number and go straight to writing a fraction for the left side of the equation. Put the *out of* number on the bottom and the other number on the top. Then, multiply by 100 to go from the decimal form of the number to the percent form.

Fast Math: Percent Benchmarks

You can calculate most percentages quickly using some combination of 50%, 10%, 5%, and 1% of the original number. These percentages are **benchmark** percentages, or common building blocks for other numbers.

For example, the previous section asked you to find 70% of 120. Note that 70% is the equivalent of 50% + 10% + 10%. Calculate 50% and 10% of the number and add up the building blocks:

100% (original number)	50%	10%	50% + 10% + 10% = 70%
120	60	12	60 + 12 + 12 = 84

Here's another way: 70% is equivalent to 10% × 7, as shown here:

100% (original number)	10%	10% × 7 = 70%
120	12	12 × 7 = 84

There are typically multiple ways to compute an ugly percent from a combination of benchmark percents. The numbers you're dealing with may mean that, one time, you'd rather do the 50% + 10% + 10% version but, another time, you'd rather to the 10% × 7 version. Pause and think about the numbers involved before rushing to do the calculation.

Try this problem:

What is 15% of 90 ?

100% = 90
10% = 9
5% = 4.5
15% = 9 + 4.5 = 13.5

Now, try this one:

What is 6% of 50 ?

$100\% = 50$

$1\% = 0.5$

$6\% = (1\%)(6) = (0.5)(6) = 3$

You can also find 5% and 1% and add them up—whatever seems easier to you. Just take a moment to think about your approach and make the best choice for you.

Test your skills on these drills:

1. What is 18% of 50 ?
2. What is 40% of 30 ?
3. What is 75% of 20 ?

Here are the answers:

1. $100\% = 50$

   $20\% = (10\%)(2) = (5)(2) = 10$

   $2\% =$ move the decimal from $20\% = 1$

   $18\% = 20\% - 2\% = 10 - 1 = 9$

2. $100\% = 30$

   $10\% = 3$

   $40\% = (4)(10\%) = (4)(3) = 12$

3. Don't forget about your fraction-conversion skills! Sometimes, it's easier to convert to fractions and cancel. $75\% = \frac{3}{4}$, so:

$$\frac{3}{{}_1\cancel{4}}\left(\overset{5}{\cancel{20}}\right) = (3)(5) = 15$$

Why is it (arguably) easier to use the benchmark method on the first two problems, but easier to use fractions on the third problem?

Most people don't memorize the fraction conversion for 18%, so converting to fractions for the first problem would be annoying.

The second problem could go either way, but because 40% is a multiple of 10%, and 10% is very easy to find, building the answer is still quick.

In the third problem, 75% would take multiple steps to build via the percent method, plus 75% also converts to a very nice fraction: $\frac{3}{4}$. In this case, it will probably be easier to use the fraction here (especially because the starting number, 20, is a multiple of 4, so the denominator will cancel entirely).

Percent Increase and Decrease

Consider this example:

> The price of a cup of coffee increased from 80 cents to 84 cents. By what percent did the price change?

If you want to find a change, whether in terms of percent or of actual value, use the following equation:

$$\textbf{Percent Change} = \frac{\textbf{Change in Value}}{\textbf{Original Value}}$$

In the coffee example, you want to find the *change* in terms of percent. Write $\frac{x}{100}$ to represent an unknown percent:

$$\text{Percent Change} = \frac{\text{Change}}{\text{Original}}$$

$$\frac{x}{100} = \frac{4}{80} = \frac{1}{20}$$

Cross-multiply to get rid of the fractions and solve:

$$\frac{x}{100} = \frac{1}{20}$$

$$20x = 100$$

$$x = 5$$

Therefore, the price increased by 5%.

If you feel comfortable thinking in percents, you can also use the benchmark approach to answer that question. The price went from 80 cents to 84 cents, an increase of 4 cents. That additional 4 cents represents what percentage of the original price, 80 cents?

Ten percent of 80 cents is 8 cents. Halve the 8 cents to get 4 cents. And this figure is half of 10%, or 5%. The percent increase is equivalent to 5%.

Alternatively, a question might ask:

> If the price of a $30 shirt is decreased by 20%, what is the final price of the shirt?

In this case, the question didn't tell you the new percent; rather, it gave the percent decrease. If the price decreases by 20%, then the new price is 100% − 20% = 80% of the original. Use the new percent, not the decrease in percent, to solve for the new price directly. You can use this equation:

$$\text{New Percent} = \frac{\text{New Value}}{\text{Original Value}}$$

Once again, use x to represent the value you want, the new price:

$$\frac{80}{100} = \frac{x}{30}$$

$$\frac{4}{5}(30) = x$$

$$24 = x$$

5

The new price of the shirt is \$24.

Alternatively, you can solve directly without setting up a proportion. The starting price is \$30 and this price is decreased by 20%. Find 20% of \$30 and subtract:

$\$30 - (20\%)(\$30)$ 20% of 30 is 6

$\$30 - \$6 = \$24$

Increasing or Decreasing from the Original

When dealing with percent change, how you calculate depends on what is considered the "original" number, or starting point. For example, if a problem asks how much *smaller* the population was in 1980 than in 1990, which is the original number—the population in 1980 or that in 1990?

Don't try to do math yet. Just think. The question says the number gets smaller, with the population in 1990 as the high point. In this case, the 1990 population is the starting point, or original number—it's the starting point of the story.

Next, when talking about a percent change made to a number, always think of the original number as 100%, or your baseline for future calculations.

For example, if you increase the number 100 by 10%, you'll get $100 + 10 = 110$. The new number will be 110% of the original number, regardless of your starting number. Here are some common language cues for this concept:

10% increase = 110% of the original

10% greater than = 110% of the original

If you decrease a number, then you subtract from 100%:

45% decrease = 55% of the original

45% less than = 55% of the original

Use this conversion to save steps on percent problems. For example:

What number is 50% greater than 60 ?

Fifty percent greater than is the same as *150% of.* So one path is to rewrite the question:

What number is 150% of 60 ?

Translate into an equation, using 1.5 or $\frac{3}{2}$ to represent 150%:

$$x = \frac{3}{2} \times 60$$

$$x = 90$$

Another path is to use benchmarks. What number is 50% greater than 60 ? Well, 50% of 60 is 30. So 50% greater than 60 is $60 + 30 = 90$.

Successive Percent Change

Some problems will ask you to calculate successive percents. For example:

> If a ticket increased in price by 20%, and then increased again by 5%, by what percent did the ticket price increase in total?

Although it may seem counterintuitive, the answer is *not* 25%. When you have *successive* percent changes, the answer will never be to just add or subtract the percentages.

Walk through this with real numbers. If the ticket originally cost \$100, then the first increase would bring the ticket price up to 100 plus 20% of 100 (or \$20) for a total of \$120.

The second increase of 5% is now based on this *new* ticket price, \$120:

$$120 + (0.05)(120) = \$126$$

The price increased from \$100 to \$126, so the percent increase is the change divided by the original, or $\frac{26}{100} = 26\%$.

Why is it 26% and not 25%? Because the second calculation is based on a larger starting number—you're taking 5% of 120, not 100. This will always be true when you are doing two percent increases in a row, so the total percent increase will always be more than the number you'd get if you just added the two percentages together.

In short, successive percents *cannot* simply be added together; instead, you have to calculate each piece separately. This holds for successive increases, successive decreases, and for combinations of increases and decreases.

125 100 0x

Try this problem:

> The cost of a plane ticket is increased by 25%. Later, the ticket goes on sale and the price is reduced 20%. What is the overall percent change in the price of the ticket?

You can *multiply* these changes together; you can't just add or subtract them. A 25% increase followed by a 20% decrease is the same as 125% of 80% of the original number:

$$\left(\frac{125}{100}\right)\left(\frac{80}{100}\right)x = ?$$

$$\left(\frac{5}{4}\right)\left(\frac{4}{5}\right)x = x$$

The 20% decrease entirely offsets the 25% increase. The new price is exactly the same as the original price. You can also work through the math using a real number, as shown in the previous problem:

$$\$100 + (25\% \text{ of } \$100) = \$125$$
$$\$125 - (20\% \text{ of } \$125) = \$100$$

Finally, remember how two successive percent increases will result in a percent change that is greater than the number you'd get if you added the two numbers together? (In that problem, the answer was 26%, not 25%.)

If you have two successive percent decreases, the overall percent decrease will be less than the number you'd get if you just added the two together. For example, if the price of a TV decreased by 10% and then decreased by another 10%, look what happens:

$$\$100 - (10\% \text{ of } \$100) = 100 - 10 = \$90$$
$$\$90 - (10\% \text{ of } \$90) = 90 - 9 = \$81$$

Why does it work that way? By definition, the second number in the calculation, \$90, is smaller than the original number, \$100. So 10% of that number is going to be smaller. Instead of a total decrease of 10% + 10% = 20%, the total decrease is actually 10% + 9% = 19%.

Problem Set

1. A stereo was marked down by 30% and sold for \$84. What was the presale price of the stereo?

   (A) \$100

   (B) \$120

2. A car loan is offered at 8% annual interest, compounded annually. After the first year, the interest due is \$24. What is the principal on the loan?

3. If x is 40% of y and 50% of y is 40, then 16 is what percent of x ?

4. A bowl is half full of water. Four cups of water are then added to the bowl, filling the bowl to 70% of its capacity. How many cups of water are now in the bowl?

5. Challenge problem! (Data Sufficiency answers not given; check the DS chapter if needed.)

   Company X has exactly two product lines and no other sources of revenue. If the consumer product line experiences a k% increase in revenue (where k is a positive integer) in 2015 from 2014 levels and the machine parts line experiences a k% decrease in revenue in 2015 from 2014 levels, did Company X's overall revenue increase or decrease in 2015 ?

   (1) In 2014, the consumer products line generated more revenue than the machine parts line.

   (2) $k = 8$

6. If 800 is increased by 50% and then decreased by 30%, what is the resulting number?

7. If 1,500 is increased by 20% and then reduced by y%, yielding 1,080, what is y ?

   (A) 20

   (B) 30

   (C) 40

8. A bottle is 80% full. The liquid in the bottle consists of 60% guava juice and 40% pineapple juice. The remainder of the bottle is then filled with 200 milliliters of rum. How much guava juice is in the bottle?

   (A) 360 ml

   (B) 480 mL

   (C) 600 mL

   (D) 720 mL

   (E) 900 mL

9. Challenge problem! Company Z sells only chairs and tables. What percent of its revenue in 2008 did Company Z derive from its sales of chairs?

   (1) In 2008, the price of tables sold by Company Z was 10% higher than the price of chairs sold by Company Z.

   (2) In 2008, Company Z sold 20% fewer tables than chairs.

Solutions

1. **(B) $120:** Understand and Plan before you try to Solve. This problem is worded in a very annoying way: It provides the answer after 30% is taken, but not the original or starting number. The original number is what you want to take 30% of though. What to do?

   Luckily, the GMAT is a multiple-choice test. The answers represent the starting number—so just try them to see which one matches the information given in the problem.

   (A) $100. Take 30%: $30. In this case, the new price would be $100 - 30 = 70$, but the problem says the new price is $84. This one's incorrect and (B) is the only remaining answer, so that one must be correct.

   Here's how to do the math, but note that on the GMAT, if you have only one answer left, stop solving. Go ahead and pick it.

   (B) $120. Take 30%: $(10\%)(3) = (12)(3) = 36$.

   $120 - 36 = 84$. Bingo! Answer **(B)** is indeed correct.

   Alternatively, you could rephrase the given information to say the following:

   $84 is 70% of the original price of the stereo.

   You could then translate this statement into an equation and solve:

$$84 = \left(\frac{70}{100}\right)x$$
$$84 = \left(\frac{7}{10}\right)x$$
$$840 = 7x$$
$$120 = x$$

5

2. **$300:** Although this looks like an interest problem, you can think of it as a percent change problem. The percent change is 8%, and the change in value is $24:

$$\text{Percent Change} = \frac{\text{Change in Value}}{\text{Original Value}}$$
$$\frac{8}{100} = \frac{24}{x}$$
$$\frac{2}{25} = \frac{24}{x}$$
$$2x = (24)(25)$$
$$x = (12)(25) = 300$$

   The principal amount of the loan is $300.

   Alternatively, you could use benchmarks. $24 represents a change of 8%:

$$8\% = 24$$
$$1\% = \frac{24}{8} = 3$$
$$10\% = 30$$
$$100\% = 300$$

Examine those two solution methods. Which one works better for you? If you would have naturally thought of the first one, but you like the second better, what do you need to practice in order to get comfortable enough with benchmarks that you think of that solution method first next time?

3. **50%:** You can translate the first two sentences directly into equations. Just slow down and reflect/Plan for a moment. Use the simplest versions of the equivalent fractions:

$$x \text{ is } 40\% \text{ of } y \rightarrow x = \left(\frac{2}{5}\right) y$$

$$50\% \text{ of } y \text{ is } 40 \rightarrow \left(\frac{1}{2}\right) y = 40$$

Reflect again. The second equation has only one variable, so solve for *y*:

$$\left(\frac{1}{2}\right) y = 40$$

$$y = 80$$

Now, replace *y* with 80 in the first equation to solve for *x*:

$$x = \left(\frac{40}{100}\right)(80)$$

$$x = \frac{4}{10} \times 80$$

$$x = 4 \times 8 = 32$$

Be careful now. The question asks, *16 is what percent of* x *?* You figured out that $x = 32$, so this question is really asking, *16 is what percent of 32 ?*

Create a new variable (z) to represent the unknown value in the question and solve:

$$16 = \frac{z}{100} \times 32$$

$$\frac{100}{32} \times 16 = z$$

$$\frac{100}{2} \times 1 = z$$

$$50 = z$$

Alternatively, use the translation shortcut. Place the "percent of" number on the bottom of the fraction and the other number on the top:

$$\frac{16}{32} \times 100 = 0.5 \times 100 = 50\%$$

Or, if you feel *really* comfortable with percents, think logically. What percent of 32 is 16 ? Sixteen is half of 32, so 16 is 50% of 32.

4. **14 cups of water:** Understand and Plan before you Solve. If the bowl was already half full of water, then it was originally 50% full. Adding 4 cups of water increased the percentage by 20% of the total capacity of the bowl.

   Use benchmarks to solve. The measurement 4 cups is equivalent to 20%. What else can you figure out?

   $20\% = 4$ cups

   $10\% = 2$ cups

   $70\% = (2)(7) = 14$ cups

   There are 14 cups of water in the bowl.

   Alternatively, you can set up a proportion. You know 4 represents 20% of the capacity. Let x represent 70% of the capacity. Set up the proportion and solve for x:

   $$\frac{4}{x} = \frac{20}{70}$$

   $$\frac{4}{x} = \frac{2}{7}$$

   $$28 = 2x$$

   $$14 = x$$

5 5. **(A):** This question requires you to employ logic about percents. No calculation is required, or even possible, since no real numbers are given.

   Here's what you know so far (use new variables c and m to keep track of your information):

   2014:

   Consumer products makes c dollars

   Machine parts makes m dollars

   Total revenue $= c + m$

   2015:

   Consumer products makes c dollars increased by k%

   Machine parts makes m dollars decreased by k%

   Total revenue = ?

   What would you need to answer the question *did Company X's overall revenue increase or decrease in 2015 ?* Certainly, if you knew the values of c, m, and k, you could achieve sufficiency, but the GMAT would never write such an easy problem. What is the *minimum* you would need to know to answer definitively?

   Since both changes involve the same percent (k), you know that c increases *by the same percent* by which m decreases. As a result, whichever number is greater (c or m) will constitute a bigger change to the overall revenue. Why?

   If c started off greater, then a k% increase in c means more new dollars coming in than you would lose due to a k% decrease in the smaller number, m. On the other hand, if c is smaller, then the k% increase would be smaller than what you would lose due to a k% decrease in the larger number, m.

   So you really need to know whether c or m is greater. You don't actually need to know k at all!

The question can be rephrased, *Which is greater,* c *or* m *?*

(1) SUFFICIENT: This statement indicates that c is greater than m. Thus, a $k\%$ increase in c is greater than a $k\%$ decrease in m, so the overall revenue went up.

(2) INSUFFICIENT: Knowing the percent change doesn't help, since you don't know whether c or m is bigger.

Note that you could try some real numbers, although this problem is probably faster with logic. Using statement (1) only:

2014:

Consumer products makes $200

Machine parts makes $100

Total revenue = $300

2015: If $k = 50$

Consumer products makes $300

Machine parts makes $50

Total revenue = $350

This one case yields an answer of Yes—the overall revenue did increase. However, you might have to test several sets of numbers to establish that this will always be true. (That's the main reason that logic is faster here!) You can experiment with different values for c and m, and you can change k to any positive integer (you don't need to know what k is). As long as c is greater than m, you will get the same result. The increase to the larger c will always be greater than the decrease to the smaller m.

The correct answer is **(A)**: Statement (1) is sufficient to answer the question, but statement (2) is not.

6. **840:** This is a successive percent question. Since the numbers in the problem are fairly nice, one approach is to calculate step-by-step.

Start with 800. Increase by 50%, or 400. Now, you have 800 + 400 = 1,200.

From 1,200, decrease by 30%. Benchmark: 10% is 120, so 30% is 360. Subtract: 1,200 − 360 = 840.

Alternatively, set up the math as follows. Increasing by 50% is the same as *150% of* something. Decreasing by 30% is the same as *70% of* something. So the full problem translates to *What is 150% of 70% of 800?*

$$\frac{150}{100} \times \frac{70}{100} \times 800 = ?$$

$$\frac{3}{2} \times \frac{7}{10} \times 800 = ?$$

$$\frac{21}{20} \times 800 = ?$$

$$21 \times 40 = 840$$

7. **(C) 40:** Break the question into two parts. First, 1,500 is increased by 20%. Find 20% percent of 1,500.

If 10% of 1,500 is 150, then 20% is 300. The new number is 1,500 + 300 = 1,800.

Next, 1,800 is reduced by *y*% to get to 1,080. The answer choices represent *y*, so try them to see which one works. Start with the middle of the three answers.

(B) 30%. Find 30% of 1,800: 10% of 1,800 is 180, so 30% is (180)(3) = 540. Next, 1,800 – 540 = 1,260. The answer is supposed to be 1,080, not 1,260, so answer (B) is incorrect.

The other two possibilities for *y* are 20% and 40%. Think about what happened with the math when trying 30%. Do you need a larger or smaller percentage?

When using 30%, the number to subtract was 540, yielding an answer of 1,260. In order to get down to 1,080, you'd need to subtract a larger number. So you're looking for a larger percentage decrease than 30%.

Only answer **(C)** is larger than 30%, so it must be correct. (You can try the math to make sure—but the GMAT is a timed test. If you feel confident in the logic, don't try the math; just select the answer and move on.)

8. **(B) 480 mL:** If the bottle was 80% full, and adding 200 milliliters of rum filled it to capacity, then 200 milliliters is equal to 20% of the bottle's total capacity.

The figure 80% is 4 times 20%, so the other 80% of the bottle represents (200mL)(4) = 800 mL.

The guava juice represents 60% of that 800 milliliters. Use benchmarks to figure out how much guava juice there is:

100% = 800 mL
10% = 80 mL
60% = (80 mL)(6) = 480 mL

The bottle contains 480 milliliters of guava juice.

Alternatively, you could work backwards to solve this problem. The answer choices represent the amount of guava juice in the mixture; also the answers are relatively "clean" numbers, making working backwards less cumbersome.

Start with answer (B) or (D), your choice. This solution will start with (B) since that number is smaller.

(B) 480 mL. This represents 60% of the liquid currently in the bottle. This problem has some intricate details. The answers represent the guava juice, which is 60% of the liquid that's currently in the bottle—but that liquid only fills 80% of the bottle. Lay out separate steps for each of these circumstances.

First, find the amount of liquid in the bottle. That represents 80% of the bottle's capacity, so find the value for the 20% that's empty and see whether it matches the figure given in the problem:

Guava = 60% of liquid	100% of liquid	Liquid = 80% of capacity	20% of capacity = 200 ?
(B) 480	60% = 480 10% = 80 100% = (80)(10) = 800	80% = 800 divide both by 4 20% = 200	Yes!

It's a match so this is the correct answer. If you had started with answer (D) and done the same math, you'd get the following:

Guava = 60% of liquid	100% of liquid	Liquid = 80% of capacity	20% of capacity = 200 ?
(D) 720	60% = 720 10% = 120 100% = (120)(10) = 1,200	80% = 1,200 10% = 150 20% = (150)(2) = 300	No!

Using answer (D), 20% of the capacity is 300 milliliters, but the problem said that it was 200 milliliters, so this is not the correct answer. Further, 300 is too much, so the answer has to be smaller. At this point, you'd cross off answers (D) and (E), then try answer (B) next.

9. **(C):** First, notice that the question is asking only for the *percent* of its revenue the company derived from chairs. The question is asking for a relative value, so you may not need to know any actual values in order to solve.

The question asks for the revenue from chairs as a fraction of the total. Also, total revenue is made up of the revenue from chairs and the revenue from tables:

$$\frac{R_C}{\text{Total Rev}} \qquad \text{Total Rev} = R_C + R_T$$

If you know the ratio of chair revenue to total revenue, you can find the requested percentage. But note also that, if you're given relationships involving table revenue, you might also be able to find the requested percentage, since that second equation is true, too.

Also, note that the GMAT will expect you to know that Revenue = Price × Quantity Sold.

The revenue derived from tables is the price per table multiplied by the number of tables sold. The revenue derived from chairs is the price per chair multiplied by the number of chairs sold. You can create some variables to represent these unknown values:

$$R_T = P_T \times Q_T$$
$$R_C = P_C \times Q_C$$

(1) INSUFFICIENT: This statement provides the relative value of the price of tables to the price of chairs. If the price of tables was 10% higher than the price of chairs, then the price of tables was 110% of the price of chairs:

$$\frac{P_T}{P_C} = 1.1$$

However, no information is given on quantity sold, so it's not possible to determine anything about the relative value of their revenues.

(2) INSUFFICIENT: If the company sold 20% fewer tables than chairs, then the number of tables sold is 80% of the number of chairs sold:

$$\frac{N_T}{N_C} = 0.8$$

However, no information is given about price, so it's not possible to determine anything about the relative value of their revenues.

(1) AND (2) SUFFICIENT: Hmm. The first statement was about price, but not quantity. The second statement was about quantity, but not price. Could they work together to find a consistent *relative* value?

$$R_T = P_T \times N_T$$

The formula above is for revenue of tables. The first statement provided info about how the price of tables relates to the price of chairs (or how P_T relates to P_C). The second statement provided information about how the number of tables relates to the number of chairs (or how N_T relates to N_C).

When you know those relative relationships for the right side of the equation, then it's possible to calculate the relative relationship for the left side of the equation—that is, how table revenue relates to chair revenue.

If you know how table revenue relates to chair revenue, then you can always figure out what percentage each represents out of total revenue. For example, if you knew that table revenue was three times as much as chair revenue, then table revenue would have to be 75% of total revenue and chair revenue would have to be 25% of total revenue, because 75% is three times as much as 25%.

In other words, you don't have to calculate anything further (since this is Data Sufficiency). You can just know that, if you know the relative relationship between price and the relative relationship between quantity, then you can find the relative relationship between revenue.

5

The correct answer is **(C)**: The two statements together are sufficient but neither one alone is sufficient.

If you really want to see how this works from a textbook math perspective, read on. But it's strongly recommended to stop right here!

Replace P_T with $1.1P_C$ and replace N_T with $0.8N_C$:

$$R_T = P_T \times N_T$$
$$R_T = 1.1P_C \times 0.8N_C$$
$$R_T = (0.88)(P_C \times N_C)$$

On the right-hand side, $P_C \times N_C = R_C$, so substitute that in:

$$R_T = 0.88R_C$$

Taken together, the two statements provide the relative value of the revenues for tables and chairs.

You can use that to find the relative value of chair revenue to total revenue. Rearrange the equation so that you can write a ratio:

$$\frac{R_T}{R_C} = \frac{0.88}{1}$$

$$\text{RevChair} : \text{RevTable} : \text{RevTotal}$$
$$1 : 0.88 : 1.88$$

Finally, use the needed parts of the ratio to solve:

$$\frac{R_C}{\text{Total Revenue}} = \frac{1}{1.88} \approx 53\%$$

Save time on DS problems by avoiding unnecessary computation. Once you know you can find the needed figure, choose your answer and move on to the next problem.

CHAPTER 6

Digits and Decimals

In This Chapter

- Digits
- Decimals
- Place Value
- Rounding to the Nearest Place Value
- Powers of 10: Shifting the Decimal
- Decimal Operations

In this chapter, you will learn how digits, decimals, and place value are tested on the GMAT, as well as how to perform the needed computations on numbers in decimal form, including rounding.

CHAPTER 6 Digits and Decimals

Digits

Every number is composed of digits. There are only 10 digits in our number system: 0, 1, 2, 3, 4, 5, 6, 7, 8, 9. The term **digit** refers to one "building block" of a number; it does not refer to the entire number. For example, 356 is a number composed of three digits: 3, 5, and 6.

Integers can be classified by the number of digits they contain. For example:

2, 7, and −8 are each single-digit numbers (they are each composed of one digit).

43, 63, and −14 are each double-digit numbers (composed of two digits).

500,000 and −468,024 are each six-digit numbers (composed of six digits).

789,526,622 is a nine-digit number (composed of nine digits).

Integers such as the above always have a nonzero digit as the first number. For instance, 2 is a single-digit number, but you can't write 02 and call that a two-digit integer. If a problem specifies a two-digit integer, then the first digit has to be some value from 1 to 9.

Non-integers are not generally classified by the number of digits they contain, since you can always add any number of zeros at the end, on the right side of the decimal point:

$9.1 = 9.10 = 9.100$

Decimals

Decimals are yet another way to write numbers that fall between integers. For example, the decimal 6.3 falls between the integers 6 and 7:

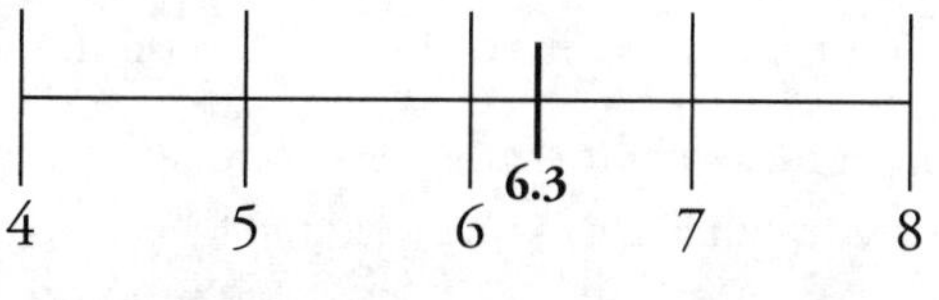

Some useful groupings of decimals include the following:

Group	Examples
Decimals less than −1:	−3.6, −12.01
Decimals between −1 and 0:	−0.65, −0.5
Decimals between 0 and 1:	0.2, 0.45
Decimals greater than 1:	2.9, 42.42

Note that an integer can be expressed as a decimal by adding the decimal point and the digit 0. For example:

$8 = 8.0 \qquad -123 = -123.0 \qquad 400 = 400.0$

Place Value

Every digit in a number has a particular **place value** depending on its location within the number. For example, in the number 452, the digit 2 is in the ones (or units) place, the digit 5 is in the tens place, and the digit 4 is in the hundreds place. The name of each location corresponds to the value of that place. Thus:

The 2 is worth two ones (i.e., $2 \times 1 = 2$).

The 5 is worth five tens (i.e., $5 \times 10 = 50$).

The 4 is worth four hundreds (i.e., $4 \times 100 = 400$).

You can write the number 452 as the *sum* of these products:

$$452 = (4 \times 100) + (5 \times 10) + (2 \times 1)$$

Millions	Hundred Thousands	Ten Thousands	Thousands	Hundreds	Tens	Units Or Ones		Tenths	Hundredths	Thousandths	Ten Thousandths
7	8	9	1	0	2	3	.	8	3	4	7

The chart to the left analyzes the place value of all the digits in the number **7,891,023.8347**.

Notice that all of the place values that end in "ths" are to the right of the decimal; these are all fractional values.

Analyze just the decimal portion of the number **0.8347**:

8 is in the tenths place, giving it a value of 8 tenths, or $\frac{8}{10}$.

3 is in the hundredths place, giving it a value of 3 hundredths, or $\frac{3}{100}$.

4 is in the thousandths place, giving it a value of 4 thousandths, or $\frac{4}{1{,}000}$.

7 is in the ten-thousandths place, giving it a value of 7 ten thousandths, or $\frac{7}{10{,}000}$.

To use a concrete example, 0.8 might mean eight tenths of one dollar, which would be 80 cents. Additionally, 0.03 might mean three hundredths of one dollar, or 3 cents.

Rounding to the Nearest Place Value

The GMAT occasionally requires you to round a number to a specific place value. For example:

What is 3.681 rounded to the nearest tenth?

First, find the digit located in the specified place value. The digit 6 is in the tenths place.

Second, look at the right-digit neighbor (the digit immediately to the right) of the digit in question. In this case, 8 is the right-digit neighbor of 6. If the right-digit neighbor is 5 or greater, round the digit in question *up*. Otherwise, leave the digit alone. In this case, the hundredths-digit number, 8, is greater than 5, so you're going to have to round up. Go back to the digit in question, 6, and round up to 7. Thus, 3.681 rounded to the nearest tenth equals 3.7. Note that all the digits to the right of the right-digit neighbor are irrelevant when rounding.

Rounding appears on the GMAT in the form of questions such as this:

> If x is the decimal 8.1d5, with d as an unknown digit, and x rounded to the nearest tenth is equal to 8.1, which digits could NOT be the value of d?

In order for x to be 8.1 when rounded to the nearest tenth, the right-digit neighbor, d, must be less than 5. Therefore, d cannot be 5, 6, 7, 8, or 9.

Powers of 10: Shifting the Decimal

What are the patterns in this table?

In words	**Thousands**	**Hundreds**	**Tens**	**Ones**	**Tenths**	**Hundredths**	**Thousandths**
In numbers	1,000	100	10	1	0.1	0.01	0.001
In powers of ten	10^3	10^2	10^1	10^0	10^{-1}	10^{-2}	10^{-3}

The place values continually decrease from left to right by powers of 10. Understanding this can help you understand the following shortcuts for multiplication and division.

When you multiply any number by a positive power of 10, move the decimal to the right of the specified number of places. This makes positive numbers larger:

$89.507 \times 10 = 895.07$ — 10 is the same as 10^1, so move the decimal to the right 1 space.

$3.9742 \times 10^3 = 3{,}974.2$ — The exponent is 3, so move the decimal to the right 3 spaces.

When you divide any number by a positive power of 10, move the decimal to the left of the specified number of places. This makes positive numbers smaller:

$89.507 \div 10 = 8.9507$ — Move the decimal to the left 1 space.

$4{,}169.2 \div 10^2 = 41.692$ — Move the decimal to the left 2 spaces.

Sometimes, you will need to add zeros in order to shift a decimal:

$2.57 \times 10^6 = 2{,}570{,}000$ — Add 4 zeros at the end.

$14.29 \div 10^5 = 0.0001429$ — Add 3 zeros at the beginning.

Finally, note that negative powers of 10 reverse the regular process: Move the decimal in the opposite direction that you'd have used for a positive power. Now, multiplication makes the number smaller and division makes the number larger:

$6{,}782.01 \times 10^{-3} = 6.78201$ $\qquad$ $53.0447 \div 10^{-2} = 5{,}304.47$

You can think about these processes as trading decimal places for powers of 10.

For instance, all of the following numbers equal 110,700:

$$110.7 \times 10^3$$
$$11.07 \times 10^4$$
$$1.107 \times 10^5$$
$$0.1107 \times 10^6$$
$$0.01107 \times 10^7$$

The number in the first column gets smaller by a factor of 10 as you move the decimal one place to the left, but the number in the second column gets bigger by a factor of 10 to compensate, so the overall number still equals 110,700.

Decimal Operations

Addition and Subtraction

To add or subtract decimals, first, check the answers to see whether you can just estimate instead. If not, line up the decimal points. Then, add zeros to make the right sides of the decimals the same length:

$4.319 + 221.8$		$10 - 0.063$	
Line up the decimal points and add zeros.	$\begin{array}{r} 4.319 \\ +\ 221.800 \\ \hline 226.119 \end{array}$	Line up the decimal points and add zeros.	$\begin{array}{r} 10.000 \\ -\ \ \ 0.063 \\ \hline 9.937 \end{array}$

Addition and subtraction: Line up the decimal points!

Multiplication

To multiply decimals, ignore the decimal point until the end. Just multiply the numbers as you would if they were whole numbers. Then count the total number of digits to the right of the decimal point in the starting numbers. The product should have the same number of digits to the right of the decimal point:

	Count the digits to the right of the decimal:	Multiply normally:	Move the decimal 3 places to the left:
0.02 × 1.4	3	$\begin{array}{r} 14 \\ \times\ 2 \\ \hline 28 \end{array}$	28 → 0.028

If the product ends with 0, that 0 still counts as a place value. For example: $0.8 \times 0.5 = 0.40$, since $8 \times 5 = 40$.

> **Multiplication:** Count all the digits to the right of the decimal point—then multiply normally, ignoring the decimals. Finally, put the same number of decimal places in the product.

If you are multiplying a very large number and a very small number, the following trick works to simplify the calculation: Move the decimals the same number of places, but *in the opposite direction*. For example:

$0.0003 \times 40{,}000 = ?$

Move the decimal point *right* four places on the $0.0003 \rightarrow 3$

Move the decimal point *left* four places on the $40{,}000 \rightarrow 4$

$0.0003 \times 40{,}000 = 3 \times 4 = 12$

This technique works because you are multiplying and then dividing by the same power of 10. In other words, you are trading decimal places in one number for decimal places in another number. This is just like trading decimal places for powers of 10, as you saw earlier.

Division

If you ever need to do long division, first. . .stop. Make sure you can't estimate or do something else that is less annoying. Here's one less annoying way: You can always simplify division problems that involve decimals by shifting the decimal point *in the same direction* in both the divisor and the dividend, even when the division problem is expressed as a fraction:

$$\frac{0.0045}{0.09} = \frac{45}{900}$$

Move the decimal 4 spaces to the right in both the numerator and the denominator to make whole numbers. Always move the same number of places in the top and bottom.

Note that this is essentially the same process as simplifying a fraction. You multiply the numerator and denominator of the fraction by the same number—in this case, 10^4, or 10,000.

> **Division:** Use whole numbers! To dump the decimals, move the decimal the same number of places in the top and the bottom of the fraction.

If you absolutely must do long division with decimals and there is a decimal point in the dividend (the number under the division sign), you can bring the decimal point straight up to the answer and divide normally:

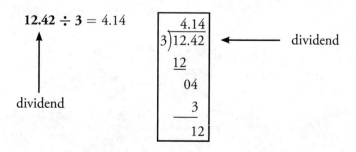

12.42 ÷ 3 = 4.14
↑
dividend

```
    4.14
3)12.42   ←——  dividend
  12
   04
    3
   ——
    12
```

However, if there is a decimal point in the divisor (the outer number), shift the decimal point the same number of times to the right in both the divisor and the dividend to make the *divisor* (the outer number) a whole number. Then, bring the decimal point up and divide:

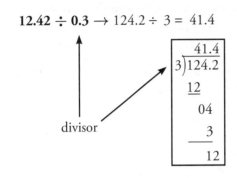

$\mathbf{12.42 \div 0.3} \rightarrow 124.2 \div 3 = 41.4$

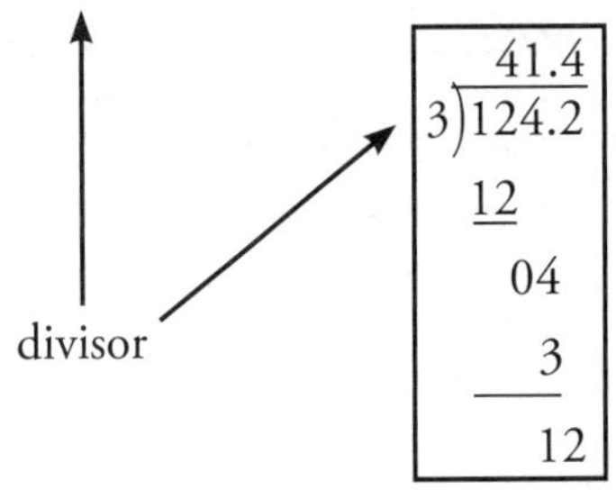

Move the decimal 1 space to the right to make 0.3 a whole number. Then, move the decimal 1 space to the right in 12.42 to make it 124.2.

> **Keep track of the decimal:** To simplify multiplication, you can move decimals in *opposite* directions. But to simplify division, move decimals in the *same* direction. Either way, make sure you're moving the decimal the same number of places to trade off equally.

Advanced material for the Fractions, Decimals, Percents, and Ratios (FDPR) unit (primarily covering additional strategies for decimals and digits) can be found in Atlas, Manhattan Prep's online learning platform. Use the online material only if you feel that you have mastered everything in the FDPR unit of this strategy guide and only if you are aiming for a Quant section score of 48 or higher.

6

Problem Set

Solve each problem, applying the concepts and rules you learned in this section.

1. In the decimal 2.4*d*7, *d* represents a digit from 0 to 9. If the value of the decimal rounded to the nearest tenth is less than 2.5, what are the possible values of *d* ?

2. Simplify: $\dfrac{0.00081}{0.09}$

3. Which integer values of *b* would give the number $2002 \div 10^b$ a value between 1 and 100 ?

   (A) $\{-1, -2\}$

   (B) $\{-2, -3\}$

   (C) $\{1, 2\}$

   (D) $\{2, 3\}$

4. Simplify: $(4 \times 10^{-2}) - (2.5 \times 10^{-3})$

5. If *k* is an integer and 0.02468×10^k is greater than 10,000, what is the least possible value of *k* ?

6. What is $4{,}563{,}021 \div 10^5$, rounded to the nearest whole number?

Solutions

1. **{0, 1, 2, 3, 4}:** The rounded decimal is less than 2.5, so it must round to 2.4. This represents rounding down, so the value of *d* must be 0, 1, 2, 3, or 4.

2. **0.009:** Shift the decimal point five spaces to eliminate the decimal points (note that this means adding zeros to the number in the denominator), then simplify:

$$\frac{0.00081}{0.09} = \frac{81}{9{,}000} = \frac{9}{1{,}000} = 0.009$$

3. **(D) {2, 3}:** Understand before you try to solve (and if you don't understand, guess and move on). Some of the answers contain positive numbers and some contain negative numbers, so should that exponent be positive or negative? The starting value is 2,002, but the ending value is between 1 and 100, so 2,002 needs to get smaller. Specifically, it will have to be either 2.002 or 20.02 in order to fall between 1 and 100. If you start from 2,002 and divide by a power of 10 to get to 20.02 or 2.002, you'd want to divide by 10 or 100 or 1,000—in other words, you want that exponent to be positive to make the divisor larger. Eliminate choices (A) and (B).

   Of the two remaining answers, both contain the value 2, so apparently 2 must be one value for *b*. Is the other value 1 or 3? $2{,}002 \div 10^1 = 200.2$. Too big! The answer must be 2 and 3.

   If you're not sure of the logic, check. $2{,}002 \div 10^3 = 2{,}002 \div 1{,}000 = 2.002$. Perfect!

   The correct answer is **(D)** {2, 3}.

4. **0.0375:** First, rewrite the numbers in standard notation by shifting the decimal point. Then, add zeros, line up the decimal points, and subtract:

$$\begin{array}{r} 0.0400 \\ -\ 0.0025 \\ \hline 0.0375 \end{array}$$

6

5. **6:** Understand and Plan before you Solve. Understand: Multiplying 0.02468 by a positive power of 10 will shift the decimal point to the right. Your goal is to make the number greater than 10,000.

   Plan: Shift the decimal point to the right until the result is greater than 10,000, keeping track of how many times you shift the decimal point.

   Solve: Shifting the decimal point five times results in 2,468. This is still less than 10,000. Shifting one more place yields 24,680, which is greater than 10,000.

6. **46:** To divide by a positive power of 10, shift the decimal point to the left. This yields 45.63021. To round to the nearest whole number, look at the tenths place. The digit in the tenths place, 6, is more than 5. Therefore, round up: The number is closest to 46.

CHAPTER 7

Strategy: Estimation

In This Chapter

- How to Estimate
- When to Estimate
- Using Benchmarks to Estimate

In this chapter, you will learn how to identify when to estimate on the GMAT, as well as how to stay within reasonable bounds and minimize errors in your estimations.

CHAPTER 7 Strategy: Estimation

You can estimate your way to an answer on problems with certain characteristics. Try these two problems:

1. $\frac{7}{13}+\frac{5}{11}$ is approximately equal to

   (A) 0

   (B) 1

   (C) 2

2. Of 450 employees at a company, 20% are managers and the rest are not managers. If 60% of the managers work in the engineering department, how many managers do not work in the engineering department?

   (A) 36

   (B) 54

   (C) 90

   (D) 180

   (E) 216

Before you look at the solutions in the next section, try to figure out how you would recognize that you *can* estimate on these two problems.

How to Estimate

Before we dive in, remember that Understand, Plan, and Solve process from Data Sufficiency? This is called the UPS process and you can use it on Problem Solving problems as well.

Here's a little graphic that helps you to know what kinds of steps to take at each stage in that process:

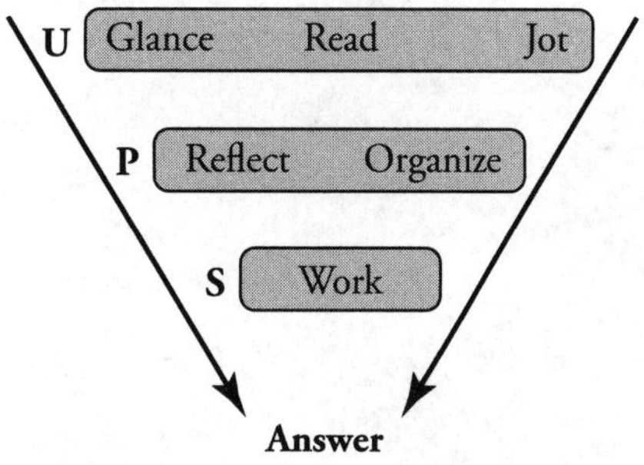

Step 1: Understand. Glance at the problem. First, notice whether it's PS or DS. If it's PS (as in this case), glance at the answers. The first one has whole, "easy" numbers.

1. $\frac{7}{13}+\frac{5}{11}$ is approximately equal to

   (A) 0

   (B) 1

   (C) 2

Then, read the problem. This problem contains the word *approximately*. It's literally telling you to estimate! When you see this kind of language, do not even try to do exact calculations. Take the problem at its word and estimate. Also, jot down the given expression.

Step 2: Plan. First, converting to common denominators here would be pretty annoying, as would converting the fractions to decimals or percents. Second, it's telling you to estimate and the answers are 0, 1, and 2. Round those annoying fractions to easier ones and estimate whether the sum is closest to 0, 1, or 2.

Step 3: Solve. $\frac{7}{13}$ is very close to $\frac{7}{14}$, or $\frac{1}{2}$, so call that first fraction 0.5.

Note that $\frac{7}{13}$ is a little *larger* than $\frac{7}{14}$ because increasing only the denominator makes a positive fraction smaller. In other words, you rounded down so your answer will be a little too small. The next time you need to estimate, if possible, round up so that you are minimizing the amount of error that you introduce.

Since $\frac{5}{11}$ is a little bit less than $\frac{1}{2}$, you can round up this time. Call the second fraction 0.5 as well.

The approximate sum is $0.5 + 0.5 = 1$, so the answer is (B).

2. Of 450 employees at a company, 20% are managers and the rest are not managers. If 60% of the managers work in the engineering department, how many managers do not work in the engineering department?

   (A) 36

   (B) 54

   (C) 90

   (D) 180

   (E) 216

7

The second problem doesn't tell you that you can estimate; nevertheless, it contains an important clue that points toward estimation.

In the Understand step, your first task is to glance at the problem:

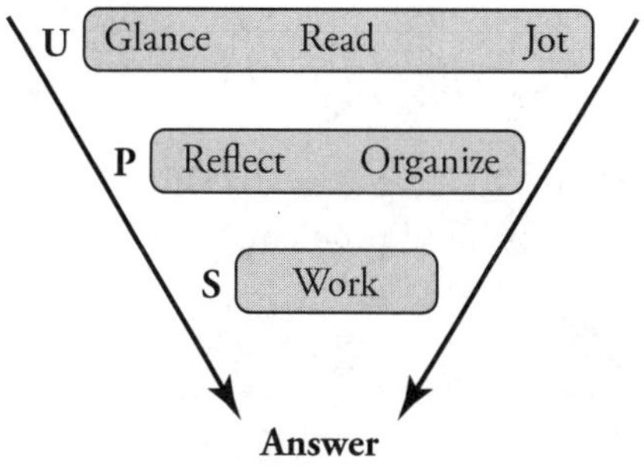

On all PS problems, get in the habit of glancing at the answers, too. In this case, the answers are pretty far apart. When that's true, you can often estimate. (Note that sometimes the numbers only need to be far apart in relative terms—in the first problem, the numbers are only 1 apart, but 2 is twice as big as 1, and there's a big relative difference between 1 and 0.)

Step 1: Understand. The answers are decently far apart, so plan to estimate wherever it makes sense in the process. Also, the question asks for the number of *managers* who do *not* work in engineering. Jot that down on your scrap paper.

Step 2: Plan. The problem provides information about certain categories of employees by percentages, as well as the total number of employees, so your task is going to be to take percentages of that 450 figure. But save yourself some time by using the answers to estimate as you go.

Step 3: Solve. First, find the number of managers, which is 20% of 450. Use benchmarks: 10% of 450 is 45, so 20% is twice as many, or 90.

There are 90 *total* managers, so a fraction of that group will be smaller. None of the answers that are 90 or greater can be the correct answer; cross off (C), (D), and (E).

Next, what percentage of these 90 managers do *not* work in engineering? If 60% of those managers *do* work in engineering, then 40% do not. You could take 40% of 90...but you don't have to. Half of 90 is 45, so the number of managers not in engineering must be less than 45. The only possible answer is (A).

The four wrong answers are all traps built into the problem. The value for managers, 90, is there. The value 54 represents 60% of the managers (instead of 40%). The value 180 represents 40% of the entire 450 employees rather than 40% of just the managers. And the value 216 represents mistakenly taking 80% and then 60% of the total number of employees, rather than 20% and then 40%.

When to Estimate

Estimate whenever the problem explicitly asks for an approximate answer. In addition, consider estimating when the answers are far apart or when they cover certain "divided" characteristics (more on this below).

In many cases, this estimation will get you all the way to the correct answer. In others, you may be able to eliminate some answers before guessing on a hard problem.

Consider these possible answers:

(A) −6

(B) −3

(C) −2

(D) 1

(E) 2

These answers can be divided into two groups: positive and negative. If you are running out of time or are not sure how to answer the question in the normal way, you may be able to tell whether the answer should be positive or negative. If so, you'll be able to eliminate two or three answers before making a guess.

Other examples of a divided characteristic: A fraction problem might have some answers greater than 1 and others less than 1. A probability problem may have some answers greater than 0.5 and some answers less than 0.5 (or greater or less than half).

Whenever you run into these divided characteristics, you may be able to estimate, so train yourself to look for these opportunities during the Understand phase.

Using Benchmarks to Estimate

The Benchmark method for calculating percents was first introduced in the Percents chapter. You can also use benchmarks to estimate.

7

The easiest percent benchmarks are 50%, 10%, and 1%. You can also use easy fraction benchmarks to estimate. The easiest fraction benchmarks are $\frac{1}{2}$, the quarters $\left(\frac{1}{4}, \frac{3}{4}\right)$, and the thirds $\left(\frac{1}{3}, \frac{2}{3}\right)$.

Try this problem:

> A television originally priced at $700 was offered at a 12% discount. What was the sale price of the television?
>
> (A) $650
>
> (B) $616
>
> (C) $560

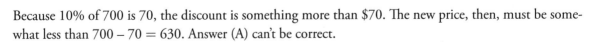

Because 10% of 700 is 70, the discount is something more than $70. The new price, then, must be somewhat less than 700 – 70 = 630. Answer (A) can't be correct.

Next, the answer does need to be somewhat smaller than 630, but not very much smaller—the difference between 10% and 12% is not that much. So answer (B) looks better than answer (C).

And, indeed, a 20% discount would result in another \$70 off, for a total \$140 discount, or a sale price of \$560. Answer (C) is definitely too small. The correct answer must be (B).

(If you check the math: $10\% + 1\% + 1\% = 70 + 7 + 7 = \$84$, and $700 - 84 = \$616$. But don't do this math on the test unless it's necessary!)

You can also use benchmark values to compare fractions:

Which is greater: $\frac{127}{261}$ or $\frac{162}{320}$?

Don't try to solve yet. First, Understand and Plan. It would be seriously annoying to use the double-cross method here without a calculator. It would be even more annoying to find common denominators. And there's your clue! When they give you math that clearly won't be done in 2 minutes without a calculator, there must be another way to approach it.

Each one is smaller than 1. Hmm. How does each fraction compare to $\frac{1}{2}$? It turns out that 127 is less than half of 261 and 162 is more than half of 320, so $\frac{162}{320}$ must be the greater fraction.

You can also use benchmark values to estimate computations involving fractions:

What is $\frac{10}{22}$ of $\frac{5}{18}$ of 2,000 ?

Again, that math is annoying, so estimate. What nicer fractions are these fractions close to?

The fraction $\frac{10}{22}$ is a little bit less than $\frac{1}{2}$ and $\frac{5}{18}$ is a little bit more than $\frac{1}{4}$. Use these to estimate:

$$\frac{1}{2} \text{ of } \frac{1}{4} \text{ of } 2{,}000 = 250$$

Therefore, $\frac{10}{22}$ of $\frac{5}{18}$ of $2{,}000 \approx 250$.

Notice that the rounding errors compensated for each other:

$\frac{10}{22} \approx \frac{10}{20} = \frac{1}{2}$ You decreased the denominator, so you rounded up: $\frac{10}{22} < \frac{1}{2}$.

$\frac{5}{18} \approx \frac{5}{20} = \frac{1}{4}$ You increased the denominator, so you rounded down: $\frac{5}{18} > \frac{1}{4}$.

If you had rounded $\frac{5}{18}$ to $\frac{6}{18} = \frac{1}{3}$ instead, then you would have rounded both fractions up. This would lead to a slight but systematic overestimation:

$$\frac{1}{2} \times \frac{1}{3} \times 2{,}000 \approx 333$$

That might be good enough, depending on how far apart the answer choices are, but it's a little risky. If possible, try to make your rounding errors cancel out. If you round up in one part of the calculation, try to round down in another (or vice versa).

7

Problem Set

Directions: On some, try doing the official math *and* estimating to see how much time and effort estimation can save you. When you're done, analyze your work. How did you know you could estimate? At which point in the problem did the estimation come into play? Could you have streamlined the process or made better estimates at any step along the way? Finally, continue to look for opportunities to estimate on every GMAT problem you do from now on!

1. At a particular school, 65% of the students have taken language classes. Of those students, 40% have studied more than one language. If there are 300 students at the school, how many have studied more than one language?

   (A) 78
   (B) 102
   (C) 120
   (D) 150
   (E) 195

2. A total of 9,180 people participated in a research study on the genetics of eye color. Of the participants, $\frac{4}{9}$ had two parents with blue eyes, and of the remaining participants, $\frac{8}{17}$ had one parent with blue eyes. How many participants, in total, had at least one blue-eyed parent?

   (A) 780
   (B) 2,700
   (C) 4,320
   (D) 6,480
   (E) 8,400

3. Every elementary school student in a certain town attends one of two schools, and at both schools, each student is assigned to a specific classroom. Broad River Academy has 29 classrooms with an average of 17 students per classroom, and Lakeside School has 19 classrooms with an average of 18 students per classroom. Approximately what percent of the town's elementary school students attend Broad River Academy?

   (A) 29%
   (B) 41%
   (C) 48%
   (D) 59%
   (E) 82%

Answers and explanations are on next page

Solutions

1. **(A) 78:** First, Understand. Glance at the problem: Problem Solving. Percentages in the question. Numerical answers. Not very close together. Jot:

$$65\% = L \quad \rightarrow 40\% \text{ OF } L > 1 \text{ lang}$$
$$300 = T$$

Next, Plan. Reflect on the info. The starting point is 300, but 65% is a bit annoying. You *can* figure out that number. Do you want to take the time to do so?

If you've noticed that the answers are decently far apart, you know you can estimate. Since 65% is very close to $\frac{2}{3}$, that's the way to go (especially with 300 as the starting point!).

Finally, Solve:

$$\frac{2}{3} \text{ of } 300 \text{ is } 200.$$

Note that you rounded up, so your estimate will be a little higher than the official number.

Benchmark to calculate 40% of that number. Find 10% of the number, then multiply by 4 to get 40%:

$$10\% \text{ of } 200 = 20, \text{ so } 40\% = 20 \times 4 = 80$$

Approximately 80 students have studied more than one language. The closest answer is 78.

2. **(D) 6,480:** The ugly fractions jump out. The first fraction isn't too bad, but $\frac{8}{17}$ is really annoying. Couple that with the starting number of 9,180 people and no calculator and this looks like a terrible problem.

7

But wait! During your Understand phase, when you did your first glance, did you glance at the answer choices? If not, start making that a part of your glance on PS problems and notice this: The answers are spread very far apart. What does that mean?

Estimate your way to the answer. Both fractions are near 50%, so you might round to that benchmark, but aim to make your rounding errors balance across all of the steps.

Of the 9,180 people, $\frac{4}{9}$ had two parents with blue eyes. If you round the number of people down to 9,000, you don't need to approximate the $\frac{4}{9}$ fraction at all: $\frac{4}{9}$ of 9,000 is 4,000. This is a slight underestimation of the number of people who had two parents with blue eyes.

Next, how many people remain? About $9{,}000 - 4{,}000 = 5{,}000$. Of these people, $\frac{8}{17}$ or approximately 50% had one parent with blue eyes. Half of 5,000 is 2,500, which is a slight overestimation of the number of people who had one parent with blue eyes.

In total, about $4{,}000 + 2{,}500 = 6{,}500$ people had at least one parent with blue eyes. The only close answer is 6,480.

3. **(D) 59%:** Glance at those answers. They contain pretty annoying percentages. If only they'd given nicer numbers—they wouldn't even have had to change them very much.

That's your big clue! The answers are basically 30%, 40%, 50%, 60%, and 80%—so estimate on this problem.

The question asks for B students as a percentage of all students. The number of B students is $(29)(17) =$ yuck. And the number of L students is $(19)(18)$. It's easy to round 29 up to 30 and 19 up to 20, but what about that 17 and 18? Can you just round everything up? Write out the math that needs to happen but don't do anything; just examine it:

$$\frac{(29)(17)}{(29)(17) + (18)(19)}$$

The 17 on the top can cancel with the one 17 on the bottom, but it also has to cancel with something in the $(18)(19)$ term. Why not have it cancel the 18? That's close enough:

$$\frac{(29)\cancel{(17)}}{(29)\cancel{(17)} + \cancel{(18)}(19)} \approx \frac{29}{29+19} \approx \frac{30}{30+20} = \frac{30}{50} = \frac{60}{100}$$

And estimate once again at the middle step. On a fraction, estimate in the *same* direction to balance out your estimations: If you estimate up on the top, also estimate up on the bottom. The closest match is 59%.

7

UNIT TWO

Algebra

In this unit, you'll learn how to process all of the algebra found on the GMAT, including exponents, roots, linear and quadratic equations, inequalities, and formulas of various kinds. You'll also learn additional strategies for the Data Sufficiency problem type, as well as for Test Cases and Choose Smart Numbers. Finally, you'll learn how to solve combo and max/min problems.

In This Unit

CHAPTER 8

PEMDAS

In This Chapter

- Subtraction of Expressions
- Fraction Bars as Grouping Symbols

In this chapter, you will learn the **order of operations**—the rules for simplifying equations.

CHAPTER 8 PEMDAS

When simplifying an algebraic expression, you have to follow a specific order of operations: Parentheses Exponents (Multiplication/Division) (Addition/Subtraction), or **PEMDAS** as it's referred to in the United States. If you learned math in other English-speaking countries, you may have memorized slightly different acronyms; however, the rules are still the same. Multiplication and division are in parentheses because they are on the *same* level of priority. The same is true of addition and subtraction. When two or more operations are at the same level of priority, work from left to right. For example:

Simplify: $5 + (2 \times 4 + 2)^2 - |7(-4)| + 18 \div 3 \times 5 - 8$

P = PARENTHESES. First, perform all of the operations that are *inside* parentheses. Note that in terms of order of operations, absolute value signs are equivalent to parentheses. In this expression, there are two groups of parentheses:

$(2 \times 4 + 2)$ and $|7(-4)|$

In the first group, there are two operations to perform, multiplication and addition. According to PEMDAS, multiplication must come before addition:

$(2 \times 4 + 2) = (8 + 2) = 10$

In the second group, perform the operation inside first (multiplication), then take the absolute value of that number:

$|7(-4)| = |-28| = 28$

Now the original expression looks like this:

$\mathbf{5 + 10^2 - 28 + 18 \div 3 \times 5 - 8}$

E = EXPONENTS. Second, take care of any exponents in the expression:

$10^2 = 100$

Now, the expression looks like this:

$\mathbf{5 + 100 - 28 + 18 \div 3 \times 5 - 8}$

M&D = MULTIPLICATION & DIVISION. Next, perform all the multiplication and division. When only multiplication and division are involved, you can do the work in any order. If that seems complicated, keep it simpler by working left to right:

$\underbrace{18 \div 3}_{6} \times 5$

$6 \times 5 = 30$

Now the expression reads:

$\mathbf{5 + 100 - 28 + 30 - 8}$

A&S = ADDITION & SUBTRACTION. Lastly, perform all the addition and subtraction. Always work from left to right when doing a mix of addition and subtraction:

$5 + 100 - 28 + 30 - 8$

$105 - 28 + 30 - 8$

$77 + 30 - 8$

$107 - 8$

The answer: **99**

Subtraction of Expressions

One of the most common errors involving the order of operations occurs when an expression with multiple terms is subtracted. The subtraction must occur across *every* term within the expression. Each term in the subtracted part must have its sign reversed. For example:

$x - (y - z) = x - y + z$	The signs of both y and $-z$ have been reversed. Note that "minus a negative" turns into a positive.
$x - (y + z) = x - y - z$	The signs of both y and z have been reversed.
$x - 2(y - 3z) = x - 2y + 6z$	The signs of both y and $-3z$ have been reversed.

Now, try another example:

What is $5x - [y - (3x - 4y)]$?

Both expressions in parentheses must be subtracted, so the signs of each term must be reversed for *each* subtraction, working from the inside out. Note that the square brackets are just fancy parentheses, used so that you avoid having double parentheses right next to each other:

$$5x - [y - (3x - 4y)] =$$
$$5x - (y - 3x + 4y) =$$
$$5x - (5y - 3x) =$$
$$5x - 5y + 3x = \mathbf{8x - 5y}$$

Fraction Bars as Grouping Symbols

In any expression with a fraction bar, pretend that there are parentheses around the numerator and denominator of the fraction. This may be obvious as long as the fraction bar remains in the expression, but it is easy to forget if you eliminate the fraction bar or add or subtract fractions. For example:

Simplify: $\frac{x-1}{2} - \frac{2x-1}{3}$

The common denominator for the two fractions is 6, so multiply the numerator and denominator of the first fraction by 3 and those of the second fraction by 2:

$$\frac{x-1}{2}\left(\frac{3}{3}\right) - \frac{2x-1}{3}\left(\frac{2}{2}\right) = \frac{3x-3}{6} - \frac{4x-2}{6}$$

For the next step, treat the expressions $3x - 3$ and $4x - 2$ as though they were enclosed in parentheses. Once you combine them, actually put in parentheses for these numerators. Then, reverse the signs of both terms in the second numerator when you distribute the subtraction:

$$\frac{(3x-3)-(4x-2)}{6} = \frac{3x-3-4x+2}{6} = \frac{-x-1}{6} = -\frac{x+1}{6}$$

The last two forms are both acceptable as the answer. You can leave the negative sign in each of the two terms in the top of the fraction. You can also pull a negative out of both terms and put that negative sign out front.

Problem Set

1. Evaluate: $(4 + 12 \div 3 - 18) - [-11 - (-4)]$

2. Evaluate: $-|-13 - (-17)|$

3. Evaluate: $\left(\dfrac{4+32}{2-(-6)}\right) - (4 + 8 \div 2 - (-6))$

4. Simplify: $x - (3 - x)$

5. Simplify: $(4 - y) - 2(2y - 3)$

8

Solutions

1. **−3:**

$$\begin{aligned}(4+12\div 3-18)-(-11-(-4)) &= && \text{Division before addition/subtraction}\\ (4+4-18)-(-11+4) &= && \\ (-10)-(-7) &= && \text{Subtraction of negative = addition}\\ -10+7 &= -3 && \text{Arithmetic—watch the signs!}\end{aligned}$$

2. **−4:**

$$\begin{aligned}-|-13-(-17)| &= && \\ -|-13+17| &= && \text{Subtraction of negative = addition}\\ -|4| &= -4 &&\end{aligned}$$

Note that the absolute value *cannot* be made into 13 + 17. You must perform the arithmetic inside grouping symbols *first*, whether inside parentheses or inside absolute value bars, *then* remove the grouping symbols.

3. **−9.5:**

$$\left[\frac{4+32}{2-(-6)}\right]-[4+8\div 2-(-6)]=$$

$$\left(\frac{4+32}{2+6}\right)-(4+8\div 2+6)=$$

$$\left(\frac{36}{8}\right)-\ 4+4+6\ =$$

$$5-14=-9.5$$

4. **2x − 3:** Reverse the signs of every term in the parentheses:

$$x-(3-x)=x-3+x=2x-3$$

5. **−5y + 10 (or 10 − 5y):** Reverse the signs of every term in the subtracted parentheses:

$$(4-y)-2(2y-3)=4-y-4y+6=-5y+10\ (\text{or } 10-5y)$$

8

CHAPTER 9

Linear Equations and Combos

In This Chapter

- Expressions vs. Equations
- Solving One-Variable Equations
- Two Variables: Solving by Substitution
- Two Variables: Solving by Elimination
- Two Variables: Solving for the Combo
- Absolute Value Equations

In this chapter, you will learn the difference between expressions and equations, as well as how to simplify and solve linear equations via various methods, including one strategy often used on the GMAT: the combo. You'll also learn how to solve equations containing absolute values.

CHAPTER 9 Linear Equations and Combos

Here's an example of a linear equation: $x - 13y = 24$.

Linear equations are equations in which all variables have an exponent of 1. In the equation above, the variable x can be written x^1. (This is always true when a variable doesn't have a "visible" exponent: The exponent is in fact 1.)

In addition, in linear equations, no variables are multiplied together.

The term **combo** is short for *combination of variables*. This is a test-taking term referring to questions such as "What is $x + y$?" The expression $x + y$ is a combo.

Expressions vs. Equations

Equations (such as $x + y = 6$) contain an equals sign, while expressions (such as $x + y$) do not.

An expression, even one that contains variables, represents a value. When manipulating or simplifying expressions, you have to follow certain rules to ensure that you don't change the value of the expression.

There are several methods for simplifying expressions. You can:

1. Combine like terms: $6z + 5z \rightarrow 11z$
2. Find a common denominator: $\frac{1}{12} + \frac{3x^3}{4} \times \left(\frac{3}{3}\right) \rightarrow \frac{1}{12} + \frac{9x^3}{12} = \frac{9x^3 + 1}{12}$
3. Pull out a common factor: $2ab + 4b \rightarrow 2b(a + 2)$
4. Cancel common factors: given $y \neq 0$, simplify $\frac{5y^3}{25y} \rightarrow \frac{y^2}{5}$

These moves are all valid because they do not change the value of the expression. In other words, if you plug numbers into both the original and simplified forms, the value stays the same. For example, replace z in the first expression with 3:

Original form	Simplified form
$6z + 5z$	$11z$
$6(3) + 5(3)$	$11(3)$
$18 + 15$	33
33	

Thus, $6z + 5z$ is equivalent to $11z$.

Since equations contain an equals sign, they behave differently. In order to keep the two sides of the equation equal, any change made to one side must also be made to the other side. Also, the change may alter the values on both sides of the equation—though the two sides will still be equal to each other. For example:

$3 = 3$	This is a valid equation: 3 equals 3.
$(2)3 = 3(2)$	Multiply both sides by 2.
$5 + 6 = 6 + 5$	Add 5 to both sides.
$11 = 11$	The two sides are still equal, but have different values.

In general, there are six operations you can perform to both sides of an equation. Remember to perform the action on the *entire* side of the equation. For example, if you were to square both sides of the equation $\sqrt{x} + 1 = x$, you would have to square the entire expression $\left(\sqrt{x} + 1\right)$, as opposed to squaring each term individually.

You can:

1. Add the same thing to both sides:

$$\begin{array}{l} z - 13 = -14 \\ \underline{\;\; +13 \quad +13} \\ z \qquad = -1 \end{array}$$

2. Subtract the same thing from both sides:

$$\begin{array}{l} x + 8 = 34 \\ \underline{\quad -8 \;\; -8} \\ x \qquad = 26 \end{array}$$

3. Multiply both sides by the same thing:

$$\frac{4}{a} = a + b$$
$$a \times \left(\frac{4}{a}\right) = (a + b) \times a$$
$$4 = a^2 + ab$$

4. Divide both sides by the same thing:

$$3x = 6y + 12$$
$$\frac{3x}{3} = \frac{6y + 12}{3}$$
$$x = 2y + 4$$

5. Raise both sides to the same power:

$$\sqrt{y} = y + 2$$
$$\left(\sqrt{y}\right)^2 = (y + 2)^2$$
$$y = (y + 2)^2$$

6. Take the same root of both sides:

$$x^3 = 125$$
$$\sqrt[3]{x^3} = \sqrt[3]{125}$$
$$x = 5$$

9

Solving One-Variable Equations

In order to solve one-variable equations, isolate the variable on one side of the equation (isolate = get the variable by itself). In doing so, make sure you perform identical operations on both sides of the equation.

Also, generally speaking, follow PEMDAS *in reverse*. Where possible, try to make moves that keep values positive, since people usually make fewer math mistakes with positive values versus negative values. Try these examples:

$3x + 5 = 26$	Subtract 5 from both sides.
$3x = 21$	Divide both sides by 3.
$x = 7$	

$w = 17w - 1$	Subtract w from both sides.
$0 = 16w - 1$	Add 1 to both sides.
$1 = 16w$	Divide both sides by 16.
$\frac{1}{16} = w$	

$\frac{p}{9} + 3 = 5$	Subtract 3 from both sides.
$\frac{p}{9} = 2$	Multiply both sides by 9.
$p = 18$	

When simplifying an *expression* (not like the examples just given), you'd follow PEMDAS, in which case multiplication and division would come before addition and subtraction. When simplifying an *equation*, by contrast, follow PEMDAS in reverse: Add and subtract first, to get the plain numbers over to the other side of the equation, then multiply or divide to move the numbers that are "attached" to the variable.

Two Variables: Solving by Substitution

Sometimes the GMAT asks you to solve a system of equations with more than one variable. You might be given two equations with two variables, or perhaps three equations with three variables. In either case, there are two primary textbook ways of solving simultaneous equations—substitution or elimination—and a third way that occurs on the GMAT, the combo. This section deals with the first method, substitution. For example:

> Use substitution to solve for y.
>
> $x + y = 9$
> $2x = 5y + 4$

First, isolate the variable you *don't* want to solve for—in this case, you don't want x. Choose the equation in which it is easier to isolate x:

$$x + y = 9$$
$$x = 9 - y$$

Next, substitute the right-hand side of that equation into the other equation. In this case, substitute $9 - y$ wherever you see x:

$$2x = 5y + 4$$
$$2(9 - y) = 5y + 4$$

Now you've got an equation with just y, the variable that you want. Solve for y:

$$2(9 - y) = 5y + 4$$
$$18 - 2y = 5y + 4$$
$$14 = 7y$$
$$2 = y$$

You can also substitute your solution for y into either of the original equations in order to solve for x—but first check whether you need to do that. Most of the time, the GMAT will ask for just one variable. Here's how to solve for the second variable, just in case:

$$x + y = 9$$
$$x + 2 = 9$$
$$x = 7$$

If the problem had asked you to solve for x, you would start by isolating y in one of the equations and then substituting into the second equation. You can choose which equation to do first versus second—and if you do have to solve for both variables, you can also choose in which order you solve. But if, as will usually be the case, you're asked to solve only for one variable, first isolate the variable you *don't* want, and then substitute to solve for the variable you do want.

Two Variables: Solving by Elimination

Alternatively, you can solve simultaneous equations by elimination. In this method, you can add or subtract the two equations to eliminate one of the variables—though you'll minimize mistakes if you plan on adding whenever you do this, not subtracting. For example:

> Solve the following for y.
>
> $x + y = 9$
> $2x = 5y + 4$

To start, line up the terms of the equations:

9

$$x + y = 9$$
$$2x - 5y = 4$$

The goal is to get the coefficient (or number) in front of the variable you *don't* want (in this case, x) to be the same *number* but the opposite sign (positive or negative). You accomplish this by multiplying one of the equations by some number. For example, multiply the first equation by -2:

$$-2(x + y = 9) \rightarrow -2x - 2y = -18$$

Now, the x coefficient in both equations is the same number (2) but opposite in sign. Next, add the equations to eliminate the undesired variable:

$$\begin{array}{r} -2x - 2y = -18 \\ +2x - 5y = 4 \\ \hline -7y = -14 \end{array}$$

Finally, solve the resulting equation for the unknown variable:

$$-7y = -14$$
$$y = 2$$

The GMAT will usually ask you to solve for just one of the two variables, but if you do have to find both, then substitute the value for the known variable into either of the starting equations to find the value for the other variable. Use whichever equation looks easier to you:

$$x + y = 9$$
$$x + 2 = 9$$
$$x = 7$$

Two Variables: Solving for the Combo

Combo questions might look, at first glance, much like certain algebra questions you were asked in school. Try this Data Sufficiency problem:

What is the value of $\frac{x}{y}$?

(1) $\frac{x+y}{y} = 3$

(2) $y = 4$

It wasn't unusual to be asked, in school, to solve for $\frac{x}{y}$, or $x + y$, or any similar combination of variables. Find x, find y, and voilà! You can calculate any desired combination of the variables, too.

GMAT combo problems, however, have one key difference: Your goal is to solve directly for the *combination* of variables, not for each individual variable. There are two steps in a combo problem: noticing the combo and manipulating to match it.

First: Notice that the question asks for a combo.

When a question asks directly for a combination of variables, you have a combo problem. (There are ways to disguise a combo—you'll learn about this later.)

Second: Manipulate any given information to try to match the combo.

In this case, the question stem doesn't contain any additional given information and the question itself is already simplified: $\frac{x}{y} = ?$

Jump into the statements:

(1) $\frac{x+y}{y} = 3$

If you weren't looking for the combo, you might start to simplify the equation by multiplying both sides by y, getting $x + y = 3y$. However, the combo contains a fraction $\left(\frac{x}{y}\right)$, so keep that denominator right where it is. How else can you manipulate the equation while preserving the fraction? Split the numerator and simplify:

$$\frac{x}{y} + \frac{y}{y} = 3$$

$$\frac{x}{y} + 1 = 3$$

$$\frac{x}{y} = 2$$

Statement (1) is sufficient!

AD
~~BCE~~

Here's statement (2):

(2) $y = 4$

The statement provides no information about x, so it is not sufficient.

Ⓐ ~~D~~
~~BCE~~

The correct answer is (A).

When you solve for a combo in Data Sufficiency (DS), your ultimate goal is to try to find a single match for the desired combo. If you can, then the statement is sufficient.

The problem above also contains a common DS trap called the C-Trap. Problems with this trap appear to work only when both statements are used together—that is, the answer appears to be (C). In actuality, one of the two statements works by itself and (C) is incorrect. Take a look at the two statements again:

(1) $\frac{x + y}{y} = 3$

(2) $y = 4$

If you are trying to solve for both x and y individually, you will realize pretty quickly that neither statement alone will get you there. Put the two statements together, however, and it is possible to find the individual values of both x and y.

There's just one hitch: The problem didn't ask for the values of x and y. It asked for the value of $\frac{x}{y}$, and statement (1) is sufficient all by itself to find that combo. Since answer (C) specifically says that you have to use both statements together and that *neither one alone is sufficient,* it cannot be correct.

Keep an eye out for the C-Trap on DS problems. If it is obvious that the two statements do work together, reexamine each one individually; one might work all by itself. Combo problems are a very common place for C-Traps to occur.

Try another combo problem:

What is the value of $x + y$?

(1) $x - y = 1$

(2) $x = 3 - y$

Notice that the question asks for a combo. The question stem asks directly for a combo: $x + y$.

Manipulate any given information to try to match the combo. Jot down $x + y = ?$ on your scratch paper. Now look at statement (1):

(1) $x - y = 1$

Hmm. How can you turn this into $x + y$? How about $x = y + 1$. Good, now there's an addition sign—but it's not between the x and y. What next?

It turns out that, no matter how you manipulate the equation, you can't change the original subtraction relationship between x and y into addition. As a general rule, if the relationship between the two variables starts out as addition, you cannot switch it to subtraction, or vice versa, without some additional information to add to the equation. Ditto if the relationship begins as multiplication—you cannot switch it to division, or vice versa, without additional information.

Statement (1) is not sufficient; cross off answers (A) and (D):

~~AD~~
BCE

Now, look at statement (2):

(2) $x = 3 - y$

This one also doesn't have $x + y$. At least, not right now. But put x and y on the same side:

$x + y = 3$

Although you can't find the individual values for x and y, you do have the value for the combo $x + y$. And that's all you need!

This statement is sufficient to answer the question. The correct answer is (B).

~~AD~~
ⒷCE

9

A question stem may also try to disguise the combo. Consider this question:

> If $a + b = c$, what is the value of c?

The question itself asks for a single variable, but it also provides given information in the form of an equation that contains three variables total. Given that equation, if you are able to find the value of the combo $a + b$, then you could also find the value of c. So the real question is this:

> What is c? Or, what is $a + b$?

Finally, while combos show up more often on DS, you may also see them on Problem Solving problems. Here's an example:

> If $2x + y = 18$ and $x + 2y = 12$, what is the value of $x + y$?
>
> (A) 2
> (B) 6
> (C) 8
> (D) 10
> (E) 12

Since you're given two equations and two variables, you could solve for the individual values of x and y—but when the question asks for a combo, it's usually faster to solve for the combo!

Note two characteristics about the combo: the R&R. First, the desired *relationship* between the variables is addition (+). Second, the desired *ratio* of the coefficients—the values in front of the variables—is 1 : 1 (you have one x and one y).

Take a look at the two equations. Do you see any way to combine them that would give you an addition relationship and a 1 : 1 ratio between the variables?

$$\begin{array}{rr} & 2x + y = 18 \\ + & x + 2y = 12 \\ \hline & 3x + 3y = 30 \end{array}$$

Add them up! Divide by 3 to solve for the combo: $x + y = 10$. The correct answer is (D).

You can also solve for x and y individually and then add them up; that will just take longer. A little time investment up front can often save you more time later on in the problem. (And if you don't see how to solve directly for the combo, you can always go ahead and solve individually.)

Notice that the question asks for a combo.

A question stem may ask for the combo directly or it may try to disguise the combo. You may have to do a little rephrasing in order to find the combo. Start training yourself to look for this feature.

Manipulate any given information to try to match the combo.

Your goal is to try to match the combination of variables (look for the R&R: relationship and ratio). Most of the time, if you try to solve for each variable individually, it will take longer and, on DS, you risk falling into a trap answer. Go for the combo!

Absolute Value Equations

Absolute value refers to the *positive* value of the expression within the absolute value brackets. For instance, if you know that $|x| = 5$, then x could be either 5 or -5 and the equation would still be true. There's exactly one circumstance in which the value isn't positive: when it's zero. In this case, $|x| = 0$, so $x = 0$.

Unless the answer is zero, equations that involve absolute value generally have two solutions. In other words, there are *two* numbers that the variable could equal in order to make the equation true, because the value of the expression inside the absolute value brackets could be *positive or negative.*

Here's how to solve an absolute value equation:

> Solve for w, given that $12 + |w - 4| = 30$.

First, isolate the absolute value expression:

$$12 + |w - 4| = 30$$
$$|w - 4| = 18$$

Second, once you have an equation of the form |variable expression| = a with $a > 0$, you know that the variable expression *without* the absolute value symbols could be ±. Remove the absolute value brackets and solve the equation for two different solutions:

CASE 1: When w is positive, $w = a$.

$$w - 4 = 18$$
$$w = 22$$

CASE 2: When w is negative, $-w = a$.

$$-(w - 4) = 18$$
$$w - 4 = -18$$
$$w = -14$$

Advanced material for the Algebra unit (primarily covering additional strategies for equations, formulas, and inequalities) can be found in Atlas, Manhattan Prep's online learning platform. Use the online material only if you feel that you have mastered everything in the Algebra unit of this strategy guide and only if you are aiming for a Quant section score of 48 or higher.

Problem Set

Now that you've finished the chapter, try the following problems.

1. Solve for x: $2(2 - 3x) - (4 + x) = 7$

2. Given $z \neq \frac{3}{2}$, solve for z: $\frac{4z-7}{3-2z} = -5$

3. What is the sum of x, y, and z ?

   $x + y = 8$
   $x + z = 11$
   $y + z = 7$

   (A) 1
   (B) 13
   (C) 26

4. Solve for y: $22 - |y + 14| = 20$

5. If $y = 2x + 9$ and $7x + 3y = -51$, what is the value of x ?

   (A) -6
   (B) -3
   (C) 0

6. If $a = 3bc$ and $abc \neq 0$, what is the value of c ?

   (1) $a = 10 - b$
   (2) $3a = 4b$

7. Every attendee at a monster truck rally paid the same admission fee. How many people attended the rally?

   (1) If the admission fee had been raised to \$15 and twice as many people had attended, the total admission fees collected would have been three times the amount actually collected.
   (2) If the admission fee had been raised to \$22.50 and two-thirds as many people had attended, the total admission fees collected would have been 150% of the actual admission fees collected.

8. If $A = \frac{\frac{x}{3}}{\frac{2}{y}}$, what is A ?

   (1) $xy = 8$
   (2) $\frac{x}{y} = 2$

9

9. If $x \neq 0$ and $x\left(x - \frac{5x+6}{x}\right) = 0$, what are all of the possible values of x ?

10. At a certain coffee shop, a mocha sells for \$3.00 and a cappuccino sells for \$2.25. In total, the shop sold \$180 worth of mochas and cappuccinos over the course of a day. How many mochas did the shop sell?

    (1) The shop sold 10 more cappuccinos than it did mochas.

    (2) The combined price of all of the cappuccinos sold was equal to the combined price of all of the mochas sold.

Solutions

1. **−1:**

$$\begin{aligned} 2(2-3x)-(4+x) &= 7 \\ 4-6x-4-x &= 7 \\ -7x &= 7 \\ x &= -1 \end{aligned}$$

2. $\mathbf{\frac{4}{3}}$**:**

$$\begin{aligned} \frac{4z-7}{3-2z} &= -5 \\ 4z-7 &= -5(3-2z) \\ 4z-7 &= -15+10z \\ 8 &= 6z \\ z &= \frac{8}{6}=\frac{4}{3} \end{aligned}$$

3. **(B) 13:** It is possible to solve for x, y, and z individually, but you can save a significant amount of time by solving for the combo: What is $x+y+z$? The equations collectively contain exactly two "copies" of each variable and these variables are always added. Add the three equations together:

$$\begin{array}{lcccl} & x+y & & & =8 \\ & x & & +z & =11 \\ + & & y & +z & =7 \\ \hline & 2x+2y+2z & & & =26 \end{array}$$

Divide the equation by 2: the combo $x+y+z=13$.

4. $\mathbf{y=\{-16,-12\}}$**:** First, isolate the expression within the absolute value brackets. Then, solve for two cases, one in which the expression is positive and one in which it is negative:

$$\begin{aligned} 22-|y+14| &= 20 \\ 2 &= |y+14| \end{aligned}$$

Case 1: $y+14=2$

$$y=-12$$

Case 2: $-(y+14)=2$

$$\begin{aligned} y+14 &= -2 \\ y &= -16 \end{aligned}$$

9

5. **(A) −6:** The question asks for x, so you need to figure out how to eliminate y. Since the first equation already has y isolated, substitute the first equation into the second equation:

$$y = 2x + 9 \qquad 7x + 3y = -51$$

$$\begin{aligned} 7x + 3(2x + 9) &= -51 \\ 7x + 6x + 27 &= -51 \\ 13x + 27 &= -51 \\ 13x &= -78 \\ x &= -6 \end{aligned}$$

Note that answer (B) is a trap. The value for y is −3, but the question asked for x, not y.

6. **(B):** Since the question asks about c and provides a given equation that contains c, solve the given equation for c:

$$c = \frac{a}{3b}$$

What would you need to know in order to calculate c? Take a look at the equation this way:

$$c = \left(\frac{1}{3}\right)\left(\frac{a}{b}\right)$$

If you can find a value for the combination $\frac{a}{b}$, then you can calculate c. This problem is a combo problem in disguise! Try to solve for the combo.

(1) INSUFFICIENT: $a = 10 - b$. Can this be manipulated into the desired combo? If you add b to both sides ($a + b = 10$), you get a combo, but not the desired one. If you divide everything by b, you partially get the desired combo: $\frac{a}{b} = \frac{10}{b} - 1$. The problem is that there's another b associated with the 10. There isn't a way to get just $\frac{a}{b}$ by itself on one side and only a numerical value (no variables) on the other side. Statement (1) is not sufficient, so cross off answers (A) and (D).

(2) SUFFICIENT: This time, the desired combo can be created: $3a = 4b \rightarrow \frac{a}{b} = \frac{4}{3}$ This statement is sufficient.

The correct answer is **(B)**: Statement (2) is sufficient, but statement (1) is not.

7. **(E):** This question asks how many people attended a monster truck rally. The total amount collected equals the number of attendees times the admission fee, or $T = A \times P$. The question asks for A.

(1) INSUFFICIENT: If the price had been $15 and twice as many people had attended, the total would be three times greater. Therefore:

$$\begin{aligned} 3T &= 2A \times 15 \\ 3T &= 30A \end{aligned}$$

The value of A depends on the unknown value of T, so more than one answer is possible, and this statement is not sufficient.

(2) INSUFFICIENT: If the price had been \$22.50 and two-thirds as many people had attended, the total would be 150% of the actual total. Therefore:

$$1.5T = \frac{2}{3}A \times 22.50$$

$$1.5T = 15A$$

The value of A depends on the unknown value of T, so more than one answer is possible, and this statement is not sufficient.

(1) AND (2) INSUFFICIENT: In order to be able to solve for the value of A, you would need two different equations. Take a look at the two equations: If you multiply the second one by 2, the two equations will be identical. In other words, they are the same; you have only one equation. Combining the two statements is therefore no more sufficient than either statement alone.

The correct answer is **(E)**: Using the two statements together is still not sufficient.

8. **(A):** This question is a combo problem in disguise. The question asks for A, but the value of A depends on x and y. Before diving into the statements, simplify the given equation:

$$A = \frac{\frac{x}{3}}{\frac{2}{y}}$$

$$A = \frac{x}{3} \times \frac{y}{2}$$

$$A = \frac{xy}{6}$$

If you can find the value of the combo xy, you can answer the question.

(1) SUFFICIENT: Statement (1) matches the rephrased question, so it is sufficient to answer the question.

(2) INSUFFICIENT: In general, it's not possible to find the value for the multiplication combo xy from the value for the division combo $\frac{x}{y}$. This is always the case, so you can memorize this rule. (Why is this the case? When given $\frac{x}{y} = 2$, the x could be 2 and the y could be 1, in which case xy is 2. Alternatively, x could be 4 and y could be 2, in which case xy is 8. There will be an infinite number of values that could work.)

The correct answer is **(A)**: Statement (1) alone is sufficient, but statement (2) is not.

9

9. **{6, –1}:** Distribute the multiplication by x. Note that, when you cancel the x in the denominator, the quantity $5x + 6$ is implicitly enclosed in parentheses:

$$x\left(x - \frac{5x+6}{x}\right) = 0$$

$$x^2 - (5x + 6) = 0$$

$$x^2 - 5x - 6 = 0$$

$$(x - 6)(x + 1) = 0$$

$$x = 6 \text{ or } -1$$

10. **(D):** Call the number of mochas m and the number of lattes c. The total revenue can be expressed as the equation $3m + 2.25c = 180$. The question asks for the value of m. If you can find the value of c, then you can find the value of m, so the question can be rephrased as this: What is the value of m or c?

(1) SUFFICIENT: This statement can be translated into the equation $m + 10 = c$. This can be substituted into the first equation: $3m + 2.25(m + 10) = 180$. This can be solved for m (though don't actually solve!).

(2) SUFFICIENT: This statement can be translated into the equation $3m = 2.25c$. Again, this can be substituted into the equation given in the question stem: $3m + 3m = 180$. This can be solved for m.

The correct answer is **(D)**: Each statement alone is sufficient.

CHAPTER 10

Data Sufficiency 201

In This Chapter

- Test Cases Redux
- The C-Trap
- Avoid Statement Carryover
- Guessing Strategies

In this chapter, you will learn more about Data Sufficiency strategies, including how to avoid certain traps and common mistakes on DS and how to eliminate wrong answers and make an educated guess.

CHAPTER 10 Data Sufficiency 201

You're ready for your next level of Data Sufficiency studies. First, refresh your DS skills.

Step 1: Understand

First, just *glance* at the problem to note the overall type—in this case, it's DS. Where does it look messy or complex? Include the question stem and both statements in your glance.

Next, *read* the problem and decide: Is this a Value or a Yes/No?

Value: The question asks for the value of an unknown (e.g., What is x?).

A statement is **Sufficient** if it provides **exactly one possible value**.

A statement is **Not Sufficient** if it provides **more than one possible value**.

Yes/No: The question asks whether a given piece of information is true (e.g., Is x even?). Most of the time, these will be in the form of Yes/No questions.

A statement is **Sufficient** when the answer is **Always Yes** or **Always No**.

A statement is **Not Sufficient** when the answer is **Sometimes Yes, Sometimes No**.

Jot down both the given information and the question itself. If the information is straightforward, it's fine to jot as you read. If the information is at all complex (especially if it's a story!), you may want to read the whole thing before you jot anything down. When you are ready to jot, draw a T-diagram on your paper; write information from the question stem above the horizontal line of the T.

Given information—that is, any information in the question stem other than the question itself—is true information that you must consider or use when answering the question. Write this information separately from the question itself. It's important to distinguish between what you were *told* is true and what you were *asked* to find. For the question stem, write facts to the left and the question more to the right, both above the line.

Step 2: Plan

Reflect on the question and the given, and rephrase the question if you can. If you have a lot of information, you may also need to decide how to *organize* your work.

Step 3: Solve

If you understand the problem and have a decent plan to solve (it doesn't need to be perfect!), go ahead and follow your plan. If, on the other hand, you realize that you don't understand the problem or you don't have a decent plan, this is an excellent time to pick any answer and move on. Save that time and mental energy for a problem that has a better chance of paying off.

Test Cases Redux

You also learned how to test cases—one of the strategies for avoiding algebra by using real numbers instead. Try this problem:

Is $b < 0$?

(1) $b^3 < b$

(2) $b^2 > b$

Step 1: Understand. DS. Yes/No. The problem is a theory problem and it's asking whether b is less than 0, so you can test some real numbers.

Asking whether b is less than 0 is the same as asking whether b is negative, so you'll almost certainly want to try some negative numbers.

Also, rephrase the question: Is b negative?

Step 2: Plan. What kind of numbers would be good to try on this problem? Where possible, try 0 or 1. Also, the statements contain exponents, so that's another vote for considering negative values. (There's also one other type of number to consider when you see exponents—did you spot it when you tried the problem? If not, feel free to play around with the statements a little before you keep reading.)

Step 3: Solve. Dive into the statements.

(1) $b^3 < b$

Reflect on this statement for a moment. You cube a number. . .and the cube is *smaller* than the starting number. That's a little weird! For what kinds of numbers does that happen?

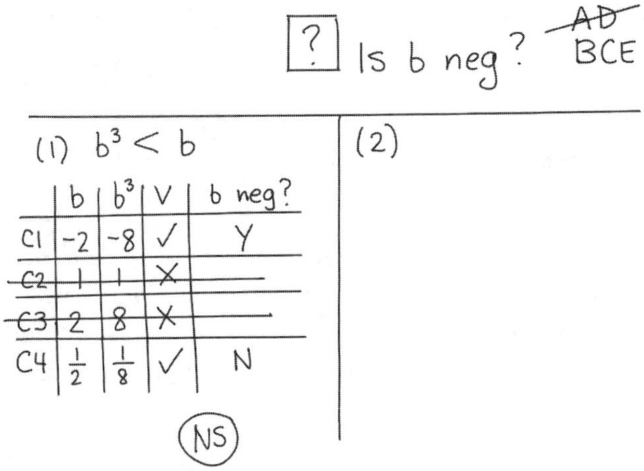

Case 1: Negatives work! If $b = -2$, then $-8 < -2$. Therefore, -2 is a possible value for b. In this case, Yes, b is negative. Next, can you get a No answer?

Cases 2 and 3 (attempts): Try a positive to see whether that makes a difference. If $b = 1$, then it is not true that $1 < 1$. Discard this case. What about a larger positive value, like $b = 2$? It's not true that $8 < 2$. Any number greater than 1 would make the statement $b^3 < b$ false, so you can't use those numbers in your cases.

Are there any other kinds of numbers that can be used? As you'll learn in the next chapter, negative numbers and fractions between 0 and 1 do funny things when raised to an exponent. You've already tried a negative; maybe it's time to try a fraction?

Case 4: Fractions between 0 and 1 also get smaller when you raise them to a power. If $b = \frac{1}{2}$, then $\frac{1}{8} < \frac{1}{2}$. Therefore, $\frac{1}{2}$ is a valid case to test for b. In this case, No, b is not a negative number.

Since there is a Yes and a No, statement (1) is not sufficient. Cross off answers (A) and (D).

(2) $b^2 > b$

Hmm. You square something, and it gets bigger. What kinds of numbers do that?

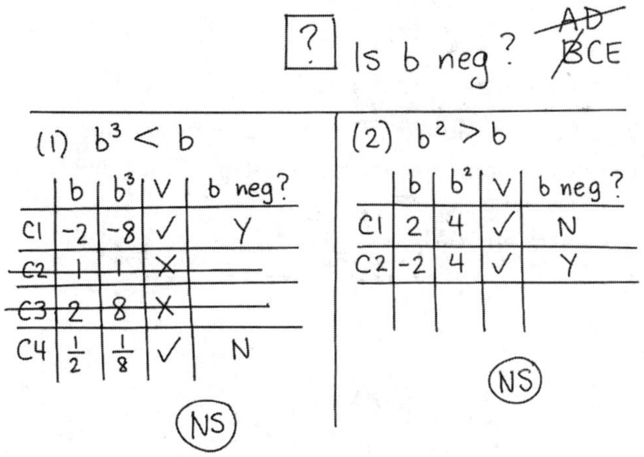

Case 1: If $b = 2$, then $4 > 2$. Therefore, 2 is a valid case and, in this case, No, b is not a negative number. Next, can you get a Yes answer?

To get a Yes answer, b has to be negative, so try a negative value next.

Case 2: If $b = -2$, then $4 > -2$. Therefore, -2 is a possible value and, in this case, Yes, b is negative.

Since there is a Yes and a No, statement (2) is not sufficient. Cross off answer (B).

Finally, try the two statements together:

(1) $b^3 < b$

(2) $b^2 > b$

The goal now is to find cases that are valid for *both* of the statements simultaneously. That's a lot of work! Rather than start from scratch, first examine the cases that you already tested; are any valid for both statements? If so, you can reuse your work.

You've already tested $b = -2$ for both. That test gave a Yes answer, so your Yes case is done. Now, can you find a case that is valid for both statements and that gives a No answer? Examine the No cases that you tried before.

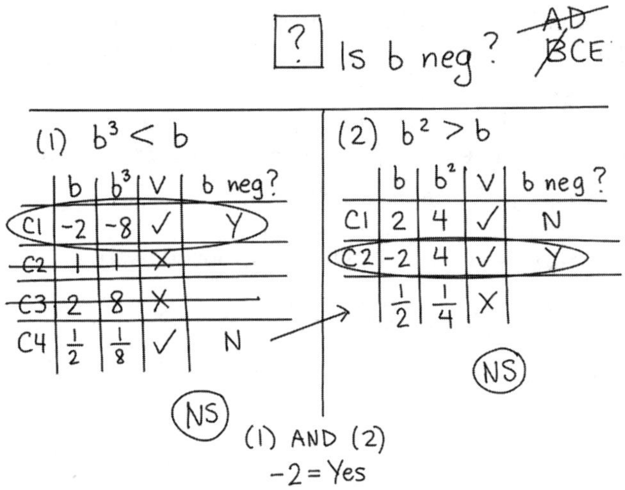

For statement (1), you tried $\frac{1}{2}$. Are you allowed to try that value for statement (2)? That would give $\frac{1}{4} > \frac{1}{2}$, which is false, so cross off this case entirely. Statement (2) doesn't allow values between 0 and 1.

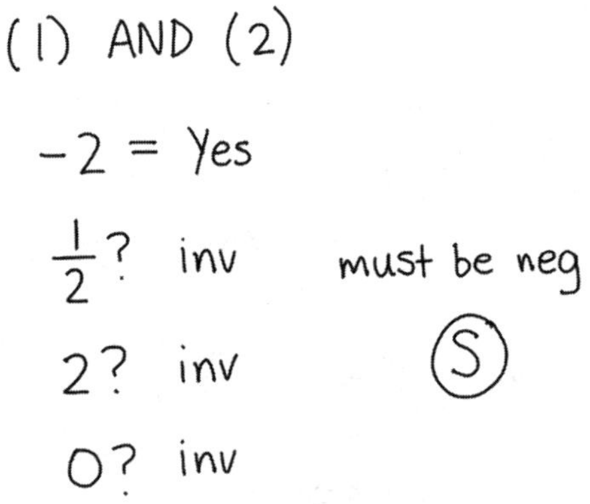

You tried $b = 2$ for statement (2), but during statement (1), you already figured out that any value greater than 1 won't be valid.

What about 0? No, that doesn't work either. The only values that work for both statements are negative, so b must be a negative number. Together, the statements are sufficient.

The correct answer is (C): Both statements together are sufficient, but neither one is sufficient by itself.

Think back over how the math played out. When you see exponents on future Test Cases problems, what kinds of numbers do you want to consider?

Start with 0 and 1, if possible. Consider whether you may want a negative. And think about fractions between 0 and 1 (or, maybe, fractions between 0 and -1). All of these characteristics can result in weird outcomes with exponents—outcomes that might serve to give you a different answer when testing cases.

Here's a summary of the Test Cases strategy for DS problems:

10

Understand: First, **recognize** that you can test cases. The question stem and the statement will allow for multiple possible values; it doesn't lock you into using one set of values.

Articulate the *facts* given in the problem and separate them from the *question* that is being asked. Remind yourself of your goal when testing cases on DS: Try to find two different answers so that you can call that statement Not Sufficient and move on.

Plan: First, **think about** any **constraints** you're given. The constraints are the facts given in the problem and can be found in *two* places: (1) the question stem and (2) the two statements. You are only allowed to try numbers that fit the given facts. (As you work on one statement alone, ignore any facts given in the *other* statement.)

Next, use the given facts as clues to figure out what kinds of numbers you *do* want to try. These clues will help you to find the kinds of numbers that can give you different answers.

Solve: Then, **test one set of numbers**. Choose your values, write them down, then check your numbers against the facts in the problem to make sure that you have chosen a valid case. If your chosen numbers "break" any of the facts—that is, make any fact in the question stem or the statement on which you're working right now false—*discard* that case. All of the given facts must be true, so any numbers you choose must go along with those facts. Cross an invalid case off on your scratch paper and start again.

If you have a valid case, solve to find an answer to the question. On a Yes/No question, you will get either a Yes or a No. On a Value question, you will get a particular value.

Then, try to find a second case that gives you a *different* answer. Remind yourself of what a different answer looks like for this problem. For example, if the question is "Is $b > 5$?" and your first answer is Yes, then you would want to find a No case. For this particular question, a No case would only occur when b is equal to or less than 5, so choose such a value for your second case.

If you can find two different answers, you're done! That statement has a Sometimes Yes/Sometimes No answer, so you can cross off the relevant answer(s) on your grid and move to the next step in your DS process.

If you keep getting the same answer, try to to articulate *why* this is happening. If you are trying the same kind of number each time, then you may need to try a different kind of number to find that opposite case—so trying to articulate what's happening can lead you to realize that you need to try a specific kind of number that will get you to a different answer.

Alternatively, articulating what's happening with the math may allow you to realize that you will always get that same answer—in other words, that this statement is sufficient.

At times, you may get the same answer after a few cases but not be able to articulate what's happening. If you're not sure why but you also don't see how to get a different answer after trying a few different kinds of numbers, don't keep sitting on this problem. Go ahead and call this statement sufficient and move on.

The C-Trap

Set a timer for 4 minutes and try these two DS problems.

What is the value of x ?

(1) $12x + 4y = 4(21 + y)$

(2) $y = 12$

If $a + b = c$, what is the value of c ?

(1) $b = 5$

(2) $2(a + c) = 22 + 2(c - b)$

10

What did you get for the first one?

> What is the value of x ?
>
> (1) $12x + 4y = 4(21 + y)$
>
> (2) $y = 12$

Step 1: **Understand.** It's a DS that asks for the value of x; it provides no additional information. Glance at the statements. Statement (1) is a lot messier. (For a reason, it turns out. It's setting a trap!)

Step 2: **Plan.** Since statement (2) is easier, start there. Make a mental note that, when you get to statement (1), you're going to want to simplify it.

Step 3: **Solve.** Statement (2) provides no information about x, so it's not sufficient. Eliminate answers (B) and (D). So far, so good (you haven't hit the trap yet).

Here's where the trap closes: You know that statement (2) gives you y. Look at statement (1): It contains an equation with both x and y. That equation doesn't look like it could possibly work by itself because it contains two variables. So you get rid of answer (A), choose answer (C), and move on...but you just fell into the C-Trap (first introduced in the prior chapter). Answer (C) is *not* the correct answer!

When you see a messy equation, first try to simplify the information. For instance, you can divide everything by 4. What else?

$$\overset{3}{\cancel{12}}x + \cancel{4}y = \cancel{4}(21 + y)$$
$$3x + y = 21 + y$$
$$3x = 21$$
$$x = 7$$

Interesting. The variable y drops completely out of the equation. This statement is enough all by itself to get a definitive value for x.

The correct answer is (A): Statement (1) alone is sufficient to answer the question, but statement (2) alone is not.

The C-Trap occurs when you (mistakenly) think that you need *both* statements to answer the question, but it turns out that *just one* of those statements is enough all by itself. The text for answer (C) states that you have to use both pieces of information and that *neither one alone is sufficient.*

It is certainly true that, if you have both pieces of information, you can find x—but you don't *need* both pieces together. Statement (1) will do the job by itself.

If you ever find yourself thinking, "Oh, it's *completely* obvious that using the two pieces of information together will get you to the answer," pause for a moment! This test isn't often super-obvious—so double-check. Ask yourself whether you might be falling for the C-Trap. It may be the case that one of the pieces of information is sufficient on its own.

Here's the second problem. Did you get (C) as your answer? If so, try it again right now:

If $a + b = c$, what is the value of c?

(1) $b = 5$

(2) $2(a + c) = 22 + 2(c - b)$

Step 1: **Understand.** It's a DS Value. It asks for the value of c, but it also gives the equation $a + b = c$. This is a combo question in disguise! If you can solve for the combo $a + b$, that will give you the value of c. So the rephrased question is this: What is c *or* what is the combo $a + b$?

Step 2: **Plan.** Statement (1) is straightforward, but statement (2) is complicated. That complexity signals that there may be some way to simplify.

Step 3: **Solve**, starting with the easier statement (1). Knowing that $b = 5$ is not enough to get to the value of the combo $a + b$. Statement (1) is not sufficient, so cross off answers (A) and (D).

Statement (2) is a lot messier, so simplify. Before you start, remind yourself of what would be sufficient: Can you find c, or can you find the combo $a + b$?

$$2(a + c) = 22 + 2(c - b)$$
$$a + c = 11 + (c - b)$$
$$a = 11 - b$$

The variable c drops out completely. Now, can you get the combo $a + b$? Yes!

$$a = 11 - b$$
$$a + b = 11$$

Statement (2) is sufficient all by itself. The correct answer is (B).

This problem sets up a C-Trap that many people will fall for even if they do figure out that the question is a combo. When the test gives you something messy, it's probably trying to hide something from you. Whenever you see an "ugly" equation (or, really, any equation!), take some time to try to simplify the messiness so that you can understand what the test is really asking or telling you.

Avoid Statement Carryover

When you first learned how to do Data Sufficiency, you learned one very important step: Evaluate each statement individually before evaluating the two statements together.

The GMAT likes to set a certain trap that plays off of this step (and you may have already fallen for this trap in the past). Take a look at this problem (you may remember seeing a similar one earlier in this guide):

If Farai is twice as old as Dmitry, how old is Farai?

(1) Samantha will be 11 years old in 5 years.

(2) Samantha is 4 years younger than Dmitry.

The question asks how old F is and provides a relationship: $F = 2D$. The rephrased question is "What is F or D?" since the equation provides a direct relationship between the two variables.

Here's how the trap works. You can find *S*'s age from statement (1), but that's not enough to get to *D* or *F*, so you cross off answers (A) and (D).

In evaluating the second statement, you realize that, since you know how old *S* is, you can find *D*, and knowing *D* is sufficient to answer! So the answer is (B).

The answer is actually *not* (B). What happened?

When working on statement (2), you used the information about *S*'s age, but that's from statement (1)—at this stage, you're supposed to be evaluating each statement individually! You're not allowed to carry over information from one statement to the other right now; this is literally called the **Statement Carryover** trap. In the heat of the test, it's very easy to do this, even when you know that you're not supposed to—especially as the math becomes more complicated (and therefore distracting).

To help avoid this trap, use the T-diagram consistently when solving DS problems. When you are working on each statement, you are not allowed to "cross the vertical line" of the T. Keep the two statements completely separate. You can only look "up the T" and use the information from the question stem:

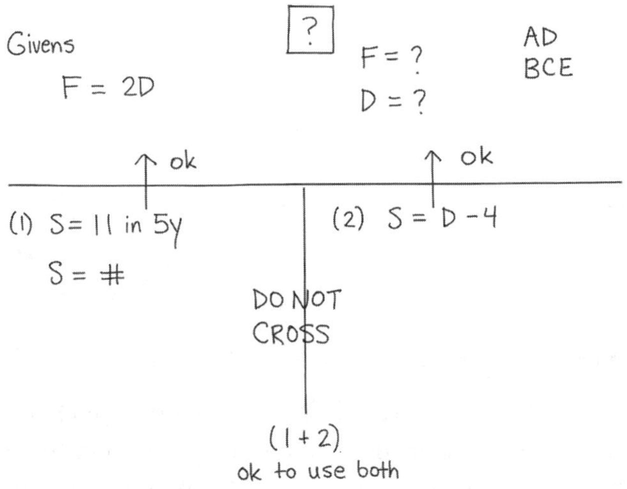

If you have eliminated answers (A), (B), and (D), you will then evaluate the two statements together. In this circumstance, go ahead and work below the two prior statements—and below the "Do Not Cross" line. Now, you're allowed to use the information from both statements.

Guessing Strategies

There are several strategies that can help you guess effectively. Even when you know how to solve and don't need to guess, you can avoid certain traps or careless mistakes by practicing these strategies.

Situation 1: The Identical Twins. Two statements provide *exactly* the same information.

Here is an example:

(1) $4y + 3x = 9$

(2) $6x - 18 = -8y$

Each statement provides an equation that contains x and y, but the variables are in a different order. When you see this, be suspicious; they are probably trying to hide something. Rearrange one of the two equations to match.

For instance, rearrange the second equation to match the placement of the variables in the first: $8y + 6x = 18$. Now, compare the two equations:

(1) $4y + 3x = 9$

(2) $8y + 6x = 18$

The second equation is exactly twice the first equation. Divide the second equation by 2 and you have the first equation. In other words, there are not two *different* equations here; there is just one equation. The statements are identical.

When the statements are identical, only two answers are possible. If the information in one statement is sufficient to answer the question, then it's sufficient in *either* statement, so the correct answer is (D).

Alternatively, if the information in one statement is *not* sufficient to answer the question, then the second statement also won't be sufficient. Further, that second statement adds no new information, so even together, the statements are insufficient, so the answer is (E).

If you see that the two statements are identical twins, immediately cross off answers (A), (B), and (C)—even if you are still working on the problem. That will forestall any careless mistakes. The answer must be either (D) or (E).

Situation 2: The Cannibal. One statement completely includes or incorporates the information given by the other.

Here is an example:

(1) $x > 20$

(2) $80 < x < 142$

The first statement indicates that x is greater than 20. The second statement indicates that x is between 80 and 142.

If x is between 80 and 142, then x must be greater than 20. Statement (2) tells you everything that statement (1) told you (x is greater than 20), plus additional information (x is between 80 and 142). Think of the second statement as the Cannibal; it cannibalized statement (1), plus it gives you additional information.

In this case, the answer cannot be (A), statement (1) alone, because statement (2) also provides that same piece of information. If the fact that x is greater than 20 is sufficient, then the answer must be (D): Each statement works alone.

The answer also cannot be (C). In order for answer (C) to be correct, each statement must contribute a *separate* piece of useful information (since you have to use them together). In the example above, statement (1) doesn't provide any *new* information relative to statement (2), so the answer cannot be (C).

The answer has to be (B), (D), or (E).

Here is another example:

(1) $x = 10$

(2) x is even.

This time, statement (1) is the Cannibal: if you know that $x = 10$, then you also know that x is even. Statement (2) gets cannibalized, so the answer cannot be (B) or (C).

If, at any point, you become aware that the information given in one statement is already 100% covered by the other statement, immediately cross off two answers: answer (C) and the answer that "goes with" the statement that was cannibalized:

- If statement (1) gets cannibalized, cross off answers (A) and (C).
- If statement (2) gets cannibalized, cross off answers (B) and (C).

If you end up having to guess, you'll be down to just three answers. Of the three remaining answers, the best guess is the one associated with the Cannibal—either (A) or (B)—since that statement provides at least two pieces of relevant information.

Situation 3: You suspect a C-Trap.

If it seems very clear to you that using the two statements together would be sufficient—it would have been obvious when you were 12 and first learning this math!—then be on the lookout for a possible C-Trap. If you suspect there may be a C-Trap even though you can't figure out why or which statement does work alone, then don't guess answers (C) or (E).

Next, decide which of the two statements contains the more complicated information. This one is the one more likely to work on its own (similar to the Cannibal), so choose the corresponding answer. For example, if statement (1) has the more complicated info, choose answer (A). If, on the other hand, statement (2) looks more complex, choose choice (B).

Problem Set

It's time to practice your Data Sufficiency skills.

1. If $y > 0$, what is the value of y ?

   (1) $y^2 \leq y$

   (2) y is an integer.

2. If $a \neq bc$, what is the value of $\frac{(a+bc)}{(a-bc)}$?

   (1) $abc = 32$

   (2) $a + b + c = 12$

3. If n is a one-digit positive integer, what is n ?

   (1) The units digit of 4^n is 4.

   (2) The units digit of n^4 is n.

4. If $x = 300 - y - z$, what is the value of x ?

   (1) $y = \frac{(x+z)}{2}$

   (2) $x = \frac{(y+z)}{2}$

5. 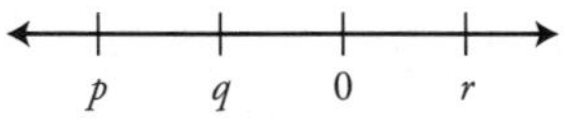

   If points p, q, and r appear on a number line as shown above, is $p < -5$?

   (1) The distance between p and r on the number line is at least 5.

   (2) The distance between p and q on the number line is at least 5.

Save the next problems for review after you finish this entire guide.

6. If x and y are integers, what is $x + y$?

   (1) $3^x = 81$

   (2) $5^x = \frac{25}{5^y}$

7. If x is a positive integer, what is the units digit of x ?

   (1) The units digit of $\frac{x}{10}$ is 4.

   (2) The tens digit of $10x$ is 5.

8. If x and y are integers, what is the value of $x^2 + 2xy + y^2$?

   (1) $x + y = 7$

   (2) $2x = \frac{28 - 4y}{2}$

Solutions

1. **(C):** The question stem allows any positive values for y, including fractions. The second statement is considerably easier than the first, so you might choose to start there.

   (2) INSUFFICIENT: The statement indicates that y is an integer. The value of y could be 1, 2, 14, 192, or any other positive integer.

   (1) INSUFFICIENT: What numbers make $y^2 \le y$ true?

   Case 1: If $y = 1$, then $1 \le 1$. Therefore, 1 is a possible value for y.

   Case 2: If $y = \frac{1}{2}$, then $\frac{1}{4} \le \frac{1}{2}$. Therefore, $\frac{1}{2}$ is a possible value for y.

   There are at least two possible values for y.

   (1) AND (2) SUFFICIENT: Together, the two statements eliminate the fraction case $y = \frac{1}{2}$, but $y = 1$ is still a valid case. In order for $y^2 \le y$ to be true, y must equal 0, 1, or a fraction between 0 and 1. Because y is a positive integer, it cannot be 0 or a fraction. The two statements together, then, are sufficient to answer the question: The value of y is 1.

   The correct answer is **(C)**: The two statements together are sufficient, but neither one works alone.

2. **(E):** Why does the problem indicate that a doesn't equal bc ? If that were true, then the bottom of the fraction could be 0—and the GMAT doesn't divide by 0. So you don't need to write that piece of information down. Do write down the question stem, and just note that it's a big combo. If you can find the value of a and bc, then you can solve. Or if you can find the whole combo $\frac{(a + bc)}{(a - bc)}$, then you can solve.

   (1) INSUFFICIENT: This statement doesn't allow you to re-create the whole big combo or to find a separately from bc.

   (2) INSUFFICIENT: This statement doesn't allow you to re-create the whole big combo or to find a separately from bc.

   (1) AND (2) INSUFFICIENT: You've got two equations with three variables, so you can't find each individual variable, and that means you can't find a separately from bc. Can you find the whole big combo? Try finding just $a + bc$ first.

   Rearrange the first equation: $a = \frac{32}{bc}$. Plug that into the second equation: $\frac{32}{bc} + b + c = 12$. Hmm. The variable a has disappeared now and there isn't a way to find the combo bc or the individual values b and c from this. There isn't a way to rearrange the information to get a by itself, bc, $a + bc$, or $a - bc$, so even using the two statement together, there's no way to solve.

   The correct answer is **(E)**: Both statements together are still not sufficient.

10

3. **(E):** If n is a one-digit positive integer, it has to be 1, 2, 3, 4, 5, 6, 7, 8, or 9.

(1) INSUFFICIENT: The units digit of 4^n is 4.

Case	n	The units digit of 4^n is 4.	What is n ?
#1	1	$4^1 = 4$ ✓	1
#2	2	~~$4^2 = 16$~~ ✗	invalid case
#3	3	$4^3 = 64$ ✓	3

Since n could be 1 or 3, statement (1) is not sufficient. (You might notice a pattern. It turns out that every n = odd will return a units digit of 4. Every n = even will return a units digit of 6.)

(2) INSUFFICIENT: The units digit of n^4 is n.

Case	n	The units digit of n^4 is n.	What is n ?
#1	1	$1^4 = 1$ ✓	1
#2	2	~~$2^4 = 16$~~ ✗	invalid case
#3	3	~~$3^4 = 81$~~ ✗	invalid case

You can continue to test each possible value for n in order, or you can think about any patterns you know for raising a number to a power.

For example, raising 5 to any power will always return a number that ends in 5. Therefore, 5^4 will end in 5, so 5 is a valid number for n:

n	The units digit of n^4 is n.	What is n ?
5	$5^4 = 625$ ✓	5

Because there are at least two possible values for n, statement (2) is not sufficient.

(1) AND (2) INSUFFICIENT: Both statements allow $n = 1$. Statement (2) does not allow 3, but does allow 5. Does $n = 5$ work for statement (1)?

n	The units digit of 4^n is 4.	What is n ?
5	4^5 = (ends in 4) ✓	4

Note that you do *not* actually multiply out 4^5. Instead, note the pattern:

4^n	Units digit
4^1	4
4^2	6
4^3	4
4^4	6

This pattern repeats to infinity: 4 to any positive odd integer has a units digit of 4.

Because both 1 and 5 work for each statement, even the two statements together are not sufficient to answer the question.

The correct answer is **(E)**: Both statements together are still not sufficient.

4. **(B):** The question asks for the value of x but gives an equation that contains two other variables, y and z. Rephrase the question in terms of y and z.

   This is a little tricky. If you place parentheses around the y and z, be careful with the signs: $x = 300 - (y + z)$. The negative sign outside applies to both the y and the z inside. So the rephrased question is: What is x, or what is the combo $y + z$?

   (1) INSUFFICIENT: There are two equations and three variables, so you can't solve for each individual variable—but rearrange to see whether you can solve for the combo.

$$y = \frac{(x + z)}{2}$$
$$2y = x + z$$
$$2y - z = x$$

   This isn't the right combo, so this statement is not sufficient.

   (2) SUFFICIENT: Rearrange to see whether you can solve for the combo:

$$x = \frac{(y + z)}{2}$$
$$2x = y + z$$

   The right side matches the combo, so plug this into the equation given in the question stem to see what happens:

$$x = 300 - (y + z)$$
$$x = 300 - (2x)$$
$$x + 2x = 300$$

   That can be solved for a single value of x, so the correct answer is **(B)**: Statement (2) is sufficient, but statement (1) is not.

5. **(B):** When the GMAT provides a number line with a specific ordering of variables, you can assume that the variables do appear in that order on the line. In this case, the p and the q are both negative, and $p < q$. And r is positive. It's a Yes/No question: Is p less than -5?

   Note a few things. The problem does not specify that the variables are integers, so anything is possible, as long as you follow the constraints noted in the previous paragraph. Also, you can test cases on this problem; specifically, try to find a case in which the value for p is less than -5 and a case in which the value for p is equal to or greater than -5.

(1) INSUFFICIENT: If p and r are at least 5 apart, then p could be -10 and r could be 10; in this case, Yes, p is less than -5. Alternatively, p could be -2 and r could be 10; in this case, No, p is not less than -5. Eliminate answers (A) and (D).

(2) SUFFICIENT: This statement is almost identical to the first one—so although you still generally want to ignore statement (1) at this point, do pay attention to the similarity. Statement (2) changes just one thing: The variable r becomes the variable p. Look at the number line and compare what the two statements indicate: (1) says that the p-to-r distance is at least 5 and (2) says that the p-to-q distance is at least 5.

The distance from p to r is greater, so if the p-to-q distance is at least 5, then the p-to-r distance must be at least 5 as well. In other words, statement (2) is a Cannibal: It already fully incorporates statement (1). As a result, the answer cannot be either (A) or (C). Cross those off on your answer grid. (Answer (A) is already crossed off, but (C) isn't crossed off yet.)

Now, process statement (2). If p and q are at least 5 apart, then p could be -10 and q could be -4; in this case, Yes, p is less than -5.

Alternatively, p could be -4 and q could be...no, that would make q positive and that's not allowed. If q is -0.01, then p would be -5.01. No matter how close to 0 you make q, it's still the case that subtracting 5 will make p less than -5, so Yes, p must be less than -5.

The correct answer is **(B)**: Statement (2) is sufficient, but statement (1) is not.

6. **(B):** The question asks for the combo $x + y$ and specifies that x and y are integers.

(1) INSUFFICIENT: $3^x = 81$

You could solve for the value of x, but the statement does not provide any information about the value of y, so this statement is not sufficient. Don't solve for x now; check statement (2) first:

(2) SUFFICIENT:

$$5^x = \frac{25}{5^y}$$
$$(5^x)(5^y) = 25$$
$$5^{x+y} = 5^2$$
$$x + y = 2$$

Note that, if you do not do the math (or you do it incorrectly), you may think that this statement is not enough to answer the question. In that case, you may have fallen into a C-Trap: The two statements together are definitely enough, but the answer cannot be (C) because one of the statements works by itself.

The correct answer is **(B)**: Statement (2) is sufficient, but statement (1) is not.

7. **(B):** The question stem establishes that x is a positive integer and asks for the units digit of x. The units digit can consist of only a single digit: 0, 1, 2, 3, 4, 5, 6, 7, 8, or 9. Glance at the statements. This is a theory problem, so you can test cases to solve. Your goal will be to try to find cases that can give you different units digits for x.

(1) INSUFFICIENT: First, note that x is a positive integer but $\frac{x}{10}$ doesn't have to be an integer. The only requirement is that the units digit of $\frac{x}{10}$ is 4. For example, if $\frac{x}{10} = 4.5$, then x would be $(4.5)(10) = 45$. What happened? When dividing by 10, the digits each move one place to the right. In order for the 4 to be in the units digit after the division, the 4 must have started out in the tens digit of x. So any integer you try for x must have a 4 in the tens digit.

Case 1: $x = 45$. First, check that this makes the statement true: x does have a 4 as the tens digit, so $x = 45$ is a valid case to test.

Next, answer the question: What is the units digit of x? It's 5.

Case 2: What can you try that fits the facts in the problem but gives a different units digit as the answer? Try $x = 46$. This is valid because there is a 4 in the tens digit of x. What's the units digit? This time it's 6—a different value. Since there are at least two different values for the units digit of x, statement (1) is not sufficient. Cross off answers (A) and (D).

(2) SUFFICIENT: First, figure out what kinds of values for x are acceptable, given that the tens digit of $10x$ is 5. For example, if $x = 35$, then $10x$ is 350. If you multiply by 10, then all of the digits move one to the left. In order for the tens digit to be 5 after that multiplication, the 5 must have started out in the units digit. So any value you try for x must have a 5 in the units digit.

Wait! Don't try any cases yet. Go back and read that last sentence again.

If any acceptable case must have 5 in the units digit, you have your answer. The units digit of x is always 5.

The correct answer is **(B)**: Statement (2) is sufficient, but statement (1) is not.

8. **(D):** The question stem specifies that x and y are integers and asks what is the value of $x^2 + 2xy + y^2$? Since the expression is one of the common quadratic identities, write down the other form of this question: What is the value of $(x + y)^2$?

(1) SUFFICIENT: The work is made much easier if you recognized the quadratic identity and wrote down both forms. Knowing the value of $x + y$ is enough to find the value of $(x + y)^2$.

(2) SUFFICIENT: Glance at the equation. It contains an x and a y, but it's written in a much more confusing form than statement (1). Be suspicious when they do this; simplify:

$$\begin{aligned} 2x &= \frac{28 - 4y}{2} \\ 4x &= 28 - 4y \\ 4x + 4y &= 28 \\ x + y &= 7 \end{aligned}$$

Note that, after rearranging the second statement, the equation is identical to the equation given in the first statement: These are Identical Twins! In this circumstance, the answer must be either (D) or (E).

The correct answer is **(D)**: Each statement is sufficient by itself.

CHAPTER 11

Exponents

In This Chapter

- All about the Base
- Combining Exponential Terms with Common Bases
- Fractions and Exponents
- Factoring Out a Common Term
- Equations with Exponents
- Same Base or Same Exponent

In this chapter, you will learn all about how to work with exponents—including when dealing with integers, fractions, positives and negatives, and so on. You'll also learn steps to simplify equations with exponents.

CHAPTER 11 Exponents

The mathematical expression 4^3 consists of a **base** (4) and an **exponent** (3).

The base (4) is multiplied by itself as many times as the power indicates (3):

$$4^3 = 4 \times 4 \times 4 = 64$$

In other words, exponents are actually shorthand for repeated multiplication.

Two exponents have special names: The exponent 2 is called the square, and the exponent 3 is called the cube:

5^2 can be read as five squared ($5^2 = 5 \times 5 = 25$).

5^3 can be read as five cubed ($5^3 = 5 \times 5 \times 5 = 125$).

All about the Base

A Variable Base

Variables can also be raised to an exponent, and they behave the same as numbers:

$$y^4 = y \times y \times y \times y$$

Base of 0 or 1

0 raised to *any* power equals 0.
1 raised to *any* power equals 1.

For example, $0^3 = 0 \times 0 \times 0 = 0$ and $0^4 = 0 \times 0 \times 0 \times 0 = 0$.

Similarly, $1^3 = 1 \times 1 \times 1 = 1$ and $1^4 = 1 \times 1 \times 1 \times 1 = 1$.

If you are told that $x = x^2$, then x must be either 0 or 1.

A Base of −1

$(-1)^1 = -1$ $\quad$ $(-1)^2 = -1 \times -1 = 1$ $\quad$ $(-1)^3 = -1 \times -1 \times -1 = -1$

This pattern repeats indefinitely. In fact:

$(-1)^{\text{ODD}} = -1$ $\quad$ $(-1)^{\text{EVEN}} = 1$

A Fractional Base

Squaring a fraction is the equivalent of multiplying the fraction by itself. You can also distribute the exponent before multiplying. For example:

$$\left(\frac{3}{4}\right)^2 = \frac{3}{4} \times \frac{3}{4} = \frac{9}{16} \qquad \left(\frac{3}{4}\right)^2 = \frac{3^2}{4^2} = \frac{9}{16}$$

When a fraction between 0 and 1 is raised to a power, an interesting thing occurs: The value gets smaller, not larger! For example:

$$\left(\frac{3}{4}\right)^1 = \frac{3}{4}$$

$$\left(\frac{3}{4}\right)^2 = \frac{3}{4} \times \frac{3}{4} = \frac{9}{16}$$

$$\left(\frac{3}{4}\right)^3 = \frac{3}{4} \times \frac{3}{4} \times \frac{3}{4} = \frac{27}{64}$$

Notice that $\frac{3}{4} > \frac{9}{16} > \frac{27}{64}$. If the fractional base is positive, as you continue to increase the value of the power, the value of the fraction continues to decrease.

If the base fraction is negative, then raising it to either an even or odd power makes the fraction *larger*, but for slightly different reasons. Raising to an even power turns the fraction positive, and a positive fraction is larger than a negative one:

$$\left(-\frac{3}{4}\right)^2 = -\frac{3}{4} \times -\frac{3}{4} = \frac{9}{16}$$

But when you raise a negative base to an odd power, it actually becomes *less* negative, or closer to 0. Because of that, the new fraction is actually larger than the original:

$$\left(-\frac{3}{4}\right)^3 = -\frac{3}{4} \times -\frac{3}{4} \times -\frac{3}{4} = -\frac{27}{64}$$

In general, remember that raising any proper fraction (fractions between -1 and 1) to any power will result in a new fraction that is *closer* to 0. This is still true for negative fractions raised to even powers. They are still closer to 0; they just happen to be closer on the positive end of the number line.

A Decimal Base

Like proper fractions, decimals between 0 and 1 decrease as their exponent increases, while negative decimals increase as the exponents increase by becoming either positive or less negative:

$$(0.6)^2 = 0.36 \qquad (0.5)^4 = 0.0625 \qquad (0.1)^5 = 0.00001$$

$$(-0.6)^2 = 0.36 \qquad (-0.5)^4 = 0.0625 \qquad (-0.1)^5 = -0.00001$$

A Compound Base

Just as an exponent can be distributed to a fraction, it can also be distributed to a product:

$$10^3 = (2 \times 5)^3 = (2)^3 \times (5)^3 = 8 \times 125 = 1{,}000$$

This also works if the base includes variables:

$$(3x)^4 = 3^4 \times x^4 = 81x^4$$

More on Negative Bases

When dealing with negative bases, pay particular attention to PEMDAS. Unless the negative sign is inside parentheses, the exponent does not distribute. For example:

$$-2^4 \neq (-2)^4$$

$$-2^4 = -1 \times 2^4 = -16 \qquad (-2)^4 = (-1)^4 \times (2)^4 = 1 \times 16 = 16$$

As with a base of -1, any negative bases raised to an odd exponent will be negative, and any negative bases raised to an even exponent will be positive.

Combining Exponential Terms with Common Bases

The rules in this section *only* apply when the terms have the *same* base. All of these rules are related to the fact that exponents are shorthand for repeated multiplication.

Multiply Terms: Add Exponents

When *multiplying* two exponential terms with the same base, *add the exponents*. This rule is true no matter what the base is:

$$z^2 \times z^3 = (z \times z) \times (z \times z \times z) = z \times z \times z \times z \times z = z^5$$

$$4 \times 4^2 = (4) \times (4 \times 4) = 4 \times 4 \times 4 = 4^3$$

Fortunately, once you know the rule, you can simplify the computation greatly:

$$z^2 \times z^3 = z^{2+3} = z^5$$

Divide Terms: Subtract Exponents

When *dividing* two exponential terms with the same base, *subtract the exponents*. This rule is true no matter what the base is:

$$\frac{5^6}{5^2} = \frac{5 \times 5 \times 5 \times 5 \times \cancel{5} \times \cancel{5}}{\cancel{5} \times \cancel{5}} = 5 \times 5 \times 5 \times 5 = 5^4$$

Fortunately, once you know the rule, you can simplify the computation greatly:

$$\frac{x^6}{x^2} = x^{6-2} = x^4$$

Anything Raised to the Zero Power is Equal to 1

This rule is an extension of the previous rule. If you divide something by itself, the quotient is 1:

$$\frac{a^3}{a^3} = \frac{\cancel{a} \times \cancel{a} \times \cancel{a}}{\cancel{a} \times \cancel{a} \times \cancel{a}} = 1$$

Look at this division by subtracting exponents:

$$\frac{a^3}{a^3} = a^{3-3} = a^0$$

Therefore, $a^0 = 1$.

Any base raised to the 0 power equals 1. The one exception is a base of 0.

Note that you cannot raise 0 to the 0 power. $0^0 = \frac{0}{0}$, which is *undefined* (but the GMAT does not test undefined numbers, so you don't need to memorize this). Although the GMAT doesn't test undefined numbers directly, you may need to use the knowledge that you cannot divide by 0 when considering values for variables in a denominator.

Negative Exponents

The behavior of negative exponents is also an extension of the rules for dividing exponential terms. For example:

$$\frac{y^2}{y^5} = \frac{\cancel{y} \times \cancel{y}}{y \times y \times y \times \cancel{y} \times \cancel{y}} = \frac{1}{y^3}$$

Look at this division by subtracting exponents:

$$\frac{y^2}{y^5} = y^{2-5} = y^{-3}$$

Therefore, $y^{-3} = \frac{1}{y^3}$.

This is the general rule: *Something with a negative exponent is just "one over" that same thing with a positive exponent.* You can rewrite y^{-3} by taking the reciprocal of y and dropping the negative sign from the exponent:

$$y^{-3} \rightarrow \left(\frac{1}{y}\right)^3 \rightarrow \frac{1}{y^3}$$

Here are some additional examples of how to take the reciprocal and drop the negative sign:

$$\frac{1}{3^{-3}} = 3^3 \qquad \left(\frac{x}{4}\right)^{-2} = \left(\frac{4}{x}\right)^2 \qquad \left(\frac{x}{2}\right)^{-2} = \left(\frac{2}{x}\right)^2$$

Note that 0 to a negative power is undefined for the same reason that 0 to the power of 0 is undefined; both result in division by 0:

$$0^{-2} = \frac{1}{(0)^2} = \frac{1}{0} = \text{undefined}$$

Nested Exponents: Multiply Exponents

How can you simplify $(z^2)^3$? Expand this term to show the repeated multiplication:

$$\left(z^2\right)^3 = \left(z^2\right)\times\left(z^2\right)\times\left(z^2\right) = z^{2+2+2} = z^6$$

When you raise an exponential term to an exponent, multiply the exponents:

$$\left(a^2\right)^3 = a^{2\times 3} = a^6$$

Fractions and Exponents

There are four broad categories of fractions that all behave differently when raised to a power. The result depends on the size and the sign of the fraction, as well as on the power. While it is not necessary to memorize all of the cases below, it is important to understand how each case works so that you know what numbers to try when testing cases, if necessary.

Divide fractions up into these four categories: less than -1, between -1 and 0, between 0 and 1, and greater than 1:

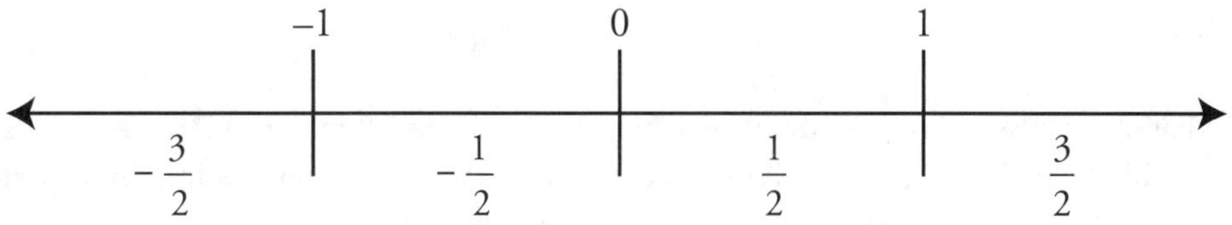

As you examine the math below, think about why the result is what it is.

Even Exponents (such as 2):

Less than -1	Between -1 and 0	Between 0 and 1	Greater than 1
$\left(-\frac{3}{2}\right)^2 = \frac{9}{4}$	$\left(-\frac{1}{2}\right)^2 = \frac{1}{4}$	$\left(\frac{1}{2}\right)^2 = \frac{1}{4}$	$\left(\frac{3}{2}\right)^2 = \frac{9}{4}$
$-\frac{3}{2} < \frac{9}{4}$	$-\frac{1}{2} < \frac{1}{4}$	$\frac{1}{2} > \frac{1}{4}$	$\frac{3}{2} < \frac{9}{4}$
Result is bigger.	Result is bigger.	Result is *smaller*.	Result is bigger.

If the exponent is even, then the fraction will get bigger in all circumstances except for one: when the fraction is between 0 and 1.

Odd Exponents (such as 3):

Less than -1	Between -1 and 0	Between 0 and 1	Greater than 1
$\left(-\frac{3}{2}\right)^3 = -\frac{27}{8}$	$\left(-\frac{1}{2}\right)^3 = -\frac{1}{8}$	$\left(\frac{1}{2}\right)^3 = \frac{1}{8}$	$\left(\frac{3}{2}\right)^3 = \frac{27}{8}$
$-\frac{3}{2} > -\frac{27}{8}$	$-\frac{1}{2} < -\frac{1}{8}$	$\frac{1}{2} > \frac{1}{8}$	$\frac{3}{2} < \frac{27}{8}$
Result is *smaller*.	Result is bigger.	Result is *smaller*.	Result is bigger.

If the exponent is odd, on the other hand, then there are two circumstances in which the fraction gets smaller: when the number is between 0 and 1 (as before) *and* when the number is less than -1.

11

Negative Exponents (such as –2):

To raise a fraction to a negative power, raise the reciprocal to the equivalent positive power:

$$\left(\frac{3}{7}\right)^{-2} = \left(\frac{7}{3}\right)^{2} = \frac{7^2}{3^2} = \frac{49}{9} \qquad \left(\frac{x}{y}\right)^{-w} = \left(\frac{y}{x}\right)^{w} = \frac{y^w}{x^w}$$

Factoring Out a Common Term

In most cases, exponential terms that are added or subtracted cannot be combined; for example, you can't combine these two terms: $2^3 + 3^4$. However, if two terms with the same base are added or subtracted, you can factor out a common term. In the following example, factor out 11^3:

$$11^3 + 11^4$$
$$11^3\left(11^0 + 11^1\right)$$
$$11^3(1 + 11)$$
$$11^3(12)$$

For any term that matches what you pulled out, an exponent of 0 is left behind; in this example, factoring 11^3 out of 11^3 leaves 11^0 behind. For all terms, the exponent becomes whatever is left behind. In the example above, 11^3 was pulled to the front, so the 11^4 term has 11^1 left over.

On the GMAT, it generally pays to factor exponential terms that have bases in common, and when doing so, factor out the smallest power. If the exponents are negative, factor out the term with the most negative exponent. Try this example:

If $x = 4^{20} + 4^{21} + 4^{22}$, what is the greatest prime factor of x?

To find the prime factors of *x*, express *x* as a product (terms multiplied together). Factor 4^{20} out of the expression on the right side of the equation:

$$x = 4^{20} + 4^{21} + 4^{22}$$
$$x = 4^{20}\left(4^0 + 4^1 + 4^2\right)$$
$$x = 4^{20}(1 + 4 + 16)$$
$$x = 4^{20}(21)$$
$$x = \left(2^2\right)^{20}(3 \times 7)$$
$$x = \left(2^{40}\right)(3)(7)$$

Now that *x* has been expressed as a product, you can see all of its prime factors: 2, 3, and 7. The greatest prime factor is 7.

If the terms are all identical, you can use a great shortcut. For example:

$$11^4 + 11^4 + 11^4$$

The official math works this way:

$$11^4 + 11^4 + 11^4$$

$$11^4\left(11^0 + 11^0 + 11^0\right)$$

$$11^4(1+1+1)$$

$$11^4(3)$$

Here's the shortcut: Count up the number of terms. In this case, there are three 11^4 terms. Multiply the term, 11^4, by the number of terms, 3: The answer is $11^4(3)$.

Equations with Exponents

Exponents can also appear in equations. In fact, the GMAT often complicates equations by including exponents or roots with unknown variables. Here are a few situations to look out for when equations contain exponents.

Even Exponents Hide the Sign of the Base

Any number raised to an even exponent becomes positive. For example:

$3^2 = 9$ AND $(-3)^2 = 9$

Another way of saying this is that an even exponent hides the sign of its base. Compare the following two equations:

$x^2 = 25$ $\quad\quad$ $|x| = 5$

Do you see what they have in common? In both cases, $x = \pm 5$. The equations share the same two solutions. In fact, there is an important relationship: **For any x,** $\sqrt{x^2} = |x|$.

Here is another example:

$a^2 - 5 = 12$ By adding 5 to both sides, you can rewrite this equation as $a^2 = 17$. This equation has two solutions: $\sqrt{17}$ and $-\sqrt{17}$.

You can also say that the equation $a^2 = 17$ has two roots (the word *root* is a synonym for the word *solution*). The GMAT will sometimes use the word *root*, so if this term is new to you, make yourself a flash card to help remember.

Also note that not all equations with even exponents have two solutions. For example:

$x^2 + 3 = 3$ By subtracting 3 from both sides, you can rewrite this equation as $x^2 = 0$, which has only one solution: 0.

Odd Exponents Keep the Sign of the Base

Equations that involve only cube roots or other odd exponents have only one solution:

$x^3 = -125$ Here, x has only one solution, -5, because $(-5)(-5)(-5) = -125$. This will not work with positive 5.

$243 = y^5$ Here, y has only one solution, 3, because $(3)(3)(3)(3)(3) = 243$. This will not work with -3.

If an equation includes some variables with odd exponents and some variables with even exponents, treat it as dangerous, as it is likely to have two solutions. Any even exponents in an equation signal two potential solutions.

Same Base or Same Exponent

In problems that involve exponential expressions on *both* sides of the equation, it is imperative to rewrite the bases so that either the same base or the same exponent appears on both sides of the equation. Once you do this, you can usually eliminate the bases or the exponents and rewrite the rest as an equation. Consider this example:

If $(4^w)^3 = 32^{w-1}$, what is the value of w?

To start, rewrite the bases so that the same base appears on both sides of the equation. Right now, the left side has a base of 4 and the right side has a base of 32. Both 4 and 32 can be expressed as powers of 2, so you can rewrite 4 as 2^2 and you can rewrite 32 as 2^5.

Next, plug the rewritten bases into the original equation:

$$\left(4^w\right)^3 = 32^{w-1}$$
$$\left(\left(2^2\right)^w\right)^3 = \left(2^5\right)^{w-1}$$

Now, simplify the equation using the rules of exponents:

$$\left(\left(2^2\right)^w\right)^3 = \left(2^5\right)^{w-1}$$
$$2^{6w} = 2^{5w-5}$$

When the bases are identical (and no other bases exist), you can drop the bases, rewrite the exponents as an equation, and solve:

$$6w = 5w - 5$$
$$w = -5$$

Be very careful if 0, 1, or -1 is the base (or could be the base), since the outcome of raising those bases to powers is not unique. For instance, $0^2 = 0^3 = 0^{29} = 0$. So if $0^x = 0^y$, you cannot claim that $x = y$.

Likewise, $1^2 = 1^3 = 1^{29} = 1$, and $(-1)^2 = (-1)^4 = (-1)^{\text{even}} = 1$, while $(-1)^3 = (-1)^5 = (-1)^{\text{odd}} = -1$. Fortunately, the GMAT rarely tries to trick you this way.

Problem Set

Now that you've finished the chapter, try the following problems.

For problems 1 and 2, determine whether the inequality is TRUE or FALSE.

1. $\left(-\frac{3}{4}\right)^3 > -\frac{3}{4}$

2. $\left(\frac{x+1}{x}\right)^{-2} > \frac{x+1}{x}$, if $x > 0$.

3. $x^3 < x^2$. Describe the possible values of x.

4. Simplify: $\frac{m^8p^7r^{12}}{m^3r^9p} \times p^2r^3m^4$

5. If $p = \frac{x^{a+b}}{x^b}$, what is the value of positive integer p ?

   (1) $x = 5$

   (2) $a = 0$

6. Which of the following expressions has the greatest value?

   (A) $(3^4)^{12}$

   (B) $\left[\left(3^{30}\right)^{12}\right]^{\frac{1}{10}}$

   (C) $3^{30} + 3^{30} + 3^{30}$

   (D) $4(3^{47})$

   (E) $\left(3^{90}\right)^{\frac{1}{2}}$

7. Simplify: $(4^y + 4^y + 4^y + 4^y)\ (3^y + 3^y + 3^y)$

   (A) $4^{4y} \times 3^{3y}$

   (B) 12^{y+1}

   (C) $16^y \times 9^y$

   (D) 12^y

   (E) $4^y \times 12^y$

8. If x and y are integers, what is $x + y$?

   (1) $3^x = 81$

   (2) $5^x = \frac{25}{5^y}$

9. If m and n are positive integers and $(2^{18})(5^m) = (20^n)$, what is the value of m ?

10. If $B^3A < 0$ and $A > 0$, which of the following must be negative?

(A) AB

(B) B^2A

(C) B^4

(D) $\frac{A}{B^2}$

(E) $-\frac{B}{A}$

11

Solutions

1. **TRUE:** Cubing a negative number will maintain the negative sign, so the left-hand side of the inequality will stay negative. Raising a fraction between 1 and -1 to a power causes that fraction to move closer to 0 on a number line. If the starting number is between 0 and 1, the fraction will get smaller as it moves closer to 0. However, if the starting number is between -1 and 0, as it is in this problem, then the number will get larger as it moves closer to 0.

   The value $\left(-\frac{3}{4}\right)^3$, therefore, will be to the right of $-\frac{3}{4}$ on the number line, or closer to 0. It is true that $\left(-\frac{3}{4}\right)^3$ is greater than $-\frac{3}{4}$.

2. **FALSE:** Test a case (a real number!) to understand what the problem is asking. Note that the problem states that x is positive. Any number $\frac{x+1}{x}$, where x is positive, will be greater than 1. Therefore, raising that number to a negative exponent will result in a number smaller than 1:

   If $x = 1$, then:

   $$\text{Is } \left(\frac{1+1}{1}\right)^{-2} > \frac{1+1}{1}\ ?$$

   $$\text{Is } (2)^{-2} > 2\ ?$$

   $$\text{Is } \left(\frac{1}{2}\right)^{2} > 2\ ?$$

   You can solve that last line, but you don't need to if you've learned how numbers work. A fraction between 0 and 1 raised to a positive exponent will always get smaller, so the left side of that inequality cannot be greater than the 2. The statement is false.

3. **Any non-zero number less than 1:** First, consider possible positive values. As positive fractions between 0 and 1 are raised to a power (multiplied together), their value decreases. For example, $\left(\frac{1}{2}\right)^3 < \left(\frac{1}{2}\right)^2$. So these types of fractions are possible values for x. The number 1 makes the inequality false, though, as does any positive number greater than 1.

   The number 0 does not work in this inequality as 0 raised to any power equals 0 (ignoring the case of 0 raised to the 0 power).

   Now consider negative numbers. A negative number cubed is negative. Any negative number squared is positive. For example, $(-3)^3 < (-3)^2$. By definition, any negative number is smaller than any positive number, so this inequality is true for all negative values.

4. $\boldsymbol{m^9p^8r^6}$**:** First, multiply the term on the right into the numerator of the fraction:

   $$\frac{m^8p^7r^{12}}{m^3r^9p} \times p^2r^3m^4 = \frac{m^{12}p^9r^{15}}{m^3r^9p}$$

   Then, simplify the top and bottom of the fraction:

   $$\frac{m^{12}p^9r^{15}}{m^3r^9p} = m^{(12-3)}p^{(9-1)}r^{(15-9)} = m^9p^8r^6$$

11

5. **(B):** Understand and Plan first. This question isn't really about p. It's about the expression $\frac{x^{a+b}}{x^b}$, which can be simplified by subtracting the exponent in the denominator from the exponent in the numerator:

$$\frac{x^{a+b}}{x^b} = x^{a+b-(b)} = x^a$$

So this question may be rephrased as a potential combo: What is x^a ?

You may need to know x and a individually in order for a statement to be sufficient. In certain cases, though, you would not need to know x and a individually. (As just one example, if x is 1, then a is not needed, because 1 to any power will always be 1.)

(1) INSUFFICIENT: Knowing that x is 5 is not sufficient without knowing a.

(2) SUFFICIENT: Anything to the 0 power is 1. The only exception to the rule is 0, because 0^0 is undefined. However, the problem states that p is a positive integer, so x cannot equal 0.

The correct answer is **(B):** Statement (2) is sufficient, but statement (1) is not.

6. **(D) 4(3^{47}):** Use the rules of exponents to simplify each expression:

(A) $(3^4)^{12} = 3^{48}$

(B) $\left[\left(3^{30}\right)^{12}\right]^{\frac{1}{10}} = 3^{\left(30\times12\times\frac{1}{10}\right)} = 3^{3\times12} = 3^{36}$

(C) $3^{30} + 3^{30} + 3^{30} = 3(3^{30}) = 3^{31}$ (Since both values have the same base, combine to get 3^{31}.)

(D) $4(3^{47})$ Cannot be simplified further.

(E) $\left(3^{90}\right)^{\frac{1}{2}} = 3^{\frac{90}{2}} = 3^{45}$

Answer choices (A) and (D) are larger than (B), (C), and (E). Compare (A) and (D):

(A) 3^{48}

(D) $4(3^{47})$

The difficult part to compare is the exponent. Is there any way to get the same exponent?

Factor one 3 out of answer (A): $3(3^{47})$. This is less than $4(3^{47})$, so answer **(D)** is greater.

11

7. **(B) 12^{y+1}:** Glance at the answers. There are no terms added together, so there must be some way to combine the individual terms in this problem. Factor out common terms from each expression. Use the terms-are-identical shortcut discussed in this chapter:

$$\left(4^y + 4^y + 4^y + 4^y\right)\left(3^y + 3^y + 3^y\right)$$
$$\left(4^y\right)(4)\left(3^y\right)(3)$$
$$\left(4^{y+1}\right)\left(3^{y+1}\right)$$
$$(4 \times 3)^{y+1}$$
$$12^{y+1}$$

8. **(B):** The question asks for the combo $x + y$ and specifies that x and y are integers.

(1) INSUFFICIENT: $3^x = 81$

You could solve for the value of x, but the statement does not provide any information about the value of y, so this statement is not sufficient. Don't solve for x now; check statement (2) first.

(2) SUFFICIENT:

$$5^x = \frac{25}{5^y}$$
$$\left(5^x\right)\left(5^y\right) = 25$$
$$5^{x+y} = 5^2$$
$$x + y = 2$$

Note that, if you do not do the math (or you do it incorrectly), you may think that this statement is not enough to answer the question. In that case, you may have fallen into a C-Trap: The two statements together are definitely enough, but the answer cannot be (C) because one of the statements works by itself.

The correct answer is **(B)**: Statement (2) is sufficient, but statement (1) is not.

9. **9:** With exponential equations such as this one, the key is to recognize that as long as the exponents are all integers, each side of the equation must have the same number of each type of prime factor. Break down each base into prime factors and set the exponents equal to each other:

$$\left(2^{18}\right)\left(5^m\right) = \left(20^n\right)$$
$$2^{18} \times 5^m = (2 \times 2 \times 5)^n$$
$$2^{18} \times 5^m = 2^{2n} \times 5^n$$
$$18 = 2n; \; m = n$$
$$n = 9; \; m = n = 9$$

Because m and n have to be integers, there must be the **same number of 2's** on either side of the equation and there must be the **same number of 5's** on either side of the equation. Thus, $18 = 2n$ and $m = n$.

10. **(A) *AB*:** This is a "must be" PS problem! You can test cases. A is positive, so call it $A = 2$. B^3A is negative. If A is positive, then the B^3 term must be negative. Call it $B = -1$.

Double-check that you chose numbers that follow the facts in the problem. A is positive and $B^3A = (-1)^3(2) = -2$. This is negative, which is what the problem states. Good, check the answers. Leave in anything that's negative. Cross off anything that's non-negative.

(A) $AB = (2)(-1) = -2$. Leave this in.

(B) $B^2A = (-1)^2(2) = 2$. Eliminate.

(C) $B^4 = (-1)^4 = 1$. Eliminate.

(D) $\frac{A}{B^2} = \frac{2}{(-1)^2} = 2$. Eliminate.

(E) $-\frac{B}{A} = -\frac{-1}{2} = \frac{1}{2}$. Eliminate.

Alternatively, you can think it through theoretically, if you feel comfortable with this math. Since A is positive, B^3 must be negative. Therefore, B must be negative. That specific answer isn't among the choices, so keep thinking. If A is positive and B is negative, the product AB must be negative.

CHAPTER 12

Roots

In This Chapter

- Roots and Fractional Exponents
- Simplifying a Root
- Imperfect vs. Perfect Squares
- Memorize: Squares and Square Roots
- Memorize: Cubes and Cube Roots

In this chapter, you will learn how exponents and roots are related, as well as how to manipulate and simplify both square and cube roots. You'll also learn about perfect squares and you'll memorize commonly used squares, cubes, square roots, and cube roots.

CHAPTER 12 Roots

Roots are the reverse of exponents. You can square something (multiply a number by itself) or you can take the square root of a number (find what number, multiplied by itself, would give you the starting number). For example, $4^2 = 16$ and $\sqrt{16} = 4$...but there's a little intricacy to the GMAT on that second part.

Compare the following two equations:

$$x^2 = 16 \qquad x = \sqrt{16}$$

Although they may seem very similar, there is an important difference. There are two solutions to the equation on the left: $x = 4$ or $x = -4$. There is only *one* solution to the equation on the right: $x = 4$.

If the GMAT itself gives you a square root symbol (e.g., $\sqrt{16}$), *only* use the positive root.

If, on the other hand, the equation contains a squared variable (e.g., x^2), and *you* take the square root, use both the positive and the negative solutions:

Given: $x^2 = 16$	$x = \sqrt{16}$
Solve: $x = \pm 4$	$x = 4$

This rule applies for any even root (square root, 4th root, 6th root, etc.). For example:

$$\sqrt[4]{81} = 3$$

Odd roots (cube root, 5th root, 7th root, etc.) also have only one solution.

Odd roots, like odd exponents, keep the sign of the base. For example:

If $\sqrt[3]{-27} = x$, what is x?

The correct answer is -3, because $(-3)(-3)(-3) = -27$.

By the way, the root symbol is also called a **radical sign**.

Roots and Fractional Exponents

Fractional exponents are the link between roots and exponents. For example:

$$\sqrt{x} = \sqrt[2]{x^1} = x^{\frac{1}{2}}$$

Any number that isn't raised to a power has an implied power of 1, so x can be written x^1. And any root can be written with that little number in the "v" of the radical sign, telling you which root to take (if no number is written there, a square root—or root of 2—is assumed).

Take those two numbers, the 1 and the 2, and write them as a fraction. The exponent of the base x is always the numerator of the fraction. The radical number is always the denominator of the fraction.

Try this problem:

What is $64^{\frac{1}{3}}$?

The numerator of the fraction is 1, so raise the base to the power of 1: 64^1. The denominator is 3, so take the cube root: $\sqrt[3]{64^1}$. In order to determine that root, break 64 down:

$$64 = 4 \times 4 \times 4 = 4^3$$

The value 64 is equal to 4^3, so $64^{\frac{1}{3}} = \sqrt[3]{64} = \sqrt[3]{4^3} = 4^{\left(\frac{3}{3}\right)} = 4^1 = 4$.

As a shortcut, if a number is raised to a certain power and also rooted to that same value, you can cancel out the power and the root. In this case, 4 is raised to the power of 3 but also cube-rooted, so cancel the two operations out to get 4.

Try another one:

What is $\left(\frac{1}{8}\right)^{-\frac{4}{3}}$?

Because the exponent is negative, first take the reciprocal of the base, $\left(\frac{1}{8}\right)$, and change the exponent to its positive equivalent. Next, deal with the root and the power. You can do them in whichever order is easier for you:

$$\left(\frac{1}{8}\right)^{-\frac{4}{3}} = 8^{\frac{4}{3}} = \sqrt[3]{8^4} = \left(\sqrt[3]{8}\right)^4 = (2)^4 = 16$$

Above, it's easier to take the cube first, so move that exponent of 4 to the outside. Take the cube root of 8 (which is 2) and then raise the result to the power of 4.

Try one more:

Express $\sqrt[4]{\sqrt{x}}$ as a fractional exponent.

Transform the individual roots into exponents. The square root is equivalent to an exponent of $\frac{1}{2}$, and the fourth root is equivalent to an exponent of $\frac{1}{4}$:

$$\sqrt[4]{\sqrt{x}} = \sqrt[4]{x^{\frac{1}{2}}} = \left(x^{\frac{1}{2}}\right)^{\frac{1}{4}} = x^{\frac{1}{8}}$$

The value $x^{\frac{1}{8}}$ can also be written as $\sqrt[8]{x}$.

Simplifying a Root

Sometimes there are two numbers inside the radical sign that you'd like to combine, if possible. Other times, you may have two different radical signs to simplify. There are certain rules to follow regarding when you can and cannot simplify.

When Can You Simplify Roots?

12

You can only simplify roots in the ways described below when the roots are connected via multiplication or division. If two roots are added or subtracted, you cannot use this method.

How Can You Simplify Roots?

When multiplying roots, you can split up a larger product into its separate factors, saving you from having to compute large numbers. For example:

$$\sqrt{25 \times 16} = \sqrt{25} \times \sqrt{16} = 5 \times 4 = 20$$

$\sqrt{25} \times \sqrt{16}$

$5 \times 4 = 20$

There are two numbers under the same radical sign and each one is a perfect square. Because they are multiplied together, you can take the square root of each first and then multiply them. Here's another example:

$$\sqrt{50} \times \sqrt{18} = \sqrt{50 \times 18} = \sqrt{2 \times 25 \times 2 \times 9} = \sqrt{4 \times 25 \times 9} = 2 \times 5 \times 3 = 30$$

First, the two numbers are not under the same radical, but because they are multiplied, you can combine them under one radical. Next, 50 and 18 are not perfect squares. In this case, break down the numbers into factors and recombine in order to find any perfect squares, then take the square root.

Division of roots works the same way. You can split a larger quotient into two parts. You can also combine two roots that are being divided into a single root. For example:

$$\sqrt{\frac{144}{16}} = \frac{\sqrt{144}}{\sqrt{16}} = \frac{12}{4} = 3$$

$$\frac{\sqrt{72}}{\sqrt{8}} = \sqrt{\frac{72}{8}} = \sqrt{9} = 3$$

However, if the two numbers are added or subtracted, you *cannot* split them apart or put them together. You have to leave them as they are. For example:

$\sqrt{16+9}$	$\rightarrow$	$\sqrt{16} + \sqrt{9}$	
$\sqrt{25}$		$4 + 3$	This move is illegal.
5	$\neq$	7	

$\sqrt{16} + \sqrt{9}$	$\rightarrow$	$\sqrt{16+9}$	So is the reverse.
7	$\neq$	5	

You may only separate or combine the *product* (×) or *quotient* (÷) of two roots. You cannot separate or combine the *sum* or *difference* of two roots.

In this case, first add the numbers together, then take the square root:

$$\sqrt{16+9} = \sqrt{25} = 5$$

In this case, first take the square root, then add:

$$\sqrt{16} + \sqrt{9} = 4 + 3 = 7$$

You *can* add two terms together if they have the same value under square root signs. Add only the numbers in front of the roots:

$$2\sqrt{3} + 4\sqrt{3} = 6\sqrt{3}$$

Treat the stuff under the root similar to a variable: $2x + 3x = 5x$. In other words, two x terms plus three x terms gives you five x terms. In the same way, above, two $\sqrt{3}$ terms plus four $\sqrt{3}$ terms gives you six $\sqrt{3}$ terms.

Imperfect vs. Perfect Squares

Not all square roots yield an integer. For example, $\sqrt{52}$ is the root of an imperfect square. It will not yield an integer answer because no integer multiplied by itself will yield 52.

Simplifying Roots of Imperfect Squares

Some imperfect squares can be simplified into multiples of smaller square roots. For an imperfect square such as $\sqrt{52}$, you can rewrite $\sqrt{52}$ as a product of primes under the radical:

$$\sqrt{52} = \sqrt{2 \times 2 \times 13}$$

Since this is a *square* root, look for *pairs* of numbers under the radical. In this case, there is a pair of 2's. Since $\sqrt{2 \times 2} = \sqrt{4} = 2$, you can rewrite $\sqrt{52}$ as follows:

$$\sqrt{52} = \sqrt{4 \times 13} = 2 \times \sqrt{13} = 2\sqrt{13}$$

Basically, identify a pair. Then, pull one of the pair out in front of the radical and eliminate the other number in the pair. Leave any unpaired numbers (13, in this case) under the radical.

Look at another example:

Simplify $\sqrt{72}$.

You can rewrite $\sqrt{72}$ as a product of primes:

$$\sqrt{72} = \sqrt{2 \times 2 \times 2 \times 3 \times 3}$$

Since there are a pair of 2's and a pair of 3's inside the radical, you can pull out one of each:

$$\sqrt{72} = 2 \times 3 \times \sqrt{2} = 6\sqrt{2}$$

Memorize: Squares and Square Roots

Memorize the following squares and square roots, as they often appear on the GMAT. If rote memorization is not a strength for you, take the time to learn the squares that are most likely to pop up on the GMAT: 1 through 12, as well as 15 and 20.

$1^2 = 1$	$\sqrt{1} = 1$
$1.4^2 \approx 2$	$\sqrt{2} \approx 1.4$
$1.7^2 \approx 3$	$\sqrt{3} \approx 1.7$
$2^2 = 4$	$\sqrt{4} = 2$
$3^2 = 9$	$\sqrt{9} = 3$
$4^2 = 16$	$\sqrt{16} = 4$
$5^2 = 25$	$\sqrt{25} = 5$
$6^2 = 36$	$\sqrt{36} = 6$
$7^2 = 49$	$\sqrt{49} = 7$
$8^2 = 64$	$\sqrt{64} = 8$
$9^2 = 81$	$\sqrt{81} = 9$
$10^2 = 100$	$\sqrt{100} = 10$
$11^2 = 121$	$\sqrt{121} = 11$
$12^2 = 144$	$\sqrt{144} = 12$
$13^2 = 169$	$\sqrt{169} = 13$
$14^2 = 196$	$\sqrt{196} = 14$
$15^2 = 225$	$\sqrt{225} = 15$
$16^2 = 256$	$\sqrt{256} = 16$
$20^2 = 400$	$\sqrt{400} = 20$
$25^2 = 625$	$\sqrt{625} = 25$
$30^2 = 900$	$\sqrt{900} = 30$

Memorize: Cubes and Cube Roots

Memorize the following cubes and cube roots, as they often appear on the GMAT:

$1^3 = 1$	$\sqrt[3]{1} = 1$
$2^3 = 8$	$\sqrt[3]{8} = 2$
$3^3 = 27$	$\sqrt[3]{27} = 3$
$4^3 = 64$	$\sqrt[3]{64} = 4$
$5^3 = 125$	$\sqrt[3]{125} = 5$
$10^3 = 1{,}000$	$\sqrt[3]{1{,}000} = 10$

Problem Set

Now that you've finished the chapter, try the following problems.

1. For each of these statements, indicate whether the statement is TRUE or FALSE:

   (a) If $x^2 = 11$, then $x = \sqrt{11}$.

   (b) If $x^3 = 11$, then $x = \sqrt[3]{11}$.

   (c) If $x^4 = 16$, then $x = 2$.

   (d) If $x^5 = 32$, then $x = 2$.

2. $\sqrt{18} \div \sqrt{2}$

3. $\left(\frac{1}{125}\right)^{-\frac{1}{3}}$

4. $\sqrt{63} + \sqrt{28}$

5. $\sqrt[3]{100 - 36}$

6. Estimate: $\sqrt{60}$

   (A) 6.5

   (B) 7.7

   (C) 8.2

7. $\sqrt{150} - \sqrt{96}$

8. $10\sqrt{12} \div 2\sqrt{3}$

   (A) 4

   (B) 10

   (C) $10\sqrt{2}$

   (D) $10\sqrt{3}$

9. $\frac{\sqrt[4]{64}}{\sqrt[4]{4}}$

10. If $xy \neq 0$ and $\sqrt{\frac{xy}{3}} = x$, what is y?

    (1) $\frac{x}{y} = \frac{1}{3}$

    (2) $x = 3$

Solutions

1. (a) **FALSE:** The problem gave you x^2, so you may have two roots, positive and negative. The exponent of 2 is even, so indeed there are both positive and negative roots. If $x^2 = 11$, then $|x| = \sqrt{11}$. Thus, x could be either $\sqrt{11}$ or $-\sqrt{11}$.

   (b) **TRUE:** Odd exponents preserve the sign of the original expression. Therefore, if x^3 is positive, then x must itself be positive. If $x^3 = 11$, then x must be $\sqrt[3]{11}$.

   (c) **FALSE:** Even exponents hide the sign of the original number, so both positive and negative answers are possible. If $x^4 = 16$, then x could be either 2 or -2.

   (d) **TRUE:** Odd exponents preserve the sign of the original expression. Therefore, if x^5 is positive, then x must itself be positive. If $x^5 = 32$, then x must be 2.

2. **3:**

$$\sqrt{18} \div \sqrt{2} = \sqrt{18 \div 2} = \sqrt{9} = 3$$

3. **5:**

$$\left(\frac{1}{125}\right)^{-\frac{1}{3}} = 125^{\frac{1}{3}} = \sqrt[3]{125} = \sqrt[3]{5 \times 5 \times 5} = 5$$

4. **$5\sqrt{7}$:** 7These two roots are added together, so you cannot combine them under one root to start. Simplify separately. At the end, you can combine them because the values under the roots are the same:

$$\sqrt{63} + \sqrt{28} = \left(\sqrt{9 \times 7}\right) + \left(\sqrt{4 \times 7}\right) = 3\sqrt{7} + 2\sqrt{7} = 5\sqrt{7}$$

5. **4:**

$$\sqrt[3]{100 - 36} = \sqrt[3]{64} = 4$$

6. **(B) 7.7:** The number 60 is in between two perfect squares—49, which is 7^2, and 64, which is 8^2. The answer, then, must be between 7 and 8 and only answer **(B)** qualifies.

   If you did have to estimate the answer more carefully, here's how: The difference between 64 and 49 is 15, so 60 is a little more than $\frac{2}{3}$ of the way toward 64 from 49. A reasonable estimate for $\sqrt{60}$, then, would be about 7.7, which is a little more than $\frac{2}{3}$ toward 8 from 7.

7. **$\sqrt{6}$:**

$$\sqrt{150} - \sqrt{96} = \left(\sqrt{25 \times 6}\right) - \left(\sqrt{16 \times 6}\right) = 5\sqrt{6} - 4\sqrt{6} = \sqrt{6}$$

8. **(B) 10:** You can solve algebraically or estimate. Here's the algebraic solution:

$$10\sqrt{12} \div 2\sqrt{3} = \frac{10\sqrt{4 \times 3}}{2\sqrt{3}} = \frac{20\sqrt{3}}{2\sqrt{3}} = 10$$

Alternatively, you could approximate the values of the square roots. Since 12 is about halfway between 3^2 and 4^2, use 3.5 as an estimate. Also, the square root of 3 is on the memorization list. It equals about 1.7:

$$\frac{10\sqrt{12}}{2\sqrt{3}} \approx \frac{10 \times 3.5}{2 \times 1.7} \approx \frac{35}{3.4} \approx 10$$

Answer **(B)** is the same as the estimate.

9. **2:**

$$\frac{\sqrt[4]{64}}{\sqrt[4]{4}} = \sqrt[4]{\frac{64}{4}} = \sqrt[4]{16} = 2$$

Note: Since the problem started you with a square root sign, solve for only the positive value.

10. **(B):** The question asks for the value of y, so isolate y in the given equation:

$$\sqrt{\frac{xy}{3}} = x$$

$$\frac{xy}{3} = x^2$$

$$xy = 3x^2 \quad \text{It's okay to divide by } x \text{ since you know that } x \text{ is not } 0.$$

$$y = 3x$$

In other words, if you can find the value of x, then you can also find the value of y. Rephrase the question: What is y or what is x?

(1) INSUFFICIENT: Statement (1) provides the value of $\frac{x}{y}$, but does not provide the value of x and y individually. For example, x could be 1 and y could be 3, or x could be 2 and y could be 6. There are at least two different values for y (or for x), so this statement is not sufficient.

(2) SUFFICIENT: Given x, you can find y.

This problem is a reminder that sometimes what might appear to be a combo question might just involve "school" algebra of solving for a single variable.

The correct answer is **(B)**: Statement (2) is sufficient, but statement (1) is not.

CHAPTER 13

Strategy: Arithmetic vs. Algebra 2

In This Chapter

- Good Numbers for Test Cases
- Good Numbers for Smart Numbers
- Problem Solving: Pop Quiz
- Avoid 0 or 1 When Choosing Smart Numbers

In this chapter, you will learn how to select good numbers when using the Test Cases or Smart Numbers strategies.

CHAPTER 13 Strategy: Arithmetic vs. Algebra 2

In an earlier strategy chapter, you learned three ways to turn an algebra problem into an arithmetic (real numbers) problem: Test Cases (TC), Smart Numbers (SN), and Work Backwards (WB). Two of these three types, TC and SN, require you to choose your own numbers and that's the focus of this chapter. (For the third, WB, you'll use the values given in the answer choices.)

One important note: At first, you may find yourself avoiding these test-taking approaches and instead using the textbook approaches that worked for you in school. You've practiced algebra for years, after all, and you've only been using these test-taking techniques for a short period of time. Keep practicing; you'll get better! Every high scorer on the Quant section will tell you that using these strategies where appropriate is invaluable to getting through Quant on time and with a sufficiently consistent performance to reach a top score.

Let's start with a summary of each of the three strategies.

Test Cases

- Data Sufficiency: Use when the problem allows multiple possible values for the unknowns. Try at least two different cases to see whether you can get a different answer (Yes *and* No; two *different* values).
- Problem Solving: Use when the problem asks a *must be* or *could be* question. Test cases until only one answer choice remains.

Choose Smart Numbers

- Problem Solving only
- When you see variable expressions or relative values (such as percents, fractions, ratios) in the answers, check the problem to see whether you can use smart numbers.
- If the problem never gives you a real number for that variable or relative value, you can use smart numbers.

Work Backwards

- Problem Solving only
- When the answer choices are relatively "nice" real numbers, check the problem to see whether you can work backwards.

- If the problem asks you to solve for what would be a single variable (if you were to set things up algebraically), you can work backwards.
- Start from answer (B) or (D).

Working backwards allows you to use the numbers given in the answer choices, but for the first two methods, you'll need to decide what numbers to use—and the guidelines can vary based on the strategy and on what that problem is testing. Knowing how to pick good numbers will save you time and mental effort on the GMAT.

Good Numbers for Test Cases

When using the Test Cases (TC) strategy, your goal is to find two valid cases that result in different answers so that you can prove a statement insufficient (on DS) or prove an answer incorrect (on PS).

When testing cases, people usually start with a small positive integer; that's often a good idea. But it can also be useful to test numbers that have "weird" properties: 0, 1, negatives, primes, fractions between 0 and 1, and so on.

Weird numbers are good ones to try because weird properties often give you a different answer to the question—for example, a Yes and a No answer (on a Yes/No problem) or two different values (on a Value problem). On DS, as soon as you can find two different answers, you've proven that the statement is insufficient.

Consider this problem:

Is $c = d$?

(1) $cd = 1$

(2) $|c| = d$

Step 1: Understand. At a glance, it's DS. The question asks whether c and d have the same value; jot that down. Glance at the statements. There's an absolute value symbol in one, so negative vs. positive is probably going to come into play.

This is a "theory" problem; it uses variables to ask or say something about certain relationships, but there are no individual numbers that you're locked into using for c and d. Choose your own numbers to test out what would happen in various scenarios (or cases). In short, you can test cases!

Step 2: Plan. Given that absolute value symbol in statement (2), try a negative number. It's also a good idea to pause and ask yourself: What kind of case will give a Yes answer and what kind of case will give a No answer?

In this problem, if c and d are the same number, the answer is Yes. If c and d are different numbers, the answer is No. Your goal when testing cases on this problem: Find one case where they are equal and one case where they're not equal.

Step 3: Solve. Now that you have a plan, do the necessary work to solve. Follow a few guidelines to set up your first case. First, you're only allowed to try numbers that make the *facts* in the problem true. (The statements are always facts. Any givens in the question stem—*not* including the question itself—are facts.)

Second, try numbers that make your job easier. Third, try anything you like for your first case, but for your second case, pause and think about what kinds of other or weird numbers might give you a *different* answer.

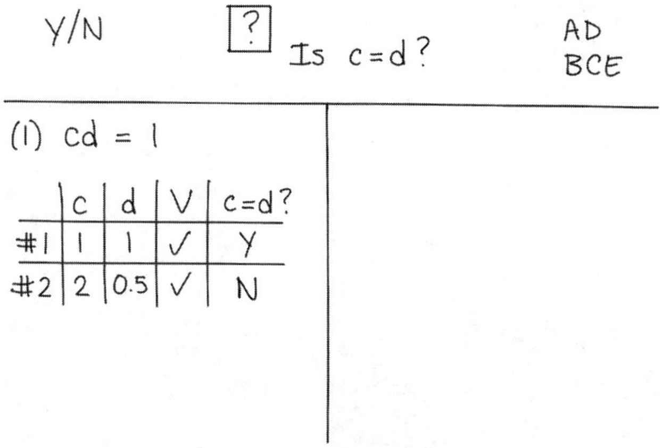

In the first case, start with the simplest weird numbers you can think of. For example, try $c = 1$ and $d = 1$. After you've chosen your numbers, pause for a moment to check that you chose Valid (V) numbers. Do your numbers fit all of the facts given in the question stem and in this statement? (Don't include the second statement.)

The only fact so far is that $cd = 1$. The chosen numbers, $c = d = 1$, correlate with this fact, so your numbers are valid. Continue solving. In this first case, the answer is Yes: $c = d$.

Time to try a second case. Pause for a second. You just got a Yes answer. What would need to happen in order to get a No answer instead?

You would need to find a case in which c does not equal d. Can you think of a case for which $c \neq d$ and they multiply to 1? The product of reciprocals equals 1: $c = 2$ and $d = 0.5$. Pause to make sure this is a valid case; it is. This case gives a No answer. There are two different answers, so statement (1) overall returns a Sometimes Yes/Sometimes No answer; statement (1) is not sufficient to answer the question.

It doesn't matter in which order you try cases, as long as you're trying valid numbers. Try the first valid case you think of and see what answer you get. Then pause to think about what kinds of numbers might give you a different result and try that case next.

Now, test the second statement:

Y/N [?] Is c = d? ~~AD~~ BCE

(1) cd = 1

	c	d	V	c=d?
#1	1	1	✓	Y
#2	2	0.5	✓	N

(NS)

(2) |c| = d

	c	d	V	c=d?
#1	1	1	✓	Y
#2	-1	1	✓	N

Since this statement contains an absolute value symbol, try negatives where you can—though it's fine to begin with the "simpler" $c = d = 1$ case, which is a valid case and yields a Yes answer for the second statement. What could give a No answer?

Try a negative! If $c = -1$ and $d = 1$, the answer is No ($c \neq d$), so statement (2) is not sufficient to answer the question. Cross off answer (B).

Put both statements together. First, scan the cases you've already tried. Did you try the same set of numbers for each statement? Yes, $c = d = 1$ worked for each statement individually, so this case will also work for the two statements together. There's your Yes case. Can you find a No?

(1 + 2)

#1: c = 1, d = 1 → Y

#2:

|c| = d

−1 or 1 → 1

−2 or 2 → 2

...

You can try some numbers to see—but first think about how the math works in order to figure out what numbers to try. Start with statement (2) because it has the weirder constraint. What kinds of numbers are allowed? The "plain" value (ignoring the positive/negative sign) must be the same for *c* and *d*—the only difference is that *c* could have a negative sign (but it might not).

What does that mean for statement (1)? This one says that they have to multiply to *positive* 1. In this case, both numbers have to have the same sign—either both positive or both negative:

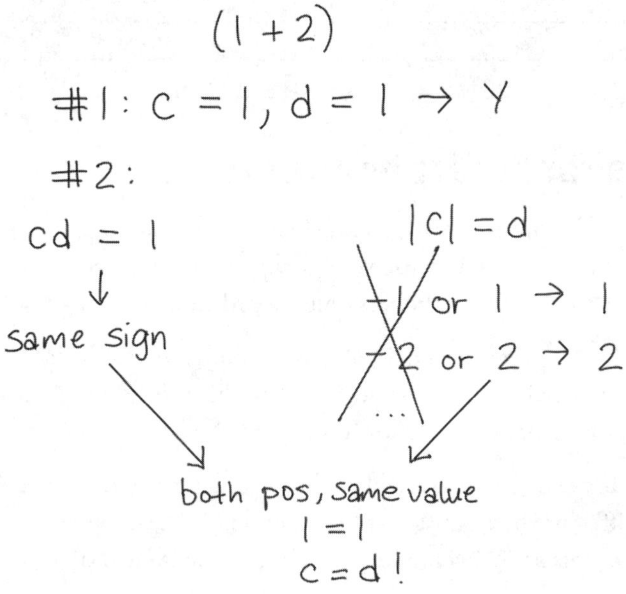

So the only possibility left from statement (2) is that the two numbers are the same. The case where *c* is negative and *d* is positive doesn't pass the test for statement (1)—that is, a negative *c* and a positive *d* would be an invalid case. And since the two values have to multiply to 1, *c* and *d* must each equal 1. Therefore, *c* must in fact equal *d*, always, using the two statements together.

The correct answer is (C).

Let's recap. When testing cases, your goal is to try to find two conflicting cases (e.g., a Yes and a No) in order to prove a statement insufficient (on DS) or an answer choice incorrect (on PS). As such, you want to try numbers that have certain weird characteristics that might serve to give you these different answers. What kinds of numbers? That will depend on clues you find in the specific problem you're trying to solve.

For example, the problem you just did had an absolute value symbol, so that was a clue to try negatives and positives.

In the Exponents chapter, you learned that squaring most numbers will make them larger—but that squaring a fraction between 0 and 1 will make that fraction smaller. In addition, squaring 0 or 1 will result in no change. So if you need to test cases on a problem that includes exponents, think about trying 0, 1, or fractions between 0 and 1 (as long as you're allowed to—you can only try numbers that are valid for the given facts in the problem).

Start keeping a list or make flash cards to help you remember the clues that will point you toward certain numbers to test.

On TC, when I see...	I'll try...
$\|x\|$	abs value: + and −
x^2	exponents: 0, 1, fractions

Good Numbers for Smart Numbers

The considerations for "good" numbers are different when you **choose smart numbers**. Here, you usually *don't* want to go for the weird numbers, because your goal is to pick numbers that will lead directly to the correct answer—so you don't want those numbers doing weird things in the middle of the problem.

When choosing numbers for SN, avoid 0 and 1. Also avoid numbers that already appear in the problem. (When you become very practiced, you may decide to break this rule and use one of these numbers for some very good reason—but for right now, follow these guidelines.)

If you have to pick values for two or more variables, choose different values for each variable. If appropriate, pick numbers that have different characteristics—for example, if the problem has some clue that causes you to think that even/odd concepts are being tested, then choose one even and one odd.

Finally, think about what's going on in the problem and try to choose numbers that will make your task easier.

Try this problem:

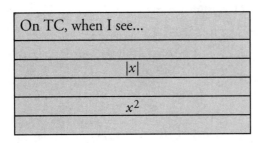

> A store sold a packet of 10 identical pens for a total of x dollars. The store originally purchased the packet of pens for 80% of the amount for which it sold the packet. In terms of x, how much profit did the store make on a single pen?
>
> (A) $\frac{x}{5}$
>
> (B) $\frac{x}{10}$
>
> (C) $\frac{4x}{5}$
>
> (D) $\frac{x}{50}$
>
> (E) $\frac{4x}{50}$

Step 1: Understand. At a glance, this is PS. The answers contain variables. Can you use smart numbers? Yes, the problem talks about a price for the pens but never mentions a real number for price anywhere along the way. The question asks how much *profit* was made on *one* pen. Finally, note that Profit = Revenue − Cost (the GMAT expects you to know this formula).

Step 2: Plan. Make your life easy and choose a number that will work nicely in the problem. You bought 10 pens for x dollars. The problem asks for the profit in terms of just 1 pen, not all 10, so you're going to need to divide by 10 at some point. Choose something that is a multiple of 10. Make this small but not 10 itself (in general, avoid choosing numbers that already appear in the problem). Try $x = \$20$.

Step 3: Solve. The store sold the 10 pens for a total of \$20, or \$2 per pen. The store earned a revenue of \$2 per pen.

Its *cost* for the pens was 80% of the sales price, so its *profit* is 20% of the sales price. Use benchmarks to find 20% of \$2:

$$100\% = \$2$$
$$10\% = \$0.20$$
$$20\% = \$0.40$$

The profit for one pen was \$0.40.

None of the answers say \$0.40 though. Plug $x = 20$ into the answers and look for the one that matches \$0.40. At any point that you can tell that a particular answer will *not* equal \$0.40, stop and cross off that answer:

(A) $\frac{x}{5} = \frac{20}{5} = \text{not } 0.4$

(B) $\frac{x}{10} = \frac{20}{10} = \text{not } 0.4$

(C) $\frac{4x}{5} = \frac{4(20)}{5} = \text{too big}$

(D) $\frac{x}{50} = \frac{20}{50} = 0.4 = \text{a match!}$

(E) $\frac{4x}{50} = \frac{4(20)}{50} = \frac{80}{50} = \text{too big}$

The correct answer is (D).

Here's the algebraic solution:

The store sold 10 pens for a total of x dollars, or $\frac{x}{10}$ dollars per pen. The store bought the pens for 80% of that sale price. Profit equals revenue minus cost:

$$(\text{Profit per pen}) = (\text{Revenue per pen}) - (\text{Cost per pen})$$
$$P = \frac{x}{10} - \frac{4}{5}\left(\frac{x}{10}\right)$$
$$P = \frac{x}{10} - \frac{4x}{50}$$
$$P = \frac{5x}{50} - \frac{4x}{50}$$
$$P = \frac{x}{50}$$

13

The correct answer is (D). That may seem like fewer steps, but it's harder to set up. And take a look at some of the wrong answers:

(A) $\frac{x}{5}$ Mistake: Assume x is cost per pen, instead of $\frac{x}{10}$.

(C) $\frac{4x}{5}$ Mistake: Assume x is cost per pen, instead of $\frac{x}{10}$, *and* solve for cost rather than profit.

(E) $\frac{4x}{50}$ Mistake: Solve for cost rather than profit.

It's very easy, when doing algebra, to make either of those mistakes—or both. And the most common algebraic mistakes are always built into the answers on PS. You have a much better chance of avoiding those mistakes when you are working with real numbers (because everybody is better at arithmetic than algebra).

As a general rule, if you find the algebra very easy, go ahead and solve that way. When the algebra becomes harder for you, though, then switch to smart numbers. If you realize you made a careless mistake with the algebra, that may be a signal to try smart numbers instead.

You can, of course, make careless mistakes whether using algebra or real numbers. Whichever approach you choose to use, do make sure to write down what your variables stand for (in the above, x = total \$) and double-check what you're solving for (profit for *one* pen).

Problem Solving: Pop Quiz

On Data Sufficiency, you can use only Test Cases. But on Problem Solving, you can use all three strategies, so part of your task will be to quickly identify which strategy is appropriate for any given question.

Pop Quiz! Take about 30 seconds to decide for both questions which strategy you could use. Then go ahead and try the two problems:

1. The price of a certain computer is increased by 10%, and then the new price is increased by an additional 5%. The new price is what percent of the original price?

   (A) 120%
   (B) 119.5%
   (C) 117%
   (D) 115.5%
   (E) 115%

2. If $ab > 0$, which of the following must be negative?

   (A) $a + b$
   (B) $|a| + b$
   (C) $b - a$
   (D) $\frac{a}{b}$
   (E) $-\frac{a}{b}$

Ready? What did you think?

Use...	When you see...
Test Cases	Data Sufficiency "theory" problem OR Problem Solving with a *must be* or *could be* question
Smart Numbers	Problem Solving with variables or relative values (percents, fractions, ratios) in the answers and *no* real numbers given for the variables or for items mentioned in the problem (e.g., number of cats, cups of sugar, dollars)
Work Backwards	Problem Solving with real values in the answers. The answer choices represent a single variable in the problem.

The first problem is a Smart Numbers problem and the second one is a Test Cases problem.

> The price of a certain computer is increased by 10%, and then the new price is increased by an additional 5%. The new price is what percent of the original price?
>
> (A) 120%
> (B) 119.5%
> (C) 117%
> (D) 115.5%
> (E) 115%

Step 1: Understand. PS with percentages in the answers. Check the problem: no real values given for the price. You can use smart numbers or solve algebraically.

Step 2: Plan. Think through what's going on. First, the price goes up 10%, and then the new price goes up another 5%. This is successive percent increase, so the increase is *not* just 10% + 5% = 15%. Further, it has to be *more* than 15% because the second (5%) increase is based on a larger starting number. Cross off answer (E).

Working algebraically on this problem is likely to be pretty annoying. Try choosing a smart number instead. Since this is a percent problem, use 100. (On percent problems in general, unless the number 100 shows up in the problem, it's a good idea to use 100 as your smart number.)

Step 3: Solve. Starting price is $100.

First increase: $100 + 10% = $100 + $10 = $110

Second increase: $110 + 5% = $110 + $5.50 = $115.50

Don't forget to use benchmarks when calculating percents! To get 5% of a number, take 10% and divide that by 2:

$$\text{Percentage: } \frac{\text{new}}{\text{orig}} \times 100 = \frac{115.5}{100} \times 100 = 115.5\%$$

Notice, at the end, how you both divide and multiply by 100, so they cancel out? This is why choosing 100 on a percent problem is a good idea.

The correct answer is (D).

The second problem was the Test Cases problem.

If $ab > 0$, which of the following must be negative?

(A) $a + b$

(B) $|a| + b$

(C) $b - a$

(D) $\frac{a}{b}$

(E) $-\frac{a}{b}$

Step 1: Understand. PS. Asks a *must be* "theory" question, so test cases. Jot down $ab > 0$.

Step 2: Plan. Think about the kinds of numbers that you could try: 0 and 1, fractions, negatives, etc. What would be good to try here?

Since the question asks what must be negative, you'd want to include negatives in the mix. Also, what does the inequality $ab > 0$ signify? Two things multiply together to be positive. First, that means neither variable can be 0, so don't try 0. It also means that the two numbers have to have the same sign, either both positive or both negative.

Step 3: Solve. Go straight for a negative-negative case:

$a = -1$

$b = -2$

(A) $a + b$	neg
(B) $\lvert a\rvert + b$	neg
(C) $b - a$	neg
~~(D) $\frac{a}{b}$~~	~~pos~~
(E) $-\frac{a}{b}$	neg

The question wants to know what must be negative, so cross off anything that's positive. When you're done, review any answers still in the mix to see what you might want to change in your next case in order to get a positive answer next time.

For example, choice (A) is negative for the first set of numbers, but you're allowed to choose positive numbers, too. And if you do, choice (A) will drop out. So will choice (B). You may even notice some of these things as you work through your first case; if so, jot down a reminder for what to use for your second case.

	$a = -1$, $b = -2$	$a = 2$, $b = 1$
~~(A) $a + b$~~	~~neg~~	~~pos~~
~~(B) $\|a\| + b$~~	~~neg~~	~~pos~~
(C) $b - a$	neg	neg
~~(D) $\frac{a}{b}$~~	~~pos~~	
(E) $-\frac{a}{b}$	neg	neg

Choices (C) and (E) both stayed negative. If you're going to use positive values, then you need variable *b* to be larger than variable *a* in order to get choice (C) to drop out. Prove it to yourself with a concrete case:

	$a = -1$, $b = -2$	$a = 2$, $b = 1$	$a = 1$, $b = 2$
~~(A) $a + b$~~	~~neg~~	~~pos~~	
~~(B) $\|a\| + b$~~	~~neg~~	~~pos~~	
~~(C) $b - a$~~	~~neg~~	~~neg~~	~~pos~~
~~(D) $\frac{a}{b}$~~	~~pos~~		
(E) $-\frac{a}{b}$	neg	neg	neg ✓

Finally! The correct answer is (E). No matter what you try, this one stays negative.

As you worked through the problem, you might have begun to "see" the theory. For instance, on that last step, you might have felt comfortable that answer (C) would drop out as soon as you made variable *b* larger than variable *a*. Any time you feel confident in your reasoning, it's okay not to plug in actual values to test. You're still testing the case—you're just using number characteristics rather than specific numbers.

Note one more thing. If you know that you're prone to careless mistakes on any specific kinds of math (e.g., absolute values or fractions), then write out the math itself, not just the "pos" and "neg" designations.

Everyone makes careless errors with some kinds of seemingly simple math. Know your own patterns to help you minimize mistakes!

Avoid 0 or 1 When Choosing Smart Numbers

For the Smart Numbers strategy, you've learned to avoid using 0, 1, or a number that appears elsewhere in the problem. Here's why. Try this example:

> A truck can carry x shipping containers and each container can hold y gallons of milk. If one truck is filled to capacity and a second truck is half full, how many gallons of milk are they carrying, in terms of x and y?
>
> (A) $x + 0.5y$
>
> (B) $x + y$
>
> (C) $0.5xy$
>
> (D) $1.5xy$
>
> (E) $2xy$

13

Step 1: Understand. PS. Variables in the answers. No real numbers in the problem. You can use smart numbers, if you like.

What's the actual story? One truck holds some number of shipping containers and each shipping container holds some number of gallons of milk. And there are two trucks. Sketch something out. It doesn't need to be pretty! Just use the sketch to help understand the story.

There are two trucks. One's full and the other is half full. Each one has the same number of shipping containers (how about 1?) and each container can carry...how about 3 gallons of milk?

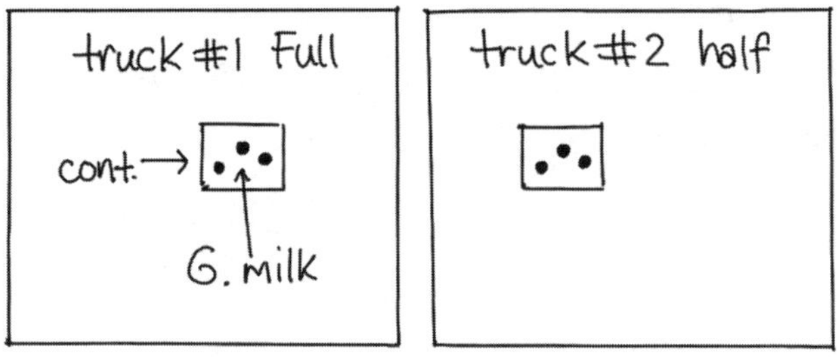

Don't worry at this stage about whether those are the right numbers to pick (it turns out that what's sketched above doesn't quite fit all the facts in the story—so you will have to adjust). Just focus on understanding the story first.

Step 2: Plan. Once you understand, you can decide what to do. The drawing shows $x = 1$ and $y = 3$. At this stage, you'd normally tell yourself, "Whoops, I'm not supposed to use 1 on smart numbers," but keep going so that you can see what could happen when you do.

Step 3: Solve. Okay, $x = 1$ and $y = 3$. Each truck has one shipping container. The first truck is filled to capacity, so it carries a total of 3 gallons of milk. The second is half full, so it carries 1.5 gallons...ugh, decimals are annoying.

That's okay! Just go back and tweak your drawing/numbers to give you integer values instead. What if $x = 1$ and $y = 2$, instead? Now, here's the scenario: The first truck is filled to capacity, so it has 2 gallons of milk. The second is half full, so it carries 1 gallon; together, the two trucks carry 3 gallons of milk.

Plug $x = 1$ and $y = 2$ into the answers to find the one that equals 3:

(A) $x + 0.5y = 1 + (0.5)(2) = 2$

(B) $x + y = 1 + 2 = 3$ Match!

(C) $0.5xy = (0.5)(1)(2) = 1$

(D) $1.5xy = (1.5)(1)(2) = 3$ Wait a second—this one matches, too!

(E) $2xy = 2(1)(2) = 4$

In rare circumstances, when using the Smart Numbers strategy, the number you choose could work for more than one answer choice. The odds are greatly increased if you choose 0, 1, or a number that already appears in the problem—so that's why you want to avoid those numbers when using the Smart Numbers strategy. (Incidentally, this is the same reason why you *do* want to use 0 or 1 when testing cases on PS. Because that can make multiple answers drop out at once!)

If you do get two answers that work, now what? If you think you've spent too much time already, guess between (B) and (D), the two answers that worked; you still have a 50/50 chance. Or, if you have time, try a different set of numbers in the problem—but you only need to check answers (B) and (D) when you get to the end.

Try $x = 2$ containers and $y = 3$ gallons of milk per container instead.

The first truck is now carrying $(2)(3) = 6$ gallons of milk. The second carries half that, or 3 gallons. Together, they carry 9 gallons of milk.

Try (B) and (D):

(B) $x + y = 2 + 3 = 5$ Not a match

(D) $1.5xy = (1.5)(2)(3) = 9$ Match!

The correct answer is (D).

If you follow the guidelines for choosing numbers, then the "two answers work!" situation is much less likely to occur:

- Avoid 0 and 1.
- Avoid numbers that appear elsewhere in the problem.
- If you have to choose multiple numbers, choose different numbers.

If you do accidentally find yourself in this situation and you have the time, then go back, change one of the numbers in your problem, and do the math again. If you don't have time, just choose one of the two answers that did work and move on.

Finally, this is important enough to repeat: At first, you may find yourself always choosing the textbook or algebraic approach. You've practiced algebra for years, after all, and you've only been using these test-taking techniques for a short period of time. Keep practicing; you'll get better!

Problem Set

Practice your test-taking strategies: Smart Numbers, Test Cases, Work Backwards. Try the algebraic/textbook way as well to compare methods. When you're done, ask yourself which way you prefer to solve *this* problem and why.

On the real test, you won't have time to try both methods; you'll have to make a decision and go with it. Learn *how* to make that decision while studying; then, the next time a new problem pops up in front of you, you'll be able to make a quick (and good!) decision about what to do.

1. Seamus has 3 times as many marbles as Ronit, and Taj has 7 times as many marbles as Ronit. If Seamus has *s* marbles, then, in terms of *s*, how many marbles do Seamus, Ronit, and Taj have together?

   (A) $\frac{3}{7}s$

   (B) $\frac{7}{3}s$

   (C) $\frac{11}{3}s$

   (D) $7s$

   (E) $11s$

2. Machine X produces cartons at a uniform rate of 90 every 3 minutes, and Machine Y produces cartons at a uniform rate of 100 every 2 minutes. Working simultaneously, the two machines would produce a total of 560 cartons in how many minutes?

   (A) 7

   (B) 6

   (C) 5

   (D) 4

   (E) 3

3. If $x = a + b$ and $y = a + 2b$, then what is $a - b$, in terms of x and y?

   (A) $2y - 3x$

   (B) $3y - 2x$

   (C) $2x - 3y$

   (D) $2x + 3y$

   (E) $3x - 2y$

4. If $x < y$, which of the following must be true?

   (A) $x < y^2$

   (B) $x^2 < y$

   (C) $x^2 < y^2$

   (D) $(x - y)^2 > 0$

   (E) $x^3 > y$

Save the next problems for review after you finish this entire guide.

5. A train travels at a constant rate. If the train takes 13 minutes to travel m kilometers, how long will the train take to travel n kilometers?

(A) $\frac{13m}{n}$

(B) $\frac{13n}{m}$

(C) $13mn$

(D) $\frac{n}{13}$

(E) $\frac{m}{13}$

6. A manager split a bonus award among four employees. The first employee received $\frac{1}{3}$ of the total, the second received $\frac{1}{4}$ of the total, the third received $\frac{1}{5}$ of the total, and the fourth received the remaining \$195. What was the total bonus amount awarded to the four employees?

(A) \$500

(B) \$600

(C) \$750

(D) \$900

(E) \$1,000

Solutions

1. **(C) $\frac{11}{3}s$:** The problem will be easier to solve if you can choose smart numbers that will give you all integers as you solve. Both Seamus and Taj have a multiple of the number of marbles that Ronit has, so begin by picking for Ronit, not for Seamus. If Ronit has 2 marbles, then Seamus has $(3)(2) = 6$ marbles and Taj has $(7)(2) = 14$ marbles. Together, the three have 22 marbles.

   Plug $s = 6$ into the answers (remember that the problem asks about Seamus's starting number, not Ronit's!), and look for a match of 22:

   (A) $\frac{3}{7}s =$ not an integer

   (B) $\frac{7}{3}s = \frac{7}{3}(6) = 14$. Not a match.

   (C) $\frac{11}{3}s = \frac{11}{3}(6) = 22$. Match!

   (D) $7s = 42$. Not a match.

   (E) $11s =$ too large

   Alternatively, you can use an algebraic approach. Begin by translating the first sentence into equations:

   $$s = 3r$$
   $$t = 7r$$

   The question asks for the sum of the three:

   $$s + r + t = ?$$

   The answers use only s, so figure out how to substitute to leave only s in the equation:

   $$r = \frac{s}{3}$$
   $$t = 7r = 7\left(\frac{s}{3}\right)$$

   Substitute those into the question:

   $$s + r + t$$
   $$s + \frac{s}{3} + 7\left(\frac{s}{3}\right)$$
   $$\frac{3s}{3} + \frac{s}{3} + \frac{7s}{3}$$
   $$\frac{11s}{3}$$

2. **(A) 7:** The answer choices are real numbers and they represent a single variable in the problem (how long it would take the two machines together to produce 560 cartons). Work backwards from the answers. Start with answer (B) or (D).

Minutes	X 90 cart in 3 min	Y 100 cart in 2 min	Total cartons produced	= 560 ?
(B) 6	180	300	480	No

Answer (B) is incorrect; in 6 minutes, the two machines will have produced only 480 cartons, not 560. Further, the number of minutes must be greater than 6 (in order for more cartons to be produced).

Only answer (A) is greater than 6, so it must be correct.

If you're not sure about that reasoning, try answer (D) next. In 4 minutes, the two machines produce 320 cartons, even fewer! This confirms the trend that a lower number of minutes will produce fewer cartons, so the answer must be **(A)**.

3. **(E) $3x - 2y$:** With so many variables, choosing smart numbers will probably be more efficient. Because x and y can be found by certain sums of a and b, pick for a and b, then calculate x and y.

If $a = 5$ and $b = 2$, then $x = 5 + 2 = 7$ and $y = 5 + 2(2) = 9$. The difference is $a - b = 5 - 2 = 3$.

Plug $x = 7$ and $y = 9$ into the answers and look for a match of 3:

(A) $2y - 3x = 2(9) - 3(7) = 18 - 21 =$ negative

(B) $3y - 2x = 3(9) - 2(7) = 27 - 14 =$ not 3

(C) $2x - 3y = 2(7) - 3(9) = 14 - 27 =$ negative

(D) $2x + 3y = 2(7) + 3(9) =$ too big

(E) $3x - 2y = 3(7) - 2(9) = 21 - 18 = 3$. Match!

You can also use an algebraic approach.

Given: $x = a + b$
Given: $y = a + 2b$
What is $a - b$?

The answers use only x and y, so figure out how to rewrite the given equations to plug into the question, using only x and y.

If you subtract the two equations, you'll get x and y in terms of b alone:

$$\begin{array}{r} y = a + 2b \\ -\,(x = a + b) \\ \hline y - x = b \end{array}$$

Multiply the $x = a + b$ equation by 2 and perform the same operation to get x and y in terms of a alone:

$$\begin{array}{r} 2x = 2a + 2b \\ -\,(y = a + 2b) \\ \hline 2x - y = a \end{array}$$

Then, find $a - b$:

$$(2x - y) - (y - x)$$

$$2x - y - y + x$$

$$3x - 2y$$

13

13

4. **(D) $(x - y)^2 > 0$:** The *must be* language signals that you can (and probably want to) test cases on this problem. The only constraint given is that x is less than y. The answers contain exponents and one contains > 0, so test negatives and fractions between 0 and 1, as well as 0 and 1 themselves.

Answer	$x = 0$, $y = 1$	$x = -1$, $y = 0$	$x = \frac{1}{4}$, $y = \frac{1}{2}$
(A) $x < y^2$	$0 < 1$ True	$-1 < 0$ True	(A) $\frac{1}{4} < \frac{1}{4}$ False
(B) $x^2 < y$	$0 < 1$ True	$1 < 0$ False	already eliminated
(C) $x^2 < y^2$	$0 < 1$ True	$1 < 0$ False	already eliminated
(D) $(x - y)^2 > 0$	$1 > 0$ True	$1 > 0$ True	(D) $\left(-\frac{1}{4}\right)^2 = \frac{1}{16} > 0$ True!
(E) $x^3 > y$	$0 > 1$ False	already eliminated	

Try the easiest combo first, something involving 0 and 1. That only knocks out one answer, but it helps you to think about what's going on with the math. Sometimes x is squared, sometimes y is squared, so put a negative number into the mix next. (Note: You no longer have to try answer (E); it drops out after the first case.)

When x is -1 and y is 0, two more answers drop out, but two are still left. Fractions between 0 and 1 do interesting things when squared, so try those next. In this final case, answer (A) is false. Answer **(D)** is true throughout all of the tests, so it's the correct answer.

5. **(B) $\frac{13n}{m}$:** The problem never provides a real number for the distance that the train travels, just the variables m and n, so you can choose your own smart number. A small number like 2 is often a good one to choose—but that turns out not to be a great number in this case. Why?

The train takes 13 minutes to travel 2 kilometers, so the train's rate is 2 kilometers per 13 minutes. That's not a nice number. Choose something that will result in an integer, such as $m = 26$ kilometers. Now, the train is going $\frac{26 \text{ km}}{13 \text{ min}} = 2\frac{\text{km}}{\text{min}}$.

Next, how long will the train take to go n kilometers? If $n = 10$, then the train will take 5 minutes to go 10 kilometers.

Find a match in the answers. Plug $m = 26$ and $n = 10$ into the answers. Your goal is to find an answer choice that equals 5. If you can tell that a certain answer will *not* equal 5, cross it off without calculating exactly what it does equal:

(A) $\frac{13m}{n} = \frac{13(26)}{10} =$ too big

(B) $\frac{13n}{m} = \frac{13(10)}{26} =$ maybe. Simplify to confirm: $\frac{1(10)}{2} = 5$ Match!

(C) $13mn = 13(10)(26) =$ too big

(D) $\frac{n}{13} = \frac{10}{13} =$ fraction

(E) $\frac{m}{13} = \frac{26}{13} = 2$. Not a match.

6. **(D) $900:** You can solve this problem algebraically or you can work backwards. You'd have to find a common denominator across three fractions to solve algebraically, so it may be faster to work backwards, since the fractions are relatively easy ones and the numbers in the answers are pretty nice. Start with answer (B).

	#1 $\left(\frac{1}{3}\right)$	#2 $\left(\frac{1}{4}\right)$	#3 $\left(\frac{1}{5}\right)$	#4 ($195)	Sum to the choice?
(B) 600	200	150	120	195	NO

To find a third, divide by 3. To find a fourth, divide by 2 twice. To find a fifth, or 20%, take 10% and double it.

The total won't be $600 because three of the numbers end in a 0 and the fourth ends in a 5, so answer (B) isn't correct. Is this answer too big or too small? Examine the first three figures—the ones that can actually change from answer choice to answer choice.

The first three figures add up to 470. If the total is 600, then the fourth person would get a bonus of 130. But the fourth person's bonus is actually 195, so this answer choice falls short. You need a larger number. Cross off answers (A) and (B) and try (D) next.

	#1 $\left(\frac{1}{3}\right)$	#2 $\left(\frac{1}{4}\right)$	#3 $\left(\frac{1}{5}\right)$	#4 ($195)	Sum to the choice?
(B) 600	200	150	120	195	NO
(D) 900	300	225	180	195	Yes!

This could be right, since two of the answers end in 5 now. Add them up, but make your job easier; 195 is an annoying value, so take 5 from the 225 and add it to the 195.

Don't do: $300 + 225 + 180 + 195$

Instead, do: $300 + 220 + 180 + 200 = 300 + 400 + 200 = 900$

The total matches the starting point, so this choice is the correct answer.

CHAPTER 14

Quadratic Equations

In This Chapter

- Factoring Quadratic Equations
- Disguised Quadratics
- Taking the Square Root
- Going in Reverse: Use FOIL
- One-Solution Quadratics
- Zero in the Denominator: Undefined
- The Three Special Products

In this chapter, you will learn how to factor and expand quadratic equations, and you'll memorize three special quadratics (known as the special products) that will save you time and mental energy on the GMAT. You'll also learn some common ways that the GMAT likes to disguise quadratic equations—and how to recognize and strip away those disguises.

CHAPTER 14 Quadratic Equations

One special type of equation is called the **quadratic equation**. Here are some examples of quadratic equations:

$$x^2 + 3x + 8 = 12 \qquad w^2 - 16w + 1 = 0 \qquad 2y^2 - y + 5 = 8$$

The standard form of a quadratic equation is $ax^2 + bx + c = 0$, where a, b, and c are constants and a does not equal 0.

Here are other ways of writing quadratics (in nonstandard form):

$$x^2 = 3x + 4 \qquad a = 5a^2 \qquad 6 - b = 7b^2$$

Like other even-exponent equations, quadratic equations generally have two solutions. That is, there are usually two possible values of x (or whatever the variable is) that make the equation *true*.

Factoring Quadratic Equations

The following example illustrates the process for solving quadratic equations:

If $x^2 + 3x + 8 = 12$, what is x?

To start, move everything to the left side of the equals sign so that the equation is equal to 0. Put the left side in the form $ax^2 + bx + c$ (where a, b, and c are typically integers on the GMAT):

$x^2 + 3x + 8 = 12$ Subtract 12 from both sides to set the right side to 0.

$x^2 + 3x - 4 = 0$

Next, factor the equation. In order to factor, you generally need to think about two terms in the equation. Assuming that $a = 1$ (which is often the case on GMAT quadratic equation problems), focus on the two terms b and c. (If a is not equal to 1, divide everything in the equation by a to make a equal to 1.)

$$x^2 + 3x - 4 = 0$$

Rewrite the equation in the form $(x + \quad)(x + \quad)$, where the blanks represent two spaces you're leaving for numbers that you're about to calculate.

In order to factor this equation, find two integers whose product is equal to c (-4 in this equation) and whose sum is equal to b (3 in this equation).

In the original equation, $a = 1$, $b = 3$, and $c = -4$. To fill in the blanks, find the pair of numbers that will *multiply* to -4 and *add* to $+3$. The GMAT will typically make these integers, so think in those terms. In order for c to be negative, the numbers in the blanks will have to have the opposite signs. Now think of the specific values that are possible:

$$x^2 + 3x - 4 = 0$$

$$(x + \quad)(x - \quad) = 0$$

For example, 2 and -2 multiply to -4, but they do not add to 3, so this is not the right pairing. The other integer possibility is some combination of 4 and 1. Which one should get the negative sign in order to add to positive 3 ?

Make the 4 positive and the 1 negative: 4 and -1 multiply to -4 and add to 3. Place these in the spaces in the parentheses:

$$x^2 + 3x - 4 = 0$$
$$(x + 4)(x - 1) = 0$$

The two terms on the left-hand side multiply to 0, so one or both of the terms must be equal to 0. As another example, if you know that $M \times N = 0$, then you know that either $M = 0$ or $N = 0$ (or both M and N are 0).

In this problem, set each factor in parentheses independently to 0 and solve for x:

$$x + 4 = 0 \qquad \text{OR} \qquad x - 1 = 0$$
$$x = -4 \qquad\qquad\qquad x = 1$$

Therefore, the two solutions of the quadratic equation $x^2 + 3x + 8 = 12$ are -4 and 1. The solutions of a quadratic equation are also sometimes called its *roots*. If you see the word *root* in conjunction with a quadratic equation, this word is a synonym for *solution*.

Disguised Quadratics

The GMAT will often attempt to disguise quadratic equations by putting them in forms that do not quite look like the traditional form of $ax^2 + bx + c = 0$.

Here is a very common "disguised" form for a quadratic:

$$3w^2 = 6w$$

This is a quadratic equation because it contains both a w^2 term and a plain w term. The classic misake is to try to solve this equation without thinking of it as a quadratic:

$3w^2 = 6w$	Divide both sides by w.
$3w = 6$	Divide both sides by 3.
$w = 2$	

The value 2 is one possible solution to this equation—but there's another! If you solve this equation without factoring it like a quadratic, you will miss one of the solutions. Here is how it should be solved:

$$3w^2 = 6w$$
$$3w^2 - 6w = 0$$
$$w(3w - 6) = 0$$

Setting both factors equal to 0 yields the following solutions:

$$w = 0 \quad \text{OR} \quad 3w - 6 = 0$$
$$3w = 6$$
$$w = 2$$

If you recognize that $3w^2 = 6w$ is a disguised quadratic, you will find both solutions instead of accidentally missing one (in this case, the solution $w = 0$).

Here is another example of a disguised quadratic:

Solve for b, given that $\frac{36}{b} = b - 5$.

At first glance, this does not look like a quadratic equation at all. But it's annoying to have a variable on the bottom of a fraction, so try to get rid of that. Watch what happens:

$\frac{36}{b} = b - 5$	Multiply both sides of the equation by b.
$36 = b^2 - 5b$	

Now this looks like a quadratic! Solve it by factoring:

$36 = b^2 - 5b$	Subtract 36 from both sides to set the equation equal to 0.
$b^2 - 5b - 36 = 0$	
$(b - 9)(b + 4) = 0$	Thus, $b = 9$ or $b = -4$.

Some quadratics are hidden within more difficult equations, such as higher order equations (in which a variable is raised to the power of 3 or more). On the GMAT, these equations can almost always be factored to find the hidden quadratic expression. For example:

Solve for x, given that $x^3 + 2x^2 - 3x = 0$.

$x^3 + 2x^2 - 3x = 0$	Factor out an x from each term.
$x\left(x^2 + 2x - 3\right) = 0$	

Now, factor the quadratic:

$$x\left(x^2 + 2x - 3\right) = 0$$
$$x(x + 3)(x - 1) = 0$$
$$x = 0 \quad \text{OR} \quad x + 3 = 0 \quad \text{OR} \quad x - 1 = 0$$

This equation has *three* solutions: 0, -3, and 1.

This example illustrates a general rule:

> If you have a quadratic expression equal to 0, *and* you can factor an x out of the expression, then $x = 0$ is a solution of the equation.

Do not just divide both sides by x. If you do so, you will eliminate the solution $x = 0$. You are only allowed to divide by a variable if you are absolutely sure that the variable does not equal 0.

Taking the Square Root

So far you have seen how to solve quadratic equations by setting one side of the equation equal to 0 and factoring. However, some quadratic problems can be solved without setting one side equal to 0. If the other side of the equation is a perfect square, the problem can be solved by taking the square root of both sides of the equation. For example:

If $(z+3)^2 = 25$, what is z?

Take the square root of both sides of the equation to solve for z. You just have to consider both the positive and the negative square root:

$$\sqrt{(z+3)^2} = \sqrt{25}$$
$$z + 3 = \pm 5$$
$$z = -3 \pm 5$$
$$z = \{2, -8\}$$

Going in Reverse: Use FOIL

Instead of starting with a quadratic equation and factoring it, you may need to start with factors and rewrite them as a quadratic equation (this is known as *expanding* the quadratic). To do this, use a multiplication process called FOIL: First, Outer, Inner, Last.

To change the expression $(x+7)(x-3)$ into a quadratic equation, use FOIL as follows:

First: Multiply the *first term* of each factor together: $(x)(x) = x^2$.

Outer: Multiply the *outer terms* of the expression together: $(x)(-3) = -3x$.

Inner: Multiply the *inner terms* of the expression together: $(7)(x) = 7x$.

Last: Multiply the *last term* of each factor together: $(7)(-3) = -21$.

Now, there are four terms: $x^2 - 3x + 7x - 21$. Combine the two middle terms for the fully simplified quadratic expression: $x^2 + 4x - 21$.

If you encounter a quadratic equation or expression, try factoring it. On the other hand, if you encounter the product of factors such as $(x+7)(x-3)$, you may need to use FOIL. Note that if the product of factors equals 0, you should be ready to *interpret* the meaning. For instance, if you are given $(x+k)(x-m) = 0$, then you know that $x = -k$ or $x = m$.

One-Solution Quadratics

Not all quadratic equations have two solutions. Some have only one solution. One-solution quadratics are also called perfect square quadratics, because both roots are the same. Consider the following examples:

$$x^2 + 8x + 16 = 0$$
$$(x + 4)(x + 4) = 0 \quad \text{Here, the only solution for } x \text{ is } -4.$$
$$(x + 4)^2 = 0$$

$$x^2 - 6x + 9 = 0$$
$$(x - 3)(x - 3) = 0 \quad \text{Here, the only solution for } x \text{ is } 3.$$
$$(x - 3)^2 = 0$$

When you see a quadratic equation, look for two solutions, but be aware that some circumstances will lead to just one solution. As long as you understand how the math works, you'll know when you should have two solutions and when you should have just one.

Zero in the Denominator: Undefined

When 0 appears in the denominator of an expression, then that expression is called *undefined*. The GMAT (thankfully!) doesn't go into this territory. Consider the following:

What are the solutions to the equation $\frac{x^2 + x - 12}{x - 2} = 0$?

For such a question, the GMAT would always first tell you that $x \neq 2$. If x did equal 2, then the bottom of that equation would be 0—and the GMAT won't allow that.

The numerator contains a quadratic equation. Since it is a good idea to start solving quadratic equations by factoring, factor this numerator as follows:

$$\frac{x^2 + x - 12}{x - 2} = 0 \rightarrow \frac{(x - 3)(x + 4)}{x - 2} = 0$$

If either of the factors in the numerator is 0, then the entire expression equals 0. Thus, the solutions (roots) to this equation are $x = 3$ or $x = -4$. (And, for the purposes of finding the roots, you can ignore the denominator, since the test will tell you that it does not equal 0.)

The Three Special Products

Three quadratic expressions called **Special Products** come up so frequently on the GMAT that it pays to memorize them. They are GMAT favorites! Make flash cards and drill them until you immediately recognize these three expressions and know how to factor (or distribute) each one automatically. This will usually put you on the path toward the solution to the problem.

Memorize these!

Special Product 1:	$x^2 - y^2 = (x + y)(x - y)$
Special Product 2:	$x^2 + 2xy + y^2 = (x + y)(x + y) = (x + y)^2$
Special Product 3:	$x^2 - 2xy + y^2 = (x - y)(x - y) = (x - y)^2$

You may also need to identify these products when they are presented in other forms. For example, $a^2 - 1$ can be factored as $(a + 1)(a - 1)$. Similarly, $(a + b)^2$ can be distributed as $a^2 + 2ab + b^2$.

14

Within an equation, you may need to recognize these special products in pieces. For instance, if you see $a^2 + b^2 = 9 + 2ab$, move the $2ab$ term to the left, yielding $a^2 - 2ab + b^2 = 9$. This quadratic can then be factored to $(a - b)^2 = 9$, or $a - b = \pm 3$. For example:

Simplify $\frac{x^2 + 4x + 4}{x^2 - 4}$, given that x does not equal 2 or −2.

Both the numerator and denominator of this fraction can be factored:

$$\frac{(x + 2)(x + 2)}{(x + 2)(x - 2)}$$

The expression $x + 2$ can be canceled out from the numerator and denominator:

$$\frac{x^2 + 4x + 4}{x^2 - 4} = \frac{x + 2}{x - 2}$$

Problem Set

Now that you've finished the chapter, try the following problems.

1. $(3-\sqrt{7})(3+\sqrt{7})=$

2. If −4 is a root for x in the equation $x^2 + kx + 8 = 0$, what is k ?

3. If 8 and −4 are the solutions for x, which of the following could be the equation?

   (A) $x^2 - 4x - 32 = 0$

   (B) $x^2 - 4x + 32 = 0$

   (C) $x^2 + 4x - 12 = 0$

   (D) $x^2 + 4x + 32 = 0$

   (E) $x^2 + 4x + 12 = 0$

4. If $x^2 + k = G$ and x is an integer, which of the following could be the value of $G - k$?

   (A) 7

   (B) 8

   (C) 9

   (D) 10

   (E) 11

5. What is y ?

   (1) $x = 4y - 4$

   (2) $xy = 8$

6. If $\frac{d}{4} + \frac{8}{d} + 3 = 0$, what is d ?

7. If $x \neq -3$ and $\frac{x^2 + 6x + 9}{x + 3} = 7$, what is x ?

8. If $z^2 - 10z + 25 = 9$, what are the possible values for z ?

9. If $a \neq 2$ and $ab \neq 0$, which of the following is equal to $\frac{b(a^2 - 4)}{ab - 2b}$?

   (A) ab

   (B) a

   (C) $a + 2$

   (D) a^2

   (E) $2b$

14

Solutions

1. **2:** You can use the special product or FOIL to simplify. The special product is faster—but you have to have it memorized.

   The original expression is in the form $(x - y)(x + y)$, which is one of the three special products. Since $(x - y)(x + y) = x^2 - y^2$, the expression in this problem simplifies to this:

   $$3^2 - \left(\sqrt{7}\right)^2 = 9 - 7 = 2$$

   Alternatively, FOIL to solve:

   $$\begin{aligned} \text{F: } 3 \times 3 &= 9 \\ \text{O: } 3 \times \sqrt{7} &= 3\sqrt{7} \\ \text{I: } -\sqrt{7} \times 3 &= -3\sqrt{7} \\ \text{L: } -\sqrt{7} \times \sqrt{7} &= -7 \\ \hline \text{FOIL: } 9 + 3\sqrt{7} - 3\sqrt{7} - 7 &= 2 \end{aligned}$$

14

2. **6:** The word *root* is a synonym for *solution*. If -4 is a solution, then $(x + 4)$ must be one of the factors of the quadratic equation. The other factor is $(x + ?)$.

   $$\begin{aligned} x^2 + kx + 8 &= 0 \\ (x + 4)(x + ?) &= 0 \end{aligned}$$

   The product of 4 and ? must be equal to 8; thus, the other factor is $(x + 2)$. Next, the sum of 4 and 2 must be equal to k. Therefore, $k = 6$.

   Alternatively, if -4 is a solution, then it is a possible value for x. Plug it into the equation for x and solve for k:

   $$\begin{aligned} x^2 + kx + 8 &= 0 \\ 16 - 4k + 8 &= 0 \\ 24 &= 4k \\ k &= 6 \end{aligned}$$

3. **(A) $x^2 - 4x - 32 = 0$:** If the solutions to the equation are 8 and -4, the factored form of the equation is $(x - 8)\ (x + 4) = 0$.

   Scan the answers. Most of them have a different c term $(-32, 32, -12, \text{or } 12)$, so check just that last part first. That's the L in FOIL: $(-8)(4) = -32$. Only answer (A) has 32 as the c term, so it must be the answer. (If more than one had that same number, then you would have to do the full FOIL.)

4. **(C) 9:** The problem states that x is an integer. It also asks for the combo $G - k$. Rearrange the expression to isolate the combo on one side:

   $$\begin{aligned} x^2 + k &= G \\ x^2 &= G - k \end{aligned}$$

Because you know that x is an integer, x^2 is a perfect square (the square of an integer). Therefore, $G - k$ is also a perfect square. The only perfect square among the answer choices is the number 9.

5. **(E):** The question asks for the value of y. You must be able to find one definitive value in order to say that a statement is sufficient.

   (1) INSUFFICIENT: This statement contains x and y, so it is not sufficient to find y alone.

   (2) INSUFFICIENT: This statement contains x and y, so it is not sufficient to find y alone.

   (1) AND (2) INSUFFICIENT: The two equations are $x = 4y - 4$ and $xy = 8$. The second equation is nonlinear (it multiplies the variables rather than adding or subtracting them), so when you combine them, you're likely to get a quadratic—which typically leads to more than one solution.

   Solve until you can tell whether you're going to get one solution or more than one. First, because the problem asked for y, isolate x in one of the equations. Luckily, this is already done in the first equation. Substitute into the second:

$$x = 4y - 4 \rightarrow (4y - 4)y = 8$$
$$4y^2 - 4y = 8$$
$$y^2 - y = 2$$
$$y^2 - y - 2 = 0$$
$$(y + 1)(y - 2) = 0$$

   If you are able to tell before that last line that you will get two different answers, you can stop at that point.

   The correct answer is **(E)**: Nothing given is sufficient to answer the question.

6. **{−8, −4}:** Multiply the entire equation by $4d$ (to eliminate the fractions) and factor:

$$d^2 + 32 + 12d = 0$$
$$d^2 + 12d + 32 = 0$$
$$(d + 8)(d + 4) = 0$$

$$d + 8 = 0 \quad \text{OR} \quad d + 4 = 0$$
$$d = -8 \qquad\qquad d = -4$$

7. **4:** The problem states that x is not -3, so you can divide out the term on the bottom of the fraction:

$$\frac{x^2 + 6x + 9}{x + 3} = 7$$
$$\frac{(x + 3)(x + 3)}{x + 3} = 7$$
$$\frac{(x + 3)\cancel{(x + 3)}}{\cancel{x + 3}} = 7$$
$$x + 3 = 7$$
$$x = 4$$

8. **{2, 8}:** The right-hand side is a perfect square (9), so check whether the left-hand side is as well. And it is!

$$z^2 - 10z + 25 = 9$$
$$(z - 5)^2 = 9$$
$$\sqrt{(z - 5)^2} = \sqrt{9}$$
$$z - 5 = \pm 3$$
$$z = 5 \pm 3$$

9. **(C) $a + 2$:** There are variables in the answers and no real values given in the problem, so choose smart numbers. The number 2 is not allowed for a and the number 4 appears in the expression, so try $a = 3$ and $b = 5$, and remember to simplify before you multiply:

$$\frac{b(a^2 - 4)}{ab - 2b} =$$
$$\frac{(5)((3)^2 - 4)}{(3)(5) - 2(5)} =$$
$$\frac{5(9 - 4)}{15 - 10} =$$
$$\frac{5(5)}{5} = 5$$

Now, plug $a = 3$ and $b = 5$ into the answer choices and look for a matching answer of 5:

(A) $ab = (3)(5) = 15$

(B) $a = (3) = 3$

(C) $a + 2 = (3) + 2 = 5$ Match!

(D) $a^2 = (3)^2 = 9$

(E) $2b = 2(5) = 10$

Alternatively, you can solve algebraically. Begin by factoring the given expression, then simplify:

$$\frac{b(a + 2)(a - 2)}{b(a - 2)} = a + 2$$

Everything divides out except for the $a + 2$ term. If you spot that quickly, then the algebraic solution is faster. If not, then the algebra can get messy and the smart numbers solution may be better.

CHAPTER 15

Formulas

In This Chapter

- Plug-In Formulas
- Functions
- Variable Substitution in Functions
- Sequence Formulas
- Recursive Sequences
- Linear Sequence Problems: Alternative Method

In this chapter, you will learn how to simplify and solve standard "plug-in" formulas, functions, and sequences (including both regular and recursive sequences).

CHAPTER 15 Formulas

Formulas are another means by which the GMAT tests your ability to work with unknowns. Formulas are specific equations that can involve multiple variables and these problems may be pure math or real-life/story problems. There are four major types of formula problems on the GMAT:

1. Plug-in formulas
2. Functions
3. Sequence formulas
4. Strange symbol formulas

The first three types are covered in this chapter. The final category is fairly rare; if you want to learn about strange symbol formulas, see the supplemental study material for this guide, found online.

Plug-In Formulas

The most basic GMAT formula problems provide you with a formula and ask you to solve for one of the variables in the formula by plugging in given values for the other variables. For example:

> The formula for determining an individual's comedic aptitude, C, on a given day is defined as $\frac{QL}{J}$, where J represents the number of jokes told, Q represents the overall joke quality on a scale of 1 to 10, and L represents the number of individual laughs generated. If Niko told 12 jokes, generated 18 laughs, and earned a comedic aptitude of 10.5, what was the overall quality of Niko's jokes?

The first sentence is providing a formula, though it may not look like it. When a variable is *defined as* a combination of some other variables, write a formula:

$$C = \frac{QL}{J}$$

Next, plug the given values into the formula in order to solve for the unknown variable Q:

$$C = \frac{QL}{J}$$

$$10.5 = \frac{18Q}{12}$$

$$Q = \frac{10.5(12)}{18}$$

$$Q = \frac{10.5(2)}{3}$$

$$Q = \frac{21}{3} = 7$$

The quality of Niko's jokes was rated a 7.

Notice that you will typically have to do some rearrangement after plugging in the numbers in order to isolate the desired unknown. The actual computations are typically not very complex (though do remember to simplify before you multiply!). Formula problems are tricky because the given formula is unfamiliar. Do not be intimidated. Figure out how to write down the equation, plug in the numbers carefully, and solve for the required unknown.

Functions

Functions are very much like the "magic boxes" you may have learned about in elementary school. For example:

> You put a 2 into the magic box, and a 7 comes out. You put a 3 into the magic box, and a 9 comes out. You put a 4 into the magic box, and an 11 comes out.

There are many possible ways to describe what the magic box is doing to your number. One possibility is that the magic box is doubling your number and adding 3:

$$2(2) + 3 = 7 \qquad 2(3) + 3 = 9 \qquad 2(4) + 3 = 11$$

Assuming that this is the case, this description would yield the following rule for this magic box: $2x + 3$. This rule can be written in function form as:

$$f(x) = 2x + 3$$

15

The function f represents the rule that the magic box is using to transform your number. The test might give you the function and say something like "What is $f(3)$?" The direction is telling you to put 3 into the function wherever you see an x, so 3 is the *input*:

$$f(3) = 2x + 3 \rightarrow 2(3) + 3 = 6 + 3 = 9$$

The answer is 9, so 9 is the *output*. By the way, that $f(x)$ form is read "f of x," not *fx*. It does *not* mean "f times x!" The letter f does not stand for a variable; rather, it stands for the rule that dictates how the input x changes into the output (answer).

Here are some other examples of functions. What do they have in common?

$$f(x) = 4x^2 - 11$$

$$g(t) = t^3 + \sqrt{t} - \frac{2t}{5}$$

They always start with that *letter*(*letter*) format. Most of the time, the first letter will be an f, g, or h. Whenever you see $f(x)$, it's saying "for the function f, follow this rule for any value of x."

The *domain* of a function indicates the possible inputs. The *range* of a function indicates the possible outputs. For instance, the function $f(x) = x^2$ can take any input (x can be anything) but never produces a negative number (because you can't square something and have the result be negative). So the domain is $x =$ all numbers, but the range is $f(x) \geq 0$.

The most basic type of function problem asks you to input the numerical value (say, 5) in place of the independent variable (x) in order to determine the value of the function. For example:

> If $f(x) = x^2 - 2$, what is the value of $f(5)$?

Apply the given rule:

$$f(5) = (5)^2 - 2 = 25 - 2 = 23$$

Variable Substitution in Functions

This type of function problem is slightly more complicated. Instead of finding the output value for a numerical input, you must find the output when the input is an algebraic expression. For example:

If $f(z) = z^2 - \frac{z}{3}$, what is the value of $f(w + 6)$?

Input the variable expression $(w + 6)$ in place of the independent variable (z) to determine the value of the function:

$$f(w + 6) = (w + 6)^2 - \frac{w + 6}{3}$$

Compare this equation to the equation for $f(z)$. The expression $(w + 6)$ has taken the place of every z in the original equation. In a sense, you are treating the expression $(w + 6)$ as one thing, as if it were a single letter or variable.

If you needed to simplify the right side, you would do so using standard algebraic simplification.

You could also be told the output and asked to find the input. For example:

If $f(x) = 3x + 2$ and $f(x) = 5$, what is x?

The first equation is the function ("given an input x, put it in the form $3x + 2$"). The second equation, though, represents an output: For some particular value of x, the output is 5. What is that value of x? To solve, set the function equal to the output:

$$3x + 2 = 5$$
$$3x = 3$$
$$x = 1$$

When $x = 1$, the output of the function is 5.

15

Sequence Formulas

A **sequence** is a collection of numbers in a set order. For example, $\{1, 4, 9, 16, 25\}$ is a sequence, as is $\{1, 1, 2, 3, 5, 8\}$. Sequences do not necessarily go in increasing order and it's possible to have repeated numbers.

Every sequence is defined by a rule, which you can use to find the values of terms:

$$A_n = 9n + 3$$

Find the first term (A_1) by plugging $n = 1$ into the equation: $A_1 = 12$.

Find the second term (A_2) by plugging $n = 2$ into the equation: $A_2 = 21$.

Find the nth term (A_n) by plugging n into the equation.

Here's another example:

> If $S_n = 15n - 7$, what is the value of $S_5 - S_3$?

This question is asking for the difference between the fifth term and the third term of the sequence, or $S_5 - S_3$:

$$\begin{aligned} S_5 - S_3 &= 15(5) - 7 - [15(3) - 7] \\ &= 75 - 7 - 45 + 7 \\ &= 75 - 45 \\ &= 30 \end{aligned}$$

Recursive Sequences

Occasionally, a sequence will be defined *recursively*. A **recursive sequence** defines each term relative to other terms in that same sequence, something like "each term is equal to the previous term plus 2."

Take a look at this example:

> If $a_n = 2a_{n-1} - 4$ and $a_6 = -4$, what is the value of a_4?

You can recognize that this is recursive because it doesn't have just an a_n term. It also has an a_{n-1} term. That second term refers to a different term in the same sequence; if you see this, you have a recursive sequence.

Solve the problem. If a_n represents the nth term, then a_{n-1} is the term right before a_n. You are given the value of the sixth term, and need to figure out the value of the fourth term. Keep track of this on your scrap paper:

		-4
a_4	a_5	a_6

Use the value of the sixth term (a_6) to find the value of the fifth term (a_5):

$$\begin{aligned} a_6 &= 2a_5 - 4 \\ (-4) &= 2a_5 - 4 \\ 0 &= 2a_5 \\ 0 &= a_5 \end{aligned}$$

The value of the fifth term is 0:

	0	-4
a_4	a_5	a_6

Now use the fifth term to find the fourth term:

$$\begin{aligned} a_5 &= 2a_4 - 4 \\ (0) &= 2a_4 - 4 \\ 4 &= 2a_4 \\ 2 &= a_4 \end{aligned}$$

The value of the fourth term is 2.

When a sequence is defined recursively, the question will have to give you the value of at least one of the terms. Use that value to find the value of the desired term.

Linear Sequence Problems: Alternative Method

For **linear sequences**, in which the same number is added to any term to yield the next term, you can use the following alternative method:

> If each number in a sequence is 3 more than the previous number, and the 6th number is 32, what is the 50th number in the sequence?

Instead of finding the rule for this sequence, consider the following reasoning: From the 6th to the 50th term, there are 44 "jumps" of 3 each. Since $44 \times 3 = 132$, there is an increase of 132 from the 6th term to the 50th term:

$32 + 132 = 164$

$a_n = a_{n-1} + 3$

$1 = 3$

$a_2 = 3 + 3$ $a_2 = 6$

$a_3 = 6 + 3 = 9$

$a_6 = 32$

$a_5 = 29$

$a_4 = 26$

$a_7 = 35$

$a_8 = 38$

$a_9 = 42$

$a_{10} = 45$

$a_{11} = 48$

$a_{12} = 52$

$a_{13} = 55$

$a_{14} = 58$

Problem Set

Now that you've finished the chapter, try the following problems.

1. If $A_n = 3 - 8n$, what is A_1 ?

2. If $A_n = 3 - 8n$, what is $A_{11} - A_9$?

3. If $f(x) = 2x^2 - 12$, what is the value of $f(2\sqrt{3})$?

4. If $a_n = \frac{a_{n-1} \times a_{n-2}}{2}$, $a_5 = -6$, and $a_6 = -18$, what is the value of a_3 ?

5. Hugo lies on top of a building, throwing pennies straight down to the street below. The formula for the height, H, that a penny falls is $H = Vt + 5t^2$, where V is the original velocity of the penny (how fast Hugo throws it when it leaves his hand) and t is equal to the time it takes to hit the ground, in seconds. Hugo throws the penny from a height of 60 meters at an initial speed of 20 meters per second. How long does it take, in seconds, for the penny to hit the ground?

   (A) 2
   (B) 20
   (C) 200

6. Life expectancy is defined by the formula $L = \frac{6SB}{G}$, where S = shoe size, B = average monthly electric bill in dollars, and G = GMAT score. If Melvin's GMAT score is twice his monthly electric bill, and his life expectancy is 75, what is his shoe size?

7. The "competitive edge" of a baseball team is defined by the formula $\sqrt{\frac{W}{L}}$, where W represents the number of the team's wins and L represents the number of the team's losses. This year, the GMAT All-Stars had 3 times as many wins and one-half as many losses as they had last year. By what factor did their "competitive edge" increase?

8. If $t(x) = 4x^3a$ and $t(3) = 27$, what is $t(2)$?

9. The first term in an arithmetic sequence is −5 and the second term is −3. What is the 50th term? (In an arithmetic sequence, the difference between successive terms is constant.)

10. Challenge problem: If $f(x) = 2x^2 - 4$ and $g(x) = 2x$, for what values of x will $f(x) = g(x)$?

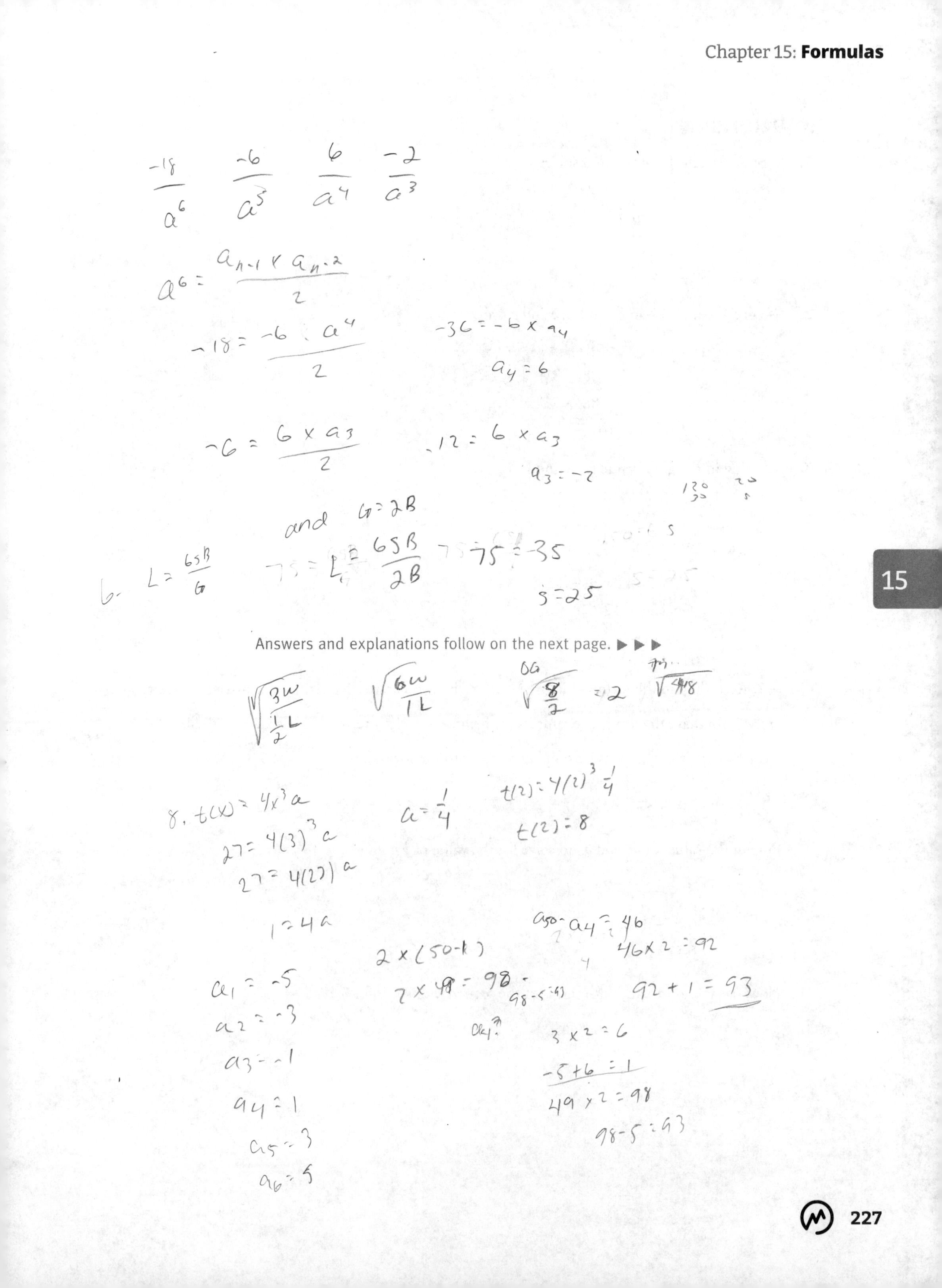

Answers and explanations follow on the next page. ▶ ▶ ▶

Solutions

1. **−5:** Substitute 1 in for n and solve:

$$\begin{aligned} A_n &= 3 - 8_n \\ A_1 &= 3 - 8(1) \\ &= 3 - 8 \\ &= -5 \end{aligned}$$

2. **−16:** Substitute 11 and 9 in for n and solve:

$$\begin{aligned} A_{11} - A_9 &= 3 - 8(11) - [3 - 8(9)] \\ &= 3 - 88 - 3 + 72 \\ &= 0 - 88 + 72 \\ &= -16 \end{aligned}$$

3. **12:** Plug in the given value for x and solve:

$$\begin{aligned} f(x) &= 2\left(2\sqrt{3}\right)^2 - 12 \\ &= 2(2)^2\left(\sqrt{3}\right)^2 - 12 \\ &= (2 \times 4 \times 3) - 12 \\ &= 24 - 12 \\ &= 12 \end{aligned}$$

15

4. **−2:** According to the formula, $a_3 = \frac{a_2 \times a_1}{2}$. But you aren't given a_1 or a_2. Instead, you're given a_5 and a_6. You have to work backwards from the fifth and sixth terms of the sequence to find the third term. Notice what happens if you plug $n = 6$ into the formula:

$$a_6 = \frac{a_5 \times a_4}{2}$$

Plug in the values of a_5 and a_6 to solve for the value of a_4:

$$\begin{aligned} -18 &= \frac{-6 \times a_4}{2} \\ -36 &= -6 \times a_4 \\ 6 &= a_4 \end{aligned}$$

Now, use the fourth and fifth terms of the sequence to solve for a_3:

$$\begin{aligned} a_5 &= \frac{a_4 \times a_3}{2} \\ -6 &= \frac{6 \times a_3}{2} \\ -12 &= 6 \times a_3 \\ -2 &= a_3 \end{aligned}$$

5. **(A) 2 seconds:** If you feel comfortable thinking through the scenario, you can estimate. The penny drops from 60 meters at a speed of 20 meters per second, so it should take no more than 3 seconds to drop. (It will take less than 3 seconds, in fact, since gravity will cause the speed to increase.) Only answer **(A)** is close. Here's how to do the algebra:

$$H = Vt + 5t^2$$
$$60 = 20t + 5t^2$$
$$5t^2 + 20t - 60 = 0$$
$$5\left(t^2 + 4t - 12\right) = 0$$
$$5(t+6)(t-2) = 0$$

$t + 6 = 0$ OR $t - 2 = 0$
$t = -6$ $\quad$ $t = 2$

Since a time must be positive, discard the negative value for t.

6. **Size 25:** The problem states that $G = 2B$, so substitute $2B$ for G in the formula, then simplify:

$$\frac{6SB}{2B} = 75$$
$$3S = 75$$
$$S = 25$$

You could also pick smart numbers for G and B as long as they fit the relationship described in the problem: G is twice B. Try $G = 4$ and $B = 2$. Then, substitute in your smart numbers and solve for S:

$$\frac{6S(2)}{4} = 75$$
$$3S = 75$$
$$S = 25$$

7. $\sqrt{6}$**:** The question says the competitive edge (call that c) *is defined by* a certain expression, so write a formula:

$$c = \sqrt{\frac{W}{L}}$$

Pick numbers to see what happens to the competitive edge when W is tripled and L is halved. If the original value of W is 4 and the original value of L is 2, the original value of c is $\sqrt{\frac{4}{2}} = \sqrt{2}$. If W triples to 12 and L is halved to 1, the new value of c is $\sqrt{\frac{12}{1}} = \sqrt{12}$. The competitive edge has increased from $\sqrt{2}$ to $\sqrt{12}$. Therefore:

$$\frac{\sqrt{12}}{\sqrt{2}} = \frac{\sqrt{12}}{\sqrt{2}} = \sqrt{6}$$

The competitive edge has increased by a factor of $\sqrt{6}$. (You can also ask yourself: What do I need to multiply $\sqrt{2}$ by to get to $\sqrt{12}$?)

8. **8:** The problem contains a function, t, into which you plug values for x. The function also contains a separate variable, a. First, use the given information $t(3) = 27$ to find the value for a:

$$t(x) = 4x^3a$$
$$t(3) \rightarrow 4(3)^3 a = 27$$
$$4(27)a = 27$$
$$4a = 1$$
$$a = \frac{1}{4}$$

Next, plug that back into the function to find the value of $t(2)$:

$$t(x) = 4x^3a$$
$$t(2) = 4(2)^3\left(\frac{1}{4}\right)$$
$$t(2) = 4(8)\left(\frac{1}{4}\right)$$
$$t(2) = 8$$

15

9. **93:** The first term is -5 and the second term is -3, so you are adding $+2$ to each successive term. How many times do you have to add 2? There are $50 - 1 = 49$ additional "steps" after the first term, so you have to add $+2$ a total of 49 times, beginning with your starting point of -5: $-5 + 2(49) = 93$.

10. **$\{-1, 2\}$:** To find the values for which $f(x) = g(x)$, set the functions equal to each other:

$$2x^2 - 4 = 2x$$
$$2x^2 - 2x - 4 = 0$$
$$2\left(x^2 - x - 2\right) = 0$$
$$2(x - 2)(x + 1) = 0$$

$$x - 2 = 0 \quad \text{OR} \quad x + 1 = 0$$
$$x = 2 \qquad\qquad x = -1$$

CHAPTER 16

Inequalities and Max/Min

In This Chapter

In this chapter, you will learn how to simplify and solve inequalities (almost the same as equations, but not quite!). You'll also learn about a common question feature that shows up on the GMAT: the max/min variation, in which you're asked to find the maximum or minimum possible value of something.

CHAPTER 16 Inequalities and Max/Min

Unlike equations, which relate two equivalent quantities, **inequalities** compare quantities that have different values. Inequalities are used to express four kinds of relationships, illustrated by the following examples:

1. x is less than 4.

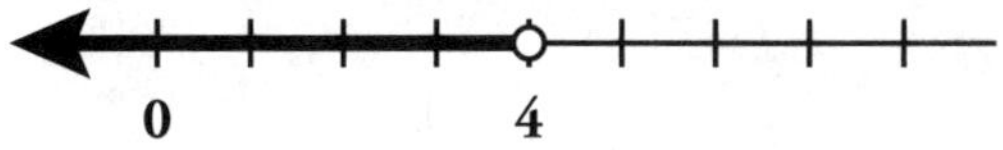

$x < 4$

2. x is less than or equal to 4.

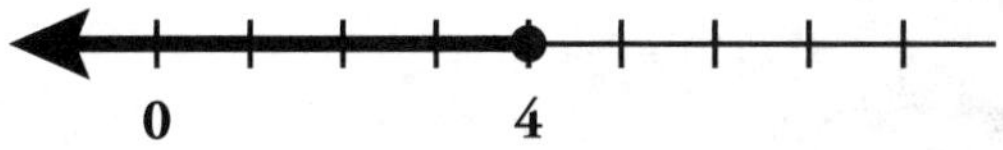

$x \leq 4$

3. x is greater than 4.

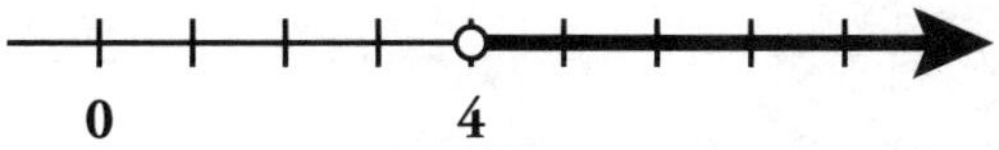

$x > 4$

4. x is greater than or equal to 4.

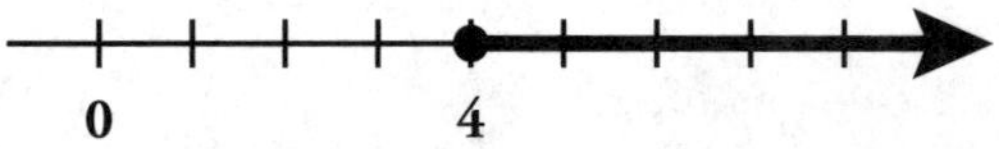

$x \geq 4$

Number lines, such as those shown above, are an excellent way to visualize exactly what a given inequality means.

When you see inequalities with 0 on one side of the inequality (> 0 or < 0), the problem is likely testing positive and negative characteristics. You'll learn more about this later.

Here are some common inequality statements on the GMAT, as well as what they imply:

Statement	Implication
$xy > 0$	x and y are *both positive* OR *both negative.*
$xy < 0$	x and y have *different signs* (one positive, one negative).
$x^2 - x < 0$ $x^2 < x$	These are two different versions of the same inequality. Both mean that $0 < x < 1$.

Why is that last one true? The inequality to the left is saying that, when you square a number, it gets smaller. Only a very narrow set of circumstances makes this true; most of the time, when you square a number it gets larger.

If you square any negative number, it becomes positive (and, therefore, larger). If you square any positive number greater than 1, it gets larger.

If you square 0, it stays 0. If you square 1, it stays 1. These are the only two numbers that stay the same when you square them.

Finally, if you square a value between 0 and 1, this is the one cirumstance in which the value gets smaller.

Flip the Sign

Most operations that can be performed on equations can be performed on inequalities. For example, in order to simplify an inequality (e.g., $2 + x < 5$), you can add or subtract a constant on both sides:

$$\begin{array}{rcl} 2 + x & < & 5 \\ \underline{-2 \quad\;} & & \underline{-2} \\ x & < & 3 \end{array} \qquad\qquad \begin{array}{rcl} x - 5 & < & 9 \\ \underline{\quad +5} & & \underline{+5} \\ x & < & 14 \end{array}$$

You can also add or subtract a variable expression on both sides:

$$\begin{array}{rcl} y + x & < & 5 \\ \underline{-y \quad\;} & & \underline{-y} \\ x & < & 5 - y \end{array} \qquad\qquad \begin{array}{rcl} x - ab & < & 9 \\ \underline{\quad + ab} & & \underline{+ ab} \\ x & < & 9 + ab \end{array}$$

You can multiply or divide by a *positive* number on both sides:

$$\begin{array}{rcl} 2x & < & 6 \\ \underline{\div 2} & & \underline{\div 2} \\ x & < & 3 \end{array} \qquad\qquad \begin{array}{rcl} 0.2x & < & 1 \\ \underline{\times 5} & & \underline{\times 5} \\ x & < & 5 \end{array}$$

One procedure, however, is very different for inequalities: When you multiply or divide an inequality by a negative number, the inequality sign flips! For example:

If $4 - 3x < 10$, what is the range of possible values for x ?

$$\begin{array}{rcl} 4 - 3x & < & 10 \\ \underline{-4 \qquad} & & \underline{-4} \\ -3x & < & 6 \\ \underline{\div -3} & & \underline{\div -3} \\ x & > & -2 \end{array}$$

First, subtract 4 from both sides.

Next, divide by -3.

Because you're dividing by a negative, flip the inequality sign.

Do not multiply or divide an inequality by a variable unless you know the sign of the number that the variable stands for. If you don't know whether that number is positive or negative, then you don't know whether to flip the inequality sign.

Combining Inequalities: Line 'Em Up!

Many GMAT inequality problems involve more than one inequality. To solve such problems, you may need to convert several inequalities to a compound inequality, which is a series of inequalities strung together, such as $2 < 3 < 4$. To convert multiple inequalities to a compound inequality, first line up the variables, then combine. For example:

> If $x > 8$, $x < 17$, and $x + 5 < 19$, what is the range of possible values for x?

First, solve any inequalities that need to be solved. In this example, only the last inequality needs to be solved:

$$x + 5 < 19$$
$$x < 14$$

Second, rearrange the inequalities so that all the inequality symbols point in the same direction, and then line up the common variables in the inequalities:

$$8 < x$$
$$x < 17$$
$$x < 14$$

Finally, put the information together. Notice that $x < 14$ is more limiting than $x < 17$ (in other words, whenever $x < 14$, x will always be less than 17, but not vice versa). The range, then, is $8 < x < 14$ rather than $8 < x < 17$. Discard the less limiting inequality, $x < 17$. Try another example:

> If $u < t$ and $b > r$ and $f < t$ and $r > t$, is $b > u$?

Combine the four given inequalities by simplifying and lining up the common variables.

First, align all inequalities in the same direction: $u < t$, $r < b$, $f < t$, and $t < r$.

Then, line up any like variables . . .	. . . and combine.
$u < t$	$u < t < r < b$
$r < b$	$f < t < r < b$
$f < t$	
$t < r$	

In this problem, it is not possible to combine all the information into a single compound inequality. Both u and f are less than t, but you do not know the relationship between u and f.

The answer to the question is yes, b is greater than u.

Manipulating Compound Inequalities

Sometimes a problem with compound inequalities will require you to manipulate the inequalities in order to solve the problem. You can perform operations on a compound inequality as long as you remember to perform those operations on every term in the inequality, not just the outside terms. For example:

$x + 3 < y < x + 5 \not\rightarrow x < y < x + 2$	**INCORRECT**: You must subtract 3 from *every* term in the inequality.
$x + 3 < y < x + 5 \rightarrow x < y - 3 < x + 2$	CORRECT
$\frac{c}{2} \leq b - 3 \leq \frac{d}{2} \rightarrow c \leq b - 3 \leq d$	**INCORRECT**: You must multiply by 2 in *every* term in the inequality.
$\frac{c}{2} \leq b - 3 \leq \frac{d}{2} \rightarrow c \leq 2b - 6 \leq d$	CORRECT

Combining Inequalities: Add 'Em Up!

You can also combine inequalities by adding the inequalities together. In order to add inequalities, the inequality signs must face in the same direction. (Don't subtract inequalities, though—ever.) For example:

Is $a + 2b < c + 2d$?

(1) $a < c$

(2) $d > b$

16

Assume that you've already tried the two statements individually and neither was sufficient by itself. In order to test the statements together, add the inequalities together to see whether they match the question. First, line up the inequalities so that they are all facing the same direction:

$$a < c$$
$$b < d$$

Then, take the sum of the two inequalities to try to prove the result. Add them up once, then take a look. It's not quite the same. What's missing? You need another b and d, so add the second inequality *again*:

$$\begin{array}{rl} & a \quad\;\; < c \\ + & \quad\;\; b < \quad\;\; d \\ \hline & a + b < c + d \\ + & \quad\;\; b < \quad\;\; d \\ \hline & a + 2b < c + 2d \end{array}$$

If you use both statements, you can answer the question. Therefore, the answer is **(C)**.

You also could have multiplied the second inequality by 2 before summing so that the result matched the original question:

$$\begin{array}{rl} & a \quad\;\; < c \\ + & \quad\;\; 2b < \quad\;\; 2d \\ \hline & a + 2b < c + 2d \end{array}$$

You might not notice that at first, though. Adding one of each inequality the first time is a good way to understand what's going on with the math; that can help you to notice that you need to double one of the inequalities (i.e., use it twice).

You can also multiply inequalities together as long as all possible values of the inequalities are positive, though this doesn't show up a lot on the GMAT.

But remember this: *Never subtract or divide inequalities.*

Maximizing and Minimizing

Some problems ask you to find the maximum or minimum of multiple possible solutions; these are called max/min problems for short.

As you work through the problem, look for the spots where you have flexibility to try multiple possible values. Then, think about what the problem asked you to do. For instance, if the problem asked you to find the maximum value for something, where else in the problem do you need to maximize or minimize values in order to accomplish your overall goal? Try an example:

If $2y + 3 \leq 11$ and $1 \leq x \leq 5$, what is the maximum possible value for xy?

Which combinations of extreme values will maximize the value of the product xy? First, simplify whatever you can. The x inequality is already simplified, but the y inequality can be simplified further:

$$2y + 3 \leq 11$$
$$2y \leq 8$$
$$y \leq 4$$

16

Next, examine the extreme ends of each range. If a range includes 0, it's also a good idea to note that, since 0 can have an unusual effect in problems:

Extreme Values for x	Extreme Values for y
The lowest value for x is 1.	There is no lower limit to y.
The highest value for x is 5.	The highest value for y is 4.
	y could be 0.

Now, consider the different scenarios for x and y that could lead to the maximum possible value for xy. The value of y could be positive or negative, but x must be positive. A positive times a negative has to be negative, and that won't be the maximum value, so ignore all negative values for y.

The value of 0 for y also won't help to maximize the value of xy. If you're restricted to positives, then you want to maximize the value of each individual number in order to get the maximum possible product.

In this case, xy is maximized when $x = 5$ and $y = 4$, with a result that $xy = 20$.

How does the situation change if this is the problem:

If $-20 \leq 2y \leq 8$ and $-3 \leq x \leq 5$, what is the maximum possible value for xy?

The first inequality simplifies to $-10 \leq y \leq 4$. Also, this time, both x and y could be negative—and a negative times a negative is positive—so you have to consider the negative scenario this time:

Extreme Values for x	**Extreme Values for y**
The lowest value for x is -3.	The lowest value for y is -10.
The highest value for x is 5.	The highest value for y is 4.
x could be 0.	y could be 0.

Max scenario 1: Positive × Positive. Use the largest possible values for each:

$x = 5$ and $y = 4$, so $xy = 20$

Max scenario 2: Negative × Negative. Use the smallest possible values for each:

$x = -3$ and $y = -10$, so $xy = 30$

In this problem, the maximum value for xy is obtained when using the smallest possible values for x and y. The maximum value is 30.

When you see max/min language in a problem, first jot down whether the problem is asking you to maximize or to minimize. Next, identify the parts of the problem where you have the flexibility to maximize or minimize some values. Finally, consider the different possible scenarios—you may need to test two or three options in order to figure out the correct answer.

Square-Rooting Inequalities

Just like equations involving even exponents, inequality problems involving even exponents require you to consider *two* scenarios. Consider this example:

If $x^2 < 4$, what are the possible values for x?

To solve this problem, recall that when given x^2 and solving for x, you'll have two solutions: the positive version and the negative version. For example, if $x^2 = 4$, then $x = \pm 2$.

Something similar happens when you solve an inequality, with one important difference:

$$x^2 < 4$$
$$x < 2 \text{ and } x > -2$$

If x is positive, then $x < 2$. So far, this is how you would normally solve.

But, if x is negative, then taking the square root is the equivalent of dividing by a negative, so you have to flip the inequality sign: $x > -2$.

Here is another example:

> If $10 + x^2 \geq 19$, what is the range of possible values for x?

$$10 + x^2 \geq 19$$
$$x^2 \geq 9$$
$$x \geq 3 \quad \text{AND} \quad x \leq -3$$

If x is positive, then $x \geq 3$, but if x is negative, then $x \leq -3$.

Advanced material for the Algebra unit (primarily covering additional strategies for equations, formulas, and inequalities) can be found in Atlas, Manhattan Prep's online learning platform. Use the online material only if you feel that you have mastered everything in the Algebra unit of this strategy guide and only if you are aiming for a Quant section score of 48 or higher.

Problem Set

Now that you've finished the chapter, try the following problems.

1. Which of the following is equivalent to $-3x + 7 \leq 2x + 32$?

   (A) $x \geq -5$

   (B) $x \geq 5$

   (C) $x \leq 5$

   (D) $x \leq -5$

2. If $G^2 < G$, which of the following could be G ?

   (A) 1

   (B) $\frac{23}{7}$

   (C) $\frac{7}{23}$

   (D) −4

   (E) −2

3. If $5B > 4B + 1$, is $B^2 > 1$?

4. If $|A| > 19$, which of the following could NOT be equal to A ?

   (A) 26

   (B) 22

   (C) 18

   (D) −20

   (E) −24

5. If $-10 \leq a \leq 5$ and $7 \leq b \leq 10$, what is the least possible value of $|a - b|$?

   (A) −2

   (B) 0

   (C) 2

   (D) 3

   (E) 5

Save the following problems for review after you finish this entire guide.

6. If $a > 7$, $a + 4 > 13$, and $2a < 30$, which of the following must be true?

   (A) $9 < a < 15$

   (B) $11 < a < 15$

   (C) $15 < a < 20$

   (D) $13 < a < 15$

7. If $d > a$ and $L < a$, which of the following cannot be true?

   (A) $d + L = 14$

   (B) $d - L = 7$

   (C) $d - L = 1$

   (D) $a - d = 9$

   (E) $a + d = 9$

8. A retailer sells only radios and clocks. If there are currently exactly 42 total items in inventory, how many of them are radios?

   (1) The retailer has more than 26 radios in inventory.

   (2) The retailer has less than twice as many radios as clocks in inventory.

9. If $4x - 12 \geq x + 9$, which of the following must be true?

   (A) $x > 6$

   (B) $x < 7$

   (C) $x > 7$

   (D) $x > 8$

   (E) $x < 8$

10. If $0 < ab < ac$, is a negative?

   (1) $c < 0$

   (2) $b > c$

Solutions

1. **(A) $x \geq -5$:**

$$\begin{aligned} -3x + 7 &\leq 2x + 32 \\ -5x &\leq 25 \\ x &\geq -5 \end{aligned}$$

2. **(C) $\frac{7}{23}$:** If G^2 is less than G, then G must be positive (since G^2 itself has to be 0 or positive). In addition, only values between 0 and 1 get smaller when you square them. Thus, $0 < G < 1$. Only the value in answer **(C)** is between 0 and 1.

3. **Yes:**

$$\begin{aligned} 5B &> 4B + 1 \\ B &> 1 \end{aligned}$$

For any number greater than 1, the square of the number is also greater than 1, so $B^2 > 1$.

4. **(C) 18:** If $|A| > 19$, then $A > 19$ OR $A < -19$. The only answer choice that does not satisfy either of these inequalities is **(C)**, 18.

5. **(C) 2:** The question asks for the least possible value, so this is a max/min problem. Take some time during the Understand and Plan phases to think about what it means to minimize the value of $|a - b|$.

How low can an absolute value go? It can never be negative. Glance at the answers—choice (A) can't be correct.

16

An absolute value can be 0 or positive. Glance at the answers again—0 is in the running. Since the question asks for the least possible value, start there. What would need to happen in order for $|a - b| = 0$ to be true?

The values for a and b would have to be identical. But this isn't possible, since a is between -10 and 5, inclusive, and b is between 7 and 10 inclusive. Eliminate choice (B) and move on to the next smallest value, 2.

In order for the absolute value to be 2, the actual difference would have to be either 2 or -2. In other words, a and b would have to be 2 apart (though it doesn't matter which one is larger than the other). Is that a possible outcome? Yes, when $a = 5$ and $b = 7$.

Alternatively, try each of the four extreme cases:

Case 1: $|-10 - 7| = 17$

Case 2: $|-10 - 10| = 20$

Case 3: $|5 - 7| = 2$

Case 4: $|5 - 10| = 5$

The least possible value is 2. Note that answer (A) is a trap. The value of $5 - 7$ is -2, but the value of $|5 - 7|$ is 2, and the question asks about the absolute value.

6. **(A) $9 < a < 15$:** First, solve the second and third inequalities. The second one, $a + 4 > 13$, becomes $a > 9$. The third one, $2a < 30$, becomes $a < 15$.

   Next, make all of the inequality symbols point in the same direction. Then, line up the inequalities based on the variable a to combine:

   $$9 < a$$
   $$a < 15 \rightarrow 9 < a < 15$$
   $$7 < a$$

   If 7 and 9 are both less than a, the limiting factor is the larger value, 9. (If a is greater than both 7 and 9, then overall a is greater than 9.) Therefore, a is between 9 and 15.

   Notice that, in all of the incorrect answers, the low end is too high. For example, answer (B) indicates that a cannot be 11, but a could in fact be 11. The correct answer will both keep out all the impossible values of a *and* include all the possible values of a.

7. **(D) $a - d = 9$:** The *cannot be true* language signals an opportunity to test cases. The wording of the question indicates that the four wrong answers all could be true—so start with answer (A) and see which cases you can create. If you get hung up on a particular answer, maybe that's the one that can't be true. Leave that one aside and keep going with the others.

   The question stem indicates that d is greater than a but L is less than a. In other words: $L < a < d$. Test cases, making sure to try only numbers that follow this constraint:

   $$L < a$$
   $$a < d \rightarrow L < a < d$$

Answers to test	Given $L < a < d$ Test	Does it work?
(A) $d + L = 14$	$d = 10, L = 4$	Yes
(B) $d - L = 7$	$d = 10, L = 3$	Yes
(C) $d - L = 1$	$d = 10, L = 9$	Yes
(D) $a - d = 9$	$a = 10, d =$ bigger...?	...?
(E) $a + d = 9$	$a = 4, d = 5$	Yes

   For four of the answers, it's possible to choose values that follow the constraint that $L < a < d$. For answer **(D)**, though, this is impossible. The value for a has to be *less* than the value for d, so whatever you try to choose will end up with a negative answer, not positive 9.

8. **(C):** First, assign variables (r = number of radios and c = number of clocks) so that you can jot down the information in the question stem:

   $$r + c = 42$$

   The question asks for r. Note that, if you can find c, then you can find r, so the rephrased question is this: What is r OR What is c?

   (1) INSUFFICIENT: This indicates that $r \geq 27$, so r could equal 27, 28, 29, etc.

16

(2) INSUFFICIENT: This statement is tricky to translate. First, pretend that it says that there are twice as many radios as clocks. That translates to $r = 2c$. Then, add in the inequality: There are *less than twice as many radios*: $r < 2c$.

Combine this information with the original equation $r + c = 42$:

$$r < 2c$$
$$r + c = 42$$

Isolate c in the second equation, then substitute into the inequality:

$$c = 42 - r$$

$$r < 2c$$
$$r < 2(42 - r)$$
$$r < 84 - 2r$$
$$3r < 84$$
$$r < 28$$

This information on its own is insufficient; r could be 27, 26, and so on.

(1) AND (2) SUFFICIENT: Statement (1) tells you $r \geq 27$, and statement (2) tells you $r < 28$. Therefore, r must equal 27.

The correct answer is **(C)**: Both statements together are sufficient, but neither one alone is sufficient.

9. **(A) $x > 6$:** What must be true? You might want to test some cases. First, though, simplify that annoying inequality:

16

$$4x - 12 \geq x + 9$$
$$3x \geq 21$$
$$x \geq 7$$

Careful. None of the answers match exactly. So test a couple of cases first before you choose something—make sure you understand what's going on. If $x \geq 7$, then x could be 7 itself.

Answers to test	Test #1: If $x = 7$ Answer true?	Test #2: If $x = 8$ Answer true?
(A) $x > 6$	Yes. Keep.	Yes. Keep.
(B) $x < 7$	No. Eliminate.	(ignore)
(C) $x > 7$	No. Eliminate.	(ignore)
(D) $x > 8$	No. Eliminate.	(ignore)
(E) $x < 8$	Yes. Keep.	No. Eliminate. Done!

The only answer that works every time is answer **(A)**.

10. **(D):** If $0 < ab < ac$, then $0 < ac$. Since ab is positive, a and b must have the same sign. Since ac is also positive, the same applies to a and c. Therefore, a, b, and c must all have the same sign.

The question stem also indicates that $ab < ac$. You can't divide out the a, though, since if a were negative, you would need to flip the inequality. Leave it for now.

(1) SUFFICIENT: Statement (1) indicates that c is negative. Therefore, since a and c share the same sign, a is negative.

(2) SUFFICIENT: Statement (2) is trickier. The statement indicates that $b > c$, but the question stem indicates that $ab < ac$. When you multiply both sides of $b > c$ by a, the inequality sign gets flipped. The only time an inequality sign flips is when you multiple or divide by a negative, so a must be negative.

Another option for statement (2) is to test cases. Pick values for b and c that adhere to the statement $b > c$, and then evaluate what values of a can make the inequality given in the question true. You also know that both ab and bc are greater than 0, so you only need to test cases where all the variables have the same sign.

Case	b	c	a	$0 < ab < ac$
1	3	2	1	$0 < 3 < 2$ ✗
2	−2	−3	−1	$0 < 2 < 3$ ✓

Only case 2, in which all the variables are negative, is valid. Thus, a must be negative; statement (2) is sufficient.

The correct answer is **(D)**: Each statement alone is sufficient.

UNIT THREE

Word Problems

In this unit, you'll learn how to translate, organize, and solve all kinds of story problems, including how to logic your way to an answer on many types of these problems; topics include rates, work, overlapping sets, statistics, and consecutive integers. You'll also learn advanced methods for the Choose Smart Numbers and Work Backwards strategies.

In This Unit

- Chapter 17: Translations
- Chapter 18: Strategy: Logic It Out
- Chapter 19: Rates and Work
- Chapter 20: Overlapping Sets
- Chapter 21: Statistics
- Chapter 22: Weighted Averages
- Chapter 23: Strategy: Arithmetic vs. Algebra 3
- Chapter 24: Consecutive Integers

CHAPTER 17

Translations

In This Chapter

- Pay Attention to Units
- Common Relationships

In this chapter, you will learn how to translate stories into math. You'll also learn certain common formulas that the GMAT expects you to know (e.g., Profit = Revenue − Cost), as well as how to convert among different types of units (e.g., meters to kilometers).

CHAPTER 17 Translations

Story problems are prevalent on the GMAT and can come in any form: Word Problems, Fractions, Percents, Algebra, and so on. Tackle story problems using your standard 3-step approach to solving: Understand, Plan, Solve.

Step 1: Understand: What's the Story?

Glance at the problem: The first thing you'll notice is a lot of text. Also note whether it is Problem Solving or Data Sufficiency. Do the answers or statements give you any quick clues about possible approaches? (Example: "Nice" real numbers in the answers on PS might lead you to work backwards. An annoying or complicated equation anywhere in the problem or statements signals a chance to rephrase or simplify.)

Often, on story problems, it's best to read the entire problem before you begin to jot down the information. In fact, you might move this task to your Plan phase.

Step 2: Plan: Choose an Approach

Your task is two-fold: Turn the story into math and then decide how you want to approach it. You can use either the Algebraic method or one of the test-taking strategies (Work Backwards, Choose Smart Numbers, Test Cases, and so on). One more thing: Choose variables that tell you what they are (more on this below).

Step 3: Solve: Go for It!

Now that you understand and have a plan, go ahead and solve. (If you don't understand or have a plan, don't try to solve. Guess and move on.)

Try this problem:

> A candy company sells premium chocolate candies at $5 per pound and regular chocolate candies at $4 per pound in increments of whole pounds only. If Bronte buys a 7-pound box of chocolate candies that costs $31, how many pounds of premium chocolate candies are in the box?
>
> (A) 1
> (B) 2
> (C) 3
> (D) 4
> (E) 5

Ready?

Step 1: **Understand.** The first glance indicates that this is a PS story problem. The answers are small whole numbers, so this might be a candidate for working backwards. Jot down WB on your scrap paper to remind yourself later.

Now, read the story and get oriented. There are two different kinds of candies. You have to buy in whole-pound increments. Bronte (abbreviate this to B from now on, even in your head) buys a 7-pound box that cost $31. It asks how many pounds were premium candies. That's a lot of information. Push the *jot* task to the Plan step.

Step 2: **Plan.** B probably bought both kinds of candies. How can you know? Glance at the answers. The choices are 1 through 5, so B had to buy *some* premium candies but couldn't have bought all 7 pounds. So, yes, B bought both kinds of candies. Call premium candies *P* and regular candies *R*. (Don't just use *x* and *y* every time. Choose variables that tell you what they are. You don't want to accidentally solve for the wrong thing!)

The question asks specifically for the number of pounds of premium candies. This represents a single variable in the problem (*P*), so working backwards would be a good strategy here.

Here's one way to organize this story on paper:

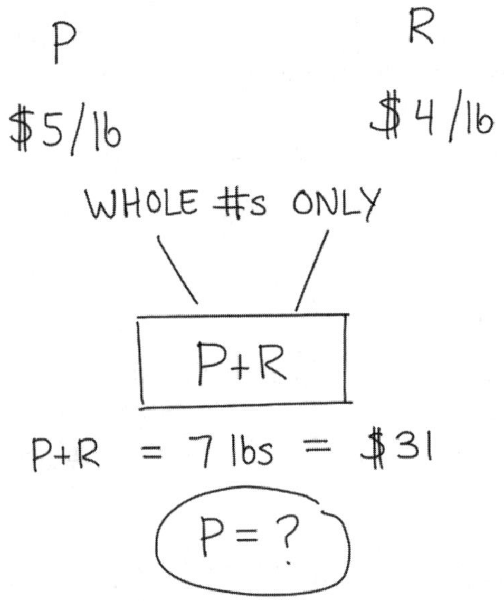

Step 3: **Solve.** Start with either answer (B) or answer (D), your choice:

	P=	R=	$P 5P	$R 4R	= $31?
(A)					
(B)	2	5	5(2)=10	4(5)=20	No. Too small.
(C)					
(D)					
(E)					

Answer (B) is incorrect. The number only added up to \$30 and it needs to add up to \$31. Which direction do you need to go to find the correct answer?

You need to add a dollar, so you need more of the more expensive chocolate. Which one is more expensive? The premium brand is, so you need more of that type. Cross off answer (A) as well, since that would mean fewer pounds of the premium brand.

Next, if you feel comfortable with this, you can actually think your way through the rest of the math. Answer (B) came to \$30, but B spent \$31, so you need to add just one more dollar. The difference in price between P and R is also just one dollar. So if you add one pound of P and take away one pound of R, you'll pay one more dollar. The answer must be (C), 3 pounds.

If you're not comfortable thinking that through, that's fine—just go back to the standard process and try answer (D) next. Use the scratch paper setup you already have, and run the new answer choice through the same process.

If P is 4, then R is 3. The cost is $(5)(4) + (4)(3) = 20 + 12 = \$32$. This is too much, so answer (D) is incorrect. Then examine the pattern. Answer (B) was too small at \$30 and answer (D) was too large at \$32, so answer (C) must be correct.

Either way, the correct answer is (C).

You can also solve algebraically, but fair warning: On this problem, since the answer choice values are such nice numbers, the algebra is probably more annoying than working backwards. It's still a good idea to know how this works, though, because you may need to use algebra on a different one. For example:

p = pounds of premium chocolate candies
r = pounds of regular chocolate candies

You would also want to write down something similar to this:

$p = \_\_\_\_?$

What else can you write down? Bronte bought a 7-pound box of the candies. Both premium and regular make up that 7 pounds, so you can write an equation:

$$p + r = 7$$

The other given concerns the total cost of the box, \$31. The total cost is equal to the cost of the premium chocolates plus the cost of the regular chocolates.

This is a relationship the GMAT expects you to know: *Total Cost* = *Unit Price* × *Quantity*. You can express total cost using information you already have:

$$\text{Total Cost of Box} = \$31$$
$$\text{Cost of Premiums} = (5\ \$/\text{pound}) \times (p\ \text{pounds}) = 5p$$
$$\text{Cost of Regulars} = (4\ \$/\text{pound}) \times (r\ \text{pounds}) = 4r$$

Note that you can translate "dollars per pound" to "\$/pound." In general, the word *per* is translated as "divided by."

Put that all together to get the second equation:

$$31 = 5p + 4r$$

Here's your current scratch paper; how can you solve?

$p = \#$ prem

$r = \#$ reg

$p + r = 7$

$31 = 5p + 4r$

$p = \_\_\_\_?$

When you have two equations with two variables, the most efficient way to find the desired value is to eliminate the unwanted variable in order to solve for the desired variable.

You're looking for p. To eliminate r, first isolate it in one of the equations. It is easier to isolate r in the first equation:

$$r + p = 7 \longrightarrow r = 7 - p$$

Now, replace r with $(7 - p)$ in the second equation and solve for p:

$$31 = 5p + 4(7 - p)$$
$$31 = 5p + 28 - 4p$$
$$3 = p$$

The correct answer is (C).

Story problems typically toss a lot of information at you, which is why it is so important to have a good process. Understand the story first—and possibly hold off on jotting down the math until you start to figure out your Plan. When you Understand and have a Plan, then you can go ahead and Solve.

One last thing: A lot of stories have what's called a *hidden integer constraint.* If the story is talking about people or cars or marbles, there's an assumption that you have only whole numbers of people or cars or marbles. You'll never have 1.2 people or half of a car.

Pay Attention to Units

Unlike problems that test pure algebra, Word Problems have a context or story. The values, both unknown and known, have a meaning. Practically, this means that every value in a Word Problem has units.

Every equation that correctly represents a relationship has units that make sense. Most relationships are either additive or multiplicative.

Additive Relationships

In the chocolates problem, there were two additive relationships:

$$\text{pounds } p + \text{pounds } r = 7 \text{ pounds}$$

$$\$31 = \text{cost of } p + \text{cost of } r$$

For each equation, the units of every term are the same; for example, pounds plus pounds equals pounds.

Multiplicative Relationships

Remember this relationship?

$$\text{Total Cost} = \text{Unit Price} \times \text{Quantity}$$

In the problem, the cost of p is \$5 per pound and the cost of r is \$4 per pound. If you're solving algebraically, it works out this way:

$$5\left(\frac{\text{dollars}}{\text{pound}}\right) \times p\ (\text{pounds}) = 5p\ (\text{dollars})$$

$$4\left(\frac{\text{dollars}}{\text{pound}}\right) \times r\ (\text{pounds}) = 4r\ (\text{dollars})$$

For multiplicative relationships, treat units like numerators and denominators. Units that are multiplied together *do* change.

In the equations above, pounds in the denominator of the first term cancel out pounds in the numerator of the second term, leaving dollars as the final units:

$$5\left(\frac{\text{dollars}}{\cancel{\text{pounds}}}\right) \times p\ \left(\cancel{\text{pounds}}\right) = 5p\ (\text{dollars})$$

Look at the formula for area to see what happens to the same units when they appear on the same side of the fraction (l = length and w = width):

$$l\ (\text{feet}) \times w\ (\text{feet}) = lw\ \left(\text{feet}^2\right)$$

Keep track of the units to stay on track in the calculation.

Common Relationships

The GMAT will assume that you have mastered the following relationships. Notice that for all of these relationships, the units follow the rules laid out in the previous section:

- Total Cost (\$) = Unit Price (\$/unit) × Quantity Purchased (units)
- Profit (\$) = Revenue (\$) − Cost (\$)
- Total Earnings (\$) = Wage Rate (\$/hour) × Hours Worked (hours)
- Miles = Miles per Hour × Hours
- Miles = Miles per Gallon × Gallons

17

Units Conversion

When values with units are multiplied or divided, the units change. This property is the basis of using **conversion factors** to convert units. A conversion factor is a fraction whose numerator and denominator have different units but the same value.

For instance, how many seconds are in 7 minutes? There are 60 seconds in a minute. In this case, $\frac{60 \text{ seconds}}{1 \text{ minute}}$ is a conversion factor. Because the numerator and denominator are the same, multiplying by a conversion factor is just a sneaky way of multiplying by 1. The multiplication looks like this:

$$7 \text{ minutes} \times \frac{60 \text{ seconds}}{1 \text{ minute}} = 420 \text{ seconds}$$

Because you are multiplying, you can cancel minutes, leaving the desired units (seconds).

Questions will occasionally center around your ability to convert units. Try the following example:

> A certain medicine requires 4 doses per day. If each dose is 150 milligrams, how many milligrams of medicine will a person have taken after the end of the third day, if the medicine is used as directed?

For any question that involves unit conversion, there will have to be some concrete value given. In this case, you were told that the time period is three days, that there are 4 doses/day, and that 1 dose equals 150 milligrams.

Now, you need to know what the question wants. It's asking for the number of milligrams of medicine that will be taken in that time. How can you combine all of those givens so that the only units that remain are milligrams?

Combine the calculations into one big expression:

$$3 \cancel{\text{days}} \times \frac{4 \cancel{\text{doses}}}{1 \cancel{\text{day}}} \times \frac{150 \text{ milligrams}}{1 \cancel{\text{dose}}} = 1{,}800 \text{ milligrams}$$

17

During the GMAT, you may not actually write out the units for each piece of multiplication. If you don't, however, make sure that your conversion factors are set up properly to cancel out the units you don't want and to leave the units you do want.

Finally, keep an eye out for more of these relationships! For instance, rate and work problems are also built on a common relationship that you're expected to know for the test; you'll learn about that relationship later.

Advanced material for the Word Problems unit (primarily covering additional strategies for overlapping sets and consecutive integers) can be found in Atlas, Manhattan Prep's online learning platform. Use the online material only if you feel that you have mastered everything in the Word Problems unit of this strategy guide and only if you are aiming for a Quant section score of 48 or higher.

Problem Set

Now that you've finished the chapter, try the following problems.

1. United Telephone charges a base rate of $10.00 for service, plus an additional charge of $0.25 per minute. Atlantic Call charges a base rate of $12.00 for service, plus an additional charge of $0.20 per minute. For what number of minutes would the bills for each telephone company be the same?

2. Caleb spends $72.50 on 50 hamburgers for the marching band. If single burgers cost $1.00 each and double burgers cost $1.50 each, how many double burgers did he buy?

3. Carina has 100 ounces of coffee divided into packages of 5 or 10 ounces. If she has 2 more 5-ounce packages than 10-ounce packages, how many 10-ounce packages does she have?

   (A) 2
   (B) 4
   (C) 6
   (D) 8
   (E) 10

4. A circus earned $150,000 in ticket revenue by selling 1,800 VIP and Standard tickets. They sold 25% more Standard tickets than VIP tickets. If the revenue from Standard tickets represents one-third of the total ticket revenue, what is the price of a VIP ticket?

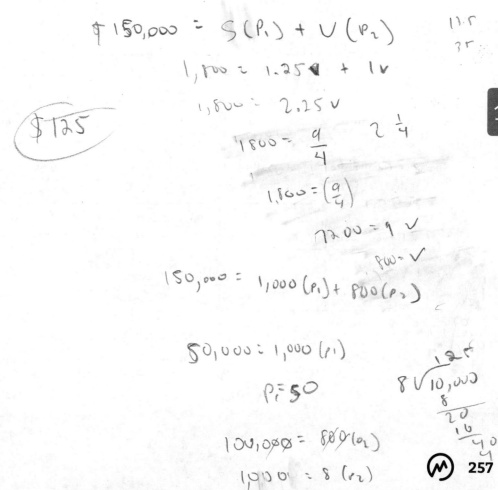

17

Solutions

1. **40 minutes:** Let $x =$ the number of minutes.

    A call made by United Telephone costs \$10.00 plus \$0.25 per minute: $10 + 0.25x$.

    A call made by Atlantic Call costs \$12.00 plus \$0.20 per minute: $12 + 0.20x$.

    Set the expressions equal to each other and solve for x:

$$\begin{aligned} 10 + 0.25x &= 12 + 0.20x \\ 0.05x &= 2 \\ x &= 40 \end{aligned}$$

    For that last math step, you can multiply both sides by 100 to get rid of the decimal ($5x = 200$), then solve. You could also recognize that 0.05 is the same as 5% and use percent benchmarks to solve. If 5% of a number equals 2, then 10% of the number equals 4, and 100% of the number equals 40.

2. **45 double burgers:** Let $s =$ the number of single burgers purchased and $d =$ the number of double burgers purchased:

    Caleb bought 50 burgers:

$$s + d = 50$$

    Caleb spent \$72.50 in all:

$$s + 1.5d = 72.5$$

    Combine the two equations by subtracting equation 1 from equation 2:

$$\begin{aligned} s + 1.5d &= 72.50 \\ -\left(s + d\right. &= \left.50\right) \\ \hline 0.5d &= 22.5 \\ d &= 45 \end{aligned}$$

17

3. **(C) 6:** The answers are small integers and represent a single variable in the problem, so work backwards to solve. Set up a table to keep your work organized as you test the answer choices. Start with answer (B) or (D).

    Let T equal the number of 10-ounce packages and F equal the number of 5-ounce packages. *Last* refers to the value in the previous column.

$T =$	Amt in 10 oz ($T \times 10$)	Amt in 5 oz (100 – last)	$F =$ (last/5)	$F - T = 2$?
(B) 4	40 oz	60 oz	12	12 – 4 = 8 No
(D) 8	80 oz	20 oz	4	4 – 8 = –4 No

    Answer (B) is too large and answer (D) is too small; the correct answer must be in between the two.

Alternatively, solve via algebra. Let F equal the number of 5-ounce packages and T equal the number of 10-ounce packages:

Carina has 100 ounces of coffee:

$$5F + 10T = 100$$

She has 2 more 5-ounce packages than 10-ounce packages:

$$F = T + 2$$

Combine the equations by substituting the value of F from equation 2 into equation 1:

$$\begin{aligned} 5(T+2) + 10T &= 100 \\ 5T + 10 + 10T &= 100 \\ 15T + 10 &= 100 \\ 15T &= 90 \\ T &= 6 \end{aligned}$$

4. **\$125:** To answer this question correctly, make sure to differentiate between the *price* of tickets and the *quantity* of tickets sold. Let V equal the number of VIP tickets sold and S equal the number of Standard tickets sold.

The question indicates that the circus sold a total of 1,800 tickets, and that the circus sold 25% more Standard tickets than VIP tickets. Create two equations:

$$V + S = 1{,}800 \qquad 1.25V = S$$

Use these equations to figure out how many VIP tickets were sold:

$$\begin{aligned} V + S &= 1{,}800 \\ V + (1.25V) &= 1{,}800 \\ 2.25V &= 1{,}800 \\ \frac{9}{4}V &= 1{,}800 \\ V &= 1{,}800\left(\frac{4}{9}\right) \\ V &= 800 \end{aligned}$$

Now, find the cost per VIP ticket. The circus earned \$150,000 in ticket revenue, and Standard tickets represented one-third of that revenue. Therefore, Standard tickets accounted for $\frac{1}{3} \times \$150{,}000 = \$50{,}000$. VIP tickets then accounted for the other \$100,000 in revenue.

Thus, $\frac{100{,}000}{800} = \frac{1{,}000}{8} = \$125$ per VIP ticket.

CHAPTER 18

Strategy: Logic It Out

In This Chapter

- Draw It Out
- Maximizing and Minimizing
- Write Out the Scenarios
- When in Doubt, Logic It Out

In this chapter, you will learn how to logic your way to answers on all kinds of story problems, including drawing out a story, listing out and testing scenarios, maximizing and minimizing, and more.

CHAPTER 18 Strategy: Logic It Out

Numerous times throughout this guide, you've learned how to use real numbers or to sketch out a story—basically, to use a more "real-world" approach to perform the necessary math.

This chapter contains more ways to **logic it out** on the GMAT.

Try this problem:

> Five identical pieces of wire are soldered together end-to-end to form one longer wire, with the pieces overlapping by 4 centimeters at each joint. If the wire thus made is exactly 1 meter long, how long, in centimeters, is each of the identical pieces? (1 meter = 100 centimeters)
>
> (A) 21.2
> (B) 22
> (C) 23.2
> (D) 24
> (E) 25.4

The setup of this problem is unusual, so draw out the scenario in order to understand what the problem is describing:

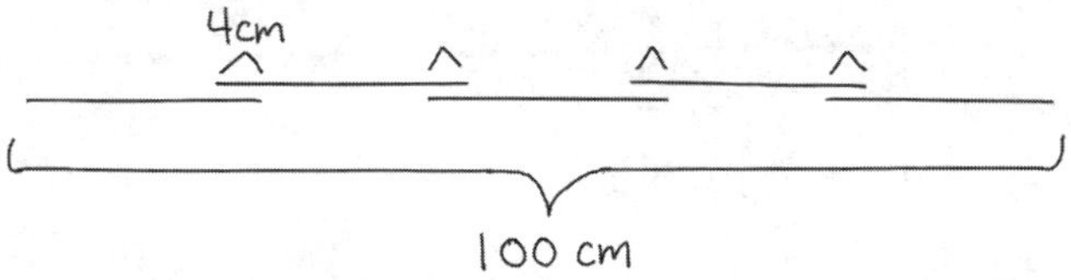

How many overlapping areas are there? Many people make the mistake of thinking that, because there are five pieces of wire, there are also five spots where the wires join. It turns out that there are only four joints! Sketch out weird scenarios to catch these kinds of details.

The total length is 100 centimeters plus those extra amounts where the wires overlap. What happens when you solder the wire together? Consider just the first two segments. Imagine that each one is 10 centimeters long (they aren't—this is just to understand what's going on and to help you figure out your plan).

If two 10-centimeter wires were laid end-to-end with no overlap, the length would be 20 centimeters. But since the two are overlapped, you'll lose a portion of that length. How much?

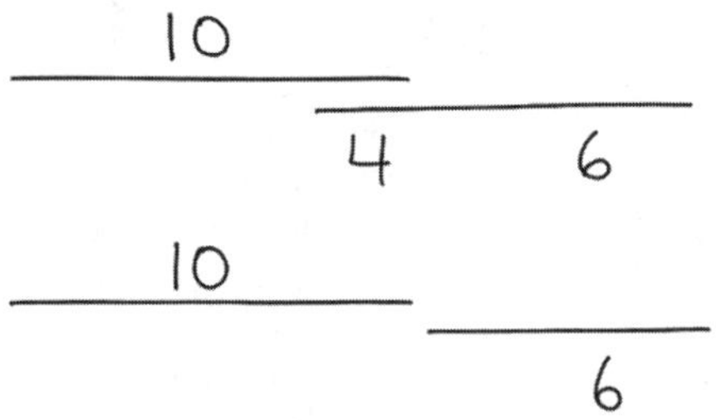

When they're soldered (melted) together, you don't lose *both* of the overlapping segments—if you did, then there would be a gap in the wire. The two pieces wouldn't actually be connected. Rather, think of it as though the top 4-centimeter segment stays, but the bottom one "disappears" (because it gets melted into the top one). So the length is $10 + 6 = 16$ centimeters. You've lost the length of *one* of the overlapping segments, or 4 centimeters.

Back to the given problem. There are four overlapping segments. You lose 4 centimeters at each connection, so you'll lose a total of 16 centimeters. The full length *before* the wires are soldered together—shown in the first picture—is $100 + 16 = 116$ centimeters.

Because there are five wires, the length of each one is $\frac{116}{5} = \ldots$ wait! That's a little annoying without a calculator. Break it into pieces that are more easily divisible by 5:

$$\frac{100 + 15 + 1}{5}$$

$$\frac{100}{5} = 20 \qquad \frac{15}{5} = 3 \qquad \frac{1}{5} = 0.2$$

The length is 23.2. Keep an eye on the answer choices as you do this math. Once you realize that the answer is 23-point-*something*, you can stop.

The correct answer is (C).

This problem can also be done algebraically; the relevant equation is $5x - 4(4) = 100$, where x is the length of each wire. Those who don't draw it out, though, are more likely to think that there are five joints and mistakenly write the equation as $5x - 5(4) = 100$, which leads to trap answer (D) 24.

Draw It Out

There are multiple ways that you can avoid "textbook" math to get to the answer more quickly and easily on the GMAT. Whenever you find a problem that could actually be happening to someone in the real world, ask yourself: If I were in this situation right now, how would I try to figure out the answer?

You almost certainly wouldn't start writing equations. Instead, you'd sketch out the situation using a combination of logic, math, and just trying out numbers or scenarios.

How could you sketch out this problem?

> A train travels at a constant rate of 90 kilometers/hour. How many hours does it take the train to travel 450,000 meters? (1 kilometer = 1,000 meters)

First, 450,000 meters is a really annoying number—but the problem gives you a conversion metric. And the rate is in kilometers per hour, so definitely convert the ugly meters figure to kilometers. Divide by 1,000 to convert this distance to 450 kilometers.

Logic it out: You're driving the train and you're going a steady 90 kilometers/hour. How long is it going to take you to go 450 kilometers? After an hour, you've gone 90 kilometers. After two hours, you've gone 180. What's the pattern?

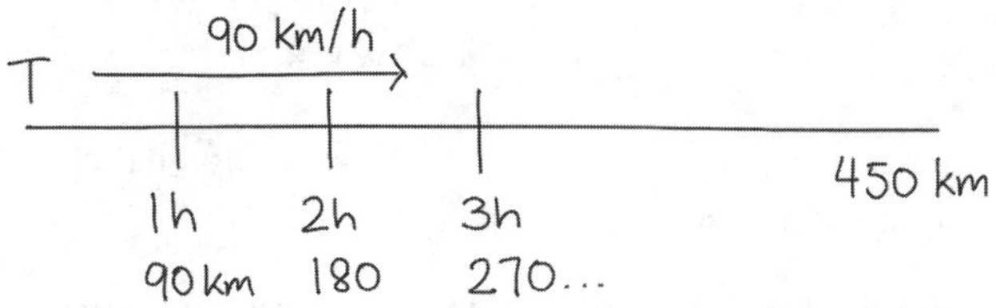

It's all in multiples of 90. It's going to take you five multiples, or 5 hours, to get to 450. (By the way, if you like, you can make the numbers easier to look at by chopping a 0 off of each one. You're driving 9 kilometers every hour and want to go 45 kilometers total. That will take 5 hours.)

A problem could also ask something like this:

> A train leaves a station at 1 p.m. and travels at a constant rate of 90 kilometers/hour. At what time does the train reach the next station, a distance of 450,000 meters? (1 kilometer = 1,000 meters)

It still takes the train 5 hours to travel that distance, but the answer is now 1 p.m. + 5 hours = 6 p.m. As on any problem, take note of what the question wants you to find; a good (and very annoying!) trap answer on this problem would be 5 p.m.

Most of the time, the GMAT will ask for the stopwatch time; occasionally, it will ask you to solve in terms of clock times.

There are usually multiple ways to draw out the problem to get to the answer, so you aren't stuck trying to figure out the main textbook math method. Put yourself in the situation and ask yourself how you would go about this in the real world. You'd almost never start writing a bunch of equations; rather, you'd use logic and estimation to get to a close-enough answer.

Rate and work problems, in particular, often lend themselves well to using logic to solve. You'll see more of these in the next chapter.

18

Maximizing and Minimizing

As you learned a little earlier in this guide, a story problem might ask you to find the minimum or maximum possible value of something.

For example:

> There are enough available spaces on a school team to select at most $\frac{1}{3}$ of the 50 students trying out for the team. What is the greatest number of students that could be rejected while still filling all available spaces for the team?
>
> (A) 16
> (B) 17
> (C) 33
> (D) 34
> (E) 35

You're asked to maximize the number of *rejected* students. Think about what else you may need to minimize (or maximize) in the problem in order to maximize this number.

First, fill all available spaces on the team. If at most $\frac{1}{3}$ of the students can be selected, then at most $\frac{50}{3}$, or $16\frac{2}{3}$, students can be selected. It's impossible to select $\frac{2}{3}$ of a person, though! Is the maximum possible 16 or 17?

If the *maximum* is 16 and a bit, then you can't go up to 17. Round down to 16. (Note that both of these values are in the answers; they're traps!)

The maximum number of rejected students, then, is $50 - 16 = 34$. The correct answer is (D).

This problem has a hidden *integer constraint*. Notice also that you have to be careful to round in the right direction—not up, but down. If the maximum number of available spaces is $16\frac{2}{3}$, then 17 students is more than that max, so round down to 16.

Try another. How would you logic this problem out?

> Orange Computers is breaking up its conference attendees into groups. Each group must have exactly 1 person from Division A, 2 people from Division B, and 3 people from Division C. There are 20 people from Division A, 30 people from Division B, and 40 people from Division C at the conference. What is the smallest number of people who will NOT be able to be assigned to a group?
>
> (A) 12
> (B) 5
> (C) 2
> (D) 1
> (E) 0

You're in charge of the conference and you have to figure this out. First, you need to **understand** what the parameters are. Jot down the given information on your scrap paper:

Div.	Total People	Per Group
A	20	1
B	30	2
C	40	3

Plan. The goal is to place as many people as possible in groups. Consider Division A. There are 20 of these people and you need 1 per group, so that's 20 groups…

Oh, wait. For 20 groups, you'd need 40 people from B and there are only 30, so that won't work. There have to be fewer than 20 groups. (And, incidentally, this proves that at least 1 person will be without a group, so the answer can't be 0.) Hmm. If starting with Division B, you'd have 15 groups, but that would require 45 people from Division C and there are only 40.

The most constrained or limited group is Division C because you need 3 in each group and you only have 40 people overall, for a maximum of 13 groups. So start there.

Solve. Division C can make 13 groups of 3, using a total of 39 people. One person is left without a group. Glance at the answers. Answer (E) can't be correct, since at least 1 person is already without a group (if you didn't already notice this earlier).

Next, Division B will use $13 \times 2 = 26$ people. There are 4 Division B people left without a group. So there are at least 5 total without a group now; eliminate answers (C) and (D).

You'll also need 13 people from Division A, leaving 7 more without a group. Look at the answers. Don't even bother to add up the numbers—the answer must be more than 5, so answer (A) must be correct.

Some max/min problems will be more like the first one, where the path of the math is fairly straightforward, but you have to make decisions along the way about maximizing or minimizing other pieces in order to get to your desired answer.

In others, the starting point won't be so obvious. As with the second problem, you'll try a couple of scenarios until you find the limiting factor, and then you'll follow the math from there.

In both cases, make sure to pay attention to any constraints, especially those not explicitly stated. People and saxophones and rabbits cannot be split into fractional parts.

Write Out the Scenarios

Here's another variation on how to use logic:

> During a week-long sale at a car dealership, the greatest number of cars sold on any one day was 12. If at least 2 cars were sold each day, was the average (arithmetic mean) daily number of cars sold during that week greater than 6 ?
>
> (1) During that week, the second fewest number of cars sold on any one day was 4.
>
> (2) During that week, the median number of cars sold was 10.

Note: The average is found by taking the sum of a set of numbers and dividing by the number of terms. The median is the middle number in a set of numbers arranged in increasing order. You'll learn more about statistics a bit later in this guide—but you can solve this problem even though you haven't relearned much of anything about stats yet!

Pretend you're the manager of the car dealership and the owner has asked you to figure this out. Your manager knows you're not a mathematician. . .and you don't need to be to do this.

You know that the highest day was 12, but you don't know which day of the week that was. And at least 2 cars were sold each day, but more cars could have been sold. The problem allows multiple possible scenarios, so how could you draw something that shows what you know but allows for flexibility?

Glance at the statements. They provide information about the fewest number of sales and the median number of sales.

Since it's asking about median, try organizing the number of sales from smallest to largest.

Draw out seven slots (one for each day) and add the information given in the question stem:

$$\underline{\geq 2}\ \ \underline{\quad}\ \ \underline{\quad}\ \ \underline{\quad}\ \ \underline{\quad}\ \ \underline{\quad}\ \ \underline{12}$$

The problem indicates that at least 2 cars were sold on each day, so the smallest number has to be at least 2 (though it could be greater). The greatest number sold on any one day was 12. The other days have to be somewhere in this range from 2 to 12, *inclusive*. You are allowed to have two days on which the same number of cars were sold.

The question asks whether the average number of daily sales for the week is more than 6. Because this is a Yes/No DS question, test each statement to see whether it can give you both a "Yes, the average is more than 6" answer and a "No, the average is not more than 6" answer. If so, then you'll know the statement is insufficient.

(1) During that week, the second smallest number of cars sold on any one day was 4.

Draw out a version of the scenario that includes statement (1):

$$\underline{\geq 2}\ \ \underline{4}\ \ \underline{\quad}\ \ \underline{\quad}\ \ \underline{\quad}\ \ \underline{\quad}\ \ \underline{12}$$

Can you find a way to make the average less than 6? Keep the first day at 2 and make the other days as small as possible. You can use the same number more than once:

$$\underline{\geq 2}\ \ \underline{4}\ \ \underline{4}\ \ \underline{4}\ \ \underline{4}\ \ \underline{4}\ \ \underline{12}$$

If the first day is 2, the sum of the numbers is 34. The average is $\frac{34}{7}$, which is a little less than 5.

Can you also make the average greater than 6? Try making the numbers as big as you can:

$$\underline{4}\ \ \underline{4}\ \ \underline{12}\ \ \underline{12}\ \ \underline{12}\ \ \underline{12}\ \ \underline{12}$$

You may be able to eyeball that and tell it will be greater than 6. If not, calculate: The sum is $8 + 5(12) = 68$, so the average is $\frac{68}{7}$, which is a bit less than 10.

Statement (1) is not sufficient because the average might be greater than or less than 6.

Cross off answers (A) and (D) and move to statement (2):

(2) During that week, the median number of cars sold was 10.

Again, draw out the scenario (using *only* the second statement this time!). The median is the middle number or slot in the list:

$$\underline{\geq 2}\quad\underline{\quad}\quad\underline{\quad}\quad\underline{10}\quad\underline{\quad}\quad\underline{\quad}\quad\underline{12}$$

Can you make the average less than 6 ? The three lowest days could each be 2. Then, the next three days could each be 10.

$$\underline{2}\quad\underline{2}\quad\underline{2}\quad\underline{10}\quad\underline{10}\quad\underline{10}\quad\underline{12}$$

The sum is $6 + 30 + 12 = 48$. The average is $\frac{48}{7}$, or just less than 7, but greater than 6. The numbers cannot be made any smaller. First, you have to have a minimum of 2 a day. Once you hit the median of 10 in the middle slot, you have to have something greater than or equal to the median for the remaining slots to the right.

The smallest possible average is greater than 6, so this statement is sufficient to answer the question. The correct answer is (B).

If a problem talks about a set of numbers but doesn't give you the value of all of those numbers, try drawing out slots to represent each number in the set and stepping through the allowed scenarios. If it's a max/min problem, you'll probably want to test the extreme scenarios (make everything as small as possible or as large as possible) to see the range of possible outcomes.

If a problem includes information about the median, you will probably want to order the numbers from least to greatest.

When in Doubt, Logic It Out

Sketching out a problem and using logic is a fantastic way to get through some especially annoying story problems—and not just when you're in doubt. As you get better at working in this way, you'll find that these methods are very effective even when you do know how to do the "textbook" version of the math.

First, put yourself in the problem; pretend that you have to figure this out in the real world. Then, ask yourself what you would do in order to find the answer—even if just to estimate and narrow down the answers.

As you work, keep your eye on the answer choices. Often, on GMAT stories, you'll be able to stop working before you reach the "true" end of the math, because the other four answers will already have been eliminated.

Problem Set

Now that you've finished the chapter, try the following problems. You'll get additional chances to practice these techniques later in this guide.

1. A bookshelf holds both paperback and hardcover books. The ratio of paperback books to hardcover books is 22 to 3. How many paperback books are on the shelf?

   (1) The number of books on the shelf is between 202 and 247, inclusive.

   (2) If 18 paperback books were removed from the shelf and replaced with 18 hardcover books, the resulting ratio of paperback books to hardcover books on the shelf would be 4 to 1.

2. a, b, and c are integers in the set $\{a, 72, b, 51, c, 85\}$. Is the median of the set greater than 70 ?

   (1) $b > c > 69$

   (2) $a < c < 71$

3. Velma has exactly one week to learn all 71 Japanese hiragana characters. If she can learn at most a dozen of them on any one day and will only have time to learn four of them on Friday, what is the least number of hiragana that Velma will have to learn on Saturday?

4. A casino uses chips in \$5 and \$7 denominations only. Which of the following amounts CANNOT be paid out using these chips?

   (A) \$31
   (B) \$29
   (C) \$26
   (D) \$23
   (E) \$21

Answers and explanations follow on the next page. ▶ ▶ ▶

Solutions

1. **(D):** The question stem states that the ratio of paperback books to hardcover books is 22 to 3 and asks for the number of paperback books. Set up a ratio table:

	P	***H***	**Total**
R	22	3	25
M			
A			

The actual number of paperbacks must be a multiple of 22, the number of hardcovers must be a multiple of 3, and the total number of books must be a multiple of 25. Use this knowledge to evaluate the statements.

(1) SUFFICIENT: There is only one multiple of 25 between 202 and 247, so the total number of books must be 225. You can find the unknown multiplier, so you can also find the number of *P*'s.

(2) SUFFICIENT: Hmm. The starting ratio can be written as an equation: $\frac{P}{H} = \frac{22}{3}$.

Then, a new ratio is given. Use this information to write a second equation: $\left(\frac{P-18}{H+18}\right) = \frac{4}{1}$. You now have two equations and two variables; can you solve?

Check to make sure that both equations are linear and that you do have two *different* equations. Cross-multiply: $3P = 22H$ and $(P - 18) = 4(H + 18)$. You might want to do one more step with the second one (but don't do more work than you have to do): $P = 4H + (18)(4) + 18$.

Yes, the equations are both linear (no squares or similar) and they are not the same equation. You can solve for the individual values of P and H.

The correct answer is **(D)**: Each statement works alone.

2. **(A):** The set is not in increasing order already, so you're going to need to do that yourself. Draw out six spaces and imagine they contain values ordered from low to high. What would the median be? Since there are an even number of numbers, the median of a set of six integers is the average of the two middle terms (the third and fourth) when the terms are placed in order from low to high.

____ ____ ____ ____ ____ ____
low   median (third and fourth)   high

Glance at the statements. Together with the question stem, many scenarios are possible, so test cases on this problem.

(1) SUFFICIENT: Since the statement establishes the smallest possible values for b and c, start with the minimum case. If c is an integer greater than 69, the smallest c can be is 70. By similar logic, the smallest b could be is 71. In this case, the set contains the values $\{a, 51, 70, 71, 72, 85\}$. The only unknown is the value of a.

Try the smallest possibility for a. If $a \leq 51$, the median is halfway between 70 and 71, which is greater than 70.

$a \leq 51$	51	$c = 70$	$b = 71$	72	85
low		median	median		high

Next, place a in the middle. If $a = 70$ or 71, then the median is either between 70 and 71 or between 71 and 71—both of which are greater than 70. Here's the 71 and 71 case:

51	$c = 70$	$a = 71$	$b = 71$	72	85
low		median	median		high

If $a > 71$, the ordered set is $\{51, 70, 71, 72, a, 85\}$, so the median is between 71 and 72, or again greater than 71:

51	$c = 70$	$b = 71$	72	$a = 72$	85
low		median	median		high

In all cases, the median is greater than 70 using the *smallest* possible values for all three variables, so the answer is a definite Yes.

(2) INSUFFICIENT: Since the statement establishes the greatest possible values for a and c, start with the maximum case. If c is an integer less than 71, the greatest c can be is 70. By similar logic, the greatest a could be is 69. In this case, the set is $\{b, 51, 69, 70, 72, 85\}$. The only unknown is the value of b.

If $b \leq 51$, the ordered set is $\{b, 51, 69, 70, 72, 85\}$ and the median is halfway between 69 and 70, which is less than 70. The answer is No, the median is not greater than 70 as shown below:

$b \leq 51$	51	$a = 69$	$c = 70$	72	85
low		median	median		high

Try to get a Yes answer next. Jump much higher for b.

If $b = 90$, the ordered set is $\{51, 69, 70, 72, 85, 90\}$, the median is between 70 and 72, which is greater than 70.

Because there are both Yes and No cases, this statement is not sufficient.

The correct answer is **(A)**: Statement (1) works alone, but statement (2) does not.

3. **7:** Draw it out! Draw seven slots and label them for the days of the week. The problem states that Velma will learn 4 hiragana on Friday and at most 12 on any other day. Finally, it asked for the least possible number that she will need to learn on Saturday:

≤ 12	≤ 12	≤ 12	≤ 12	≤ 12	4	least?
Sun	M	Tu	W	Th	F	Sat

18

Since she'll learn 4 on Friday, she has 67 more to learn. To minimize the number of hiragana that she will have to learn on Saturday, *maximize* the number that she learns on the other days. If Velma learns the maximum of 12 hiragana from Sunday to Thursday, then she will have 67 − 5(12) = 7 left for Saturday:

12	12	12	12	12	4	7
Sun	M	Tu	W	Th	F	Sat

4. **(D) $23:** The payouts will have to be in the sum of some integer number of $5 chips and some integer number of $7 chips. Which of the answer choices *cannot* be the sum? First, check the answers for any multiples of 7 and/or 5; this eliminates answer (E). Glance at the answers. The numbers are not that large, so you could try to re-create them. Write out some multiples of 5 and 7 and try to combine them to create the remaining four answers:

5	7
10	14
15	21
20	

You don't need to go higher than 20 for the multiples of 5. If that went up to 25 and you added 7 more, you'd be above the greatest number in the answers. Ditto, if you went up to 28 for the multiples of 7, then added 5 more, you'd be beyond the range of answers.

Now, pair up the numbers systematically and see which answer choices you can match. 5 + 7, 5 + 14, 5 + 21 ? Bingo, that last one equals 26. Eliminate answer (C).

Next, 10 + 7, 10 + 14, 10 + 21 ? Bingo again, the last one equals 31. Eliminate answer (A).

Keep going; 15 + 14 = 29, so eliminate answer (B). The only remaining value is 23; by process of elimination, it must be the sum that cannot be paid out in these chips, so **(D)** is the correct answer.

CHAPTER 19

Rates and Work

In This Chapter

- Basic Motion: The RTD Chart
- Matching Units in the RTD Chart
- Multiple Rates
- Relative Rates
- Average Rate: Find the Total Time
- Basic Work Problems
- Working Together: Add the Rates

In this chapter, you will learn how to set up and solve a variety of rate and work problems, both algebraically and by using logic. (The latter approach is often the easier one!) You'll also learn what to do with more complicated scenarios such as relative rates, average rates, and working together.

CHAPTER 19 Rates and Work

Rate problems come in a variety of forms on the GMAT, but all are marked by three primary components: *rate*, *time*, and either *distance* or *work*.

These three elements are related by the following equations:

Rate × Time = Distance

Rate × Time = Work

These equations can be abbreviated as $RT = D$ or as $RT = W$.

This chapter will discuss the ways in which the GMAT makes rate situations more complicated. Often, $RT = D$ problems, also known as RTD problems, will involve more than one person or vehicle traveling. Similarly, many $RT = W$ problems will involve more than one worker.

Let's get started with a review of some fundamental properties of rate problems.

Basic Motion: The RTD Chart

All basic motion problems involve three elements: rate, time, and distance.

Rate is expressed as a ratio of distance and time, with two corresponding units. Some examples of rates include 30 miles per hour, 10 meters/second, and 15 kilometers/day.

Time is expressed using a unit of time. Some examples of times include 6 hours, 23 seconds, and 5 months.

Distance is expressed using a unit of distance. Some examples of distances include 18 miles, 20 meters, and 100 kilometers.

You can make an RTD chart to organize the information for a basic motion problem. Read the problem and fill in two of the variables. Then, use the $RT = D$ formula to find the missing variable. For example:

If a car is traveling at 30 miles per hour, how long does it take to travel 75 miles?

Fill in your RTD chart with the given information. Then, solve for the time:

	Rate (miles/hour)	×	*Time* (hours)	=	*Distance* (miles)
Car	30	×		=	75

$30t = 75$, or $t = 2.5$ hours

Up next is a much more complicated problem. Pretend you're Annika, actually hiking right now, and see what you can do with the Logic It Out approach from the prior chapter.

Annika hikes at a constant rate of 12 minutes per kilometer. She has hiked 2.75 kilometers east from the start of a hiking trail when she realizes that she has to be back at the start of the trail in 45 minutes. If Annika continues east, then turns around and retraces her path to reach the start of the trail in exactly 45 minutes, for how many kilometers total did she hike east?

(A) 2.25
(B) 2.75
(C) 3.25
(D) 3.75
(E) 4.25

This is a pretty nasty problem. You could use an RTD chart to solve algebraically. But to set that up correctly, you've got to understand the weird scenario, so start by sketching it out. (And then, it turns out, you can just keep going and solve fully that way!)

Here's Annika partway down her hiking trail, suddenly realizing that she's got 45 minutes till she needs to get back:

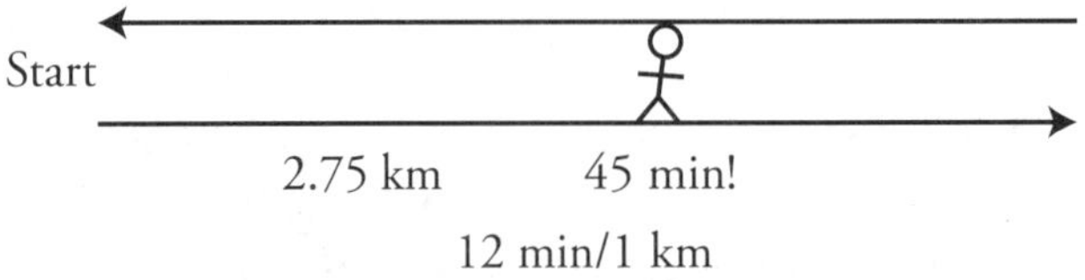

Pretend that isn't Annika at all—now, it's you. Are you going to whip out paper and pencil to start doing some algebra to figure out when to turn around? No way. You're going to use real-world logic to figure out what to do.

What do you want to figure out? The question asks how far you will have traveled east. The first part of the distance is 2.75 kilometers, but you don't know how much *farther* east you can go before turning around. Glance at the answers. Hey, the answer can't be (A) because you've already gone more than 2.25 kilometers. And the answer can only be (B) if you have to turn around right now. Do you?

First, if you didn't go a step farther, how long would it take to get back?

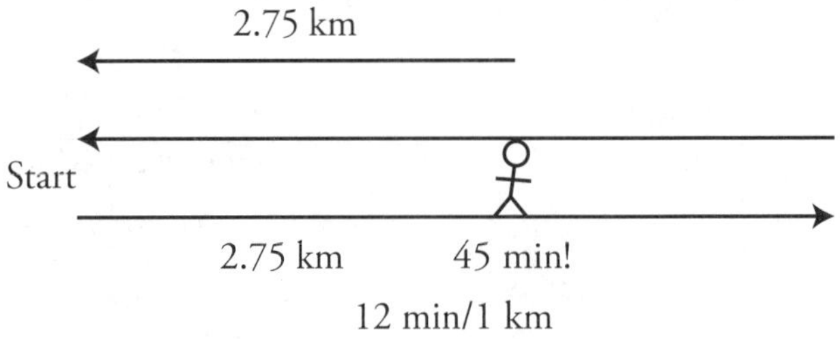

You're going to need 2.75 kilometers to get back. How long is that going to take if you're going 1 kilometer every 12 minutes? Let's see, you can go 3 kilometers in (count it out) 12, 24, 36 minutes. So if you turn around right now (at 2.75 kilometers), you'll be back in less than 36 minutes. But you still have 45 minutes to go, so answer (B) isn't correct.

The next possible answer is 3.25 kilometers. If you go that far east in total, you'd have to go another half a kilometer right now, then turn around and hike 3.25 kilometers back. How long does it take you to go 0.5 kilometer? If it takes 12 minutes to go 1 kilometer, then you'll need 6 minutes to go 0.5 kilometer.

So, first, you'd continue east for another 6 minutes. Then you'd turn around and hike back 3.25 kilometers. You can go 3 kilometers in 36 minutes, and you'd need another 3 minutes to go that last 0.25 kilometer, for a total of 39 minutes hiking west.

Therefore, 6 minutes east + 39 minutes west = 45 minutes total and you're back at your car. The correct answer is (C).

Here's another way to draw it out:

Go back to the beginning.

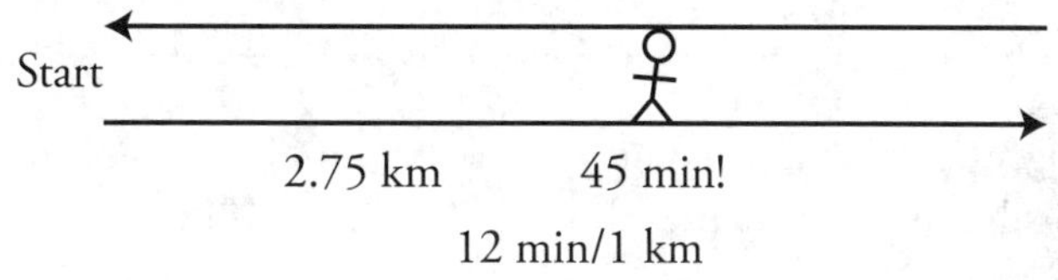

Step back from the problem for a second—forget that you want 2.75 kilometers plus some unknown distance. Look at your diagram. You're asking yourself how far you can travel east before you turn around and go back; that is, you want to know how far *half* of the trip is. If you can calculate the total distance, you can find the halfway mark.

To start, you travel 2.75 kilometers. Then, you travel another 45 minutes at 12 minutes per kilometer. You can count it out again or do the straight math—$12 \times 4 = 48$—so it takes 48 minutes to go 4 kilometers. How can you find the distance for 45 minutes?

If you hike 1 kilometer in 12 minutes, then you hike 0.25 kilometer in 3 minutes. Subtract: You hike $4 - 0.25 = 3.75$ kilometers in $48 - 3 = 45$ minutes.

Therefore, you travel $2.75 + 3.75 = 6.5$ kilometers total. Half of that, 3.25 kilometers, is spent hiking east. The correct answer is (C).

There are usually multiple ways to logic out the problem to get to the answer; you can do whatever feels easiest to you. Put yourself in the situation and ask yourself how you would go about this in the real world. You'd almost never start writing a bunch of equations; rather, you'd start just sketching out scenarios, using real-world logic and estimation to get to the answer (or close enough!).

Whenever you run across a rate or work problem, try sketching out the problem to gain practice. At first, you'll likely feel slow, but you'll gain efficiency and accuracy with practice!

Matching Units in the RTD Chart

All the units in your RTD chart must match up with one another. The two units in the rate should match up with the unit of time and the unit of distance. For example:

> An elevator operates at a constant rate of 4 seconds to rise one floor. How many floors will the elevator rise in 2 minutes?

The elevator moves 1 floor every 4 seconds: $\frac{1 \text{ floor}}{4 \text{ seconds}} = \frac{1}{4}$ floor/second.

There are two common potential mistakes people make. First, always express the rate as per *one* unit of time: one second, one minute, one hour. In the case above, the rate is the fraction $\frac{1}{4}$ of a floor per one second, not 1 floor per 4 seconds.

Second, the rate is *not* $\frac{4 \text{ seconds}}{1 \text{ floor}}$. Always express rates as *distance over time*, not as *time over distance*.

Given the rate of $\frac{1}{4}$ floor per second, how many floors will the elevator rise in 2 minutes?

Watch out! There is a problem with the RTD chart below. The rate is expressed in floors per second, but the time is expressed in minutes. This will yield an incorrect answer.

	R **(floors/second)**	×	***T*** **(minutes)**	=	***D*** **(floors)**
Elevator	0.25	×	2	=	?

To correct this table, change the time into seconds. To convert minutes to seconds, multiply 2 minutes by 60 seconds per minute, yielding 120 seconds, as shown in the chart below:

	R **(floors/second)**	×	***T*** **(seconds)**	=	***D*** **(floors)**
Elevator	0.25	×	120	=	?

Once the time has been converted from 2 minutes to 120 seconds, the time unit will match the rate unit, and you can solve for the distance using the $RT = D$ equation:

$$0.25(120) = d$$
$$d = 30 \text{ floors}$$

Thus, the elevator will go up 30 floors in 2 minutes.

You can also try to logic it out. Sketch out the answer as though it's happening in the real world.

You're on the elevator. Every 4 seconds, you're going to go up one floor, and you'll be on the elevator for 2 minutes. After 8 seconds, you're at floor 2. After 12 seconds, you're at floor 3. It's annoying to keep going up by increments of 4; what would be easier?

After 40 seconds, you're at floor 10. After 80 seconds, you're at floor 20. And after 120 seconds (or 2 minutes), you're at floor 30.

The RTD chart or the sketch-it-out approach may seem like overkill for problems in which you need to set up just one equation ($RT = D$ or $RT = W$) and then substitute. However, these two methods will help you to address more complicated scenarios, as you'll see in the next section.

Multiple Rates

Some rate problems on the GMAT will involve *more than one trip or traveler*. To deal with this, you will need to deal with multiple $RT = D$ relationships. Try this example:

> Amal runs a 30-mile course at a constant rate of 6 miles per hour. If Cahaya runs the same course at a constant rate and completes the course in 60 fewer minutes, how fast did Cahaya run?

Draw the scenario. This is a good idea whether you plan to continue with a logic-it-out approach or whether you plan to use an RTD chart; sketching the scenario will help you to keep the moving parts straight:

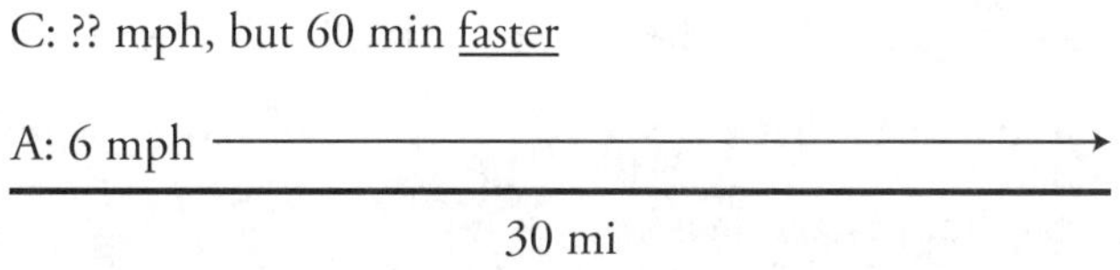

Start thinking logically. What's the connection between A and C? The time: C was 60 minutes faster than A. What can you figure out around this connection? You can figure out how fast A went. If A ran 6 miles every hour and had to cover 30 miles, then A took 5 hours to go the whole 30 miles.

Therefore, C took $5 - 1 = 4$ hours to run the 30 miles. If C covered 30 miles in 4 hours, then C ran $\frac{30}{4} = 7.5$ miles in 1 hour, or 7.5 miles per hour.

Alternatively, create an RTD chart. A chart for this question has two rows, one for Amal and one for Cahaya, as shown below:

	R **(miles/hour)**	×	***T*** **(hours)**	=	***D*** **(miles)**
Amal					
Cahaya					

Pay attention to the relationships between these two equations. Try to use the minimum necessary number of variables.

For example, Cahaya ran for 60 fewer minutes, so use t and $t - 60$ minutes for the two times. To make units match, convert 60 minutes to 1 hour. If Amal ran t hours, then Cahaya ran $(t - 1)$ hours. The distance they both ran was 30 miles. Fill in this information on your chart:

	R **(miles/hour)**	×	***T*** **(hours)**	=	***D*** **(miles)**
A	6		t		30
C	?		$t - 1$		30

Now, solve for t:

$$6t = 30$$
$$t = 5$$

If $t = 5$, then Cahaya ran for $5 - 1 = 4$ hours. Now, solve for Cahaya's rate:

$$r \times 4 = 30$$
$$r = 7.5$$

For questions that involve multiple rates, start by sketching the situation. From there, decide whether you would rather logic it out or whether you would rather set up the $RT = D$ equations. Either way, look for connections, or relationships, between the different parts of the problem. These relationships will help you to be able to solve efficiently.

Relative Rates

Relative rate problems are a subset of multiple rate problems. The defining aspect of relative rate problems is that two bodies are traveling *at the same time*. There are three possible scenarios:

1. The bodies move *toward* each other.
2. The bodies move *away* from each other.
3. The bodies move in the *same direction* on the same path.

These questions can be dangerous because they can take a long time to solve using the conventional multiple rates strategy (discussed in the last section). You can save valuable time and energy by considering the *combined* rate at which the distance between the bodies changes:

Toward each other:

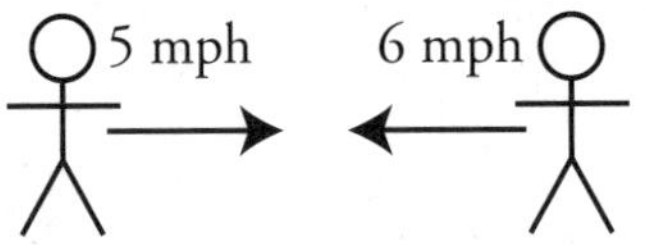

Two people decrease the distance between themselves at a rate of $5 + 6 = 11$ mph.

Away from each other:

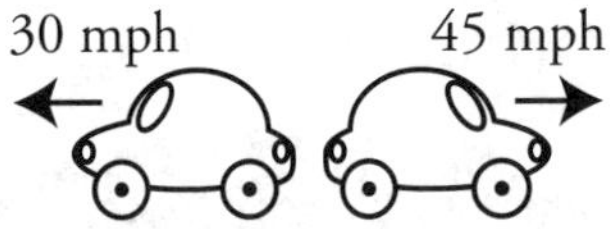

Two cars increase the distance between themselves at a rate of $30 + 45 = 75$ mph.

Same direction:

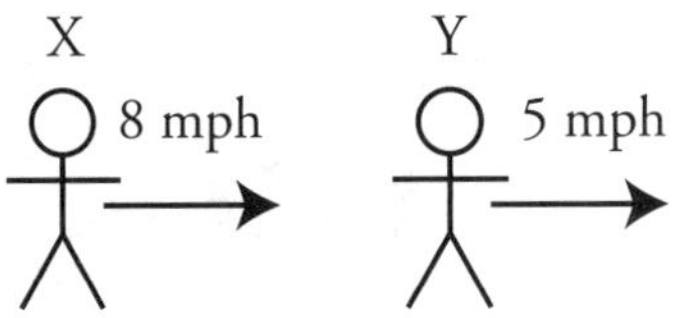

Persons X and Y decrease the distance between themselves at a rate of $8 - 5 = 3$ mph.

Try an example:

> Two people are 14 miles apart and begin walking toward each other. Person A walks 3 miles per hour, and Person B walks 4 miles per hour. How long will it take them to reach each other?

What is the combined rate of the two people? Since they are walking toward each other, they are both contributing to getting closer together at a rate of $3 + 4 = 7$ miles per hour. For every hour that they both walk, they get 7 miles closer together.

How long will it take to cover the 14 mile distance between them? Walking 7 miles an hour for 2 hours will bring them together, so the answer is 2 hours. You can literally sketch out all of the movement:

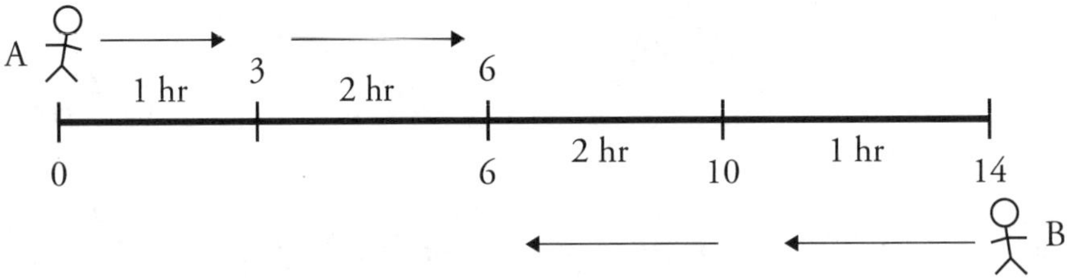

Some people might prefer an RTD chart (though the logical approach used above works on a surprising number of GMAT problems, even harder ones). Create an $RT = D$ equation for the combined rate: $3 + 4 = 7$ miles per hour.

	R (miles/hour)	×	*T* (hours)	=	*D* (miles)
A + B	7		t		14

$$7t = 14$$
$$t = 2$$

Note that the draw-it-out technique will still work even when the answer isn't an integer. Let's say that Person B is walking at a rate of 5 miles per hour:

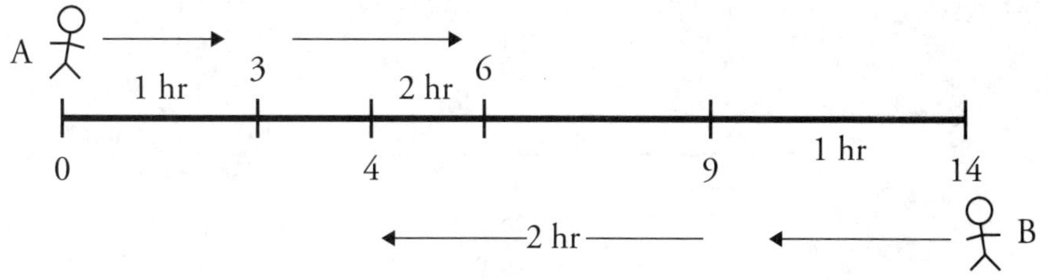

They haven't passed at 1 hour, but they have at 2 hours. You would typically be able to eliminate two or three multiple-choice answers at this stage. Next, try 1.5 hours:

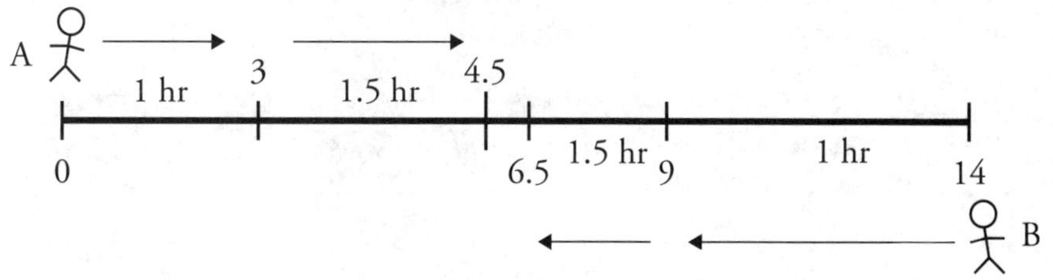

They haven't passed yet. This is usually enough for you to narrow the choices down to a single answer, though it depends on the exact mix of answer choices.

Average Rate: Find the Total Time

Consider the following problem:

> If Lior walks to work at a rate of 4 miles per hour and walks home by the same route at a rate of 6 miles per hour, what is Lior's average walking rate for the round trip?

It is very tempting to find an average rate as you would find any other average: add and divide. Thus, you might say that Lior's average rate is 5 miles per hour ($4 + 6 = 10$ and $10 \div 2 = 5$). However, this is incorrect!

If an object moves over the same distance twice, but at different rates each time, then *the average rate will NEVER be the "straight" average of the two rates given for the two legs of the journey*. Instead, because the object spends more time traveling at the slower rate, *the average rate will ALWAYS be closer to the slower of the two rates than to the faster.* Basically, the slower trip is weighted more heavily in the calculations (this is called a weighted average and you'll learn more about this in a few chapters). On DS problems, that knowledge may be enough to answer the question.

In order to find the average rate, first find the *total* combined distance for the trips and the *total* combined time for the trips. Use this formula:

$$\textbf{Average Speed} = \frac{\textbf{Total Distance}}{\textbf{Total Time}}$$

The problem above never establishes a specific distance. Because Lior walks the *same* route to work and back home, the average does not depend upon the specific distance. Whether the person or vehicle in the question goes 1 mile or 15, the *average* will be the same, so pick your own smart number for the distance.

Since 12 is a multiple of the two rates in the problem, 4 and 6, 12 is a good number to use.

Set up an RTD chart or draw out the scenario, your choice. Both approaches are shown here:

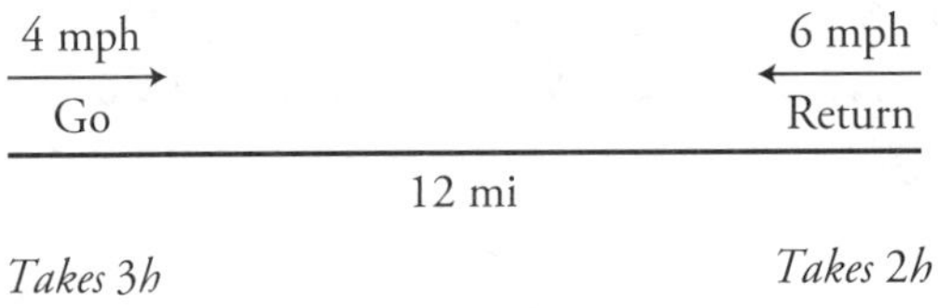

$$\frac{\text{Dist}}{\text{Time}} = \frac{24}{5} = 4.8$$

The calculations are shown in the chart, but you would typically perform these outside of the chart and then enter the information into your chart:

	Rate (miles/hour)	×	*Time* (hours)	=	*Distance* (miles)
Going	4	×	$\frac{12}{4} = 3$	=	12
Return	6	×	$\frac{12}{6} = 2$	=	12
Total	$\frac{24}{5} = 4.8$	×	$3 + 2 = 5$	=	$12 + 12 = 24$

If you like, test different numbers for the distance (try 24 or 36) to prove that you will get the same answer, regardless of the number you choose for the distance.

Basic Work Problems

Work problems are just another type of rate problem. These questions are concerned with the amount of work of some type performed rather than the distance traveled.

Work: Work takes the place of distance. Instead of $RT = D$, use the equation $RT = W$. The amount of work done is often a number of jobs completed or a number of items produced.

Time: This is the time spent working.

Rate: In work problems, the rate expresses the amount of work done in a given amount of time.

$$R = \frac{W}{T}$$

As with rate problems, always express a rate as work per unit time $\left(\frac{W}{T}\right)$. For example, if a machine produces pencils at a constant rate of 120 pencils every 30 seconds, the rate at which the machine works is $\frac{120 \text{ pencils}}{30 \text{ seconds}} = 4$ pencils/second.

Many work problems will require you to calculate a rate. Try the following problem:

> Malak can paint $\frac{2}{9}$ of a room in 40 minutes. At this rate, how long will it take Malak to paint the entire room?
>
> (A) 2 hours
>
> (B) 3 hours
>
> (C) 4 hours

You can use an RTW chart or logic it out, your choice. Both approaches are shown here.

The question asks how long it takes Malak to paint the whole room. In terms of the fraction given in the question stem, the whole job is $\frac{9}{9}$.

If Malak takes 40 minutes to paint $\frac{2}{9}$ of a room, how long would is take to paint $\frac{1}{9}$ of the room? Since $\frac{1}{9}$ is half as much as $\frac{2}{9}$, it would take half as long, or 20 minutes.

If it takes 20 minutes to paint $\frac{1}{9}$ of the room, then it takes 9 times as long to paint the whole room: $(20)(9) = 180$ minutes, or 3 hours. The correct answer is (B).

Alternatively, set up an RTW chart with your known information to find Malak's rate; note that the given information is in minutes but the question asks for hours, so at some point you'll need to convert from minutes to hours:

	R (rooms/hour)	×	*T* (hours)	=	*W* (rooms)
Malak	r		$\frac{2}{3}$		$\frac{2}{9}$

Now, solve for the rate:

$$r \times \frac{2}{3} = \frac{2}{9}$$

$$r = \frac{2}{9} \times \frac{3}{2} = \frac{1}{3}$$

Malak paints $\frac{1}{3}$ of the room every hour. Painting the whole room is the same as doing $\frac{3}{3}$ of the job, so it will take a total of 3 hours to complete. The correct answer is (B).

One interesting item. Malak's rate is $\frac{1}{3}$ and the time to complete the whole job is 3. These two numbers, $\frac{1}{3}$ and 3, are reciprocals. It will always be the case that the rate and the time it takes to do 100% of the job are reciprocals—that knowledge may save you some calculation time on some problems.

Working Together: Add the Rates

More often than not, work problems will involve more than one worker. When two or more workers are performing the same task, their rates can be added together. For instance, if Machine A can make 5 boxes in an hour, and Machine B can make 12 boxes in an hour, then working together the two machines can make $5 + 12 = 17$ boxes per hour.

Likewise, if Ren can complete $\frac{1}{3}$ of a task in an hour and Serena can complete $\frac{1}{2}$ of that task in an hour, then working together they can complete $\frac{1}{3} + \frac{1}{2} = \frac{5}{6}$ of the task every hour.

If, on the other hand, one worker is undoing the work of the other, subtract the rates. For example, if one hose is filling a pool at a rate of 3 gallons per minute, but another hose is draining the pool at a rate of 1 gallon per minute, the pool is being filled at a rate of $3 - 1 = 2$ gallons per minute.

Try the following problem:

> Machine A fills soda bottles at a constant rate of 60 bottles every 12 minutes, and Machine B fills soda bottles at a constant rate of 120 bottles every 8 minutes. How many bottles can both machines working together at their respective rates fill in 25 minutes?

First, check the given rate information against the question. It's asking about a 25-minute time frame. It would be easy to take the given information and "scale it up" for a 24-minute time frame (Machine A fills 120 bottles every 24 minutes, and Machine B fills 360 bottles every 24 minutes). If this problem had multiple-choice answers, you would want to glance at them at this point to see whether you can get away with rounding from here.

That's not the case on this problem, though. Instead, begin by putting the rates in proper form (per 1 unit of time):

$$\text{Rate}_{\text{Machine A}} = \frac{60 \text{ bottles}}{12 \text{ minutes}} = 5 \text{ bottles/minute}$$

$$\text{Rate}_{\text{Machine B}} = \frac{120 \text{ bottles}}{8 \text{ minutes}} = 15 \text{ bottles/minute}$$

Working together, they fill $5 + 15 = 20$ bottles every minute. In 25 minutes, then, they would fill $(20)(25) = 500$ bottles.

If you're not sure about that final calculation, you can fill out an RTW chart. Let b be the number of bottles filled:

	R (bottles/minute)	×	*T* (minutes)	=	*W* (bottles)
A + B	20		25		*b*

$b = 20 \times 25 = 500$ bottles

Even as work problems become more complex, there are still only a few relevant relationships:

- $RT = W$
- When two machines (or similar) are both contributing to the same job, add the rates.
- If one machine is undermining or taking away from a job, subtract the rate of that machine.

Try another example:

> Alejandro, working alone, can build a doghouse in 4 hours. Betty can build the same doghouse in 3 hours. If Betty and Carey, working together, can build the doghouse twice as fast as Alejandro can alone, how long would it take Carey, working alone, to build the doghouse?

Begin by solving for the rate that each person works. Let c represent the number of hours it takes Carey to build the doghouse.

Alejandro can build $\frac{1}{4}$ of the doghouse every hour, Betty can build $\frac{1}{3}$ of the doghouse every hour, and Carey can build $\frac{1}{c}$ of the doghouse every hour.

The problem states that Betty and Carey, working together, can build the doghouse twice as fast as Alejandro. In other words, their rate is twice Alejandro's rate:

$$\begin{aligned}\text{Rate}_B + \text{Rate}_C &= 2(\text{Rate}_A)\\ \frac{1}{3} + \frac{1}{c} &= 2\left(\frac{1}{4}\right)\\ \frac{1}{c} &= \frac{1}{2} - \frac{1}{3} = \frac{1}{6}\\ c &= 6\end{aligned}$$

It takes Carey 6 hours to build the doghouse alone.

You can also logic it out. Alejandro takes 4 hours to build the doghouse, and Betty takes 3 hours.

Betty and Carey together can build the doghouse twice as fast as Alejandro. It takes Alejandro 4 hours, so Betty and Carey together take 2 hours.

What portion of the doghouse will Betty do in that 2 hours? Since she can do the whole thing in 3 hours, she'll have $\frac{2}{3}$ of it done in 2 hours. Therefore, Carey will have to do the other $\frac{1}{3}$ of the doghouse in 2 hours.

That's Carey's rate; use it to figure out how long Carey will take to do the whole job alone:

$$2 \text{ hours} \rightarrow \frac{1}{3} \text{ of job}$$

$$6 \text{ hours} \rightarrow \frac{3}{3} \text{ of job}$$

When dealing with multiple rates, be sure to express rates per unit time. When the work involves completing a task, treat completing the task as doing 100% of the work. Once you know the rates of every worker, add the rates of workers who work together to complete the same task.

Problem Set

Now that you've finished the chapter, try the following problems.

1. An empty bucket is filled with paint at a constant rate, and after 6 minutes the bucket is filled to $\frac{3}{10}$ of its capacity. How much more time will it take to fill the bucket to full capacity?

2. Two hoses are pouring water into an empty pool. Hose 1 alone would fill up the pool in 6 hours. Hose 2 alone would fill up the pool in 4 hours. How long would it take for both hoses to fill up two-thirds of the pool?

   (A) 1 hour 36 minutes
   (B) 2 hours 24 minutes
   (C) 5 hours

3. Did it take a certain ship less than 3 hours to travel 9 kilometers? (1 kilometer = 1,000 meters)

   (1) The ship's average speed over the 9 kilometers was greater than 55 meters per minute.
   (2) The ship's average speed over the 9 kilometers was less than 60 meters per minute.

4. Twelve identical machines, running continuously at the same constant rate, take 8 days to complete a shipment. How many additional machines, each running at the same constant rate, would be needed to reduce the time required to complete a shipment by 2 days?

   (A) 2
   (B) 3
   (C) 4
   (D) 6
   (E) 9

5. Al and Barb shared the driving on a certain trip. What fraction of the total distance did Al drive?

   (1) Al drove for $\frac{3}{4}$ as much time as Barb did.
   (2) Al's average driving speed for the entire trip was $\frac{4}{5}$ of Barb's average driving speed for the trip.

6. Nicky and Chadi begin running a race at the same time, though Nicky starts the race 36 meters ahead of Chadi. If Chadi runs at a pace of 5 meters per second and Nicky runs at a pace of only 3 meters per second, how many seconds will Nicky have run by the time Chadi passes him?

   (A) 15 seconds
   (B) 18 seconds
   (C) 25 seconds
   (D) 30 seconds
   (E) 45 seconds.

7. Mary, working at a steady rate, can perform a task in m hours. Nadir, working at a steady rate, can perform the same task in n hours. Is $m < n$?

(1) The time it would take Mary and Nadir to perform the task together, each working at their respective constant rates, is greater than $\frac{m}{2}$.

(2) The time it would take Mary and Nadir to perform the task together, each working at their respective constant rates, is less than $\frac{n}{2}$.

Solutions

1. **14 minutes:** The question asks how much more time it will take to finish filling the bucket. You would need another $\frac{7}{10}$ to fill the bucket. One way to go from $\frac{3}{10}$ to $\frac{7}{10}$ is this:

$$\frac{3}{10} \text{ capacity} \rightarrow 6 \text{ minutes}$$

$$\frac{1}{10} \text{ capacity} \rightarrow 2 \text{ minutes}$$

To get to $\frac{7}{10}$ capacity, multiply by 7: It will take (2 minutes)(7) = 14 minutes.

Alternatively, assign a smart number for the capacity of the bucket. The logic is the same, but this approach allows you to work with more whole numbers and fewer fractions. The bucket is initially filled to $\frac{3}{10}$ of its capacity, so pick a multiple of 10.

If the capacity is 20 (call it gallons), then the bucket is currently $\frac{3}{10} \times 20 = 6$ gallons full. It took 6 minutes for the bucket to get this full, so the bucket is filling at a rate of 1 gallon per minute.

There are $20 - 6 = 14$ more gallons to go until the bucket is full, so it will take another 14 minutes to fill.

2. **(A) 1 hour 36 minutes:** The question is a bit unusual. It doesn't ask how long it will take to fill the pool to capacity but how long it will take to fill the pool to *two-thirds* of capacity. Ideally, try to solve directly for this value.

To start, glance at the answers. First, they're fairly far apart, so you may be able to estimate. Second, if the second hose alone can fill the pool completely in 4 hours, then it can't take more time than that for the two hoses together to fill the pool to two-thirds of capacity. Eliminate answer (C). There are only two answers left; take the math as far as you need to in order to tell whether it will take more or less than 2 hours.

If Hose 1 can fill the pool in 6 hours, its rate is $\frac{1}{6}$ "pool per hour," or the fraction of the job it can do in 1 hour. Likewise, if Hose 2 can fill the pool in 4 hours, its rate is $\frac{1}{4}$ pool per hour. Therefore, the combined rate is $\frac{5}{12}$ pool per hour $\left(\frac{1}{4} + \frac{1}{6} = \frac{5}{12}\right)$.

Convert $\frac{2}{3}$ of capacity to have the same denominator: $\frac{2}{3} \rightarrow \frac{8}{12}$.

After 1 hour, the pool is $\frac{5}{12}$ full. After 2 hours, the pool is $\frac{10}{12}$ full. This is too much! It takes less than 2 hours to get to $\frac{8}{12}$ full. The only possible answer is **(A)**.

3. **(A):** The statements provide rates in meters per minute but the question asks how many hours it takes to go a certain number of kilometers. A good first step here is to figure out how fast the ship would have to travel to cover 9 kilometers in 3 hours. Create an RTD chart, and convert kilometers to meters and hours to minutes:

	R (meters/minute)	×	*T* (minutes)	=	*D* (meters)
	r		180		9,000

$$180r = 9{,}000$$
$$r = 50$$

The question asks whether the ship traveled 9 kilometers in *less than* 3 hours. If it took less time, the ship would have to have traveled *faster* than 50 meters/minute. Therefore, the question is really asking, was $r > 50$ meters/minute?

(1) SUFFICIENT: If the average speed of the ship was greater than 55 meters per minute, then $r > 55$. Thus, r is definitely greater than 50.

(2) INSUFFICIENT: If the average speed of the ship was less than 60 meters per minute, then $r < 60$. The value of r could be greater or less than 50.

The correct answer is **(A)**: Statement (1) alone is sufficient, but statement (2) is not.

4. **(C) 4:** This is a complicated story. Lay it out carefully before you figure out how to solve. All the machines run at the same rate, so you can ignore that potential aspect of things. There are 12 machines to start and they take 8 days to do the job. The problem states that the time required will be reduced *by* 2 days—so that's a total of 6 days. (Note the trap: The problem writer is hoping you'll think the time was reduced *to* 2 days.)

If you feel really comfortable with work problems, there's a neat shortcut you can use. Twelve machines complete the job in 8 days, or $(12r)(8) = 1$ job. An unknown number of machines (call it n) completes the job in 6 days, or $(nr)(6) = 1$ job. The left sides of those two equations equal the same thing, so you can set them equal to each other and solve:

$$(12r)(8) = (nr)(6)$$
$$\frac{(12)(8)}{6} = \frac{nr}{r}$$
$$(2)(8) = n$$
$$n = 16$$

The *new* number of machines is 16. The *added* number of machines is $16 - 12 = 4$.

If that doesn't work for you, use the standard RTW approach. Let the work rate of 1 machine be r. Then the work rate of 12 machines is $12r$, and you can set up an RTW chart:

	R	×	*T*	=	*W*
Original	12*r*		8		96*r*

The shipment work is then $96r$. To figure out how many machines are needed to complete this work in $8 - 2 = 6$ days, set up another row and solve for the unknown rate:

	R	×	*T*	=	*W*
Original	$12r$		8		$96r$
New	⬭		6		$96r$

Therefore, there are $\frac{96r}{6} = 16r$ machines in total, or $16 - 12 = 4$ additional machines.

5. **(C):** The problem asks for a relative value, not the actual value. Rephrase the question as follows: What is the ratio of Al's driving distance to the entire distance driven? Alternatively, since the entire distance is the sum of only Al's distance and Barb's distance, you can find the ratio of Al's distance to Barb's distance:

(1) INSUFFICIENT: Knowing only the relative amount of time each drove indicates nothing about distance driven.

(2) INSUFFICIENT: Knowing only the relative rates at which each drove indicates nothing about distance driven.

(1) AND (2) SUFFICIENT: Set up an RTD chart to combine the information:

	R	×	*T*	=	*D*
Al	$\left(\frac{4}{5}\right)r$		$\left(\frac{3}{4}\right)t$		$\left(\frac{3}{5}\right)rt$
Barb	r		t		rt
Total					$\left(\frac{8}{5}\right)rt$

Call the distance measurement *miles*. The total trip distance was $\frac{8}{5}$ miles or 1.6 miles (ignore the *rt*, since that's identical for all three entries for distance). Bob drove 0.6 miles of the total distance, so he drove $\frac{0.6}{1.6}$ of the distance.

The correct answer is **(C)**: The two statements work together, but neither one works alone.

6. **(B) 18 seconds:** Save time on this problem by considering the rate at which Chadi closes the gap with Nicky. If Nicky runs at a rate of 3 meters per second and Chadi runs at a rate of 5 meters per second, then Chadi catches up at a rate of $5 - 3 = 2$ meters per second. Since Nicky starts off 36 meters ahead of Chadi, Chadi needs to make up 36 meters to catch up to Nicky. If Chadi closes the gap by 2 meters per second, then it will take Chadi $\frac{36}{2} = 18$ seconds to catch up to Nicky.

Alternatively, use a single $RT = D$ equation. The rate at which Chadi catches up to Nicky is 2 meters per second, and the distance is 36 meters (because that's how far apart Nicky and Chadi are):

	R **(meters/second)**	×	***T*** **(seconds)**	=	***D*** **(meters)**
	2		*t*		36

$$2t = 36$$

$$t = 18$$

A third way to solve this problem is to draw it out. Draw Nicky and Chadi's starting points:

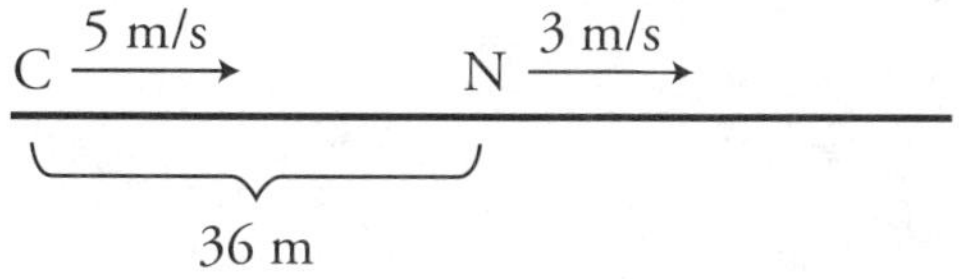

Next, map out how their positions will change over time. It will take a while for Chadi to catch up to Nicky; Chadi runs 5 meters per second and needs to make up 36 meters. Map out their progress in increments of 10 seconds rather than 1 second (looking at the answer choices is another way to get this hint; the smallest answer is 15):

Seconds	**Nicky's Position = 36 + 3 meters/second**	**Chadi's position = 5 meters/second**
0	36	0
10	36 + 3(10) = 66	5(10) = 50
20	36 + 3(20) = 96	5(20) = 100

After 20 seconds, Chadi has just passed Nicky, so Chadi overtook Nicky at some time between 10 and 20 seconds. Only answers (A) and (B) are in this range. You could test answer (A) at this point or logic it out. The two runners are much closer together after 20 seconds ($100 - 96 = 4$ meters) than they are after 10 seconds ($66 - 50 = 16$ meters). Thus, the exact time Chadi passed Nicki must be closer to 20 seconds than 10 seconds.

7. (D): The question asks whether $m < n$, or whether Mary is faster than Nadir. There are three possibilities: They work at the same rate, Mary is faster, or Nadir is faster. If the two people work at exactly the same rate, then together they would complete the job in half the time it would take to work alone.

(1) SUFFICIENT: What does $\frac{m}{2}$ represent? Since m is the time it takes Mary to do the job alone, $\frac{m}{2}$ is half of that—or the time it would take two identical Mary clones to do the job. This statement indicates that, when Mary and Nadir do the job, they will spend *more* time than two Mary clones would take—so Nadir must be slowing down the job. In other words, Yes, $m < n$.

Put some concrete numbers on this to help understand. For example, say that Mary can do the job in 5 hours, or $m = 5$. Two Mary clones would do the job in 2.5 hours, or $\frac{m}{2} = 2.5$. But this statement says that Mary and Nadir take *longer* than $\frac{m}{2}$, so Nadir must be slowing down the job. In other words, Yes, $m < n$.

(2) SUFFICIENT: Use similar logic. Since n is the time it takes Nadir to do the job alone, $\frac{n}{2}$ is half of that—or the time it would take two identical Nadir clones to do the job. This statement indicates that, when Mary and Nadir do the job, they will spend *less* time than two Nadir clones would take—so Mary must be speeding up the job. In other words, Yes, $m < n$.

Use some concrete numbers again to check the logic: If Nadir can do the job in 6 hours, or $n = 6$, then two Nadir clones would do the job in 3 hours, or $\frac{n}{2} = 3$. But this statement says that Mary and Nadir take *less* than $\frac{n}{2}$, so Mary must be speeding up the job. In other words, Yes, $m < n$.

The correct answer is **(D)**: Each statement alone is sufficient.

CHAPTER 20

Overlapping Sets

In This Chapter

- The Double-Set Matrix
- Overlapping Sets and Percents
- Overlapping Sets and Algebraic Representation

In this chapter, you will learn how to organize and solve overlapping set stories in both percent and algebraic form.

CHAPTER 20 Overlapping Sets

Stories that involve two (or more) given sets of data that partially intersect with each other are termed **overlapping sets**. For example:

> Of 30 integers, 15 are in set *A*, 22 are in set *B*, and 8 are in both sets *A* and *B*. How many of the integers are in NEITHER set *A* nor set *B* ?

This problem involves two sets, *A* and *B*. The two sets overlap because some of the numbers are in both sets. Thus, these two sets can actually be divided into four categories:

1. Numbers in set *A*
2. Numbers in set *B*
3. Numbers in both *A* and *B*
4. Numbers in neither *A* nor *B*

Solving double-set GMAT problems, such as in the example above, involves finding values for one of these four categories.

The Double-Set Matrix

For GMAT problems involving only *two* sets of data, the most efficient tool is the **double-set matrix**. Here's how to set one up, using the previous example:

> Of 30 integers, 15 are in set *A*, 22 are in set *B*, and 8 are in both set *A* and *B*. How many of the integers are in NEITHER set *A* nor set *B* ?

First, set up a table:

	A	**Not *A***	**Total**
B			
Not *B*			
Total			

For two data sets, you'll always have four columns and four rows. The final column and the final row will always be labeled Total. Next, ask yourself what the two data sets are. In this case, the sets are *A* and *B*. A particular value can be either in set *A* or not in set *A*. These are called *mutually exclusive*, a term you'll hear in graduate school. Label the columns so that the mutually exclusive options *A* and not *A* are side by side. Likewise, a particular value can be either in set *B* or not in set *B*.

	A	Not *A*	Total
B	8		22
Not *B*			
Total	15		30

This box shows the overlap. (→ *B*/*A* box)

This box shows the total members in set *B*. (→ *B*/Total box)

This box in the lower right corner is the key. This tells you how many distinct members exist in the overall group. (→ Total/Total box)

This box shows the total members in set *A*. (→ Total/*A* box)

This box shows the members in NEITHER set. (→ Not *B*/Not *A* box)

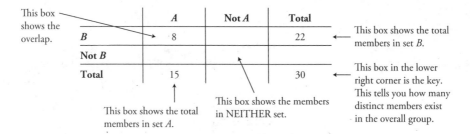

Once the information given in the problem has been filled in, as in the chart below, complete the rest of the chart. Each row and each column sum to a total value as shown here:

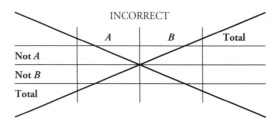

	A	+ Not *A*	= Total
B	8	14	22
+ Not *B*	7	1	8
= Total	15	15	30

The question asks for the number of integers that are in *neither* set. Look at the chart to find the number of integers that are Not *A* and Not *B*; the answer is 1.

There are two important points to remember. First, you likely will not need to fill in the entire chart; you only have to fill in enough to get the particular value that the question asked you to find. To that end, before you start solving, put a circle in the box that you want to find.

Second, when you construct a double-set matrix, the rows must correspond to the *mutually exclusive options* for one decision: You have *A* or you don't have *A*. Likewise, the columns should correspond to the mutually exclusive options for the other decision: You have *B* or you don't have *B*. Do *not* draw the table this way:

INCORRECT

	A	*B*	Total
Not *A*			
Not *B*			
Total			

Once you've set up the matrix, take a moment to check the logic of a couple of the boxes. In the incorrect example, the first open box shows the intersection of *A* and Not *A*. How many items can be both in *A* and not in *A* at the same time? Zero. The same is true of *B* and Not *B*. It's also the case that you could have some items in both *A* and *B*, but the matrix doesn't contain any box that allows that combination. Logically, then, this cannot be the correct set-up for the matrix.

One final note: Venn diagrams (overlapping circles) can also be used for these problems, but the double-set matrix is strongly recommended for problems with only two sets of data points. The double-set matrix conveniently displays *all* possible combinations of options, including the totals, whereas the Venn diagram displays only a subset of the combinations.

Overlapping Sets and Percents

Many overlapping sets problems involve *percents* or *fractions*. The double-set matrix is still effective on these problems, especially if you choose a smart number for the grand total. For problems involving percents, choose a total of 100. For problems involving fractions, choose a common denominator for the total. For example, choose 15 if the problem mentions categories that are $\frac{1}{3}$ and $\frac{2}{5}$ of the total. For example:

> The books on a bookshelf are either hardcover or paperback. Sixty percent of the books are paperback and half of the hardcover books are fiction. If 40% of the paperback books are fiction, what percent of the books are nonfiction?
>
> (A) 30
> (B) 40
> (C) 44
> (D) 56
> (E) 60

First, set up your chart. The two groups are fiction/nonfiction and hardcover/paperback. Because the problem uses only percentages, no real numbers, choose 100 for the total number of books. The problem asks for the percentage that are nonfiction; put a circle in that box.

Then, begin to fill in the other information given in the problem. The second sentence indicates that 60% of the books are paperback. That allows you to figure out the portion that are hardcover, since the two have to add up to 100. You also know that half of the hardcover books are fiction; therefore, half of the hardcover books are nonfiction. Fill in the table:

	F	NF	Total
HC	50% Tot HC = 20	50% Tot HC = 20	100 – 60 = 40
PB	40% Tot PB = 24		60
Total		( )	100

Next, add the information from the third sentence and solve for the desired box. Of the paperbacks, 40% are fiction; there are 60 paperbacks, so 40% is 24. (Take 10%, then multiply by 4: $(6)(4) = 24$.) Now, you have a choice. You can solve to the right or solve down in order to get to the circle. Here's how to solve down:

	F	NF	Total
HC	50% Tot HC = 20	50% Tot HC = 20	$x = 40$
PB	40% Tot PB = 24		60
Total	20 + 24 = 44	(100 – 44 = 56)	100

You don't need to complete the entire chart, since you have already answered the question asked in the problem. If you want to check your work—and you have the time!—you can complete the matrix. The last box you fill in must work both vertically and horizontally.

The correct answer is (D), 56. There are some traps built into the answer choices. The last number before the answer, 44, is in the answer choices; this number represents an adjacent category, fiction, rather than the desired category, nonfiction. Someone choosing (C) solved for the wrong box.

Note one important thing about this pair of answers, 44 and 56: They add up to 100%! Trap answer (C) has a name: It's an evil twin. One of the most common careless mistakes people make is to solve for the wrong thing. In this case, you would do everything correctly, right up to the end, and then just choose the wrong answer.

Evil twins pop up on all kinds of story problems, not just ones that involve percents. When you see that a story problem contains two adjacent things you could have solved for (nonfiction *or* fiction, in this case, or the number of cats vs. the number of dogs), and the answers contain real numbers, glance at those answers first to see whether evil twins are present. In this case, there are *two* pairs of evil twins adding up to 100: the pair 44/56 and the pair 40/60. Answer choice (A), 30, is the odd one out, so if you have to guess, don't guess that one.

The other pairing, 40/60, is the result of a calculation error along the way. The problem states that 40% of the paperbacks are fiction. If someone mistakenly reads that as 40% of *all* of the books are fiction, then she would put 40 in the fiction total box and calculate the final answer as 60. Alternatively, if someone did place the 40% properly in the paperback fiction box but mistakenly took 40% of 100 rather than 40% of 60, then she would put 60 in the fiction total box and calculate the final answer as 40.

As with any problem, only use smart numbers if the problem contains only relative values (such as fractions and/or percents), but no actual *numbers* of items or people. In that case, go ahead and pick a total of 100 (for percent problems) or a common denominator (for fraction problems). If actual quantities appear anywhere in the problem, though, then all the totals are already determined. In that case, you cannot assign numbers, but must solve for them instead.

Overlapping Sets and Algebraic Representation

When solving overlapping sets problems, pay close attention to the wording of the problem. For example, consider this problem:

> A researcher estimates that 10% of the children in the world are between the ages of 8 and 18 and dislike soccer, and that 50% of the children who like soccer are between the ages of 8 and 18. If 40% of the children in the world are between the ages of 8 and 18, what percentage of children in the world are under age 8 and dislike the game of soccer? (Assume all children are between the ages of 0 and 18.)

It is tempting to fill in the number 50 to represent the percent of children aged 8 to 18 who like soccer. However, this approach is incorrect:

WRONG

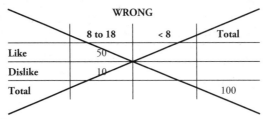

	8 to 18	< 8	Total
Like	50		
Dislike	10		
Total			100

You'll need some of your Sentence Correction skills here. The sentence says that 50% of the children *who like soccer* are between the ages of 8 and 18. This is different from saying that 50% of the children *in the world* are between the ages of 8 and 18. The children *who like soccer* are a subset—a smaller number—of *all* of the children in the world.

You do not yet know how many children like soccer, so you can't actually find the 50% figure (yet!). Instead, represent the unknown total number of children who like soccer with the variable x. Then, represent the number of children aged 8 to 18 who like soccer with the expression $0.5x$:

	8 to 18	**< 8**	**Total**
Like	$0.5x$		x
Dislike	10	◯	
Total	40		100

The "8 to 18 + Like" box must equal $40 - 10 = 30$; set up an equation to solve for x:

$$0.5x = 30$$
$$x = 60$$

Fill in whatever you need to get to the desired cell. Here's one possible path:

	8 to 18	**< 8**	**Total**
Like	**$0.5x = 30$**		**$x = 60$**
Dislike	10	**(30)**	**40**
Total	40		100

Therefore, 30% of the children are under age 8 and dislike soccer.

Problem Set

Now that you've finished the chapter, try the following problems.

1. Set *A* contains 16 even integers, and set *B* contains 22 integers that are all multiples of 3. If 7 of the integers fall into both sets *A* and *B*, how many integers are in exactly one of the two sets?

2. Of the 28 people in a park, 12 are children and the rest are adults. Eight people have to leave the park at 3 p.m.; the rest will stay. If, after 3 p.m., there are 6 children still in the park, how many adults are still in the park?

   (A) 2

   (B) 8

   (C) 11

   (D) 14

   (E) 20

Save the following problems for review after you finish this entire guide.

3. Of the students at a certain high school, 40% take physics. Of those students who don't take physics, 20% do take calculus. What percentage of students take neither physics nor calculus?

4. Of 30 snakes at the reptile house, 10 have stripes, 21 are poisonous, and 5 have no stripes and are not poisonous. How many of the snakes both have stripes and are poisonous?

5. At a car dealership, 10% of all cars are red and have heated seats, and 75% of cars without heated seats are red. If 40% of all of the cars are red, what percent of the cars have heated seats?

   (A) 25%

   (B) 40%

   (C) 60%

   (D) 75%

   (E) 85%

	Even	Not even	Total
×3	7	(15)	22
Not ×3	(9)		
Total	16		

1. 24

	Adult	Child	Total
Leaving			8
Staying 3pm	(14)	6	20
Total	16	12	28

Answers and explanations follow on the next page. ▶ ▶ ▶

Solutions

1. **24 integers:** Use a double-set matrix to solve this problem. First, fill in the numbers given in the problem: 16 integers total in set A and 22 integers total in set B. There are 7 integers in the overlap of sets A and B. Next, use subtraction to solve for the number of integers in set A but not in set B (9) and the number of integers in set B but not in set A (15). Finally, add those two numbers: $9 + 15 = 24$.

	A	Not *A*	Total
B	7	**15**	22
Not *B*	**9**		
Total	16		

2. **(D) 14:** Use a double-set matrix to solve this problem. First, fill in the numbers given in the problem: There are 28 people total; 12 are children, and the rest ($28 - 12 = 16$) are adults; 8 leave at 3 p.m. and the rest ($28 - 8 = 20$) stay. Next, 6 children stay in the park after 3 p.m. Since there are a total of 20 people in the park after 3 p.m., the remaining 14 people who stay must be adults. Here is the table:

	C	A	Total
Leave			8
Stay	6	**14**	**20**
Total	12	**16**	28

Notice that there are two pairs of evil twins in the answers choices. Answers (A) and (D) sum to 16, the total number of adults. If you thought the question asked how many adults left the park, rather than stayed, you would come up with answer (A).

Answers (B) and (E) sum to 28, the total number of people in the park. If you thought the question asked for the total number of people who stayed in the park, rather than just the adults who stayed, you might choose answer (E).

3. **48%:** Since all the numbers in this problem are given in percentages, assign a grand total of 100 students. The problem indicates that 40% of all high school students take physics, so fill in 40 for this total. The number who don't take physics must be $100 - 40 = 60$.

Next, 20% of those students who do not take physics do take calculus. (It does not say that 20% of *all* students take calculus!) According to the table, 60 students do not take physics, so 20% of those, or 12, do take calculus. Therefore, fill in 12 for the students who take calculus but not physics. Finally, subtract: $60 - 12 = 48$ students take neither physics nor calculus.

	P	No P	Total
C		**12**	
No C		**48**	
Total	40	**60**	100

4. **6:** Use a double-set matrix to solve this problem. First, fill in the numbers given in the problem: 30 snakes total, 10 with stripes (and therefore 20 without), 21 that are poisonous (and therefore 9 that are not), and 5 that are neither striped nor poisonous. Use subtraction to fill in enough of the chart to answer the question (one way is shown below). A total of 6 snakes have stripes and are poisonous.

	S	**Not S**	**Total**
P	**6**		21
Not P	**4**	5	**9**
Total	10	**20**	30

5. **(C) 60%:** Use a double-set matrix to solve this problem. Since all the numbers in this problem are given in percentages, assign a grand total of 100 cars. The problem indicates that 10% of all cars are red and have heated seats, so enter 10 in the R + HS cell. It also indicates that 75% *of cars without heated seats* are red. At this point, you don't know how many cars don't have heated seats, so assign the variable x to represent the Total Not HS. Of these cars, 75% are red, so enter $0.75x$ in the R + Not HS cell.

Next, 40% of all cars are red, so enter 40 in the Total R cell. Column R has to add up ($10 + 0.75x = 40$), so the R + Not HS cell ($0.75x$) must equal 30. Solve the equation to find that $x = 40$. If 40 cars do not have heated seats, then 60 have heated seats. Therefore, 60% of all of the cars have heated seats as shown in the table below:

	R	**Not R**	**Total**
HS	10		**60**
Not HS	$0.75x =$ **30**		$x =$ **40**
Total	40		100

Did you notice the two pairs of evil twins that add to 100 in this problem? Answers (A) and (D) are one pair, and answers (B) and (C) are the other. You might get answer (B) if you solved for the cars without, rather than with, heated seats. You could get answers (A) or (D) if you focused on red cars as opposed to all cars.

CHAPTER 21

Statistics

In This Chapter

- Averages
- Using the Average Formula
- Median: The Middle Number
- Standard Deviation

In this chapter, you will learn how to calculate averages in a variety of situations, as well as how to lay out median problems and how to logic your way through standard deviation problems.

CHAPTER 21 Statistics

Averages

The **average** (or the **arithmetic mean**) of a set is given by the following formula:

$$\textbf{Average} = \frac{\textbf{Sum}}{\textbf{\# of terms}}, \text{ which is abbreviated as } A = \frac{S}{n}.$$

The sum, S, refers to the sum of all the terms in the set.
The number, n, refers to the number of terms that are in the set.
The average, A, refers to the average value (arithmetic mean) of the terms in the set.

The language in an average problem will often refer to an arithmetic mean. However, occasionally, the concept is implied. "The cost per employee, if equally shared, is \$20" means that the *average* cost per employee is \$20. Likewise, the "per capita income" is the average income per person in an area.

Here's a commonly used variation of the average formula:

$$\text{Average} \times \text{Number of terms} = \text{Sum, or } A \times n = S$$

Using the Average Formula

Every GMAT problem dealing with averages can be solved using some form of the average formula. In general, if the average is unknown, the first formula, $A = \frac{S}{n}$, will solve the problem more directly. If the average is known, the second formula, $A \times n = S$, is better.

When you see any GMAT average problem, write down the average formula. Then, fill in any of the three variables (S, n, and A) that are given in the problem. Try an example:

The sum of 6 numbers is 90. What is the average term?

$A = \frac{S}{n}$ The sum, S, is given as 90. The number of terms, n, is given as 6.
By plugging in, you can solve for the average: $\frac{90}{6} = 15$.

Notice that you do *not* need to know each term in the set to find the average!

Sometimes, using the average formula will be more involved. For example:

If the average of the set {2, 5, 5, 7, 8, 9, x} is 6.1, what is the value of x?

Plug the given information into the average formula, and solve for x:

$A \times n = S$ $\quad (6.1)(7 \text{ terms}) = 2 + 5 + 5 + 7 + 8 + 9 + x$

$$42.7 = 36 + x$$
$$6.7 = x$$

More complex average problems involve setting up two average formulas. For example:

> Sam earned a $2,000 commission on a big sale, raising his average commission by $100. If Sam's new average commission is $900, how many sales has he made?

To keep track of two average formulas in the same problem, you can set up a table. Sam's new average commission is $900, and this is $100 higher than his old average, so his old average was $800.

Note that the Number and Sum columns add up to give the new cumulative values, but the values in the Average column do *not* add up:

	Average	×	Number	=	Sum
Old total	800	×	n	=	$800n$
This sale	2,000	×	1	=	2,000
New total	900	×	$n+1$	=	$900(n+1)$
	DON'T add vertically		add vertically		add vertically

The right-hand (Sum) column gives the equation you need:

$$800n + 2{,}000 = 900(n + 1)$$
$$800n + 2{,}000 = 900n + 900$$
$$1{,}100 = 100n$$
$$11 = n$$

Since you are looking for the new number of sales, which is $n + 1$, Sam has made a total of 12 sales.

Median: The Middle Number

Some GMAT problems feature another stats concept: The **median**, or middle value in a list of values placed in increasing order. The median is calculated in one of two ways, depending on the number of data points in the set:

1. For sets containing an *odd* number of values, the median is the *unique middle value* when the data are arranged in increasing (or decreasing) order. For example, the median of the set {5, 17, 24, 25, 28} is the unique middle number, 24.

2. For sets containing an *even* number of values, the median is the *average (arithmetic mean) of the two middle values* when the data are arranged in increasing (or decreasing) order. For example, the median of the set {3, 4, 9, 9} is the mean of the two middle values (4 and 9), or 6.5.

Notice that the median of a set containing an *odd* number of values must be an actual value in the set. However, the median of a set containing an *even* number of values does not have to be in the set—and indeed will not be, unless the two middle values are equal.

Medians of Sets Containing Unknown Values

Unlike the arithmetic mean, the median of a set depends only on the one or two values in the middle of the ordered set. Therefore, you may be able to determine a specific value for the median of a set *even if one or more unknowns are present.*

For example, consider the unordered set {x, 2, 5, 11, 11, 12, 33}. No matter whether x is less than 11, equal to 11, or greater than 11, the median of the resulting set will be 11. (Try substituting different values of x to see why the median does not change.)

By contrast, the median of the unordered set {x, 2, 5, 11, 12, 12, 33} depends on x. If x is 11 or less, the median is 11. If x is between 11 and 12, the median is x. Finally, if x is 12 or more, the median is 12.

Standard Deviation

The mean and median both give *average* or *representative* values for a set, but they do not tell the whole story. It is possible for two sets to have the same average but to differ widely in how spread out their values are. For example, both of these sets have an average and median of 5: {2, 4, 6, 8} and {0, 0, 10, 10}.

To describe the spread, or variation, of the data in a set, use a different measure: the **Standard Deviation** (SD).

Standard deviation indicates how far from the average (mean) the data points typically fall. Therefore:

- A small SD indicates that a set is clustered closely around the average (arithmetic mean) value. In the two sets given earlier, the set {2, 4, 6, 8} has the smaller SD.
- A large SD indicates that the set is spread out widely, with some points appearing far from the mean. In the two sets given earlier, the set {0, 0, 10, 10} has the larger SD.

What about the set {5, 5, 5, 5}? When a set contains all the same value, the numbers are not spread out at all, so the SD is 0.

For most sets, even if you know both the average and the SD of a set, you cannot tell what the numbers are in that set. Multiple possible combinations of numbers can result in the same average and the same SD. The exception is any set with an SD of 0. For example, if the SD is 0 and the average is 13, then all of the members of that set must equal 13. (You still don't know, though, how many instances of 13 are in the set; There might be 1 or 1,000.)

	Set 1	Set 2	Set 3
Mean = 5 Median = 5	{5, 5, 5, 5}	{2, 4, 6, 8}	{0, 0, 10, 10}
Difference from the mean of 5 (in absolute terms)	{0, 0, 0, 0} SD = 0 An SD of 0 means that all the numbers in the set are equal.	{3, 1, 1, 3} moderately spread out SD = moderate (technically, SD = $\sqrt{5} \approx 2.24$ but you won't have to calculate this!)	{5, 5, 5, 5} more spread out (technically, SD = 5) If every absolute difference from the mean is equal, then the SD equals that difference.

You might be asking how to calculate the $\sqrt{5}$ shown as the SD for the second set. The good news is that you do not need to know—the GMAT will not ask you to calculate a specific SD unless a shortcut exists, such as knowing that the SD is 0 if all of the numbers in the set are identical. If you just pay attention to what the *average spread* is doing, you'll be able to answer all GMAT standard deviation problems, which involve either 1) *changes* in the SD when a set is transformed or 2) *comparisons* of the SDs of two or more sets. Just remember that the more spread out the numbers, the larger the SD.

If you see a problem focusing on changes in the SD, ask yourself whether the changes move the data closer to the mean, farther from the mean, or neither. If you see a problem requiring comparisons, ask yourself which set is more spread out from its mean.

Following are some sample problems to help illustrate SD properties:

1. Which set has the greater standard deviation: {1, 2, 3, 4, 6} or {441, 442, 443, 444, 445}?
2. If each data point in a set is increased by 7, does the set's standard deviation increase, decrease, or remain constant?
3. If each data point in a set is increased by a factor of 7, does the set's standard deviation increase, decrease, or remain constant? (Assume that the set consists of different numbers.)

Answers and explanations follow on the next page. ▶ ▶ ▶

Answer Key

1. **The first set has the greater SD.** One way to understand this is to observe that the gaps between its numbers are, on average, slightly bigger than the gaps in the second set (because the last two numbers are 2 units apart). Another way to resolve the issue is to observe that the set {441, 442, 443, 444, 445} would have the same standard deviation as {1, 2, 3, 4, 5}. Replacing 5 with 6, which is farther from the mean, will increase the SD of that set.

2. **The SD will not change.** "Increased by 7" means that the number 7 is *added* to each data point in the set. This transformation will not affect any of the gaps between the data points, and thus it will not affect how far the data points are from the mean. If the set were plotted on a number line, this transformation would merely slide the points 7 units to the right, taking all the gaps and the mean along with them.

3. **The SD will increase.** "Increased by a *factor* of 7" means that each data point is multiplied by 7. This transformation will make all the gaps between points 7 times as big as they originally were. Thus, each point will fall 7 times as far from the mean. The SD will increase by a factor of 7. Why did the problem specify that the set consists of different numbers? If each data point in the set was the same, then the SD would be 0. Multiplying each data point by 7 would still result in a set of identical numbers and an identical SD of 0.

Problem Set

Now that you've finished the chapter, try the following problems.

1. The average (arithmetic mean) of 11 numbers is 10. When one number is eliminated, the average of the remaining numbers is 9.3. What is the eliminated number? 17

2. Given the set of numbers {4, 5, 5, 6, 7, 8, 21}, how much higher is the mean than the median?

3. For an entire class of students, the mean score on a test was 60, and the standard deviation was 15. If Eike's score was within 2 standard deviations of the mean, what is the lowest score Eike could have received?

4. Matt earned a $1,000 commission on a big sale, raising his average commission by $150. If Matt's new average commission is $400, how many sales has he made?

Save the following problems for review after you finish this entire guide.

5. If the average of x and y is 50, and the average of y and z is 80, what is the value of $z - x$?

   (A) 20
   (B) 30
   (C) 50
   (D) 60
   (E) 80

6. The median price of all houses sold in the Seaside Hills neighborhood last year was $450,000. Was the average (arithmetic mean) price of the houses sold last year greater than $400,000 ?

   (1) The most expensive house sold in Seaside Hills last year was sold for $800,000.
   (2) Exactly three houses were sold in Seaside Hills last year.

Solutions

1. **17:** If the average of 11 numbers is 10, their sum is $11 \times 10 = 110$. After one number is eliminated, the average is 9.3, so the sum of the 10 remaining numbers is $10 \times 9.3 = 93$. The number eliminated is the difference between these sums: $110 - 93 = 17$.

2. **2:** The mean of the set is the sum of the numbers divided by the number of terms. First, group numbers to make it easier to add them up. For example, $4 + 6 = 10$, $5 + 5 = 10$ and $7 + 8 = 15$. The mean is $56 \div 7 = 8$. The median is the middle number in the set, which is 6. The difference between the two numbers is 2.

3. **30:** Eike's score was within 2 standard deviations of the mean. Since 1 standard deviation is 15, her score is no more than $15 \times 2 = 30$ points from the mean. The lowest possible score she could have received, then, is $60 - 30$, which is equal to 30.

4. **5:** For this kind of problem, you can do your calculations just in terms of the "extra" money that Matt made, over his prior average.

   Before the big sale, Matt's average commission was \$250. For the big sale, he got a commission of \$1,000. Count the first \$250 toward his original average and the other \$750 as his "extra" money. If he hadn't made any extra money, then his average would have stayed at \$250. But he did make \$750 extra, so how does that impact the average?

   Imagine that, prior to the big sale, Matt had made exactly one other sale. Then, the big sale with an extra \$750 would increase his average across two sales by $\frac{750}{2} = 375$. His average actually increased by only \$150, so he must have made more than two sales. If he had had two prior sales with an average of \$250, then adding the extra \$750 from the third sale would increase the average by $\frac{750}{3} = 250$. In short, you can calculate the increase in the average using this shortcut:

   $$\frac{\text{Extra Amount}}{\text{\# of Sales}} = \text{Increase in Average}$$

   In this problem, $\frac{750}{\text{\# of sales}} = 150$, so Matt had 5 total sales.

   Alternatively, you can solve algebraically. Before the big sale, Matt's average commission was \$250, so the sum of the previous sales was $S = 250n$. After the sale, three things happened: The sum of Matt's commissions increased by \$1,000, the number of sales he made increased by 1, and his average commission was \$400. Express this algebraically with the following equation:

   $$\begin{aligned} S + 1{,}000 &= 400(n + 1) \\ 250n + 1{,}000 &= 400(n + 1) \\ 250n + 1{,}000 &= 400n + 400 \\ 150n &= 600 \\ n &= 4 \end{aligned}$$

   Before the big commission, Matt had made 4 sales. Including the big commission, Matt made 5 sales.

5. **(D) 60:** This is an interesting hybrid problem. At first glance, it may seem like a candidate for working backwards, since the answers are real numbers. However, it asks for a relative value: the difference betweeen z and x. In this case, you can choose smart numbers for the values of the individual variables, as long as those numbers make the given facts true.

   Let $x = 40$ and $y = 60$ (the average must be equal to 50). Next, the average of y and z must be 80. If $y = 60$, then z has to be 100. Therefore, $z - x = 100 - 40 = 60$.

   You can also solve algebraically, though that is more cumbersome on this problem. First, translate the given information:

$$\frac{x + y}{2} = 50 \qquad \frac{y + z}{2} = 80$$

   The first equation can be rearranged to give $x = 100 - y$. The second equation can be rearranged to give $z = 160 - y$. Plug the information into $z - x$ and solve:

$$\begin{aligned} z - x &= (160 - y) - (100 - y) \\ &= 160 - y - 100 + y \\ &= 160 - 100 \\ &= 60 \end{aligned}$$

6. **(C):** The question stem provides information about a median for a data set and asks whether the average of the same data set was greater than \$400,000, which can be abbreviated \$400K. When you're given a median, it's often a good idea to draw out dashes for each item in the set (e.g., for a three-item set: __ __ __), but this question stem doesn't indicate how many items are in the set. And that's your first clue as to how to think about this information.

   If the set contains exactly one item, then that item is \$450K and the average is also \$450K. If the set contains two items, then the two items must again average to \$450K, since the median of a two-item set is found by averaging the two items. So if you know that the set has one or two items, then the average matches the median (\$450K).

   If the set contains exactly three items, then the middle item is \$450K, but the least expensive item could be anything between 0 and \$450K and the most-expensive item could be anything from \$450K to infinity. That flexibility would allow an average below or above \$400K. The same will be true for a four-item set, a five-item set, and so on. If the set has three or more items, then you'd have to be given more information in order to be able to find the average.

   Glance at the statements. Begin with statement (2) on this one.

   (2) INSUFFICIENT: Three houses were sold, but no additional information is given. It's not possible, therefore, to calculate anything about the average price for all three houses.

   (1) INSUFFICIENT: The most expensive house was \$800K, but how many houses were sold? It could have been two, in which case the average equals the median, \$450K. In this case, the answer to the question is Yes, the average is greater than \$400K.

But there could also have been more houses sold. Imagine that five houses were sold for the following prices: \$1, \$1, \$450K, \$450K, and \$800K. The average would be approximately $\frac{\$1{,}700K}{5}$. That value is less than \$400K, so the answer is No. (For the average to be \$400K, the numerator would have to be \$2,000K.)

(1) AND (2) SUFFICIENT: If three houses (an odd number) were sold, then the median must be the price of one of the houses, so two of the three houses were sold for \$450K and \$800K, respectively. If the third house sold for \$1 (almost the minimum, which is actually \$0), the average would be $\frac{\$1 + \$450K + \$800K}{3}$. Is that value going to be greater than \$400K or less than \$400K? The sum of the prices is greater than \$1,200K, so the average of the three prices is greater than \$400K. This is the minimum average possible, so the answer is Always Yes.

The correct answer is **(C)**: The two statements are sufficient when used together, but neither one works alone.

CHAPTER 22

Weighted Averages

In This Chapter

- The Algebraic Method
- The Teeter-Totter Method
- Mixtures, Percents, and Ratios

In this chapter, you will learn how to recognize weighted average and mixture problems and how to use both logical and algebraic approaches to solve.

CHAPTER 22 Weighted Averages

The concept of **weighted averages** will come up all the time in graduate school—and in the general business world. It's worth spending some extra time digging in to understand this topic. If you can get to the point that you can think logically about weighted averages, as this chapter shows, you'll be in a strong position to talk about similar quant topics in grad school and beyond.

The regular formula for averages, $A = \frac{S}{n}$, applies only to sets of data consisting of individual values that are equally weighted—that is, all of the values "count" equally toward the average. For example, if you earn 100 on one exam and 80 on another exam, an equally weighted average of your scores is 90.

Some averages, however, are weighted more heavily toward certain data points. For example, imagine that your teacher tells you that your midterm exam will count for 40% of your grade and your final exam will count for 60% of your grade. If you can score a perfect 100 on only one of those components, which one would you want it to be?

Your final exam, of course! It counts more heavily toward your final grade. Next, imagine that you score 100 on your final exam but only 80 on your midterm exam. What is the weighted average of those two scores?

Any average has to be between the two starting points, in this case 100 and 80. The *regular* average would be 90. Is the weighted average higher or lower than the regular average of 90?

The final exam counts for more than 50% of your final score, so the weighted average must be closer to the final exam score of 100 than to 80. The weighted average must be between 90 and 100.

That knowledge is usually enough to get you to the right answer on a Data Sufficiency problem and it can often be enough to get to the right answer even on a Problem Solving problem. If you do need to calculate further, there are two ways to calculate the exact value: *algebraically* or via the *Teeter-Totter*.

The Algebraic Method

The **algebraic method** can be time-consuming without a calculator. It's usually only worth using if you have two data points and relatively easy numbers. It is worth *understanding*, though, because this will allow you to understand and remember the faster method introduced in the next section.

First, think about how a regular (nonweighted) average works. In a regular average, each item has exactly equal weight. For example, if there are two items, both are weighted $\frac{1}{2}$. If your teacher weighted your two exams equally, then this would be the calculation:

$$100\left(\frac{1}{2}\right) + 80\left(\frac{1}{2}\right) = 50 + 40 = 90$$

That is, the average is 90, exactly halfway between 80 and 100. The initial equation could be rearranged in this way:

$$100\left(\frac{1}{2}\right) + 80\left(\frac{1}{2}\right) = \frac{1}{2}(100 + 80) = \frac{100 + 80}{2}$$

Is that starting to look familiar? That's the average formula: Find the sum of the two numbers and divide by 2. Technically, regular averages all have these equal weightings, so you can always write the equation in the simplified form: $\frac{\text{Sum}}{\text{\# of Terms}}$

Weighted averages are solved using the same initial formula, but the weightings are not $\frac{1}{2}$ for each of the two terms.

You scored 100 on your final exam and it has a 60%, or $\frac{3}{5}$, weighting. You scored 80 on your midterm and it has a 40%, or $\frac{2}{5}$, weighting. Here's what that looks like:

$$100\left(\frac{3}{5}\right) + 80\left(\frac{2}{5}\right) = ?$$
$$60 + 32 = 92$$

The weighted average is 92.

If you're going to solve algebraically for a weighted average, you always have to use the "long" form of the average equation. You'll always have a component multiplied by its weighting, and then the next component multiplied by its weighting, and so on:

$$\text{Weighted Average} = (\text{Component 1})(\text{Weighting 1}) + (\text{Component 2})(\text{Weighting 2})$$

You can have more than two components. The GMAT typically sticks to two or three.

The Teeter-Totter Method

The **Teeter-Totter method** is very efficient as long as you understand what a weighted average is and how the concept works in general. If you struggle with the concept, then you may want to stick with the algebraic method—and just guess if you get a complicated one that's too annoying to solve algebraically.

The problem is the same: You scored 100 on your final exam and it has a $\frac{3}{5}$ weighting. You scored 80 on your midterm and it has a $\frac{2}{5}$ weighting. What is your final grade?

As with the algebraic method, begin by thinking about what would happen if you had two evenly weighted scores:

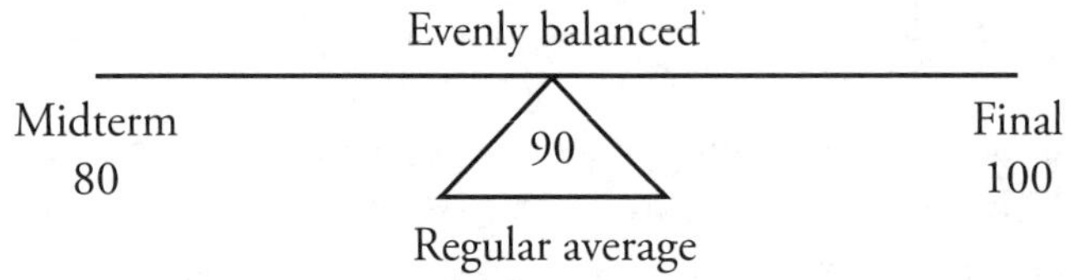

If you had a "regular" average, then the teeter-totter would be perfectly balanced and you would have an average of 90, halfway between 80 and 100.

In this case, though, you have a weighted average. Which way does the teeter-totter tilt?

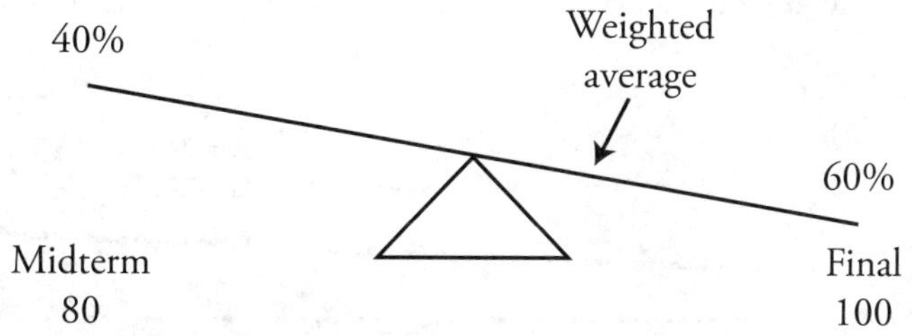

The final exam is weighted more heavily. The weighted average "slips" down toward the heavier end of the teeter-totter, so you know that the weighted average must be between 90 and 100. On DS problems, this is usually enough to determine whether a statement is sufficient!

On a PS problem, you might have a mix of answers such as the following: 82, 90, 92, 98, 105. You can knock out 82, 90, and 105 immediately, since they aren't between 90 and 100.

The two remaining answers, 92 and 98, are at opposite ends of the possible spectrum. Look at the weightings you were given: Are they pretty close to the regular weighting of $\frac{1}{2}$ or 50/50? If so, then the answer should be closer to the regular average (90 in this case).

Or are the given weightings really far from the 50/50 regular average calculation? If so, then the answer should be farther away from the regular average.

In this problem, the weightings are $\frac{3}{5}$ and $\frac{2}{5}$, or 60/40. This is pretty close to the 50/50 case, so the answer should be closer to 90—and, indeed, 92 is the correct answer.

If you do have to calculate the exact weighted average, here's what you do: The two ends of the teeter-totter are 80 and 100, and the difference between them is 20. Write that down. The final exam has a weighting of 60%, so it is responsible for 60% of that length of 20. Find 60% of 20: It is equal to 12. The average will weigh down the 100 end of the teeter totter more:

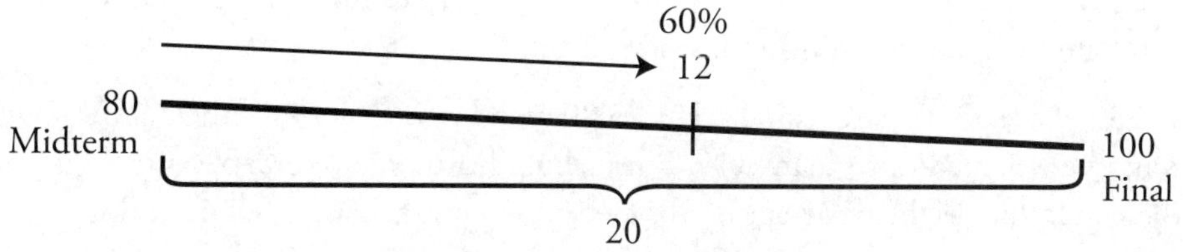

Therefore, the average is 80 + 12, which sums to 92 (and this makes logical sense; the value is between 90 and 100).

You don't need to draw out a full teeter-totter, but do draw at least the sloped line. Use logic to know which side is heavier. Calculate the "length" of the line (the difference between the two ends) and use it to calculate the value of the heavier weighting (in this case, 12); then, add that weight to the lighter side to see how far it tilts the teeter-totter down to the heavier side.

Imagine the situation were reversed: The score of 80 had the 60% weighting and the score of 100 had only a 40% weighting. In this case, you would start from the lighter end of the teeter-totter (the 100 end) and subtract instead:

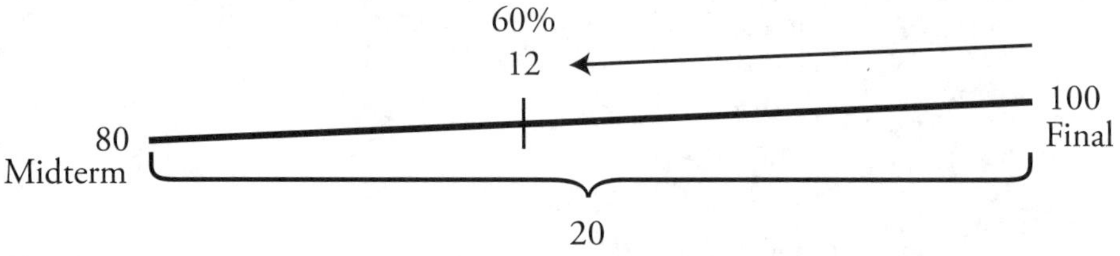

In this case, the average needs to be closer to the midterm end, so start from the higher (lighter) end, 100. Subtract from that end: $100 - 12 = 88$. Again, this makes logical sense: This time, the answer should be between 80 and 90.

In both cases, draw the sloped line and place the final number in roughly the appropriate position. That step will tell you which end is the lighter end and whether you'll need to add from the smaller end $(80 + 12)$ or subtract from the larger end $(100 - 12)$.

What if the problem changed the given information? Try this:

> You score 80 on your midterm exam and 100 on your final exam. Only these two exams make up your final grade of 92. How heavily did your teacher weight the final exam?

First, draw your teeter-totter:

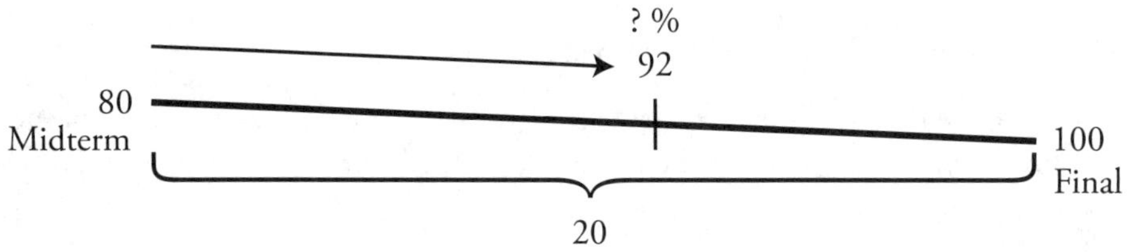

In this case, you still know the two end points (and the length), but now you're given the final average of 92 and you have to figure out the weighting that results in that average.

Because the weighted average is closer to 100 than to 80, you know that 100 is the heavier weight, so your final exam should be weighted more than 50%. But it shouldn't be a lot more, because 92 is not that much higher than the regular/unweighted average of 90. Depending on the answer choices, this might be enough to find the correct answer.

If you do need to calculate more precisely, find the longer of the two distances. In this case, that's between 80 and 92:

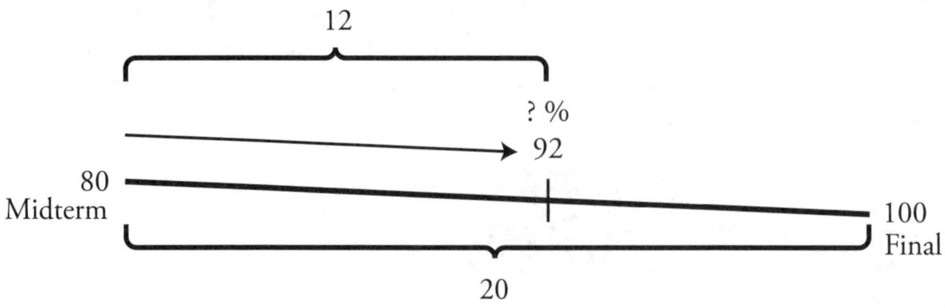

The weighting of the heavier (final exam) side is the fractional part 12 over the total length 20: $\frac{12}{20} = \frac{3}{5}$, which is equal to 60%.

If the problem had asked you to calculate the weighting of the *less*-heavily weighted value, the midterm exam, then you would find the *shorter* of the two distances, 8, and divide by the total distance, 20: $\frac{8}{20} = \frac{2}{5}$, which is equal to 40%.

Try this DS problem:

> The average number of students per class at School X is 25 and the average number of students per class at School Y is 33. Is the average number of students per class for both schools combined less than 29 ?
>
> (1) There are 12 classes in School X.
>
> (2) There are more classes in School X than in School Y.

Because this is a DS problem, there's a very good chance that you will not have to complete the calculations. In this case, try the teeter-totter method.

First, the question stem provides this information:

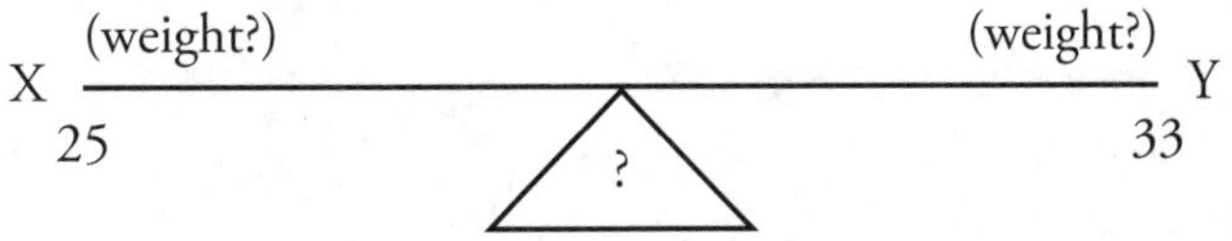

You don't know how to tilt the teeter-totter, because you don't know enough information yet. The question itself, though, implies something very intriguing.

If the two schools are equally weighted, then the regular average would be 29. What would have to be true to make the average *less* than 29?

The teeter-totter would have to be tilted down toward School X; this school would be weighted more heavily. Keep this in mind as you examine the statements:

> (1) There are 12 classes in School X.

This statement doesn't provide any information about School Y, so it's impossible to tell whether one school is weighted more heavily. Statement (1) is not sufficient. Eliminate answers (A) and (D).

> (2) There are more classes in School X than in School Y.

If there are more classes over at School X, then the weighted average has to tilt down toward this school:

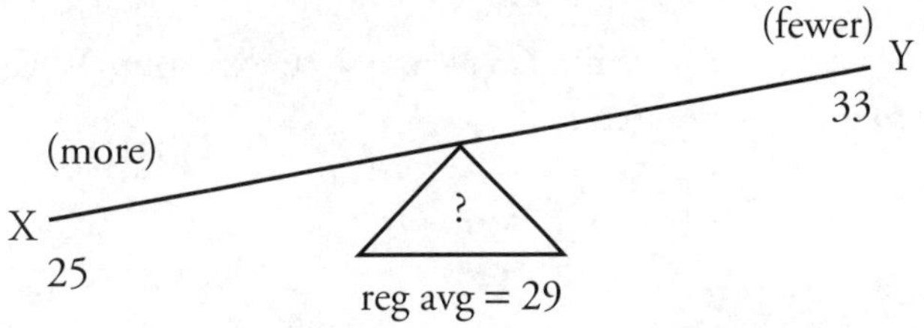

As a result, the weighted average has to be less than the regular average of 29.

Statement (2) is sufficient; the correct answer is (B).

On weighted average problems, you can choose whether to use the algebraic method or the teeter-totter method. The teeter-totter method is generally faster—*if* you really understand how weighted averages work. Try both methods out on some *Official Guide* problems and decide which one is better for you.

Mixtures, Percents, and Ratios

Percents and ratios can also show up in weighted average problems, particularly in the form of mixtures.

First, try this regular mixtures problem (you don't need to calculate a weighted average for this one):

A 400 milliliter solution is 20% alcohol by volume. If 100 milliliters of water is added, what is the new concentration of alcohol, as a percent of volume?

(A) 5%

(B) 10%

(C) 12%

(D) 12.5%

(E) 16%

To start, you have two liquid solutions: a 400 milliliter solution that is 20% alcohol and 80% something else and a 100 milliliter solution that is 100% water (and therefore 0% alcohol).

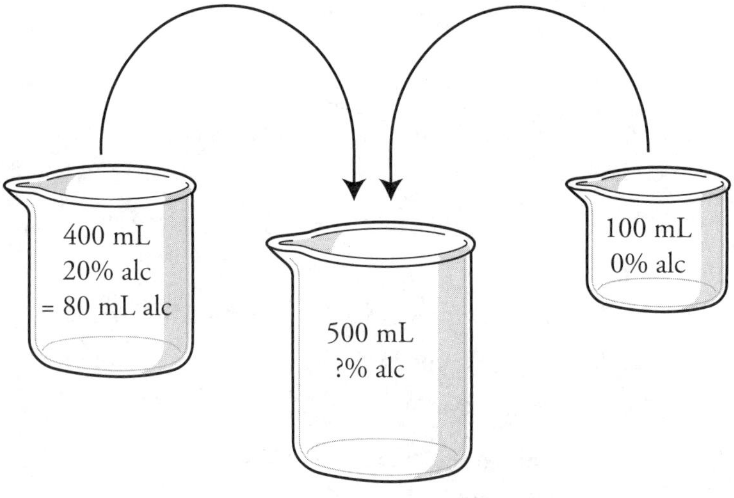

You can actually calculate the milliliters of alcohol in the 400 milliliter beaker: 20% of 400 is 80 milliliters. The 100 milliliter beaker doesn't contribute any alcohol at all, so the 500 milliliter beaker contains a total of 80 milliliters of alcohol. The big beaker, then, is $\frac{80}{500} = \frac{8}{50} = \frac{16}{100}$ = 16% alcohol. The correct answer is (E).

In this case, only one of the two beakers contributed alcohol to the mixture. What happens when both parts of the problem contribute to the desired mixture?

Try this example:

> Kris-P cereal is 10% sugar by weight, whereas healthier but less delicious Bran-O cereal is 2% sugar by weight. To make a delicious and healthy mixture that is 4% sugar, what should be the ratio of Kris-P cereal to Bran-O cereal, by weight?
>
> (A) 1 : 2
>
> (B) 1 : 3
>
> (C) 1 : 4
>
> (D) 3 : 1
>
> (E) 4 : 1

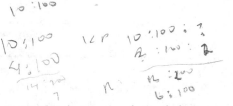

You can use the algebraic method or the teeter-totter—your choice. Both solutions are shown below.

The question asks for a ratio. Note that you don't necessarily need to know the real values of something in order to find a ratio. Call the weight of Kris-P cereal K and the weight of Bran-O cereal B.

To solve algebraically, set up an equation:

$$0.1K + 0.02B = 0.04(K + B)$$

Kris-P is weighted 10% and Bran-O is weighted 2%. The final mixture (the sum of the two components K and B) is weighted 4%.

Because the question asks for the ratio of K to B, manipulate the equation to solve for $\frac{K}{B}$. First, multiply the whole equation by 100 to get rid of the decimals. Then, simplify from there:

$$\begin{aligned} 10K + 2B &= 4(K + B) \\ 10K + 2B &= 4K + 4B \\ 6K &= 2B \\ \frac{K}{B} &= \frac{2}{6} = \frac{1}{3} \end{aligned}$$

The ratio of Kris-P to Bran-O is 1 : 3. The correct answer is (B).

To use your teeter-totter, start drawing:

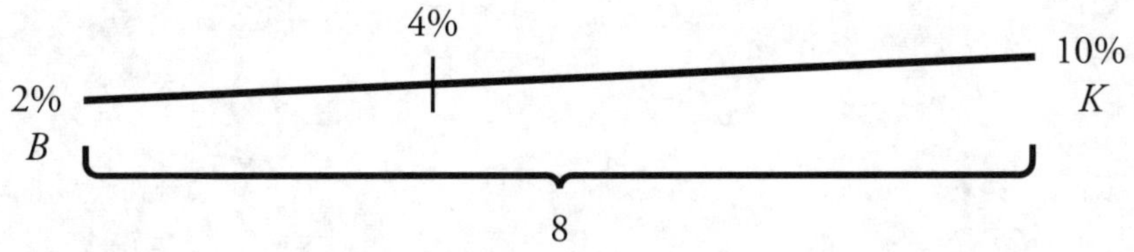

Because 4% is closer to 2%, the Bran-O side is heavier. Calculate the distance between the two ends: $10 - 2 = 8$. Finally, find the distances of the two subparts of the line:

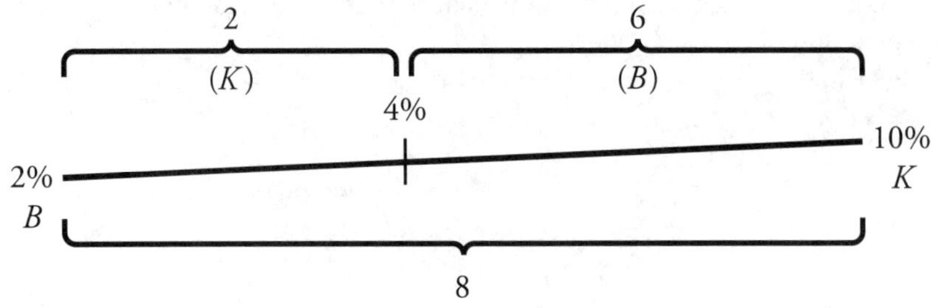

The smaller number, 2, is associated with the less-heavily weighted end (Kris-P, 10%). Note that the 10% *K* figure is on the other end of the teeter-totter; it will always be the case that the subpart is associated with the opposite end of the teeter-totter.

The larger number, 6, is associated with the more heavily weighted end (Bran-O, 2%). Again, it will always be the case that the subpart is associated with the opposite end of the teeter-totter.

Therefore, the ratio of Kris-P to Bran-O is 2 : 6, or 1 : 3, which is answer (B).

You can choose whether to use algebra or the teeter-totter; try out both to see which works best for you in various circumstances.

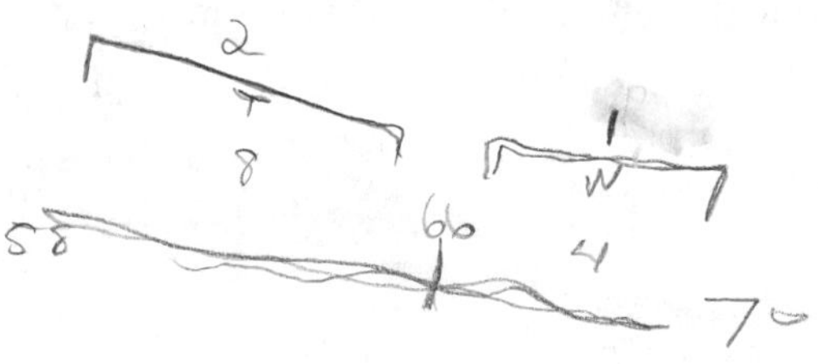

Problem Set

Now that you've finished the chapter, try these problems.

1. Imani has won 40% of the first 25 poker games she played this week. If she wins 80% of the remaining games she plays this week, how many additional games must Imani play in order to win 60% of all games for the week?

2. Hot dog vendors sold an average of 66 hot dogs per stand. Trainee vendors averaged 70 hot dogs sold. The ratio of non-trainee vendors to trainee vendors was 1 : 2. What was the average number of hot dogs sold by the non-trainee vendors?

Save these problems for review after you finish this entire guide.

3. Tickets to a play cost $10 for children and $25 for adults. If 100 tickets were sold, were more adult tickets sold than children's tickets?

   (1) The average revenue per ticket was $18.25.

   (2) The revenue from ticket sales exceeded $1,800.

4. A feed store sells two varieties of birdseed: Brand A, which is 40% millet and 60% sunflower, and Brand B, which is 65% millet and 35% safflower. If a customer purchases a mix of the two types of birdseed that is 50% millet, what percent of the mix is Brand A?

   (A) 15%

   (B) 40%

   (C) 50%

   (D) 60%

   (E) 85%

5. On a particular exam, the seniors in a history class averaged 86 points and the juniors in the class averaged 80 points. If the overall class average was 82 points, what was the ratio of seniors to juniors in the class?

6. A mixture of lean ground beef (10% fat) and super-lean ground beef (3% fat) has a total fat content of 8%. What is the ratio of lean ground beef to super-lean ground beef?

Solutions

1. **25 additional games:** This is a weighted averages problem. You can calculate this algebraically, but sketch it out first to understand the moving parts:

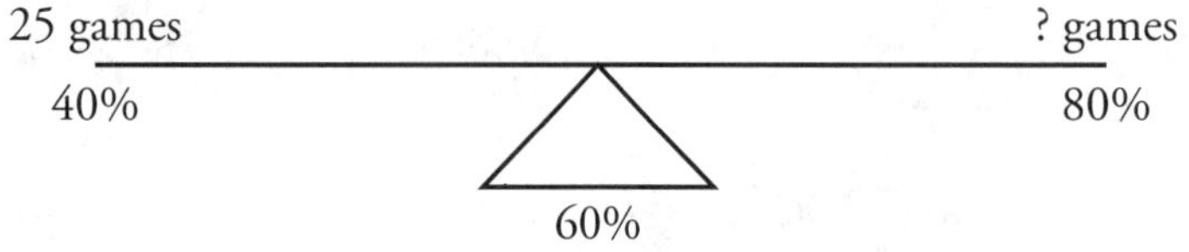

Which way should the teeter-totter tilt, to the right or to the left?

Actually, it doesn't tilt at all. Since 60% is exactly halfway between 40% and 80%, this isn't a weighted average at all; it's a regular average, where the two sides are equally weighted.

Since that's the case, the number of games at each end should match. Since Imani played 25 games for the 40%-win-rate group, she must also have played 25 games for the 80%-win-rate group. No algebra needed!

2. **58 hot dogs:** You can save yourself some calculation time by using smart numbers for part of this problem. The overall average of hot dogs sold is 66; trainees sold an average of 70. The ratio of non-trainees to trainees is 1 : 2, so just assume there was one actual non-trainee and two actual trainees (these are your smart numbers):

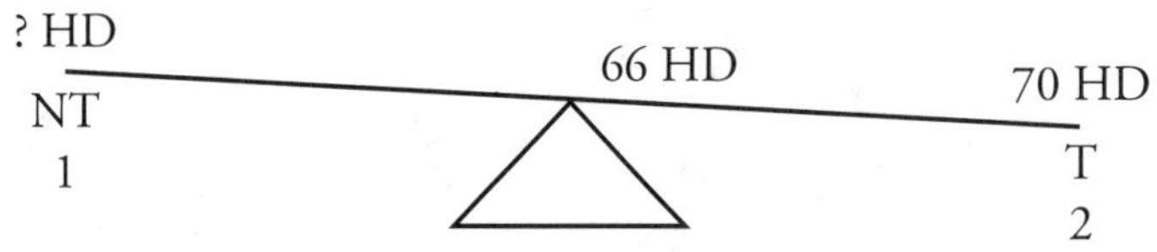

The teeter-totter is tilted toward the trainees. If those two trainees sold 70 hot dogs each, then those two people sold 140 hot dogs together. The overall average is 66 hot dogs and there were three people selling hot dogs, so there was an overall total of $(66)(3) = 198$ hot dogs sold. The one non-trainee, then, must have sold $198 - 140 = 58$ hot dogs.

But this can be solved in an even more streamlined way. The overall sum of $(66)(3)$ hot dogs sold must stay constant. If the two trainees sold 70 hot dogs each, then each one sold 4 hot dogs above the average, for a total of 8 extra hot dogs above the average of 66. In order for the overall average to be 66, those 8 extra hot dogs have to be taken away from the other group—in this case, the one non-trainee. The non-trainee, therefore, must have sold $66 - 8 = 58$ hot dogs.

3. **(D):** First things first: How would you recognize that this question is about weighted averages? The two different prices for tickets are like two different data points, and the number of tickets sold will act as the weight. If more adult tickets were sold, then the average ticket price will be closer to $25. If more children's tickets were sold, then the average ticket price will be closer to $10.

(1) SUFFICIENT: $18.25 is closer to $25 than to $10, so there must have been more adult tickets sold than children's tickets. Statement (1) is sufficient.

(2) SUFFICIENT: The total revenue from ticket sales exceeded $1,800. How are ticket sales calculated?

To figure that out, look at the information in the question stem again. One hundred tickets were sold. Consider two extreme scenarios:

$$100 \text{ children's tickets sold} = 100 \times \$10 = \$1{,}000 \text{ revenue}$$
$$100 \text{ adult tickets sold} = 100 \times \$25 = \$2{,}500 \text{ revenue}$$

If there were an equal number of adult and children's tickets sold, the revenue would be an average of $1,000 and $2,500, or $1,750. That's the connection to weighted averages. If the revenue is greater than $1,800, it is closer to $2,500 than to $1,000, which means more adult tickets must have been sold. Statement (2) is also sufficient.

The correct answer is **(D)**: Each statement works alone.

4. **(D) 60%:** The mixtures contain various things, but the question is only about the percent of millet, so ignore the other ingredients. Brand A is 40% millet and Brand B is 65% millet. The mixture is 50% millet, so this is a weighted averages problem. Sketch it out:

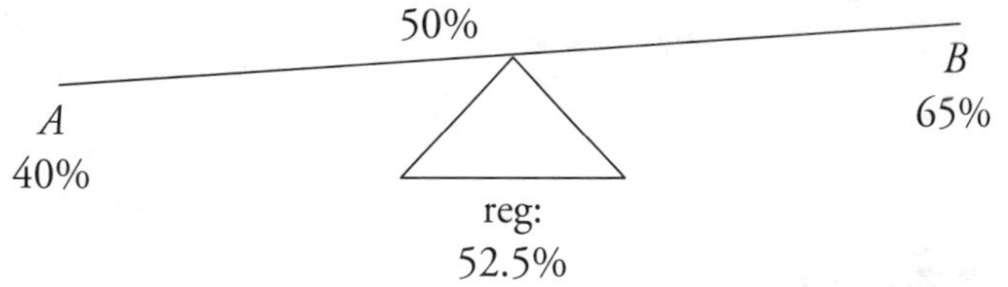

The regular average of 40% and 65% is halfway between, or 52.5%. If there were 50% of each brand in the mix, then the percentage of millet would be 52.5%.

The actual weighted average is 50%; this is closer to 40%, so there's more of Brand A in the mix. The correct answer has to be more than 50%, so eliminate answers (A), (B), and (C).

Compare the diagram to the two remaining answers. Is the given average of 50% closer to the regular average in the middle or closer to the extreme end of 40%? Since it's closer to the regular average (which represents a 50/50 mixture), the correct answer must be 60%, not 85%.

5. **1 : 2:** The seniors in the class scored 4 points higher on average than the entire class. Similarly, the juniors scored 2 points lower on average than the class. Draw a teeter-totter to solve:

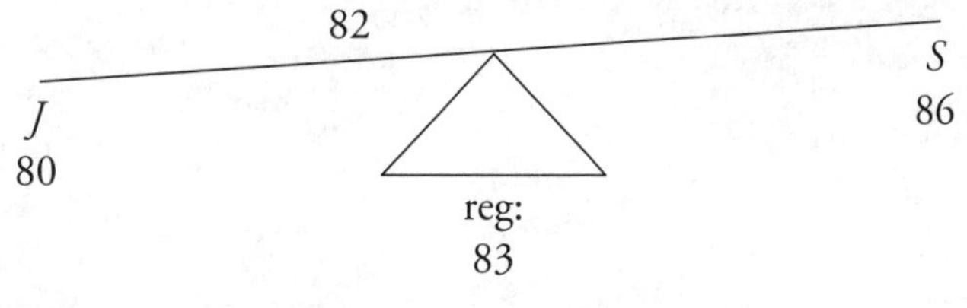

There are more juniors because the weighted average is closer to the 80 side of the teeter-totter. What's the ratio of the two parts?

The total distance of the line is 6, broken down into two portions of 2 and 4. Which is which?

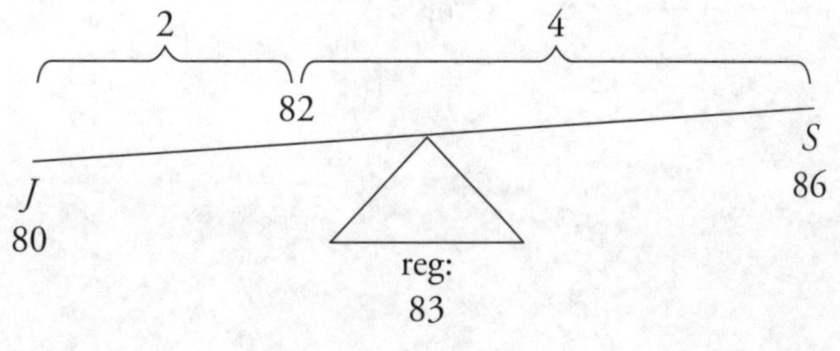

Think logically: There are fewer seniors than juniors, so the ratio of seniors to juniors must be 2 : 4, or 1 : 2. (You might also remember that these parts are always associated with the opposite end of the teeter-totter, so the 2 portion is associated with seniors and the 4 portion is associated with juniors.)

6. **5 : 2:** The question asks for the ratio of the two types of beef, so you don't need to worry about the actual amount of beef.

To set up this problem algebraically, first set up an equation, letting L be lean beef and S be super-lean beef:

$$0.1L + 0.03S = 0.08(L + S)$$

The question asks for the ratio of L to S, or $\frac{L}{S}$. First, multiply the equation by 100 to get rid of the decimals, then solve:

$$10L + 3S = 8(L + S)$$
$$10L + 3S = 8L + 8S$$
$$2L = 5S$$
$$\frac{L}{S} = \frac{5}{2}$$

Alternatively, draw a teeter-totter:

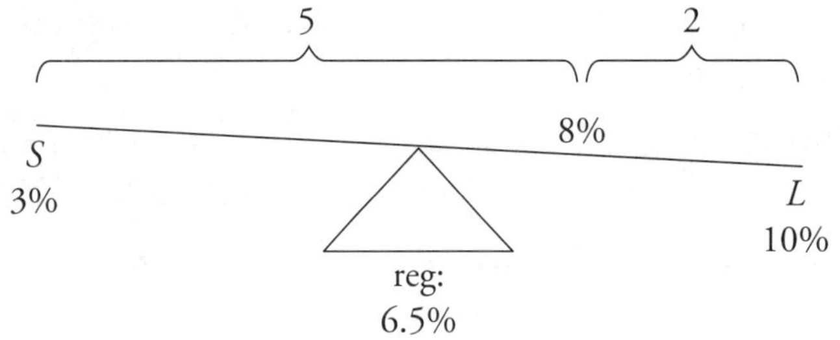

There's more lean ground beef, because 8% is closer to 10%. What's the ratio?

The "length" of the line is $10 - 3 = 7$. The lean (L) side is associated with the larger number, 5, and the super-lean (S) side is associated with the smaller number, 2. The ratio of $L : S = 5 : 2$.

CHAPTER 23

Strategy: Arithmetic vs. Algebra 3

In This Chapter

- Choosing Numbers for Smart Numbers
- Pick for Any Unknown on Smart Numbers
- Smart Numbers Disguised as Working Backwards
- Logic It Out and Work Backwards

In this chapter, you will learn more advanced approaches for the Choose Smart Numbers, Work Backwards, and Logic It Out strategies, including when to choose certain kinds of numbers, how to work more flexibly with smart numbers, and how to both work backwards and logic it out on the same problem.

CHAPTER 23 Strategy: Arithmetic vs. Algebra 3

This chapter focuses on more advanced techniques for handling harder Smart Numbers, Work Backwards, and Logic It Out problems. (The Arithmetic vs. Algebra 4 chapter will cover advanced techniques for the Test Cases strategy.)

Try this problem:

> Cost is expressed by the formula tb^4. If b is doubled and t remains the same, the new cost is how many times greater than the original cost?
>
> (A) 1.2
> (B) 2
> (C) 6
> (D) 8
> (E) 16

You can use an algebraic approach on this problem—and the algebraic approach is really streamlined *if* you know how to set it up. Here's how:

$$\text{Original} = tb^4$$

$$\text{New} = t(2b)^4 = 16tb^4$$

$$\frac{\text{New}}{\text{Old}} = \frac{16tb^4}{tb^4} = 16$$

The correct answer is (E). If you feel comfortable with this algebraic approach, go for it. More people, though, will be unsure about that approach or setup. Instead, use one of the approaches built for standardized tests.

At first glance, the problem might seem like a candidate for working backwards—there are real numbers in the answer choices. In fact, though, those numbers are *relative* values, not actual ones: They represent the multiplier to go from the original cost to the new cost. If the multiplier were 5, then it wouldn't matter whether your original cost was \$10 or \$10 million—you'd still multiply the original cost by 5 to get the new one.

Further, there are never any real values given for the cost. This is actually a Smart Numbers problem!

The original cost is defined as tb^4. Choose something for b that isn't very large, since you're going to have to raise it to a power of 4. Try $b = 2$ and $t = 3$:

$$\text{Original cost} = tb^4 = 3\left(2^4\right)$$

The numbers are a little annoying, so don't keep multiplying that out. Just leave it for now; later, you may be able to simplify before you multiply. (This applies in general to the whole test. Don't do math that you might not have to do! Defer the work.) Keep in mind that you're looking for opportunities to divide out either the 3 or the 2^4 or both!

Next, figure out the new cost. The value of b doubles, but t stays the same:

$$\begin{aligned}\text{New cost} &= t(2b)^4 \\ &= 3(2 \times 2)^4 \\ &= (3)(2^4)(2^4)\end{aligned}$$

Since you're looking for opportunities to divide out a 3 or a 2^4, don't combine the bases 2 and 2 to make a 4^4. Instead, distribute the exponent to each 2 and keep them separate.

The question asks how many times greater the new cost is than the old one, or New = y(Old). In other words, divide the new by the old to find the multiplier:

$$\frac{\text{New}}{\text{Old}} = \frac{(\cancel{3})(\cancel{2^4})(2^4)}{(\cancel{3})(\cancel{2^4})} = 2^4 = 16$$

The math with real numbers is the same math as the algebra—in both cases, everything cancels out except for the 16. Using real numbers can just help you to see how the math works and to set it up correctly.

Choosing Numbers for Smart Numbers

Earlier in this guide, you learned how to choose good numbers for certain strategies. This section summarizes the earlier guidelines for the Smart Numbers strategy and adds some new ones.

First, you always have to follow any constraints given in a problem. For example, if the problem says that x is a positive integer, then you can only try positive integers for x.

When using the Smart Numbers strategy on Problem Solving problems, the general guidelines are to avoid 0, 1, and numbers that appear in the problem. If you have to choose for more than one variable, choose different numbers for each variable.

In addition to the above, try to choose numbers that will work well in the problem. Here are some of the most common ways in which you'll choose numbers on the exam.

Choosing Smart Numbers	
When I see...	*I'll choose...*
Percents	100 or 50
Fractions (part to whole)	A common denominator for all of the fractions
Ratios (even if in fraction form)	The parts of the ratio e.g. The number of dogs is $\frac{3}{4}$ the number of cats. e.g. The ratio of dogs to cats is 3 : 4. Use 3 dogs to 4 cats.

Choosing Smart Numbers	
That I'll need to divide	A multiple of the divisor e.g. Someone bought 8 pens for x dollars. Use a multiple of 8; if $x = 16$, then the pens were $2 each.
Variation of dividing: Rate or work problems	Values that will give integers when calculating a rate Rate = Distance (or Work) divided by Time
A lot of multiplication or exponents	Smaller numbers (e.g. 2)
A variable under a square root sign A variable under a cube root sign	A perfect square, such as 4 A perfect cube, such as 8
2 or more variables; choosing for one will determine the value of the other(s)	*Don't* default to choosing for the first variable mentioned. Think about it. What's the easiest starting point? e.g. If $x + y = a$ and $x - y = b$, it's easier to choose x and y than a and b. e.g. If Pool A's capacity is twice Pool B's capacity, choose for the smaller capacity first, then multiply by 2 to get the larger capacity.

On more advanced problems, you may see two such clues and have to decide which one to use first. This is what your Plan phase is for—to figure out which characteristic you should prioritize.

As you study, continue adding to the list above as you come across more examples of smart numbers and find your own ways to decide how to choose specific numbers.

Pick for Any Unknown on Smart Numbers

On a Smart Numbers problem, it's often easiest to pick for the actual variables in the problem. Sometimes, though, it's easier to pick for a different unknown, *not* the variable that shows up in the problem and answer choices.

Here's an example:

> A truck is filled to $\frac{1}{4}$ of its maximum weight capacity. An additional y pounds are added such that the truck is now filled to $\frac{7}{8}$ of its capacity. In terms of y, what is the maximum weight capacity of the truck, in pounds?
>
> (A) $\frac{5}{8}y$
>
> (B) $\frac{5}{4}y$
>
> (C) $\frac{8}{5}y$

Understand. This is a PS problem with variable expressions in the answers and no real value ever given for the weight. You can choose smart numbers. The question asks for the maximum capacity. The variable y represents the additional weight added to the truck to go from $\frac{1}{4}$ to $\frac{7}{8}$ of capacity.

Plan. What kind of value for y would be a "good" number, given that y covers the gap between $\frac{1}{4}$ and $\frac{7}{8}$ of the truck's capacity? That's an annoying question. This problem would be a lot easier if it *gave* the maximum capacity and *asked* you to find y.

Guess what? You're actually allowed to choose for whatever unknown you would like. If you think it's easier to choose for the answer/ending value and then work from the end of the problem to the beginning to solve for the starting variable, go right ahead!

The two fractions have denominators of 4 and 8, so choose a value for the total capacity that works nicely with both: 8.

Solve. If the total capacity of the truck is 8 pounds (it's a *really* small truck!), then at first it contains 2 pounds of material. Later, it contains 7 pounds, so $y = 5$ pounds were added. Plug this value into the answers and look for the answer that equals the total capacity of 8:

(A) $\frac{5}{8}y = \frac{5}{8}(5) \neq 8$ Eliminate

(B) $\frac{5}{4}y = \frac{5}{4}(5) \neq 8$ Eliminate

(C) $\frac{8}{5}y = \frac{8}{5}(5) = 8$ Match!

The correct answer is (C).

When using smart numbers, you can always choose where to start. Most of the time, it will be easier to choose for the given variable, but if you ever find yourself thinking that the math would be easier if they had given the end value, go ahead and reverse the process. Choose your own value for that ending point and work your way to the variable.

By the way, one of the answer choices doesn't make logical sense—though most people don't stop to consider the problem in this way. The variable y represents a subset of the truck's capacity, since it's the amount of capacity that allows the truck to go from $\frac{1}{4}$ to $\frac{7}{8}$ full. The answer choices represent the total capacity of the truck. Logically, the total capacity must be greater than a subset of the capacity, so the correct answer must be y times a number greater than 1. Answer (A) is illogical because the value of the fraction is less than 1.

You don't absolutely have to learn to spot those kinds of traps—but if you do, that can help you to narrow down answers when you need to guess. It can also help you to avoid careless mistakes—if you know logically that the fraction should be greater than 1, but you end up getting answer (A), you'll know to check your work.

Smart Numbers Disguised as Working Backwards

Some problems do have real numbers in the answer choices, but can still be solved via smart numbers.

Try this problem:

> A company pays the same hourly rate to all of its employees. Four people work for 8 hours each and earn a total of y dollars collectively. How many people need to work for 20 hours each in order to earn a total of $1.25y$ dollars collectively?
>
> (A) 1
>
> (B) 2
>
> (C) 3

Understand. This problem fits all of the hallmarks of a working backwards problem—"nice" real numbers in the answers, and those answers represent a single variable in the problem—but there's a hitch. What do you do with that variable y in the story?

The y represents the dollars earned for a certain number of hours worked. Later, the problem uses $1.25y$ to represent the dollars earned for a different number of hours worked. The problem also states that the hourly pay rate is the same for everyone, but it *never* gives a real number for rate of pay or for dollars anywhere in the problem.

That's a characteristic of smart numbers! If the problem keeps talking about something but never gives you a real number for that something, you're allowed to choose your own number—so go for it!

Plan. Choose your own pay rate and work through the problem accordingly. How about \$10/hour? (You may be tempted to go with something like \$15. Don't think real world. Make your task as easy as you can.)

Solve. The pay rate is \$10 per hour. In the first scenario, four people work for 8 hours each, or a total of 32 hours. Collectively, they are paid $(32)(10) = \$320$. This is y.

The problem asks about a second scenario in which the workers earn $1.25y$. This is 25% greater than y itself, so take 25%, or $\frac{1}{4}$, of y and add to y: $320 + 80 = \$400$.

Aside: To find 25%, you can benchmark: $25\% = 10\% + 10\% + 5\% = 32 + 32 + 16 = 80$. Alternatively, to find $\frac{1}{4}$, divide by 2 twice: $\frac{320}{2} = \frac{160}{2} = 80$.

In order to earn a total of \$400 at a pay rate of \$10 per hour, the workers must have collectively worked a total of 40 hours. For the second scenario, the problem states that the workers worked 20 hours each, so there must have been 2 workers to work a total of 40 hours.

The correct answer is (B).

Note: You can also solve this problem by choosing a value for the variable y and then calculating the pay rate. You'd need to divide y by both 4 (people) and 8 (hours each) to find the hourly rate, so $y = 32$ might be a good fit. (This would work out to a pay rate of \$1/hour.) As on any Smart Numbers problem, start with whatever seems easiest or most natural to you.

Whenever a problem talks about some variable and never gives you a real value for that variable, you can choose your own number for that thing—even if the problem gives you real numbers for other items in the problem, including the answer choices.

Logic It Out and Work Backwards

Try this problem:

> Train X is traveling at a constant speed of 30 miles per hour, and Train Y is traveling at a constant speed of 40 miles per hour. If the two trains are traveling in the same direction along the same route but Train X is 25 miles ahead of Train Y, how many hours will pass before Train Y is 10 miles ahead of Train X ?
>
> (A) 1.5
> (B) 2.0
> (C) 2.5
> (D) 3.0
> (E) 3.5

Understand. Glance at the answers before reading the problem. They're all small numbers—so when you read the problem, check whether you can work backwards. The problem itself involves two trains moving in certain ways, so sketch out the story. The question does ask for a single variable in the problem (the number of hours it will take for a certain scenario to happen), so you can work backwards. Sketch the story out to make sure you know all of the moving parts:

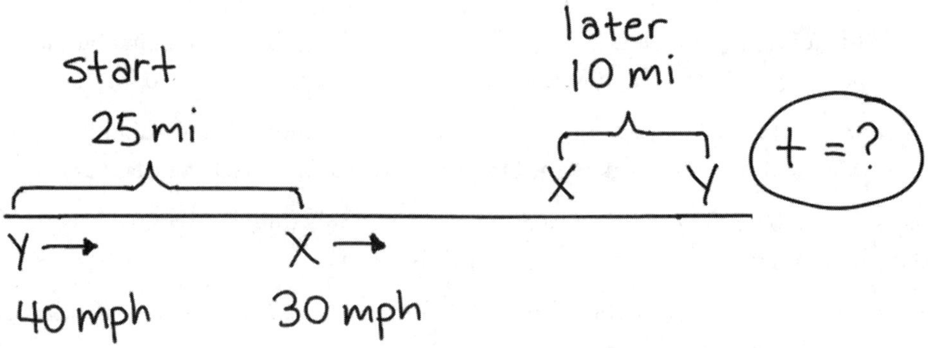

Plan. Think about how to use the sketch to make it easier to work backwards. The answer choices represent the amount of time that both trains move. You know the rates of both trains, so for each answer choice that you try, you could sketch another line below and map out how the trains move each hour (or half hour) of the trip.

Solve. Try answer (B) first:

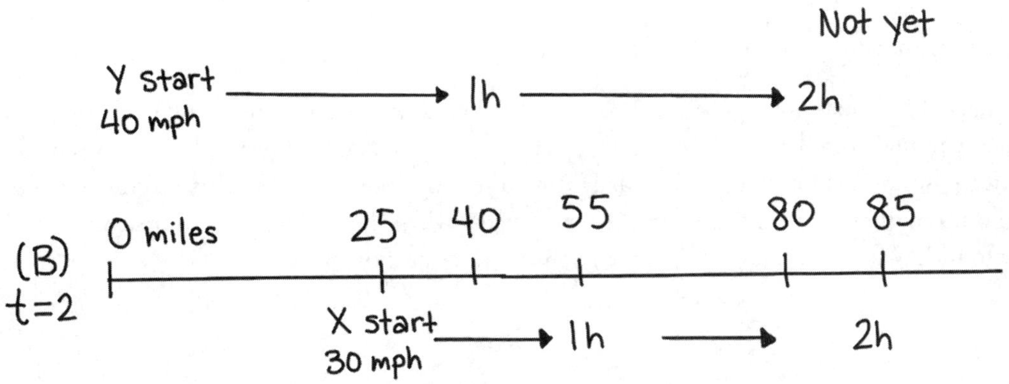

Train Y hasn't passed Train X yet by the 2-hour mark, so answer (B) is incorrect and answer (A) must be wrong, too. Cross off both.

Glance at the answers. Answer (D) is 3 hours, so just extend the line a little farther to find where the trains are after 1 more hour:

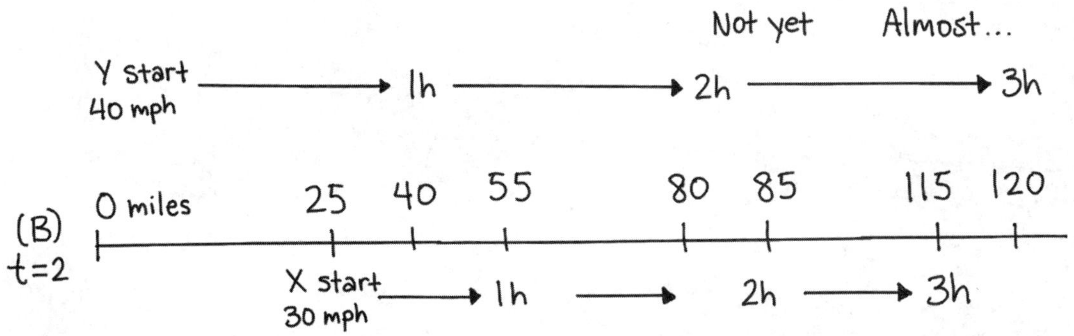

Close! But not quite. Train Y has passed Train X, but it is not yet 10 miles ahead of Train X. So (D) isn't long enough.

Only answer (E) represents a longer time, so it must be the correct answer.

You can also solve algebraically. The most efficient algebraic method is shown below.

Because the problem focuses on the difference in movement between the two trains, find the difference in distance and the difference in rate, then plug into the Rate-Time-Distance (RTD) formula.

The two trains are currently 25 miles apart, with X ahead of Y. The problem asks you to solve for the time at which Y has moved 10 miles ahead of X. Therefore, Y has to catch up to X to erase that initial 25-mile deficit and then move an additional 10 miles beyond X. In other words, Y has to travel an additional $25 + 10 = 35$ miles farther than X travels. Use 35 as the distance in the RTD formula.

For every hour that the two trains travel, Y goes 10 miles per hour faster (since it travels 40 miles per hour to X's 30 miles per hour). Use 10 miles per hour as the rate in the RTD formula:

$$\frac{35\text{ miles}}{10\text{ miles per hour}} = 3.5\text{ hours}$$

When the algebra for a particular problem feels easier for you, that solution can be quite efficient—but on a problem that you find complex, it's easy to mess up the equation. As you study, think about when you would want to use an algebraic approach (usually when the problem feels straightforward to you) and when you would want to draw it out and work backwards (usually when the problem feels more complex). If you study how to make the best choice for you, then you can react quickly on test day.

Problem Set

Pop quiz! The problems in this set may cover any strategies from the entire guide up to this point.

1. In a college class, each student's overall grade is calculated by averaging the student's grades on t different exams. Up until the last exam, Wei had earned an average exam grade of $0.75g$. After earning a grade of g on the last exam, Wei's overall grade in the class was $0.8g$. What is the value of t ?

   (A) 2
   (B) 3
   (C) 4
   (D) 5
   (E) 6

2. If $a = 2.4d7$, and d represents a digit from 0 to 9, is d greater than 4 ?

   (1) If a were rounded to the nearest hundredth, the new number would be greater than a.
   (2) If a were rounded to the nearest tenth, the new number would be greater than a.

3. The Crandall's hot tub has a capacity of x liters and is half full. Their swimming pool, which has a capacity of y liters, is filled to four-fifths of its capacity. If enough water is drained from the swimming pool to fill the hot tub to capacity, the pool is now how many liters short of full capacity, in terms of x and y ?

   (A) $0.8y - 0.5x$
   (B) $0.8y + 0.5x$
   (C) $0.2y + 0.5x$
   (D) $0.3(y - x)$
   (E) $0.3(y + x)$

4. Four brothers split a sum of money between them. The first brother received 50% of the total, the second received 25% of the total, the third received 20% of the total, and the fourth received the remaining \$4. The first brother received how much more money than the third brother received?

   (A) \$4
   (B) \$16
   (C) \$20
   (D) \$24
   (E) \$36

5. A rental car agency owns a total of $5x$ cars and $2x$ trucks, where x is a positive integer. If the agency purchases c new cars, will the new ratio of cars to trucks be at least 3 to 1 ?

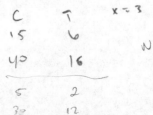

   (1) $c = x + 5$
   (2) $x = 11$

Save the following problems for review after you finish this entire guide.

6. Teachers and students at a school are solving problems. There are twice as many students as teachers, and each student solves 3 more problems than each teacher. If teachers solve 24 of the 90 total problems solved, how many problems does each teacher solve?

    (A) 3
    (B) 4
    (C) 5
    (D) 6
    (E) 8

7. If b is an integer, is 1.3 multiplied by b an integer?

    (1) b is a multiple of 3.
    (2) 0.7 multiplied by b is an integer.

8. Vimbai spends $\frac{3}{8}$ of her monthly paycheck on rent and $\frac{1}{4}$ on food. Her roommate, Carrie, who earns twice as much as Vimbai, spends $\frac{1}{4}$ of her monthly paycheck on rent and $\frac{1}{2}$ on food. If the two roommates decide to donate the remainder of their money to charity each month, what fraction of their combined monthly income will they donate?

    (A) $\frac{5}{24}$
    (B) $\frac{7}{24}$
    (C) $\frac{11}{24}$
    (D) $\frac{17}{24}$
    (E) $\frac{19}{24}$

Solutions

1. **(D) 5:** The answer choices contain real numbers, represented by t in the problem, but the problem also contains an unspecified value, g. No real value is ever given for g, so choose your own. You'll need to take both 0.75 and 0.8 of g, so chose a value that will work well in both calculations.

   Let $g = 100$. Wei's average for all but the last exam (or $t - 1$ exams) was 75. The last exam grade was 100. The sum of all of the grades is $75(t - 1) + 100$. The total number of tests is t. Plug these values and variables into the average formula and solve for t:

$$\begin{aligned} \text{Average} &= \frac{\text{Sum}}{\text{\# of Terms}} \\ 80 &= \frac{75(t-1)+100}{t} \\ 80t &= 75(t-1)+100 \\ 80t &= 75t - 75 + 100 \\ 5t &= 25 \\ t &= 5 \end{aligned}$$

   Wei took a total of 5 exams.

2. **(B):** The variable d represents a single digit, so it could be any digit from 0 to 9. The question doesn't ask for the value of d; rather, it asks whether d is greater than 4. This is a Yes/No question. What would be sufficient and what would not? If you can tell that $d > 4$, the information is sufficient. If you can tell that $d \leq 4$, the information is sufficient. If d could cross over the "barrier" of 4 (that is, it could be 4 or 5), the information is not sufficient—so you may want to test the numbers 4 and 5 specifically.

   (1) INSUFFICIENT: In the representation $a = 2.4d7$, the hundredths digit is the variable d. Test some cases to see what happens to a when you round to d.

   This statement is complex, so think about what you're allowed to try. If $d = 5$, then $a = 2.457$. Rounding to the nearest hundredth produces 2.46, which is indeed greater than 2.457. It's valid, then, to choose $d = 5$. In this case, is d greater than 4 ? Yes.

   Can you think of another case that would give a No answer?

   Try $d = 4$. In this case, $a = 2.447$. Rounding to the nearest hundredth produces 2.45, which is indeed greater than 2.447. It's valid to choose $d = 4$. In this case, is d greater than 4 ? No.

   Because the answer is Sometimes Yes/Sometimes No, this statement is not sufficient.

   (2) SUFFICIENT: The tenths digit of $a = 2.4d7$ is 4. Two outcomes are possible when rounding to the tenths digit: 2.4 or 2.5. The value 2.4 would be smaller than the starting number; only the value 2.5 would be greater. In order to make the rounded value 2.5, the value of the next digit to the right, d, has to be 5 or greater. According to this statement, Yes, d is always greater than 4.

   The correct answer is **(B)**: Statement (2) is sufficient, but statement (1) is not.

3. **(C) $0.2y + 0.5x$:** The answers contain the variables x and y; the question stem never offers real values for these variables, so you can choose your own smart numbers.The problem contains two fractions: The hot tub is *half* full and the pool is filled to *four-fifths* of its capacity. The two capacities are not related (that is, once you pick for one variable, the other variable is not automatically determined), so you'll have to pick two numbers. Pick something divisible by 2 for x and divisible by 5 for y.
Try $x = 4$ and $y = 10$:

$x = \text{H cap} = 4$	Half full $= 2$
$y = \text{P cap} = 10$	$\frac{4}{5}$ full $= 8$

The hot tub, with a capacity of 4, is half full, so there are 2 liters of water in the hot tub. The pool, with a capacity of 10, is four-fifths full, so there are 8 liters in the pool.

Next, the problem says that water is siphoned off from the pool and put into the hot tub. How much? The hot tub needs 2 more liters to be full, so subtract 2 from the pool. The pool now has only 6 liters, so it is 4 liters short of its capacity of 10.

Plug $x = 4$ and $y = 10$ into the answer choices and look for an answer that matches: 4 liters short.

(A) $0.8y - 0.5x = (0.8)(10) - (0.5)(4) = 8 - 2 = 6$

(B) $0.8y + 0.5x = (0.8)(10) + (0.5)(4) =$ too big, since (A) was too big.

(C) $0.2y + 0.5x = (0.2)(10) + (0.5)(4) = 2 + 2 = 4$ Match!

(D) $0.3(y - x) = 0.3(10 - 4) = 0.3(6) =$ not an integer

(E) $0.3(y + x) = 0.3(10 + 4) = 0.3(14) =$ not an integer

4. **(D) \$24:** The answer choices are "nice" integers; check the question stem to see whether you can work backwards.

The question asks for the difference between Brother 1 and Brother 3. If you started with answer (B), 16, what values would you choose for each brother? They can be anything, as long as the difference is 16.

Don't work backwards on this problem. (This is why the strategy specifies that the question should ask for a single variable in the problem.) Do the actual math to solve.

The first three brothers got 50% + 25% + 20% = 95% of the money. The fourth brother, then, got the remaining 5%, and that 5% is equal to \$4.

If 5% = \$4, then 10% = \$8, and 100% = \$80. The total amount of money is \$80. The first brother got 50%, or \$40, and the third brother got 20%, or \$16. The difference is \$40 – \$16 = \$24.

5. **(A):** This is a Yes/No question and it asks an *at least* question, so expect to use an inequality to translate into math. The story problem discusses ratios using the variables c and x. Glance at the statements. The second statement provides a value for the unknown x. The first statement would allow you to find c if you know x. So is the answer (C)?

That's probably too good to be true. Be suspicious—this might be a C-Trap. Jot down the information from the question stem. The current number of cars to trucks is $5x$ to $2x$, or a ratio of $5 : 2$. If there are c more cars, then there are a total of $5x + c$ cars. The question asks whether this new situation has a car-to-truck ratio of *at least* $3 : 1$. Use this information to set up a proportion for the question: Is the ratio of the new number of cars to the number of trucks at least 3 to 1 ?

$$\text{Is } \frac{\text{Cars}}{\text{Trucks}} = \frac{5x + c}{2x} \geq \frac{3}{1}\,?$$

The left-hand side shows the real-number representation for cars and trucks after c cars are added. The right-hand side shows the ratio for the same scenario. The question asks whether that ratio is *at least* 3 : 1, so use the greater-than-or-equal-to symbol.

Fractions are annoying; can you cross-multiply to simplify the equation? Yes, the problem indicates that x is positive, so don't switch the direction of the inequality sign when you cross-multiply:

Is $5x + c \geq 6x$?

Is $c \geq x$?

This is the rephrased question. Statement (2) is easier, so start there.

(2) INSUFFICIENT: This statement provides no information about c, so it's not possible to tell whether $c \geq x$.

(1) SUFFICIENT: The question stem states that x is a positive integer. Take any positive integer and add 5; what happens? The number gets larger, so c does have to be greater than x. (In fact, this would work with any number, positive or negative, integer or fraction.) This information is sufficient to answer the question Always Yes.

The correct answer is **(A)**: Statement (1) is sufficient alone, but statement (2) is not.

6. **(E) 8:** The answers contain easy integers, so check whether you can work backwards. The question does ask for a single variable, so you can. (Note: The problem might seem pretty straightforward at first glance, but there are three variables: number of teachers, number of students, and number of problems solved. This will make for a very messy algebraic solution. Even if you really like algebra, consider working backwards on this problem.)

The problem gives enough information to solve for the total number of problems solved by students. If teachers solve 24 out of the 90 problems, then the students must solve $90 - 24 = 66$ problems.

The answers represent the number of problems solved by each teacher. Each student solves 3 more than each teacher, so start by adding 3 to each answer choice:

	Prob per T:	→	Prob per S:
(A)	3	→	6
(B)	4	→	7
(C)	5	→	8
(D)	6	→	9
(E)	8	→	11

(# of students)(# problems solved per student) = 66

The students solve a total of 66 problems, and there must be an integer-number of students (no partial people!), so the number of problems solved per student must be a factor of 66. Only answers (A) and (E) qualify; eliminate the other three.

Try either remaining answer. If the one you try is incorrect, then the correct answer has to be the other one.

Prob per T	Prob per S (Prob per T + 3)	# S (66 ÷ prior)	# S = twice # T
(A) 3	6	$\frac{66}{6} = 11$	5.5 teachers...

There are supposed to be twice as many students as teachers, so that would be 5.5 teachers ... no good! The only remaining answer is **(E)**. (If you try it: problems per teacher = 8, problems per student = 11, # of students = 6, # of teachers = 3. The teachers solve (8)(3) = 24 problems, which is what the problem said, so this answer is correct.)

7. **(B):** This is a Yes/No question. The question stem establishes that b is an integer and asks whether 1.3 multiplied by b is an integer. Before jumping to the statements, think about what kinds of values for b would allow $1.3b$ to be an integer.

For example, if $b = 10$, then $1.3b$ would be 13. Any multiple of 10 would also return a Yes answer. The value 5 would not return an integer, but 10 (a multiple of 5) would. The value 3 would not return an integer, but 30 (a multiple of 3) would ...

(1) INSUFFICIENT: If b is a multiple of 3, then b could be 3 itself, so $1.3b$ would not be an integer, and the answer is No. (You don't necessarily need to find the value in order to tell that it won't be an integer, but $(3)(1.3) = 3.9$.)

Alternatively, b could be 30, and then $1.3b$ would be $(1.3)(10)(3)$. This is an integer, so the answer is Yes. The answer is Sometimes Yes/Sometimes No, so this statement is not sufficient.

(2) SUFFICIENT: If 0.7 multiplied by b is an integer, then b could be 10. In this case, $1.3b$ is also an integer, and the answer is Yes.

Try to find a No answer. If $b = 1$, then $0.7b$ is not an integer, so this is an invalid case. Discard it. If $b = 2$, then $0.7b$ is also not an integer, so this is another invalid case. Discard it. In fact, none of the integers 1 through 9 will make $0.7b$ an integer. Why not?

When multiplying a decimal by an integer, you'll always need to insert the same number of decimal places into the product: for example, $(0.7)(2) = 1.4$ and $(0.7)(3) = 2.1$. When you get up to $(0.7)(10)$, the answer is technically 7.0—but that digit after the decimal place is a 0, so now you have an integer. In other words, in order for $0.7b$ to be an integer, b has to contain a multiple of 10. And since b contains a multiple of 10, the value of $1.3b$ has to be an integer as well. Using statement (2), the answer to the question *Is 1.3b an integer?* is Always Yes.

The correct answer is **(B)**: Statement (2) alone is sufficient, but statement (1) alone is not.

8. **(B)** $\frac{7}{24}$**:** The answer choices represent a relative amount, so use smart numbers to solve. The question asks what fraction of their total income Vimbai and Carrie will donate, or $\frac{\text{combined donation}}{\text{combined total}}$.

Since the denominators in the problem are 8, 4, and 2, assign Vimbai a monthly paycheck of \$8. Assign Carrie, who earns twice as much, a monthly paycheck of \$16. Total income is \$8 + \$16 = \$24. The roommates' monthly expenses break down as follows:

	Rent	Food	Left over/to donate
V	$\frac{3}{8}$ of 8 = 3	$\frac{1}{4}$ of 8 = 2	8 − (3 + 2) = 3
C	$\frac{1}{4}$ of 16 = 4	$\frac{1}{2}$ of 16 = 8	16 − (4 + 8) = 4

Vimbai and Carrie will donate a total of \$3 + \$4 = \$7 out of their combined monthly income of \$24.

Notice the two pairs of evil twins: Answers (A) and (E) sum to 1, as do answers (B) and (D). Answer (D) represents the fraction of total income that Vimbai and Carrie *spend*, rather than donate, a classic GMAT trap on this kind of question. Answer (A) results from using the same income for Vimbai and Carrie (but doing everything else correctly). And answer (E) makes both of those mistakes. Avoid guessing (C) on this problem, since it does not have an evil twin at all.

23

CHAPTER 24

Consecutive Integers

In This Chapter

- Evenly Spaced Sets
- Counting Integers: Add 1 before You Are Done
- Properties of Evenly Spaced Sets
- The Sum of Consecutive Integers

In this chapter,you will learn how to recognize and solve problems involving consecutive integers and other evenly spaced sets, as well as how to determine the number of integers in a large set and the sum of the integers in a set.

CHAPTER 24 Consecutive Integers

Consecutive integers are integers that follow one after another from a given starting point, without skipping any integers. For example, 4, 5, 6, and 7 are consecutive integers, but 4, 6, 7, and 9 are not. There are many other types of consecutive patterns. For example:

Consecutive even integers: 8, 10, 12, 14

(8, 10, 14, and 16 is incorrect, as it skips 12)

Consecutive primes: 11, 13, 17, 19

(11, 13, 15, and 17 is incorrect, as 15 is not prime)

Evenly Spaced Sets

In **evenly spaced sets**, the values of the numbers in the set go up or down by the same amount (or **increment**) from one item in the sequence to the next. For example, the set {4, 7, 10, 13, 16} is evenly spaced because each value increases by 3 over the previous value. Think of this as the broadest grouping—the biggest circle in the diagram shown below:

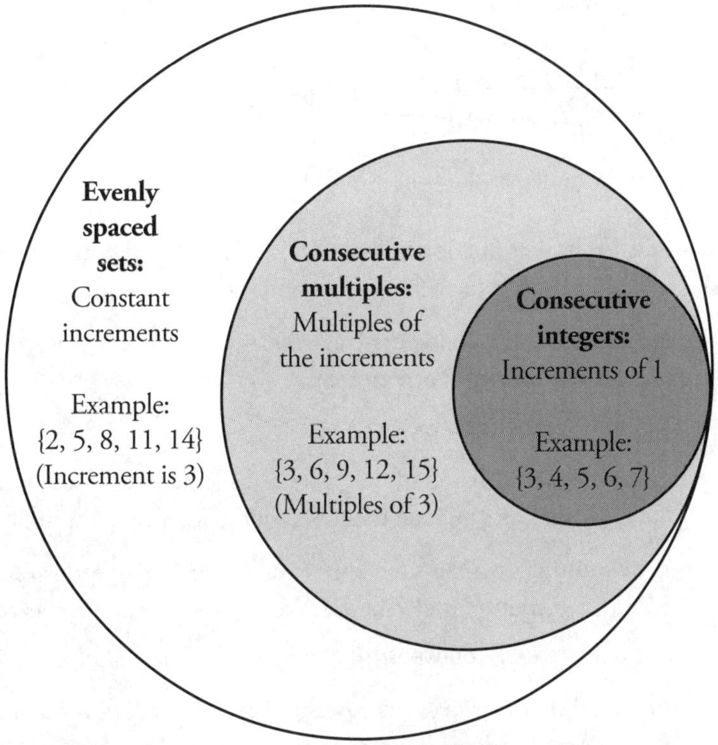

Within that circle is the subset **consecutive multiples**. These are special cases of evenly spaced sets in which all of the values in the set are multiples of the increment. For example, in the set {12, 16, 20, 24}, the values increase from one to the next by 4, and each element is a multiple of 4. Sets of consecutive multiples must be composed of integers.

The inner circle, **consecutive integers**, holds special cases of consecutive multiples: All of the values in the set increase by 1, and all integers are multiples of 1. For example, $\{12, 13, 14, 15, 16\}$ is a set of consecutive integers.

Counting Integers: Add 1 before You Are Done

How many integers are there from 6 to 10, inclusive? Four, right? No! There are actually *five* integers from 6 to 10. Count them: 6, 7, 8, 9, 10.

How did that happen? When you subtract $(10 - 6 = 4)$, you are actually subtracting out the lower extreme, 6; that number is not included in the count. If you *do* want to include it in the count, then add 1 before you're done. For example:

How many integers are there from 14 to 765, inclusive?

The word *inclusive* indicates that you need to include both numbers at the ends of the range in your count. The formula is **(Last − First + 1)**: $765 - 14 + 1 = 752$.

This is straightforward when you are dealing with consecutive integers. Sometimes, however, the question will ask about consecutive multiples.

In this case, if you subtract the greatest number from the least and add 1, you will be overcounting. For example, "All of the even integers between 12 and 24, inclusive" yields seven integers: 12, 14, 16, 18, 20, 22, and 24. However, (Last − First + 1) would yield $(24 - 12 + 1) = 13$, which is too big. How do you amend this? Since the items in the list are going up by increments of 2 (you are counting only the even numbers), divide (Last − First) by 2. Then, add the 1 before you're done:

$$\frac{(\text{Last} - \text{First})}{\text{Increment}} + 1 = \frac{(24 - 12)}{2} + 1 = 6 + 1 = 7$$

For consecutive multiples, the formula is $\dfrac{(\text{Last} - \text{First})}{\text{Increment}} + 1$.

The bigger the increment, the lower that fraction will go. This makes logical sense, since a bigger increment between numbers in the range means that there are fewer numbers to be counted in that range.

Sometimes, it is easier to list the terms of a consecutive pattern and count them, especially if the list is short or if one or both of the extremes are omitted. For example:

How many multiples of 7 are there between 10 and 40 ?

First, note that the question says *between* 10 and 40 but does not include the word *inclusive*. So don't include 10 or 40 in this count. (Also, don't include them because neither one is a multiple of 7!)

Second, there aren't that many multiples of 7 in such a short range, so it may be fastest to just write them down: 14, 21, 28, 35. There are four multiples of 7 in the given range. Try another example:

How many multiples of 7 are there between 10 and 80 ?

This time, it would be more annoying to write out the possibilities. Instead, find the least multiple of 7 and the greatest multiple of 7 in that range and use those as your First and Last numbers. The least one is 14 and the greatest is 77. Now use the formula:

$$\frac{(\text{Last} - \text{First})}{\text{Increment}} + 1 = \frac{(77 - 14)}{7} + 1 = \frac{63}{7} + 1 = 9 + 1 = 10$$

Properties of Evenly Spaced Sets

The following properties apply to all **evenly spaced sets**:

1. The average (arithmetic mean) and median are equal to each other. For example:

    What is the arithmetic mean of 4, 8, 12, 16, and 20 ?

    In this example, the median is 12. Since this is an evenly spaced set, the arithmetic mean (average) is also 12. Now, try another example:

    What is the arithmetic mean of 4, 8, 12, 16, 20, and 24 ?

    In this example, the median is the average (arithmetic mean) of the two middle numbers, or the average of 12 and 16. Thus, the median is 14. Since this is an evenly spaced set, the average of the set is also 14.

    In a set with an odd number of evenly spaced integers, such as the first example above, the median/average will always be a member of the set (and, therefore, an integer).

    In a set with an even number of evenly spaced integers, such as the second example above, the median/average will *not* be a member of the set, since you'll always have to average the two middle numbers of the set in order to find the median.

2. The mean and median of the set are equal to the average of the First and Last terms. For example:

    What is the arithmetic mean of 4, 8, 12, 16, and 20 ?

    In this example, the arithmetic mean and median are both equal to $\frac{(4 + 20)}{2} = 12$. Now, try another example:

    What is the arithmetic mean of 4, 8, 12, 16, 20, and 24 ?

    In this example, the arithmetic mean and median are both equal to $\frac{(4 + 24)}{2} = 14$.

    For all evenly spaced sets, the average equals $\frac{\textbf{First + Last}}{\textbf{2}}$.

The Sum of Consecutive Integers

Consider this problem:

What is the sum of all the integers from 20 to 50, inclusive?

(A) 990

(B) 1,085

(C) 1,167

Adding all those integers would take much more time than you have for a GMAT problem. Since the set is evenly spaced, though, there's a way to calculate the sum:

Sum of Evenly Spaced Set = Average × Number of Terms

First, use the first and last terms of the set to find the average:

$\frac{20 + 50}{2} = 35$

Find the number of terms: 50 – 20 + 1 = 31. Then, plug these values into the formula to find the sum:

Sum = (35)(31)

Glance at the answer choices to see how far you have to go with the calculation. The answers are fairly close together, so standard estimation doesn't seem like a great bet.

But the math you have to do is multiplication, so check the units digits of the answers. All three are different, so you can find just the units digits of (35)(31) and you're done. In multiplication, the units digit of the answer depends only on the units digits of the starting numbers. In this case, (5)(1) = 5, so choose the answer with a units digit of 5.

The correct answer is (B).

Advanced material for the Word Problems unit (primarily covering additional strategies for overlapping sets and consecutive integers) can be found in Atlas, Manhattan Prep's online learning platform. Use the online material only if you feel that you have mastered everything in the Word Problems unit of this strategy guide and only if you are aiming for a Quant section score of 48 or higher.

Problem Set

Now that you've finished the chapter, try these problems.

1. How many terms are there in the set of consecutive integers from –18 to 33, inclusive?

2. What is the sum of all the positive integers up to 100, inclusive?

Save the following problems for review after you finish this entire guide.

3. In a sequence of eight consecutive integers, how much greater is the sum of the last four integers than the sum of the first four integers?

4. If the sum of the last three integers in a set of six consecutive integers is 624, what is the sum of the first three integers of the set?

5. The operation $x \Rightarrow y$ is defined as the sum of all integers from x to y, inclusive. For example, $3 \Rightarrow 7 = 3 + 4 + 5 + 6 + 7$. What is the value of $(100 \Rightarrow 150) - (125 \Rightarrow 150)$?

Solutions

1. **52:** Number of terms = First − Last + 1:

$$33 - (-18) + 1 = 52$$

2. **5,050:** Sum = (Average)(Number of Terms). To find the average, take the average of the first and last terms in the set: $\frac{1+100}{2} = 50.5$. To find the sum, find the difference between the last and the first and then add 1 before you're done: $(100 - 1) + 1$. Finally, multiply 100 by 50.5 to find the sum of all the integers in the set: $100 \times 50.5 = 5{,}050$.

3. **16:** The problem never specifies a set of numbers, so it must be the case that you get the same outcome no matter what numbers you use. In that case, choose your own set of numbers!

For example, try 1, 2, 3, 4, 5, 6, 7, and 8. The sum of the first four integers is 10. The sum of the last four integers is 26. The difference is $26 - 10 = 16$.

If you want to get extra fancy, line up those eight numbers in two rows as follows:

1	2	3	4
5	6	7	8

What is the problem asking you? Find the difference between the sum of the top row and the sum of the bottom row. Make this easier by first finding the *differences*, not the sums. For instance, the difference between 1 and 5 is +4. Likewise, the difference between 2 and 6 is +4. The same is true for all numbers in the set (since they're all consecutive!), so the total difference is $4 + 4 + 4 + 4 = (4)(4) = 16$.

Here's how to solve algebraically. The numbers can be represented as follows: n, $(n + 1)$, $(n + 2)$, $(n + 3)$, $(n + 4)$, $(n + 5)$, $(n + 6)$, and $(n + 7)$.

First, find the sum of the first four integers:

$$n + (n + 1) + (n + 2) + (n + 3) = 4n + 6$$

Then, find the sum of the next four integers:

$$(n + 4) + (n + 5) + (n + 6) + (n + 7) = 4n + 22$$

The difference between these two partial sums is:

$$(4n + 22) - (4n + 6) = 22 - 6 = 16$$

4. **615:** Think of the set of integers as n, $(n + 1)$, $(n + 2)$, $(n + 3)$, $(n + 4)$, and $(n + 5)$. Thus, $(n + 3) + (n + 4) + (n + 5) = 3n + 12 = 624$. Don't solve that quite yet, though—it's a little annoying. What does the problem want you to find?

It asks for $n + (n + 1) + (n + 2) = 3n + 3$. Look back at the other equation.

If $3n + 12 = 624$, then $3n + 3$ is 9 less than 624, or $624 - 9 = 615$.

Alternatively, another way you could solve this algebraically is to line up the algebraic expressions for each number so that you can subtract one from the other directly:

Sum of the last three integers		$(n+3) + (n+4) + (n+5)$
Less the sum of the first three integers	$-$	$[n + (n+1) + (n+2)]$
		$3 + 3 + 3 = 9$

Thus, the sum of the last three numbers is 9 greater than the sum of the first three numbers, so the sum of the first three numbers is $624 - 9 = 615$.

5. **2,800:** Definitely take your time to understand what's going on. This problem contains two components: the sum of all the numbers from 100 to 150 and the sum of all the numbers from 125 to 150. Since the problem asks for the *difference* between these components, you are essentially finding just the sum of all the numbers from 100 to 124 (because you will subtract out the value of the numbers from 125 to 150). You can think of this logically by visualizing a simpler problem: Find the difference $(1 \Rightarrow 5) - (3 \Rightarrow 5)$. Set up an equation:

$$\begin{array}{r} 1+2+3+4+5 \\ -\qquad\quad 3+4+5 \\ \hline 1+2\qquad\qquad \end{array}$$

Back to the given problem. Find the sum of the integers from 100 to 124. Use the Sum = Average × Number of Terms formula.

There are 25 numbers from 100 to 124 $(124 - 100 + 1)$. To find the sum of these numbers, multiply by the average term:

$$\text{Average: } \frac{100+124}{2} = 112$$

$$\text{Sum: } 25 \times 112 = 25 \times 100 + 25 \times 12 = 2{,}500 + 300 = 2{,}800$$

UNIT FOUR

Number Properties

In this unit, you'll learn all about number properties, including how to handle divisibility, primes, odds and evens, positives and negatives, combinatorics, and probability. You'll also learn advanced strategies for testing cases on number properties problems.

In This Unit

CHAPTER 25

Divisibility and Primes

In This Chapter

- Arithmetic Rules
- Rules of Divisibility by Certain Integers
- Factors and Multiples
- Fewer Factors, More Multiples
- Divisibility and Addition/Subtraction
- Primes
- Prime Factorization
- Factor Foundation Rule
- The Prime Box
- Remainders

In this chapter, you will learn number property rules specific to positive integers, including a special subset of positive integers called primes. You'll learn how to find multiples, factor pairs, and prime factors of integers and how to address divisibility topics. Finally, you'll learn different ways that the GMAT will present this information and how the test might disguise the information—as well as how to strip away the disguise!

CHAPTER 25 Divisibility and Primes

The special properties of integers form the basis of most number properties problems on the GMAT. **Integers** are whole numbers, such as 0, 1, 2, and 3, that have no fractional part. Integers include positive numbers (1, 2, 3 ...), negative numbers (−1, −2, −3 ...), and the number 0.

Arithmetic Rules

Most arithmetic operations on integers will result in an integer. For example:

$4 + 5 = 9$	$(-2) + 1 = -1$	The sum of two integers is always an integer.
$4 - 5 = -1$	$(-2) - (-3) = 1$	The difference of two integers is always an integer.
$4 \times 5 = 20$	$(-2) \times 3 = -6$	The product of two integers is always an integer.

Division, however, is different. Sometimes the result is an integer, and sometimes it is not:

$8 \div 2 = 4$	This result is an integer ...
$2 \div 8 = \frac{1}{4}$	... but this one isn't. (By the way, the result of division is called the **quotient**.)

An integer is said to be **divisible** by another number if the result, or quotient, is an integer.

For example, 21 is divisible by 3 because 21 divided by 3 results in an integer $(21 \div 3 = 7)$. However, 21 is not divisible by 4 because 21 divided by 4 results in a non-integer $(21 \div 4 = 5.25)$.

You can also talk about divisibility in terms of remainders. One number is divisible by another if the result has a remainder of 0. For example, 21 is divisible by 3 because 21 divided by 3 yields 7 with a remainder of 0. On the other hand, 21 is not divisible by 4 because 21 divided by 4 yields 5 with a remainder of 1.

Here are some more examples:

$8 \div 2 = 4$	Therefore, 8 is divisible by 2.
	You can also say that 2 is a **divisor** or **factor** of 8.
$2 \div 8 = 0.25$	Therefore, 2 is *not* divisible by 8.
$(-6) \div 2 = -3$	Therefore, −6 is divisible by 2.
$(-6) \div (-4) = 1.5$	Therefore, −6 is *not* divisible by −4.

Rules of Divisibility by Certain Integers

The **divisibility rules** are very useful shortcuts to determine whether an integer is divisible by 2, 3, 4, 5, 6, 8, 9, and 10.

An integer is divisible by

2 if the integer is even.
For example, 12 is divisible by 2, but 13 is not. Integers that are divisible by 2 are called **even**, and integers that are not divisible by 2 are called **odd**. You can tell whether a number is even by checking to see whether the units (ones) digit is 0, 2, 4, 6, or 8. For example, 1,234,567 is odd, because 7 is odd, whereas 2,345,678 is even, because 8 is even.

3 if the sum of the integer's digits is divisible by 3.
For example, 72 is divisible by 3 because the sum of its digits is $7 + 2 = 9$, which is divisible by 3. By contrast, 83 is not divisible by 3, because the sum of its digits is 11, which is not divisible by 3.

4 if the integer is divisible by 2 *twice* or if the last two digits are divisible by 4.
For example, 28 is divisible by 4 because you can divide it by 2 twice and get an integer result ($28 \div 2 = 14$ and $14 \div 2 = 7$). For larger numbers, check only the last two digits. For example, 23,456 is divisible by 4 because 56 is divisible by 4, but 25,678 is not divisible by 4 because 78 is not divisible by 4.

5 if the integer ends in 0 or 5.
For example, 75 and 80 are divisible by 5, but 77 and 83 are not.

6 if the integer is divisible by *both* 2 and 3.
For example, 48 is divisible by 6 since it is divisible by 2 (it ends with an 8, which is even) AND by 3 ($4 + 8 = 12$, which is divisible by 3).

8 if the integer is divisible by 2 three times or if the last three digits are divisible by 8.
For example, 32 is divisible by 8 since you can divide it by 2 three times and get an integer result ($32 \div 2 = 16$, $16 \div 2 = 8$, and $8 \div 2 = 4$). For larger numbers, check only the last three digits. For example, 23,456 is divisible by 8 because 456 is divisible by 8, whereas 23,556 is not divisible by 8 because 556 is not divisible by 8.

9 if the sum of the integer's digits is divisible by 9.
Since the sum of the digits of 4,185 is $4 + 1 + 8 + 5 = 18$, it is divisible by 9. By contrast, 3,459 is not divisible by 9, because the sum of its digits is 21, which is not divisible by 9.

10 if the integer ends in 0.
Because it ends in a zero, 670 is divisible by 10, but 675 is not.

The GMAT can also test these divisibility rules in reverse. For example, if you are told that a number has a ones digit equal to 0, you can infer that that number is divisible by 2, by 5, and by 10. Similarly, if you are told that the sum of the digits of x is equal to 21, you can infer that x is divisible by 3 but *not* by 9.

There is no rule listed for divisibility by 7 because there isn't a relatively easy rule for this. The simplest way to check for divisibility by 7, or by any other number not found in this list, is to perform long division—that is, if you have to divide at all. First, check whether you can estimate or otherwise avoid annoying math!

Factors and Multiples

Factors and multiples are essentially opposite terms.

A **factor** is a positive integer that divides evenly into an integer. For example, what are the factors of 8? The factors (or divisors) are 1, 2, 4, and 8. A factor of an integer is smaller than or equal to that integer.

A **multiple** of an integer is formed by multiplying that integer by any integer. What are the multiples of 8? The multiples include 8, 16, 24, and 32 (and keep going forever). On the GMAT, multiples of an integer are equal to or larger than that integer.

Note that an integer is always both a factor and a multiple of itself; for example, 8 is both a factor of and a multiple of 8. In addition, 1 is a factor of *every* integer.

An easy way to find all the factors of *small* integers is to use **factor pairs**. Factor pairs for any integer are the pairs of factors that, when multiplied together, yield that integer. For example, the factor pairs of 8 are (1, 8) and (2, 4).

To find the factor pairs of a number such as 72, start with the most basic factors: 1 and 72. Then, "walk upwards" from 1, testing to see whether different numbers are factors of 72. Once you find a number that is a factor of 72, find its partner by dividing 72 by the factor. Keep walking upwards until all factors are exhausted.

Here's how to find factor pairs, step-by-step:

1. Make a table with two columns labeled *Small* and *Large*.
2. Start with 1 in the Small column and 72 in the Large column.
3. Test the next possible factor of 72 (which is 2); 2 is a factor of 72, so write 2 underneath the 1 in your table. Divide 72 by 2 to find the factor pair: 36. Write 36 in the Large column.
4. Repeat this process until the numbers in the Small and the Large columns run into each other. In this case, once you have tested 8 and found that 9 is its paired factor, you can stop.

Small	Large
1	72
2	36
3	24
4	18
6	12
8	9

Fewer Factors, More Multiples

It can be easy to confuse factors and multiples. Use the mnemonic **Fewer Factors, More Multiples** to help remember the difference. Every positive integer has a limited number of factors. Factors divide into the integer and are therefore less than or equal to the integer. For example, there are only four factors of 8: 1, 2, 4, and 8.

By contrast, every positive integer has infinite multiples. These multiply out from the integer and are therefore greater than or equal to the integer. For example, the first five multiples of 8 are 8, 16, 24, 32, and 40, but you could go on listing multiples of 8 forever.

Factors, multiples, and divisibility are very closely related concepts. For example, 3 is a factor (or a divisor) of 12. This is the same as saying that 12 is a multiple of 3 or that 12 is divisible by 3.

On the GMAT, this terminology is often used interchangeably in order to make the problem seem harder than it actually is. Be aware of the different ways that the GMAT can phrase information about divisibility. Moreover, try to convert all such statements to the same terminology. For example, all of the following statements *say exactly the same thing*:

- 12 is divisible by 3.
- 12 is a multiple of 3.
- $\frac{12}{3}$ is an integer.
- 12 is equal to $3n$, where n is an integer.
- 12 items can be shared among 3 people so that each person has the same number of items.
- 3 is a divisor of 12, or 3 is a factor of 12.
- 3 divides 12.
- $\frac{12}{3}$ yields a remainder of 0.
- 3 goes into 12 evenly.

When you see language similar to the above, you can translate it and write it down in whatever form works best for your brain. Practice recognizing that all of these forms are really telling you the same piece of information.

Divisibility and Addition/Subtraction

If you add two multiples of 7, you get another multiple of 7. Try it: $35 + 21 = 56$. This is always mathematically valid because this is the math that's happening: $(5 \times 7) + (3 \times 7) = (5 + 3) \times 7 = 8 \times 7$.

Likewise, if you subtract two multiples of 7, you get another multiple of 7. Try it: $35 - 21 = 14$. Again, this is what's happening with the math: $(5 \times 7) - (3 \times 7) = (5 - 3) \times 7 = 2 \times 7$.

This pattern holds true for the multiples of any integer N. If you add or subtract multiples of N, the result is a multiple of N. You can restate this principle using any of the disguises noted earlier: For example, if N is a divisor of x and of y, then N is a divisor of $x + y$.

Primes

Prime numbers are a very important topic on the GMAT. A prime number is any positive integer with *exactly two* different factors: 1 and itself. In other words, a prime number has *no* factors *other* than 1 and itself. For example, 7 is prime because the only factors of 7 are 1 and 7. However, 8 is not prime because it has more than two factors: 1, 2, 4, and 8.

The number 1 is a special case. It has exactly one factor (itself), so it does not qualify as prime (which needs exactly two factors). The number 1 is unique in that 1 has just one factor, while all the other non-prime positive integers (officially known as *composite* numbers) have three or more factors.

1	Primes (2, 3, 5, 7, . . .)	Composites (4, 6, 8, 9, . . .)
Exactly one factor: 1	Exactly two factors: 1 Itself	Three or more factors: 1 Itself Other(s) between 1 and itself

The first prime number is 2, which is also the only even prime. The first ten prime numbers are 2, 3, 5, 7, 11, 13, 17, 19, 23, and 29. Memorizing these primes will save you time on the test.

Prime Factorization

Earlier, you learned how to find the factor pairs of a number. You can also find the **prime factors** of a number. Every number has its own unique mix of prime factors, so breaking a number down to its prime factors can be very useful on the GMAT.

Create a prime factor tree, as shown below with the number 72. Test different numbers to find one that goes into 72 without leaving a remainder. Once you find such a number, split 72 into factors, as shown here:

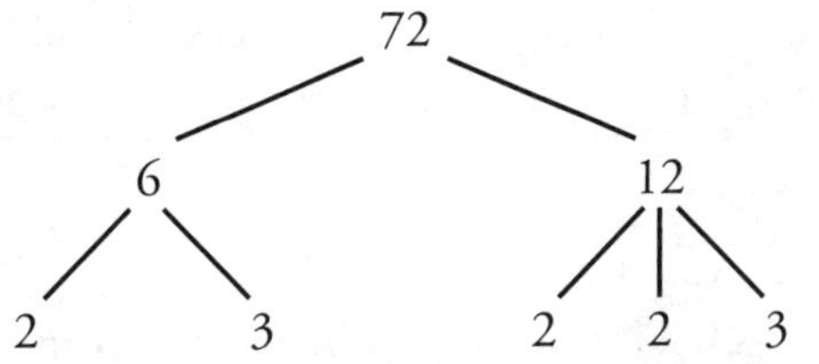

For example, 72 is divisible by 6, so it can be split into 6 and $72 \div 6 = 12$. Then, repeat this process on 6 and 12 until every branch on the tree ends at a prime number. Once you have only primes, stop, because you cannot split prime numbers into two smaller factors. In this example, 72 splits into 5 total prime factors (including repeats): $2 \times 2 \times 2 \times 3 \times 3$. In general, write prime factors for a number in increasing order, as shown.

Prime factorization is an extremely important tool to use on the GMAT. Once you know the prime factors of a number, you can determine *all* the factors of that number, even for large numbers. The factors can be found by building all the possible products of the prime factors; the next section shows how.

Factor Foundation Rule

The GMAT expects you to know the factor foundation rule: **If *a* is a factor of *b*, and *b* is a factor of *c*, then *a* is a factor of *c*.** In other words, any integer is divisible by all of its factors—and it is also divisible by all of the factors of its factors.

For example, if 72 is divisible by 12, then 72 is also divisible by all the factors of 12 (1, 2, 3, 4, 6, and 12). Written another way, if 12 is a factor of 72, then all the factors of 12 are also factors of 72. The factor foundation rule allows you to conceive of factors as building blocks in a foundation; for example, 12 and 6 are factors, or building blocks, of 72 (because 12×6 builds 72).

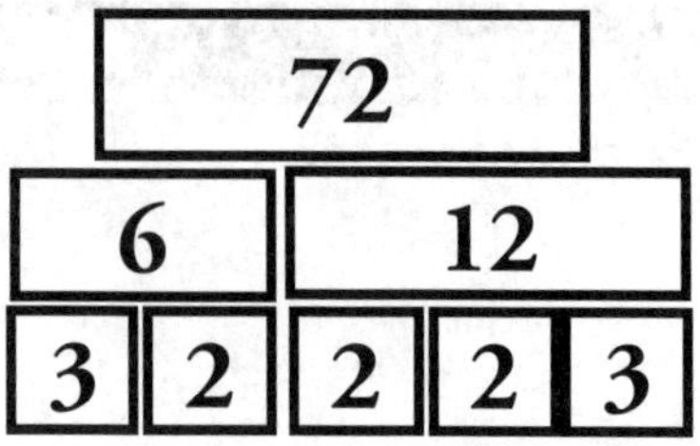

The number 12, in turn, is built from its own factors; for example, 4×3 builds 12. Thus, if 12 is part of the foundation of 72 and 12 in turn rests on the foundation built by its prime factors (2, 2, and 3), then 72 is also built on the foundation of 2, 2, and 3.

You can use the bottom level—the prime building blocks—to find (almost) any factor of 72. First, write them in increasing order: $2 \times 2 \times 2 \times 3 \times 3$. (The one factor you won't find here is the factor of 1. Just remember that all numbers always have 1 as a factor.)

Back to the building blocks. First, 2 and 3 are factors of 72. Next, you can multiply any combination of the building blocks to find larger factors. For example, $2 \times 2 = 4$ is a factor of 72. So is $2 \times 3 = 6$.

You can combine any of the prime factors you like to find any factors of 72. For example, if the test asks you whether 24 is a factor of 72, you could divide to find out—but that would get annoying as the numbers get larger. Instead, find the prime factors of 24 (which are 2, 2, 2, and 3), and check whether they're on the list for 72. They are, so 24 is also a factor of 72.

The Prime Box

You can organize this information with a tool called a prime box. A **prime box** is exactly what its name implies: a box that holds all the prime factors of a number (in other words, the lowest-level building blocks). Here are prime boxes for 72, 12, and 125:

72	**12**	**125**
2, 2, 2, 3, 3	2, 2, 3	5, 5, 5

Do repeat copies of the prime factors if the number has multiple copies of that prime factor. What goes in the box should actually multiply up to the main number.

You can use the prime box to test whether or not a specific number is a factor of another number. For example:

Is 27 a factor of 72 ?

72
2, 2, 2, 3, 3

$27 = 3 \times 3 \times 3$, but 72 only has *two* 3's in its prime box. It's not possible to make 27 from the prime factors of 72, so 27 is not a factor of 72.

Now, try another example:

> If the integer n is divisible by 8 and 15, is n divisible by 12 ?

n

2, 2, 2,
3, 5,
. . . ?

First, factor both numbers: $8 = 2 \times 2 \times 2$ and $15 = 3 \times 5$. Although you don't know what n is, n has to be divisible by any number made up of those primes.

$12 = 2 \times 2 \times 3$. All of those factors appear in n's box, so yes, n is also divisible by 12.

What if integer k is divisible by 8 and by 10? First, factor: $8 = 2 \times 2 \times 2$ and $10 = 2 \times 5$. Next, combine. . .actually, wait. Don't combine yet. If the two numbers have any *overlapping* factors, then you first have to strip out any overlap. The number 10 has one factor of 2 and the number 8 has three factors of 2, so they overlap on one factor of 2. Strip out that one factor. The prime box for k is $2 \times 2 \times 2 \times 5$.

Notice the ellipses and question mark ("... ?") in the prime box of n. This indicates that you have created a **partial prime box** of n. Whereas the *complete* set of prime factors of 72 can be calculated and put into its prime box, you only have a *partial* list of prime factors of n, because n is an unknown number. You know that n is divisible by 8 and 15, but you do *not* know what additional primes, if any, n has in its prime box.

Most of the time, when building a prime box for a *variable*, you will use a partial prime box, but when building a prime box for a *number*, you will use a complete prime box.

25

Remainders

Most of this chapter has focused on numbers that are divisible by other numbers (factors)—that is, numbers that have an integer result. This section, however, discusses what happens when a number, such as 8, is divided by a *non*-factor, such as 5.

Every division has four parts:

1. The **dividend** is the number being divided. In $8 \div 5$, the dividend is 8.
2. The **divisor** is the number that is dividing. In $8 \div 5$, the divisor is 5.
3. The **quotient** is the number of times that the divisor goes into the dividend *completely*. The quotient is always an integer. In $8 \div 5$, the quotient is 1 because 5 goes into 8 one (1) time completely.
4. The **remainder** is what is left over. In $8 \div 5$, the remainder is 3 because 3 is left over after 5 goes into 8 once.

Putting it all together, you have $8 \div 5 = 1$, with a remainder of 3.

On the GMAT, it's not unusual to see the word *remainder*. The other terms (*dividend, divisor*, and *quotient*) are much less common; they could appear but most people won't see them. Factor that knowledge into your decision as to whether to memorize these terms.

As another example, the number 17 is not divisible by 5. When you divide 17 by 5 using long division, you get 3 with a remainder of 2:

```
   3
5)17
 -15
   2
```

The quotient is 3 because 15 is the largest multiple of 5 smaller than 17, and 15 ÷ 5 = 3. The remainder is 2 because 17 is 2 more than a multiple of 5 (15).

You can also express this relationship as a general formula:

Dividend = Quotient × Divisor + Remainder
(or, Dividend = Multiple of Divisor + Remainder)

Finally, it is possible to have a remainder of 0. A remainder of 0 occurs when one number actually is divisible by another. For example, 20 ÷ 5 = 4 remainder 0. Most of the time, you won't need to notice that something has a remainder of 0, but the GMAT might use this to disguise information. If the test tells you that *n* divided by 5 has a remainder of 0, it's really telling you that *n* is divisible by 5. (You could also say it's telling you that *n* is a multiple of 5.)

Advanced material for the Number Properties unit (primarily covering additional strategies for divisibility and primes, combinatorics, and probability) can be found in Atlas, Manhattan Prep's online learning platform. Use the online material only if you feel that you have mastered everything in the Number Properties unit of this strategy guide and only if you are aiming for a Quant section score of 48 or higher.

Problem Set

For questions 1–6, answer each question with one of three responses: Always Yes, Always No, or Sometimes Yes/Sometimes No. If your answer is Sometimes, use two numerical examples to show how to get a Yes and a No.

All variables in problems 1–6 are integers.

1. If a is divided by 7 or by 18, an integer results. Is $\frac{a}{42}$ an integer?

2. If 80 is a factor of r, is 15 a factor of r ?

3. If 7 is a factor of n and 7 is a factor of p, is $n + p$ divisible by 7 ?

4. If j is divisible by 12 and 10, is j divisible by 24 ?

5. If 6 is a divisor of r and r is a factor of s, is 6 a factor of s ?

6. If s is a multiple of 12 and t is a multiple of 12, is $7s + 5t$ a multiple of 12 ?

Save the following problem set for review after you finish this entire guide.

7. A skeet shooting competition awards points for each round as follows: The first-place finisher receives 11 points, the second-place finisher receives 7 points, the third-place finisher receives 5 points, and the fourth-place finisher receives 2 points. No other points are awarded. Jordan competes in several rounds of the skeet shooting competition and receives points in each round. If the product of all of the points Jordan receives equals 84,700, in how many rounds does Jordan participate?

   (A) 2

   (B) 3

   (C) 7

   (D) 9

   (E) 11

8. If x, y, and z are integers, is x even?

   (1) $10^x = (4^y)(5^z)$

   (2) $3^{x+5} = 27^{y+1}$

Solutions

1. **Always Yes:**

a

2, 3, 3, 7, . . . ?

If a is divisible by 7 and by 18, its prime factors include all of the factors of those two numbers: 2, 3, 3, and 7, as shown in the prime box. Therefore, any integer that can be constructed as a product of any of these prime factors is also a factor of a. $42 = 2 \times 3 \times 7$, all of which are in the prime box, so 42 is also a factor of a.

2. **Sometimes Yes/Sometimes No:**

r

2, 2, 2, 2, 5, . . . ?

If r is divisible by 80, its prime factors include 2, 2, 2, 2, and 5, as shown in the prime box. Therefore, any integer that can be constructed as a product of any of these prime factors is also a factor of r. $15 = 3 \times 5$. The factor 5 is in the prime box, but the 3 may or may not be. For example, if $r = 80$, then No, 15 is *not* a factor of r, but if $r = 240$ (which is 80×3), then Yes, 15 *is* a factor of r.

3. **Always Yes:** If two numbers are both multiples of the same number, then their *sum* is also a multiple of that same number. Since n and p share the common factor 7, the sum of n and p must also be divisible by 7.

4. **Sometimes Yes/Sometimes No:**

j	*j*	*j*
2, 2, 3, . . . ?	2, 5, . . . ?	2, 2, 3, 5, . . . ?

Careful! The number 12 contains 2, 2, and 3. The number 10 contains 2 and 5. But you can't (necessarily) put all of those numbers in the combined prime box for j. First, check for overlap. The two boxes overlap on one factor of 2, so strip out one 2, leaving you with $2 \times 2 \times 3 \times 5$ for j's prime box.

Next, the question asks whether j is divisible by 24, which equals $2 \times 2 \times 2 \times 3$. The prime box of j contains at least two 2's and *could* contain more but it doesn't have to. The number 24 requires three 2's. Therefore, you may or may not be able to create 24 from j's prime box; 24 is not necessarily a factor of j.

Prove it with numbers. The smallest possible value of j is $2 \times 2 \times 3 \times 5 = 60$. This number is *not* divisible by 24, so if $j = 60$, the answer is No. Alternatively, j could equal 120 (which is 60×2), in which case j is divisible by 24 and the answer is Yes.

5. **Always Yes:** By the factor foundation rule, if 6 is a factor of r and r is a factor of s, then 6 is a factor of s.

6. **Always Yes:** If s is a multiple of 12, then so is $7s$. If t is a multiple of 12, then so is $5t$. Since $7s$ and $5t$ are both multiples of 12, then their sum $(7s + 5t)$ is also a multiple of 12.

7. **(C) 7:** The values for scoring first, second, third, and fourth place in the competition are all prime numbers—when this happens, it is never a coincidence. Notice also that the problem mentions a *product* involving those prime numbers. Those two pieces together signal a prime factor problem. Take that ugly number and break it down into its prime factors:

$$84{,}700 = 847 \times 100$$

847 is a pretty annoying number to have to break down. But the problem indicates that it must be some combination of 2, 5, 7, and 11. It doesn't contain any 2s or 5s, so it must be some combination of 7 and/or 11.

Break the number into parts that are more easily divisible by 7:

$$700 = 7 \times 100$$
$$140 = 7 \times 20$$
$$7 = 7 \times 1$$

700 + 140 + 7 adds up to 847. To get there, you need a total of $100 + 20 + 1 = 121 \times 7$. The 7 part of that is a prime, but the 121 can be broken down further. (And don't forget about the initial value of 100—that still needs to be broken down, too!)

$$847 = 7 \times 121 = 7 \times 11 \times 11$$

$$100 = 10 \times 10 = 2 \times 2 \times 5 \times 5$$

Thus, Jordan received first place twice (11 points each), second place once (7 points each), third place twice (5 points each), and fourth place twice (2 points each). Jordan competed in a total of 7 rounds.

8. **(A):** The question stem establishes that x, y, and z are all integers and asks whether x is even. This is a Yes/No question. An even integer will end in 0, 2, 4, 6, or 8.

(1) SUFFICIENT: Statement (1) indicates that $10^x = (4^y)(5^z)$. The variables are all in the exponents, so break the bases down to primes so that you can get the variables out of the exponents:

$$10^x = (4^y)(5^z)$$
$$(2 \times 5)^x = (2^2)^y(5^z)$$
$$2^x 5^x = 2^{2y} 5^z$$

Next, drop the bases and set the corresponding exponents equal to each other: $x = 2y$ and $x = z$. (You're allowed to do this even with multiple variables as long as everything is broken down into primes.) If $x = 2y$, and y is an integer (as given in the question stem), x must be even, since it equals 2 times an integer. The answer is Always Yes.

(2) INSUFFICIENT: Statement (2) indicates that $3^{x+5} = 27^{y+1}$. Break the bases down to primes so that you can get the variables out of the exponents. Since y is an integer, x must be 2 smaller than a multiple of 3, but that does not tell you whether x is even. If $y = 1$, then $x = 1$ (odd), but if $y = 2$, then $x = 4$ (even). Therefore:

$$3^{x+5} = 27^{y+1}$$

$$3^{x+5} = \left(3^3\right)^{y+1}$$

$$3^{x+5} = 3^{3y+3}$$

Drop the bases and set the corresponding exponents equal to each other: $x + 5 = 3y + 3$. Simplify: $x = 3y - 2$. The variable y is an integer but it could be odd or even. If y is odd, then $3y$ is also odd, as is $3y - 2$. In this case, x would be odd. However, if y is even, then $3y$ is also even, as is $3y - 2$. In this case, x would be even.

The correct answer is **(A)**: Statement (1) alone is sufficient, but statement (2) is not.

CHAPTER 26

Odds, Evens, Positives, and Negatives

In This Chapter

- Arithmetic Rules of Odds and Evens
- Representing Odds and Evens Algebraically
- Positives and Negatives
- Absolute Value: Absolutely Positive
- A Double Negative = A Positive
- Multiplying and Dividing Signed Numbers
- Disguised Positives and Negatives
- The Sum of Two Primes

In this chapter, you will learn how positive and negative concepts are tested on the exam for both integers and non-integers. You will also learn about odd and even rules, which apply only to integers. Finally, you'll learn how to recognize these topics when the GMAT disguises them at times.

CHAPTER 26 Odds, Evens, Positives, and Negatives

Even numbers are integers that are divisible by 2. Odd numbers are integers that are not divisible by 2. All integers are either even or odd. For example:

Evens: 0, 2, 4, 6, 8, 10, 12 . . . Odds: 1, 3, 5, 7, 9, 11 . . .

Note that 0 is an even integer. When 0 is divided by 2, the result is an integer—so 0 is even.

Consecutive integers alternate between even and odd: 9, 10, 11, 12, 13 . . .

O, E, O, E, O . . .

Negative integers are also either even or odd:

Evens: −2, −4, −6, −8, −10, −12 . . . Odds: −1, −3, −5, −7, −9, −11 . . .

Arithmetic Rules of Odds and Evens

The GMAT tests your knowledge of how odd and even numbers combine through addition, subtraction, multiplication, and division. Rules for adding, subtracting, multiplying, and dividing odd and even numbers can be derived by testing out simple numbers, but it pays to memorize the following rules for operating with odds and evens, as they are extremely useful for certain GMAT math questions.

Addition and subtraction:

Even ± Even = Even $8 + 6 = 14$

Odd ± Odd = Even $7 + 9 = 16$

Even ± Odd = Odd $7 + 8 = 15$

If they're the same, the sum (or difference) will be even. If they're different, the sum (or difference) will be odd.

Multiplication:

Even × Even = Even $2 \times 4 = 8$

Even × Odd = Even $4 \times 3 = 12$

Odd × Odd = Odd $3 \times 5 = 15$

If one even number is present, the product will be even. If you have only odd numbers, the product will be odd.

If you multiply together several even integers, the result will be divisible by higher and higher powers of 2 because each even number will contribute at least one 2 to the factors of the product.

For example, if there are two even integers in a set of integers being multiplied together, the result will be divisible by (at least) 4:

$\mathbf{2} \times 5 \times \mathbf{6} = 60$ (divisible by 4)

If there are three even integers in a set of integers being multiplied together, the result will be divisible by (at least) 8:

$\mathbf{2} \times 5 \times \mathbf{6} \times \mathbf{10} = 600$ (divisible by 8)

Division:

There are no guaranteed outcomes in division, because the division of two integers may not yield an integer result. In these cases, you'll have to try the actual numbers given. The divisibility tools outlined in Chapter 1 can help you determine the outcome.

Representing Odds and Evens Algebraically

Try this problem:

Is positive integer m odd?

(1) $m = 2k + 1$, where k is an integer.

(2) m is a multiple of 3.

Statement (2) is easier to attack. The variable m could be 3, which is odd, or 6, which is even. This statement is NOT sufficient to determine whether m is odd.

Statement (1) is a bit trickier. An even number is a multiple of 2, so any even number can be represented as $2n$, where n is an integer. An odd number is always one more than an even number, so the subsequent odd number could be written $2n + 1$. When you see this notation in future (even if the variable is different, as it is in the given problem), note that the problem is signaling that something is odd.

Statement (1) indicates that $m = 2k + 1$, where k is an integer, so m must be odd. Statement (1) is sufficient to answer the question: Yes, m is odd.

The answer is (A): Statement (1) is sufficient alone, but statement (2) is not.

The GMAT will sometimes use this notation to disguise information about odds and evens; add it to your list of "GMAT codes" to know for the test.

Positives and Negatives

Numbers can be either positive or negative (except the number 0, which is neither):

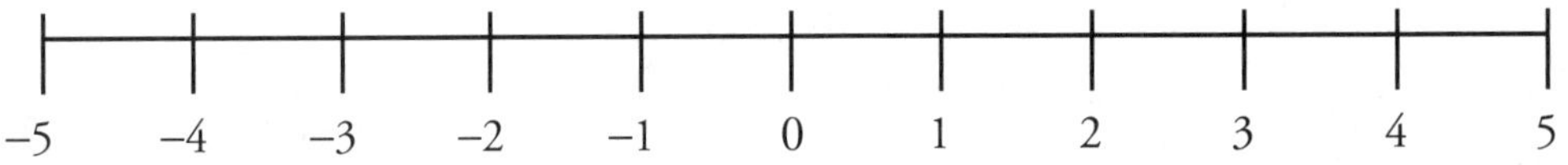

On the number line, negative numbers are all to the left of the number 0. Positive numbers are all to the right of the number 0.

Note that a variable (such as x) can have either a positive or a negative value, unless there is evidence otherwise. The variable x is not necessarily positive, nor is $-x$ necessarily negative. For example, if $x = -3$, then $-x = 3$.

Absolute Value: Absolutely Positive

Absolute value can be a component of positive/negative problems. The **absolute value** of a number answers this question: How far away is the number from 0 on the number line? For example, the number 5 is exactly 5 units away from 0, so the absolute value of 5 equals 5. Mathematically, this is written using the symbol for absolute value: $|5| = 5$. To find the absolute value of -5, look at the number line again: -5 is also exactly 5 units away from 0. Thus, the absolute value of -5 equals 5, or, in mathematical symbols, $|-5| = 5$.

Absolute value is always positive, because it disregards the direction (positive or negative) from which the number approaches 0 on the number line. When you interpret a number in an absolute value sign, just think: absolutely positive! (Except, of course, for 0, because $|0| = 0$. This is the smallest possible absolute value.)

One more thing: 5 and -5 are the same distance from 0; in other words, 0 is located halfway between them. In general, if two numbers are opposites of each other, then they have the same absolute value, and 0 is halfway between. If $x = -y$, then one of the two scenarios below is true:

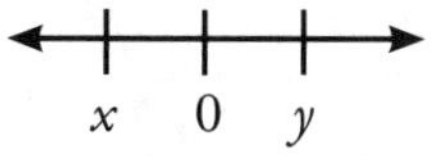

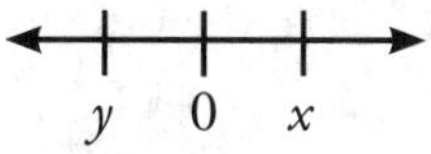

(You cannot tell which variable is positive and which is negative without more information.)

A Double Negative = A Positive

A **double negative** occurs when a minus sign is in front of a negative number (which already has its own negative sign). For example:

What is $7 - (-3)$?

As you learned in English class, two negatives yield a positive:

$$7 - (-3) = 7 + 3 = 10$$

This is a very easy step to miss, especially when the double negative is somewhat hidden. For example:

What is $7 - (12 - x)$?

Many people will make the mistake of computing this as $7 - 12 - x$. However, notice the first minus sign has to be distributed to both terms in the parentheses, so the second term ends up with a double minus sign. This expression is simplified as $7 - 12 - (-x) = 7 - 12 + x$.

Multiplying and Dividing Signed Numbers

When you multiply or divide numbers, positive or negative, follow these rules to keep the signs straight:

Even number of negative signs = **positive**	0 negative signs: $7 \times 8 = 56$	2 negative signs: $(-7) \times (-2) = 14$
Odd number of negative signs = **negative**	1 negative sign: $-7 \times 8 = -56$	3 negative signs: $(-1) \times (-2) \times (-3) = -6$

Try this Data Sufficiency problem:

Is the product of all of the elements in set *S* negative?

(1) All of the elements in set *S* are negative.

(2) There are 5 negative numbers in set *S*.

The problem asks whether the product of all of the elements is negative. Based on the rule above, it seems as though you just need to know whether there are an odd or even number of negative numbers in the set. There is one other number, though, to consider: 0. If you forgot about that while doing the problem, try it again right now.

Statement (1) indicates that everything in set *S* is negative, but you don't know whether there are an odd or even number of terms in the set, so this information is not sufficient to answer the question.

Statement (2) indicates that there are 5 negative numbers in the set. When the GMAT says something like this, you *can* conclude that there are exactly 5 negative numbers in the set (and no more). There could also be other numbers in the set (such as 0 or positive numbers). If there are 5 negative numbers and no others, then the product would be negative. If there are 5 negative numbers and other positive numbers, then the product would still be negative. But if 0 is in the mix, then the product is 0, which is not negative. So this statement is also not sufficient by itself.

Combined, set *S* contains 5 negative numbers *and nothing else*, so this information is sufficient to know that the product of the elements in set *S* must be negative. The correct answer is (C): The two statements are sufficient together, but neither one works alone.

Disguised Positives and Negatives

Some Positive/Negative questions are disguised as inequalities. This generally occurs whenever a problem tells you that a quantity is greater than or less than 0, or asks you whether a quantity is greater than or less than 0. For example:

If $\frac{a-b}{c} < 0$, is $a > b$?

(1) $c < 0$

(2) $a + b < 0$

The fact that $\frac{a-b}{c} < 0$ indicates that the numerator and denominator have *different* signs. That is, either the entire numerator $(a - b)$ is positive and the denominator c is negative, or vice versa.

Statement (1) establishes that c is negative. Therefore, $a - b$ must be positive:

$$a - b > 0$$
$$a > b$$

Statement (1) is sufficient: Yes, a must be greater than b.

Statement (2) indicates that the sum of a and b is negative. Test some cases. If a is 2 and b is -5, then the sum is negative (so this is a valid case). In this case, Yes, $a > b$. If, on the other hand, a is -5 and b is 2, then the sum is negative (so this is a valid case). In this case, No, a is not greater than b. This statement is not sufficient to answer the question.

The correct answer is (A): Statement (1) is sufficient by itself, but statement (2) is not.

Generally speaking, whenever you see inequalities with the number 0 on either side of the inequality, test positive and negative cases to help solve the problem.

The Sum of Two Primes

All prime numbers are odd, except the number 2. (All even numbers greater than 2 are divisible by 2, so they cannot be prime.) Thus, the sum of any two primes will be even (odd + odd = even), *unless* one of those primes is the number 2.

If a problem tells you that the sum of two primes is odd, one of those primes must be the number 2 and the other prime must not be 2. Conversely, if you know that 2 *cannot* be one of the primes in the sum, then the sum of the two primes must be even. Try an example:

> If *a* and *b* are both prime numbers greater than 10, which of the following CANNOT be true?
>
> I. *ab* is an even number.
>
> II. The difference between *a* and *b* equals 117.
>
> III. The sum of *a* and *b* is even.
>
> (A) I only
>
> (B) I and II only
>
> (C) I and III only
>
> (D) II and III only
>
> (E) I, II, and III

The question asks what cannot be true; jot that down. Since *a* and *b* are both prime numbers greater than 10, they must both be odd. Therefore, *ab* must be an odd number, so statement I cannot be true. This statement has to be included in the correct answer, so eliminate answer (D).

Similarly, if *a* and *b* are both odd, then $a - b$ cannot equal 117 (an odd number). The difference between two odd numbers must be even. Therefore, statement II cannot be true. Eliminate answers (A) and (C).

Finally, since *a* and *b* are both odd, $a + b$ must be even, so statement III will always be true. Statements I and II cannot be true, so the correct answer is (B).

Problem Set

For questions 1–6, answer each question with one of three responses: Always Yes, Always No, or Sometimes Yes/Sometimes No. Try to explain each answer using the rules you learned in this section.

All variables in questions 1–6 are integers.

1. If $x \div y$ yields an odd integer, is x odd?

2. If $a + b$ is even, is ab even?

3. If c, d, and e are consecutive integers, is cde even?

4. If h is even, j is odd, and k is odd, is $k(h + j)$ odd?

5. If n, p, q, and r are consecutive integers, is their sum even?

6. If xy is even and z is even, is $x + z$ even?

7. Simplify $\frac{-30}{5} - \frac{18-9}{-3}$.

8. Simplify $\frac{20 \times (-7)}{-35 \times (-2)}$.

9. If x, y, and z are prime numbers and $x < y < z$, what is the value of x?

   (1) xy is even.

   (2) xz is even.

Save the following problem set for review after you finish this entire guide.

10. If c and d are integers, is $c - 3d$ even?

    (1) c and d are odd.

    (2) $c - 2d$ is odd.

11. Is the integer x odd?

    (1) $2(y + x)$ is an odd integer.

    (2) $2y$ is an odd integer.

Answers and explanations follow on the next page. ▶ ▶ ▶

Solutions

1. **Sometimes Yes/Sometimes No:** There are no guaranteed outcomes in division. For example, if $x = 6$ and $y = 2$, then $6 \div 2 = 3$ and x is even. Alternatively, if $x = 9$ and $y = 3$, then $9 \div 3 = 3$ and x is odd.

2. **Sometimes Yes/Sometimes No:** If $a + b$ is even, a and b are either both odd or both even. If they are both odd, ab is odd. If they are both even, ab is even.

3. **Always Yes:** Since all integers alternate between even and odd, at least one of the consecutive integers, c, d, or e, must be even. Therefore, the product cde must be even.

4. **Always Yes:** If h is even and j is odd, then $h + j$ must be odd, since E + O = O. Therefore, $k(h + j)$ = odd(odd), which is always odd.

5. **Always Yes:** If n, p, q, and r are consecutive integers, two of them must be odd and two of them must be even. Pair them up to add them: O + O = E and E + E = E. Finally, add those two results: E + E = E.

6. **Sometimes Yes/Sometimes No:** If xy is even, then either x or y (or both x and y) must be even. Given that z is even, $x + z$ could be either O + E or E + E. If $x + z$ = O + E = O, the answer is No. If $x + z$ = E + E = E, the answer is Yes.

7. **−3:** This is a two-step subtraction problem. First, simplify each fraction. The first fraction simplifies to $\frac{-30}{5} = -6$, and the second fraction simplifies to $\frac{9}{-3} = -3$. The final answer is $-6 - (-3) = -6 + 3 = -3$.

8. **−2:** The sign of the first product, $20 \times (-7)$, is negative. The sign of the second product, $-35 \times (-2)$, is positive. Therefore, −140 divided by 70 is −2.

26

9. **(D):** This is a Value question. The value of each variable is prime and x is the smallest of the three.

   (1) SUFFICIENT: If xy is even, then x is even or y is even. Only one prime number is even: the number 2. Since $x < y$, x must equal 2, since that's the smallest prime number.

   (2) SUFFICIENT: Similarly, if xz is even, then x is even or z is even. Since $x < z$, x must equal 2, because 2 is the smallest and only even prime number.

   The correct answer is **(D)**: Each statement is sufficient by itself.

10. **(A):** This is a Yes/No question. The two variables are both integers. In order for the difference $c - 3d$ to be even, the two terms (c and $3d$) either both have to be even or both have to be odd.

    (1) SUFFICIENT: If both c and d are odd, then $c - 3d$ equals O − (3 × O) = O − O = E.

    (2) INSUFFICIENT: If $c - 2d$ is odd, then c must be odd, because $2d$ will always be even. However, this indicates nothing about d. If d is also odd, then the difference $c - 3d$ is even. But if d is even, then the difference $c - 3d$ is odd.

    The correct answer is **(A)**: Statement (1) is sufficient by itself, but statement (2) is not.

11. (E): This is a Yes/No question. The stem establishes that x is an integer and asks whether it's odd. Glance at the two statements. The second one provides no information about x, so start with this one.

(2) INSUFFICIENT: This statement indicates nothing about x. The question stem also doesn't provide any facts about the relationship between x and y, so this statement is not sufficient.

(1) INSUFFICIENT: $2(y + x)$ is an odd integer. The standard rule states that 2 multiplied by any integer is even, so how is it possible that 2 multiplied by something could yield an odd integer? The value in the parentheses must not be an integer itself. For example, the decimal 1.5 times 2 yields the odd integer 3. List some other possibilities:

$$2(y + x) = 1, 3, 5, 7, 9, \text{etc.}$$
$$(y + x) = \frac{1}{2}, \frac{3}{2}, \frac{5}{2}, \frac{7}{2}, \frac{9}{2}, \text{etc.}$$

The variable x is an integer, so y must be a fraction in order to get such a fractional sum.

Case 1: If $y = 0.5$ and $x = 0$, then $2(y + x) = 2(0.5) = 1$, so this is a valid case to test. In this case, No, x is not odd. (The number 0 is even.)

Case 2: If $y = 0.5$ and $x = 1$, then $2(y + x) = 2(1.5) = 3$, so this is a valid case to test. In this case, Yes, x is odd.

(1) AND (2) INSUFFICIENT: Statement (1) indicates that y must be a fraction or decimal in the pattern 0.5, 1.5, 2.5, etc. How does statement (2) add to this information?

$$2y = \text{odd}$$
$$y = \frac{\text{odd}}{2}$$

Odd integers divided by 2 will turn into fractions: $\frac{1}{2}, \frac{3}{2}, \frac{5}{2}, \ldots$

This is the same information conveyed by statement (1); the two statements are identical twins. Identical twins must be either answer (D) or (E). Answer (D) has already been knocked out, so the answer must be (E).

The correct answer is **(E)**: Using the two together is still not sufficient to answer the question.

CHAPTER 27

Strategy: Arithmetic vs. Algebra 4

In This Chapter

- How to Test Cases
- Choosing Numbers for Testing Cases
- Review Your Work

In this chapter, you will learn advanced strategies for testing cases as well as methods for reviewing your work on problems and pushing your learning as far as you can. The review methods can be used on all GMAT problems—quant, verbal, and integrated reasoning.

CHAPTER 27 Strategy: Arithmetic vs. Algebra 4

Number Properties concepts lend themselves very well to testing cases, so it's common to see these on the GMAT. Most will be in the form of Data Sufficiency, though you may see one or two Problem Solving versions.

Set a timer for 8 minutes and try the following four-problem set under official exam conditions. Do the problems in order. Choose an answer before moving to the next problem (even if you have to guess).

Your main goal is to finish the set. Have an answer—any answer!—for all four problems by the time your timer goes off (i.e., by the time the test ends). Ready? Go!

1. Does positive integer b have a factor n such that $1 < n < b$?

    (1) $b = 2k$, where k is an integer greater than 1.

    (2) k is a factor of b, where k is an integer greater than 1.

2. If $xy \neq 0$, is $\frac{x}{y} < \frac{2x}{y}$?

    (1) y is positive.

    (2) xy is positive.

3. If x and y are integers and $1 < x < y$, what is the value of y?

    (1) $xy = 15$

    (2) The product of 42 and x is 126.

4. Is integer p even?

    (1) $2p + 1$ is odd.

    (2) $\frac{p}{2}$ is even.

Before you read further, how do you think that went?

Do you have an answer for each question? On the real test, there's a penalty for not answering all of the questions.

How was your time management? In hindsight, do you think you should have cut off a particular problem more quickly or spent more time on a particular problem?

Full disclosure: Most people will find the first two problems harder than the last two. Did you spend too much time on either or both and then have to rush to finish? This can easily happen on the real test as well, so think about whether you should have bailed on one of the problems in order to be able to finish the set. Everyone needs to do this on the real test, so practice doing so!

Do you think you chose the best solution methods (for you)? Do you have any ideas for alternative approaches that you could have tried? Feel free to try any of the problems again using any other approaches that you would like.

Before checking the solutions to the problem set, review how to test cases and then analyze the process you used on the problem set.

How to Test Cases

This section summarizes how to test cases on Data Sufficiency problems and on Problem Solving problems.

Don't look yet, but the solutions to the problem set are a little later in this chapter. Consider how your process compared to the testing cases summary below. You may want to try the problems again before you look at the solutions.

Testing Cases on Data Sufficiency

Understand: First, **recognize** that you can test cases. The question stem and the statement will allow for multiple possible values; they don't lock you into using one set of values.

Articulate the *facts* given in the problem and separate them from the *question* that is being asked. Remind yourself of your goal when testing cases on DS: Try to find two different answers so that you can call that statement Not Sufficient and move on.

Plan: First, **think about** any **constraints** you're given. The constraints are the facts given in the problem and can be found in *two* places: (1) the question stem and (2) the two statements. You are only allowed to try numbers that fit the given facts. (As you work on one statement alone, ignore any facts given in the *other* statement.)

Next, use the given facts as clues to figure out what kinds of numbers you *do* want to try. These clues will help you to find the kinds of numbers that will give you different answers (more on this in the next section of this chapter).

Solve: Then, **test one set of numbers**. Choose your values, write them down, then check your numbers against the facts in the problem to make sure that you have chosen a valid case. If your chosen numbers "break" any of the facts—that is, make any fact in the question stem or the statement on which you're working right now false—*discard* that case. All of the given facts must be true, so any numbers you choose must go along with those facts. Cross an invalid case off on your scratch paper and start again.

If you have a valid case, solve to find an answer to the question. On a Yes/No question, you will get either a Yes or a No. On a Value question, you will get a particular value.

Then, try to find a second case that gives you a *different* answer. Remind yourself of what a "different" answer looks like for this problem. For example, if the question is "Is $b > 5$?" and your first answer is Yes, then you would want to find a No case. For this particular question, a No case would only occur when b is equal to or less than 5, so choose such a value for your second case.

If you can find two different answers, you're done! That statement has a Sometimes Yes/Sometimes No answer, so you can cross off the relevant answer(s) on your grid and move to the next step in your DS process.

If you keep getting the same answer, try to to articulate *why* this is happening. If you are trying the same kind of number each time, then you may need to try a different kind of number to find that opposite case—so trying to articulate what's happening can prompt you to try a specific kind of number that will yield a different answer.

Alternatively, articulating what's happening with the math may demonstrate that you will always get that same answer—in other words, that this statement is sufficient.

At times, you may get the same answer after a few cases but not be able to articulate what's happening. If you're not sure why but you also don't see how to get a different answer after trying a few different kinds of numbers, don't keep sitting on this problem. Go ahead and call this statement sufficient and move on.

Testing Cases on Problem Solving

There weren't any PS problems in the set, but it's still a good idea to review that process.

Understand: First, during the Understand step, **recognize** that you can test cases. The question will ask what *must* or *could be* a certain thing (true, false, or a certain characteristic).

Articulate the *facts* given in the problem and separate them from the *question* that is being asked. Remind yourself of your goal when testing cases on PS: to try to find a value that takes this answer choice out of the running. (For example, if it asks what could be *true*, try to find a value to make an answer *false,* and then you know you can cross it off forever.)

Plan: During the Plan step, first **think about** any **constraints** you're given. The constraints are the facts given in the problem. You are only allowed to try numbers that fit the given facts.

Next, use the given facts as clues to figure out what kinds of numbers you *do* want to try. These clues will help you to find the kinds of numbers that will give you the result you're looking for.

Solve: Then, **test one set of numbers**. Choose your values, write them down, then check your numbers against the facts in the problem to make sure that you have chosen a valid case. If your chosen numbers "break" any given facts, *discard* that case. Cross it off on your scratch paper and start again.

If you have a valid case, test it across all five answer choices and cross off any answers that fail the test. Then, look at the remaining answer choices and think about what kind of case to try next. What might help you to knock out one (or more) of the remaining choices? Repeat until you're down to one answer (or you get stuck; in that case, guess from the remaining answers and move on).

Choosing Numbers for Testing Cases

One more thing before diving into the solutions for the problem set: Review the guidelines for good numbers to use when testing cases. If this sparks any ideas for the problems in that set, feel free to retry any of them before looking at the solutions.

First, you always have to follow any constraints given in a problem. For example, if the problem says that x is positive, then you can only try positive values for x—but you may want to try both integers and non-integers.

When using the Test Cases strategy on either Data Sufficiency or Problem Solving problems, the general guidelines are to try numbers that are really easy to use and are likely to give you opposite, or different, answers.

The table below contains some common clues that can help you to decide what kinds of numbers to test. The first column refers to a given or fact, not the question. Only the givens or facts constrain what you're allowed to try. Also, some entries will show both mathematical symbols and words for the same concept—the test can tell you something in math or in words.

Testing Cases	
When I see (given/fact) . . .	*I'll choose . . .*
That I can test cases	0 and 1 if I can
Positive	Integers if possible/easy; fractions if needed
Non-negative	0 and positive (don't forget 0!)
(A) > 0 or greater than 0 (B) < 0 or less than 0 (C) $\|x\|$	(A) Positive (B) Negative (C) Positive and negative
Divisible by 2 or 4 x and y are integers and $x = y + 1$	Even Odd and even
(A) x^2 (B) x^3 (C) $x^2 < x$	(A) hides sign (could be pos or neg); 0 and 1 (stay same); fractions between 0 and 1 get smaller (B) keeps sign; 0 and 1 (stay same); fractions between 0 and 1 get smaller (C) Fractions between 0 and 1
x and y are positive integers, and either $xy =$ (some number) or the product of x and y is (some number)	x and y are factors of the number (write out factor pairs)
(A) A number has exactly two factors. (B) A number has a factor between itself and 1. (C) $1 < n < p$, where n is a factor of p. (D) A number has more than two factors.	(A) Prime (B) Not prime (C) Not prime (D) Not prime
x and y are integers, and (A) $x + y > 0$ (B) $x + y < 0$ (C) $xy > 0$ or $x \div y > 0$ (D) $xy < 0$ or $x \div y < 0$	 (A) At least one is positive. (B) At least one is negative. (C) Same sign: both positive or both negative (D) Opposite signs: one positive, one negative
x and y are integers, and (A) $x + y =$ even (B) $x + y =$ odd (C) $xy =$ even (D) $xy =$ odd	 (A) Same parity: both even or both odd (B) Opposite parity: one even, one odd (C) At least one is even. (D) Both are odd.

You have to choose numbers that fit all of the facts given in a problem. Often, this is straightforward. For example, if the problem tells you that x is a positive integer and that x is divisible by 3, it's not terribly difficult to process all of those facts at once and realize that you can choose 3, 6, 9, and so on.

Other combinations of facts will require additional thought. For example, a problem might say that x is an integer and that $x + 3$ is prime. If you begin by thinking about possible integer values for x, you might easily choose something that isn't prime when you add 3. It's probably safer to think of a prime number first (e.g., 7) and then figure out that x would have to be 4 in this case.

Try another one:

> If y is an integer and the remainder is 0 when $y + 2$ is divided by 5 . . . what could you use for y?

In order to get a remainder of 0, $y + 2$ must be divisible by 5. So $y + 2$ could be 5, in which case $y = 3$. Alternatively, $y + 2$ could be 10, in which case $y = 8$. Again, it's easier to start by choosing a value for $y + 2$, not for y by itself.

When you have multiple facts to account for, take your time during the Plan phase to figure out where to start your thinking as you choose values for your cases.

Now, are you ready? It's time to take a look at the solutions to the problem set.

Review Your Work

Use these solutions as a series of hints to help you review the problems. First, check just the correct answer; if you got it wrong, does knowing the right answer give you any ideas? If so, try those ideas before you read the solution.

Then, start reading the solution. The moment you read anything that gives you an idea about what to do, immediately *stop* reading the solution and try those next steps on your own. See what you can figure out for yourself. Whenever you get stuck, return to the solution—but when you get another idea, *stop* reading the solution again and push your thinking as far as you can on your own.

As you work, if you find any new "When I see *X*, I'll do *Y*" clues, add them to your flash cards or notes immediately.

Problem 1

> Does positive integer b have a factor n such that $1 < n < b$?
>
> (1) $b = 2k$, where k is an integer greater than 1.
>
> (2) k is a factor of b, where k is an integer greater than 1.

The correct answer is (A).

The question stem indicates that b is a positive integer and asks whether b has a factor smaller than b itself but larger than 1. The problem is a theoretical one—no real numbers are given, so you may want to test cases. First, though, take some time to understand that unusual question.

Can you think of a number that does have this trait? (You're not actually solving the problem or testing cases at this point. You're just trying to understand what they're talking about.)

The number 10 fits the description. It has a factor of 2. It also has a factor of 5. Both of those are less than 10 but greater than 1.

Can you think of a positive integer for which this description does *not* work? That is, a positive integer that does *not* have a factor less than itself but greater than 1?

Consider the number 7, a prime number, which by definition has exactly two factors: itself and 1. Any prime number would give a No answer to the question. Any composite number would give a Yes answer. (Composite numbers are all of the positive integers *besides* prime numbers and the number 1. The number 1 is the only positive integer that is neither prime nor composite. You don't need to know the term *composite* for the GMAT; you just need to know the concept.)

So the question is really asking whether b is a composite number. (If you don't want to use that term, you can also ask whether b is a "non-prime" number. That term isn't really proper from a math standpoint—but the GMAT isn't really a math test!)

Now that you understand what the question is asking, you can come up with a plan. The statements contain b and n, as well as a third variable, k. Testing cases is probably the best approach. Look at statement 1:

(1) $b = 2k$, where k is an integer greater than 1.

(1) SUFFICIENT: The statement introduces a third variable that wasn't in the question stem. This statement also says nothing about n. So it can't be sufficient, right?

Wait. It's pretty unusual for the statements to introduce a variable that didn't appear in the question stem. Examine this more closely. Given that k is an integer greater than 1, what are some possible values for b?

Case 1: If $k = 2$, then $b = 4$. Is b composite (or non-prime)? Yes.

Case 2: If $k = 3$, then $b = 6$. Is b composite (or non-prime)? Yes.

Can you get a No answer? Is there a value for k that would allow b to be prime?

It's not possible. First, b equals k multiplied by 2, so b will always be even. Second, k is at least 2, so b is at least 4. The only even prime number is 2, so if b is even and at least 4, it cannot be prime.

Statement (1) is sufficient to answer the question. Eliminate answers (B), (C), and (E).

(2) k is a factor of b, where k is an integer greater than 1.

(2) INSUFFICIENT: Try some cases.

Case 1: If $k = 2$, then b could be 4. In this case, is b composite (or non-prime)? Yes.

Given that same starting point, $k = 2$, b itself could also be 2, since any number has itself as a factor (in other words, 2 is a factor of 2).

Case 2: If $k = 2$, then b could be 2. In this case, is b composite (or non-prime)? No, in this case b is prime.

A Sometimes Yes/Sometimes No answer is not sufficient.

The correct answer is (A): Statement (1) works alone, but statement (2) does not.

Problem 2

If $xy \neq 0$, is $\frac{x}{y} < \frac{2x}{y}$?

(1) y is positive.

(2) xy is positive.

The correct answer is (B).

The question stem is annoying. The statements are pretty straightforward and the reference to *positive* indicates that this might be a Positive/Negative problem. Can you simplify or rephrase the question? Your initial instinct may be to cross-multiply to get rid of the fractions, but the question stem does not indicate whether y is positive or negative. As a result, you wouldn't know whether to flip the inequality sign when performing the multiplication, so taking this action is likely to make the rephrase more complicated, not less. Don't go there.

Instead, compare the two sides of the inequality. They're almost identical; the only difference is multiplying the numerator by 2. The statements hinted at a positive/negative approach, so test some cases with some easy positive and negative numbers. Note the constraint: Don't use 0 for either variable.

Statement (1) indicates that y is positive but says nothing about x. Statement (2) indicates that x and y are either both positive or both negative. It's your choice as to which seems like an easier starting point; this solution will start with statement (1).

(1) INSUFFICIENT: This statement indicates that y is positive but says nothing about x. Try cases in which x is both positive and negative.

Case 1: $x = 1, y = 2$. (Pause to verify that your numbers fit all of the facts given in the problem. They do? Carry on.)

$$\text{Is } \frac{1}{2} < \frac{2(1)}{2} \text{ ?}$$

$$\text{Is } \frac{1}{2} < 1 \text{ ? Yes.}$$

This is a Yes case. Try a negative value for x to see what answer that returns.

Case 2: $x = -1, y = 2$. (Pause. Does this fit all of the facts? Carry on.)

$$\text{Is } \frac{-1}{2} < \frac{2(-1)}{2} \text{ ?}$$

$$\text{Is } -\frac{1}{2} < -1 \text{ ? No.}$$

When x is negative and y is positive, the answer is No. Because the answer is Sometimes Yes/Sometimes No, this statement is not sufficient. 27

(2) SUFFICIENT: The statement indicates that x and y are either both positive or both negative. Try both cases.

First, examine the cases that you tried for statement (1) (but don't use that statement itself!). You can reuse any cases that also fit statement (2). The two variables have the same sign. The first case ($x = 1$ and $y = 2$) fits this scenario, so this case will also work for statement (2). That's your Yes case.

Note: If you use the same starting numbers for the case, the answer will always be the same—Yes, in this case—because the two statements never contradict. So when you see that you can reuse the numbers for the other statement, don't actually do the whole case. The answer will be the same.

The second case for statement (1), though, used a negative x and positive y, so that one can't be reused here. Instead, try the negative-negative case for statement (2).

Case 1: Reused from statement (1). Yes.

Case 2: $x = -1$, $y = -2$. (Pause. Did you fulfill all constraints? Carry on.)

$$\text{Is } \frac{-1}{-2} < \frac{2(-1)}{-2}\ ?$$

$$\text{Is } \frac{1}{2} < 1\text{? Yes.}$$

Hmm. That also returned a Yes case. Try to articulate what's happening with the math. The left side has $\frac{x}{y}$ and the right side has almost the same thing, $\frac{2x}{y}$. The right side can also be written $2\left(\frac{x}{y}\right)$. In other words, you're just multiplying the original fraction by 2.

If you start with any *positive* fraction and multiply it by 2, you're going to get a larger value. So when x and y are both positive, you'll always get a Yes answer.

What about when they're both negative? If they're both negative, those negative signs will actually cancel out, so you'll end up with a positive fraction. And any positive fraction multiplied by 2 will get larger. This statement is sufficient because the only possible answer is Yes.

The correct answer is (B): Statement (2) works alone, but statement (1) does not.

Problem 3

If x and y are integers and $1 < x < y$, what is the value of y?

(1) $xy = 15$

(2) The product of 42 and x is 126.

The correct answer is (A).

The question stem doesn't have a lot of complexity. Both variables are integers and both are greater than 1. Also, y is greater than x. The question asks for the value of y.

27

At first, the problem might not appear to contain any of the usual clues that can help you to tell what kind of problem is being tested. The statements talk about basic multiplication. There's nothing indicating the dividing line between positive and negative or odd and even.

Go back to the multiplication part. Both statements multiply two integers together to get a third integer. This is a clue! The two smaller numbers are factors of the larger number.

(1) SUFFICIENT: The factor pairs of 15 are (1, 15) and (3, 5). Both variables are greater than 1, so cross off the (1, 15) factor pair. And y is greater than x, so y must be 5 (and x must be 3). You have a definitive value for y, so this statement is sufficient.

(2) INSUFFICIENT: This statement allows you to find the value of x, but it indicates nothing about y.

The correct answer is (A): Statement (1) works alone, but statement (2) does not.

This problem is setting up a C-Trap. You can get the value of x from statement (2), and you could plug that into the equation in statement (1) to get the value of y. If the question stem hadn't provided the additional facts that it did, then (C) would have been the answer. But, given the question stem, statement (1) is enough on its own.

Problem 4

Is integer p even?

(1) $2p + 1$ is odd.

(2) $\frac{p}{2}$ is even.

The correct answer is (B).

The question stem establishes that p is an integer and asks whether p is even.

(1) INSUFFICIENT: If $2p + 1$ is odd, then $2p$ is even. Any integer multiplied by 2 is even, though, so p itself could be either even or odd. (If you're not sure, test a couple of numbers to see.)

(2) SUFFICIENT: Any odd number divided by 2 will result in a non-integer. So if $\frac{p}{2}$ is even, then p itself must be even. You can literally write an equation to show this:

$$\frac{p}{2} = \text{even}$$
$$p = 2(\text{even})$$

If p equals 2 times another even, then p itself must be even. (You can also test actual values to figure this out, if you prefer.)

The correct answer is (B): Statement (2) is sufficient by itself, but statement (1) is not.

Now that you've reviewed the four problems, what are your major takeaways?

How will you make better decisions around time management next time you do a problem set? Do you need to build any better habits around your DS process, how you write things down on your scratch paper, or how you solve?

Problem Set

Now that you've finished the chapter, try the following problems.

1. Is $pqr > 0$?

   (1) $pq > 0$

   (2) $\frac{q}{r} < 0$

2. If x is a positive integer, is $x^2 + 6x + 10$ odd?

   (1) $x^2 + 4x + 5$ is odd.

   (2) $x^2 + 3x + 4$ is even.

3. If x is a positive integer and $3x + 2$ is divisible by 5, then which of the following must be true?

   (A) x is divisible by 3.

   (B) $3x$ is divisible by 10.

   (C) $x - 1$ is divisible by 5.

   (D) x is odd.

   (E) $3x$ is even.

4. If p, q, and r are integers, is $pq + r$ even?

   (1) $p + r$ is even.

   (2) $q + r$ is odd.

Save these problems for review after you finish this entire guide.

5. If x is an integer and $0 < x < 24$, is $\frac{24}{x}$ an integer?

   (1) $\frac{28}{x}$ is an integer.

   (2) $\frac{x}{4}$ is an integer.

6. The length of a certain rectangle is a multiple of 18, and the width of the rectangle is a multiple of 12. Which of the following CANNOT be the perimeter of the rectangle?

   (A) 60

   (B) 72

   (C) 84

   (D) 96

   (E) 108

7. A university badminton club has both students and professors as members. Is the number of students in the club at least 45?

   (1) The number of professors in the club is a multiple of 8.

   (2) The number of students in the club is exactly 20% greater than the number of professors in the club.

Answers and explanations follow on the next page. ▶ ▶ ▶

Solutions

1. **(E):** The question stem asks whether the product of three numbers is greater than 0, so this is a Yes/No question focusing on the concept of positive and negative. First, figure out what would need to be true in order for the product of three numbers to be positive.

   First, if any of the variables is 0, the answer is No. Next, if all three variables are positive, then the product will be positive. If exactly two are negative and one is positive, then the product will be positive. Finally, if exactly one or exactly three are negative, then the product will be negative.

   (1) INSUFFICIENT: If pq is greater than 0, then p and q have the same sign, either both positive or both negative. This statement says nothing about r, so r could be positive, negative, or 0. Test cases; try to get different answers.

	p	q	r	Valid?	Is $pqr > 0$?
Case 1	+	+	0	✓	No
Case 2	+	+	+	✓	Yes

   (2) INSUFFICIENT: If q divided by r is less than 0, then q and r have opposite signs. This statement says nothing about p, so p could be positive, negative, or 0. Test cases; try to get different answers.

	p	q	r	Valid?	Is $pqr > 0$?
Case 1	0	+	–	✓	No
Case 2	–	+	–	✓	Yes

   (1) AND (2) INSUFFICIENT: Using both statements together, p and q have the same sign (either both positive or both negative) and q and r have opposite signs. In other words, two of the variables have the same sign and the third has opposite signs.

27

	p	q	r	Valid?	Is $pqr > 0$?
Case 1	+	+	–	✓	No
Case 2	–	–	+	✓	Yes

   The correct answer is **(E)**: Using the two statements together, there is still not enough information to answer the question.

2. **(A):** The question can first be simplified by noting that if x is even, $x^2 + 6x + 10$ will be even (a No answer), and if x is odd, $x^2 + 6x + 10$ will be odd (a Yes answer). Thus, you can simplify this question: Is x odd?

   (A couple of shortcuts to save time in reaching that conclusion: The exponent on the first term can be ignored, since an even squared is still even and an odd squared is still odd. You know $6x$ will be even no matter what, since 6 is even, and obviously 10 is even no matter what. So an even plus two evens is even, and an odd plus two evens is odd.)

(1) SUFFICIENT: You can test odd and even cases or simply use number theory. If x is even, you get even + even + odd = odd, and if x is odd, you get odd + even + odd = even. Thus, since $x^2 + 4x + 5$ is odd, x is even. The answer to the rephrased question is Always No, so this statement is sufficient.

(2) INSUFFICIENT: $x^2 + 3x + 4$ is actually even regardless of what integer is plugged in for x. If x is even, you get even + even + even = even, and if x is odd, you get odd + odd + even = even. Thus, x could be odd or even, and the answer is Sometimes Yes/Sometimes No. Plugging in numbers will yield the same conclusion—x could be any integer.

Note that you should *not* factor any of the expressions above. If you wasted time factoring, remember: Factoring is meaningless if you don't have an equation set equal to 0! This problem was about number theory (or number testing), not factoring.

The correct answer is **(A)**: Statement (1) is sufficient by itself, but statement (2) is not.

3. **(C) $x - 1$ is divisible by 5:** The question stem is asking a *must be* question, so test cases on this problem. Use positive integers for x that make the following equation true:

$$\frac{3x+2}{5} = \text{integer}$$

If $x = 1$, then $3(1) + 2 = 5$, which is divisible by 5. So this is a valid case to test. Check $x = 1$ against the answer choices. Answers (A), (B), and (E) are all false for this case, so eliminate them.

Try another case. If $x = 2$, then $3(2) + 2 = 8$, which is not divisible by 5. This is an invalid case; discard it. What about $x = 3$? In this case, $3(3) + 2 = 11$. Still invalid. You can continue to try increasing integers or take a moment to think about what's happening with the math to help you find the next case. Rearrange that starting equation a little:

$$\frac{3x+2}{5} = \text{int}$$

$$3x + 2 = (5)(\text{int})$$

$$3x = (5)(\text{int}) - 2$$

In other words, $3x$ must equal a multiple of 5 minus 2. Multiples of 5 are 5, 10, 15, 20, 25, and so on. Subtract 2 from these multiples of 5 to find the potential values of $3x$, which are 3, 8, 13, 18, 23, and so on.

Because x itself must be an integer, $3x$ must be a multiple of 3. This narrows down the list of potential values of $3x$ to 3, 18, and so on, and the corresponding x values are 1, 6, and so on. The first case, $x = 1$, has already been tested, so the next one to try is $x = 6$.

Case 2: $x = 6$. Verify that this is valid: $(3)(6) + 2 = 20$. This is divisible by 5, so proceed. Answers (A), (B), and (E) have already been eliminated, so test only answers (C) and (D). In this case, answer (D) is false so eliminate it. The only remaining answer is **(C)**.

4. **(E):** The Yes/No question asks whether $pq + r$ is even. What would need to be true in order for the answer to be Yes? Either both pq and r need to be even or both pq and r need to be odd.

(1) INSUFFICIENT: You are told that $p + r$ is even. To stay organized, test all the cases that make the statement true. Both p and r are even, or both p and r are odd. For each of those scenarios, q could be odd or even. Set up a table to keep track of all of these possibilities:

27

Scenario	p	q	r	$pq + r$
1	Odd	Odd	Odd	$O \times O + O = E$
2	Odd	Even	Odd	$O \times E + O = O$
3	Even	Odd	Even	$E \times O + E = E$
4	Even	Even	Even	$E \times E + E = E$

Since $pq + r$ could be odd or even, statement (1) is not sufficient. Note that you can stop as soon as you have found contradictory cases (one odd and one even); above, for example, you could have stopped after scenario 2.

(2) INSUFFICIENT: As in statement (1), you can organize the information from statement (2) with a table. Either q is even and r is odd or q is odd and r is even, and p can be odd or even:

Scenario	p	q	r	$pq + r$
5	Odd	Even	Odd	$O \times E + O = O$
6	Even	Even	Odd	$E \times E + O = O$
7	Odd	Odd	Even	$O \times O + E = O$
8	Even	Odd	Even	$E \times O + E = E$

(1) AND (2) INSUFFICIENT: Notice that scenarios 2 and 5 are identical, as are scenarios 3 and 8. Therefore, both sets of scenarios meet the criteria laid forth in statements (1) and (2), but they yield opposite answers to the question:

Scenario	p	q	r	$pq + r$
2 & 5	Odd	Even	Odd	$O \times E + O = O$
3 & 8	Even	Odd	Even	$E \times O + E = E$

The correct answer is **(E)**: The statements are not sufficient alone or together.

5. **(C):** This Yes/No question indicates that x is an integer between (but *not* including) 0 and 24. It asks whether 24 divided by x is an integer, or $\frac{24}{x} = \text{int}$?

The value of x would need to be a factor of 24 in order for the result to be an integer; there are a limited number of possibilities. The factor pairs for 24 are (1, 24), (2, 12), (3, 8), and (4, 6). Keep this in mind as you test cases.

(1) INSUFFICIENT: If 28 is divisible by x, then x is a factor of 28. The factors of 28 are (1, 28), (2, 14), and (4, 7). Also follow the constraints given in the question stem: x is an integer between 0 and 24. So try anything on the factors-of-28 list besides the number 28.

Case 1: If $x = 4$, then $\frac{24}{4}$ is an integer. This is a Yes case.

Case 2: Can you get a different answer? Look over the list of factors for 28 (not including 28 itself!) and try to find one that will result in a non-integer when divided into 24. If $x = 7$, then $\frac{24}{7}$ is not an integer. This is a No case.

(2) INSUFFICIENT: If x is divisible by 4, then x is a multiple of 4, so it could be 4, 8, 12, 16, and so on. Try values only from that list.

Case 1: $x = 4$, in which case the answer to the question is Yes, $\frac{24}{4}$ is an integer.

Case 2: $x = 16$, in which case the answer to the question is No, $\frac{24}{16}$ is not an integer.

(1) AND (2) SUFFICIENT: Using both statements together, x must be both a factor of 28 and divisible by 4. First, review the factor pairs of 28. (You don't need to rewrite them—you can look at what you wrote down for the second statement.) Cross off all of the numbers that are not divisible by 4 and that are not between 0 and 24: $(\not{1}, \not{28})(\not{2}, \not{14})(4, \not{7})$. The only value left is $x = 4$, and the answer to the question is Yes, $\frac{24}{4}$ is an integer.

The correct answer is **(C)**: The two statements together are sufficient, but neither one works alone.

6. **(B) 72:** The length could be 18, 36, 54, and so on. The width could be 12, 24, 36, and so on. The question stem asks what *cannot* be the perimeter. This wording signals that there are multiple possible values that will work, so test cases on this problem. First, set up the information. The perimeter of a rectangle is $2(w + l)$. What's the smallest possible perimeter?

   Let $l = 18$ and $w = 12$. In this case, the perimeter is $2(18 + 12) = 2(30) = 60$. Cross off answer (A).

   What's the next possible case? You could double both values, the length to 36 and the width to 24, which would significantly increase the perimeter...but glance at those answers. They're not that much greater than 60, yet three of the four remaining answers must also work. That's your clue to first double only one of the dimensions, but leave the other the same.

   The next smallest case will be to double the width to become 24 but leave the length at 18. (Ignore the fact that this makes the width longer than the length; that's okay.) In this case, the perimeter is $2(24 + 18) = 2(42) = 84$. Eliminate answer (C).

   That skipped over answer (B). Is there another, smaller case you could have tried to get 72 as the perimeter? The length is a multiple of 18, so doubling that one (and leaving the width at 12) would lead to a larger perimeter than 84. There is no other case possible between 60 and 84, so 72 is not a possible length for the perimeter.

7. **(C):** Let s and p be the number of students and professors in the club, respectively. The question asks whether $s \geq 45$.

   (1) INSUFFICIENT: This statement provides information about the professors but not the students. The question stem did not provide any additional information about the relationship between p and s, so this statement is not sufficient to answer the question.

   (2) INSUFFICIENT: This statement provides a *relative* relationship between the number of professors and the number of students but no actual values. There is a hidden integer constraint here—both p and s must be integers—so this limits the values that could work for the given relationship. What integers will allow you to take 20% and get another integer?

Case 1: Try 100 first since this is a percent problem. Let $p = 100$ and $s = 120$. (To find 20%, take 10% and double it.) In this case, Yes, $s \geq 45$.

A No case would require an integer less than 45 that will still yield an integer when you take 20%. Benchmark your way to the smallest possible integer that will work: If 20% = 1, then 100% = (1)(5) = 5. Now put this number formally through the test to make sure the logic worked.

Case 2: Try $p = 5$. In this case, 20% of 5 is 1, so $s = 6$. In this case, s is less than 45, so the answer is No.

(1) AND (2) SUFFICIENT: According to statement (1), the value of p has to be 8, 16, 24, 32, and so on. According to statement (2), the smallest possible value of p is 5; the other possible values of p will be multiples of 5, or 5, 10, 15, 20, and so on.

Put the information together. The first value that is both a multiple of 8 and a multiple of 5 is $p = 40$. Now find s: 20% of 40 = 4 + 4 = 8, so $s = 48$. This is the smallest possible value for s, so the answer is always Yes, $s \geq 45$.

The correct answer is **(C)**: Both statements together are sufficient, but neither one works alone.

CHAPTER 28

Combinatorics

In This Chapter

- The Words *OR* and *AND*
- Arranging Groups
- Arranging Groups Using the Anagram Grid
- Multiple Groups

In this chapter, you will learn how to set up and solve combination, or counting, problems. These questions are not very common on the GMAT and many people dislike them, so you may choose not to study certain material; the chapter will guide you in making this choice.

CHAPTER 28 Combinatorics

The Words *OR* and *AND*

Suppose you are at a restaurant that offers a free side dish of soup or salad with any main dish. How many possible side dishes can you order?

You have two options: the soup OR the salad. The most important part of the example is this: The word *or* means *add*. You will see this word show up again and again in both combinatorics and probability problems.

If the same restaurant offers three main dishes (steak, salmon, or pasta), then how many possible combinations of main dish and side dish are there?

There are two decisions that need to be made: a main dish AND a side dish. List out all the possible combinations:

Steak - Soup	Steak - Salad	Salmon - Soup
Salmon - Salad	Pasta - Soup	Pasta - Salad

There are six possible combinations. For a problem without many options, you can literally just write out the possibilities. You can also do some math if you know that the word *and* means *multiply*.

When you make two decisions, you make decision 1 AND decision 2. This is true whether the decisions are simultaneous (e.g., choosing a main dish and a side dish) or sequential (e.g., choosing among routes between successive towns on a road trip).

In this example, you have three options for main dishes AND two options for side dishes:

$$\begin{array}{ccccc} \text{(steak OR chicken OR salmon)} & \text{AND} & \text{(soup OR salad)} & & \\ (1 + 1 + 1) & \times & (1 + 1) & = & 6 \\ 3 & \times & 2 & = & 6 \end{array}$$

More straightforward combinatorics (also known as counting) problems can be solved using these two principles:

1. *OR* means *add.*
2. *AND* means *multiply.*

GMAT questions will get more complicated, of course. Try the following example:

> An office manager must choose a four-digit lock code for the office door. The first and last digits of the code must be odd, and no repetition of digits is allowed. How many different lock codes are possible?

When a question asks how many possible ways something can happen, you have a combinatorics or counting problem. In this case, the manager has to make four decisions to get a four-digit lock code. To keep track, make a slot for each digit:

	$\times$		$\times$		$\times$	
Digit 1	AND	Digit 2	AND	Digit 3	AND	Digit 4

Next, fill in the number of options for each slot. This is known as the **slot method**.

How many options are there for each digit? Start with the most constrained decisions first. There are restrictions on the first and last numbers so start there.

The first digit must be odd, so it can be 1 OR 3 OR 5 OR 7 OR 9. There are five options for the first digit. The problem also indicated that there can be no repeated numbers. Now that you have chosen the first digit (even though you don't know what the actual value will be), there are only four odd numbers remaining for the last digit. Fill in both slots:

5	$\times$		$\times$		$\times$	4
Digit 1	AND	Digit 2	AND	Digit 3	AND	Digit 4

Now, fill in the other two slots. Make sure to account for the lack of repetition. Ten digits exist in total (0 through 9), but two have already been used, so there are eight options remaining for the second digit and seven options for the third digit:

5	$\times$	8	$\times$	7	$\times$	4
Digit 1	AND	Digit 2	AND	Digit 3	AND	Digit 4

Finally, multiply this out. Look to multiply multiples of 5s and 2s together (because $5 \times 2 = 10$ and 10 is easier to multiply into other numbers). In this case, $5 \times 4 = 20$ and $8 \times 7 = 56$. The number 20 can be thought of as 2×10, so multiply $(56)(2)(10) = 1{,}120$.

When making decisions, there are two main cases:

1. Decision 1 OR Decision 2: ADD the possibilities.
2. Decision 1 AND Decision 2: MULTIPLY the possibilities.

Finally, the rest of this chapter deals with more complex scenarios. Many test-takers really dislike combinatorics; if you are one of them, you can decide to bail (guess immediately) on most combinatorics problems on the GMAT. It is possible to score well into the 700s while bailing on most combinatorics problems on the test.

If you see a more straightforward problem for which you can write out a small number of combinations, go ahead and logic it out. If you see a problem that has anything more complicated, choose your favorite letter and move on. (And, if you want to do that, you don't have to learn how to do anything else in this chapter.)

Arranging Groups

Another very common type of combinatorics problem asks how many different ways there are to arrange a group.

The number of ways of arranging n distinct objects, if there are no restrictions, is $n!$ (n factorial).

The term ***n* factorial** ($n!$) refers to the product of all the integers from 1 to n, inclusive. If you are going to go for it on medium to harder combinatorics questions, memorize the first six factorials, shown here:

$1! = 1$	$4! = 4 \times 3 \times 2 \times 1 = 24$
$2! = 2 \times 1 = 2$	$5! = 5 \times 4 \times 3 \times 2 \times 1 = 120$
$3! = 3 \times 2 \times 1 = 6$	$6! = 6 \times 5 \times 4 \times 3 \times 2 \times 1 = 720$

For example, how many ways are there to arrange four people in four chairs in a row? Using the **slot method**, there is one slot for each position in the row. If you place any one of four people in the first chair, then you can place any one of the remaining three people in the second chair. For the third and fourth chairs you have two choices and then one choice.

$$\underline{\quad 4 \quad} \times \underline{\quad 3 \quad} \times \underline{\quad 2 \quad} \times \underline{\quad 1 \quad} = 24 \text{ arrangements}$$

If you know how to think that through, you can just say, "The number of ways to arrange four people equals 4 factorial, which equals 24."

Arranging Groups Using the Anagram Grid

How many arrangements are there of the letters in the word EEL?

There are three letters, so according to the factorial formula, there should be $3! = 6$ arrangements, as follows (the two E's have subscripts to keep them straight):

E_1E_2L	E_1LE_2	LE_1E_2
E_2E_1L	E_2LE_1	LE_2E_1

The two arrangements in each column are considered identical. For example, E_1E_2L is the same thing as E_2E_1L; they're both EEL. There are really only three distinct arrangements:

EEL ELE LEE

Sometimes, you have to divide out a subset of the possible arrangements because they are identical to others in the set.

Here's how that would play out on a more GMAT-like problem:

> Seven people enter a race. There are 4 types of medals given as prizes for completing the race. The winner gets a platinum medal, the runner-up gets a gold medal, the next 2 racers each get a silver medal, and the last 3 racers all get bronze medals. What is the number of different ways the medals can be awarded?

In order to keep track of all the different categories, create an **anagram grid**. Anagram grids can be used whenever you are arranging members of a group.

The number of columns in the grid will always be equal to the number of members of the group. There are 7 runners in the race, so make 7 columns (labeled 1 through 7). Next, categorize each member of the group. There are 1 platinum medal, 1 gold medal, 2 silver medals, and 3 bronze medals. Note: Use only letters for the bottom row, never numbers (you'll see why in a minute).

1	2	3	4	5	6	7
P	G	S	S	B	B	B

Just as the two E's in EEL were indistinguishable, the 2 silver medals and the 3 bronze medals are indistinguishable, so 7! is not the answer. Use the top and bottom rows to create a fraction:

$$\frac{\text{Top row}}{\text{Bottom row}} = \frac{7!}{1!1!2!3!}$$

The numerator of the fraction is always the factorial of the largest number in the top row (in this case, 7!). The denominator is the product of the factorials of each *different* kind of letter in the bottom row. In this case, there are one P, one G, two S's, and three B's. (Use only letters in the bottom row to avoid mixing up the number of repeats with the numbers themselves.)

The bottom row of the fraction shows the 1! terms for both P and G, but in practice, you don't have to write out any 1! terms, since they don't make a difference to the calculation. As you simplify the fraction, look for ways to cancel out numbers in the denominator with numbers in the numerator:

$$\frac{7!}{2!3!} = \frac{7\times6\times5\times\overset{2}{\cancel{4}}\times\cancel{3!}}{{}_1\cancel{2}\times1\times\cancel{3!}} = 7\times6\times5\times2 = 420$$

Try another problem:

> A local card club will send 3 representatives to the national conference. If the local club has 8 members, how many different groups of representatives could the club send?

The problem talks about 8 members, so draw 8 columns for the anagram grid. There are 3 representatives chosen; represent them with Y. Use N to represent the 5 members of the group who are not chosen.

1	2	3	4	5	6	7	8
Y	Y	Y	N	N	N	N	N

Set up your fraction:

$$\frac{8!}{3!5!} = \frac{8\times7\times\cancel{6}\times\cancel{5!}}{(\cancel{3}\times\cancel{2}\times1)\cancel{5!}} = 8\times7 = 56$$

On the top of the fraction, only write out the numbers down to the largest factorial that also appears on the bottom of the fraction. In the fraction above, you can cancel out the two 5! terms without having to write them out.

Multiple Groups

So far, the discussion has revolved around two main themes: (1) making decisions and (2) arranging groups. More difficult combinatorics problems will actually combine the two topics. In other words, you may have to make multiple decisions, each of which will involve arranging different groups.

Try the following problem:

> The I Eta Pi fraternity must choose a delegation of 3 senior members and 2 junior members for an annual interfraternity conference. If I Eta Pi has 6 senior members and 5 junior members, how many different delegations are possible?

First, note that you are choosing senior members AND junior members. These are different decisions, so determine each separately and then multiply the possible arrangements.

You have to pick 3 seniors out of a group of 6. That means that 3 are chosen (and identical) and the remaining 3 are not chosen (and also identical):

$$\frac{6!}{3!3!} = \frac{\cancel{6} \times 5 \times 4 \times \cancel{3!}}{(\cancel{3} \times \cancel{2} \times 1)\cancel{3!}} = 5 \times 4 = 20$$

Similarly, pick 2 juniors out of a group of 5, where 2 members are chosen (and identical) and the remaining 3 members are not chosen (and also identical):

$$\frac{5!}{2!3!} = \frac{5 \times \overset{2}{\cancel{4}} \times \cancel{3!}}{({}_{1}\cancel{2} \times 1)\cancel{3!}} = 5 \times 2 = 10$$

There are 20 possible senior delegations AND 10 possible junior delegations. Since *AND* means *multiply*, there are $20 \times 10 = 200$ possible delegations.

Problems will not always make it clear that you are dealing with multiple decisions. Try the following problem:

> The yearbook committee has to pick a color scheme for this year's yearbook. There are 7 colors to choose from (red, orange, yellow, green, blue, indigo, and violet). How many different color schemes are possible if the committee can select at most 2 colors?

Although this question concerns only one group (colors), it also involves multiple decisions. The question states there can be *at most* 2 colors chosen. In other words, the color scheme can contain 1 color OR 2 colors. 28

Figure out how many combinations are possible if 1 color is chosen, as well as how many are possible if 2 colors are chosen, and then add them together:

$$\text{1 color chosen and 6 colors not chosen} = \frac{7!}{1!6!} = 7$$

$$\text{2 colors chosen and 5 colors not chosen} = \frac{7!}{2!5!} = 21$$

Together, there are $7 + 21 = 28$ possible color schemes.

Problem Set

Now that you've finished the chapter, try the following problems.

1. In how many different ways can the letters in the word *LEVEL* be arranged?

2. A company makes 5 different types of truffles. If one package contains exactly 2 truffles of different types, how may different combinations are possible?

Save the following problems for review after you finish this entire guide.

3. A pod of 6 dolphins always swims single file, with 3 females at the front and 3 males in the rear. In how many different arrangements can the dolphins swim?

4. Mario's Pizza offers a choice of 2 types of crust, 2 types of cheese, and 5 different types of vegetables. If Linda's volleyball team decides to order a pizza with 4 types of vegetables, how many different choices do the teammates have at Mario's Pizza?

5. What is the sum of all the possible three-digit numbers that can be constructed using the digits 3, 4, and 5 if each digit can be used only once in each number?

Answers and explanations follow on the next page. ▶ ▶ ▶

Solutions

1. **30 ways:** There are two repeated E's and two repeated L's in the word *LEVEL*. To find the number of ways this word can be arranged, set up a fraction in which the numerator is the factorial of the number of letters and the denominator is the factorial of the number of each repeated letter:

$$\frac{5!}{2!2!} = \frac{5 \times \overset{2}{\cancel{4}} \times 3 \times \cancel{2!}}{\cancel{2} \times 1 \times \cancel{2!}} = 5 \times 2 \times 3 = 30$$

Alternatively, you can solve this problem using the slot method, as long as you correct for over-counting (since there are some identical elements). There are five choices for the first letter, four for the second, and so on, making the product $5 \times 4 \times 3 \times 2 \times 1 = 120$. However, there are two sets of two indistinguishable elements each, so you must divide by 2! to account for each of these. Thus, the total number of combinations is as shown in the calculation above.

2. **10:** In every combination, 2 types of truffles will be in the package and 3 types of truffles will not. Therefore, this problem is a question about the number of anagrams that can be made from the "word" YYNNN:

1	2	3	4	5
Y	Y	N	N	N

$$\frac{5!}{2!3!} = \frac{5 \times \overset{2}{\cancel{4}} \times \cancel{3!}}{\cancel{2} \times \cancel{3!}} = 5 \times 2 = 10$$

3. **36:** This is a multiple arrangements problem, in which you have two separate pools (females AND males). There are 3! ways in which the 3 females can swim. There are 3! ways in which the 3 males can swim. Therefore, there are $3! \times 3!$ ways in which the entire pod can swim:

$$3! \times 3! = 6 \times 6 = 36$$

4. **20 choices:** Consider the vegetables first. Model them with the "word" YYYYN, in which four of the types are on the pizza and one is not. The number of anagrams for this "word" is in the table below:

1	2	3	4	5
Y	Y	Y	Y	N

$$\frac{5!}{4!} = 5$$

If each of these pizzas can also be offered in 2 choices of crust, there are $5 \times 2 = 10$ choices of pizza. The same logic applies for the cheese so there are $10 \times 2 = 20$ choices.

28

5. **2,664:** There are six ways in which to arrange these digits:

3	4	5
3	5	4
4	3	5
4	5	3
5	3	4
5	4	3

Notice that each digit appears twice in the hundreds column, twice in the tens column, and twice in the ones column. Use place value to find the sum. The sum of each digit in the hundreds column is $3 + 3 + 4 + 4 + 5 + 5 = 24$. Since this is the hundreds column, multiply this sum by 100 to get the sum of just the hundreds part of each number. Repeat this reasoning for the tens column and the ones column:

$$100(24) + 10(24) + 1(24) = 2,400 + 240 + 24 = 2,664$$

CHAPTER 29

Probability

In This Chapter

- Calculate the Numerator and Denominator Separately
- More Than One Event: AND vs. OR
- P(A) + P(Not A) = 1
- The 1 – x Probability Trick

In this chapter, you will learn how to set up and solve probability problems for both single and multiple events. You'll also learn a very useful shortcut for tackling multi-part probabilities: calculating the probability of the outcome that you *don't* want (otherwise known as the $1 - x$ trick).

CHAPTER 29 Probability

Probability is a quantity that expresses the chance, or likelihood, of an event.

Think of probability as a fraction:

$$\text{Probability} = \frac{\text{Number of } \textit{desired} \text{ or } \textit{successful} \text{ outcomes}}{\text{Total number of } \textit{possible} \text{ outcomes}}$$

For instance, if you flip a coin (one side heads, the other tails), what is the probability that heads turns up? There are two possible outcomes (heads or tails), but only one of them is considered desirable (heads), so the probability is $\frac{1}{2}$.

Notice that the numerator of the fraction is *always* a subset of the denominator. If there are n possible outcomes, then the number of desirable outcomes must be between 0 and n (the number of outcomes cannot be negative). As a result, *any probability will be between 0 and 1.*

An impossible event has a probability of 0 when the desired outcome cannot happen. For example, if you flip a coin (one side heads, the other tails), what is the probability that a dragon turns up? There are no dragons on the coin, so $\frac{0}{2} = 0$. By contrast, a certain event has a probability of 1 when the number of desired outcomes is equal to the number of possible outcomes. If you flip a coin (heads or tails), what is the probability that either heads or tails turns up? $\frac{2}{2} = 1$. Those are the only two possible outcomes.

Additionally, probability can be expressed as a fraction, a decimal, or a percent. For example, $\frac{3}{4} = 0.75 = 75\%$. Depending on the problem, you can solve in any one of these forms; sometimes, you'll need to use the percent form in order to think about the number of desired outcomes and the number of possible outcomes.

Calculate the Numerator and Denominator Separately

Numerators and denominators of probabilities are related, but they must be calculated separately. Often, it will be easier to begin by calculating the denominator.

There are two ways to calculate a number of outcomes for either the numerator or the denominator:

1. Manually count the number of outcomes (if there aren't that many).
2. Use an appropriate combinatorics formula. These problems tend to be harder; if you dislike probability, you may decide to bail immediately on these kinds of problems (as there aren't typically that many on the test).

Try the following problem:

> Two number cubes with faces numbered 1 to 6 are rolled. What is the probability that the sum of the rolls is 8 ?

Start with the total number of possible outcomes (the denominator). For this calculation, you can use combinatorics. Notice that rolling two number cubes is like rolling cube 1 AND rolling cube 2. For each of these rolls, there are six possible outcomes (the numbers 1 to 6). Since AND equals multiply, there are $6 \times 6 = 36$ possible outcomes. This is the denominator of the fraction.

Next, figure out how many of those 36 possible rolls represent the desired outcome (a sum of 8). It would be complicated to come up with an appropriate combinatorics formula—and not worth the time it would take because only a limited number of combinations would work. Count them up! If the first cube turns up a 1, the other cube would need to roll a 7. This isn't possible, so eliminate that possibility. Keep counting; here are the rolls that work, in order (first roll and second roll):

2 and 6   3 and 5   4 and 4   5 and 3   6 and 2

You do actually need to include the final two in that list; a roll of 3 and then 5 is a different outcome than a roll of 5 and then 3 because both of those outcomes were counted separately in the 6×6 calculation.

There are 5 combinations that work, so the probability of a sum of 8 is $\frac{5}{36}$.

More Than One Event: AND vs. OR

Combinatorics and probability have another connection: the meaning of the words *AND* and *OR*. In probability, as well as in combinatorics, the word *AND* means multiply and the word *OR* means add. Try this example:

> There is a $\frac{1}{2}$ probability that a certain coin will turn up heads on any given toss. What is the probability that two tosses of the coin will yield heads both times?

To answer this question, calculate the probability that the coin lands on heads on the first flip AND heads on the second flip. The probability of heads on the first flip is $\frac{1}{2}$. The probability of heads on the second flip is also $\frac{1}{2}$. Since AND means multiply, the probability is $\frac{1}{2} \times \frac{1}{2} = \frac{1}{4}$.

Try another example:

> The weather report for today states that there is a 40% chance of sun, a 25% chance of rain, and a 35% chance of hail. Assuming only one of the three outcomes can happen, what is the probability that it rains or hails today?

The question is asking for the probability of rain OR hail. Therefore, the probability is $25\% + 35\% = 60\%$. The calculation would change if *both* rain and hail can happen, but don't worry about that for now.

P(A) + P(Not A) = 1

29

P(A) + P(Not A) = 1 is a fancy way of saying that the probability of something happening plus the probability of that thing *not* happening must sum to 1. For example, the probability that it either rains or does not rain is equal to 1: If there's a 25% chance of rain, then there must be a 75% chance that it will *not* rain. Try an example:

> A person has a 40% chance of winning a game every time he or she plays it. If there are no ties, what is the probability that Asha loses the first game played and wins the second game?

If the probability of winning the game is 40%, then the odds of *not* winning the game (losing) are $100\% - 40\% = 60\%$. Calculate the odds that Asha loses the game the first time AND wins the game the second time:

$$(60\%) \times (40\%) = 0.6 \times 0.4 = 0.24$$

The probability is 0.24, or 24%.

The 1 - *x* Probability Trick

Suppose that a salesperson makes 5 sales calls, and you want to find the likelihood that he or she makes *at least 1* sale. If you try to calculate this probability directly, you will have to confront 5 separate possibilities that constitute "success": exactly 1 sale, exactly 2 sales, exactly 3 sales, exactly 4 sales, or exactly 5 sales. This would almost certainly be more work than you can reasonably do in two minutes.

There is, however, another option. Instead of calculating the probability that the salesperson makes at least 1 sale, you can calculate the probability that the salesperson does *not* make at least 1 sale.

$$\begin{aligned} \text{Prob of at least 1 sale} + \text{prob of 0 sales} &= 1 \\ P(\geq 1) \quad + \quad P(0) &= 1 \\ P(\geq 1) &= 1 - P(0) \end{aligned}$$

These two outcomes (at least 1 sale or 0 sales) make up all of the possible outcomes. So if you know the probability of making 0 sales, you can subtract that from 1 to find the probability of making at least 1 sale. This is the **1 - *x* shortcut.**

Calculating just a single probability and subtracting from 1 is a lot faster than calculating 5 probabilities and adding them up. When a probability problem sets up an *at least* or *at most* scenario, look for this 1 - *x* shortcut.

For complicated probability problems, decide whether it is easier to calculate the probability you want or the probability you do *not* want. On the GMAT, most of the time, it will be faster to calculate the probability that the problem did not ask for. Try an example:

> A bag contains equal numbers of red, green, and yellow marbles. If Gurdeep pulls three marbles out of the bag, replacing each marble after picking it, what is the probability that at least one will be red?

Since the question asks whether at least one will be red, there are three possible cases to calculate: one red, two red, or three red. Instead, calculate the probability that *none* of the marbles are red. Each time Gurdeep picks a marble, there is a $\frac{2}{3}$ probability that the marble will *not* be red. The probability that all three marbles will not be red is $\frac{2}{3} \times \frac{2}{3} \times \frac{2}{3} = \frac{8}{27}$.

If the probability that *none* of the marbles is red is $\frac{8}{27}$, then the probability that at least one marble is red is $1 - \frac{8}{27} = \frac{19}{27}$.

If you need to calculate the probability of an event (P(A)), there are two ways to calculate the probability:

$$\text{P(A)} \qquad \text{or} \qquad 1 - \text{P(Not A)}$$

When the question includes *at least* or *at most* language, the 1 - P(Not A) method is usually faster.

Advanced material for the Number Properties unit (primarily covering additional strategies for divisibility and primes, combinatorics, and probability) can be found in Atlas, Manhattan Prep's online learning platform. Use the online material only if you feel that you have mastered everything in the Number Properties unit of this strategy guide and only if you are aiming for a Quant section score of 48 or higher.

Problem Set

Now that you've finished the chapter, try the following problems. For problems 1 and 2, assume that each number cube has six sides with faces numbered 1 to 6.

1. Two number cubes are rolled. What is the probability that the sum of the two numbers will yield a 10 or lower?

2. What is the probability that the sum of two number cubes will yield a 7 on their first roll, and then when both are rolled again, their sum will again yield a 7 ?

Save the remaining problems for review after you finish this entire guide.

3. On the planned day of a picnic, there is a 30% chance of rain. If it rains, there is a 50% chance that the picnic will be canceled, but if it doesn't rain, the picnic will take place. What is the chance that the picnic will take place?

4. In a diving competition, each diver has a 20% chance of a perfect dive. The first perfect dive of the competition, but no subsequent dives, will receive a perfect score. What are the chances that the third diver will receive a perfect score on that dive? (Assume that each diver can perform only one dive.)

5. A magician has five animals in a magic hat: 3 doves and 2 rabbits. If the magician pulls two animals out of the hat at random, what is the chance that the two will be the same type of animal?

Answers and explanations follow on the next page. ▶ ▶ ▶

Solutions

1. $\frac{11}{12}$**:** There are a total of $6 \times 6 = 36$ possible outcomes. There are many possible ways to get the desired outcome of a sum of 10 or lower. Solve this problem by calculating the probability that the sum will be *higher* than 10 and subtracting that probability from 1. There are three combinations of two number cubes that yield a sum higher than 10: $5 + 6$, $6 + 5$, and $6 + 6$. Therefore, the probability that the sum will be higher than 10 is $\frac{3}{36}$, or $\frac{1}{12}$. The probability that the sum will be 10 or lower is $1 - \frac{1}{12} = \frac{11}{12}$.

2. $\frac{1}{36}$**:** There are 36 ways in which two number cubes can be thrown ($6 \times 6 = 36$). The combinations that yield a sum of 7 are $1 + 6$, $2 + 5$, $3 + 4$, $4 + 3$, $5 + 2$, and $6 + 1$, or six different combinations. Therefore, the probability of rolling a 7 is $\frac{6}{36}$, or $\frac{1}{6}$. To find the probability that this will happen twice in a row (an outcome of 7 AND 7), multiply: $\frac{1}{6} \times \frac{1}{6} = \frac{1}{36}$.

3. **85%:** There are two possible ways in which the picnic can take place:

   1. It doesn't rain: $P = 70\%$ OR
   2. It rains AND the picnic is held anyway:

   $$P = 30\%\left(\frac{1}{2}\right) = 15\%$$

   Add the probabilities together to find the total probability that the picnic will take place:

   $$70\% + 15\% = 85\%$$

4. $\frac{16}{125}$**:** In order for the third diver to receive a perfect score, neither of the previous two divers can receive one. Therefore, you are finding the probability of a chain of three events: that diver one will *not* get a perfect score AND diver two will *not* get a perfect score AND diver three *will* get a perfect score. Multiply the probabilities:

   $$\frac{4}{5} \times \frac{4}{5} \times \frac{1}{5} = \frac{16}{125}.$$

   The probability is $\frac{16}{125}$ that the third diver will receive a perfect score.

5. $\frac{4}{10}$ **or 40%:** Use an anagram model to determine the total number of different pairs the magician can pull out of the hat. Since two animals will be in the pair and the other three will not, use the "word" YYNNN.

A	B	C	D	E
Y	Y	N	N	N

$$\frac{5!}{2!3!} = \frac{5 \times 4}{2 \times 1} = 10$$

Thus, there are 10 possible pairs; this is the bottom of the probability fraction.

29

Then, list the pairs in which the animals will match. Represent the rabbits with the subscript letters *a* and *b*, and the doves with the letters *x*, *y*, and *z*.

Matched Pairs:	$R_a\ R_b$	$D_x\ D_y$	There are four pairs in which the animals will be a matched set: one way in which the rabbits can be chosen and three ways in which the doves can be chosen.
	$D_x\ D_z$	$D_y\ D_z$	

Therefore, the probability that the magician will randomly draw a matched set is $\frac{4}{10} = 40\%$.

UNIT FIVE

Geometry

In this unit, you will learn all of the geometry topics you need to know for the GMAT, including line and angle rules; definitions, formulas, and rules for polygons, triangles, and circles; and various rules associated with coordinate planes. You'll also find a cheat sheet at the end of this unit containing all of the major geometry rules and formulas on a single page. Feel free to tear it out of the book (or photocopy it) to have handy during your studies.

In This Unit

- Chapter 30: Geometry Strategy
- Chapter 31: Lines and Angles
- Chapter 32: Polygons
- Chapter 33: Triangles and Diagonals
- Chapter 34: Circles and Cylinders
- Chapter 35: Coordinate Plane

CHAPTER 30

Geometry Strategy

In This Chapter

- The Three Principles
- Understand–Plan–Solve
- Estimation

In this chapter, you will learn how to adapt the Understand–Plan–Solve process for geometry problems in particular and you'll learn how to estimate on geometry problems.

CHAPTER 30 Geometry Strategy

Before diving into the rules and formulas, take a few minutes to learn some important guidelines that will help you approach every geometry problem you will do on the GMAT.

The Three Principles

Use three general principles to succeed on geometry problems:

1. **If they don't tell you, don't assume.**

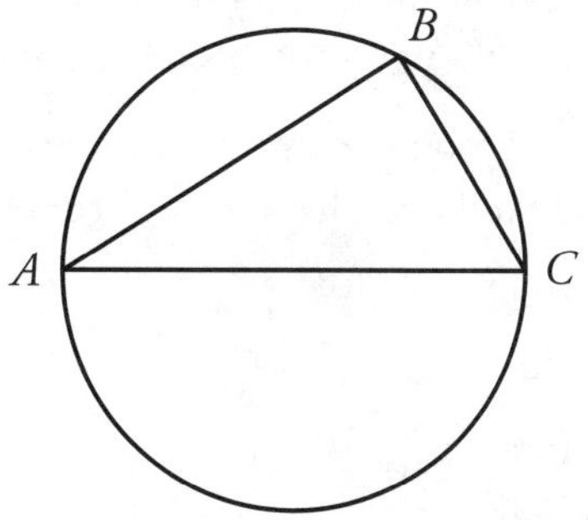

Points *A*, *B*, and *C* lie on the circle and form a triangle. Is line segment *AC* a diameter of the circle?

In the figure above, line segment *AC* does look like a diameter of the circle, but it could be just slightly off and not a diameter at all. Don't make any assumptions; just *looking* like a diameter doesn't make *AC* a diameter on the GMAT.

> **Vocab Lesson:** When a triangle lies inside a circle and the "points" (or *vertices*) of a triangle touch the circle, then the triangle is said to be *inscribed* in the circle.

2. If they give you a piece of information, use it.

Line segment *AC* passes through the center of the circle.

What can you infer from that piece of information?

If a line segment passes from one side to the other of a circle through the center, then that line segment must be a diameter of the circle. Now, you've got a connection between the triangle and the circle: The longest side of the triangle is also a diameter of the circle.

How does that help? Read on—but note that, any time you're given multiple shapes, the trick to solving the problem usually revolves around finding connections between those shapes.

3. Know your rules and formulas.

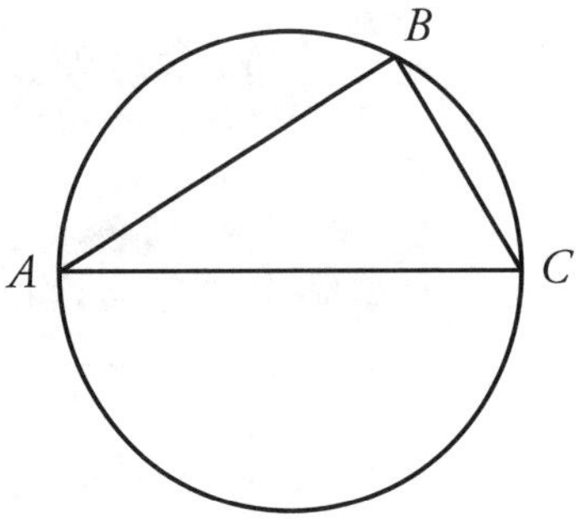

Rule:
If one of the sides of a triangle inscribed in a circle is a diameter of the circle, then the triangle must be a right triangle.

If you inscribe a triangle in a circle (as in the figure shown above), and one side of that triangle is also a diameter of the circle, then the opposite angle (angle *B* in this diagram) has to be a right angle. It doesn't matter where you place *B* on the circle; it will still be a right angle. (Well, if you place *B* right on *A* or *C*, then *B* won't be a right angle. In that case, though, *ABC* also won't be a triangle!)

In short, it is not enough just to memorize a bunch of rules. The test writers are going to "cut up" the rules and give them to you in pieces. You need to know the rules well enough that you can put those pieces back together.

To recap:

1. If they don't tell you, don't assume.
2. If they give you a piece of information, use it.
3. Know your rules and formulas.

One last thing: It turns out, thankfully, that there are a few small things you *can* take for granted on GMAT Geometry.

If the problem describes a shape as a triangle, then it really is a triangle. If the problem discusses a line, then you really do have a 180° straight line. If lines look as if they touch, they do. In other words, you can take the test at its word—it will use the word *line* in the official geometry sense—but you can't add in any extra assumptions.

If the GMAT gives you a figure or number line with points, you can assume that the points will always be in the order shown in the diagram. For instance, consider the figure below:

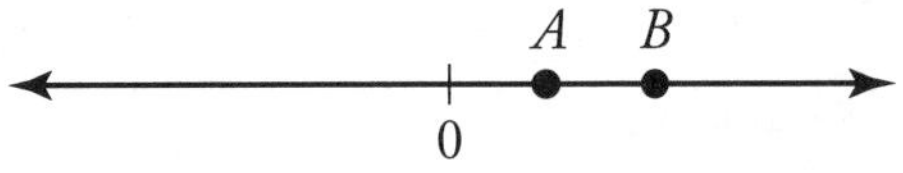

You can trust that both *A* and *B* are positive (because both are shown to the right of 0) and that *B* is greater than *A* (because *B* is to the right of *A*).

30

Figures on Problem Solving questions will be drawn to scale unless noted. Figures on Data Sufficiency questions, however, are *not* necessarily drawn to scale (and they will *not* be noted accordingly). You can still trust that lines are lines and that intersecting lines or shapes actually do intersect, including the relative positions of points, angles, and regions.

Understand–Plan–Solve

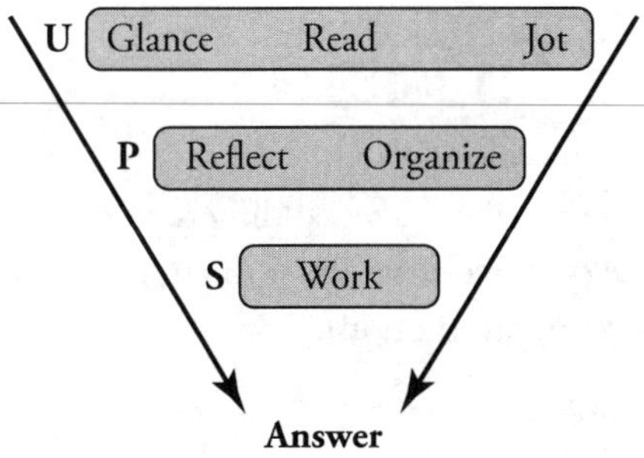

As with all other Quant problems, use the Understand–Plan–Solve approach. This will include some special steps for geometry problems.

1. Understand

If the problem mentions something for which you know a formula (e.g., the area of a circle), write down the formula. If the problem gives you a figure, redraw it on your scrap paper. If a geometry problem doesn't give you a figure, draw one anyway.

You have graph paper, so make the figure decently precise. Don't waste time or space, of course, but make the figure big enough that you can see what you're doing and accurate enough to prevent careless mistakes. For instance, if you know one side of a triangle is longer than another, draw the figure so that the longer side *looks* longer.

Finally, mark clearly what you're trying to find. Perhaps the question asks you to find the measure of angle x, which has already been labeled on the figure. Put a symbol, such as a star, next to the x to remind yourself that this is your goal. (You can use any symbol you want, as long as you use the same symbol consistently and as long as you use a symbol that will never be used by the test writers themselves.)

Perhaps the question asks you to find the perimeter of a rectangle. It would be tough to show that on the figure, so instead, write the formula for perimeter and put a star next to the P:

$$\star P = 2l + 2w$$

Alternatively, write something like:

$$P = \_\_\_\_\_ ?$$

2. Plan

Are there overlapping shapes? Think about the connections between the shapes during your Plan phase.

The givens, or starting information, will allow you to infer certain other things that must be true. Are there multiple directions in which you could start to infer new information from the givens? Take a little time to think about which path looks most efficient to get you to your goal.

30

Not sure what to do first? That's okay. Go ahead and infer two or three things, even if you're not sure yet how that might help to get you to the answer. (If you can't find anything to infer, now might be a good time to guess and move on.)

3. Solve

As you proceed through the rest of the problem, keep adding to your drawing. Every time you infer something new, write or draw it in. (Make sure, when you first draw the figure, that you give yourself enough space to draw and write additional information on it!)

Try out the 3-step process on this problem:

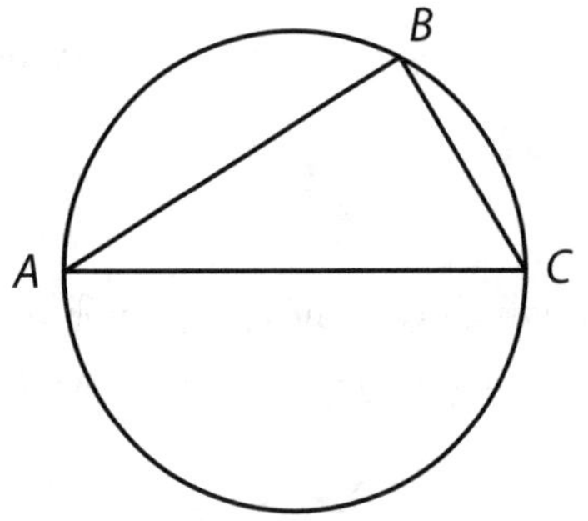

Triangle *ABC* is inscribed in the circle and line segment *AC* passes through the center of the circle. If the length of line segment *AB* is 3 and the length of line segment *AC* is 5, then what is the length of line segment *BC* ?

(A) 2
(B) 3
(C) 4
(D) 6
(E) 8

Understand. Draw the figure on your scratch paper and add the given lengths. Mark the wanted information, line segment *BC*.

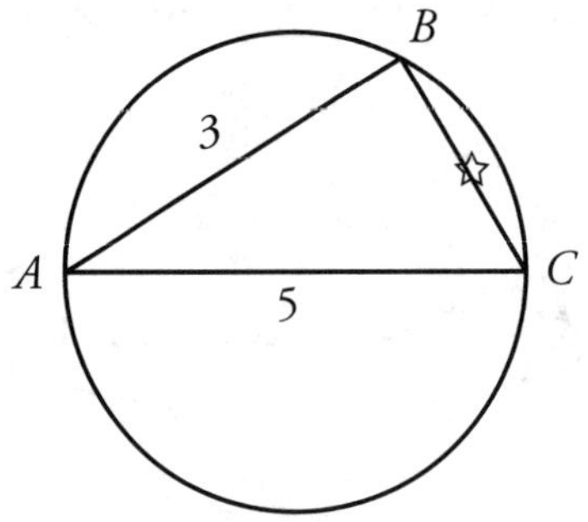

Plan. They want the length of *BC*. There are two overlapping shapes; what's the connection between the shapes? The diameter *AC* is also the hypotenuse of the triangle. What does that mean?

30

Solve. Given that AC is a diameter, ABC must be a right triangle and angle B must be the right angle. Great! You can use the Pythagorean theorem to solve:

$$a^2 + b^2 = c^2$$
$$3^2 + b^2 = 5^2$$
$$9 + b^2 = 25$$
$$b^2 = 16$$
$$b = 4$$

The correct answer is (C).

Don't worry if you've completely forgotten about the Pythagorean theorem or any of the other math needed to answer this question. You'll relearn how to do it all while working through this section of the guide.

Estimation

You can estimate your way to an answer on problems with certain characteristics; this technique is often helpful on geometry problems in particular.

First, it's important that the problem gives you either a figure drawn to scale or enough information to draw a figure reasonably to scale yourself. Remember that your scrap paper will be graph paper, so you can draw right angles, squares, and other dimensions reasonably accurately.

Second, the answers need to be spread far enough apart that estimating an answer will still keep you in the range of the one correct answer.

For instance, say you are given these answer choices:

(A) 25°
(B) 45°
(C) 60°
(D) 90°
(E) 110°

You might not know how to calculate the correct answer, but you might be able to tell, for example, that the desired angle is less than 90°, which will eliminate (D) and (E). Alternatively, you might be able to tell that the answer is close to 90°, allowing you to chop out (A) and (B) and possibly (C).

Try this problem, inspired by one from *The GMAT Official Guide*:

A square has a 10-centimeter diagonal. What is the area of the square, in square centimeters?

(A) 50
(B) 64
(C) 100
(D) 144
(E) 200

First, draw a square on your scrap paper. Remember, you'll have graph paper, so you can make a true square. Draw a diagonal and label it 10:

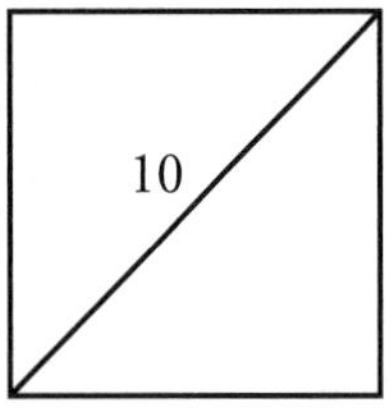

First, if the diagonal is 10, then the length of one side must be less than 10.

Next, the area of a square is s^2, where s is the length of one side. If the length of a side were 10, then the area would be 10^2, which equals 100. But the length is less than 10, so the area must also be less than 100. Eliminate answers (C), (D), and (E). There are only two answers left!

You might be thinking, That's too good to be true. . .the real test won't do that. It does; as noted, this problem and set of answer choices were inspired by a real question that was published by the makers of the GMAT.

You might also be thinking: I can just do the math, so why would I need to estimate to make a guess?

There are two reasons. First, you learn how to do harder problems by practicing your skills on easier ones, so even if you find this problem easy, learning how to estimate here will help you to do so on harder ones that you can't do the "textbook" way.

Second, you can use the rough estimation to check your work. Say that you made a calculation error and called the length of one side $10\sqrt{2}$. (There is a specific reason why someone might be susceptible to that particular mistake. If you're not sure what it is, look at this problem again after you've studied the Triangles and Diagonals chapter.)

If you accidentally call one side $10\sqrt{2}$, then you're going to calculate the area as 200, which is answer (E). If you then double-check your work via estimation, you'll realize that 200 is too big.

Advanced material for the Geometry unit can be found in Atlas, Manhattan Prep's online learning platform. Use the online material only if you feel that you have mastered everything in the Geometry unit of this strategy guide and only if you are aiming for a Quant section score of 48 or higher.

Problem Set

If you think you remember some (or many!) geometry rules, use this problem set as a diagnostic quiz to see where you need to review. On the other hand, if you've totally forgotten all of your geometry rules, skip this set for now and come back to the problems after working through the relevant chapters in this book.

1. If the length of an edge of cube A is one-third the length of an edge of cube B, what is the ratio of the volume of cube A to the volume of cube B ?

2. 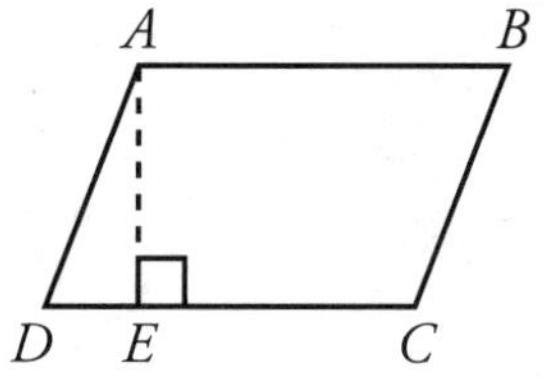

In the figure shown above, *ABCD* is a parallelogram. The ratio of *DE* to *EC* is 1 : 3. Height *AE* has a length of 3. If quadrilateral *ABCE* has an area of 21, what is the area of *ABCD* ?

3. 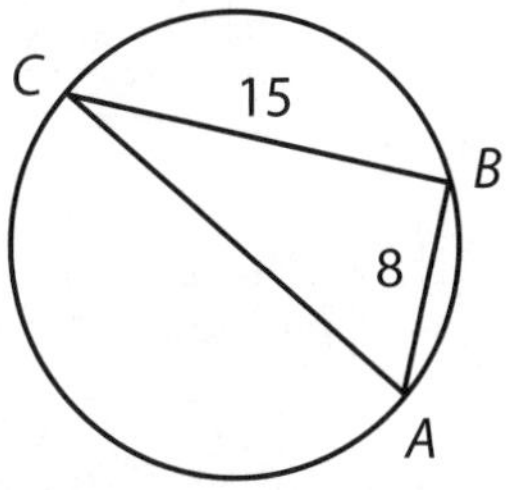

In the figure shown above, triangle *ABC* is inscribed in a circle, such that *AC* is a diameter of the circle. If line segment *AB* has a length of 8 and line segment *BC* has a length of 15, what is the circumference of the circle?

4. 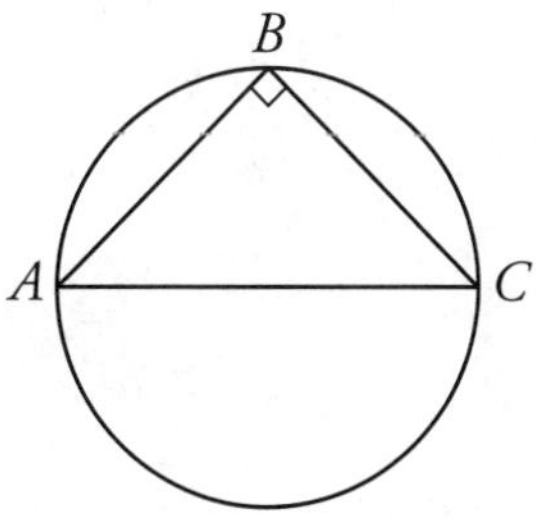

As shown in the figure, triangle *ABC* is inscribed in a circle. Line segment *AC* is a diameter of the circle and angle *BAC* is 45°. If the area of triangle *ABC* is 72 square units, how much larger is the area of the circle than the area of triangle *ABC* ?

5. 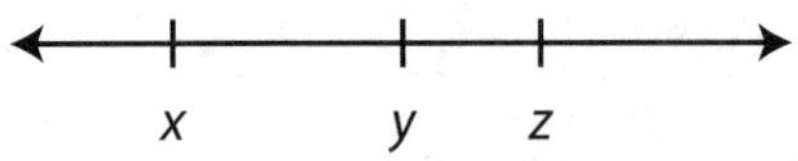

On the number line shown above, is $xy < 0$?

(1) Zero is to the left of y on the number line above.

(2) xy and yz have opposite signs.

6. 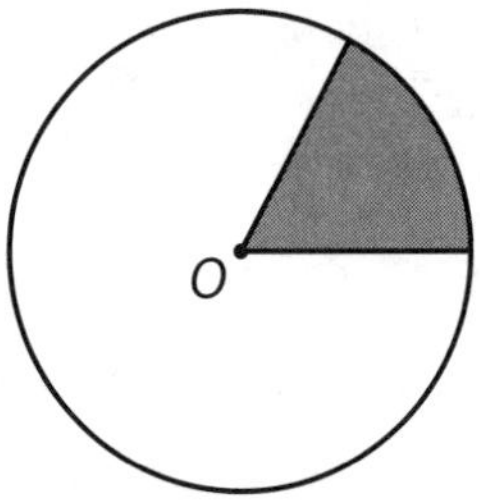

In the figure shown above, O represents the center of a circular 60-minute timer. If the minute-hand moves through the shaded region shown, does the shaded region represent more than 10 minutes on the timer?

(1) The minute-hand has a length of 10.

(2) The area of the sector is greater than 16π.

7. The side of an equilateral triangle has the same length as the diagonal of a square. What is the area of the square?

(1) The height of the equilateral triangle is equal to $6\sqrt{3}$.

(2) The area of the equilateral triangle is equal to $36\sqrt{3}$.

8. 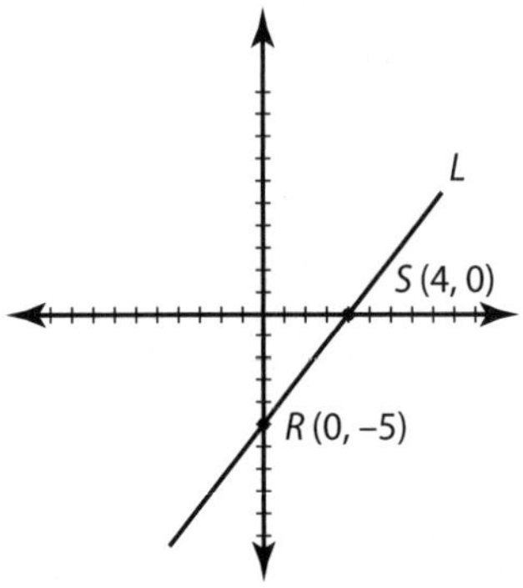

Line L passes through points R (0, –5) and S (4, 0) in the figure shown. Point P with coordinates (x, y) is a point on line L and does not overlap with points R or S. Is $xy > 0$?

(1) $x > 4$

(2) $y > -5$

Solutions

1. **1 to 27:** There are no specified amounts in this question, so pick numbers. Let cube A have sides of length 1 and cube B have sides of length 3:

$$\text{Volume of cube A} = 1 \times 1 \times 1 = 1$$
$$\text{Volume of cube B} = 3 \times 3 \times 3 = 27$$

Therefore, the ratio of the volume of cube A to the volume of cube B is $\frac{1}{27}$, or 1 : 27.

2. **24:** First, label the lengths with the given ratio and break quadrilateral *ABCE* into two pieces: a 3 by $3x$ rectangle and a right triangle with a base of x and a height of 3. Add the area of each shape to get the area of quadrilateral *ABCE*:

$$(3 \times 3x) + \frac{3 \times x}{2} = 9x + 1.5x = 10.5x$$

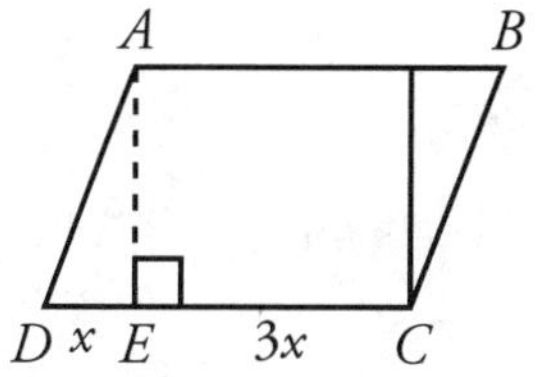

If *ABCE* has an area of 21, then $21 = 10.5x$, which reduces to $x = 2$. Quadrilateral *ABCD* is a parallelogram, so use the formula for area: Area = Base × Height, or $4x \times 3$. Substitute the known value of 2 for x and simplify:

$$A = 4(2) \times 3 = 24$$

3. **17π:** If line segment *AC* is a diameter of the circle, then inscribed triangle *ABC* is a right triangle, with *AC* as the hypotenuse. Use the Pythagorean theorem to find the hypotenuse:

$$8^2 + 15^2 = c^2$$
$$64 + 225 = c^2$$
$$289 = c^2$$
$$c = 17$$

The 8–15–17 right triangle is also one of the "common" right triangles; if you have it memorized, then you don't have to use the Pythagorean theorem to find diameter *AC*.

The circumference of the circle is πd, or 17π.

4. **$72\pi - 72$:** Draw a picture. If AC is a diameter of the circle, then angle ABC is a right angle. Therefore, triangle ABC is a 45–45–90 triangle, and the base and the height are equal. Assign the variable x to represent both the base and height:

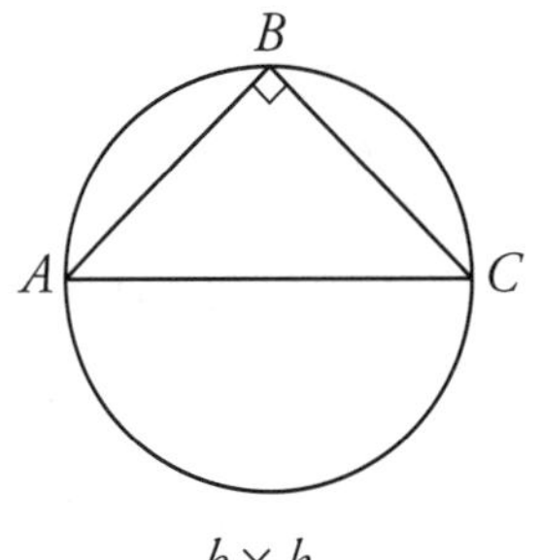

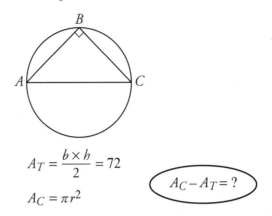

$$A_T = \frac{b \times h}{2} = 72$$

$$A_C = \pi r^2$$

$$A_C - A_T = ?$$

Use the formula for the area of a triangle to find the value of x:

$$A = \frac{bh}{2}$$

$$72 = \frac{(x)(x)}{2}$$

$$144 = x^2$$

$$x = 12$$

A 45–45–90 triangle's sides are always in the ratio $x : x : x\sqrt{2}$. Since the two legs are equal to 12, the hypotenuse, which is also the diameter of the circle, is $12\sqrt{2}$. Therefore, the radius is equal to $6\sqrt{2}$ and the area of the circle, πr^2, equals 72π. The area of the circle is $72\pi - 72$ square units larger than the area of triangle ABC.

5. **(C):** This is a Yes/No Data Sufficiency question. For xy to be negative, x and y need to have opposite signs.

On the number line shown, this would only happen if 0 falls between x and y. If 0 is to the left of x on the number line shown, both x and y would be positive, so $xy > 0$. If 0 is to the right of y on the number line shown, both x and y would be negative, so $xy > 0$. So the real question is: Does 0 fall between x and y on the number line?

(1) INSUFFICIENT: Test a couple of cases. If zero is to the left of y on the number line, zero could be between x and y. In that case, $xy < 0$ and the answer to the question is Yes. However, 0 could also be to the left of x. In that case, both x and y would be positive, so $xy > 0$ and the answer is No.

(2) INSUFFICIENT: The fact that xy and yz have opposite signs implies that one of the three variables has a different sign than the other two. If x, y, and z all have the same sign, xy and yz would have the same sign. Thus, this statement implies that 0 does not fall to the left of x (which would make all three variables, as well as xy and yz, positive) nor to the right of z (which would make all three variables negative and both xy and yz positive). The only two cases this statement allows are:

0 is between x and y: In this case, yz is positive and xy is negative, and the answer is Yes.

0 is between y and z: In this case, yz is negative and xy is positive, and the answer is No.

(1) AND (2) SUFFICIENT: Statement (1) restricts 0 to the left of y on the number line. This rules out one of the two cases allowed by statement (2), leaving only the case in which 0 is between x and y. Thus, xy is negative, and the answer is a definite Yes.

The correct answer is **(C)**: The two statements together are sufficient, but neither one works alone.

6. **(E):** This is a Yes/No Data Sufficiency question. The question "Does the shaded region represent more than 10 minutes on the timer?" is really asking about the area of a sector of a circle.

Since 10 minutes is $\frac{1}{6}$ of the total 60 minutes, the question is asking whether the shaded region is equal to more than $\frac{1}{6}$ of the area of the circle.

(1) INSUFFICIENT: The minute-hand is equal to the radius. If the radius is 10, the entire area of the circle is 100π. Is the area of the shaded region more than one-sixth of 100π? This statement doesn't provide any information about the size of the shaded region relative to the whole circle.

(2) INSUFFICIENT: The area of the *sector* is more than 16π, but no information is given as to the area of the whole circle.

(1) AND (2) INSUFFICIENT: The area of the entire circle is 100π, and the area of the sector is more than 16π. Is the area of the shaded region more than one-sixth of 100π? Find $\frac{1}{6}$ of 100π:

$$\frac{100\pi}{6} = \frac{50\pi}{3} = 16.\overline{6}\pi$$

Since $\frac{1}{6}$ of the area of the circle is actually $16.\overline{6}\pi$, knowing that the area of the sector is more than 16π is still insufficient—the area of the sector could be 16.1π or something much larger.

The correct answer is **(E)**: Both statements together are still not sufficient.

7. **(D):** Both equilateral triangles and squares are **regular figures**. Regular figures (squares, equilaterals, circles, spheres, cubes, 45–45–90 triangles, 30–60–90 triangles, and others) are those for which you only need one measurement to know *every* measurement. For instance, if you have the radius of a circle, you can get the diameter, circumference, and area. If you have a 45–45–90 or 30–60–90 triangle, you only need *one* side to get all three. In this problem, if you have the side of an equilateral triangle, you could get the height, area, and perimeter. If you have the side of a square, you could get the diagonal, area, and perimeter.

If you have *two* regular figures, as you do in this problem, and you know how they are related numerically (*the side of an equilateral triangle has the same length as the diagonal of a square*), then you can safely conclude that *any* measurement for *either* figure will give you *any* measurement for either figure.

The question can be rephrased: What is the value of any part of either figure?

(1) SUFFICIENT: This provides one length of the figure (the height of the triangle).

(2) SUFFICIENT: The area of the triangle can be used to find the length of one side of the triangle.

The correct answer is **(D)**: Each statement is sufficient by itself.

8. **(A):** This is a Yes/No question. Line L passes through three quadrants:

1. Quadrant I, where x and y are both positive, so $xy > 0$ and the answer is Yes.
2. Quadrant III, where x and y are both negative, so $xy > 0$ and the answer is Yes.
3. Quadrant IV, where x is positive and y is negative, so $xy < 0$ and the answer is No.

If you can determine what quadrant point P is in, you will have sufficient information to answer the question. Also, Quadrant I or Quadrant III both return a Yes answer, so knowing that point P is in either of those two quadrants (even if you don't know which one) would be sufficient.

(1) SUFFICIENT: If $x > 4$, then point P is in Quadrant I. As a result, Yes, $xy > 0$.

(2) INSUFFICIENT: If $y > -5$, then point P could be in either Quadrant I $(xy > 0)$ or Quadrant IV $(xy < 0)$.

The correct answer is **(A)**: Statement (1) alone works, but statement (2) does not.

CHAPTER 31

Lines and Angles

In This Chapter

- Intersecting Lines
- Parallel Lines Cut by a Transversal

In this chapter, you will learn the necessary fundamental properties of lines and angles, including for parallel lines.

CHAPTER 31 Lines and Angles

A straight line is the shortest distance between two points. As an angle, a line measures 180° as shown here:

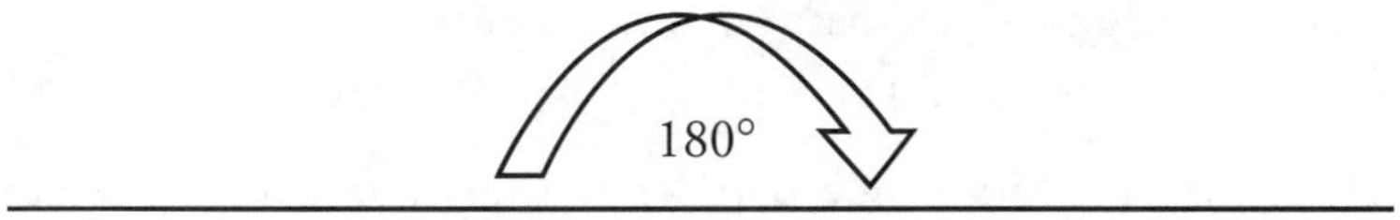

Parallel lines are lines that lie in a plane and that never intersect. No matter how far you extend the lines, they never meet:

Perpendicular lines are lines that intersect at a 90° angle. Two perpendicular lines are shown below:

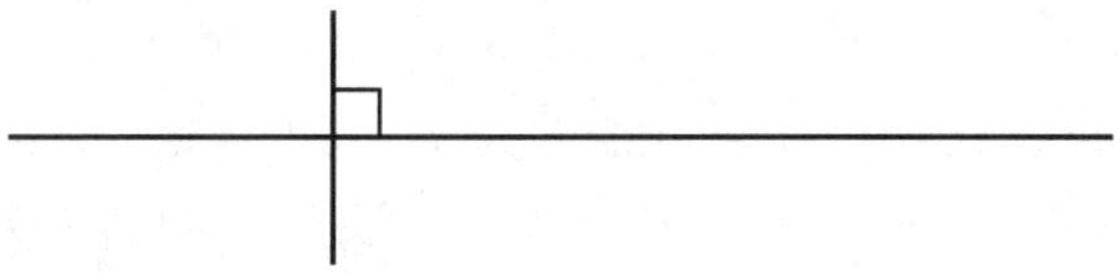

There are two major line–angle relationships to know for the GMAT. You'll learn about both in this chapter:

1. The angles formed by any intersecting lines
2. The angles formed by parallel lines cut by a transversal (a third line)

Intersecting Lines

Intersecting lines have three important properties.

First, the interior angles formed by intersecting lines form a circle, so the sum of these angles is 360°. In the figure: $a + b + c + d = 360$.

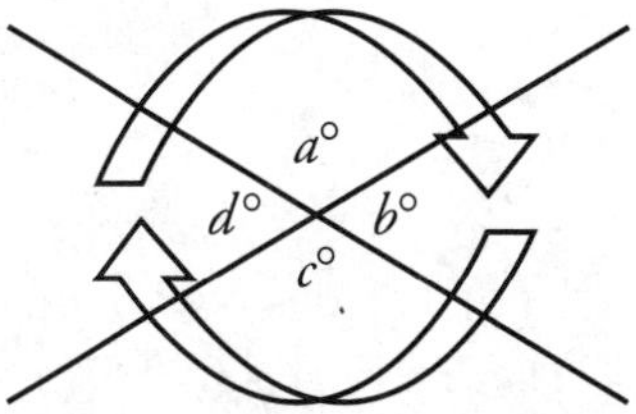

Second, interior angles that combine to form a line sum to 180°. For example, in the figure shown to the right, $a + b = 180$, because angles a and b form a line together. Other pairs of angles are $b + c = 180$, $c + d = 180$, and $d + a = 180$.

Third, when two lines intersect, angles found opposite each other are equal. These are called **vertical angles.** Thus, in the figure above, $a = c$, because these angles are opposite each other and are formed from the same two lines. Additionally, $b = d$ for the same reason.

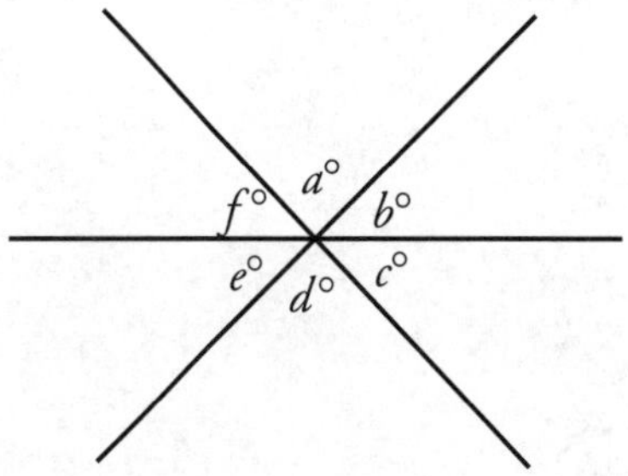

These rules apply to more than two lines that intersect at a point, as shown in the figure to the right. Here, $a + b + c + d + e + f = 360$, because these angles combine to form a circle. In addition, $a + b + c = 180$, because these three angles combine to form a line. Finally, $a = d$, $b = e$, and $c = f$, because they are pairs of vertical angles.

31

Parallel Lines Cut by a Transversal

The GMAT makes frequent use of figures that include parallel lines cut by a transversal.

Notice that there are eight angles formed by this construction, but there are only two *different* angle measures (a and b, as shown in the figure). All the **acute** angles (less than 90°) in this figure are equal. Likewise, all the **obtuse** angles (greater than 90° but less than 180°) are equal. Any acute angle plus any obtuse angle equals 180°.

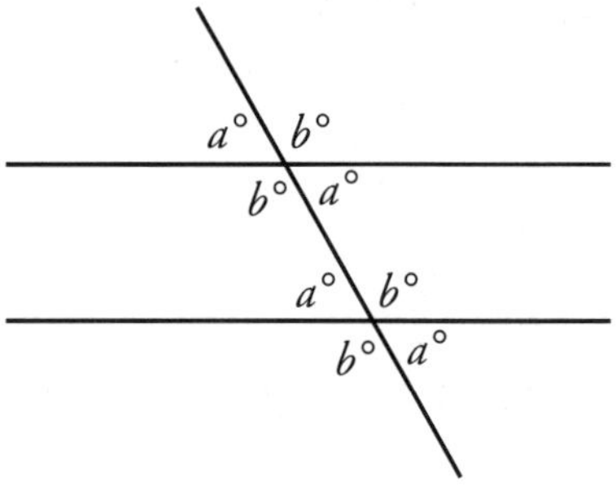

Thus, $a + b = 180$.

When you see a transversal cutting two lines that you know to be parallel, fill in all the a (acute) and b (obtuse) angles.

Sometimes the GMAT disguises the parallel lines and the transversal so that they are not readily apparent. In the first Z figure, the two horizontal lines are parallel and the angled line is the transversal, but the various angles created aren't fully apparent because the lines are truncated.

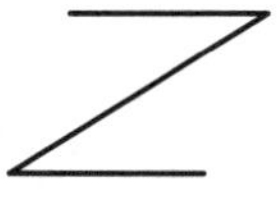

In these disguised cases, redraw the figure and extend the lines yourself so that you can more easily see all of the angles created, as shown in the second Z figure. You might also mark the parallel lines with arrows, as shown, in order to indicate that the two lines are parallel.

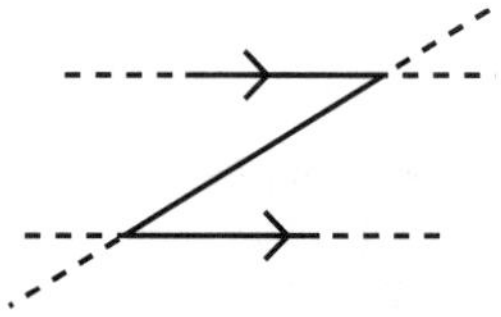

The GMAT uses the symbol || to indicate in text that two lines or line segments are parallel. For example, if you see $MN \parallel OP$ in a problem, you know that line segment MN is parallel to line segment OP.

Problem Set

Problems 1 and 2 refer to the given figure, where line *AB* is parallel to line *CD*.

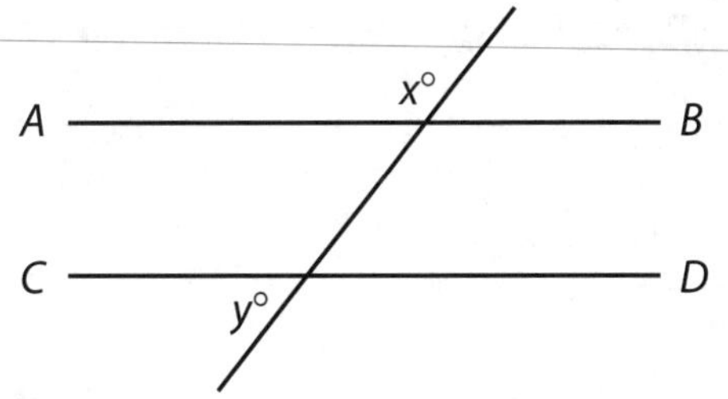

1. If $x - y = 10$, what is x ?
2. If $x + (x + y) = 320$, what is x ?

Problems 3–4 refer to the figure to the figure below.

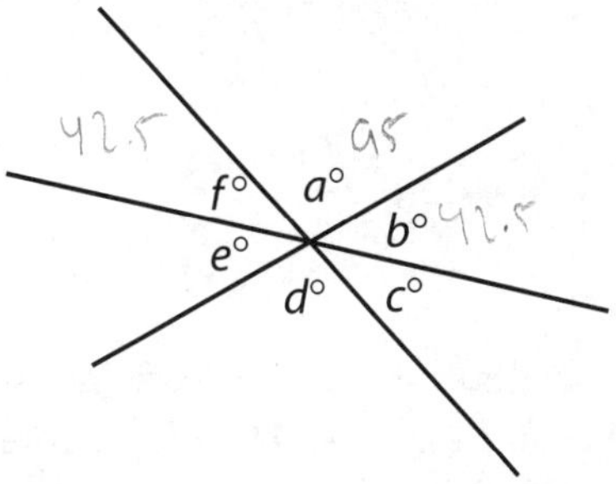

3. If a is 95, what is $b + d - e$?
4. If $c + f = 70$ and $d = 80$, what is b ?

Challenge! Problems 5–7 refer to the figure to the figure below.

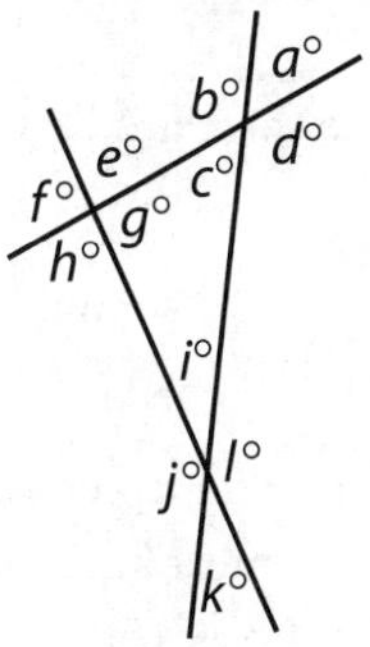

5. If $c + g = 140$, what is k ?
6. If $g = 90$, what is $a + k$?
7. If $f + k = 150$, what is b ?

Solutions

1. **95°:** The figure shows two parallel lines cut by a third, so $x + y = 180$. Add the two equations together to eliminate the y variable and solve for x:

$$\begin{array}{rr} & x + y = 180 \\ + & x - y = \ \ 10 \\ \hline & 2x = 190 \\ & x = 95 \end{array}$$

2. **140°:** The figure shows two parallel lines cut by a third, so $x + y = 180$. Substitute $x + y = 180$ into the given equation of $x + (x + y) = 320$ to solve for x:

$$x + 180 = 320$$
$$x = 140$$

Alternatively, subtract the equation $x + y = 180$ from $2x + y = 320$ to eliminate y and solve for x:

$$\begin{array}{r} 2x + y = 320 \\ -(x + y = 180) \\ \hline x = 140 \end{array}$$

3. **95°:** Because a and d are vertical angles, they have the same measure: $a = d = 95$. Likewise, since b and e are vertical angles, they have the same measure: $b = e$. Therefore, $b + d - e = b + d - b = d = 95$.

4. **65°:** Because c and f are vertical angles, they have the same measure: $c + f = 70$, so $c = f = 35$. Notice that b, c, and d form a straight line: $b + c + d = 180$. Substitute the known values of c and d into this equation:

$$b + 35 + 80 = 180$$
$$b + 115 = 180$$
$$b = 65$$

5. **40°:** If $c + g = 140$, then $i = 40$, because there are 180° in a triangle. Since k and i are vertical angles, k is also equal to 40.

6. **90°:** If $g = 90$, then the other two angles in the triangle, c and i, sum to 90. Since a and k are vertical angles to c and i, they sum to 90 as well.

7. **150°:** Angles f and k are vertical to angles g and i. The latter two angles, then, must also sum to 150. Therefore, the third angle in the triangle, c, must be $180 - 150$, so $c = 30$. Then, c and b create a straight line, or 180, so $30 + b = 180$, and $b = 150$.

CHAPTER 32

Polygons

In This Chapter

- Quadrilaterals: An Overview
- Polygons and Interior Angles
- Polygons and Perimeter
- Polygons and Area
- Three Dimensions: Surface Area
- Three Dimensions: Volume

In this chapter, you will learn about angle measures, perimeter, and area for certain two-dimensional shapes, including squares, rectangles, parallelograms, and trapezoids. You'll also learn about surface area and volume for certain three-dimensional shapes, including cubes and boxes.

CHAPTER 32 Polygons

A **polygon** is defined as a closed, two-dimensional shape formed by line segments. The polygons tested on the GMAT include the following:

- Three-sided shapes (triangles)
- Four-sided shapes (quadrilaterals)
- Other polygons with *n* sides (where *n* is five or more)

This section will focus on polygons of four or more sides. On the GMAT, the most commonly tested polygons of this category are squares and rectangles. Other shapes, such as trapezoids and parallelograms, can show up but are less common.

Quadrilaterals: An Overview

The most common polygon tested on the GMAT, aside from the triangle, is the **quadrilateral** (any four-sided polygon). Almost all GMAT polygon problems involve the special types of quadrilaterals shown below:

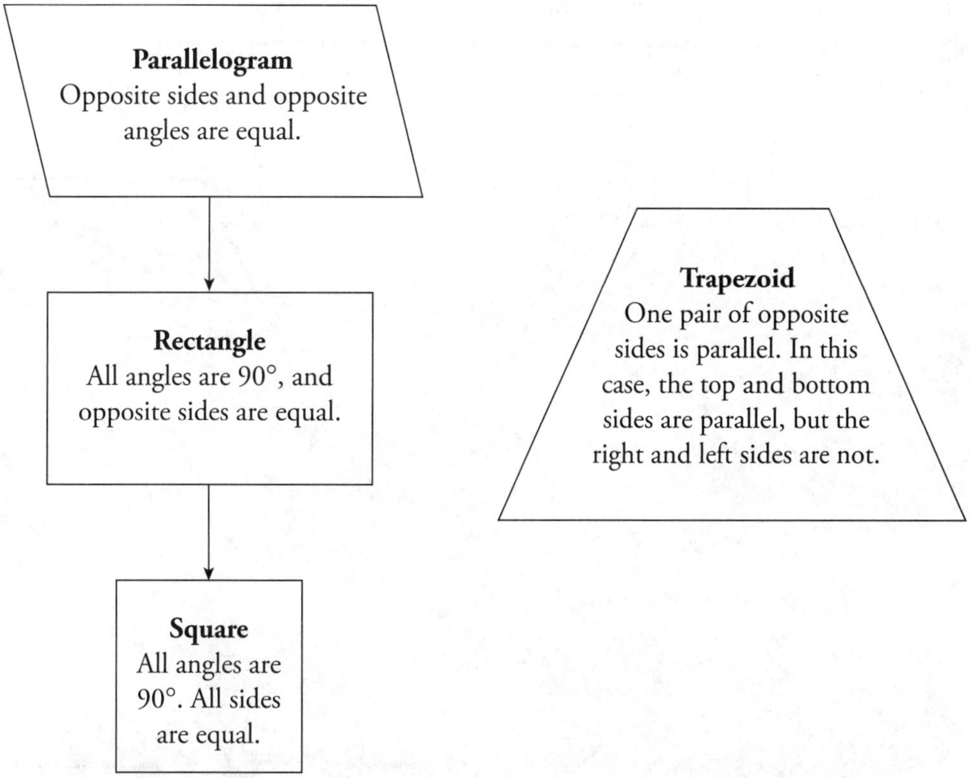
Parallelogram
Opposite sides and opposite angles are equal.
Rectangle
All angles are 90°, and opposite sides are equal.
Square
All angles are 90°. All sides are equal.
Trapezoid
One pair of opposite sides is parallel. In this case, the top and bottom sides are parallel, but the right and left sides are not.

Squares are a special subset of rectangles: They have all of the characteristics of rectangles plus the special additional characteristic that all sides are equal.

Likewise, rectangles are a special subset of parallelograms: They have all of the characteristics of parallelograms plus the special additional characteristic that all angles are 90°.

Polygons and Interior Angles

The sum of the interior angles of a given polygon depends only on the **number of sides in the polygon**. The following table displays the relationship between the type of polygon and the sum of its interior angles:

Polygon	# of Sides	Sum of Interior Angles
Triangle	3	180°
Quadrilateral	4	360°
Pentagon	5	540°
Hexagon	6	720°

This pattern can be expressed as the number of sides minus 2, multiplied by 180:

$$(n - 2) \times 180 = \textbf{Sum of Interior Angles of a Polygon}$$

Since this polygon has four sides, the sum of its interior angles is $(4 - 2)180 = 2(180) = 360°$. The interior angles of all four-sided polygons will always sum to 360°. This is true for squares, rectangles, trapezoids—anything with four sides.

Alternatively, a quadrilateral can be cut into two triangles by a line connecting opposite corners. Thus, the sum of the angles is $2(180) = 360°$.

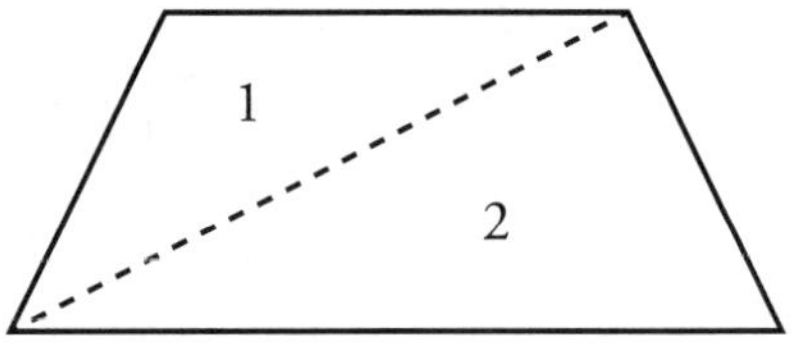

In the polygon with six sides, the sum of the interior angles is $(6 - 2)180 = 4(180) = 720°$.

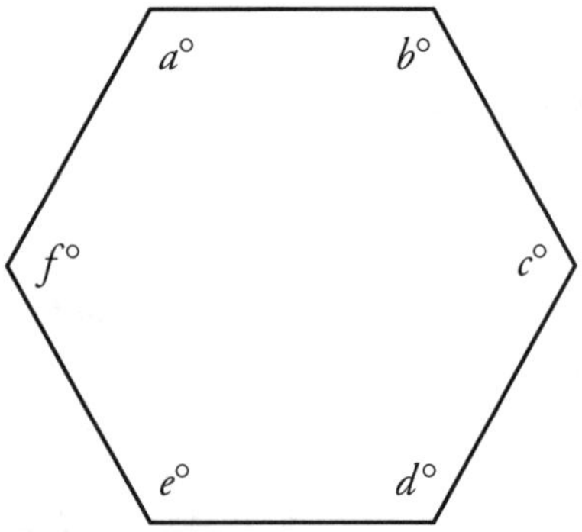

Alternatively, note that a hexagon can be cut into four triangles by three lines connecting corners:

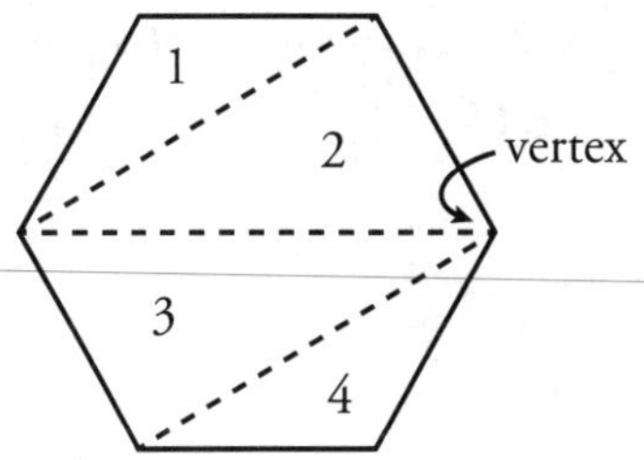

Thus, the sum of the angles is $4(180) = 720°$.

By the way, the corners of polygons are also known as vertices (singular: vertex).

Polygons and Perimeter

The **perimeter** refers to the distance around a polygon, or the sum of the lengths of all the sides. The amount of fencing needed to surround a yard would be equivalent to the perimeter of that yard (the sum of all the sides).

The perimeter of the pentagon to the right is $9 + 7 + 4 + 6 + 5 = 31$.

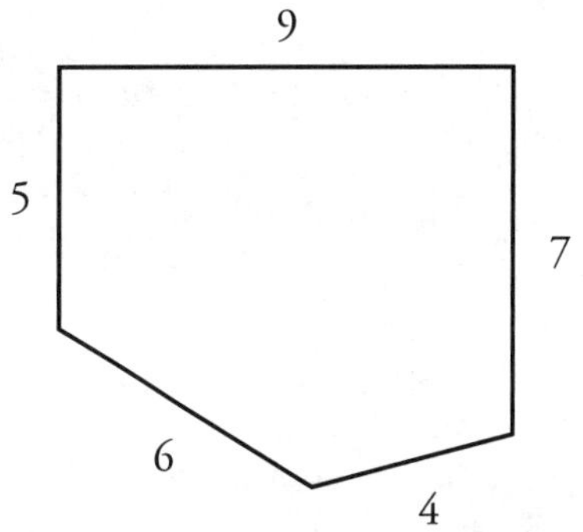

Polygons and Area

The area of a polygon refers to the space inside the polygon. Area is measured in square units, such as cm^2 (square centimeters), m^2 (square meters), or ft^2 (square feet). For example, the amount of space that a garden occupies is the area of that garden.

For the GMAT, definitely memorize the first two area formulas:

1. **Area of a Square = Side × Side = Side²**

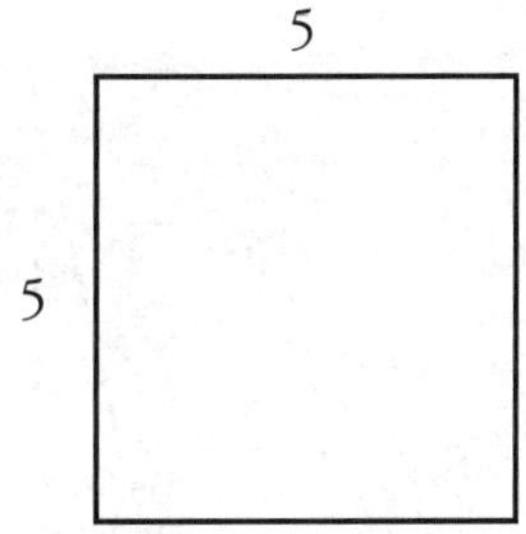

The side length of this square is 5. Therefore, the area is $5^2 = 25$.

2. **Area of a Rectangle = Length × Width**

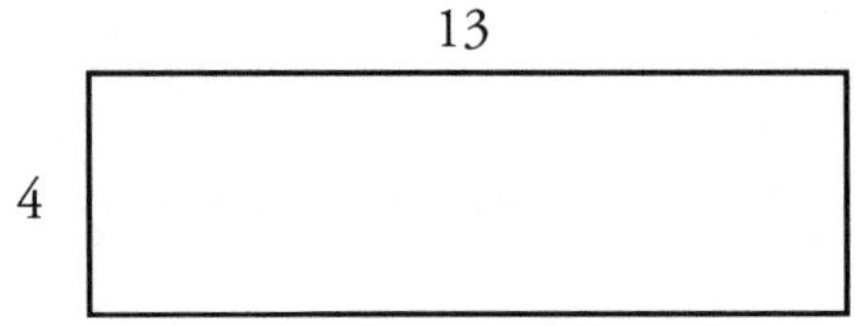

The length of this rectangle is 13 and the width is 4. Therefore, the area is $13 \times 4 = 52$.

The GMAT will occasionally ask you to find the area of a polygon more complex than a square or rectangle. The following formulas can be used to find the areas of other types of quadrilaterals. You may or may not see these shapes on the exam, so you'll need to decide whether you want to take the time to memorize the formulas.

3. **Area of a Trapezoid** $= \dfrac{(\text{Base}_1 + \text{Base}_2)(\text{Height})}{2}$

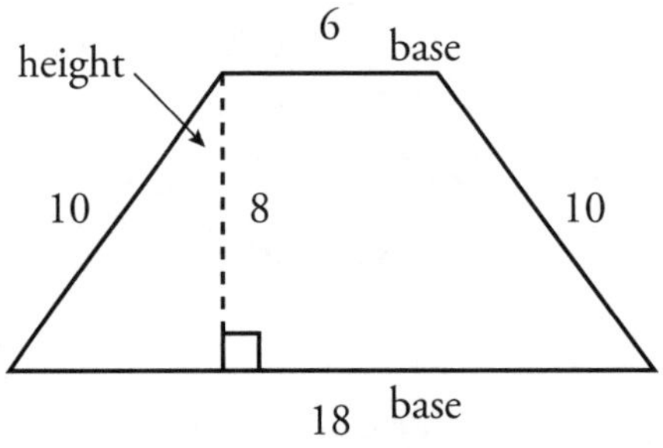

The bases are the two parallel lines. The height refers to a line perpendicular to the two bases. (You often have to draw in the height, as in this case.) In the trapezoid shown, $\text{base}_1 = 18$, $\text{base}_2 = 6$, and the height = 8. Another way to think about this formula is to take the *average* of the two bases and multiply it by the height: $\dfrac{(18+6)}{2}(8) = (12)(8) = 96$.

4. **Area of any Parallelogram = Base × Height**

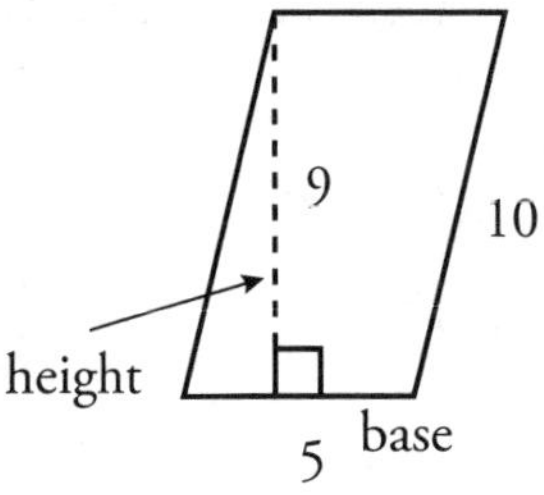

Note that the height refers to the line perpendicular to the base. (As with the trapezoid, you often have to draw in the height.) In the parallelogram shown, the base is 5 and the height is 9. Therefore, the area is $5 \times 9 = 45$.

Note that some more complex shapes can be divided into a combination of rectangles and right triangles. For example:

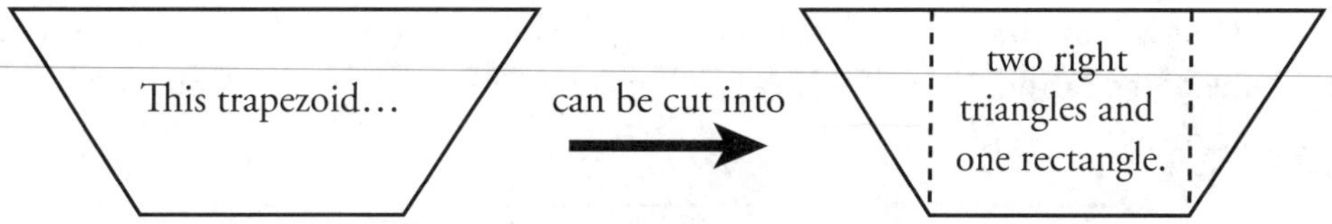

32

Solving in this way will take longer than using the real formula, but trapezoids are infrequent enough that you might be willing to take that risk in order to avoid having to memorize yet another formula.

Three Dimensions: Surface Area

You may see a problem involving either a rectangular solid or a cube. (Or you may not. Three-dimensional geometry is not all that common on the GMAT.)

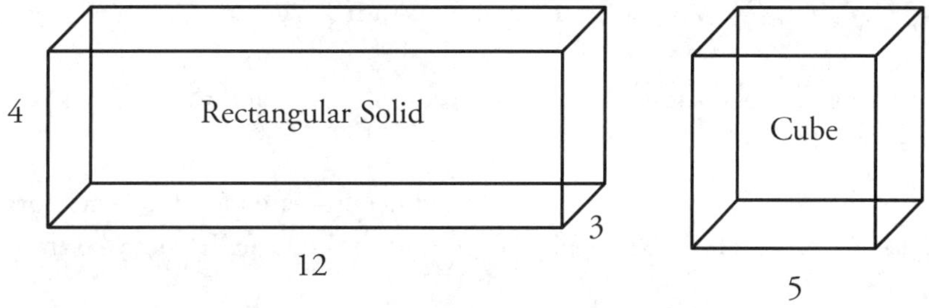

The surface area of a three-dimensional shape is the amount of space on the surface of that particular object. For example, the amount of paint that it would take to fully cover a rectangular box could be determined by finding the surface area of that box. As with simple area, surface area is measured in square units such as in^2 (square inches) or ft^2 (square feet).

Surface Area = The *Sum* of the Areas of *All* of the Faces

Both a rectangular solid and a cube have six faces.

To determine the surface area of a rectangular solid, you'll need to find the area of each face—but you don't need to find six separate faces.

In a rectangular solid, the front and back faces have the same area, the top and bottom faces have the same area, and the two side faces have the same area. In the solid shown, the area of the front face is equal to $12 \times 4 = 48$. Thus, the back face also has an area of 48. The area of the bottom face is equal to $12 \times 3 = 36$, so the top face also has an area of 36. Finally, each side face has an area of $3 \times 4 = 12$. Therefore, the surface area, or the sum of the areas of all six faces, equals $48(2) + 36(2) + 12(2) = 192$.

To determine the surface area of a cube, you need the length of one side. First, find the area of one face: $5 \times 5 = 25$. Then, multiply by six to account for all of the faces: $6 \times 25 = 150$.

Three Dimensions: Volume

The **volume** of a three-dimensional shape is the amount of "stuff" it can hold. *Capacity* is another word for volume. For example, the amount of liquid that a rectangular milk carton holds can be determined by finding the volume of the carton. Volume is measured in cubic units such as in^3 (cubic inches), ft^3 (cubic feet), or m^3 (cubic meters).

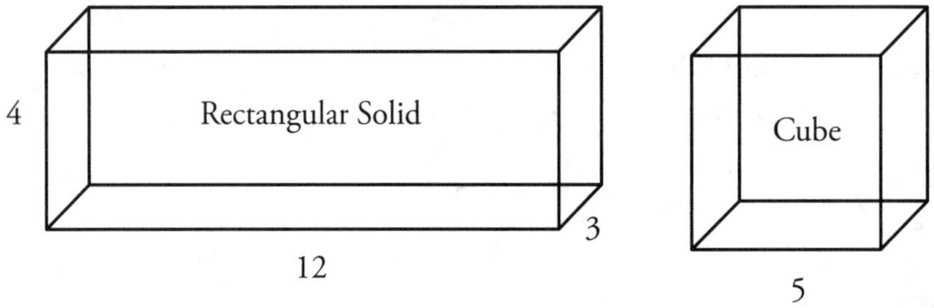

Volume = Length × Width × Height

The length of the rectangular solid shown above is 12, the width is 3, and the height is 4. Therefore, the volume is $12 \times 3 \times 4 = 144$.

In a cube, all three of the dimensions—length, width, and height—are identical. Therefore, knowing the measurement of just one side of the cube is sufficient to find the volume. In the cube above, the volume is $5 \times 5 \times 5 = 125$.

Beware of a GMAT volume trick, as in this example:

> How many books, each with a volume of 100 in^3, can be packed into a crate with a volume of 5,000 in^3?

It is tempting to answer "50 books" (since $50 \times 100 = 5{,}000$). However, this is incorrect, because you do not know the exact dimensions of each book! One book might be $5 \times 5 \times 4$, while another book might be $20 \times 5 \times 1$. Even though both have a volume of 100 in^3, they have different rectangular shapes. Without knowing the exact shapes of all the books, you cannot tell whether they would all fit into the crate or whether there would be empty space because the 50 books don't fill the crate perfectly.

When you are fitting three-dimensional objects into other three-dimensional objects, knowing the respective volumes is not enough. You must know the specific dimensions (length, width, and height) of each object to determine whether the objects can fit without leaving gaps.

Problem Set

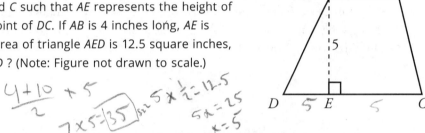

Now that you've finished the chapter, try these problems.

1. If 40 percent of Andrea's living room floor is covered by a carpet that is 4 feet by 9 feet, what is the area of her living room floor?

2. A pentagon has three sides with length x and two sides with length $3x$. If x is $\frac{2}{3}$ of an inch, what is the perimeter of the pentagon?

3. Francis fences in three of the four sides of a rectangular yard. The unfenced side of the yard is 40 feet long. The yard has an area of 280 square feet. What is the length, in feet, of the fence that Francis installs?

4. In the figure shown, $ABCD$ is a quadrilateral, with AB parallel to DC. Point E is between D and C such that AE represents the height of $ABCD$ and E is the midpoint of DC. If AB is 4 inches long, AE is 5 inches long, and the area of triangle AED is 12.5 square inches, what is the area of $ABCD$? (Note: Figure not drawn to scale.)

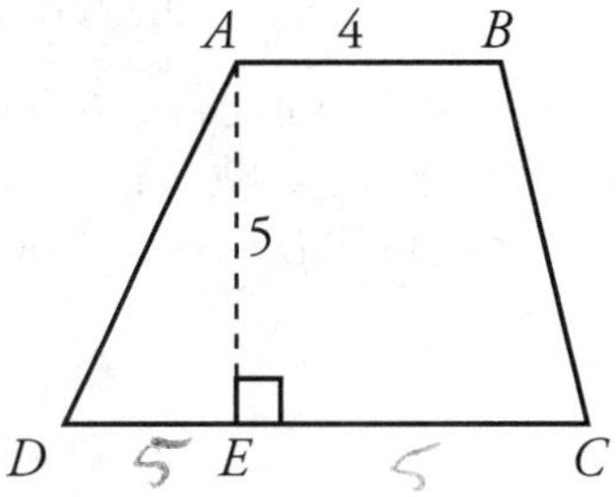

5. A rectangular solid has a square base, with each side of the base measuring 4 meters. If the volume of the solid is 48 cubic meters, what is the surface area of the solid?

6. If the perimeter of a rectangular flower bed is 30 feet, and its area is 44 square feet, what is the length of each of its shorter sides?

7. A rectangular swimming pool has a length of 30 meters, a width of 10 meters, and an average depth of 2 meters. If a hose can fill the pool at a rate of 0.5 cubic meters per minute, how many hours will it take the hose to fill the pool?

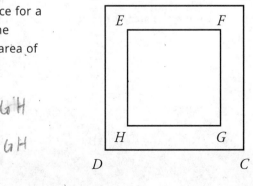

8. A rectangular tank needs to be coated with insulation. The tank has dimensions of 4 feet, 5 feet, and 2.5 feet. Each square foot of insulation costs $20. How much will it cost to cover the surface of the tank with insulation?

9. There is a rectangular parking lot with a length of $2x$ and a width of x. What is the ratio of the perimeter of the parking lot to the area of the parking lot, in terms of x ?

10. $ABCD$ is a square picture frame, as shown in the diagram. $EFGH$ is a square hole cut into the frame $ABCD$ as a space for a picture. The area of $EFGH$ (for the picture) is equal to the area of the picture frame (the area of $ABCD$ minus the area of $EFGH$). If $AB = 6$, what is the length of EF ?

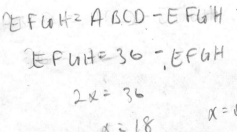

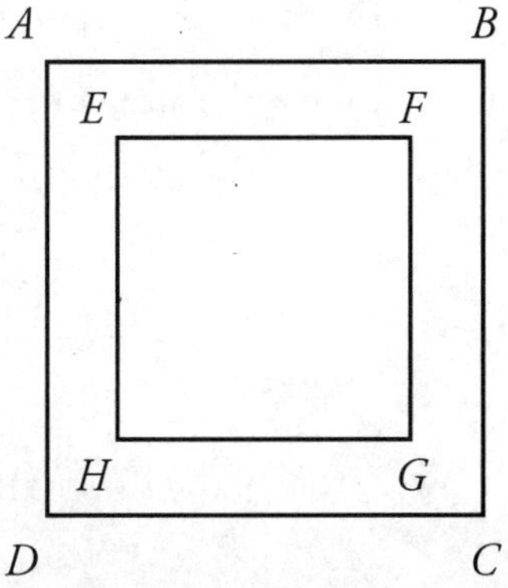

Solutions

1. **90 ft^2:** The area of the carpet is equal to $l \times w$, or $4 \times 9 = 36$ ft^2. Set up a proportion to find the area of the whole living room floor. Use the simplified fraction for 40% to save time.

$$\frac{2}{5} = \frac{36}{x}$$

$$2x = 180 \qquad \text{Cross-multiply to solve.}$$

$$x = 90\,\text{ft}^2$$

2. **6 inches:** The perimeter of a pentagon is the sum of its five sides: $x + x + x + 3x + 3x = 9x$. If x is $\frac{2}{3}$ of an inch, the perimeter is $9\left(\frac{2}{3}\right)$, or 6 inches.

3. **54 feet:** In order to find the perimeter, you need the length and width of the yard. One side of the yard is 40 feet long; call this the length. The area of the yard is 280 square feet. Use this information to find the width of the yard:

$$A = l \times w$$

$$280 = 40w$$

$$w = \frac{280}{40}$$

$$= 7 \text{ feet}$$

Francis fences in the two 7-foot sides and one of the 40-foot sides. Thus, Francis needs $40 + 7 + 7 = 54$ feet of fencing.

4. **35 in^2:** If E is the midpoint of DC, then $DE = EC = x$. Determine the length of x by using what you know about the area of triangle AED:

$$A = \frac{b \times h}{2}$$

$$12.5 = \frac{5x}{2}$$

$$25 = 5x$$

$$x = 5$$

Therefore, the length of DC is $2x$, or 10.

To find the area of the trapezoid, use the formula:

$$A = \frac{b_1 + b_2}{2} \times h$$

$$= \frac{4 + 10}{2} \times 5$$

$$= 35 \text{ in}^2$$

5. **80 m^2:** The volume of a rectangular solid is equal to length × width × height. The length and width are both 4 meters long. Substitute values into the formulas as shown:

$$48 = 4 \times 4 \times h$$
$$h = 3$$

To find the surface area of a rectangular solid, sum the individual areas of all six faces:

	Area of One Face		**Total Area of Identical Faces**
Top and bottom:	$4 \times 4 = 16$	→	$2 \times 16 = 32$
Four sides:	$4 \times 3 = 12$	→	$4 \times 12 = 48$
	All 6 faces	→	$32 + 48 = 80\text{ m}^2$

6. **4 feet:** Set up equations to represent the area and perimeter of the flower bed:

$$A = l \times w \qquad P = 2(l + w)$$

Then, substitute the known values for the variables *A* and *P*:

$$44 = l \times w \qquad 30 = 2(l + w)$$

Solve the two equations using the substitution method:

$$l = \frac{44}{w}$$

$$30 = 2\left(\frac{44}{w} + w\right)$$

$$15w = 44 + w^2$$ Multiply the entire equation by $\frac{w}{2}$.

$$w^2 - 15w + 44 = 0$$
$$(w - 11)(w - 4) = 0$$
$$w = \{4, 11\}$$

Solving the quadratic equation yields two solutions: 4 and 11. Each represents a possible side length. Since you were asked to find the length of the shorter side, the answer is 4.

Alternatively, you can arrive at the correct solution by testing numbers. What length and width add up to 15 (half of the perimeter) and multiply to produce 44 (the area)? Some experimentation will demonstrate that the longer side must be 11 and the shorter side must be 4.

7. **20 hours:** The volume of the pool is length × width × height, or $30 \times 10 \times 2 = 600$ cubic meters. Use a standard work equation, $RT = W$, where W represents the total work of 600 m^3:

$$0.5t = 600$$
$$t = 1,200 \text{ minutes}$$

Convert this time to hours by dividing by 60: $1,200 \div 60 = 20$ hours.

Alternatively, you could convert to the hourly rate first:

$$\frac{0.5 \text{ m}^3}{\text{min}} \times \frac{60 \text{ min}}{\text{hr}} = \frac{30 \text{ m}^3}{\text{hr}}$$

Next, use the standard work equation:

$$30t = 600$$
$$t = 20 \text{ hours}$$

8. **$1,700:** To find the surface area of a rectangular solid, sum the individual areas of all six faces:

	Area of One Face		Total Area of Identical Faces
Top and bottom:	$5 \times 4 = 20$	→	$20 \times 2 = 40$
Side 1:	$5 \times 2.5 = 12.5$	→	$12.5 \times 2 = 25$
Side 2:	$4 \times 2.5 = 10$	→	$10 \times 2 = 20$
	All 6 faces	→	$40 + 25 + 20 = 85$ ft^2

Thus, covering the entire tank will cost 85 × $20, which equals $1,700.

9. $\mathbf{\frac{3}{x}}$ **or 3 : x:** The length of the parking lot is $2x$ and the width is x. The perimeter is $2(2x + x)$ and the area is $(2x)(x)$. Set up a fraction to represent the ratio of the perimeter to the area:

$$\frac{\text{Perimeter}}{\text{Area}} = \frac{2(2x + x)}{(2x)(x)} = \frac{6x}{2x^2} = \frac{3}{x}$$

10. $\sqrt{18}$ **or** $3\sqrt{2}$**:** The area of the frame and the area of the picture sum to the total area of the image, which is 6^2, or 36. Therefore, the area of the frame and the picture are each equal to half of 36, or 18. Since $EFGH$ is a square, the length of EF is $\sqrt{18}$, or $3\sqrt{2}$.

CHAPTER 33

Triangles and Diagonals

In This Chapter

- The Angles of a Triangle
- The Sides of a Triangle
- The Pythagorean Theorem
- Common Right Triangles
- Isosceles Triangles and the 45–45–90 Triangle
- Equilateral Triangles and the 30–60–90 Triangle
- Exterior Angles of a Triangle
- Triangles and Area
- Similar Triangles

In this chapter, you will learn all of the needed properties of triangles, including angle measures, perimeter, and area, as well as the rules for special triangles: isosceles, equilateral, and right. You'll also learn when and how to use the Pythagorean theorem.

CHAPTER 33 Triangles and Diagonals

The triangle is typically the most commonly tested polygon on the GMAT.

Right triangles (those with a 90° angle) require particular attention, because they have special properties that are useful for solving many GMAT geometry problems.

The most important property of a right triangle is the unique relationship of the three sides. Given the lengths of any two of the sides of a right triangle, you can determine the length of the third side using the Pythagorean theorem. There are even two special types of right triangles—the 30–60–90 triangle and the 45–45–90 triangle—for which you only need the length of *one* side to determine the lengths of the other two sides.

Finally, right triangles are essential for solving problems involving other polygons. For example, you might cut a square or rectangle into right triangles. Or, you might have a triangle inscribed in a circle or other shape.

The Angles of a Triangle

The angles in any given triangle have two key properties:

1. **The sum of the three angles of a triangle equals 180°.**

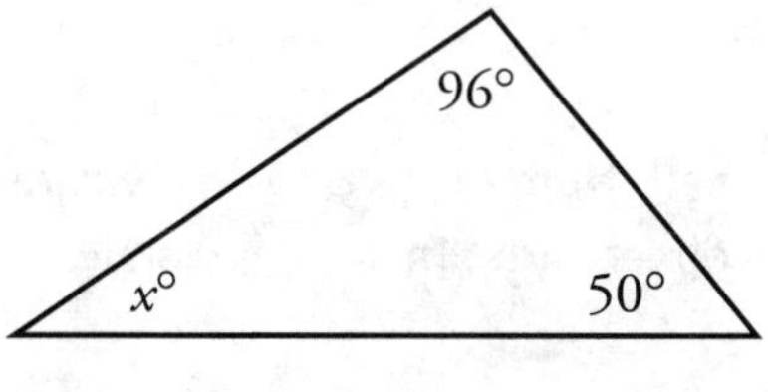

What is x ? Since the sum of the three angles must be 180°, you can solve for x as follows:

$x = 180 - 96 - 50 = 34$

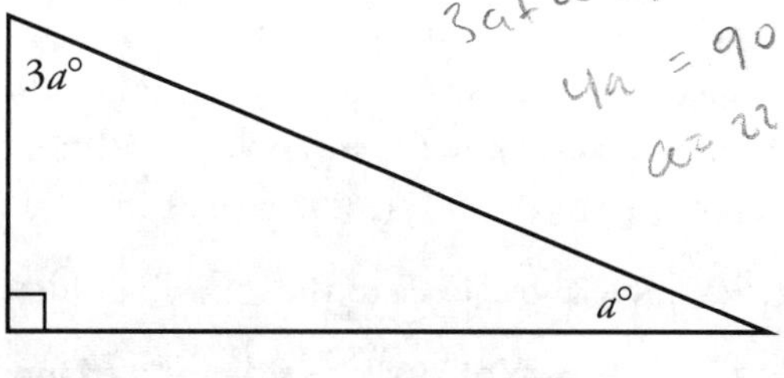

What is a ? Since the sum of the three angles must be 180°, you can solve for a as follows:

$90 + 3a + a = 180 \rightarrow a = 22.5$

2. **Angles correspond to their opposite sides.** This means that the largest angle is opposite the longest side, while the smallest angle is opposite the shortest side. Additionally, **if two sides are equal, their opposite angles are also equal.**

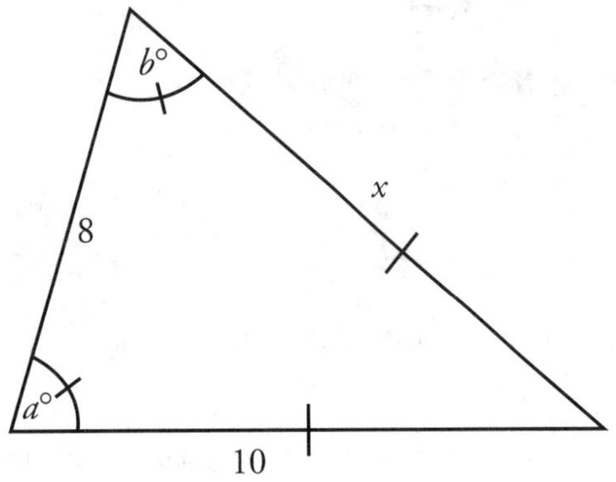

If $a = b$, what is the length of side x?

Since the side opposite angle b has a length of 10, the side opposite angle a must have the same length. Therefore, x is equal to 10.

Mark equal angles and equal sides with a slash, as shown. Also don't hesitate to redraw; if a figure is very different from the dimensions you were given, redraw the triangle closer to scale.

33

The Sides of a Triangle

Consider the following "impossible" triangle ABC and what it reveals about the relationship between the three sides of any triangle:

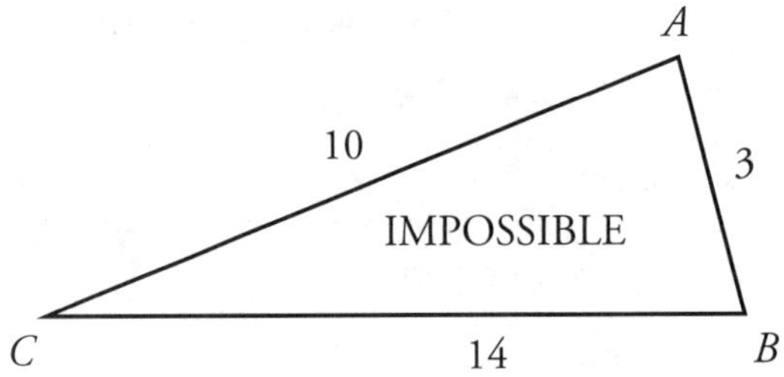

The triangle above could never be drawn with the given measurements. Why? Consider that the shortest distance between any two points is a straight line. According to the triangle shown, the direct straight line distance between point C and point B is 14; however, the indirect path from point C to B (the path that goes from C to A to B) is $10 + 3$, or 13, which is shorter than the direct path. This is impossible!

The example above leads to the following rule:

The sum of any two sides of a triangle must be greater than the third side.

If side CA is 10 and side AB is 3, then the maximum integer distance for side BC in the triangle above is 12. If the length of side BC is not restricted to integers, then this length is *less than* 13.

Any side must also be *greater than* the difference between the lengths of the other two sides. In this case, side BC must be longer than $10 - 3$, or 7.

Consider the following triangle and the proof that the given measurements are possible:

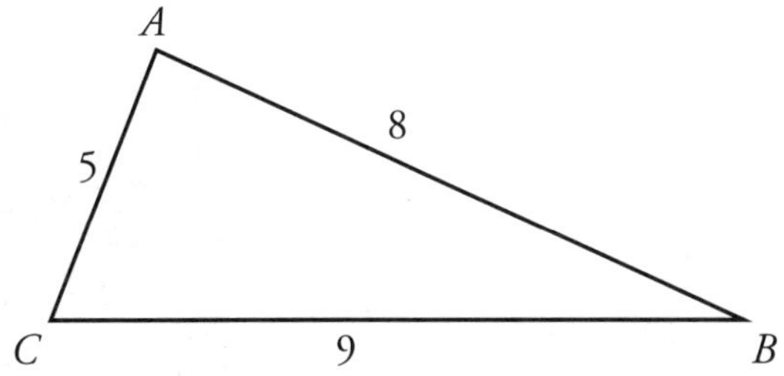

Test each combination of sides to prove that the measurements of this triangle are possible.

$8 + 5 > 9$	$8 - 5 < 9$
$9 + 5 > 8$	$9 - 5 < 8$
$9 + 8 > 5$	$9 - 8 < 5$

Note that the sum of two sides cannot be equal to the third side. The sum of two sides must always be *greater than* the third side. Likewise, the difference cannot be equal to the third side. The difference between two sides must be *less than* the third side.

If you are given two sides of a triangle, the length of the third side must lie between the difference and the sum of the two given sides. For example, if you are told that two sides are of lengths 3 and 4, then the length of the third side must be between $4 - 3 = 1$ and $4 + 3 = 7$, as shown here:

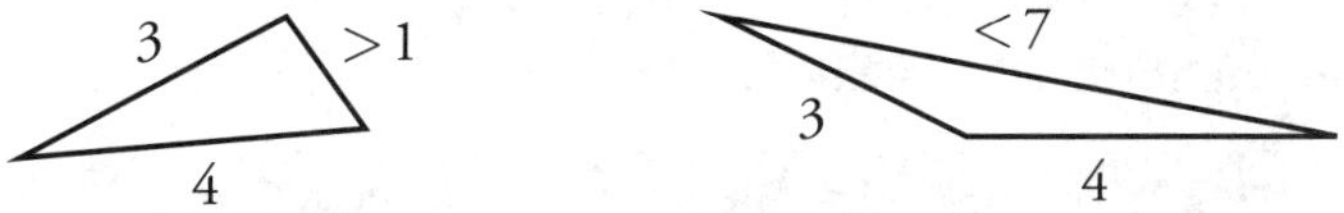

The Pythagorean Theorem

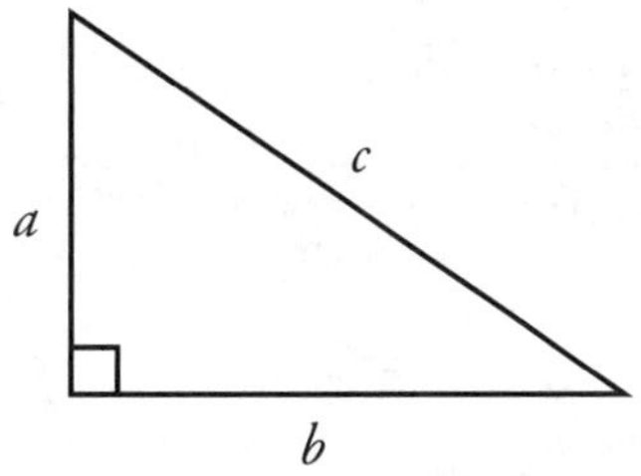

A **right triangle** is a triangle with one right angle (90°). Every right triangle is composed of two **legs** and a **hypotenuse**. The hypotenuse is the side opposite the largest angle (in this case, the right angle) and is often assigned the letter c. The two legs that form the right angle are often called a and b (it does not matter which leg is a and which leg is b).

Given the lengths of two sides of a ... f the third side? Use the Pythagorean theorem:

memorize

$$a^2 + b^2 = c^2$$

What is x?

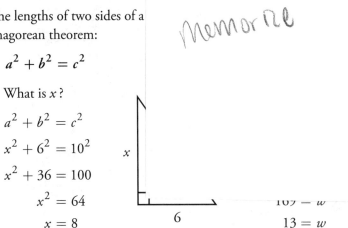

$$a^2 + b^2 = c^2$$
$$x^2 + 6^2 = 10^2$$
$$x^2 + 36 = 100$$
$$x^2 = 64$$
$$x = 8$$

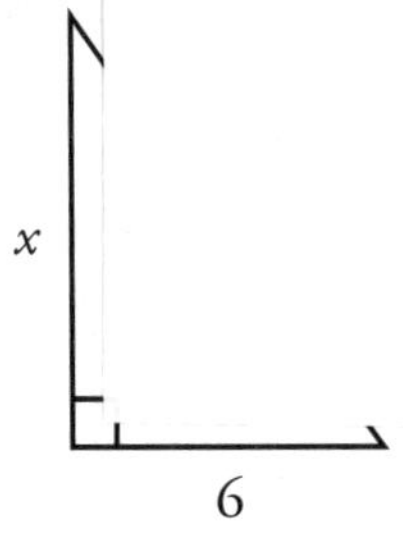

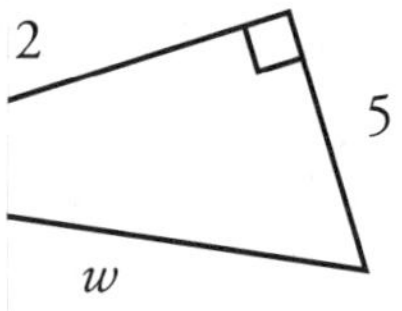

$$13 = w$$

33

Common Right Triangles

Certain right triangles appear over and over on the GMAT. It pays to memorize these common combinations in order to save time on the exam. Instead of using the Pythagorean theorem to solve for the lengths of the sides of these common right triangles, memorize the following Pythagorean triples:

Common Combinations	Key Multiples
3–4–5 The most popular of all right triangles $3^2 + 4^2 = 5^2$ $(9 + 16 = 25)$	6–8–10 9–12–15 12–16–20
5–12–13 Also quite popular on the GMAT $5^2 + 12^2 = 13^2$ $(25 + 144 = 169)$	10–24–26
8–15–17 Appears less frequently $8^2 + 15^2 = 17^2$ $(64 + 225 = 289)$	None

Watch out for impostor triangles! A non-right triangle with one side equal to 3 and another side equal to 4 does not have a third side of length 5. Likewise, if a right triangle has a side of 3 and a hypotenuse of 4, then the other leg is not 5; a leg can't be longer than the hypotenuse.

Isosceles Triangles and the 45–45–90 Triangle

An **isosceles triangle** is one in which two of the three sides are equal. The two angles opposite those two sides will also be equal. The most important isosceles triangle on the GMAT is the isosceles right triangle.

An isosceles right triangle has one 90° angle (opposite the hypotenuse) and two 45° angles (opposite the two equal legs). This triangle is called the 45–45–90 triangle.

The lengths of the legs of every 45–45–90 triangle have a set ratio; memorize this:

leg	leg	hypotenuse
45°	45°	90°
x	x	$x\sqrt{2}$

Try an example:

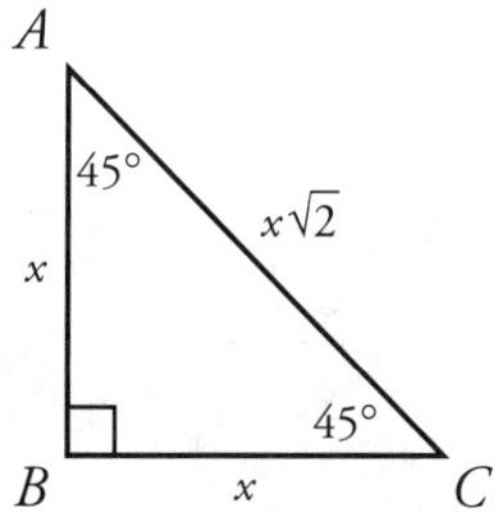

If the length of side *AB* is 5, what are the lengths of sides *BC* and *AC*?

The question indicates that *AB* is 5, so $x = 5$. Use the ratio $x : x : x\sqrt{2}$ for sides $AB : BC : AC$ to determine that the sides of the triangle have lengths $5 : 5 : 5\sqrt{2}$. Therefore, the length of side $BC = 5$ and the length of side $AC = 5\sqrt{2}$. Try another example:

For a 45–45–90 triangle, if the length of side *AC* is $\sqrt{18}$, what are the lengths of sides *AB* and *BC*?

Since the hypotenuse *AC* is $\sqrt{18}$:

$$x\sqrt{2} = \sqrt{18}$$

$$x = \frac{\sqrt{18}}{\sqrt{2}} = \sqrt{\frac{18}{2}}$$

$$x = \sqrt{9} = 3$$

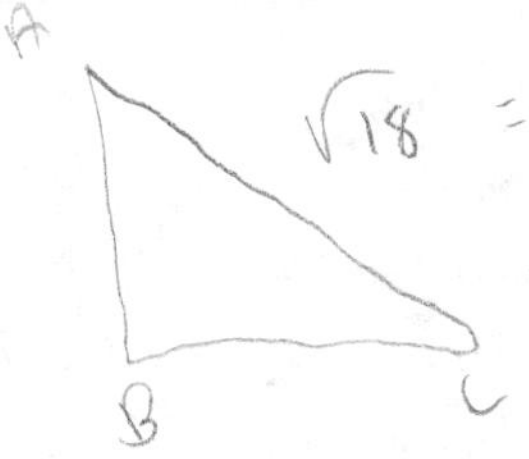

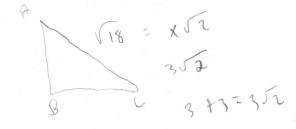

Thus, the sides *AB* and *BC* are each equal to *x*, or 3.

Interestingly, the 45–45–90 triangle is exactly half of a square. That is, two 45–45–90 triangles put together make up a square. Thus, if you are given the diagonal of a square, you can use the 45–45–90 ratio to find the length of a side of the square:

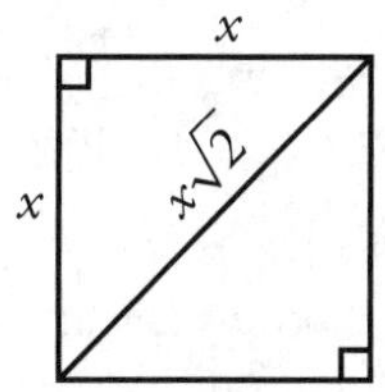

33

Equilateral Triangles and the

An **equilateral triangle** is one in which all three side
equilateral triangle is 60° (because all three angles mı
triangle is the 30–60–90 triangle. Notice that two of eral
triangle:

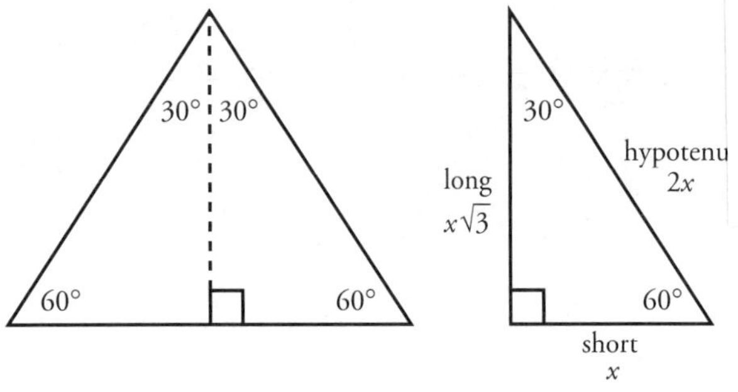

Equilateral Triangle 30–60–90 Triangle

The lengths of the legs of every 30–60–90 triangle have a set ratio; memorize this:

Leg	Leg	Hypotenuse
30°	60°	90°
x	$x\sqrt{3}$	$2x$

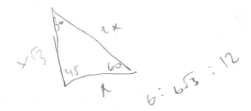

Try an example:

> If the short leg of a 30–60–90 triangle has a length of 6, what are the lengths of the long leg and the hypotenuse?

The question indicates that the short leg, which is opposite the 30° angle, is 6. Use the ratio $x : x\sqrt{3} : 2x$ to determine that the sides of the triangle have lengths $6 : 6\sqrt{3} : 12$. The long leg measures $6\sqrt{3}$ and the hypotenuse measures 12. Try another example:

> If an equilateral triangle has a side of length 10, what is its height?

The side of an equilateral triangle is the hypotenuse of a 30–60–90 triangle created when the height of the equilateral triangle is drawn (the dotted line in the equilateral triangle shown). Additionally, the height of an equilateral triangle is the same as the long leg of a 30–60–90 triangle. Since the hypotenuse is 10, use the ratio $x : x\sqrt{3} : 2x$ to set $2x = 10$ and determine that the value of x is 5. Therefore, the sides of the 30–60–90 triangle have lengths $5 : 5\sqrt{3} : 10$. The long leg has a length of $5\sqrt{3}$, which is the height of the equilateral triangle.

You may find it useful to estimate on some problems, in which case it will be good to know the approximate decimal forms for $\sqrt{2}$ and $\sqrt{3}$. If you're able to estimate aggressively, you can call either one 1.5. If you need to be more precise with your estimation, then $\sqrt{2} \approx 1.4$ and $\sqrt{3} \approx 1.7$. (A neat little mnemonic to help remember these: 2/14 is Valentine's Day and 3/17 is St. Patrick's Day.)

If you see a 45–45–90 triangle, use the ratio $x : x : x\sqrt{2}$. You can remember this ratio by always calling the smallest angle x (in this case, the two 45° angles) and then making the largest angle $x\sqrt{2}$ because there are two kinds of angles in this triangle, 45 and 90. (This isn't actually *why* the value is $\sqrt{2}$; it's just a way to remember the value.)

If you see a 30–60–90 triangle, use the ratio $x : x\sqrt{3} : 2x$. Remember this ratio by always calling the smallest angle x (in this case, the 30° angle) and the largest $2x$. The middle angle is $x\sqrt{3}$ because there are three kinds of angles in this triangle (30, 60, and 90).

If you get turned around on which side gets the 2 and which one gets the $\sqrt{3}$, compare the numbers: $\sqrt{3}$ is approximately 1.7. The value 2 is greater than 1.7, so 2 must go with the longest side.

Exterior Angles of a Triangle

An **exterior angle** of a triangle (x in the diagram shown) is equal in measure to the sum of the two non-adjacent (opposite) **interior angles** of the triangle (a and c in the diagram shown), as shown here:

$a + b + c = 180$ (sum of angles in a triangle).

$b + x = 180$ (form a straight line).

Therefore, $x = a + c$.

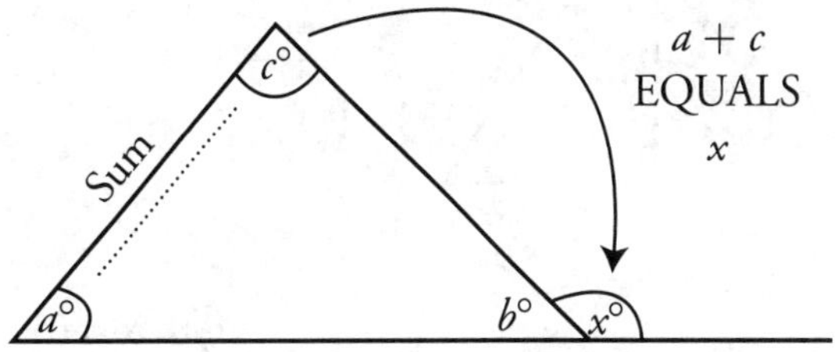

In particular, look for exterior angles within more complicated figures. You might even redraw the figure with certain lines removed to isolate the triangle and exterior angle you need:

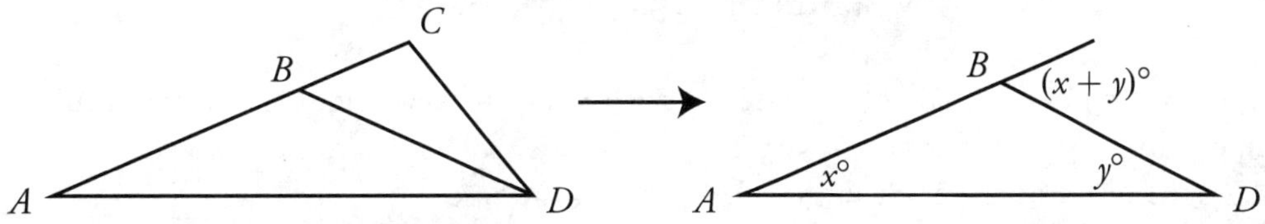

Triangles and Area

You are very likely to be asked to find the area of a triangle on the GMAT:

$$\text{Area of a Triangle} = \frac{\text{Base} \times \text{Height}}{2}$$

The **base** refers to the bottom side of the triangle. The **height** *always* refers to a line drawn from the opposite vertex to the base, creating a 90° angle.

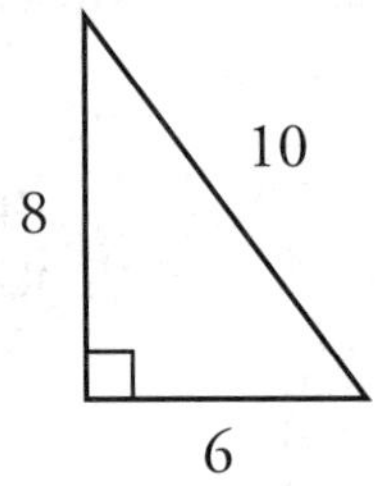

In the triangle on the left, the base is 6 and the height (perpendicular to the base) is 8. Therefore, the area is $(6 \times 8) \div 2 = 48 \div 2 = 24$.

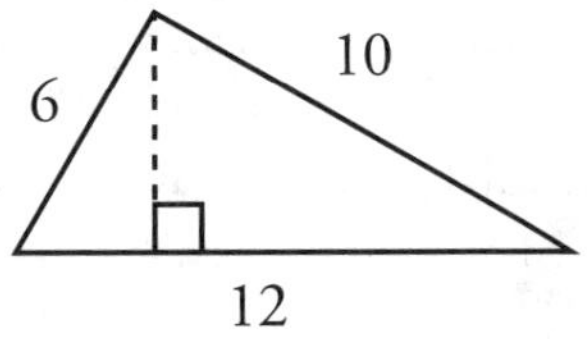

In this triangle, the base is 12, but the height is not shown. Neither of the other two sides of the triangle is perpendicular to the base. In order to find the area of this triangle, you would first need to determine the height, which is represented by the dotted line.

Although you may commonly think of the base of a triangle as whichever side is drawn horizontally or at the bottom, you can designate any side of a triangle as the base. For example, the following three figures show the same triangle, with each side in turn designated as the base:

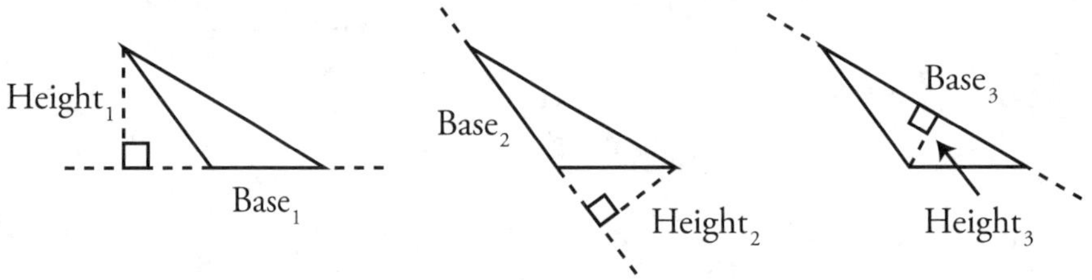

Since a triangle has only one area, the area must be the same regardless of the side chosen as the base. You can choose any pairing of height and base that you like, as long as the height is a perpendicular line drawn from the opposite vertex to the base that you've chosen.

Right triangles have three possible bases just as other triangles do, but they are special because their two legs are perpendicular. Therefore, if one of the legs is chosen as the base, then the other leg is the height. You can also choose the hypotenuse as the base, if that's easier for the problem.

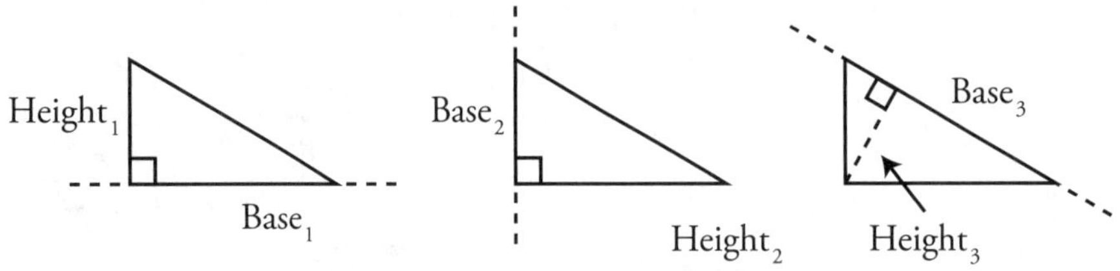

Similar Triangles

One final tool that you can use for GMAT triangle problems is the **similar triangle** strategy. Often, looking for similar triangles can help you solve complex problems.

In similar triangles, all of the **corresponding angles are equal** and the **corresponding sides are in proportion**, as in the triangles below:

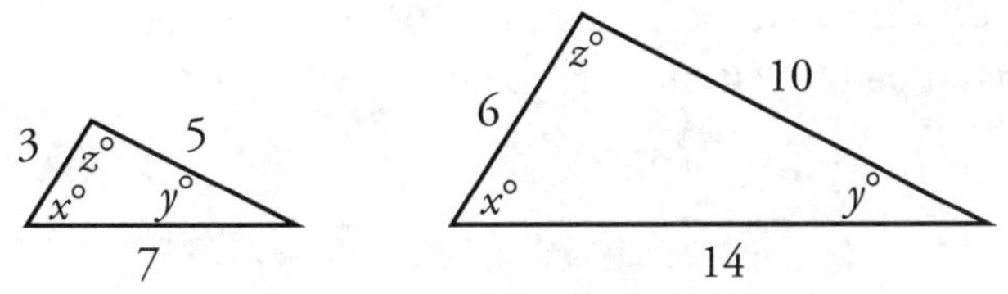

Once you find that two triangles have two pairs of equal (or congruent) angles, you know that the triangles are similar. If two sets of angles are congruent, then the third set of angles must be congruent, since the sum of the angles in any triangle is 180°.

Try an example:

What is the length of side *EF*?

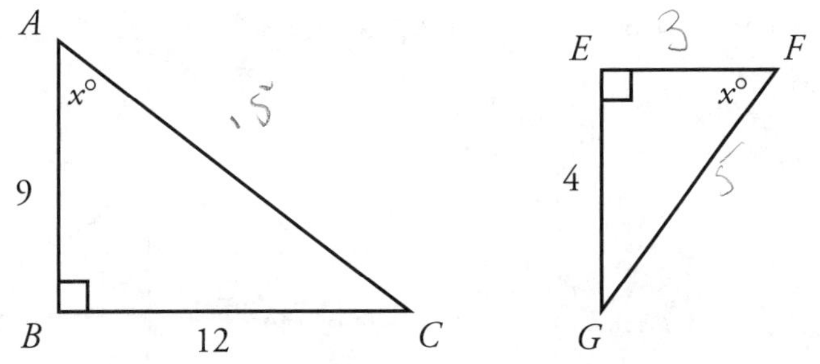

The two triangles above are similar because they have two angles in common (x and the right angle). Since they are similar triangles, their corresponding sides must be in proportion.

Side *BC* corresponds to side *EG* (since they both are opposite angle x). Because these sides are in the ratio of 12 : 4, you can determine that the large triangle is three times bigger than the smaller one. That is, the triangles are in the ratio of 3 : 1. Since side *AB* corresponds to side *EF*, and *AB* has a length of 9, you can conclude that side *EF* has a length of 3.

Problem Set

Now that you've finished the chapter, try these problems.

1. Two sides of a triangle have lengths 4 and 10. If the third side has a length of integer x, how many possible values are there for x ?

2. In the figure shown, $AD = DB = DC$. If angle DCB is 60° and angle ACD is 20°, what is the value of x ? (Note: Figure not drawn to scale.)

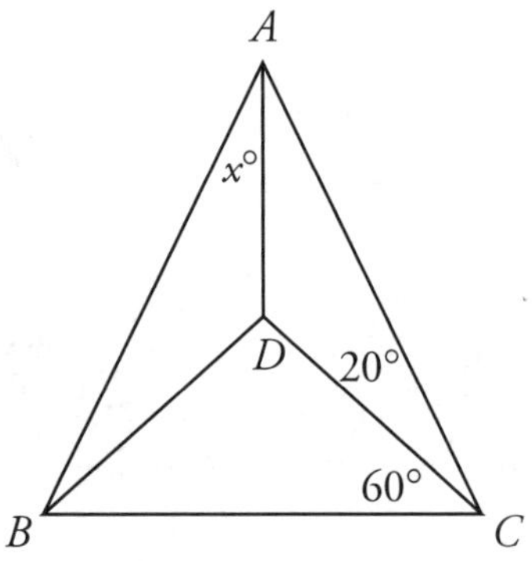

3. Beginning in Town A, Brogan rides a bike 10 miles west, 3 miles north, 5 miles east, and then 9 miles north, to Town B. What is the shortest distance between Town A and Town B? (Assume perfectly flat terrain.)

4. A square is bisected into two equal triangles, as shown in the figure. If the length of BD is $16\sqrt{2}$ inches, what is the area of the square?

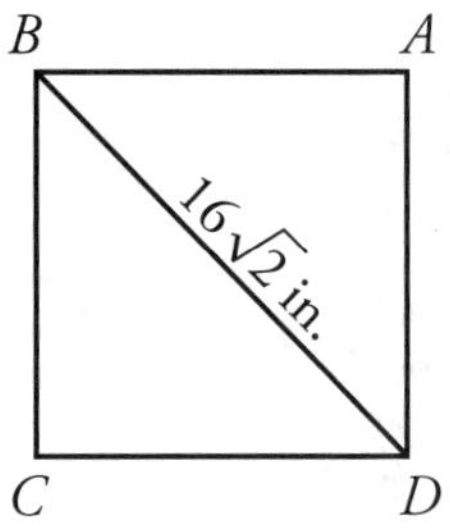

5. What is the value of x in the figure shown?

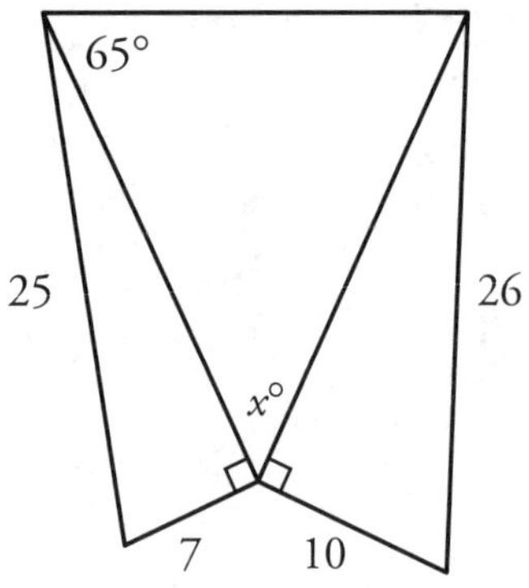

6. The size of a square computer screen is measured by the length of its diagonal. How much bigger is the visible area of a square 24-inch screen than the area of a square 20-inch screen?

Answers and explanations follow on the next page. ▶ ▶ ▶

Solutions

1. **Seven:** If two sides of a triangle are 4 and 10, the third side must be between 10 − 4 and 10 + 4. Therefore, the possible integer values for x are {7, 8, 9, 10, 11, 12, and 13}.

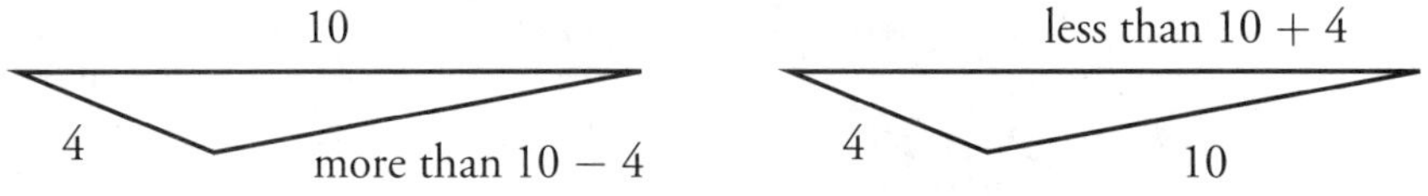

2. **10°:** If $AD = DB = DC$, then the three triangular regions in this figure are all isosceles triangles. Therefore, you can fill in some of the missing angle measurements as shown. Next, there are 180° in the large triangle ACB. Write the following equation for the three angles of the large triangle ACB:

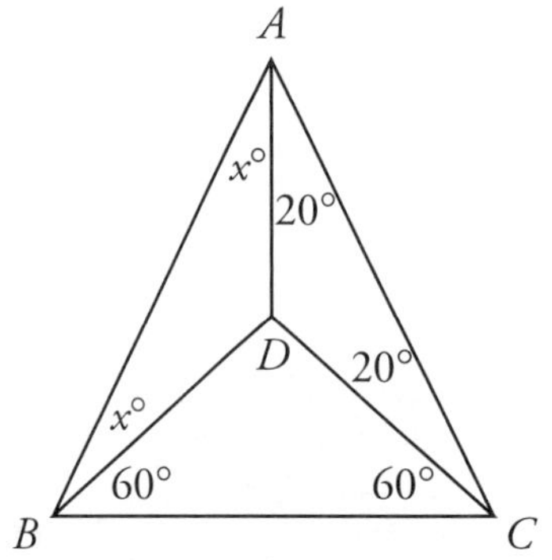

$$x + x + 20 + 20 + 60 + 60 = 180$$
$$2x + 160 = 180$$
$$x = 10$$

3. **13 miles:** Draw a rough sketch of the path Brogan takes, as shown. The direct distance from A to B forms the hypotenuse of a right triangle. The short leg (horizontal) is 10 − 5 = 5 miles and the long leg (vertical) is 9 + 3 = 12 miles. This is a common right triangle with dimensions 5–12–13. If you don't have that common triangle memorized, use the Pythagorean theorem to find the direct distance from A to B:

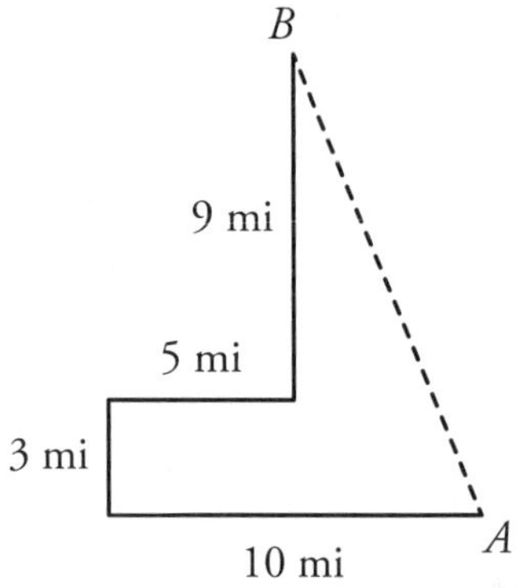

$$5^2 + 12^2 = c^2$$
$$25 + 144 = c^2$$
$$c^2 = 169$$
$$c = 13$$

4. **256 in^2:** A square is formed from two 45–45–90 triangles. The diagonal of a square is $s\sqrt{2}$ and the given length of the diagonal in the problem is $16\sqrt{2}$. Therefore, the side length of square *ABCD* is $s = 16$ inches. The area of the square is s^2, or $16^2 = 256$.

5. **50°:** Find the missing lengths of the two right triangles on the left and right sides of the figure. The right-hand triangle (10–*y*–26) is the 5–12–13 triangle multiplied by 2. The missing length, therefore, is $12 \times 2 = 24$. Use the Pythagorean theorem to find the value for the left-hand triangle:

$$\begin{aligned} 7^2 + b^2 &= 25^2 \\ 49 + b^2 &= 625 \\ b^2 &= 576 \\ b &= 24 \end{aligned}$$

Since the two sides are the same length, the inner triangle is isosceles. Therefore, both angles opposite the equal sides measure 65°. Since there are 180° in a right triangle, $x = 180 - 2(65) = 50$.

6. **88 in^2:** The diagonal of the larger screen is 24 inches. For a square, $d = s\sqrt{2}$, so:

$$\begin{aligned} 24 &= s\sqrt{2} \\ s &= \frac{24}{\sqrt{2}} \end{aligned}$$

You may have learned in school not to leave a root on the bottom of a fraction, but don't do anything about this yet. (In general, if you see annoying math, hold off on doing it as long as you can.) First, find the equivalent value for the smaller screen:

$$\begin{aligned} 20 &= s\sqrt{2} \\ s &= \frac{20}{\sqrt{2}} \end{aligned}$$

The area of a square is s^2, so do that math:

Large screen:

$$\begin{aligned} A &= \frac{24}{\sqrt{2}} \times \frac{24}{\sqrt{2}} \\ &= \frac{24 \times 24}{2} \\ &= 24 \times 12 \\ &= 2 \times 12 \times 12 \\ &= 288 \end{aligned}$$

Small screen:

$$\begin{aligned} A &= \frac{20}{\sqrt{2}} \times \frac{20}{\sqrt{2}} \\ &= \frac{20 \times 20}{2} \\ &= 20 \times 10 \\ &= 200 \end{aligned}$$

The square roots disappear on their own! The visible area of the larger screen is $288 - 200 = 88$ square inches bigger than the visible area of the smaller screen.

CHAPTER 34

Circles and Cylinders

In This Chapter

- Radius, Diameter, Circumference, and Area
- Area of a Sector
- Inscribed vs. Central Angles
- Inscribed Triangles
- Cylinders and Volume

In this chapter, you will learn how to use the radius and diameter of a circle to find circumference and area, as well as how to find the area or circumference of just a portion of a circle. You'll also learn the difference between inscribed and central angles and how to use them. Finally, you'll learn about three-dimensional shapes related to circles, including cylinders and spheres.

CHAPTER 34 Circles and Cylinders

A **circle** is defined as the set of points in a plane that are equidistant from a fixed center point. A circle contains 360°.

Any line segment that connects the center point to a point on the circle is termed a **radius** of the circle. If point *O* is the center of the circle shown, then segment *OC* is a radius:

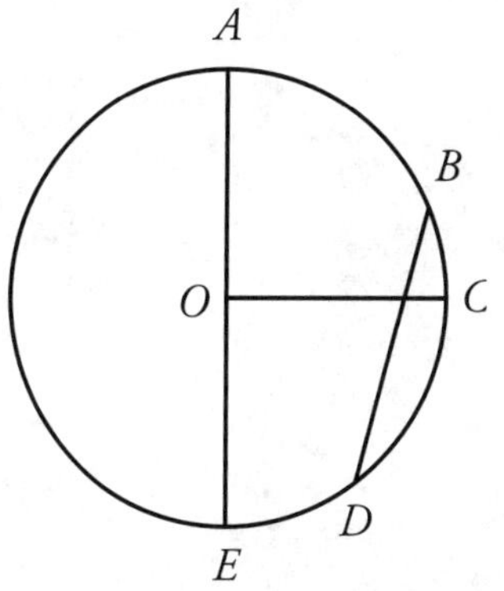

Any line segment that connects two points on a circle is called a **chord**, such as line *BD*. Any chord that passes through the center of the circle is called a **diameter**, such as line *AE*. The diameter is always two times the length of the radius.

The GMAT tests your ability to find the circumference and the area of whole and partial circles. In addition, some advanced problems may test **cylinders**, which are three-dimensional shapes made, in part, of circles. The GMAT may test your ability to find the volume of cylinders.

Radius, Diameter, Circumference, and Area

The relationships between the radius, diameter, circumference, and area remain constant for every circle. If you know any one of these values, you can find all of the rest.

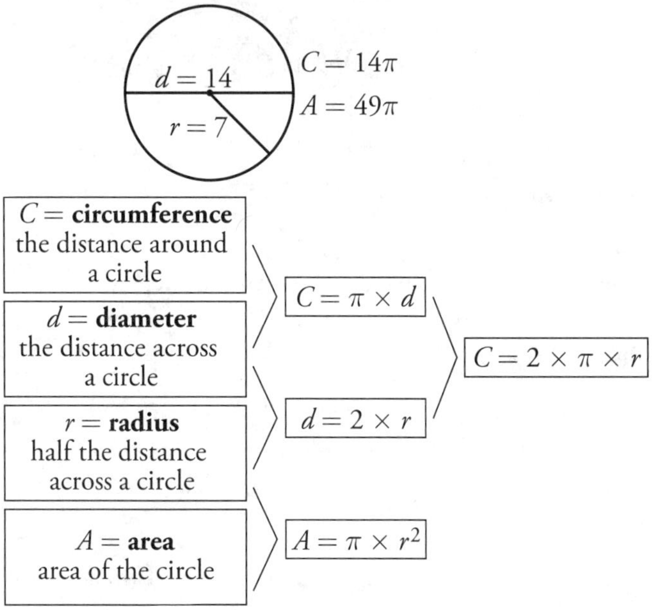

For Problem Solving questions, you will often need to use one of these values to solve for one of the other three. For Data Sufficiency questions, just knowing that you have one of these values is enough to know that you can find any of the others—so you may not have to do very much math at all.

The value of π is approximately 3.14. Most of the time, the GMAT will keep π in the answer, so you don't need to know what it is. Occasionally, you may need to estimate an answer; use 3 as the estimated value for π. Try an example:

> What is the area of a circle with a circumference of 16π?

In order to find the area of a circle, find the radius. The circumference of the circle is 16π and $C = 2\pi r$, so the radius must be 8. Plug this into the area formula:

$$A = \pi r^2 = \pi\left(8^2\right) = 64\pi$$

Area of a Sector

The GMAT may ask you to solve for the area of a sector of a circle instead of the area of the entire circle. You can find the area of a sector by determining the fraction of the entire area that the sector occupies. Try an example:

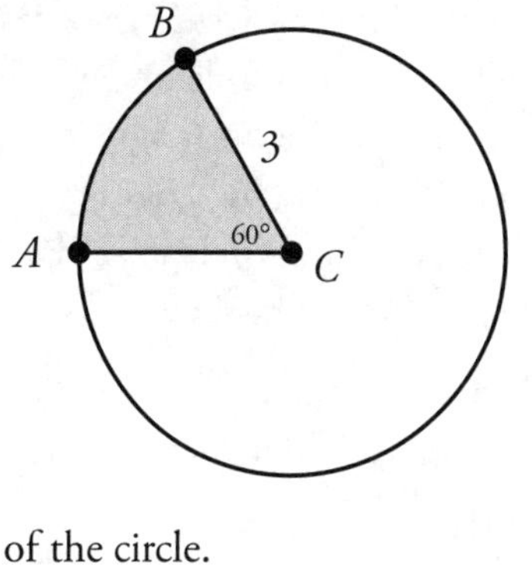

What is the area of sector *BCA* (the shaded region) in the figure?

First, find the area of the entire circle:

$$A = \pi r^2 = \pi\left(3^2\right) = 9\pi$$

Then, use the central angle to determine what fraction of the entire circle is represented by the sector. Since the sector is defined by the central angle of 60°, and the entire circle is 360°, the sector occupies $\frac{60^\circ}{360^\circ} = \frac{1}{6}$ of the area of the circle.

Therefore, the area of sector *BCA* is $\left(\frac{1}{6}\right)(9\pi) = 1.5\pi$.

Inscribed vs. Central Angles

The **central angle** is defined as an angle whose vertex lies at the center point of a circle. Another type of angle is termed an **inscribed angle**. An inscribed angle has its vertex on the circle itself.

The following figures illustrate the difference between a central angle and an inscribed angle:

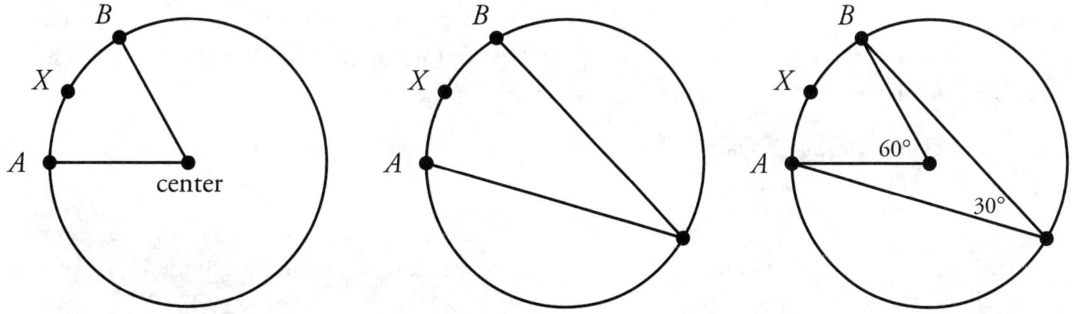

Central Angle   Inscribed Angle

In both cases, the angle defines both an arc (*AXB*, a portion of the circumference) and a sector (the pie-shaped wedge, a portion of the area).

In the circle at the far right, there is a central angle and an inscribed angle, both of which intercept arc *AXB*. The central angle for the arc is 60° (or one-sixth of the complete 360° circle). **An inscribed angle is equal to half of the equivalent central angle**, in degrees. In this case, the inscribed angle is 30°, which is half of 60°.

Inscribed Triangles

Related to this idea of an inscribed angle is that of an **inscribed triangle**. A triangle is said to be inscribed in a circle if all of the vertices of the triangle are points on the circle. The important rule to remember is this: **If one of the sides of an inscribed triangle is a *diameter* of the circle, then the triangle *must* be a right triangle.** Conversely, any right triangle inscribed in a circle must have the diameter of the circle as one of its sides (thereby splitting the circle in half).

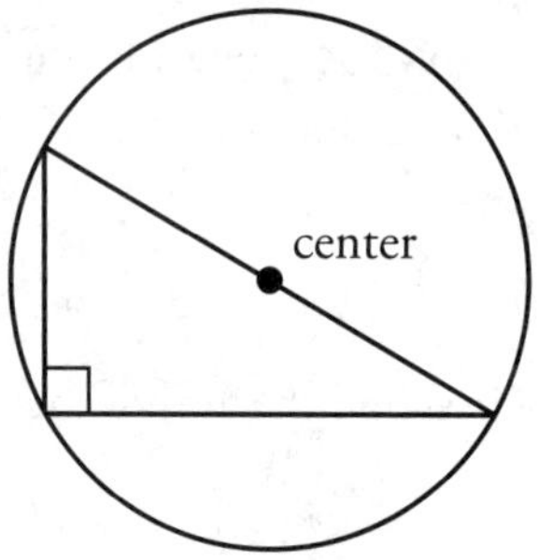

In the second figure, triangle *ABC* must be a right triangle, since *AC* is a diameter of the circle.

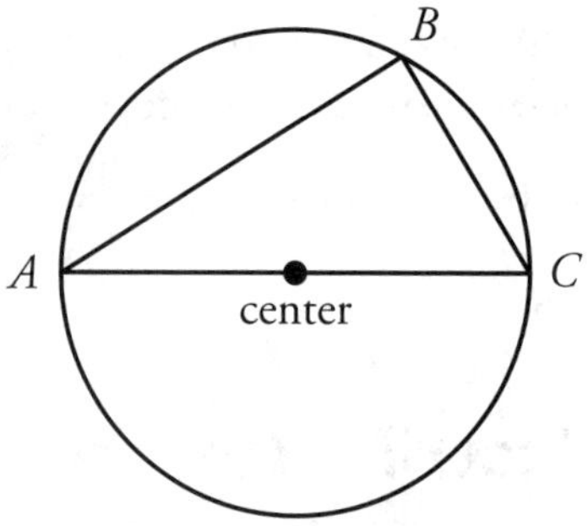

34

Cylinders and Volume

Cylinder questions are not especially common on the GMAT; you probably won't see any, but, if you do, you might not see more than one. If geometry is a weaker area for you, consider not studying this material and guessing immediately if you do see a cylinder problem on the exam.

The volume of a cylinder measures how much "stuff" it can hold inside. In order to find the volume of a cylinder, use the following formula:

$V = \pi r^2 h$ *V* is the volume, *r* is the radius, and *h* is the height of the cylinder.

Determining the volume of a cylinder requires two pieces of information: 1) the radius of the cylinder and 2) the height of the cylinder.

The figures below show that two cylinders can have the same volume but different shapes (and therefore each would fit differently inside a larger object):

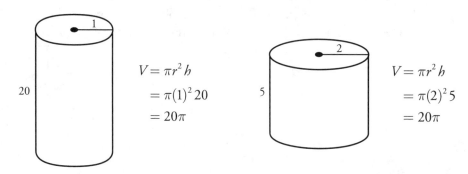

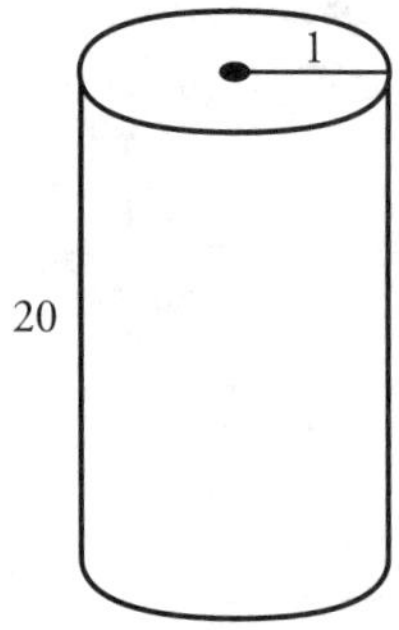

$$\begin{aligned} V &= \pi r^2 h \\ &= \pi(1)^2 20 \\ &= 20\pi \end{aligned}$$

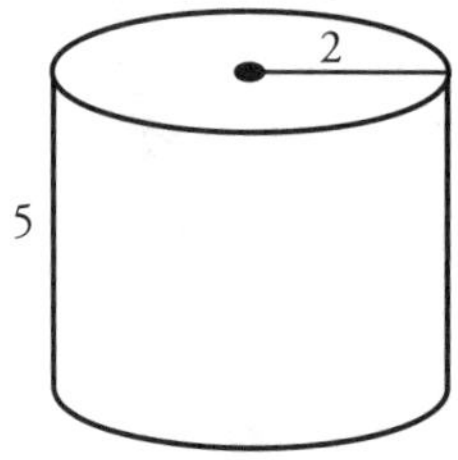

$$\begin{aligned} V &= \pi r^2 h \\ &= \pi(2)^2 5 \\ &= 20\pi \end{aligned}$$

Problem Set

Now that you've finished the chapter, try these problems.

1. As shown in the figure, a circular lawn with a radius of 5 meters is surrounded by a circular walkway that is 4 meters wide. What is the area of the walkway, in square meters?

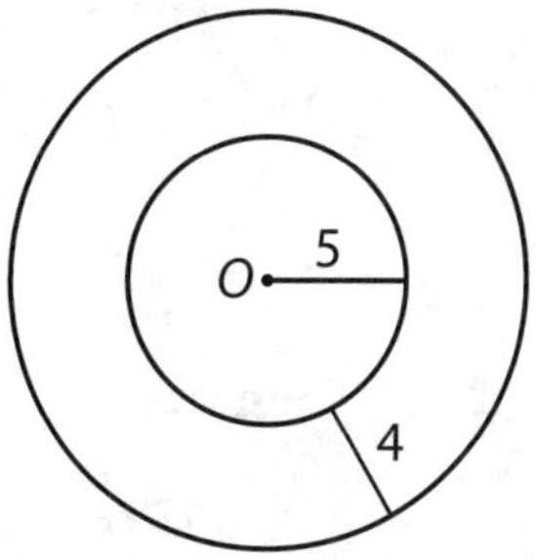

2. Ren can run π meters every 2 seconds. If a circular track has a radius of 75 meters, how many minutes does it take Ren to run twice around the track?

3. As shown in the figure, *BE* and *CD* are both diameters of a circle with center *A*. If the area of the circle is 180, what is the total area of the shaded regions?

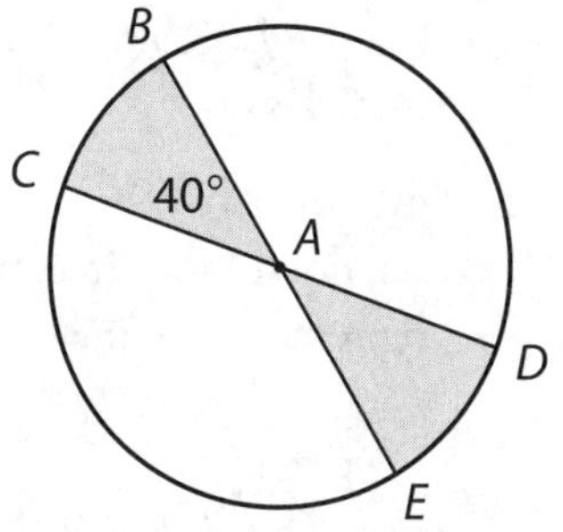

4. A cylindrical water tank has a diameter of 4 meters and a height of 20 meters. A water truck can fill π cubic meters of the tank every minute. How many minutes will it take the water truck to fill the water tank from empty to half full?

5. A Hydrogenator water gun has a cylindrical water tank, which is 30 centimeters long. A hose can fill the Hydrogenator with π cubic centimeters of water every second. If it takes 8 minutes to fill the tank with water, what is the diameter of the circular base of the gun's water tank, in centimeters?

Solutions

1. **56π m^2:** The area of the walkway is the area of the entire image (walkway + lawn) minus the area of the lawn. Find the area of each circle and subtract:

Large circle: $A = \pi r^2 = \pi(9)^2 = 81\pi$

Small circle: $A = \pi r^2 = \pi(5)^2 = 25\pi$ Subtract: $81\pi - 25\pi = 56\pi$ m^2

2. **10 minutes:** The distance around the track is the circumference of the circle:

$$C = 2\pi r$$
$$C = 2\pi(75)$$
$$C = 150\pi$$

Running twice around the circle would equal a distance of 300π meters. At a rate of π meters every 2 seconds, Ren runs 30π meters every minute. Therefore, it will take Ren 10 minutes to run 300π meters.

3. **40:** The two central angles of the shaded sectors cover a total of $40° + 40° = 80°$. Figure out what fraction of the circle this represents, then use that fraction to solve for the portion of the area represented by the shaded regions:

$\frac{80}{360} = \frac{2}{9}$ $\frac{2}{9}$ of 180 is 40.

4. **40 minutes:** First, find the volume of the cylindrical tank:

$$V = \pi r^2 \times h$$
$$= \pi(2)^2 \times 20$$
$$= 80\pi$$

If the water truck can fill π cubic meters of the tank every minute, it will take 80 minutes to fill the tank completely; therefore, it will take $80 \div 2 = 40$ minutes to fill the tank halfway.

5. **8 centimeters:** In 8 minutes, or 480 seconds, 480π cm^3 of water flows into the tank. Therefore, the volume of the tank is 480π. Use the height of 30 to solve for the radius:

$$V = \pi r^2 \times h$$
$$480\pi = 30\pi r^2$$
$$r^2 = 16$$
$$r = 4$$

Therefore, the diameter of the tank's base is 8 centimeters.

CHAPTER 35

Coordinate Plane

In This Chapter

- Positive and Negative Quadrants
- The Slope of a Line
- The Four Types of Slopes
- The Intercepts of a Line
- Slope-Intercept Equation: $y = mx + b$
- Horizontal and Vertical Lines
- The Distance Between Two Points

In this chapter, you will learn how to find the slope of a line and how to map a line onto a coordinate plane. You'll learn how to use the slope-intercept form of the equation of a line, as well as how to find the distance between any two points in a coordinate plane.

CHAPTER 35 Coordinate Plane

The **coordinate plane** is formed by a horizontal axis or reference line (the ***x*-axis**) and a vertical axis (the ***y*-axis**), as shown below. These axes are each marked off like a number line, with both positive and negative numbers. The axes cross at right angles at the number zero.

Points in the plane are identified by using an ordered pair of numbers, such as the point shown, which is written as $(2, -3)$. The first number in the ordered pair (2) is the ***x*-coordinate**, which corresponds to the point's horizontal location, as measured by the x-axis. The second number in the ordered pair (-3) is the ***y*-coordinate**, which corresponds to the point's vertical location, as indicated by the y-axis. The point $(0, 0)$, where the axes cross, is called the **origin**.

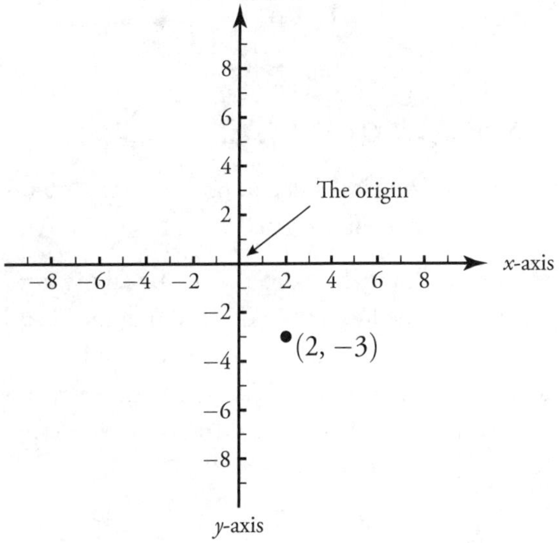

A line in the plane is formed by the connection of two or more points. Also, along the x-axis line, the y-coordinate is 0. Likewise, along the y-axis line, the x-coordinate is 0.

If the GMAT gives you coordinates with other variables, match them to x and y. For instance, if you have point (a, b), a is the x-coordinate and b is the y-coordinate.

Positive and Negative Quadrants

There are four quadrants in the coordinate plane, as shown in the figure below. Start in the upper-right corner and move *counter*clockwise.

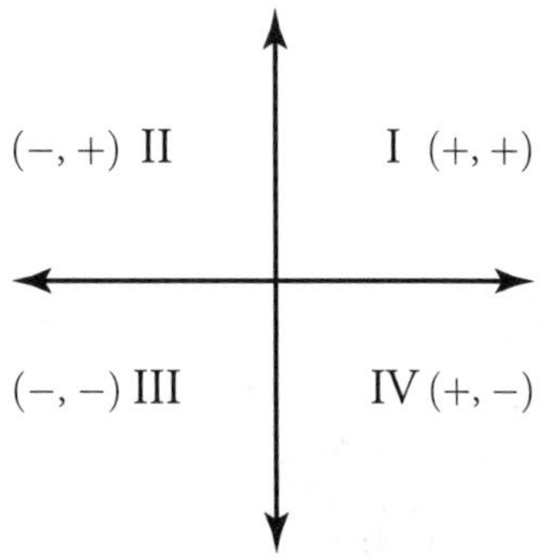

Quadrant I contains only those points with a **positive** *x*-coordinate and a **positive** *y*-coordinate.

Quadrant II contains only those points with a **negative** *x*-coordinate and a **positive** *y*-coordinate.

Quadrant III contains only those points with a **negative** *x*-coordinate and a **negative** *y*-coordinate.

Quadrant IV contains only those points with a **positive** *x*-coordinate and a **negative** *y*-coordinate.

The Slope of a Line

The **slope** of a line is defined as *rise over run*—that is, how much the line *rises* vertically divided by how much the line *runs* horizontally.

The slope of a line can be determined by taking any two points on the line and 1) determining the **rise**, or difference between their *y*-coordinates, and 2) determining the **run**, or difference between their *x*-coordinates. You can use the formula below to find a slope:

$$\textbf{Slope} = \frac{\textbf{Rise}}{\textbf{Run}}$$

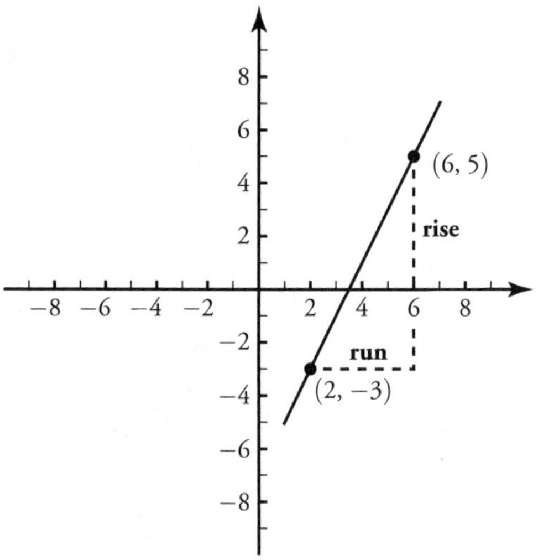

For example, in the graph shown, the line rises vertically from -3 to $+5$. To find the vertical distance, subtract the *y*-coordinates: $5 - (-3) = 8$. Thus, the line rises 8 units. The line also runs horizontally from 2 to 6. To find the horizontal distance, subtract the *x*-coordinates: $6 - 2 = 4$. Thus, the line runs 4 units.

Put the results together to find the slope of the line: $\frac{\text{Rise}}{\text{Run}} = \frac{8}{4} = 2$.

Two other points on the same line may have a different rise and run, but the slope will be the same. The rise over run will always be 2 because a line has a constant slope.

The slope of a line is equal to $\frac{y_2 - y_1}{x_2 - x_1}$.

For a different line, if you are given the two points (2, 3) and (4, −1), then you can find the slope:

$$\frac{-1-3}{4-2} = \frac{-4}{2} = -2$$

You can use the two points in either order, but make sure that y_2 and x_2 always come from the same point (and that y_1 and x_1 always come from the same point). Here's the slope for the same two points but used in reverse order, $(4, -1)$ and $(2, 3)$:

$$\frac{3-(-1)}{2-4} = \frac{4}{-2} = -2$$

Either way, the slope is the same.

The Four Types of Slopes

A line can have one of four types of slopes:

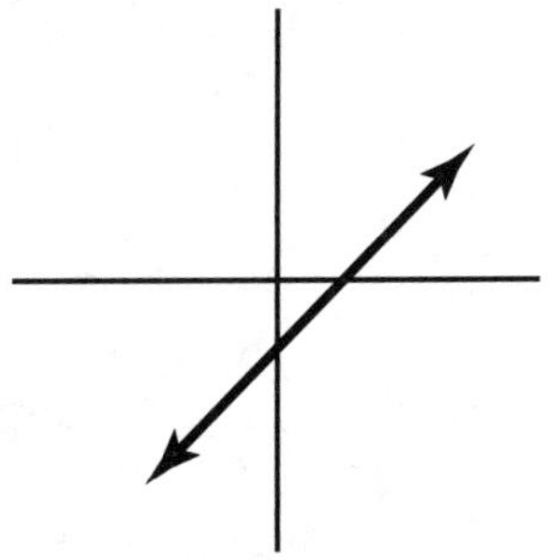

Positive Slope

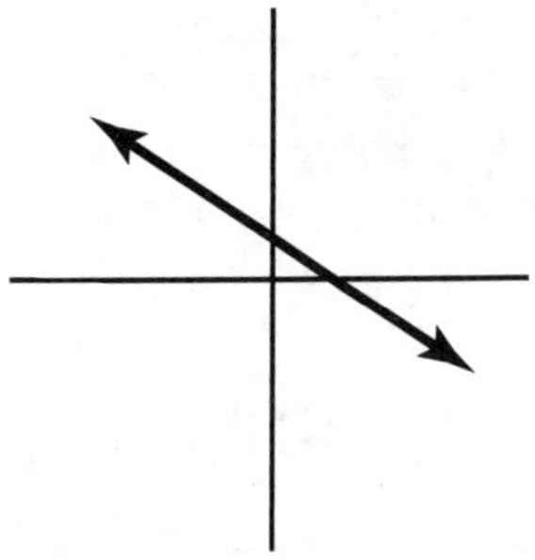

Negative Slope

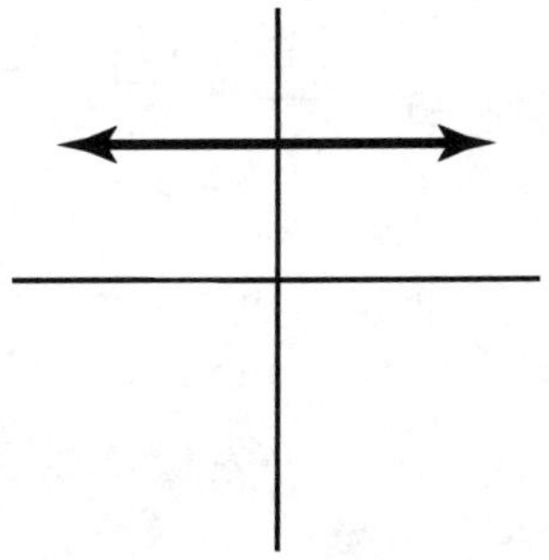

Zero Slope

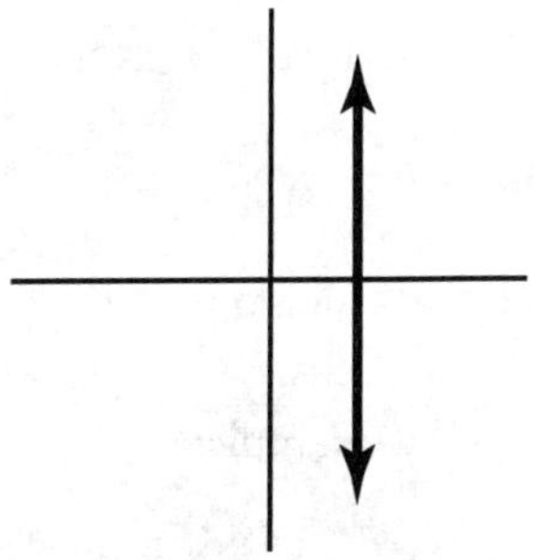

Undefined Slope

A line with positive slope rises upward from left to right. A line with negative slope falls downward from left to right. A horizontal line has zero slope. A vertical line has undefined slope. Notice that the *x*-axis has zero slope, while the *y*-axis has undefined slope.

The Intercepts of a Line

A point where a line intersects a coordinate axis is called an **intercept**. There are two types of intercepts: the x-intercept, where the line intersects the x-axis, and the y-intercept, where the line intersects the y-axis.

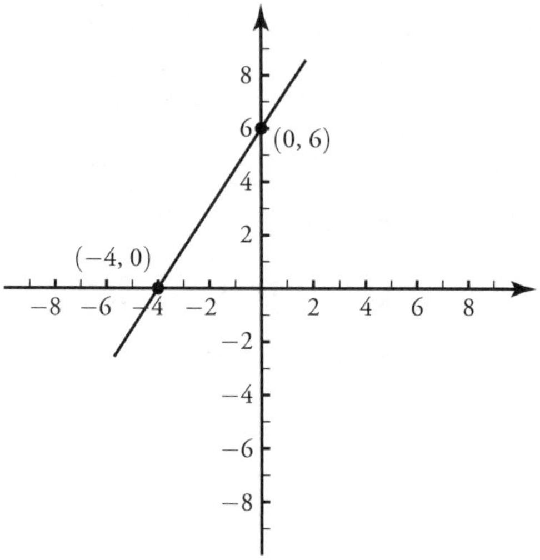

The x-intercept is expressed using the ordered pair $(x, 0)$, where x is the point where the line intersects the x-axis. **The x-intercept is the point on the line at which $y = 0$.** In this graph, the x-intercept is -4, as expressed by the ordered pair $(-4, 0)$.

The y-intercept is expressed using the ordered pair $(0, y)$, where y is the point where the line intersects the y-axis. **The y-intercept is the point on the line at which $x = 0$.** In this graph, the y-intercept is 6, as expressed by the ordered pair $(0, 6)$.

Slope-Intercept Equation: $y = mx + b$

Linear equations represent lines in the coordinate plane. Linear equations often look like this: $Ax + By = C$, where A, B, and C are numbers. For instance, $6x + 3y = 18$ is a linear equation. Linear equations never involve terms such as x^2, $\sqrt{x}$, or xy.

In coordinate plane problems, it can be useful to write linear equations in the slope-intercept form:

$$y = mx + b$$

In this equation, m represents the slope of the line and b represents the y-intercept of the line, or the point at which the line crosses the y-axis. When you want to graph a linear equation, rewrite the equation in the slope-intercept form. Try this example:

What is the slope-intercept form for a line with the equation $6x + 3y = 18$?

$3y = 18 - 6x$
$3y = -6x + 18$
$y = -2x + 6$

Rewrite the equation by solving for y as follows:

$$6x + 3y = 18$$

$3y = 18 - 6x$	Subtract $6x$ from both sides.
$y = 6 - 2x$	Divide both sides by 3.
$y = -2x + 6$	Rearrange. The y-intercept is $(0, 6)$, and the slope is -2.

$6x + 3y = 18$
$6x = -3y + 18$
$x = -\frac{1}{2}y + 3$

To graph this line, first put a point at +6 on the y-axis (because the y-intercept, b, equals 6).

Then, count down 2 units (because the slope is negative) and to the right 1 unit. Place another point.

Now, draw a line between the two points.

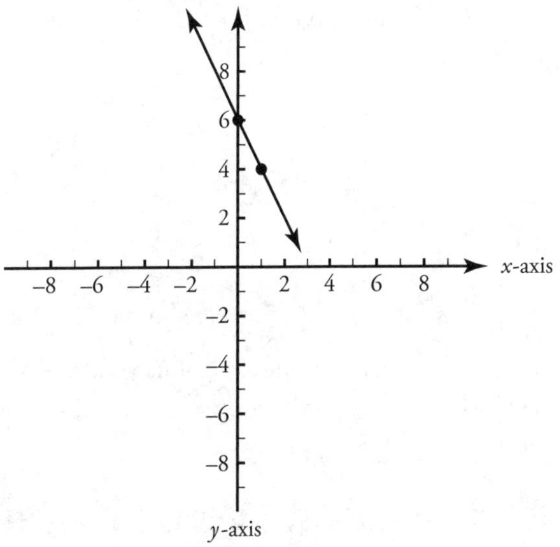

The GMAT sometimes asks you to determine which quadrants a given line passes through. For example:

> Which quadrants does the line $2x + y = 5$ pass through?

First, rewrite the line in the form $y = mx + b$:

$$2x + y = 5$$
$$y = 5 - 2x$$
$$y = -2x + 5$$

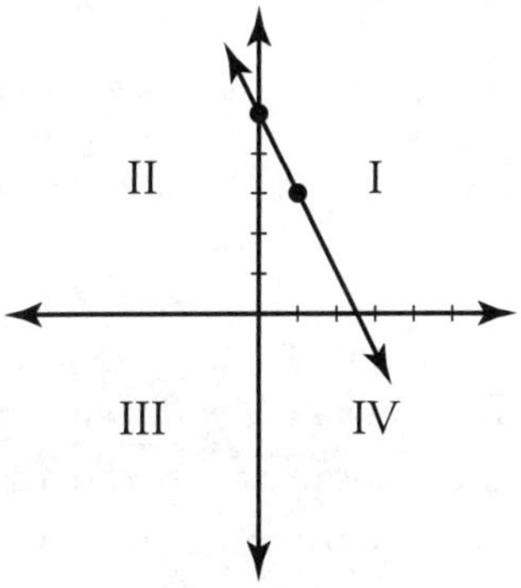

Next, sketch the line. Since $b = 5$, the y-intercept is the point (0, 5). The slope is -2, so the line slopes downward to the right from the y-intercept. A slope of -2 is the equivalent of $\frac{-2}{1}$. Count two places down from the intercept (the rise of a negative slope) and one place to the right (the run). Draw a second point, then connect the two points with a line. You can now see that the line passes through quadrants I, II, and IV.

Alternatively, find two points on the line by setting x and y equal to 0 in the original equation. In this way, you find the x- and y-intercepts:

$$\begin{aligned} x &= 0 \\ 2x + y &= 5 \\ 2(0) + y &= 5 \\ y &= 5 \end{aligned}$$

$$\begin{aligned} y &= 0 \\ 2x + y &= 5 \\ 2x + (0) &= 5 \\ x &= 2.5 \end{aligned}$$

The points (0, 5) and (2.5, 0) are both on the line.

Now, sketch the line using the points you have identified. If you plot (0, 5) and (2.5, 0) on the coordinate plane, you can connect them to see the position of the line. Again, the line passes through quadrants I, II, and IV.

Horizontal and Vertical Lines

Horizontal and vertical lines are not expressed in the $y = mx + b$ form. Instead, they are expressed as simpler one-variable equations.

Horizontal lines are expressed in the form:

$y =$ *some number*, such as $y = 2$ or $y = -7$

Vertical lines are expressed in the form:

$x =$ *some number*, such as $x = 3$ or $x = 5$

All the points on a vertical line have the same x-coordinate. This is why the equation of a vertical line is defined only by x. The y-axis itself corresponds to the equation $x = 0$. Likewise, all the points on a horizontal line have the same y-coordinate. This is why the equation of a horizontal line is defined only by y. The x-axis itself corresponds to the equation $y = 0$.

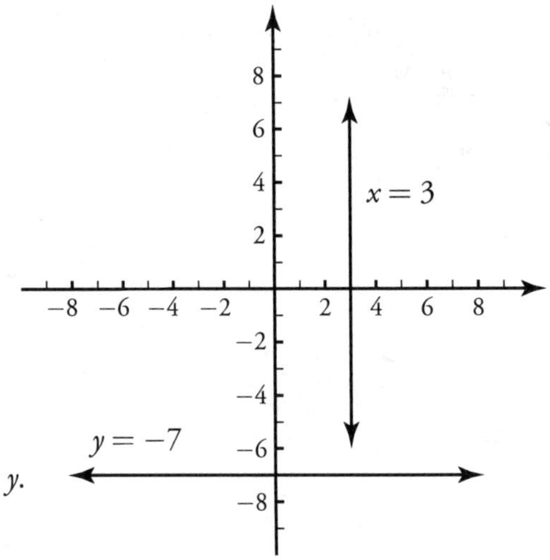

The Distance between Two Points

The distance between any two points in the coordinate plane can be calculated by using the Pythagorean theorem. For example:

What is the distance between the points (1, 3) and (7, −5) ?

Start by drawing a right triangle connecting the points, as shown here:

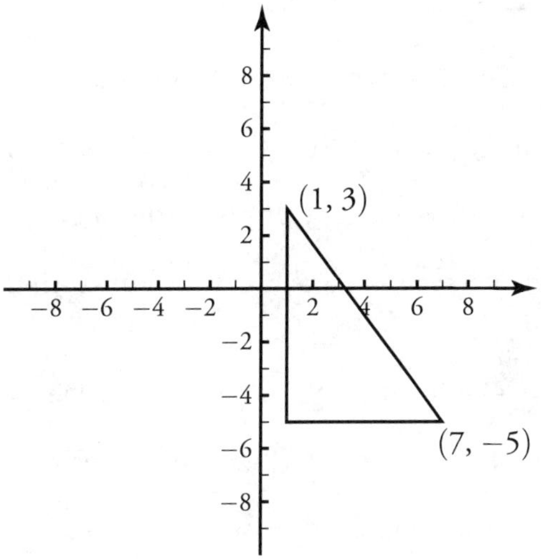

Next, find the lengths of the two legs of the triangle by calculating the rise and the run.

The y-coordinate changes from 3 to -5, a difference of 8 (the vertical leg).

The x-coordinate changes from 1 to 7, a difference of 6 (the horizontal leg).

Now, if you have a common right triangle, use what you've memorized. In this case, the triangle is a multiple of the common 3–4–5 triangle: 6–8–10. The hypotenuse of the triangle is 10, so the distance between the two points is 10 units.

Alternatively, use the Pythagorean theorem to calculate the length of the diagonal, which is the distance between the points:

$$6^2 + 8^2 = c^2$$
$$36 + 64 = c^2$$
$$100 = c^2$$
$$c = 10$$

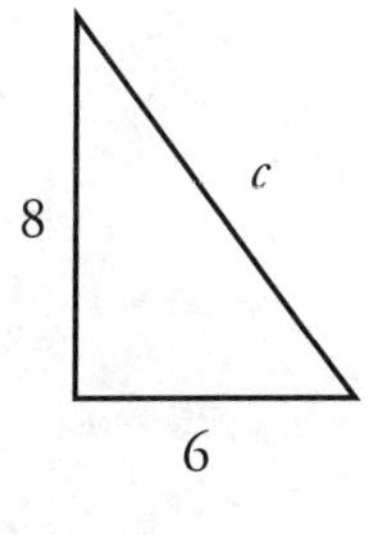

Advanced material for the Geometry unit can be found in Atlas, Manhattan Prep's online learning platform. Use the online material only if you feel that you have mastered everything in the Geometry unit of this strategy guide and only if you are aiming for a Quant section score of 48 or higher.

Problem Set

Now that you've finished the chapter, try these problems.

1. A line has the equation $y = 3x + 7$. At which point does this line intersect the y-axis?

2. A line has the equation $x = -2y + z$. If (3, 2) is a point on the line, what is z ?

3. Which quadrants, if any, do NOT contain any points on the line represented by $x - y = 18$?

4. A line has a slope of $\frac{1}{6}$ and intersects the x-axis at $(-24, 0)$. At which point does this line intersect the y-axis?

5. A line has the equation $x = \frac{y}{80} - 20$. At which point does this line intersect the x-axis?

6. Which quadrants, if any, do NOT contain any points on the line represented by $x = 10y$?

7. Which quadrants, if any, contain points on the line represented by $x + 18 = 2y$?

8. A line has a slope of $\frac{3}{4}$ and intersects the point $(-12, -39)$. At which point does this line intersect the x-axis?

Answers and explanations follow on the next page. ▶ ▶ ▶

Solutions

1. **(0, 7):** A line intersects the y-axis at the y-intercept. Since this equation is written in slope-intercept form, $y = mx + b$, the y-intercept is the b portion of the equation: 7. Thus, the line intersects the y-axis at the point $(0, 7)$.

2. **7:** Substitute the coordinates $(3, 2)$ for x and y and solve for z:

$$3 = -2(2) + z$$
$$3 = -4 + z$$
$$z = 7$$

3. **Quadrant II:** First, rewrite the line in slope-intercept form:

$$y = x - 18$$

Find the intercepts by setting x equal to 0 and y equal to 0:

$$y = 0 - 18 \qquad 0 = x - 18$$
$$y = -18 \qquad x = 18$$

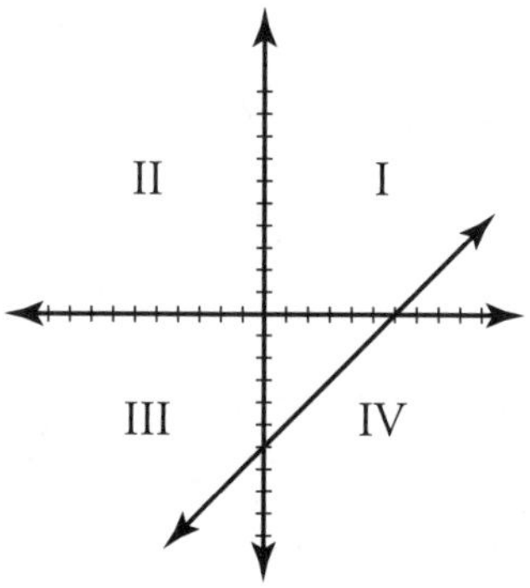

Plot the points: $(0, -18)$ and $(18, 0)$. (In the diagram shown, each tick mark represents three units: 3, 6, 9, . . .) The line does not pass through quadrant II.

4. **(0, 4):** Plug the slope in for m. Then, use the given point to find the value of b:

$$y = \frac{1}{6}x + b$$
$$0 = \frac{1}{6}(-24) + b$$
$$0 = -4 + b$$
$$b = 4$$

The variable b represents the y-intercept. Therefore, the line intersects the y-axis at $(0, 4)$.

5. **(−20, 0):** A line intersects the x-axis at the x-intercept or when the y-coordinate is equal to 0. Substitute 0 for y and solve for x:

$$x = 0 - 20$$
$$x = -20$$

The line crosses the x-intercept at the point $(-20, 0)$.

6. **Quadrants II and IV:** First, rewrite the line in slope-intercept form: $y = \frac{x}{10}$

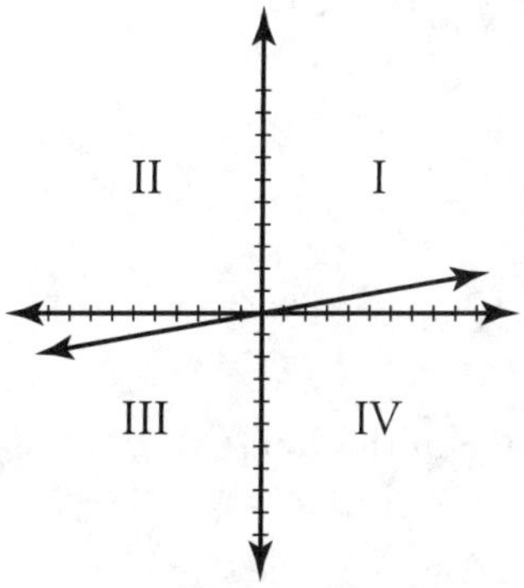

If you plug in 0 for either variable, the other variable will also equal 0. The line crosses the y-intercept at the origin (0, 0). To find another point on the line, substitute any convenient number for x; given the equation, 10 would be a good number to choose:

$y = \frac{10}{10} = 1$ The point (10, 1) is on the line.

Plot the points: (0, 0) and (10, 1). The line does not pass through quadrants II or IV.

7. **Quadrants I, II, and III:** First, rewrite the line in slope-intercept form: $y = \frac{x}{2} + 9$

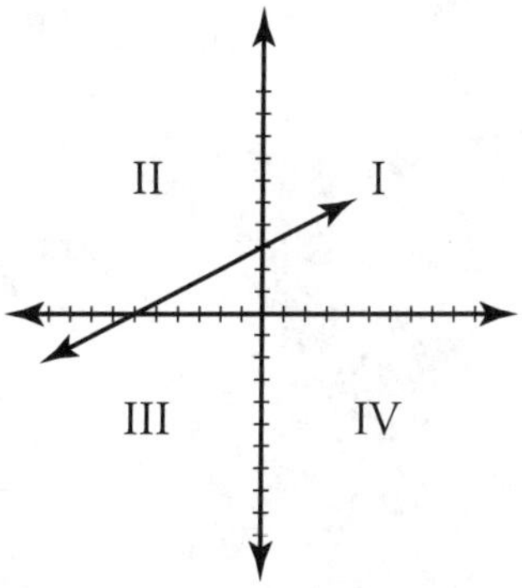

Find the intercepts by setting x equal to 0 and y equal to 0:

$0 = \frac{x}{2} + 9$ $y = \frac{0}{2} + 9$

$x = -18$ $y = 9$

Plot the points: (−18, 0) and (0, 9). (In the diagram shown, each tick mark represents three units: 3, 6, 9, …) The line passes through quadrants I, II, and III.

8. **(40, 0):** First, plug the information given into the slope-intercept equation to find the value of b:

$$y = \frac{3}{4}x + b$$
$$-39 = \frac{3}{4}(-12) + b$$
$$-39 = -9 + b$$
$$b = -30$$

This allows you to write the equation of this line:

$$y = \frac{3}{4}x - 30$$

The line intersects the x-axis when $y = 0$. Set y equal to 0 and solve for x:

$$0 = \frac{3}{4}x - 30$$
$$\frac{3}{4}x = 30$$
$$x = 40$$

The line intersects the x-axis at $(40, 0)$.

Geometry Cheat Sheet

Use the cheat sheet, shown on the reverse, to help memorize geometry rules and formulas. Feel free to cut or tear out this page to keep as a reference.

Area

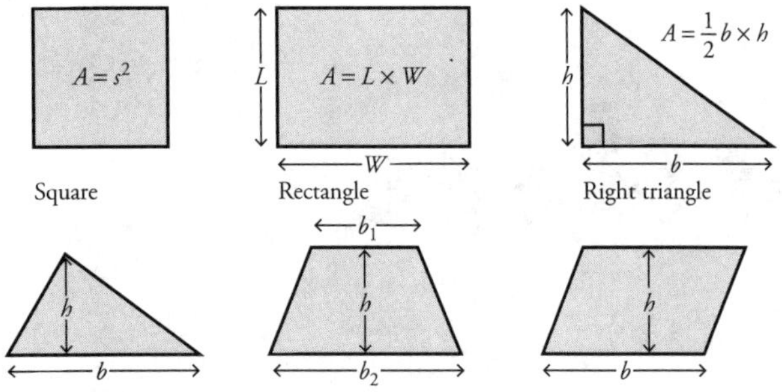

$A = \frac{1}{2} b \times h$
Triangle

$A = \left(\frac{b_1 + b_2}{2}\right) \times h$
Trapezoid

$A = b \times h$
Parallelogram

Perimeter

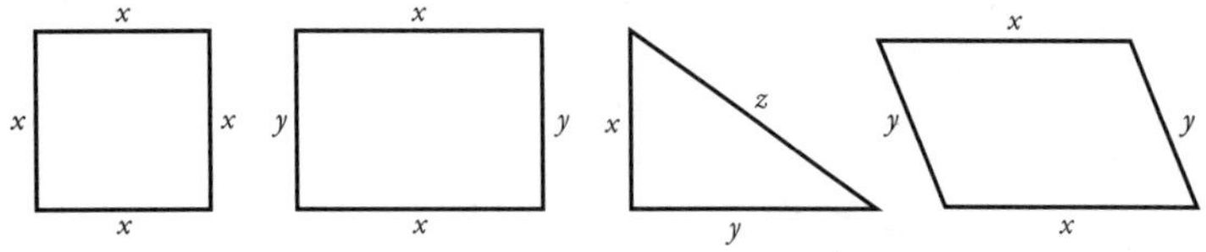

$P = 4x$

$P = 2x + 2y$

$P = x + y + z$

$P = 2x + 2y$

Circles

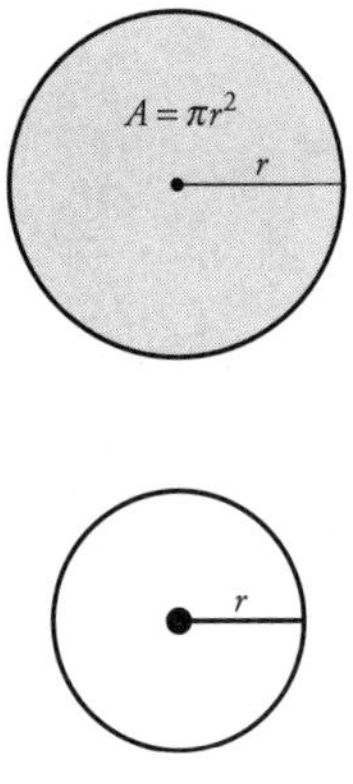

$C = 2\pi r$

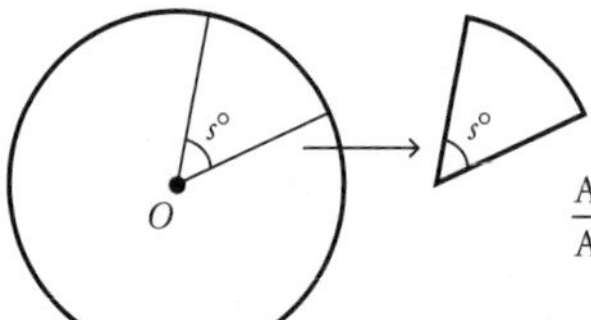

$$\frac{\text{Area}_{\text{sector}}}{\text{Area}_{\text{circle}}} = \frac{s}{360}$$

Inscribed Angles

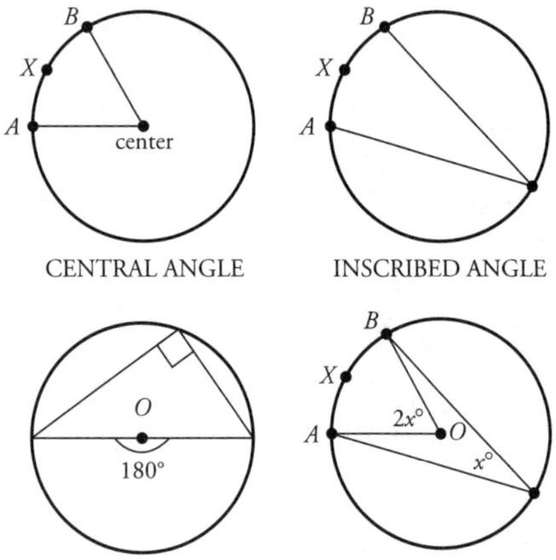

Coordinate Plane

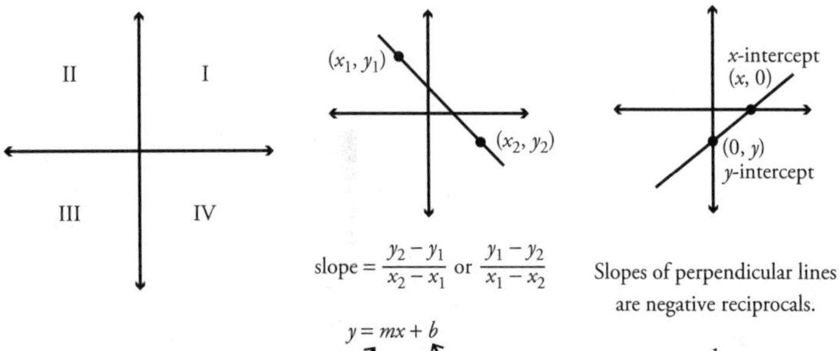

$$\text{slope} = \frac{y_2 - y_1}{x_2 - x_1} \text{ or } \frac{y_1 - y_2}{x_1 - x_2}$$

$y = mx + b$
slope ↗ ↖ y-intercept

Slopes of perpendicular lines are negative reciprocals.

ex. l_1 slope $= \frac{1}{2}$, l_2 slope $= -2$

Special Right Triangles

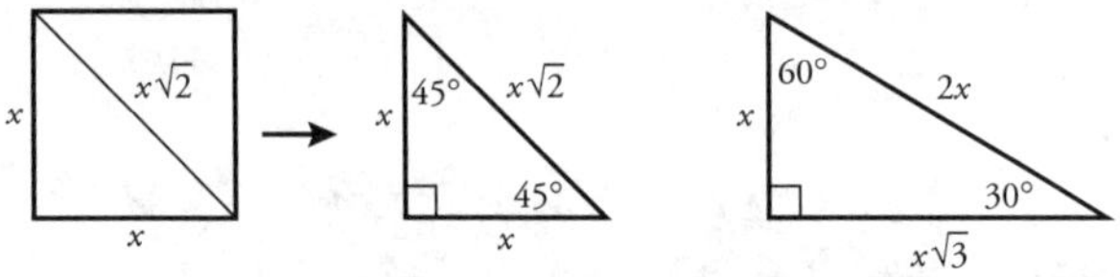

leg	leg	hypotenuse
45°	45°	90°
x	x	$x\sqrt{2}$

leg	leg	hypotenuse
30°	60°	90°
x	$x\sqrt{3}$	$2x$

Triangles

Pythagorean Triples
3–4–5
6–8–10
5–12–13
8–15–17

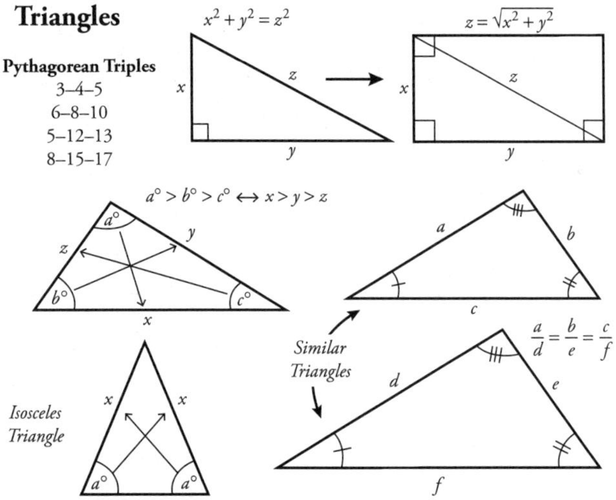

3-D Shapes

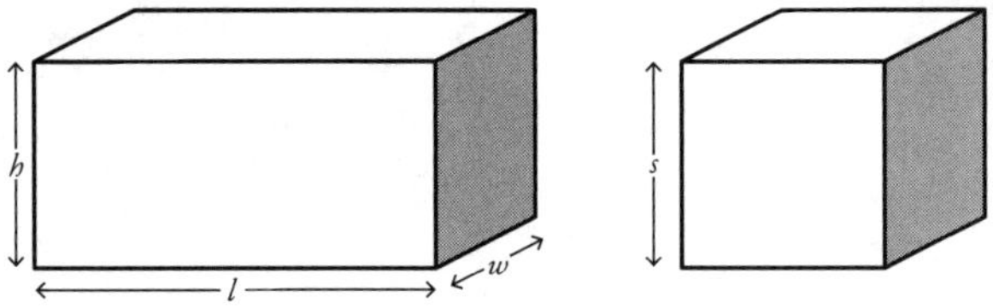

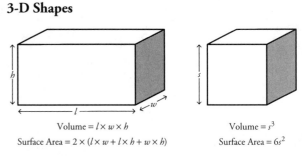

Volume $= l \times w \times h$
Surface Area $= 2 \times (l \times w + l \times h + w \times h)$

Volume $= s^3$
Surface Area $= 6s^2$

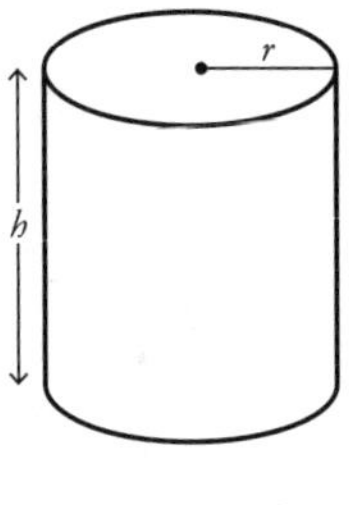

Volume $= \pi r^2 h$
Surface Area $= 2(\pi r^2) + 2\pi rh$

Slopes

$\frac{\text{rise}}{\text{run}}$ = slope

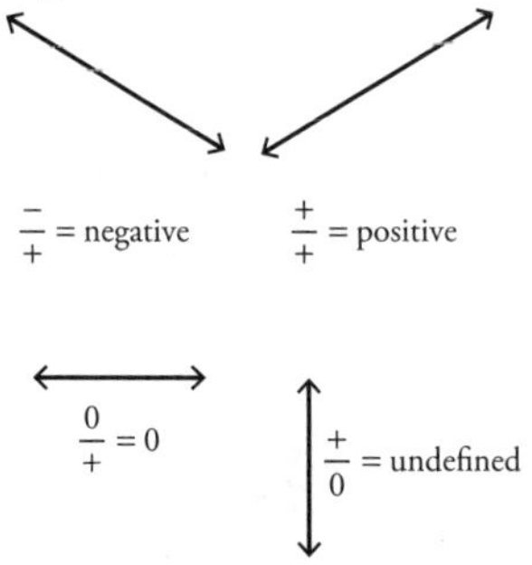

l_1 parallel to l_2

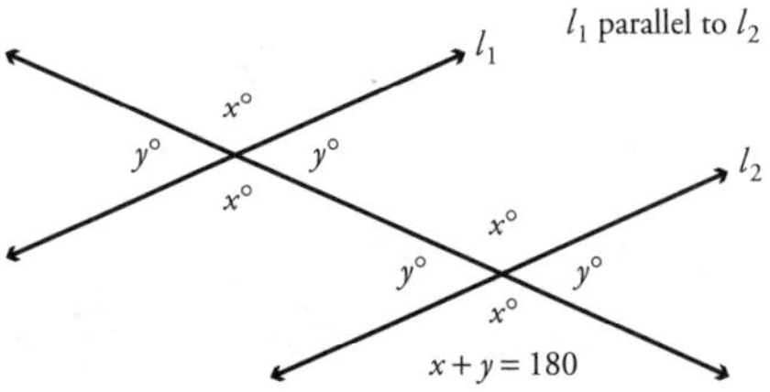

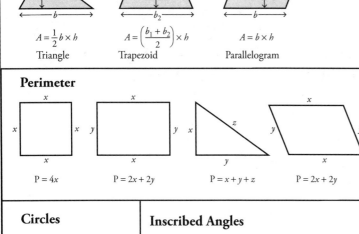

$x + y = 180$